ENCYCLOPEDIA OF WITCHCRAFT

ENCYCLOPEDIA OF WITCHCRAFT

THE WESTERN TRADITION

Volume 3, K–P

Richard M. Golden, Editor

ABC-CLIO

Santa Barbara,
Denver, CO
Oxford, UK

Cataloging-in-Publication Data is available from the Library of Congress

08 07 06 10 9 8 7 6 5 4 3 2 1

This book is also available on the World Wide Web as an eBook. Visit abc-clio.com for details.

ABC-CLIO, Inc.
130 Cremona Drive, P.O. Box 1911
Santa Barbara, California 93116-1911

Production Team:

Acquisitions Editor	*Patience Melnik*
Project Manager	*Wendy Roseth*
Media Editor	*Ellen Rasmussen*
Media Manager	*Caroline Price*
Production Editor	*Martha Whitt*
Editorial Assistant	*Alisha Martinez*
Production Manager	*Don Schmidt*
Manufacturing Coordinator	*George Smyser*

Typeset in 11/12 Garamond

This book is printed on acid-free paper. ∞

Manufactured in the United States of America

CONTENTS

ENCYCLOPEDIA OF WITCHCRAFT: THE WESTERN TRADITION

EDITOR AND
EDITORIAL BOARD

LIST OF CONTRIBUTORS

Ray G. Abrahams
Churchill College
University of Cambridge
Cambridge
United Kingdom

Michael D. Bailey
Assistant Professor
Department of History
Iowa State University
Ames, IA

Jonathan Barry
Senior Lecturer in History
University of Exeter
Exeter
United Kingdom

Thomas Becker
Director, Archives
University of Bonn
Bonn
Germany

Wolfgang Behringer
Professor and Chair in Early Modern History
Historisches Institut
Universität des Saarlandes
Saarbrücken
Germany

Edward Bever
Associate Professor
State University of New York, College at Old
  Westbury
Old Westbury, NY

Stephen Bowd
Lecturer in European History
University of Edinburgh
Edinburgh
United Kingdom

John Bradley
Senior Lecturer
Department of Modern History
National University of Ireland
Maynooth, Co. Kildare
Ireland

Robin Briggs
Senior Research Fellow
All Souls College
University of Oxford
Oxford
United Kingdom

Ivan Bunn
Lowestoft
United Kingdom

John Callow
Research Fellow
Lancaster University
Lancaster
United Kingdom

Andrew Cambers
Lecturer
Department of History
Oxford Brookes University
Oxford
United Kingdom

Nicholas Campion
Principal Lecturer
Department of History
Bath Spa University
Bath
United Kingdom

Hilary M. Carey
Keith Cameron Professor of Australian History
University College Dublin
Dublin
Ireland

Carmel Cassar
Senior Lecturer in History
University of Malta
Msida
Malta

J. H. Chajes
Lecturer in Jewish History
University of Haifa
Haifa
Israel

Stuart Clark
Professor of Early Modern Cultural and Intellectual
   History
University of Wales
Swansea
United Kingdom

Annibale Cogliano
Prof. Storia e filosofia
Direttore Centro studi e documentazione Carlo
   Gesualdo
Gesualdo
Italy

Lesley Coote
Lecturer in Medieval and Renaissance
   Studies
Department of English
University of Hull
Hull
United Kingdom

Allison P. Coudert
Paul and Marie Castelranco Chair in Religious
   Studies
University of California, Davis
Davis, CA

Guido Dall'Olio
Professore Associato
Università di Urbino "Carlo Bo"
Urbino
Italy

Jane P. Davidson
Professor of History of Art
University of Nevada, Reno
Reno, NV

Owen Davies
Reader in Social History
University of Hertfordshire
Hatfield, Hertfordshire
United Kingdom

Rainer Decker
Studiendirektor
Studienseminar Paderborn II
Paderborn
Germany

Andrea Del Col
Professor
Università degli Studi di Trieste
Trieste
Italy

Oscar Di Simplicio
Professor
University of Florence
Florence
Italy

Johannes Dillinger
FB III Neuere Geschichte
Universität Trier
Trier
Germany

Peter Dinzelbacher
Honararprofessor am Institut für Wirtschafts - und
   Sozialgeschichte
Universität Wien
Vienna
Austria

Frances E. Dolan
Professor of English
University of California, Davis
Davis, CA

Matteo Duni
Professor of History
Syracuse University in Florence
Florence
Italy

Jonathan Durrant
Senior Lecturer in Early Modern History
School of History, Law, & Social Sciences
University of Glamorgan
Pontypridd, Wales
United Kingdom

Kateryna Dysa
Lecturer
History Department
National University of "Kiev-Mohyla Academy"
Kiev
Ukraine

Kathryn A. Edwards
Associate Professor
University of South Carolina
Columbia, SC

Peter Elmer
Senior Lecturer
The Open University
Milton Keynes
United Kingdom

Germana Ernst
Professor
Dipartimento di Filosofia
Università di Roma Tre
Rome
Italy

Sarah Ferber
School of History, Philosophy, Religion & Classics
University of Queensland
Brisbane
Australia

Andrew Fix
Charles A. Dana Professor of History
Lafayette College
Easton, PA

Gunther Franz
Stadtbibliothek
Trier
Germany

Nils Freytag
Assistant Professor
Department of History
Universität München
Munich
Germany

Ralf-Peter Fuchs
Ludwig-Maximilians-Universität
Munich
Germany

Ronald Füssel
Marburg
Germany

Iris Gareis
Institut für Historische Ethnologie
Johann Wolfgang Goethe-Universität
Frankfurt am Main
Germany

Benoît Garnot
Professeur d'histoire moderne
Université de Bourgogne
Dijon
France

Malcolm Gaskill
Fellow and Director of Studies in
    History
Churchill College
Cambridge
United Kingdom

Gilbert Geis
Professor Emeritus
University of California, Irvine
Irvine, CA

Gudrun Gersmann
Universität zu Köln
Cologne
Germany

Marion Gibson
University of Exeter
Exeter
United Kingdom

Raymond Gillespie
Associate Professor
Department of Modern History
National University of Ireland, Maynooth
Maynooth
Ireland

Richard Godbeer
Professor of History
University of Miami
Coral Gables, FL

Richard M. Golden
Professor of History
Director, Jewish Studies Program
University of North Texas
Denton, TX

Julian Goodare
University of Edinburgh
Edinburgh
Scotland
United Kingdom

Klaus Graf
Freiburg im Breisgau/Aachen
Germany

Jeremy A. Greene
Fellow, Department of Social Medicine
Harvard Medical School
Boston, MA

Daniela Hacke
Historisches Seminar
Universität Zürich
Zürich
Switzerland

Rune Blix Hagen
Academic Librarian
University of Tromsø
Tromsø
Norway

Zakiya Hanafi
University of Ca' Foscari
Venice
Italy

Jörg Haustein (deceased)
Rheinische Friedrich-Wilhelms-Universität
Bonn
Germany

Gustav Henningsen
Research Director
Danish Folklore Archives
Copenhagen
Denmark

Tamar Herzig
The Hebrew University
Jerusalem
Israel

Robert Irwin
London University
London
United Kingdom

Michael J. Jarvis
Assistant Professor
University of Rochester
Rochester, NY

Günter Jerouschek
Chair of Penal Law, Criminal Procedure, and
    History of Law
Friedrich-Schiller-Universität
Jena
Germany

Jens Chr. V. Johansen
Københavns universitet, Saxo-instituttet, Afd.
    for historie
Copenhagen
Denmark

Marguerite Johnson
School of Humanities
University of Newcastle
Newcastle, New South Wales
Australia

Heinrich Kaak
Berlin
Germany

Louise Nyholm Kallestrup
Aalborg University
Aalborg
Denmark

Henry Kamen
Higher Council for Scientific Research
Barcelona
Spain

Edmund M. Kern
Associate Professor
Department of History
Lawrence University
Appleton, WI

Valerie A. Kivelson
Professor
University of Michigan
Ann Arbor, MI

Elisabeth Korrodi-Aebli
Lic.Phil.Psychologin FSP
Schulpsychologischer Dienst
Schaffhausen
Switzerland

Matevž Kosir
Arhiv Republike Slovenije
Ljubljana
Slovenia

Petr Kreuz
Prague City Archives
Prague
Czech Republic

Ildikó Sz. Kristóf
Senior Research Fellow
Institute of Ethnology
Hungarian Academy of Sciences
Budapest
Hungary

Richard Landes
Professor
Department of History
Boston University
Boston, MA

Thomas Lange
Hessisches Staatsarchiv Darmstadt
Darmstadt
Germany

Diana Laulainen-Schein
Faculty Associate
Arizona State University
Tempe, AZ

Vincenzo Lavenia
Assegnista
Scuola Normale Superiore
Pisa
Italy

David Lederer
Lecturer
National University of Ireland, Maynooth
Maynooth
Ireland

Christopher I. Lehrich
Boston University
Boston, MA

Brian P. Levack
John E. Green Regents Professor in
    History
Department of History
University of Texas at Austin
Austin, TX

Nicole K. Longen
Universität Trier
Trier
Germany

Sönke Lorenz
Institut für Geschichtliche Landeskunde und
    Historische Hilfswissenschaften der
    Eberhard-Karls-Universität-Tübingen
Tübingen
Germany

Machteld Löwensteyn
Free University
Amsterdam
Netherlands

T.M. Luhrmann
Max Palevsky Professor
University of Chicago
Chicago, IL

Eric-Oliver Mader
Universität des Saarlandes
Saarbrücken
Germany

Armando Maggi
Associate Professor
University of Chicago
Chicago, IL

Wolfgang Mährle
Hauptstaatsarchiv Stuttgart
Stuttgart
Germany

Victor H. Matthews
Professor of Religious Studies and Associate Dean
Missouri State University
Springfield, MO

Peter G. Maxwell-Stuart
Department of Modern History
University of St. Andrews
St. Andrews
United Kingdom

Georg Modestin
Monumenta Germaniae Historica
Munich
Germany

Katrin Moeller
Martin-Luther-Universität Halle-Wittenberg
Halle
Germany

Lynn Wood Mollenauer
Assistant Professor
University of North Carolina–Wilmington
Wilmington, NC

William Monter
Professor
Department of History
Northwestern University
Evanston, IL

Marina Montesano
Università di Genova
Genoa
Italy

Franco Mormando
Associate Professor, Italian Studies
Boston College
Chestnut Hill, MA

Robert Muchembled
Professor
Université de Paris XIII (Paris-Nord)
Paris
France

Gerald Mülleder
Vienna
Austria

Hans Eyvind Naess
Professor of History Senior Advisor, National Archives of Norway
Oslo
Norway

William G. Naphy
Senior Lecturer
University of Aberdeen
Aberdeen
Scotland
United Kingdom

Franco Nardon
Arta Terme, UD
Italy

Marko Nenonen
Assistant Professor
Department of History
University of Tampere
Tampere
Finland

Lawrence Normand
Principal Lecturer in English Literary Studies
Middlesex University
London
United Kingdom

Maximillian E. Novak
Distinguished Professor of English, Emeritus
University of California, Los Angeles
Los Angeles, CA

Jutta Nowosadtko
Universität GH Essen
Essen
Germany

Caroline Oates
Information Officer/Librarian
The Folklore Society
London
United Kingdom

Peter Oestmann
Director, Institut für
    Rechtsgeschichte
Münster
Germany

Daniel Ogden
Reader in Ancient History
University of Exeter
Exeter
United Kingdom

Mary R. O'Neil
Associate Professor
Department of History
University of Washington
Seattle, WA

Martine Ostorero
Université de Lausanne
Lausanne
Switzerland

José Pedro Paiva
Professor
University of Coimbra
Coimbra
Portugal

Gian Maria Panizza
Ministero per i Beni e le Attività Culturali:
    Archivio di Stato di Alessandria
Alessandria
Italy

Jonathan L. Pearl
Associate Professor
University of Toronto
Toronto, Ontario
Canada

Ludolf Pelizaeus
Assistant Professor
Department of General and Modern History
Johannes Gutenberg-Universität Mainz
Mainz
Germany

Edward Peters
Henry Charles Lea Professor of History
University of Pennsylvania
Philadelphia, PA

Parsla Petersone
Riga
Latvia

Giovanni Pizza
Senior Researcher, Lecturer in Medical Anthropology
Università di Perugia, Dipartimento
    Uomo & Territorio
Perugia
Italy

Éva Pócs
Professor
Department of Ethnology and Cultural
    Anthropology
University of Pécs
Pécs
Hungary

Paolo Portone
Società Storica Comense
Como
Italy

Diane Purkiss
Senior English Fellow
Keble College
University of Oxford
Oxford
United Kingdom

Anita Raith
Head, Documentary Film Centre Archive
Stuttgart
Germany

Robert Rapley
Independent Scholar
Ottawa, Ontario
Canada

Francesc Riera
Majorca
Spain

Alison Rowlands
Senior Lecturer in European History
University of Essex
Colchester
United Kingdom

Walter Rummel
Landeshauptarchiv Koblenz
Koblenz
Germany

Jeffrey Burton Russell
Professor of History, Emeritus
University of California, Santa Barbara
Santa Barbara, CA

W. F. Ryan
Warburg Institute, School of Advanced
    Study
University of London
London
United Kingdom

Geoffrey Scarre
Department of Philosophy
University of Durham
Durham
United Kingdom

Jürgen Michael Schmidt
Institut für Geschichtliche Landeskunde
    und Historische
Universität Tübingen
Tübingen
Germany

Corinna Schneider
Historikerin
Tübingen
Germany

Rolf Schulte
Chrisitan-Albrechts-Universität zu Kiel
Kiel
Germany

James Sharpe
Professor
Department of History
University of York
York
United Kingdom

David J. Silverman
Assistant Professor
Department of History
George Washington
    University
Washington, DC

Maryse Simon
History Faculty
University of Oxford
Oxford
United Kingdom

Jacqueline Simpson
The Folklore Society
London
United Kingdom

Gordon Andreas Singer
Greenbelt, MD

Natalia Uladzimirauna Slizh
Associate Professor
Intitute of Modern Knowledge
Grodna
Belarus

Per Sörlin
Department of Humanities
Mid Sweden University
Härnösand
Sweden

Walter Stephens
Charles S. Singleton Professor of Italian
    Studies
Johns Hopkins University
Baltimore, MD

Constanze Störk-Biber
Universität Tübingen
Tübingen
Germany

Krzysztof Szkurlatowski
Collegium Gedanense
Gdáńsk
Poland

María Tausiet
IES "Prado de Santo Domingo"
Madrid
Spain

Olina Thorvardardottir
Principal
Junior College of Isafjordur
Isafjordur
Iceland

Robert W. Thurston
Phillip R. Shriver Professor of History
Miami University
Oxford, OH

Daniel Tollet
Ingénieur de recherche et Directeur de recherches
Secrétaire général, Institut de recherches pour
    l'étude des religions
Université de Paris IV Sorbonne
Paris
France

E.R. Truitt
Harvard University
Cambridge, MA

Manfred Tschaikner
Vorarlberger Landesarchiv
Bregenz
Austria

Christa Agnes Tuczay
Österreichische Akademie der Wissenschaften
Universität Wien
Vienna
Austria

Kathrin Utz Tremp
Université de Lausanne, Switzerland
Stoatsarchiv Freiburg,
Switzerland

Michaela Valente
Università "La Sapienza"
Rome
Italy

Dries Vanysacker
Professor
Katholieke Universiteit Leuven
Louvain
Belgium

Trpimir Vedriš
History Department
University of Zagreb
Zagreb
Croatia

Rita Voltmer
Lecturer
Department of History
Universität Trier
Trier
Germany

Hans de Waardt
Vrije Universiteit
Amsterdam
Netherlands

Gary K. Waite
Professor of Medieval and Early Modern
    History
University of New Brunswick
Fredericton, New Brunswick
Canada

Robert Walinski-Kiehl
Senior Lecturer, School of Social, Historical
    and Literary Studies
University of Portsmouth
Portsmouth
United Kingdom

Rainer Walz
Professor
Ruhr-Universität Bochum
Fakultät für Geschichtswissenschaft
Lehrstuhl Neuere Geschichte I
Bochum
Germany

Richard Weisman
Associate Professor
York University
Toronto, Ontario
Canada

Merry Wiesner-Hanks
Professor
Department of History
University of Wisconsin-Milwaukee
Milwaukee, WI

Manfred Wilde
Head of Museum, Castle of Delitzsch
Delitzsch
Germany

Gerhild Scholz Williams
Thomas Professor in the Humanities
Washington University
St. Louis, MO

Melvyn Willin
Post-Doctoral Researcher
Great Leighs
United Kingdom

Karin Wohlschlegel
Bretzfeld
Germany

Elliot R. Wolfson
Abraham Lieberman Professor of Hebrew
    and Judaic Studies
New York University
New York, NY

Juliette Wood
Cardiff University
Cardiff
Wales
United Kingdom

David Wootton
Anniversary Professor of History
University of York
York
United Kingdom

Thomas Worcester
Associate Professor
College of the Holy Cross
Worcester, MA

Wanda Wyporska
Hertford College
Oxford
United Kingdom

Avihu Zakai
Professor of Early Modern History and Early
    American History
The Hebrew University of Jerusalem
Jerusalem
Israel

Gabriella Zarri
Professor of Modern History
Università di Firenze
Florence
Italy

Charles Zika
Professor
University of Melbourne
Melbourne
Australia

FOREWORD

The *Encyclopedia of Witchcraft: The Western Tradition* is an indispensable resource at the dawn of the third millennium. Above all, it provides reliable answers to satisfy the sharp curiosity of our contemporaries, who are surrounded by an atmosphere that is softly but strongly tinted with magic—the magic of dreams, of successful books such as *Harry Potter,* and of innumerable films and television series featuring witches, werewolves (**lycanthropy**), and **vampire**s. This new work will be both necessary and extremely useful in bringing order to an often incomprehensible flood of information and misinformation and providing meaning for a vast river of symbols, emotions, and ideas that carry some truths but also a great many errors. It will also help readers locate the elements of truth within the vast **literature** devoted to diabolical sensationalism by distinguishing between hysterical fantasy and historical truth, enabling them to understand better the ways in which magic and witchcraft have left a profound cultural imprint on today's Western world.

Moreover, this encyclopedia appears at an appropriate moment to fill a huge void. In its breadth of subject matter, its international and collective character, and its completeness, it has no equivalent. A few dictionaries of diabolism and magic exist in various languages; in 1959, for example, **Rossell Hope Robbins** published the 570-page *Encyclopedia of Witchcraft and Demonology.* But until now, no multivolume survey, bringing together contributions from 172 specialists representing twenty-eight countries, has ever been attempted. Like Denis Diderot's famous eighteenth-century *Encylopédie,* this work offers mature collective wisdom about the topics it surveys. The time has finally come to consider carefully and seriously the greatest enigma of Western civilization between the 1420s and 1750: the **executions** of witches, whose flamboyant traces still haunt our imaginations in both Europe and America. We know today that there were not 100,000 executions, as **Voltaire** claimed, but barely one-third as many. Most of them occurred within the boundaries of present-day **Germany**, and most witches died in western Europe between 1560 and 1630.

Witchcraft and magic are universal human phenomena; they can be found on any continent at any time. However, only the West has ever burned great numbers of witches, after legally constituted **trials** that were approved by political authorities and fully accepted by established churches. Women generally constituted around 80 percent—at times more—of those accused and condemned, although there were exceptions to this rule in places such as **Finland** or the French province of **Normandy**. This astounding imbalance between the genders makes the mystery even more impenetrable, because at that time, witchcraft (along with **infanticide**) became the female capital crime par excellence; generally, women accounted for only a very small minority of all defendants in courtroom trials, rarely exceeding 20 percent.

*****

The past is not dead. It weighs on those living today—and not just in vivid sensations that remain deeply embedded in our memories or in museum collections such as those at **Salem**. It endures more subtly through the impact of strong images, which I prefer to call cultural matrices, that carry their symbolic baggage from century to century. One of the most powerful of these images, the great European enigma of the witch at the stake, drives this encyclopedia. No one person can resolve this enigma in such a short space. I simply want to direct readers' attention to some paths of research and give them a desire to sample this work in the same way that Voltaire tried to guide readers of his *Dictionnaire philosophique* (Philosophical Dictionary, 1764): Here also, one article refers to another, and readers can best absorb their ultimate meanings by linking together multiple entries.

The problem at the heart of these volumes is enormously complicated, and no single answer or approach can resolve it. But like any great question, it can be simplified by seeking its most basic core: The **witch hunts** were so terrible and so intense that simply retelling their history reveals something fundamental about the mentality of the western Europeans who conducted them. And without any general consensus among historians for explaining the persecution of witches, I hope to enrich its significance by placing it among the formative myths that slowly but profoundly shaped the cultural and social foundations of early modern Europe.

*****

Attempts to explain the persecution of witches have multiplied since the end of the witchcraft trials. Obviously, the judges and most other people believed purely and simply that witchcraft demonstrated the unleashed power of the **Devil**, a kind of prelude to the **Apocalypse;** in their eyes, the witches constituted a secret society of deviant devil-worshippers, paying homage to Satan and fornicating with him at their **Sabbat**s. Those who dared to express doubts on this topic, as **Johann Weyer** did, were few. The eighteenth-century *philosophes* tried to eradicate such **superstition**s by talking about madness or, more cleverly, about diabolical suggestion; skeptics such as **Daniel Defoe** argued that the Devil had no physical power but simply insinuated his venom into human minds. Nevertheless, a residue of **demonology** has survived at various intellectual levels; it ranges from today's abundant overtly satanic literature to historical accounts and theological discussions, with each genre serving the specific needs and cultural conventions of its special audience. Until 1960 (and sometimes later), the dominant explanation in the Anglo-Saxon world came from the works of the Egyptologist **Margaret Murray,** who saw the witches' Sabbat as a very real but secret ceremony demonstrating the clandestine survival of a cult of a pre-Christian horned god. Without going that far, **Carlo Ginzburg** followed a parallel path when investigating the ***benandanti*** of Friuli and suggested, unconvincingly, that **shamanism** profoundly influenced the witches' Sabbat.

A major turning point occurred in the 1970s. Influenced by events such as opposition to the Vietnam War or the French student uprising of 1968, some researchers followed smoke signals from the Devil's grass (cannabis or peyote) and explained the experiences of witches as **hallucinogen**ically induced dreams. Others took more novel paths. In **France**, **Robert Mandrou** explained the end of witchcraft persecutions long before the **Enlightenment** through increasing **skepticism** among the ruling classes. In **England**, **Alan Macfarlane** and **Keith Thomas** built an anthropological model, in which witches were often accused of casting **spells** on people who had previously refused them charity. For these British scholars, neighborhood and a sense of guilt seemed more important than the Devil, whose presence was never elicited through **torture**, as it was on the Continent. A response followed quickly from **H. C. Erik Midelfort**, who used massive statistical information from an epicenter of persecution in **southwestern Germany** to build a highly useful model describing the variations in witchcraft persecution within a region where confessional rivalry appeared to multiply witch burnings. With youthful enthusiasm, I devised a two-sided **acculturation** model, using witchcraft trials from the Spanish-ruled **southern Netherlands**. One part merged the British/anthropological explanation with a then-fashionable type of Marxism, stressing that the richer inhabitants of villages encouraged their overlords to persecute poorer residents by offering to pay the costs of witchcraft trials. The other part described how confessional churches and emerging absolutist states targeted witches as prime and particularly dangerous transmitters of an outdated oral culture, heavily charged with what these authorities called superstitions. My model proved too schematic to apply successfully throughout Europe, but it contained some still-valid elements, including an explanation for the predominance of women among witches.

While the effervescent intellectual climate of the 1970s led to some intellectual collisions, other researchers working in the Jura region, **Scotland,** the Spanish **Basque Country**, and **New England** patiently collected information that enabled us to gain a better overall grasp of the dimensions of the witch hunt in some widely scattered places. However, too much archival work of the 1970s was carried out in parts of western Europe other than Germany—the "mother of so many witches," in **Friedrich Spee**'s evocative phrase. A major revival of interest in witchcraft trials occurred in West Germany only after 1980, when the amazing collection made by the Nazi *Hexenkommando* finally came to scholars' attention. Subsequently, this material has been used to shape some fresh and persuasive interpretations of the phenomenon in its heartland, most prominently **Wolfgang Behringer**'s correlations between climatic disasters, famine, and major witchcraft persecutions.

The years since 1990 have marked a new stage in the journey down this long road. Several general accounts of the witch hunt have been published, usually without privileging any single interpretation. Even the outstanding **Lorraine**-based investigation emphasizing quarrels within villages (Briggs 2001) offers "many reasons why" when trying to explain witchcraft persecutions throughout Europe. But if a historian's most fundamental task is to establish some hierarchy for the information he or she provides, then a multiplicity of explanations, each of roughly equal weight, ultimately remains unsatisfactory. Moreover, some recent developments have significantly clarified our knowledge of this topic, including works highlighting the idea that witchcraft persecution had a center with several peripheries, the specificity of **demonic possession** in convents such as **Loudun** and its hidden connections to witchcraft prosecutions, and especially the fundamental importance of **gender** for comprehending this theme.

The **geography** of witch hunting now seems clear: The phenomenon was centered in the German-speaking **Holy Roman Empire** (plus **Switzerland**). This core region also produced the **Protestant Reformation**, pioneered the system of confessionalism, and endured Europe's bloodiest religious war until 1648. But there were also various types of "witchcraft peripheries," three of which should be noted in particular. Most of Protestant northern Europe, apart from **Scotland** and northern **Sweden** after 1668, seems to have been relatively immune to extensive witch hunting; one exceptionally prosperous region, the United Provinces of the **Netherlands**, abandoned witch hunting much sooner than any other area. Another little-affected region comprised the solidly Catholic lands of southern Europe (**Spain, Italy,** and **Portugal**), where Inquisitions avoided putting witches to death, and France, whose appellate courts permitted relatively few executions for this crime. Finally, eastern Europe constituted a very different sort of periphery. There, trials and executions of witches occurred much later than in western Europe, but they were confined to Latin Christianity; **Orthodox** Christendom remained almost entirely impervious to this phenomenon, and **Islam**ic regions were completely so.

It is abundantly clear that witch hunts were very unevenly distributed throughout Europe. The heartlands of witchcraft persecutions lay mostly in parts of west-central Europe, which were sharply disputed between Protestants and Catholics between 1560 and 1630, and there were later prolongations in eastern Europe during the post-1650 Catholic reconquest and in a few overseas colonies such as New England. Major outbreaks of witchcraft trials were distributed widely among both Protestants and Catholics during the apogee of confessionalization, but few obvious subpatterns emerged along confessional fault lines. Europe's

very worst witchcraft **panics** tended to cluster between 1585 and 1630 in Germany's Catholic **ecclesiastical territories** (principalities), especially those, such as **Cologne,** ruled by electoral prince-archbishops. Meanwhile, the most intensive (per capita) and regular (per annum) witchcraft trials in western Europe afflicted the Protestant **Pays de Vaud.** The best general rule one can discover is a negative correlation: The lay judges who burned most of Europe's witches were usually the furthest removed from the centers of political power in major monarchies such as France or Spain.

The theme of witchcraft probably requires the sort of multilayered approach pioneered by Fernand Braudel (Braudel 1900). At the short term or "conjunctural" level, we must identify the local circumstances: Sometimes, the most serious outbreaks of witch hunting were prompted by climate changes and harvest failures, and at other times, they were triggered by the actions of unusually zealous judges, among them **Pierre de Lancre** or **Henri Boguet.** At a multigenerational intermediate level, they developed against a background of prolonged confessional rivalry and strife, which seems to have been most intense in the Holy Roman Empire. The lion's share of the prosecutions occurred in regions ruled by Catholics, who, in one sense, had a head start because the papacy had apparently endorsed the **Malleus Maleficarum** (The Hammer of Witches, 1486) a century before the worst outbreaks began; after the Council of Trent, **Jesuits** including **Juan Maldonado** rediscovered and emphasized the profound links between **heresy** and diabolical witchcraft. The purely Catholic phenomenon of demonic possession in nunneries led to some spectacular dramas: For example, at least two nuns from the convent of the Verger in Artois were burned as witches around 1614 (Muchembled 2003a, 250–263), after which Catholic authorities made a much stronger separation between witches and "possessed" women.

At the deepest, long-term level of explanations for witchcraft, the subject of gender relations in Europe between the fifteenth and eighteenth centuries—and beyond—deserves very close attention, not just because books on the subject seem to multiply, giving one the impression of a passing fashion, but also because if the overwhelming majority of convicted witches were women, it is impossible not to ask why. Back in the 1970s, a few male scholars, myself included, made timid allusions to this problem, without attracting much attention. Only recently has feminist scholarship emphasized the strongly feminine character of the crime of *lèse-majesté divine* or treason against god—and some current defenders of this approach have not improved its credibility by talking about "gynocide" or grossly exaggerating the **number**s of women killed for this crime at a time when religious massacres, not to mention famines and **plague**, truly decimated European populations.

My own reading of European cultural and social history in the early modern period suggests a slow and subtle modification, at the very deepest level, in the relationship between the sexes. The onset of witchcraft persecution at the end of the Middle Ages, which has been analyzed less thoroughly than its peak, coincided with what feminists describe as the development of a "paternalist-misogynist" model. One might just as easily call it a reinforcement of masculine privilege, an attempt to confine women more strictly than before within the bounds of "propriety," meaning, first and foremost, the control of their sexual impulses. Except for a handful of princesses and fashionable courtisans, women of that period were subjected to a more intensive and intrusive surveillance of their sexual behavior, which was insistently defined as naturally malevolent and sinful. Any woman found guilty of disposing freely of her own sexuality suffered extreme consequences. Extramarital sexual activity enhanced a man's reputation, but it invariably had tragic consequences for any woman unlucky enough to be caught concealing her pregnancy; for example, in France, following a royal edict of Henry II in 1557, women were fifteen times likelier to be executed for this crime than burned as a witch in the vast district of the *Parlement* **of Paris**.

Moreover, only during the sixteenth and seventeenth centuries did the consensus of European thinkers agree that a **pact with the Devil** could not be broken. Instead of the famous medieval miracle of **Theophilus,** who outwitted the Devil, the dominant motif became the pact of Dr. Faustus (**Johann Georg Faust**), who was eternally damned (Muchembled 2003b). Although both Theophilus and Faustus were men, the consequences of the change weighed overwhelmingly on women. The ultimate metaphor became the one-sided and unbreakable pact between an old woman and the Devil, confirmed not in writing but by an act of sexual intercourse, which male authors and judges invariably described as painful.

*****

Of course, no single explanation can cover a phenomenon so important, so spectacular, and so terrifying as witchcraft persecution, which has left indelible traces on Western civilization. But we must not shrug our shoulders in defeat or retreat behind a confusing multiplicity of causes. In fact, European witchcraft between the fifteenth and eighteenth centuries offers an excellent terrain for attempting a total history, at every level from local to global. The *Encyclopedia of Witchcraft* thus comes at the right time to shine a spotlight on many things, especially two notions that have been too often neglected recently: first, the essential role of Christianity in encouraging the persecution of witches, and second, the reinforced legal subordination and surveillance of women in early modern European society. The evidence for both phenomena is so overwhelming that they have all too often remained hidden in plain view, obscured by multicausal approaches and thus minimized by even the best specialists. The deepest reason for this neglect probably lies in the ways in which great cultural myths usually work: They touch essential matters but without drawing attention to them because a myth that is too easily understood has little effect on any given society.

I believe that Western witchcraft from the 1420s to around 1750 carried the cultural baggage of one of our greatest myths: male supremacy, powerfully reinforced at that time by a religious ethic that placed increasing emphasis on a man's duty to supervise his female companions, whose cold and damp natures were inclined toward evil and were dangerous for the collective salvation of humanity. A witchcraft trial involved a woman, frequently widowed or otherwise unsupervised by male kin, who was accused of giving herself—in both body and soul—to the Devil. This fact cannot be understood without setting it in the religious context of that age, as different confessional churches rivaled each other in increasing supervision over the female **imagination** (including a stronger indoctrination of **children**). Burning a witch in public concealed a veritable forest of symbols, the most essential being the relationship between genders. The idea of the evil woman was one of the most fundamental Western myths until the eighteenth century—and beyond. Myths die hard. Imaginative cinematographers such as Alfred Hitchcock or David Lynch re-created an image of the dangerously perverse blonde, capable of the very worst sexual transgressions, closely resembling the figure of the witch punished by early modern European males.

Have we reached a crossroads? In this millennium, the social and cultural importance of Christianity is declining at an accelerated rate in Europe, although much more slowly in the United States, while in both places, women are increasingly demanding their place in the sun. After more than five centuries, the myth of the witch as the sexual slave of Satan, eating babies and raising hailstorms, seems to be disintegrating. Radical and profound mutations in gender relations, including marital relations and **family** values, have surely played a major role in this disintegration. When civilizations shift at their deepest levels, fundamental myths shift with them. In both Europe and the United States, now safely insulated from infant mortality and food shortages, the old myth of a happier life after death is increasingly challenged by the contemporary myth of immediate and total individual gratification: I want it here, I want it now, I want it all . . .

For anyone seeking reliable information about this basic Western myth, the *Encyclopedia of Witchcraft* provides exactly that: We have it here, we have it now, and we have it all.

—*Robert Muchembled*
Institute for Advanced Study, Princeton
October 2003

References and further reading:

Braudel, Fernand. 1980. *On History.* Translated by Sarah Matthews. Chicago: University of Chicago Press.

Briggs, Robin. 2001. *Witches and Neighbors: The Social and Cultural Context of European Witchcraft.* 2nd ed. Oxford: Blackwell.

Muchembled, Robert. 2003a. *Passions des femmes au temps de la Reine Margot, 1553–1615.* Paris: Seuil.

———. 2003b. *A History of the Devil: From the Middle Ages to the Present.* Translated by Jean Birrell. Cambridge: Polity.

Note: Words marked in bold refer to the encyclopedia's entries.

ACKNOWLEDGMENTS

This encyclopedia entailed more work than I could have imagined and required more help than I had expected. So many people have assisted me over these past six years that I fear I will omit someone here; if I do, I hope that person will forgive me. Those I must thank comprise three groups: scholars, ABC-CLIO staff, and family.

I have been fortunate indeed to have had a superb editorial board consisting of excellent scholars: Wolfgang Behringer, Gustav Henningsen, Brian P. Levack, William Monter, James Sharpe, and Merry Wiesner-Hanks. The members of the board helped me develop the initial lists of entries by correspondence and in two meetings at the University of York in April 2001. They wrote entries themselves, provided advice, and answered questions. I and at least one member of the editorial board read each entry in the encyclopedia. While I did the final editing, the comments of the board members proved invaluable, and they will see much of their handiwork when they read the published encyclopedia.

Three historians provided me with exceptional help and saved me from innumerable missteps. Bill Monter read every entry, and he did so quickly, week to week, month to month, and year to year. He was, as he likes to say, my *éminence grise*. He is a master of comparative history, and he frequently improved entries by calling my attention to issues that contributors might well include in their articles. Bill more than once volunteered to write entries when contributors reneged or when I could not locate suitable authors. Finally, after declining to be editor himself, he had the wisdom or folly to recommend me to ABC-CLIO. Wolfgang Behringer put his enormous knowledge of witchcraft at my disposal; whenever I had a question, often arcane, he responded immediately and correctly. He is, in large part, responsible for the blanket coverage of Germany in our encyclopedia

and for the multiplicity of Germans who wrote entries. In addition, he authored more entries than anyone else. My fellow Texan Brian Levack also served as a sounding board, contributed entries when I despaired of locating authors, and settled many witchcraft matters in long telephone conversations. His expertise in legal history proved invaluable. He, along with Bill Monter, even helped by reading some of the page proofs.

In my career, I have found that historians of Europe have been friendlier and kinder than most other groups of people I have encountered. My work on this encyclopedia confirmed that view. The contributors to the encyclopedia have been affable and cooperative. Certain contributors warmed my heart with their eagerness to help and their supreme kindness. These *Menschen* include Michael Bailey, Robin Briggs, Carmel Cassar, Yossi Chajes, Jane P. Davidson, Oscar Di Simplicio, Johannes Dillinger, Sarah Ferber, Julian Goodare, Rune Hagen, Tamar Herzig, Valerie Kivelson, David Lederer, Victor Matthews, Georg Modestin, Caroline Oates, Martine Ostorero, Edward Peters, Alison Rowlands, Will Ryan, Jürgen-Michael Schmidt, Walter Stephens, Michaela Valente, Dries Vanysacker, Rita Voltmer, and Charles Zika. Edward Bever gave me extraordinary help throughout but especially by writing some difficult entries on short notice during the final stages of production.

Numerous were those who did not write entries but who patiently answered my questions, suggested contributors, and helped me in other ways: Guy Chet, Harvey Chisick, Geoffrey Dennis, Chad Gunnoe, Tom Kuehn, Dan Magilow, Alfred Mierzejewski, David Nicholas, Carles Salazar, Jonathan Schick, Laura Stern, John Tedeschi, Carmen Terry, and Martin Yaffe.

Many at ABC-CLIO have participated in this extensive project. Todd Hallman, acquisitions editor, approached me about editing the encyclopedia after speaking to Bill Monter. I have worked closely with Allison Miller, assistant developmental editor, and then Patience Melnik, developmental editor. Both have been utterly professional, smart, and efficient. Martha Whitt and Anna Kaltenbach, production editors, have been on top of their jobs. Cisca Schreefel, associate production editor, gave great help, as did production editor Martha Gray. The copy editors caught some mistakes and often rightly asked for more information: Silvine Farnell, Anne Friedman, Beth Partin, Kathy Delfosse, and Joan Sherman. Ellen Rasmussen, media editor, facilitated my selecting the encyclopedia's illustrations. Elaine Vanater in marketing did her job extremely well. Terry Buss and then Wendy Roseth handled contributor relations after Patience Melnik. Art Stickney and Don Schmidt, editorial directors, watched over this project. Ron Boehm, chief executive officer of ABC-CLIO, has been gracious and supportive in my conversations with him.

I am grateful to the University of North Texas for giving me a semester's Faculty Development Leave to work on this encyclopedia.

Finally, I owe—I really do—gargantuan amounts of gratitude to my family. My wife, Hilda, allowed me to withdraw to my upstairs office days, nights, and weekends to work on the encyclopedia. The house deteriorated somewhat during my seemingly ceaseless and grinding work, but she rarely called upstairs for me to do a chore or to come up (down) for air. She demonstrated great marital wisdom by never asking me when I would finish or when we could go on a decent vacation. Love is never having to badger. My children, Davina, Irene, and Jeremy, also never complained (about the encyclopedia, anyway), and while they did not stop making demands on my time, they did show greater forbearance. I owe all of my family much time, which I shall duly repay with interest.

INTRODUCTION

Witchcraft is a topic of enduring interest for a variety of reasons. Many and probably most human societies, from primitive bands through civilizations, have practiced and still practice forms of witchcraft (and its close relations magic and religion) and/or believe in the concept of a witch, defined as someone who uses supernatural means to cause harm or misfortune. When beneficent as well as malevolent power is subsumed in the definition of witchcraft, then the concept of witchcraft is universal, historically and geographically.[1] For societies or segments of societies that mistakenly believe only "the Other" employs witchcraft, the topic may have interest as an entrée into the minds and behaviors of the backward, the superstitious, or the ignorant. Witchcraft, a part of the occult, fascinates, perplexes, and offers vicarious experience with the dark, deadly, and dangerous. Thus, in Western civilization, some skeptical Romans, medieval and early modern peoples, and the transoceanic societies that comprise the contemporary West have expressed their feelings of superiority as well as their fascination and fear of witchcraft, perceived to be joined to its Siamese twin, evil. The perception of witchcraft can function to mark cultural and religious boundaries, to label or cleanse a society of the socially and/or the religiously indigestible, and to distinguish the good from the bad, offering a partial theodicy to cope with humankind's Hobbesian lives.

All topics are on the scholars' table, although they do not always realize the seemingly endless varieties of approaches and subjects—hence, historiography and spectacular alterations in scholarship that can often bewilder those more comfortable with static knowledge and with understanding through faith in authority. Our comprehension of perceptions of witchcraft—historically and culturally—and witchcraft itself changes temporally and geographically. The *Encyclopedia of Witchcraft: The Western Tradition,* approximately six years from conception to publication, reflects these fast-paced changes in research, knowledge, and approach. Indeed, in editing the 757 entries, I found that articles often had to be reworked because contributors did not and frequently could not know results of new research that has appeared in a wide variety of languages and that subsequently has been incorporated into different entries.

Scholars, to be sure, have studied witchcraft across the planet and from prehistory to the present. However, since the eighteenth century, arguably more research on witchcraft (and related subjects) has been done in the West than elsewhere. Such research and writing has taken place in Western societies, spread now over the world, because the West is where the more than two dozen democracies exist and thus where relative freedom of expression and research is possible. The twenty-eight nations represented by the 172 contributors to this encyclopedia are all in the West—and not only because the volumes deal with the Western tradition. An encyclopedia of witchcraft that covers the globe would doubtless have Westerners as the overwhelming majority of contributors.

*****

Witchcraft interests the academic world partly because it is extraordinarily interdisciplinary: Anthropologists, ethnologists, folklorists, historians, linguists, philosophers, political scientists, sociologists, and scholars of literature, medicine, religion, and theology have contributed to this encyclopedia. The central focus of the encyclopedia is the European witch hunts that occurred between the early fifteenth century and the late eighteenth century. These centuries encompassed those developments that make the Western witchcraft experience unique: the emergence of the so-called cumulative concept of witchcraft and the prosecution of upwards of 100,000 people for witchcraft, most of them for diabolical witchcraft—meeting with the Devil (sometimes at Sabbats, which witches usually traveled to by flight), signing a pact with the Evil One, and subsequently working *maleficium* (harmful magic) in a revolt that aimed to topple Christian civilization.

Many scholars have come to the period of the witch hunts to investigate persecution and religious intolerance, linking the pursuit of witches in the "persecuting society" that was late medieval and early modern Europe to the maltreatment of Jews, lepers, homosexuals, and those Christians labeled as heretics by other Christians. In fact, there was little persecution of diabolic witches, for those prosecuted as serving the Devil did not (and could not) do so. There is absolutely no evidence of a devil-worshipping sect in late medieval and early modern Europe, but empirical evidence, of course, is irrelevant to faith (or prejudice). Yet diabolic witches, like the Islamic Ottoman Empire entrenched in southeastern Europe and often expanding into central Europe, instilled great fear in Latin Christendom as threats that could literally destroy Christian society. Somewhere between 35,000 and 50,000 accused witches were executed or lynched; we will never know the exact number. Anyone, even a pope, could be accused as a witch, though in this, as in all of life, probability counted: People were more plausibly denounced as witches if they were women, related to another accused witch, old, single, and possessed of a quarrelsome reputation. But there was no certain safety; many entries in the *Encyclopedia of Witchcraft* detail exceptions to the familiar image of the witch and note the urban and high social status of some of those executed. Given these fears, superimposed on the omnipresent structural threats of hunger and cold, scholars have lately wondered why many more witches were not killed. After all, the numbers of individuals who were institutionally or extralegally killed as witches pale in comparison to the millions of victims of twentieth-century genocides.

The issue of the persecution of women as witches has attracted feminist scholars (not to mention Neo-Pagans) to the topic, and they have significantly increased our knowledge of gender relations and sexuality, even though women were not prosecuted simply for being women, unlike Jews victimized for being Jews, lepers for having leprosy, or homosexuals for behaving as homosexuals. Nevertheless, the prosecution of thousands for concluding a pact with the Devil, kissing his anus, flying to his Sabbat, and having frigid and painful intercourse with him explains much of the attraction of the subject of witch hunts because the prosecutions and the lynchings were of people judged guilty of an impossible crime. While Jews, heretics, and homosexuals were guilty of being Jewish, heretical, and homosexual—common enough states and sometimes chosen voluntarily—no one can meet or mate with a concept such as the Devil. Thus, scholars have sought to understand the exotic, neurotic, and erotic mind-sets of Europeans, so seemingly different from those among our contemporaries influenced by the Enlightenment.[2] Along with trying to comprehend the mental structures of Europeans in the fifteenth to eighteenth centuries, historians and others have researched legal, political, social, and cultural systems in order to explain the playing out and representations of early modern belief systems.

*****

The *Encyclopedia of Witchcraft's* entries investigate the origins of the beliefs and practices of the early modern witch hunts; thus, many entries, certainly important in their own right, cover antiquity (the Hebrew Bible, Greece, and Rome); primitive Christianity; and the Early, central (High), and late Middle Ages. Some articles provide comparative perspectives (for example, "Africa, Sub-Saharan," "Native Americans," and "Islam"), but this is definitely not an encyclopedia of worldwide witchcraft, which would have required many more entries and would have taken several more years to finish. I dismissed the idea of such an encyclopedia because it would have turned the focus away from Europe's witch hunts, leaving several peripheries in search of a core. This encyclopedia excludes modern witchcraft, except for entries necessary to understand the period of the witch hunts (such as "Nazi Interest in Witch Persecution," "Halloween," and "Contemporary Witchcraft [Post-1800]") and for coverage at the end of some entries of the modern West.

There are diverse types of entries: biographies, elements of folklore, religion and theology, art, music, film, literature, theater, gender and sexuality, law, politics, institutions, and geography (cities, regions, states). The geographic entries usually include the dates of the first and last witchcraft trials and executions, the total number of accused witches executed, the gender of the accused or executed, and the population (in order to measure the intensity of prosecutions). However, the sources necessary to provide these types of information may not be extant, and the sources available do not always answer the questions scholars pose; thus, many entries could not incorporate all these data. There were inevitable limitations to the list of entries: Some subjects or areas have not been researched; for other topics, I could not locate contributors. To give one example, there are several entries on drama (England, Spain, and so forth), but other regions did not find their contributors.

The starting point for this encyclopedia was Rossell Hope Robbins's 1959 *Encyclopedia of Witchcraft and Demonology.* This magnificent, single-authored work reflects the scholarship current in the 1950s, is Anglocentric, and, as we know currently, is often incorrect. Research on the age of the witch hunts has rendered Robbins's encyclopedia obsolete, but it remains useful as a source of some factual information and as a good read. Subsequent encyclopedias in English have been less ambitious than Robbins's. The *Encyclopedia of Witchcraft: The Western Tradition,* however, contains both broader coverage geographically and historically on the witch hunts and more entries than any previous encyclopedia or dictionary of witchcraft. For instance, it more than triples the number of entries in Robbins's *Encyclopedia of Witchcraft and Demonology,* which, moreover, omits most of Europe behind the Iron Curtain. Rosemary Eileen Guiley's *Encyclopedia of Witches and Witchcraft* (1989) has 416 entries, but it offers as much if not more on modern witchcraft as on the era of the witch hunts. Two fine recent works are also limited by size and by being single-authored: Michael Bailey's *Historical Dictionary of Witchcraft* (2003) has brief entries on fewer than 200 pages, while William E. Burns's *Witch Hunts in Europe and America* (2003) is less than one-fifth the size of our *Encyclopedia of Witchcraft: The Western Tradition,* and does not have its range of entries.

Robbins's 227 entries provided the starting point for the six members of our editorial board and for me as editor. We then went to indexes in major books on witchcraft and compiled a list of possible entries, from which we selected those we thought appropriate. We added other topics. Finally, many contributors suggested entries. In actuality, the selection of entries continued while time permitted. Like early modern political absolutism, the encyclopedia seemed always to be in the making.

Germany, known famously as the heartland of the witch hunts, is the subject of the most entries (both geographical and biographical)—127. There are 70 entries covering England and Scotland; 62 on France; 50 on Italy; 24 on the Iberian Peninsula; 20 on eastern and southeastern Europe (Poland, Russia, Hungary, the Balkans, Slovenia, Croatia, Ukraine, Estonia, Latvia, and Lithuania); 20 on Austria, present-day Liechtenstein, the Czech Republic, and Slovakia; 18 on today's Low Countries; 17 on Switzerland; 17 on Scandinavia (including Iceland); 15 on the Americas; 2 on Ireland; and 1 on Malta. There would have been additional entries on eastern Europe and some other of Europe's islands had I been able to locate scholars to make those contributions.

While the bulk of entries covers the late Middle Ages and early modern Europe, the idol of origins will be appeased by the 25 entries on antiquity and 17 on the Early and High Middle Ages. These numbers significantly underplay the scope of the coverage of the periods prior to the witch hunts because numerous thematic and geographic entries discuss the ancient and medieval background.

Beyond exploring the subject matter contained in the entries, readers of the *Encyclopedia of Witchcraft: The Western Tradition* should appreciate the type of questions scholars now ask about the field of witchcraft studies, see what areas recent scholarship has examined, and hopefully perceive what topics and areas still need to be researched. This encyclopedia is very much a product of the first years of the twenty-first century; many cities and regions in the West need to be explored, new sources consulted, and coverage of wide-ranging topics expanded beyond the scope of a single scholar's expertise. The encyclopedia reflects the areas of expertise of its contributors, who (without false academic modesty) represent most of the leading experts in the Western world professing this specialization. Of course, solid experts on a subject in one geographic area, say France, England, or Germany, were often reluctant to venture beyond those boundaries to make entries truly Continent-wide. Their reluctance is understandable, given the explosion of contemporary scholarship, the difficulty in keeping abreast of research in any topic, and the rightful and well-considered hesitation of academics to discuss areas in which they lack significant knowledge grounded in their personal research. One can contrast this humble realization of limitations with the eagerness of talking heads, movie stars, politicians, "the person on the street," letter writers to newspapers and magazines, and random citizens to offer opinions on just about any subject, regardless of their knowledge. A truly ignorant person is one who does not know his or her own ignorance.

This encyclopedia has great value not only in showcasing witchcraft scholarship at one point in time but also in allowing anyone to compare rather quickly the skills, approaches, methodologies, and contributions of most of the best witchcraft scholars in the West. Such comparison was previously possible only through great and time-consuming efforts, if at all. It is my hope that the *Encyclopedia of Witchcraft: The Western Tradition* will bridge the gap between scholars and the general public by making the vast scholarship on witchcraft readily accessible. This encyclopedia offers a means for enjoyment, a singularly instructive (if mostly pessimistic) exploration of the human condition, and a milepost for our successors to see where they can now advance the field of witchcraft and witch-hunt studies.

—*Richard M. Golden*

Notes

1. Ronald Hutton, reviewing recent anthropological and historical studies on witchcraft, has constructed a model of a witch that has the following characteristics: a person who employs nonphysical means to bring misfortune or injury; harms neighbors or kin, not strangers; reaps social disapproval; works within a tradi-

tion; and can be opposed by others. Hutton did not consider "good" witchcraft, which is discussed in numerous entries in the *Encyclopedia of Witchcraft*. See his "Anthropological and Historical Approaches to Witchcraft: Potential for a New Collaboration?" *Historical Journal* 4, no. 2 (2004): 413–434.

2. While witchcraft scholars do not discuss the possibility of the Devil's existence in history (at least in this encyclopedia), polls in 2004 indicated that 70 percent of Americans believed in the Devil and that 78 percent believed in angels. See *Dallas Morning News*, July 3, 2004, G1.

K

KABBALAH

By the late Middle Ages, the occult tradition of Judaism was referred to most frequently by the generic term "Kabbalah," literally, "that which has been received." The term reflects the universally accepted attitude among Kabbalists that their teachings form part of the rabbinically sanctioned oral Torah, which complements the written Torah. Kabbalah is not monolithic, but comprises a collage of disparate doctrines and practices cultivated by elite circles within medieval rabbinic society.

Contemporary scholarship ordinarily distinguishes two major typological trends within the history of medieval Jewish mysticism: prophetic and theosophic Kabbalah. Prophetic Kabbalah, as expounded by Abraham Abulafia (thirteenth century) cultivates meditative practices centered on the permutation of letters (*tseruf ha-otiyyot*) of the Hebrew alphabet to attain ritual and moral purity. These exercises attempt to unfetter the rational soul from the body and facilitate its conjunction (*devequt*) with the divine intellect, a state also referred to as cleaving to the Name, that is, YHWH, which was thought to be the one true reality that encompassed all the other letters. Moreover, following Maimonides, Abulafia and his disciples viewed this unitive state as the true meaning of prophecy; for them the goal of Kabbalah was to overcome differentiation and be incorporated into the divine Name, which is the spiritual essence of the messianic ideal and the true meaning of the eschatological world-to-come.

Theosophic Kabbalah, by contrast, is concerned primarily with the visual contemplation of ten luminous emanations that collectively represent the configuration of *Ein Sof,* the infinite Godhead beyond all linguistic and iconic representation. The most emblematic term for these emanations was *sefirot,* initially employed in the first section of an older anthology of cosmological speculation, *Sefer Yesirah* (Book of Formation). Over time, Kabbalists developed allegedly new and more intricate images, based at least in part on principles from earlier sources, including, most importantly, the idea that the *sefirot* are comprised within the Tetragrammaton and thus are the name by which the nameless is called. Additionally, the *sefirot* assume the form of an anthropos in the human imagination; because Adam was created male and female, this divinely human image is androgynous. Therefore, Kabbalists portray the unity of God in the explicitly erotic language of heterosexual coupling. In the *Sefer ha-Zohar* (Book of Splendor, the major repository of Kabbalistic writings attributed to the mystical fraternity headed by Simeon bar Yohai of second-century Palestine, but actually composed in thirteenth- and fourteenth-century Castile), the coupling of male and female is the mystery of faith (*raza di-meheimanuta*).

Complex as Kabbalistic symbolism can be, it views gender very simply: the potency to overflow is masculine and the capacity to withhold feminine. Adopting an earlier rabbinic tradition, Kabbalists further link the male and female potencies, respectively, with the attributes of mercy and judgment, and their designated names *YHWH* and *Elohim.* Kabbalists interpret the traditional religious obligation to unify the God of Israel as the harmonizing of male and female, a pairing of the will to bestow and the desire to contain.

One must not oversimplify. Careful textual scrutiny indicates both that Kabbalists identified as "theosophic" had ecstatic experiences of union, and that Kabbalists labeled "ecstatic" presumed that esoteric gnosis imparted theosophic wisdom. Here, we shall concentrate on the convergence of the ecstatic and theurgic aspects of the experience of enlightenment cultivated by the so-called theosophic Kabbalists.

The Kabbalist's goal—what justifies calling him a Kabbalist—is to receive the secret of the Name; that is, to cleave to *YHWH,* the archaic Deuteronomistic injunction interpreted by Kabbalists (in a manner very close to twelfth-century Andalucian Neoplatonist philosopher-poets) as conjunction of thought (*devequt ha-mahshavah*), the true mystical intent (*kawwanah*) of liturgical worship, and Torah study. In another crucial way, this Kabbalistic ideal betrays crucial affinities to views in Islamic and other Jewish philosophical sources. Twelfth- and thirteenth-century Kabbalists, like later generations, understood this conjunction of intellectual and imaginative components as an expression of prophecy. However, in their case, the contemplative ascent is emphatically a personal experience of *unio mystica,* a more deeply expressed existential sense that the fragmented soul can attain wholeness by being reincorporated into the Godhead. Union with the divine

Name is a psychic transport (after having cleared mundane matters from the mind) that in turn facilitates the theurgical unification of the divine potencies signified by letters of the Name.

Although the mystical conjunction facilitates the theurgical task, it seems preferable to imagine a core experience of ecstasy with two facets, reintegration of the soul in the divine and fusion of the sefirotic potencies. It is tempting to align these two phases in causal sequence, the former occasioning the latter. However, viewed morphologically, as opposed to typologically, that is, under the semblance of form rather than type, ecstasy and theurgy become two manifestations of the same phenomenon.

The consonance of these two elements, too sharply bifurcated in dominant critical studies of Jewish mysticism, is necessitated by the ontological assumption regarding the divine/angelic status of the Jewish soul. This idea assumes that the righteous or holy ones of Israel have been endowed with an angelomorphic nature, a conception that evolved in late-second temple Judaism, probably based on still older ancient near-eastern forms of angelic or divine kingship. Medieval Kabbalists presumed that, because God and Israel are circumscribed within a monopsychic unity that flattens the difference between cause and effect, it follows that mystical union and theurgic unification are concurrent processes that have been artificially separated for extraneous reasons. In the final analysis, the two schools of Kabbalah shared many features: traditions about the secret names of God, particularly the most sacred name, *YHWH;* the unique status of Hebrew, the one language considered "natural" rather than conventional; the understanding of sefirotic potencies as the means to attain mystical communion; and the theurgical interpretation of ritual as the way to maintain the unity of multiple potencies within God.

One of the most significant elements shared by all Kabbalists is their inordinate emphasis on secrecy. Kabbalah is usually studied as a form of mysticism, but a far better term to capture its nature may be esotericism, although the two terms are not easily differentiated, especially with Kabbalistic material. Kabbalah's mystical dimensions are embedded within a hermeneutical framework of esotericism, and its esoteric dimensions within a phenomenological framework of mysticism.

With respect to secrecy, Kabbalists embrace a fundamental paradox also found in other religious cultures, but expressed in ways that reflect different theological, anthropological, and cosmological assumptions. Although truth is transmitted from generation to generation in a continuous chain—hence the term "Kabbalah"—it is a secret truth that cannot be disclosed in its entirety. These restrictions are not based on any need to hide the truth from those unworthy to receive it, a stance affirmed by Kabbalists, but are due

to the enigmatic nature of the mystery, the doubling of secrecy engendered by the fact that, to remain secret, it can be divulged only if it is concealed in its disclosure. This orientation, probably inherent in the esoteric texture of Kabbalah, was enunciated explicitly by sixteenth-century Kabbalists in Safed, utilizing a maxim taken from the Muslim philosopher Avicenna, "disclosure is the cause of concealment and concealment the cause of disclosure" (Wolfson 2002, 113–114).

Kabbalistic sources often justify secrecy with the biblical verse, "To investigate the matter is the glory of kings, but to conceal the matter is the glory of God" (Ps. 25:2). It is no exaggeration to say that Psalmist's text served as an oracle posted on the walls of the small elitist circles, where specific secrets concerning both symbols and rites have been transmitted orally and in writing, although the eventual proliferation of the latter usually posed a challenge to the explicit injunction against disclosing secrets publicly. Of course, not every written exposition of occult knowledge defies this injunction; some Kabbalists mastered the art of concealing secrets by revealing them. One might say that the form of esoteric writing—to conceal in the exposition and expose in the concealment—is the hermeneutical method that allowed Kabbalists to explicate their esoteric knowledge. As Abulafia elegantly expressed it, "My intention is to hide and to reveal, to reveal and to hide, for the truth is deep for the enlightened and how much more so for the ignorant!" (Sitrei Torah, MS Paris, Bibliothèque Nationale 774, fol. 149a).

The same principle characterizes Zoharic literature. Mysteries of Torah are disclosed through being hidden, an exegetical pattern perceptible in the Torah. Its exoteric and esoteric layers of meaning are distinguishable, but the latter can only be expressed through the former. The initiated in the mystical teaching sees the secret through the garment of the text, rather than discarding it to behold the naked truth. The greatest of veils would be for one to think that one could see the face of God unveiled; the final veil to remove, therefore, is the veil of thinking it possible to see without any veil. For Kabbalists, the ultimate veil is the Tetragrammaton, the name that is the Torah in its mystical essence.

The minds of Kabbalists, again without distinguishing between theosophic and prophetic camps, reveal an intricate nexus between esotericism and eroticism. Indeed, it would be no exaggeration to say that one enters the heart of Kabbalah by marking the precise spot where the erotic and the esoteric intersect—a spot providing entry into the garden of mystical secrets. From the Kabbalists' vantage point, the ecstatic experience of enlightenment facilitates knowing the eros of mystery wrapped in the exposé of the mystery of eros.

ELLIOT R. WOLFSON

See also: BIBLE; JEWS, WITCHCRAFT, AND MAGIC; OCCULT.

References and further reading:
Hallamish, Moshe. 1999. *An Introduction to the Kabbalah.*
Translated by Ruth Bar-Ilan and Ora Wiskind-Elper. Albany:
State University of New York Press.
Idel, Moshe. 1988a. *Kabbalah: New Perspectives.* New Haven and
London: Yale University Press.
———. 1988b. *The Mystical Experience in Abraham Abulafia.*
Translated by Jonathan Chipman. Albany: State University of
New York Press.
Scholem, Gershom. 1954. *Major Trends in Jewish Mysticism.* New
York: Schocken Books.
———. 1969. *On the Kabbalah and Its Symbolism.* Translated by
Ralph Manheim. New York: Schocken Books.
———. 1987. *Origins of the Kabbalah.* Edited by R. J. Zwi
Werblowsky. Translated by Allan Arkush. Princeton, NJ:
Princeton University Press.
———. 1991. *On the Mystical Shape of the Godhead: Basic Concepts
in the Kabbalah.* Translated by Joachim Neugroschel, edited
and revised by Jonathan Chipman. New York: Schocken Books.
Wolfson, Elliot. 1994. *Through a Speculum That Shines: Vision and
Imagination in Medieval Jewish Mysticism.* Princeton, NJ:
Princeton University Press.
———. 2000. *Abraham Abulafia—Kabbalist and Prophet:
Hermeneutics, Theosophy, and Theurgy.* Los Angeles: Cherub.
———. 2002. "Divine Suffering and the Hermeneutics of
Reading: Philosophical Reflections on Lurianic Mythology."
Pp. 101–162 in *Suffering Religion.* Edited by Robert Gibbs and
Elliot R. Wolfson. London and New York: Routledge.

KEMPTEN, PRINCE-ABBEY OF

The imperial abbey (*Fürstabtei* or *Fürststift*) of
Kempten is famous for a very late execution, usually
labeled the last legal execution of a witch in the Holy
Roman Empire. The case was mentioned already in the
mid-nineteenth century (Haas 1865) and widely popularized by Soldan and Heppe's history of witchcraft
trials (Soldan and Heppe 1880). In 1892, Von Wachter reliably paraphrased the surviving contemporary copy of a
legal opinion—still in place in the Kempten archive in
the late 1980s, but which seems to have disappeared
recently. According to the document, a death sentence
was issued in 1775. This legal opinion referred to the
prehistory of the case in much detail and described the
entire life story of a mentally disturbed woman of about
forty, who had suffered considerable hardships
(orphanage, leprosy, lameness), and had converted,
hoping to marry a Protestant lover, who abandoned her
soon afterward. She gained the impression that he
might have been a diabolical seducer, and felt great guilt
for renouncing the saints, and the Virgin Mary in particular. Because of her incapacities, she was put in a
workhouse at Langenegg, where she incited other
female inmates with her fantasies. At some stage she
was accused by a possessed five-year-old girl and beaten
by other female inmates. The director of the workhouse
tried to calm the tumult, but in consequence of their
shared fantasies, one of the female inmates eventually
delivered her to the authorities. If we can trust the
records, torture was not used in her trial. The criminal
court of the prince-abbey dealt with her case from
February 20. Because she maintained her stories of devilish possession, a Devil's pact, and apostasy, the high
judge came to the conclusion that she had to be convicted according to criminal law, although she denied
harmful magic. The prince-abbot, Honorius Roth von
Schreckenstein (ruled 1760–1785), signed the death
sentence on April 11, adding the words: *fiat iustitia* (let
justice be done)! This is exactly what one could expect
from a prince-abbot who in 1774 had invited the controversial exorcist Johann Joseph Gassner, notorious for
claiming that all diseases were caused by witchcraft.
Gassner's booklet on how to fight the Devil effectively,
Nützlicher Unterricht wider den Teufel zu streiten (Useful
Instruction on How to Struggle Against the Devil), was
first printed at Kempten in 1774.

Although no newspaper reported her execution,
there seemed little doubt that it actually took place. A
local lawyer even published a booklet on the case in the
early 1890s, amplifying the whole story with more
details. However, a local archivist recently started digging deeper in local sources and found that her death
sentence was never carried out. Although a conservative
faction within the government supported the conviction, another faction fiercely denied the possibility of
witchcraft and the legality of the trial, even if witchcraft
remained in the law codes. But in the decade after the
Bavarian War of the Witches, under the rule of the
enlightened emperor Joseph II, even Benedictine
monks were able to attack witchcraft publicly. The
already convicted witch, Maria Anna Schwägelin
(1734–1781), was imprisoned and died six years later.
Hers was a witchcraft trial, but can no longer exemplify
the final execution in the Holy Roman Empire. In his
legal opinion, the high judge, named Treichlinger,
referred to an earlier execution of a witch in 1755, in
which he had participated, as a precedent within the
prince-abbey. Even if this case cannot yet be verified
from other sources (and no other local case was referred
to in this legal opinion), it implied that the
prince-abbey of Kempten shared the experience of late
executions with a few other southern German ecclesiastical territories, but also that they must have been
extremely rare events.

This surprising turn enables us to tell a completely
different story of witchcraft trials in the prince-abbey,
setting the events of 1775 in perspective. A thousand
years earlier, in 772, the Benedictine abbot of St. Gallen
founded a monastery at Kempten, near the ruins of an
ancient Roman town, which had succeeded a Celtic settlement. The Carolingians used the monastery as a
bridgehead in an Alemannic region. In 1062, the Holy
Roman Emperor Henry IV made Kempten an imperial
abbey; in 1360, Emperor Charles IV elevated it to the
status of a prince-abbey. Its prince-abbots managed a

territory of about 50,000 inhabitants, making Kempten one of the largest monastic lands within the Holy Roman Empire. However, its road to state formation was rocky. By 1289, the town of Kempten became an imperial city and escaped the abbot's rule. After 1525, this imperial city of just about 4,000 inhabitants became Protestant. Likewise, the local nobility managed to become independent, and joined the Imperial Knighthood of Swabia. The abbacy was thus reduced to seven market towns and eighty-five villages. And because other estates were lacking, peasants sat in the parliament (*Landschaft*) of this extraordinary territory. These peasants were particularly self-confident and challenged their feudal overlords in numerous rebellions, including the great peasant war in 1524/1525.

Through the activities of capable local historians and an interested local public, Kempten's history has been particularly well explored. Extensive publications on the history of the imperial city and the imperial abbey revealed few incidents of sorcery or witchcraft, and almost no executions for witchcraft. In an early case of 1484, presumably linked to the activities of Heinrich Kramer, author of the *Malleus Maleficarum* (The Hammer of Witches, 1486), in the region, an accuser—not the witch—was punished in the market town of Unterthingau. In 1549, a village collectively accused a woman of damaging their crops by making hailstorms. The local lord, Veit Werdenstein von Eberspach, tried to convince the witch to retract her spells, but the peasant woman ridiculed him publicly. The nobleman and his villagers appealed to the prince-abbot's government. The Kempten high court scrutinized the case, but concluded that it was impossible to substantiate the accusation and open a formal criminal trial. Under Abbot Wolfgang von Grünenstein (ruled 1535–1557), the prince-abbey's government withstood repeated attempts by villagers to imprison or to punish this alleged witch, because there was no convincing circumstantial evidence; it eventually threatened the villagers with severe punishment if they did not stop harassing her. When witch hunting peaked in the region around 1590, the prince-abbey did not participate in the persecutions. When the prince-bishop of Augsburg tried to extend his persecution into Kempten's territory, Prince-Abbot Johann Erhard Blarer von Wartensee (ruled 1587–1594) was prepared to offer military resistance to invasions by foreign troops.

In 1673, we hear for the first time that a woman was burned for witchcraft within the prince-abbey, at Martinszell. A few years later, in 1687, after witchcraft trials had shaken the imperial city for the second time since 1664–1665, Prince-Abbot Rupert Bodman (ruled 1678–1728) denied the extradition of a peasant woman, because his government considered the circumstantial evidence against her insufficient. By then,

Bodman had already gained deep insights into the treatment of witchcraft. When Count Ferdinand Carl Franz von Hohenems resumed massive persecution between 1677–1680, burning large numbers of subjects within the county of Vaduz, the imperial administration of Leopold I (ruled 1658–1705) intervened and appointed Prince-Abbot Bodman to investigate. He condemned the lack of circumstantial evidence, the "unchristian torture," and the obvious financial interest the count had taken in his persecutions. Bodman took on not just the responsibility of inquiring the case and suggesting an appropriate sentence, but even took care that this severe sentence was indeed enacted.

After convicting the count in the *Reichshofrat* (imperial aulic court), the emperor commissioned the prince-abbot of Kempten to lead a Habsburg army that eventually captured Count von Hohenems in 1681. The emperor stripped the count of Vaduz of his rights in 1684, and had him imprisoned in the prince-abbot's dungeon, where he died after years of confinement. From 1681 to 1712, the Benedictine abbot of Kempten administered the count's territories, before they were awarded to the princes of Liechtenstein, who still rule it. Rich and noble as the Kempten Benedictines were, at least this abbot did not hesitate to convict another rich and noble ruler for his crimes, and to enforce the most drastic treatment of an aristocratic witch hunter anywhere in the history of the Holy Roman Empire. Possibly Bodman was the most qualified of all Kempten's abbots: he had studied at the universities of Strasbourg, Salzburg, and Padua, and spoke fluent French, Italian, and Spanish in addition to Latin and German.

The prince-abbey of Kempten, formerly stigmatized for its late executions, can now serve as an example for ecclesiastical territories that carefully avoided witch hunts. If we look for explanations, we find a striking absence of religious zeal during the period of the Counter-Reformation and the Thirty Years' War. The Benedictines were certainly Catholic, but they clearly did not share the austerity that characterized Catholic piety elsewhere in this period. For instance, all prince-abbots of Kempten had concubines and children, as the chroniclers in the neighboring Protestant imperial city of Kempten meticulously and maliciously recorded. In 1594, papal visitors lamented that the Benedictines of Kempten all lived in private houses instead of cells, that they wore secular clothes with rich jewelry, and that they spent their time on drinking, hunting, gambling, and women. The abbots of this wealthy sinecure were usually not religious zealots, and their attitude toward sin, like their attitude toward women, seems noticeably more relaxed than those of most Counter-Reformation bishops. Although Abbot Bodman was more serious in his religious attitude, his government seems to have been characterized by a relaxed attitude, because he granted his subjects the pleasure of smoking and founded new breweries. Furthermore, he improved his territory by commissioning water pipelines and bridges, postal services, and fishing ponds; he replaced feudal services by taxes, regulated social relationships within his territories by means of contracts, and introduced professional health service and firefighters in his prince-abbey.

WOLFGANG BEHRINGER

See also: BAVARIAN WAR OF THE WITCHES; ECCLESIASTICAL TERRITORIES (HOLY ROMAN EMPIRE); EXECUTIONS; GASSNER, JOHANN JOSEPH; HISTORIOGRAPHY; HOLY ROMAN EMPIRE; JOSEPH II, HOLY ROMAN EMPEROR; KRAMER, HEINRICH; VADUZ, COUNTY OF.

References and further reading:
Behringer, Wolfgang. 1997. *Witchcraft Persecutions in Bavaria. Popular Magic, Religious Zealotry and Reason of State in Early Modern Europe.* Translated by J. C. Grayson and David Lederer. Cambridge: Cambridge University Press.
Haas, Carl. 1865. *Die Hexenprozesse. Ein culturhistorischer Versuch nebst Dokumenten.* Tübingen: H. Laupp'schen Buchhandlung.
Petz, Wolfgang. 1998. "Das Schicksal der Maria Anna Schwegele [. . .]," Pp. 225–227 in *"Bürgerfleiss und Fürstenglanz." Reichsstadt und Fürstabtei Kempten.* Edited by Wolfgang Jahn. Augsburg: Haus der bayrischen Geschichte.
Soldan, Wilhelm Georg, and Heinrich Heppe. 1880. *Geschichte der Hexenprozesse.* Stuttgart: Cotta.
Wachter, Georg Friedrich von. 1892. "Der letzte Hexenprozess des Stifts Kempten." *Allgäuer Geschichtsfreund,* NF. 5: 8–63.

KEPLER, JOHANNES (1571–1630)

One of the most intriguing episodes of the Scientific Revolution was Galileo Galilei's trial before the Roman Inquisition, but hardly less significant was the fate of Johannes Kepler, who had to flee the Catholic Counter-Reformation at several places, was exiled from his Lutheran homeland Württemberg for refusing to sign the Formula of Concord, and eventually became entangled in an endless witchcraft trial against his mother, Katharina Kepler.

His father Heinrich Kepler (1547–1590) owned the tavern *Zum Engel* in the tiny imperial free city Weil der Stadt; his mother Katharina (1551–1621) was the daughter of an innkeeper and village judge at Eltingen, Melchior Guldenmann. Kepler's parents settled in Leonberg, a Württemberg town, but family life was strained, and Heinrich left in 1589, leaving behind Katharina and four children. In 1608, Margaretha, the lone daughter, married a Protestant theologian, Georg Binder, who became pastor in nearby Heumaden (today a suburb of Stuttgart). One son, Christoph, became an artisan, married a woman from Eltingen, and settled in Leonberg. Another son, Heinrich, became a soldier and died young, after returning to his mother's house.

Their brother Johannes was allowed to study at the University of Tübingen. The astronomer Michael Mästlin (1550–1631) aroused his enthusiasm for astronomy and mathematics, and, after graduating in 1594, Kepler was hired as a professor of mathematics by the estates of Inner Austria at Graz, a Habsburg territory with Protestant nobility and close links to Tübingen. There Kepler published his *Mysterium Cosmographicum* (Mystery of the Cosmos, 1596), attempting to combine the Copernican system with Neoplatonic ideas. Under the impact of the Counter-Reformation—Martín Del Rio was teaching at the Jesuit College in Graz—Kepler was exiled. Supported by the Bavarian chancellor Johann Georg Herwarth von Hohenburg, a long-standing correspondent, Kepler managed to succeed Tycho Brahe as imperial court astronomer in Prague. In this position, Kepler suggested that God spoke in the language of mathematics and interpreted the movements of the planets in mathematical equations (Kepler's Laws), one of the major achievements of the Scientific Revolution. He published some important books on Copernican cosmology, the *Astronomia Nova* (New Astronomy, 1609), a *Dissertatio cum Nuncio Sidereo* (Discussion of the Starry Messenger, 1610), and *Dioptrice,* a book about optics (1611). During this period, Kepler invited Galileo to settle in Germany, where everybody was free to think and publish whatever he wished. However, Kepler's situation deteriorated sooner than Galileo's. After the death of the Holy Roman Emperor Rudolf II (ruled 1576–1612), his position as imperial astronomer was confirmed by Emperor Mathias I (ruled 1612–1619), and even by Ferdinand II (ruled 1619–1637), who had exiled him from Graz. But Kepler preferred to settle at Linz, where the Protestant estates of Lower Austria employed him as professor of mathematics.

In 1615, his sister Margaretha informed him that their mother was involved in a bitter feud with neighbors at Leonberg, who had accused her of witchcraft. There were no extensive witch hunts in the duchy of Württemberg, but precisely in 1615 a number of women were burned at Leonberg. When a neighbor, Ursula Reinbold, accused his mother of witchcraft, Christoph Kepler sued her for slander. However, the litigation was delayed, since the Reinbold family found an ally in the district judge, Luther Einhorn, who had been rejected by Katharina Kepler as a husband for her daughter. Another ally was a local doctor who had become court physician to Prince Achilles Friedrich of Württemberg. The Reinbold faction began threatening Katharina Kepler physically, and eventually claimed material damages for the harm done to their children through her maleficent witchcraft. In autumn 1616, Johannes Kepler brought his mother to Linz. However, the stubborn lady returned to Heumaden in Württemberg, where the quarrels continued. Kepler tried to protect his mother by intensifying his contacts with Württemberg's ruling elite. The famous lawyer Dr. Christoph Besold (1577–1638) and the theologian Wilhelm Bidembach served as informants and supporters. However, because Kepler had refused to sign the Formula of Concord, the duchy's orthodox Lutherans, including his former teacher Mathias Hafenreffer, emphasized Kepler's dissidence.

At this point, Johannes Kepler traveled to Württemberg, attempting to influence the decision of its *Hofgericht* (high court). Besold urged Kepler to take his mother back to Linz, and in November 1617, Kepler obtained official assurance that her departure did not constitute "flight," providing circumstantial evidence for her guilt. However, Katharina Kepler decided to stay in Württemberg, even returning to her house at Leonberg in June 1618. Besold kept warning Johannes Kepler about the machinations of Judge Einhorn. Seeking her estate, the Reinbold family commissioned a lawyer, Dr. Philipp Jacob Weyhenmayer, to compile evidence of Katherina Kepler's witchcraft. In August 1619, he presented fifty-two articles, and a formal inquisition into her case was started in winter 1619–1620, hearing numerous witnesses, while Judge Einhorn delayed the Kepler family's countersuit for slander.

On July 24, 1620, the Württemberg aulic council decided to imprison Katharina Kepler, and on August 7, 1620, she was jailed at Leonberg. Christoph Kepler immediately protested and succeeded in having her transferred to a prison in Güglingen. Johannes Kepler tried to intervene through Christoph Besold, before reaching Güglingen himself in September 1620. He commissioned a formal defense, presumably supported or authored by Besold and/or Bidembach, which was submitted to the *Hofgericht* on May 7, 1621, The ducal vice-chancellor, Dr. Sebastian Faber, arranged that this case reached the court's agenda within a few weeks. Councilor Hieronymus Gabelkover gave his opinion by July 14, and the case went to the legal faculty of the University of Tübingen (to which Besold belonged) in August 1621. On September 10, 1621, they ruled that Katharina Kepler was to be tortured at the lowest grade, the *territio,* which in practice meant that the instruments of torture were shown to her before a formal interrogation. Their very precise decision explicitly forbade the hangman to touch her, or even bind her. Under these circumstances, Katharina Kepler would not confess, and on October 3, 1621, Duke Johann Friedrich von Württemberg (ruled 1608–1628) ordered her set free. When the local court finally complied some days later, Katharina Kepler had been imprisoned for 405 days. She died six months later, in April 1622.

Like many contemporaries, Johannes Kepler was acutely aware of freedom of conscience and suppression. He must have been deeply impressed by his mother's fate, although he admitted openly that, like many old people, she was indeed quarrelsome, difficult, and stubborn. It is striking that his own stubbornness caused him enormous difficulties, since the Lutheran superintendent of Linz, a Württemberger, suspected him of being Calvinist while simultaneously conspiring with the Jesuits. These accusations provoked fierce debate within the parliament of Lower Austria before a precarious favorable decision saved his position at Linz.

About the same time, Kepler published his *Harmonice Mundi Libri Quinque* (Five Books of the Harmony of the World, 1619), dedicated to King James I of England, a Neoplatonic interpretation of the universe as inspired by eternal harmony. His claim that God spoke in the language of mathematics implied that orthodox (but mathematically illiterate) theologians were unable to understand God's word. By Easter 1626, the Counter-Reformation in Lower Austria drove Kepler from Linz. He retired to the imperial city of Ulm, where he published the *Tabulae Rudolphinae* (Rudolphine Tables, 1627), then to Regensburg, both Protestant towns. In 1628, Imperial Generalissimo Albrecht von Wallenstein employed Kepler, and he moved to Sagan in Silesia. In autumn 1630, Kepler decided to return to Austria, but died en route.

Four years later his son Ludwig Kepler (1607–1663) published a manuscript that had played a role in his grandmother's witchcraft trial. After the invention of the telescope, Johannes Kepler had written his *Somnium seu Astronomia lunari* (Dream, or Lunar Astronomy, 1634). Influenced by Plutarch and Lucian, Kepler invented a literary framework for descriptions of the moon, where the possibilities of getting there were discussed ironically. According to Aristotelian physics, dry and thin Spaniards were likely to be attracted by the moon, but Kepler preferred employing an old hag to beam his hero up—and in this story the hero calls his mother a witch. In 1611, Kepler sent copies of this manuscript to Tübingen and other places, where they were recopied and circulated. Kepler suspected that readers identified him with the hero of his story and that his intellectual joke had played a role in the witchcraft trial against his mother.

WOLFGANG BEHRINGER

See also: AUSTRIA; FERDINAND II, HOLY ROMAN EMPEROR; RUDOLF II, HOLY ROMAN EMPEROR; SCIENCE AND MAGIC; WÜRTTEMBERG, DUCHY OF.

References and further reading:

Baumgardt, Carola. 1951. *Johannes Kepler. Life and Letters.* Introduction by Albert Einstein. New York: Philosophical Library.
Caspar, Max. 1993. *Kepler.* Translated by Owen Gingerich. New York: Dover.
Conner, James A. 2004. *Kepler's Witch: An Astronomer's Discovery of Cosmic Order Amid Religious War, Political Intrigue, and the Heresy Trial of His Mother.* New York: HarperCollins.

Hemleben, Johannes. 1971. *Johannes Kepler.* Hamburg: Rowohlt.

Kepler, Johannes. 1634. *Somnium seu Opus posthumum de Astronomia Lunari.* Frankfurt/Main.

———. 1929. *Astronomia Nova.* Edited by Max Caspar. Berlin: R. Oldenbourg.

———. 1937–1959. *Gesammelte Werke.* Edited by Max Caspar. 20 vols. Munich: C. H. Beck.

———. 1965. *Kepler's Dream.* With the full text and notes of *Somnium, sive Astronomia lunaris Joannis Kepleri.* Edited by John Lear. Translated by Patricia Frueh Kirkwood. Berkeley, CA: University of California Press.

———. 1997. *The Harmony of the World.* Edited by E. J. Aiton, A. M. Duncan, and J. V. Field. Philadelphia: American Philosophical Society.

Sutter, Berthold. 1979. *Der Hexenprozess gegen Katharina Kepler.* Weil der Stadt: Scharpf.

KISS OF SHAME

The kiss of shame, also known as the *osculum infame* or the obscene kiss, was believed to be an act of worship performed at the witches' Sabbat. The Devil appeared to the witches in the form of a goat or other animal and his followers kissed him on the anus, genitals, or feet. The kiss had its origins in Roman propaganda against Jews, conspirators, and early Christians. Christian authorities later used the kiss against medieval heretics. It appeared in depictions of the witches' Sabbat used to illustrate early modern demonological texts, and in medieval and early modern literature, notably Geoffrey Chaucer's *Miller's Tale* (late fourteenth century) and Hans (Johann) Jakob Christoph von Grimmelshausen's *Simplicissimus* (The Adventures of Simplicius Simplicissimus, 1669). The kiss of shame had several functions: as a parody of the kiss of peace in the Christian Eucharist; an act of fealty; an act of illicit sexual activity (premarital fornication, adultery, or bestiality); a humiliation; and a means of denoting the dishonor of the performer.

In his *Octavius* (late second century), Minucius Felix, a Christian apologist, recorded the rumor that Christians worshipped the head of a donkey and reverenced the genitals of their priests. He separated the two essential elements of the kiss of shame, which were later

Witches at a Sabbat offer the kiss of shame to the Devil's anus. (Art Archive/Dagli Orti)

conflated: worship of an animal considered to be abject in the dominant culture; and adoration of an unclean part of the body. The English cleric Walter Map in the late twelfth century and Pope Gregory IX in 1233 both claimed that contemporary heretics worshipped a large black cat by kissing it on the feet, under the tail, or on the genitals. The Waldensians, Gregory stated, had also to kiss a huge toad (or a goose or a duck) on the behind or the mouth, and afterward a mysterious pale, ice-cold being. The notion that Waldensians worshipped the Devil in the form of an animal persisted into the fifteenth century. Illustrations to Johann Tinctor's (Johannes Tinctoris; Jean Taincture) *Contra sectam Valdensium* (Against the Waldensian Sect, ca. 1460) depicted a heretic about to kiss a goat on the anus. King Philip IV of France used this propaganda in his attack on the Knights Templar in 1307. He accused the knights of revering a Satanic cat by removing their hats, bowing to it, and kissing it on the anus.

Although the kiss of shame cannot be found in the *Malleus Maleficarum* (The Hammer of Witches, 1486), at the height of the witch persecutions it was incorporated into later demonological texts, pamphlet accounts of trials, and images depicting the heretical witches' Sabbat. For example, the kiss appeared in a colored woodcut in a news-sheet reporting the witchcraft trials in Geneva in 1570, now in the Zürich collection known as the *Wickiana*, and a century later it was still the central image of an illustration for Johannes Prätorius's *Blockes-Berges Verrichtung* (Performance at the Blocksberg, 1668). In these images, the kiss of shame (clearly a parody of the kiss of peace) illustrated the fealty of the witch heretic to the Devil, and therefore her abandonment of God and the inversion of spiritual norms. It also indicated her sexual promiscuity and lack of chastity: if single, she could not marry the Devil; if married, she was committing adultery with him. The pamphlet *Newes from Scotland* (1591) introduced English readers to a different version of the kiss of shame. It reported that the North Berwick witches were forced to kiss the Devil's buttocks as a humiliating penance because they had "tarried overlong" in performing their evil duties. Both Chaucer and Grimmelshausen also used the kiss as a gesture of humiliation in their works. In *The Miller's Tale*, Alison granted her suitor Absalon a kiss, but he ended up kissing her "naked arse." In *Simplicissimus*, some soldiers were forced to kiss the backsides of the peasants who had captured them before being shot. In a further episode, an impersonator of the eponymous hero refused a duel and was forced instead to kiss the backsides of the sheep he had intended to steal. The duel provided an honorable means of resolving conflict; kissing sheep, or goats in the case of witches, was an act of bestiality that

incurred personal dishonor, social exclusion, and the punishment of exile or death.

JONATHAN DURRANT

See also: BLACK MASS; CATS; GOAT; GREGORY IX, POPE; NORTH BERWICK WITCHES; PAMPHLETS AND NEWSPAPERS; PRÄTORIUS, JOHANNES; SABBAT; TEMPLARS; TINCTOR, JOHANN; *VAUDOIS* (WALDENSIANS).

References and further reading:

Chaucer, Geoffrey. 1971. *The Canterbury Tales.* Harmondsworth: Penguin.
Cohn, Norman. 1975. *Europe's Inner Demons: An Enquiry Inspired by the Great Witch-Hunt.* New York: Basic Books.
Gregory IX. 2001. "*Vox in Rama (1233).*" Pp. 114–116 in *Witchcraft in Europe 400–1700. A Documentary History.* 2d ed. Edited by Alan Charles Kors and Edward Peters. Revised by Edward Peters. Philadelphia: University of Pennsylvania Press.
Grimmelshausen, Johann Jakob Christoffel von. 1999. *Simplicissimus.* Translated by Mike Mitchell. Sawtry: Dedalus.
Russell, Jeffrey Burton. 1972. *Witchcraft in the Middle Ages.* Ithaca, NY: Cornell University Press.

KRAMER (INSTITORIS), HEINRICH (CA. 1430–1505)

Kramer (in Latin, Institoris), a Dominican friar and inquisitor, achieved a dubious kind of immortality by publishing the first comprehensive handbook for witch hunters, the *Malleus Maleficarum* (The Hammer of Witches, 1486), which not only described the crime luridly but gave detailed instructions to help lay judges as well as inquisitors conduct witchcraft trials and also did much to associate the crime of witchcraft with women. His career as a witch-hunting inquisitor, however, suggests a pattern of failure and frustration.

Born in Sélestat (Schlettstadt), an imperial city in Alsace, Kramer's father may have been a retailer, as his German name suggests. That Institoris is the Latin form of his original German name is proved by the *Nürnberger Hexenhammer* (Nuremberg Witches' Hammer), a secular witch hunt instruction from 1491 written in his own hand, where he named himself Heinrich Kramer. He probably entered the Dominican monastery of his native city about the age of fifteen, rising through the order and becoming master of theology by 1474. Being well suited for this profession, he was also appointed inquisitor that same year. By 1475, he was involved in gathering evidence about earlier Jewish ritual murders in south Germany to help with the famous Jew-baiting ritual murder case of the "child-saint" Simon at Trent (the capital of the prince-bishopric of Trent, now Trento in Italy). In 1478, he was promoted to inquisitor of upper (i.e., southern) Germany.

Kramer's first experiences with witchcraft trials date from the 1480s in the Rhineland, mainly in his homeland, Alsace. Encountering some opposition, he went to Rome and obtained the famous bull *Summis desiderantes*

(Desiring with Supreme Ardor) from the new Pope Innocent VIII in December 1484, directed at the bishop of Strasbourg. Afterward, named papal inquisitor in upper Germany, he moved to the diocese of Constance, which covered the greater part of southern Swabia. However, his attempted persecutions of witches in the imperial city of Ravensburg, and especially the Tyrolean capital Innsbruck, miscarried dramatically.

Starting in July 1485, Kramer's inquisition at Innsbruck was conducted through intimidation, limitless torture, denial of legal defense, and distorted reports. Not just the relatives of the accused, but also the citizens of the capital, the clergy, and the Tyrolean nobility protested against Kramer's procedures. The bishop of Brixen, Georg Golser, appointed a commission to investigate his inquisition, which interrogated seven imprisoned women on October 4. Over Kramer's desperate resistance, the bishop stopped the persecution on October 29, nullified its results, and, with the Tyrolean archduke's approval, liberated all the imprisoned women on November 2. Nine days later, the bishop formally requested the inquisitor to leave his diocese; by February 1486, Golser threatened to use force if Kramer did not leave Tyrol immediately.

Kramer sought revenge for such bitter defeats by composing his notorious treatise *Malleus Maleficarum*, published in 1486, with a second edition in 1487 that included the 1484 papal bull. The formerly assumed coauthorship of Jacob Sprenger has been convincingly refuted, and the notarial document giving approval from the theological faculty of the University of Cologne was a forgery.

There was evidence of pathological elements in Kramer's personality; Bishop Golser thought he was mad. Everywhere he picked quarrels and became disliked; soon the wandering inquisitor departed, sometimes exiled. Kramer's misogyny was extreme even for a medieval monk, and his sadism was mixed with prurience; he was accused of illegally investigating sexual affairs of women. In his *Nuremberg Witches' Hammer*, Kramer approved a "reserved" use of torture to avoid releasing women who did not confess after undergoing it. Kramer's boasts of having burned 200 women at the stake in 1491 seem greatly exaggerated. At first, popes protected him, but the jurists at the Roman Curia did not share his opinions and hindered his activities with uncomfortable bulls.

In 1500, Pope Alexander VI, at the instigation of the bishop of Olomouc, Stanislav Thurzo, named Kramer papal inquisitor to Moravia and Bohemia. He moved to Olomouc (Olmütz), which boasted an important Dominican monastery, and devoted himself to literary polemics. In April 1501, he published two tracts at Olomouc against Czech heresies, but never began any inquisitorial trials against them; and so far as we know, he made no further attempt to conduct witchcraft trials. He died in Olomouc in 1505, but his grave has not yet been found.

GÜNTER JEROUSCHEK

See also: GOLSER, GEORG; INNOCENT VIII, POPE; INNSBRUCK; *MALLEUS MALEFICARUM;* MORAVIA; RITUAL MURDER.
References and further reading:
Broedel, Hans Peter. 2003. *The* Malleus Maleficarum *and the Construction of Witchcraft: Theology and Popular Belief.* Manchester and New York: Manchester University Press.
Jerouschek, Günter, ed. 1992. *Malleus Maleficarum.* Zürich, Hildesheim, and New York: Olms.
———. 1992. *Nürnberger Hexenhammer.* Zürich, Hildesheim, and New York: Olms.
———. 2003. "Heinrich Kramer—Zur Psychologie des Hexenjägers." Pp. 113–137 in *Gewalt und ihre Legitimation im Mittelalter.* Edited by Guenther Mensching. Würzburg: Koenigshausen and Neumann.
Kramer (Institoris), Heinrich. 2003. *Malleus Maleficarum. KommentierteNeübersetzung* [new German translation from Latin]. Edited by Wolfgang Behringer, Günter Jerouschek, and Werner Tschacher. Introduction by Wolfgang Behringer and Günter Jerouschek. 3d ed. Munich: DTV.
Segl, Peter, ed. 1988. *Der Hexenhammer. Entstehung und Umfeld des Malleus Maleficarum.* Cologne and Vienna: Bohlau.
Stephens, Walter. 2002. *Demon Lovers: Witchcraft, Sex, and the Crisis of Belief.* Chicago: University of Chicago Press.

KYTELER, ALICE
(CA. 1260/1265–AFTER 1324)

The trial of Alice Kyteler for heresy and sorcery in 1324 is the only such case known from medieval Ireland. It was significant for three reasons. First, it was one of the earliest trials in European history to link sorcery with heresy. Second, it was the first to treat the defendants as members of an organized group. Third, it was the first to accuse a woman of having acquired the power of sorcery by means of sexual intercourse with a demon. Our information about the trial derives from a single manuscript, generally referred to as the *Narrative* because of the title (A Narrative of the Proceedings Against Dame Alice Kyteler) given to it by Thomas Wright in his edition of 1843. Although the *Narrative* is unsigned, it is clear from internal evidence that its author was Alice Kyteler's accuser, Richard Ledrede, bishop of Ossory (1317–ca. 1360).

We know little about Alice. William Outlaw, the son of her first marriage was appointed "sovereign" (equivalent to mayor) of Kilkenny in 1305, suggesting that she was born ca. 1260–1265. Her family was Flemish. In 1277, William le Kyteler of Ieper (Ypres) was granted a safe conduct to trade in Ireland. He settled there and, by 1303, had become sheriff of the liberty of Kilkenny. Joseph de Ketteler (perhaps William's son or brother) died in 1286/1287 and was buried at Kilkenny. Alice was presumably the daughter of one of these men. She married William Outlaw, a wealthy Kilkenny money lender and merchant, ca. 1280. Their son, also called

William Outlaw, inherited the family business after his father's death, which had occurred by 1303. By then Alice had married again, this time to another wealthy man, Adam le Blund. In 1307, Blund's heirs renounced all claims on their inheritance in favor of William Outlaw. By 1309, Blund was dead and Alice had married a third husband, Richard de Valle, the owner of six manors in the neighboring county of Tipperary. William Outlaw was appointed to look after de Valle's business interests, but his heirs refused to surrender their inheritance. On de Valle's death ca. 1316, Alice was forced to take legal proceedings against her stepson, Richard de Valle junior, in order to gain her widow's dower of a third part of the estate. Sometime between 1316 and 1324 she married a fourth husband, Sir John le Poer, a member of a prominent Anglo-Irish aristocratic family. By 1324 Lady (or Dame) Alice, as she had become, was a very wealthy woman. She also had influential connections. Roger Outlaw, a kinsman of her first husband, was the chancellor of Ireland. William Douce, mayor of Dublin, was a close friend, while Walter de Islip, the treasurer of Ireland, and Arnold le Poer, the seneschal (and, therefore, chief legal officer) of the liberties of Kilkenny and Carlow, were her son's trusted friends.

In 1324, Alice and five other women were accused of being heretical sorceresses. There were seven charges. These alleged that (1) they denied the Christian faith for a month or a year, depending on the scale of what they desired to attain through sorcery; during this time they neither heard mass, nor received communion, nor entered any church. (2) They sacrificed to "son of Art," one of the inferior demons of hell, at a crossroads near Kilkenny, using live animals that they dismembered and scattered there. (3) They asked advice and sought responses from demons through sorcery. (4) They usurped the authority and jurisdiction of the Church by excommunicating their husbands at nightly gatherings. Using lighted candles, they named, spat on, and cursed each part of their husband's bodies, extinguishing their candles at the end with the words: "fi, fi, fi [perhaps a manuscript abbreviation of *fiat,* "let it be"], "amen" (Davidson and Ward 1993, 28). (5) They made powders, ointments, potions, and candles, which they used to arouse love and hate, to maim, and to kill. They prepared these from a stew that consisted of a thief's decapitated head, dismembered cockerels, dead men's nails, pubic hair, spiders, disfigured worms, milfoil, and the brains and clothing [perhaps the caul] of boys who had died unbaptized. (6) The sons and daughters of her four husbands had commenced litigation at the bishop's court. They openly accused Alice of using sorcery to kill some of their fathers and infatuate others to such an extent that they gave all their possessions to her and to William Outlaw. Her present husband, Sir John le Poer, had been reduced by sorcery to such a state that he was totally emaciated, his nails had fallen out, and there was no hair on any part of his body. (7) Alice had a demon incubus, called "son of Art" or "Robin son of Art," who had sexual intercourse with her. He appeared sometimes in the form of a cat, other times as a shaggy black dog, or as a black man with two companions. She had given herself and all her possessions to this incubus, and she acknowledged that she had received all her wealth and everything that she possessed from him. One of Alice's accomplices, Petronilla of Meath, later confessed that, with her own eyes, in full daylight, she had seen Robin materialize in the form of three black men bearing iron rods in their hands and had watched the apparition, thus armed, having sexual intercourse with Alice. Indeed, she added that she had dried the place with a bedcover after their departure.

The local bishop, Richard Ledrede, an English Franciscan schooled at Avignon and a personal appointee of Pope John XXII, formulated the charges. Ledrede requested the chancellor of Ireland to arrest Alice because of the public accusation of heresy and sorcery. But the chancellor was her relation, Roger Outlaw, and he replied by urging the bishop to drop the case. When Ledrede persisted and summoned her to appear before his own ecclesiastical court, his summons was ignored. A second date was set; but Alice, using her influence with the seneschal, Arnold le Poer, had the bishop arrested instead and committed to prison in Kilkenny Castle. If they hoped that a spell in prison would cool the bishop's ardor, it had precisely the opposite effect. He appealed in person at the seneschal's court, reading out the papal bulls that required the secular power to pursue heretics. Ledrede was told bluntly to "go to the church and preach there" (Davidson and Ward 1993, 46)

The case appeared to be lost but, by chance, John Darcy, the justiciar (chief governor) of Ireland, passed through Kilkenny in July 1324 and Ledrede succeeded in having the issue brought before him. Guilty verdicts were returned, but Alice managed to slip away. Her son, William Outlaw, publicly renounced his heresy, accepted penance, and promised to atone by providing monies for the repair of the cathedral. Petronilla of Meath confessed to all the charges after she had been flogged six times and tortured until she was senseless. Refusing to accept penance or abjure her heresies, she was paraded through the streets of Kilkenny and burned alive on November 2, 1324.

Although some commentators detected political motives behind Ledrede's actions, there can be little doubt but that he was endeavoring to introduce the Inquisition's methods into the judicial practice of Ireland and England, where convictions on the basis of confession alone were prohibited. The charges, which have many similarities with those placed against the Templars seventeen years earlier, originated because of a combination of disaffected stepchildren and a religious zealot. The description of John le Poer's body as emaciated and devoid of body hair fits the symptoms of arsenic poisoning. Together with the allegation that Alice had killed her previous husbands, her stepchildren suspected that she was slowly murdering the current one. The property and wealth of heretics did not pass to their blood heirs but reverted to the family's next of kin. Because both Alice and her son, William Outlaw, would have been dispossessed by her conviction, John le Poer would have inherited her property and wealth.

Instead, Ledrede was forced to flee from his diocese in 1327. He sheltered at Avignon, returning only in 1349 when he again started to pursue heretics. Subsequently he was accused of trumping-up charges against the "decent, simple, faithful people" as a means of extorting money (Colledge 1974, xxxi). Ledrede survived the accusations, however, and died of old age in 1360 or 1361. We have no idea what happened to Alice Kyteler after 1324.

JOHN BRADLEY

See also: COURTS, ECCLESIASTICAL; CROSSROADS; HERESY; INCUBUS AND SUCCUBUS; INQUISITION, MEDIEVAL; IRELAND; JOHN XXII, POPE; PAPACY AND PAPAL BULLS; POTIONS; TEMPLARS.

References and further reading:
Cohn, Norman. 1993. *Europe's Inner Demons: The Demonization of Christians in Medieval Christendom.* Revised edition. London: Pimlico.
Colledge, Edmund, ed. 1974. *The Latin Poems of Richard Ledrede, O.F.M., Bishop of Ossory, 1317–1360.* Toronto: Pontifical Institute of Medieval Studies.
Davidson, L. S., and Ward, J. O., eds. 1993. *The Sorcery Trial of Alice Kyteler.* Binghamton, NY: State University Press. [A translation of the Latin text, with an excellent introduction and notes together with appendices of the relevant papal decretals and contemporary historical documents.]
Massey, Eithne. 2000. *Prior Roger Outlaw of Kilmainham.* Dublin: Irish Academic.
Neary, Anne. 1983. "The Origins and Character of the Kilkenny Witchcraft Case of 1324." *Proceedings of the Royal Irish Academy* 83, sect. C, 333–350.
Williams, Bernadette. 2000. "'She Was Usually Placed with the Great Men and Leaders of the Land in Public Assemblies'—Alice Kyteler: A Woman of Considerable Power." Pp. 67–83 in *Women in Renaissance and Early Modern Europe.* Edited by Christine Meek. Dublin: Four Courts.
Wright, Thomas. 1843. *A Contemporary Narrative of the Proceedings Against Dame Alice Kyteler Prosecuted for Sorcery in 1324, by Richard de Ledrede, Bishop of Ossory.* London: Camden Society. [The only edition of the Latin text.]

L

LAMBE, DR. JOHN (CA. 1545–1628)

Lambe was a notorious English conjuror, magician, and astrologer who in the 1620s became an adviser to the king's favorite, Sir George Villiers, first duke of Buckingham. The fortunes of the two men became intertwined, their ambition and vanity spread murderous hatred among political elites and common people alike.

Lambe began working as a tutor to the sons of the gentry but turned to medicine and was licensed by the bishop of Durham. Lambe used sorcery, conjurations, and cunning magic. His career ended in 1608 after he was prosecuted at Worcester for bewitching Thomas Lord Windsor. He was also charged with invoking spirits. Although found guilty on both counts, he escaped execution. Initially held in Worcester Castle, he was moved to London after some participants in the trial died. He remained in the King's Bench Prison until June 1623, styling himself "Doctor" and continuing to practice magic for wealthy clients. In 1622, the duke of Buckingham accompanied his mother at a consultation session with Lambe to determine whether sorcery had caused his brother John's insanity. Buckingham became Lambe's patron, quashing his conviction for raping an eleven-year-old girl while in jail. Shortly before he was to be hanged, Lambe told the Lord Chief Justice, in an interview arranged by Buckingham, that he had important information about the gunpowder plot. The attorney general was instructed to issue a pardon.

How close Lambe became to Buckingham is unclear. A letter of 1624 from the duke to the king at least pretended to mock him. In 1625, Lady Purbeck, who had been forced by her father to marry the insane John Villiers, reportedly visited Lambe accompanied by her lover Sir Robert Howard. Upon hearing a rumor of this, Buckingham tried to compel Lambe to divulge what had been said in order to prove that her infant son was a bastard. Nevertheless, Lambe became a symbol of malign influence when the duke's popularity waned. In June 1626, before the king dissolved Parliament for trying to impeach Buckingham, a terrible storm broke over the River Thames. Gossip spread that "Buckingham's Wizard" had caused it. In 1626–1628, tension over parliamentary subsidies accompanied ballads attacking Lambe for both witchcraft and sexual scandal, suggesting that he used magic to procure women for Buckingham. Meanwhile, rumors abounded that Buckingham's mother had consulted Lambe about her son's fate, and even that Lambe was responsible when Lady Purbeck faced charges not only of adultery but also of witchcraft after the discovery of a wax image of Buckingham. In 1627, Lambe was examined by the Royal College of Physicians and found ignorant of the principles of astrology.

In June 1628, a mob spotted Lambe leaving a London theater. Reviling him as "witch," "devil," and "the duke's conjuror," they chased him and beat him so severely that he died the next day. News of his death caused popular rejoicing and inspired ballads. Martin Parker, in his ballad, *The Tragedy of Doctor Lambe, the great suposed Conjurer,* damned Lambe as "the Devill of our Nation," hated him just for his magic, but also for his greed (his last meal had been half a suckling pig). The final verses treat Lambe's death as an act of providential deliverance from treachery, corruption, and immorality. A popular pamphlet ridiculed Lambe in his ribboned knee-points (that hold stockings up), striped silks, and deep lace ruff, pathetically trying to repel his assailants with the sword he carried to affect the appearance of a gentleman. London's authorities made little effort to trace Lambe's killers, earning them a rebuke and a fine from King Charles I.

Mocking verses circulated in the London crowd that Buckingham's authority was bound up with Lambe's magic and that Buckingham would soon share his much-loathed magician's fate. Buckingham was assassinated in August of the same year. The link between Buckingham and Lambe, and their association with witchcraft, was revived in the 1650s during the well-publicized witchcraft trial of Anne Bodenham, who claimed to have been Lambe's servant.

MALCOLM J. GASKILL

See also: ASTROLOGY; CUNNING FOLK; ENGLAND; JAMES VI AND I, KING OF SCOTLAND AND ENGLAND; MALE WITCHES; PAMPHLETS AND NEWSPAPERS; SORCERY.

References and further reading:

A Briefe Description of the Notorious Life of John Lambe, otherwise called Doctor Lambe. Together with his Ignominious Death. Amsterdam (London), 1628. Facsimile reprint, Amsterdam: Theatrum Orbis Terrarum.

Goldstein, Leba M. 1979. "The Life and Death of John Lambe." *Guildhall Studies in London History* 4: 19–32.

Parker, Martin. [1628?]. "The Tragedy of Doctor Lambe, the great suposed Conjurer." Pp. 278–282 in *A Pepysian Garland: Black-Letter Broadside Ballads for the Years 1595–1639, Chiefly from the Collection of Samuel Pepys.* Edited by Hyder E. Rollins. Cambridge: Cambridge University Press, 1922.

LAMIA

According to late Greek tradition, Lamia was a very beautiful Libyan queen. Zeus, king of the gods, fell in love with her, but his wife, Hera, full of jealousy, robbed her of her children. In despair, Lamia began to steal other people's children and murder them, and this appalling behavior warped her face and made her extremely ugly. Accordingly, she became the bogey-woman of the nursery. Horace, for example, suggests that a poet should not ask his audience to believe impossibilities such as drawing a child still alive from Lamia's stomach (Horace, *Ars Poetica,* 340). Other late Greek and Roman authors, such as Philostratus, conceived *lamiae* as nonhuman females who seduced young men so that they could eat their flesh and drink their blood—hence their development, in modern Greek folklore, to beautiful women with monstrous feet or half-woman, half-fish creatures who drown people who go swimming in the sea.

Lamia quickly became a term used insultingly about female magical operators. Apuleius of Madaura (second century C.E.) has the hero of his *Metamorphoses* describe how two elderly women entered the room as he lay in bed, drenched him with urine, and tore out his traveling companion's heart. And in his famous story of Psyche and Cupid, Psyche's two sisters, creatures endowed, according to the tale, with more than natural envy and malice, are called "wicked" and "treacherous little wolves," as well as *lamiae* (Apuleius, 5.11). These, then, are the associations that the word *lamia* carried forward into later times, deriving in part, perhaps, from men's memories of elderly women in the family who dominated their childhood and played a prominent role in the magical rituals attending almost every act of consequence in family life.

Isidore of Seville made a greater impression on the Middle Ages by deriving the word *lamia* from a Latin verb, *laniare,* meaning "to tear, savage, mutilate"—ingenious but inaccurate: The term is originally Greek. But Isidore's mistaken derivation became popular; Gervase of Tilbury repeated it. A thousand years after Apuleius, Gervase knew *lamiae* as a type of mischievous fairy, describing them as "women who run about all over the place, never still for a moment, looking for a way to get into people's houses. Once in, they empty jars, baskets, and dishes, and peer into pots. They drag babies out of their cradles, light candles or tapers, and often hit people while they are asleep" (Gervase of Tilbury, *De otiis imperialibus* part 3, chap. 87). A few

centuries later, the title page of Ulrich Molitor's treatise on witches, *De laniis et phitonicis mulieribus* (Concerning Witches and Fortune-tellers, 1489), contained an interesting misprint, since *lamiis* (witches) there appears as *laniis* (butchers), a variation corrected in later editions.

Lamiae was picked up by later writers on magic and witchcraft, who tried, not altogether successfully, to use it as a technical rather than a general term for "witch." Johann Weyer, for example, offered to explain *lamia* to his readers, only to identify it with *striga* and *saga* (two words with very different histories and implications), before saying that he is going to use it to refer to a woman who enters into a pact with an evil spirit and thereafter worked maleficent magic with his help (Weyer, *De praestigiis daemonum* [On the Tricks of Devils], book 3, chap. 1). His contemporary, Johann Georg Goedelmann, went somewhat further, describing *lamiae* as ignorant old women who, unlike magicians (magi) and workers of poisonous magic (*venefici*), did not learn their magical techniques from books but were cozened by the Devil into believing they could work wonders (Goedelmann, *De magis, veneficis, et lamiis* [On Sorcerers, Poisoners, and Witches], book 1, chap. 2). The Jesuit Martín Del Rio, however, mocked Weyer's claim to distinguish among the various names given to workers of harmful magic on the grounds that what was important about such people were their deeds and not their names, By now, he asserted, it had become accepted custom to lump together the various magical practitioners, regardless of what they were called, and to treat them as though there were no differences among them (Del Rio, *Disquisitiones Magicae Libri Sex* [Six Books on Investigations into Magic] book 5, section 16). This is the position adopted by many, perhaps most, early modern authors writing on magic and witchcraft.

P. G. MAXWELL-STUART

See also: APULEIUS OF MADAURA; DEL RIO, MARTIN; FAIRIES; GOEDELMANN, JOHANN GEORG; ISIDORE OF SEVILLE; MOLITOR, ULRICH; STRIX, STRIGA, STRIA.

References and further reading:
Burriss, E. E. 1936. "The Terminology of Witchcraft." *Classical Philology* 31: 137–145.

Henderson, J. 1987. "Older Women in Attic Old Comedy." *Transactions of the American Philological Association* 117: 105–130.

LAMOTHE-LANGON, ETIENNE-LÉON DE (1786–1852)

An impoverished nobleman from Toulouse, whose father had been killed in 1794 during the "Terror" of the French Revolution, Etienne-Léon de Lamothe perpetrated the most spectacular hoax in the historiography of witchcraft. Lacking formal schooling, he earned his living as a freelance author and Romantic novelist with "a marked taste for the sinister, the mysterious, and the melodramatic" (Cohn 1975, 132), becoming one of the most productive French writers of this period. He began writing at three o'clock in the morning and managed to publish no fewer than 400 books (or 1,500 volumes in manuscript) in fifty years.

His work includes a celebrated three-volume *Histoire de l'Inquisition en France* (History of the French Inquisition) of 1829, presumably inspired by Juan Antonio Llorente's *Histoire critique de l'Inquisition d'Espagne* (Critical History of the Spanish Inquisition, 1817–1818), a best seller throughout Europe. Lamothe allegedly wrote his history from archival sources. However, Lamothe had no time for archival research. In 1829 alone, he published twenty-two volumes, including novels like *La Vampire ou la Vierge de Hongrie* (The Vampire, or The Virgin of Hungary), and he had no training in paleography. Only recently has it become clear that he not only amplified his own name into "Lamothe-Houdancourt" (from 1815–1817) and "Baron de Lamothe-Langon" (after 1817) but also invented his "sources." They included the earliest reports about the witches' Sabbat, allegedly from 1275, as well as the earliest reports of a large-scale witch hunt, allegedly conducted between 1300 and 1350. His accounts of mass persecutions seemed plausible, because Pope John XXII in a bull of 1320 had indeed empowered the Inquisitions of Toulouse and Carcassonne to proceed against practitioners of certain kinds of magic.

Lamothe's forgeries became universally accepted after Wilhelm Gottlieb Soldan quoted them in his authoritative *Geschichte der Hexenprozesse* (History of Witch Trials, 1843), and even more so after Joseph Hansen quoted them fully in both his history of witchcraft in the Middle Ages (1900) and in his source collection (1901). Thereafter, scholars universally took the authenticity of these sources for granted. It was only in the mid-1970s that two historians (Cohn 1975, 126–146; Kieckhefer 1976, 16–20) independently demolished Lamothe's allegations. Neither Lamothe's alleged inquisitors of Carcassonne and Toulouse nor their witch hunts could be substantiated from any surviving sources. Lamothe had simply fabricated the victims and their confessions in order to sell his publications and perhaps in order to amplify the importance of France in the history of witchcraft. But even Pope John XXII had withdrawn his authorization in 1330, and thereafter, inquisitors were no longer responsible for sorcery trials in France. With Lamothe's forgeries eliminated, it became clear that it was only circa 1400–1430 that different aspects of witchcraft and heresy were assembled into a specifically European "cumulative" concept of witchcraft, which allowed witch hunts of unprecedented severity. The case of Lamothe remains a warning to historians not to accept "sources" just because they appear to be plausible. After 1835, Lamothe specialized in forging sources, and he fabricated (among many others) the memoirs of Louis XVIII and Napoleon Bonaparte. Furthermore, Lamothe's fraud demonstrated the efficacy of traditional source criticism: In a masterful intellectual exercise, Norman Cohn suggested that Lamothe had simply copied his account of the witches' Sabbat from a seventeenth-century French demonologist, Pierre de Lancre.

WOLFGANG BEHRINGER

See also: FRANCE; HANSEN, JOSEPH; HISTORIOGRAPHY; INQUISITION, MEDIEVAL; JOHN XXII, POPE; LANCRE, PIERRE DE; ORIGINS OF THE WITCH HUNTS; SOLDAN, WILHELM GOTTLIEB.
References and further reading:
Behringer, Wolfgang. 2004. "Geschichte der Hexenforschung." Pp. 485–680 in *Wider alle Zauberei und Teufelswerk: Die europäische Hexenverfolgung und ihre Auswirkung auf Südwestdeutschland.* Edited by Sönke Lorenz and Jürgen Michael Schmidt. Ostfildern: Jan Thorbecke.
Cohn, Norman. 1975. *Europe's Inner Demons: An Enquiry Inspired by the Great Witch-Hunt.* New York: Basic Books.
Hansen, Joseph. 1900. *Zauberwahn, Inquisition und Hexenprozess im Mittelalter und die Entstehung der grossen Hexenverfolgung.* Munich: R. Oldenbourg.
———. 1901. *Quellen und Untersuchungen zur Geschichte des Hexenwahns und der Hexenverfolgung im Mittelalter.* Bonn: C. Georgi. Reprint, Hildesheim: Georg Olms, 1963.
Kieckhefer, Richard. 1976. *European Witch Trials: Their Foundations in Popular and Learned Culture, 1300–1500.* Berkeley and Los Angeles: University of California Press.
Lamothe-Langon, Etienne Léon de. 1829. *Histoire de l'Inquisition en France.* 3 vols. Paris.
Soldan, Wilhelm Gottlieb. 1843. *Geschichte der Hexenprozesse.* Stuttgart and Tübingen.
Switzer, Richard. 1962. *Etienne-Léon de Lamothe-Langon et le roman populaire français de 1800 à 1830.* Toulouse: Privat.

LANCASHIRE WITCHES

The term *Lancashire witches* (sometimes called the *Pendle witches*) usually refers to a group of sixteen alleged witches from the Pendle region of Lancashire who were tried at the Lancaster assizes August 18–19, 1612. This Lancashire outbreak was, at the time, the most serious witch hunt yet experienced in England. Ten of the accused were executed, and another was sentenced to a year's imprisonment punctuated by four sessions on the pillory. Another woman associated with this group, Jennet Preston, had been tried and executed in the neighboring county of Yorkshire three weeks previously.

Thomas Potts, the clerk of the court that tried the witches, soon recorded the Lancashire outbreak in a lengthy tract, published in 1613. This tract, which reproduced the examinations of the witches and of those giving witness against them, is a major source for the events of 1612. Unusual for an English case, the 1612 Lancashire trials have passed into local legend, and their memory endures in the local tourist

Ten witches from Pendle in Lancashire were hanged in what was England's largest witch hunt up to that time. The witch on the left may be the octogenarian Elizabeth Southerns ("Old Demdike"), while the fear that a Sabbat had taken place was represented by the female witch, male witch, and devil riding on broomsticks to the witches' gathering. (TopFoto.co.uk)

and heritage industries. This probably owes much to *The Lancashire Witches,* a novel based on the 1612 trials, published in 1849 by William Harrison Ainsworth, one of the most popular Victorian writers, and still in print. Robert Neill in 1951 published another novel based on the 1612 Lancashire witches, *Mist over Pendle.*

The train of events behind the Lancashire witch scare began on March 21, 1612, when a woman named Alizon Device met a peddler called John Law. Device asked to see some of the goods in his pack and grew angry when he refused her. Law instantly went into what was regarded as a witchcraft-induced illness (to the modern reader, his affliction looks much like a stroke), and he and his relatives decided to report the matter to the authorities. On March 30, the justice of

the peace, Roger Nowell, took depositions from Alizon Device, her mother Elizabeth, and her brother James and from John Law's son, Abraham. Three days later, Nowell examined Elizabeth Device's mother, the octogenarian Elizabeth Southerns (alias "Old Demdike"), Anne Whittle (alias "Chattox"), and three witnesses. On April 4, Nowell committed Alizon Device, Old Demdike, Chattox, and Chattox's daughter, Anne Redferne, to the jail at Lancaster Castle to await trial for witchcraft. Rumors of witchcraft continued to burgeon, especially after a group of suspects met together at the Malkin Tower, apparently to discuss tactics in the face of the developing witch craze and also to plot blowing up Lancaster Castle in order to release their friends. News of this meeting, which looked very like a Sabbat to contemporaries, convinced Nowell and his fellow justices of the peace that they were confronting a major outbreak of witchcraft, and investigations intensified. Sir Edward Bromley and Sir James Altham, experienced judges who had been responsible for convicting Jennet Preston in Yorkshire, presided over the trials. Both judges had been well briefed by the Lancashire authorities, and the trials, notable particularly for an unusual dependence on child witnesses, were heavily weighted against the accused.

Because the Lancashire trials were the largest yet seen in England, contemporaries regarded them as noteworthy and possibly controversial: Potts's tract was apparently written at the request of the judges and can be read as a justification of their conduct of the trial. Although, as we have noted, the trials have continued to attract considerable attention, they have not become the subject of a full-scale scholarly investigation, despite some useful studies by local historians (for example, Lumby 1995) and an important recent collection of essays (Poole 2002). Many questions about the trials remain unanswered. Most importantly, it is very unclear why such a large-scale outbreak of witchcraft occurred in this place at a time when witchcraft cases in other parts of England were in decline. This problem awaits investigation, but the answer probably lies in the peculiar state of religious affairs in the county. Lancashire was one of the strongholds of Catholicism in England, but it also had an active Protestant county elite, who were anxious both to check popery and to impose greater godliness on the population at large. The parish of Whalley, within which Pendle lay, was typical of upland England, being large and full of scattered settlements, the kind of area to which it was difficult to bring the message of the Reformation. Much responsibility for the development of this witch craze rests with Nowell, who seems to have played an important part in orchestrating the examination of the suspected witches. Nowell was an experienced local administrator, aged sixty-two at the time, who was not only a justice of the peace but had also served as sheriff of Lancashire. Through his family connections, Nowell also had contacts with advanced Protestantism. He was related to another gentry family, the Starkies of Cleworth, whose household had been in 1595 the center of one of the typical demonic possession-cum-witchcraft cases of the period. He was also close to the Lister family, one of whose members was victim of Jennet Preston, the Yorkshire witch executed in 1612. In Nowell, we have an unusual local justice of the peace who had a strong animus against witches and whose influence was very marked, both in the pretrial investigations of the 1612 witches and on the assize judges.

Although it was the Pendle witches who passed into legend after the 1612 trials, three more women from the nearby village of Salmesbury were also tried at the Lancaster assizes in 1612 (hence the nineteen witches referred to in Potts's tract). They were prosecuted through evidence given by Grace Sowerbutts, who accused them of offering her various forms of physical abuse, of tempting her to commit suicide, of killing a child whose body they later exhumed and ate, and of transporting her to the River Ribble to participate in what was in effect a Sabbat, where she and the three alleged witches danced with "foure black things" and then had sexual intercourse with them after the dancing. The Pendle witches were tried and, in the relevant instances, convicted of standard malefic witchcraft, but Sowerbutts's evidence was very different from that offered by witnesses in the main series of trials. The court, which was in the process of sentencing ten alleged witches to death, totally rejected Sowerbutts's allegations and acquitted the three women she named. The judges would not countenance allegations of this type, especially after they learned that a Jesuit priest had schooled Sowerbutts in her witchcraft beliefs. In 1612 Lancashire, malefic witches were dangerous, but popish delusions about the Sabbat and cannibalistic witches were superstitions.

After the 1612 trials, rumors of witchcraft evidently continued in the Pendle area, and reentered the historical record in a less-well-known witch scare of 1633–1634. At the center of this episode lay an eleven-year old boy named Edmund Robinson, who claimed that shape-changing witches had taken him to the Sabbat and that he there saw a large number of local people whom he recognized. The 1633–1634 outbreak was badly documented, but one source suggested that sixty people were suspected. Certainly, a large-scale witch panic threatened, with Robinson and his father touring settlements in the area offering their services as witch hunters. But there was to be no replay of 1612. The judge presiding over the trials, clearly worried by what was happening, contacted the central government at Westminster. Apparently no trials were held, and the bishop of Chester, within whose diocese Pendle lay, was sent in to investigate. Robinson and his father were taken to London, along with five of the suspected witches, who were given medical examinations. Robinson withdrew his evidence, claiming that he had made everything up because he was late getting the cattle home and feared being chastised by his mother. The incident demonstrated both the persistence of witch beliefs in rural England in the 1630s and a growing reluctance among British authorities to countenance witch hunting, in stark contrast to the situation in 1612.

JAMES SHARPE

See also: CHILDREN; ENGLAND; PANICS; RURAL WITCHCRAFT.
References and further reading:
Lumby, Jonathan. 1995. *The Lancashire Witch-Craze: Jennet Preston and the Lancashire Witches, 1612.* Preston, Lancashire: Carnegie.

Poole, Robert, ed. 2002. *The Lancashire Witches: Histories and Stories.* Manchester: Manchester University Press.

Potts, Thomas. 1613. *The Wonderfull Discoverie of Witches in the Countie of Lancaster. With the Arraignment and Triall of nine-teene notorious Witches, at the Assizes and Generall Gaole Deliverie, holden at the Castle of Lancaster, upon Munday, the seventeenth of August last, 1612.* London.

LANCRE, PIERRE DE (1533–1630)

In 1609, Pierre de Lancre conducted trials that resulted in dozens of executions for witchcraft—the largest mass witchcraft trial in early modern France, until the Languedoc-Ardennes panic of the 1640s. Frustrated by the persistent skepticism of his colleagues at the *Parlement* (sovereign judicial court) of Bordeaux, Lancre then wrote three lengthy treatises on the subject, defending his actions and arguing that witchcraft was real, that witches constituted a dangerous heretical sect, and that the sect had to be stamped out with severity.

Lancre was born around 1533 to an influential Bordeaux family. He was related by birth and marriage to several well-known Bordeaux authors, including Florimond de Raemond and Michel de Montaigne. On the way to his long legal career, Lancre attended the Jesuit *collège* of Clermont in Paris in the early 1570s. He (and Martín Del Rio) probably heard Juan Maldonado's influential lectures on witches in 1571. Throughout his life, Lancre was inspired by the intense Catholic spirituality encouraged by the Jesuits.

In 1579, Lancre received his doctorate of law. He joined the *Parlement* of Bordeaux in 1582. In the early seventeenth century, when he was in his fifties, he began a prolific writing career that lasted almost up to his death in 1630. In 1607, he published a long work of neostoicist philosophy. He devoted about a third of this book to the exalted role of judges in the grave, almost divine, function of dispensing justice. He opposed cruelty and the too-easy recourse to torture he had observed among some of his colleagues. He firmly supported the French legal tradition of trials being conducted by groups of judges to avoid abuses that could occur if one person held the power of life and death. Such judicial caution was an especially powerful tradition among his parlementary colleagues at Bordeaux, who were apparently the last appellate tribunal in France to approve an execution for witchcraft. Another central theme of this work was the weakness and inconstancy of women. He described women as dishonorable, licentious, and, following the example of Eve, inclined by nature to follow the Devil.

The following year brought the judicial assignment that made Lancre famous. In late 1608 or early 1609, complaints from the Labourd region, a Basque area south of Bordeaux, reached King Henry IV, stating that witchcraft was out of control in the region. The king named two special commissioners, Pierre de Lancre and Jean d'Espaignet, to conduct a four-month judicial mission to the Labourd to investigate the problem and to conduct trials as they saw fit. They had full powers to convict and execute anyone they found guilty of the heinous crime of witchcraft. Both judges found widespread belief that huge witches' Sabbats were taking place, and they heard hundreds of confessions, apparently without torture, from people who claimed they had attended these diabolical gatherings. Meanwhile, as suspected witches fled for safety across the border, the Spanish Inquisition received similar complaints and began investigating the problem in the Spanish Basque areas.

For four months, Lancre and d'Espaignet traveled throughout the region. As they interrogated people, their goal was to distinguish the witches who had renounced Christianity and to offer clemency to the women and children who had merely attended Sabbats, using their testimony to identify the ringleaders and organizers who were seen to be active members of a demonic sect. The existence of the Devil's heretical sect became Lancre's obsession, inspiring his subsequent writings on witches. The two judges conducted interrogations and trials and carried out executions with speed and efficiency. They seem to have executed between fifty and eighty witches, although we cannot be certain of more than two dozen, including at least three "ringleader priests." When the judges' commission expired in November 1609, those whom Lancre thought were guilty but whom he had not been able to deal with were sent to Bordeaux for trial by the *parlement*. Lancre's verdicts were based on his perception that the real problem in the Labourd was the sect of Devil worshipers. He based his findings on testimony and confessions about participation in Sabbats. But the *Parlement* of Bordeaux never adopted his views and discounted his evidence. Applying its normal criminal procedures and upholding its traditions about suspected witches (which Michel de Montaigne, a former Bordeaux judge, had eloquently expressed), the judges insisted on evidence of actual crimes (*maleficia*) committed by the accused. On this basis, the court convicted a few of Lancre's witches and released many others.

Lancre's colleagues' professional rebuff, which showed they were unwilling to take seriously testimony on Sabbats and to see it as proof of the existence of a demonic sect threatening godly society, motivated Lancre to write his best-known book, *Tableau de l'Inconstance des mauvais anges et demons* (Description of the Inconstancy of Evil Angels and Demons, 1612). He put great energy into trying to convince his readers that "there was no way to cast doubt on [the reality] of witchcraft and that the Devil actually and bodily transports witches to Sabbats. . . . Sixty or eighty certain witches and five hundred witnesses . . . have stated that Satan had done this" (Lancre 1982, 2). Lancre was concerned that if judges did not take these matters seriously, their blindness and weakness would help the Devil's power grow.

Central to this book, and to Lancre's concept of witchcraft, was the Sabbat. For Lancre, basing his arguments on Martín Del Rio's recent synthesis, the Devil's transportation of people to Sabbats, in body or in spirit, was real. Belief in this idea was required of Christians. The details of what happened at the Sabbats were shocking. All the attendees practiced unnatural sexual acts and committed horrible blasphemies. Lancre stated, "I can say of the women and girls of the Labourd who have gone to Sabbats, that instead of being quiet about this damnable coupling [with demons], or of blushing or crying about it, they tell the dirtiest and most immodest circumstances with such great freedom and gaiety that they glory in it and take pleasure talking about it" (Lancre 1982, 142). One even called the Sabbat a "Paradise." Of course, this fit in with Lancre's view that women were inclined to witchcraft "because of their imbecilic nature" and basic inclination to evil. For Lancre, aspects of Basque society made the Labourd region especially vulnerable to the Devil's work. He saw these people as foreign, barely civilized, and poorly educated as Christians. The fact that most adult men were sailors meant that normal agricultural life was not present there. Furthermore, it meant that the women were far too independent, so that the proper, male-dominated family life did not exist. "They are Eves," he wrote, "who easily seduce the children of Adam" (Lancre 1982, 43). Although Lancre welcomed testimony from children as part of gathering evidence, he disagreed with Nicolas Rémy's opinion that prepubescent witches should be executed.

Lancre's position on the Devil's power, based on Del Rio, was carefully orthodox. Satan could not do anything really supernatural, such as transforming people into animals (in contrast to what Jean Bodin argued). But he could create illusions of these sorts of changes. For Lancre, witches who joined the Devil "have fallen into heresy and apostasy" (Lancre 1982, 531). In the fight against them, judges had to be vigilant and severe. Although witchcraft and heresy were closely related, Lancre held that witchcraft was more dangerous than ordinary heresy because it was hidden in darkness and because innocent people were victims of witches' evil spells. He went to great length to argue that these evildoers should be put to death.

Because the parlementary judges at Bordeaux and Paris continued to ignore his opinions about witches and witchcraft, Lancre published another long work on witchcraft in 1622, *L'incredulité et mescréance du sortilege* (Incredulity and Misbelief of Enchantment). This book was entirely devoted to the problem of judicial incredulity about witchcraft. He stated that he had written "to dislodge whatever incredulity the *Parlements,* all judges and other important people might have . . . who sustain that there is no truth in what is said of witches and witchcraft but that it is only an illusion" (Lancre 1622, 4). This work was very defensive in tone. He reiterated the main arguments of his earlier work, referring often to his experiences as a judge.

In 1627, Lancre wrote his final book on witchcraft: *Du sortilege* (About Witchcraft). But no matter how many books he published, Lancre remained a voice crying in a French judicial wilderness. It is clear that French *parlements* seldom prosecuted witchcraft severely or paid much attention to testimony about Sabbats after 1610. Between 1610 and 1625, although most of the thirteen people executed by the *Parlement* of Paris were charged with having been present at Sabbats, only one was put to death for attending a Sabbat. It is clear that the career and writings of Pierre de Lancre did little to reverse a clearly visible trend in French jurisprudence.

JONATHAN L. PEARL

See also: BASQUE COUNTRY; BODIN, JEAN; CHILDREN; DEL RIO, MARTÍN; FLIGHT OF WITCHES; FRANCE; INQUISITION, SPANISH; MALDONADO, JUAN; METAMORPHOSIS; MONTAIGNE, MICHEL DE; *PARLEMENT* OF PARIS; RÉMY, NICHOLAS; SABBAT.

References and further reading:
Houdard, Sophie. 1990. "Frontière et altérité dans le *Tableau de l'inconstance des mauvais anges et démons* de Pierre de Lancre." *Frénésie: Histoire, psychiatrie, psychanalyse* 9: 23–32.
———. 1992. *Les Sciences du diable: Quatre Discourses sur la sorcellerie, XVe–XVIIe siècle.* Paris: Cerf.
Lancre, Pierre de. 1622. *L'incredulité et mescréance du sortilege.* Paris.
———. 1982. *Tableau de l'inconstance des mauvais anges et démons: ou il est amplement traité des sorciers et de la sorcellerie.* 1612. Edited by Nicole Jacques-Chaquin. Paris: Aubier Montaigne.
McGowan, Margaret. 1977. "Pierre de Lancre's *Tableau des l'inconstance des mauvais anges et démons:* The Sabbath Sensationalized." Pp. 182–201 in *The Damned Art: Essays in the Literature of Witchcraft.* Edited by Sydney Anglo. London: Routledge and Kegan Paul.
Pearl, Jonathan L. 1999. *The Crime of Crimes: Demonology and Politics in France, 1560–1620.* Waterloo, Ontario: Wilfred Laurier University Press.

LANGTON, WALTER (D.–1321)

Treasurer (1295–1307) of King Edward I of England and bishop of Coventry and Lichfield (1296–1321), Walter Langton was accused of sorcery, entering into a pact with the Devil (frequently offering the kiss of shame to Satan), murder, adultery, and simony and was tried from 1301 to 1303. Pope Boniface VII suspended Langton from his episcopal duties and ordered him tried by an ecclesiastical court presided over by the archbishop of Canterbury, Winchelsea, Langton's personal enemy. The case was soon transferred to

Rome. Edward I wrote four letters to the pope in Langton's defense and charged that his accuser, Sir John Lovetot, had acted out of personal animosity. Lovetot believed Langton was responsible for his stepfather's murder and that he had maintained an adulterous affair with Lovetot's stepmother, subsequently keeping her as his mistress after her husband's strangulation. The Roman Curia found Langton innocent in June 1303, owing in part to his thirty-seven compurgators.

After his acquittal, Langton returned to England, where he became Edward I's principal adviser. But in 1307, as soon as Edward I was dead, his son King Edward II had Langton arrested, charging him with malfeasance as royal treasurer. Langton was imprisoned, and his lands and wealth were confiscated. However, he was released, became treasurer again, and was subsequently excommunicated by the archbishop of Canterbury. After the archbishop's death in 1315, Langton joined the royal council, until Parliament called for his dismissal two years later, thus ending a tumultuous political career.

Although Langton's trial took place a century before the emergence of the cumulative concept of witchcraft and fully developed witch hunts, it set precedents for a number of political witchcraft trials in the early fourteenth century in which members of the elite were targeted. It slightly preceded the notorious trial of the Templars in France and occurred just two decades before the most notorious of these trials in the British Isles, that of Alice Kyteler in Ireland.

RICHARD M. GOLDEN

See also: KISS OF SHAME; KYTELER, ALICE; ORIGINS OF THE TEMPLARS WITCH HUNTS.

References and further reading:
Beardwood, Alice. 1964. *The Trial of Walter Langton, Bishop of Lichfield, 1307–1312.* Philadelphia: American Philosophical Society.
———, ed. 1969. *Records of the Trial of Walter Langeton, Bishop of Coventry and Lichfield, 1307–1312.* London: Royal Historical Society.
Ewen, Cecil L'Estrange. 1933. *Witchcraft and Demonianism: A Concise Account Derived from Sworn Depositions and Confessions Obtained in the Courts of England and Wales.* London: Heath Cranton.
Kieckhefer, Richard. 1976. *European Witch Trials: Their Foundations in Popular and Learned Culture, 1300–1500.* Berkeley and Los Angeles: University of California Press.
Kittredge, George Lyman. 1929. *Witchcraft in Old and New England.* Cambridge, MA: Harvard University Press.

LANGUEDOC

The French province of Languedoc, the heart of southern France, was once believed to be the site of Europe's earliest witches' Sabbats, in the mid-fourteenth century, until the "document" on which this opinion rested was shown to be a forgery (Cohn 1975, 126–138). Actually, witch hunting in Languedoc has a very different history.

Recorded witchcraft trials in this province reach back to the end of the Hundred Years' War. After an apparent pause, they resumed at the outbreak of the French Wars of Religion and peaked when Languedoc experienced the single largest recorded witch craze in France in the 1640s. However, from the mid-fifteenth century until the age of Louis XIV, the *Parlement* of Toulouse, France's second-oldest and second-largest appellate court, consistently played a major role in reducing the severity of punishments of accused witches.

Shortly after its installation in 1443, the *Parlement* of Toulouse investigated various irregularities committed in some witchcraft trials at Millau. It cleared a plaintiff from Millau charged with witchcraft because the written evidence against her was obviously perjured. The *parlement*'s investigator discovered other irregularities in this witch hunt as well: An accused witch who had died under atrocious tortures without confessing had been illegally buried in profane ground; the judge ordered a stake put up for another witch before pronouncing sentence against her. All told, at least three witches were burned at Millau in autumn of 1444, two others died before sentence was pronounced, and at least three other women were accused of attending Sabbats and killing babies. The episode reveals how quickly the new crime of witchcraft had spread southwest from Dauphiné, and the *parlement*'s attitude anticipated the better-known skepticism of their Parisian colleagues when investigating the *Vauderie* of Arras in 1491.

But the *parlement* could not prevent other burnings of accused witches in Languedoc. Around 1490, a woman was burned for sorcery and diabolism in Vivarais. Shortly afterward, we catch glimpses in notarial records of three women burned as witches by seigneurial courts near Nîmes and of two other women burned in the same region in 1493 (Girard 1995). Then comes a long silence, finally broken in 1555 when the seneschal of Bigorre, in the Pyrenees, asked the Toulouse *parlement* to send commissioners to judge several prisoners charged with witchcraft "in order to extirpate such scandalous and pernicious people from this region" (ADHG, B 3408). The court brusquely dismissed his request, on the grounds that people who "fell into such diabolical errors and illusions" had been improperly educated, and turned the whole business over to their local parish priests.

Only seven years later, the Toulouse *parlement* took witchcraft accusations seriously enough to uphold some death sentences for this crime from Pyrenean Languedoc. In the spring and summer of 1562, amid the turmoil surrounding the first French War of Religion, it approved at least three burnings for witchcraft (Le Nail 1976). However, the *parlement* soon reverted to its previous practice and decreed lesser punishments for the next thirty women from this region also accused of witchcraft.

Afterward, more executions certainly occurred in a region as large as Languedoc during the time when most witches were burned elsewhere in France (roughly 1580–1625). However, we cannot trace the Toulouse *parlement's* judgments in witchcraft trials because of the exceptional laconism of its criminal records. A "notable warlock" and five women witches were executed in southern Languedoc in 1586, but the sovereign court for the county of Foix had judged them. However, at some unknown date, the *Parlement* of Toulouse copied the Parisian custom of requiring all local judgments in witchcraft trials to be automatically appealed to it. So when the greatest witch panic in French history struck Languedoc in 1643, it left an enormous paper trail, and an ingenious study (Vidal 1987) examined its actions.

From spring of 1643 until spring of 1645, the *Parlement* of Toulouse judged at least 641 accused witches, only 8 percent of whom were men. It behaved much as it had in 1562. For several months, it upheld many local decisions, and probably some fifty or sixty witches were burned. But by December 1643, the *parlement* became aware of the activities of professional witch finders in several parts of Languedoc. It ordered some of them arrested; by summer of 1644, three men had been hanged for forging commissions from the Privy Council or the *parlement* to hunt witches, and others had been sent to the galleys. At the same time, the *parlement* sharply reduced almost all punishments for accused witches; extremely few were burned, over a hundred were banished for periods of one to five years, and almost two-thirds of these 600 prisoners were released, often because of insufficient evidence. Meanwhile, this witch hunt even inspired a chapbook, the *Historia maravellosa del sabbat de las bruxes y bruxots* (Wondrous History of the Witches Sabbat), supposedly translated from French and printed in 1645 at Barcelona (which was then under French occupation). It described the adventures of "Señor Barbasta," a mythical super-heroic Languedoc witch finder, who had reputedly identified over 3,000 witches throughout the kingdom of France, including his own wife.

After this panic subsided, as late as 1680 the Toulouse *parlement* was still trying to investigate witchcraft cases in the Pyrenees (at Bigorre, the same region affected in 1555). There was an instance of demonic possession in Toulouse in 1681–1682, but there was no further talk of burning witches in Languedoc (Mandrou 1968, 473–478).

WILLIAM MONTER

See also: ARRAS; FRANCE; ORIGINS OF THE WITCH HUNTS; PANICS; WARS OF RELIGION (FRANCE); WITCH FINDERS.

References and further reading:

Archives Départmentales de la Haute-Garonne (ADHG), Toulouse, B 3408, 3440–3444, 3658–3662.

Cohn, Norman. 1975. *Europe's Inner Demons: An Enquiry Inspired by the Great Witch-Hunt.* London: Basic Books.

Girard, René de. 1995. *Boucoiran au XVe siècle: Une sorcière; Martiale Espaze.* Montpellier: Mémoire d'Oc series, #44.

Le Nail, Jean-François. 1976. "Procédures contre des sorcières à Seix en 1562." *Bulletin de la Société Ariégoise des Sciences, Lettres et Arts* 31: 155–232.

Mandrou, Robert. 1968. *Magistrats et sorciers en France au XVIIe siècle.* Paris: Plon.

Vidal, Jacques. 1987. "Le Parlement de Toulouse et la répression de la sorcellerie au milieu du XVIIe siècle." Pp. 511–527 in *Hommages à Gérard Boulvert.* Nice: Université de Nice.

LAPLAND

Lapland's witches were famous throughout early modern Europe. From ancient times, the Lapland sorcerers had a strong reputation for wind magic, shape shifting (metamorphosis), employment of familiars, the ability to move objects (such as small darts) across great distances, and for their wicked drum playing. Portrayals of the evil witches from Lapland became a favorite motif in demonology, travel narratives, and literary fiction between the sixteenth and eighteenth centuries. The expression *Lapland witches* appeared in the work of such renowned English writers as William Shakespeare, John Milton, Daniel Defoe, Henry More, and Jonathan Swift. In 1796, the Swiss painter Johann Heinrich Füssli depicted them in a rather dismal painting, *The Night-Hag Visiting the Lapland Witches,* illustrating some passages from Milton's *Paradise Lost* (1667). By the end of the eighteenth century, the mention of Lapland witches had become a cliché.

The concept "Lapland witches" refers to the indigenous people of northernmost Scandinavia and Russia, the Sami (formerly known as Laplanders or Lapps). Today, the Sami call their land Sapmi, and their whole area is often named the North Calotte. The notion of the far northern regions of Europe as centers of witchcraft and idolatry reduced to the question of Sami sorcery. "For practice of witchcraft and sorcery, they pass all nations in the world" (Anderson 1958, 13), wrote the English ambassador to Russia, Sir Giles Fletcher, in 1591, describing the life and manners of the "wild" Sami in northern Russia. The Lapland witches and the knotted winds had already become somewhat notorious by then, because authors like Olaus Magnus and Jean Bodin had already told Europe that the Sami were immensely dangerous magicians and sorcerers. The conjuring of these Lapland witches was so great that people believed they could use sorcery instead of weapons while in combat with their enemies. Rumors indicating that the Swedes used the techniques of Sami sorcery in warfare dogged Swedish military forces throughout the seventeenth century. When they won several significant battles and advanced deep into German territory during the Thirty Years' War, it was insinuated that their success was due to sorcery by Sami troops assisting them.

RUNEBOMME—THE MAGIC DRUM; SHAMANISM

Educated Europeans of the early modern age believed that Sami witchcraft entailed three characteristics: First, the Sami were famous for their ability to tell fortunes and predict future events. Ever since the recording of the Nordic sagas, this feature of the indigenous populations of the far North was well known. In general, Old Norse sources give the impression that all Sami were great sorcerers. Ancient Norwegian laws forbade people to travel to Finnmark's Sami to have their fortunes told. Closely associated with their powers of prophecy were their abilities to narrate events. By the use of a magic drum (*runebomme*) and other rituals, a Sami shaman (*noaidi*) would allow himself to fall into some kind of a trance (*ecstasis diabolica*), at which time his spirit would be led far away. Upon awakening, he could describe events that had occurred at the places to which his spirit had traveled. Christians immersed in demonological concepts of shamanism believed that Satan himself gave these drums to the Sami. The drum, an instrument of the Devil, enabled a sorcerer to summon his demons, which were believed to reside in it and were revived by striking it. In this manner, each drumbeat—to quote a Swedish missionary working among the Sami whose discourse helped to "diabolize" them—was intended for Satan in hell. The singing among the Sami, called *Joik,* which accompanied the beating of the drum, was regarded as a diabolical, monotonous cacophony.

While under the spell of his satanic trance, a shaman communicated with his attendant demon that, because of its tremendous acuity and faculty for moving swiftly, could divulge global events to its master. As a result, seventeenth-century Lutheran missionaries to the Sami regions made arrangements to burn these drums and thereby destroy the Sami pagan gods. The demonizing of this pantheistic religion continued throughout the seventeenth century, and Sami who believed they could predict the future were accused of being satanic prophets.

DIABOLICUS GANDUS

The ancient idea of "elf-shot" (in German, *Hexenschuss*) was the third kind of sorcery attributed to the Sami. This kind of spell casting, or *gand* (*diabolicus gandus,* in Sami sorcery trials of the seventeenth century), was what pious Norwegians feared most during the sixteenth century and the beginning of the seventeenth century. The witches of Lapland were known to cast their evil spells across vast distances. Their spells could even be carried upon the northern winds and could provoke illnesses among people far to the south in Europe. "Shooting," or the conjuring of spells "on the wind," was a well-known *maleficium* (harmful magic) across most of northern Scandinavia and was asserted with great conviction by some leading European intellectuals. Among others, the famous French jurist and demonologist Jean Bodin had much to say about the evil magic of Lapland's witches. The *gand* was imagined to be something physical. "Lapp shots" were perceived as small leaden darts, which the Sami could shoot across great distances. In the mid-sixteenth century, Olaus Magnus described them as small leaden arrows. At the end of the seventeenth century, a Norwegian vicar, Petter Dass, later described the Sami spell as vile, dark blue flies, or "Beelzebub's flies." Court records from northern Norwegian witchcraft trials offer explicit descriptions and actual illustrations of the Sami *gand.* One of the passages even mentions that the *gand* resembles a mouse with heads at both front and rear. What we today call shamanism among the Sami was regarded by the Lutheran confessional church as the worst type of superstition and witchcraft. A few witchcraft trials in Norwegian, Finnish, and Swedish Lapland contained elements of shamanism.

LAPLAND WITCHES AND THE WITCH HUNT

As a collective group living in the borderlands, moving and trading within three countries at the same time, the Sami posed a threat to the territorial expansion of Nordic countries and their endeavors to spread Christian civilization in the North. This was especially the case for the conflicts among Russia, Sweden, and Denmark-Norway at a time of territorial state formation. All of them considered the Sami as subjects in need of proper integration. Fearful of Sami sorcery, the Norwegians, according to reports forwarded to King Christian IV in 1608, dared not inhabit the fjords of Finnmark that were populated by the "wild and wicked" Sami. In response, the king in 1609 commanded the governors of his northern-Norwegian districts to hunt down and eradicate all kinds of Sami sorcery. Those who practiced it would be put to death. In the three counties that comprise Arctic Norway, civil courts held witchcraft trials for thirty-seven individual Sami between 1593 and 1692 (Hagen 1999). Of these, twenty men and eight women were burned at the stake. Suspicion of sorcery was one of the charges that arose every time serious conflicts emerged between the Sami and the Danish-Norwegian authorities during this period. But still, it should be pointed out that there were many more Norwegian women involved in the hunt than people from the indigenous group.

TABLE L-1 WITCHCRAFT TRIALS IN NORTHERN NORWAY (ARCTIC NORWAY) 1593-1692

Gender and ethnicity	Total	Death sentences
Female—Sami	11	8
Male—Sami	26	20
Female—Norwegian	120	87
Male—Norwegian	14	5
Unknown	6	6
Total	177	126

Meanwhile, in Swedish regions of Lapland, seventy-three Sami males and three Sami females were prosecuted between 1639 and 1749 on charges of using drums and practicing sacrificial rituals (Granqvist 1998). Few of them received death penalties, however.

In both Norway and Sweden, it was primarily Sami men who were accused of witchcraft. The notion of witchcraft, with few exceptions, was primarily a male phenomenon in Sami society. At the same time, in small northern Norwegian coastal villages, witchcraft was basically a crime committed by Norwegian women. Legal sources thus confirm that Sami men were the basic cultural bearers of their traditional ritual magic. And the witchcraft trials of the far north were distinctive in a European context because of the simultaneous prosecutions of wives of seasonal Norwegian fishermen and of Sami shamans.

RUNE HAGEN;

TRANSLATED BY MARK LEDINGHAM

See also: BODIN, JEAN; CHRISTIAN IV; DENMARK; FAMILIARS; FINLAND; GENDER; MAGNUS, OLAUS; MALE WITCHES; METAMORPHOSIS; NORWAY; SHAMANISM; SORCERY; SPELLS; SWEDEN; WIND KNOTS.

References and further reading:

Ahlbäck, Tore, and Jan Bergman, eds. 1991. *The Saami Shaman Drum.* Åbo Scripta Instituti Donneriani Åboensis Series, 14.

Anderson, M.S. 1958. *Britain's Discovery of Russia, 1553–1815.* London: MacMillan and New York: St. Martin's.

Granqvist, Karin. 1998. "'Thou shalt have no other Gods before me' (Exodus 20:3): Witchcraft and Superstition Trials in Seventeenth- and Eighteenth-Century Swedish Lapland." Pp. 13–29 in *Kulturkonfrontation i Lappmarken,* edited by P. Sköld and K. Kram. Umeå: Kulturgräns Norr.

Hagen, Rune. 1999. "The Witch Hunt in Early Modern Finnmark." *Acta Borealia: A Norwegian Journal of Circumpolar Societies* (Oslo: Novus Forlag) 16, no. 1: 43–62.

———. 2002. "Early Modern Representations of the Far North: The 1670 Voyage of La Martinière." *ARV—Nordic Yearbook of Folklore* 58: 19–42.

———. 2003. "At the Edge of Civilisation: John Cunningham, Lensmann of Finnmark, 1619–51." Pp. 29–51 in *Military Governors and Imperial Frontiers c. 1600–1800.* Edited by A. Mackillop and Steve Murdoch. Boston and Leiden: Brill.

Moyer, Ernest J. 1981. *Raising the Wind: The Legend of Lapland and Finland Wizards in Literature,* edited by Wayne R. Kime. Newark: University of Delaware Press.

Mundal, Else. 1996. "The Perception of the Saamis and Their Religion in Old Norse Sources." Pp. 97–116 in *Shamanism and Northern Ecology.* Edited by Juha Pentikäinen. Berlin and New York: de Gruyter.

Nenonen, Marko. 1993. "Envious Are All the People, Witches Watch at Every Gate: Finnish Witches and Witch Trials in the Seventeenth Century." *Scandinavian Journal of History* 18, no. 1: 77–92.

Rydving, Håkan. 1995. *The End of Drum-Time: Religious Change among the Lule Saami, 1670s–1740s.* 2nd rev. ed. Uppsala: Almqvist and Wiksell International.

LARNER, CHRISTINA (1934–1983)

A preeminent historian of the Scottish witch hunt. Larner's main book, *Enemies of God* (1981), is a beacon of methodological clarity that ranks among the most influential and widely cited regional studies of European witch hunting.

Larner, a sociologist at the University of Glasgow, taught not only in her own department but also in those of history and politics, and she was appointed to a personal chair shortly before her tragically early death. She wrote her PhD thesis (1962) on Scottish witchcraft, and in 1970 Norman Cohn encouraged her to resume work on this. A new anthropological perspective on village-level witchcraft was opening up, which Larner was well placed to exploit. However, she first studied an elite witch hunter and demonologist, publishing "James VI and I and Witchcraft" in 1973 in a volume edited by Glasgow historian Alan Smith. (It was republished, along with most of the rest of her articles, in the 1984 collection, *Witchcraft and Religion: The Politics of Popular Belief.*) Although her idea that James imported the demonic pact to Scotland from Denmark in 1590 has been questioned, her article remains essential for the development of James's views.

Larner then obtained funding for a project to collect information on all recorded cases of witchcraft in Scotland. The results, published by her research team in 1977, listed 3,069 witchcraft "cases" with their place, date, and trial status. Although an imperfect work (riddled with miscitations, several hundred duplicate cases, and other errors), it exploited hitherto-unused manuscript sources and provided a firmer statistical basis for the Scottish witch hunt than had ever been available before. The best estimates for numbers of executions had hitherto ranged between 3,000 and 4,500; Larner pared away layers of speculation to show that the number must have been much lower. More than half of these "cases" (the exact proportion was unknown) ended in acquittals or other noncapital outcomes, suggesting a figure of probably fewer than

1,500 executions with a maximum of 2,000 (Larner 1984, 28). More recent research has explored further sources and has tended to raise the numbers somewhat but has also endorsed the soundness of Larner's basic approach.

Larner's masterpiece, *Enemies of God,* was also written at this time. It combined statistics with a detailed reading of individual cases. Many seminal works are characterized by a single penetrating idea, but Larner's work stood out in its balanced use of complementary methodologies. She reconstructed peasant networks of accusation with the same verve that she brought to beliefs about the Devil or theories of social control. She confirmed the quarrelsomeness of many accused witches while showing that Scotland did not fully fit the "Thomas-Macfarlane" model, whereby English witches were accused after a denial of charity was followed by misfortune. Distinguishing between "English" and "continental" patterns of witch hunting, she placed Scotland between the two. Subsequent research, although refining the "continental" pattern, has not significantly modified Larner's conclusion. She was alive to the hitherto-neglected issue of women as witches, but she resisted the tendency of some feminist contemporaries to turn the witch hunt into a "woman hunt."

As well as peasant quarrelsomeness, Larner emphasized the responsibility of governmental authorities. She came to believe that *witch hunting* was an apt term because witches did have to be sought out and labeled. She had not yet reached that point when she wrote in her 1962 thesis, "There are those who claim that the witchcraft persecution originated at the end of the fifteenth century precisely because this was the era of the creation of the modern state. . . . Yet most historians today would not give that importance to the late fifteenth and early sixteenth centuries in the creation of fully developed administrative systems which writers of an earlier generation did." But she later changed her mind, adding a pencil note in the margin: "But I think I would now (1971) plus literacy" (Larner 1962, 15). She was, in fact, moving toward what she called "the Christianization of the people" (Larner 1981, chap. 12), a process taken up by local elites seeking to inculcate godly discipline; after the godly King James VI succeeded the godly state. A few of its details were problematic—her much-quoted "general commission" or "standing commissions" of the 1590s have proved illusory—but later research has borne out the general soundness of her approach.

What most distinguished Larner's book was its methodological sophistication. She was far more familiar with social theory than most empiricist historians; she could write about the problems of "treating seventeenth-century culture as an alien belief system" (Larner 1981, 134) from within the rich conceptual framework of the social sciences. She took a particular interest in the belief system of preindustrial Europe, characterizing it as a "middle ground" society, neither primitive nor dominated by belief in science and technology.

After *Enemies of God,* Larner gave the 1982 Gifford Lectures, "Relativism and Ethnocentrism: Popular and Educated Belief in Pre-Industrial Culture." These lectures, by a sociologist intervening in a debate "among philosophers and anthropologists" (Larner 1984, 97), are vital for historians of witchcraft, who need to decide how to respond to beliefs that seem alien. She provided a powerful corrective, both to condescending accounts of past "ignorance" and "superstition" and to extreme relativist interpretations in which all beliefs are equally valid. Larner's clear, jargon-free prose sparkled with erudite wit and humor. Arguing against reductionist explanations for witchcraft beliefs, she asked, "Was the social structure of hell feudal or was it more likely 'hydraulic' (the term given by Karl Wittfogel to despotic regimes organized in relation to permanent water shortage)?" (Larner 1981, 202). She not only knew her subject, she also knew how to communicate it.

JULIAN GOODARE

See also: FEMINISM; GENDER; HISTORIOGRAPHY; JAMES VI AND I, KING OF SCOTLAND AND ENGLAND; SCOTLAND.

References and further reading:
Goodare, Julian. 2002. "Introduction." Pp. 1–15 in *The Scottish Witch-Hunt in Context.* Edited by Julian Goodare. Manchester: Manchester University Press.
Larner (née Ross), Christina. 1962. "Scottish Demonology in the Sixteenth and Seventeenth Centuries and Its Theological Background." PhD diss., University of Edinburgh.
———. 1977. "Two Late Scottish Witchcraft Tracts: *Witch-Craft Proven* and *The Tryal of Witchcraft.*" Pp. 227–245 in *The Damned Art: Essays in the Literature of Witchcraft.* Edited by Sydney Anglo. London: Routledge and Kegan Paul.
———. 1981. *Enemies of God: The Witch-Hunt in Scotland.* London: Chatto and Windus.
———. 1984. *Witchcraft and Religion: The Politics of Popular Belief.* Edited by Alan Macfarlane. Oxford: Blackwell.
Larner (née Ross), Christina, Christopher H. Lee, and Hugh V. McLachlan, comps. 1977. *A Source-Book of Scottish Witchcraft.* Glasgow: Department of Sociology, University of Glasgow.

LATVIA

Witchcraft trials occurred between 1548 and 1699 in Latvia, which was partitioned and dominated by Poland, Sweden, and Russia in the early modern period.

Latvian folklore preserves extremely rich evidence about witches in its folktales, legends, stories, customs, sayings, riddles, beliefs, incantations, and folk songs. In folktales, the witch's husband is the Devil. She herself eats people and kills her own daughters. Latvian witches live in strange houses with one leg, dance with devils in hell, can change their form, and cast spells that turn people into animals or objects. They have tails, which not everyone can see. Like sorcerers, they do not die easily. Folklorists have preserved other traditions concerning Latvian witches. Evil people turn into witches, having given up their souls to the Devil. Anyone can become a witch by putting drugs in a mortar and grinding them up while making an incantation; one must also wear appropriate clothes and walk in a circle around the mortar, until one flies away through the air. Or one can become a witch by smearing a special ointment on the body, particularly in the armpits. On the Saturday of Whitsuntide, a woman can wash in the bathhouse, wrap herself in a white cloth, and lie down to sleep in the bushes on her stomach. An evil force will fly down in the form of a bee, crawl into the sleeping woman, and she will become a witch. By a single look, witches can harm newborn babies, often exchanging the children for their own.

According to folklore, milk witches were especially widespread throughout Latvia. They milk cows belonging to others and collect dew from fields to bewitch their neighbors' livestock, transferring the milk to themselves. Witches are particularly active on June 23 (Midsummer Night), but animals also need protection from them on other special nights. Milk witches have their own servants, the milk carriers, whom they feed and maintain.

Although Livonia was famous as a land of witches, sorcerers, and werewolves, its recorded witchcraft trials only began in the mid-sixteenth century and never reached the scale seen in most European countries. Witches and sorceresses were well known in medieval Latvia, under the Livonian Order (a crusading order). Several of Latvia's earliest law codes contained articles dealing with witches, and their punishment was that of heretics—burning—but no trials were recorded. Regulations issued at Valmiera in 1537 charged territorial overlords and church authorities with prohibiting and eradicating sorcery, superstition, and idolatry. The death penalty for malignant sorcery was also envisaged in the Carolina Code (1532) of the Holy Roman Empire, which became law in Livonia soon after being issued in 1532. We know about witchcraft trials from Cçsis in 1548 and from Courland in 1550 (Augstkalns 1938, 169). In 1559, the bailiff of Grobiòa ordered a witch to be burned, the first such instance known in Latvia (Arbusow 1910, 104).

However, after the area came under Polish rule in the second half of the sixteenth century, witchcraft trials attained their typical form in Latvia, with an inquisitorial procedure, examining witches, torture, and irregular institution of proceedings. Much of our evidence comes from sources in Riga and the surrounding area, where twelve sorcerers and witches were burned between 1577 and 1590. Almost as many victims were recorded from the first decades of the seventeenth century (Svelpis 1984, 182).

Latvian legal practice made extensive use of so-called ducking (also known as the swimming test or the water ordeal) to identify witches. It was mentioned in Latvia's first documented witchcraft trial, in 1548, when the master of the Livonian Order, Hermann von Brüggenei, submitted a legal opinion regarding ducking to the Cçsis town council (Augstkalns 1938, 197). The method was as follows: An executioner undressed the accused, tied her arms and legs crosswise, and, holding her by a rope, submerged her three times in cold water, repeating the ducking in case of doubt. According to the records, the accused usually "floated on the water like a duck" or "like a blade of grass," providing sufficient proof of guilt. Some sources also mentioned complaints that executioners, by tugging on the rope or by various other means, had not allowed the accused to sink. If during the ducking the accused died in the icy water, the court recorded that the Devil had killed the witch to prevent him or her from betraying associates. In Riga and the area that later became Courland, ducking was used rarely at first, beginning in the mid-sixteenth century, because neither local custom nor general German law envisaged this form of interrogation. But by the first half of the seventeenth century, witch ducking was practiced throughout Latvia, being abandoned only at the close of the century.

After 1621, Latvia was divided. In the west, the duchy of Courland and Semigallia made up a vassal state of Poland; in the center, the lands on the right bank of the River Daugava along with Riga became the Swedish province of Livland; and the eastern part, Latgale, belonged to Poland. These regions differed in their handling of witchcraft trials.

In Livland, the largest number of witchcraft trials took place in the 1630s. Legends about covens and corporations of sorcerers and witches, who were thought to meet in a bog or on a hill and who could harm livestock, people, and crops with the aid of Satan, were widespread in all sections of society. Pastors and judges also believed in them. Hermann Samson (1579–1643), senior pastor of St. Peter's Church in Riga and superintendent of Livland, demanded in his sermons that all malignant witches be put to death. He also reported that in the course of church inspections, many people had complained to him about witches and sorcerers. Evidence of frequent witchcraft trials can be found in the records of Livland's High Court, which show that forty such proceedings were begun between 1630 and 1640; most of them ended with the burning of the accused. Witchcraft trials also took place at almost every session of the Land Court. Often, the accused named her supposed associates, so the proceedings included groups of defendants. One case tried in 1646 at Riga's Land Court involved fifty accused witches (Arbusow 1910, 118).

In the second half of the seventeenth century, the number of witchcraft trials in Livland fell, and the death penalty was seldom invoked. This resulted partly from Swedish royal decrees from 1665 and 1687 stating that the death penalty could only be applied for malignant sorcery and a pact with Satan; divination, fortunetelling, quackery, and other superstitions were punishable only with fines and corporal punishments, along with public confession and putting in the stocks during the church service.

After torture was forbidden in the courts of Livland in 1686, the number of sorcerers and witches fell sharply. Courts in Livland often complained that they could no longer force accused witches and sorcerers to confess and that the accused had to be acquitted or punished for superstition with quite light, arbitrary penalties, which usually meant beating peasants with ten or twenty blows from rods, followed by confession and being locked in the stocks or pillory. After 1686, Livland's High Court imposed very few death penalties. The last case of witch burning in Livland occurred in 1692 and the last beheading of a witch in 1699 (Svelpis 1984, 183).

By the eighteenth century, when Russia annexed Livland, belief in witches and sorcery had declined significantly. In the court records from before 1731, one still finds a few such cases, but now the guilty were punished only for superstition, and the most severe penalty was a sentence of life imprisonment passed in 1724. In 1731, the Senate, in order to eradicate the superstition of supposed sorcerers, stated that such deceivers were to be burned alive, and those who requested help from witches and sorcerers should be whipped severely or even executed. Afterward, trials connected with sorcery and witches came to an end in Livland.

In the duchy of Courland and Semigallia, persecution of witches, based on Article 209 of the Statute of Courland and on the General German Law, continued unhindered throughout the seventeenth and eighteenth centuries. Court archives show witches being punished by burning, beheading, or banishment. Thus, for example, in the Sçlpils district alone, a total of thirty-one witchcraft trials were held at the Senior Castellan's Court between 1630 and 1720; fifteen executions took place, the last witch being burned in 1718. At Blankenfelde in Semigallia, two witches were burned as late as 1721 (Arbusow 1910, 117–119).

There is very meager information about witchcraft trials in Latgale, the part of Latvia under direct Polish rule. However, witchcraft trials may have been just as frequent there as elsewhere. Poland only repealed the death penalty for witches in 1776, that is, after Latgale had been annexed to Russia.

Belief in sorcery and witches long persisted in the popular mind, as Latvia's rich folklore testifies. Thus, as late as 1808, a noblewoman in Livland ordered her maidservant to be flogged mercilessly for casting a spell on the manor's livestock and for keeping a "dragon" at home. An 1848 issue of the newspaper *Inland* expressed the opinion that witches existed and suggested that they should be stoned.

PÂRSLA PÇTERSONE

See also: CAROLINA CODE (*CONSTITUTIO CRIMINALIS CAROLINA*); FOLKLORE; LYCANTHROPY; MILK; POLAND; RUSSIA; SWIMMING TEST; TRIALS.

References and further reading:
Arbusow, Leonid. 1910. "Zauber- und Hexenwahn in den baltischen Provinzen." Pp. 101–126 in *Rigascher Almanach für 1911*. Riga.
Augstkalns, Alvils. 1938. "Dapas 16. gadsimta Rîgas raganu un burvju prâvas." Pp. 167–197 in *Tautas vçsturei*. Riga: Ansis Gulbis.
Brastiòô, Ernests. 1963. *Mûsu dievestîbu tûkstôgadîgâ apkarôana*. Chicago: Latvju Dievturu Draudze.
Latvijas PSR Zinâtòu Akadçmijas Vçstures Institûts. 1978. *Feodâlâ Rîga*. Riga: Zinâtne.
Samson, Hermann. 1626. *Neun ausserlesen und wolgegründete Hexen Predigt*. Riga.
Straubergs, Kârlis. 1941. *Latvieôu buramie vârdi*. Riga: Latvju folkloras krâtuve.
Svelpis, Alnis. 1984. Latvieôu raganas un viòu tiesas. Pp. 180–183 in *Dabas un vçstures kalendârs*. Riga: Zinâtne.

LAUSANNE, DIOCESE OF (FIFTEENTH CENTURY)

The diocese of Lausanne, in the center of French Switzerland, covered most of the present cantons of Vaud, Fribourg, Bern, and Neuchâtel. Together with Dauphiné, the Valais, the Val d'Aosta, and the Bernese Oberland (all in the western Alps), it became a center for persecutions of the new heresy of witches and devil worshipers in the fifteenth century. Its first witchcraft trials took place in the 1430s, with many local witch hunts following later in the century. Nearly fifty records of fifteenth-century witchcraft trials are preserved from the diocese of Lausanne. Many recent microanalyses and critical editions have helped clarify both the local and judicial implications of this phenomenon. Dominican inquisitors conducted these trials, using inquisitorial procedure, that is, relying on denunciations and local rumor (*fama*) when arresting suspects, making secret investigations, and employing torture. An element specific to the fifteenth-century witchcraft trials in the diocese of Lausanne is their detailed descriptions of the witches' Sabbat, called the "synagogue," including secret gatherings of the sect around a demon, banquets, cannibalism of children, night flight on brooms or sticks, and evil ointments.

CHRONOLOGICAL SURVEY

The first well-documented witch hunt occurred in 1448 near Vevey. The three trial records preserved establish that at least seven sorcerers and witches were condemned and that forty other persons were denounced and probably prosecuted (Ostorero 1995). Thirty years later, the same Riviera region of Lake Geneva experienced a second witch craze, often involving the same families, in which at least a dozen victims were condemned to the stake (Maier 1996). Around 1460, a witch hunt affected some territories of the prince-bishop of Lausanne, Georges de Saluces (Saluzzo), located in the eastern part of his diocese (Henniez, La Roche, and Bulle). His persecution of devil worshipers formed part of a larger movement of spiritual reform he initiated in his diocese (Modestin 1999).

The village of Dommartin, north of Lausanne, appeared to be a nest of sorcerers and witches. Relatively important hunts happened here twice, in 1498 and again around 1525—the first carried out by a Dominican inquisitor, the second by the area's local landlords, the cathedral chapter of Lausanne. Microanalyses have shown that the victims of Dommartin's persecution were mostly rich farmers, well integrated into their community but engaged in conflicts either with neighbors, with their own families over inheritances, or with the local authorities. Accusations of witchcraft reveal local tensions and conflicts that led to unusually dramatic resolutions, that is, the inquisitors and the stake (Chollet 1989; Pfister 1997).

In the northern part of the diocese of Lausanne, the region of Neuchâtel experienced two witch hunts: first around 1439, then from 1480 to 1499 (Andenmatten and Utz Tremp 1992). In the east, around Fribourg, the first witchcraft cases appeared between 1438 and 1442; it is the only situation in the diocese of Lausanne when witches were judged not by the Inquisition but by local secular authorities (Utz Tremp 1995, 42–47).

CONTEMPORARY ECHOES OF THE WITCH HUNTS

Apart from the judicial records, both the novelty of the phenomenon and its importance in the diocese of Lausanne were amply attested. In 1438, Aymonet Maugetaz, a young man of the wine-growing village Epesses, went "spontaneously" to the inquisitor Ulric de Torrenté to confess that he belonged to a sect of Devil worshipers who committed *maleficia* (harmful magic). He told how witches stole ice from the mountains in order to make it fall on the crops as hail. This anecdote reappeared almost verbatim in a second version of the anonymous treatise *Errores gazariorum* (Errors of the Gazars or Gazarii [Cathars—a common term for heretics and later witches]), first written around 1436 in the Val d'Aosta. That clue proved that this text, which contained one of the first descriptions of the witches' Sabbat, was also used by inquisitors in the diocese of Lausanne. In his *Formicarius* (The Anthill, 1437–1438), the Dominican theologian

Johannes Nider, a professor at the University of Vienna, related facts of witchcraft that had taken place *recently* in the diocese of Lausanne, that is to say, around 1435–1438. Nider took most of his examples from trials held in the diocese of Lausanne, mostly in the Bernese territories. Unfortunately, no judicial evidence has been found yet (Chène 1999, 223–248). Martin Le Franc, the secretary of the Savoyard antipope Felix V, described the new crimes associated with witches in his lengthy poem *Le Champion des dames* (The Defender of Ladies, 1440–1442). Although he referred to a valley in Dauphiné (*Valpute, Vallouise*), Le Franc must also have known about the first witch hunts in the diocese of Lausanne, because he was then provost of the chapter of Lausanne. In a bull of 1440 against duke Amadeus VIII of Savoy, elected by the Council of Basel as the antipope Felix V (1439–1449), Eugenius IV connected his rival's pontificate with all the heresies and sorcery in his lands. Therefore, from Vienna to Rome, the diocese of Lausanne (mostly a Savoyard possession), had the dubious reputation of a land filled with devil worshipers as early as 1440.

INQUISITION AND JUDICIAL FRAMEWORK

In the diocese of Lausanne, Dominican inquisitors conducted all trials in collaboration with the vicar of the bishop of Lausanne. Their intervention began only upon request from local authorities, who were present in court. The local population played an important role by denouncing suspects. Between 1450 and 1480, inquisitors conducted most of these trials in the castle of Ouchy, in Lausanne, where suspects were brought. Their archives were conserved in this castle as the episcopal Inquisition became increasingly effective.

The longtime prince-bishop of Lausanne, Georges de Saluces (Saluzzo), began the first witch hunts in his diocese, after having done the same in the diocese of Aosta before moving to Lausanne. The struggle against heretics was part of his program of spiritual reform. A major regional power in the fifteenth century, he had the favor of his close relative, the Duke of Savoy, Amadeus VIII, overlord of the Pays de Vaud.

MEN OR WOMEN?

One particularity of the witchcraft phenomenon in the diocese of Lausanne was the high rate of men sentenced, amounting to 60 percent of all fifteenth-century cases. The most frequent explanation offered is that in this region, the Inquisition was actively pursuing Waldensians, both men and women, at the beginning of this century. The image of the witch and devil worshiper had been fashioned from the figure of the heretic. For example, the persons persecuted for witchcraft in 1448 at Vevey were defined as "modern Waldensians heretics" (*heretici moderni valdenses)*. Witchcraft implied a pact with the Devil, making it a crime against God; therefore, the sorcerer was above all a heretic. In the first phase of witch persecutions, this crime, like Waldensianism, was often charged to men.

MARTINE OSTORERO

See also: *ERRORES GAZARIORUM;* BASEL, COUNCIL OF; DAUPHINE; DOMINICAN ORDER; EUGENIUS IV; GENDER; HERESY; INQUISITION MEDIEVAL; INQUISITORIAL PROCEDURE; LE FRANC, MARTIN; MALE WITCHES; MOUNTAINS AND THE ORIGINS OF WITCHCRAFT; NIDER, JOHANNES; ORIGINS OF THE WITCH HUNTS; SABBAT; SAVOY, DUCHY OF; VALAIS; *VADAI* (WALDENSIANS) VAUD, PAYS DE;.

References and further reading:
Andenmatten, Bernard, and Kathrin Utz Tremp. 1992. "De l'hérésie à la sorcellerie: l'inquisiteur Ulric de Torrenté OP (vers 1420–1445) et l'affermissement de l'inquisition en Suisee romande." *Revue d'histoire ecclésiastique suisse* 86: 69–119.
Blauert, Andreas. 1989. *Frühe Hexenverfolgungen: Ketzer-, Zauberei- und Hexenprozesse des 15. Jahrhunderts.* Hamburg: Sozialgeschichtliche Bibliothek bei Junius.
Chène, Catherine. 1999. "Johannes Nider, Formicarius (livre II, chap. 4 et livre V, chaps. 3, 4 et 7)." Pp. 99–266 in *L'imaginaire du sabbat: Editions critique des textes les plus anciens (1430–1440)."* Edited by Martine Ostorero, Agostino Paravicini Bagliani, Kathrin Utz, and Catherine Chene. Lausanne: Cahiers lausannois d'historie medievale, 26. Section d'Historie, Faculte des Lettres.
Choffat, Pierre-Han. 1989. *La sorcellerie comme exutoire: Tensions et conflits locaux, Dommartin 1524–1528.* Cahiers lausannois d'histoire médiévale 1. Lausanne: Section d'Histoire, Faculté des Lettres.
Maier, Eva. 1996. *Trente ans avec le diable: Une deuxième chasse aux sorciers sur la Riviera lémanique (1477–1484).* Cahiers lausannois d'histoire médiévale 17. Lausanne: Section d'Histoire, Faculté des Lettres.
Maier, Eva, Martine Ostorero, and Kathrin Utz Tremp. 1997. "Le pouvoir de l'inquisition." Pp. 247–258 in *Les pays romands au Moyen Age.* Edited by Agostino Paravicini Bagliani, Jean-Pierre Felber, Jean-Daniel Morerod, and Véronique Pasche. Lausanne: Payot.
Modestin, Georg. 1999. *Le diable chez l'évêque: Chasse aux sorciers dans le diocèse de Lausanne vers 1460.* Cahiers lausannois d'histoire médiévale 25. Lausanne: Section d'Histoire, Faculté des Lettres.
Ostorero, Martine. 1995. *"Folâtrer avec les démons": Sabbat et chasse aux sorciers à Vevey en 1448.* Cahiers lausannois d'histoire médiévale 15. Lausanne: Section d'Histoire, Faculté des Lettres.
Ostorero, Martine, Agostino Paravicini Bagliani, Kathrin Utz Tremp, and Catherine Chène, eds. 1999. *L'imaginaire du sabbat: Edition critique des textes les plus anciens (1430 c.–1440 c.).* Lausanne: Cahiers lausannois d'histoire médiévale 26. Section d'Histoire, Faculté des Lettres.
Pfister, Laurence. 1997. *L'enfer sur terre: Sorcellerie à Dommartin (1498).* Cahiers lausannois d'histoire médiévale 20. Lausanne: Section d'Histoire, Faculté des Lettres.
Utz Tremp, Kathrin. 1995. "Ist Glaubenssache Frauensache? Zu den Anfängen der Hexenverfolgungen in Freiburg (um 1440)." *Freiburger Geschichtsblätter* 72: 9–50.

LAWS ON WITCHCRAFT (ANCIENT)

Laws against the practice of magic in the ancient world were more numerous, specific, and punitive in Rome than in Greece.

GREEK LAW

Few traces remain of legislation of any kind against magic by any Greek state. Indeed, it seems the Greeks never outlawed (or defined) magic as a category, although it may have been possible to prosecute harmful acts of magic under more general laws. A common source of ambiguity in ancient law, for the ancients themselves and for modern interpreters alike, has been equivocation of the Greek word *pharmakon* and its Latin equivalent *venenum* between "poison," "drug," and "spell."

Shortly after 479 B.C.E., Teos in Asia Minor erected an inscription known as the *Dirae Teiorum* (Curses of the Teians), which began with the imprecation "If anyone makes harmful spells/poisons [*pharmaka dêlêtêria*] against the Teian state or against individuals of it, he is to die, himself and his family with him" (Meiggs and Lewis 1969, no. 30). The fact that the state was contemplated as an object of possible attack guarantees that *pharmaka* here included spells. The text generally resembled an early law code in style, layout, and phraseology, and it may therefore have prescribed in trials. But the demand that the perpetrator's family should also die suggested rather the deterrent technique of a curse and an ill-defined magical defense against an ill-defined magical attack.

It is sometimes speculated that one could seek redress against harmful magic in fifth- and fourth-century B.C.E. Athens through a "public prosecution for damage" (*dikê blabês*). When, in that city, Philoneos's concubine supposedly poisoned him accidentally in the belief that she was giving him a love potion, she was charged with (and executed for) murder, pure and simple, according to Antiphon. The circumstances of the condemnation and execution of the "witch" (*pharmakis*) Theoris remain obscure, but the charge was one of impiety, as Demosthenes tells us.

In the first century B.C.E., the private rules of a religious cult in Philadelphia in Lydia required its members, among other things, to "swear an oath by all the gods not to use trickery against men or women, not to devise or perform a wicked spell [*pharmakon*] against people, nor wicked incantations [*epôidai*], nor a love charm [*philtron*], nor an abortifacient, nor a contraceptive" (Dittenberger 1915–1924, no. 985).

Beyond this, we can only turn to the imaginary regulations Plato composed for an ideal state in his *Laws* in the fourth-century B.C.E. First he prescribed that those found guilty of the evocation of the dead, of trying to bring compulsion upon the gods through sorcery (*goêteia*), or of trying to destroy families for money were to be jailed for life and deprived of contact with free men; when they died, their bodies were to be cast out without burial. But then he prescribed execution for those found guilty of producing binding spells, charms, or incantations. It remains unclear whether these laws resembled any on the statute books of any Greek state of Plato's day, but the philosopher does seem to have been particularly hostile to sorcerers inasmuch as they were rival soul-technicians.

It seems, however, that magic was much used in association with the law. Numerous classical Athenian "tongue-binding" curse-tablets, or *defixiones,* manufactured against opponents in lawsuits have been discovered in the city's civic center and its Ceramicus Cemetery. A number of protective amulets for use in lawsuits also survive from the wider ancient world.

ROMAN LAW

Roman law is a more fertile area of study. The original Roman law code of 451 B.C.E., the *Twelve Tables,* included laws against the singing of evil incantations (*malum carmen*) and against the charming of crops from one field into another (*excantatio cultorum*), but we have no indication of the assigned penalties. The specification here of "evil" suggests that harmless varieties of incantation were permitted; certainly Cato the Elder was able to publish a healing incantation in his *De agricultura* of circa 160 B.C.E. In the first-century C.E., Pliny the Elder recounted an apocryphal tale about the unsuccessful prosecution of the honest freedman Cresimus for crop charming in his *Natural History* (77).

The principal law against magic in the Late Republic and after seems to have been Lucius Cornelius Sulla's 81 B.C.E. *Lex Cornelia de sicariis et veneficis* (Law of Cornelius on Assassins and Poisoners/Sorcerers). Once again, the key Latin term is equivocal, but the later jurists leave us in no doubt about the law's scope; they also specify that it outlawed, among other things, the selling, buying, possession, and administering of harmful drugs. It is usually believed that it was in reply to a prosecution under this law that Apuleius of Madaura made his famous ironic *Apology,* or "defense speech," on a capital charge at Sabratha in 158–159 C.E. Apuleius had arrived in the North African town of Oea and persuaded its most desirable rich widow, Pudentilla, to marry him, to the chagrin of her family, who wished to retain control of her money. They accordingly brought him to trial, primarily on the grounds that he had used erotic magic to seduce Pudentilla, but the case was built up with many further allegations of magical practice, such as the use of voodoo dolls and the infliction of trances upon boys for divination. A second-century C.E. rhetorical exercise by Hadrian of Tyre may have indicated that it was usual to burn witches at the stake, in a remarkable anticipation of more-modern ages.

The events of the so-called Bacchanalian conspiracy, resulting in the Senatorial Decree on Bacchanals of 186 B.C.E., and the subsequent execution, supposedly, of some 5,000 people for sorcery (according to Livy) showed the Roman government for the first time linking magic, divination, and foreign cults and considering all alike to be threats to the state. Cassius Dio later imagines Agrippa explaining the relationship to the new emperor Augustus:

> You should hate and punish those who introduce foreign elements into our religion . . . because men of this sort, by importing new powers, persuade many people to take up foreign customs, and from this are born conspiracies and gatherings and secret clubs, which are the last thing a monarchy needs. Do not then permit people to be atheists or sorcerers [*goêtes*] . . . it is proper that there should be no mages [*mageutai*] whatsoever. For such men often incite many to revolution, either by telling the truth, or, as more often, by telling lies. (*Roman History* 52.36.1–2)

Executions or expulsions from the city of individuals branded as "Chaldaeans," "astrologers," "sorcerers," or "mages," together with burnings of their books, became frequent. Large groups were again targeted under the Republic in 139 B.C.E, and under the earlier empire in 33 B.C.E. (Augustus), 45 C.E. (Tiberius), 52 C.E. (Nero), and 69 C.E. (Vitellius). The emperors were particularly sensitive to the conspiratorial implications of divinations made to individuals and divinations on the subject of death, their own death in particular. Augustus, Tiberius, Nero, and Valens took special measures to ban this.

Under the Christian empire (for the relevant laws of which see the ninth book of the Theodosian Code), Constantine legislated in 319 C.E. against soothsaying and magic, making special mention of magic to create erotic attraction but excepting measures taken for healing or for agricultural weather control. In 357 C.E., Constantius II legislated against soothsayers, astrologers, diviners, augurs, seers, Chaldaeans, mages, and evildoers (*maleficii*) in general. The effects of Constantius's legislation were far-reaching. It resulted, Ammianus Marcellinus tells us, in the execution of individuals merely for wearing amulets or for passing by graves at night. Further legislation followed under Valentinian between 368 and 389 C.E. and under Honorius in 409.

In his *Apology,* Apuleius cleverly argued that there were no circumstances under which a charge of magic should be brought: If a charge was false, it should not be brought for that reason alone, but if it was true, then the accuser would fall victim to the magician's terrible power, which was inevitably greater than that of the court.

DANIEL OGDEN

See also: AMULET AND TALISMAN; APULEIUS OF MADAURA; *DEFIXIONE;* DIVINATION; LOVE MAGIC; POISON; POTIONS; ROMAN LAW; SPELLS.

References and further reading:

Clerk, Jean-Benoît. 1995. *Homines magici: Etude sur la sorcellerie et la magie dans la société romaine impériale.* Berne: Lang.

Collins, Derek. 2001. "Theoris of Lemnos and the Criminalization of Magic in Fourth-Century Athens." *Classical Quarterly* 51: 477–493.

Dittenberger, Wilhelm, ed. 1915–1924. *Sylloge inscriptionum graecarum.* 3rd ed. 4 vols. Leipzig: Hirzel.

Gordon, Richard L. 1999. "Imagining Greek and Roman Magic." Pp. 159–275 in *Witchcraft and Magic in Europe: Ancient Greece and Rome.* Edited by Bengt Ankarloo and Stuart Clark. Philadelphia: University of Pennsylvania Press.

Graf, Fritz. 1997. *Magic in the Ancient World.* Cambridge, MA: Harvard University Press.

Hunink, Vincent, ed. 1997. *Apuleius of Madauros: Pro se de magia (Apologia).* 2 vols. Amsterdam: Gieben.

Kippenberg, Hans G. 1997. "Magic in Roman Civil Discourse: Why Rituals Could Be Illegal." Pp. 137–163 in *Envisioning Magic: A Princeton Seminar and Symposium.* Edited by Peter Schäfer and Hans G. Kippenberg. Studies in the History of Religions 75. Leiden: Brill.

Massoneau, Elaine. 1934. *La magie dans l'antiquité romaine.* Paris: Recueil Sirey.

Meiggs, Russel, and David Lewis. 1969. *A Selection of Greek Historical Inscriptions.* Oxford: Oxford University Press.

Ogden, Daniel. 2002. *Magic, Witchcraft and Ghosts in the Graeco-Roman World.* New York: Oxford University Press.

Pharr, Clyde. 1932. "The Interdiction of Magic in Roman Law." *Transactions of the American Philological Association* 63: 269–295.

Phillips, C. R., III. 1991. "*Nullum crimen sine lege:* Socioreligious Sanctions on Magic." Pp. 260–276 in *Magika Hiera: Ancient Greek Magic and Religion.* Edited by Christopher A. Faraone and Dirk Obbink. New York: Oxford University Press.

Xella, Paola, ed. 1976. *Magia: Studi di storia delle religioni in memoria di Rafaella Garosi.* Rome: Bulzoni.

LAWS ON WITCHCRAFT (EARLY MODERN)

Although it has recently been claimed that laws on witchcraft constituted a "judicial revolution" in the early modern period (Ankarloo 2002, 63–64), this is clearly not the case. Witchcraft can be considered one of the oldest crimes in the history of mankind, going as far back in history as we can see. From the earliest surviving law code (1792–1750 B.C.E.) of ancient Mesopotamia, literate societies with codified law have severely punished sorcery or witchcraft. The Code of Hammurabi imposed a river ordeal (swimming test) if such charges could not be proved by means of witnesses. This offered an effective remedy against too frequent accusations: According to the principle of talion, the accuser had to face the punishment the accused would have suffered if the ordeal failed to prove the suspect's guilt. In cases of witchcraft, this was the death penalty.

We know similar laws from the Middle Assyrian Empire, and one can assume that the death penalty was imposed on both male and female witches throughout the ancient Middle East (Thomsen 2001, 25–26). The most comprehensive set of texts from the struggle against witchcraft, about 100 incantations and prayers compiled during the rule of King Esarhaddon (680–669 B.C.E.), bore a title significant for the treatment of witches: *Maqlu,* which literally means "Burning." The laws of the Hebrews include the rule that witches (or poisoners) must be killed (Exod. 22:17), that those employing a spirit should be stoned to death (Lev. 20:27), and generally that diviners and prophets were to be killed (Deut. 13:5). Biblical law remained the most important legal source for witchcraft throughout the Christian history in Europe.

How much European perceptions of witchcraft were also molded by long-standing secular law becomes perfectly clear seen against the backdrop of ancient Rome. From the earliest Roman law codes (ca. 450 B.C.E.) to late-imperial legislation, the possibility of magic was generally admitted and its misuse (*maleficium*) penalized (Luck 1990, 147–151). Witchcraft panics generated a rising awareness in Roman law, starting with the *Lex Cornelia de sicariis et veneficiis* (Law of Cornelius on Assassins and Poisoners/Sorcerers), promulgated by Lucius Cornelius Sulla (138–178 B.C.E.), one of the most important sources of European laws on witchcraft in the late medieval and early modern periods (Ferrary 1991, 417–434).

According to a decree of Emperor Diocletian (ruled 284–305 C.E.), harmful sorcerers were to be burned alive, but those who practiced beneficial magic were to remain unpunished. By the later fourth century, the equating of *veneficium* (poisoning), *maleficium* (harmful magic), and divination paved the way for collective actions against evildoers in the Roman Empire. In book 16, chapter 8, Ammianus Marcellinus (330–ca. 395 C.E.) in his *Roman History* reported a sorcery scare from the reign of Emperor Constantius II (ruled 337–361 C.E.) during a period of famines and diseases: "If anyone consulted a soothsayer . . . , or if he used an old wives' charm to relieve pain . . . , he was denounced through some agency which he could not guess, brought to trial, and punished with death" (*The Later Roman Empire,* book 16, chapter 8).

Contrary to the Greco-Roman distinction between bad and good magic or between black and white magic, Christians questioned the efficacy of all magic, but they considered any kind of sorcery as diabolical. During the era of Emperor Constantius II, magicians were labeled "enemies of mankind" (*humani generis inimici*), and the death penalty was imposed for black and white magic alike in a series of laws from 357 (*Lex Nemo; Lex Multi*) and 358 (Fögen 1997, 223–232). This paradigm shift soon had other consequences. When the synod of

Zaragoza (380) condemned the scholar Priscillian as a heretic, he was also subjected to an imperial investigation. Found guilty of magical practices, he and six followers were sentenced to death for *maleficium*. The first convicted Christian heretic was thus actually punished for magic and, against the protest of several bishops, executed in 385. The consequences can also be seen in such late Roman codes as the *Codex Theodosianus* of Theodosius I (ruled 379–395), or the *Codex Justinianus* of Justinian I (ruled 527–565). With the reception of Roman law in medieval Europe, these imperial decrees had a lasting legacy. Their impact was increased by the semiotic theory of magic developed by St. Augustine (Harmening 1979, 303–308).

Early medieval penal codes imposed severe penalties for witchcraft, for example, the Salic law, "if a *stria* shall devour a man and it shall be proved against her . . ." (Hansen 1900, 58–59). Legislation remained contradictory, however; Frankish, Lombard, and Alemannic laws all treated the subject differently. Alemannic law, compiled around 600 C.E., forbade burning *strigae* (witches), which probably indicated that this was the customary procedure. Likewise, the Lombard king Rothari decreed in 643 that Christians must not believe that women devour a human being ("*ut mulier hominem vivum intrinsecus possit comedere*") and therefore supposed *strigae* must neither be killed nor convicted in court. A capitulary of Charlemagne (ruled 768–814) for the Saxons in 787 imposed the death penalty on and burned those who, like pagans, believed that someone could be a *striga* who devours humans. Around 800, an Irish synod likewise condemned belief in witches, and particularly those who slandered people for being *lamiae* (witches; "*que interpretatur striga*"). Clearly, there was an increase in official skepticism during the Carolingian period, even allowing for an increase in surviving sources.

The most important text on the subject was the *Canon Episcopi,* officially attributed to a fourth-century Church council but in fact formulated and perhaps conceived by Abbot Regino of Prüm in an early tenth-century penitentiary, which admonished bishops (*episcopi*) to proceed against sorcerers in their dioceses. It was later adopted by the most important contemporary authorities, first by Bishop Burchard of Worms and then, around 1140, by Gratian of Bologna. Regino's canon was important not only for its rejection of the efficacy of sorcery but also for its denial of certain witch beliefs. After an introductory paragraph about the need to fight against sorcerers, male as well as female, suggesting lenient sentences, Regino inserted a long paragraph about women who believed that they experienced nocturnal flights with the pagan goddess Diana. He condemned believers in such fantastical tales for implicitly accepting a supernatural power rivaling God. Bishops should fight against these beliefs through

their clergy and should make clear that these flights were not real, but only dreams and devilish illusions. The canon became part of the *Corpus Juris Canonici,* the Church law of Latin Christendom, and proved influential during the following centuries. The harsh implications of Mosaic law (Exod. 22:17: "Thou shalt not suffer a witch to live") were reinterpreted by such Carolingian theologians as Archbishop Rabanus Maurus of Mainz, who suggested as punishment mere exclusion from the community instead of physical extinction (Haustein 1990, 69). The idea that "the official church stance regarding magic shifted from a demonic association with paganism to a demonic association with heresy" (Jolly 2002, 21) seems compelling.

Of course, medieval reality was more complex. Harmful magic was considered devilish: According to St. Augustine, it implied a demonic pact, and according to Roman law, it deserved the death penalty. Both traditions influenced the development of European law. For instance, the laws of Alfred the Great of Wessex (ruled 871–899) clearly used the same biblical reference as had Rabanus Maurus to impose the death penalty on women who frequented sorcerers or magicians: Here, witchcraft was considered real. Nor does it sound like "skepticism" when the Carolingian king Charles II decreed in 873 that witches—men and women alike—had caused illness and death in different parts of his realm and should therefore be put to death, together with their accomplices and supporters. Killing witches was obviously practiced among Germanic peoples. The laws of the Franks, Ostrogoths, and Visigoths rejected only the belief in *strigae,* rarely questioning the danger of harmful magic. "Carolingian skepticism" notwithstanding, Charlemagne was quite clear about the punishment of *maleficium.* In his *Admonitio Generalis* (General Warning) of 789, the future emperor, commenting on several papal decrees from Hadrian I (ruled 772–795), decreed that sorcerers and witches (*maleficii, incantatores,* and *incantatrices*) must not be tolerated, explicitly referring to Mosaic law; in later versions of this list, *tempestarii* (witches who raise storms) were added (Hansen 1900, 63–64).

In Frankish and Anglo-Saxon law, harmful magic was frequently placed together with murder, which makes perfect sense if we consider present-day African ideas about witchcraft. According to the *Lex Salica* (Salic Law), those who could not pay for their magical crimes should be burned ("*certe ignem tradatur*") (Hansen 1900, 55–56). Numerous decrees from the later Carolingian period implied the death penalty for harmful sorcery. Such sorcerers were liable to suffer capital punishment under Norman rule in England (Ewen 1933, 26), as well as in Sicily. The Venetian Republic issued draconian laws against *maleficium* in 1181, as did many Italian towns in the thirteenth century. Medieval German law codes imposed burning at the stake as the customary penalty for harmful magic. The *Schwabenspiegel* (Swabian Legal Mirror; ca. 1240), one of the most influential medieval compilations of imperial law, suggested that sorcery implied apostasy and a pact with the Devil (Hansen 1900, 387). The author, probably a jurist close to the Franciscans at Augsburg, merely combined secular law with Christian theology. Demonic witchcraft was no new invention but required only basic knowledge of theology. In a famous legal opinion of 1398, Jean Gerson and the University of Paris came to exactly the same conclusion (Hansen 1900, 283–284).

The decisive step toward mass persecutions of witches in Europe was the construction of a cumulative concept of witchcraft during the late fourteenth and early fifteenth centuries, when the first large-scale witch hunts and major persecutions were launched in some Alpine valleys. Only around 1400 were different aspects of witchcraft and heresy assembled into the specific European concept of witchcraft, which allowed witch hunts of previously unprecedented severity. Harmful magic combined with the pact with the Devil to form the core of the new cumulative crime, the first aspect crucial for secular law, the second for its qualification as a heresy. Around these crystallized a group of what were even by medieval perceptions exotic accusations: apostasy, flying through the air to nocturnal gatherings at remote places, the witches' dance, sexual intercourse with demons, and adoration of the Devil.

In legal practice, accusations of nocturnal flights turned out to be the most destructive, because suspects were asked to name their accomplices, whom they supposedly met at these gatherings. Combined with the use of torture, such questions could generate chain reactions, resulting in massive witch hunts, reminiscent of similar events in Roman antiquity. Inquisitorial procedure was a legacy of Roman law that had survived within the Latin Church; first revived for disciplining the higher clergy, it was later applied in heresy trials. At the Fourth Lateran Council (1215), the Roman Church accepted torture in trials run by inquisitors in order to obtain confessions from suspects, while forbidding archaic rituals like ordeals by hot iron or cold water (the swimming test). Although subsequently illegal, ordeals were nevertheless practiced in lynchings throughout northern and eastern Europe and were occasionally even commissioned by lower courts.

Because legal torture aimed to achieve material truth rationally rather than through mystical intervention, as in ordeals, it was initially considered an improvement to legal procedure. We must keep in mind that the meaning of legal torture differed decisively from modern perceptions. Although torture had been meant to replace ordeals, in practice judges sometimes used unlimited torture as if it were an ordeal, particularly in heresy trials. A blend of physical coercion, systematizing

all kinds of real or false information, and mere fantasy or projection led to the idea that dissidents belonged to a devilish sect and worshipped the Devil.

Harmful magic and heresy were first fused into a new cumulative crime of witchcraft in Savoy under Duke Amadeus VIII (ruled 1416–1451). This new state dominated the eastern Alps. When Duke Amadeus felt bewitched, the persecution of Jews, Waldensians, and witches gained momentum. It was in Savoy that the fusion of heresy, anti-Judaism, and sorcery took place, and the new cumulative crime of witchcraft was born. Amadeus VIII's ambitious law code of 1430, the *Statuta Sabaudie* (Statutes of Savoy), emphasized the crime of sorcery, although still in traditional language. Ten years later, witchcraft surfaced in a much more prominent form when Pope Eugenius IV (ruled 1431–1447) mentioned in a decree that Savoy bristled with "*stregule vel stregones seu Waudenses*"—female and male witches, or Waldensians (Hansen 1900, 18–19).

In Savoy, trials of sorcery fueled heresy trials and eventually, by the late 1420s, produced large-scale witch hunts. The persecution in neighboring Dauphiné never reached this massive level but was characterized by a steady flow of "small panic" trials. One explanation for this contrast could be the different judicial system. In Dauphiné, subject to France since 1349, only secular courts were responsible for witchcraft trials, with judges referring mainly to secular law, to French jurists, or to Roman law. Therefore, they ignored both witches' flight and synagogues or Sabbats, which were still considered to be devilish illusions. Several late medieval territories accepted the services of papal inquisitors, but, with a few exceptions, they generally observed existing or customary laws on witchcraft. When Tyrol, an independent duchy of the Holy Roman Empire, suffered Heinrich Kramer's attempt to launch a major witch hunt in 1485, both government and parliament were extremely reluctant to accept indictments for witchcraft. "Witchcraft" was in fact never mentioned in its law codes, and when "sorcery" was first mentioned in the *Tiroler Landesordnung* (Tyrol government regulation) of 1544, it was classified as a form of fraud. Likewise, the imperial city of Nuremberg defined witchcraft as fraud as late as 1536.

Spanish and German traditions merged in the legislation of the Holy Roman Emperor Charles V (ruled 1519–1556), the leading ruler of his age. His criminal law of 1532, promulgated as *Constitutio Criminalis Carolina* (the Carolina Code), had been negotiated long before among the imperial estates. This code, which remained virtually unchanged until the Holy Roman Empire collapsed in 1806, completely ignored the cumulative crime of witchcraft as defined by the *Malleus Maleficarum* (The Hammer of Witches, 1486). It contained a paragraph against harmful magic (par. 109), the treatment of which was regulated scrupulously in three paragraphs on procedural law (pars. 21, 44, 52). Capital punishment was confined to cases where harmful magic could be proven beyond doubt, whereas nonharmful magic of any sort was left to the arbitrary judgment of the courts.

The inquisitorial procedure of the Carolina Code avoided the worst shortcomings of Inquisition courts by granting suspects clearly defined rights and ruling out the arbitrary use of violence. In order to avoid arbitrary acts by local courts, every capital sentence had to be submitted to a high court or a law faculty. Within the boundaries of the *processus ordinarius* (ordinary procedure), as later jurists called it, torture could only be used in cases of evident guilt, when a suspect already stood convicted by two independent witnesses, or in cases of clear evidence. Torture could not be employed in order to extract confessions on the basis of mere denunciation or suspicion.

Later witch hunters complained that under these conditions, hardly anyone could be convicted of witchcraft. Indeed, this may have been one purpose of this legislation. Its main author, the Franconian baron Johann von Schwarzenberg (1463–1528), a humanist translator of Cicero and an early follower of Luther's Reformation in 1521, becoming one of the first lords to forbid Catholic rites in his territory—had belonged to Maximilian I's entourage in the late 1480s and was presumably familiar with discussions about the scandalous inquisitor Heinrich Kramer, the author of the *Malleus*. In contrast to an earlier law code designed by Schwarzenberg before the Reformation, in the Carolina Code he now eliminated any mention of interference by good or evil spirits and any trace of heresy laws. The Carolina Code clearly signaled its disapproval of Inquisition courts, whose activities were no longer tolerated by German estates, thus marking a clear difference from Charles's Spanish and Italian territories. The Carolina Code was accepted even in the most remote corners of the Holy Roman Empire, for instance, Switzerland or the Spanish Netherlands.

Like the Holy Roman Empire, many other states introduced witchcraft into their penal codes during the sixteenth century, either in order to limit the power of ecclesiastical courts or to underline the achievements of the Protestant Reformation. Even in countries where Roman law was never applied, traces of this development can be found. In Tudor England, a new Witchcraft Act was promulgated in 1563. It superseded an earlier attempt of 1542, which had been repealed after five years (Sharpe 2001, 99–100). Like the penal code of Charles V, the Elizabethan witchcraft statute focused on harmful magic, but it also provided extensive details on minor punishments for cases of magic causing harm less than death, or even causing no harm at all. The bill had already been introduced in the House of Commons in 1559, and it received a second

reading in the House of Lords before being revived in 1563, in the context of the Protestant restoration after Elizabeth I's accession. Although historians have not yet discovered related English trials until 1566, we can assume that the act was not enacted without reason. In the Channel Islands, the first recorded death penalties for witchcraft occur exactly at this time, on Jersey in 1562 and on Guernsey in 1563. The English witchcraft bill fits neatly into the general picture of rising awareness about witchcraft in Europe during the 1560s. In Scotland, legislation was also introduced in 1563, accompanied by a Calvinist Reformation and a sudden rise in the number of accusations. Claims that the Scottish Witchcraft Act might indicate skepticism (Larner 1981, 66) are ludicrous. Its wording clearly stated that according to divine law, those who used witchcraft, sorcery, or necromancy must receive the death penalty (Normand and Roberts 2000, 89), as must those who sought help from witches, sorcerers, or necromancers. After 1563, numerous laws dealt with superstition, sorcery, and witchcraft in general; it will be difficult to provide a comprehensive list for all European territories.

Furthermore, after 1563, numerous laws and decrees dealt with certain aspects of the witchcraft trials. In August 1563, the Council of Luxembourg promulgated an ordinance on August 13, 1563, in order to limit ongoing prosecutions in this province of the Spanish Netherlands. Laws on witchcraft became more numerous in subsequent years, usually attempting to curb legal abuses in witchcraft trials or to stop actual witch hunts. Massive witch hunts alerted the government of Luxembourg to promulgate more laws on witchcraft in 1570 and 1573, and frequently from April 1591 onward. Decrees of King Philip II for the Spanish Netherlands in 1592, 1595, and 1606 also affected Franche-Comté and Luxembourg.

Continuing legislation on aspects of witchcraft trials was by no means confined to Catholic governments. King Frederick II of Denmark (ruled 1559–1588) tried to limit executions for witchcraft through a 1576 decree making the ratification of such judgments by the high court compulsory, although there are no indications that this law had any more effect than later Danish decrees. Many German territories tried to curb the persecutions of supposed witches, even states with massive persecutions such as the archbishop-electorate of Trier, which in 1591 and again in 1630 attempted to reduce the power of witch-hunting village committees. Numerous decrees, for example, in electoral Mainz in 1612 or in the prince-bishopric of Würzburg in 1627, limited the extent of confiscations of convicted witches' property. Other laws, as in the imperial free city of Kaufbeuren in 1591 or the prince-bishopric of Bamberg in 1627 and 1628, tried to curb witchcraft persecutions by punishing gossip. But other territories, like the principality of Saxe-Coburg in 1629, simply tried to regulate court procedures in order to avoid disturbances during witchcraft trials.

A third category of legislation on witchcraft tried to redefine the crime in the spirit of St. Augustine. Not surprisingly, this development began in the duchy of Württemberg, a stronghold of Lutheran orthodoxy, whose reformer Johann Brenz had been attacked by Johann Weyer in 1563 for inconsistencies when discussing witchcraft. Like Weyer, Brenz claimed that witchcraft was ineffective, but Brenz nevertheless wanted to see witches burned because of their apostasy. The legislative process apparently began after Weyer ridiculed Brenz by emphasizing that apostasy was not a crime in secular law. Unsurprisingly, in Württemberg's new law code (*Landrecht*) of 1567, for the first time harmful magic was no longer required when defining the crime of witchcraft. Within a few years, this radical reinterpretation was adopted by other Lutheran states. In 1572, the Lutheran prince-electorate of Saxony's new penal code (*Kursächsische Kriminalordnung*) shifted emphasis entirely to the spiritual aspects of witchcraft: The witch's compact with the Devil now stood at the crime's core. This redefinition of witchcraft explicitly denied the importance of harmful magic and implicitly denied the meaning of both ancient and modern imperial law (Behringer 1988, 79).

The Saxon lawyers drew the consequence of a prolonged Protestant debate over the efficacy of harmful magic, building on both common sense and the theological tradition of the *Canon Episcopi*. Unlike the insulted Württembergers, the Saxons argued directly against Weyer, whose arguments they considered worthless, because he was a doctor of medicine, not of law. The Saxon code was the more consistent piece of Lutheran legislation, because it required no proof of harmful magic for conviction. The then-Lutheran electoral Palatinate followed in 1582 (*Kurpfälzisches Landrecht*), but it soon returned to Calvinism, thus becoming the first Calvinist state with a spiritualized definition of witchcraft in its law code. Other Protestant penal codes showed similar spiritualizing tendencies, enabling us to identify an overall tendency. In Norway, subject to Denmark, the Lutheran clergy got royal approval of a 1584 statute that imposed the death penalty for superstition. This punishment was reduced to exile in Denmark's subsequent comprehensive 1617 witchcraft statute (Ankarloo 2002, 69), while those who made a pact with the Devil were to be burned. This Danish statute was extended to Iceland in the 1630s. Similarly, the famous English Witchcraft Act of 1604 imposed the death penalty not just for the witch's pact but also for harmful magic; it included a broader variety of harm than the 1563 statute. But clearly there was a shift in emphasis from *maleficium* to demonolatry throughout the laws of Protestant Europe.

Similar tendencies can also be observed in Catholic states. In 1588, the Counter-Reformation territory of Baden-Baden (then under Bavarian guardianship because of the minority of its ruler) no longer required proof of *maleficium* for a death penalty, focusing instead on apostasy and the Devil's pact. Interestingly, its government took this wording from the 1582 code of the Calvinist Palatinate (*Kurpfälzisches Landrecht*), although adding several "Catholic" notions (such as the witches' flight) in an appendix that contained an extensive questionnaire. The duchy of Bavaria followed in practice in 1590 and de jure in 1612; electoral Cologne followed in 1607, and the prince-bishopric of Bamberg in 1610.

The Bavarian statute promulgated by Duke Maximilian I in 1612 offered by far the most comprehensive example of legislation on witchcraft, covering no fewer than forty printed pages (Behringer 1988, 165–191). Bavarian lawyers had argued that because the government had failed to explain what witchcraft actually meant, it was unpunishable in principle. So this extensive law first explained why witchcraft must be punished (1–7), then it defined witchcraft as opposed to sorcery and mere superstition (8–29), and, finally, it published sanctions for all forms of witchcraft, sorcery, and superstition (30–40). Although seeming insane from our modern viewpoint, it clearly represented a courageous attempt to impose some order on the chaos of contemporary views about witchcraft. Furthermore, it attempted to protect superstitious peasants from persecutions by Counter-Reformation zealots. Whereas demonologists like Peter Binsfeld and Martín Del Rio suggested that according to Augustinian theology, wearing amulets indicated an implicit compact with the Devil, the Bavarian law clearly considered such customary superstitions completely separate from witchcraft. First published in 1612, this witchcraft statute was reissued in 1665 and again as late as 1746—by then an outstanding example of Bavarian stubbornness and backwardness.

Like the criminalization of witchcraft, the repeal of witchcraft laws has yet to be researched on a comparative level in Europe. With the outstanding exception of the British witchcraft act of 1736 (Bostridge 1997, 180–203), we lack thorough studies. Clearly, the formal British repeal via parliamentary decision was unique. The kings of France and Prussia, the tsar of Russia, and Empress Maria Theresa of Austria-Hungary suppressed witchcraft trials without changes in legislation, just as the Spanish Inquisition and the Dutch Estates General had done earlier. In this context, we should notice that after the massive witch hunts of the 1620s, many German princes and prince-bishops had simply forbidden further witchcraft trials, for example, Carl Caspar von der Leyen, archbishop-elector of Trier in 1659 (Rummel 1991, 246). The first European government to start crushing witchcraft accusations as early as 1572, the electoral Palatinate, despite its disgruntled clergy and its 1582 penal code, never issued a death sentence for witchcraft. But because such conduct can only be detected by reading archival sources instead of published law codes, there may be further discoveries in the future.

Only shortly before the French Revolution did a landslide start. In 1766, Maria Theresa intervened decisively in Hungary. Witchcraft laws were repealed in Poland in 1776 and in Sweden in 1779. A Swiss "judicial murder" of 1782 provoked action in Germany. In 1787, Emperor Joseph II simply omitted all articles about sorcery or witchcraft from his new criminal code for the Austrian-Hungarian monarchy. French laws against *magie et sortilège* (magic and witchcraft) remained in place, albeit limited by a 1682 royal edict. However, France experienced trials well into the Enlightenment, with the Devil playing an important role (Bostridge 1997, 227–231); only during the French Revolution, in 1791, were these *crimes imaginaires* (imaginary crimes) abandoned.

Some states never formally introduced laws on sorcery or witchcraft and therefore never needed to remove them, but most countries only disposed of those laws during the social and political upheaval around 1800, when new criminal law codes were introduced in the wake of general reforms, often in such newly created states as the Kingdom of Bavaria (1813). A late repeal of witchcraft laws meant nothing. Such legislation remained intact longest in the European country with the fewest known witchcraft executions: Ireland's 1587 Witchcraft Act remained in force until 1821. The public debates about its abolition remind us that even in the British Isles, a minority continued to believe in witchcraft and were convinced that witches must be punished.

European legislation on witchcraft was exported during the prolonged period of European expansion, not least through such ideologies as Marxism, functionalism, and modernization theory. The Soviet rulers of Russia and China, claiming to dictate their subjects' belief as had previous rulers of these empires, tried to extirpate beliefs in witchcraft, shamanism, and official religion simultaneously. But more often, disbelief in witchcraft was introduced under foreign colonial rule—in the Americas, Australia, and large parts of Africa and Asia.

However, modern European legislation on witchcraft was not welcomed or universally accepted, and it sometimes even created major problems. Following Christian tradition, such colonial laws not only forbade persecution of evil witches but also criminalized witch doctors. When Dutch legislation was introduced in Indonesia in 1905 or British legislation in eastern Africa in 1922, many natives understood them as laws to protect witches; European law inverted traditional values. Because the European elites had stopped believing in witchcraft and had exported their laws to the colonies, legal prosecution suddenly became impossible, with the ritual killing of witches classified as murder. Poison ordeals and oracles were prohibited, witch doctors were prosecuted as legal offenders, while witches were protected. The colonized could not believe this inversion of norms: Why would their foreign rulers protect evil witches?

Some postcolonial African countries have begun to legalize witch persecution. In 1965, newly independent Uganda introduced legislation that replaced the colonial witchcraft ordinance with an "Act to Make Provision for the Prevention of Witchcraft and the Punishment of Persons Practising Witchcraft." This act laid considerable emphasis on "repute" as valid evidence. This repeal may have encouraged the subsequent witch hunts in northern Uganda, launched in the home region of President Milton Obote (ruled 1962–1971, 1980–1985) during a time when he had decided to destroy the traditional Bugandan monarchy and introduce socialist reforms. Obote's supporters took his Five-Year Economic Plan of 1966/1967 as a model for a "five-year antisorcery plan" and began rounding up suspected witches, many of them educated or wealthy (Abrahams 1985, 32–45).

In Cameroon and Malawi, diviners testified in court against suspected witches. It has become acceptable to decide cases of suspected witchcraft through such occult practices as divination, with the accused risking physical punishment and prison sentences. If witches may be officially accused and tried, it is no longer necessary to kill them clandestinely. During the late 1970s, under President Ahmadou Ahidjo of Cameroon, the official tribunal of the eastern province (home of the Maka people) regularly sentenced accused witches, sometimes even without their admission of guilt. Traditional healers, the *nganga,* testified to the witches' guilt through their mystical knowledge; on that basis, courts issued sentences of up to ten years in prison, the legal maximum under the 1965 penal code. The interesting aspect is that this law is similar to the English Witchcraft Act of 1736 and to colonial law codes that were meant to punish witch doctors. However, legal practice turned their meaning upside down.

WOLFGANG BEHRINGER

See also: ACCUSATORIAL PROCEDURE; AFRICA (SUB-SAHARAN); BIBLE; *CANON EPISCOPI;* CAROLINA CODE (*CONSTITUTIO CRIMINALIS CAROLINA*); COURTS, ECCLESIASTICAL; COURTS, INQUISITORIAL; COURTS, SECULAR; DECLINE OF THE WITCH HUNTS; EXODUS 22:18 (22:17); HERESY; INQUISITORIAL PROCEDURE; LAWS ON WITCHCRAFT (ANCIENT); LAWS ON WITCHCRAFT (MEDIEVAL); LAWYERS; *MALEFICIUM;* ORDEAL; ORIGINS OF THE WITCH HUNTS; PAPACY AND PAPAL BULLS; ROMAN LAW; SWIMMING TEST; TORTURE; TRIALS; UNIVERSITIES.

References and further reading:

Abrahams, Ray. 1985. "A Modern Witch Hunt." *Cambridge Anthropology* 10: 32–45.

Ankarloo, Bengt. 2002. "Witch-Trials in Northern Europe, 1450–1700." Pp. 53–96 in *The Period of the Witch Trials*, vol 4 of *The Athlone History of Witchcraft and Magic in Europe.* Edited by Bengt Ankarloo and Stuart Clark. London and Philadelphia: Athlone and University of Pennsylvania Press.

Behringer, Wolfgang. 1988. *Mit dem Feuer vom Leben zum Tod: Hexengesetzgebung in Bayern.* Munich: Hugendubel.

———. 2004. *Witches and Witch Hunts: A Global History.* Cambridge: Polity.

Bostridge, Ian. 1997. *Witchcraft and Its Transformations, ca. 1650–ca. 1750.* Oxford: Oxford University Press.

Ewen, Cecil L'Estrange. 1933. *Witchcraft and Demonianism: A Concise Account Derived from Sworn Depositions and Confessions Obtained in the Courts of England and Wales.* London: Heath Cranton.

Ferrary, J. 1991. "Lex Cornelia de sicariis et veneficiis." *Athenaeum* 69: 417–434.

Fögen, Marie Theresa. 1997. *Die Enteignung der Wahrsager.* Frankfurt am Main: Suhrkamp.

Hansen, Joseph. 1900. *Zauberwahn, Inquisition und Hexenprozess im Mittelalter und die Entstehung der grossen Hexenverfolgung.* Munich: Oldenbourg.

Harmening, Dieter. 1979. *Superstitio.* Berlin: E. Schmidt.

Haustein, Jörg. 1990. *Martin Luthers Stellung zum Zauber-und Hexenwesen.* Stuttgart: W. Kohlhammer.

Jolly, Karen. 2002. "Medieval Magic." Pp. 1–72 in *The Middle Ages,* vol. 3 of *The Athlone History of Witchcraft and Magic in Europe.* Edited by Bengt Ankarloo and Stuart Clark. London and Philadelphia: Athlone and University of Pennsylvania Press.

Lambrecht, Karen. 1995. *Hexenverfolgungen und Zaubereiprozesse in den schlesischen Territorien.* Cologne and Vienna: Böhlau.

Larner, Christina. 1981. *Enemies of God: The Witch-Hunt in Scotland.* London: Chatto and Windus.

Lorenz, Sönke, ed. 1994. *Hexen und Hexenverfolgung im deutschen Südwesten.* Ostfildern: Cantz.

Luck, Georg. 1990. *Magie und andere Geheimlehren der Antike.* Munich: Kröner.

Merzbacher, Friedrich. 1971. "Schwarzenberg." *Fränkische Lebensbilder* 4: 173–185.

Muchembled, Robert. 1993. *Le roi et la sorcière.* Paris: Desclée.

Normand, Lawrence, and Gareth Roberts. 2000. *Witchcraft in Early Modern Scotland.* Exeter: University of Exeter Press.

Paravy, Pierrette. 1993. *De la Chrétienté romaine à la Réforme en Dauphiné: Evêques, fidèles, et déviants (vers 1340–vers 1530).* 2 vols. Rome: Ecole Française de Rome.

Peters, Edward. 1985. *Torture.* Philadelphia: University of Pennsylvania Press.

Rummel, Walter. 1991. *Bauern, Herren, Hexen.* Göttingen: Vandenhoeck and Ruprecht.

Sharpe, James. 2001. *Witchcraft in Early Modern England.* 2nd ed. London: Longmans.

Thomas, Keith. 1971. *Religion and the Decline of Magic.* London: Weidenfeld and Nicolson.

Thomsen, Marie-Louise. 2001. "Witchcraft in Ancient Mesopotamia." Pp. 1–95 in *Witchcraft and Magic in Europe: Biblical and Pagan Societies.* Edited by Bengt Ankarloo and Stuart Clark. Philadelphia: University of Pennsylvania Press.

LAWS ON WITCHCRAFT (MEDIEVAL)

During the centuries conventionally defined as the Middle Ages, laws concerning witchcraft cannot be easily separated from those condemning magical practices and beliefs or surviving pagan habits. Unlike the laws of later centuries, medieval laws often aimed to condemn not witches but rather those who believed their powers were real.

Laws constitute one of the better sources for studying magic and witchcraft during the Early Middle Ages. Nearly all of them fall into one of two categories: secular Germanic legal codes and ecclesiastical legislation. To the former belong all the codes produced in different European regions during the reigns formed with the contribution of Germanic and Latin elements. In the latter there are numerous regulations (canons, synods, decrees, penitentials) decreed by the Church during its first centuries as an official state religion. Not all of them have the same purpose: Some were meant to impose or forbid a habit; others just instituted penalties. Only in the twelfth century, with the *Concordantia discordantium canonum* (Concord of Discordant Canons, better known as the *Decretum*) of the monk Gratian, did there appear a revision that harmonized the entire ecclesiastical legislative tradition.

It is not easy to discern exactly what "witchcraft" was in those early sources because most of them express, in Latin, notions emerging from Germanic (and sometimes Celtic or even Asiatic) culture. The long-term result of interchanges among those many traditions ultimately led to the formation of the early modern notion of witchcraft, involving the idea of a diabolical pact or at least some intervention by the Devil. But early legislation dealt with a complex of traditions concerning deadly spells, weather magic, residues of pagan cults, and men and women thought to have certain powers over things or people; many of the laws are not easy to decipher and relate to cultural contexts that we can detect.

The early Christian world inherited two main traditions about witchcraft: one from Scripture, the other from the legislation of the Roman Empire. Both considered practices of witchcraft to be real rather than fraudulent. In the Bible, Deuteronomy (18:10–12) condemns all forms of magic as abominations: 10: "There shall not be found among you any one who burns his son or his daughter as an offering, any one who practices divination, a soothsayer, or an augur, or a sorcerer," 11: "or a charmer, or a medium, or a wizard, or a necromancer." 12: "For whoever does these things is an abomination to the Lord; and because of these abominable practices the Lord your God is driving them out before you" (*The Holy Bible: Revised Standard Version.* London: Nelson, 1966.) Wizards and witches deserve death for their practices, as stated explicitly in Exodus (22:17: "You shall not permit a sorceress to live") and reaffirmed in Leviticus (20:27: "A man or a woman who is a medium or a wizard shall be put to death; they shall be stoned with stones, their blood shall be upon them"). The whole episode of Saul's visit to the witch of Endor (1 Kings 28; now 1 Samuel 28) presupposes the reality of the evocation of Samuel.

Roman imperial legislation toward *maleficia* (harmful magic) was severe as well, showing the same level of belief in the reality of witches' powers. In the third century C.E., the punishment of burning alive was prescribed for people who had provoked someone's death through spells. The first Christian councils, held in late antiquity, merged the Roman with the biblical traditions and took witchcraft with the same seriousness. For instance, Canon 6 of the Council of Elvira (306) refused the Viaticum to those who had killed a man *per maleficium* (through harmful magic), adding that such a crime could not be perpetrated "without idolatry": The worship of pagan idols was already equated with worship of the Devil, as became general in following centuries. Also, Canon 24 of the Council of Ancyra (314) imposed five years' penance for the lesser crime of seeking advice from magicians. But this ruling seems to refer to the survival of pagan practices and beliefs, especially in rural settings. We have many such indications of this: Throughout the Early Middle Ages, councils held across Europe provided evidence that peasants, even those who were baptized, still worshiped trees, rocks, and springs once linked to some deity. Many "rustics" also required help from figures whom our sources, following the Romans, called *sortilegi* (sorcerers), *auguri* (augurs), *arioli* (diviners), and *incantatores* (spellbinders). But the attitude of the Church councils toward these beliefs was generally "disenchanted": They were considered "superstitions" rather than real menaces.

During the Early Middle Ages, many Germanic kingdoms provided themselves with written codes, usually collected from their common traditions and more or less influenced by Roman legislation. Some of these codes punished practices of magic and witchcraft, but they also contained law that only censured those who believed those practices have real effects or those who accused someone of being a witch or a wizard. For example, in the Salic law, issued by the Franks, those found guilty of *maleficia* had to pay sixty-two and a half golden *solidi* (coins; all Germanic codes refer to this measure, issued from the Roman world, though golden coins were no longer produced and silver coins had replaced them everywhere in Europe); the penalty rose to 200 golden *solidi* for a witch (*malefica*) who had eaten a man. The power of witches was recognized as real, and making an unproved accusation of being a witch drew a fine of eighty-seven gold coins.

The Visigothic Code was harsher because it did not always allow *Wergild* ("man price," that is, financial damages as the only punishment for crimes): Those

who had done serious *maleficia* could lose their freedom and become slaves; if the *maleficium* had caused someone's death, the perpetrator could receive the death penalty. Weather magic with bad consequences, invocations, and worshiping of the Devil were punished with severe whippings (up to 200 strokes) and public humiliation. The Lombard laws showed fewer worries about the real effects of magical acts, merely condemning those who call a woman *striga* or *masca* (clearly both names for "witch," though the second was previously unknown); we must suppose that the Lombard legislators wanted to discourage any beliefs of this kind.

The many codes created in the Carolingian era show little uniformity. The Council of Lipsia (743) prescribed a fine of only fifteen *solidi* for those found guilty of *maleficium*. Another council, held in Paderborn (785), was more detailed, though being partially self-contradictory. Sorcerers were condemned to submit themselves as servants to the Church, but those who, blinded by the Devil and infected with pagan errors, held another person to be a witch who ate human flesh and who therefore burned her, ate her flesh, or gave it to others to eat would themselves be punished with death. We should note that these measures were meant for a particular region, recently conquered by Charlemagne: The Saxons who lived there were still pagans and strongly resisted conversion to Christianity.

Among the laws issued directly by the Frankish kings, called *capitularia* (capitularies), some condemned surviving pagan traditions; they mentioned divine sorcerers, witches who raise storms (*tempestarii*), and, more peculiarly, "women who eat the moon and rip men's hearts off" (*Monumenta Germaniae Historica* 1883, I, n. 108, p. 223).

In the Church's prolonged fight against surviving pagan habits, diminishing ancient cults could sometimes be discouraged as useless superstitions, including beliefs and practices about witchcraft. Medieval penitentials shed light upon the various ways Christianity sought to overwhelm paganism. In the Irish world, the penitentials of Finnian (written in mid-sixth-century Ireland) and St. Columba (written slightly later in Europe by an Irish author) showed a certain moderation: Forty days of fasting were prescribed for those who joined pagan or diabolical rites; those who repeated the same sin would observe penitence for three Lents; three years' penance was suggested for those who persisted in their crime. As usual in such sources, penalties for Christian clerics were harsher: doubled for deacons, tripled for priests. One year of penitence was the price for fabricating a love potion, and inducing an abortion by magical means could cost up to six Lents of fasting or a penance of half a year with just bread and water (plus two years without wine or meat).

In late-seventh-century England, the penitential of Theodore, archbishop of Canterbury, threatened three years' penance to those who sacrificed to demons (presumably referring to pagan survivals), but in the most serious cases, the penance rose to ten years. If a woman performed diabolical incantations or divinations, she was condemned to a penance of one year. Another English penitential, named for the Venerable Bede but probably belonging to the eighth century, prescribed five years' penance for clerics and three to five for laymen who performed different forms of magic, such as fabricating amulets or consulting diviners. The early-ninth-century French penitential called "of Halitgar" contained interesting details because many of its prescriptions involved surviving pagan traditions: A wizard found guilty of taking away the mind of a man by invoking demons was condemned to a penance of five years; a conjurer of storms received an even harsher penance of seven years, three of them on bread and water, or exactly the same as for those who caused the death of someone performing magic arts. The early-ninth-century Spanish penitential of Silos was more severe: Those who made images of demons or consulted them were condemned to eight years' penance, and a woman who burned grain where a man had died, seeking relief for the health of the living, had to do penance for one year.

Post-Carolingian society produced few written law codes. Sometimes we can discover crimes and punishments indirectly: For example, in tenth-century Anglo-Saxon England, under King Edgar, a woman and her son were condemned to death by drowning for having employed magical figurines, or *defixiones.* Pope Gregory VII wrote to King Harold of Denmark in 1080, forbidding him to put to death those who were believed to have caused storms, damaged harvests, or spread pestilence. In this era, our most important legislative corpus came from three Hungarian kings: Stephen I (997–1038), Ladislas I (1077–1095), and Coloman (1095–1116). Their laws separate magical practices punishable by civil legislation (such as those related to poisoning or *maleficia*) from those that included invoking demons or divination, which were left to ecclesiastical judgment. It is also important to recall that King Coloman, deeply engaged in the fight against the still very widespread pagan practices among his people, refused to issue laws condemning witches (though it is unclear exactly what he meant by the word) because he thought witches did not exist.

After the tenth century, our sources start to show a theme—the "game of Diana"—that would become important in forming the image of the modern witch. It appears in a penitential known as *De ecclesiasticis disciplinis* (About Ecclesiastical Discipline), ascribed to Regino of Prüm and dated to the first decade of the tenth century. Among the usual prescriptions against magical practices, the author inserted a text later known as *Canon Episcopi,* which dismisses the belief that women, seduced by the illusions of demons, could follow Satan and ride at night upon beasts along with the pagan goddess Diana. Slightly more than a century later, another penitential, the *Decretorum libri XX* (The Twenty Books of Decisions) of Burchard, bishop of Worms (about 1015), returned to this subject in its nineteenth book, often known separately as the *Corrector et medicus* (Corrector, or the Physician). Burchard paid attention to many forms of magic, including magical potions that could produce impotence or abortion, ceremonies for inducing fertility, and love charms. But he also rejected the reality of the nocturnal ride through the air, along with the control of thunder, rain, and sunshine, the transformation of a man into an animal, and the intercourse of *incubi* and *succubi* with human beings (unlike what Scholastics commonly held in later centuries). The beliefs denounced by Regino and Burchard nevertheless soon found acceptance in other legislative sources, such as the English penitential of Bartholomew Iscanus, from the second half of the twelfth century. The author seemed to acknowledge the reality of some magical powers; for instance, those who took away another's supply of milk or honey or of other things by any incantation were condemned to a penance of three years; conjurors of storms or those who, by invoking demons, led someone to insanity had to do five years' penance. But people who believed in the nocturnal rides or in the transformation of men and women into wolves got, respectively, one year and ten days of penance.

Many of the confused norms that had accumulated during the Early Middle Ages were reconsidered and reordered in the twelfth century by the monk Gratian. His *Decretum* included a section devoted to acts of sorcery (*De sortilegiis*), kept separate from the section about heresy, where the belief in nocturnal rides with Diana was included. Meanwhile, about the same time, the rise of the papal Inquisition began a new era for legislation about witchcraft. Though in 1258 Pope Alexander IV stated that the inquisitors should limit their intervention to cases involving a clear supposition of heretical belief, it was often hard to separate heresy from witchcraft. For example, a few years earlier, in 1233, Pope Gregory IX issued the bull *Vox in Rama* (A Voice in Rama), promoting a crusade against the Stedinger, peasants of a northern Germanic region (Steding) who refused to pay taxes to the archbishop of Bremen. The pope excommunicated the Stedinger and accused them of both heresy and magical practices, among them orgies; worshiping the Devil in the shape of beasts (a black cat and a toad) in many ways, including the *osculum infame* (kiss of shame, obscene kiss); and profaning the holy host.

Because inquisitors had to deal increasingly with cases connected with magical beliefs and practices, Pope

Alexander IV stated in both 1258 and 1260 that they had to consider those accusations carefully and that only crimes dealing with divination and sorcery—obviously considered as involving the Devil—should be prosecuted. Consequently, at Toulouse in 1275, where the Cathar heresy had been strong, prosecutions ended with the condemnation of a woman; she was burned to death for having given birth to a creature after intercourse with demons and then nourishing it with babies' flesh, which she procured during her nocturnal rides. The fourteenth century witnessed further enlargement of inquisitors' powers, though not without some opposition: King Philip IV of France forbade inquisitors to prosecute crimes of magic. Under the papacy of John XXII, the Inquisition's authority over magicians and witchcraft became almost boundless. With his *Super illius specula* (Upon His Watchtower) in 1326, Pope John XXII excommunicated anyone who made a pact with the Devil.

In the fourteenth and fifteenth centuries, many jurists, especially in Italy and France, gave opinions about the reality of magical powers. It must be remembered that the most famous among them, the Italian Bartolo of Sassoferrato (1313–1357), a professor at the University of Perugia and an adviser to the Holy Roman Emperor Charles IV, gave a *consilium* (juridical advice) for the bishop and the inquisitor of Novara during their trial of a woman who had confessed to having worshiped the Devil, profaned the holy cross, and bewitched children who consequently died. Bartolo suggested she deserved the death penalty for her heretical crimes (unless she were to repent), as stated by the Roman *Lex Cornelia de sicariis et veneficiis* (Law of Cornelius on Assassins and Poisoners/Sorcerers, 81 B.C.E.), but he doubted that these women could kill with just their looks and touches because of their pact with the Devil.

Increasing inquisitorial activity against magic also pushed many authorities to include laws against magical activities in their codes—though most seemed more worried about frauds than about the real damages these practices could do, and none of them specified punishments against witchcraft. One of the earliest came from the city of Florence, with the *Constitutiones* of its bishop Antonio degli Orsi in 1310–1311. At that time, the Inquisition had many problems in Florence and did not begin to work effectively until the middle of the century. The attention paid by the *Constitutiones* to magical practices probably offered a way to handle the situation without external interference. A chapter about acts of sorcery (*De sortilegiis*) condemned crimes achieved through magic, divination, poisoning intended to hurt or kill (*veneficia*), and amulets (*brevia*). Later collections of laws (*statuta*) issued by different towns contained similar prescriptions.

In the fifteenth century, legislation about witchcraft became tighter. Civil authorities began to judge acts of witchcraft as distinct from other kinds of magical practices. This situation emerged clearly from the trial of a woman called Matteuccia, held in Todi in 1428 without the intervention of the inquisitor, who lived nearby in Perugia. During her trial, she was accused of many magical activities but also specifically of being a *strega*, or witch, and of flying to the southern town of Benevento with other women, where they met the Devil, had intercourse with him, turned into animals, and went around Todi and nearby villages killing children in their cradles. Matteuccia was found guilty and burned.

In 1451, Pope Nicholas V issued a bull that, reversing precedents from the previous century, explicitly asked inquisitors to involve themselves in cases of witchcraft, even when the link to heresy was not clear. The route leading to the witch hunts was now traced out, and it culminated with the *Summis desiderantes affectibus* (Desiring with Supreme Ardor) promulgated by Innocent VIII in 1484.

MARINA MONTESANO

References and further reading:
Attenborough, Frederick Levi. 1974. *The Laws of the Earliest English Kings.* 3rd ed. New York: AMS.
Cardini, Franco. 1979. *Magia, stregoneria, superstizioni nell' Occidente medievale.* Florence: Nuova Italia.
Conrat, Max von. 1963. *Breviarium Alaricianum.* Aalen: Scientia.
Drew, Katherine Fischer. 1976. *The Lombard Laws.* Philadelphia: University of Pennsylvania Press.
Dumville, David. 1997. *Councils and Synods of the Gaelic Early and Central Middle Ages.* Cambridge: Cambridge University Press.
Flint, Valerie I. J. 1991. *The Rise of Magic in Early Medieval Europe.* Princeton: Princeton University Press.
Habiger-Tuczay, Christa. 1992. *Magie und Magier im Mittelalter.* Munich: Diederichs.
Hansen, Joseph. 1963. *Quellen und Untersuchungen zur Geschichte des Hexenwahns und der Hexenverfolgungen im Mittelalter.* 2nd ed. Hildesheim: Olms.
———. 1964. *Zauberwhan, Inquisition und Hexenprozess im Mittelalter, und die Entstehung der grossen Hexenwerfolgung.* 2nd ed. Aalen: Scientia.
Kieckhefer, Richard. 1976. *European Witch Trials: Their Foundations in Popular and Learned Culture, 1300–1500.* London: Routledge.
Lea, Henry Charles. 1986. *Materials Toward a History of Witchcraft in the Middle Ages.* 3rd ed. New York: AMS.
McNeill, John, and Helena M. Thomas-Gamer. 1990. *Medieval Handbooks of Penance.* 3rd ed. New York: Columbia University Press.

Montesano, Marina. 1999. *Supra acqua et supra ad vento: "Superstizioni, maleficia e incantamenta nei predicatori francescani osservanti (Italia, sec. XV).* Rome: Istituto Storico Italiano per il Medio Evo.

Monumenta Germaniae historica Leges. Capitularia regum Francorum. 1883. Hanover.

Peters, Edward. 1978. *The Magician, the Witch and the Law.* Philadelphia: University of Pennsylvania Press.

Rivers, Theodore John. 1986. *Laws of the Salian and Ripuarian Franks.* New York: AMS.

Roberton, Agnes Jane. 1974. *The Laws of the Kings of England from Edmund to Henry I.* 2nd ed. New York: AMS.

Russel, Jeffrey Burton. 1972. *Witchcraft in the Middle Ages.* Ithaca, NY, and London: Cornell University Press.

Scott, Samuel Parsons. 1982. *The Visigothic Code.* 2nd ed. Littleton: F. B. Rothman.

Vogel, Cyrille. 1974. "Pratiques superstitieuses au début du XIe siècle d'après le 'Corrector sive Medicus' de Burchard, évêque de Worms (965–1025)." Pp. 751–761 in *Etudes de civilisation médiévale (IX–XII siècles): Mélanges offerts à Édmond-René Labande.* Poitiers: Centre d'Etudes Supérieurs de Civilisation Médiévale.

———. 1978. *Les "libri paenitentiales."* Turnhout: Brepols.

LAWYERS

Lawyers, broadly defined as men trained or educated in the law, played a variety of roles in witchcraft prosecutions. Their most visible function was as judges in witchcraft trials, especially in the central or upper-level courts of European states. Many of the court officials who assisted in the investigation and prosecution of witchcraft also had legal training. Some of the most prominent authors of witchcraft treatises, including Jean Bodin, Benedict Carpzov, Henri Boguet, Nicolas Rémy, and Christian Thomasius, possessed law degrees and had served in some official judicial capacity. In Germany, members of the university faculties of law regularly consulted with officials in local jurisdictions regarding witchcraft prosecutions.

The most controversial and sensitive role lawyers played in witchcraft trials was representing those accused of the crime. Although witches were entitled to defense counsel in all continental European and Scottish trials, few lawyers took such cases during the peak periods of witch hunting. Not only was legal counsel too costly for the typical lower-class witch (only the major Inquisitions provided lawyers gratis for defendants), but lawyers were reluctant to defend witches on the grounds that they might thereby encourage the Devil's activities and incur suspicion themselves. The *Malleus Maleficarum* (The Hammer of Witches), while admitting the right of the judge to appoint an advocate for the accused, insisted that those appointed be convinced of the justice of their client's cause. If a lawyer were to unduly defend a person accused of heresy or witchcraft, he would become a patron of that crime and would come under strong suspicion himself. Concerns regarding the religious orthodoxy of lawyers reinforced the old German saying, "Lawyers are wicked Christians" (Stolleis 2002, 1).

Although we cannot gain any kind of accurate figures regarding the number of witches who had the benefit of counsel, there is a sufficiently large record of legal representation in the seventeenth century to suggest that the number of cases in which lawyers defended the accused was increasing. The large volume of business that was directed to the appellate courts of France by itself accounts for a great part of this increase, because legal representation at appeals was mandatory. Even in trials in the first instance, however, lawyers started pleading for witches in greater numbers during the seventeenth century. In Scotland, lawyers began to defend witches in the Court of Justiciary in the 1620s, and they succeeded in securing acquittals in some cases. Most of those acquittals came after 1670, such as that of the witch known as Maevia, whom Sir George Mackenzie successfully defended before the High Court of Justiciary. To this can be added the acquittals of Margaret Clerk in 1674 and Bessie Gibb in 1680, each of whom had an attorney, in Gibb's case, her husband. By the 1660s, the legal representation of German witches also seems to have become fairly common. In Hungary, counsel for accused witches appeared in the records as early as the 1650s and received frequent mention in eighteenth-century cases, when the number of trials finally began to decline. In England, lawyers could be assigned to defendants only to advise them on points of law. This happened occasionally, such as in 1630, when Chief Justice John Finch assigned four barristers to counsel a poor woman accused of witchcraft.

Legal assistance of this sort benefited witches more than those accused of any other crime, precisely because the evidence in witchcraft cases was so vulnerable to challenge by a person skilled in the law. Lawyers in witchcraft cases could easily raise doubts regarding the supernatural causes of alleged *maleficia* (harmful magic), demand evidence of the corpus delicti, and impeach the credibility of witnesses who would not have been allowed to testify in the trial of ordinary crimes. They could also point out the insufficiency of the evidence, especially when it was hearsay, and the irrelevancy of the evidence that was presented to the indictment or the libel. They could even go so far as to deny the existence of witchcraft and call for a ban on the trials, as one Hungarian lawyer did in 1671. No wonder that in the previous century, Martin Luther, in one of his outbursts regarding the crime of witchcraft, complained that lawyers wanted too much evidence and refused to accept clear proofs of witchcraft. It was doubtless a similar frustration with the tactics of lawyers that led members of the Spanish Inquisition to complain in 1526 that none of the jurists in Castile believed in witchcraft. Nor should it surprise us that the one person acquitted of witchcraft in the central Scottish courts between 1605 and 1622 had been wealthy enough to hire no fewer than three lawyers.

BRIAN P. LEVACK

See also: BODIN, JEAN; CARPZOV, BENEDICT; MACKENZIE, SIR GEORGE; *MALLEUS MALEFICARUM;* RÉMY, NICOLAS; THOMASIUS, CHRISTIAN; TRIALS.

References and further reading:

Cockburn, J. S. 1972. *A History of English Assizes, 1558–1714.* Cambridge: Cambridge University Press.

Levack, Brian P. 1999. "The Decline and End of Witchcraft Prosecutions." Pp. 1–93 in *Witchcraft and Magic in Europe: The Eighteenth and Nineteenth Centuries.* Edited by Bengt Ankarloo and Stuart Clark. Philadelphia: University of Pennsylvania Press.

Peters, Edward. 1978. *The Magician, the Witch and the Law.* Philadelphia: University of Pennsylvania Press.

Stolleis, Michael. 2002. *Reluctance to Glance in the Mirror: The Changing Face of German Jurisprudence after 1933 and post-1945.* Chicago: University of Chicago Law School.

LAYENSPIEGEL (1509)

Layenspiegel is a handbook for lay judges, written by Ulrich Tengler (1447–1511), a clerk serving both the chancery of the Bavarian duke and the imperial free city of Nördlingen, who later became high bailiff and even a count palatine (*Reichspius*). Recognizing the need for a vernacular manual on practical juridical matters, in 1509 Tengler published his *Layenspiegel* (A Mirror [of Law] for Laymen; *Spiegel,* "mirror," was a frequent title for such books), which he dedicated to Holy Roman Emperor Maximilian I. It was an eclectic compilation of helpful materials, written for his colleagues and selected from many sources chosen among German, Roman, and canon laws. The humanist Sebastian Brant, author of the famous *Ship of Fools,* contributed an introduction of recommendation. The first edition, embellished by interesting woodcuts of high quality, was printed by Johann Rynmann in Augsburg and was followed by a second edition only a year later. It was reprinted, with alterations, thirteen times before 1560 and was much used both by Catholics and Protestants during the sixteenth century (there is, however, no recent edition nor any modern translation). The first part of the *Layenspiegel* comprised civil and police law; the second dealt with civil legal process; the third was about criminal law. How firmly Tengler was rooted in the traditional Catholic mentality that saw law as a religious problem became evident through several additions to the legal text, for example, a poem about the *Processus Sathanae contra genus humanum* (an invention of fourteenth-century Italian jurists dealing with the sinfulness of mankind, the Devil's rights, and redemption, in the form of a canonical trial) or a religious play about the last judgment (another fourteenth-century text). The book's main impact for the history of Germanic law consisted in its dissemination of Roman jurisprudence.

Tengler was the first layman to deal with the witchcraft trials in form of a textbook. Given his practical concerns, in part 3 he discussed the subject "*Von kätzerey, warsagen, schwarzer kunst, zauberey, unholden,* etc." (On heresy, soothsaying, black magic, sorcery, witches, etc.) (Tengler 1511, chap. CIV, p. v). In the second and later editions, he was much more severe against these crimes, having been influenced by his son Christopher, a theologian at the university of Ingolstadt. Whereas Tengler saw necromancy as being based on forbidden contact with demons, he saw astrology and similar arts as possibly being regarded as legal as long as they were practiced as natural sciences and without superstition. Regarding witchcraft, the *Layenspiegel* transmitted the teachings of the *Malleus Maleficarum* (The Hammer of Witches), which it recommended for further details on this subject. Tengler offered a *Forma Citation wider Unholden,* that is, a schedule for bringing witches to trial, with a list for questioning them: "Why do your cows give more milk than the neighbors' cows? What did you do in the field during a thunderstorm? Do you believe in witches? Why do you think people are scared of you? Why did you do this or that during your neighbor's delivery?" and so on. It also showed how to record the witnesses' testimonies, how to search the house of the accused, how to interrogate the alleged sorceress, and the like. Many details of the practice of German criminal courts when dealing with witches were codified here, for example, the use of blessed salt, water, and wax; the practice of fetching the accused into court with her back to the judge; or the complete removal of all hair.

Through Tengler's *Layenspiegel,* both the idea of a pact with the Devil and the inquisitorial procedure of canon law were spread far and wide among juridical practitioners in sixteenth-century Germany. Undoubtedly, this book did much to intensify and brutalize the persecution of witches by offering an abridged vernacular version of the *Malleus Maleficarum* to everybody who could read but remained an *illiteratus* with no Latin.

PETER DINZELBACHER

See also: LAWS ON WITCHCRAFT (EARLY MODERN); *MALLEUS MALEFICARUM;* ROMAN LAW; TRIALS.

References and further reading:

Erler, Adalbert. 1998. "Tengler." Pp. 145–146 in *Handwörterbuch zur deutschen Rechtsgeschichte.* Edited by Adalbert Erler and Ekkehard Kaufman. 5, Berlin: E. Schmidt.

Hansen, Joseph, ed. 1901. *Quellen und Untersuchungen zur Geschichte des Hexenwahns und der Hexenverfolgung im Mittelalter.* Bonn: C. Georgi, 1901. Reprint, Hildesheim: Georg Olms, 1963.

Kleinschmidt, Erich. 1977. "Das 'Epitaphium Ulrici Tenngler.'" *Daphnis* 6: 41–64.

———. 1995. "Tenngler, Ulrich." Pp. 9: 690–696 in *Die deutsche Literatur des Mittelalters: Verfasserlexikon.* 2nd ed. Berlin: de Gruyter.

Stintzing, Johann August Roderich von. 1867. *Geschichte der populären Literatur des römisch-kanonischen Rechts in Deutschland am Ende des fünfzehnten und im Anfang des sechszehnten Jahrhunderts.* Leipzig: Hirzel.

Tengler, Ulrich. 1511. *Der neü Layenspiegel.* 2nd ed. Augsburg.

LAYMANN, PAUL (1574–1635)

Laymann was the Jesuit author of the *Theologia Moralis* (Moral Theology; Munich, 1625), a standard textbook on witchcraft and magic that influenced the great critic of witchcraft trials, Friedrich Spee. Born near Innsbruck in Tyrol, Laymann joined the Jesuit order in 1594 and spent most of his life in Bavarian Jesuit colleges. He was a novice in the college of Landsberg on the Lech, a student in Ingolstadt, and a gymnasium teacher in Dillingen, capital of the prince-bishops of Augsburg. From 1603 to 1609, he taught philosophy at Ingolstadt, then, from 1609 to 1625, he taught moral theology at the large college in Munich, and he then became professor of canon law at the University of Dillingen, where he stayed from 1625 to 1632. Fleeing from Swedish invaders during the Thirty Years' War, Laymann died of plague at Constance.

The *Theologia Moralis* was reprinted many times well into the eighteenth century. Whereas its first edition touched only briefly upon how confessors should treat witches, Laymann's third edition (Ingolstadt, 1630) borrowed widely from Adam Tanner, as did all subsequent editions. Laymann's foreword to the 1630 edition emphasized that its section "De iustitia" (Of Justice) had been enlarged to discuss witchcraft trials. Like his Bavarian fellow Jesuit Tanner, Laymann recommended utmost caution, because the Devil could deceive the senses, and very many cruelties had occurred. Laymann denied that denunciations had any legal value in witchcraft trials and suggested that many innocent people had already fallen victim to illegal witch hunts. Clearly distancing himself from Martín Del Rio, Laymann copied whole passages verbatim from Tanner. In 1631, Spee, in his *Cautio Criminalis seu de processibus contra sagas liber* (A Warning on Criminal Justice, or a Book on Witch Trials), used Laymann to double the number of Catholic authorities he could quote to support his position. Laymann's works were present in every better monastic library, where it was well known that his arguments about witchcraft were in fact Tanner's; usually they were quoted like twins, "Tanner and Laymann."

In 1629, at the climax of witch hunting in Germany, Laymann's chapter on witchcraft in his *Theologia Moralis* was allegedly published separately at Aschaffenburg, in German, although under a Latin title. However, as its subtitle demonstrated (a translation into German, amplified with useful examples and other things), Laymann had little to do with this pamphlet. Someone (probably Hermann Goehausen, a lawyer serving Ferdinand of Bavaria, archbishop-elector of Cologne) used Laymann's authority in moral theology to justify the massive witch hunts in the Rhineland by translating, amplifying, and reshaping some bits of text from the first edition of Laymann's *Theologia Moralis.* It was merely a forgery, not a translation, possibly commissioned by the printer Quirin Botzer, who published other pamphlets of similarly dubious quality. Presumably the interests of Goehausen and some authorities coincided perfectly with Botzer's. The absence of approval by the Jesuit superiors demonstrated clearly that this publication was unauthorized.

This misuse may have provoked Laymann to reshape and clarify his ideas on witchcraft trials in his third and subsequent editions of his *Theologia Moralis.* After three years of intensive witch hunting in many parts of Germany, witchcraft trials had expanded beyond moral theology into a political and partisan issue. By clearly articulating that he and Tanner approved a lenient attitude and opposed Del Rio's rigidity (Laymann 1630, 1:524), Laymann repudiated any claim that the 1629 pamphlet represented his ideas. Nevertheless, the false claims to authenticity of Botzer's Aschaffenburg pamphlet, reprinted in Cologne, confused Laymann's first Jesuit biographers and provoked a sharp debate around 1900 between a Jesuit historian and a liberal Catholic about Laymann's real position, where the Jesuit's interpretation was more nearly correct. In 1909, Henry Charles Lea (who owned a copy of Botzer's pamphlet) was careful enough to notice that the same text, with few additions, was reprinted in Cologne in 1629 under Goehausen's name; his discussion (Lea 1939, 2:670–689) remains the most extensive account in English. However, a medical historian and early biographer of Johann Weyer (Binz 1901) found that an eighteenth-century bibliographer ascribed the pamphlet to Dr. Johannes Jordanaeus, a canon and parish priest at Bonn, who reportedly assembled the text anonymously, commissioned by Archbishop-Elector Ferdinand. In any case, the evidence points to the authorities of electoral Cologne, and it seems more likely that Goehausen was the author.

But Sigmund Riezler emphasized that Tanner was clearly the primary precursor of Friedrich Spee, especially considering Laymann's defense of the imperial Edict of Restitution (March 6, 1629) during a bitter feud among Catholic orders. And even without confusing Laymann's ideas with those of the 1629 pamphlet, "we do not have to look far elsewhere in Laymann's writings to find complete demonological orthodoxy" (Clark 1996, 206). Laymann was indeed conventional about magic and witchcraft. However, it was significant that he supported Tanner's criticisms of witch hunting in 1630, thereby providing another major Jesuit authority for Spee.

WOLFGANG BEHRINGER

See also: AUGSBURG, PRINCE-BISHOPRIC OF; BAVARIA, DUCHY OF; DEL RIO, MARTÍN; DUHR, BERNHARD, SJ; FERDINAND OF COLOGNE; INGOLSTADT, UNIVERSITY OF; JESUITS (SOCIETY OF JESUS); LEA, HENRY CHARLES; RIEZLER, SIGMUND; SPEE, FRIEDRICH; TANNER, ADAM; TYROL, COUNTY OF.

References and further reading:
Binz, Carl. 1901. "Pater P. Laymann SJ und die Hexenprozesse: Zur weiteren Aufklärung." *Historische Zeitschrift* 85: 290–292.
Bireley, Robert. 1979. "The Origins of the '*Ravis Compositio*' (1629): A Text of Paul Laymann, S.J." *Archivium Historicum Societatis Jesu* 42: 106–127.
Clark, Stuart. 1996. *Thinking with Demons: The Idea of Witchcraft in Early Modern Europe.* Oxford: Oxford University Press.
Duhr, Bernhard, SJ. 1899. "Paul Laymann und die Hexenprozesse." *Zeitschrift für katholische Theologie* 23: 733–744.
———. 1900. *Die Stellung der Jesuiten in den deutschen Hexenprozessen.* Cologne: Bachem.
Goehausen, Hermann. 1629. *Processus Juridicus contra Sagas et Veneficos.* Cologne.
Laymann, Paul, SJ. 1625. *Theologia Moralis, in quinque libros partita.* Munich: Nicolaus Henricus (3rd ed.: Ingolstadt, 1630; 4th ed.: Antwerp, 1634).
———. 1629. *De processu juridico contra sagas et veneficos, das ist. Ein Rechtlicher Prozess gegen die Unholden und Zauberische Persohnen, ... Jetzt den Gerichtshaltern . . . zum besten verteutscht, auch mit bewehrten Historien und andern Umbständen vermehrt, und in unterschidliche Titul ordentlich abgetheilet,* Quirin Botzer. Aschaffenburg, Germany: Quirin Botzer.
———. 1630. *Theologia Moralis, in quinque libros partita.* 3rd ed. Ingolstadt.
Lea, Henry Charles. 1939. *Materials Toward a History of Witchcraft.* Edited by Arthur C. Howland. 3 vols. Philadelphia: Thomas Yoseloff.
Riezler, Sigmund. 1896. *Geschichte der Hexenprozesse in Baiern, im Lichte der allgemeinen Entwickelung dargestellt.* Stuttgart.
———. 1900. "Paul Laymann und die Hexenprozesse." *Historische Zeitschrift* 84: 244–256.

LE FRANC, MARTIN (1410–1461)

Le Franc was one of the most accomplished French-language poets of the fifteenth century, secretary of Duke Amadeus VIII of Savoy, provost of the cathedral of Lausanne, and later administrator of the monastery at Novalese. While attending the Council of Basel (1431–1449) in the service of Amadeus VIII (whom the council elected pope as Felix V), Le Franc wrote his long (24,384 lines) poem *Le Champion des dames* (The Defender of Ladies). It included an important discussion of contemporary ideas of diabolical sorcery and witchcraft within the context of a poetic debate on women's virtues and vices. A Paris manuscript of Le Franc's poem, copied around 1450 for Philip the Good,

Duke of Burgundy, to whom the entire poem is dedicated, contained the earliest known illustration of witches riding broomsticks. Around the turn of the twentieth century, first the Cologne archivist Joseph Hansen and then the great Dutch historian Johan Huizinga, in his classic study *The Autumn of the Middle Ages* (1919), recognized Le Franc's importance in the development of ideas of witchcraft (Huizinga 1996, 286–293).

The 823-line discussion of witchcraft (Le Franc 1999, 4:113–146) between the "Adversary" (of women) and "Free Will," the "Defender" (of women), was part of Le Franc's contribution to the fifteenth-century moral and poetic debate known as "the quarrel over the *Roman de la Rose*," a series of literary works dealing with the misogynistic treatment of women by the thirteenth century poet Jean de Meung, in which Christine de Pizan was one of the most notable participants.

In Book 4 of LeFranc's poem, as the Defender describes the achievements of illustrious women of antiquity and later ages in metalwork, painting, and other arts, the Adversary interrupts, insisting that the Defender also consider women's sorcery, flight to the Sabbat, and cannibalism. The Defender abruptly dismisses the challenge with the argument that men invented sorcery and says that the charges made by the Adversary are only delusions. Instead of responding with traditional misogyny, however, the Adversary begins to cite recent trial records and confessions concerning the recently formulated idea of "classical" witchcraft: flight to the Sabbat, apostasy (renouncing Jesus), idolatry (demon worship), sexual orgies, demonic discipline, and the infliction of various injuries upon humans. Among the latter, the Adversary cites sexual impotence and infertility, injurious weather magic, and sexual intercourse with demons.

The Defender responds with what becomes the initial skeptical argument, citing St. Augustine, Gregory the Great, St. Ambrose, and St. Jerome—as well as the life of St. Germanus from *The Golden Legend*—to insist that these were only mental illusions created by the demons, who were in Hell and could not roam the world seeking the ruin of souls. But the Adversary responds with the biblical story of Simon Magus, reinforced with references to Apuleius of Madaura, the legendary Circe, the Roman ethnographer Solinus, the Sybil, the fairy Melusine, St. Augustine, and Albertus Magnus (Albert the Great), to emphasize that such things may be done with God's permission.

The Defender then launches a long and fierce attack on contemporary clerical ignorance, corruption, and incompetence that have permitted such erroneous beliefs to flourish, citing a number of recent instances of misguided laity, including the very recent case of Gilles de Rais, to which the Adversary responds with his past point: that the case of Gilles de Rais only proved that it was easier for the Devil to tempt men than women.

These arguments located Le Franc in the broad contemporary movement of ecclesiastical reform of the clergy and laity and attacks on what they termed "superstition" associated with Jean Gerson, who had also participated in the debates over the *Roman de la Rose.*

EDWARD PETERS

See also: APULEIUS OF MADAURA; BASEL, COUNCIL OF; CIRCE; EUGENIUS IV.
References and further reading:
Barbey, Léon. 1985. *Martin Le Franc, prévôt de Lausanne et avocat de l'amour et de la femme au XVe siècle.* Fribourg, Switzerland: Editions Universitaires.
Huizinga, Johan. 1996. *The Autumn of the Middle Ages.* 1919. Translated by Rodney J. Payton and Ulrich Mammitzsch. Chicago: University of Chicago Press.
Le Franc, Martin. 1999. *Le champion des dames.* Edited by Robert Deschaux. 5 vols. Paris: Champion. 4:113–146.
Lea, Henry C. 1957. *Materials Toward a History of Witchcraft.* Reprint of 1939 ed. Edited by Arthur C. Howland. 3 vols. New York: Thomas Yoseloff.

LEA, HENRY CHARLES (1825–1909)

Lea was the most erudite American historian of the nineteenth century; author of still-valuable studies of the Inquisitions of the Middle Ages and early modern Spain, sacerdotal celibacy, and auricular confession and indulgences; and compiler of an immense, posthumously published collection of sources for the history of witchcraft, *Materials Toward a History of Witchcraft.* Lea was born into a publishing family in Philadelphia in 1825, was tutored at home until he joined the firm in 1843, and was a productive and frequently published literary critic and scientist until he suffered a breakdown from overwork in 1847. Lea turned his attention to history, first historical memoirs and then chronicles, developing a serious interest in medieval Europe, to which his considerable intellectual energies turned as he spent his days working in and then directing the publishing house until his retirement in 1880. During his life, he was politically active in the Union cause in the Civil War and subsequently in both local and national civic affairs until his death.

Lea's early historical works focused on the history of law, which he considered the most reliable guide to what he termed the "inner life" of past peoples, and the history of the Latin Christian Church. His early works on legal procedure and sacerdotal celibacy were remarkable for their period, and extraordinary for a scholar working in the United States, using information taken exclusively from his own growing private library and a network of European libraries and booksellers.

Lea kept a sharp eye on political Roman Catholicism in his own time, both in the United States and in Europe, and he strove in his historical work to distinguish between dogma and personal devotion, on the one hand, and institutional history and prelacy, on the other. Lea criticized both the Episcopalian bishop of Vermont for justifying slavery on the basis of arguments from the Bible and Catholic bishops for their separation from society and the danger of their powers of ecclesiastical discipline in civil matters. From 1884 until his death, Lea turned these subjects into material for his historical works, *A History of the Inquisition of the Middle Ages* of 1888 and *A History of the Inquisition of Spain* in four volumes of 1906–1907. Lord Acton, who admired Lea greatly, invited him to write the chapter "The Eve of the Reformation" for the first volume of *The Cambridge Modern History.*

Lea wrote several other long and important works during the last quarter of the nineteenth century, but his last great project was to have been a history of witchcraft, which he died without having completed. Arthur C. Howland edited his notes, and the work was published as *Materials Toward a History of Witchcraft* in three volumes in 1939. *Materials* is a treasure trove of both original sources and Lea's reading notes, including extensive translations into English from many languages. Lea's range of reading was immense, and he read original sources closely, since he argued that only from these could reliable history be written. His work remains invaluable for students and historians of the subject.

The first of the three consecutively paged volumes contains Parts 1 and 2 of Lea's notes: Part 1 deals with demonology, magic, and sorcery from antiquity to the sixteenth century, and with learned and popular beliefs, including the Sabbat. Part 2 treats the assimilation of sorcery to heresy and provides brief accounts of all known trials for witchcraft to the mid-sixteenth century. The second volume contains the beginning of Part 3, on the demonological literature, canon law, and secular legal procedures, as well as the literature of the Roman Inquisition. The third volume contains the rest of Part 3, demonic possession and a survey of witchcraft by regions, as well as Part 4, texts illustrating the decline of the beliefs, final controversies, and survivals of witchcraft beliefs into the nineteenth century. The entire work offers eloquent testimony to Lea's astonishing scholarly energy and to the genius of one of the greatest historians who ever investigated this subject.

EDWARD PETERS

See also: BURR, GEORGE LINCOLN; HISTORIOGRAPHY; INQUISITION, MEDIEVAL; INQUISITION, SPANISH.
References and further reading:
Bradley, Edward Sculley. 1931. *Henry Charles Lea: A Biography.* Philadelphia: University of Pennsylvania Press.
Lea, Henry C. 1957. *Materials Toward a History of Witchcraft.* 1939. Edited by Arthur C. Howland. 3 vols. New York: Thomas Yoseloff.
O'Brien, John M. 1967. "Henry Charles Lea: The Historian as Reformer." *American Quarterly* 19: 104–113.

Peters, Edward. 1984. "Henry Charles Lea and the 'Abode of Monsters.'" Pp. 577–608 in *The Spanish Inquisition and the Inquisitorial Mind.* Edited by Angel Alcalá. New York: Columbia University Press.

———. 1995. "Henry Charles Lea (1825–1909)." Pp. 89–99 in *History.* Vol. 1 of *Medieval Scholarship: Biographical Studies of the Formation of a Discipline.* Edited by Helen Damico and Joseph Zavadil. New York and London: Garland.

———. 2000. "Henry Charles Lea and the Libraries Within a Library." Pp. 33–60 in *The Penn Library Collections at 250: From Franklin to the Web.* Philadelphia: University of Pennsylvania Library.

LEMNIUS, LEVINUS (1505–1568)

An Erasmian and Galenist physician, Lemnius gave preference to natural causes and cures in cases of diseases that were usually attributed to demonic interference. Born in Zierikzee, a town in the Dutch province of Zeeland, he matriculated at the University of Louvain in 1521, first studying arts and letters. In addition to Latin, Lemnius also learned Greek and Hebrew, probably at the Collegium Trilingue, an independent institute outside the university. Founded in 1517, it was instrumental in spreading the humanist study of classical letters in northwestern Europe. Lemnius also studied medicine at Louvain, but he received his medical doctorate elsewhere, probably from an Italian university. He returned to Zierikzee around 1527, where he married and began practicing medicine. He stayed Catholic, while maintaining contact with Protestants. After ending his practice, Lemnius traveled to London in 1560 to visit his son Willem, who had turned Protestant and therefore moved to England. There, Lemnius met the humanist Thomas Newton, who later translated one of Lemnius's books, and probably also the botanist William Turner, who was in close contact with Dutch Protestant exiles. In 1560, Lemnius also traveled to Italy and Switzerland. He died at Zierikzee.

As a physician, Lemnius was a convinced Galenist but also an admirer of Vesalius, whom he had met personally, probably in 1558. His publications showed that he knew the works of such contemporary physicians as the Frenchman Jean Fernel, the Swiss Conrad Gesner, and the Italian Girolamo Fracastoro. He was also familiar with the work of Girolamo Cardano, but he never mentioned Paracelsus. In his view of astrology, Lemnius was a typical transitional figure. He rejected the idea that one could predict future events by interpreting the position of the planets. Nor did he believe that the time and location of medical interventions such as bloodletting should be chosen on the basis of astrological calculations. Nevertheless, he accepted that comets could change the physical and mental condition of human beings—but believed that the influence of food and drink, rest, physical exercise, sleeping and waking, or the quality of the air was far more important. Their effects depended on individuals' constitution, the character of their humors, the geographic circumstances in which they lived, and their mental state.

A similarly mixed attitude characterized his ideas concerning demonic possession. While admitting that this affliction could occur, he preferred purely somatic explanations such as "melancholy, frenzy, madness, epilepsy and horrible diseases that in the case of young women and widows clearly result from uterine disturbances, either when their first menstruation begins very late, or when they marry at advanced age. Then their mind is so afflicted by dark and dense vapors that they seem to be harassed by an evil spirit, as if the devil has conquered their mind and has driven them to abnormal fantasies" (Lemnius 1593, 573). To free patients of these "poisonous vapors, or the devil, or fantasy," they should be bled and treated with herbal medicines. Not demons but unbalanced humors caused illness. Demons could, however, mingle with the humors to incite the mind to things wicked. The use of superstitious prayers or strange formulas was quite unacceptable. Concerning witchcraft, Lemnius admitted its existence in principle and even acknowledged that witches should be burned. But he also stressed that the effects of witchcraft should be cured by the use of the appropriate herbal medicines, whose effectiveness resulted from God's benevolence and not from some superstitious ritual.

In the course of the sixteenth and seventeenth centuries, Lemnius's books were frequently reprinted. French, German, and Italian translations of his main work, *Occulta naturae miracula* (The Secret Miracles of Nature), first printed in 1559, already appeared with variations in the title by the sixteenth century. An English version was published in 1658. In his *Anatomy of Melancholy,* Robert Burton frequently quoted Lemnius's Latin original, which apparently also influenced views on melancholy, the philosophy of Horace, and the prophetic power of dying human beings as they were presented in Shakespeare's *Hamlet.*

HANS DE WAARDT

See also: ASTROLOGY; ERASMUS, DESIDERIUS; HERBAL MEDICINE; MEDICINE, MEDICAL THEORY; MELANCHOLY; POSSESSION, DEMONIC.

References and further reading:
Burton, Robert. 1621. *The Anatomy of Melancholy.* Oxford: Cripps.

Clark, Stuart. 1997. *Thinking with Demons: The Idea of Witchcraft in Early Modern Europe.* Oxford: Clarendon.

Hoorn, Carel Maaijo van. 1978. *Levinus Lemnius, 1505–1568: Zestiende-eeuws Zeeuws geneesheer.* [n.p.]: C. M. van Hoorn.

Lemnius, Levinus. 1593. *De miraculis occultis naturae.* Frankfurt am Main: Wechelus.

———. 1658. *The Secret Miracles of Nature.* London: Moseley.

Otten, Charlotte F. 1994. "Hamlet and *The Secret Miracles of Nature*." *Notes and Queries* 239: 38–41.

LEVACK, BRIAN (1943–)

Brian P. Levack is a leading historian of the European witch hunt. He studied at Yale under the legendary J. H. Hexter, earning his PhD in 1970. The work that he did for it later emerged as his first book, *The Civil Lawyers in England, 1603–1641* (1973). He has continued to publish extensively on legal history, with a particular interest in the Anglo-Scottish union; a book on this appeared in 1987.

He was appointed to the University of Texas at Austin, where he became John Green Regents Professor of History. He began teaching on the European witch hunt in the 1970s, a subject related to his judicial interests. The appearance of Christina Larner's *Source-Book of Scottish Witchcraft* in 1977 aided his research for "The Great Scottish Witch-Hunt of 1661–1662," a seminal article of 1980 on the last and greatest of Scotland's witchcraft panics.

Then came *The Witch-Hunt in Early Modern Europe* (1987), the book that established his reputation as a leading scholar on the subject. Several syntheses on the witch hunts were published in the 1980s, but Levack's was arguably the best and was reissued in a revised edition in 1995. Noted for the clarity and accessibility of its exposition and for the breadth of up-to-date knowledge that it displayed, it proved invaluable in teaching and research. By showing that witch hunting could not be ascribed to a single cause but arose from a conjunction of factors, it cleared up much misunderstanding and placed subsequent research on a firmer footing. Levack paid much attention to the complex origins of the witch hunt, analyzing intellectual, legal, and religious causes and well as the social context. His emphasis on the judicial nature of witch hunting was welcome, and his dissection of the composite intellectual stereotype of the witch has stood the test of time particularly well. Levack stressed most of all the legal changes that led to the witch persecutions, especially the transition from accusatorial to inquisitorial procedure and the growing use of torture to extract confessions. He set such legal developments against the background of state building and saw a correlation between state control of the judiciary and the absence of witch persecution. Thus, witch hunting was most severe where local courts could act without hindrance from appellate courts and central governments. Levack later developed this theme extensively (1996).

More than a synthesis, *The Witch-Hunt in Early Modern Europe* is noteworthy because many of its approaches and theses have become the standard explanations for scholars. Levack paid close attention to geography, including all of Europe in his discussion, whereas previously scholars had let England, Scotland, and western Europe drive discussions of witchcraft, ignoring, for the most part, Scandinavia and eastern Europe. This close scrutiny of regions enabled him to develop more accurate totals for the number of witchcraft cases, reducing the number of executions to 60,000 (a figure that other historians have subsequently reduced further).

By contrast, the way this book distinguished between magic and religion was arguably outdated, and the book was sketchy on the crucial question of women and witch hunting. But these are minor criticisms of a comprehensive book that offers a great deal both to beginners in the subject and to experts. At the time of the writing of this entry, a third edition is in the press, further developing a number of themes, including demonic possession and the revival of witch hunting in the modern world.

Levack has remained in the forefront of the trends in witchcraft scholarship, as his more recent articles and the second edition of *The Witch-Hunt in Early Modern Europe* demonstrate. He has recognized the importance of community pressures and has taken a particular interest in the decline of witch hunting—something that earlier scholars had neglected. As befits a scholar who is a specialist in other fields too, he has always taken a broad view of the subject of witchcraft. Some of his recent publications have explored related areas, notably judicial torture and demonic possession.

In 1992, he compiled *Articles on Witchcraft, Magic, and Demonology*, a multivolume collection of reprints of articles on witchcraft, containing some of the best recent work as well as a number of gems of older scholarship. A second multivolume collection, published in 2001, made accessible some of the many works on the subject from the 1990s. Each collection contained well over 100 articles in English. Levack's most recent work is *The Witchcraft Sourcebook* (2004), a collection of sixty-one selections of primary sources, raging from antiquity to the late seventeenth century and including selections from literature and drama, theologians, demonologists, and skeptics. This work is one of the two major collections of primary documents available in English, the other being Alan Kors and Edward Peters's *Witchcraft in Europe, 400–1700: A Documentary History*.

JULIAN GOODARE

See also: HISTORIOGRAPHY; WITCH HUNTS.

References and further reading:
Gijswijt-Hofstra, Marijke, Brian P. Levack, and Roy Porter. 1999. *Witchcraft and Magic in Europe: The Eighteenth and Nineteenth Centuries.* London: Athlone.
Kors, Alan, and Edward Peters. 2001. *Witchcraft in Europe, 400–1700: A Documentary History.* 2nd ed. Philadelphia: University of Pennsylvania Press.
Levack, Brian P. 1980. "The Great Scottish Witch-Hunt of 1661–1662." *Journal of British Studies* 20: 90–108.
———. 1995. *The Witch-Hunt in Early Modern Europe.* 2nd ed. London: Longman.
———, ed. 1992. *Articles on Witchcraft, Magic, and Demonology.* 12 vols. Vol. 1, *Anthropological Studies of Witchcraft, Magic,*

and Religion. Vol. 2, *Witchcraft in the Ancient World and the Middle Ages.* Vol. 3, *Witch-Hunting in Early Modern Europe: General Studies.* Vol. 4, *The Literature of Witchcraft.* Vol. 5, *Witch-Hunting in Continental Europe: Local and Regional Studies.* Vol. 6, *Witchcraft in England.* Vol. 7, *Witchcraft in Scotland.* Vol. 8, *Witchcraft in Colonial America.* Vol. 9, *Possession and Exorcism.* Vol. 10, *Witchcraft, Women, and Society.* Vol. 11, *Renaissance Magic.* Vol. 12, *Witchcraft and Demonology in Art and Literature.* New York: Garland.

———. 1995. "Possession, Witchcraft, and the Law in Jacobean England." *Washington and Lee University Law Review* 52: 1613–1640.

———. 1996. "State-Building and Witch Hunting in Early Modern Europe." Pp. 96–115 in *Witchcraft in Early Modern Europe: Studies in Culture and Belief.* Edited by Jonathan Barry, Marianne Hester, and Gareth Roberts. Cambridge: Cambridge University Press.

———, ed. 2001. *New Perspectives on Magic, Witchcraft, and Demonology.* 6 vols. Vol. 1, *Demonology, Religion and Witchcraft.* Vol. 2, *Witchcraft in Continental Europe.* Vol. 3, *Witchcraft in the British Isles and New England.* Vol. 4, *Gender and Witchcraft.* Vol. 5, *Witchcraft, Healing, and Popular Diseases.* Vol. 6, *Witchcraft in the Modern World.* London: Routledge.

———. 2002a. "The Decline and End of Scottish Witch-Hunting." Pp. 166–181 in *The Scottish Witch-Hunt in Context.* Edited by Julian Goodare. Manchester: Manchester University Press.

———. 2002b. "Judicial Torture in Scotland During the Age of Mackenzie." Pp. 185–198 in *Miscellany IV.* Edited by Hector L. MacQueen. Edinburgh: Stair Society.

———, ed. 2004. *The Witchcraft Sourcebook.* London: Routledge.

The female demon Lilith, who stole and killed children. Terracotta relief, Mesopotamia, ca. 300 B.C.E. (Art Archive/Christies/Eileen Tweedy)

LILITH

Lilith was a female demon that preyed on unsuspecting men and infants. Her origins are linked to Mesopotamian mythology, which made references to male and female demons called *Lilu* and *Lilitu,* respectively. These were storm or wind demons, with names that are etymologically based on the Sumerian word *lil,* literally meaning "wind." Lilith, the Hebrew form of *Lilitu,* occupies an important position in Jewish folklore and demonology. Hebrew Scripture contains one reference to Lilith, the night hag (Isaiah 34:14), in a passage describing Yahweh's day of retribution. In the aftermath of this vengeance, when the land is turned into a wilderness, Lilith is referred to as one of the creatures that will be tamed.

In postbiblical literature, Lilith was mentioned in the Babylonian Talmud. It was there that her demonic characteristics were developed: She had long hair (Erubin 100b); she had the form of a woman but was winged (Nidda 24b); she preyed on men who slept alone (Shabbat 151b). The story of Lilith as the wife of Adam was first evidenced in the *Alphabet of Ben Sira,* which was in part a version of earlier accounts of Lilith from the Midrashic tradition. Of uncertain date, possibly between the eighth and tenth centuries C.E., the *Alphabet* named Lilith as Adam's original wife and stated that she refused to submit to his authority, particularly in terms of sexual union (disobeying his expectation that she lay beneath him). Lilith eventually fled, pursued by three angels (Senoy, Sanseoy, and Semangelof) who, at God's behest, explained that she must return or have 100 of her offspring perish each day. Lilith defied the order and exclaimed that she was made to bring death to infants.

The story went on to describe the existence of amulets designed to protect the young from child-stealing demons such as Lilith, which suggests, to some extent, its etiological nature. Protective charms against Lilith are evidenced in archaeology, particularly in the form of incantation bowls, from a Jewish community at Nippur, dating from the early centuries C.E. It may be assumed that these bowls had a function similar to that of the amulets mentioned in the *Alphabet,* although they usually functioned in a broader context, namely to keep Lilith or other demons from harming the household in general. From these traditions developed the role of Lilith in the Kabbalah. In the thirteenth-century kabbalistic text *Treatise on the Left Emanation,* for example, Lilith was born as one half of an androgynous being, the other half of which was Samael (the diabolic angel who, on falling from Heaven, assumed the name Lucifer or Satan). This text also named a second Lilith, the wife of Asmodeus, another demon king; hence, the two female spirits were distinguished by the titles Lilith the Elder and Lilith the Younger.

The collection of fourteenth-century writings known as the *Zohar* augmented Lilith's demonic aspects. In *Zohar* 3:76b–77a, Lilith and the demon Naamah (Charmer), were presented as succubi who appeared to men as they experienced wet dreams and collected their semen for the purpose of producing demonic offspring. Here Lilith's role as a baby-snatching demon was also reiterated. A combination of both the amulet and the Kabbalistic traditions concerning Lilith was best exemplified in the *Book of Raziel* written in about 1100 C.E., which contained several amulets to ward off evil spirits, particularly Lilith, who threatened to harm mothers and their newly born. These recipes were to be inscribed on parchment or on the door and walls of the room occupied by the mother and child. Less detailed rituals involved a protective spell for a boy-child in which a circle was drawn on the wall of the birthing room with the words "Adam and Eve. Out Lilith" inscribed within; this practice continued until the nineteenth century.

MARGUERITE JOHNSON

See also: AMULET AND TALISMAN; ANGELS; BIBLE; DEMONS; JEWS, WITCHCRAFT, AND MAGIC; KABBALAH.

References and further reading:

Budge, E. A. Wallis. 1930. *Amulets and Superstitions.* Oxford: Oxford University Press.
Gager, John G. 1992. *Curse Tablets and Binding Spells from the Ancient World.* Oxford: Oxford University Press.
Gaster, Moses. 1900. "Two Thousand Years of a Charm against the Child-Stealing Witch." *Folk-Lore* 11: 129–161.
Montgomery, James Alan. 1913. *Aramaic Incantation Texts from Nippur.* Philadelphia: University of Pennsylvania Press.
Oesterley, W. O. E., and Theodore H. Robinson. 1966. *Hebrew Religion: Its Origin and Development.* London: Society for Promoting Christian Knowledge.
Patai, Raphael. 1990. *The Hebrew Goddess.* 3rd ed. Detroit: Wayne State University Press.

LILLE NUNS

In 1612–1614, possession cases at a Brigittine convent in Lille, in the Spanish Netherlands, generated controversial but largely ineffectual witchcraft accusations.

In a case of convent possession that began as an attempted "copycat" of the notorious Aix-en-Provence case of 1609–1611, two possessed "nun-witches" accused their convent almoner of witchcraft. A papal nuncio defended the priest in Rome, and the pope rejected the accusations. The French lay author Jean Le Normant described the Lille cases in 1623 in a controversial book that depicted the outbreak of diabolical activities at the convent as evidence of the Antichrist's coming.

Early in 1612, several nuns at the convent started to go into convulsions, to dance on the altar of their chapel, and to fall into states of torpor. Following accusations by the possessed nuns, Marie de Sains, a nun who had been renowned for her piety, confessed she was a witch. She in turn accused a young novice, Simone Dourlet, of being her accomplice. Both were imprisoned at the *officialité* (diocesan prison) of Tournai but soon retracted their confessions. Nicolas de Montmorency, a powerful local noble and a patron of the convent, requested the *official* (presiding judge of the diocesan court) of Tournai to invite Sebastien Michaelis and François Domptius, the Dominican exorcists made famous by the recent Aix-en-Provence case, to exorcise the possessed women at the convent. In May 1612, three prominent possessed nuns alleged that Marie de Sains had caused their possessions by means of charms. De Sains was obliged to confess and display Devil's marks on her body. But events now took a different turn from similar cases: Although a self-confessed witch, de Sains began to play the role of the prophetic possessed, while her possessed sisters received less public exposure.

Under exorcism, de Sains delivered revelations about the coming of the Antichrist and claimed to have participated at a Sabbat with Father Louis Gaufridy, the priest executed at Aix-en-Provence in 1611. She had been vowed to the Devil at birth, and a governess had made her "princess of magicians" (thus the companion of Gaufridy, "prince of magicians"). Her devil, she said, had been infuriated by the foundation of the Brigittine house in Lille and had ordered her to enter it to undermine it. She claimed that she and Dourlet had caused all the illnesses and other problems at the house, the possession being their crowning achievement. She also admitted to making Nicolas de Montmorency and his wife infertile.

In mid-1613, de Sains made a witchcraft accusation against Canon Jean Leduc, almoner of the convent and *écolâtre* (priest in charge of teaching at a cathedral) of the chapter of St.-Pierre in Lille. The chapter persuaded the papal nuncio, Guido Bentivoglio, to intercede with Rome. In early autumn of 1613, Bentivoglio appointed the *official* of Malines, Father Jacques Boonen, to investigate the case, over the protests of Montmorency, who simply wanted the alleged witches prosecuted. Boonen cleared the canon of witchcraft, and Pope Paul V pointedly gave Leduc a more important benefice. While Montmorency pursued avenues of appeal against the decision, Bentivoglio had Michaelis's account of the Aix-en-Provence case, *Histoire admirable de la possession et conversion d'une pénitente, séduite par un magicien* (The Admirable History of the Possession and

Conversion of a Penitent Woman, Seduced by a Magician, 1614) examined by the faculty of theology of Louvain, who put it under interdict. The bishop of Tournai ordered all copies surrendered to him. In 1623, when Jean Le Normant published his account of the Lille case, the *Histoire veritable et memorable de ce qvi c'est passé sovs l'exorcisme de trois filles possedées és païs de Flandre* (True and Memorable History of What Took Place in the Exorcism of Three Possessed Girls in Flanders), the Sorbonne censured it.

The nuns were much less fortunate than the canon. Although Bentivoglio informed Rome that he was returning the women to their convent, he was unable to effect this, and subsequently he suspected Montmorency of harboring them. Marie de Sains probably died in custody in 1630, after spending many years in the episcopal prison in Tournai and subsequently at a prison in Vilvorde. The claim that Simone Dourlet was burned for witchcraft has been refuted (Lottin 1984, 170–177), but she probably spent the remainder of her life in prison. They were, however, far more fortunate than two of their convent sisters in nearby Artois, who really were burned as witches immediately afterwards, in 1615 (Muchembled 2003, 250–265).

This episode revealed two deeply contrary tendencies in the upper echelons of Catholicism at this time. One the one hand, a vigorous and at times lethal passion for the fruits of exorcism was at work, and, on the other hand, a humane and skeptical spirit existed. To be sure, jurisdictional differences could from time to time affect who was on which side, but it remains that this division was representative of the tensions within early modern reforming Catholicism. Beyond this, the role of Montmorency and the layman Le Normant show that a Church-secular distinction, which might assume the Church to be the more likely to accuse witches, did not apply here. The caution of the papacy also seems to have been characteristic.

SARAH FERBER

See also: AIX-EN-PROVENCE NUNS; ANTICHRIST; BINSFELD, PETER; DEL RIO, MARTÍN; DEVIL'S MARK; DUVAL, ANDRÉ; EXORCISM; LOUDUN NUNS; LOUVIERS NUNS; NETHERLANDS, SOUTHERN; POSSESSION, DEMONIC; SABBAT.

References and further reading:

Le Normant, Jean. 1623. *Histoire veritable et memorable de ce qvi c'est passé sovs l'exorcisme de trois filles possedées és païs de Flandre;* [and] *De la vocation des magiciens et magiciennes par le ministre des demons.* 2 vols. Paris: Buon. Reel 52:471 in *Witchcraft in Europe and America Microfilm* (1983). Woodbridge, CT: Research Publications.
Lottin, Alain. 1984. *Lille: Citadelle de la Contre-Réforme? (1598–1668).* Dunkirk: Westhoek.
———. 1985. "Sorcellerie, possessions diaboliques et crise conventuelle." Pp. 111–132 in *L'histoire des faits de la sorcellerie.* Publications de Centre de Recherches d'Histoire Religieuse et d'Histoire des Idées 8. Angers: Presses de l'Université d'Angers.
Michaelis, Sebastien. 1613. *The Admirable Historie of the Possession and Conversion of a Penitent woman. Sedvced by a magician that made her to become a Witch . . . Wherevnto is annexed a Pnevmology, or Discourse of Spirits.* Translated by W. B. London: Aspley. Reel 69:663 in *Witchcraft in Europe and America Microfilm* (1983). Woodbridge, CT: Research Publications.
Muchembled, Robert. 2003. *Passions de femmes au temps de la Reine Margot 1553–1615.* Paris: Seuil.

LIPPE, COUNTY OF

A small county (*Grafschaft*) of the Holy Roman Empire, Lippe was an important center of witch hunts. It covered approximately 1,200 square kilometers and had about 40,000 inhabitants around 1600, of whom some 10,000 lived in small towns (Lippe became a protoindustrial region in the seventeenth and eighteenth centuries). Its capital, Lemgo, preserved a certain autonomy from the count, including the right to condemn criminals to death; there were bitter conflicts between Lemgo and its lords. Around 1540, Lippe became Lutheran and then, about 1600, under Count Simon VI (ruled 1563–1613), Calvinist, although Lemgo remained Lutheran. Simon VI carried through important reforms in Lippe, including of its law courts. Simon's heirs quarreled, and the administration of his lands was partly divided.

Apart from Lemgo, we can find 221 persons involved in witchcraft trials between 1550 and 1686, including 41 in the town of Horn. Half of the 221 were tried during the most intensive hunt, which occurred between 1653 and 1661; only 8 were accused later, between 1670 and 1678. In Lemgo, the number of victims was about 250, with great waves of trials taking place in 1565, 1583–1605, 1628–1637, and 1653–1681.

Apart from trials of women, the usual victims, Lemgo also saw many trials against both men and children. More than fifty children were arrested between 1654 and 1676; some were imprisoned for eleven years, and some were even tortured. Most, but not all, were connected with the trial against a sorcerer-teacher, Hermann Beschorn, who had worked in Lemgo. Children "seduced" by him were usually re-educated by the teacher Henkhausen, but some children (older than fourteen) were executed as hopeless witches. Some of the Lippe clergy gave infamous advice in this difficult matter. When the clergy suggested these children be killed secretly while they were praying, in order to secure their salvation, the government did not follow their counsel.

The trials in Lemgo were Lippe's most famous because they were connected with the fight among political factions. They were also expressions of economic depression and of political upheaval during the Thirty Years' War. Lemgo's mayor, Hermann Cothmann, whose mother had been executed as a witch, was a main figure in the persecution. The previous mayor, Heinrich

Kerkmann, had also persecuted witches relentlessly. Lemgo's *Hexenbürgermeisterhaus* (house of the witch mayor), today a museum, is a witness to Cothmann's activities.

The Lippe witchcraft trials are well documented. There are comprehensive depositions of witnesses, making a microanalysis possible. The surviving protocols of the lower courts allow us in many cases to observe the "career" of a witch before her trial, sometimes for decades. These documents make it possible to show the behavior of both accused and accusers. We can discover whether or not the accused women had shown deviant behavior, compared with other suspected women who were not prosecuted. These patterns have been described in detail (Walz 1993). Witch finders played a great part in the defense against witches, but gypsies were also consulted. The Lippe population frequently consulted one of the most famous witch finders around 1650, Wicken Klaus; his magical practices were described in detail at his trial.

The local criminal procedure, codified in 1593, provided the foundation of the trials. The procedure was split into inquisition and accusation. Advocates were permitted. By about 1600, their counsels already showed arguments similar to those used by Friedrich Spee von Langenfeld some decades later, but they had no visible effect. Though Simon VI had forbidden the water ordeal (swimming test), it was applied in many trials, very often in order to shock the accused person into making a confession. Before a person was arrested and again before torture was employed, officials consulted universities, generally the law faculty of the nearby University of Rinteln. After being sentenced to death by fire, convicted witches were often "pardoned" to death by sword. In all probability, the slowdown in Lippe's witch hunts after 1660 was due more to the dysfunctional contradictions of an out-of-control epidemic than to any kind of "enlightenment."

RAINER WALZ

See also: CHILDREN; GERMANY, WEST AND NORTHWEST; SPEE, FRIEDRICH; SWIMMING TEST; UNIVERSITIES; WITCH FINDERS.

References and further reading:

Ahrendt-Schulte, Ingrid. 1997. *Zauberinnen in der Stadt Horn (1554–1603)*. Frankfurt am Main: Campus.

Koppenborg, Ingo. 2003. *Hexen in Detmold: Die lippische Residenzstadt, 1599–1669*. Bielefeld: Verlag für Regionalgeschichte.

Schormann, Gerhard. 1977. *Hexenprozesse in Nordwestdeutschland*. Hildesheim: Lax.

Walz, Rainer. 1993. *Hexenglaube und magische Kommunikation*. Paderborn: Schöningh.

Wilbertz, Gisela, and Jürgen Scheffler, eds. 2000. *Biographieforschung und Stadtgeschichte: Lemgo in der Spätphase der Hexenverfolgung*. Bielefeld: Verlag für Regionalgeschichte.

Wilbertz, Gisela, Gerd Schwerhoff, and Jürgen Scheffler, eds. 1994. *Hexenverfolgung und Regionalgeschichte: Die Grafschaft Lippe im Vergleich*. Bielefeld: Verlag für Regionalgeschichte.

LITERATURE

Texts provide the bulk of our information about the place of witchcraft in larger cultural contexts, particularly for the past. Witchcraft has achieved a relatively stable range of definitions in recent decades. But careful interpretation requires defining the spectrum of relations between texts and the themes or topics of witchcraft they display. Most importantly, do literary texts present witchcraft reliably? And what do we mean by *literature* and *literary?* The terms evade succinct definition. Equating literature with fiction oversimplifies many witchcraft texts: As wholes or in part, they resist categories like "factual," "historical," "fictive," or "fictitious." Understanding how texts represent witchcraft requires considering how they are produced (including conventions of genre and rhetoric) and how actual or plausibly conjectured audiences "consumed" them.

PRODUCTION

Witchcraft has been called a species of narrative, a statement that opens two possibilities.

The first possibility is that witchcraft always implied a narrative: It was a kind of "story" told about physical causation or human deviance, so "witchcraft literature" could comprise all texts mentioning *maleficium* (harmful magic), interaction with demons, and so on. By this definition, instructions for performing witchcraft could qualify as a hypothetical narrative in the second person and the future tense: "If you do this, that will happen." Similarly, an indictment for witchcraft would be a hypothetical second- or third-person narrative in the past tense: "You/She did this." These examples seem forced, however, and such an all-inclusive category would be useless.

The second possibility is that only explicit narratives—stories—describing *maleficium,* interactions with demons, or the like qualify as witchcraft literature. This is not strictly true; versified instructions about such activity would strike most readers as literature. Besides, many actual charms and spells had meter and rhyme. Yet many witchcraft texts were narratives. They told stories about persons not identifiable as the reader and were set in places and times different from the reader's (though the displacement may have been minimal, if events were presented as "news").

Stories have, in Aristotle's phrase, a beginning, a middle, and an end. The chronological sequence required by a story differentiates witchcraft narratives from witchcraft treatises, which depended on criteria other than temporal sequence, such as typologies of behavior or appearance. Analytical precision and classificatory arrangement precluded ambiguity and indeterminacy, the basis for many aesthetic effects characteristic of narrative, as well as indulgence in emotion for ends other than condemning specific individuals or groups.

These are not absolute distinctions. In fact, few witchcraft treatises were entirely analytical; most presented anecdotes about witches as evidence. Yet anecdotes never simply illustrated witchcraft analyses: They frequently told something more or something different. Narrative rhetorically exploited conditioned responses (such as the evil witch, the innocent victim), it rescued or replaced analysis when logic broke down, or threatened to (Stephens 2002, 235–238). But narrative's richness can derail analysis. Often in Francesco Maria Guazzo's *Compendium Maleficarum* (A Summary of Witches, 1608), so many various and strange anecdotes were cited to illustrate an argument that they blurred or even contradicted it.

In summary, witchcraft was not reducible to narrative, but narrative was essential to writings about witchcraft, even at their most unliterary. For the purposes of this encyclopedia, "witchcraft literature" has been separated from theatrical texts about witchcraft. Excluding theatrical texts from a conventional history of literature would be indefensible: Tragedies and comedies are no less literary than narrative poems, romances, or novels. And theatrical texts about witchcraft were numerous, as the entries on Drama attest.

But differences in consumption between theatrical texts and other storytelling media are unusually crucial for witchcraft. On stage, theatrical texts are intensely appropriate to witchcraft. In Aristotelian terms, theatrical texts predispose impersonation by their almost exclusively mimetic character. They display little diegesis—descriptive or explanatory narration—and abundant mimesis, or lines intended to be spoken, with accompanying gestures, by impersonating actors. Therefore, when a text presents its characters as dramatis personae to be physically impersonated by actors, even a solitary reader experiences the text differently from narrative. Early modern demons also engaged in a kind of theatrical impersonation, through possession or apparition, animating bodies perceptible by human senses.

Film presents comparable characteristics, but amplified and expanded. Constant technological advances make cinematic special effects ever more appropriate for presenting the wonders and illusions (*praestigia*) of demons.

Conversely, narration evokes readers' experience of listening to a single "voice." Voice and the illusory presence of a narrator are effects of grammar, produced by scenic description and indirect reportage of dialogue. Here again, differences are not absolute: A narrating voice can create mental "theater" when the reader visualizes the scenes it describes.

The dialogue, a genre adopted by many writers on witchcraft, presents a special case. Dialogue resembles theater by minimizing or excluding the utterances of a narrator, yet it must be consumed like narrative: An abundance of direct speech and a paucity of action make impersonation difficult or impossible. Dialogues, like treatises, approached witchcraft scientifically. By replacing sequential analysis with debate, dialogue added a dimension of lifelikeness, and some early authors, such as Ulrich Molitor, even cast historical persons as interlocutors. Most witchcraft dialogues became treatises in disguise by preordaining the triumph of one viewpoint: The subject required that they either defend or oppose its reality. Gianfrancesco Pico della Mirandola's dialogue *Strix, sive de ludificatione daemonum* (The Witch, or the Deceptions of Demons, 1523) accomplished this through a strong narrative line (three interlocutors successfully convince a fourth that witchcraft is real) and novel characterization (the pro-witchcraft interlocutors include an inquisitor and a confessed witch).

Understanding how texts were consumed requires identifying their implied readers. What knowledge do texts require for comprehension: Latin? specialized legal, medical, or theological expertise? Pico della Mirandola's *Strix* was written originally in Latin, and its cultural references implied an erudite, skeptical humanist reader. It made arcane references to classical scholarship and mythology, but presupposed only superficial acquaintance with contemporary controversies over witchcraft. A year later (1524), Leandro Alberti translated *Strix* into vernacular Italian for a bourgeois and peasant audience, paraphrasing difficult vocabulary and explicating most of its arcane references. Along with implied readers, Alberti envisioned implied listeners, unable to read even simple Italian yet capable of comparing their folkloric witchcraft ideas with Pico della Mirandola's "scientific" explanations.

The implied reader of a text exists symbiotically with an implied author. Even when the empirical author—the historical individual who put pen to paper—remains anonymous, his or her intellectual and attitudinal profile remains. If the knowledge presumed or explained identifies an implied reader, it also delineates an implied author, as does the rhetorical temperature of the writing—objective and confident, hysterical and overwrought, compassionate, judgmental, skeptical, ironic, and so on. The implied author necessarily forecasts a reader receptive or resistant to the reality of witchcraft.

The implied author attempts to influence the implied reader's presumed reaction, in part by accepting or manipulating the conventions of genre. As treatise, Heinrich Kramer's *Malleus Maleficarum* (The Hammer of Witches, 1486) presupposed an audience of magistrates and inquisitors schooled in syllogistic argument and worried about such things as heresy or infant mortality. The *Malleus*'s third book, demonstrating how to entrap, prosecute, and execute witches, presumed that its previous demonstrations of witches' responsibility had been convincing. The skeptical implied reader of Pico della Mirandola's *Strix* was expected to come to prize witchcraft for plausibly explaining the realities behind classical myth by revealing pagan deities as the demons of Christianity. Thus, he or she should have more readily accepted the reality of witchcraft, for Pico della Mirandola's classical erudition should have salvaged the intellectual respectability of the supernatural order. The scholarly alternative, a euhemeristic "deconstruction" of pagan gods as mythologized kings and warriors, would have damaged the case for witchcraft.

Aristotle's *Poetics* required probability or verisimilitude in representation. In modern philosophical terms, literature creates possible worlds. A possible world maximally resembles the actual reader's experience but is not identical to it, differing in one or more aspects. The extent of difference has generic implications for texts about witchcraft. In a treatise, an implied reader was fully expected to identify the world outside as the one described in the witchcraft text. "How-to" manuals for conjuring demons and demonological tracts describing how to discover and prosecute witches shared this trait. When a text postulated less perfect accord between the implied author's world and that of the implied reader, the latter was expected to modify belief, not take action: Rather than become a witch or witch hunter, he or she had to choose sides in the witchcraft controversy.

Two conditions make witchcraft texts seem fully "literary": The worlds of text and implied reader coincided quite imperfectly, yet ambiguity, allusion, and indirection prompted the reader to entertain an indecisive attitude toward witchcraft, neither accepting nor rejecting its reality.

Recognizably literary witchcraft texts characteristically encouraged this attitude by exploiting the theme of imagination, systematically refusing to present phenomena as either factual or imaginary, real or unreal. Nathaniel Hawthorne's "Young Goodman Brown" (1835) described a possible world where beloved elders and ethereally pure newlywed wives may be witches, the Devil may be lurking on every footpath, neighbors may be flying above the overcast clouds, and the outward appearances of "Faith"—the newlywed wife or the Christian religion—may mask the perfidious reality of witchcraft. Updated, sensationalized, and gender-reversed, the same premise animated Ira Levin's *Rosemary's Baby* (1967), in which husband, neighbors, and physician seemed to be conspiring against the heroine.

These examples display individualized psychology, attention to such aesthetic factors as narrative coherence and linguistic appropriateness, and other commonly agreed upon indices of literariness. However, witchcraft narrative necessarily explored ambiguous appearances, so literary features were not always indispensable. Though crude, anecdotes in

witchcraft indictments and treatises often resembled modern literary modes of uncanny or fantastic narration, such as in Franz Kafka's *Metamorphosis* (1915).

If the implied author suggested that witchcraft described an impossible world, his narrative would be recognizable as satire or parody. An example is Laurent Bordelon's *Histoire des imaginations extravagantes de monsieur Oufle: Causees par la lecture des lives qui traitent de la magie, du grimoire, des demoniaques, sorciers* (The History of the Ridiculous Extravagances of Monsieur Oufle, Occasioned by His Reading Books Treating Magic, the Demonic Arts, Demoniacs, Witches, 1710), whose protagonist lost his reason by reading demonologies, as Don Quixote had a century earlier with chivalric romances. Oufle's name, an anagram of *le fou* (madman), reflects his upside-down worldview.

Is a precise typology of witchcraft and literature necessary? Would a laundry list of texts with witchcraft content be more useful? Literary genres are notoriously fluid; characteristics of "literariness" itself formerly occasioned endless, fruitless wrangling. Other classifications (such as ones accounting for gender, social class, or religious creed) might be equally or more valid. But to discuss literature in the specialized context of witchcraft, some concept of "literariness" is necessary.

Implied authors, implied readers, possible worlds, and modes of production and consumption vary considerably in any cultural context. Curse-tablets, Tacitus's description of the maleficent objects found after Germanicus's death, and Lucan's episode of Erichtho are all datable to early imperial Rome, but they differ literarily as well as magically. Even greater divergence is observable among medieval necromantic manuals, the fifth book of Caesarius of Heisterbach's *Dialogus Miraculorum* (Dialogue on Miracles, ca. 1225), and Giovanni Boccaccio's story (1352) of Bruno, Buffalmacco, and Maestro Simone (*Decameron* 8.9). Since the consolidation of witchcraft mythology around 1500, the range of variation has expanded constantly: Consider, among writers included in this encyclopedia, the sixteenth-century works of John Dee, Jean Bodin, Reginald Scot, and Torquato Tasso. The twentieth-century books by Aleister Crowley, Montague Summers, Arthur Miller, and Aldous Huxley differ among themselves comparably, and the decades since the 1950s have witnessed a publication explosion in witchcraft texts, including Wiccan how-to manuals, barely disguised demonologies like Daniel Ryder's *Breaking the Circle of Satanic Ritual Abuse*, novels such as Leslie Wilson's *Malefice*, and Umberto Eco's best-selling *The Name of the Rose*.

Outside of film (one thinks of the "witch" sketch in *Monty Python and the Holy Grail*), burlesque and satirical treatments of witchcraft appear to have declined; as in the Romantic period, witchcraft is now a subject for nostalgic or exploitative treatment. J. K. Rowling's Harry Potter novels offer the singular case of a fantasy world of "witchcraft" (mostly natural magic), in which the supernatural allegorized questions of diversity and adolescent development. Anne Rice's witch and vampire fiction performs a comparable service for a more urbane or disenchanted audience.

Historical change rearranges typologies and recontextualizes texts. Capital examples are trial records and news-mongering pamphlets or broadsheets, such as the Fugger newsletter about Walpurga Hausmännin (1587) and the numerous Elizabethan and Jacobean pamphlets. Pamphlets originally provided news and entertainment; scholars now read them for purposes of cultural anthropology, to recover neglected information about women, the poor, and the legal system. Since the 1980s, trial records have inspired microhistory, the narrative, sometimes novelistic reconstruction of common people's lives and lived realities.

Literary study is increasingly interdisciplinary, ever less purely aesthetic, ever more anthropological. In the 1960s and 1970s, structuralism, poststructuralism, and feminism prepared the revolution in attitudes to literary canons that triumphed in the 1980s and 1990s: *Literature* and *great* no longer imply each other in professional literary study. Even in literature departments, university courses increasingly scrutinize ephemeral and legal texts.

The motives of inquisitors, prosecutors, and magistrates who constructed the stereotype of the witch are overdue for attention comparable to that accorded defendants and accusers. Scholars have often regarded these men's motives as obvious, but what counts as "obvious" has changed over time. From about 1700 until the 1960s, condescension and sarcasm often inflected scholarly descriptions of inquisitorial ideology. More recently, Carlo Ginzburg has taken the opposite position, suggesting that witchcraft scholars involuntarily reproduce the inquisitors' and magistrates' ideologies and positions of power, asking the same questions they asked (Ginzburg 1989, 162–163).

But neither unintended sympathy nor facile contempt is inevitable. The concepts of the implied author and implied reader, coupled with more traditional techniques of close reading and rhetorical analysis, sharpen our perception of the type of person likely to write a particular text or set of assertions. Underneath overt expressions of smugness and prejudice, assertions about witches frequently imply enthusiasms, concerns, or dreads that remain unarticulated. Assertions are repeated within a text or among several texts; variations—or the lack of them—in witchcraft commonplaces could yield social insight under literary analysis. Texts contemporary or anterior to a given witchcraft text may discuss witchcraft only marginally or not at all, yet demonstrate related concerns and worries. More highly literary (or philosophical or theological) texts can provide valuable perspective on unadorned official documents (Stephens 2002, 1–11, 27–31).

In *Europe's Inner Demons* (1975), Norman Cohn provided a model for tracking witchcraft stereotypes from culture to culture over many centuries, revealing submerged or implicit anxieties. Continued attention to the specific literary means used to express (or repress) such anxieties can further enrich our understanding of why witchcraft accusations were so seductive to writers in the literate subcultures of early modern Europe.

Any attempted census of witchcraft and (or in) literature will be partial—both too brief and somewhat biased. Recent collections of texts and histories of witchcraft, listed below, make the task less daunting.

WALTER STEPHENS

See also: BORDELON, LAUREN; DRAMA, DUTCH; DRAMA, ITALIAN; DRAMA, SPANISH; FILM (CINEMA); FUGGER FAMILY; GINZBURG, CAROL; WALPURGA HAUSMÄNNIN; HISTORIOGRAPHY; *MALLEUS MALEFICARUM;* PAMPHLETS AND NEWSPAPERS; PICO DELLA MIRANDOLA, GIANFRANCESCO; RENAISSANCE DRAMA, ENGLAND; WITCH HUNTS.

References and further reading:

Collections and Studies of Witchcraft Literature

Anglo, Sydney, ed. 1977. *The Damned Art: Essays in the Literature of Witchcraft.* London: Routledge and Kegan Paul.

Kors, Alan Charles, and Edward Peters, eds. 2001. *Witchcraft in Europe, 400–1700.* 2nd ed. Philadelphia: University of Pennsylvania Press.

Luck, Georg, ed. 1985. *Arcana Mundi: Magic and the Occult in the Greek and Roman Worlds.* Baltimore: Johns Hopkins University Press.

———. 1997. *Arcana mundi: Magia e occulto nel mondo greco e romano.* Translated by Claudio Tartaglini. 2 vols. Milan: Fondazione Lorenzo Valla/Arnaldo Mondadori.

Maxwell-Stuart, P. G. 1999. *The Occult in Early Modern Europe.* New York: St. Martin's.

Ogden, Daniel. 2001. *Greek and Roman Necromancy.* Princeton: Princeton University Press.

———. 2002. *Magic, Witchcraft, and Ghosts in the Greek and Roman Worlds: A Sourcebook.* Oxford: Oxford University Press.

Porter, Roy. 1999. "Survival: Art and Literature." Pp. 245–250 in *Witchcraft and Magic in Europe: The Eighteenth and Nineteenth Centuries.* Edited by Bengt Ankarloo and Stuart Clark. Philadelphia: University of Pennsylvania Press.

Purkiss, Diane. 1996. *The Witch in History: Early Modern and Twentieth-Century Representations.* London: Routledge.

Roberts, Gareth. 1996. "The Descendants of Circe: Witches and Renaissance Fictions." Pp. 183–206 in *Witchcraft in Early Modern Europe: Studies in Culture and Belief.* Edited by Jonathan Barry, Marianne Hester, and Gareth Roberts. Cambridge: Cambridge University Press.

Rowlands, Alison. 1998. "Telling Witchcraft Stories: New Perspectives on Witchcraft and Witches in the Early Modern Period." *Gender and History* 19: 294–302.

General Works on Literature and Philosophy

Aristotle. 1984. *Poetics.* Pp. 2:2316–2340 in *The Complete Works of Aristotle: The Revised Oxford Translation.* Edited by Jonathan Barnes. 2 vols. Princeton: Princeton University Press.

Childers, Joseph, and Gary Hentzi. 1995. *The Columbia Dictionary of Modern Literary and Cultural Criticism.* New York: Columbia University Press.

Eagleton, Terry. 1996. *Literary Theory: An Introduction.* 2nd ed. Minneapolis: University of Minnesota Press.

Eco, Umberto. 1994. *The Limits of Interpretation.* 1990. Reprint, Bloomington: Indiana University Press.

Martin, Robert M. 1994. *The Philosopher's Dictionary.* 2nd ed. Peterborough, Ontario: Broadview.

TEXTS DISCUSSED

Boccaccio, Giovanni. 1982. *The Decameron.* 1352. Translated by Mark Musa and Peter Bondanella. New York: Mentor.

Caesarius of Heisterbach. 1929. *The Dialogue on Miracles.* Ca. 1225. Translated by Henry von Essen Scott and Charles Cooke Swinton Bland. 2 vols. London: Routledge.

Cohn, Norman. 1975. *Europe's Inner Demons: An Enquiry Inspired by the Great Witch-Hunt.* New York: Basic Books.

Eco, Umberto. 1994. *The Name of the Rose.* 1983. Translated by William Weaver. Reprint, San Diego: Harcourt, Brace.

Ginzburg, Carlo. 1989. *Clues, Myths, and the Historical Method.* Translated by John and Anne C. Tedeschi. Baltimore: Johns Hopkins University Press.

Guazzo, Francesco Maria. 1988. *Compendium Maleficarum.* 1608. Translated from 1st ed. by E. A. Ashwin. New York: Dover.

Hawthorne, Nathaniel. 1987. "Young Goodman Brown." 1835. In *Young Goodman Brown, and Other Tales.* Edited by Brian Harding. Oxford: Oxford University Press.

Huxley, Aldous. 1996. *The Devils of Loudun.* 1952. Reprint, New York: Carrol and Graf.

Kafka, Franz. 1988. *The Metamorphosis.* 1915. Translated by Stanley Corngold. New York: Bantam Books.

Levin, Ira. 1997. *Rosemary's Baby.* 1967. Reprint, New York: Signet Books.

Ryder, Daniel. 1992. *Breaking the Circle of Satanic Ritual Abuse: Recognizing and Recovering from the Hidden Trauma.* Minneapolis: CompCare.

Stephens, Walter. 2002. *Demon Lovers: Witchcraft, Sex, and the Crisis of Belief.* Chicago: University of Chicago Press.

Wilson, Leslie. 1992. *Malefice.* New York: Pantheon.

LITHUANIA, GRAND DUCHY OF

From the thirteenth until the eighteenth century, the Grand Duchy of Lithuania covered the entire territory of what is now Belarus, Ukraine, Lithuania, Latvia, and parts of Russia (Smolensk and Briansk provinces), Poland (Belastok province), and Latvia (Daugavpils province). This vast and thinly populated region, with its bewildering variety of religions and complicated mixture of law courts, recorded remarkably few witchcraft trials. It is difficult to offer complete statistics, but even allowing for lacunae, no more than fifty witches perished throughout the whole territory between the fifteenth and eighteenth centuries.

Although most of these Slavic regions were soon converted to Orthodox Christianity, the Baltic territories of the Grand Duchy of Lithuania remained pagan—in 1394, visiting missionaries noted that the local population practiced a cult of fire—until the end of the fourteenth century, when its ruler, Grand Duke Jahaila (Jogaila), became Catholic in order to acquire the crown of Poland in 1386. Protestant ideas had spread over the grand duchy by the mid-sixteenth century. The majority of noblemen (*shlyachta*) and part of the petty bourgeoisie became Protestant. Beginning in the late sixteenth century, Catholicism's influence grew. Although Catholicism became dominant, Orthodox, Protestant, and Greek Catholic Christian Churches, Islam, Judaism, and paganism still were practiced. This religious pluralism did not result in serious conflicts like those that occurred between different religions in western Europe.

One reason we know of so few witchcraft trials in the Grand Duchy is that we have only erratic records from most of its courts. A more important reason is the fact that there were fewer trials: Although the rulers were Catholic, much of the population was Orthodox—a religion that virtually ignored diabolical pacts and therefore very rarely prosecuted witches. The temporal power of the grand duchy's rulers was great, and they practiced toleration of Lithuania's inhabitants owing to its multinational society and the diversity of religions.

In the Grand Duchy of Lithuania, secular tribunals, without any ecclesiastical interference, tried all cases of witchcraft. Defendants were judged solely for damage caused by sorcery. But the system of courts in the grand duchy was complex. From the bottom up, it included communal *Kopny* courts for peasants; town council courts for municipal citizens; and *Zemski* courts for district nobles. Regional castle courts handled appeals from both nobles and commoners, and at the top sat the grand duchy's highest tribunal, the Court of Appeal.

The Grand Duchy of Lithuania had no laws against witchcraft until the sixteenth century. In 1529, the first statue dealing with witchcraft held that a criminal who through sorcery did not feel pain when tortured had to pay a fine to the plaintiff. In 1566, another statute confirmed the 1529 law. After the Third Statute of 1588 (part 4, article 30) defined sorcery as a criminal charge, these provisions passed into judicial practice. A special provision (part 14, article 18) allowed the use of torture three times a day. In Lithuania, where sorcery remained a criminal offense until 1776, Roman or canon law and Magdeburg law (which provided for towns' having their own courts) occasionally supplemented such statutes (see, for example, Collection of Early Texts 1867b, 119–120).

The date of the very first witchcraft trial in the grand duchy is unknown. One of them first happened in 1436, but there is little information preserved about witchcraft trials until the sixteenth century, when the Catholic Counter-Reformation changed the situation and the number of trials increased. A statement that there had been damage was necessary to initiate a case. Overall, evidence about witchcraft trials is sparse. Even in the seventeenth century, for which evidence is relatively abundant, we know of only thirteen trials between 1615 and 1699 that definitely ended by burning a witch.

Complaints varied greatly. At a trial held in the castle court of Brest in 1614, Rafal Andreeuski and his wife's brothers testified that Matsei Matseevich Rakitski's wife had killed Rafal's wife with a doll (Schedule of Documents 1913, 434–435). In 1630, the *voiski* (a court official in *Zemski* courts) of Pinsk and his wife complained in Pinsk's castle court that Fyodora Vysotski, the wife of the *vozny* (a court official) of Pinsk, had given her maidservant "sorcery" (bones, nails, and sand from a village grave) to injure them (Acts of Vilna Commission 1891, 304–310). In 1638, at the *Kopny* court of Balotchychy, Homa Zhylechovets blamed a maidservant for killing his wife by putting a toad in her mistress's food (Acts of Vilna Commission 1891, 333–334). Witches used many methods of sorcery, ranging from taking milk from cows by gathering dew from fields to causing illness or death to others. Many different complaints about damage caused by witches reached courts in the Grand Duchy, but few of them explain the beginning of a trial.

Interrogation was used in witchcraft investigations. A list of questions (which have rarely been preserved) from 1630–1631 shows two *voznies* of Navahradak, Adam Tseraivich and Mikalai Petrovich, and other noblemen asking Raina Gramychyna about witchcraft. Questioned about other witches, she named two men and a woman. Raina had met them at Anderei Afanasavich's estate, because his wife had skills in sorcery. They had tried to prevent the *marshalok* (an official at the Diet) Jan Sapega from marrying by injuring his health. Raina herself admitted putting the evil eye on the *marshalok*. When the *voznies* asked why she had not confessed this before, she answered that her mouth had been shut (Collection of Early Texts 1867b, 99–100, 143–146). At the end of the interrogation, she admitted that she could heal and gave recipes. Raina was burned, but the other witches she named were not arrested.

A statute from 1566 (part 11, article 16) stipulated that defendants who had magical spells in their mouth, armpits, or hair must pay a fine. In a 1595 incident, an executioner removed the shirt of a peasant accused of stealing horses and oxen; a crust of bread fell from the peasant's armpit. This constituted proof of sorcery; without the protection of the spell, the defendant died under torture (Schedule of Documents 1913, 254–246, 248, 276).

As in neighboring Latvia, witches were sometimes "ducked" in the grand duchy. In 1615, Jurgel's wife Sofia Sunyan, her son Gasul, and Tumelis Paulavich Daradyndzenas underwent the ordeal by water (swimming test) in a peasant or *Kopny* court in a village in Braslau province—and all three of them floated, leading to the execution of Sofia and Tumelis. Torture was usually necessary to make a witch admit guilt.

Some documentary information suggests that here, as in Russia, men were considered more powerful sorcerers than women. At least half of those burned were men. The first, Tumelis Paulavich Daradyndzenas, was accused of belonging to a clan of notorious sorcerers. Sources show Maxim Znak (burned in 1691) to have been a powerful sorcerer who named other witches; Rasul from Vertialishki was both the oldest and strongest magician in the Grodno region in 1691 (Jodkowski 1932).

Witchcraft trials ended in different ways. Some well-known sorcerers were banished from the region and burned elsewhere. Condemned to death by fire were Jurgel's wife Sofia Sunyan and Tumelis Paulavich Daradyndzenas (1615), Barys Slavinavich (1622), Hanna Paulukova Krotka (1629), Fyadora Vysotskaya (1630), Raina Gromychyna (1631), Vasil Brykun (1643), Maxim Znak (1691), Kiril Adamovich, his son Fyodor, and Palashka Seiginava (1699), and others. Lithuanian witches often remained unpunished because private owners refused to present them in court; for example, in 1670, Ieranim Buchavecki protected his peasant Charchykha from a *Kopny* court.

In the Grand Duchy of Lithuania, pagan beliefs strongly influenced everyday life among nobility, townspeople, and peasants alike, but pacts with the Devil were practically unknown. For both pagans and Orthodox, as a criminal act "witchcraft" meant sorcery, and people of all strata were seldom put on trial for causing harm by such methods.

NATALIA SLIZH

See also: LATVIA; MALE WITCHES; RUSSIA; SORCERY; SPELLS; SWIMMING TEST; TRIALS.

NOTE:

All proper names are given according to Belarussian transcription, and in the references, English translations of the titles are given in parentheses.

References and further reading:
PRIMARY SOURCES
Акты издаваемые Виленскою археографическою комиссиею. 1865. Т. 18. Вильна. (Acts of Vilna Commission of Study and Publication of Early Texts. 1891. Vol. 18. Vilna.)
Archiwum Komisyi prawniczej. 1900. Vol. 7. Cracow. (Archives of the Law Commission. 1900. Vol. 7. Cracow.)
Археографический сборник документов относящихся к истории Северо-западной Руси. 1867а. Т. 1. Вильна. (The Collection of Early Texts Concerning the History of North Western Russia. 1867a. Vol. I. Vilna.)

Археогра ический сборник документов относящихся к истории Северо-западной Руси. 1867b. Т. 3. Вильна. (The Collection of Early Texts Concerning the History of North Western Russia. 1867b. Vol. 3. Vilna.)

Опись докуменмов Виленскою ченмрального Архива древних акмовых книг. 1913. Вып. 10. Вильна. (Schedule of Documents of Vilna Central Archive of Early Official Books. 1913. Vol. 10. Vilna.)

Собрание государственных и частных актов, касающихся истории Литвы и соединённых с ней владений (от 1387 до 1710 года). 1858. Вильна. (The Collection of Official and Private Documents Concerning the History of Litva and the Nearest Territories [from 1387 to 1710]. 1858. Vilna.)

Статут Великого кня ества Литовского 1529. 1960. Минск: издательство Академии Наук БССР. (Statute of Grand Duchy of Lithuania of 1529. 1960. Minsk: Academy of Science of BSSR.)

Статут Вялікага княтсва Літоўскага 1588. 1989. Мінск: БелСЭ. (Statute of Grand Duchy of Lithuania of 1588. 1989. Minsk: BelSE.)

SECONDARY SOURCES

Бабко Вольга. "Чарадзейства." *Наша Ніва.* 23, no. 2 (верасня) . (Babkova, Volga. 1996. "Witchery." Nasha Niva 23, no. 2 (September))

Gloser, Zygimunt. 1958. *Encyklopedia Staropolska Ilustrowana.* Vol. 1. Warsaw.

Jodkowski, Josef. 1932. *O czarowniku Znaku na inkwizicji w Grodnie w 1691 r.* Lwów. Lwów, Ukraine.

Лобач, Уладзімір. 1996a. "Паганства і хрысціянства ў сярэнявечнай Беларуі." *Весці Полакага дзяр аўнага універітэта. Гуманімарные навукі* 2:3–11. (Lobach, Uladzimir. 1996. "Paganism and Christianity in Medieval Belerus [14–18 cc.]." Polatsk Research Reports. Humanities. 2: 3–11.)

———. 1996b. *"Чарадзейства на Полаччыне: гістоыка-культурны кантэкст."* Pp. 50–59 in *Полауік: карані нашага радавода* (Lobach, Uladzimir. 1996. "Witchery in Polatsk Region: Historical and Cultural Context." Pp. 50–59 in Polatsk: Roots of Our History. Polatsk.)

———. 1997. "Браслаўская судовая справа 1615 г.: да характарыстыкі чардзейства ў сярэднявечнай Беларусі." Pp. 69–73 in *Браслаўскія чыманні: матэрыяы 4-й навукова-краязнаўчай краязнаўчай кан ярэнуіі 24–25 красавіка 1997.* Браслаў. (Lobach, Uladzimir, 1997. "Witchcraft process in Braslau in 1615: Characteristic of witchery in Medieval Belarus." Pp. 69–73 in Braslau readings: Materials of the 4th scientific and regional conference, 24–25 April 1997. Braslau.)

Маслыка, Г. 1989. *Чары in Статут Вялікага княтсва Літоўскага 1588.* Мінск: БелСЭ. С. 542. (Maslyka, G. 1989. Statute of Grand Duchy of Lithuania of 1588. Minsk: BelSE. Pp. 542.)

LITTLE ICE AGE

The core period of the Little Ice Age coincided exactly with the climax of witch hunting in central Europe. Not yet well defined, the concept of a Little Ice Age was invented in 1939. Subsequently, its proposed duration—originally large parts of the Holocene (the present geological epoch, beginning about 10,000 years ago)—has shrunk to an epoch between 1300 and the 1880s, in recognition of the fact that these almost 600 years of coldness were interrupted by more favorable periods. Using Swiss data, Christian Pfister and others (1996) have identified two core phases of the Little Ice Age in the fourteenth and the seventeenth centuries. The periodizations are usually drawn from remains of the physical environment (dendrochronology, glaciology, sedimentation, pollen analysis, and the like), but witch hunts also seem to be a sensitive indicator. Climatic deterioration in the Northern Hemisphere had its greatest impact between 1560 and 1630, when the effects of global cooling were worsened by an increase in precipitation, a combination that severely hampered both wine making and wheat harvests. It has frequently been remarked that marginal wine-growing areas (Franconia, the Rhineland, Alsace, Franche-Comté, the Valais, Styria) were particularly prone to severe witch hunting.

Though persecutions for heresy were known already in high medieval Europe (circa 1000–1300), persecutions of internal enemies for their supposed influence on the physical environment began after 1300: In the early 1320s, lepers and Jews were held collectively responsible for the poisoning of wells, and Jews were held responsible for the Europe-wide epidemics of 1348–1350 known as the Black Death and for the subsequent recurrences of plague later in the fourteenth century. Famine, flooding, and high mortality in the early 1340s preceded the arrival of the Black Death in December 1347. During these decades of the first half of the fourteenth century, when a sequence of cold and long winters indicated the return of Little Ice Age conditions, the interdependence among climatic factors, crop failures, rising prices, hunger, the outbreak of epidemics, and the classical pattern of subsistence crises of Old Europe became more visible. Thus, attention shifted from epidemics to weather, and it is striking to see that the gradual emergence of the new crime of cumulative witchcraft was closely connected to the waves of climatic hardship and agrarian crises during the earlier phases of the Little Ice Age, particularly the 1420s and 1430s, when the new cumulative idea of witchcraft was fabricated in the western Alps, or the 1480s, when the *Malleus Maleficarum* (The Hammer of Witches, 1486) was compiled.

The impact of the Little Ice Age began to be felt again in the 1560s. Contemporary chroniclers such as Johann Jacob Wick from Zurich reported that the summer of 1560 was unusually wet. The following winter was the coldest and longest winter since

1515–1516. For the first time in generations, large Alpine lakes like Lake Constance froze ("*Seegfrörni*"), and the vegetation period shortened decisively. The following winter (1561–1562) was not only similarly cold but also included an immense snowfall, mentioned in a broadsheet printed at Leipzig in 1562. Orthodox Lutheran theology interpreted these events as signs that God was furious at the people because of their sins. The coincidence of coldness and wetness harmed this agrarian society by damaging the harvest, while rising prices worsened the living conditions for poorer people. During the spring and summer of 1562, a thaw and heavy rainfall caused flooding in various parts of Germany, poisoned the fields, and led to cattle diseases, rising infant mortality, and the outbreak of epidemics. After unusually severe thunderstorms hit central Europe, a fierce debate on weather making involved some leading Lutheran reformers in Germany (Johann Brenz, Thomas Naogeorgus, Jacob Heerbrand) and Johann Weyer, who exchanged the principal arguments on the subject. Simultaneously, severe witch hunts started in southwestern Germany. The mechanism of torture, confession, and denunciation turned single cases of witchcraft into witch hunts. The largest hunt occurred in the small territory of Wiesensteig, belonging to the Lutheran counts of Helfenstein, where sixty-three women were burned as witches within a year. A contemporary newsletter reported this event, making the witch hunt well known throughout the Holy Roman Empire.

Starting in the 1560s, a series of witch panics shook several European societies, followed by attempts to legalize witchcraft persecutions (for example, the English and Scottish witchcraft statutes of 1563). After the initial witch hunts of 1562 and 1563, a wave of persecutions followed the hunger crisis of the years around 1570, following the catastrophic coldness of the previous two years. But a totally new persecutorial zeal could be observed during the 1580s. At the end of the 1570s, crop failures and price increases again caused hunger in parts of central Europe, stimulating witch burnings in many places. After 1580, the persecutions began to reach levels previously unknown. Between 1580 and 1620 in the Pays de Vaud, which was under the rule of the reformed Swiss city-state of Bern since 1536, subject of the reformed Swiss town of Bern, more than 1,000 persons were burned for witchcraft. Between 1580 and 1595, hundreds of witches were burned in the duchy of Lorraine, subjects of their Catholic dukes who were heavily involved in the power struggles of the French Wars of Religion. The Lorraine witch hunts closely coincided with those in the neighboring Spanish Netherlands and in the archbishopric of Trier, where hundreds of witches were also burned between 1581 and 1595. A local chronicler, Johann Linden, canon of St. Simeon in Trier, explains in his *Gesta Treverorum* (The History of Trier) the reasons for that witch hunt, the largest in German-speaking territories in the sixteenth century, which occurred under Archbishop Johann VII von Schönenberg (governed 1581–1599):

> Hardly any of the Archbishops governed their diocese under such hardships, such sorrows and such extreme difficulties as Johann. . . . During the whole period he and his subjects had to endure a continuous shortage of grain, a rigorous climate and crop failures. Only two of these nineteen years were fertile, 1584 and 1590. . . . Since everybody thought that the continuous crop-failure was caused by witches from devilish hatred, the whole country wished for their eradication. (Linden 1964, 7:13–14)

Until recently, this explanation was not taken seriously, but research has demonstrated that the persecution was indeed not only demanded but also organized by the population. Because the legal administration of this territory was inefficient and officials were reluctant to prosecute, village committees began to extend their competence and organized the witch hunts themselves. Elected committees collected information, captured and tried the suspected witches, and delivered them to the authorities only after they had already confessed. The persecution thus resembled a popular uprising in which the people usurped functions usually reserved to state authorities. Only in 1591, when popular acceptance of the persecution in his archbishopric declined, did the electoral prince try to deprive the local committees of their power and recover his authority. A woodcut on a contemporary broadsheet hinted at the reason for these persecutions: It showed a panorama with three tremendous thunderstorms falling on villages and fields while witches flew through the air casting their spells (*Sigfriedus*, ca. 1590). Similarly, a broadsheet printed in 1590 about the witch hunt in southern Germany reads like a collection of meteorological disasters and their consequences on physical and mental health (*Erweytterte Unholden Zeyttung* 1590).

After 1586, long and cold winters were complemented by cold and wet springs and summers, thus causing hunger and epidemics and creating enormous psychological stress. In 1586, the famous collection of Fugger newsletters reported a "great fear" among ordinary people, terminology that reminds us of *la grande peur* preceding the French Revolution. These early witch hunts indeed acquired revolutionary dimensions, implicating some members of the ruling oligarchies—magistrates, clerics, even noblemen. Unlike the hunger crisis of 1570, the crisis of the 1580s endured for ten or more years. Socioeconomic explanations of the crises indicate that since the 1560s a general decline in living standards resulted from a combination of continuous population growth and a diminishing food supply because of ecological crisis. In addition, the wine-growing areas of central Europe, from Hungary, Austria, Switzerland, and Germany into northern France, experienced a permanent decline in income due to the deterioration of wine harvests (*Landsteiner*). Basket-of-goods calculations on the basis of statistical data from the imperial city of Augsburg demonstrate that after 1586, an average craftsman with a family of four could no longer earn the necessary living costs without help from other members of his family.

The socioeconomic disaster affected society as a whole. But meteorological disfavor fell hardest on such disadvantaged areas as the Bernese highlands, the Scottish highlands, the mountainous regions of Lorraine and Alsace, the archbishopric of Trier, or the Ardennes in northern France. In these marginal agricultural regions, increasing wetness, falling temperatures, shorter growing seasons, and the increased frequency of hailstorms endangered the production of cereals and wine. After 1586, the impact of a series of cold and prolonged winters was sharpened by a period of wet and cold springs and summers. In Switzerland, snow covered the ground until late spring in 1587; snowfall returned on July 4 down to 400 meters on the Swiss plateau. Again, 1588, the year the Invincible Armada failed in heavy mid-September storms, was one of the rainiest years in history. A Swiss chronicler, Renward Cysat, reported severe thunderstorms almost daily, starting in June. It was during these two years, 1587–1588, that witchcraft accusations reached their climax in England and northern France, while large-scale witch hunts began in Scotland and Germany.

The synchronicity of accusations and persecutions in countries that were not connected by dynastic, confessional, or economic links demonstrates the importance of the climatic factor for explanation. Many individual witchcraft trials show that meteorological events contributed decisively to suspicions and accusations. These events were often supraregional or even supranational. Areas of low pressure can cover large regions; the advance of arctic air can at times harm the northern part of the Continent or even the Northern Hemisphere. What we can learn from this is that contemporary laments about decreasing fruitfulness of the fields, of cattle, and even of people were far from merely rhetorical devices; rather, they rested on empirical observation. The rising tide of demonological literature reinforced such lamentations. By the 1590s, members of contemporary elites, such as the famous French jurist Jean Bodin, the suffragan bishop of Treves Peter Binsfeld, the chief public prosecutor of Lorraine Nicolas Rémy, or the king of Scotland James VI (soon to become James I of England), all shared

the idea that witches could be responsible for the weather. In his *Daemonologie* (Demonology, 1597), James claimed that witches

> can rayse stormes and tempestes in the aire either upon Sea or land, though not universally, but in such a particular place and prescribed boundes, as God will permite them so to trouble. Which likewise is verie easie to be discerned from any other naturall tempestes that are meteores, in respect of the suddaine and violent raising thereof, together with the short induring of the same. And this is likewise very possible to their master to do . . . . (James VI 1597, 46)

Rémy, like an ethnographer, reported detailed weather magic from Lorraine witchcraft trials that he had judged. Although Binsfeld certainly emphasized theological reasons for bad weather, his best arguments came from empirical data from his persecution in the archbishopric of Trier.

At the end of the sixteenth century, a few European states managed to escape the circle of witch belief and witchcraft persecution, since their elites stopped feeling threatened and became strong enough to suppress popular demands for witch hunts. In central Europe, however, where demographic pressure and economic depression lingered on, unstable governments remained vulnerable to new demands for persecution. Large-scale witch hunts occurred, for instance, around 1600 in Franche-Comté and some ecclesiastical territories in Germany, in the Basque region and parts of Germany from 1608–1612, and in Franconia between 1616 and 1618. Contemporary court records and broadsheets described the importance of meteorological events as triggering factors behind these persecutions.

During the third decade of the seventeenth century, when the Thirty Years' War preoccupied governing elites, organized witch hunts reached their peak in the ecclesiastical territories of the Holy Roman Empire. Once again the climax of witch hunting coincided with some extraordinarily dramatic meteorological events. It is noteworthy that contemporary accounts almost never connected these witch hunts with war, confessional strife, state building, changes in the medical or judicial system, gender relations, or whatever historians might imagine. Instead, court records dwelled upon disease and death of children and cattle, destruction of crops and vineyards. Chroniclers related such misfortunes to general meteorological developments. And historians of climate confirm their observations, in general as well as in particular. The 1620s were characterized by long and cold winters, late springs, and cold and wet summers and autumns, leading to crop failures and price increases. In 1626, during the last week of May, in the middle of the vegetation period, winter returned; temperatures fell so low that lakes and rivers froze overnight and trees and bushes lost their leaves. Severe frost destroyed cereals and grapes, and even the grapevines. Such an event had not been recorded in the preceding 500 years (Pfister et al. 1996). The uniqueness and devastating effects of this climatic anomaly confirmed contemporary impressions that it was an "unnatural" event.

A chronicler in the Franconian town of Zeil reported:

On 27th May 1626, all the vineyards were completely destroyed by frost within the prince-bishoprics of Bamberg and Würzburg, together with the dear grain which had already sprouted. . . . Everything was frozen, which had not happened as long as one could remember. And it caused a great rise in prices . . . consequently, pleading and begging began among the rabble, questioning why the authorities continued to tolerate the destruction of crops by witches and sorcerers. Therefore the prince-bishop punished these crimes, and the persecution began in this year. (Behringer 2001, 250)

In the following years, broadsheets emphasized the supposed responsibility of witches for these severe frosts, adding later events like hailstorms, cattle diseases, and epidemics. Confessions under torture claimed to have detected a devilish conspiracy to destroy vineyards and grains for several years in order to create hunger and disease to the extent that people would be forced to eat each other. Only drastic measures by the authorities seemed capable of stopping these plans—and the measures taken were indeed dramatic. In the tiny prince-bishopric of Bamberg, 600 persons were burned for suspected witchcraft; in the neighboring prince-bishopric of Würzburg, 900; in the electorate of Mainz, another 900; and under the rule of prince-archbishop and elector Ferdinand of Cologne in the Rhineland and Westphalia, nearly 2,000.

Wherever the power of central governments, prosperity, and Cartesian rationalism increased, witch hunts were terminated during the seventeenth century. However, in large areas of central Europe, the link between climate and witch hunting remained intact. While scientists have debated the causal effects of the Maunder Minimum (the near absence of sunspot activity between 1645 and 1715), which occurred alongside the coldest part of the Little Ice Age, persecution of witches peaked around 1690, reaching its climax then in Austria, the Baltic region, and Scandinavia, and in Poland and Hungary during the first decades of the eighteenth century. In some Catholic areas of central Europe, every year with Little Ice Age types of events led to another cycle of witchcraft trials. It is more than just a metaphor that the sun of Enlightenment melted the cold era of witch hunting. From the 1730s on, the climate, though still cold, was more stable than during previous decades. In a few backward areas of Germany, France, and Austria, witchcraft trials lasted into the 1740s, and in remote corners of Switzerland, Hungary, and Poland even into the 1770s.

Above all in central Europe, the age of witch hunting seems congruent with the era of the Little Ice Age. The peaks of persecution coincided with years of sharp climatic deterioration. Witches were traditionally held responsible for bad weather that was so dangerous to the precarious agricultural surpluses of the preindustrial period. But only in the fifteenth century did ecclesiastical and secular authorities accept the reality of this crime. The 1420s, the 1450s, and the last two decades of the fifteenth century, well-known to historians of climate, were decisive times when secular and ecclesiastical authorities increasingly accepted the existence of weather-making witches. During the "cumulative sequences of coldness" in the years 1560–1574, 1583–1589, 1623–1630, and 1678–1698 (Pfister 1984, 150), people demanded the eradication of the witches they held responsible for such climatic aberrations. The impact of the Little Ice Age increased the pressure from below and convinced some members of the intellectual elites of the existence of witchcraft. Therefore, we can conclude that witchcraft was the characteristic crime of the Little Ice Age.

WOLFGANG BEHRINGER

See also: AGRARIAN CRISES; BAMBERG, PRINCE-BISHOPRIC OF; BINSFELD, PETER; BODIN, JEAN; BRENZ, JOHANN; HOLY ROMAN EMPIRE; JAMES VI AND I, KING OF SCOTLAND AND ENGLAND; LORRAINE, DUCHY OF; *MALLEUS MALEFICARUM*; MOLITOR, ULRICH; PLAGUE; POPULAR PERSECUTION; SCOTLAND; SWITZERLAND; TRIER, ELECTORATE OF; VALAIS; WEATHER MAGIC; WEYER, JOHANN.

References and further reading:
Behringer, Wolfgang. 1995. "Weather, Hunger and Fear: The Origins of the European Witch Persecution in Climate, Society and Mentality." *German History* 13: 1–27.
———. 1999. "Climatic Change and Witch-Hunting: The Impact of the Little Ice Age on Mentalities." Pp. 335–351 in *Climatic Variability in Sixteenth Century Europe and Its Social Dimension.* Edited by Christian Pfister, Rudolf Brazdil, and Rüdiger Glaser, first published as a special issue of *Climatic Change: An Interdisciplinary, International Journal Devoted to the Description, Causes and Implications of Climatic Change* 43, no. 1 (September, 1999). Dordrecht, Boston, and London: Kluwer Academic.
———. 2001. *Hexen und Hexenprozesse in Deutschland.* 5th ed. Munich: Deutscher Taschenbuch.
James I. 1597. *Daemonologie.* Edinburgh. Reprint 1969. New York and Amsterdam: Da Capo.
Kamber, Peter. 1982. "La chasse aux sorciers et aux sorcières dans le pays de Vaud: Aspects quantitatives (1581–1620)." *Revue historique vaudoise* 90: 21–33.

Linden, Johann. 1964. *Gesta Treverorum*. Ed. Emil Zenz. Trier.

Pfister, Christian. 1980. "The Little Ice Age: Thermal and Wetness Indices for Central Europe." *Journal of Interdisciplinary History* 10: 665–696.

———. 1984. *Klimageschichte der Schweiz 1525–1860*. Bern: Paul Haupt.

Pfister, Christian, et al. 1996. "Winter Severity in Europe: The Fourteenth Century." *Climatic Change* 34: 91–108.

LIVING SAINTS

Many religions have revered people who, for different reasons, were venerated by their contemporaries as living saints. Some experienced extraordinarily intensive contacts with the deity; some worked miracles, especially healing; sometimes their position within the religious hierarchy assimilated them to the gods. We know about such individuals in Europe since pre-Christian antiquity. The sacred kings of the Celts and Germans had some qualities of living saints, upon whom the welfare of their peoples depended. Nor was the phenomenon unknown to Jews or early Christians (Brown 1981), but its heyday was the Middle Ages. The fame of many a saint, like Bernard of Clairvaux (1090–1153), lay in his thaumaturgic miracle-working, powers. When he left his monastery to visit a town, we are told, the faithful thronged around him praying for help, mostly to relieve illness or demonic obsession, and trying to pluck threads from his robe as relics. The number of living saints increased with the flowering of mysticism from the thirteenth century onward; from then until the eighteenth century, most living saints were women. Their charisma often included, besides the power to heal, stigmata, anorexia, telepathy, or the gift of prophecy. What mattered most, however, were their ecstasies, during which they received divine revelations. One can hardly imagine the throngs of admirers assembled to greet a famous visionary like Catherine of Siena (1347–1380). The phenomenon was especially widespread in Latin countries, where many kings kept a living saint at court, as Louis IX and Charles VIII of France did with the famous thaumaturge Francesco di Paula.

In the thirteenth and fourteenth centuries, such saints encountered little resistance from ecclesiastical authorities. Later, however, things changed; a general skepticism arose toward their charisma, in part because visionaries propagandistically supported both popes (at Avignon and at Rome) during the Great Schism (1378–1417) of the Catholic Church. Especially from discussing the authenticity of the revelations of Bridgit of Sweden (1307–1373), the clergy developed an "art of discernment of the spirits," a set of theological rules to discover whether a revelation came from divine intervention or from an evil spirit. From then on, living saints were carefully tested for the possibility of human deception or, more menacingly, diabolical fraud. The Holy Office tried many living saints because it seemed so difficult to separate thaumaturgy from witchcraft. A charismatic leader, Joan of Arc was burned as a witch in 1431, but many thought her to be a saint (and it took nearly 500 years to certify that she was). The papacy had Girolamo Savonarola, who had claimed divine inspiration while criticizing the pope, burned in 1498.

When Reformed theologians denied the possibility of private revelations and rejected the cult of saints, the phenomenon of living saints ceased in large parts of Europe. Meanwhile, in Catholic territories, the post-Tridentine clergy exerted strict control over women who manifested charisma, and only the cults of a few mystics such as Teresa of Avila or Theresa of Lisieux found official acceptance. Now, ecstasies and revelations mattered less in the canonization processes than obedient subordination to male ecclesiastics.

Because the phenomena on which the pious based the veneration of living saints were so ambiguous, many living saints were considered demoniacs or were accused of heresy and witchcraft, even if exonerated later. This happened, for instance, to Dorothea of Montau (d. 1394), Colomba of Rieti (d. 1503), Gentile of Ravenna (d. 1530), and Domenica da Paradiso (d. 1553), all of whom the Church beatified or canonized after many centuries. Why was it so easy to mistake a living saint for a witch? Because both operated similarly in many respects and because the Devil could appear disguised as an angel, one could never know which a person was. Both pious visionaries and malignant sorceresses encountered apparitions of nonhuman men. Both told of erotic encounters: the saints of the mystical union, often narrated in undeniably sexual terms, and the witches of intercourse with an incubus. The result might even be an extranatural pregnancy—for example, St. Bridgit of Sweden showed bodily signs of bearing the Christ child each Christmas—but there were also cases of alleged pregnancies by incubi, including the Catholic claim that the Devil had impregnated Martin Luther's mother. Saints and witches both received painful corporal marks from nonhuman lovers: the saints the stigmata, and the witches the Devil's mark. Whereas the saints often claimed to have been wedded ceremoniously to Jesus (the "mystical marriage"), the witches, too, confessed to have made a solemn pact with the Devil. Both often met their supernatural or superhuman lover at a feast, be it in heaven or at the Sabbat. The same kinds of miracles were associated with both groups, especially paranormal healing and flight experiences.

In the late Middle Ages and the early modern period, therefore, a woman who manifested paranormal faculties had a chance of being seen as a living saint, but she also ran the risk of being mistaken for a heretic and witch. How she was judged depended very strongly on her social situation and whether or not she had supporters in the ecclesiastical hierarchy.

PETER DINZELBACHER

See also: DEVIL'S MARK; DISCERNMENT OF SPIRITS; HOLINESS; INCUBUS AND SUCCUBUS; JOAN OF ARC; MIRACLES; PACT WITH THE DEVIL; SEXUAL ACTIVITY, DIABOLIC; VISIONS.

References and further reading:
Brown, Peter. 1981. *The Cult of the Saints.* Chicago: University of Chicago Press.
Caciola, Nancy. 2003. *Discerning Spirits: Divine and Demonic Possession in the Middle Ages.* Ithaca, NY, and London: Cornell University Press.
Craveri, Marcello. 1980. *Sante e streghe.* Milan: Feltrinelli.
Dinzelbacher, Peter. 2001. *Heilige oder Hexen? Schicksale auffälliger Frauen in Mittelalter und Frühneuzeit.* 4th ed. Düsseldorf: Albatros.
Schulte van Kessel, Elijsa, ed. 1986. *Women and Men in Spiritual Culture.* The Hague: Staatsuitgevereij.
Thurston, Herbert. 1955. *Surprising Mystics.* London: Burns and Oates.
Zarri, Gabriella, ed. 1991. *Finzione e santità tra medioevo ed età moderna.* Turin: Rosenberg and Sellier.

LÖHER, HERMAN (1595–1678)

Herman Löher has left us a detailed account of his personal involvement, both as a judge and as a victim, with the brutal witch hunts that swept over the German Rhineland in the second quarter of the seventeenth century in an extremely rare book of 1676. The book is one of extremely few ego-documents (memoirs, autobiographics, diaries, or personal correspondence where the writer is continuously present in the text) containing firsthand information about the ways people experienced the terror of the witchcraft trials. Born in Munster Eiffel, a small town in the duchy of Jülich not far from Bonn, Löher moved with his family in 1601 to nearby Rheinbach in the lands of the archbishop of Cologne. At fifteen, Löher joined his father in the textile trade. In 1621, he was elected burgomaster (chief magistrate) of Rheinbach; ten years later, he became one of its seven aldermen. In that year, 1631, Rheinbach became the scene of a real witch hunt under the direction of the *Hexenkommissar* (Witch Commissioner) Franz Buirmann. After 1626, witch commissioners like Buirmann played a major role in many of the trials in the archbishopric of Cologne. Local courts were powerless against these commissioners.

The first two people executed at Rheinbach in 1631 were poor and powerless. This changed, however, with the third defendant, the widow of a former burgomaster and alderman. She died during the horrible torture Buirmann had ordered. After her, an alderman and the wife of another alderman fell victim to the commissioner's brutality. As the hunt went on, it became clear that it was being used to replace the town's governing oligarchy with a new faction. During interrogations, Buirmann forced the accused to name members of this elite as accomplices.

After a few months, when the wave was already slackening, rumors spread that there were also witches within the household of Herman Löher. By bribing Buirmann's superior, Löher could prevent himself or other members of his family from being arrested. However, in August 1636, a new series of trials began under the direction of another commissioner, Johann (Jan) Möden, and Löher realized that he had to flee if he wanted to survive. He, his wife, and his mother-in-law left Rheinbach secretly on August 3, 1636. They went first to Cologne, in order to collect the money Löher had stashed away there, before moving to Amsterdam. In the Dutch Republic, no witch had been executed since 1608, and in Amsterdam none for over forty years. Amsterdam was nominally a Protestant city, but Löher always remained Catholic. He had already acquired full citizenship in Amsterdam in November 1636 and repeatedly showed pride in the commercial success of his new hometown in his book, but this did not lead him to change his religion. In Amsterdam, all sorts of religions and confessions could worship God as they saw fit. Even though the city magistrates were required to be Reformed, they never questioned the loyalty of citizens whose beliefs differed from theirs.

Löher published his autobiographical *Hochnötige Unterthanige Wemütige Klage der Frommen Unschültigen* (Much Needed, Humble, and Woeful Complaint of the Pious Innocent) in 1676. Any hope that it would persuade authorities in the Rhineland to allow his return proved futile. In his discussion of the supporters of the trials, Löher concentrated on the works of Agricola of Sittard, Jean Bodin, and Pseudo-Laymann (so-called because a book advocating harsh treatment of witchcraft suspects was incorrectly attributed to Paul Laymann)—the same authors that his Mennonite friend and fellow textile trader Abraham Palingh had singled out in his book. In appealing to the authorities to prevent witchcraft trials, Palingh had summarized Löher's experiences. Löher in turn borrowed stories from Palingh's book. Unlike Palingh, Löher also quoted the work of such opponents as Adam Tanner, Friedrich Spee, and Daniel Jonctys, and he inserted a treatise from the Catholic priest Michael Stappert, who as a confessor had observed firsthand the injustice and cruelty with which so many witchcraft trials abounded.

At the time of his death in 1678, Löher's financial situation was rather difficult. After his death, all remaining copies of his book were confiscated by a creditor, a paper trader who probably recycled them; thus, only two copies survive today. In his book, Löher repeatedly admitted that he had little formal education, which helps explain why his book was written in a peculiar mixture of Dutch and Low German, making it a valuable source for sociological linguists as well as for historians of witchcraft trials.

HANS DE WAARDT

See also: AMSTERDAM; BODIN, JEAN; BUIRMANN, FRANZ; COLOGNE; JONCTYS, DANIEL; LAYMANN, PAUL; MODEN, JOHANN GANZ; NETHERLANDS, NORTHERN; PALINGH, ABRAHAM; SKEPTICISM; SPEE, FRIEDRICH; TANNER, ADAM.

References and further reading:
Gibbons, Lois Oliphant. 1931. "A Seventeenth Century Humanitarian: Herman Löher." Pp. 335–359 in *Persecution and Liberty. Essays in Honor of George Lincoln Burr.* Edited by John Franklin Jameson. New York: Century.
Löher, Herman. 1676. *Hochnötige Unterthanige Wemütige Klage der Frommen Unschültigen.* Amsterdam: Jacob de Jonge. Also available online: *Hochnötige Unterthanige Wemütige Klage der Frommen Unschültigen.* Edited by Thomas P. Becker and Theresia Becker with comments by Thomas Becker, Rainer Decker, and Hans de Waardt. University of Munich, http://www.sfn.uni-muenchen.de/loeher.

LOOS, CORNELIUS (1540 TO 1546–1596?)

A Dutch Catholic theologian, Loos was one of the most prominent opponents of witch belief and witchcraft trials. His written criticism of the persecution of witches, entitled *De vera et falsa magia* (On True and False Magic, perhaps partially published in 1592), was confiscated in 1592 by the censor; he was forced to recant his arguments in 1593. Thereafter, every criticism of the belief in witchcraft was regarded as heresy.

The son of a distinguished citizen of Gouda, Loos was born in the early 1540s. He studied theology at Louvain, earning the degree of licentiate in 1564. Ten years later, he was banished permanently after his family was involved in an unsuccessful royalist conspiracy. By 1578, Loos was apparently studying with the theology faculty of the University of Mainz. He published two anti-Protestant polemics in 1579, calling for a war of annihilation against the rebellious Dutch provinces. Around 1585, Loos moved from Mainz to Trier. Probably by autumn 1589, he was working on a rebuttal of the *Tractatus de confessionibus maleficorum et sagarum* (Treatise on Confessions of Sorcerers and Witches, 1589), which had been recently published by the suffragan bishop of Trier, Peter Binsfeld, in favor of witch hunting.

Binsfeld wanted to silence Loos's criticisms and to ensure that the *De vera et falsa magia* was not published. The official Catholic party was on Binsfeld's side; in April 1590 in Munich and Ingolstadt, it drew up statements of principle that, based partially on Binsfeld's *Tractatus de confessionibus maleficorum et sagarum* and with the participation of the Jesuits, favored severe witch persecutions and recommended the application of strict legal criminal procedures in witchcraft trials.

Binsfeld also found support in Cologne from the papal nuncio Ottavio Frangipani, who asked the archbishop of Trier to intervene and stop the publication of *De vera et falsa magia,* which Loos had already sent to a publisher in Cologne. Loos had also written letters to the city council of Trier, to highly placed churchmen, and to other unnamed individuals in which he questioned both the legality of the witchcraft trials that had taken place in Trier and the belief in witches generally. He specifically accused the elector of Trier of tyranny. Frangipani accused Loos of having sent his book—which allegedly contained both errors and new ideas—to be published without the approval from the censor, and he demanded that he be given a copy to examine. After the nuncio had read the text, he ordered that its printing cease immediately.

Nothing remains of *De vera et falsa magia* except a few publisher's proofs, discovered in 1888. The complete manuscript has disappeared; only one handwritten section survives in the City Library in Trier, which contains the first two of what the index indicates would have been four books. In his text, Loos referred to witchcraft trials that had occurred in Trier and also attacked Binsfeld's arguments with scathing derision. Drawing almost exclusively on the Bible, the Church Fathers, and classical authorities, Loos argued that it was impossible for the Devil to appear to humans in corporeal form or to have sexual intercourse with them; he also denied such other elements of witchcraft belief as the supposed ability of witches to fly and to cause bad weather. In a radically critical rejection of the scholastic mode of thinking adopted by Binsfeld, Loos showed himself an adherent of humanist philological textual analysis.

Loos was particularly skeptical about the value of the confessions and denunciations against their alleged coconspirators made by accused witches, thus destroying the basis of Binsfeld's arguments in favor of witch hunts. In Loos's opinion, such confessions and denunciations either came from mentally disturbed individuals or were the result of horrible torture. In emotional tones, Loos emphasized that by means of the witch-trial "machine," innocent people had been executed. He also hinted at the possibility that accusations of witchcraft and witchcraft trials could be manipulated for purposes other than the ostensible persecution of witches. Territorial lords who tolerated witch hunts Loos labeled tyrants. For this Dutch theologian, witch beliefs—along with Protestantism—constituted tools by means of which the Devil sought to imperil the spiritual welfare of true Christians. Those who persecuted witches were thus, according to Loos, the real adherents of the Devil, who damned their souls by shedding innocent blood.

Arrested and imprisoned in the prince-abbey of St. Maximin, Loos had to recant his ideas formally on

March 15, 1593. In 1599, Martín Del Rio published a copy of the recantation, attested by a notary. Its consequences are clear: Together with the theological statements drawn up at Munich and Ingolstadt in 1590, Loos's recantation made it impossible for any Catholic to criticize witch belief without being branded a heretic. New ways of arguing against witchcraft trials thus had to be found, such as those presented by other Jesuits, by Adam Tanner, and especially by Friedrich Spee in his fundamental criticism of witchcraft trials, *Cautio criminalis* (A Warning on Criminal Justice), in 1631. Banned from the diocese of Trier, Loos went to Brussels, where he was given a prebend in the cathedral. Here, he repeated his arguments against belief in witches and witchcraft trials; as a result, he was again incarcerated and was put on a diet of bread and water, although he was released after a relatively short time. Loos died before action could be taken for a third time against his criticisms of witchcraft trials.

RITA VOLTMER;

TRANSLATED BY ALISON ROWLANDS

See also: BAVARIA, DUCHY OF; BINSFELD, PETER; DEL RIO, MARTÍN; JESUITS (SOCIETY OF JESUS); SKEPTICISM; SPEE, FRIEDRICH; ST. MAXIMIN, PRINCE-ABBEY OF; TANNER, ADAM; TRIER, ELECTORATE OF.

References and further reading:
Behringer, Wolfgang. 1988. *Mit dem Feuer vom Leben zum Tod. Hexengesetzgebung in Bayern.* Munich: Hugendubel.
Scholer, Othon. 1998a. "'O Kehricht des Aberglaubens, ô leerer Wahn der Täuschungen und Gespenster der Nacht!' Der Angriff des Cornelius Loos auf Petrus Binsfeld." Pp. 254–276 in *Methoden und Konzepte der historischen Hexenforschung.* Edited by Gunther Franz and Franz Irsigler. Trier: Spee.
———. 1998b. "Die Trierer und Luxemburger Hexenprozesse in der dämonologischen Literatur." Pp. 303–327 in *Methoden und Konzepte der historischen Hexenforschung.* Edited by Gunther Franz and Franz Irsigler. Trier: Spee.
Van der Eerden, P. C. 1992. "Cornelius Loos und *die magia falsa.*" Pp. 139–160 in *"Vom Unfug der Hexenprozesse": Vom Unfug des Hexen-Processes; Gegner der Hexenverfolgung von Johann Weyer bis Friedrich von Spee.* Edited by Hartmut Lehmann and Otto Ulbricht. Wiesbaden: Harrossowitz.
———. 1996. "Der Teufelspakt bei Petrus Binsfeld und Cornelius Loos." Pp. 51–71 in *Hexenglaube und Hexenprozesse im Raum Rhein-Mosel-Saar.* Edited by Gunther Franz and Franz Irsigler. 2nd ed. Trier: Spee.

LORD'S PRAYER

In the New Testament, the Lord's Prayer is transmitted in two versions: Matthew 6:9–13 and Luke 11:2–4. It is related to Jewish prayers (for example, the Kaddish). The last bidding (numbered as the sixth or seventh) is "but deliver us from evil." *The evil* is a genitive (*apo tou ponerou*), so it has been discussed since ancient times whether it should be understood as a masculine form (referring to the Devil) or as a neuter form (referring to evil in general). The Greek Fathers interpreted it as masculine, St. Augustine as neuter. Even during the Reformation, the debate continued.

Prayer, in general, is related to incantation. And the prayer of a developed religion, which is communication with a god as supplication or thanksgiving, can easily be used in magical contexts, giving it the primitive function of a spell. The bidding mentioned above suggests that the Lord's Prayer was especially suitable for use in apotropaic contexts, and it was used so in many functions and forms against demons and witches. It could be spoken, written on amulets, or even buried in the ground. It could protect harvests from hailstorms by speaking only the fourth bidding ("Give us this day our daily bread"). It was also prayed to protect newborn children. Above all, it was thought efficacious for driving away demons and witches, often combined with the sign of the cross. Inscribed in a magic circle around a person, it would protect him from demons.

Its magical function became especially clear if it was prayed backward: Then, it worked as black magic, causing harm to somebody. The magical function is also shown in the fact that it usually worked only in combination with a certain rite, for instance, spitting or using rue against witches. Often it was said as a conclusion to a series of incantations. Its use in incantations against disease was very common and departed from the normal form by leaving out the "Amen." Repetition (three, seven, nine times) also shows its magical function; there was even a superstition that praying it seventy-seven times healed every disease. It was often used against fever and for stopping blood, but it was also used for the salvation of the dead. The exceptional holiness of this prayer is shown in the belief that if a person interrupted it by noise when it was being spoken in church, he or she would die.

RAINER WALZ

See also: AMULET AND TALISMAN; HOLINESS; MAGIC AND RELIGION; MAGIC CIRCLE; SPELLS; SUPERSTITION.

References and further reading:
Brown, Michael J. 2000. "'Panem Nostrum': The Problem of Petition and the Lord's Prayer." *Journal of Religion* 80, no. 4: 595–614.
Cullmann, Oscar. 1995. *Prayer in the New Testament.* Translated by John Bowden. Minneapolis: Fortress.
Schneider, A. M. 1937. "Vaterunser." Vol. 8, col. 1513–1515 in *Handwörterbuch des deutschen Aberglaubens.* Edited by Hanns Bächtold-Stäubli and Eduard Hoffmann-Krayer. 10 vols. Berlin and Leipzig: de Gruyter, 1927–1942.

LORRAINE, DUCHY OF

Records of nearly 2,000 trials and over 1,400 executions for witchcraft have been preserved from the duchy of Lorraine, omitting the duchy of Bar and numerous enclaves belonging mainly to the prince-bishops of Metz, Toul, and Verdun (for which relatively few records survive). Such figures place this independent bilingual duchy, a buffer state separating the Holy Roman Empire from the Kingdom of France, with a total population of approximately 400,000, among the worst witch-hunting regions of Europe; Lorraine's rate of executions per thousand population in its French-speaking heartland ranks second in French-speaking Europe. Lorraine was permanently united after 1506 with the smaller duchy of Bar to the west, and the dukes of Lorraine owed fedual allegiance to the Holy Roman Empire for most of their lands, but they also owed homage to the kings of France for half of Bar.

Unusually rich local financial records record expenses from over 1,000 executions in Lorraine between the 1470s and 1630s. During the peak era of trials (1570–1630), these records are almost 90 percent complete for Lorraine's Francophone parts, and because every execution represented a justifiable public expense, local officials invariably recorded whenever witches were burned. Included among these same financial records, in order to justify claims for reimbursement, are partial trial records for over 350 defendants. Lacunae push the probable total number of executions to about 1,600—slightly more than half as many as previously supposed. Although Lorraine's probable overall total of witchcraft executions matched or even exceeded the estimated totals from many of the "superhunts" sponsored by Catholic prelates in western Germany, the numbers from its French-speaking heartland were lower than those from the Pays de Vaud in French Switzerland. During the peak of witch hunting in both places (1590–1630), Protestant Vaud, with a population much smaller than that of Francophone Lorraine, averaged thirty recorded witchcraft executions per year against only eighteen for Catholic Lorraine.

Several scholars have demonstrated recently just how heavily this region was affected by witchcraft trials (Biesel 1997; Briggs 2002). Its earliest known executions for witchcraft occurred in both the duchy of Bar and Lorraine itself, from the 1470s until the beginning of the sixteenth century. After a long hiatus, a few dozen witchcraft executions took place in mid-sixteenth-century Lorraine. Apart from these episodes, Lorraine's witchcraft executions were spread uninterruptedly over two generations (1570–1635). However, these executions were distributed unevenly across its three principal geographic parts. Most of them occurred in the Francophone heartland *bailliages* (bailiwicks) of Nancy and Vosges; there were hundreds more in the Germanophone *bailliage d'Allemagne* in the northeast. However, there were relatively few executions in the western duchy of Bar, about half of which belonged to the huge zone supervised by the *Parlement* of Paris (a sovereign judicial court, with jurisdiction over approximately one-half of France).

There is one key explanation for Lorraine's grim record. This bilingual but solidly Catholic duchy produced a well-known demonologist, Nicolas Rémy. Rémy composed his witch-hunting manual, the *Daemonolatria* (Demonolatry), soon after being appointed Lorraine's *procureur-général* (public prosecutor), in 1591, and he published it four years later at Lyons. Having previously served fifteen years on the duchy's highest court, the *Change de Nancy,* he had practical experience that no other author on witchcraft could match. (Lorraine had no true appellate court: The *Change* merely exercised an ill-defined supervision over the proceedings in the local courts, which regarded its comments as advisory and occasionally disregarded them.)

With typical late-humanist bombast, Rémy boasted in his preface that he had prosecuted more than 900 people who had been executed as witches during the previous fifteen years, but he named only about 125 defendants, extremely few of whom can be traced in Lorraine's abundant fiscal archives (and some of them were not executed). Instead, Rémy's significance lies in the fact that he and his son Claude-Marcel occupied the post of *procureur-général* to the duchy of Lorraine for forty consecutive years after 1591, thereby making it the largest European state with chief prosecutors who consistently encouraged rather than curbed witchcraft prosecutions throughout the worst period of witch hunting in western Europe. The influence of both Rémys was indirect but real: Their commitment ensured that the dukes would not question the persecution, while the *Change* was highly unlikely to challenge local courts on witchcraft when the public prosecutor held such a high-profile public position.

Lorraine's remarkably abundant local financial records, supplemented by hundreds of trial fragments, describe more than twenty trials and executions for witchcraft between 1477 and 1486 and another cluster of witchcraft trials in its Francophone heartlands between 1544 and 1552: Ten witches were burned in four districts in 1545, six more in 1550. After stopping completely between 1555 and 1569, witchcraft trials resumed there during the 1570s; for the first time, they included Germanophone Lorraine. Despite very incomplete financial records, at least seventeen different districts recorded witch burnings during the 1570s; overall totals averaged almost six executions annually. In the following decade, financial records improved and the number of recorded witch burnings more than doubled, accelerating to about thirteen victims per year across Lorraine's Francophone areas, with Germanophone districts adding another four or five executions per year. For the first time, more than ten people were burned as witches in one year in a few districts (in St.-Dié in 1583; in Homburg in 1586; in Bitche in 1588; and possibly in Dieuze in 1586).

After Rémy's appointment as *procureur-général,* nearly complete financial records show a further increase to about eighteen executions per year from 1591 to 1600 in Francophone Lorraine, although the highest totals of the early 1590s came from Germanophone districts (Dieuze, Wallerfangen, Val-de-Lièpvre, and Homburg). While the two generations of Rémys ran Lorraine's prosecutorial apparatus, recorded executions for witchcraft in Francophone Lorraine remained at approximately constant levels: From 1591 until 1630, one can locate almost 740 recorded burnings, over eighteen per year. As in the neighboring bilingual duchy of Luxembourg, Lorraine's Germanophone districts, the sparsely populated *bailliage d'Allemagne* (Hiegel 1961), seem proportionately more heavily affected by witchcraft trials than its Francophone regions, especially in the early 1590s and again from 1618 to 1621. Meanwhile, far sketchier financial records from the autonomous duchy of Bar, where the Rémys had no authority, suggest a probable total of fewer than four witchcraft executions per year between 1580 and 1630, in a region midway in size and population between Lorraine's Germanophone districts and its Francophone heartland.

One southeastern district, produced a disproportionate share of Lorraine's executions for witchcraft. St.-Dié, with less than 10 percent of Lorraine's Francophone population, accounted for over 35 percent of the recorded totals of executed witches from two dozen Francophone districts during the major persecutions between 1591 and 1630. Overall, 900 people from this single district were burned as witches, all but ten of them between 1580 and 1632. One possible explanation for this grim record is that, unlike most other parts of Lorraine, much of this district belonged to three great ecclesiastical lords (the cathedral chapter of St.-Dié and the abbeys of Etival and Moyenmoutier). Each possessed the right of high justice and hunted witches enthusiastically, but they all used ducal officials to endorse their sentences and—because ecclesiastical officials should never shed blood—paid them to carry out the actual burnings.

In Lorraine, witchcraft persecutions extended upward to the ducal household after 1600 and became notable for the high rank of those accused. In 1604, after Bernabite experts, a cardinal and a papal legate, had been brought from Italy to conduct prolonged exorcisms on the duke's crippled second son, a minor court official was finally accused and burned for bewitching the child. A few years later, the same monks exorcised the cardinal's cousin, a bishop of Verdun who had been bewitched into marriage (because of his kinship with the ducal house, the bishop's career was unaffected by this peccadillo). In the 1620s, as Lorraine's annual averages of witchcraft executions dropped off to about ten per year before their final surge in 1629–1630, two other prominent men were burned for this offense. The first, a physician attached to the ducal family, was convicted of causing the demonic possession of an extremely devout noblewoman with pretensions to sainthood (Delcambre and Lhermitte 1956). During her exorcisms, she also accused a high-ranking Franciscan, who fled to France in order to avoid arrest and then defended himself in a pamphlet. In a transparently political trial of 1625, a courtier and key adviser to the former duke was burned soon after his patron's death, charged with bewitching the new duke's marriage to the previous duke's heiress four years before; another official of the former duke met the same fate in 1631.

Lorraine's new ruler soon confronted the novel problem of a demonically possessed village, Mattaincourt. Its parish priest, a key adviser to Duke Charles IV and now venerated as a saint, ultimately had to resign because neither he nor anyone else could control the Devil's public scandals in his church whenever Mass was celebrated. Before this scandal ended, it had evolved from unsuccessful exorcisms into the largest single witch hunt in Lorraine's history. Over forty people were burned for witchcraft, most of them accused by demonically possessed adolescents. In order to end this panic, eight underaged witches, too young to be executed, had to be quarantined for over a year. Mattaincourt's hitherto-unknown tragedy offered a Catholic version that foreshadowed the all-too-famous developments sixty years later among the Puritans of Salem village in Massachusetts. Widespread attacks of plague, coupled with the French invasion and occupation of Lorraine, effectively ended Lorraine's prolonged witch hunts in the early 1630s.

WILLIAM MONTER

See also: FOURIER, ST. PIERRE; NUMBER OF WITCHES; *PARLEMENT* OF PARIS; RÉMY, NICOLAS; VAUD, PAYS DE.
References and further reading:
Biesel, Elizabeth. 1997. *Hexenjustiz, Volksmagie und soziale Konflikte im lothringischen Raum.* Trier: Spee.
Briggs, Robin. 1989. "Witchcraft and Popular Mentality in Lorraine, 1580–1630 –1630." Pp. 66–82 in *Communities of Belief: Cultural and Social Tensions in Early Modern France.* Oxford: Clarendon.
———. 1991. "Women as Victims? Witches, Judges and the Community." *French History* 5: 438–450.
———. 2002. *Witches and Neighbors: The Social and Cultural Context of European Witchcraft.* 2nd ed. Malden, MA, and Oxford: Blackwell.
Delcambre, Etienne, and Jean Lhermitte. 1956. *Un cas enigmatique de possession diabolique en Lorraine au XVIIe siècle: Elisabeth de Ranfaing.* Nancy: Société d'Archéologie Lorraine.
Hiegel, Henri. 1961–1968. *Le bailliage d'Allemagne de 1600 à 1632.* 2 vols. Sarreguemines: Pierron.
Monter, William. forthcoming. "The Catholic Salem, or How the Devil Destroyed a Saint's Parish (Mattaincourt 1627–31)." In *Witchcraft in Context.* Edited by Wolfgang Behringer and James Sharpe. Manchester: Manchester University Press.

LOUDUN NUNS

The spectacular exorcisms of Loudun's Ursuline nuns in the 1630s played an essential role in the most famous witchcraft trial of seventeenth-century France. It is arguably the best-known witchcraft case in European history, its historical fascination paralleling that of the Salem witchcraft events in America. Recent generations have portrayed the nuns' torments on stage, in films, and even in an opera. The episode became so famous for at least two reasons: in part because thousands of people observed the extraordinary recorded behavior of the nuns in very unusual public exorcisms, and in part because a prominent priest, whom many believed innocent, was executed for causing the possessions. Moreover, there has been continuing debate ever since over what roles the principal characters played and why, up to and including King Louis XIII and his first minister, Cardinal Richelieu. Furthermore, this case does not stand alone; it was the second of four connected French cases of convent "possessions," preceded by one in Aix-en-Provence and followed by cases in Louviers and Auxonne.

In the western French town of Loudun, the Ursuline convent began experiencing multiple assaults of demonic possession in 1632. Led by their mother superior, Jeanne des Anges, the nuns accused a local parish priest, Urbain Grandier, of being the author of these possessions. He fought against these accusations but was eventually arrested, tried, and, in the words of his sentence, found guilty "of the crime of sorcery, evil spells, and the possession visited upon some Ursuline nuns of this town" (Bibliothèque Nationale, Fds fr. 24163).

Grandier was a brilliant young parish priest assigned to Loudun in 1617. At this time the town was part Catholic, part Huguenot, each fearing the strength and intentions of the other. Catholics hoped that the handsome, charismatic young priest would win many converts. For twelve years he was a great success; but then, almost certainly, he seduced Philippe, the daughter of his friend, Louis Trincant, one of Loudun's foremost citizens and a man whose widespread family connections reached up to Cardinal Richelieu. The whole Trincant clan suddenly became Grandier's implacable enemy. He could not be accused of Philippe's seduction without ruining her name; Trincant avoided this by accusing him of a hidden life of lechery with his female parishioners. The priest, constantly under attack during the coming years, ultimately fought off these accusations. But in the meantime, his reputation and the stories about him had reached inside Loudun's Ursuline convent.

The convent had opened in 1626 and had grown quickly. The nuns were very young, including their mother superior, Jeanne des Anges, who at the beginning of the possessions in 1632 was still only thirty years old. She was a clever, strong-willed leader, ambitious and determined to make her convent a great success. She was also a manipulator and had a tendency to severe nervous problems under stress, for which she had to be treated from time to time by Loudun doctors.

In late September 1632, one of her young nuns had a nighttime apparition. The priest who gave religious direction to the convent had recently died of the plague; one night his ghost appeared to the nun and begged for prayers. Shaken, she reported this the following morning. Jeanne des Anges accepted the apparition as genuine. The frightened nuns, obsessed by the thought of the specter night and day, prayed earnestly, but within a few days the old priest was forgotten and the charismatic but supposedly libertine Grandier, whom the nuns had never met or even seen, had taken his place in their thoughts. From now on, the nightly invasions became decidedly erotic. Jeanne des Anges said in her autobiography that "after the demons had fully aroused in us the passion of love for this man, he did not fail to come at night into our house and into our chambers to solicit us to sin" (Legué and Tourette 1985, 67). Soon the nuns began to experience extraordinary convulsions, uncontrolled laughter, running, swearing, screaming, and blaspheming. They lost all self-possession. They spoke in strange voices. These shocking events were happening to young women who were related to leading families in the town. Clearly, in the minds of most observers, they were possessed by devils. Exorcisms were begun, and Jeanne des Anges's "demons" accused Grandier of having brought all this about.

One of the chief exorcists was Trincant's nephew. It was he who first compared the case of Grandier to that of Louis Gaufridy, the priest who had allegedly caused the demonic possession of another convent of Ursuline nuns at Aix-en-Provence in 1611. The Loudun exorcisms, initially started in secrecy, were then extended to include an audience of local gentry and ultimately became public extravaganzas open to crowds from far and wide. The onlookers, as many as 2,000 at a time, were amazed at the contortions, the obscenities, and the immodesty of the young women. A highlight of one performance came when Jeanne des Anges vomited up a piece of paper, allegedly a pact that Grandier had made with the Devil and signed with his blood. It still exists in the Bibliothèque Nationale in Paris (BN, Fds fr. 7618). Many believed everything they saw and were told, although some were skeptical and thought the exorcists were manipulating the nuns. Then the exorcists claimed that the Devil could be forced to tell the truth under exorcism—a proposition opposed by leading Catholic theologians of the time. This led to accusations of witchcraft against some of Grandier's friends, made by devils under exorcism, and created a widespread fear that a general witch hunt was about to begin. Fortunately, Grandier's friends were too powerful to be successfully attacked. Meanwhile, Grandier fought back against his accusers. By late 1633, the case was becoming a national drama.

Trincant and his supporters now appealed to Richelieu and the king to intervene. The question as to

The 1634 execution at Loudun of the French parish priest Urbain Grandier, the victim of the most famous witchcraft trial in Europe. To the left are the demonically possessed nuns being exorcized. (TopFoto.co.uk)

why the Crown acted is still unresolved. Perhaps it was important to avoid widening a breach between Huguenots and Catholics in Loudun; perhaps the moral issue of a priest seducing a parishioner and going unpunished was a factor. Whatever his motivation, the king ordered an inquiry, with the explicit purpose of finding Grandier guilty as a sorcerer and punishing him. In the trial some months later, seventy-two witnesses came before an assembly of experienced judges and testified against Grandier. The court found him guilty, and he was burned at the stake the same day before a crowd of thousands.

It was thought the possessions would end when their alleged instigator was dead, but they did not. This raised some doubts about the validity of all that had happened. Meanwhile, the nuns were left in poverty, with their school closed, no money coming in, and their reputations in tatters. They were exorcized for months and sometimes years; Jeanne des Anges was only finally cured in 1638. Some supporters came to their aid, but it was Jeanne des

Anges who saved her convent. As she recovered, "miracles" occurred, and she became famous. To those who believed her, she was no longer a woman attacked by the Devil for her weakness and sins but rather a prey chosen as worthy of all he could inflict. Her convent, and she herself, became a center for visitors and pilgrims. Many regarded her death as that of a saint. Like many other French convents, the Loudun Ursulines later fell on hard financial times, and their house closed in 1772.

UNRESOLVED ISSUES

Since the day of Grandier's execution on August 18, 1634, debates have raged over this case. Time has answered some questions; many are still in doubt. The very first issue raised was whether the nuns were truly possessed or sick or charlatans—or some combination of these. If they were sick, what was the cause? If they were charlatans, who was instructing them and teaching them what to do? Then there are questions about why Richelieu involved himself so deeply in this case. Were his primary concerns reasons of state, moral issues, or personal revenge? All have been put forward.

And was Grandier really the libertine he was accused of being? Both direct and indirect evidence suggests that he was, but was that sufficient reason to put him to death if he had not caused the possessions? Was he eliminated to avoid an open and perhaps murderous rift developing in Loudun between the Huguenots and Catholics? Then there are the questions relating to the Church. Why was his bishop so determined to ruin him? Why were the exorcists permitted to perform public exorcisms, contrary to well-established general practice? To what extent were all these events simply reflections of family and personal conflicts in a provincial town at a time of great tension?

What we do know is that the questions raised about the case played their part in the eventual decline of witch hunts in France.

—ROBERT RAPLEY

See also: AIX-EN-PROVENCE NUNS; AUXONNE NUNS; BEWITCHMENT; CONVENT CASES; EXORCISM; FRANCE; GHOSTS; LOUVIERS NUNS; PACT WITH THE DEVIL; POSSESSION, DEMONIC.

References and further reading:

Carmona, Michel. 1988. *Les diables de Loudun: Sorcellerie et politique sous Richelieu*. Paris: Fayard.
Certeau, Michel de. 2000. *The Possession at Loudun*. Translated by Michael B. Smith. Chicago and London: University of Chicago Press.
Ferber, Sarah. 2004. *Demonic Possession and Exorcism in Early Modern France*. London and New York: Routledge.
Huxley, Aldous. 1952. *The Devils of Loudun*. London: Chatto and Windus.
Legué, Gabriel, and Gilles de la Tourette. 1985. *Soeur Jeanne des Anges, supérieure des Ursulines de Loudon (XVIIe siècle): Autobiographie d'une hystérique possédée*. Paris: Millon.
Rapley, Robert. 1998. *A Case of Witchcraft: The Trial of Urbain Grandier*. Montreal and Kingston: McGill-Queen's University Press.
Villeneuve, Roland. 1980. *La mystérieuse affaire Grandier: Le diable à Loudun*. Paris: Payot.

LOUVIERS NUNS

An outbreak of demonic possession in a convent at Louviers in Normandy in the 1640s became the last in a French series of incidents in which possessed nuns made successful accusations of witchcraft against their spiritual directors.

In late 1642, at the Hospitaller convent of Ste.-Elisabeth and St.-Louis, several nuns began to display symptoms of demonic possession. They claimed the cause was the body of their recently deceased spiritual director, Father Mathurin Picard, who they said had been a witch. They also accused another nun, Madeleine Bavent, of witchcraft. Public exorcisms ensued, at which the nuns accused another priest, Father Thomas Boullé, and a former mother superior, Françoise de la Croix. The *Parlement* (sovereign judicial court) of Rouen executed Father Boullé for witchcraft in 1647; Father Picard's bones were exhumed and burned with Father Boullé. The case against Madeleine Bavent was left unresolved; she died in an asylum in 1653. The accusations against Mother de la Croix never reached court. For exorcists, the case was a *succès de scandale* that promoted the value of exorcism.

Major possessions at Ursuline convents in Aix-en-Provence (1609–1611) and in Loudun in the 1630s provided a model for the incidents at Louviers. For nearly two years, exorcists flocked to the convent from Normandy and beyond to confront the possessed nuns, performing over 100 public exorcisms. These were scenes of high drama, in which the women writhed and wailed—behavior supposedly signaling torture by demons. Exorcists themselves also resorted to violence at times, seeing the women as no longer human but merely shelters for devils who must be obliged to submit to the Catholic Church. Manuscript and printed accounts of the case appeared over a period of twelve years (1643–1654). It inspired around thirty-five printed works, a number exceeded only by the Loudun case, which led to fifty-four works. The tragedy of Louviers is that of the considerable literature the possession generated, very little concerned Thomas Boullé, its chief victim. Instead, exorcists, their supporters, and their opponents brought to Louviers their own polemic agendas, and a widespread fascination with lurid possession cases in this period ensured a readership for their works. Some major texts merit analysis.

According to one exorcist, Esprit du Bosroger, a Capuchin priest, the trouble had started in the 1620s, when the convent's first spiritual director, Father Pierre David, had supposedly spread "diabolical" devotional practices of "illuminism" (meaning overzealous, mystical, and unapproved spiritual practices) in the convent. Bosroger published a full account of the case in 1652, entitled *La pieté affligee, ov Discovrs historiqve & theologique de la possession des religieuses dittes de Saincte Elizabeth de Louuiers* (Piety Afflicted, or Historic and Theological Discourse of the Possession of the St. Elizabeth Nuns of Louviers). The supposed illuminism–witchcraft link became a distinctive feature of this case. Both illuminism and public exorcism are typical aspects of the intense Catholic spiritual revival characteristic of baroque France.

Another exorcist, Father Thomas Le Gauffre, saw the possessions as an opportunity to promote the cult of his deceased friend, the influential Father Claude Bernard (d. 1641), known as the "poor priest." Bernard had successfully performed exorcisms in his lifetime, and Le Gauffre sought both to emulate and venerate Bernard by using some of his personal relics to exorcise the nuns of Louviers. Le Gauffre published several accounts of successful exorcisms using Bernard's relics, but the sainthood campaign did not advance very far.

After Boullé's execution in 1647, Madeleine Bavent remained in jail, her own fate still undecided despite her confessions of witchcraft. An Oratorian priest named Charles Desmarets undertook to defend her reputation—and make his own—by publishing *Histoire de Magdelaine Bavent, Religieuse du Monastère de St. Loüis de Louviers* (The Story of Magdelaine Bavent, Nun of the St.-Louis Convent of Louviers). The book mixed excerpted interrogations of Bavent with a long autobiographical piece, reputedly dictated by Bavent at her request. Desmarets's account tried to demonstrate, first, that Bavent's confessions to the *Parlement* of Rouen had been obtained under duress due to the pressure of continuous new accusations put forward under exorcism by the convent's "demons" (principally the demon of sister Anne Barré, named "Leviathan"); and second, that her new confession was in effect the first time Bavent had been able to confess fully and honestly, having been obstructed by a succession of corrupt spiritual directors and hostile female superiors at her convent.

Some French critics again argued, as at Loudun, that exorcists were frauds, exploiting exorcism for malicious or self-promotional ends. Pierre Yvelin, a doctor at the court of the regent, Anne of Austria, had visited the convent early in the case and wrote two short skeptical accounts. At this time, French physicians were divided over the question of possession, all allowing it as a possibility but often refuting individual cases. Two local Norman doctors, Pierre Maignart and Jean Lempèrière, who supported the diagnosis of possession at Louviers, replied aggressively to their Parisian colleague in print. The increasingly spiteful debate was only curtailed when the court in Paris intervened.

SARAH FERBER

See also: AIX-EN-PROVENCE NUNS; CONVENT CASES; EXORCISM; LILLE NUNS; LOUDUN NUNS; POSSESSION, DEMONIC.

References and further reading:

Barbe, Lucien. 1899. "Histoire du couvent de Saint Louis et de Sainte Elizabeth de Louviers et de la possession des religieuses de ce monastère." *Bulletin de la Société d'études diverses de l'arondissement de Louviers* (1898) 5: 103–434.

[Bavent, Madeleine, and Charles Desmarets]. 1652. *Histoire de Magdelaine Bavent, Religieuse du Monastère de Saint Loüis de Louviers.* Paris: Jacques Le Gentil.

Du Bosroger, Esprit. 1652. *La pieté affligee, ov discovrs historiqve & Theologique de la Possession des Religieuses dittes de Saincte Elizabeth de Louuiers.* Rouen: Jean Le Boulenger.

Mandrou, Robert. 1968. *Magistrats et sorciers en France au XVIIe siècle: Une analyse de psychologie historique.* Paris: Plon.

Vidal, Daniel. 1990. *Critique de la raison mystique: Bénoît de Canfield, possession et dépossession au XVIIe siècle.* Grenoble: Millon.

LOVE MAGIC

Multifarious magical rituals devised to gain power over other people's emotions (especially sexual desire) through the subversion of free will constituted love magic. As the term reveals, love magic was commonly used to arouse passion and to bind unwilling lovers. In more aggressive forms, it was aimed at destroying unfaithful lovers. The experiments or techniques of love magic could be learned by anyone, female or male, young or old. In practice, however, one can detect a noticeable gender bias: The practitioners and users of love magic in Mediterranean Europe were commonly female laypeople, or less frequently, male ecclesiastics; only in southern Italy do users seem to have been predominantly male and from the laity. Its many practices make it difficult to draw any strict boundary here between learned and popular culture or between religion and magic. Everything rests on the beliefs that feelings can be manipulated through external events and that lovers can be entirely controlled by the arousal of discomfort and love sickness. The rituals rely on both holy and demonic sources.

FUNCTIONS AND USERS

Love magic functioned as a means to cope with emotional insecurity and with the anxieties of everyday life by transforming unlucky circumstances into better ones. Often love magic involved a threat of physical distress: Victims should suffer and be deprived of food, drink, sleep, and power until the user's desires were met. Love magic was an attempt to gain power over the feelings and actions of another person with the aid of the supernatural. Behind this aspiration at gaining such power stood emotional anxieties, especially of women in Mediterranean Europe. Their amorous anxieties were reflected through a wide array of practices that revealed the "different stages of love" and the "psychological states" (Sánchez Ortega 1991, 63) experienced in a sexual relationship or in marriage.

Divinatory experiments promised useful information after a lover, or more rarely a husband, had disappeared. More generally, a woman could assess her chances on the marriage market. Primarily, however, practitioners of love magic sought to arouse affection, love, or even hatred. They intended to compel unwilling lovers to appear and to fulfill their erotic and amorous desires. Love magic was used not only to bind people (and male members) and force them into marriage but also to destroy already-existing relationships. Rituals of love magic were appropriate when a man and a woman had just met, but they could be applied at any time during a partnership or marriage. Married women relied on love magic to bind their lovers or to make their husbands treat them with greater respect and care; prostitutes used different techniques to attract and hold clients.

BELIEFS AND PRACTICES

Love magic covered a multitude of differing practices that are not easily categorized because they often overlapped. Divinatory experiments, for example, encompassed elements of necromancy or conjuration; others were merely superstitious rituals. They all had, however, the advantage of being simple and cheap. The easiest way was to count out a handful of beans while chanting "He loves me, he does not love me." Another, even more popular experiment in northern Italy and Spain was casting beans or casting a rope. The pattern in which the beans or the rope landed after being thrown into the air symbolized the degree of intimacy between two lovers. This ritual was commonly preceded by a prayer to St. Helen or to St. Ursula and by making the sign of the cross over the beans. Alternatively, other fortunetellers used fire, a sieve, special cards, or scissors for the same ends.

Charms, incantations, and conjurations were more acquisitive in nature. Some of them were spread throughout Europe, whereas others were particular to a specific place. Some love charms and incantations were inspired by official rituals of the Church, such as praying on a rosary or saying a "prayer" (Key of David). They might call on the Virgin Mary, the saints, or the Holy Spirit, and they might require the use of blessed candles or other religious apparatus for their efficacy. They might appeal to events of religious legends or sacred history, pleading, for example, that the Virgin Mary make a certain person feel the love she felt when giving birth to her son. Like this example of sympathetic magic, many recitations were based on well-known aspects of biblical teachings and Christian doctrine. In early modern Venice, for example, Jesus's holy passion became a common cultural image to induce pain and make the beloved suffer for the lover just as Jesus had suffered for mankind. Additionally, devotional or simple wax or pasta statutes were made (or bought) in the name of the person against whom the magic should work. They were punctured with pins or bound with string, but the action was always accompanied by words—such as the incantation of Sant'Orsola to cause impotence—creating an analogy between the object and the victim. In this cosmology, "Emotions, like physical pains, could be the result of external events and could readily be ascribed to other people, their source sought outside rather than in the self" (Roper 1994, 213).

Assistance was sometimes sought from priests—not always with their knowledge. "Prayers" were secretly spoken during Mass when the priest was making the sign of the cross over the Eucharist. Objects and magical formulas were placed under the altar, attempting in this way to absorb the liturgical power of the Mass. Some priests also willingly performed masses over magical objects or baptized profane things, most commonly a magnet. Baptized in the name of the desired person, such magnets would attract the beloved through their innate power. Bodily fluids, like menstrual blood, were mixed with the wine of the Eucharist or with herbs like sage or rue (picked at dawn). When drunk by the desired person, they were believed to be an excellent aphrodisiac. Alternatively, a consecrated host was added to the food or wine of the desired person. Not only the ritual expertise of priests but sacramental objects in general (holy oil, holy water) were central to a variety of love magical practices.

Other magical rituals, conjurations especially, derived their power more clearly from demons and spirits (demonic magic). Unlike necromancy, which appealed to God in order to force the demons into obedience, in conjurations God and Christian elements were excluded from the ritual proceedings. Images of saints were removed from the room where the conjuration took place, as was the cross from the rosary. It was by the power of words alone that the evil spirits fulfilled the sorceress's will. Spells that were placed on body and mind would command the spirits (with variations) to make a certain person unable to eat, sleep, think, write, read, or have sex unless he came to the woman and complied with her will. The aggressiveness of these practices lay in the attempt to destroy the will of another person entirely through especially violent metaphors.

PROSECUTION

The vast bulk of documentation of prosecution for love magic comes from Mediterranean Europe, mainly from northern Italy and the Iberian peninsula in the late sixteenth and early seventeenth centuries. However, love magic was a common allegation in fourteenth-century France and in medieval England. Two women were burned for using love magic in 1390 by the *Parlement* of Paris (sovereign judicial court, with jurisdiction over approximately one-half of France). The Mediterranean Inquisitions prosecuted love magic with increasing frequency in the climate of the post-Tritendine reform and convicted people of various offenses, from the holding of heretical opinions to coercion of free will to apostasy. These "superstitions" were prosecuted with a comparatively lenient approach by the Holy Office, which distinguished between professional sorceresses (who often claimed economic motives) and simple users of love magic. Whereas the former had to endure exile and whipping, the latter were commonly freed after an abjuration.

DANIELA HACKE

See also: CHARMS; GENDER; MAGIC, LEARNED; MAGIC, NATURAL; MAGIC, POPULAR; MAGIC AND RELIGION; MARY THE VIRGIN; NECROMANCY; RITUAL MAGIC; SPELLS; SUPERSTITION; WATER, HOLY; WORDS, POWER OF.

References and further reading:
Gentilcore, David. 1992. *From Bishop to Witch: The System of the Sacred in Early Modern Terra d'Otranto.* Manchester: Manchester University Press.

Hacke, Daniela. 2001. "Von der Wirkungsmächtigkeit des Heiligen: Magische Liebeszauberpraktiken und die religiöse Mentalität venezianischer Laien." *Historische Anthropologie* 2: 311–332.

———. 2002. "Aus Liebe und aus Not: Eine Geschichte des Gefühls anhand frühneuzeitlicher Liebeszauberprozesse in Venedig." *Zeitschrift für historische Forschung* 3: 359–382.

Kieckhefer, Richard. 1989. *Magic in the Middle Ages.* Cambridge: Cambridge University Press.

Martin, Ruth. 1989. *Witchcraft and the Inquisition in Venice, 1550–1650.* Oxford: Blackwell.

O'Neil, Mary. 1987. "Magical Healing, Love Magic and the Inquisition in Late Sixteenth-Century Modena." Pp. 88–114 in *Inquisition and Society in Early Modern Europe.* Edited by Stephen Haliczer. Totowa, NJ, and New York: Barnes and Noble.

Roper, Lyndal. 1994. *Oedipus and the Devil. Witchcraft, Sexuality and Religion in Early Modern Europe.* London and New York: Routledge.

Ruggiero, Guido. 1993. *Binding Passions: Tales of Magic, Marriage, and Power at the End of the Renaissance.* New York and Oxford: Oxford University Press.

Sánchez Ortega, María Helena. 1991. "Sorcery and Eroticism in Love Magic." Pp. 58–92 in *Cultural Encounters: The Impact of the Inquisition in Spain and the New World.* Edited by Mary E. Perry and Anne J. Cruz. Berkeley and Los Angeles: University of California Press.

Thomas, Keith. 1973. *Religion and the Decline of Magic.* 1971. Reprint, Harmondsworth, UK, Penguin.

LOWES, JOHN (CA. 1565–1645)

Vicar of Brandeston in Suffolk, the most prominent victim of the 1645 panic instigated by the self-appointed "Witch Finder General," Matthew Hopkins. Although male defendants were relatively rare in English witchcraft cases, and men of gentry status rarer still, the case of John Lowes fits patterns from continental witch panics by proving that no one was exempt from accusation when faced with an investigator of Hopkins's tenacity at a time of enormous unrest in England.

Lowes was a highly unusual vicar. Educated at St. John's College, Cambridge, he began preaching at Bury St. Edmunds in 1594. Appointed to a living at Brandeston in 1596, he married a local woman in 1599. In the next half-century, Lowes was rarely at peace with his neighbors. He insisted on a type and intensity of preaching that annoyed his parishioners. Accusations of Catholicism and sorcery were made against Lowes when he was in his forties, and he was later accused of accompanying a cunning man to a fair to buy "popish" trinkets. But these charges were probably unfounded; it seems more likely that his leanings were Puritan. As early as 1594, he had been summoned before a synod at Ipswich for failing to adhere to the rites of the Church of England. Complaints from his parishioners about his preaching and doctrine even reached the prestigious Court of the Star Chamber in Westminster.

Although Lowes was indicted (and acquitted) twice for witchcraft, his offenses were mostly secular. In the Star Chamber, it was alleged that Lowes fought with his neighbors and launched many lawsuits. In the early 1630s, he was also indicted in the Court of King's Bench for "barratry," or vexatious litigation. In 1642, a pamphlet entitled *A Magazine of Scandall* noted that a petition had been raised to eject Lowes as a scandalous minister. It also damned Lowes as a "common Barrettor," adding that he kept company with witches and used their services. It even alleged that he had threatened to burn the houses of anyone who accused him of witchcraft. The fact that he had protected an accused witch in Brandeston thirty years earlier made him even more suspicious.

The arrival of Matthew Hopkins at Brandeston in 1645 provided the catalyst for accusations that would destroy Lowes. His neighbors charged him with a range of *maleficia.* For example, a Brandeston deponent, Nathaniel Man, testified that Lowes had threatened him. Man's child sickened and died soon afterward, a direct result of the witness's previous dealings with Lowes.

Lowes—by this time in his eighties—was taken to Framlingham Castle, where he underwent the swimming ordeal in the moat. Subsequently, he was chased around a room until exhausted and, like other East Anglian suspects in these trials, deprived of sleep so that delirious confessions could be extracted. Lowes finally admitted that he kept seven diabolical imps, the largest of which he suckled, but he denied sealing a contract with the Devil. He used the imps to kill cattle and imperil shipping out of Great Yarmouth. To Hopkins himself, Lowes reportedly confessed that he had indeed compacted with Satan and that to test out his imps, he had sunk a ship, drowning fourteen men. Lowes was indicted and convicted at Bury St. Edmunds. Devoutly maintaining his innocence to the last, he was hanged on August 27, 1645, with several others condemned at the same trial. Lowes read the lesson at the execution himself.

Afterward, the steward of the manor noted that everyone was glad Lowes was finally out of the way. Others upheld his innocence but recognized the power of the parish to get its way against a common enemy.

MALCOLM J. GASKILL

See also: AGE OF ACCUSED WITCHES; CONFESSIONS; FAMILIARS; HOPKINS, MATTHEW; MALE WITCHES; PAMPHLETS AND NEWSPAPERS; PROTESTANT REFORMATION; PURITANISM; STEARNE, JOHN; SWIMMING TEST.

References and further reading:

Deacon, Richard. 1976. *Matthew Hopkins: Witch Finder General.* London: Muller.

Ewen, C. L'Estrange. 1938. *Witchcraft in the Star Chamber.* N.p.: Printed privately for the author.

Gaskill, Malcolm J. 2005. *Witchfinders: A Seventeenth-Century English Tragedy.* London: John Murray.

Sharpe, James. 1996. *Instruments of Darkness: Witchcraft in England, 1550–1750.* London: Hamilton.

Stearne, John. 1973. *A Confirmation and Discovery of Witchcraft.* 1648. Facsimile edition. Exeter: Rota, University of Exeter.

LUTHER, MARTIN
(1483–1546)

Luther's attitude toward witchcraft is significant not only in itself but particularly because of its influence on early modern Protestantism. Luther was undoubtedly the greatest Protestant authority of early modern times. Abundant sources permit a comprehensive review of Luther's statements on the subject. This, however, does not facilitate a straightforward assessment of his views and his role in the history of witchcraft trials. The background to Luther's attitude to almost everything, including witchcraft, was that of the late Middle Ages. Early academic biographies contained a few vague references to his parents, particularly his mother, being superstitious, but they provided no explanation for Luther's lifelong preoccupation with theologically complicated issues associated with witchcraft.

Luther's first academic encounters with the subject of witchcraft must have occurred while he was studying theology in Erfurt. There is a marginal note *"Incubus"* in the copy of St. Augustine's *De civitate Dei* (On the City of God) that Luther used in 1509. Luther's sermons on the Ten Commandments, which he preached at Wittenberg's municipal church in 1516–1517, provide an abundance of material. They contain an extensive rendering of contemporary views; such detailed knowledge presupposed a thorough investigation of the subject, including some witchcraft manuals. Luther explicitly mentioned the Strasbourg clergyman Johann Geiler von Kaysersberg and employed motifs from his *Die Emeis* (The Ants, 1516–1517). One can assume that Luther was familiar with expositions of the Decalogue by such other Augustinian friars as Gottschalk Hollen. Luther's *Decem praecepta Wittenbergensi praedicata populo* of 1518, printed in German in 1520 as *Der Zehn Gebot ein nützliche Erklärung* (A Useful Explanation of the Ten Commandments), seems to represent the tenth-century *"Canon Episcopi* tradition," recognizing the possibility of the evil arts (*maleficium*) while rejecting the idea of witches flying.

Like other contemporary representatives of this tradition, such as Martin Plantsch or Ulrich Molitor, Luther claimed that harmful magic was possible only with God's permission. The Devil and his witches had no independent and autonomous power. Luther retained this fundamental attitude toward *maleficium* and witches flying throughout his life, as he also maintained his attitudes toward two other key elements of witchcraft: the pact with the Devil and sexual inter-course with demons. Basing his understanding on scholastic demonology, Luther considered intercourse with demons a possibility, whereas making a pact with the Devil played a subordinate role in his work.

Luther never demanded punishment for witches in any of his early sermons on the Ten Commandments. Later in life, Luther repeatedly approached the subject of sorcery and witchcraft with reference to the first (and sometimes the second) commandment, but never with the same intensity as in 1516. In his catechisms of 1529, Luther briefly prohibited sorcery: In the Large Catechism, he related it to the first commandment, and in the Small Catechism, to the second commandment. This context obviously makes sorcery a primarily religious offense to Luther, eventually resulting in demands for increasingly severe penalties for witches.

Luther's exegetical works provide a continuous but less accessible source for the evaluating of his views on witchcraft. He discussed the crucial biblical references to witchcraft in many sermons, university lectures, and Bible commentaries, interpreting them both traditionally and with a new accentuation. For example, in both sermons and lectures, Luther used Genesis 6:1–4 to support the incubus notion. In a sermon expounding Exodus 7 (Pharaoh's sorcerers and Moses), he mentioned the fundamental fact that magic could only be performed with God's permission. In his treatise *Misuse of the Mass,* Luther used 1 Samuel 28 (on the witch of Endor) to support his rejection of physical metamorphosis, indicating that Samuel appeared to Saul only as a spirit but not *corporaliter* (bodily). In this way, Luther never abandoned the framework of medieval demonology derived ultimately from St. Augustine.

Commenting upon Deuteronomy 18:10–12, which deals with the subject of witchcraft and magic in more depth, Luther applied the Hebrew terms for magical practices to witchcraft practices of his time. Within this context, he translated the word *Mecasheph* as *witch* and explained: "Witches are the evil whores of the devil who steal milk, make bad weather, ride on goats and broomsticks, . . . slaughter infants in their cribs, bewitch the marriage bed, etc." (*Kirchenpostille,* in Luther 1883ff, vol. 10, book I/1, 591). This statement did not prove, despite previous claims, that Luther believed in the reality of witches' flying. Rather, it defined the term *witch,* as used by both theologians and ordinary people in the sixteenth century.

In 1526, in a series of sermons on Exodus, Luther devoted one sermon to a detailed exposition of the best-known biblical text about witchcraft, Exodus 22:18 ("You shall not permit a sorceress to live" [*The Holy Bible,* Revised Standard Version. London: Nelson, 1966]). Without discussing flying, metamorphosis, or the witches' Sabbats, Luther repeatedly demanded the death penalty for sorcery, because of the *maleficium* and the pact with the Devil but above all because it violated the first commandment. This sermon was not printed and had no further impact. It is important that Luther did not use the word *Hexe* (witch) in any of his Bible translations.

The Wittenberg reformers rarely took public action on such matters. It is of particular interest that Luther personally excommunicated two supposed witches in Wittenberg after preaching on witchcraft in 1529. Apparently, however, no secular prosecutions ensued. In 1540, a witchcraft trial did take place in Wittenberg; four people were condemned to death and burned at the stake. Luther was not involved directly but may have expressed approval. In his *Table Talk,* Luther occasionally mentioned magic and witchcraft but introduced no new aspects. It is striking that none of Luther's numerous letters ever mentioned witchcraft.

Luther's attitude toward witchcraft did not agree with the new "cumulative" picture propagated by the *Malleus Maleficarum* (The Hammer of Witches, 1486), which Luther never read. Throughout his entire work, Luther rejected the notions of flying, metamorphosis, and the Sabbat. Like Ulrich Molitor and other "conservative" witchcraft theorists, Luther followed the *Canon Episcopi* tradition. It must be stressed, however, that Luther was no moderate representative of this tradition: He was not reluctant to condone punishment for witches. The essentially theological crimes of witches and sorcerers (who violated the first commandment and turned to other gods, in this case to the Devil) demanded prosecution and punishment—in most cases, death. Among Lutherans, this aspect provided sufficient encouragement for witchcraft trials, as could Luther's uncompromising opposition to and repeated criminalization of "white magic," that is, harmless sorcery with Christian motives.

However, in his sermons and catechistic writings, Luther deprived early modern witchcraft trials of one of their essential motives: He forbade hunting for scapegoats in the form of sorcerers when unexplained misfortune struck; instead, he referred the afflicted person to the will of God. Thus, he applied the theological notion that sorcery required God's permission to everyday life. Luther was not interested in "witch hunting" but in the existence of man before God. Since his own attitude remained ambivalent, responses to his position varied; both supporters and opponents of witchcraft trials claimed allegiance to Luther. His rejection of the notion that witches flew and held Sabbats required Lutheran advocates of severe prosecutions for witches and sorcerers to avoid discussing these issues when citing the biblical commandment to put such offenders to death.

In the late nineteenth century contexts of "Higher Criticism" and the *Kulturkampf* (culture war), Luther's position on witchcraft became the subject of heated controversy between Catholic and Protestant church historians. In 1888, Johannes Diefenbach first put the main responsibility for witchcraft prosecutions on Luther; twelve years later, Rudolf Ohle denied Luther's involvement entirely; finally, a Catholic scholar, Nikolaus Paulus (Paulus 1910), succeeded in pronouncing a comparatively fair-minded judgment by placing Luther within the theological framework of his time.

JÖRG HAUSTEIN;

TRANSLATED BY HELEN SIEGBURG

See also: AUGUSTINE, ST.; BIBLE; *CANON EPISCOPI;* CORPOREALITY, ANGELIC AND DEMONIC; ENDOR, WITCH OF; EXODUS 22:18 (22:17); GEILER VON KAYSERSBERG, JOHAN; INCUBUS AND SUCCUBUS; *MALLEUS MALEFICARUM; MALEFICIUM;* MOLITOR, ULRICH; PACT WITH THE DEVIL; PLANTSCH, MARTIN; PROTESTANT REFORMATION; SEXUAL ACTIVITY, DIABOLIC; SORCERY.

References and further reading:
Brauner, Sigrid. 1989. "Martin Luther on Witchcraft: A True Reformer?" Pp. 29–42 in *The Politics of Gender in Early Modern Europe.* Edited by Jean R. Brink, Allison P. Coudert, and Maryanne C. Horowitz. Kirksville, MO: Sixteenth Century Journal.
Clark, Stuart. 1997. *Thinking with Demons. The Idea of Witchcraft in Early Modern Europe.* Oxford: Clarendon.
Frank, Beatrice. 1984. "Etiam loqui volo vom Zaubern." *Archiv zur Weimarer Ausgabe* 5: 291–297.
Haustein, Jörg. 1990. *Martin Luthers Stellung zum Zauber- und Hexenwesen.* Stuttgart: Kohlhammer.
Luther, Martin. 1883ff. *Werke: Kritische Gesamtausgabe.* 58 volumes. Weimar: Hermann Böhlau and Hermann Böhlau's successor, Weimarer Ausgabe.
———. 1955–1986. *Works.* General editor, Helmut T. Lehmann. 55 vols. St. Louis, MO: Concordia.
Paulus, Nikolaus. 1910. *Hexenwahn und Hexenprozess, vornehmlich im 16. Jahrhundert.* Freiburg im Breisgau: Herder.

LUXEMBOURG, DUCHY OF

Between 1560 and 1683, approximately 2,500–3,000 witchcraft trials took place in the duchy of Luxembourg, one of the seventeen provinces of the Habsburg Netherlands. At least 2,000 ended with the execution of the accused, making Luxembourg's witch hunts among the most savage anywhere in western Europe. The figures cited in older research are either far too high (van Werveke 1983–1984 claimed 20,000–30,000 executions) or far too low (Dupont-Bouchat 1978 listed only 355). The rate of execution was clearly lower in the Walloon, the French-speaking parts of Luxembourg, than in the German-speaking regions, where witch hunts were pursued by special secret committees (*monopoles, Hexenausschüsse*) working in conjunction with minor territorial lords. Often, only marginal notes in account books documented trials in the so-called *Oberpropsteien* (Luxembourg's seventeen administrative districts), but manuscript records survive from some trials in small territorial lordships, such as Neuerburg and Hamm. The richest source on Luxembourg's witchcraft trials is the *Fonds van Werweke:* At the start of the twentieth century, the archivist and historian Nicolas van Werveke collected around 1,700 references to witchcraft trials from the records of Luxembourg's Provincial Council (*Provinzialrat*), portions of which have since disappeared.

TERRITORIAL AND CONSTITUTIONAL HISTORY OF LUXEMBOURG

In order to understand Luxembourg's severe witch hunts, it is essential to look at the duchy's territorial and constitutional history. From 1441, Luxembourg belonged to the Netherlands, which was divided into seventeen nominally sovereign territories or provinces in 1531, with its central government in Brussels and its highest court, the *Grand Conseil* (Great Council), in Malines (Mecheln). King Philip II of Spain inherited this loose confederation of provinces in 1556.

At the apex of Luxembourg's government was a governor, holding office for life. The Ducal Council, its highest administrative and legal authority, became a Provincial Council. It served as the highest appellate court in civil cases; families or individuals could bring nullity suits before it on account of legal abuses in criminal cases. The Provincial Council received many petitions and supplications; it issued so-called *lettres de purges,* certificates confirming the good reputation of individuals who had been cleared of witchcraft slanders. It was not a sovereign court: Its verdicts could always be appealed before the *Grand Conseil* in Malines. Although we have no documented evidence that the Carolina Code (the 1532 code of criminal law procedure for the Holy Roman Empire) was observed even in Luxembourg's German-speaking areas, the influence of French as well as German law was apparent in Luxembourg. Through its ad hoc promulgation of numerous administrative and criminal law ordinances that shaped local practice, the Provincial Council ensured that Roman law had wide influence in Luxembourg.

At the end of the sixteenth century, the province was divided into seventeen administrative districts (*Oberpropsteien*), each headed by a subgovernor (*Propst*), who also presided over its criminal law court. Within these districts lay more than fifty territorial enclaves belonging to minor lords, over whose courts the Luxembourg government only gradually obtained influence during the sixteenth and seventeenth centuries, partly as a result of the witch hunts. In these courts, uneducated jurors, mostly illiterate, judged cases on the basis of a still mainly oral tradition of customary law. Witchcraft trials occurred more frequently in these small lordships, often containing from one to three villages, than in areas belonging to an *Oberpropstei*. Furthermore, some of these minuscule noble or monastic lordships were fragmented by subdivision or mortgaged portions. In addition, some village communities also possessed criminal law rights, and the provosts (appointed by Luxembourg's governor) were often local noblemen using their position to further their private interests. Ecclesiastically, most of the provinces belonged to the archdiocese of Trier. Luxembourg was divided linguistically into German- and French-speaking areas.

LEGAL PRACTICES IN LUXEMBOURG WITCHCRAFT TRIALS

In Luxembourg, accusations in criminal cases (including witchcraft trials) could be made by a private individual (*partie formelle*), who had to produce evidence and witnesses and pay costs if his accusation was rejected. At the beginning of a criminal trial, both accuser and accused were imprisoned by court authorities. The accuser was released only after providing sufficient sureties for the duration of the trial. In German-speaking parts of Luxembourg, private accusation was the more common method for making witchcraft accusations; in French-speaking areas, judges or other officials initiated most such cases.

In both systems, however, the peasantry played a significant role in spreading witch hunts. In Walloon districts, witchcraft trials were initiated by a so-called *enquêtes generales* (general investigations) ordered by the authorities, requiring their subjects to denounce people who were reputedly witches to local courts. Local officials could then begin witchcraft trials on the basis of these denunciations. Some evidence suggests that *monopoles* (committees formed at the village level for the express purpose of bringing alleged witches to court) were formed in both German- and French-speaking parts of Luxembourg belonging to the archdiocese of Trier even earlier than in electoral Trier or the prince-abbey of St. Maximin. These committees were characterized by secret deals, corruption, and bribery (to the detriment of the accused witches), and they often used violent means to raise taxes in their villages to finance their witch hunts.

After being arrested, alleged witches were interrogated without torture and confronted with the witnesses against them. Sometimes an accused witch was allowed to name defense lawyers. However, many defendants did not use this opportunity, either because they believed firmly in their own innocence or because using a lawyer only increased the costs of the trial. In the end, it was the application of torture that produced the required confession from the accused. After implementation of the sentence, the convicted witch's property was confiscated and auctioned off. After the trial costs and a stipulated fine had been paid, a third of the property belonged to the lord who presided over the local criminal law court.

Records of Luxembourg's Provincial Council and ordinances issued by the Brussels government provide some detailed evidence about flagrant legal abuses occurring during witchcraft trials. At the beginning of the sixteenth century, Luxembourg's provincial government tried to restrain the autonomy of local courts in its administrative districts and minor lordships by stipulating that they risked punishment if they arrested or tortured an accused witch without first sending the pertinent evidence to the provincial government for approval, or if they used, paid, or bribed private accusers to circumvent the regulations of accusatorial legal procedure. For example, an ordinance of August 13, 1563, decreed that no one could be arrested and tortured merely on the basis of only one denunciation and without a legal opinion on the case being provided by a lawyer of the Provincial Council.

The mass persecutions of the 1580s and 1590s produced so many scandalous breaches of the law that on April 6, 1591, the provincial government published a lengthy decree that severely censured the corruption and abuses evident in making both private and official accusations of witchcraft at local courts. It explicitly prohibited consortia of accusers, *monopoles* (the witch-hunting committees) and "front men" who brought accusations on behalf of others. Guaranteeing the financial position of private accusers became punishable: Apart from official accusations, only private accusations made at the accuser's personal risk were allowed. It was again stipulated that legal advice must be sought from Luxembourg's Provincial Council at every stage of the pretrial investigation. In addition, torturers could not conduct interrogations in the absence of judges and the court scribe. Leading questions and particularly the suggestion of possible accomplices were prohibited, as was the public proclamation of lists of accomplices at executions. Trial costs were to be kept as low as possible.

Neither the Provincial Council in Luxembourg nor the central government in Brussels intended or desired a complete cessation of witchcraft trials. The latter issued decrees in 1592 and 1606 calling for the merciless persecution of soothsayers, workers of black magic, heretics, witches, and sorcerers. Of greater significance was a reorganization of criminal law implementation, aiming to deprive noble and ecclesiastical lords of their power to exercise criminal law by subjecting them more firmly to the authority of the provincial government.

However, the many nullity suits and petitions brought before the Luxembourg provincial courts show that the centralizing efforts of the provincial government did not enjoy rapid success. Both local lords with the right to exercise criminal justice and village witch-hunting committees continued to resist its decrees. The Provincial Council repeatedly issued new mandates—for example, in 1598, 1605, and 1606—

forbidding the use of consortia of accusers or paid private accusers and reminding local lords of their duty to send witchcraft trial records to them for scrutiny and to use only lawyers approved by them when drawing up and assessing such records. Finally, in 1623, the Provincial Council promulgated a general ordinance of criminal law procedure, placing particular emphasis on procedures used in witchcraft trials. In addition to repeating stipulations from previous ordinances, this decree sought to give clear preference to official accusations and to limit the practice of private accusation. However, evidence of significant legal abuses in Luxembourg witchcraft trials can still be found until the trials ceased in 1683.

COURSE AND END OF THE WITCHCRAFT TRIALS

After a few isolated cases in the middle and late fifteenth century, witchcraft trials in Luxembourg increased after 1500. The most severe phase of persecution began in 1560. From then until 1636, continual waves of persecution affected various areas. The Provincial Council's attempts to impose centrally stipulated norms and procedures on arbitrarily pursued local witch hunts were insufficient to stem the rising tide of trials. Crises caused by the sixteenth-century economic decline of the province and intensive attempts to impose new Counter Reformation standards of discipline triggered repeated calls from the inhabitants of Luxembourg for the destruction of witches. Minor territorial lords, who felt themselves to be victims of witchcraft, hoped to grow rich on the proceeds of witchcraft trials, or wanted to further their political ambitions, supported the efforts of village witch-hunting committees in German-speaking Luxembourg. The result was a local environment in favor of persecution, which the provincial government could influence only with difficulty. Moreover, the provincial government's decrees were circumvented by an ordinance of Philip II in September 1592, urging that the vice of witchcraft be fought on all fronts: Ecclesiastical and secular authorities should zealously persecute popular magic, soothsaying, magical healing, and witchcraft. This ordinance by no means triggered the Luxembourg witchcraft trials, as older research suggested (Dupont-Bouchat 1978), but it did provide additional legitimacy for the persecution.

A woman was burned as a witch in Arlon as late as 1675; a final phase of witch persecution arose in Echternach around 1680, resulting in several executions before ending in 1683. After the partial occupation of Luxembourg by the French in 1684, Louis XIV's 1682 edict issued for France came into effect, decreeing that sorcery could be punished with death only when accompanied by sacrilege. At this point, trials for witchcraft ended in Luxembourg, although cases of witchcraft slanders and possession continued to be heard. Belief that witches could work *maleficium* (harmful magic) remained widespread, however.

RITA VOLTMER;

TRANSLATED BY ALISON ROWLANDS

See also: ACCUSATIONS; ACCUSATIONAL PROCEDURE; DECLINE OF THE WITCH HUNTS; LAWS ON WITCHCRAFT (EARLY MODERN); LAWYERS; LORRAINE, DUCHY OF; NETHERLANDS, SOUTHERN; NUMBER OF WITCHES; POPULAR PERSECUTION; RURAL WITCHCRAFT; ST. MAXIMIN, PRINCE-ABBEY OF; TORTURE; TRIALS; TRIER, ELECTORATE OF; WITCH HUNTS.

References and further reading:
Dupont-Bouchat, Marie-Sylvie. 1978. "La répression de la sorcellerie dans le duché de Luxembourg aux XVIe et XVIIe siècles: Une analyse des structures de pouvoir et de leur fonctionnement dans le cadre de la chasse aux sorcières." Pp. 40–154 in *Prophètes et sorciers dans les Pays-Bas XVIe-XVIIe siècle.* Edited by Marie-Sylvie Dupont-Bouchat, Willem Frijhoff, and Robert Muchembled. Paris: Hachette.
———. 1999. "Démonologie, démonomanie, démonolâtrie et procès de sorcellerie à Saint-Hubert au XVIIe siècle." Pp. 237–252 in *La bibliothèque de L'abbaye de Saint-Hubert en Ardenne au dix-septième siècle: Première partie; Vie intellectuelle et religieuse d'une communauté Bénédictine.* Edited by Luc Knapen. Louvain: Bibliotheek van de Faculteit der Godgeleerdheid.
Kmec, Sonja. 2002. "Hexenprozesse im Herzogtum Luxemburg: Echternach 1679/1680." *Hémecht: Zeitschrift für Luxemburger Geschichte/Revue d'Histoire Luxembourgeoise* 54: 89–130.
van Werveke, Nicolas. 1898. "Deux sentences du conseil de Luxembourg, en matière de sorcellerie." *Publications de la Section Historique de l'Institut grand-ducal de Luxembourg* 46: 361–369.
———. 1983–1984. *Kulturgeschichte des Luxemburger Landes: Neue Auflage.* Edited by Carlo Huy. 2 vols. Esch-sur-Alzette: Schortgen.
Voltmer, Rita. 2002a. "Abläufe, Ursachen und Hintergründe der grossen Hexenverfolgungen in den Territorien zwischen Reich und Frankreich im späten 16. und im 17. Jahrhundert." Pp. 84–95 in *Hexenwahn: Ängste der Neuzeit.* Edited by Rosmarie Beier-De Haan, Rita Voltmer, and Franz Irsigler. Berlin: Minerva Farnung.
———. 2002b. "Rechtsnormen, Gerichts- und Herrschaftspraxis bei Hexereiverfahren in Lothringen, Luxemburg, Kurtrier und St. Maximin während des 16. und 17. Jahrhunderts." Pp. 60–71 in *Hexenwahn: Ängste der Neuzeit.* Edited by Rosmarie Beier-de Haan, Rita Voltmer, and Franz Irsigler. Berlin: Minerva Farnung.
———. 2002c. "Monopole, Ausschüsse, Formalparteien: Vorbereitung, Finanzierung und Manipulation von Hexenprozessen durch private Klagekonsortien." Pp. 5–67 in *Hexenprozesse und Gerichtspraxis.* Edited by Herbert Eiden and Rita Voltmer. Trierer Hexenprozesse—Quellen und Darstellungen 6. Trier: Paulinus.
———. 2002d. "Hochgerichte und Hexenprozesse: Zur herrschaftlich-politischen Instrumentalisierung von Hexenverfolgungen." Pp. 475–525 in *Hexenprozesse und Gerichtspraxis.* Edited by Herbert Eiden and Rita Voltmer. Trierer Hexenprozesse—Quellen und Darstellungen 6. Trier: Paulinus.
———. 2004. ". . . ce tant exécrable et détestable crime de sortilège. Der 'Bürgerkrieg' gegen Hexen und Hexenmeister im Herzogtum Luxemburg (16. und 17. Jahrhundert)." *Hémecht: Zeitschrift für Luxemburger Geschichte* 56, no. 1: 57–92.

LYCANTHROPY

The theme of the transformation of human beings into animals can be found in the imaginary worlds of all societies. Lycanthropy is the special case of transforming a man into a wolf: The Greek-derived word *lycanthropy* means "wolf-man," as does its English, German, Danish, or Italian counterparts. The Romans used an especially telling word for werewolf, namely *versipellis* or skin-changer.

There seem to be several possible roots for this belief. It might derive from numerous myths, folktales, and rituals that postulate a time when humans felt no clear boundaries between themselves and the animal world, assuming, rather, some permeability between them. Second, it may be a relic of belief in an animal-shaped external double of the soul, which often appeared in Old Norse sources (*hamr*). Third, totemistic structures also seem to have existed in prehistoric European societies (compare the Greek *Hirpi Sorani* who, clad in wolf skins, venerated Apollo Soranus, originally a wolf god). Secret societies using wolf skins for disguise may have infested some European regions, like the cannibalistic secret societies in Africa whose members disguised themselves as lions or leopards in order to kill men. Fourth, lycanthropy is a known, specific form of mental aberration, a psychic disease akin to schizophrenia, forcing the patient to act like the animal. Fifth, animal transmutations also figure in dreams and drug-induced ecstasies.

In the European traditions, two versions of this transmutation are known: Either it happens spontaneously, or else it is induced by another person without the victim's approval. These were already the usual patterns in classical antiquity: for example, on the one hand, Virgil's Moeris, a shepherd-sorcerer who became a wolf by eating special herbs; or, on the other hand, King Lycaon of Arcadia, whose impiety Zeus punished by changing him into a wolf. Among the Vikings, transformation into a bear was more common than transformation into a wolf: Their most formidable troops, the berserkers, were clad in bear skins and, falling into a trancelike state, fought like bears. However, the *Haraldskvaedhi* (Harold's Song; ca. 900 C.E.) also mentioned "wolf-frocks," warriors howling like beasts. *Eigil's saga Skalla Grímssonar* (The Saga of Egil Skalla-Grimsson, ca. 1230) described a berserker named Kveld-Úlfr who lived as a man during daytime, while at night he became a wolf (as his name—Evening

Wolf—implies). According to Olaus Magnus (1555), werewolves had become an epidemic in the Baltic, where they gathered by preference during Christmas time in order to undertake raids against the foresters (probably cases of criminal gangs acting under folkloric disguise).

The wolf-man figured as the subject of several medieval literary texts, the most famous of which was the Old French poem *Bisclavet* by Marie de France (ca. 1200). When the hero's wife recognized that the knight Bisclavet changed into a wolf for three days each week, she has his clothing hidden so that he could not become a man again. The king, however, brought the wolf to his court and helped him punish his wife. The werewolf in the anonymous romance *Guillaume de Palerne* (early thirteenth century) was a positive figure, helping other persons several times. Small wonder, as he was the son of the king of Spain transformed by a malignant sorceress.

In perfect synchronicity with the increasing persecution of witches, the old beliefs about werewolves were adapted to demonological models. Once the doctrine of the pact with the Devil became prominent, werewolves brought to trial had to confess to have received their abnormal powers from the Devil. Theologians such as Heinrich Kramer, the author of the *Malleus Maleficarum* (Part II, Question 1, Chap. 8–9), and many others discussed whether the Devil caused real animals to perpetuate those cruelties that were supposedly committed by men and women in animal form, men and women who were in reality lying asleep and dreaming. Or should one rather think that the Devil, appearing in the form of a wolf, committed the crimes the lycanthrope only dreamt of? Or did he only cause an illusion to that effect in the people's mind? The problem was that any real transformation into a wolf had been declared impossible by the unsurpassable authority of St. Augustine.

From the early sixteenth century, records of a considerable number of trials against werewolves have been preserved, the common accusations being slaughter of animals and men, committed in lupine form, and pact with the Devil. An inquisitorial trial held in the diocese of Besançon in 1521 against two werewolves, Pierre Bourgot and Michel Verdung, mentioned by Johann Weyer, is one of the earliest instances, and one of the last seems to have been a trial before a jury of the archbishop of Salzburg in 1720. During the two centuries between these dates, dozens of such trials were carried out; the French judge Henri Boguet boasted of trying several lycanthropes in his *Discours des sorciers* (Discourse on the Execrable Speech of the Witches, 1602). Boguet's Franche-Comté, apparently, was the center of the early modern hunt for werewolves. It is remarkable that no juridical persecution directed against a real wolf has been found, whereas not a few

animal trials have been documented from the thirteenth to the eighteenth century in which dangerous animals, especially pigs, were hanged by secular courts for the homicide of small children. People molested by vermin and parasites regularly sought redress from ecclesiastical courts against noxious pests like cockchafers or mice. In the case of the werewolves, both the religious and the secular authorities could be interested. Though the trials against this kind of delinquents were clearly a special form of witchcraft trials, sometimes even combined with the accusation of participation in the Sabbat, a marked difference consisted in the fact that the accused were nearly all men, although some of the werewolves burned by Boguet were women.

An instance of a case clearly referring to pathological lycanthropy occurred in 1603 when the *Parlement* (sovereign judicial court) of Bordeaux proceeded against a fourteen-year-old shepherd, Jean Grenier, who confessed to using a wolf skin and an ointment when roaming through the woods and hamlets, killing animals and children. Both devices were given to him by a gentleman in black who had marked him. Other werewolves, including his father, accompanied him. Grenier's hands and his way of moving and of eating were described as congruent with that of a wild beast, and what pleased him most was watching wolves. Because he was under adult age, this apparently semi-imbecilic adolescent was not executed but sentenced to lifelong imprisonment in a monastery, where he died in 1610.

More common was the fate of one Peter Stumpf, who changed himself into a wolf through a belt that the Devil had given to him. Having murdered and devoured thirteen children—including his own son—two pregnant women, and many sheep and cows, he was hunted down, tortured, condemned, and executed with exemplary cruelty at Bedburg near Cologne in 1589, together with his lover and a daughter with whom he had had incestuous relations. This is an example of a werewolf confession by a man tortured on suspicion of multiple homicides. Generally recurrent patterns were the following: The transmutation was effected through magic formulas, an ointment, a skin, a shirt, a belt, a drink, all provided by the Devil; often the magic worked only for a certain time; there was some connection with the phases of the moon. The gravest crimes committed were the slaughter of men and animals and cannibalism. If such a being received a wound while a wolf, it appeared on the very same part of his human body.

Especially in the sixteenth century, the werewolf, or rather certain "historical" werewolves, became the subject of artistic treatment in the manner of handbills, the most famous example being a woodcut of 1512 by Lucas Cranach the Elder. The eighteenth-century

Enlightenment put an end to the persecution of werewolves, who were henceforth treated as madmen. Nineteenth-century romantic literature was full of such creatures, and in the twentieth century a number of films were produced about them.

PETER DINZELBACHER

See Also: ANIMALISTIC AND MAGICAL THINKING; ANIMALS; AUGUSTINE, ST.; BOGUET, HENRI; FRANCHE-COMTÉ; MAGNUS, OLAUS: *MALLEUS MALEFICARUM;* METAMORPHOSIS; WEYER, JOHANN.

References and further reading:
Dinzelbacher, Peter. 2002. "Animal Trials: A Multidisciplinary Approach." *Journal of Interdisciplinary History* 32, no. 3: 405–421.

Douglas, Adam. 1992. *The Beast Within: A History of the Werewolf.* New York: Avon Books.

Dunn, C. W. 1980. *The Foundling and the Werewolf: A Literary History of Guillaume de Palerne.* Toronto: University of Toronto Press.

Edwards. Kathryn A. 2002. *Werewolves, Witches, and Wandering Saints: Traditional Belief and Folklore in Early Modern Europe.* Kirksville, MO: Truman State University Press.

Höfler, Otto. 1973. *Verwandlungskulte, Volkssagen und Mythen.* Vienna: Österreichische Akademie der Wissenschaften.

Lecouteux, Claude. 1992. *Fées, sorcières et loups-garous.* Paris: Imago.

Lorey, Elmar M. 1998. *Heinrich der Werwolf: Eine Geschichte aus der Zeit der Hexenprozesse mit Dokumenten und Analysen.* Frankfurt am Main: Anabas.

MacCulloch, J. A. 1915. "Lycanthropy." Pp. 8:206–220 in *The Encyclopaedia of Religion and Ethics.* Edited by James Hastings. Edinburgh: Clark.

Mandrou, Robert. 1979. *Possession et sorcellerie au XVIIe siècle.* Paris: Fayard. Pp. 33–109.

Odstedt, Ella. 1943. *Varulfen i svensk folktradition: Mit deutscher Zusammenfassung.* Uppsala: Lundequistka Bokhandeln.

Otten, Charlotte F., ed. 1986. *A Lycanthropy Reader: Werewolves in Western Culture.* Syracuse, NY: Syracuse University Press.

Roberts, Keith. 1999. "Eine Werwolf-Formel: Eine kleine Kulturgeschichte des Werwolfs." Pp. 2:565–581 in *Mittelaltermythen.* Edited by Ulrich Müller and Werner Wunderlich. Saint Gall, Switzerland: UVK.

South, Malcolm, ed. 1987. *Mythical and Fabulous Creatures. A Source Book and Research Guide.* New York: Greenwood.

LYNCHING

Illegal witch hunts, or lynchings, are an important yet poorly explored issue. It is difficult to provide sound overall estimates of the relation between legal and illegal executions of witches because official records documented exclusively the actions of secular and the ecclesiastical authorities, and refer to vigilantism only if *post facto* legal action was taken against the murderers. Surprisingly, this problem occurred right at the beginning of Europe's witch hunts, when a man named Gögler was punished for accusing women of witchcraft in Lucerne (Switzerland) in 1419. According to Joseph Hansen, this incident was the first time that the German term for witchcraft—*Hexereye* (*Hexerei*)—appeared in court records. But there certainly were many earlier examples of lynchings of female and male sorcerers. As a general rule, lynchings served as a safety valve in areas where people believed in witchcraft but authorities would not, for whatever reasons (religion, law, laziness, Western rationalism), comply with their demand for persecution.

A number of spectacular lynchings are known from the period before legal witch hunting in Europe. In his famous sermon on hailstorms, Agobard of Lyons reported frequent lynchings of supposed *tempestarii* (witches who raise storms), as well as killings of sorcerers who were held responsible for diseases of livestock in the year 810. According to Agobard, the common people in their fury over crop failure developed the extravagant idea that foreigners were secretly coming with airships to strip crops from their fields and transport them to Magonia (the home of witches). Such anxieties led to severe aggression; on one occasion around 816, Agobard barely prevented a crowd from killing three foreign men and a woman, whom they considered to be Magonians. As their supposed airships and their country's name suggest, crop failures were blamed on magic. Bishop Agobard therefore emphasized that thunderstorms were always caused by natural or divine agencies. His account of the popular backdrop of these stories may have been distorted, since some of its details appear highly unusual for European witchcraft. For example, in 1080 Pope Gregory VII (ruled 1073–1085) admonished King Harald of Denmark not to hold old women and priests responsible for storms and diseases and not to slaughter them. The pope explained that these catastrophes were God's punishment for human sins and that killing innocent people would only increase his fury. No other source confirms these Danish witch hunts, but there is no reason to doubt the contents of this papal letter.

In 1090, a complex situation can be observed in Bavaria with the burning of three women, who had been convicted of harming or poisoning people (*veneficae*) and of having spoiled or destroyed the crops (*perditrices frugum*), presumably by causing hailstorms. According to the Benedictine chronicler of Weihenstephan, only the fact that the nearby bishop's see was vacant, together with related political tensions, enabled the rabble to carry out their persecution. The chronicler considered this procedure as essentially illegal and called the victims "martyrs." Their corpses were recovered and buried by the monks within the walls of the monastery.

The report was sufficiently detailed to reveal that the supposed lynching must have been a rather elaborate procedure. After being captured, the suspected witches first had to undergo an ordeal by water, a swimming test. Unexpectedly, they passed it and could therefore not be executed. Thereafter they were publicly tortured, in order to force them into confessions, again unsuccessfully. The villagers turned next to the nearby episcopal city of Freising, where two men of "high rank," presumably nobles, summoned a public meeting. The women were transferred to Freising and tortured again. Although the suspects still refused to confess, they were carried to the banks of the river and ritually burned to death (Monumenta Germaniae Historica, *Scriptores*, XIII, 52). However illegal the procedure may now appear, the persecutors obviously respected some procedural rules. More important, the authorities remained passive in the face of a grassroots movement.

For the High Middle Ages, our sources are scanty and difficult to interpret. In 1115, for instance, a Styrian chronicle laconically reported that thirty women were burned at Graz in one day (*concrematae sunt triginta mulieres in Greez una die*). Capital punishment for females was highly unusual throughout European history, and burning was restricted to a very few crimes, such as arson, sodomy, counterfeiting, or domestic incest. None of these, however, were typical female crimes; nor were they likely to trigger a large-scale persecution. In cases of heresy, a more even gender distribution could be expected. Witchcraft therefore was a likely candidate for the cause of this mass burning, particularly in conjunction with major subsistence crises or epidemics of "unnatural" diseases. The scarcity of surviving sources suggests that there were some sporadic witch hunts during the High Middle Ages. Given the tensions between popular witch beliefs and the reluctance of the authorities, ecclesiastical or secular, to accept demands for persecution, we would expect acts of lynching rather than legal persecutions, especially in Alpine regions, Scandinavia, or Russia.

In the early modern period, Denmark under King Christian III (ruled 1534–1559) offered the most surprising case of lynching. After a tumultuous period of civil war, territorial expansion, and rapid political, social, and religious reforms, a witch panic—the first one in a Protestant territory—became a major, large-scale persecution. Peasants hunted witches in the open fields "like wolves," as was reported approvingly by Peder Palladius, royal adviser and leading Danish churchman of his age as superintendent of ecclesiastical affairs for Norway, Iceland, and the Faeroe Islands. In Jutland alone, fifty-two women were killed in 1543; lynchings were reported in other parts of Denmark and in Danish-ruled southern Sweden as well. By 1547, the government in Copenhagen tried to curb the persecution through restrictive laws.

Illegal persecutions were not confined to northern Europe. The relative leniency of the Spanish or Roman Inquisitions also led to occasional lynchings. One finds them, for instance, at Reggio Emilia in Italy, where a woman was stoned to death in 1599 after the inquisitors had released her after her public abjuration. In Spain, the same scene was repeated almost a century later, in 1691, in the Canary Islands. Meanwhile, in the "Enlightened" Netherlands, where capital punishment of witches ended sooner than anywhere else in Europe, lynchings took place in Amsterdam in 1624, in Rotterdam in 1628, and in Huizen, a village southeast of Amsterdam, in 1746. In "enlightened" England, a woman was lynched in 1751—five years later than in Huizen.

Lynchings are known from France to Poland, wherever legal systems made it difficult or impossible to punish known witches with death. The famous skepticism of French lawyers and the reluctance of judges in most French *parlements* to confirm death penalties for witchcraft left the rural population dissatisfied and apparently provoked numerous illegal executions, which we now call lynchings. In the 1580s, processions of "White Penitents" in the Ardennes and Champagne triggered massive but often illegal witch hunts. Many similar instances occurred over a wide zone from Languedoc to the Ardennes during the last great French witch panic in the 1640s, when the crime of witchcraft had been virtually "decriminalized" by the *parlements* (sovereign judicial courts). Sometimes sheer cost seems to have triggered such behavior. For example, in the easternmost zone subject to the *Parlement of Paris*, the *Barrois mouvant* (that area in the French sphere of influence in the duchy of Lorraine), from which it was prohibitively expensive to appeal to Paris, sporadic lynchings have been recorded in pardons from the dukes of Lorraine.

Eastern Europe saw much illegal witch hunting. For example, in the parts of Hungary under Ottoman rule, lynchings were the only way of punishing witches, because the Turkish authorities never accepted accusations of witchcraft in the courts. Incidents like the lynching in Wolhynia of a nobleman, who was put to the stake by an agitated rabble, led by the parish priest, because he was blamed for an epidemic, were recorded only because his widow afterward sued the murderers. A Polish historian, Janusz Tazbir, claimed that half of all victims in Poland and the Ukraine were burned in lynchings, although he provided no supporting evidence.

If lynchings occurred in Europe long before witchcraft became a capital crime, one could expect that they did not stop after witchcraft laws were repealed. Previously, Church law had denied the capacity of supposed witches to cause harm, and now secular law did so, in both instances leaving people alone with their misery and fear and punishing those who dared to challenge the authorities. The results were predictable. In England, numerous incidents of swimming witches—the swimming test—illustrated the continuing discrepancy between popular perceptions and legal practices (Davies 1999). In 1808, Cambridgeshire villagers broke into the cottage of Ann Izzard, restrained her husband from protecting her, dragged her out of bed, threw her naked into the yard, scratched her arms with pins, and beat her stomach, breasts, and face with a length of wood. The parish constable refused to help, but a compassionate neighbor, Alice Russel, gave her shelter. On hearing this, the villagers returned, arguing that "the protectors of witches are as bad as a witch and deserve the same treatment" (Davies 1999, 111)—an argument reminiscent of the demonologist Martín Del Rio—and attacked Russel as a harborer of witches; she died a few days later from her wounds. The mob threatened Izzard with ducking, but the fifty-six-year-old woman managed to flee from the village and subsequently sued her attackers. The murderers received short prison sentences, and the constable remained unpunished. In Dorset, a young farmer named John Bird was tried as late as 1871 for severely beating Charlotte Griffin, an eighty-five-year-old woman, with a stick because he believed she was bewitching him and "hag-riding" him at night. A surgeon classified Bird as a "simple, weak-minded, monomaniac," (Davies 1999, 41) but the judge found that Bird acted mainly because he believed in witches. Four years later, Ann Tennant was killed in Warwickshire with a pitchfork because her attacker, James Haywood, believed that she had bewitched him. The killer claimed that he had not intended to kill the old woman but had meant merely "to draw her blood in order to break her power over him" (Davies 1999, 41). On a different occasion he said that he considered it his duty to kill witches and that there were fifteen more in his village. Haywood was charged with murder, but a surgeon considered him insane, and the jury acquitted him on that ground. If all believers in witchcraft had been diagnosed as insane, English asylums would have been overflowing with inmates.

In the United States, witch killings were not confined to the Native Americans. A man and his wife, both citizens of Texas, attributed his incurable disease to Antonia Alanis, a woman in a neighboring village. In February 1860, his father, one of the wealthiest Mexican landowners in the area, hired several men to kidnap the witch. They killed one of her daughters, who was trying to protect her mother, wounded another, "lassoed" the suspected witch, and "dragged her on the ground" (*The Times,* April 17, 1860, 12) toward the village of Camargo (Nueva Villa). There she was kept prisoner for two weeks and repeatedly beaten. Because the bewitched man's health failed to improve, a witch doctor suggested that the witch had to be burned (*The Times,* April 17, 1860, 12). Another lynching was reported from Arkansas, where a widow named Hill had been murdered together with a slave woman and

her house burned down in order to conceal the murder. The *New York Tribune* reported that a slave was forced through severe torture to confess to the murders in November 1859. He was subsequently burned at the stake. But the report strongly suggested that he had indeed been innocent and that the instant execution had been staged to protect the true culprits.

Witch huntings were frequently reported from Mexico and Russia in the second half of the nineteenth century—both countries at the periphery of Western civilization but certainly both independent, or postcolonial and governed by elites educated in the spirit of the Enlightenment. However, among Russian peasants, belief in witchcraft remained strong. Lynchings were mostly linked to crop failures, drought, epidemics, lack of milk, or love magic, particularly around 1880, with four killings recorded in this year alone. These lynchings often included a swimming test, severe beatings, and mutilation of the corpse of the deceased. Although there is no consistent body of sources, researchers have collected over 100 cases of lynchings from ethnographic, juridical, psychiatric, and newspaper reports, reaching from urban areas in the Ukraine to remote rural areas of European Russia. Countermeasures against witchcraft included disinterring the bodies of suspected witches and transporting their dangerous remains to remote forests. The witch craze was fueled by cases of demonic possession (*klikushestvo*), which could be seen as an antiwitchcraft movement, because the aim of the female peasant demoniacs, that is, "shriekers," was to identify witches.

Some recent postcolonial African examples show extreme discrepancies between Western and native perceptions. The South African Witchcraft Suppression Act of 1895, refurbished in 1957 and amended in 1970, seemed completely pointless from an African point of view. Instead of persecuting the evildoers, it prevented their chiefs from handling cases of witchcraft properly, thus damaging their authority. Traditional healers, diviners, or other people who could detect witches were outlawed, and the witches were protected instead. As a consequence, the people took the law into their own hands and started to kill those whom they suspected of having harmed their children or livestock, either secretly or in mob lynchings. Gruesome dimensions were reached in Tanzania, where antiwitchcraft movements had already been active during the colonial period. According to Simeon Mesaki, an anthropologist from the University of Dar es Salaam, between 1970 and 1984 3,692 persons were killed as witches in Tanzania, 69 percent of them female. In this Swahili-speaking country, the Bantu people of Sukuma, living under traditional conditions in the northern provinces of Mwanza and Shinyanga, were particularly affected. With 2,246 witch killings, plus another 826 lynchings between 1985 and 1988, Mesaki offered a grand total of 3,072 from this area between 1970 and 1988 (Mesaki 1994, 52).

Mesaki considered the "witch-killing in Sukumaland" as an indirect result of the villagization program imposed in the 1960s by the socialist government of Julius Kambarage Nyerere (party leader until 1987). However, there are many parallel examples from other parts of sub-Saharan Africa. In the late 1970s, the persecution in the People's Republic of Benin (formerly Dahomey) was linked to a tetanus epidemic, and the witch hunts in Ghana in 1997 accompanied an outbreak of meningitis. Protests by human rights organizations against these lynchings caused the military government of Jerry Rawlings (ruled 1981–2001) to allocate four camps, or "sanctuaries," for the protection of suspected witches in October 1997, presumably following the example of South Africa. Like sub-Saharan Africa, Southeast Asia seems to count among contemporary hotspots of witch hunting. Newspaper reports mentioned mob lynchings in the late 1980s in both Java and Papua New Guinea.

WOLFGANG BEHRINGER

See also: AFRICA (SUB-SAHARAN); AGOBARD OF LYONS; CONTEMPORARY WITCHCRAFT (POST 1800); HANSEN, JOSEPH; LANGUEDOC; PANICS; *PARLEMENT* OF PARIS; POPULAR PERSECUTION; SWIMMING TEST; WEATHER MAGIC.

References and further reading:

Behringer, Wolfgang. 2004. *Witches and Witch Hunts: A Global History.* Cambridge: Polity.

Davies, Owen. 1999. *Witchcraft, Magic and Culture, 1736–1951.* Manchester: Manchester University Press.

Gijswijt-Hofstra, Marijke. 1999. "Witchcraft After the Witch Trials." Pp. 95–189 in *The Eighteenth and Nineteenth Centuries* Vol. 5 of *The Athlone History of Witchcraft and Magic in Europe.* Edited by Bengt Ankarloo and Stuart Clark. London and Philadelphia: Athlone and University of Pennsylvania.

Levack, Brian P. 1999. "The Decline and End of Witchcraft Prosecutions." Pp. 1–93 in *The Eighteenth and Nineteenth Centuries,* Vol. 5 of *The Athlone History of Witchcraft and Magic in Europe.* Edited by Bengt Ankarloo and Stuart Clark. London and Philadelphia: Athlone and University of Pennsylvania.

Mesaki, Simeon. 1994. "Witch-Killings in Sukumaland." Pp. 47–60 in *Witchcraft in Contemporary Tanzania.* Edited by Ray Abrams. Cambridge: African Studies Centre.

Monumenta Germaniae historica. Scriptores rerum Germanicarum. Welmar, Germany. 13:52.

Soman, Alfred. 1986. "Witch Lynching at Juniville." *Natural History* 95: 8–15.

Tazbir, Janusz. 1966. "Z dziejow falszerstw historycznych w Polsce w pierwszej polowie XIX wieku." *Przeglad Historyczny* 57: 580–598.

M

MACFARLANE, ALAN (1941–)

Alan Douglas James Macfarlane's place among witchcraft historians was established in 1970 by his first (and subsequently reissued) book, *Witchcraft in Tudor and Stuart England: A Regional and Comparative Study*, the published version of his Oxford DPhil thesis. This thesis was completed under the supervision of Keith Thomas, who then published his own major work on witchcraft and related beliefs in 1971. Macfarlane has published extensively on both history and anthropology and has, among other things, written works challenging standard interpretations of English historical development. Macfarlane was educated at Worcester College, Oxford, where he earned his BA, MA, and DPhil degrees, subsequently gaining an MPhil at the London School of Economics and a PhD at London University's School of Oriental and African Studies. He subsequently worked at the University of Cambridge, where he has been professor of anthropological sciences since 1991.

Macfarlane's *Witchcraft in Tudor and Stuart England* reestablished witchcraft as a serious topic of study among historians of England and has proved influential among historians of witchcraft more generally. It was a work that entirely changed perceptions of early modern European witchcraft. Its novelty lay in three main directions. First, Macfarlane had worked through all of the main court records for England's most witchcraft-ridden county, Essex. The courts in question included the assizes, which tried most cases of witchcraft, defined as felony by statutes of 1563 and 1604; Essex borough courts; the county Quarter Sessions; and the Essex ecclesiastical courts. These court records, together with a series of pamphlets about Essex witchcraft trials, provided him with a massive body of evidence. Second, on the strength of these materials, he demonstrated that the motivating force for witchcraft accusations lay not in the activities of clergy or judges but rather in disputes between villagers. Most frequently, Macfarlane argued, a witchcraft accusation occurred after a slightly richer villager had turned away a poorer, and usually female, neighbor who had come begging at his door. The woman, possibly with an existing reputation for being a witch, would go away muttering or cursing in her disappointment. If misfortune befell the household of the person refusing charity a little later (for example, the inexplicable death of cattle or illness of a child), that misfortune would be attributed to the suspected witch's malevolence. Macfarlane argued further that this pattern of witchcraft accusations was attributable to changes in the nature of the village community. Population pressure was increasing competition for resources, and the spread of market forces and agrarian capitalism was eroding traditional community values. More particularly, richer villagers were ambivalent in their attitudes toward an ever more numerous poor, a situation that eased as the poor law became an established part of English culture in the seventeenth century. The accuser of the witch thus transferred any guilty feelings about not giving charity by accusing the person to whom he had refused alms of witchcraft. Third, Macfarlane added anthropological insights to historical materials, not least those that interpreted witchcraft in terms of the breaking and reformulating of social relationships.

Macfarlane's thesis can be criticized on a number of levels. He tended, perhaps, to write the elite too much out of his model of accusations. The supposed relationship between witchcraft and socioeconomic change is rendered problematic by the experience of a number of other counties in southeastern England, notably Kent, Surrey, and Middlesex, that underwent essentially the same socioeconomic changes as Essex but experienced massively lower levels of witchcraft accusations. And the applicability of essentially non-Western anthropological models to early modern European witchcraft evidence has been questioned (it is noteworthy that little subsequent work on early modern witchcraft has followed Macfarlane's lead here). Indeed, Macfarlane has retreated from some of the positions he established in 1970, especially those suggesting links between witchcraft accusations and the supposed breakup of the traditional village community. Nevertheless, the originality of his focus on village disputes and interpersonal tensions as the background to witchcraft accusations remains a major conceptual breakthrough that has informed numerous subsequent studies.

JAMES SHARPE

See also: AFRICA (SUB-SAHARAN); ANTHROPOLOGY; ENGLAND; ESSEX; HISTORIOGRAPHY; THOMAS, KEITH; WITCH HUNTS.

References and further reading:
Macfarlane, Alan. 1987. *The Culture of Capitalism.* Oxford: Basil Blackwell: chap. 5, "Evil: the Root of All Evil."
———. 1999. *Witchcraft in Tudor and Stuart England: A Regional and Comparative Analysis.* 1970. London: Routledge and Kegan Paul: reissued with introduction by James Sharpe.

MACHIAVELLIANISM

Machiavellianism was a political doctrine that venerated the power and security of the state, disparaging religion and religious morality except insofar as they proved useful to the state, thus contributing to a perspective that regarded the belief in witchcraft as superstitious nonsense.

The printing revolution created new audiences that the Church could not control and fostered the rise of public opinion. Administrative institutions of emerging European states, such as courts, councils, academies, and universities, provided platforms for discussion and bred new attitudes toward spiritual affairs. Niccolò Machiavelli (1469–1527) saw the full potential of Renaissance politics. His classic *Il Principe* (The Prince), written in 1513 and published posthumously in 1531, reduced religion to an instrument of a rational ruler. In his *Discourses* (also published in 1531), the former Florentine official implied that religion served only to frighten and discipline the populace. The implications of such an attitude marked a paradigm shift, whereby politics moved to the center of history and divine predestination became irrelevant, if not nonexistent. Machiavelli's contemporary, the Paduan philosopher Pietro Pomponazzi, who denied the immortality of the soul and the existence of hell, similarly emphasized the political usefulness of religion for rulers. In such a context, magic and witchcraft were just other inventions, ridiculous to a man of virtue, a rational ruler, or an official who acted from necessity and "reason of state." Machiavelli's books, although put on the Roman Catholic Church's *Index librorum prohibitorum* (Index of Prohibited Books), molded the debate about politics throughout the early modern period. Even in the confessional age of the sixteenth and seventeenth centuries, religious zealots continually complained about Epicureans, Pyrrhonians, libertines, or atheists, usually meaning anyone conspicuously lacking in religious zeal, and displayed a common-sense attitude toward such things as witchcraft.

The antagonism between religious zeal and "politics" was already visible in Italy during Machiavelli's lifetime. The bishop of Brescia triggered a large-scale persecution of witches in the Valcamonica in the summer of 1518. The valley's worldly overlord, the Republic of Venice, stopped the persecution almost as soon as the news arrived. The Council of Ten summoned the inquisitors to Venice, provoking conflict between the republic and Pope Leo X, who tried to protect the authority of his inquisitors. Venetian politicians like Vice-Doge Luca Tron bluntly branded all stories of flying witches as "nonsense," and lesser citizens like the famous diarist Marino Sanudo called the executed people "martyrs." The conflict dragged on for three years, with local inquisitors continuing to capture "witches" and the Venetian government immediately blocking any trials, until July 1521, when the Venetian government finally managed to terminate all trials (Decker 2003, 55–66). By then Italy's leading jurist, Andrea Alciati became the first secular author to brand the witch hunts as a *nova holocausta* (new holocaust) in his essay *De lamiis et strigibus* (On Witches and Evil Spirits). Alciati, inspired by Machiavellianism, indeed invented the almost Durkheimian interpretation that the Inquisition was not fighting witchcraft but was creating the witches instead (see Hansen 1901, 310–312).

It seems unnecessary here to summarize the early modern debates on Machiavelli, who was considered an atheist by theologians of all denominations and could therefore hardly be used officially as a source of interpretation in the confessional age. Admirers of his way of analyzing politics thus resorted to quoting Cornelius Tacitus, whose *Histories* Machiavelli had commented upon in his *Discorsi* (Discourses). This indirect reference to Machiavelli is usually called "Tacitism," a hidden form of Machiavellianism. Meanwhile, religious authors of all confessions condemned any predominantly political decision as inspired by Machiavelli, in contrast to decisions motivated by religious considerations. Around 1600, when the first chairs of politics were established at universities (a consequence of the progressive formation of national bureaucracies), the term *politician* was equated with *Machiavellianism* by religious authors. For Martín Del Rio, himself a former chief prosecutor of the Spanish Netherlands before joining the Jesuit order and becoming a leading demonologist, *politici* were officials and advisers who tried to stop witch hunts for secular or "political" reasons.

Del Rio certainly knew of the contemporary attack on Machiavellianism launched by his fellow Spanish Jesuit Pedro de Ribadeneira (1526–1611). However, in his *Disquisitiones Magicae libiri sex* (Six Books on Investigations into Magic, 1599–1600), Del Rio also referred to debates about witchcraft in Bavaria, where the opponents of witch hunting were called "cold and political Christians" or "politicians." In Counter-Reformation Bavaria, it is striking to see the sharp rift between two parties—zealots and moderates—within the Catholic camp. The same "politicians" who opposed witch hunting domestically also suggested entering negotiations with their Protestant enemies to prevent further bloodshed. The hard-liners, however, whom even Pope Urban VIII labeled *zelanti,* preferred to have their enemies killed first and to make peace afterward. The *politici* employed an Erasmian interpretation of the parable of the wheat and the tares (Matthew 13:29), later adopted by the Jesuits Adam

Tanner and Friedrich Spee, whereas the zealots wished to root out the weeds regardless of the damage, in order to prevent future heresies and crimes and avoid God's vengeance. It seems fair to call their approach radical, because the idea of getting to the root (Latin *radix*) of crime, or heresy, dominated their thinking. The interdependence of their fantasies of eradication and their adherence to radical measures, whether unlimited torture in criminal trials or wars of conquest in foreign policy, linked these ideas with a certain type of religiosity.

In contrast, the politicians sought balanced judgments in the service of their prince and country. Bavaria's politicians were led by such jurists as the chancellor of the privy council, Dr. Johann Georg Herwarth von Hohenburg (1553–1626), who was succeeded by his ally Dr. Joachim Donnersberger (1565–1650). Both came from urban patrician backgrounds, Donnersberger from the Bavarian capital of Munich and Herwarth from the imperial city of Augsburg. Both had received a solid academic education at foreign universities, a doctorate in France or Italy, and had practiced law at the *Reichskammergericht* (imperial chamber court). The Herwarths were a banking dynasty, with Protestant branches in Augsburg, France, and England, and the Catholic branch had entered princely service in Bavaria, eventually joining the landed nobility and becoming leaders of the Bavarian parliament. Herwarth recruited able officials from the Bavarian high nobility as well as members of the imperial aristocracy, including the Hohenzollern and Wolkeinstein dynasties. Herwarth personified an open Catholicism, keeping international contacts even beyond confessional boundaries. These "cold and political Christians" managed to end Bavarian persecution and launched a political debate instead.

Machiavellianism played an important role throughout Europe during the period of witch hunting and, for obvious reasons, frequently encountered the burning issue of witchcraft as an extreme symbol of religiously inspired policy. Beyond Italy, it was France where secular policy developed first; for example, Guillaume Farel equated Machiavellism, libertinism, and Epicureanism (Schneider 1970, 105). We must understand Jean Bodin's attacks against Epicureans, skeptics, and Pyrrhonists in these terms. Clearly the insult "politique" emerged to censure those, like Chancellor Michel de l'Hôpital, who shunned religious radicalism (either Catholic or Huguenot) during the French Wars of Religion, following the maxim that peace with two religions was preferable to war with none. After a generation of civil war, religious radicalism became more discredited in France than anywhere else in Europe. Clearly the strongest opponents of witch hunting in France are to be sought among "libertines" like Gabriel Naudé, the defender of accused sorcerers (Naudé 1625).

In England, similar conflicts emerged during and after the Civil War, when a high-ranking member of the Royal Society, Joseph Glanvill, defended the existence of witchcraft. Even before a last series of witchcraft trials occurred under heavy popular pressure in the early 1680s, several intellectuals, embarrassed by Glanvill's equating disbelief in witchcraft with atheism, attacked him harshly. Aggressive rebuttals came from John Wagstaffe, who sailed in the waters of Machiavellian and Hobbesian atheism. Suddenly it was no longer the question of witchcraft alone that was being debated, but a much wider issue: religion. More credibly, John Webster, a Nonconformist chaplain in the Civil War, and later a physician, attacked Glanvill for attempting to "defend these false, absurd, impossible, impious and bloody opinions" (Webster 1677, 36).

Ironically, those considered godless by Christian theologians—Machiavellians, libertines, atheists—were moderate in their attitudes toward unnecessary bloodshed, whereas ardent supporters of confessional orthodoxies were responsible for the worst persecutions. But in western Europe the witch hunts faded or were forcibly stopped as the powers of the central governments increased. France was, of course, the model case, where political centralization successfully suffocated not only popular unrest but also popular witch hunting. French *parlements* usually controlled their districts tightly, and the *Parlement* of Paris upheld few death penalties after 1625. Louis XIV (ruled 1643–1715) brought these executions to an end by royal decree in 1682. By and large, France mirrored general European developments, somewhere in the middle ground.

All over western Europe, executions of witches petered out in the 1680s, in England as well as Denmark, Norway, and Iceland; in the formerly panic- stricken duchies of Holstein and Mecklenburg; in all of northern Germany; in the Swedish realm in the Baltic; in the Spanish Netherlands; and in the Rhineland and the Saar region, where particularly fierce hunts had been common only decades before. National, regional, or parochial historians offered tales of local heroes—professors, theologians, lawyers, or princes—successfully fighting the sea of superstition. However, the executions even stopped in places without a single hero. A new generation of politicians, educated at the same universities—whether Catholic or Protestant—and usually raised in the spirit of Cartesian rationalism, suppressed any attempt at witch hunting, if necessary by sending in troops, an instrument of power their predecessors had lacked. With the rise of nation-states, "reason of state" replaced religious zeal. However, the term *politician* retained connotations of Machiavellianism, still visible in works by other authors on witchcraft like Christian Thomasius or even in the articles in Johann Heinrich Zedler's *Universal-Lexicon* in the mid-eighteenth century.

WOLFGANG BEHRINGER

See also: ALCIATI, ANDREA; BAVARIA, DUCHY OF; DECLINE OF THE WITCH HUNTS; DEL RIO, MARTÍN; ERASMOS, DESIDERIOUS; GLANVILL, JOSEPH; HOBBES, THOMAS; *PARLEMENT* OF PARIS; POMPONAZZI, PIETRO; SKEPTICISM; SPEE, FRIEDRICH; TANNER, ADAM; THOMASIUS, CHRISTIAN; WAGSTAFFE, JOHN; WARS OF RELIGION (FRANCE); WEBSTER, JOHN.

References and further reading:

Behringer, Wolfgang. 2004. *Witches and Witch Hunts: A Global History.* Cambridge: Polity.

Bireley, Robert. 1990. *The Counter-Reformation Prince: Anti-Machiavellianism or Catholic Statecraft in Early Modern Europe.* Chapel Hill: University of North Carolina Press.

Clark, Stuart. 1996. *Thinking with Demons. The Idea of Witchcraft in Early Modern Europe.* Oxford: Clarendon.

Decker, Rainer. 2003. *Die Päpste und die Hexen.* Darmstadt: Wissenschaftliche Buchgesellschaft.

Del Rio, Martín. 1599–1600. *Disquisitiones Magicarum libri sex.* Lourain.

Glanvill, Joseph. 1665. *Some Philosophical Considerations Touching the Being of Witches and Witchcraft.* London.

———. 1681. *Sadducismus Triumphatus, or Full and Plain Evidence Concerning Witches and Apparitions.* London.

Hansen, Joseph, ed. 1963. *Quellen und Untersuchungen zur Geschichte des Hexenwahns und der Hexenverfolgungen im Mittelalter.* Bonn: C. Georgi. 1901. Reprint, Hildesheim: Georg Olms.

Hunter, Michael, and David Wootton, eds. 1992. *Atheism from the Reformation to the Enlightenment.* Oxford and New York: Oxford University Press.

Naudé, Gabriel. 1625. *Apologie pour tous les grands personnages, qui ont esté sopconnez de magie.* Paris. Translated as *The History of Magic by Way of Apology for All the Wise Men Who Have Unjustly Been Reputed Magicians.* London, 1657.

Pomponazzi, Pietro. 1925. *De immortalitate animae* [1516]. Messina: Giuseppe Principato.

Schneider, Gerhard. 1970. *Der Libertin.* Stuttgart: J. B. Metzler.

Stolleis, Michael. 1988. *Geschichte des öffentlichen Rechts in Deutschland, Erster Band: Reichspublicistik und Policeywissenschaft, 1600–1800.* Munich: C. H. Beck.

Thomasius, Christian. 1701. *De Crimine Magiae.* Halle.

———. 1712. *Disputatio Juris Canonici de Origine ac Progressu Processus Inquisitorii contra Sagas.* Halle.

Wagstaffe, John. 1669. *The Question of Witchcraft Debated: Or a Discourse Against Their Opinion That Affirm Witches.* London.

Webster, John. 1677. *The Displaying of Supposed Witchcraft.* London.

Wootton, David. 1984. "The Fear of God in Early Modern Political Theory." Pp. 56–80 in *Canadian Historical Association: Historical Papers 1983.* Ottawa: Canadian Historical Association.

Zedler, Johann Heinrich, ed. 1732–1750. *Grosses vollständiges Universal-Lexicon aller Wissenschaften und Künste.* 64 vols. Halle: J. H. Zedler.

MACKENZIE, SIR GEORGE (CA. 1636–1691)

As lord advocate of Scotland, Sir George Mackenzie of Rosehaugh played a crucial role in the decline of Scottish witch hunting. Sometimes called "Bloody Mackenzie" for his relentless persecution of the Presbyterian Covenanters, Mackenzie was far more sympathetic to accused witches. More than anyone else, he was responsible for the decline in the number of witchcraft convictions and executions in Scotland during the late seventeenth century.

Mackenzie's initial involvement in witchcraft trials occurred during the large Scottish witch hunt of 1661–1662, when he was appointed to serve as a judge at a number of trials in Midlothian and East Lothian. This hunt was marked by a great many procedural abuses, including the pricking and torturing of witches by local authorities. Mackenzie made frequent references to these trials in his writings, and it is likely this experience shaped his conviction that only trained judges should try witches. In *The Laws and Customs of Scotland in Matters Criminal* (1678), he objected that many witches were tried by "country men" who received conciliar or parliamentary commissions to try witches in the localities. He also attacked the trade of the prickers who were employed to locate the Devil's mark as a "horrid cheat" (Mackenzie 1678, 90–91).

Mackenzie served as an advocate in the High Court of Justiciary during the 1670s and in 1677 was appointed lord advocate, a position he held until 1686. In this capacity he secured a number of acquittals of accused witches. In 1680, for example, he directed the acquittal of Bessie Gibb, mainly on the grounds that the magistrates and the bailie of the burgh of Bo'ness who had proceeded against her were not competent to try her. Mackenzie was likewise critical of the use of torture in Scottish witchcraft trials. Upon his recommendation in 1680, five witches whose confessions were shown to have been the product of several types of torture were set at liberty. Mackenzie did not object to torture as such: he defended his own use of the practice in treason trials on the basis of reason of state and claimed that its use was authorized by the law of nations. But he insisted that its use be restricted to the Privy Council and the justice general (who presided over the Justiciary Court, the central court at Edinburgh), a policy similar to that declared by the *Parlement* of Paris in 1624.

Mackenzie apparently harbored no doubts regarding the existence of witches. He introduced the section on witchcraft in *Laws and Customs* by responding to the sixteenth-century skeptic Johann Weyer, whom he referred to as "that great patron of witchcraft" (Mackenzie 1678, 81). Mackenzie claimed that witches should suffer death, not just for poisoning and murder but also for "enchanting and deluding the world." Even charmers, who served as healers, were in his eyes guilty of at least apostasy and heresy. Nevertheless, he claimed that witches were not so numerous as in the past, and as an advocate and judge he tended to doubt the validity of the charges brought against most witches. This judicial skepticism underlay his demand for adherence to due process and the use of caution in the trial of witches. He would accept confessions only if they were in no way extorted, if they contained nothing that was impossible or improbable, and if the person confessing was neither melancholic nor suicidal. His skepticism was particularly apparent when he defended the accused witch Maevia before the High Court of Justiciary during the 1670s. In this pleading, he argued that acts of maleficent magic could only be proved by either confession or the testimony of two respectable eyewitnesses. He also insisted that diseases could not be said to have been inflicted by magical means just because those diseases had no known natural causes.

In defending Maevia, Mackenzie relied heavily upon Scripture and the works of theologians to support his client's cause. He made an eloquent statement of the Protestant belief in the sovereignty of God, citing scriptural passages regarding Jesus's casting out of the Devil and asked rhetorically how God could have allowed Satan "to reign like a Sovereign, as our fabulous representations would now persuade us" (Mackenzie 1672, 185). In discrediting the belief in witches' flight, he invoked the authority of the *Canon Episcopi,* St. Augustine, and even the Jesuit Martín Del Rio, insisting that flight, like metamorphosis, was the product of illusion. These citations were calculated to disarm his critics and ward off charges of atheism, but they also reveal how critics of the trials could use religious arguments to reinforce their positions.

BRIAN P. LEVACK

See also: ACQUITTALS; *CANON EPISCOPI;* CONFESSIONS; DECLINE OF THE WITCH HUNTS; DEVIL'S MARK; FLIGHT OF WITCHES; PRICKING OF SUSPECTED WITCHES; SCOTLAND; SKEPTICISM; TORTURE; TRIALS; WEYER, JOHANN; WITCH HUNTS.

References and further reading:
Lang Andrew. 1909. *Sir George Mackenzie: King's Advocate, of Rosehaugh: His Life and Times 1636(?)–1691.* London: Longman, Green.
Levack, Brian P. 2002a. "Judicial Torture in Scotland During the Age of Mackenzie." Pp. 185–198 in *Miscellany Four.* Edited by Hector L. MacQueen. Edinburgh: Stair Society.
———. 2002b. "The Decline and End of Scottish Witch-Hunting." Pp. 166–181 in *The Scottish Witch-Hunt in Context.* Edited by Julian Goodare. Manchester: Manchester University Press.
Mackenzie, Sir George. 1672. *Pleadings in Some Remarkable Cases.* Edinburgh: George Swintoun.
———. 1678. *The Laws and Customs of Scotland in Matters Criminal.* Edinburgh: George Swintoun.

MAFFEI, SCIPIONE (1675–1755)

An Italian skeptic about witchcraft and an Enlightenment thinker, born into a noble family of Verona, Maffei is probably best known as the editor of the periodical *Giornale de Letterati d'Italia* (Journal of the Literati of Italy). His life was filled with wide-ranging activities. He devoted several years to archaeological investigations and artistic studies, including poetry; he also joined the Bavarian army and participated in a battle. Following contemporary aristocratic fashion, he traveled around the European continent seeking antiques for his collections. Like his contemporary, Voltaire, he was a famous playwright who was also fascinated by scientific research.

Maffei engaged in empirical research and read widely; his interests reached from philology to natural science and from archaeology to tragedy to magic. Jonathan Israel called Maffei called "one of the chief heralds of the Venetian Enlightenment" (*Radical Enlightenment* 2001, 142); his rich correspondence reveals various sides of the Italian and European Enlightenment. Maffei's eclectic approach to culture typified Italy's emerging Enlightenment, that had as its main concerns the discovery, encouragement, publication, and advancement of rational scholarship. After composing short essays on various scientific topics, Maffei wrote about the causes of lightning (*Della formazione dei fulmini;* or On the Formation of Lightning) in 1747. Meanwhile, he engaged in religious controversy, defending the Jesuit point of view against the Jansenists in 1742 with his *Theological History of the Doctrines and Opinions Expressed by the Church on Divine Grace, Free Will and Predestination.*

Before analyzing his polemics against superstition and magic between 1749 and 1754, it seems useful to recall that Maffei engaged in controversies among scholars and historians on many different subjects. For example, he argued about history with Montesquieu and debated tragedy with Voltaire. Maffei's polemical talents were also displayed in three works against magic. The first, *Arte magica dileguata* (Magical Arts Vanished, 1749), argued mainly against Girolamo Tartarotti (whom Maffei appreciated, as did Ludovico Muratori). Maffei contested Tartarotti's main assertions about the definition and reality of demonic magic; he claimed that fourteen other authors had also opposed its existence. The second, *Arte magica distrutta* (Magical Arts Destroyed, 1750), was written under a pseudonym to defend his previous work. The third, *Arte magica annichilata* (Magical Arts Annihilated, 1754) refuted accusations of heresy by Tartarotti and others. His polemic against Tartarotti went beyond the witches' Sabbat (or *congresso notturno*) to attack the whole theory. Maffei denied the existence of both witchcraft and magic because both were impossible in nature. Maffei also rejected any apparent proof from scriptural sources, stressing the deep diversity of practices described there. According to Henry Charles Lea (1957: III, p. 1449), he overcame Johann Weyer's inconsistencies by asserting that, even before Jesus, there was no magic and no witchcraft. Maffei defined all such evidence as fables and ridiculed anyone who defended their reality. No sane intellect can believe in magic or witchcraft, he claimed; all "miracles" can be explained by natural laws. Maffei claimed that Pliny the Elder, to him the most important ancient author, rejected magic on the basis of his philosophical theories rather than because of atheism, as Tartarotti asserted. But when Maffei tried to persuade his opponents to reject tales of magic and witchcraft found in ancient sources, they charged him with impiety.

Maffei was anxious to provide plausible natural explanations for all supernatural phenomena. Rejecting any moderate position about magic and witchcraft, he employed skeptical arguments and offered natural explanations in pursuit of a scientific theory. Maffei was particularly acute in denouncing supposedly rational judgments that were shaped as orthodox. Hidden fables, as he showed in surveying both scriptural and literary sources, were utterly unreliable. His position was original for his time and place.

MICHAELA VALENTE

See also: ENLIGHTENMENT; MIRACLES; MURATORI, LUDOVICO; SKEPTICISM; TARTAROTTI, GIROLAMO; VOLTAIRE; WEYER, JOHANN.

References and further reading:
Ferrone, Vincenzo. 1995. *The Intellectual Roots of the Italian Enlightenment: Newtonian Science, Religion, and Politics in the Early Eighteenth Century.* Atlantic Highlands, NJ: Humanities Press.
Israel, Jonathan. 2001. *Radical Enlightenment: Philosophy and the Making of Modernity, 1650–1750.* Oxford: Oxford University Press.
Lea, Henry Charles. 1957. *Materials Toward a History of Witchcraft.* Edited by Arthur C. Howland. 3 vols. New York and London: Thomas Yoseloff.
Maffei, Scipione. 1749. *Arte magica dileguata: Lettera . . . al padre Innocente Ansaldi.* Verona.
———. 1750. *Arte magica distrutta risposta di don Antonio Fiorio veronese arciprete di Tignale, e Valvestino, vicario foraneo.* Trent: G. A. Brunati.
———. 1754. *Arte magica annichilata.* Verona: Antonio Andreoni.
Parinetto, Luciano. 1998. *I lumi e le streghe: Una polemica italiana intorno al 1750.* Paterno: Dugnano.
Romagnoli, Gian Paolo, ed. 1998. *Scipione Maffei nell'Europa del Settecento.* Verona: Consorzio editori veneti.

MAGIC AND RELIGION

Both the words *magic* and *religion* are products of a specific process of historical development within a specific culture, and attempts to employ them as generalized categories of human activity have generated increasing controversy. The word *magic* has proved particularly problematic because of its negative moral connotations. The common assumption that magic represents a binary opposite to religion, a practice in which spirits can be coerced, whereas religion more modestly supplicates its god(s), has been found inadequate because not all religions involve a conscious deity, and even when they do, the line between coercion and supplication is difficult to discern or is even explicitly crossed.

Such difficulties have led many scholars to focus on elucidating the words' specific meanings in the circumstances in which they were employed. Although this solution threatens to leave us with no vocabulary for discussing phenomena that, however ill-defined, are generally acknowledged to be more or less universal, this approach seems justified in the current context because the "Western tradition" is the culture from which these words derived their meanings and within which the opposition between them was defined. Furthermore, the latest chapter in the relationship between them in the Western tradition is the social sciences' attempt to formulate them as generalized categories of human activity and apply them to other cultures—an approach that ultimately leads back to the issue of their general applicability.

Even within Western tradition, definitions of magic and religion pose difficulties because both concepts changed over time and have meant different things to different groups in society. In order to proceed with this entry, minimal definitions will be required as a basis for the following discussion of their specific development. Here, *magic* will signify the manipulation of spirits and occult forces to produce material effects, whereas *religion* involves the worship of god(s) and obedience to their moral instructions with the hope of gaining material rewards and a favorable situation in the afterlife. It should be noted that although these definitions preserve the Western tradition's formal polarization of magic and religion, the ambiguity and overlap between the concepts of manipulation and worship open up the possibility of magical practices within religion, which in fact frequently occurred.

JUDAISM, PAGANISM, AND MAGIC

One root of the Western distinction between magic and religion and of their antagonism was the Hebrew God's insistence that his people worship only him. The Hebrew Bible contains numerous prohibitions of divination and other activities presumed to involve other gods and spirits, which are often interpreted as a repudiation of magic. However, the Bible also contains stories of Hebrew priests producing magical effects in competition with foreign magicians in order to demonstrate the superior power of their god, and the Hebrew people from the lowest to the highest levels of society engaged in prophesy, divination, exorcism, incantations, cursing, protective spells, use of amulets, oaths, and ordeals similar to the magic forbidden by the Bible. The religious authorities accepted these practices so long as their acknowledged source of power was Yahweh and they did not compromise the priests' dominance of the community's spiritual life. Similar magical or folk-religious practices persisted in Jewish popular culture through the Middle Ages into modern times, and the learned mystical tradition embracing Merkavah and Kabbalah was open to magical influences as well. Both the folk and the mystical traditions existed at the edge of Jewish orthodoxy, always in danger of straying from monotheism or of presuming too much power, so their existence only added ambiguity to, instead of undercutting, the biblical injunctions against magic.

The other root of the Western distinction between magic and religion, and the specific root of the term *magic*, lies in Greco-Roman culture. Specifically, the English word "magic" derives from the Latin *magia*, borrowed from the Greek *mageia*, which itself came from the Persian *magu*, or priest. The Persian term entered Greek as *mago* around the time of the Persian Wars as an insult associating Greeks who practiced magical arts like healing or belonged to ecstatic cults with hostile foreigners. The term *mageia* came into common use during the Hellenistic period and was adopted by the Romans during the last century B.C.E. Although not always used in a derogatory way originally, over time magic's negative connotations became fixed, gradually increasing both cultural opprobrium and legal restrictions. As with the Hebrew proscription of magic, the Greco-Roman denigration did not imply denial of its power, although the potential of fraud was noted, nor did it amount to a repudiation of its practices and beliefs, which were quite similar to those of official religion. Instead, the issue was the danger that unregulated spiritual activity was perceived to pose to the community. The earliest Greek condemnations concerned the disruption it threatened to introduce into the community's relationship to its gods, whereas the Romans were concerned with its potential damage to private citizens' health and property, the way it empowered women and thereby undercut patriarchy, and, later, its potential to damage imperial authority.

Not all magicians accepted this intensifying vilification. Philosophers interested in magic, Neoplatonists in particular, called their practices *theurgy*, differentiating them from lesser traditions called *goetia*. They argued that magic and prayer alike work through the natural sympathetic bonds that permeate the universe and emphasized the extent to which magic operates through occult natural processes, thereby beginning a tradition known as "natural magic." At its extreme, their concept of magic resembled a form of mysticism. However, by the time they developed their theories, their main opposition no longer came from traditional pagan religions but instead from a new creed, Christianity, which would prove far more hostile to magic.

MAGIC AND CHRISTIANITY

Christianity inherited Judaism's rejection of magic, but Jesus, the early Apostles, and Christian saints also followed Hebrew tradition by producing magical effects, and the Christian sacraments had magical connotations as well. The resolution of this paradox was to assert that magical effects produced by Christian actions were miracles, manifestations of God's power freely exercised, whereas magic depended on evoking the power of demons. The concept of demons was derived from both Greco-Roman *daimones*, spirits that could be good, bad, or indifferent, and that played a significant role in magic, and Jewish demons, who were inherently bad spirits (angels were good ones) that undermined God and harmed humans. Early Christianity associated demons with Satan, who acquired increased prominence as the leader of God's enemies, and turned magicians into the Devil's foot soldiers.

While this process of demonization increased the moral menace posed by magic, Christianity simultaneously argued against its practical threat. The difference between miracles and magic was not simply that miracles were good and magic was bad but also that miracles were genuine and magic was false. For centuries, some pagan philosophies had questioned the efficacy of magic, attributing its effects to fraud, illusion, and natural processes, but Christians, who believed in miracles, denied its efficacy on different grounds. Like the Jews, they considered their God to be omnipotent: therefore he, and only he, could contravene the laws of nature. Borrowing arguments from the pagan philosophers, they emphasized the extent to which magic relied on natural processes, illusion, and fraud and argued that any additional power demons had was granted them by God.

These two intertwined themes—that magic involves the idolatrous worship of evil demons and that its power is ultimately illusory—were developed in late antiquity and reiterated and elaborated down through the Middle Ages. However, their exact implications were subject to changing interpretations, and the balance between them shifted as well. Focusing on the demonic basis of magic could heighten the threat it posed, whereas emphasizing its illusory nature could diminish its importance. However, just because magic often involved natural processes and trickery and demons deceived people into thinking they, not God, had power, did not mean magic could not harm people: it was perfectly possible to see magic as both illusory and dangerous. Similarly, the demonic element could be seen as either a purely moral issue (idolatry) to be punished with penance or excommunication, rather than as a public danger requiring criminal prosecution and secular punishment. Thus, in late antiquity, Christian emperors, influenced by the clergy's desire to expurgate paganism and confident in their own power, made all practice of magic a capital offense. In the Early Middle Ages, in contrast, St. Boniface declared belief in witches and werewolves to be un-Christian, and the *Canon Episcopi* condemned the belief of some women that they flew at night on the backs of animals with the goddess Diana as an illusion and punished it with penance. Such variations in emphasis reflect not only changing intellectual fashions but also the worldly power available to Christian authorities: when the opportunity permitted it, they readily suppressed magic by force as well as decrying it as vain; where secular rule was weak, they simply disparaged it and punished its practitioners with penance.

Even with the might of the Roman Empire at their disposal, the Christians could not expunge magic or magicians from their midst. By the time the western empire fell, they had largely succeeded in eradicating formal pagan cults, but they were far less successful in eliminating magic from popular culture. Furthermore, the conversion of the Germans, while similarly eliminating formal pagan opposition, was even less successful at the popular level, because in the process of conversion, Christian missionaries pragmatically tried to win acceptance by superimposing their religion on existing forms as much as possible. To some extent, Christian clergymen took over magical roles previously played by pagan priests, like blessing fields and animals, and to a much greater extent they simply continued time-honored practices after purging them of explicit paganism. For its part, the European populace gradually accommodated its traditions to the new creed, substituting God, Jesus, the Virgin Mary, and the saints for pagan deities in their spells and Christian symbols for pagan signs in their charms. This process introduced significant changes into both popular magic and Christianity. Because popular magic was amorphous and routinely adapted to and adopted from other spiritual systems, whereas Christianity was more rigid, these changes created a disjunction between formal doctrines and accepted rituals and actual beliefs and practices. The resulting tensions remained latent for centuries but eventually came to a head when secular power reached levels that made their resolution seem practicable.

Before that day of reckoning, though, new elements entered the mix in the High Middle Ages, when the importation of Arabic scholarship and revival of classical learning prompted a revival of learned natural magic. This system claimed to avoid demonic agency by manipulating hidden forces of nature rather than spirits. Alchemy and astrology, in particular, lent themselves to this interpretation, and generations of learned magicians from the twelfth-century Renaissance through the Neoplatonic movement in the High Renaissance to the early Scientific Revolution in the seventeenth century dreamed that they could gain acceptance in the Christian community. They pointed to the value of their arts in revealing the secrets of nature and argued that their cultivation would lead to a fuller understanding of the Christian God.

Unfortunately, natural magic posited that the universe is an organic, living whole bound together and permeated by an incorporeal spirit that seemed suspiciously close to a god. Furthermore, a certain amount of natural magic involved invocation of spirits that, despite the magicians' protestations that they were neutral, almost mechanical connectors in the celestial system, sounded much like demons to the uninitiated. The Christian community already had a variety of less dubious means of approaching its God and understanding nature and an array of specialists engaged in them. Theologians therefore reiterated that any invocation of spirits was idolatry, that there were no good or neutral demons, that no form of magic leads to knowledge of God or the Holy Spirit, and that there is a fundamental difference between miracles and magic. For several centuries, natural magic enjoyed general acceptance as a body of knowledge within natural philosophy concerned with hidden processes in nature, but it never gained general acceptance as a set of practices or as a legitimate source of more general wisdom or approach to God.

The refutation of natural magic's religious claims formed one part of a much larger process by which medieval Christianity rationalized its beliefs, the intellectual movement known as Scholasticism that systematized ideas about the supernatural dimension of evil into the demonology that underlay the early modern persecution of witches. Belief in the immanent operation of a hierarchy of demons working against the Christian community under the overall dominion of the Devil became an integral part of late medieval culture even as it became more aware of the disparity between approved and actual beliefs and practices. Not just malevolent witches, who were thought to be primarily women, but all practitioners of magic, no matter how beneficent their activities or high-minded their intentions, were perceived as human agents of this dangerous diabolic conspiracy. Even among the elite, only a minority followed this reasoning to its logical conclusion, so at the height of the witch persecutions, local healers and learned astrologers and alchemists continued to practice, and ordinary people continued to employ a vast array of magical remedies and protections, but nevertheless, the demonological paradigm shaped law codes, informed jurists and magistrates, inspired artists and writers, frightened ordinary peasants and townspeople, gave malicious or vengeful people a weapon against anyone (particularly women) who could plausibly be accused of magic, and forced everyone (and again particularly women) to be more conscious of gaps between the dictates of their religion and their actual beliefs and practices. The witch persecutions reflected a number of trends and tensions in European society: one of the most important was the desire, inherited from late antiquity, to purge the culture of magic and society of its various practitioners.

Even as the early modern witch persecutions got underway, Europe was rent by the Protestant Reformation, which affected the relationship between religion and magic in several important ways. To begin with, by replacing the Church, with its sacraments, saints, and good works, with individual faith as the key to salvation, Protestantism heightened the importance of the purity of each individual's beliefs and practices. It became more problematic for Christians to go to a cunning woman on Thursday and church on Sunday if they could not just confess and do penance in between. Second, just as Protestantism eliminated the spiritual hierarchy that mediated between the individual and God, so too it reduced the importance of demons in magic in favor of the direct involvement of the Devil, strengthening the connection between magic and evil. Third, the religious conflict intensified the scrutiny of popular practices on both sides of the confessional divide, as Protestants and Catholics competed in their zeal to prove their spiritual superiority. Finally, by denigrating Catholicism as rife with magical rituals and doctrines and minimizing its own magical elements, Protestantism codified the division between religion and magic. Some Protestant sects tried to eliminate all traces of magic, regarding rituals as symbolic only, consigning miracles to biblical times, and disparaging any claims of miraculous processes or supernatural effects in the present as rank magic no different from the pretenses of marketplace charlatans.

The decline of the witch persecutions in the seventeenth century involved another shift in the relationship of Christianity to magic. Faced with the disorder and injustices the witch persecutions created and perhaps reacting to their success in curbing if not eliminating magical practices, Europe's civil and, somewhat more reluctantly, its religious authorities gradually abandoned their concern about the danger posed by the Devil and malevolent magicians and placed increasing stress on the illusory nature of magic, both in terms of its efficacy and of its ultimate cause. While maintaining the theoretical possibility of magical effects and the Devil's involvement in human affairs, they increasingly questioned the likelihood of magic having caused harm in any particular instance, and they emphasized that since the Devil is subservient to God, any power he or his servants manifest is a sign of God's displeasure and should lead people to scrutinize their own consciences rather than punish the apparent perpetrators. They still opposed magical practices, but now (again) for their impiety and fraudulent claims. Without abandoning their fundamental belief in magic and the reality of the Devil, they shifted emphasis away from the danger they posed to their illusory nature—this time not because they lacked the power to combat them forcefully, but rather because they realized that they had too much of it.

MAGIC, RELIGION, SCIENCE, AND THE SOCIAL SCIENCES

As the witch persecutions ended because of a shift of emphasis within the traditional framework bequeathed by antiquity, the relationship between magic and religion soon began to be affected by a radically new factor, the rising importance of science and, particularly, the new mechanical philosophy. Recent research has shown that the traditional Whig interpretation of the rising scientific worldview as the implacable foe of magic contains considerable oversimplification, for natural magic was an integral part of the natural philosophy out of which science emerged and played a role in scientific thought well into the eighteenth century. However, mechanical philosophy rejected the notions of occult causation, spiritual agency, and an organic unity to the physical universe, putting it at odds not only with magic but with Christianity as well. To some extent, this common opponent pushed magic and religion together, so, for example, defenders of witchcraft beliefs argued that denial of witches' magical powers and the Devil's immanence logically undercut other supernatural beliefs more central to Christianity, like miracles, angels, and the afterlife. Religion enjoyed the protection of powerful social patrons, though, whereas magic was a social orphan, so Enlightenment thinkers could rebut and lampoon magical beliefs far more openly and caustically than they could religious ones. Disbelief in magic (though not in religion) became a sociocultural marker of membership in the intellectual elite, and social pressure, class snobbery, and sycophantism played at least as great a role as experimentation and reasoned argument in the ultimate triumph of science. The *philosophes* used the vulnerability of magic, which Christianity had done so much to create, not only to deprecate magic but also to attack religion indirectly. Theologians generally responded to this scientific assault by de-emphasizing the magical aspects of religion and highlighting its moral message. During the eighteenth century magic disappeared entirely from learned discourse, and Christianity lost its central place in intellectual life, relegated to the role of metaphorical narrative and ethical adviser.

Rumors of the death of God and assumptions about the end of magic have proved greatly exaggerated: belief in the reality and power of both survived education, ridicule, and repression (in the case of magic) in popular culture, and both have revived in recent decades—even, in the New Age movement, together. Nevertheless, what intellectuals contested in the eighteenth century, their descendents in the nineteenth and twentieth centuries assumed they had won, and so they turned from scientific debates about the reality of magic to social-scientific explanations of magical and religious beliefs. Individual belief in magic and religious enthusiasm were pathologized by the emergent discipline of psychology, and psychologists competed with philosophers, historians, sociologists, and anthropologists in constructing sociocultural theories to explain magico-religious thinking's long hold on human consciousness and to celebrate its eventual demise. Nineteenth-century theorists like Auguste Comte, G. W. F. Hegel, and Karl Marx pioneered an etic approach to the problem, proposing grand narratives in which different formulations of magic, religion, and science formed succeeding stages in the evolution of human cognition linked to the development of material civilization. Somewhat later, Max Weber championed a more emic approach that insisted on the need to understand what peoples' religious beliefs meant to them, and, in opposition to Marx, pointed to the ways they could shape the development of socioeconomic structures.

By the late twentieth century, at least eight major interpretive approaches had emerged, which have been termed the intellectualist, the emotionalist, the phenomenological, the structural-functional, the symbolic, the structuralist, the feminist, and the cognitive (Cunningham 1999).

The intellectualist interpretation (whose exponents include Herbert Spencer, E. B. Tyler, J. B. Frazer, and a number of British anthropologists since World War II) regards magical and religious thinking as prescientific attempts to explain otherwise inexplicable phenomena and magical and religious rituals as attempts to influence otherwise uncontrollable processes. Early intellectualists distinguished magic from religion as different stages in the evolution of conceptualization, whereas later ones were more concerned with the relationship of both to science. The emotionalist approach (exemplified by R. R. Marett, Sigmund Freud, and Bronislaw Malinowski) explains both magical and religious beliefs as ways of coping with stressful emotions, whether the frustration caused by an inability to control an important situation, long-repressed infantile conflicts, or the need to express feelings generated by significant life events. The phenomenological approach (including Rudolf Otto, Karl Jung, and Mircea Eliade) seeks to study the contents of consciousness as people experience them, with Otto treating the transition from magic to religion not as a product of material development but as a widening of the range of human feelings, whereas Jung and Eliade treat magic and religion as a unitary set of symbols either inherited or recognized in nature that represent and help resolve critical life events and foster psychological development.

Although these three schools of thought have made contributions that have been assimilated into the current understanding of magic and religion, the mainstream of contemporary thought focuses on their relationship to the larger society and culture. The first such approach, structural-functionalism, began with Emile Durkheim's insistence that social phenomena be explained in social rather than psychological terms. He applied that idea to religion by saying it symbolizes social structures in a way that serves as a general classificatory system linking individual consciousness, social relations, and the larger environment and that integrates society by reaffirming social identity. Durkheim paid less attention to magic because he felt it was distinguished by its private intent and secret execution from religion's public purpose and open practice and therefore revealed relatively little about the larger social reality. Following Durkheim's sociological approach, Marcel Mauss, his nephew, actually first worked out this distinction between religion and magic. A. R. Radcliffe-Brown took the tradition in another direction, opposing any distinction between religion and magic and focusing on the relationship between their rituals and other aspects of society, an approach that became the norm among anthropologists in the mid-twentieth century. Radcliffe-Brown's student E. E. Evans-Pritchard continued to link religious forms to social structure but broadened his approach to include the idea that the Africans he studied utilized two modes of thought, mystical and empirical, in explaining events and reacting to them, for he found that structural-functionalist explanations clarified only limited aspects of his subjects' magico-religious beliefs.

Evans-Pritchard's theory about two complementary modes of thought echoed the ideas of Lucien Levy-Bruhl, who first proposed an evolutionary schema involving a progression from primitive mystical consciousness into modern rational thought but later modified it to the notion that the two modes of understanding coexist. Because of his focus on the content of thought, as opposed to the process of thinking, Levy-Bruhl was an early exemplar of the symbolist approach in anthropology. From this point of view, structural-functionalism's portrayal of religion as an expression of social structure is just one possible type of symbolization. Anthropologists like Mary Douglas, J. H. M. Beattie, Victor Turner, Arnold Van Gennep, and Clifford Geertz broadened symbolic interpretations to include the ways that the rituals and beliefs of magic and religion symbolize basic biological and psychological processes, social transitions, and the cosmic order. They also emphasized that symbol systems can actually shape the social order. The anthropologist S. J. Tambiah has gone one step further by approaching magic as a rhetorical art in which performative acts and utterances do not just symbolize or guide but actually constitute transferences of (social) qualities and changes of (social) state.

Tambiah's focus on magico-religious symbolism as a form of performative rhetoric is rooted in semiotics, the science of symbol systems, which is the basis for the approach called structuralism. Primarily associated with Claude Levi-Strauss but also including Edmund Leach and Maurice Godelier, it approaches culture from the point of view of Saussurean linguistics, treating it as a set of communications systems exemplified by language in which the relationship of symbols to each other is paramount. Leach's early work was characterized by a particularly direct reliance on linguistic structuralism, but Levi-Strauss put more emphasis on the unconscious structures of the human mind, and Godelier attempted to synthesize structuralism's focus on culture and language with Marxism's concern for socioeconomic realities. Following Marx's repudiation of religion as the "opium of the people," Godelier regarded religion and magic as inextricably linked, with religion an illusory explanatory system and magic an imaginary method for causing effects. Levi-Strauss also regarded magic and religion as complementary, although in very different terms: he posited that religion involves treating physical reality as if it has human characteristics, whereas magic involves treating human ritual actions as if they have a direct connection to physical reality. Lesch, in contrast, came to question whether words like *religion* and *magic* can be used to discuss cultures that do not include cognates, and has expressed doubts whether *magic* in particular has any meaning at all.

Feminist interpretations of magic and religion focus on the links between gender, power, and the legitimacy of spiritual activity. Because religions since antiquity have been patriarchal, both in their conceptualizations of spiritual reality and in their secular structures, women have tended to be particularly linked to magic, the illicit, or at least unofficial, practice of spirituality. Furthermore, because men dominated scholarship on this topic until the 1980s, early theories about religion and magic overlooked the role of and the impact on women. Feminist scholars in a variety of disciplines have worked to correct this imbalance, with a historian of religion like Ross Shepard Kraemer, for example, critiquing classicists' traditional reliance on male-centered sources when studying Greco-Roman religion; the anthropologist Julia Kristeva critiquing anthropology for its neglect of matriarchal Neolithic religions and the process of repression by which patriarchal cults supplanted them; and the theologian and philosopher Mary Daly launching a much broader attack on patriarchal religion as part of a broader critique of patriarchal institutions generally.

Finally, the cognitive approach has developed from dissatisfaction with Saussurean assumptions about the workings of the human mind, in particular, the reliance on semiotics and privileging of linguistics. Instead of seeing meaning as coming from the relationship between signs, it adopts generative linguistics' focus on the relationship between deep structures rooted in the brain and their specific manifestations in speech. Furthermore, it rejects the assumption that language determines people's perception of reality, instead treating language as one of several specialized mental processes that structure perception and mentation. For example, Dan Sperber argues that symbolism is a mechanism for handling irregular types of information that makes use of a specialized cognitive process separate from language that interacts with perceptual and conceptual mechanisms in constructing knowledge and consolidating memories. E. Thomas Lawson and Robert McCauley have focused more specifically on religious and magical ritual, arguing that specific rituals are surface manifestations of three underlying cognitive mechanisms. Pascal Boyar argues that many ideas about magical causation and the resultant ritual actions are relatively mundane consequences of the normal functioning of our system for making inferences, while Patrick McNamara suggests that perception of the hidden workings of spirits, gods, or karma is triggered by our mechanisms for detecting intentionality and the subsequent application of our "theory of mind." What these last two theories, in particular, indicate is that magico-religious beliefs may stem not from some malfunction of the nervous system but from its regular functioning. We repeat things associated with success, avoid things associated with failure, and deal with the world on the assumption that it is sentient, because in a dangerous world it is safer to treat something as smart that is not than vice versa.

One final approach goes beyond cognitive psychology to explore the physiology of trance states and mystical communion. For example, the recent research of Eugene d'Aquili and Andrew Newburg has found that if either the sympathetic (arousing) or the parasympathetic (quieting) nervous system is pushed too far, it activates the other, and this simultaneous activation of the two opposing systems results in an ecstatic state and the suppression of the brain center that maintains our awareness of the border between ourselves and the external world. This, in their estimation, accounts for the sensation of mystical communion, and it can be achieved, as experience suggests, by either an overload or prolonged deprivation of activity and sensory stimulation. A different approach to trance states has been pursued by Michael Winkelman, who has connected the physiological, psychological, and anthropological dimensions of shamanistic healing to develop a rich understanding of how that form of magic works. Finally, in an older set of studies, d'Aquili and another set of collaborators focused on the effects of rhythmic group rituals on their participants, arguing that they "tune" the participants' nervous systems to common neural rhythms, inducing group harmony to facilitate collective action or promote intramural accord. This concept of "tuning" the nervous system seems to hold particular promise for expanding our understanding of religion and magic, suggesting that ritual actions, incantations, fasting, hallucinogenic drugs, meditation, and similar practices provide an array of techniques for physiologically "tuning" our processes of perception and cognition so that we apprehend and interact with the world in different and, in different contexts, useful ways.

More generally, the physiological and cognitive approaches together suggest that although the distinction between magic and religion may be an artifact of the historical development of the Western tradition, and specific magico-religious practices and beliefs are manifestations of specific cultures, the terms refer not simply to cultural constructs, but rather to cultural constructs built upon the common foundations of more basic human processes and experiences.

EDWARD BEVER

See also: ANGELS; ANTHROPOLOGY; BIBLE; *CANON EPISCOPI;* CLERICAL MAGIC; DEMONOLOGY; DEMONS; DEVIL; DOUGLAS, MARY; ENLIGHTENMENT; EVANS-PRITCHARD, EDWARD E.; FREUD, SIGMUND; IDOLATRY; INVOCATIONS; JESUS; JEWS, WITCHCRAFT, AND MAGIC; KABBALAH; MAGIC, LEARNED; MAGIC, NATURAL; MAGIC, POPULAR; MALINOWSKY, BRONISLAW KASPER; MECHANICAL PHILOSOPHY; MIRACLES; OCCULT; PROTESTANT REFORMATION; ROMAN CATHOLIC CHURCH; SCIENCE AND MAGIC; SHAMANISM.

References and further reading:
Ankarloo, Bengt, and Stuart Clark, eds. 1999–2002. *The Athlone History of Witchcraft and Magic in Europe.* 6 vols. London and Philadelphia: Athlone and University of Pennsylvania Press.
Boyer, Pascal. 2001. *Religion Explained: The Evolutionary Origins of Religious Thought.* New York: Basic Books.
Clark, Stuart. 1997. *Thinking with Demons: The Idea of Witchcraft in Early Modern Europe.* Oxford: Clarendon.
Cunningham, Graham. 1999. *Religion and Magic: Approaches and Theories.* New York: New York University Press.
D'Aquili, Eugene G., et al. 1979. *The Spectrum of Ritual: A Biogenetic Structural Analysis.* New York: Columbia University Press.
Flint, Valerie. 1991. *The Rise of Magic in Early Modern Europe.* Princeton, NJ: Princeton University Press.
Glucklick, Ariel. 1997. *The End of Magic.* New York: Oxford University Press.
Janowitz, Naomi. 2002. *Icons of Power: Ritual Practices in Late Antiquity.* University Park: Pennsylvania State University Press.
Kieckhefer, Richard. 2000. *Magic in the Middle Ages.* Cambridge: Cambridge University Press.
Levack, Brian. 1995. *The Witch-Hunt in Early Modern Europe.* 2nd ed. London: Longman.
Luck, George. 2003. *Ancient Pathways and Hidden Pursuits: Religion, Morals, and Magic in the Ancient World.* Ann Arbor: University of Michigan Press.
McNamara, Patrick. 2001. "Religion and the Frontal Lobes." Pp. 237–256 in *Religion in Mind: Cognitive Perspectives on Religious Beliefs, Ritual, and Experience.* Edited by Jensine Andresen. Cambridge: Cambridge University Press.
Neusner, Jacob, et al. 1989. *Religion, Science, and Magic in Concert and in Conflict.* Oxford: Oxford University Press.
Newberg, Andrew, Eugene G. d'Aquili, and Vince Rause. 2001. *Why God Won't Go Away: Brain Science and the Biology of Belief.* New York: Ballantine.
Noegel, Scott, et al. 2003. *Prayer, Magic, and the Stars in the Ancient World.* University Park: Pennsylvania State University Press.
Peters, Edward. 1978. *The Magician, the Witch, and the Law.* Philadelphia: University of Pennsylvania Press.
Styers, Randall. 2004. *Making Magic: Religion, Magic, and Science in the Modern World.* Oxford: Oxford University Press.
Thomas, Keith. 1971. *Religion and the Decline of Magic.* New York: Schribner's.
Trachtenberg, Joshua. 1977. *Jewish Magic and Superstition: A Study in Folk Religion.* New York: Atheneum.
Winkelman, Michael. 2000. *Shamanism: The Neural Ecology of Consciousness and Healing.* London: Bergin and Garvey.

MAGIC CIRCLE

A sacred space creating a physical barrier to the environment within which many magical rites, such as invocations of demons and other similar ceremonies, are performed is called a magic circle.

Embodying wholeness, perfection, and unity, the circle had not only magical but also universal religious significance. Remnants of cult circles, not unlike the well-known Stonehenge, exist throughout the world, proving their ancient origins. Circular forms were used in old Babylonian magic. Medieval and Renaissance ceremonial magicians employed them; Rembrandt van Rijn's famous etching of Dr. Faustus shows the scholar focusing on a magical circle on the ground, which is reflected in the window panes. Some American Indian tribes or, for that matter, today's Wiccans, have used magic circles, but for different reasons.

ANCIENT AND MEDIEVAL MAGIC CIRCLES

To summon an angel, a spirit, or a demon, a magician generally requires a magic circle. The German monk Caesarius of Heisterbach, a rich source for both learned and folk magic, included a story in his *Dialogus Miraculorum* (Dialogue on Miracles, ca. 1225) about a knight who denied that demons exist and was dramatically refuted by a monk, who drew a magic circle and conjured demons. In his *Autobiography,* Benevenuto Cellini vividly described experiencing a similar episode in the Roman Colosseum in the 1520s.

Handbooks of ceremonial magic from late antiquity to the present dealt repeatedly with the matter, although the form of the circle was not invariable and almost every *grimoire* showed a different form of magic circle. The well-known, widely adapted, and relatively ancient *Key of Solomon* described the essential clothing and requirements (knife, rings, scepter, fire, parchment, ink) needed to create a properly equipped magical circle from which an operator might safely evoke a demon. As the book instructed, the circle had to be 9 feet in diameter and traced with the consecrated knife. Four pentacles were to be engraved with the names of the Creator, inscribed with the same knife. The characters inscribed in the circle were Greek and Hebrew; the formula "alpha–omega," the first and last letters of the Greek alphabet, had to be repeated several times.

Johann Georg Faust invoking a demon while inside a magic circle. (Stapleton Collection/Corbis)

A few other examples show how more recent imitators have twisted this formula. The *grimoire Le Dragon rouge* (Red Dragon), supposedly dating from 1522 but originally printed in 1822, called the circle the "Triangle of the Pacts." It had to be made with the skin of a kid lamb nailed with four nails, and the triangle within the circle had to be traced with an enameled stone. *The Magus,* published in London in 1801 by Francis Barrett, who attempted to renew occultism in England, instructed the operator to engrave the letters *alpha* and *omega* and various divine names. His pentacles inscribed within the circles contained mostly Hebrew names and formulas.

MAGICAL CIRCLES IN NEOPAGAN RITUALS

In much of Wicca today, a circle becomes a sacred space to meet the gods and goddesses. Human mental energy creates the circle, which restricts negative energy and spirits. The circle, usually 9 feet in diameter, simply marks the point where the sphere touches the earth (or floor) and continues beneath. Some kind of marking is often placed on the ground to show where the circle bisects the earth: a cord laid in roughly circular shape, a lightly drawn circle of chalk, or objects (even tarot cards) showing its outlines. Details like knives and pentacles recall Solomon's ancient key.

CHRISTA TUCZAY

See also: CONTEMPORARY WITCHCRAFT (POST 1800); DEMONS; FAUST, JOHANN GEORG; *GRIMOIRES;* INVOCATIONS; RITUAL MAGIC.

References and further reading:

Butler, E. M. 1949. *Ritual Magic.* Cambridge: Cambridge University Press.

Fanger, Claire, ed. 1998. *Conjuring Spirits: Texts and Traditions of Medieval Ritual Magic.* University Park: Pennsylvania State University Press.

Guiley, Rosemary Ellen. 1989. *The Encyclopedia of Witches and Witchcraft.* New York and Oxford: Facts on File.

Luhrmann, T. M. 1989. *Persuasions of the Witch's Craft: Ritual Magic in Contemporary England.* Cambridge, MA: Harvard University Press.

Pearson, Joanne Elizabeth. 2000. *Religion and the Return of Magic. Wicca as Esoteric Spirituality.* Lancaster: University of Lancaster.

Thorndike, Lynn. 1923. *The First Thirteen Centuries.* Vol. 2 of *The History of Magic and Experimental Sciences.* New York: Columbia University Press.

Waite, Arthur Edward. 1969. *The Book of Ceremonial Magic.* 1911. London: Rider. Reprint, New York: Bell Publishing.

MAGIC, LEARNED

Since the Early Middle Ages, European culture has contained a tradition of literate or "learned" magic as well as the orally transmitted traditions of "popular" magic. The two differed both in their content as well as their mode of transmission, but they were connected by a reciprocal exchange of influences. Furthermore, like popular magic, learned magic encompassed a number of disparate traditions. Although written texts were fewer and more interconnected than the innumerable local and regional popular traditions, they were more widely accessible, particularly after the invention of the printing press in the late Middle Ages brought a quantum jump in the availability of texts. The printing press also accelerated the interaction between learned and popular traditions, gradually merging them to the point at which they are barely distinguishable today.

The roots of the learned tradition lay in antiquity, with magical techniques and theories transmitted directly through a small number of texts preserved in the European provinces of the western Roman Empire and indirectly through a much larger number of texts preserved and elaborated on in Byzantine, Arab, and Jewish cultures, which western Europeans increasingly encountered in the High and late Middle Ages. During the Renaissance, learned magic reached a high point in the Neoplatonic movement, which saw "natural" magic, or knowledge of the hidden forces of nature, as a route not simply to power but also to transcendent knowledge, comparable in many ways to religious mysticism. At the same time, western European learned magic descended into necromancy, or the deliberate summoning of demons through complex esoteric rituals, which contributed significantly to fears of a conspiracy of diabolic magicians that motivated early modern witch persecutions. Such fears put a significant damper on open involvement with many forms of learned magic, especially those involving spirits as opposed to occult natural mechanisms. Forms of the latter, like astrology and alchemy, continued to be practiced openly through the early modern period, and popular magical practitioners utilized books drawn from the learned tradition with increasing frequency, but in elite circles, open involvement with spiritual magic virtually disappeared. Covert practices probably declined as well, given the dangers involved, but some residual activity appears to have remained. In the nineteenth and twentieth centuries, the open practice of learned magic revived and evolved, mixing with non-Western traditions, popular practices, mysticism, and fringe science to form the magico-religious New Age movement.

ROOTS OF EUROPEAN LEARNED MAGIC

Early medieval culture, including magic, combined two basic influences: the traditions of the Germanic peoples who overran much of the western Roman Empire and the traditions of the "Romans" themselves, that is, the earlier inhabitants of the late western empire. Germanic traditions were almost exclusively oral and affected early medieval popular culture more than they did the learned culture. Much of Roman culture was also oral, but two of its strands were written and became the basis of medieval learned culture: the texts of pagan writers and of the Judeo-Christian tradition.

Of the two, pagan writers contributed more substantially to early medieval learned magic. The Bible, of course, confirmed the existence and power of magical forces, chiefly in the form of miracles, and some late Roman Christian commentators recorded some magical practices with evident approval. In general, though, the Judeo-Christian tradition, from the Hebrew Bible to the late-Roman Church Fathers, disparaged the apparent power of magic as illusory and warned its adherents to shun such practices as deliberate or implicit trafficking with demons. A few pagan authors similarly disputed the power of magic, but the vast majority accepted the existence of hidden, or occult, forces that directly influenced the material world. They recorded some of the wide variety of beliefs and practices held across the Mediterranean world, including both simple popular practices and complex learned systems like astrology. Proponents of philosophically grounded systems typically valued their magic as far superior to the mundane practices of village healers and marketplace fortunetellers, theurgy as opposed to goetia, which anticipated the divide between learned and popular magic in later European culture. The pagan writers whose writings influenced learned medieval magic included not only philosophers, historians, and others who intended to record and evaluate actual magical practices but also poets and storytellers whose fictional accounts (whether or not they reflected actual beliefs and practices) were accepted as real during the Middle Ages.

EARLY MEDIEVAL LEARNED MAGIC

Only a small number of texts survived the collapse of the Roman Empire in the west, so no coherent system of learned magic was preserved there. The few miscellaneous surviving works containing knowledge of magic were consulted, and through use, their knowledge gradually diffused into popular culture. They were supplemented by a growing body of texts recording popular practices, often mixed with classical knowledge, so rather than forming a distinct tradition, the surviving texts contributed a learned component to what has been called the "common tradition" of medieval magic, which included healing, divination, talismans, love magic, and sorcery (Kieckhefer 2000, 56).

With the twelfth-century Renaissance, this situation changed. Growing contact with the Byzantine and especially the Arab world introduced educated Europeans to increasingly specialized knowledge, including complex and sophisticated forms of magic rooted in antiquity and further elaborated over the intervening centuries. These techniques required highly developed literacy and mathematical skills, and they were grounded in Aristotelian physics, Ptolemaic astronomy, and Galenic medicine. In particular, astrology (fortune telling based on the relative positions of the stars), astral magic (harnessing the power thought to emanate from the heavens), and alchemy (transmuting one element into another, particularly, changing base metals into gold) all required intensive study of texts, careful calculations, and, in the last case, elaborate equipment. Later, practice of the Jewish magical and mystical tradition known as the Kabbalah required a precise knowledge of Hebrew, and necromancy, the conjuring of spirits, involved complex rituals following elaborate written scripts. Such arts both influenced and were influenced by popular practices, but each of these traditions constituted an intricate, autonomous system. Together, their content as well as their mode of transmission made them a separate variety of magic, distinct from the popular traditions practiced in innumerable European localities.

APOGEE OF LEARNED MAGIC: THE RENAISSANCE

The high point of learned magic undoubtedly came during the Renaissance, when a group of humanists revived Neoplatonism and linked it to writings ascribed to a mythical ancient *magus,* Hermes Trismegistus. Neoplatonism, founded by the philosopher Plotinus in the third century C.E., held that a network of natural sympathetic bonds connects all things in the universe and can be manipulated through complex rituals. The Hermetic writings were thought to go back to ancient Egypt but were actually a collection of second- and third-century-C.E. Greek treatises on philosophy, astronomy, alchemy, and magic. The leaders of the Renaissance movement included Marsilio Ficino, who translated Hermetic manuscripts and wrote original works on astrological medicine and astral magic, and Giovanni Francesco Pico della Mirandola, who went to Rome and set forth for public debate 900 theses that asserted the underlying compatibility of all religions, defended the value of Neoplatonic magic as a means of understanding the inner workings of nature, and claimed to have found a higher and more potent form

of magic in the Jewish Kabbalah, in which the magician, speaking God's own language (Hebrew), can gain both wisdom and power. For Renaissance magi such as Ficino and Pico, magic was a quasi-mystical way to approach God.

Such Renaissance magi practiced and publicized their magic in the face of Christianity's traditional hostility to any supernatural phenomenon beyond the miracles ascribed to God and subsumed within the doctrine and rituals of the Church. They argued that their magic was fundamentally different from the magical practices that the Church opposed. These had traditionally relied on spirits, conscious incorporeal entities, which in Christian doctrine could only be agents of God, angels, or demons (agents of the Devil); and, because God's supernatural work was generally done through the Church, any independent operator working through nonapproved spiritual channels was almost certainly working consciously or unconsciously with demons. However, the tradition in which these Renaissance magi worked styled itself as "natural magic" or the "occult sciences," the study and manipulation of hidden natural forces. This concept of magic dated from the introduction of the learned magical systems during the twelfth-century Renaissance; it was one aspect of that much larger reintroduction of classical knowledge, particularly natural philosophy. While conceiving the universe as an organic, living whole permeated and bound together by incorporeal spirit, natural magic de-emphasized the role of individual conscious spirits in favor of a more mechanistic concept of the occult dimension of nature. To the extent that Renaissance magi still invoked spirits, they insisted that they were not demonic and could be manipulated like any other natural phenomenon, without recourse to a diabolical pact. Natural magic was, in their estimation, the alternative to demonic magic and hence was perfectly compatible with Christianity. Ficino, in particular, attempted to fuse Christianity and magic in what he called "Platonic theology."

NECROMANCY AND THE PROSCRIPTION OF WITCHCRAFT

Although natural magic won widespread acceptance as the branch of natural philosophy that dealt with hidden processes in nature, learned magicians still faced formidable obstacles in their broader quest to gain legitimacy for their practices. One barrier was the Church's deeply rooted suspicion of any heterodox spiritual system. Another was the fact that, as the learned magicians had to admit, their beliefs and practices were closely related to other forms of magic that were malign or even explicitly demonic, some of which also belonged to the learned tradition—particularly necromancy, which originally meant divination by conjuring the spirits of the dead but had come to mean conjuring spirits, including demons, for any magical purpose. Necromancy, which involved complex rituals contained in illicit books, enjoyed considerable popularity in the late Middle Ages, especially in an underworld on the fringe of clerical and courtly circles. Many necromantic rituals appealed specifically for God's permission, and most necromancers probably rationalized their activities as within the bounds of Christian behavior, but many of their rituals were unquestionably performed for destructive or exploitative ends, and some explicitly invoked evil spirits.

The witch persecutions that began in the late Middle Ages and climaxed in the early modern period stemmed from multiple causes, but one was surely the actual practice of necromancy by members of the educated elite. A good number of the late medieval sorcery trials that contributed to the growth of witch fears and the consolidation of belief in a conspiracy of Devil-worshipping evil magicians involved people who had actually practiced harmful magic. Necromancy was particularly important, both because it tended to be practiced by people with the wealth to buy books and the education to read them and because it made the link between malefic magic and diabolism particularly clear. Not only did it involve the explicit invocation of demons, but also it often made illicit use of Christian symbols, prayers, and rites in the process. Furthermore, at times, necromancy was practiced by small groups of people, supporting the notion that evil magicians met in secret. There is no evidence that necromancers formed a widespread underground conspiracy that had renounced God and signed on with the Devil, but their actual beliefs and practices helped make fears about such a sect plausible.

LEARNED MAGIC, WITCHCRAFT PERSECUTIONS, AND THE SCIENTIFIC REVOLUTION

Necromancy was not the only way that learned magic contributed to witchcraft beliefs, for learned magicians participated vigorously in the sixteenth-century debate about witchcraft. Several voiced skepticism about the notion that witchcraft was a diabolic counterreligion of malevolent magicians, like Cornelius Agrippa, who defended a peasant woman accused of witchcraft in 1519 and who reportedly called witchcraft a delusion and a dream; Paracelsus, Girolamo Cardano, and Jean-Baptiste Van Helmont all tried to explain witches' powers in nondemonic terms. After a "witch" let him observe her anointing herself with a mixture (which he described), then fell into a profound sleep and upon awakening, claimed to have flown away, Giambattista Della Porta argued that witches' flights to Sabbats were hallucinogenic dreams. Of course, all of them accepted that magic could work, and their opposition to witch beliefs was at most conditional. Other learned magicians, like Johannes Trithemius, denounced witches and

witchcraft as vehemently as any demonologist, whereas Johann Weyer, who had once been Agrippa's assistant, coupled skepticism about witchcraft and defense of accused witches with a harsh condemnation of learned magicians! In the end, the position each took probably mattered less than their collective contribution to the sheer volume of discussions of witchcraft, for quibbles about the source and extent of witches' powers or the nature of their congress with the Devil mattered less in the late sixteenth and early seventeenth centuries than the apparent consensus that some people had given themselves over to the Devil and sought to harm others by practicing *maleficium* (harmful magic).

Weyer's attack on learned magicians was echoed by numerous demonologists, who denounced their activities as frequently as they denounced their popular counterparts, insisting that their magic probably involved demons, whatever the magicians claimed about natural magic, and arguing that even if it did not, it was still irreligious and probably fraudulent. In this age, even benign magic, although less serious than witchcraft, was still subject to penalties like fines, incarceration, and banishment, and there was always a chance that it could lead to an accusation of witchcraft. Consequently, being known as a learned magician became increasingly dangerous during the sixteenth century, and the number of prominent men who identified themselves as such appears to have declined significantly during the height of the witch persecutions from 1550 to 1650. Astrologers and, to a lesser extent, alchemists continued to practice, for their occult arts clearly involved natural forces, and local cunning folk and provincial wizards continued to offer their services, increasingly furtively, but learned magicians practicing the invocation of spirits had largely disappeared from the European stage by the seventeenth century. Nostradamus, for example, insisted that he was not a magician and claimed he had burned his magic books even as he cultivated a European-wide reputation for prophesying. Similarly, John Dee insisted that he was not a magician even as he studied the occult arts and employed scryers to communicate with spirits in hopes of attaining transcendent insights. In all probability, a few individuals on the fringes of upper-class society secretly practiced learned magic, hoping to harness occult powers for their own or their clients' purposes, but they kept a low profile and have left few traces.

Although natural magicians disappeared rather abruptly from the European scene, natural magic did not. As a body of explanations about the more obscure workings of the physical world, it held a respected place in natural philosophy. Natural magic played a role in all medieval philosophies of nature and continued to do so in the professional activities and conceptual schemes of many early modern scientists. Both William Gilbert and Van Helmont took magic very seriously, and

Johannes Kepler and Galileo Galilei cast horoscopes professionally. Kepler was deeply influenced by Hermeticism and Neoplatonism, and his research on planetary motion was encouraged by his faith in the existence of a magical geometry of the planets and a unifying spirit in the universe. Isaac Newton studied alchemy as well as optics, and his greatest achievement, the universal laws of gravitation, involved the acceptance of an essentially occult force in nature, gravity. However, because natural magic was so closely integrated into medieval natural philosophy, its explanatory power declined as science changed. Astrology, for example, had been explained in terms of Aristotelian cosmology, and the idea of occult influences on health and disease fit with Galenic medicine, but the magical systems lost their intellectual underpinnings as venerable scientific systems fell out of favor. Furthermore, the most vehement advocates of the new mechanical philosophy objected to any notion of action at a distance, so even though gravitation and magnetism made this position impossible to sustain in the long run, in the short run, mechanical philosophers argued strenuously against magical notions like the physical power of sympathy and antipathy or the ability of the heavens to directly influence human affairs. More fundamentally, and perhaps most importantly, the magical notion of a purposive universe held together by conscious forces ultimately could not be reconciled with the new scientific conception of an inanimate universe governed by mechanical processes.

LEARNED MAGIC AFTER THE WITCH PERSECUTIONS

Except for astrology, the practice of learned magic languished in Europe for the better part of two centuries, from the mid-1600s to the mid-1800s. The devout regarded it as irreligious if not diabolical; scientists rejected it as they embraced the new mechanical philosophy; the *philosophes* ridiculed it; and the upper classes in general adopted disbelief as a cultural marker distinguishing themselves from the common herd. Popular practitioners now used books, including texts adapted from learned magical traditions, but it is uncertain how many indulged in the more complex and arcane rituals. Whatever they did, like whatever isolated members of the elite did, was furtive and left few traces. A few famous eighteenth-century figures like Emanuel Swedenborg and Franz Anton Mesmer are sometimes considered magicians, but Swedenborg was a mystic who did not practice magic, whereas Mesmer combined modern technology and magnetic instruments with instinctive showmanship rather than practicing any esoteric tradition. Figures like Casanova and "Count Cagliostro" were merely adventurers and charlatans who used magic to perpetrate conscious frauds. Of course, their ability to perpetrate frauds demonstrates the continuing attraction of magical beliefs, even for a significant portion of the elite. It seems certain that some people read surviving treatises on learned magic and attempted to practice what they read, but learned magic had been pushed to the outermost margins of European intellectual life by the combination of religious disapproval, intellectual disregard, and social disdain.

The open and serious practice of learned magic only revived in the middle of the nineteenth century, when Alphonse Louis Constant began publishing books on learned magic under the pseudonym of Eliphaz Levi and quickly gathered a circle of disciples and pupils. This revival gained momentum when it was institutionalized in a number of secret societies modeled on Freemasonry, which was at that point already well over a century old. The first of these, the Societas Rosicruciana, was founded in 1866 to study the Kabbalah, the Hermetic texts, and other ancient traditions. It was soon followed by the Theosophical Society, which started in 1875 and focused on introducing non-Western esoteric traditions to Europe and the United States. The process culminated in 1888 with the founding of the Hermetic Order of the Golden Dawn, which had the express purpose of practicing the magic that such older groups were merely studying. In the following decades, books about the practice of venerable magical traditions spread gradually, stimulated by a series of charismatic magicians like Aleister Crowley and George Ivanovitch Gurdjieff and supported by attempts to study occult phenomena scientifically that appeared to confirm their existence. However, their following and impact remained limited until the passing of the Fraudulent Mediums Act that eliminated witchcraft from British law in 1951 and the rise of the psychedelic "counterculture" in the late 1960s opened the floodgates to widespread incorporation of a variety of magical traditions, including those that had made up European learned magic, into the New Age culture that involves a range of magical practitioners and whose books comprise a section of virtually every contemporary bookstore.

EDWARD BEVER

See also: AGRIPPA VON NETTESHEIM, HEINRICH CORNELIUS; ALCHEMY; APULEIUS OF MADAURA; ASTROLOGY; CARDANO, GIROLAMO; CONTEMPORARY WITCHCRAFT (POST 1800); DEE, JOHN; DELLA PORTA, GIAMBATTISTA; DEMONOLOGY; ENLIGHTENMENT; FAUST, JOHANN GEORG; HERMETICISM; INVOCATIONS; KABBALAH; KEPLER, JOHANNES; MAGIC, NATURAL; MAGIC, POPULAR; MECHANICAL PHILOSOPHY; MEDICINE AND MEDICAL THEORY; NECROMANCY; OCCULT; PARACELSUS, THEOPHRASTUS BOMBASTUS VON HOHENHEIM; RITUAL MAGIC; SCIENCE AND MAGIC; SKEPTICISM; SYMPATHY; THORNDIKE, LYNN; TRITHEMIUS, JOHANNES; WEYER, JOHANN.

References and further reading:
Ankarloo, Bengt, and Stuart Clark, eds. 1999–2002. *The Athlone History of Witchcraft and Magic in Europe.* 6 vols. London and Philadelphia: Athlone and University of Pennsylvania Press.

Clark, Stuart. 1997. *Thinking with Demons: The Idea of Witchcraft in Early Modern Europe.* Oxford: Clarendon.

Evans, R. J. W. 1973. *Rudolf II and His World: A Study in Intellectual History, 1576–1612.* Oxford: Oxford University Press.

Fanger, Claire, ed. 1998. *Conjuring Spirits: Texts and Traditions of Medieval Ritual Magic.* University Park: Pennsylvania State University Press.

Flint, Valatie. 1991. *The Rise of Magic in Early Medieval Europe.* Princeton, NJ: Princeton University Press.

Gibbons, B. J. 2001. *Spirituality and the Occult: From the Renaissance to the Modern Age.* London: Routledge.

Gouk, Penelope. 1999. *Music, Science, and Natural Magic in Seventeenth-Century England.* New Haven: Yale University Press.

Grafton, Anthony. 1999. *Cardano's Cosmos: The World and Works of a Renaissance Astrologer.* Cambridge, MA: Harvard University Press.

Kieckhefer, Richard. 1998. *Forbidden Rites: A Necromancer's Manual of the Fifteenth Century.* University Park: Pennsylvania State University Press.

———. 2000. *Magic in the Middle Ages.* Cambridge: Cambridge University Press.

Maxwell-Stuart, P. G., ed. and trans. 1998. *The Occult in Early Modern Europe: A Documentary History.* New York: St. Martin's.

Thomas, Keith. 1971. *Religion and the Decline of Magic.* New York: Scribner's.

Vickers, Brian, ed. 1984. *Occult and Scientific Mentalities in the Renaissance.* Cambridge: Cambridge University Press.

Walker, D. P. 1958. *Spiritual and Demonic Magic from Ficino to Campanella.* London: Warburg Institute.

Webster, Charles. 1982. *From Paracelsus to Newton: Magic and the Making of Modern Science.* Cambridge: Cambridge University Press.

Yates, Francis. 1964. *Giordano Bruno and the Hermetic Tradition.* London: Routledge.

MAGIC, NATURAL

A set of beliefs and practices relating to the ability of human beings to affect their condition for the better and to create helpful objects through the manipulation of natural forces. *Natural* magic, which worked with and within the laws of nature for useful and licit purposes, was distinguished by its practitioners from *artificial* magic, which made use of machines and technological processes, and from *demonic* magic, which superseded natural laws through intervention of supernatural beings and was considered wicked and illicit. (*Divine* magic, through which God created miracles and prodigies, had no relation whatsoever to human understanding.) The natural magician, or magus, was a learned man who sought to explore the workings of nature for speculative or mystical purposes (e.g., Marsilio Ficino in the fifteenth century), for domestic or utilitarian aids (e.g., Giambattista Della Porta in the sixteenth century), or as a pseudoscientific experimental research program (e.g., Athanasius Kircher in the seventeenth century). The philosophical roots of natural magic grew out of the same mystical Hermetic and Neoplatonic tradition that inspired astrology, geomancy, and alchemy. Many of the recipes, spells, and beauty and household tips that were presented in Books of Secrets (as works on magic were sometimes called) also passed into manuals of natural magic. Its practical, use-oriented bias and the organized appearance of the discipline in early modern academies, along with publications that allowed for verification and repeatability of experiments, have led some historians to view natural magic as a precursor to science proper. Apart from a shared belief in hidden forces affecting objects at a distance, the forms or curative and love magic practiced by wise women and the black magic practiced by witches had little or nothing to do with the aims of natural magic, which sought not to influence people or fate but rather to understand better the workings of nature and to create useful products for the benefit of human society.

BASIC BELIEF STRUCTURE

At the base of natural magic lies the founding belief that the world is infused with a soul, or *anima mundi* (world soul), emanating directly from the Divine Mind and endowing all material forms with spirit. According to this Hermetic and Neoplatonic tradition, there is a correspondence between microcosm (all earthly things and beings as well as the little microcosm of the human body) and macrocosm (the planets and stars) that links all things together through sympathies and antipathies, creating a harmonious cosmic consensus. These resonances between sublunary and celestial beings are similar in their workings to how we understand modern physical forces like gravity, causing things to be attracted to or repelled by each other.

Magnetism, as described by Athanasius Kircher (1667), for example, was an immaterial sympathy that bound all beings and all levels of existence together in a hierarchical chain held in the hand of God. According to Kircher, the same force governed the declination of the magnet, the resurgence of plants, the association of animals with sun (cock) and moon (stag), the phenomena of heliotropic and selenotropic flowers, and the virtues of the snake-stone, a homeopathic remedy for snakebite (Godwin 1979, 74). Parts and qualities of earthly things, including the organs of the body and their ailments, were classified along with their corresponding celestial counterparts according to various theoretical schemas based on active versus passive, male versus female, solar versus lunar, and so forth. A magus strove to identify hidden "signatures" that revealed the exact place of things in the cosmic order so as to be able to manipulate their properties for his benefit.

For example, the early Renaissance practitioner of natural magic might construct a talisman out of gold (a solar metal) in the shape of an animal under the celestial reign of the sun's influence, such as a rooster or a hawk. By engraving an image of the sun on it with characters to signify Jove (representing the penetrative solar power) and setting a solar gem like a carbuncle or ruby into it, he could induce healthful influxes into the formed metal. In order to benefit from the solar spirit thus called into the talisman, he could wear it around his neck, thereby allowing the celestial influence to permeate his body.

The art of the magus lay in gathering particular natural materials while the planet whose influx they contained was reigning; he then formed them according to their planetary resonance and obtained for himself the gifts that the heavens had to offer. What nature provided, he manipulated or operated on, turning it to his uses. This interventionist attitude toward nature and natural products, which the magus saw as being perfected by human knowledge and skill, is also at the basis of the technological attitude. In fact, by the end of the seventeenth century, natural magic had a solidly technical bias to it and gradually became assimilated into the new sciences.

THE MAGUS
Natural magicians took pains to distinguish their arts from the diabolical crafts of common conjurers, witches, and diviners, although the distinction was not always clear to some contemporaries who marveled at their arcane feats. Giambattista Della Porta, for instance, was denounced to the Inquisition several times, along with his fellow members of the Academy of the Secrets of Nature, for dabbling in the occult and resorting to demonic aid. Like others who were accused of straying into impious and dangerous practices in their pursuit of knowledge, he responded to the charges by pointing out that all technological inventions are classified as magic by the vulgar until their functioning is explained and their prodigious quality subsides.

Perhaps that is why, in the late sixteenth century, Della Porta also described the preparation and learning needed to become a natural magician as very arduous and wide-ranging: the adept must be "a very perfect Philosopher" and "a skillful Physician": "moreover it is required of him that he be an Herbalist," "and as there is no greater inconvenience to any Artificer, than not to know his tools that he must work with," he must be equally proficient "in the nature of Metals, Minerals, Gems and Stones." "Furthermore, what cunning he must have in the art of Distillation . . . no man will doubt of it: for it yields daily very strange inventions, and most witty devices." Beyond that, "he must also know the Mathematical Sciences, and especially Astrologie," and, finally, optics (Della Porta 1957, 3).

As is apparent from this curriculum, the late Renaissance magus was typically a scholarly person engaged in experimental research with his colleagues or working alone in his laboratory. Some examples of the experiments of a natural magician from this period include stuffing live geese into boiling water, building furnaces for coloring plates, fabricating damask knives, preserving apples in sawdust, transforming spectators into monsters by boiling an ass's head in oil, constructing a talking head, breeding animals to produce creative hybrid races, or creating a quasi-perpetual motion machine.

ZAKIYA HANAFI

See also: ALCHEMY; AMULET AND TALISMAN; ASTROLOGY; DEE, JOHN; DELLA PORTA, GIAMBATTISTA; HERMETICISM; MAGIC, LEARNED; MAGIC, POPULAR; OCCULT.

References and further reading:
Agrippa Von Nettesheim, Henry Cornelius. 1982. *Occult Philosophy or Magic* (Translation of Book 1 of *De occulta philosophia,* 1533). Translated by W. F. Whitehead, using 1651 English translation. Reprint of Hahn and Whitehead edition (Chicago, 1898). New York: AMS.
Della Porta, Giambattista. 1957. *Natural Magick.* Edited by Derek J. Price. London, 1658. Reprint, New York: Basic Books.
Ficino, Marsilio. 1980. *The Book of Life* [*De Vita Triplici*]. Translated by Charles Boer. Irving, TX: Spring Publications.
Godwin, Joscelyn. 1979. *Athanasius Kircher: A Renaissance Man and the Quest for Lost Knowledge.* London: Thames and Hudson.
Hanafi, Zakiya. 2000. *The Monster in the Machine: Magic, Medicine, and the Marvelous in the Time of the Scientific Revolution.* Durham, NC, and London: Duke University Press.
Schumaker, Wayne. 1989. *Natural Magic and Modern Science.* Vol. 63. Binghamton, NY: Medieval and Renaissance Texts and Studies.

MAGIC, POPULAR
Witchcraft beliefs belong to a larger constellation of magical concepts that were articulated in related but distinct ways by learned and popular traditions in literate premodern societies. Magical concepts take many different forms but share a belief that the world is influenced by occult or hidden forces (spirits) that can be manipulated through words, ritual actions, or spiritually potent objects. Popular magic describes the set of beliefs current among the general populace (as opposed to specialist magical practitioners in the literate elite) about the nature of these forces and the rituals and objects that can be used to influence them. Magic was a pervasive part of early modern European popular culture, and early modern witch beliefs were strongly influenced by this tradition both directly and through its interaction with Christian theology.

THE CULTURAL CONTEXT OF POPULAR MAGIC
Magic is the oldest system for understanding and influencing the unseen processes that affect human life and has been an important part of almost all cultures. It has traditionally been distinguished from science by its belief that the nonmaterial forces that drive the universe are conscious, and from religion by the belief that these forces can nevertheless be controlled rather than merely supplicated, although this distinction is less clear-cut

than it once seemed. Both religion and science condemn magic as superstitious, and social elites have sometimes tried to suppress it, but traditions of popular magic have generally adapted and endured.

There is not much distinction between learned and popular magic in simple societies, although there are often adepts with special knowledge and powers (shamans) in them. As class structures and literacy developed, specialists (priests) dedicated their lives to mastering esoteric knowledge and ritual skills, creating a body of written records that preserved and elaborated them. Learned magic thus separated from popular practices, though they remained heavily interconnected. However, not all specialists necessarily became part of the elite, so in many civilizations popular magic involved both the beliefs and practices of low-status practitioners who performed services that the formal priesthood either could not or would not, and the everyday magical beliefs and practices of the general populace.

The rise of the world religions challenged the learned magic of earlier priesthoods and popular magic alike. In addition, sleight-of-hand and other forms of illusion that were often used by magical specialists as part of their rituals were also utilized and developed by entertainers and con artists to amuse paying audiences and defraud the credulous. By the late Middle Ages in Europe, the popular magic of local practitioners and ordinary people thus existed alongside a tradition of conjuring as entertainment and theft, in a mutually enriching relationship with learned magic (although learned magicians often scorned their popular counterparts) and in an antagonistic relationship with the official religion (even though popular magic contained many religious elements and the priesthood participated semiofficially in some popular practices).

POPULAR MAGIC IN EARLY MODERN CULTURE

Popular magical beliefs and practices in early modern Europe were extraordinarily diverse. Peasants in the British Isles, for example, believed that fairies or elves, diminutive people with magical powers, lived in the wild areas between and beyond the cultivated fields. Hungarian peasants believed that babies born with teeth would grow up to be magically adept shamans capable of rendering diverse magical services to the community. Peasants in other parts of the Balkans nearby believed that such infants would die and come back as vampires unless decapitated before being buried. The poor of Venice frequently named their children "Nane" and "Marita" because they believed people with these names could not be bewitched, and Scandinavians believed that the ghosts of victims of infanticide haunted watery places unless they were baptized. Such examples could be multiplied a thousand-fold and would still convey only a partial impression of the range of magical beliefs particular to specific places and times across Europe.

Although the content of early modern popular magic varied enormously, certain common purposes, modes of thought, and practices can be discerned. First, popular magic sought both agricultural productivity and human health and reproduction. Agricultural productivity was fostered through a series of rituals tied to the yearly cycle, supplemented by additional rituals to deal with specific problems like adverse weather and disease in animals. Similarly, human health and reproduction were promoted through rituals tied to the life cycle, especially the points of greatest vulnerability: birth, infancy, marriage, procreation, pregnancy, and death (to help the soul's transition to the afterlife). A huge array of additional magical rituals supplemented these to combat specific maladies. Diagnosis often involved some form of magical divination, which was also used to identify thieves, locate lost objects, and foretell the future. Other common forms of popular magic were used to foster love, promote good luck, locate hidden treasures, ward off evil magic, or inflict harm on others. Across the Continent, these activities involved the ritual use of words, gestures, and objects (sometimes combined with natural agents), which were understood to operate through nonmaterial spirits.

Within particular localities, popular beliefs tended to comprise an aggregate of long-standing local traditions, more recent arrivals from adjacent territories via oral transmission, elements of learned magical traditions conveyed by a combination of written and oral communication, related religious notions imported by the clerical elite, innovations developed by authoritative practitioners, and mutations introduced by the vagaries of oral transmission and unconscious adaptation to changing circumstances. Individual beliefs existed in the context of the local magical cosmology and the larger popular culture, and they both expressed and helped shape social relationships.

POPULAR MAGIC, CHRISTIAN AUTHORITY, AND WITCHCRAFT FEARS

Because Christianity supplied early modern Europe's overall cosmology, popular beliefs and rituals, even those that originated in paganism, were at least loosely framed in Christian terms, or their implications were simply ignored. A larger intellectual framework for popular magic remained largely unarticulated, for any attempt would have constituted heresy. Meanwhile, working in the opposite direction, late medieval theologians assimilated both learned and popular magic into Christian doctrine by asserting that both inherently involved evil spirits or demons, thus making all magic diabolical and all magicians agents of the Devil. Only a minority of Europeans accepted this line of reasoning entirely, and civil authorities generally treated beneficent magicians less harshly than people thought to practice harmful or explicitly diabolical magic, but this reductionist process of systematic diabolization nevertheless became an important part of the early modern belief in a wide-spread conspiracy of diabolical witches.

There was, as far as we can determine, no conspiracy of Devil-worshiping sorcerers in late medieval Europe. Nor was there any underground pagan religion with a theology and priestly hierarchy. There was, however, an immense body of popular magic that existed outside, and in some cases against, the formal doctrines of the established church. The desire to root this out, as disobedience and moral laxity if not as diabolism, was incorporated into many law codes. From this point of view, the witch persecutions were only the most severe component of a much broader campaign to suppress popular magic, which itself was a component of an even broader campaign to rid popular culture of all non-Christian elements. This campaign achieved only partial success overall, but it made life difficult for generations of specialized practitioners and distanced the sociopolitical elite from magical beliefs and practices, perhaps thereby contributing to the decline of magic and the rise of science during the same period.

Popular magic contributed in two other ways to early modern European concerns about witchcraft. First, fear of witchcraft, in the sense of hostile magic rather than diabolism, was a long-standing element of popular culture, and "un-witchers," or healers who specialized in detecting and countering witches, were common among popular practitioners. Second, popular magical traditions contained techniques that people could use to attempt to inflict harm on others—and some people used them, either alone or in combination with other agents like poisons. Consequently, the accusation that a person was a victim of some form of harmful magic, while difficult to prove and open to significant abuse, was neither inherently absurd nor necessarily wrong. In fact, popular magical traditions also included many other elements of the witchcraft demonology. Not only did people believe that some people flew through the air, congregated with other similar people, and could raise storms or change into animals, but also some people thought they themselves did these things. Popular magic was no mere backdrop for witchcraft beliefs, helping to make them plausible; it was the source for most of them. The demonologists did not invent their evidence, but rather they conflated many disparate and disjointed elements of popular magic and mixed them with literate traditions about magic and deviancy and with Christian theology in a way that distorted both their significance and their substance.

EDWARD BEVER

See also: CHARMS; CLERICAL MAGIC; COUNTERMAGIC; CUNNING FOLK; CURSES; DIABOLISM; DIVINATION; EVIL EYE; FAIRIES; FOLKLORE; GHOSTS; LOVE MAGIC; MAGIC AND RELIGION; *MALEFICIUM;* OCCULT; PEOPLE OF THE NIGHT; SCIENCE AND MAGIC; SHAMANISM; SPELLS; SUPERSTITION; VAMPIRE; WEATHER MAGIC; WORDS, POWER OF.

References and further reading:
Burke, Peter. 1978. *Popular Culture in Early Modern Europe.* New York: Harper and Row.
Devlin, Judith. 1987. *The Superstitious Mind: French Peasants and the Supernatural in the Nineteenth Century.* New Haven: Yale University Press.
Ginzburg, Carlo. 1983. *The Night Battles: Witchcraft and Agrarian Cults in the Sixteenth and Seventeenth Centuries.* Baltimore: Johns Hopkins University Press.
Kieckhefer, Richard. 1976. *European Witch Trials: Their Foundation in Popular and Learned Culture, 1300–1500.* Berkeley: University of California Press.
Klaniczay, Gàbor. 1990. *The Uses of Supernatural Power: The Transformation of Popular Religion in Medieval and Early Modern Europe.* Cambridge: Polity.
Martin, Ruth. 1989. *Witchcraft and the Inquisition in Venice 1550–1650.* Oxford: Blackwell.
Pócs, Éva. 1999. *Between the Living and the Dead: A Perspective on Witches and Seers in the Early Modern Age.* Budapest: Central European Press.
Ryan, W. F. 1999. *The Bathhouse at Midnight: An Historical Survey of Magic and Divination in Russia.* University Park: Pennsylvania State University Press.
Thomas, Keith. 1971. *Religion and the Decline of Magic.* New York: Scribner's.
Wilson, Stephen. 2000. *The Magical Universe: Everyday Ritual and Magic in Pre-Modern Europe.* London and New York: Hambledon and London.

MAGNUS, OLAUS (1490–1557)

Magnus was a Swedish geographer and historian whose chapters on sorcery and supernatural powers, even though occupying only miniscule space in his vast description of the Nordic peoples, *Historia de Gentibus Septentrionalibus* (History of the Northern Peoples, 1555), received the most attention in Europe and stunned readers.

Born in Lindköping, Sweden, Olaus Magnus was a Catholic who chose to live in voluntary exile after Sweden's conversion to Lutheranism in 1524. Together with his elder brother Johannes Magnus, he traveled and studied widely in Europe. From 1544 onward, he performed the duties of a titular Swedish bishop from Rome, where he had settled by 1541, and died sixteen years later.

The original Latin edition of *Historia de Gentibus Septentrionalibus,* made of 22 parts comprising nearly 770 chapters in 816 folio pages, actually began as a detailed commentary to the *Carta Marina* (sometimes called the *Carta Gotica*), a 1539 map that Magnus had made and published in Venice, showing the vast territory the Catholic Church had lost through the Reformation. This work was based upon a journey that Magnus took to Norrland (the northern part of Sweden) in 1518–1519. He visited Nidaros (Trondheim) in Norway and traveled as far north as Pello, in Övertorneå. He described Torneå as a meeting place for people trading in northern Scandinavia. Olaus Magnus was one of the first to mention and to locate Blåkulla, a famous Nordic mountain believed to be the site of witches' meetings.

Following typical conventions of the time, his book had an extensive subtitle: readers would learn about the northern people's "different positions, customs, habits, ways of life, superstitions methods of instruction, activities, government, food, wars, buildings, implements, metal mines, and marvels, together with almost all the living creatures that dwell in the North, and their characteristics." Scandinavia had been called the septentrionale region since ancient times in Europe. Its literal translation is "The History of the Peoples Living Under the Seven Plow-Oxen or Under the Plough [the Big Dipper]." It was the first report that thoroughly described the Nordic countries to a geographically interested Renaissance Europe, and it remained the most important work on Scandinavia until the mid-eighteenth century. It contained about 500 illustrations, many made by the author, some of which are still used to illustrate Nordic customs and witchcraft. Abridgements of the original text were translated into French, Italian, Spanish, German, Dutch, and English during the sixteenth and seventeenth centuries, although no Swedish translation appeared until the 1920s, and the first complete English translation appeared quite recently (Magnus 1996–1998).

Magnus emphasized three characteristics of the Nordic countries: they were the cradle of warfare, the haunt of demons, and the realm of immeasurable cold. The author wrote about everything Scandinavian: about the rich catches of fish off the coast of northern Norway, Lofoten's engulfing maelstrom, the invincible Vardø fortress, the lifestyle of northern Scandinavia's Sami, and sea monsters that tore human beings apart with their teeth. Exceptional depictions abound; the North was both the Arctic Eden and the ancient home of evil. Its climate produced a hardy people known for their courage, bravery, and strength. Knowledge and control of the natural elements not only helped the Swedes in warfare but also assisted northern Norwegian fishermen, who avoided shipwreck by their knowledge of the winds. By showing the reciprocal interactions between nature and northern peoples and their talents in the arts of war, Magnus wished to warn European leaders of what they faced if they planned to invade his homeland.

The book was published at the right time to fill geographical gaps in sixteenth-century demonological information. Nordic witches had permanent meeting grounds for holding Sabbats, and throughout northern Scandinavia, wrote Jean Bodin in 1580, alluding to Magnus's work, one could hear incantations and the tongue of the Devil. Sorcery was particularly widespread among the inhabitants of Lapland. They were adept at fortunetelling, wind magic, and other shameful works of the Devil. Satan reigned over the people of the North, and evil and misfortune arrived on the northern winds. Lycanthropy plagued vast regions of the Nordic countries, and many werewolves resided in the Baltic nations—and all this came from Magnus.

RUNE HAGEN;

TRANSLATED BY MARK LEDINGHAM

See also: BLÅKULLA; BODIN, JEAN; DEMONOLOGY; FINLAND; LAPLAND; NORWAY; SWEDEN; WEATHER MAGIC; WIND KNOTS.

References and further reading:
Bodin, Jean. 1580. *De la démonomanie des sorciers,* Paris. Translated as *On the Demon-Mania of Witches.* Abridged with an introduction by Jonathan L. Pearl. Translated by Randy A. Scott. Toronto: Centre for Reformation and Renaissance Studies, 1995.
Hagen, Rune. *Historien om Folkene under de syv Plogoksene.* http://www.ub.uit.no/fag/historie/olaus.htm (accessed April 4, 2003).
Magnus, Olaus. 1996–1998. *Historia de Gentibus Septentrionalibus (Description of the Northern Peoples),* Rome, 1555. Translated by Peter Fisher and Humphrey Higgens, edited by Peter Foote; with annotation derived from the commentary by John Granlund, abridged and augmented. 3 vols. London: Hakluyt Society.
Urness, Carol. 1999. *The Olaus Magnus Map of Scandinavia. 1539.* Minneapolis: James Ford Bell Library, University of Minnesota.
———. 2001. "Olaus Magnus: His Map and His Book." *Mercator's World* 6, no. 1: 26–33.

MAINZ, ELECTORATE OF

With approximately 2,000 victims in a territory of approximately 7,000 square kilometers, the ecclesiastical electorate of Mainz ranks among the most strongly affected states of the Holy Roman Empire (Pohl 1998, 41; Gebhard 1991, 65). Its main period of witch hunting lasted only from 1593 to 1630, in four main waves, until the occupation of the electorate of Mainz by Swedish troops brought the trials to an abrupt end as Elector Anselm Kasimir fled to Cologne. Under his successor, Johann Philipp von Schönborn, who was influenced by Friedrich Spee, only a few trials occurred. It is not true, as one often reads, that under his rule witchcraft trials ended; the last executions took place in 1684 at Worbis (in the district of Eichsfeld in Thuringia) (Pelizaeus 2004). Afterward, Mainz had individual trials for witchcraft insults until 1739.

The electorate of Mainz, whose territorial lord was not only an elector but also an archbishop and the imperial arch-chancellor, had an outstanding position within the Holy Roman Empire; therefore, witchcraft trials in this territory possessed a certain model character for other ecclesiastical territories. Like the other two archbishop-electors, his territory was scattered across possessions on the Rhine (the Unterstift, or lower archbishopric), in the Spessart, Odenwald, Main, and Tauber River area (the Oberstift, or upper archbishopric), in Hesse and around Erfurt, and in Thuringia (Eichsfeld). The witchcraft trials affected the upper archbishopric more than its possessions in the Unterstift, in Hesse, and in Thuringia. Most trials were promoted by local populations and local officials, whose zeal the electoral government tried repeatedly to moderate. However, the archbishop's government made no serious attempt to prevent the trials.

The principal literature agreed that there were four waves of pursuit but dated them differently, although agreeing that the last and largest wave occurred from 1627 to 1629, parallel to those in the Franconian dioceses of Würzburg and Bamberg. Most victims died during these waves. Pohl (1998, 39) dated the first wave from 1593 to 1595, the second one in 1603, and the third in 1615–1616; Gebhard (1991, 303) dated the first wave from 1601 to 1604, the next from 1611 to 1614, and the third in 1616–1617. However, Gebhard ignored the trials in the 1590s and overestimated the intensity of pursuit, so Pohl's dates seem preferable. Due to the unsatisfactory state of sources (only 404 criminal procedures survive), estimates of the distribution of the victims for the entire electorate are impossible and must be limited to certain districts. The large majority of those executed were female and married, although the proportion of men seems relatively high at 17–30 percent (Pohl 1998, 212–219). Victims were most commonly aged 41–60, followed by the 26–40 year olds. In the city of Dieburg, the average age of victims was about 55 (Gebhard 1991, 239–249; Pohl 1998, 214–219). Trials against children leading to execution were very rare.

The electoral government made no profits from these trials, particularly because a 1612 regulation expressly forbade the confiscation of goods intended for the victims' children. Many professions were involved in Mainz witchcraft trials. As elsewhere, outsiders like shepherds, musicians, or groups like migrants or widows (who because of their social status were in greater danger than other groups) were affected first. Midwives are repeatedly mentioned in trials, but no firm statistics exist about the frequency with which they were tried. Some large-scale trials of the final wave, particularly in the city of Dieburg, also reached into the urban upper class, including councilmen. However, clergy, scholars, or noblemen were never affected, even by the final wave of pursuit. Therefore, the majority of victims were artisans or came from rural groups. Although there is no evidence that special Counter-Reformation attacks lie behind these trials, it is noteworthy that districts bordering Protestant areas were particularly affected, as was Dieburg, where tensions between Catholic clergy and the partially Protestant population ran high.

LEGISLATION

Because Elector and Arch-chancellor Berthold of Henneberg (1484–1504) had a relevant role in planning what became the Carolina Code, already introduced in the electorate of Mainz during the reign of Albrecht of Brandenburg (1514–1545) in 1527–1528, five years before its official proclamation for the entire Holy Roman Empire, the Carolina Code always regulated criminal procedure at Mainz. All witchcraft trials had to be judged by the archbishop's *Weltlicher Rat* (Secular Council), which, despite its name, included a majority of clergymen. Nevertheless, during the seventeenth century such lower territorial instances as the *Keller* (Cellar) tended to accomplish many measures on their own. In order to cover themselves, they dispatched documents to the Secular Council in Mainz or at least corresponded with higher authorities before passing judgment. However, law faculties, including the University of Mainz, were almost never consulted. Therefore the influence of lawyers on the trials remained comparatively small, especially because only two lawyers generally sat on the Secular Council.

In 1612, Elector Johann Schweickart von Kronberg (1604–1626) published a detailed questionnaire and regulations about detention and confiscation. Although the new procedures were intended to provide greater equity, in fact they aggravated the situation. The questionnaire, consisting of 113 questions, enabled even lower local instances to proceed against witches without any legal advice and to convict suspects simply for confessing under torture to the questionnaire. This change allowed very rapid procedures and condemnations of suspects, which proved particularly fatal during the waves of 1612–1613 and 1627–1629. The new regulations for detention did improve the situation in individual cases, but with mass trials, the situation remained catastrophic after 1612. Therefore only the regulations for confiscation, compared to the previous regulations of Elector Wolfgang von Dalberg, may be regarded as beneficial.

CHRONOLOGY

In 1511, the first provable witchcraft trial before the city council of Mainz still involved nondiabolical *maleficium* (harmful magic), as did everything else until the last quarter of the sixteenth century. Only in the city of Steinheim did executions occur before 1550. In the last quarter of the sixteenth century, the behavior of the authorities changed fundamentally; from that point, they felt themselves obliged to intervene directly in cases of witchcraft accusations. Around 1570, during the reign of Elector Wolfgang von Dalberg (1582–1601), pursuit began to intensify, first in the upper bishopric. From there it reached the whole electorate, where trials occurred continuously after 1590, with varying intensity.

During the short reign of Johann Adam von Bicken (1601–1604), trials received a sharp stimulus. Bicken continued von Dalberg's proceedings, and trials multiplied rapidly, particularly in the upper bishopric and especially in some places that would also be affected later: Dieburg, Aschaffenburg, Miltenberg, and Lohr. After Bicken's sudden death, trials came to a nearly complete halt for about six years. The new elector, Johann Schweickart von Kronberg, responsible for the 1612 regulations, held himself back at first, apparently giving special attention to steering the trials into better-regulated courses. But when the population and local authorities again demanded trials, the elector complied with their desires. These trials gained momentum through re-arresting people already accused in 1604 and now included the lower bishopric as well.

Toward the end of Schweickart von Kronberg's reign, the trials decreased again, probably because of the parallel decrease in the neighboring bishopric of Würzburg. However, the largest wave, with the most victims, began immediately under his successor, Georg Friedrich of Greiffenclau (ruled 1626–1629). Like Schweikart von Kronberg , he yielded to local demands for resumption of the witchcraft trials. After his death in 1629, trials decreased substantially under Anselm Kasimir Walmbold of Umstadt (ruled 1629–1647) and almost stopped with the conquest of the electorate by Swedish troops in 1631. After the elector fled to exile in Cologne, only isolated trials continued; with his return, they did not revive. His successor Johann Philipp von Schönborn (ruled 1647–1673), who was also prince-bishop of Würzburg from 1642, marked a clear break. His government prevented the wave of trials from 1660–1670, which afflicted most of the Holy Roman Empire, from again disturbing the electorate. Isolated trials still occurred under Schönborn, but the elector always made an exact examination of each case and thereby prevented any expansion of the trials. Schönborn's actions were on the one hand considerably affected by the views of Friedrich Spee's *Cautio Criminalis seu de processibus contra sagas liber* (A Warning on Criminal Justice, or a Book on Witch Trials, 1631) and on the other hand by his political support from Louis XIV's France. The last two executions for witchcraft occurred in 1684 at Worbis; accusations can be found afterward, but they never led to executions.

LUDOLF PELIZAEUS

See also: CAROLINA CODE (*CONSTITIO CRIMINALIS CAROLINA*); ECCLESIASTICAL TERRITORIES (HOLY ROMAN EMPIRE); GERMANY, SOUTHEASTERN; HESSE; HOLY ROMAN EMPIRE; SPEE, FRIEDRICH; THURINGIA; UNIVERSITIES; WITCH-BISHOPS (HOLY ROMAN EMPIRE); WÜRZBURG, PRINCE-BISHOPRIC OF.

References and further reading:

Behringer, Wolfgang. 1999. "Witchcraft Studies in Austria, Germany, Switzerland." Pp. 64–95 in *Witchcraft in Early Modern Europe. Studies in Culture and Belief*. Edited by Jonathan Barry, Marianne Hester, and Gareth Roberts. Cambridge: Cambridge University Press.

Gebhard, Horst. 1991. *Hexenprozesse im Kurfürstentum Mainz des 17. Jahrhunderts*. Aschaffenburg: Geschichts- und Kunstvereins Aschaffenburg. (Veröffentlichungen des Geschichts- und Kunstvereins Aschaffenburg e.V. 31).

Keller, Wilhelm Otto, ed. 1989. *Hexer und Hexen in Miltenberg und der Cent Bürgstadt: "Man soll sie dehnen, bis die Sonn' durch sie scheint!" Beträge zur Geschichte der Hexenprozesse am südlichen Untermain*. Miltenberg: Stadt Miltenberg.

Larner, Christina. 1984. *Witchcraft and Religion: The Politics of Popular Belief*. Oxford: Blackwell.

Midelfort, H. C. Erik. 1972. *Witch Hunting in Southwestern Germany: 1562–1684: The Social and Intellectual Foundations*. Stanford: Stanford University Press.

Pelizaeus, Ludolf, ed. 2004. *Hexenprozesse in Kurmainz*. 2004. CD-Rom. Dieburg, AVA Dieburg.

Pohl, Herbert. 1998. *Zauberglaube und Hexenangst im Kurfürstentum Mainz: ein Beitrag zur Hexenfrage im 16. und beginnenden 17. Jahrhundert*. 2nd ed. Stuttgart: Steiner.

MALDONADO, JUAN (1534–1583)

Known in France as Jean Maldonat, this Jesuit became a significant figure in the development of European demonology. His well-attended Paris lectures of 1571–1572, which presented a militant, highly political approach to demons and witches, became very influential in France and helped shape Jesuit thought on these subjects before the great synthesis by his former student, Martín Del Rio, early in the seventeenth century.

A native of Seville, Maldonado studied at the University of Salamanca, where he became a professor of philosophy and theology in 1562. Ordained as a priest in the Jesuit order in 1563, he was soon sent to Paris to become professor of theology at the newly founded *collège* of Clermont. Staffed by Jesuits and patronized by the powerful Guise family, it was able to open its doors only after winning a bitter lawsuit brought by their French enemies.

Maldonado soon proved a popular and successful teacher. His ability to attract students probably explains the vehemence of his opponents in the University of Paris. But even those who opposed his intellectual and political positions considered his learning and holiness impeccable. Maldonado tried to create a revived Aristotelian Catholic theology and trained men to argue and defend it. Typically for a Spaniard, he described himself as a soldier in the religious combat of his age, and from his first days in Paris, he joined the Catholic polemicists who attacked the growth and spread of the French Reformed Church.

In 1569, during the third French War of Religion, Maldonado participated in a Catholic mission to reconvert people to Roman Catholicism in a region near Poitiers that had been deeply penetrated by Protestant heresy. After returning to Paris, he gave a series of public lectures that became crucial to the development of a confessionalized French Catholic demonology. We know their contents only because one of his students published them thirty-five years later. Delivered in simple Latin to appeal to a wide audience and informed by his recent mission in Poitou, his lectures were enormously popular, attracting hundreds of auditors.

The theological thread running through all Maldonado's Paris lectures, including his series on witches, was the immortality of the soul. Seeing this doctrine as central to Christian belief, he accused Protestants of denying or seriously underplaying it; for him, that could only be diabolically inspired heresy. Maldonado tied the growth of heresy closely to the spread of demons, "In Bohemia and Germany," he claimed, "the Hussite heresy was accompanied by such a storm of demons that witches were busier than heretics" (Maldonado 1605, 156). Then Geneva became infected, then France. One of the greatest sins of contemporary heretics was to deny the reality of demons and angels; Maldonado considered doing so equivalent to atheism. He emphasized the reality and orthodoxy of beliefs like the transportation of witches to Sabbats. To deny such things, as he accused Calvin's followers of doing, only confirmed their heretical and diabolical atheism.

A brilliant lecturer and inspiring teacher, Maldonado's influence stretched far beyond his 1571–1572 lectures. His auditors and students included several men who became important Catholic spokesmen and carried his ideas about the connections between witchcraft and heresy well into the seventeenth century. The prolific Jesuit author Louis Richeome was Maldonado's student, as was Martín Del Rio, the best-known Jesuit authority on witchcraft, whose subsequent career took place mainly in Flanders and whose influence was greatest in the Holy Roman Empire. Another listener at Clermont in 1571–1572 was Pierre de Lancre, who subsequently conducted the biggest witchcraft trials in French history; he was then in Paris studying law.

JONATHAN L. PEARL

See also: DEL RIO, MARTÍN; FRANCE; LANCRE, PIERRE DE; WARS OF RELIGION (FRANCE).

References and further reading:

Maldonado, Jean. 1605. *Traicté des anges et demons, mis en Français par Maistre François de la Borie.* Paris.

Pearl, Jonathan L. 1999: *The Crime of Crimes: Demonology and Politics in France, 1560–1620.* Waterloo, Ontario: Wilfred Laurier University Press.

MALE WITCHES

The crime of witchcraft was sex-linked, but it was certainly not sex-specific. With the large amount of scholarship devoted in recent years to the connections between women and witchcraft, we have almost lost

A male witch frolics with demons, who dance and play music around a magic circle at a Sabbat. From Olaus Magnus, Historia de Gentibus Septentrionalibus (*History of the Northern Peoples*), *1555. (Cornell University Library)*

sight of the fact that a great many witches were men. In fact, probably somewhere around 6,000 men were executed for witchcraft in early modern Europe, which means that far more European men were burned as witches than were executed for heresy during the Protestant Reformation. Men were well-represented in the very earliest European witch hunts; for example, men formed at least one-third of the identifiable witches tried in Valais in 1428 and 28 percent of the 250-plus witches tried in the Alpine valleys of Dauphiné between 1424 and 1448. In a few places, like Neuchâtel in French Switzerland, men even formed a majority of the earliest recorded witches. If the *Malleus Maleficarum* (The Hammer of Witches, 1486) insisted that witches were almost invariably women, the (probably forged) papal bull that preceded it specified that men and women alike were guilty of witchcraft.

Although the link between women and witchcraft accusations remained strong almost everywhere in Europe during the most intensive period of witch hunting between 1570 and 1660, some men were punished for practicing witchcraft almost everywhere. Very few places imitated the Inquisition of Siena, which heard testimony about male witches, or *stregoni,* but arrested only women; indeed, other branches of the Roman Inquisition behaved quite differently toward men who were magical healers, as the well-known history of the mostly male Friulian *benandanti* (do-gooders) testifies. At the opposite extreme from Siena was Europe's westernmost outpost, Iceland, where women comprised less than 10 percent of witchcraft defendants, and only one of the twenty-two people executed for witchcraft in the seventeenth century was a woman, burned together with her son. We need to realize that there were places as extreme as Siena or Iceland about gendering witches, but in fact, almost everyplace else fell somewhere in between—and they were usually much closer to the example of Siena than of Iceland.

In order to shed some light on the problem of male witches, it seems helpful to start by trying to answer some simple questions, such as *where* men were most frequently found among accused witches, and *what kinds* of men seem to have been most frequently accused of witchcraft, before trying to tackle the ultimate problem of *why,* despite the opinions of some witchcraft theorists and some modern authors, so many thousands of men were punished for witchcraft. If we imagine a geographical list that reverses the usual gender priorities about witches and proceeds from Iceland toward Siena rather than vice versa, we encounter a few places with sizable samples of recorded witchcraft trials where men comprised a clear majority of accused witches: seventeenth-century Muscovy, with about 150 men in 200 witchcraft trials (Zguta 1977;

Kivelson 1991), and Normandy in northwestern France, with almost 300 men in 400-plus witchcraft trials between 1560 and 1700 (Monter 1997). If seventeenth-century Muscovy saw three men arrested for witchcraft for every woman, this disproportion was even greater in seventeenth-century Normandy, with at least four male witches for every female witch; by mid-century, when this province averaged one or two witchcraft cases per year, women had almost disappeared.

In the areas discussed in this paragraph, men and women were represented approximately evenly among accused witches. They include two places near Muscovy: Finland, with almost-equal numbers of men and women, and Estonia, with a majority of men among its 200 indicted witches (Ankarloo and Henningsen 1990, 321, 267)—but in both places, the majority of executed witches were women. In some Austrian provinces, particularly Styria and Carinthia, men also comprised a majority of people arrested for witchcraft (Labouvie 1990, 57–58). In western Europe, we find similar percentages on Normandy's borders among the 1,000-plus witches judged by the *Parlement* of Paris between 1560 and 1640 (Soman 1977, 798–799); here, if we combine witchcraft with maleficent magic, men comprised a majority of those condemned to death by Europe's most prestigious appellate court.

Beneath such widely scattered half-male samples, we find a cluster of contiguous states along what were then the western edges of the Holy Roman Empire, west of the Rhine and extending south from modern Belgium to the French Alps, where men comprised a sizable minority of the very large groups of people tried and frequently burned as witches. Men accounted for between 27 percent and 33 percent of all witches in such German-speaking places as Luxembourg or Saarland and such French-speaking places as Lorraine, Franche-Comté, or the Pays de Vaud in western Switzerland; smaller samples from Alsace and the electorate of Trier confirm the impression that we are dealing with a regional phenomenon. Farther east, in the Germanic heartlands of the witch hunts, the percentage of men usually drops below one-fourth; for modern Germany as a whole, it was probably around 20 percent. And, of course, there were also several places, including the British Isles, Sweden, or parts of modern Belgium, where male witches were very rare, comprising less than one-tenth of accused witches.

In the handful of places where most witches were men, the *kinds* of men arrested for this crime seem extremely different. In Muscovy, the single most common feature among men charged with witchcraft is that they were vagrants, recent immigrants, or often-fugitive serfs; several other witches were non-Christians, Finns, or Turks. However, in Normandy, a cheese-producing region, by far the most feared male witches were shepherds, some of whom possessed veritable arsenals suitable for performing both offensive and defensive magic. Unlike Muscovy, Normandy's witches included many priests, at least seven of whom were burned for *sortilège* (diabolic magic), while another went to the galleys and several more were permanently banished (Monter 1997, 582–583). Normandy's blacksmiths provided a third dangerous occupational category because of their skill in harming as well as healing horses.

There was, however, one important characteristic shared between seventeenth-century Muscovite and Norman male witches: Many men in both places practiced magical healing. Early modern European folk healers included large numbers of both men and women; it seems significant that the ordinary English phrase for them, "cunning folk," is not sex-specific. Male healers could be found throughout Europe, including Sienese *stregoni* who, unlike many of their counterparts elsewhere, were never charged with witchcraft by the inquisitors. However, we should realize that male magicians rarely tried to heal very young children; in the age of witch hunting, "neonatal medicine" and "pediatrics" were almost exclusively female specialties. And because the very worst crimes attributed to witches involved harming or even killing very young children (for example, this was almost the only reason for hanging witches in England), women were overwhelmingly predominant among the usual suspects in such circumstances. Almost the only way men killed young children was in the form of werewolves, and such cases were extremely rare almost everywhere in Europe.

But if men rarely practiced pediatrics or inflicted *maleficia* (harmful magic) on small children, they had a near-monopoly on veterinary medicine, especially in connection with horses and cows, the largest and most valuable animals on any farm in early modern Europe. The whole western Alpine zone, where men comprised upwards of one-third of all witches, were afflicted with bewitched cattle. The blacksmiths of Normandy (and perhaps elsewhere) also fit here.

There were certainly other reasons why men were targeted as witches. Many men were drawn into the net of witchcraft suspects through being related to female witches, their mothers or sisters as well as their wives. In places such as England where men comprised an extremely small share of accused witches, kinship with other witches through blood or marriage provides the principal explanation for which men were accused. As with women, various personal attributes such as spitefulness, a penchant for making threats, or some other forms of criminal behavior, also increased some men's vulnerability to charges of witchcraft.

It has been demonstrated (Midelfort 1972, 182) that men even became a majority of those executed during the latter phases of some of the very largest German witch hunts in the 1620s, as traditional stereotypes of witches began to break down; but it has also been argued that this very development led to a crisis of confidence in the legal system. Even more remarkably, the final phase of witch hunting in present-day Austria, the *Zauberer-Jackl* (Sorcerer-Jack) panic of Salzburg at the end of the 1670s, involved mostly very young men rather than old women, and this pattern carried over into some of eighteenth-century witchcraft trials in Bavaria (Behringer 1997, 336–344). But a great deal of work remains to be done on this topic, as the exploratory nature of this sketch shows.

WILLIAM MONTER

See also: AUSTRIA; *BENANDANTI*; CHILDREN; CUNNING FOLK; ESTONIA; FEMALE WITCHES; FINLAND; FRANCHE-COMTÉ; GENDER; ICELAND; LUXEMBOURG, DUCHY OF; NORMANDY; *PARLEMENT* OF PARIS; RUSSIA; SALZBURG, PRINCE-ARCHBISHOPRIC OF; SIENESE NEW STATE; TRIER, ELECTORATE OF; VAUD, PAYS DE.

References and further reading:
Ankarloo, Bengt, and Gustav Henningsen, eds. 1990. *European Witchcraft: Centres and Peripheries.* Oxford: Clarendon.
Apps, Lara, and Andrew Gow. 2003. *Male Witches in Early Modern Europe.* Manchester: Manchester University Press.
Behringer, Wolfgang. 1997. *Witchcraft Persecutions in Bavaria: Popular Magic, Religious Zealotry and Reason of State in Early Modern Europe.* Translated by J. C. Grayson and David Lederer. Cambridge: Cambridge University Press.
Kivelson, Valerie. 1991. "Through the Prism of Witchcraft: Gender and Social Change in Seventeenth-Century Muscovy." Pp. 74–94 in *Russia's Women: Accommodation, Resistance, Transformation.* Edited by Barbara Evans Clements, Barbara Alpern Engel, and Christine D. Worobec. Berkeley: University of California Press.
———. 2003. "Male Witches and Gendered Categories in Seventeenth-Century Russia." *Comparative Studies in Society and History* 45: 606–631.
Labouvie, Eva. 1990. "Männer im Hexenprozess: Zur sozialantropologie eines 'männlichen' Verständnisses von Magie und Hexerei." *Geschichte und Gesellschaft* 16: 56–78.
Midelfort, H. C. Erik. 1972. *Witch Hunting in Southwestern Germany, 1562–1684. The Social and Intellectual Foundations.* Stanford, CA: Stanford University Press.
Monter, William. 1997. "Toads and the Eucharist: The Male Witches of Normandy." *French Historical Studies* 20: 563–595.
Soman, Alfred. 1977. "Les procès de sorcellerie au Parlement de Paris (1565–1640)." *Annales: Economies, Sociétés, Civilisations* 32: 790–814.
Walinski-Kiehl, Robert. 2004. "Males, 'Masculine Honor,' and Witch Hunting in Seventeenth-Century Germany." *Men and Masculinities* 6: 254–271.
Zguta, Russell. 1977. "Witchcraft Trials in Seventeenth-Century Russia." *American Historical Review* 82: 1187–1207.

MALEFICIUM

Maleficium, harm inflicted through occult means, was one of the two main ingredients of early modern witchcraft, along with a pact with the Devil. In theory, any harmful magic required the assistance of the Devil and therefore implied a pact with him, but in practice the two were generally distinguished. Learned commentators stressed the primacy of the pact, and some law codes made it alone a capital offense, but generally evidence of both diabolism and some form of *maleficium* was needed for prosecution to be carried through to execution. Commoners, who made most accusations and testified about prior offenses, focused on *maleficia,* which included both sorcery, or harmful ritual magic, and witchcraft, an inherent ability to cause magical harm. While diabolism was a particular, and in many ways peculiar, feature of early modern European witchcraft, *maleficium* linked it to the much broader fears of harmful magic that haunt people in many societies worldwide. No good evidence of the kind of widespread Devil-worship feared by the demonologists has been found, but there is no question that malefic magic was practiced, and there is reason to think that some of the activities it involved constituted a real threat to other peoples' health and well-being.

FORMS OF *MALEFICIUM*

As in many other cultures, harmful magic took two main forms in Europe: ritual magic intended to cause various sorts of damage, which social scientists call sorcery, and an inherent power to inflict harm that certain people were thought to have, called witchcraft. The specific rituals employed in sorcery vary widely from culture to culture, but the basic elements and forms of damage they are thought to inflict do not. Sorcerers, in early modern Europe as elsewhere, worked through the use of spells and incantations, ritual actions and gestures, potions (poisons), and spiritually potent objects. The damage they were thought to cause included first and foremost bodily injury (illness, impotence, and death in people and animals) and disruption of natural processes (storms and hail; stunted crops; and impeded production of butter, cheese, or beer). Love magic was sometimes considered a form of sorcery but could also be regarded as beneficent magic, depending on the circumstances.

Innate witchcraft was thought to manifest the witch's ill will directly, but as in many other cultures it was transmitted via a look (the evil eye), a touch, or a spontaneous word or gesture. Some cultures held that it could occur without the witch being aware that he or she was causing injury or even consciously wanting to do so, but early modern Europeans generally treated it as a manifestation of the witch's conscious desire to cause harm. In fact, the witch demonology insisted that the power came from an explicit pact with the Devil, and magistrates used torture to compel suspects accused of manifesting this power to confess to having made one. This innate witchcraft was held responsible for damages similar to sorcery, although bodily maladies and small-scale, localized physical effects like butter not churning were featured more prominently than larger-scale natural processes like storms and stunted harvests, which were more likely to be ascribed to ritual magic.

MALEFICIUM, THE DEVIL, AND THE LAW

The idea that malign magical powers are closely related to a malign personality is deeply rooted. The word *maleficium* originally meant simply "wrongdoing" or "mischief," yet it was linked specifically to harmful magic even in pagan Rome. This association intensified with the rise of Christianity, which saw any recourse to magic as a moral failing. Roman law had proscribed sorcery as a source of injury to individuals from the earliest times, and the Roman Empire prosecuted magic as a source of politically destabilizing intrigue as well; Moses had enjoined his people not to "suffer a witch [or magician; the Hebrew is ambiguous] to live amongst you," and the Vulgate frequently referred to *maleficium*. The Theodosian Code joined these two traditions together, using *maleficium* in place of the earlier, more neutral *magia*.

Early medieval Germanic law codes contained punishments for sorcerers both because of the injuries they caused and because they employed pagan rites, and trials focusing on the harms caused by sorcery took place sporadically through the Middle Ages. The connection between harm and moral character was not lost, however, and late medieval theologians strengthened it considerably by reviving the argument first made in late antiquity that all magic requires some sort of spiritual agent, and illicit, especially malevolent, magic therefore must involve demons and at least an implicit pact with their master, the Devil. In the fifteenth century, this pact became linked with the notion that the Devil organized his followers into an underground conspiracy with perverted nocturnal orgies and the power and obligation to perpetrate various forms of *maleficium*.

The gradual adoption of this image of witchcraft by much of Europe's elites over the next century had the effect of not only making allegiance to the Devil a capital offense, on par with *maleficium,* but also, more subtly, changed the legal nature of *maleficium*. Until this point, prosecutions for *maleficium* generally concerned sorcery, magic that by definition had to be practiced deliberately, with some sort of external manifestation. Now, with the suspect's moral orientation the focus of attention, prosecution no longer hinged on proof of an explicit ritual attack or even the evidence of a reputation for practicing magic. Evidence of *maleficium* remained important, but in sixteenth- and seventeenth-century trials, this requirement was frequently met with allegations (and tortured confessions) of apparently spontaneous infliction of harm with no ritual mechanism specified or implied. In some cases this may reflect just an oversight in the investigation or the record, but in many it seems clear that the witch was thought to be guilty of spontaneous witchcraft as defined by anthropologists. Because the general populace generally did not concern itself with diabolism and there were only a limited number of magical practitioners, particularly malevolent ones, it would seem that opening the legal process to accusations of spontaneous witchcraft was at least as important as the criminalization of a pact with the Devil in multiplying persecutions during the early modern period.

MALEFICIUM AND COMMUNITY

With or without a link to the Devil, people in most cultures fear *maleficium,* that some of their neighbors harbor ill will and that this ill will can be manifested in injury to them, their dependents, animals, or property. Social scientists, working in the tradition of the Enlightenment, which rejected late medieval beliefs about witchcraft, have generally treated these fears as credulous superstitions manifesting some sort of psychological, social, or cultural displacement mechanism. Belief in *maleficium* has been variously explained as a fraudulent means of victimizing one's enemies, a way of accounting for otherwise inexplicable misfortune, a mechanism for displacing anger or guilt from an accuser onto a suspect, and, most recently, as an element in a self-referencing symbol system. All of these explanations start from the assumption that *maleficium* is illusory, that attempts to inflict harm through occult means did not happen and could not have posed a threat if they did, or only posed a threat because of the beliefs of the people who feared them.

Careful consideration of what *maleficium* was supposed to involve and the evidence presented in late medieval and early modern sources, however, suggest that some people certainly did attempt to inflict harm on their enemies or opponents through occult, or hidden, means; that some of these means had the potential to deal real damage; and that this power was not simply an artifact of peoples' belief in it. First, early modern trial records contain ample evidence of popular malefic practices—image magic, curses, and the like—that some people employed occasionally and other people utilized as a more routine part of their social relations. Second, the early modern concept of *maleficium* did not correspond exactly to our notion of magic, for it included the secret employment of means that we consider natural—poisons, in particular, and also surreptitious battery against children and animals—and there is no question that these practices could indeed be used to injure other members of the community. Third, most allegations of *maleficium* involved injury to people or animals, and beyond the chemical and mechanical means suggested above, recent research into the relationship of interpersonal conflict and physiological stress suggests not only that manifestations of hostility, whether ritual attacks or spontaneous expressions, can cause or contribute to a wide variety of maladies, including disease, impotence, accidental injury, and death, but also that this effect is not dependent on prior belief in or fear of the power of magic.

Fear of *maleficium* could intensify the psychophysical reaction causing injury, and the charge certainly was made fraudulently against opponents in interpersonal conflicts. Charges of *maleficium* were often unfounded, did manifest social tensions arising from other sources, and were part of the narrative structure of early modern culture, but not all fears were illusory and not all charges unfounded. There were numerous connections between one person's ill will and another person's misfortune, some open and some hidden, some material and some psychological. Unlike diabolism, *maleficium* was not at bottom an illusory crime, but instead was a real feature of early modern life that people coped with as best they could.

EDWARD BEVER

See also: BEWITCHMENT; CURSES; DISEASE; EVIL EYE; FEAR; IMAGE MAGIC; IMPOTENCE, SEXUAL; LAWS ON WITCHCRAFT (ANCIENT); LAWS ON WITCHCRAFT (MEDIEVAL); PACT WITH THE DEVIL; PERSONALITY OF WITCHES; SORCERY; SPELLS.

References and further reading:

Arendt-Schulte, Ingrid. 1994. *Weise Frauen—böse Weiber: Die Geschichte der Hexen der Frühen Neuzeit.* Freiburg: Herder.
Bever, Edward. 2002. "Women, Witchcraft, and Power in the Early Modern Community." *Journal of Social History* 36: 955–988.
Björkqvist, Kaj, and Pirkko Niemelä, eds. 1992. *Of Mice and Women: Aspects of Female Aggression.* San Diego: Academic.
Briggs, Robin. 1989. "Ill Will and Magical Power in Lorraine Witchcraft." Pp. 83–105 in *Communities of Belief: Culture and Social Tension in Early Modern France.* Edited by Robin Briggs. Oxford: Clarendon.

Witches causing arson to a town in the duchy of Württemberg. (Fortean Picture Library)

Fiume, Giovanna. 1997. "The Old Vinegar Lady, or the Judicial Modernization of the Crime of Witchcraft." Pp. 65–87 in *History from Crime.* Edited by Edward Muir and Guido Ruggiero. Translated by Corrada Curry et al. Baltimore: Johns Hopkins University Press.

Kramer, Karl. 1983. "Schaden- und Gegenzauber in Alltagsleben des 16.–18. Jahrhunderts nach Archivalischen Quellen aus Holstein." Pp. 223–239 in *Hexenprozesse: Deutsche und Skandinavische Beitrage.* Edited by Christian Degen et al. Neumünster: Karl Wachholtz.

Levack, Brian P. 1995. *The Witch-Hunt in Early Modern Europe.* 2nd ed. London: Longman.

MALINOWSKI, BRONISLAW KASPER (1884–1942)

Polish-born British social anthropologist, regarded as the father of modern social anthropology, Malinowski explored the rationality of witchcraft and magical practices in contemporary "primitive" societies. He was among the first to argue for the centrality of fieldwork in anthropological research, and his method of "participant-observation" is now canonical in social and cultural anthropology. This technique enabled him to produce ethnographic writings steeped in the rhythms of daily life and to articulate a theory of magic as a "sacred" yet fundamentally pragmatic activity, distinct from, yet tightly entwined with empirical knowledge and techniques surrounding everyday "profane" practices.

Born in Krakow, Malinowski earned his doctorate in philosophy from Jagiellonian University in 1908 and later trained in social sciences at Leipzig and in anthropology at the London School of Economics. Having spent the better part of World War I conducting fieldwork in southeastern New Guinea, he occupied teaching posts at the London School of Economics and the University of London before taking a position at Yale University in 1938. Malinowski's insistence that the world was sensible "from the native's point of view" contradicted Lucien Lévy-Bruhl's *mentalité primitif,* his appeal to a psychological and sociological "functionalism" emergent from the "psycho-physiological" needs of individuals broke openly with the holistic and evolutionary sociology of Émile Durkheim, and his insistence on the centrality of ethnographic fieldwork would later be considered a decisive break from the "armchair" methodology of Victorian anthropology. A quarter-century after Malinowski died at New Haven, Connecticut, the 1967 publication of his private diaries caused a scandal by revealing that this seemingly egalitarian and tolerant ethnographer was, in fact, often frustrated by and condescending toward his subjects in explicitly racist terms. Far from unseating Malinowski from his central position in anthropology, however, this gap between professional presentation and private life has only served to heighten the mystique around the man and the methodology he championed.

Malinowski's interest in magic was present in his early ethnographic works, *Argonauts of the Western Pacific* (1922) and *The Sexual Life of Savages in Northwestern Melanesia* (1929), which described the *kula* magic invested in objects of ritual trade and aspects of sexual magic. However, his most significant material about magic and its practitioners came in *Coral Gardens and Their Magic* (1935), an ethnographic narrative that painstakingly delineated the everyday "monotony" of magic in the cycles of productive life. Malinowski's pragmatic theory of magic was most explicitly presented in his posthumously published *Magic, Science, and Religion* (1948), which argued against prevailing understandings of magic as a clumsy and inefficient proto-science. This conventional wisdom, best articulated by Sir Edward Tylor and Sir James Frazer, structured magic as the lowest rung on a developmental sequence rising through religious to scientific means of knowing the natural world. Malinowski never conflated magic with religion (magic, he insisted, was always a pragmatic *means,* whereas religion was an end in itself), but he took great pains to separate magic from such "primitive" scientific practices as the empirical knowledge of fluid dynamics involved in Trobriand canoe-building. Such everyday, predictable concerns were placed in the sphere of the profane, but magical activities occupied the affect-laden domain of the sacred. He illustrated this with an account of Trobriand fishing practices: boating in the lagoon was safe and its yield relatively predictable; such trips involved no magic at all. Yet fishing on the open seas, which could result in a fantastic bounty, an empty net, or the death of all involved, was associated with extensive magical ritual to secure safety and good results. Magic was therefore a complement to, not a substitute for, empirical knowledge, useful in situations involving extreme risk, high stakes, emotional commitment, or lack of control.

Although Malinowski's functional explanations of human behavior have been criticized for their "thinness" and transparent teleology, it is important to note that his ethnographic descriptions are rich with details not explained by his theories. Furthermore, Malinowski argued strongly for the importance of context in understanding magical practices, and his explicitly performative analysis of magic—in particular, his linguistic theory of the power of magical words—can be seen as prefiguring the ordinary-language philosophers. Malinowski's willingness to generalize from the Trobriand Islands to humanity at large led him to construct a general theory of the "meanings of meaningless words" and the "coefficient of weirdness" necessary to elevate magical discourse beyond mundane levels without rendering it completely unintelligible. Malinowski used this principle to suggest magical belief as a human universal, equally present in the advertising and "beauty magic of Helena Rubinstein and Elizabeth Arden" as in the practices of medieval Europeans or early twentieth-century Trobrianders.

Perhaps more far-reaching than his own writings, however, was Malinowski's impact as an educator. If he has retrospectively been dubbed the father of modern anthropology, it is chiefly because he tutored many of the best minds of the next generation of British social anthropologists. In the context of anthropological debates on rationality and magical belief, it seems particularly significant that he taught E. E. Evans-Pritchard, whose *Witchcraft, Oracles, and Magic Among the Azande* would become a landmark in the field.

JEREMY GREENE

See also: ANTHROPOLOGY; EVANS-PRITCHARD, EDWARD E.; MAGIC AND RELIGION; SCIENCE AND MAGIC; WORDS, POWER OF.

References and further reading:
Geertz, Clifford. "Under the Mosquito Net." *New York Review of Books,* September 14, 1967, 15: 3–4.
Malinowski, Bronislaw. 1922. *Argonauts of the Western Pacific.* London: G. Routledge and Sons.
———. 1929. *The Sexual Life of Savages in Northwestern Melanesia.* London: G. Routledge and Sons.
———. 1935. *Coral Gardens and Their Magic.* London: Unwin Brothers.
———. 1948. *Magic, Science, and Religion.* Boston: Free Press.
———. 1967. *A Diary in the Strict Sense of the Term.* London: Routledge and Kegan Paul.
Nadel, S. F. 1957. "Malinowski on Magic and Religion." Pp. 189–208 in *Man and Culture: An Evaluation of the Work of Bronislaw Malinowski.* Edited by Raymond Firth. London: Routledge and Kegan Paul.
Stocking, George. 1995. *After Tylor: British Social Anthropology 1888–1951.* Madison: University of Wisconsin Press.
Tambiah, Jeyraja Stanley. 1984. *Magic, Science, Religion, and the Scope of Rationality.* Cambridge: Cambridge University Press.

MALLEUS MALEFICARUM

Some late medieval theologians, like the Dominican inquisitor Heinrich Kramer (Institoris), author of the *Malleus Maleficarum* (The Hammer of Witches, 1486), imagined witches to be members of a vast conspiracy directed against Christian society that was allowed by God to cause immense physical and spiritual hardship. The witches' power, supported by the Devil with God's permission, was real. Witches therefore had to be physically eradicated, according to divine and secular law, by virtually any means, because exceptional crimes require exceptional measures. The *Malleus* was the result of Kramer's experience with witchcraft trials in his designated area as a papal inquisitor for "Upper Germany" (i.e., southwestern Germany, western Austria, Switzerland, and his homeland, Alsace).

Evidence survives from some of his trials in this region, particularly from 1482 to 1484. Kramer's activities were generally not well received by the local

MALLEVS MALEFICARVM, MALEFICAS ET EARVM hæresim frameâ conterens,

Title page of the 1669 edition of Heinrich Kramer's *Malleus Maleficarum* (The Hammer of Witches), *1486, the most notorious book on witchcraft. (Fortean Picture Library)*

authorities, who disliked his interference with their administration of justice, and the populace, who sometimes initially welcomed him, soon tired of his persecutory zeal. Annoyed by such resistance, Kramer obtained papal authorization for his inquisitorial rights over the prosecution of witchcraft from Innocent VIII (ruled 1484–1492) through the papal bull *Summis desiderantes affectibus* (Desiring with Supreme Ardor, 1484), which authorized formal inquisitions against witches in all German Church provinces. Now invested with carte blanche, Kramer decided to start a paradigmatic witch hunt. Innsbruck, capital of the duchy of Tyrol, was a significant place, since its Archduke Sigmund was a powerful Habsburg prince, ruling over a patchwork of territories stretching from northern Italy and southwestern Germany into Alsace (present-day eastern France). Innsbruck was Kramer's gateway to the Holy Roman Empire.

Kramer's Inquisition in Innsbruck, starting in July 1485, employed intimidation, brutal force, and unlimited torture; denied legal defense; and issued distorted reports of his interrogations: scandalous conduct, even by late-fifteenth-century legal standards. Therefore, not only the relatives of the accused but also citizens of Innsbruck, together with the clergy, the Tyrolean nobility and eventually the local bishop, protested against his illegal procedures. Bishop Georg II Golser, successor of the philosopher Nicolaus of Cusa at the see of Brixen, appointed a commission to scrutinize Kramer's Inquisition. Despite desperate resistance from the inquisitor's side, the bishop stopped the persecution immediately, nullified its results and (after having secured the archduke's support), liberated all suspected women.

It is worth remembering that both the secular and ecclesiastical authorities of Tyrol decided to resist this papal inquisitor and that they successfully prevented a witch persecution within their jurisdiction. Kramer was branded a fanatic, and Bishop Golser (who called Kramer senile and crazy in his correspondence) even threatened him with force if he failed to leave his diocese voluntarily. The prince-bishops of Brixen never allowed a witch persecution in their territory, and, even more importantly, the Tyrolean government had learned a lasting lesson and subsequently suppressed any attempts by lower courts to launch witch hunts. In short, the Innsbruck Inquisition was a crushing defeat for the papal inquisitor.

His failure at Innsbruck and his apocalyptic fears drove Kramer to develop his ideas further. Starting from his reports to Bishop Golser (Ammann 1911), he hastily systematized his notes into a lengthy manuscript. This papal inquisitor was among the first of his profession to recognize the importance of the printing revolution, and with this manuscript he tried to turn his defeat into victory by demonstrating the existence of witchcraft. Using his authority and experience, he urged the necessity of a campaign to eradicate witchcraft. The result was the *Malleus Maleficarum.*

Much confusion persists about the author, place of print, and date of print of this crucial publication on witchcraft. Even recently, scholars have claimed that the *Malleus* was at least coauthored by Jacob Sprenger (1437–1495). Only in 1519, decades after Sprenger's death, was he named as author on a front page, first in an edition by the Nuremberg (Nürnberg) printer Friedrich Peypus. Two generations later, in 1574, Giovanni Antonio Bertanus, a Venetian printer, even named Sprenger as its sole author. Later German and French printers adopted Bertanus's mistake. However, no contemporary evidence suggests that Sprenger had anything to do with the *Malleus,* or with witchcraft trials, or with executions of any kind as a result of inquisition trials.

The author of the *Malleus* stated that forty-eight women had been burned as witches in the diocese of Constance; there is no reason to doubt this number, especially because he indicated that he himself had searched this diocese more than any other. All these remarks pointed directly to "frater Henricus de Sletstat," or "Heinrich Institoris," as Kramer often Latinized himself. The historian Sönke Lorenz found a hitherto unknown letter of this inquisitor from 1484, announcing his arrival at Wolfegg, a Swabian castle of Count Johann von Waldburg-Trauchburg (ruled 1460–1505)—close relatives to the ruling prince-bishop of Constance—for the purpose of witch hunting. Numerous documents survive concerning Kramer's inquisition in the Imperial City of Ravensburg, mentioned in the first (Speyer 1486) edition of the *Malleus* (fol. 44r). After his crushing failure at Innsbruck, Kramer turned his attention toward Alsace, particularly in the vicinity of his convent. The expulsion of the Jews from his hometown of Sélestat should be placed in this context. In 1488 Kramer tried to incite witch hunts in the neighboring diocese of Trier; that year, thirty-five witches were burned in the nearby imperial city of Metz. In an expert opinion for the imperial city of Nuremberg, "Bruder Heinrich Kramer Prediger Ordens" boasted in October 1491 that "more than 200 witches" had been burned thus far due to his inquisitions, and in the same document he revealed his single authorship of the *Malleus* (Jerouschek 1991).

Further actions of this inquisitor remain shrouded in darkness, and recent research suggests that his own superior may have silenced him. Jacob Sprenger turned out to have been Kramer's most bitter enemy. In complete contrast to the Alsatian fanatic, a maverick who managed to get into trouble wherever he went and who had developed into a wandering inquisitor and persecution specialist, Sprenger was a prominent figure among the "observant" reform wing of the Dominicans. He was appointed prior of the large Cologne convent, then leader of the "Teutonic" province; Sprenger was also an influential theologian, promoting veneration of the Virgin Mary and introducing rosary brotherhoods organized by friars and secular clergy for lay people. It seems likely that Sprenger was involuntarily included in both the papal bull of 1484 and the foreword of the *Malleus* in 1486. Wilson (1990, 130) doubted that Kramer tried deliberately to deceive the public and Sprenger, but this must have been the case. Sprenger had tried to suppress Kramer's activities in every possible way. He forbade the convents of his province to host him, he forbade Kramer to preach, and even tried to interfere directly in the affairs of Kramer's Sélestat convent. Not one single fact or incident associated Sprenger with witchcraft prosecutions, and he apparently managed to drive the author of the *Malleus* from his province. Kramer spent his final years in Italy and Moravia, where he died. Kramer successfully deceived many modern scholars with his misrepresentations and outright lies. But one need only read the surviving Innsbruck trial records (Ammann 1890) and compare them with his accounts of the Innsbruck inquisition in the *Malleus* to realize that Kramer was ready to use any deception that served his purpose. His career offers numerous examples, but this one seems sufficient (Segl 1988).

As to date and place of print, a printer's account book (Geldner 1964) demonstrated that the *Malleus* was first printed in autumn 1486 in the imperial city of Speyer, by then a medium-size town on the Rhine with about 8,000 inhabitants. The printer was Peter Drach (ca. 1450–1504), who delivered the "treatise against sorcerers" to booksellers by December 1486. The original text of the *Malleus* comprised 129 leaves (258 pages) in folio; given the usual production of a small printer (about 900 folio pages a day), Drach could have printed 150 copies a month. If the first edition was meant to have 300 copies, the manuscript must have been delivered to Drach by mid-October 1486, with more copies even earlier. Like many early books, it had no title page at that stage, so descriptions of the *Malleus* vary in the account book. The *Malleus* was called a "treatise against sorceresses," or "against sorcery," until Kramer added a foreword to the text, his *apologia auctoris in malleum maleficarum,* around Easter 1487 (Behringer and Jerouschek in Kramer 2000, 22–31). Afterward, the book's title was fixed and appears regularly this way in the account book, even without the *Malleus* having a title page.

Kramer promoted his publication in every possible way, notably by adding the papal bull of 1484 and a reference to its approval by the University of Cologne from April 1487. The latter was at least partly a forgery, because two of its supposed authors (Thomas de Scotia and Johann von Wörde) later denied any participation. These additions were not printed by Drach but by an immediate apprentice of Johannes Gutenberg at Mainz, Peter Schöffer (ca. 1425–1503), with a separate pagination. These parts were probably added in late May 1487 and bound together with the existing main body of the text. Henceforth, the author's *Apologia,* the papal bull *Summis desiderantes affectibus,* and the Cologne *Approbatio* remained part of the *Malleus.* In early December 1486, when Speyer hosted a meeting of representatives of the imperial cities (*Städtetag*), and Emperor Frederick III (whom Kramer had insulted some years earlier, to the great displeasure of the Dominican order) was due to arrive, Kramer apparently traveled to the Burgundian capital at Brussels in order to obtain a privilege from King Maximilian I (1459–1519), the future emperor. The response must have been so unfavorable that it was not inserted into the foreword, although it was mentioned there, thus conveying the impression that the highest ecclesiastical, academic, and secular authorities backed the *Malleus.* Kramer's strategy was aimed at the princes and their law courts. However, educated theologians and lawyers must have noticed that authoritative authors, like St. Augustine and St. Thomas Aquinas, as well as Roman law, were deliberately twisted and misquoted in the

Malleus. Moreover, Kramer brazenly emphasized the success of his inquisition at Innsbruck and even thanked the archduke for his support. He was correct in assuming that few would check his claims.

By reconstructing Kramer's itinerary, it becomes clear that the *Malleus* was assembled hastily, within nine months. Starting with his opinions and apologies to the bishop of Brixen and the archduke of Tyrol, Kramer, after his expulsion from Innsbruck in February 1486, mined some standard textbooks of scholastic theology (Thomas Aquinas, Antonius of Florence), a few inquisitors' manuals (Nicolas Eymeric), and earlier sermon notes. These indispensable texts were only available in the libraries of larger Dominican monasteries like Salzburg, Augsburg (Slemer 1936), Speyer, or his own convent at Sélestat. At one of these places, the *Malleus* must have been assembled. In the first edition (Speyer 1486, fol. 44r), Kramer told us that at least parts of it were written in the imperial city of Speyer, where he was physically present in autumn 1486, because Peter Drach had agreed to publish his text without delay. Kramer may have been unable to publish it at a more important printing center like Augsburg or Strasbourg.

Kramer's haste explains why the *Malleus* bristled with inconsistencies throughout. Contradictions and mistakes of all kinds (meaning, grammar, spelling) abounded; even the gender of the witches (*malefica/maleficus*) varied continuously, although the text was clearly directed against female witches. The most striking evidence for this haste comes from the *Malleus* itself. According to its contents, forty-eight questions were to be treated, but Kramer completely ignored this structure and ended with eighty-six chapters, unevenly distributed over three "parts," two of them further subdivided. Part 1 supposedly contained sixteen chapters, but it actually had eighteen. The additional chapters, with new examples, were obviously added afterward; Chapter 17 claimed to be an extension of chapter 14, which had presumably been printed already. Part 2 supposedly contained sixteen chapters but ended up with twenty-five. Large chunks of its text were never mentioned in its table of contents; its headings hardly ever matched; whole chapters advertised in the contents were lacking; some were wrongly numbered; cross-references usually led nowhere.

It was obviously a work in progress, its author continually adding more evidence until the last possible moment, but without proofreading. The practical difficulties of compiling such a massive text under extreme time pressure and premodern conditions can hardly be underestimated. We can only guess why the maverick inquisitor became a maverick author and wrote a desperate book under such desperate conditions. Perhaps he feared more important dangers from the approaching emperor or from Jacob Sprenger, whose name he was again about to misuse and whose election as provincial superior of the German Dominicans was imminent. The same day Sprenger became successor to Jacob Strubach as provincial superior (October 19, 1487), he obtained permission from his general, Joaquino Turriani, to lash out *adversus m[agistrum] Henricum Institoris inquisitorem* (against Master Heinrich Kramer, inquisitor). But perhaps the source of Kramer's haste should be sought in the realm of the irrational; apocalypticism seemed a good guess, if we took the author's *Apologia* seriously. If the end of the world was nigh, grammar became unimportant.

Kramer's main concern was witchcraft, or the heresy of witchcraft, but we must still explain his particular obsession with female witches. One likely explanation is the legacy of Christian theology, with its long-standing assertion of increased female susceptibility to temptations of the Devil, starting with Eve. This was certainly the starting point for the misogyny of the *Malleus,* whose author devoted several pages to explaining female inclinations to witchcraft, and recommended the subject for preaching, because women had a particular desire for instruction. His first demonstration of the malice of females was the Bible; he then cited instances of female credulity and their physical qualities, in particular the changeability of their complexion, leading to a vacillating nature. He then referred to their slippery tongues, which made them share their magic with friends, with whom they employed *maleficium* (harmful magic) because they were too weak to take revenge otherwise. Worst of all, however, because of their changeability, women were less inclined to believe in God. At this point, Kramer inserted a unique "realist" etymology of *femina:* "fe" is taken as an abbreviation of "fides" (belief); combined with the suffix "minus," it literally translates into "she who believes less." In the eyes of the Dominican inquisitor, a woman's lack of belief was the basis for her apostasy and witchcraft (Speyer 1486, fol. 20–21).

Kramer's paranoid emphasis on the dangers triggered by females contrasts strikingly with the attitude of his main opponent within the German Dominicans, the Cologne prior Jacob Sprenger, who instead emphasized the positive aspects of female religious devotion, recruiting them for the veneration of Mary. It is characteristic to find Kramer—a persecution specialist whose obsessions might be described in terms of "purity and danger"—engaged in an inquisition in Augsburg against women who desired the Eucharist too frequently, who were in turn defended by a local supporter of Sprenger (Koeniger 1923).

The *Malleus Maleficarum* was divided into three parts. The first treated theological issues and the second practical problems; the third offered advice on legal procedures, referring constantly to the author's extensive experience with witchcraft trials. The first part of the original edition (fols. 4r–43r) on theological questions, designed to prove the reality and danger of witchcraft, was interesting in several respects and showed Kramer's erudition as an educated Dominican. Founded upon Augustine and Aquinas, its description of the crime of witchcraft was entirely conventional: witches could not themselves harm anyone through magic, but their abilities derived from a contract with a demon, which in turn was empowered by God. Both the *permissio Dei* (God's permission), and (wo)man's free will were crucial elements. At the core of witchcraft theory lay Augustine's semiotic theory that demons and (wo)men communicated via signs, amplified here by Kramer's perception that human deeds and natural phenomena were hardly ever what they appeared to be, but must rather be interpreted through a demonological theory of signs.

Like postmodern theorists, Kramer concluded that human beings could never be certain about reality; any phenomenon could be different from what it appeared to be and could be a demonic delusion. In contrast to modern philosophers, who denied the reality of demons, Kramer denied the reality of reality. He suspected demons were omnipresent and (with God's permission) extraordinarily powerful. Although witches believed they could do harm, it was actually demons who conducted supernatural interventions in order to fulfill their pact and to seduce them. The witch's crime thus in fact became her desire to harm. But no secular law imposed the death penalty for mere intentions, so witchcraft must therefore be considered essentially as heresy. For Kramer, heresy and apostasy lay at the core of witchcraft; although the witches themselves might have thought otherwise, their basic crime was spiritual. His conclusions were subsequently developed through examples of specific aspects of witchcraft, including sexual intercourse between humans and demons (either succubi or incubi), shape shifting, the sacrifice of babies, and the preparation of witches' unguents. According to Kramer, witches intended their harm to be real, although the demons actually did the damage by interfering in the real world in order to deceive the witches.

Kramer's conclusions were theologically correct but entailed serious practical contradictions. If harmful magic had no physical agent, it could not be prosecuted. If witches were seduced and deceived by demons, they became victims rather than perpetrators. If circumstantial evidence or direct observations could be discarded as devilish illusions (*praestigia daemonum,* as Johann Weyer later called them), witches could never be tried by a secular court because it was impossible to prove they had committed any crime whatsoever.

Surprisingly, after denying the possibility of judging the reality of evidence, Kramer's sharpest weapon (as he must have thought) was his reference to personal experience. Besides theological authorities, firsthand examples provided Kramer's foremost evidence for the reality of witchcraft. Among roughly 250 examples in the *Malleus*, mostly from the Bible or ancient authors, at least 75 (nearly 30 percent) refer to recent events, which Kramer took from trustworthy contemporaries or from personal experience. About 10 percent of them came from Speyer or its immediate vicinity, further indication that Kramer completed the manuscript of the *Malleus* in this imperial city. Most of the rest came from Swabia, Alsace, or Tyrol; a few examples came from further abroad, usually towns with Dominican monasteries where Kramer had stayed (Rome, Cologne, Augsburg, Salzburg, Landshut in Bavaria).

The second part of the original *Malleus* (fols. 43r–92v) was split into two sections. The first (2.1) described how to protect oneself against witchcraft, specifically against impotence and infertility, weather making, and milk theft; the second (2.2) treated how bewitching could be cured. Again Kramer discussed demonically caused impotence, infertility, and weather magic, as well as love magic and demonic possession. The third part of the *Malleus* (fols. 92v–129v) explored the legal treatment of witches in great detail, recommending inquisitorial procedure as superior to trials based upon accusations, and paying attention to circumstantial evidence. In this part, Kramer literally copied large chunks of text from such inquisition manuals as Nicolas Eymerich *Directorium Inquisitorum* (Directory of Inquisitors) of 1376 to provide the necessary legal formulas for inexperienced judges.

Pioneers of the intellectual history of demonology like Joseph Hansen emphasized that the *Malleus* contained almost nothing that could not be found in earlier demonologies or inquisitors' manuals. Because Kramer was a Dominican doctor of theology and papal inquisitor, and considering the conditions under which he assembled the *Malleus,* that was hardly surprising. However, five points in his *Malleus* could be called original. First, it stressed that witchcraft was a real crime, not just a spiritual one, and that witches therefore must be prosecuted and deserve capital punishment. Among earlier inquisitors, this had been a minority position. Second, Kramer claimed that witchcraft is the worst of all crimes because it combines heresy, including apostasy and adoration of the Devil, with the most terrible secular crimes such as murder, theft, and sodomy. Again, this point was not entirely new, but Kramer focused attention on it.

Third, because witchcraft was not only the worst of all crimes but also occult and difficult to trace, legal inhibitions must be abandoned. This idea was original in the sense that no serious lawyer in Europe normally suggested transgressing legal boundaries. His conflicts with local authorities had made Kramer keenly aware that this position was completely unacceptable under normal circumstances. Therefore, he resorted to the claim that witchcraft was an exceptional crime, in whose pursuit persecutory zeal was preferable to routine legality. Thus Kramer claimed the superiority of apocalyptic theology over law.

Fourth, witches were primarily women. Despite the misogyny of the times, this idea was still uncommon in theology but was widespread in popular thought, so here Kramer's personal obsessions might have gained some popular support. Finally, he believed that secular courts should prosecute the crime; here again, the inquisitor drew conclusions from his own experience because he knew how unpopular inquisitors often were in Europe north of the Alps. However, this idea was also paradoxical because secular courts were reluctant to prosecute spiritual crimes.

A curious, literate public welcomed the *Malleus Maleficarum* as the first printed handbook of witch demonology and persecution. Although largely dependent on earlier theologians and inquisitorial handbooks, it was a fresh product by an erudite and experienced author. With twelve Latin editions printed in Germany and France between 1486 and 1523, *The Hammer of Witches* could be considered a success, although public interest was clearly strongest in the first ten years when the subject was still novel and the book was almost a best seller. Just after the Protestant Reformation, the demand for reprints broke down completely. Two generations later, with the Counter-Reformation accelerating, two Venetian printers saw a renewed demand for the *Malleus* in 1574 and 1576; in the 1580s, three new editions were printed in Protestant Frankfurt, followed by a fourth in 1600.

It was France that became the stronghold of *Malleus* reprints after the Reformation. Demand grew in the 1580s, with two editions printed at Lyons in 1584 and 1595; after 1600, seven further editions were published at Lyons, the last in 1669. Significantly, the *Malleus* was never translated fully into any vernacular language during the period of witch hunting; the partial translation into Polish in 1614 omitted its legal parts. Its reception remained confined to highly educated theologians, physicians, and lawyers. Its contents had to be spread, if at all, through sermons.

The upsurge of witchcraft trials in the early 1490s in central Europe has traditionally been interpreted as a result of the publication of the *Malleus,* and some incidents indicate that it had a direct impact. A monastic chronicler at Eberhardsklausen, on the Mosel River, reported that witches had plagued this region for some time, but great uncertainty about the matter had made it impossible to prosecute them. Only after reading the *Malleus* did local authorities see how they could proceed against witches—which they did. Here we see a kind of "conversion experience," but that was a rare example, and how the *Malleus* was generally received remains unclear (Rummel 1990).

It is noteworthy that an early opposition publication was reprinted even more frequently in the 1490s.

Ulrich Molitor, a lawyer for the bishop of Constance and a minor official at Archduke Sigmund's court in Innsbruck, challenged the central assumptions of the *Malleus*. Molitor fashioned his text as a conversation between a fanatic believer in witchcraft, Molitor himself as an opponent, and Archduke Sigmund as the wise arbiter, always reaching reasonable conclusions and bluntly denying the possibility of the witches' flight, the witches' Sabbat, and shape shifting. Molitor merely repeated the traditional attitude of the Catholic Church and indeed promoted a conservative attitude toward sorcery. But this attitude had hitherto prevented witchcraft persecutions. Moreover, Molitor went one step further. By excluding theologians from his discourse, he implies that Dominicans or inquisitors should not interfere with legal questions. Illustrated by many exciting woodcuts, Molitor's dialogue quickly went through ten reprints in the 1490s, including, unlike the *Malleus*, translations into vernacular German. Molitor presumably witnessed Kramer's inquisitions in both the diocese of Constance and the diocese of Brixen. If this *juris utriusque doctor* (doctor of both laws, i.e., of canon and civil laws) opposed the *Malleus*, it was presumably because he knew its author and his illegal methods.

And there are other examples of people rejecting Kramer's views, either after reading the *Malleus* or after meeting him personally. In 1491, the imperial city of Nuremberg ordered a summary of the *Malleus* from Kramer because of some serious cases of sorcery; the famous publisher Anton Koberger, who printed three editions of the *Malleus*, was an immediate neighbor of Nuremberg's Dominican convent. However, Nuremberg's magistrates never followed Kramer's advice, and it may not be coincidence that the ideas of the *Malleus* were ridiculed publicly by leading Nuremberg humanists like Willibald Pirckheimer. In the imperial city of Augsburg, where Kramer stayed when traveling between Italy and Alsace and where he became involved in serious quarrels with the local representative of Jacob Sprenger's rosary brotherhood, the inquisitor was labeled a drunkard by the leading humanist Konrad Peutinger, and it may be no coincidence that the *Malleus* was never printed in this leading Upper German communications center. One of the most interesting reactions came from a close friend of the recently deceased Jacob Sprenger, who sharply rejected the idea that Sprenger had any connection to the *Malleus* (Klose 1972). By the early sixteenth century, the *Malleus* had clearly become a point of reference in intellectual debates: in 1509, defending a woman accused of witchcraft at Metz against the machinations of the local Dominican inquisitor, Agrippa von Nettesheim reacted equally sharply against the nonsense proposed in the *Malleus*. About the same time, Erasmus of Rotterdam satirized a zealous inquisitor in his *Praise of Folly*, and leading Italian jurist Andrea Alciati, labeled witch hunts in northern Italy as *nova holocausta*. It was certainly not an arbitrary decision of the Spanish Inquisition in 1526 to deny any authority to the *Malleus*.

Rather than provoking the rising witchcraft persecutions at the end of the fifteenth century, the publication of the *Malleus* by this troublesome inquisitor may have simply tried to exploit preexisting popular fears. Between the 1480s and about 1520, witch burnings or small panic trials occurred not only in places where Dominican inquisitors incited the populace or where the town council had purchased a copy of the *Malleus*, but in many places throughout upper Italy, northern Spain, eastern France, Switzerland, western Germany, and the Burgundian Netherlands, even prior to its publication. In the decades between 1470 and 1520, there were severe mortality crises, and scapegoats were sought. In the early 1480s, plague rampaged widely through Upper Germany, Switzerland, and eastern France, and the original edition of the *Malleus* even linked witchcraft to plague in one particular case, in which a deceased witch had spread the disease from her grave (fol. 38r–38v). Imperial cities like Memmingen or Ravensburg lost much of their population in these years, and fears of sudden death were justifiably widespread.

Not only witchcraft anxieties but popular piety in general soared, as we can see in the iconographical representations of the "Dance of Death," or in the rise of millennial fears, with the idea that humanity was living in the last age—a time characterized by bitter hardships and terrifying signs of the end of the world. Like other fundamentalist prophets, the author of the *Malleus* points to the book of *Revelation* in his *Apologia* to argue that the emergence of the witches' sect was one sign of the imminence of the Antichrist.

WOLFGANG BEHRINGER

See also: AGRIPPA VON NETTESHEIM, HEINRICH CORNELIUS; ALCIATI, ANDREA; ANTICHRIST; APOCALYPSE; AQUINAS, THOMAS; AUGUSTINE, ST.; BOOKS; CORPOREALITY, ANGELIC AND DEMONIC; DEMONOLOGY; DEMONS; DOMINICAN ORDER; ERASMUS, DESIDERIUS; EYMERIC, NICOLAS; GENDER; GOLSER, GEORG; INNOCENT VIII, POPE; INNSBRUCK; KRAMER, HEINRICH; MOLITOR, ULRICH; SEXUAL ACTIVITY, DIABOLIC; TYROL, COUNTY OF; WANN, PAULUS.

References and further reading:
Ammann, Hartmann. 1890. "Der Innsbrucker Hexenprozess von 1485." *Zeitschrift des Ferdinandeums für Tirol und Vorarlberg* 34: 1–87.
———. 1911. " Eine Vorarbeit des Heinrich Institoris für den *Malleus Maleficarum.*" *Mitteilungen des Instituts für Österreichische Geschichtsforschung*, Ergänzungsband 8: 461–504.
Anglo, Sydney. 1977. "Evident Authority and Authoritative Evidence: The *Malleus Maleficarum.*" Pp. 1–32 in *The Damned Art: Essays in the Literature of Witchcraft*. Edited by Sydney Anglo. London: Routledge and Kegan Paul.

Broedel, Hans Peter. 2003. *The* Malleus Maleficarum *and the Construction of Witchcraft*. Manchester, UK, and New York: Manchester University Press.

Geldner, Ferdinand. 1964. "Das Rechnungsbuch des Speyrer Druckherrn, Verlegers und Grossbuchhändlers Peter Drach. Mit Einleitung, Erläuterungen und Identifizierungslisten." *Archiv für die Geschichte des Buchwesens* 5 (reprint from 1962): 1–196.

Hansen, Joseph. 1898. "Der *Malleus maleficarum,* seine Druckausgaben und die gefälschte Kölner Approbation vom Jahre 1487." *Westdeutsche Zeitschrift für Geschichte und Kunst* 17: 119–168.

———. 1907a. "Heinrich Institoris, der Verfasser des Hexenhammers, und seine Tätigkeit an der Mosel im Jahre 1488." *Westdeutsche Zeitschrift für Geschichte und Kunst* 26: 110–118.

———. 1907b. "Der Hexenhammer, seine Bedeutung und die gefälschte Kölner Approbation vom Jahre 1487." *Westdeutsche Zeitschrift für Geschichte und Kunst* 26: 372–404.

Jerouschek, Günter, ed. and trans. 1991. "'Nürnberger Hexenhammer' von Heinrich Kramer: Faksimile der Handschrift von 1491. Hildesheim, Zürich, and New York: Olms.

———, ed. 1992. *Malleus Maleficarum* [*Speyer 1486*]. Hildesheim: Olms.

Klose, Hans-Christian. 1972. "Die angebliche Mitarbeit des Dominikaners Jakob Sprenger am Hexenhammer, nach einem alten Abdinghofer Brief." Pp. 197–205 in *Paderbornensia Ecclesia, Beiträge zur Geschichte des Erzbistums Paderborn. Festschrift für Lorenz Kardinal Jäger zum 80. Geburtstag*. Edited by Paul-Werner Scheele. Paderborn: Schöningh.

Koeniger, Albert Maria. 1923. *Ein Inquisitionsprozess in Sachen der täglichen Kommunion*. Bonn and Leipzig: Verlag Schröder.

Kramer (Institoris), Heinrich. 2000. *Der Hexenhammer: Malleus Maleficarum. Kommentierte Neuübersetzung*. Edited and translated by Wolfgang Behringer, Günter Jerouschek, and Werner Tschacher. Introduction by Wolfgang Behringer and Günter Jerouschek. Munich: Deutscher Taschenbuch.

———. 2004. *Der Hexenhammer: Malleus Maleficarum*. Edited and translated by Wolfgang Behringer, Günter Jerouschek, and Werner Tschacher. 4th ed. Munich: Deutscher Taschenbuch.

Kramer (Institoris), Heinrich, and James [sic] Sprenger. 1928. *Malleus Maleficarum: The Classic Study of Witchcraft (1484)*. Edited by Montague Summers. London: Pushkin. Reprints, Arrow, 1971; Bracken Books, 1996. Also published as *The Malleus Maleficarum* by Heinrich Kramer and James [sic] Sprenger. Translated by Montague Summers. London: Peter Smith, 1990.

Müller, Karl Otto. 1910. "Heinrich Institoris, der Verfasser des Hexenhammers und seine Tätigkeit als Hexeninquisitor in Ravensburg im Herbst 1484." *Württembergische Vierteljahreshefte für Landesgeschichte* NF 19: 397–417.

Petersohn, Jürgen. 1988. "Konziliaristen und Hexen: Ein unbekannter Brief des Inquisitors Heinrich Institoris an Papst Sixtus IV. aus dem Jahr 1484." *Deutsches Archiv zur Erforschung des Mittelalters* 44: 120–160.

Rummel, Walter. 1990. "Gutenberg, der Teufel und die Muttergottes von Eberhardsklausen: Erste Hexenverfolgung im Trierer Land." Pp. 91–117 in *Ketzer, Zauberer, Hexen. Die Anfänge der europäischen Hexenverfolgungen*. Edited by Andreas Blauert. Frankfurt am Main: Suhrkamp.

Schmauder, Andreas, ed. 2001. *Frühe Hexenverfolgung in Ravensburg*. Constance: UVK Verlagsgesellschaft.

Schnyder, André. 1993. Malleus Maleficarum *von Heinrich Institoris (alias Kramer), unter Mithilfe Jakob Sprengers aufgrund der dämonologischen Tradition zusammengestellt: Kommentar zur Wiedergabe des Erstdrucks von 1487 (Hain 9238)*. Göppingen: Kümmerle.

Segl, Peter, ed. 1988. *Der "Hexenhammer": Entstehung und Umfall des "Malleus Maleficarum" von 1487*. Cologne and Berlin: Böhlau.

———. 1991. "*Malefice . . . non sunt . . . heretice nuncupande* zu Heinrich Kramers Wiederlegung der Ansichten *aliorum inquisitorum in diversis regnis hispanie*." Pp. 369–382 in *Papsttum, Kirche und Recht im Mittelalter. Festschrift für Horst Fuhrmann zum 65*. Edited by Hubert Mordek. Geburtstag, Tübingen: M. Niemeyer.

Siemer, Polycarp M., O. P. 1936. *Geschichte des Dominikanerklosters Sankt Magdalena in Augsburg (1225–1808)*. Vechta: Albertus-Magnus-Verlag der Dominikaner.

Stephens, Walter. 2002. *Demon Lovers: Witchcraft, Sex, and the Crisis of Belief*. Chicago and London: University of Chicago Press.

Wilson, Eric. 1990. "The Text and Context of the *Malleus Maleficarum*." PhD diss., Cambridge University.

MALTA

Information on witchcraft practices in Malta comes from its Inquisition tribunal archives, luckily saved from total destruction during the French occupation of Malta (1798–1800). Witchcraft became a significant preoccupation of the Malta Inquisition after the arrival of the Apostolic Visitor Monsignor Pietro Dusina in 1574. Witchcraft-related proceedings rose in importance in the mid-1590s. By the early seventeenth century, witchcraft cases accounted for one-third of the Inquisition's caseload—a level approximately maintained until the late eighteenth century.

Two main factors influenced the ways the Maltese adapted and shaped their witchcraft beliefs. First, Malta's crowded urban harbor area was constantly receiving people from neighboring Mediterranean lands and beyond. Second, Malta was an intensely Catholic society, a situation that inevitably colored the beliefs and thinking of its inhabitants.

Malta's harbor towns were crowded, with neighbors able to spy on each other, leaving little room for secrecy. Therefore, the more exotic types of witchcraft, such as cannibalism or night flying, occured only in occasional denunciations by rural villagers in the late sixteenth and early seventeenth centuries. But the fact that any potentially useful witness would be acquainted with the accused and that the accused could not have done these things without being observed meant that Maltese Inquisitors rarely took accusations of exotic types of witchcraft seriously.

Meanwhile, sophisticated foreign travelers and traders introduced new ideas into Maltese society. The presence of many people of different cultural backgrounds made residents of Malta harbor towns more tolerant of strange ideas and less threatened by them.

Maltese Holy Office records reveal a steady increase in witchcraft cases from the 1590s, with the flow of accusations remaining high until the end of the eighteenth century, when the tribunal was abolished. The punishments inflicted until the early 1630s were rather harsh, although they never ended with the execution of the accused. Subsequently, however, there was no significant trend toward either severity or leniency. By the time of Inquisitor Fabio Chigi (1634–1639)—later Pope Alexander VII—the tribunal came to adopt a more bureaucratic approach, with more thorough examinations of witnesses and more formal and detailed recording procedures. The tribunal settled into a routine that enabled it to look conscientiously into each case. Nonetheless, its basic methods for handling witchcraft remained unchanged throughout the tribunal's existence.

MALTESE WITCHCRAFT PRACTICES

A fairly clear distinction separated the type of witchcraft pursued by men from that practiced by women. Men, both clerics and others, concentrated on such potentially profitable brands of magic as treasure hunting. Perhaps the best Maltese necromancer of the early seventeenth century was the military engineer and member of the Order of St. John, Fra Vittorio Cassar. Women also shared men's fascination for buried treasure, but they almost monopolized most types of divination, conjuration, and *maleficium* (harmful magic), especially those aimed at love magic. Healing was also largely undertaken by women, although a few clerics and some slaves—largely Muslims, as well as a few members of the Jewish minority—attempted it for profit. Maltese men and women displayed fundamentally divergent motives in their attempts to manipulate supernatural forces: basically, men merely sought gain, whereas women's motives were more varied and complex.

Love magic was practiced primarily by unmarried women, including widows (who were not always elderly). Married women occasionally resorted to love magic to win a husband back from another woman (though some simply accused the other woman of love magic herself). Married women also resorted to divination to ascertain whether or not their husbands, away at sea, were still alive and, if so, if they had remained faithful. Others used more passive forms of love magic to soften a husband's harsh treatment of them. Conversely, the fact that a woman was in a stable marriage argued greatly in her favor if denounced, particularly since women under male supervision could be better controlled.

Poor moral behavior contributed greatly toward suspicions of witchcraft. This was one reason why courtesans featured so much in the list of those denounced. Living outside recognized moral norms, courtesans were expected to have few scruples about violating conventional religious standards. They also had more reason to resort to witchcraft in order to entice men, thus earning the name of *meretrice* (prostitute). As with most witchcraft, the courtesan's motives can generally be reduced to love or gain. But it is clear that the courtesan-witch did not make a fortune from her witchcraft.

Another factor featuring prominently in the tribunal's thinking, and perhaps even more so in the thinking of the Maltese urban populace, was the nationality or place of origin of the "suspect." A good number of those accused in Malta's witchcraft trials were in fact foreign-born. The English traveler George Sandys, who visited Malta in 1610, commented how Malta was a place that saw an influx of people of all kinds. Many of them had moved into the harbor area, particularly Valletta, from the Maltese countryside. Many residents of Valletta came from Sicily, other parts of Italy, Greece, or elsewhere, not counting the large number of Muslim slaves. Four main groups stand out: Greeks, Sicilians, French, and male Muslim slaves serving the Order of St. John. It was mainly foreigners residing in Malta, rather than transients, who were accused of witchcraft. Such foreigners were more likely to practice certain types of witchcraft in order to gain a living in a strange environment. Male Muslim slaves were experts in divination, healing, and to some extent even love magic. But in the latter category, women of Greek origin seem to have been particularly sought after—and also to bring about impotence. Moreover, for the elderly, unmarried, or widowed popular healers of the countryside, witchcraft offered a way of gaining a certain prestige as well as providing a means of survival. A similar pattern emerged from the accusations against the male Muslim slaves, who were out to amass enough money to ransom themselves from slavery and return home.

PUNISHMENTS

As in other branches of the Roman Inquisition, the sudden increase of witchcraft-related cases in the 1590s marked a pronounced shift in the Inquisition's priorities, which is more easily identified than explained. Sixtus V's 1586 bull against magic was clearly significant in this context, describing the types of activity most commonly dealt with by the Inquisition in the 1590s and early 1600s, although the first serious clampdown on witchcraft in Malta appears to have taken place immediately after the terrible outbreak of plague in 1592–1593 and more specifically from 1595 onward.

The Inquisition's public punishments for witchcraft offenses certainly succeeded in advertising its disapproval of such activities, although they did not dissuade people from practicing such beliefs, as the continual flow of accusations throughout the late seventeenth and eighteenth centuries shows. On such occasions, the methods used were meant to ensure adequate publicity and humiliation for the penitent. Penitents were made to stand at the Annunciation Church run by the Dominican friars or, more rarely, at the parish Church of St. Lawrence, both in Vittoriosa, holding a lighted candle during High Mass, usually on a feast day, to ensure that the largest possible audience witnessed the event. Public scourging, the tribunal's other main form of punishment, was inflicted in the main squares of Vittoriosa, and the penitent was then usually exiled. However, the tribunal's primary aim was to correct rather than punish. Hence, torture was generally reserved for those unwilling to accept this correction; Malta's witches were never executed, not even in the mass trials of the early seventeenth century.

By the late 1640s, the tribunal had almost accepted witchcraft as a fact of life in Malta and had established its own routines for dealing with it. The number of voluntary confessions for witchcraft increased by the mid-seventeenth century and remained steady right up to the last years of the tribunal. Nonetheless, it appears that Maltese society began to frown upon witchcraft practices, indicating that the tribunal's policy of publicizing its dealings with known offenders had indeed paid off. Obviously, the Inquisition had not been successful in eradicating witchcraft from Maltese society. Some witches saw little to fear from the Holy Office. They either believed they would never be caught, or even if they were, the mild punishment did not deter them. Popular magic outlasted the tribunal, which was suppressed in 1798. Some Maltese even seem to have been virtually addicted to witchcraft as a way of life. Thus, it continued to be practiced in the form of healing and as a way to ward off the evil eye, right into the twentieth century.

CARMEL CASSAR

See also: INQUISITION, ROMAN; LOVE MAGIC.

References and further reading:
Bonnici, Alexander. 1990–1994. *Storja tà l-Inkizizzjoni.* 3 vols. Malta: Religjon u Hajja.
Cassar, Carmel. 1993. "Witchcraft Beliefs and Social Control in Seventeenth-Century Malta." *Journal of Mediterranean Studies* 3, no. 2: 316–334.
———. 1996. *Witchcraft, Sorcery, and the Inquisition. A Study of Cultural Values in Early Modern Malta.* Malta: Mireva Publications.
———. 2000. *Sex, Magic, and the Periwinkle. A Trial at the Malta Inquisition Tribunal, 1617.* Malta: Pin Publications.
———. 2002. *Daughters of Eve: Women, Gender Roles, and the Impact of the Council of Trent in Catholic Malta.* Malta: Mireva Publications.
Cassar-Pullicino, Joseph. 1976. *Studies in Maltese Folklore.* Malta: University of Malta.
Ciappara, Frans. 2001. *Society and the Inquisition in Early Modern Malta.* Malta: Publishers Enterprises Group.
Douglas, Mary, ed. 1970. *Witchcraft: Confessions and Accusations.* London: Tavistock Publications.
Marwick, Max, ed. 1970. *Witchcraft and Sorcery.* Harmondsworth, England: Penguin Education.
Salelles, Sebastianus. 1651–1656. *De Materiis Tribunalium S. Inquisitionis.* 3 vols. Rome: Collinius.
Sandys, George. 1637. *A Relation of a Journey Begun An. Dom. 1610. Foure Bookes. Containing a description of the Turkish Empire, of Aegypt, of the Holy Land, of the remote parts of Italy and ilands adjoyning.* London: Andrew Crooke.

MANDRAKE

The mandrake plant, *Mandragora officinarum,* is probably the best-known poisonous herb found in the witches' pharmacopoeia. Mandrakes were the subjects of much folkloric herbal beliefs, including the concept that the plants generated at the foot of a gallows from the semen of the executed. Mandrake plants were thus considered to be partially "human" and to have roots that resembled either the lower limbs or genitalia of human males or females. Sixteenth-century herbals commonly presented the "male" and "female" varieties of the plants. For example, such plants are shown in Johannes de Cuba's *Hortus Sanitatus,* a sixteenth-century herbal published in Frankfort.

Being partly human, mandrake plants were thought to emit horrible screams when harvested, which gave rise to the folk belief that a dog should be employed to draw up the root because the scream of the plant could kill a human. Early herbals sometimes show this method of harvest employing such "drug-sniffing

Poisonous plant linked to witches and thought to grow under gallows from the semen of the executed. Because the mandrake was partly human, it emitted screams when pulled. (TopFoto.co.uk)

dogs." Other items of mandrake folklore stated that one should not dig up the herb until sunset and that one should not dig if it was windy. Witches digging mandrake roots at night at the foot of a gallows are shown in a painting from about 1650 by David Teniers the Younger (found today in the Staatliche Kunsthalle in Karlsruhe, Germany). Teniers depicted a witch busily digging up a root while a freshly harvested mandrake root stands nearby, looking very humanoid in its appearance.

Like other poisonous plants thought to be used by witches, mandrake contains hyoscyamine, atropine, and scopolamine. These drugs affect the cardiovascular system and can produce hallucinations or make the individual think he or she is flying or floating. As with other poisonous herbs used by witches, mandrake could also be manipulated by a witch without causing her death, or it could be simply made up into a poison. Oddly, although mandrake was considered the very epitome of a poisonous plant used by witches, it was also believed that it could be used effectively to treat someone who was possessed. (One presumes that this was due to the herb's sedative effects.)

Mandrake roots are probably the witches' poisonous herbs most commonly depicted in the visual arts of the sixteenth and seventeenth centuries. Aside from their presence in herbals, one also finds mandrake roots in various seventeenth-century paintings. Apart from the Teniers painting, they include *Witches' Sabbat* by the Flemish artist Frans Francken the Younger, completed in 1607 and owned by the Kunsthistorisches Museum in Vienna. A male mandrake root is prominently shown in the painting's central area, close to several witches who are working *maleficia*. Two of these poisonous herbs also appear in a drawing by the seventeenth-century Dutch artist Jacques de Gheyn, entitled *Witches' Scene,* now in the Musée des Beaux-Arts, Rennes, France.

JANE P. DAVIDSON

See also: DOGS; DRUGS AND HALLUCINOGENS; HERBAL MEDICINE; TENIERS, DAVID THE YOUNGER.

References and further reading:

Davidson, Jane P. 1987. *The Witch in Northern European Art, 1470–1750.* Freren, Germany: Luca.

Grieve, M. 1931. *A Modern Herbal.* London: Jonathan Cape.

Lewis, Walter H., and M. P. F. Elvin-Lewis. 1977. *Medical Botany.* New York: John Wiley and Sons.

Müller-Ebeling, Claudia, Christian Rätch, and Wolf-Dieter Storl. 2003. *Witchcraft Medicine: Healing Arts, Shamanic Practices, and Forbidden Plants.* Translated by Annabel Lee. Rochester, VT: Inner Traditions.

MANDROU, ROBERT (1921–1984)

One of extremely few distinguished French academics from a working-class background, Mandrou made the single most important twentieth-century French contribution to the history of witchcraft with his 1968 doctoral thesis, *Magistrats et sorciers en France au XVIIe siècle* (Magistrates and Witches in Seventeenth-Century France).

Secretary of the cutting-edge French journal *Annales: Economie, Sociétés, Civilisations* from 1954 to 1962 and then Lucien Febvre's successor at the prestigious École Pratique des Hautes Études before becoming professor of history at the University of Paris-X (Nanterre) in the revolutionary year of 1968, Mandrou is best remembered today as a prolific scholar. He published many widely read books, starting with *A History of French Civilization* that he coauthored with Georges Duby in 1958 (English translation, 1964). Three years later came Mandrou's pioneering exercise in the history of *mentalités* (mentalities—the ideas and values that a society shares), his *Introduction to Modern France, 1500–1640: An Essay in Historical Psychology* (English translation, 1975), which has remained in print continuously for forty years. In 1964 came another pioneering work, not yet translated, analyzing French popular culture in the sixteenth and seventeenth centuries through the contents of chapbooks from the Bibliothèque bleue (Blue Library) of Troyes. Another synthetic work, *France in the Sixteenth and Seventeenth Centuries* (1967), preceded Mandrou's thesis on witchcraft. An interesting monograph on the Fuggers as landed gentlemen in Swabia (translated into German in 1997) followed it in 1969. (A forced laborer in Germany during World War II, Mandrou admired many things German and often spent his vacations there.) *Louis XIV in His Time* (1973) completes the list of Mandrou's major titles. His final book, an edited collection of texts titled *Possession and Witchcraft in Seventeenth-Century France* (1979), returned to the topic of his dissertation.

A generation after it first appeared, only parts of Mandrou's sprawling investigation of the treatment of witchcraft by French appellate judges—above all, those who sat on the bench of the *Parlement* of Paris, probably the most prestigious secular court in sixteenth- and seventeenth-century Christendom—have endured as authoritative contributions to witchcraft scholarship. Of its three parts (the medieval heritage to 1600; the major scandalous trials of the early 1600s, often linked to demonic possession; and the progressive abandonment of the crime of witchcraft at the appellate level after 1640), one can say that its scholarly credibility has been utterly eroded at the front but barely affected at the back. Mandrou's first section is now completely discredited, but his second part retains partial validity, and his final section has suffered only minor damage from subsequent critics.

Despite its impressive bibliographical apparatus (345 published primary sources plus a survey of French parliamentary archives), the greatest weakness of Mandrou's thesis has been its inadequate use of primary sources from French *parlements,* above all the *Parlement* of Paris. Believing—incorrectly—that its *plumitifs,* or draft minutes of deliberations in criminal cases, were unreadable, Mandrou blandly assumed that Parisian appellate judges routinely confirmed upward of 90 percent of all death sentences for witchcraft until well into the seventeenth century, when Cartesian skepticism took hold. Unfortunately for Mandrou, within a decade of publishing his thesis, an expatriate American had successfully deciphered over 1,000 of these *plumitifs* from cases of witchcraft and demonstrated that the *Parlement* of Paris had *always*—ever since the fifteenth-century *Vauderie d'Arras*—practiced the level of judicial skepticism about witchcraft that Mandrou assumed it had acquired only by 1640 (Soman 1977). Subsequently, additional work in provincial French *parlements* has similarly shown persistent judicial skepticism about witch hunting at the appellate level throughout the French kingdom. The early-seventeenth-century "crisis of Satanism" lying at the center of Mandrou's second section never occurred, at least not at the level of French appellate courts.

However, Mandrou saw correctly that a few spectacular, well-publicized cases of demonic possession did much to change educated public opinion about witchcraft in France by the mid-seventeenth century; subsequent scholarship continues to highlight such cases as Urbain Grandier, the Jesuit parish priest of Loudun who was accused of bewitching an entire convent of Ursuline nuns—and now we understand far better why Cardinal Richelieu never permitted the *Parlement* of Paris to intervene in his trial. Similarly, Mandrou's final section on the decriminalization of witchcraft throughout France slighted its close connection with the scandalous "Affair of the Poisons" (1679–1682) but remains an otherwise authoritative account.

WILLIAM MONTER

See also: AFFAIR OF THE POISONS; ARRAS; FRANCE; FUGGER FAMILY; HISTORIOGRAPHY; LOUDUN NUNS; *PARLEMENT* OF PARIS; POSSESSION, DEMONIC.

References and further reading:

Mandrou, Robert. 1968. *Magistrats et sorciers en France au XVIIe siècle.* Paris: Plon.

———, ed. 1979. *Possession et sorcellerie en France au XVIIe siècle.* Paris: Pluriel.

Soman, Alfred. 1977. "Les procès de sorcellerie au Parlement de Paris (1565–1640)." *Annales: Economies, Sociétés, Civilisations* 32: 790–814.

MANICHAEISM

During the Middle Ages, ideas derived from Manichaeism, a Near Eastern religious movement, influenced the formation of the inquisitorial stereotype of the witch. Based on Gnostic principles and founded by the Iranian prophet Mani (216–277 C.E.), Manichaeism spread east as far as China and west into North Africa and southern Europe. Although described as a Christian heresy (see the influential fourth-century text *Acta Archelai*), its roots were in Zoroastrianism, with influences from Christianity and Buddhism. Mani described himself as the promised Paraclete of God (Kephalaia 1:9–14) and the ultimate prophet (the title "Seal of the Prophets" is later used by Mohammed [Sura 30:44]), who had received a final, angelic revelation of the divine character of the universe at the age of twenty-four and then had begun an aggressive evangelism across the Persian Empire. Among the factors that helped spread his faith was its simplicity, its emphasis on a dualistic universe, and the injunction to translate his teaching to all peoples in their own language.

In his conception of the human predicament, Mani described three ages (past, present, and future) and a dualistic universe in which a continuous struggle occurred between the Kingdom of Light, with its focus being the Father of Greatness, and the Kingdom of Darkness, ruled by the Prince of Darkness and his five evil archons (demon, lion, eagle, fish, and dragon). At the heart of this struggle was the desire of the Father of Greatness to separate and return all his particles of light that had become trapped within the flesh of animals and plants during the process of the creation of the earth. It was the task of the evil forces coextensive with the forces of light to excite sexual lust and gluttony within all created beings, keeping the light particles impossibly commingled and thus lost to the Kingdom of Light. When their efforts failed, small pieces of light became disentangled from the darkness, and the sun and the moon functioned as two chariots bringing these pieces back from the world to the Father of Greatness. In the final age, a total conflagration of the earth would occur, ending with a complete separation of light from darkness, with the forces of evil sealed away forever within a bottomless pit.

Following the creation of the earth, Eve was seduced by an evil archon and subsequently gave birth to Cain. She then engaged in an incestuous relationship with both Cain and Abel, endangering humanity. Adam and his first son Seth were taught by "Jesus of Light" to adopt an ascetic lifestyle, which would protect the light particles within them. This discipline was then proposed by Mani as the basis for the rule of life of the elect, a select body within his community whose minds had been freed by the divine spirit *Nous* (knowledge) and who maintained strict ascetic practices, including sexual abstinence, poverty, and vegetarianism. The elect were not allowed to practice magic, own property, engage in commerce, kill animals, or even cut or step on plants because these living beings contained particles of light (referred to as the substance of the divine "Suffering Jesus"). The elect were assisted by a group of auditors who prepared their meals and performed all mundane tasks for the religious community. The auditors had a less rigid regimen but would not be directly freed at death to join with the Father of Greatness; instead, they would have to be reincarnated as vegetable matter. All those who were not brought to this revelation were reincarnated as animals and eventually sank into the dark regions of the Netherworld.

Christianity found Manichaeism heretical for many reasons, starting with Mani's teaching that the soul suffered not from a weak and corrupt will but from contact with matter, which entrapped the light within the flesh. Evil was not the result of human sin but a physical reality; personal misfortunes were miseries to be endured, not the result of sins. The independent power of the evil forces also clashed with God's omnipotence and was refuted by several Church Fathers (Serapion of Thmuis, Tertullian, Titus of Bostra) on the grounds of human free will versus dualistic determinism. Among the arguments made against the passive avoidance or abhorrence of evil in Manichaeism is that it did not allow credit for the human ability to overcome evil.

Ultimately, it became the practice in the Middle Ages to label as Manichaeism any dualist Christian heresy, such as the tenth-century Bogomils (founded among the Slavic peasants of the Balkans) and the Cathars. It is clear that both of these groups adopted aspects of Manichaeism, including strict vegetarianism, abstinence from sexual intercourse, and drinking wine as a way of avoiding contact with the abominable. The contrast between the opulent wealth of the Orthodox Church and nobility and the physical misery of the Slavic peasants made them ready converts to Bogomilism's ascetic dogma and allowed them to participate in passive resistance, abstaining from violence against animals or humans.

The Cathars, strict dualists and iconoclasts, appeared first in the 1140s in Italy and spread across southern France and Spain. Although there were a number of sects identified as Cathars, they all shared the belief that the destruction of war and natural catastrophes were evidence of the Devil's rule over the world and that God either could not or did not choose to interfere. The battles between divine forces took place on a cosmic rather than an earthly level. The Cathar community, divided into auditors, believers, and the perfect, therefore battled against matter (even to the extent of replacing water baptism with the *consolamentum,* laying on of hands by a perfect). All flesh or earthly product was considered the essence of evil, and thus procreation was avoided because it would result in another soul being trapped in a bodily prison. The goal was to achieve perfection and liberation from the world through the obtaining of knowledge first revealed by Jesus, the messenger. Because the Cathars identified the official Church as a lying institution established by the Devil to keep humanity enslaved within the body, they were fiercely attacked and condemned as a danger to the Church and to civil order.

In constructing the stereotype of the witch, medieval demonologists drew upon and also misrepresented a number of Manichaean ideas as developed by the Cathars. In describing witches as heretics, inquisitors claimed that they, in the manner of dualist heretic, had exaggerated the power of the Devil, so much so that they actually worshipped him. The description of sexual promiscuity and gluttony at the witches' Sabbat derived ultimately from the Manichaean belief that evil forces had excited these passions in order to keep light entrapped in matter. St. Augustine's description of sexual irregularities at the assemblies of Manichaeans gave medieval demonologists an authoritative source for such accusations. The claim that witches trampled on the cross as a symbol of their rejection of Christianity when making a pact with the Devil derived ultimately from the Manichaean and Cathar rejection of all physical material as evil.

VICTOR H. MATTHEWS

See also: DEVIL; HERESY; SEXUAL ACTIVITY, DIABOLIC.

References and further reading:
Barber, Malcolm. 2000. *The Cathars: Dualist Heretics in Languedoc in the High Middle Ages.* Harlow, UK: Longman.
Lieu, Samuel N. C. 1999. *Manichaeism in Mesopotamia and the Roman East.* Leiden: Brill.
Mirecki, Paul A. 1992. "Manichaeans and Manichaeism." Pp. iv: 502–511 in *The Anchor Bible Dictionary.* Edited by David N. Freedman. New York: Doubleday.
Polotsky, Hans J., and Alexander Böhlig, eds. 1940. *Manichäische Handschriften der Staatlichen Museen Berlin* I. *Kephalaia,* pt. 1. Stuttgart: W. Kohlhammer.
Russell, Jeffrey B. 1992. *Dissent and Order in the Middle Ages.* New York: Twayne.
Spencer, Colin. 1995. *The Heretic's Feast: A History of Vegetarianism.* Hanover, NH: University Press of New England.

MARCHTAL, IMPERIAL ABBEY OF

As in several other small states in southwestern Germany, witch hunting at Marchtal reached a peak between 1586 and 1596, but an extremely late witch panic took place between 1745 and 1757 that resulted in the execution of six women and the death of another in jail. This self-governing Premonstratensian Abbey, refounded in 1171 by Pfalzgraf Hugo II of Tübingen and his wife Elisabeth, had its seat on the edge of the Swabian Alb and belonged to the Swabian Circle of the Holy Roman Empire. Its abbots, who were authorized to establish a *Hochgericht* (high court) to hear capital trials in 1518, gradually enlarged their properties and rights until Marchtal controlled over twenty villages with a total population of about 2,700 by the eighteenth century. Marchtal developed a three-level jurisdiction, with a chief justice in Obermarchtal as the highest secular magistrate.

Marchtal's witchcraft trials share one salient characteristic: accusations of *maleficium* (harmful magic) originated especially in one village, Alleshausen, located on the Federsee, where the peasants possessed a significant

portion of the land and often defied the abbot's control. At the initial trials in 1586, the *Vogt* (governor), Bernhart Bitterlin (who unsurprisingly came from the Federsee area), played a decisive role. He investigated the charges of witchcraft in Alleshausen and used torture to obtain the names of the witches' accomplices. Under the government of Abbot Konrad Frey (1571–1591) and his successor Johannes Riedgasser (1591–1600), Marchtal's witchcraft trials were most intense and resulted in the death of at least forty-nine people. The abbots gave their secular magistrates plenty of rope, not accelerating or preventing or alleviating witchcraft trials in their territory. Later, around 1627–1628, at least five more women were convicted. Witchcraft accusations in Marchtal usually followed the same pattern, but the responses of the authorities to the accusations were less predictable. Especially after the Thirty Years' War (1618–1648), the authorities rejected several denunciations from Alleshausen and punished the accusers. In 1745, the political and economic elite of Alleshausen, who officiated at the local court, once again assumed the role of the primary prosecutors. During the lawsuit, they also became influential members of the high court in Obermarchtal. They complained that a poor woman, Catharina Schmid, had used witchcraft to destroy her affluent neighbors' property because of a grudge against them. Schmid was arrested but did not confess. So Josef von Sättelin (mayor of the Catholic part of the imperial city of Biberach from 1741–1764) was consulted as a *Gutachter* (judicial expert) to advise the court in the conduct of the trial. At first, von Sättelin proposed to release Catharina Schmid from jail and to reintegrate her into Alleshausen; according to the Carolina Code (the imperial law code, 1532), he stated, there had not been sufficient evidence to justify the application of torture, only rumors. But the prominent inhabitants of Alleshausen ignored this unwelcome advice and expanded her trial with new accusations, now also directed against the accused's daughter, Maria Tornhäuser. They wanted both women convicted, and they finally succeeded: after languishing in jail for nine months, the mother accepted her daughter's denunciation. Despite his scruples, Josef von Sättelin no longer objected to their execution, which took place on March 9, 1746.

During the rule of a new abbot, Edmund Sartor (1746–1768), another five suspected women were accused. Four of them were convicted of witchcraft and executed, two in March 1747 and two more in November 1747, and the fifth died in jail in October 1747. Von Sättelin's *Gutachten* (judicial opinions) revealed an interesting transformation. His later *Gutachten* were no longer informed by the Carolina Code. Instead, he now made additional trials possible by arguing that witchcraft was caused by a pact with the Devil, as demonologists said, and necessarily stemmed from diabolical malice. Later he argued that reason dictates the existence of witchcraft. His final argument implied that neither secular laws nor scientific logic was decisive, but that witchcraft was constituted by nature.

In the end, it was the same elite of Alleshausen, who had begun this cycle of persecutions, who brought an end to witch hunting. The *Amtmann* (bailiff) of Alleshausen offered a new interpretation of the damages attributed to witchcraft: the harm to livestock, he said, was not provoked by witches but caused by the peasants through their disregard for proper animal husbandry. In this way, the concept of witchcraft no longer provided an adequate explanation. Afterward, two newly appointed *Gutachter* from Schussenried and Ulm took the same position regarding the reality of witchcraft. No further trials were opened after 1757.

CONSTANZE STÖRK

See also: CAROLINA CODE (*CONSTITIO CRIMINALIS CAROLINA*); ECCLESIASTICAL TERRITORIES (HOLY ROMAN EMPIRE); GERMANY, SOUTHWESTERN; HOLY ROMAN EMPIRE; PANICS.

References and further reading:
Dengler, Robert. 1953. "Das Hexenwesen im Stifte Obermarchtal von 1581–1756." PhD diss., University of Erlangen.
Midelfort, H. C. Erik. 1972. *Witch Hunting in Southwestern Germany, 1562–1648: The Social and Intellectual Foundations*. Stanford: Stanford University Press.
Störk, Constanze. 2003. "'Mithin die natürliche Vernunnfft selbst dictiert, das Es hexen gebe.' Hexenverfolgung in der Reichsabtei Marchtal 1586–1757." Master's thesis, University of Tübingen.

MARIA THERESA, HOLY ROMAN EMPRESS (1717–1780; RULED 1740–1780)

Maria Theresa was a reforming empress whose skepticism regarding witchcraft contributed to its decriminalization in Austria, Hungary, and Bohemia.

As the eldest daughter of Holy Roman Emperor Charles VI, who had no male heir, Maria Theresa was heiress of the house of Habsburg, archduchess of Austria, and queen of both Hungary and Bohemia; but she became empress only through her husband, Duke Francis of Lorraine, who was elected Holy Roman Emperor in 1745. She had married him before beginning to rule after her father died in 1740. Although the major European powers had officially accepted Charles VI's Pragmatic Sanction (which guaranteed the right of female succession within Habsburg lands) at the time of its proclamation in 1713, Prussian challenges to Maria Theresa's succession provoked a seven-year war and at first prevented her husband from becoming emperor. Ultimately, she fended off these and additional affronts to emerge as one of the Habsburgs' longest-reigning and most successful monarchs. As the only woman Habsburg ruler, she is best remembered for her successful defense of her realm; her Catholic

piety; and an enlightened commitment to political, legal, social, and educational reform.

This commitment emerged clearly in her attitude toward witchcraft. As early as the mid-1750s, we have evidence of Maria Theresa's personal skepticism regarding magical crimes through her reaction to accounts of vampires and witches in Moravia and Bohemia. In response, she dispatched an investigative commission that included two physicians, Johannes Gasser and Christian Vabst. After receiving their report, she consulted her own principal court physician, Gerard van Swieten, director of the Hofbibliothek (National Library) and reformer of the University of Vienna, who concurred with the recommendations of his medical colleagues: crush such superstitions through political power. It is worth noting that, like Maria Theresa's later witchcraft patent, van Swieten's 1755 treatise on vampires affirmed the reality of miracles and Satan's earthly powers before it upheld the virtues of natural science and exposed the dangers of ignorance. In March 1755, the empress forbade her subjects from following their customary practices when fears of the supernatural led to specific allegations of harm. Instead, the authorities must investigate all cases involving vampires (*magia postuma*), apparitions, witchcraft, treasure hunting, or diabolical possessions using rational means. By January 1756, the government of Maria Theresa ordered that the royal appeals court in Hungary automatically review all decisions by lower courts involving charges of witchcraft. In response to such a trial in the Tabor district of Bohemia, she issued a resolution on July 30, 1756, stating, "It is certain that witches are found only where ignorance is; correct this and no more will be found. [The accused] is no more a witch than I" (Kern 1999, 170).

The empress's attitude toward witchcraft is best reflected in her government's *Artikel von der Zauberey, Hexerey, Wahrsagerey, und dergleichen* (An Article on Sorcery, Witchcraft, Divination, and Similar Activities), issued on November 5, 1766 (Kern 1999). Although trials for witchcraft had been on the wane for decades in the western lands of the Habsburg monarchy, they persisted in the eastern kingdoms of Bohemia and Hungary. By the 1750s, Maria Theresa had already begun to take steps to suppress trials for witchcraft, but this edict made them virtually impossible to prosecute by the late 1760s. Compiled by a court commission directed by Count Michael Johann von Althann for inclusion in a forthcoming penal code, the patent fills seventeen printed pages, in which the empress's legal advisers defined the prohibited activities and outlined their prosecution.

Although the *Artikel* nowhere denied the reality of diabolical magic, it had the overall effect of severely limiting the possibility of prosecuting anyone for witchcraft. Its text and tone suggest that although diabolical sorcery was possible, it certainly did not occur in the Habsburg lands. The contradictory purposes of the patent became clear from the titles of its first few sections, which juxtaposed the outlawed activities in question ("the offense of sorcery") with a series of qualifiers stressing the frivolity of the threat: "delusion," "credulity," "false," "fraud," and "madness" (Kern 1999, 165–166). Its following sections contributed variously to a basic dichotomy informing all legal proceedings concerned with magical events: extremely rare diabolical crimes versus widespread and potentially criminal illusionary beliefs. Sections 1 and 2 established the practice of magic as an outlawed activity.

Nonetheless, section 3 reformulated the way magical crimes should be understood in a skeptical tone, implying that most matters concerning sorcery or witchcraft coming before the courts stemmed from popular ignorance. It accordingly established a legal basis for proceeding in such cases with a considerable degree of doubt. Sections 4 and 5, which created the possibility of distinguishing legitimate from illegitimate cases, directly emphasized this issue; section 6 firmly prohibited investigators from using superstitious methods in their inquiries. The decree further indicated that only the sovereign had the authority to investigate and decide cases that might have legitimate merit; thus, sections 7 and 12 created exclusive legal prerogatives for the sovereign and her legal counselors. The remainder (sections 8–11, 13, and 14) delineated careful guidelines for proceeding with investigations, emphasizing the need for skeptical inquiry. Its final two sections (15 and 16) extended those guidelines to the investigation and suppression of continuing widespread popular superstitions. Not only were witchcraft trials to be stopped, but also the folkloric beliefs sustaining accusations of witchcraft should be stamped out.

The paradoxical message of Maria Theresa's "Article on Sorcery" hinged on a reassessment by state authorities of the threat that magical activities posed to Austrian society and a new conception of the state's role in addressing it. Policy-makers did not see the Devil or his minions as real threats to social order, and beliefs in the Devil's powers had lost currency among most, but not all, the educated and politically powerful elites in Habsburg lands. Because of the stronghold of state-sponsored Catholic orthodoxy on Austrian religious practice, skeptical medical and legal scholars like van Swieten or von Althann could not denounce demonic magic and witchcraft outright, because the manifest powers of the Devil and the possibility of his malevolent intercession remained tenets of Christian faith. Instead, officials sought to downplay the powers of the Devil, attributing beliefs in demonic magic and malefice to the inherently superstitious populace. Although the impetus for constructing the 1766 patent emerged from Maria Theresa's efforts to reform criminal and civil law and create a judicial system based on

the abstract principle of justice, Bohemian and Hungarian witch and vampire cases during the 1750s and 1760s provided a more concrete stimulus.

EDMUND M. KERN

See also: AUSTRIA; BOHEMIA; DECLINE OF THE WITCH HUNTS; HOLY ROMAN EMPIRE; HUNGARY; SKEPTICISM; SWIETEN, GERARD VAN; VAMPIRE.

References and further reading:
Kern, Edmund M. 1999. "An End to Witch Trials in Austria: Reconsidering the Enlightened State." *Austrian History Yearbook* 30: 159–185.
Klaniczay, Gabor. 1990. *The Uses of Supernatural Power: The Transformation of Popular Religion in Medieval and Early-Modern Europe*. Princeton, NJ: Princeton University Press.

MARY, THE VIRGIN

Though there are only a few references to the mother of Jesus in the New Testament and Jesus himself had a rather distanced relation to her, Mary became, at least from the Carolingian epoch onward, the second most important holy figure in Christianity, with her cult reaching its peak in the late Middle Ages. Some late medieval prayers addressed Mary as more powerful than Jesus because he has to be obedient to his mother. She was painted as Virgin of Mercy, beneath whose mantle her adepts found protection not only against demons but also especially against the wrath of God the Father, who desires to destroy sinful mankind. Many *exempla* taught that Jesus could forgive a sinner who had offended him, but never one who had offended his mother. The Virgin, more than other saints, was used to exorcise and Christianize places vowed to another religion; after anti-Jewish pogroms, for example, Marian sanctuaries were regularly erected on the place of the former synagogue.

In connection with witchcraft, several aspects are of interest: Did the Virgin appear in charms and magic? What did the witches think of her? Could she protect even a sorceress?

The protection of the Virgin was thought to be of the greatest power against the Evil One; her name can be found in many an apotropaic charm. Mary helped even those who made a pact with Satan, the most famous proof of which was the miracle story of Theophilus, told in all European tongues. This originally Byzantine motif could even apply to rueful sorceresses. In the Dutch play *Marieken van Nieumegen* (ca. 1500), the protagonist Marieken (i.e., "little Mary") made a pact with an incubus, but she had to change her name in order to stop the power of her patron saint. She, however, chose Emma (where the first letter of Mary's name appears twice) and was saved in the end.

Although the confrontation between the Virgin Mary and demons was a standard motif of preachers, she did not play any important role in specialized antiwitchcraft theology or practices of the Church. For women of all kinds, their relation to the Virgin was of central importance. It became especially obvious on those occasions in the late Middle Ages and the early modern epoch when a woman showed signs both of being a mystic and a witch. The peasant Chiara Signorini, condemned in 1519 at Modena, manifested a complex mixture of veneration of the Virgin Mary and magical practices. Signorini conceded under torture that she had caused many people to fall ill by demonic help. However, she also confessed to being close to the Virgin, who (and not a demon) actually caused these maladies, in order to revenge herself after being offended. In late-seventeenth-century Normandy, Marie Benoist de la Boucaille was a famous healer and ecstatic who claimed to have had many visions of Mary, Jesus, and God, but she also showed a Devil's mark and was condemned for witchcraft and false prophecy. "Real" witches usually avoided any veneration for the Virgin, at least according to their confessions. Many of them, when denying Jesus, had to abuse his mother also. According to the *Malleus Maleficarum* (The Hammer of Witches, 2.2), witches called her the "fat woman."

Especially from the fifteenth century onward, a huge number of popular blessings have been recorded that address the Mother of God, the Virgin, or the suffering mother, sometimes begging for help in love affairs but more often seeking protection from illness and dangerous animals (especially snakes, because the Devil seduced Eve in that form and Mary was called the second, sinless Eve). To further this aim, apocryphal situations were created, as in the following early modern High German charm: When Jesus was wounded by the arrows of two demons, his mother came and agreed to help him, if he would give her half of the earth and half of heaven. Jesus promised, and Mary called fifty-five angels and healed her son; in the same way, the pains of the person saying this charm would be healed. From the standpoint of religious psychology, male-centered Christianity obviously required a female "goddess" nearly as mighty as the male god himself, a superhuman woman onto whom cravings for motherly nurture and understanding can be projected. Therefore, the thirteenth-century mystic Mechthild of Magdeburg literally called her *goettinne* (goddess) in her work *The Flowing Light of the Godhead* (Mechthild of Magdeburg 1998, 3.1; 3.4). Meanwhile, Lollards abused the Virgin as a witch, and Luther reversed Mechthild by calling her an *Abgöttin* (idol) (Luther 7: 568, 573 f.). Mary, also, like her son, became a rich subject for blasphemies, for example, cursing "by Mary's limbs" or "by the Virgin's cunt," and was often abused as a whore in Italy. But there is also evidence that the Virgin became the object of male sexual fantasies, expressed in many miracles with visions of Mary kissing or even lactating her celibate admirer.

Mary's cult provoked a definitely negative reaction from Protestant reformers. In Tridentine Catholicism,

Mary's glory was exalted even higher as she became the patroness of every anti-Protestant action, including military ones. The triumphant Catholic Church spread the iconography of the Immaculate Conception—the woman of the Apocalypse crushing the snake underfoot—over all countries under her rule, and her famous apparitions and miracles at Lourdes and Fatima have helped maintain her veneration until the present day.

PETER DINZELBACHER

See also: CHARMS; CURSES; JESUS; THEOPHILUS.

References and further reading:
Algermissen, Konrad, et al., eds. 1967. *Lexikon der Marienkunde.* Regensburg: F. Pustet.
Beinert, Wolfgang, and Heinrich Petri. 1984. *Handbuch der Marienkunde.* Regensburg: Pustet.
De Fiores, Stefano. 1986. *Nuovo dizionario di Mariologia.* Cinisello Balsamo: Editiones Paulinae.
Dinzelbacher, Peter. 2000. *Handbuch der Religionsgeschichte im deutschsprachigen Raum. Band 2. Hoch- und Spätmittelalter.* Paderborn: Schöningh.
———. 2001. *Heilige oder Hexen? Schicksale auffälliger Frauen in Mittelalter und Frühneuzeit.* 4th ed. Düsseldorf: Albatros.
Graef, Hilda. 1965. *Mary: A History of Doctrine and Devotion.* London: Sheed and Ward.
Luther, Martin. 1883ff. *Werke: Kritische Gesamtausgabe.* 58 vols. Weimar: Herman Böhlau and successor, Weimarer Ausgabe.
Mechthild of Magdeburg. 1998. *The Flowing Light of the Godhead.* Translated by Frank Tobin. New York: Paulist.
Orth. 1933. "Maria in den Segen." Pp. 1,663–1,671 in *Handwörterbuch des deutschen Aberglaubens* 5. Berlin: de Gruyter.
Roscini, Gabriele M. 1960. *Dizionario di Mariologia.* Rome: Editrice Studium.
Schreiner, Klaus. 1994. *Maria: Jungfrau, Mutter, Herrscherin.* Munich: Hanser.
Warner, Marina. 1976. *Alone of All Her Sex: The Myth and Cult of the Virgin Mary.* New York: Knopf.

MATHER, COTTON (1663–1728)

Cotton Matter was New England's most celebrated Puritan and a staunch believer in the reality of witchcraft.

Mather played an important role in the case of the Goodwin children in Boston in 1688 and later in the witch hunting in Salem in 1692–1693. During these years, Cotton Mather advanced his views on witchcraft in private correspondence, sermons, and books: *A Discourse on Witchcraft* (1689), *Memorable Providences, Relating to Witchcrafts and Possessions* (1689), and *The Wonders of the Invisible World* (1692). Mather preached that witches represented the Devil's special war against New England, but his actions usually discouraged witch hunting.

The son of Increase Mather, minister of the Second Church in Boston and president of Harvard College, Cotton Mather (named for his grandfather, John Cotton) entered Harvard College at the age of twelve and earned his MA in 1681, at age eighteen. In 1685 he was installed as his father's assistant at Second Church in Boston. During Increase Mather's long mission in England (1688–1692) negotiating a new charter for Massachusetts, Cotton at the age of twenty-five was left in charge of the largest congregation in New England.

The author of over 400 works, Cotton Mather combined modern scientific interests, or "rational philosophy," with a strong belief in the existence of witchcraft. No Puritan better displayed the seventeenth-century New England curiosity about the physical universe than Mather did in his *Curiosa Americana* (1712–1724). An avid reader of current scientific literature, Cotton Mather was familiar with the writings of such mechanistic philosophers as René Descartes, Pierre Gassendi, and Robert Boyle. His lifelong interest in scientific issues earned him membership in the Royal Society of London, and his account of the smallpox inoculation episode of 1721 was published in the society's transactions. The best example of Cotton Mather's scientific attitude is his *Christian Philosopher: A Collection of the Best Discoveries in Nature, with Religious Improvements* (1721), where he pronounced Isaac Newton "the *Perpetual Dictator* of the Learned World in the Principles of Natural Philosophy" (p. 65). His magnum opus was *Magnalia Christi Americana* (1702), an ecclesiastical history of New England from its founding to his own time.

Cotton Mather's belief in witchcraft was influenced most by William Perkins, the prominent English Puritan preacher and demonologist, whose *Discourse of the Damned Art of Witchcraft* (1608) made him the chief authority in seventeenth-century England on witchcraft; by the Cambridge Platonist Henry More, whose *Antidote Against Atheism* (1653) not only accepted the reality of witches but even upheld their sexual intercourse with the Devil; by the famous Puritan preacher Richard Baxter, whose *Certainty of the World of Spirits* (1691) related many abnormal events as evidence of the invisible power of spirits; and lastly by Joseph Glanvill's *Saducismus Triumphatus, or Full and Plain Evidence Concerning Witches and Apparitions* (1681), which attempted to ground the belief in witchcraft scientifically on the basis of unshakable evidence.

To the thought of these authorities on witchcraft, Mather added a uniquely American perspective; he was obsessed with the view that the Devil had waged a war against Puritan New England since its founding: "*The New Englanders* are a People of God" settled in America, which was "once the *Devil* Territories" (emphasis in the original). Hence it was "a rousing *alarm* to the Devil, when a great Company of English *Protestants* and *Puritans,* came to erect Evangelical churches" in America. The Devil, accordingly, "tried all sorts of Methods to overturn" New England. Events in Salem proved that an "Army of the *Devils* is horribly broke in upon" the land, and the witches found there are evidence of an "An Horrible Plot" on the part of the

"Devil against New England" (Mather 1693c, 13–14, 74). New England therefore played a crucial role in fighting the Devil; as Jesus resisted the Devil in the wilderness, so now New England should stand against the Devil's temptation in the wilderness of America (Mather 1693c, 174–178).

Cotton Mather's first practical encounter with witchcraft came in the case of the Goodwin children in Boston in the summer of 1688, a story he described in *Memorable Providences, Relating to Witchcrafts and Possessions* (1689). An old Irish widow, Mary Glover, had confessed to be in league with the Devil, bewitching the four children of John Goodwin and practicing image magic. Before she was hanged in Boston in November 1688, Mather twice visited Mary Glover in jail; he claimed "she never denied" her guilt of "witchcraft," or of "her confederacies with the devils," or "her covenant with hell" (Hall 1991, 272). Following her execution, Cotton Mather preached a suitably damning sermon on the threat of witchcraft, asserting that "Witchcraft is the most Monstrous and Horrid Evil" because it is 'a Renouncing of God, and Advancing of the filthy *Devil* into the Throne of the Most High. . . . *Witchcraft* is a renouncing of *Christ,* and preferring the Communion of a loathsome lying *Devil.*" And given "there are witches, we are to suppose that there are devils too" (Mather 1689b, 98–99).

Four years later, Cotton Mather was caught up in the drama of the largest witch hunt in New England. But we must remember two things about his role. First, his father Increase had returned from England in May 1692, and the younger Mather deferred to his leadership. Second, Cotton Mather's behavior (not unlike that of many European Protestant ministers facing witch hunts) displayed a curious mixture of public endorsement for these prosecutions and private warnings about their dangers.

Seventeenth-century New England exhibited many signs of a witch craze: a large witch hunt claiming twenty deaths, more than half of the total victims for all New England, occurred in Salem in 1692 (nineteen Massachusetts men and women and two dogs were hanged for witchcraft, and one man was pressed to death for refusing to plead to the indictment). The first witchcraft accusations occurred in Salem Village, a parish of the town of Salem, in early February 1692. Two young girls fell into strange fits, much like those in the case of the Goodwin children in Boston, and soon other girls in the village exhibited the same behavior. Claiming that witches were afflicting them, the girls provided names of villagers, who were arrested and put in jail on charges of witchcraft. Facing a growing witchcraft hysteria, the new governor of Massachusetts, Sir William Phips, established a special court of Oyer and Terminer on May 27, 1692, to hear and determine the witchcraft cases in Salem. On June 10 the first execution occurred. The trial

and its outcome troubled so many that in June the governor turned to leading ministers for advice. In response, Cotton Mather composed "The Return of Several Ministers," which urged caution in relying on the use of spectral evidence (an image of a person visible only to the witchcraft victim whom the specter was said to have attacked in some way) in court. However, the report nonetheless urged "the speedy and vigorous Prosecution" of those guilty of witchcraft (Mather 1693b, 291). The judges paid more attention to the second recommendation than to the first, giving the girls enormous power to manipulate the court. Accordingly, by July 19 five more women had been executed.

Cotton Mather's eschatological visions ran high during that time; events in Salem signified that "there never was a poor plantation, more pursued by the *wrath* of the *Devil,* than our poor *New England*" (Mather 1693c, 74). On August 4, 1692, he delivered a sermon warning that the Last Judgment was at hand. Calculating from Biblical evidence that the year 1697 would be the year of the End, he deemed New England as leading the final charge against the Devil and his minions. Seeing the affairs in Salem as proof of an "Horrible Plot against the Country by Witchcraft" aiming to "Blow up, and pull down all the churches in the Country," Mather urged New Englanders not to "allow the Mad Dogs of Hell" to have the upper hand (Mather 1693c, 14, 22).

By late September 1692, the witchcraft hysteria reached its peak, and eight more women had been hanged. Worried about the trials, Phips again turned to the spiritual leaders for advice. In October, Increase Mather composed his *Cases of Conscience,* challenging the court's procedures head-on by denouncing the use of spectral evidence and arguing that it was better for ten suspected witches to escape than one innocent person be condemned, a view endorsed by many ministers. However, Cotton Mather was given the official trial transcripts and in the same month composed *The Wonders of the Invisible World,* which described the court proceedings favorably. The governor, however, accepted Increase Mather's views and abolished the special court. Soon the storm was over.

Robert Calef, a Boston merchant who hated Cotton Mather, read *The Wonders of the Invisible World* as both a justification of the trials and an attempt to minimize Mather's own role. Calef claimed that Cotton Mather was constantly warning that "the Devils were walking about our Streets with lengthen Chains making a dreadful noise in our Ears" (Calef 1700, preface). The truth, of course, was more complicated. The younger Mather never repudiated his father's loathing of spectral evidence, which had fueled the Salem witch hunt. If Cotton Mather persuaded authorities to proceed with the execution of George Burroughs, a former Salem minister, despite Burroughs's ability to recite the Lord's Prayer perfectly while on the gallows, this intervention must be set against Cotton Mather's visible desire to avoid turning Mercy Short's "unnatural afflictions" into a witchcraft case at Boston during 1692–1693 (Boyer and Nissenbaum 1974, 24–26). Although Cotton Mather repeated his original views on the Salem trials in his *Magnalia Christi Americana* (1702), his later diaries reveal regret for his role in the trials and executions.

AVIHU ZAKAI

See also: BAXTER, RICHARD; GLANVILL, JOSEPH; GOODWIN CHILDREN; MATHER, INCREASE; MORE, HENRY; NEW ENGLAND; PERKINS, WILLIAM; SALEM; SPECTRAL EVIDENCE.

References and further reading:
Boyer, Paul, and Stephen Nissenbaum. 1974. *Salem Possessed: The Social Origins of Witchcraft.* Cambridge: Harvard University Press.

Calef, Robert. 1700. *More Wonders of the Invisible World.* London.

Demos, John P. 1982. *Entertaining Satan: Witchcraft and the Culture of Early New England.* New York: Oxford University Press.

Hall, David, ed. 1991. *Witch-Hunting in Seventeenth-Century New England: A Documentary History, 1638–1692.* Boston: Northeastern University Press.

Levin, David, ed. 1960. *What Happened in Salem? Documents Pertaining to the Seventeenth-Century Witchcraft Trials.* 2nd ed. New York: Harcourt, Brace and World.

Mather, Cotton. 1688. "The Possessions of the Goodwin Children." Pp. 267–275 in *Witch-Hunting in Seventeenth-Century New England: A Documentary History, 1638–1692.* Edited by David Hall. Boston: Northeastern University Press, 1991.

———. 1689a. *Memorable Providences, Relating to Witchcrafts and Possessions.* Boston.

———. 1689b. "A Discourse on Witchcraft." Pp. 96–106 in *What Happened in Salem? Documents Pertaining to the Seventeenth-Century Witchcraft Trials.* 2nd ed. Edited by David Levin. New York Harcourt, Brace and World, 1960

———. 1693a. "The Return of Several Ministers . . . upon the present Witchcraft in Salem." Pp. 288–291 in *The Wonders of the Invisible World: Being an Account of the Tryals of Several Witches Lately executed in New England.* London, 1862.

———. 1693b. *The Wonders of the Invisible World: Being an Account of the Tryals of Several Witches Lately executed in New England.* London, 1862.

———. 1693c. *The Wonders of the Invisible World: Observations as Well as Historical as Theological, upon the Nature, the Number, and the Operation of the Devils.* Boston.

———. 1721. *The Christian Philosopher.* Edited by Winton U. Solberg. Urbana: University of Illinois Press, 1994.

Mather, Increase. 1693. *Cases of Conscience Concerning Evil Spirit Personating Men.* Boston.

Middlekauff, Robert. 1971 *The Mathers: Three Generations of Puritan Intellectuals, 1596–1728.* New York: Oxford University Press.

Smolinski, Reiner, ed. *The Threefold Paradise of Cotton Mather: An Edition of "Triparadisus."* Athens: University of Georgia Press.

MATHER, INCREASE (1639–1723)

Increase Mather was an American Puritan minister, theologian, and demonologist; president of Harvard College from 1685 to 1701 whose *Cases of Conscience Concerning Evil Spirits Personating Men* (1693), a response to the Salem trials, quoted numerous witchcraft treatises, some now neglected.

Evidence of demonic activity at Salem divided pastoral opinion in the Massachusetts Colony. Judges appeared naively to dismiss the possibility that God could allow the Devil to assume the shape of an innocent person to perform evil. On June 15, 1692, several Cambridge ministers wrote to the Salem judges, warning that "a demon may, by God's permission, appear even to ill purposes, in the shape of an innocent, yea, and a virtuous man" (I. Mather 1980, 290). On August 1 the conclave commissioned Mather to write *Cases of Conscience.* By the time Governor William Phips received it, the trials were essentially over.

Increase and his son Cotton Mather disagreed over Salem. Cotton conceded that spectral evidence was unreliable but defended confessions as sufficient proof of guilt (C. Mather 1980, 14–16). His *Wonders of the Invisible World* was rushed into print before Increase's *Cases of Conscience,* though he had begun the former after the completion of his father's work. Cotton seemed to rebut his father's arguments preemptively (Hall 1988, 262–263). Contemporaries evidently thought so: Increase formally denied in a postscript to *Cases of Conscience* that the two books disagreed (I. Mather 1980, 288–290).

They did agree on the fascination of the "invisible world." In 1696 Increase published *Angelographia* and *A Disquisition Concerning Angelical Apparitions,* with a subtitle that revealed intimate connections with Salem: "In Answer to a Case of Conscience, Showing that Demons Often Appear Like Angels of Light, and What Is the Best and Only Way to Prevent Deception by Them."

Like Joseph Glanvill, Henry More, and others, the Mathers considered proofs of witchcraft necessary to rebut modern "Sadducees," who reputedly doubted the reality of "spirit"—angels, demons, ghosts, and the immortal human soul. "Sadducism [*sic*] is a degree of atheism, and commonly ends therein" (I. Mather 1696b, sig. K3v). *Angelographia* begins: "There are such beings as angels. They are not mere *entia rationis* [beings defined by reason alone], imaginary beings, or apparitions. . . . The Sadducees said. . . that the angels are not real beings, but only apparitions and impressions made in the minds of men" (I. Mather 1696a, 5).

Allusions to Salem (which was never mentioned by name) implied proof of demonic reality: "some who object that the age wherein we live has no demoniacks, or possessed persons, do from thence suspect the whole Gospel of fabulosity or imposture. That there are in this age energumens, late examples amongst ourselves (and more than a few of them) are an awful

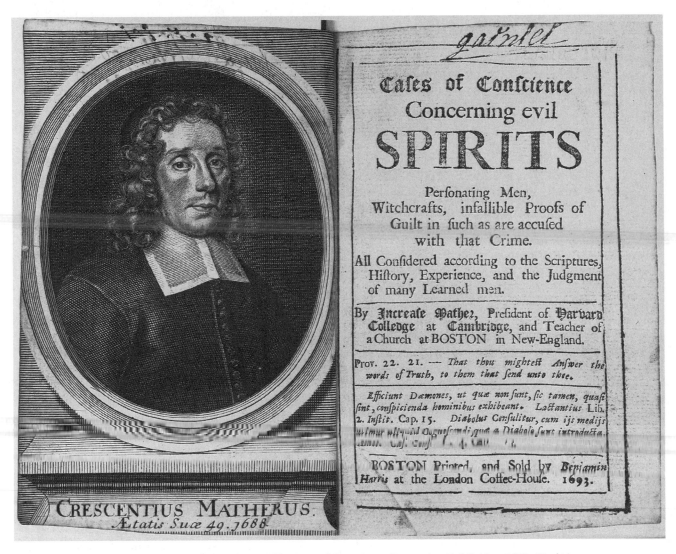

The Puritan minister Increase Mather and the title page of his Cases of Conscience Concerning Evil Spirits, *1693. (Corbis)*

conviction. . . ." (I. Mather 1696b, sigs. K3v–K4r). Evil demons implied good angels: "there are evil angels: men cannot but perceive that. . . from the bodily possessions. . . if there are evil angels, reason saith they were once good. . . . And if the evil angels were once good, we may rationally conclude that there are some who are, as originally they were, holy spirits" (I. Mather 1696a, 7).

Good angels are still present: "Their appearings are in a great measure ceased, but their working is not" (I. Mather 1696a, 63). Both Mathers sought apparitions of good angels soon after Salem: Increase convinced himself of experiencing one in September 1693, and Cotton soon followed suit (Hall 1988, 273).

WALTER STEPHENS

See also: ANGELS; CONFESSIONS; CORPOREALITY, ANGELIC AND DEMONIC; DEMONS; MATHER, COTTON; SALEM; SPECTRAL EVIDENCE.

References and further reading:

Hall, Michael G. 1988. *The Last American Puritan: The Life of Increase Mather.* Hanover, NH: University Press of New England for Wesleyan University Press.

Hoffer, Peter Charles. 1996. *The Devil's Disciples: Makers of the Salem Witch Trials.* Baltimore: Johns Hopkins University Press.

Mather, Cotton. 1980. *The Wonders of the Invisible World: Being an Account of the Tryals of Several Witches Lately Executed in New-England.* Amherst, WI: Amherst Press. Reprint of 1862 reprint of 1693 original.

Mather, Increase. 1696a. *Angelographia, or A Discourse Concerning the Nature and Power of the Holy Angels, and the Great Benefit Which True Fearers of God Receive by Their Ministry, Delivered in Several Sermons. To Which Is Added a Sermon Concerning the Sin and Misery of the Fallen Angels; Also a Disquisition Concerning Angelical Apparitions.* Boston: B. Green and J. Allen.

———. 1696b. *A Disquisition Concerning Angelical Apparitions. Sigs. K3r–M8v in Angelographia. or A Discourse Concerning the Nature and Power of the Holy Angels.* Boston: B. Green and

J. Allen.

———. 1980. *Cases of Conscience Concerning Evil Spirits Personating Men.* Pp. 218–291 in *The Wonders of the Invisible World: Being an Account of the Tryals of Several Witches Lately Executed in New-England.* By Cotton Mather. Amherst, WI: Amherst Press. Reprint of 1862 reprint of 1693 original.

"Salem Witch Trials: Documentary Archive and Transcription Project." University of Virginia. http://etext.virginia.edu/salem/witchcraft/home.html (accessed November 11, 2003).

MAXIMILIAN I, DUKE OF BAVARIA (1573–1651, RULED 1597–1651)

Educated as a witch hunter, the cautious Duke Maximilian never became one because he could not readily determine the guilty witch from the innocent accused. Bavaria's iron prince-elector had replaced his father Wilhelm V "the Pious" of the Wittelsbach dynasty (1548–1626, r. 1579–1594/1597) during the 1590s, when Bavaria was close to bankruptcy, before formally succeeding him in 1597. Maximilian became one of very few German princes who ruled before, during, and after the Thirty Years' War. As the founder and head of the Catholic League, he took action against Frederick V in 1618, when this prince-elector of the Palatineline of the Wittelsbachs was elected king of Bohemia. Maximilian's army crushed the Protestant army in 1620 at the battle at the White Mountain near Prague, terminating Frederick's kingship after only one winter. Holy Roman Emperor Ferdinand II subsequently rewarded his cousin Maximilian's support by transferring the Palatine electoral vote to the Bavarian Wittelsbachs in 1623. As leader of the Catholic League, Maximilian became so deeply embroiled in warfare that his duchy was occupied twice during the war by foreign troops and lost about half of its population, mainly through epidemic diseases rather than military action. Bavaria emerged from the war exhausted but intact, while Maximilian secured both the title of prince-elector and the territory of the Upper Palatinate for his successor. In his political testament, however, he recommended to his son Ferdinand Maria never to wage war except for the purpose of national defense because it placed too heavy a burden on the people.

The Spanish Jesuit Gregory of Valencia, a zealous demonologist, prepared Maximilian to be a witch hunter. Gregory literally spent days with his young pupil in the torture chambers, as we learn from Maximilian's letters to his father in Munich. At the age of sixteen, Maximilian had to watch the trials of witches at Ingolstadt. Throughout his long life, Maximilian was ready to support witch hunts. Many of his councilors and officials, some educated at the University of Ingolstadt in the same years, harbored similar ideas; many of the Franconian prince-bishops whom Maximilian recruited into the Catholic League had also matriculated at Ingolstadt. Maximilian and his Austrian cousin, who would become Emperor Ferdinand II (1578–1637) were the most prominent rulers during a generation of witch hunters. Furthermore, Maximilian, like his father, was married to a Lorraine princess, Elisabeth Renée (1574–1635), and thus closely allied with the rulers of this prolific witch-hunting duchy.

Despite all his zeal, however, Maximilian was a very cautious ruler, consuming his energies in the service of his people and spending many hours each day studying mountains of files. He was unwilling to tolerate administrative sloppiness, especially in the administration of the law. These positive aspects of Maximilian's personality may have motivated Bavaria's estates to secure his father's early resignation, thus ending the terrible witch hunt of the years around 1590 and securing a more capable young ruler.

This calculation worked out, at least to some extent. Maximilian knew how to use witch-hunting rhetoric but never turned into a witch hunter himself. After some executions in 1600, when zealous councilors attempted to launch a general witch hunt throughout Bavaria, representatives of the estates and the Privy Council stopped them, and Maximilian conceded a review of the legal procedure. As a result of obvious irregularities and after heated debates within his government, Maximilian agreed to the expensive procedure for asking legal opinions from different parts of Europe, including German governments and law faculties, two Italian universities, and demonologists from Lorraine (Nicolas Rémy) and the Spanish Netherlands (Martín Del Rio), all of which had to be discussed by his councilors in written legal opinions. In conclusion, the witch hunt was terminated, and legal procedures in general were reviewed. The Court Council, whose detailed minutes recorded its sessions, controlled the lower courts more tightly. No torture was to be applied in Bavaria without the Court Council's written consent. A general legal reform was begun, including the most detailed legislation anywhere in Europe against superstition, magic, and witchcraft, forty printed pages altogether, compiled between 1608 and 1612. A local judge, who had deceived the Court Council in order to conduct a local witch hunt in the Bavarian exclave of Wemding, was sentenced to death in 1613.

Although hundreds of cases of magic and witchcraft were scrutinized in Bavaria during Maximilian's long reign, there were few executions. To the great disappointment of some of his councilors, particularly his Jesuit confessor Adam Contzen and the faction around the zealous court councilor Dr. Johann Sigmund Wagnereckh, Maximilian never became a witch hunter, despite all his verbal radicalism. His hesitation was motivated not by doubts regarding the reality of witchcraft or the existence of witches, but by the difficulties of distinguishing genuine witches from innocent people who were exposed to suspicion by the enemy of mankind, the

Devil. The degree to which reason of state entered into the prince-elector's motivation is difficult to estimate. For the members of his Privy Council and the leaders of the estates, the general welfare of Bavaria's people was the guiding principle; it seems likely that Maximilian shared their opinion, although he never said so in public.

WOLFGANG BEHRINGER

See also: BAVARIA, DUCHY OF; CONTZEN, ADAM, SJ; DEL RIO, MARTÍN; FERDINAND II, HOLY ROMAN EMPEROR; GERMANY; GREGORY OF VALENCIA; HOLY ROMAN EMPIRE; INGOLSTADT, UNIVERSITY OF; JESUITS (SOCIETY OF JESUS), LAWS ON WITCHCRAFT (EARLY MODERN); LORRAINE, DUCHY OF; PALATINATE, ELECTORATE OF; RÉMY, NICOLAS.

References and further reading:
Albrecht, Dieter. 1998. *Maximilian I von Bayern.* Munich: C. H. Beck.
Behringer, Wolfgang. 1988. *Mit dem Feuer vom Leben zum Tod: Hexengesetzgebung in Bayern.* Munich: Hugendubel.
———. 1997. *Witchcraft Persecutions in Bavaria. Popular Magic, Religious Zealotry and Reason of State in Early Modern Europe.* Translated by J. C. Grayson and David Lederer. Cambridge: Cambridge University Press.
Bireley, Robert. 1975. *Maximilian von Bayern, Adam Contzen SJ und die Gegenreformation in Deutschland 1625–1635.* Göttingen: Vandenhoeck and Ruprecht.

MAXIMILIAN I, HOLY ROMAN EMPEROR (1459–1519, RULED 1486/1493–1519)

The son of Emperor Frederick III and Eleanor of Portugal, Maximilian laid the foundations for the rise of the Habsburg dynasty to world historical importance. Married in 1477 to Mary of Burgundy, heiress of Charles the Bold, he was elected "king of the Romans" in 1486 and succeeded his father as Holy Roman Emperor of the German Nation in 1493, although his coronation took place only in 1508. After his wife's death in 1482, Maximilian secured the Low Countries for their son Philip I of Burgundy, whom he married to Juana of Castile and Aragon in 1496. Maximilian's oldest grandson, Philip's son Charles (1500–1558), became king of Spain (1516), duke of Burgundy, and Holy Roman Emperor (1519); his second grandson Ferdinand (named for the Aragonese grandfather who raised him) acquired Habsburg Austria and later became king of Bohemia and Hungary (1526) and finally Holy Roman Emperor (1556). At least two demonologists tried to gain Maximilian's support. Heinrich Kramer traveled to Brussels in November 1486 to gain the king's approval for his book *Malleus Maleficarum* (The Hammer of Witches, 1486). The result must have been disappointing: only Kramer's petition is mentioned in an appendix to the *Malleus,* with the text of Maximilian's response suppressed. In 1508, Johannes Trithemius (1462–1516), abbot of the Benedictine monastery St. Jacob in Würzburg and a specialist on occult affairs, answered eight theological questions asked by Emperor Maximilian at the town of Boppard on the Rhine. Three of these (nos. 5–7) concerned witchcraft. Although Trithemius's answers were published during Maximilian's lifetime (*Liber octo questionum ad Maximilaneum Caesarem* [Book of Eight Questions to Emperor Maximilian], Oppenheim, 1515), both the circumstances of the event and the emperor's interests remain unclear. Maximilian's curiosity regarding cultural phenomena was insatiable, which was one of the reasons he was so tremendously popular in Upper Germany and Austria. But there is no evidence that Maximilian ever encouraged witchcraft trials in his possessions. Neither Tyrol nor Austria saw any executions during his reign, although the emperor was concerned about the frequent clusters of witchcraft trials in the Netherlands, his Burgundian heritage.

WOLFGANG BEHRINGER

See also: AUSTRIA; HOLY ROMAN EMPIRE; *MALLEUS MALEFICARUM;* TRITHEMIUS, JOHANNES; TYROL, COUNTY OF.

References and further reading:
Benecke, Gerhard. 1982. *Maximilian I (1459–1519): An Analytical Biography.* London and Boston: Routledge and Kegan Paul.
Grössing, Maria. 2002. *Maximilian I: Kaiser, Künstler, Kämpfer.* Vienna: Amalthea.
Wiesflecker, Hermann. 1971–1986. *Kaiser Maximilian I; Das Reich, Österreich und Europa an der Wende zur Neuzeit.* 5 vols. Munich: R. Oldenbourg.

MECHANICAL PHILOSOPHY

Seventeenth- and early eighteenth-century mechanical philosophy, which held that nature operated like a machine in accordance with the laws of nature, led some educated men to question their belief in witchcraft. The mechanical philosophy provided one of the main philosophical foundations for the Scientific Revolution. It is most closely associated with the work of the French philosopher and mathematician René Descartes, although many other scientists, including Galileo Galilei and Johannes Kepler, subscribed to its basic elements. Mechanists argued that nature operated mechanically, just like a clock or some other piece of machinery. According to mechanists, nature consisted of many machines, some of them extremely small. The human body was itself a machine, and its center, the heart, was likewise a piece of machinery that moved other parts of the body. Because God made the human body, it was superior to any human-made machine, but it was still nothing more than a machine. The only part of a human being that was not a machine was the mind or the soul, which according to Descartes was immaterial and therefore completely different from the body and the rest of the natural world.

Descartes argued that matter was completely inert or passive. It had neither a soul nor any innate purpose. Its only property was extension, by which Descartes meant its physical dimensions, such as length, width, and depth. Without a spirit or any other internal force directing its action, matter simply responded to the power of the other bodies with which it came in contact. According to Descartes, "There exist no occult forces in stones or plants, no amazing and marvellous sympathies and antipathies, in fact there exists nothing in the whole of nature which cannot be explained in terms of purely corporeal causes, totally devoid of mind and thought" (Easlea 1980, 111). This view of nature posed a direct challenge to Neoplatonism, which held that the natural world was charged with various occult forces and therefore provided the main philosophical foundation for the practice of natural magic.

The mechanical philosophy also presented a challenge to the belief in witchcraft. The view that nature operated in a regular, predictable way, in accordance with immutable laws, called into question the belief that witches used the power of the Devil to intervene in the operation of the natural world. Those who adopted Descartes' philosophy, known as Cartesianism, did not necessarily deny the existence of good or evil spirits, but they did reject the view that those spirits could change the course of nature. The English philosopher Thomas Hobbes, who differed with Descartes on many issues but nevertheless also subscribed to a mechanical view of the universe, went so far as to deny the existence of spirits altogether. For Hobbes, even God was material, and the spirits and demons mentioned in the Bible had thin bodies that were incapable of being perceived by human beings.

Nevertheless, the mechanical philosophy had only limited success in undermining the belief in witchcraft among educated people. The main reason was that other natural philosophers modified Descartes' mechanical view of nature to allow for the intervention of spiritual forces. The English philosopher Henry More, who had originally been an admirer of Descartes, and the scientist Joseph Glanvill both claimed that spiritual or occult forces were necessary to explain various natural phenomena, including the motion of matter. Glanvill argued that spirits played an active role in nature and that scientists could acquire empirical evidence of their activities. He contended that the phenomena attributed to witchcraft provided evidence for a mechanistic natural theology, in which the Devil, like God, worked through the normal course of nature. For Glanvill, the Devil was part of nature, and the empirical study of demons had scientific validity.

The limited influence of the mechanical philosophy on the decline of witch beliefs among educated people can best be seen in the work of the Dutch Reformed minister and theologian Balthasar Bekker. Bekker was one of the most radical skeptics regarding witchcraft in the late seventeenth century. In his four-volume treatise, *De Betoverde Weereld* (The World Bewitched, 1691–1693), Bekker denied that the Devil could intervene in the operation of the material world. Once the Devil was denied this ability, the possibility that a human being could commit the crime of witchcraft vanished. Bekker was admittedly a follower of Descartes, and he clearly accepted a Cartesian view of the sharp distinction between spirit and matter. But Bekker did not rely primarily on the mechanical philosophy or any other scientific evidence to attack the belief in witchcraft; the main foundation for his skepticism was his biblical scholarship, which he used to show that God maintained sovereignty over the world and had never allowed the Devil to exercise power within it.

Although the mechanical philosophy called into question the *beliefs* of some educated people in witchcraft, it had little influence on the decline of witchcraft *prosecutions*. The decline in the number of trials began in some European countries as early as 1600 and in most regions of western Europe by 1670. These were the years when the mechanical philosophy first made its appearance. Its spread, however, was a gradual process, and it was controversial. It took some time for this new mental outlook to make its mark in the universities, the legal profession, and state bureaucracies. It is unlikely that the judges and officials who applied the early brakes on witch hunting during the first seventy years of the seventeenth century were even exposed to, let alone influenced by, these new ideas.

The critical period in the reception of the mechanical philosophy appears to have been the years between 1690 and 1720, the period of the early Enlightenment. Thus, mechanism did not appreciably affect the mental outlook of the educated classes until well after prosecutions had begun to decline and, in some cases, until after they had stopped altogether. In Geneva, for example, the first magistrate to profess an adherence to Cartesian ideas, Robert Chouet, wrote a critical commentary on Geneva's prosecution of witches in 1690, almost forty years after the last witch had been executed in that republic, although only nine years after the last Genevan witch had been banished. Even in France, where the mechanical philosophy may have taken root somewhat earlier than in Geneva, Cartesianism probably did not have the negative influence on the level of prosecutions that scholars have often attributed to it. Certainly the members of the *Parlement* of Paris, who played a decisive role in the decline of French witch hunting after 1624, could not have been influenced by Cartesianism until long after they had brought executions for witchcraft to an end.

If the mechanical philosophy played any role at all in the decline of witch hunting, it was at the end of the process in the late seventeenth and early eighteenth centuries, when the last trials took place and witchcraft was decriminalized, but not in the earlier decades of the seventeenth century, when some dramatic reductions in the number of trials occurred. Even during the later period, however, the influence of philosophical ideas on the conduct of prosecutions was limited. Witchcraft trials ended mainly because authorities came to the realization that it was impossible to prove the crime, not because they denied its reality.

BRIAN P. LEVACK

See also: BEKKER, BALTHASAR; DECLINE OF THE WITCH HUNTS; DEMONOLOGY; DESCARTES, RENÉ; ENLIGHTENMENT; GLANVILL, JOSEPH; HOBBES, THOMAS; KEPLER, JOHANNES; MORE, HENRY; OCCULT; *PARLEMENT* OF PARIS; SCIENCE AND MAGIC; SKEPTICISM.

References and further reading:
Attfield, Robin, 1985. "Balthasar Bekker and the Decline of the Witch-Craze: The Old Demonology and the New Philosophy." *Annals of Science* 42: 383–395.
Bostridge, Ian. 1997. *Witchcraft and Its Transformations, c. 1650–c. 1750.* Oxford: Clarendon.
Brann, Noel. 1980. "The Conflict Between Reason and Magic in Seventeenth-Century England: A Case Study of the Vaughan–More Debate." *Huntington Library Quarterly* 47: 103–126.
Clark, Stuart. 1984. "The Scientific Status of Demonology." Pp. 351–374 in *Occult and Scientific Mentalities in the Renaissance.* Edited by Brian Vickers. Cambridge: Cambridge University Press.
———. 1997. *Thinking with Demons: The Idea of Witchcraft in Early Modern Europe.* Oxford: Clarendon.
Laslea, Brian. 1980. *Witch Hunting, Magic, and the New Philosophy: An Introduction to the Debates of the Scientific Revolution 1450–1750.* Brighton: Harvester.
Hutton, Sarah, ed. 1990. *Henry More (1614–1989): Tercentenary Studies.* Dordrecht: Kluwer Academic Publishers.
Jobe, Thomas Harmon. 1981. "The Devil in Restoration Science: The Glanvill-Webster Witchcraft Debate." *Isis* 72: 343–356.
Levack, Brian P. 1999. "The Decline and End of Witchcraft Prosecutions." Pp. 1–93 in *Witchcraft and Magic in Europe: The Eighteenth and Nineteenth Centuries.* Vol. 5 of *The Athlone History of Witchcraft and Magic in Europe.* Edited by Stuart Clark and Bengt Ankarloo. London and Philadelphia: Athlone University of Pennsylvania Press.
Thomas, Keith. 1971. *Religion and the Decline of Magic.* New York: Scribner's.

MECKLENBURG, DUCHY OF

Mecklenburg, a Lutheran duchy in the northeastern part of the Holy Roman Empire, had more than its share of intensive persecution of witches between 1560 and 1700. In a region with a population of roughly 200,000 around 1600, there were more than 4,000 witchcraft trials, at least half of them ending with the death of the accused. The worst persecutions came in two large waves, cresting between 1599 and 1614 and again between 1661 and 1675.

These two times of persecution were quite different in nature. In the first phase, when Mecklenburg was politically unified, the victims were primarily members of fringe groups or groups caught in the midst of local social conflicts. The second, later phase, coming after

Mecklenburg had been divided into two duchies in 1621, grew into mass persecutions that sought to wipe out witchcraft by eliminating anyone suspected of it. The expanding and intensifying persecutions provoked resistance from some of the families affected and from several of Mecklenburg's religious leaders. At the same time, the shift away from fear of diabolical witchcraft and criticisms of the trials led to the end of the persecutions between 1681 and 1683 in Mecklenburg-Güstrow and around 1700 in Mecklenburg-Schwerin.

Early sorcery trials can be traced back to around 1480. In such trials, it is sometimes difficult to draw a clear line between trials aimed at persecuting witches for the damages they caused (*maleficium*) and later cases that saw the Devil as partner of the sorceress. In 1558 we find the first evidence of true witchcraft hearings. Archival sources show that Mecklenburg held about ten witchcraft trials per year by 1570. The massive increases in the early phases of prosecution came with attempts to enforce Mecklenburg's evangelical ecclesiastical ordinances of 1562 and 1572. Crimes were defined largely according to the terms of the Carolina Code (1532), with some of its standards intensified.

Local rulers could now follow through on chasing down and punishing witches, using stricter regulations and penalties for breaches of law. At the same time, the Lutheran rulers also prosecuted fortunetellers, treasure hunters, and people who earned their living by counteracting witchcraft (*Hexenbanner*) on the basis of confessional considerations. Mecklenburg's late-sixteenth-century witch persecution was based on complaints from individual farmers and municipalities; their claims of evil magic were mainly directed against people from families that were already stigmatized.

Around 1600, Mecklenburg's persecutions reached their highest point. Between 1604 and 1615, there were an average of thirty witchcraft trials per year in the region, which was also suffering from epidemics and crop failures. Witch prosecution usually took the form of small groups of trials clustered together. Because magistrates were required by law to send the briefs and documentation to the faculties of law and the judiciary chancelleries, a system of relatively mild verdicts became the norm. Sentencing in Mecklenburg did not employ full force against all of the criminal aspects of witchcraft. A rather skeptical Protestant providentialism led to a relatively temperate interpretation of witchcraft. Certain elements of the cumulative concept of witchcraft were abandoned; for example, witches who flew and were transformed into animals were not part of confessions elicited, nor did Mecklenburg's clergy or judges accept them.

More important than the theoretical differentiations was the practice of following the *processus ordinarius* (ordinary procedure). Witchcraft was not considered a *crimen exceptum* (the excepted crime) in Mecklenburg in the early stages of trials. On the contrary, the tendency was to lean toward moderation and caution in dealing with circumstantial evidence and torture. Prominent Mecklenburg jurists like Johann Georg Goedelmann and Ernst Cothmann symbolized the attitudes of the region's ruling classes and administrators, who adhered to humanistic principles of thought. Thus the use of defense lawyers was always allowed in witchcraft trials, and they appear in roughly one in five court cases regarding witchcraft. Rumors of witchcraft were treated with reservation, and a single accusation never sufficed to open a proceeding. Additional evidence was also treated cautiously. In slightly more than half (55 percent) of these cases, torture and the death penalty were permitted.

Local courts were less scrupulous about enforcing these strict codes, and they offer numerous examples of breaches of law in witchcraft cases before 1600. The systems of serfdom and farmers' loss of property rights to manorial lords ran parallel to the early witch persecutions in a sparsely populated region with several types of seigneurial and lesser manorial courts. At the same time, the regional government strove for better discipline and professionalism in local law courts. They dismissed various members of small town and district courts from their offices after investigations into breaches of law.

A specific type of persecution of witches developed in different jurisdictions—both the smaller and larger autonomous cities, and the noble and district courts. It focused primarily on those groups of the population caught in the middle of social tensions and conflicts. In the larger cities and offices, this meant primarily the poor and people from fringe groups. In the smaller towns, it was often people associated with the municipal elite; in noble courts, it was members of the farming community who had protested against the loss of their power and rights. Seigneurial courts, reflecting conflicts between the nobility and their subjects under the new social and legal manorial system, primarily conducted witchcraft trials in the first period. However, the intensity of these disagreements diminished considerably during and after the end of the Thirty Years' War. The noble court leaders and civic judges in the lake areas both lost interest in witchcraft trials and consequently dismissed accusations from ordinary people.

These social differences in addressing conflict leveled out after Mecklenburg's mass persecutions began. The late-seventeenth-century persecutions also reflected other changes. Unlike the earlier persecution, witchcraft no longer manifested itself in the practice of magic or in neighborhood quarrels; rather, ties to witchcraft were now sought through kinship and association with other witches. Trials no longer targeted small fringe groups and poorer people but expanded significantly to include middle- and upper-class defendants. Similarly, witchcraft became less gender-specific; the longer these persecutions continued, the more likely they were to accuse men and children.

Mecklenburg experienced numerous intense waves of persecution following the end of the Thirty Years' War. At this time, its largest chain of trials took place, involving more than eighty people in the village districts of Redentin and Bukow. The governments in both parts of the duchy (Schwerin and Güstrow) actively supported these trials, but they used very different means. In Mecklenburg-Schwerin, the government increasingly discarded the stricter safeguards of public law and minimized the legal prerequisites for circumstantial evidence in witchcraft trials, thus allowing for chains of trials to develop. A witch's accusations toward her conspirators were accepted uncritically and used as the basis for new trials against "accomplices." One's chances of being cleared of such charges and released were minimal. Instead, in cases in which witchcraft was not proved, the basic suspicion was cause for banishment from the duchy. There was little supervision of local courts, because Schwerin law often employed special commissions. Even though its sovereign, Christian Louis I, personally called for an end to all witchcraft trials, he lived abroad; his chief civil servants, Chancellor Hans Heinrich Wedemann and later Adolf Friedrich zur Nedden, ignored his order and continued to issue commissions. Only after the death of Chancellor Nedden in May 1700 could the persecutions of witches be ended in Schwerin.

Meanwhile, persecution of magic and superstition became the core elements of an intensive campaign of confessional Lutheran discipline in Mecklenburg-Güstrow. As a result, every rumor of witchcraft was investigated—but not with the same legal procedures or standards as in Schwerin. The elimination of witchcraft was pursued with equal determination in Güstrow, but its extensive inquisitions and visitations were accompanied by rigorous controls over its local courts by upper-level and professional judges.

Mecklenburg's learned and pious experts studied each piece of evidence from each case with a high degree of exactness, often resulting in long periods of imprisonment for the accused without the case ever being decided. Many died in prison or were not released until the early 1680s. Meanwhile, because of their experiences in dealing with these trials, members of the clergy were quick to develop a more critical attitude toward witchcraft trials. In the long run, they were able to delay or prevent chains of new trials caused by accusations from those convicted, and they finally devalued the confessions of pacts with the Devil and the witches' Sabbats. Witchcraft was dismissed as a "superstition," and the persecution of witches ended by 1700.

KATRIN MOELLER

See also: ACCUSATIONS; CAROLINA CODE (*CONSTITIO CRIMINALIS CAROLINA*); COURTS, SECULAR; *CRIMEN EXCEPTUM;* GERMANY, NORTHEASTERN; GOEDELMANN, JOHANN GEORG; LAWYERS.

References and further reading:

Ankarloo, Bengt, and Gustav Henningsen, eds. 1990. *Early Modern European Witchcraft: Centres and Peripheries.* Oxford: Clarendon.

Katrin Moeller. 2002a. *"Das Willkür über Recht ginge": Hexenverfolgung im Mecklenburg des 16. und 17. Jahrhunderts.* Rostock: University Press.

———. 2002b. "Es ist ein überaus gerechtes Gesetz, dass die Zauberinnen getötet werden: Hexenverfolgung im protestantis- chen Norddeutschland." Pp. 96–107 in *Hexenwahn: Ängste der Neuzeit, Begleitband zur gleichnamigen Ausstellung des Deutschen Historischen Museums.* Edited by Rosmarie Beier-de Haan, Rita Voltmer, and Franz Irsigler. Berlin: Minerva Hermann Farnung.

Lorenz, Sönke. 1981. "Johann Georg Godelmann—Ein Gegner des Hexenwahns." Pp. 61–105 in *Beiträge zur pommerschen und mecklenburgischen Geschichte.* Edited by Roderich Schmidt. Marburg: J. G. Herder-Institut.

———. 1982. *Aktenversendung und Hexenprozess: Dargestellt am Beispiel der Juristenfakultäten Rostock und Greifswald (1570/82–1630).* Frankfurt am Main: Lang.

———. 1991. "Ernst Cothmann (1557–1624) aus Lemgo in Westfalen: Ein Jurisconsultus Rostockiensis in Sachen Hexenprozess." Pp. 437–449 in *Das andere Wahrnehmen: Beiträge zur europäischen Geschichte, August Nitschke zum 65. Geburtstag gewidmet.* Edited by Martin Kintzinger, Wolfgang Stürner, and Johannes Zahlten. Cologne: Böhlau.

Lubinski, Axel. 1997. "Hexenverfolgung im toten Winkel Magie, dörfliche Konflikte und Gutsherrschaft im nordwestlichen Mecklenburg (Amt Grevesmühlen) gegen Ende des 17. Jahrhunderts." Pp. 119–158 in *Hexenverfolgung in Mecklenburg: Regionale und überregionale Aspekte.* Edited by Dieter Harmening and Andrea Rudolph. Dettelbach: J. H. Röll.

Nedden, August Johann Carl zur. 1880–1881. "Beiträge zur Geschichte der Großherzoglichen Justiz-Canzlei zu Schwerin." *Mecklenburger Jahrbücher* 45: 177–262 and 46: 169–283.

MEDEA

Medea is one of the great paradigms of the classical magi- cian, and hence of the female witch in later times. Granddaughter of the sun and niece of the divine magi- cian Circe, she fell in love with Jason during his search for the Golden Fleece and aided him with her magic. A woman of violent emotions, her enmity could be fatal. When she abandoned her family for love of Jason and her brother tried to pursue her, she killed him without com- punction; when Jason fell in love with another woman, Medea sent her a robe anointed with an unguent intend- ed to kill; and having restored the youth of Jason's father by cutting him into pieces and boiling them in a pot with magical herbs, she persuaded the daughters of Pelias (the king who had sent Jason on his expedition for the Golden Fleece) to attempt the same, but made sure they failed by giving them inefficacious herbs. This was an aspect of her magic that early modern writers particularly noted. Marsilio Ficino and Johann Weyer, for example, drew attention to it; Cornelius Agrippa remarked in *De Occulta Philosophia* (On Occult Philosophy, Book 1: 15) that some physicians were claiming to be able to restore a per- son's youth by giving him or her a concoction made from viper's flesh and hellebore. Medea could also control the weather by calming storm and sea and blight fruitful nature by piercing the liver of a doll made for just this purpose, and she had the evil eye. When a bronze giant called Talos menaced Jason and the Argonauts, Medea uttered invocations and then fixed the giant with the power of her evil eye and killed him.

Medea came from Colchis, a region just south of the Caucasus Mountains, and so was not a Greek. Consequently, Euripides, in *Medea* or *Andromache,* portrayed her in the light of the Greeks' view of the world that was divided between civilized people like themselves and barbarians, who indulged their passions with murder or occasionally with incest. Ancient authors frequently underlined two characteristics of her magic. She used *pharmaka,* herbs or minerals with preternatural powers, making her a *venefica,* a woman who either poisons others or works poisonous magic against them; and she worshipped Hecate, a goddess associated with the earth and the moon and hence the deity par excellence of magic. Significantly, then, we are told by the third-century-B.C.E. Greek poet Apollonius Rhodius (*Argonautica* 4.50–4.53) that Medea was well-acquainted with graveyards, having spent much time wandering through them.

The story of Medea, therefore, contained several fea- tures reminiscent of the medieval and early modern scholarly image of the witch. Her emotions were both strong and malicious; she indulged herself with illicit love and sex; she employed herbs for magical purposes, which might be beneficent or maleficent according to the prompting of the emotion that currently ruled her; she had the evil eye; she worked weather and crop magic by piercing enchanted dolls; she belonged, as it were, to a society other than that which is regular and civilized; and her magic was performed in conjunction with a deity who had power over the spirits of the dead and was capable of producing extraordinary phenome- na. The portrait by Ovid (*Metamorphoses* 7.180–191) of her working a necromantic ritual was particularly vivid and highly theatrical. Medea let her hair and dress float free; she paced barefoot up and down with- out apparent purpose; she operated at night; and instead of uttering comprehensible words, she shrieked and howled almost like an animal. The marks of civi- lization had disappeared, and in their place she exhibit- ed the signs of a person who had willingly cast aside the usual restraints observed by the rest of society. Medea thus became alien and frightening as she sought to rend the veil normally dividing the realm of the living from that of the dead. Later writers on witches and demonology, all educated in the Greek and Latin classics, therefore had little to do to develop their portrait of a witch. All they needed to add were the purely Christian elements.

P. G. MAXWELL-STUART

See also: CIRCE; EVIL EYE; HECATE; PERSONALITY OF WITCHES.
References and further reading:
Arafat, Karim W. 1996. "Medea." P. 944 in *Oxford Classical Dictionary.* Edited by Simon Hornblower and Anthony Spawforth. 3rd ed. Oxford: Oxford University Press.
Dickie, Matthew. 2001. *Magic and Magicians in the Greco-Roman World.* London: Routledge.
Maxwell-Stuart, P. G. 2000. *Witchcraft, A History.* Stroud, UK, and Charleston, SC: Tempus.

MEDER, DAVID (1545–1616)

At the beginning of the seventeenth century, David Meder, a Lutheran minister in Saxony, passionately propagated the existence of an aggressive witch cult on earth and called for its extinction. Despite his fierce zeal, he desired only moderate witch hunts. Meder was close to the official mainstream in the early seventeenth-century electorate of Saxony, which crafted extremely severe legislation against witchcraft yet followed a relatively mild and scrupulous policy in witchcraft trials.

Born in Naumburg in the electorate of Saxony, Meder studied theology at the University of Leipzig and became a general inspector of Lutheran churches and schools for the small county of Hohenlohe (in southwestern Germany) in 1577. He returned to his place of birth as a preacher in 1595, later moving to the nearby Saxon town of Nebra, where he died.

Because of the divided views on witchcraft trials between the general population, who wished to eliminate witches, and the judges who pronounced sentences, who needed proof to justify them, Meder tried to influence public opinion through a series of sermons. Together with other material, his witch sermons were published in 1605, with a second edition in 1615.

In Meder's opinion, the main reason for the growth of witchcraft was the deteriorating state of mankind, manifested in increasing wickedness to which too many Christians yielded. This deterioration was further exacerbated by attacks on true Christianity from Catholics, Muslims, and Calvinists.

In his sermons, the Lutheran theologian cited the Hebrew Bible, the Church Fathers, and Martin Luther, all of whom accepted that witches existed on earth. Meder passionately opposed all skeptics of witch hunting; in his eyes, witchcraft was a capital crime, which surpassed all other sins. Witches, he believed, caused much damage; they were responsible for murder, diseases among humans and livestock, theft, and poor harvests. Their destructive undertakings were based on a pact with the Devil, who granted them powers. The pact was supposedly complemented by copulation with the Devil. Unlike many other Protestant authors, Meder accepted the witches' Sabbat, the collective element in the witch paradigm, as true. He used certain recent trials as evidence that sorcery was not confined to women. Men and even children performed this destructive art. Because this capital crime encompassed the Seven Deadly Sins and violated almost all Ten Commandments, this Lutheran preacher called upon the authorities to take action by conducting witchcraft trials—including handing out death sentences.

Despite his vehemence, Meder called for relatively modest witch hunts. He dismissed imposing death sentences for conviction of nondiabolical sorcery, believing that imposing penance was a fair punishment for such offenses. He criticized excessively harsh torture and largely dismissed denunciations from convicted witches. Meder opposed the swimming test and accepted only testimonies of respectable Christians or unforced confessions as proof. Meder exemplified the providentialist tradition within Lutheranism stemming from the Württemberg school of Johann Brenz, which saw the growth of witchcraft as a kind of godly providence (Midelfort 1972, 36–66). Thus God permitted witchcraft through the Devil's agency in order to chasten sinful mankind and warn the faithful, but, nevertheless, God allowed Satan no independent power. Thus, the powers of witches were horrible, but—because only God reigns—limited.

Meder's approach was not exempt from contradictions, for he could not reconcile his implicit clamor for an extinction policy in the first part of the book with his explicit demands for relatively mild treatment of alleged witches. His explanations also followed providential theology on another level. Because this school rejected the reality of weather spells, Meder's assertions on this very important topic for contemporaries were contradictory. On one page he attributed the obliteration of harvests by hailstorms to the magic of witches but rejected such thinking on another page. Meder's two editions of his eight witch sermons demonstrate the degree of reception of his thoughts.

ROLF SCHULTE;

TRANSLATED BY JAN VAN DER CRABBEN

See also: APOCALYPSE; BRENZ, JOHANN; DEMONOLOGY; EVIDENCE; LUTHER, MARTIN; *MALEFICIUM;* PACT WITH THE DEVIL; PROOF, PROBLEM OF; SABBAT; SAXONY, ELECTORATE OF; WEATHER MAGIC.
References and further reading:
Meder, David. 1605. *Acht Hexenpredigten.* Leipzig. 2nd ed. 1615.
Midelfort, H. C. Erik. 1972. *Witch Hunting in Southwestern Germany, 1562–1684: The Social and Intellectual Foundations.* Stanford: Stanford University Press.

MEDICINE AND MEDICAL THEORY

Spider webs, ant eggs, snakeskin, extract of wood lice, extract of foxglove, beetle's blood, and an elixir with seventy-nine different ingredients . . . "This was not, as would be reasonable to suppose, the first aid kit of a local witch left behind and found after her arrest. It was part of the pharmacopoeia of the University of Glasgow found by William Cullen on taking up an appointment as professor of medicine in 1751" (Larner 1984, 142). Astonishing as it might seem, it would be nonetheless simplistic to assume from this evidence that early modern learned medicine was rooted in a seedbed of misconceptions, that its practitioners had a poor understanding of the workings of the human body, and that the contents of their medicine chests were useless and most of their prescriptions potentially harmful. In *A Midsummer Night's Dream*, Bottom's words remind us of the curative power of a spider's web against hemorrhages: "I shall desire you of more acquaintance, good master Cobweb: if I hurt my finger, I shall make bold with you" (III, I, 164–165). In terms of therapeutics, learned and popular medicine substantially overlapped, and both were powerless to heal serious illnesses.

Despite notable developments in the history of medicine during the last few decades, its nexus with early modern witchcraft still awaits a global assessment. The spectrum of questions raised by this intricate relationship is discouragingly wide. It has recently been held that the idea of witchcraft, "a composite subject consisting of discussions" about all facets of human civilization (Clark 1997, viii), was inherent in the moods, minds, and culture of early modern people. Nevertheless, from the vantage point of the treatment of sick people in early modern Europe, two broad questions can be formulated. First, how did an age commonly defined by historians as one of scientific advancements adjust itself to widespread beliefs about diseases of demonic origin? Second, how did learned medicine of this period succeed, if at all, in imposing its intellectual superiority and forcing cures that relied on magic and religion into a corner?

MEDICINE AND CHRISTIANITY

Christianity had always been a healing religion with a strong affinity between saving souls and healing bodies. Illnesses came ultimately from an offended God as a result of sin. When early modern people fell ill, they did not generally assume that their ailments were caused by witchcraft. However, if the signs of disease appeared weird and suspicious, both common belief and Holy Scriptures allowed that it might have been engendered by bewitchment cast by malevolent persons with the help of the Devil. Curative remedies, nevertheless, should not be magical, and their healing power must be implemented through prayer by both patients and doctors. Only Church hierarchies could establish the orthodoxy of a prayer. After the mid-sixteenth century, ecclesiastical hierarchies increasingly disavowed the centuries-old healing practice of divines, although much ambiguity persisted about the practice of exorcism in Catholic lands. No doubt, when the sixteenth-century physicians

Girolamo Cardano and Johann Weyer asserted that diseases apparently caused by witches could be traced to natural origins, they were anticipating the secularization of a discipline; but the separation of functions between medicine and religion occurred very slowly.

THEORETICAL FOUNDATIONS OF EARLY MODERN MEDICINE

Recent works in the history of medicine have demolished Whiggish notions of scientific advancements, emphasizing elements that appear progressive in a modern sense. Much of the attention of historians now concentrates on how early modern people experienced medicine in terms of therapeutics and relief from anxiety and pain.

A preliminary digression on the theoretical mold of ancient medicine seems necessary before dealing with medical practitioners and patients. Unquestionably, any changes in sixteenth- and seventeenth-century medicine took place within these deep-rooted assumptions. The Hippocratic/Galenic tradition retained its preeminence throughout Renaissance, baroque, and Enlightenment Europe. Galenic physicians followed humoral theories, understanding the human body as composed of masses of four fluids: blood, phlegm, yellow bile, and black bile. It was a microcosm related to the larger macrocosm of the universe. Humors were linked to the seasons, to the four ages of humankind (childhood, youth, adulthood, and old age), and were the product of the four Aristotelian qualities (hot, cold, dry, and fire). Good health resulted from a balance among these four humors, and any alterations in their nature might jeopardize a person's physical condition. The putrefaction of humors through contagion from some poison, as in plague, could also cause illness. Therefore all treatments aimed at blocking corruption and readjusting imbalances through bleeding, purging, vomiting, and evacuating. Healing meant restoring a harmony between macrocosm and microcosm. The best means of maintaining health was to practice moderation by avoiding exhaustion, overeating, overdrinking, overheating, and immoderate passions. Immorality and a vicious life were perceived as causes of disease.

The most challenging break with the Galenic paradigm came from the physician Theophrastus Bombastus von Hohenheim, called Paracelsus (ca. 1493–1541), who carried out a head-on attack on tradition by proposing a novel physiology and anatomy. Contrary to Galenic wisdom, which ignored the existence of specific diseases, he taught that an *archeus* (vital force) external to the human body caused disease and offered a basis for understanding that illnesses were real entities. Paracelsus's chemically based medicine emphasized the process of fermentation and putrefaction at the basis of physiology. After him, iatrochemistry gained much prestige in the treatment of illnesses, in opposition to the herbal remedies mostly used by

Galenists. Iatrochemistry was soon joined by another feature of medical examination, iatromechanics, contending that human body processes obeyed the same laws of physics ruling earth and the planets. A description of sixteenth- and seventeenth-century medicine must include the many breakthroughs in anatomy (with decisive influence on forensic medicine), physiology, and pathology by Jan Baptista van Helmont (1579–1644) and his son Franciscus Mercurius van Helmont (1614?–1699), Théophraste Renaudot (1586–1653), Giorgio Baglivi (1668–1707), or Friedrich Hoffmann (1660–1742). But all these advances cannot conceal a stronger reality: throughout early modern times, methods of treatment remained overwhelmingly Galenic, and "few of the theoretical changes introduced, even the Paracelsian ones, made much difference in how illnesses were treated and none, by itself, contributed to cures" (Lindemann 1999, 88).

LEARNED DOCTORS

There seems to be an almost perfect correlation between mid- and late-seventeenth-century post-Galenic medicine and the end of witchcraft persecutions. But how can we reconcile this temporal coincidence with the fact that no radical epistemological changes characterized the birth of the new medicine? In fact, the decline of witchcraft was a complex sociocultural event, unrelated in any direct way to progress in medical science. What most recent studies have shown is that an empiricism that stressed observation and experience became the dominant theory among physicians, an investigative paradigm previously inconceivable within a community of Christian physicians.

The strongest challenges to the belief in witchcraft among university-trained scholars of the sixteenth century had come from physicians. And yet many of them, like Giovan Battista Codronchi, Pietro Piperno, or William Drage, championed the causation of illnesses by witchcraft. But unlike lawyers, philosophers, and theologians, physicians received a professional training that eventually allowed them to make a different diagnosis and provide naturalistic explanations for diseases. From correspondence in 1653 between a New Haven physician, Nicholas Augur, and John Winthrop Jr., medical doctor in Connecticut and later fellow of the Royal Society, we can observe the shaping of a different diagnosis. The illness of four young girls displayed symptoms similar to their counterparts in Salem forty years later, but these physicians ignored the girls' narrative of diabolical bewitchment. Instead, Augur searched for natural explanations for their fits, and his differential diagnosis included three possibilities: "I must needs say that strange and various accidents and distempers do arise both from the obstruction of the spleen as well as from hysterical passions, and sometimes from the retention of overflowing of the menses. . . ." (Gevitz

2000, 24). The writings of such well-known early modern doctors as Johann Weyer, Jean Fernel, Ambrose Paré, Girolamo Cardano, Daniel Sennert, Edward Jorden, or John Cotta tried to clarify the nature of odd and puzzling symptoms in patients. However, many of them rejected both the Paracelsian paradigm and the entire Hippocratic/Galenic tradition. The dividing line between tradition and modernity remained uncertain, and the dominant ethos of every scientific corporation avoided the most radical positions.

For skeptical physicians, this caution meant that almost nobody would attempt to disprove the authority of Holy Scriptures in matters of witchcraft, with the probable exception of Weyer. Practically things fared quite differently, because we know from several cases that physicians did not accept witchcraft as a serious possibility when natural causes could explain suspicious possessions, illnesses, or deaths. The "long" sixteenth century was an era dominated by antagonistic forces that tended to blur in complex ways. The erudition of some medical doctors encompassed a variety of subjects: magic, philosophy, religion, alchemy, and occult studies. Some became astrological physicians, believing that heavenly bodies could affect the human body and cause illness.

No early modern medical practice better reveals this synthesis of late Renaissance learning than the amazing career of Richard Napier, an Anglican theologian, master of arts at the University of Oxford, and parson of a rural parish in Buckinghamshire. His detailed casebooks of some 60,000 consultations from 1597 to 1634 shed light on multiple health problems of all social classes (Macdonald 1981). Apparently, sick people used to go to doctors mainly to receive physical treatment; only 5 percent of Napier's patients suffered from mental as distinct from bodily illness. In this age, few people from any social class would have questioned Napier's medical advice, his mix of astrology, magic, Christianity, and science. But by the waning years of the seventeenth century, academically trained doctors had largely succeeded in branding medical astrologers as quacks.

CAUSES CÉLÈBRES AND NEW PARADIGMS

It seems self-evident to admit that there was no incongruity at all between a "scientific" age and medical diagnoses based on demonological beliefs. The presence of demonic pathologies in academic medical milieus was no marginal and exotic aberration (Clark 1997). However, the guiding principle governing medical studies, namely differential analysis, proved to be the most intractable among all fields of learning to reconcile with the presence of a demonic agency. Historians know that it is difficult to reconstruct a coherent picture explaining the establishment of a new scientific paradigm. Regarding medical care and the etiology of illnesses, witchcraft could be discerned as an interpretive proposition based on the principle of irradiation from a center. It has been argued that the Mary Glover and Anne Gunter cases (1601–1604) marked a turning point in the history of witchcraft in England because the unveiling of both women's simulated illnesses "encouraged medical sceptics to advance their cause . . . and helped to increase the burden of proof" (Macdonald 1991, li). And in France, a similar emergence of ideas emphasizing empirical medical explanations for simulated cases of diabolical possessions extended from the Marthe Brossier case (1598) through the great scandals of Loudun (1633–1634) and Louviers (1643–1644), all of which spawned major controversies, including alternative diagnoses challenging the apparent proofs of diabolical illnesses and encouraging skeptical explanations.

PATIENTS AND PRACTITIONERS

Was the world of university-trained and town-based physicians representative of the reality of medicine and medical care in early modern Europe? Because 80 percent of its inhabitants did not live in cities, a meaningful understanding of health care systems in the past requires some knowledge of how they worked in the countryside. Unfortunately, our information is far from satisfactory with regard to where, when, and how healing practices were implemented in European villages.

In old Europe, medical care began within the household and the neighborhood, where older, experienced women practiced midwifery and pooled their wisdom to cure minor bodily afflictions. It is more difficult for social historians to assess how many health workers were available beyond the circle of neighborly first aid to cure the sick in rural areas. And certainly, numbers matter. We know, for instance, that the rural district of Veluwe in Holland had one medical practitioner for every 1,400–1,700 inhabitants in the sixteenth century. In the more urbanized parts of north Holland, this ratio was 1 to 500, and late sixteenth-century Norwich had ratios of 1 to 200. Clearly, the early modern European health system was not a total disaster.

But we must not forget the inadequate sanitation of old Europe. In seventeenth-century Tuscany, for instance, which enjoyed a relatively good sanitary system, numerous village communities petitioned the Grand Duke to find them a reliable *cerusico* (barber). Of course, in attempting to assess the medical context of witchcraft, numbers matter less than the quality of the medical care offered, and the range of healers, especially in rural areas, could be extremely diverse. University-trained physicians were rare, but there was a fair supply of less well theoretically trained medical practitioners. Beyond the circle of first aid, a net of surgeons, barber-surgeons, apothecaries, and licensed mountebanks came into play to heal fractures, wounds, abscesses, and a range of minor afflictions.

Alongside these authorized health workers, an unofficial (and illegal) health system flourished: a net of male and female healers able to identify ordinary illnesses and to prescribe medicines for them, thereby providing an additional, sometimes substitutive health service. Workers in both systems generally drew on a common pharmacopoeia, based on herbal lore, minerals, and specific prayers. Admittedly, the practice of learned physicians was more interventionist and painful, but the principal difference between medical practitioners of these two systems was gender: official medical practitioners were all male, whereas most illegal healers were female. We have much evidence that people tried all the medical options locally available in their attempts to recover health, but it is difficult to say which system enjoyed a larger clientele and better reputation. To be sure, one reason why the unauthorized health service appealed to so many people in the past must have been the shortage of stable official, village-based medical practitioners, whose fees were probably also higher.

CURATIVE MAGIC

Whenever infants suffered a sudden illness or anyone experienced a prolonged wasting away of the body, such misfortunes could be contextualized in a scenario emphasizing personal enmities; in such cases people had stronger reasons to see themselves as victims of spells and to consult a cunning woman or man with a reputation for discovering witches. Heinrich Kramer wrote in the *Malleus Maleficarum* (The Hammer of Witches, 1486) that "such witches . . . can always be found at interval of one or two German miles and they seem able to cure anyone who has been bewitched by another witch" (Kramer 1996, 159). He was describing cunning women or men, whose very ubiquity greatly deepened the problem of the medical aspect of witchcraft. Kramer's calculations could be generalized throughout early modern Europe, but it would be misleading to follow either his or the later and much stricter Reformation-era theological condemnations of such people as "witches."

Cunning men and women were not "witches" but merely pundits of an illegal health system, and their polyvalent skills were not restricted to curing magical illnesses. They were rooted in their local communities, and people stubbornly sought their services despite all prohibitions by public authorities. Historians have learned about some famous healers who attracted patients from large areas. In sixteenth-century Tyrol, a magician who worked as an innkeeper and coppersmith drew clients from a zone extending from eastern Tyrol

Physicians treat victims of witchcraft, including one suffering from demonic possession who vomits toads and snakes. To the right, a witch invokes a demon while other witches attend a Sabbat. From G. A. Mercklin, Tractatus Physico Medicus, *1715.*

to Bolzano and Merano in south Tyrol. The *stregoni* (male witches) of the Tuscan village of Galatrona, whose clientele ranged from Lorenzo the Magnificent to very ordinary Sienese people, extended their activity over a good part of early seventeenth-century Tuscany and probably passed their skills down. Unfortunately, we have no way of knowing the ratio between diseases reportedly caused by witchcraft and the surely much larger general morbidity anywhere in Europe.

COULD MEDICINE WORK?

If early modern medical prescriptions were effective against minor ailments, it is beyond doubt that its remedies and procedures were "ill-equipped to deal with organic disorders through drugs or surgery. Many men . . . died from incompetent diagnosis or treatment whose lives would have been saved today" (Thomas 1973, 251). Should this overt neglect of sanitation in the past suggest that our early modern ancestors did not "go to the doctor" with the same expectation to recover health as people living today? To decode the medical stories recounted by patients, mostly illiterate, and discover inner psychological meaning behind their "going to the doctor" is not an easy task. What remedies did they request? If medicine was often powerless to heal, did the sick really expect that a recovery was likely to

happen after narrating their misfortunes to doctors? This assumption has been questioned on several grounds: early modern people had a different mental equipment to face misfortune; their threshold of pain was higher, and their attitude about death more fatalist. "They might crave release from their illness, but they also recognized that the length of their days was measured by God" (Brockliss and Jones 1997, 305). No matter whether their disease was of natural or preternatural origin, early modern patients apparently consulted any kind of doctor who could offer them some psychological support.

Many medical practitioners provided effective therapy, whether orthodox or magical, to cure diseases that might have psychosomatic origins. Edward Jorden, discussing the medical value of charms, amulets, and holy water, observed that their success was due "to the confident persuasion which melancholic and passionate people may have in them" (Thomas 1973, 249). The best chance of any medical practitioner lay in a patient's imagination, enhanced by the secret rituals with which cunning men surrounded their practice. Indeed, the knowledge of the placebo effect must have been familiar to both health systems.

THE TWO SYSTEMS SEPARATE

If therapeutics of the period achieved no substantial improvements, did the increase in medical knowledge induce any changes in the relation between medical practitioners and patients? We possess scattered but meaningful evidence about the evolution of the medical aspect of witchcraft, which suggests that it was the quality of medical service being offered that mattered most. It has been recently argued that as more advanced medical knowledge and official healing penetrated local communities, "the more the latitude and rationale for thinking and acting in terms of witchcraft decreased" (Gijswijt-Hofstra 1991, 110). This is certainly true as far as witchcraft accusations were concerned. There are also indications that increases in medical knowledge eventually changed the balance between the two health care systems. Early modern historians have tried to discern where and when, if at all, the clientele of the unofficial health system shrank as the web of authorized medical practitioners grew. Early-eighteenth-century Europe certainly witnessed a progressive masculinization of the discipline, and there are traces of professionalism that widened the gap between learned and popular medicine. It was a slow but steady parting of ways about curative magic that separated ordinary people from educated ones. Recent studies have shown a shift in cultural psychology stimulated by changes in material realities, including the rise of medicine as a commodity market, as a part of the birth of a consumer society. Another process of diffusion can also be discerned as new fashions and lifestyles eventually spread from urban centers. There, educated and affluent patients sought out socially respectable university-trained physicians as a symbol of their distance from ordinary people.

OSCAR DI SIMPLICIO

See also: AGRIPPA VON NETTESHEIM, HEINRICH CORNELIUS; BROSSIER, MARTHE; CARDANO, GIROLAMO; CESALPINO, ANDREA; COUNTERMAGIC; COTTA, JOHN; CUNNING FOLK; GOODWIN CHILDREN; GUNTER, ANNE; HERBAL MEDICINE; JORDEN, EDWARD; LAUDUN NUNS; LOUVIER NUNS; MELANCHOLY; MENTAL ILLNESS; PARACELSUS, THEOPHRASTUS BOMBASTUS VON HOHENHEIM; PIPERNO, PIETRO; SHAMANISM; WEYER, JOHANN.

References and further reading:
Behringer, Wolfgang. 1998. *Shaman of Oberstdorf: Conrad Stoeckhlin and the Phantoms of the Night*. Charlottesville: University Press of Virginia.
Brockliss, Laurence, and Colin Jones. 1997. *The Medical World of Early Modern France*. Oxford: Oxford University Press.
Clark, Stuart. 1997. *Thinking with Demons: The Idea of Witchcraft in Early Modern Europe*. Oxford: Clarendon.
Di Simplicio, Oscar. 2000. *Inquisizione, stregoneria, medicina: Siena e il suo stato (1580–1721)*. Monteriggioni (Siena): Il Leccio.
Gevitz, Norman. 2000. "'The Devil Hath Laughed at the Physicians': Witchcraft and Medical Practice in Seventeenth-Century New England." *Journal of the History of Medicine* 55, January: 5–36.
Gijswijt-Hofstra, Marijke. 1991. "Six Centuries of Witchcraft in the Netherlands: Themes, Outlines, and Interpretations." Pp. 1–36 in *Witchcraft in the Netherlands from the Fourteenth to the Twentieth Century*. Edited by Marijke Gijswijt-Hofstra and Willem Frijhoff. Rotterdam: Universitaire Pers.
Kramer (Institoris), Heinrich, and James Sprenger [sic]. 1996. *Malleus Maleficarum: The Classic Study of Witchcraft (1484 [sic])*. Edited by Montague Summers. London: Bracken.
Larner, Christina. 1984. *Witchcraft and Religion: The Politics of Popular Belief*. Oxford: Blackwell.
Lindemann, Mary. 1999. *Medicine and Society in Early Modern Europe*. Cambridge: Cambridge University Press.
Macdonald, Michael. 1981. *Mystical Bedlam: Madness, Anxiety, and Healing in Seventeenth-Century England*. Cambridge: Cambridge University Press.
———, ed. 1991. *Witchcraft and Hysteria in Elizabethan London: Edward Jorden and the Mary Glover Case*. London and New York: Tavistock/Routledge.
Porter, Roy. 2000. *Quacks: Fakers and Charlatans in English Medicine*. Stroud: Tempus.
Thomas, Keith. 1973. *Religion and the Decline of Magic: Studies in Popular Beliefs in Sixteenth- and Seventeenth-Century England*. Harmondsworth, UK: Penguin.
Wear, Andrew. 2000. *Knowledge and Practice in English Medicine, 1550–1680*. Cambridge: Cambridge University Press.

MELANCHOLY

A disease in early modern Europe that was synonymous with a nonviolent form of madness. The word *melancholy* has an extremely long and famous history that from ancient Greece crosses the Christian old regime and enters the contemporary *Diagnostic and Statistical Manual of Mental Disorders* (4th ed., "Depression with Melancholy"). In the original sense it referred to a disease and a temperament. The Anglican divine Robert Burton summarized this latter implication in 1621 as follows: "Melancholy . . . is either in disposition, or habit. In disposition is that transitory melancholy which goes and comes upon every small occasion of sorrow, need, sickness, trouble, fear, grief, passion or perturbation of the mind. . . . In which equivocal and improper sense we call him melancholy that is dull, sad, sour, lumpish ill-disposed, solitary, and any way moved or displeased. And from these melancholy dispositions no man living is free" (Burton 2001, 143). An equation of the melancholic with the commonplace harmless mad would be a misleading oversimplification, incapable of grasping the assortment of characteristics included within that catchall mental disorder described by the melancholy syndrome.

Literally, melancholy was the "black bile," one of the four humors flowing within the human body. It imitates earth, increases in the autumn, and prevails in adulthood. A balance of humors assures good health, but melancholics were thought to suffer from an excess of black bile. It could also favor the development of exceptional intellectual faculties. The Bordeaux judge and demonologist Pierre de Lancre was certainly not alone to maintain that black blood, from which the melancholy mood comes, is so sour that it may corrupt the brain, and its color, a symbol of darkness, makes Satan take advantage of melancholics. The interpretative power of melancholy was immense in literature, drama, and painting. Being a cultural artifact, it was highly changeable, and over time, it came to be characterized by a contrasting variety of attitudes and behaviors. For instance, the earliest opponents of religious enthusiasm in seventeenth-century England argued that it was caused by melancholy, but during the eighteenth century, orthodox controversialists claimed that such enthusiasm was a sort of madness.

Among other things, the melancholy syndrome became a European-wide mark of gentility. In England, it became a fashionable disease for late Renaissance courtiers after the appearance of Burton's *Anatomy of Melancholy* in 1621: British patients of rank preferred to be melancholic rather than merely sad or troubled. Between 1597 and 1634, two-thirds (forty of sixty-two) of all of the mentally disturbed gentry patients of the Buckinghamshire physician Richard Napier complained of black bile, whereas only one-sixth of his ordinary patients bemoaned melancholy. Since Napier "sought also to articulate his patients' maladies into categories that were at once scientifically useful and consistent with popular usage . . . Ordinary people merited more often the rude and common word mopish" (MacDonald 1981, 164). In Germany, in the course of the sixteenth century, "melancholy declined as a theme for painters and became increasingly common in literature and life toward the end of the century" (Midelfort 1984, 114). As a medical diagnosis, melancholy became prominent through the growing influence of Galen's humoral theories among German academic psychiatrists. This change is particularly evident with the treatment of mad princes. Humoral-based therapy replaced "the common practice around 1500 of simply locking or chaining an offensive prince. . . . By the late sixteenth century, princes were regularly subjected to . . . purging, bleeding, change of diet and were expected to change," whereas poorer Germans, not unlike Napier's ordinary English patients, "went mad with a difference" (Midelfort 1984, 125). In 1575 a Protestant landgrave (count) reported that a woman thought to be possessed was "more likely suffering from weakness in her head and silly melancholy thoughts"; however, this suggestion of melancholy came from a prince, not a villager (Midelfort 1984, 130). After 1600, most of the 200 male and female insane admitted to Juliusspital of Catholic Würzburg were described as "melancholic" (Midelfort 1984, 377).

Melancholy people, surrendering to the power of the Devil, might have been more prone to commit suicide; this phenomenon is well attested in England by the notable increase of suicides reported to the King's Bench between 1500 and 1650. In sixteenth-century France also, suicides were frequently blamed on anxiety and melancholy.

MELANCHOLY AND FEMALE WITCHES

Because, according to the Scriptures, the agency of Satan could not be denied, early modern skeptics argued that the signs of disease caused by morbid humor, above all by black bile, revealed his work. In cases of bewitchment, all kinds of visions and hallucinations were much debated by physicians, theologians, and judges who maintained that senses could be cheated by passions and alteration of physical condition due to humoral unbalances. By the late sixteenth century, the very concept of witchcraft became an intellectual, religious, and political battleground, where melancholy eventually occupied a pivotal position.

The Dutch physician Johann Weyer first used melancholy for the strategic purpose of making witchcraft a sex-specific (and age-specific) crime. "Most often . . . that crafty schemer the Devil thus influences the female sex, which by reason of temperament is inconstant, credulous, wicked, uncontrolled in spirit, and (because of its feelings and affections, which it governs only with difficulty) melancholic; he especially seduces stupid, worn out, unstable old women. . . . Now . . . consider the thoughts, words, sights, and actions of melancholics, and you will understand how in these persons all the senses are often distorted when the melancholic humor seizes control of the brain and alters the mind" (Weyer 1991, 181, 183). Trying to

demolish the reality of the demonic pact and the Sabbat, Weyer wanted to show that the witches' confessions were caused by disturbed minds. "For clinical reasons he linked delusion to gender; but at least this led him to exclude all women from the witchcraft population" (Clark 1997, 199–200). The medicalization of witchcraft was also championed by the Kentish intellectual Reginald Scot in 1584: "melancolie abuseth old women . . . abounding in their head, and occupieng their braine, hath deprived or rather depraved their judgement and all their senses" (Scot 1972, 30). Borrowing melancholy from Weyer, Scot similarly planned to employ it in order to discredit the confessions of old women.

But Weyer's stance was not flawless and could not be adapted to a large number of accused witches. Such was the contention of Thomas Erastus and Jean Bodin: the former (a fellow physician) denied in 1572 that women's brains were dulled by melancholy vapors; the latter refuted Weyer's melancholia thesis shortly afterward within the context of a global demolition job. In *De la démonomanie des sorciers* (On the Demon-Mania of Witches, 1580), Bodin called Weyer an ignorant physician who did not even know that, according to Galen, women's humor is contrary to adult melancholy because it derives from heat and dryness, whereas women are by nature cold and wet.

GENDER

Did more women than men suffer from milder forms of mental illness in early modern Europe? Is a superabundance of melancholic women confirmed by contemporary statistics? Of course, conclusive statistical evidence is hard for historians to get. According to Erik Midelfort (1999), in the Renaissance the medical language of melancholy and madness was not highly gendered; except for hysteria, physicians expected to find roughly the same maladies among men and women. However, the casebooks of Richard Napier registered more women than men among his mentally disturbed patients. We know that, on a European average, between 75 and 85 percent of all those accused of witchcraft were women. Frailty of mind, fickleness of behavior, and notorious lustfulness: such physical deficiencies, when combined with mental delusion engendered by melancholy, made the weaker sex the Devil's favorite targets. From witchcraft trials comes much evidence both of women who felt themselves bewitched and of female witches who confessed they had made a pact with the Devil, lived with him as man and wife, flown to the Sabbat, and so on. In the former cases, historians might still be inclined to consider possessions as evidence of hysterical syndromes. In the latter cases, interpreting such narratives, when they are not clear and simple products of torture, poses a continuous challenge. Some seventeenth-century physicians, magistrates, or theologians diagnosed these women, who were suffering from melancholy, as being mentally deranged. Today's psychologists and psychiatrists have sometimes speculated about the psychic balance of the accused. Certainly, it does not seem that European magistrates, even if they had trouble distinguishing demonic possession from madness, ever confused mad people—female or male—with witches.

Can one learn more by digging deeper in such material? Will clues emerge to better define the psychic identity of womanhood within the melancholic tendencies of women under trials? No doubt, witchcraft material will continue to provide grist to psychoanalytically minded historians.

OSCAR DI SIMPLICIO

See also: BEWITCHMENT; BODIN, JEAN; DISEASE; ERASTUS, THOMAS; EXORCISM; FEMALE WITCHES; FREUD, SIGMUND; GENDER; LANCRE, PIERRE DE; MEDICINE AND MEDICAL THEORY; MENTAL ILLNESS; POSSESSION, DEMONIC; PSYCHOANALYSIS; SCOT, REGINALD; SKEPTICISM; VISIONS; WEYER, JOHANN.

References and further reading:
Burton, Richard. 2001. *The Anatomy of Melancholy (1621)*. Edited by Holbrook Jackson, and with a new Introduction by William H. Gaas. New York: The New York Review of Books.
Clark, Stuart. 1997. *Thinking with Demons: The Idea of Witchcraft in Early Modern Europe*. Oxford: Clarendon.
Macdonald, Michael. 1981. *Mystical Bedlam: Madness, Anxiety, and Healing in Seventeenth-Century England*. Cambridge: Cambridge University Press.
———, ed. 1991. *Witchcraft and Hysteria in Elizabethan London: Edward Jorden and the Mary Glover Case*. London and New York: Tavistock/Routledge.
Midelfort, Erik. 1984. "Sin, Melancholy, Obsession: Insanity and Culture in Sixteenth-Century Germany." Pp. 113–145 in *Understanding Popular Culture: Europe From the Middle Ages to the Nineteenth Century*. Edited by Steven Kaplan. Amsterdam: Mouton.
———. 1999. *A History of Madness in Sixteenth-Century Germany*. Stanford: Stanford University Press.
Porter, Roy. 1987. *Mind-Forg'd Manacles. A History of Madness in England from the Restoration to the Regency*. Harmondsworth: Penguin.
Scot, Reginald. 1972. *The Discovery of Witchcraft*. Edited by Montague Summers. New York: Dover.
Themkin, Owsei. 1971. *The Falling Sickness: A History of Epilepsy from the Greeks to the beginning of Modern Neurology*. 2nd ed. Baltimore and London: John Hopkins University Press.
Wear, Andrew. 2000. *Knowledge and Practice in English Medicine, 1550–1680*. Cambridge: Cambridge University Press.
Weyer, Johannes. 1991. *Witches, Devils, and Doctors in the Renaissance: De praestigiis daemonum*. Edited by George Mora. Tempe, AZ: Medieval and Renaissance Texts and Studies.

MENGHI, GIROLAMO (1529–1609)

Menghi was the most prominent exponent of exorcist theory and practice in Counter-Reformation Italy.

Called "Il Viadana" after his birthplace in the diocese of Cremona, Menghi entered the Observant Franciscan order around 1550. His career as a practicing exorcist and writer was spent in Bologna and Lombardy, bringing him the rewards of office: Pope Clement VIII appointed Menghi head of the Franciscan Province of Bologna from 1598 to 1602. He died in 1609 in his native town of Viadana; the inscription on his tombstone relates the joy of the infernal hosts at the death of their most rigorous assailant and describes him as the greatest exorcist of his century.

Certainly he was the most prolific. Not long after his entrance into the Franciscan order, Menghi composed the first of many exorcist manuals, the vernacular *Esorcismo mirabile da disfare ogni sorte de maleficii per un devoto religioso composto* (Wonderful Exorcism to Undo Any Kind of Maleficium, Composed by a Devout Religious), published in Venice in 1555. The novel aspect of this work was its announced focus on using exorcism as a weapon, not only against demonic possession but also against the more common negative effects of bewitchment or *maleficium* (harmful magic). Although he never took a university degree, Menghi did edit the unpublished Latin exorcist writings of the Dominican inquisitor Sylvestro Prierias (1456–1523), an anti-Lutheran polemicist and master of the sacred palace under Pope Leo X. Menghi's future work would draw heavily on Prierias and on other experts in demonology and witchcraft, especially Michael Psellus, Johannes Nider, and the *Malleus Maleficarum* (The Hammer of Witches, 1486).

The most successful of Menghi's works was the Italian *Compendio dell'arte essorcista* (Compendium of the Exorcist's Art) first published at Bologna in 1576. Literally a compendium, assembling opinions, stories, and examples from earlier authorities, it went through twelve editions by 1605 (fourteen, including two Latin editions in 1580 and 1601). His 1577 Latin *Flagellum daemonum* (Whip of Demons) appeared in twenty-one editions by 1608, with another eight between 1626 and 1727. These numerous editions and the many surviving copies testify to the popularity and wide demand for Menghi's writings. Inventories of books owned by parish priests throughout Italy invariably included at least one of Menghi's works, which served as basic manuals for the pastoral work of bringing relief to people suffering from the effects of *maleficium* or possession. He presented exorcism as just one of the "ecclesiastical medicines" offered by the Church; this category, which included blessings, sacramentals, and other clerical weapons against harm of negative supernatural origin, was central to the functionalist appeal of his work.

His later works, *Fustis Daemonum* (Club of Demons) of 1584 and *Fuga Daemonum* (Expelling Demons) of 1596, drew heavily from his own work in the field and appealed frequently to his own experience. The repeated statement, "Vidi con occhi miei" ("I saw with my own eyes"), asserted the authority of his position as an expert and an eyewitness to vouch for the reality of the events he describes. There is a curiously empirical side to this type of argument from experience that, no matter how fantastic the alleged occurrence, was probably more compelling to his audience than his sophisticated scholastic arguments. Menghi described public dispossessions, some in front of learned audiences, including skeptical "enemies of adjuration" who were won over by the performance they witnessed. Throughout it was the expert, accomplished practitioner, the *esorcista perito,* who spoke, and his firsthand anecdotes were clearly designed to remind the reader of this fact. Clerics testifying in sixteenth- and seventeenth-century Roman Inquisition trials frequently cited his works as an authoritative, learned source supporting their diagnoses of *maleficium* or possession.

Menghi's career coincided with the post-Tridentine effort to reform the Church in "head and members," which put special emphasis on the clergy. His works were aimed at correcting abuses in the practice of exorcism by providing clear guidelines as well as a theoretical justification for the efficacy and legitimacy of this office. The dedication of the *Flagellum Daemonum* of 1576 to the reforming cardinal of Bologna, Gabriele Paleotti, was indicative of the official and institutional context within which Menghi worked. The tactic of publishing both Latin and Italian versions indicated a reformer's zeal to reach the widest possible audience. The revival of exorcism and the promotion of ecclesiastical remedies in late sixteenth-century Italy, a movement led by Menghi, provided an approved orthodox means of addressing popular fears of *maleficium* and thus contributed to the low level of witch hunting in Italy.

MARY R. O'NEIL

See also: BEWITCHMENT; EXORCISM; ITALY; *MALEFICIUM; MALLEUS MALEFICARUM;* NIDER, JOHANNES; POSSESSION, DEMONIC; PRIERIAS, SYLVESTRO.

References and further reading:
Gentilcore, David. 1992. *From Bishop to Witch: The System of the Sacred in Early Modern Terra d'Otranto.* Manchester: Manchester University Press.
Maggi, Armando. 2001. *Satan's Rhetoric: A Study of Renaissance Demonology.* Chicago and London: University of Chicago Press.
O'Neil, Mary R. 1984. "*Sacerdote ovvero strione:* Ecclesiastical and Superstitious Remedies in Sixteenth-Century Italy." Pp. 53–83 in *Understanding Popular Culture: Europe from the Middle Ages to the Nineteenth Century.* Edited by Steven Kaplan. New York: Mouton.
Petrocchi, Massimo. 1957. *Esorcismi e magia nell'Italia del Cinquecento e del Seicento.* Naples: Libreria Scientifica.
Romeo, Giovanni. 1990. *Inquisitori, esorcisti e streghe nell'Italia della Controriforma.* Florence: Sansoni.

MENNONITES

With their highly spiritualized view of the relation between God and human beings, Mennonites allowed the Devil no real influence in the natural world and attached very little importance to witchcraft.

In 1536 Menno Simons (Simonsz, 1496–1561) reorganized an Anabaptist community in deep disarray, one year after the disastrous failure to found a chiliastic New Jerusalem in the German town of Munster. Menno was a former Catholic priest who became an Anabaptist but rejected the millenarianism of the Munsterians and taught that the use of force was forbidden to Christians who wanted to lead a godly life. The only way to find God was through a spiritual search leading to a rebirth in Jesus. In the Mennonite perception, the Devil was not an anthropomorphic spirit but an almost abstract principle of evil. Within the parameters of this cosmology, it was impossible to conclude a pact with a demon, let alone have sexual intercourse with him.

By the end of the sixteenth century, most Mennonites lived in the Dutch Republic, where they were a tolerated religious minority. By the following century, the Mennonites had split over a variety of dogmatic disagreements, eventually forming three main groups, all with geographical names: the Frisians, the Flemish, and the Waterlanders (named from the region directly north of Amsterdam). The Frisians were the most orthodox group, the second was somewhat less stringent, and the Waterlanders were relatively the most flexible. It should be noted that these three groups were themselves subdivided into a multitude of microconfessions. It was their usual practice to ban anyone who refused to accept the interpretation of the religious dogmas of his or her particular congregation. The implications were quite serious: other members refused to speak with someone who was excommunicated. Despite this harsh ostracism, Mennonites never demanded the application of physical force against members who had gone astray; a person could be banned but should not be persecuted. In this sense, tolerance remained a leading principle.

Their immaterial perception of the Devil and their readiness to allow other people to choose their own road in matters of religion remained essential elements of Mennonite faith. To them, witchcraft was not really an issue; consequently, few of them ever took the effort to put his or her views on this matter on paper. Pieter Twisck (1565–1636), minister of a Frisian congregation in the Dutch town of Hoorn, did take witchcraft seriously, however. In 1620 he published a chronicle about "the downfall of the tyrants" in which he related numerous stories he had found in pamphlets and other sources from abroad, combined with some incidents he had witnessed himself. In 1639 Jan Jansz Deutel, a Mennonite printer, also from Hoorn, wrote a short treatise against witchcraft that was published only in 1670 by his son. In Deutel's eyes, all stories about witchcraft were "fables, jokes, twaddle, lies and conceit." God would never allow anybody, neither the Devil nor a human being, to alter nature. A heartfelt trust in God was incompatible with a belief in witchcraft.

Abraham Palingh, a textile trader from Hoorn and member of its Waterlander congregation, expressed a similar view in a book he published in 1659. Antonius van Dale (1638–1708), a medical doctor from Haarlem, became the fourth Mennonite to write about these matters. An exponent of the early Enlightenment that blossomed in the Dutch Republic with the philosophy of Baruch Spinoza, van Dale's *De oraculis* (On Oracles) of 1683 tried to combat superstitious beliefs in oracles, demonic possession, and witchcraft. In the 1690s van Dale was involved—though indirectly—in the uproar that followed on the publication of Balthasar Bekker's *De Betoverde Weereld* (The World Bewitched, 1691–1693). *De oraculis* was translated into French (1687), English (1689), and German (1730). Voltaire used it as the basis for the entry on "Oracles" in his *Dictionnaire philosophique.*

HANS DE WAARDT

See also: ANABAPTISTS; BEKKER, BALTHASAR; DEVIL; ENLIGHTENMENT; MILLENARIANISM; NETHERLANDS, NORTHERN; ORACLES; PALINGH, ABRAHAM; VOLTAIRE.

References and further reading:

Dale, Antonius van. 1683. *De oraculis ethnicorum dissertationes duae.* Amsterdam: Boom.

Deutel, J. J. 1670. *Een kort tractaetje tegen de toovery.* Hoorn: Jan Jansz Deutel.

Evers, Meindert. 1981. "Die 'Orakel' von Antonius van Dale (1638–1708): Eine Streitschrift." *Lias* 8: 225–267.

Gijswijt-Hofstra, Marijke. 1989. "Doperse geluiden over magie en toverij: Twisck, Deutel, Palingh en Van Dale." Pp. 69–83 in *Oecumenismen.* Ed. by A. Lambo. Hilversum: Algemene Doopsgezinde Sociëteit.

Waite, Gary K. 2003. *Heresy, Magic and Witchcraft in Early Modern Europe.* Basingstoke, UK: Palgrave.

MENTAL ILLNESS

Many early modern Europeans included the Devil among the possible causes of madness, thus illustrating that the symptoms of mental illness are culturally relative and viewed as violations of conventional social norms and that mental illness is notoriously difficult to define. In 1810, a London physician registered the causes of insanity among admissions to Bethlem Hospital ("Bedlam"): *A Table of the Causes of Insanity of about one third of the patients admitted into Bedlam:* Misfortunes, Troubles, Disappointments, Grief (206); Religion and Methodism (90); Love (74); Jealousy (9); Pride (8); Study (15); Fright (51); Drink and Intoxication (58); Fevers (110); Childbed (79); Obstruction (10); Family and Heredity (115); Contusions and Fractures of the Skull (12); Venereal (14); Small pox (7); Ulcers and Scabs dried up (5)" (Porter 1987, 33–34). Earlier diagnosticians would have given an even longer list and included bewitchment.

Identifying the insane is easier than defining them. Which actions, thoughts, or emotions were considered abnormal? Not surprisingly, early modern people recognized the insane by the way they behaved: strange motions of the body, threatening or harming people, or going naked were commonplace indicators of madness. Lunatics were considered ill, but might be beaten if unmanageable or locked up if considered dangerous. The deranged were believed to be deprived of their souls and therefore no better than animals. In the late sixteenth century, London's Bethlem Hospital held about twenty babbling manacled madmen who attracted thousands of tourists each year. Figures on the insane are hard to get. Between 1597 and 1634, some 60,000 patients flocked to the "consulting room" of Richard Napier, physician and parson of a rural parish in Buckinghamshire; about 5 percent of them, 1,286 females and 748 males, appear to have been mentally disturbed (Macdonald 1981).

But were such unfortunates curable? Some hospitals were available for them, where they received mostly religious consolation. Therefore, no doubt for the poor, it seems difficult to prove Richard Burton wrong: "For the diseases of the mind, we take no note of them" (Burton 2001, 69). Was this omission regrettable? In recent decades, the "storm over psychiatry" has projected his influence onto historians. Was the eighteenth century really a disaster for the insane (MacDonald 1981)? Should the two centuries before Michel Foucault's "great confinement" of 1656 be viewed as a world relatively safe for lunatics, when the treatment of madness depended mostly on family care?

Our best information about the actual treatment of poor people's madness in early modern asylums overturns now-conventional Foucaultian wisdom about first venerating madmen as holy fools and then confining them en masse. Two converted rural monasteries in Protestant Hesse with extremely careful records from 1550 to the Thirty Years' War show a clear increase in the number of mentally ill patients admitted after 1580, rising from 13 percent to 28 percent of all residents. This post-Reformation transformation of medieval piety and charity "provided comfort for the helpless in ways so attractive that people clamored to be admitted" (Midelfort 1999, 358–365). Interestingly, they admitted about four times as many insane men (141) as insane women (33)—almost the exact reverse of the percentage of male and female witches— although the male/female disproportion was much less (8 to 5) in the Juliusspital of Catholic Würzburg over the same period (Midelfort 1999, 376–377).

Not unlike contemporary neuropsychiatry, early modern medicine identified madness as an organic disease. In fact, according to Galenic medicine, afflictions of the mind were closely connected with bodily "distempers" and resulted from an alteration of proper humoral balance. Minor psychic disturbances were considered as forms of melancholy and treated with purging and bloodletting until the late seventeenth century, when research on the nervous system pioneered by Thomas Willis signaled the decline of humoralism.

MENTAL ILLNESS AND WITCHCRAFT
Although none of the poor madmen admitted to Hessian asylums was considered demonically possessed and although Tudor and Stuart Essex showed only "a very slight connection between mental derangement and witchcraft beliefs" (Macfarlane 1999, 183), possession by the Devil was, theoretically, a distinct phenomenon. It was admitted that a melancholic temperament might make the Devil's work easier. But because a witch could have sent an evil spirit into a victim, the notions of possession and bewitchment were amalgamated. And unless fraud was involved, diabolical intervention offered a plausible explanation for the symptoms of possession: the afflicted person would fall into convulsions and contortions, displaying abnormal strength, vomiting pins, and speaking languages previously unknown. If demonic possession might explain any kind of insanity, tracing the history of madness becomes even harder.

Yet it seems clear that the heyday of witchcraft persecutions (ca. 1580–ca. 1660) deserves the label of a golden age of demoniacs. Close scrutiny of witchcraft and possession cases occasionally made physicians think that some demoniacs (and even witches) were mentally ill. In women, acute neuroses were attributed to a "wandering womb": under pressure of internal vapors, "the womb moves up or sideways to crush the organs around it . . . physical and mental illness, fits of unconsciousness or hysteria, were likely to follow" (Wear 2000, 142). Around 1600, skeptical physicians like Michel Marescot in France or Edward Jorden in England blamed the symptoms of demonic possession on hysteria rather than witchcraft. Johann Weyer, in order to defend witches through an insanity defense, had previously "seized upon the exclusively legal language of *furor* and infused it with the medical discourse of melancholy" (Midelfort 1999, 226).

OSCAR DI SIMPLICIO

See also: BEWITCHMENT; EXORCISM; FREUD, SIGMUND; JORDEN, EDWARD; MEDICINE AND MEDICAL THEORY; MELANCHOLY; POSSESSION, DEMONIC; PSYCHOANALYSIS; WEYER, JOHANN.

References and further reading:
Burton, Richard. 2001. *The Anatomy of Melancholy (1621).* Edited by Holbrook Jackson, with a new Introduction by William H. Gaas. New York: New York Review of Books.
Macdonald, Michael. 1981. *Mystical Bedlam: Madness, Anxiety, and Healing in Seventeenth-Century England.* Cambridge: Cambridge University Press.
Macfarlane, Alan. 1999. *Witchcraft in Tudor and Stuart England. A Regional and Comparative Study.* 2nd ed. London: Routledge.
Midelfort, H. C. Erik. 1999. *A History of Madness in Sixteenth-Century Germany.* Stanford: Stanford University Press.
Porter, Roy. 1987. *Mind-Forg'd Manacles. A History of Madness in England from the Restoration to the Regency.* Harmondsworth, UK: Penguin.
Temkin, Oswei. 1971. *The Falling Sickness. A History of Epilepsy from the Greeks to the beginning of Modern Neurology.* 2nd ed. Baltimore and London: John Hopkins University Press.
Wear, Andrew. 2000. *Knowledge and Practice in English Medicine, 1550–1680.* Cambridge: Cambridge University Press.

MERGENTHEIM, ECCLESIASTICAL TERRITORY OF
Within forty years, from 1590 to 1631, approximately 500 persons were executed for witchcraft in the region of Mergentheim, a small ecclesiastical possession in southwestern Germany owned by the Teutonic Order. Before the Great Plague ("Pest") of 1626, the two major cities, Mergentheim and Markolsheim, had about 3,200 inhabitants. Half of them died in the Great Plague.

The Teutonic Order was an ecclesiastical order of knights whose extensive lands along the Baltic were secularized by Prussia during the Reformation in 1525; its surviving Catholic members continued to govern a few territories within the Holy Roman Empire, covering approximately 77 square miles. The Teutonic Order moved its seat from Prussia to Mergentheim, a little town located between Stuttgart and Würzburg of around 2,000 inhabitants (the order still exists today, with its seat in Vienna).

Four major witch hunts took place in the area of Mergentheim. They all followed the same course, typical for most parts of Germany. A witch hunt started with a single complaint of *maleficium* (harmful magic), often against someone whose family had been involved in a previous case of witchcraft. This person was arrested, tortured, and forced to name other persons she (or he) had met during the witches' Sabbat. These persons were then arrested and questioned about further participants. A chain of denunciations developed and continued to expand until the witch hunt finally collapsed, for various reasons that have never been examined accurately.

During Mergentheim's first campaign, in 1590, a total of 68 people were arrested. We know that 9 of them were executed and 7 were released, but we do not know what happened to the other 52 people. In the second episode, during the years 1601–1602, 52 people were arrested and 43 were executed; the fate of the others is not known. In the third campaign, which took place in 1617–1618, no fewer than 213 persons were arrested. All but 13 of them were executed, and 3 of them died during their imprisonment. In the fourth and final witch hunt, from 1628 to 1631, another 136 people were arrested: 122 of them were executed, 10 were dismissed, and the other 4 died in prison. Overall, of the 584 people who were arrested, 493 (or 84 percent) were female (Wohlschlegel 1990).

So far, only the last wave of persecution between 1628 and 1631 has been examined systematically (Midelfort 1972, 143–155; Wohlschlegel 1990), using records at Ludwigsburg and Stuttgart. Details about the first three waves of witch hunts are available in the so-called *Hexenkartothek,* drawn up by Nazi SS. Despite some double naming, its data about Mergentheim seem generally reliable:

arrested: 493 females + 91 males = 584
executed: 333 + 54 = 387
dismissed: 21 + 6 = 27
died in prison: 8 + 0 = 8
unknown: 83 + 10 = 93

The archives of the Teutonic Order in Vienna, which contain a great number of files, have not been evaluated systematically for evidence about Mergentheim's witch hunts.

Some details have been established: more than half of these women were married. Socially, these women came from all walks of life except the nobility; many of them came from mayoral and craftsmen families, and families of tavern owners made up a disproportionately large part. Their ages ranged from twenty to sixty. The ninety-one masculine defendants, whose ages ranged from eleven to seventy-five, came exclusively from the two larger towns, Mergentheim and Markelsheim; in the smaller villages, only women were arrested. A closer examination of the kinship networks among arrested people showed that "witch families" existed, in which up to eight people were arrested. It is interesting that a large share of the people who had previously profited from these witchcraft trials were themselves accused and arrested as the persecution continued.

Although Mergentheim's witch hunting occurred at times typical for these regions (the 1628–1631 cycle in particular corresponds to the greatest wave in southwestern Germany), neither the first major European persecution wave of the 1560s nor the last a century later affected Mergentheim. The causes for Germany's witch hunts, as discussed in recent literature, such as famines resulting from agrarian crises associated with the Little Ice Age, seem relevant in the case of Mergentheim, although we cannot prove the immediate cause of any of these four outbreaks of witch hunting.

Witchcraft trials were carried out in this area using the extremely formal procedure specified by imperial law. Judges were required to ask over 100 prescribed questions, and the answers were recorded. The judiciary of the Teutonic Order (whose lands were surrounded by Protestant territories) considered itself unable to carry out such procedures without assistance. In the last two witch-hunting campaigns, Mergentheim's government

consulted the largest nearby ecclesiastical ruler, the prince-bishop of Bamberg, who sent a judge with experience in witch procedures. The Bamberg judge worked remarkably quickly. Normally, only ten days elapsed between a suspect's arrest and her execution; it took longer only if the accused were pregnant or ill. As was customary at the time, the convicted witch or her heirs paid the costs of the procedure. However, although the financial records are unusually rich for the 1628–1631 wave, we have no evidence that the Teutonic Order profited in any way from this affair, despite the claim still made by people in Mergentheim that *Hexengeld* (witch money) financed the tower of their town church.

KARIN WOHLSCHLEGEL

See also: BAMBERG, PRINCE-BISHOPRIC OF; ECCLESIASTICAL TERRITORIES (HOLY ROMAN EMPIRE); FAMILY; FEMALE WITCHES; GENDER; GERMANY, SOUTHWESTERN; LITTLE ICE AGE; NAZI INTEREST IN WITCH PERSECUTION; SOCIAL AND ECONOMIC STATUS OF WITCHES.

References and further reading:
Midelfort, H. C. Erik. 1972. *Witch Hunting in Southwestern Germany, 1562–1684: The Social and Intellectual Foundations.* Stanford: Stanford University Press.
Wohlschlegel, Karin. 1990. "Die letzten Hexen von Mergentheim: Auswertung der Verhörprotokolle aus den Jahren 1628 bis 1631." *Württembergisch Franken* 80: 41–115.

MERLIN

Merlin is the legendary magician who advised King Arthur. Merlin's origins lay in two Welsh figures, Myrddin, the author of bardic poetry, and Ambrosius, a wonder child and prophet from a medieval Welsh-Latin source. Geoffrey of Monmouth's *Historia Regum Britanniae* (History of the Kings of Britain) combined them to create Merlin, who is a central figure in the Arthurian legend and an exemplar of the all-powerful magician. Merlin explains the riddle of the dragons underneath a falling tower, transports Stonehenge to Salisbury Plain, and engineers Arthur's conception by transforming his father's (Uther Pendragon's) appearance.

Geoffrey of Monmouth used Merlin again as a wild man and prophet in *Vita Merlini* (Life of Merlin, ca. 1150), where he interacted with more localizsed Welsh characters rather than Arthurian heroes. Another Welsh-Latin source linked *Merlinus Sylvestris* (Merlin of the Woods) to *awenyddion* (the inspired) who prophesied while in a state of trance. These Welsh references formed the basis for the modern transformation of Merlin into a shaman figure. However, Geoffrey's Merlin was already an established narrative type combining elements of the wonder child/prophet who triumphed against impossible odds, the magician-engineer who created marvels, and the wise protector.

An independent tradition of Merlin romances began about 1200. Although indebted to Geoffrey, they added magical transformations, prophetic dreams, and material from the Antichrist legend. A devil raped a nun in order to create a diabolical child. The baby Merlin was baptized and saved but was often referred to as "son of Satan." Merlin possessed magic power, but he was a long way from the omnipotent figure of modern treatments, and a woman magician who took on the role of Arthur's protector eventually imprisoned him.

Undoubtedly, some episodes were rooted in folk tradition, for example, the wonder child without a father, the building that could not stand until some secret was revealed, the mysterious helper-figure, the motif of the triple death, tears and laughter provoked by ironic occurrences, and shape shifting. Their very familiarity must have added to the impact of the Merlin figure and given an air of authority to pseudohistorical works such as Geoffrey's. Merlin became important again during the nineteenth-century Arthurian revival. Here, he was unequivocally a powerful magician, and this image permeated subsequent reworkings in which the Arthurian legend functioned as an image of a lost world. Increasingly Merlin, and his spiritual descendents such as J. R. R. Tolkien's magician Gandalf, were situated in a fantastic and romantic Dark Age Britain, which was viewed as a context for magic or for a struggle between ancient and modern ways of life. Often the Welsh sources and the romances were treated as a coherent tradition in which the remnants of a pre-Christian figure could be discovered. This ignored Merlin's links with other figures and variations within the narrative material but remained an important feature in modern New Age reconstructions.

JULIETTE WOOD

See also: ANTICHRIST, THE; DIVINATION; FOLKLORE; SHAMANISM.

References and further reading:

Clarke, Basil, ed. 1973. *Vita Merlini*. Cardiff: University of Wales Press.
Dean, Christopher. 1992. *A Study of Merlin in English Literature from the Middle Ages to the Present*. Lewiston: Edwin Mellon.
Geoffrey of Monmouth. 1987. *The History of the Kings of Britain*. Translated by Lewis Thorpe. Middlesex: Penguin.
Jarman, A. O. H. 1991. "The Merlin Legend and the Welsh Tradition of Prophecy." Pp. 117–146 in *The Arthur of the Welsh*. Edited by Rachel Bromwich, A. O. H. Jarman and Brynley F. Roberts. Cardiff: University of Wales Press.

METAMORPHOSIS

Assuming another shape or transforming a victim is called metamorphosis. Metamorphosis was usually an innate capacity, but it could also be acquired, either from the Devil or from another witch.

European witches mainly took the shapes of hares, cats, wolves, dogs, mice, bees, toads, flies, and certain types of birds, but they could also appear as inanimate objects (wisps of straw, cartwheels) or natural phenomena (lights, mists, small whirlwinds). A rough gender distinction is discernible in folk traditions,

though less so in trials: hares, cats, and the nightmare tended to be female witches, but werewolves were mostly male. According to one edition of the fifteenth-century *Evangiles des quenouilles* (Gospel of the Distaves), a werewolf's son would inherit the same destiny, but his daughter would be a nightmare (Jeay 1985, 143–144).

Shape changing was recorded in folk traditions in parts of Europe from antiquity to the modern period, and it was mentioned in some of the earliest recorded confessions of witches: Matteuccia of Todi admitted going to the Sabbat in the shape of a fly in 1428 (Ginzburg 1990, 70–73, 299). Early modern courts often paid little attention to allegations of transformation, sometimes due to skepticism (or to mainstream Christian theology, which denied that metamorphosis was possible), but mainly because they were impossible to prove unless defendants confessed, which many did not (Briggs 2000, 90–91). Though witches' metamorphoses have often been attributed to pathological delusions, drug-induced hallucinations, mistakes of perception, or irrational credulity, shared traditions about shape changing appear to have arisen from different cultural understandings of personhood and of human relations with the world of spirits (Napier 1986, 4–29).

Recent scholars have looked more closely at the cognitive systems, both intellectual and folkloric, in which metamorphosis was intelligible as a rational proposition. As Stuart Clark has demonstrated, the place and powers assigned to demons in the natural world enabled intellectuals to make sense of reported transformations by classifying them as illusions; though demons had no power to transform miraculously a human being, it was within their natural capacity to surround bodies with illusory forms and interfere with people's senses and imaginations, so that transformations could be true in appearance but not in reality (Clark 1997, 157–167). Carlo Ginzburg situated shape-changing traditions within an archaic, shamanistic belief system relating to mediators who fell into trances and dreamed that their souls went out in animal shapes to the otherworld to secure benefits for their community (Ginzburg 1990). Eva Pócs emphasized the ambivalence of such ecstatic mediators in central, eastern, and southeastern Europe: they were capable of harm as well as good and were part of a dualistic system in which individuals born with cauls had spirit doubles in animal shapes and were opposed to supernatural figures with similar attributes (Pócs 1999). These traditions are well delineated in eastern, central, and southeastern Europe, as well as parts of the Baltic.

Western European shape-changing traditions show enough similarities to indicate common ancestry at some stage, but they are less often connected with clearly

Metamorphosis (shape changing) is common in European folklore. Witches assumed the body of animals, fish, and insects, but also of inanimate objects. Here witches have become on the left, various animals, and, on the right, a wolf. From Ulrich Molitor, De Laniis et phitonicis mulieribus *(Concerning Witches and Fortunetellers, 1489). (Stapleton Collection/Corbis)*

defined, potentially beneficial roles like those of the *benandanti* (do-gooders) or the Livonian werewolves. Scandinavian folklorists' research indicated that shape changing there was part of a wider scale of extracorporeal manifestations of aspects of the self in altered form; they were not confined to mediators or witches but could happen with variable degrees of intensity and visibility to almost anyone and did not require trances. A person's *hug* (thought, feeling, will) could wander away from the body in certain circumstances (such as intense longing) and be perceptible elsewhere, either invisibly or, if very strong, apparent in a shape (*ham*). One of the projections of the *hug* was the *fylgje* that accompanied a person as a sort of guardian spirit, which could take animal shape and was visible to people with second sight (Kvideland and Sehmsdorf 1991, 41–81). Anthropological studies of shape changing in contemporary societies related it to different cultural constructions of personhood, particularly where social role was a vital component, and states

of personal crisis could precipitate a corresponding instability of shape that may be both visible to others and experienced as a bodily transformation by the shape changers themselves (Jackson 1989, 102–118).

Shape changing was deeply rooted in narrative traditions. Personal experience stories were the most persuasive genre, but because transformations were always more told of than witnessed or experienced, the genre with the widest influence was the legend, a story told as a true report of specific people's experiences, which might be reported as news yet followed a traditional narrative pattern. Some of these memorably simple but highly adaptable story schemas endured over very long periods, in literature as well as oral tradition, and were sometimes reported as personal experiences by witches or their victims. St. Augustine's fifth-century account of Italian witches transforming travelers into pack horses by feeding them bewitched cheese (*City of God,* XVIII.xviii) belongs to the same family as Homer's story of Circe transforming Ulysses's companions (*Odyssey*, X), Apuleius's *Golden Ass,* and a later medieval "true" story reported in the *Malleus Maleficarum* (The Hammer of Witches, 2.2.4) about a witch in Cyprus transforming a sailor into a horse by giving him eggs to eat (Roberts 1996, 192–194). A related motif, of witches using a magic bridle to transform their victims into horses and riding them, was common in European legends from the Middle Ages and surfaced in the accusations of witnesses against witches in the early modern period (Thompson 1955–1958, Motif G241.2.1.1). Anne Armstrong testified in Northumberland in 1673 that she had been transformed into a horse in spirit by a witch who put a bridle on her head and rode her to the witches' meeting, where they appeared in the shapes of hares, cats, mice, and bees; a Cambridgeshire woman had made a similar accusation in 1659, but the judge refused to believe her (Ewen 1933, 358–361, 457). Witches' victims in eighteenth-century Hungary also told their own versions of this story, sometimes even with the same minor detail about the horse being tied to a post outside the meeting, which Anne Armstrong had also mentioned (Pócs 1999, 79–80, 93). A regular motif in legends about shape changers was the "analog injury" (or "repercussion"): a wound inflicted on the animal shape produced a corresponding mark on the human body (Thompson 1955–1958, Motif G252). It occasionally featured in trial records: one witness against Gerard Horiel of Jonvelle in 1610–1611 said she thumped a cat with a stick when it attacked her in bed one night, and afterward Horiel had a bruise on his nose for a month (Oates 1993, 282). However, it was also a detail that often crept into news reports of encounters with shape changers, as specific details were forgotten in transmission and replaced by the typical elements of familiar narratives (Oates 1989, 314–315).

Such stories were all the more persuasive when reported by credible informants; it was this that prompted St. Augustine to formulate a theory of illusory transformations provoked by demons (with God's permission), which accepted that witnesses reported truthfully, accounted for any effects observed, and at the same time denied that either the human soul or body could be really transformed except by God (*City of God,* 18.18). The *Canon Episcopi* (ca. 906) emphatically condemned the belief in shape changing, and that became the standard position in penitential texts. Twelfth- and thirteenth-century interpretations of transformations, including those of Gerald of Wales, Gervase of Tilbury, and Thomas Aquinas, built on St. Augustine's foundations and enlarged on the ways demons could make them seem to happen, for example, by borrowing

animals' bodies (Bynum 2001, 93–109). Commentators did not suggest that demons caused these deceptions in response to culpable human intentions until after the establishment of the idea of the witches' pact with the Devil. On the contrary, William of Auvergne in the mid-thirteenth century sought to demonstrate that suspected werewolves were unjustly blamed for eating people and were themselves innocent victims of the deceptions of demons (*De universo* [On the Universe], 2.3.13). It was not until the late fifteenth century that writers made any serious effort to account for the apparent transformations of diabolical witches and to explain away the *Canon Episcopi* (e.g., *Malleus maleficarum,* 1.10; 2.1.8).

With the proliferation of trials in the late sixteenth century came fresh reports of transformations, leading to more publications interpreting them. Intellectuals expressed varying degrees of belief, ranging from Jean Bodin's conviction that physical transformations were possible to Reginald Scot's skeptical dismissal of all the reports as untrue; however, few writers shared such extreme views (Clark 1997, 195–213). Some followed medical tradition, as Johann Weyer did, in attributing confessed transformations to melancholic delusions or the effects of drugs, though demons might sometimes be involved. Others, including the magistrates Nicolas Rémy, Pierre de Lancre, and Henry Boguet, refined the theory of demonic illusions to explain how witnesses saw the shapes that witches confessed they took (which medical theory could not easily account for). Either the demon went about in animal form committing harm and altered the witches' imaginations so that they dreamed they did those things in other shapes; or the witches were there in person and the demon altered observers' perceptions so they saw the witch as something other; or else he surrounded the witch with a cunningly fitted animal skin or an airy likeness of another species that would deceive observers' eyes.

Multiple interpretations of transformations were current in early modern Europe, and there was no single, unified folk view any more than there was unity among the learned. Aspects of demonology became common knowledge at all social levels: witches confessed that demons transformed them or gave them their magic wolf skins. Where some understood it as a roving spirit double in animal shape, others took it to be a form of magical disguise of the body or even a physical transmogrification, as a boy in Franche-Comté did in 1643, when he testified that after hitting a wolf with a stick he saw it immediately turn back into the shape of a beggar, Claude Chastelan, who was executed after confessing (Oates 1989, 352–354).

Legends about shape changing continued to be told until the twentieth century in some areas. Scholarly interest in them did not disappear altogether with the gradual exclusion of demons from the material world during and after the seventeenth century; the occult revival of the nineteenth century and the emergence of the disciplines of psychology, ethnography, anthropology, and folklore all stimulated new interpretations. But the emphasis was no longer on explaining how transformation could appear to happen, visibly and with material consequences, which, in the case of werewolves, were illusions that could bite.

CAROLINE F. OATES

See also: ANIMALISTIC AND MAGICAL THINKING; ANIMALS; APULEIUS OF MADAURA; AUGUSTINE, ST.; *BENANDANTI;* BODIN, JEAN; BOGUET, HENRI; *CANON EPISCOPI;* CAUL; CIRCE; CORPOREALITY, ANGELIC AND DEMONIC; DEMONOLOGY; DEMONS; FOLKLORE; HUNGARY AND SOUTHEASTERN EUROPE, MAGIC; HUNGARY AND SOUTHEASTERN EUROPE, WITCHCRAFT; LANCRE, PIERRE DE; LYCANTHROPY; MALE WITCHES; NIGHTMARES; RÉMY, NICOLAS; TODI, WITCH OF; WEYER, JOHANN.

References and further reading:
Briggs, Robin. 2000. *Witches and Neighbours: The Social and Cultural Context of European Witchcraft.* 2nd ed. Oxford: Blackwell.
Bynum, Caroline Walker. 2001. *Metamorphosis and Identity.* New York: Zone.
Clark, Stuart. 1997. *Thinking with Demons: The Idea of Witchcraft in Early Modern Europe.* Oxford: Clarendon.
Ewen. Cecil L'Estrange. 1933. *Witchcraft and Demonianism: A Concise Account Derived from Sworn Depositions and Confessions Obtained in the Courts of England and Wales.* London: Heath Cranton.
Ginzburg, Carlo. 1990. *Ecstasies: Deciphering the Witches' Sabbath.* Translated by Raymond Rosenthal; edited by Gregory Elliott. London: Hutchinson Radius.
Jackson, Michael. 1989. *Paths Toward a Clearing: Radical Empiricism and Ethnographic Enquiry.* Bloomington and Indianapolis: Indiana University Press.
Jeay, Madeleine, ed. 1985. *Les Evangiles des quenouilles: Edition critique.* Montréal, Québec: Presses de l'Université de Montréal.
Kvideland, Reimund, and Henning K. Sehmsdorf, eds. 1991. *Scandinavian Folk Belief and Legend.* Oslo: Norwegian University Press.
Napier. A. David. 1986. *Masks, Transformation, and Paradox.* Berkeley: University of California Press.
Oates, Caroline F. 1989. "Metamorphosis and Lycanthropy in Franche-Comté, 1521–1643." I: 304–363 in *Fragments for a History of the Human Body.* Edited by Michel Feher. 3 vols. New York: Zone.
———. 1993. "Trials of Werewolves in the Franche-Comté in the Early Modern Period." PhD diss., University of London, Warburg Institute.
Pócs, Eva. 1999. *Between the Living and the Dead: A Perspective on Witches and Seers in the Early Modern Age.* Translated by Szilvia Rédey and Michael Webb. Budapest: Central European University Press.
Roberts, Gareth. 1996. "The Descendants of Circe." Pp. 183–206 in *Witchcraft in Early Modern Europe: Studies in Culture and Belief.* Edited by Jonathan Barry, Marianne Hester, and Gareth Roberts. Cambridge: Cambridge University Press.
Thompson, Stith. 1955–1958. *Motif-Index of Folk-Literature . . . Revised and Enlarged Edition.* 6 vols. Bloomington and London: Indiana University Press.

MEYFART (MEYFAHRT), JOHANN MATTHÄUS (1590–1642)

Author of the *Christliche Erinnerung an gewaltige Regenten* (A Christian Reminder to Powerful Princes, 1635), Meyfart opposed witch hunting by underscoring the cruelties of witchcraft trials. Among all opponents of witch hunting, Meyfart was by far the most emotional, and his outrage was not just personal attitude but was inspired by specific cases in his environment. An orthodox Lutheran, he fervently accused the princes for their lack of compassion and their officials for inhumane cruelty. Although not the first author to attack witch hunters in the German vernacular under his full name (Trunz 1987, 212) (Johann Weyer and Anton Prätorius did this earlier), Meyfart's literary skills enabled him to invent the most powerful metaphors for this purpose. Whereas Weyer, Adam Tanner, and Friedrich Spee became entangled in juridical and theological discussions and appealed primarily to the reader's reason, Meyfart portrayed the hardships of the trials in full detail, constantly appealing to the reader's compassion. His descriptions of contemporary prisons were unprecedented, as was his ability to make the reader identify with those poor victims suffering all the fear and anguish of imminent torture. Meyfart not only taught rhetoric: he was a master of language, a poet, at times displaying the fervor of Jewish prophets.

Born in Jena, the son of a Lutheran pastor, Meyfart spent his youth in Thuringian villages where his father served as a pastor, attended the princely gymnasium at Gotha, and studied at Jena. He graduated in 1611 and turned to theology. In 1614, Meyfart matriculated at Wittenberg but returned to his father's house at Jena after contracting an infectious disease. Meyfart claimed later that his *melancholia hypochondrica*, which plagued him for the rest of his life, also began then. Meyfart became *adjunctus* at Jena's philosophical faculty before being appointed professor in 1616 at the Gymnasium Casimirianum of Coburg, the upper school of Prince Johann Casimir of Saxe-Coburg (ruled 1596–1633), where he taught for sixteen years. In order to become its director in 1623, Meyfart had to acquire a doctoral degree from Jena.

Now married, with children, Meyfart was a successful theologian and a public figure. However, he became entangled in a permanent feud with General Superintendent Caspar Finck (1578–1631). Relations worsened after 1626, as tensions and morbidity rose when Franconia experienced crop failure. Court preacher Nikolaus Hugo felt personally insulted by Meyfart's attacks against the clergy and particularly its conduct in witchcraft trials. In 1632, deeply embroiled in these quarrels, Meyfart received a call from the University of Erfurt, belonging to the prince-elector of Mainz, but recently conquered by Gustav II Adolf of Sweden. Meyfart became dean and eventually chancellor of the

Swedish university at Erfurt, where he spent the rest of his life, despite being stripped of his office during a Catholic interlude.

Although staunchly Lutheran, the tiny principality of Saxe-Coburg suffered a surprising number of witchcraft trials, about 178 during Johann Casimir's reign. Not just its clergy, but even more its lawyers and officials, the prince included, were supporters of witch hunting. In February 1629, Johann Casimir issued *Gerichts-Ordnung, die Hexerey betreffend* (Regulations for Witchcraft Trials) resembling those in neighboring prince-bishoprics. Meyfart wrote *Christliche Erinnerung* in 1631, when these terrible persecutions had already ceased in the Catholic bishoprics but continued uninterruptedly in Saxe-Coburg and peaked that very year. The driving force behind the persecutions was the court preacher Hugo, who publicly attacked the *Schöppenstuhl* (court of lay judges) for its complacency. By 1631 the lawyers of the *Schöppenstuhl* had started referring to Meyfart's opinion.

However, his *Christliche Erinnerung* was not published until 1635, when Meyfart had reached the safety of Erfurt and witch hunting was over: therefore, it was no longer necessary. A generation later, when witchcraft trials resumed in Thuringia, it was forgotten; another generation later, when Christian Thomasius commissioned a reprint in 1703, witchcraft trials had already ebbed in Protestant northern Germany. It is hardly surprising that Meyfart saw the Jesuit Martín Del Rio as the main defender of gruesome witchcraft persecutions. More surprisingly, he hardly ever referred to Protestant authorities and instead quoted other Jesuits (Tanner and Spee) as defenders of humanity. Because Meyfart clearly aimed his book at a Protestant audience, it seems likely that he tried to become the Protestant Spee. But since his publication came too late, his emotional tone was—and to a modern reader, still is—irritatingly overwrought.

WOLFGANG BEHRINGER

See also: DEL RIO, MARTÍN; GERMANY, NORTHEASTERN; PRÄTORIUS, ANTON; SKEPTICISM; SPEE, FRIEDRICH; TANNER, ADAM; THOMASIUS, CHRISTIAN; THURINGIA; WEYER, JOHANN.

References and further reading:
Clark, Stuart. 1997. *Thinking with Demons: The Idea of Witchcraft in Early Modern Europe,* Oxford: Clarendon.
Füssel, Roland. 2003. *Die Hexenverfolgungen im Thüringer Raum.* Hamburg: DoBu Verlag.
Hallier, Christian. 1982. *Johann Matthäus Meyfahrt: Ein Schriftsteller, Pädagoge und Theologe des 17 Jahrhunderts.* Neumünster: Wachholtz.
Kretz, Hans-Jürgen. 1972. *Der Schöppenstuhl zu Coburg.* Diss. jur. Würzburg.
Lea, Henry Charles. 1939. *Materials Toward a History of Witchcraft.* Edited by Arthur C. Howland. 3 vols. Philadelphia: Thomas Yoseloff.
Meyfart, Johann Matthäus. 1626. *Tuba novissima: Das ist von den vier letzten Dingen des Menschen.* Coburg.
———. 1632. *Das hellische Sodoma.* 2 vols. Nuremberg.
———. 1634. *Teutsche Rhetorica oder Redekunst.* Coburg.
———. 1635. *Christliche Erinnerung an Gewaltige Regenten und Gewissenhafte Praedicanten/wie das abschewliche Laster der Hexerey mit Ernst auszurotten/aber in Verfolgung desselbigen auff Cantzeln und in gerichtsheusern sehr bescheidenlich zu handeln sey/Vorlengstens aus hochdringenden Ursachen gestellet.* Schleusingen.
Trunz, Erich. 1987. *Johann Matthäus Meyfahrt: Theologe und Schriftsteller in der Zeit des Driessigjährigen Krieges.* Munich: Verlag C. H. Beck.
Wölfel, Dieter. 1983. "Die Krankheit von Johann Matthäus Meyfahrt." *Zeitschrift für Bayerische Kirchengeschichte,* pp. 53–59.

MICHELET, JULES (1798–1874)

Michelet was author of *La sorcière* (The Witch, 1862), an account of witchcraft in European history that stands outside of any known historical canon and yet addresses itself directly to the historian's task.

Michelet grew up in a poor Parisian family that struggled unsuccessfully to maintain a print shop founded during the French Revolution but blighted by Napoleonic censorship. A brilliant example of people newly empowered by the meritocratic standards of postrevolutionary France, he rose rapidly within the educational system, becoming a professor at the École Normale, chief of the historical section at the Royal (now National) Archives, and professor at the Collège de France by the time he was forty. His charismatic style of teaching won him the admiration of students, in whom he inculcated the values of the Revolution of 1789 in the hopes that they would form the generation capable of completing its work (Wilson 1972: I, chaps. 1–5). But his enthusiasm for the Revolution of 1848, and his refusal to take an oath of loyalty to Louis Napoleon's imperial government gave ammunition to the many historians who disliked his poetic historical imagination, poetic style, and radically liberal values. Driven from both teaching and archival positions, with no access to documents, Michelet composed a series of brilliant meditations in mythical naturalism—*The People, Woman, The Bird, The Insect, The Mountain, The Sea,* and so on.

In 1862, Michelet returned to a historical topic and composed one of his most famous and challenging books, *La sorcière,* which combined his extraordinary narrative abilities and his mythic voice with a wide knowledge of the documentation of earlier periods in French history. Book 1 traces the (imagined) experience of a serf's wife, at the bottom rung of feudal society, and follows her on her discovery of the magical forces of nature, forces unknown to the nobles and priests who dominated the social world. Her contact with this other world moved from the companionship of a helpful if mischievous imp to the great Satan, whose penetrating embrace transformed her vision of the world. All this was set out against the background of a viciously intrusive Church, inflamed by the projections of its own moral corruption. This exceptional historical novel, in which Michelet never once questioned the existence of magic (indeed, he described it as real), defied all historical canons of narration and left many conventional historians at once fascinated and appalled.

Book 2, however, consists of three early modern cases of witch persecutions, well documented and well reconstructed. (One served as inspiration for both Aldous Huxley's 1952 book *The Devils of Loudun* and Ken Russell's 1971 movie *The Devils*.) By making an abrupt transition from a kind of imaginative mythical anthropology to the kind of detailed and masterful historical reconstruction that even the most positivist historian could admire, he wed his mythical vision to the historical documentation through his understanding of the moral madness that underlay the discourse of witchcraft persecution. The book's two parts were tied together mainly through Michelet's relentless anticlerical bias; *La sorcière* was, above all, a meditation on the corruption of the Church that could produce such inquisitorial minds and institutions and on the (profoundly Christian) understanding that suffering and humiliation could bring empowerment. For him, witchcraft and rebellion represented the two major forms of popular resistance: "From there [disappointed expectations that God would intervene in history and rid them of the brutal aristocracy that embittered their lives] the Black Mass and the *Jacquerie* [peasant rebellion]" (Michelet, 1959, 101).

In a sense, the book represented a mirror image of the *Malleus Maleficarum* (The Hammer of Witches, 1486). Indeed, Michelet had a chapter on that demonology. It validated both his mythic heroine's rejection of her dominant culture and the counterreality she then discovered. At a time when conventional historians unanimously shunned this topic, Michelet permitted himself a bold and judgmental discourse that anticipated Nietzsche in assaulting the moral imagination of the Church:

As long as God punished himself, *brought his own hand down,* or struck with *the sword of an angel* (according to the noble antique formula), there was less horror; this hand was severe, that of a judge, and yet of a father. The angel, in striking remained pure and clear, like his sword. It was nothing like this, when the execution was done by disgusting demons. They did not imitate at all the angel that burned Sodom, but who first left. They stayed, and their hell is a horrible Sodom where the spirits, more soiled than the sinners handed over to them, draw odious joys from these tortures they inflicted. That is the teaching one finds on the *naïve* sculptures spread out over the doors of churches. They taught the horrible lesson of voluptuous pain.

Under the pretext of these torments, the devils pour out on their victims the most revolting caprices. Immoral notion (and profoundly guilty!) of a supposed justice that favors the worst, gives dominion to its perversity in giving it a toy, and corrupts the demon himself! (Michelet 1959, 46) (emphasis in the original)

In his journals at the time of *La Sorcière*'s publication, Michelet wrote that he had announced the death of Christianity, a necessary precondition for making the best of what it had to offer possible.

The book met immediate resistance; after losing a legal case, Michelet had to eliminate two passages (in one he referred to the doctrine of the Trinity as boring and saints' lives as insipid) and find a new publisher. And yet, *La Sorcière* was Michelet's most popular book. As Roland Barthes pointed out (Barthes 1959), it was uncannily modern. What Michelet's positivist critics considered an insult—his *poésie*—reflected a level of empathy and understanding that finds far more appreciative audiences among modern historians, who are more familiar with the anthropologist's craft, more willing to link deeds to the *mentalités* of an age, and equally, but safely, anticlerical.

RICHARD LANDES

See also: HISTORIOGRAPHY; MALLEUS MALEFICARUM

References and further reading:
Barthes, Roland. 1959. "Introduction." In *La Sorcière*. Paris: Club Français du Livre.
Haac, Oscar A. 1982. *Jules Michelet*. Boston: Twayne.
Michelet, Jules. 1959. *La Sorcière*. Paris: Club Français du Livre. English edition, 1965. *Satanism and Witchcraft: A Study in Medieval Superstition*. Translated by A. R. Allinson. New York: Citadel.
Mitzman, Arthur. 1990. *Michelet, Historian: Rebirth and Romanticism in Nineteenth-Century France*. New Haven: Yale University Press.
Wilson, Edmund. 1972. *To the Finland Station: A Study in the Writing and Acting of History*. 2nd ed. New York: Farrar, Straus, and Giroux.

MIDELFORT, H. C. ERIK (1942–)

An American-born historian, Midelfort's publications have molded the research of the current generation of scholars of witchcraft. Born into a family of physicians of Norwegian origin, he became interested in the problem of witchcraft while an undergraduate at Yale University (BA, 1964): the more he studied it, the less he understood. Bearing this experience in mind, as a graduate student choosing a dissertation subject, he picked witchcraft, then still considered a weird subject. However, there was the example of Wallace Notestein, whose dissertation on English witchcraft (1908) had not damaged his career as a major historian of Tudor-Stuart England, and who was still accessible at Yale University in the mid-1960s. A year at Tübingen (1967–1968) proved to be most productive: there Midelfort confronted the puzzling microcosm of the German southwest, one of the most fragmented regions of the former Holy Roman Empire. Receiving little help from his academic adviser, Midelfort immersed himself in the literature and the sources and defined the topics and the geographical and temporal boundaries of his dissertation himself, completing his PhD at Yale in 1970.

The results of his research proved immediately influential. In 1968, he published the first international survey of witchcraft literature since the days of George Lincoln Burr. Its title, "Recent Witch Hunting Research, or Where Do We Go from Here?" sounds as unusual as its approach then indeed was. His comparative regional study of southwestern Germany (Midelfort 1972) has proved a classic. It not only surveyed all the major and minor witch hunts of this witch-ridden area but also analyzed the region's lively contemporary debates. It put texts into social context, thus breathing life into an important area of early modern intellectual history. Keeping modern interpretations of social theory in the background, Midelfort conjured up a lively and more adequate picture of early modern debates. He was the first to acknowledge in English the overwhelming importance of Johann Weyer, who had endeavored to invent a comprehensive defense of accused "witches" prior to Reginald Scot and later opponents of witch hunting and witch beliefs by attacking the sixteenth-century Protestant orthodoxies head-on. Weyer's claim that those who confessed to being witches—the most persuasive argument for the existence of witchcraft—were simply insane triggered Midelfort's long-standing interest in demonic possession and the history of madness in early modern Europe, ultimately leading to what is perhaps his most ambitious work (Midelfort 1999).

The application of psychological theory proved even more difficult than the application of social theory. By analyzing contemporary descriptions of these diseases, Midelfort abandoned the idea of using anachronistic diagnoses and tried to understand how contemporary physicians, lawyers, and divines interpreted these symptoms. Again, his method of contextualizing contemporary texts, such as an intriguing microstudy on Germany's "mad princes" (Midelfort 1994), proved to be highly successful and were certainly suited to demolishing light-handed anachronistic interpretations, especially those by Michel Foucault. Another recent study on the late-eighteenth-century exorcist Johann Joseph Gassner, who used witchcraft to explain diseases, shattered a number of facile assumptions about the Enlightenment.

In 1970 Midelfort joined the History Department at the University of Virginia, becoming professor in 1987 and obtaining an endowed chair in 1996. Throughout this period, Midelfort mediated masterfully between the academic cultures of the United States and Germany, producing English translations of major German scholars (e.g., Bernd Moeller, Peter Blickle, and Wolfgang Behringer) and, of course, Johann Weyer (Midelfort and Kohl 1998), while alerting U.S. students to the attractions of central European history. In Germany, Midelfort is a member of an international workshop on the history of witchcraft (AKIH) and coeditor of the publication series *Hexenforschung* (Witchcraft Research, 1995ff.) and of the *Dictionary of Early Modern Europe*. During his numerous stays in Germany, at conferences, as a visiting scholar, and as a research fellow, his accessibility, wit, and thought-provoking contributions have stimulated scores of younger German scholars. In the United States, he won many fellowships, and each of his major publications received awards, including two Roland Bainton prizes (1995 and 1999) and the Phi Beta Kappa Ralph Waldo Emerson Award for history (1999).

WOLFGANG BEHRINGER

See also: GERMANY, SOUTHWESTERN; HISTORIOGRAPHY.
References and further reading:
Midelfort, H. C. Erik 1968. "Recent Witch Hunting Research, or Where Do We Go from Here?" *The Papers of the Bibliographical Society of America* 62: 373–420.
———. 1972. *Witch-Hunting in Southwestern Germany, 1582–1684: The Social and Intellectual Foundations.* Stanford: Stanford University Press.
———. 1981. "Madness and the Problems of Psychological History in the Sixteenth Century." *Sixteenth Century Journal* 12: 5–12.
———. 1994. *Mad Princes of Renaissance Germany.* Charlottesville: University Press of Virginia.
———. 1999. *A History of Madness in Sixteenth-Century Germany.* Stanford: Stanford University Press.
———. 2005. *Exorcism and Enlightenment: Johann Joseph Gassner and the Demons of Enlightenment Germany.* New Haven, CT: Yale University Press.
Midelfort, H. C. Erik, and Benjamin Kohl, eds. 1998. *On Witchcraft: An Abridged Translation of Johann Weyer's "De Praestigiis Daemonum."* Asheville, NC: Pegasus Press.

MIDSUMMER EVE

According to folklore, the evening and night before summer solstice are filled with all kinds of magic. Good and evil forces were known to be more active on this evening than at other times of the year. Herbs, dew, and water from wells should be collected on this evening because of their healing qualities. But Midsummer Eve is also regarded as one of the year's most important dates for black magic and witch merrymaking. Witches were thought to be particularly dangerous on Midsummer Eve, when they traveled through the air to their gatherings; that is why bonfires were lit to protect animals, crops, and humans against potential harm by keeping witches, trolls, and dragons at bay.

ST. JOHN'S DAY

Because Midsummer Eve was associated with many heathen practices, the Christian Church tried to ban many of the evening's traditional festivities while simultaneously giving the summer festival a Christian meaning. During the time of St. Augustine, around 400 C.E., the feast day of St. John the Baptist was moved close to the summer solstice in order to supplant pre-Christian celebrations.

Most traditional celebrations surrounding Midsummer Eve fell on June 23 (according to Christians, one day before St. John's birth), two days later than the actual summer solstice. Given the close proximity of these events, midsummer celebrations by both the people and the Church covered the entire period of June 21–24. The two traditions gradually merged with each other. Thus the magical significance of St. John the Baptist's Eve could result in a variety of rites—most commonly setting bonfires, rolling wheels of fire, and gathering magical herbs.

FOLKLORE AND MIDSUMMER

Throughout Europe, ancient folk narratives offered profuse descriptions of midsummer themes, in which all nature was filled with maximum-strength magical force on the longest day of the year. In late-fifteenth-century southern France, Canon Martin of Arles described how Basques lit Midsummer Eve bonfires, attempting to protect themselves and their crops from the destructive forces of witchcraft. Similar midsummer bonfires as antisorcery rituals have profoundly deep roots in several parts of Europe.

Especially in Slavic and Orthodox Europe, stories abounded of naked witches, oiled in witch lotions, who climbed up chimneys and flew through the air to witch Sabbats on the eve preceding St. John's Day. For such reasons, Midsummer Eve celebrations frequently occurred on Bald Mountain in the vicinity of Kiev. Witches were also said to have poured water, boiled with embers from Kupala's midsummer bonfire, over themselves or to have used an ointment made from gentian to improve their flying skills (Ryan 1999).

Other herbs, too, should be gathered on Midsummer Eve because of their professed magical powers. Such traditions can be discovered in both recipes and criminal cases from the Middle Ages. Herbs collected on the eve of St. John the Baptist were especially useful for their magical powers over love and human destiny. (For example, magical plants played a significant role in Shakespeare's *A Midsummer Night's Dream,* written at the end of the sixteenth century.) Herbs picked on this evening could be used for a number of different purposes: they could cure sterility and impotence, but they could also *cause* impotence. In a 1539 Swiss witchcraft trial near Geneva, the accused witch had fed her neighbor's cow a special kind of herb on Midsummer Eve, after which the cow suddenly died (Monter 1976, 56).

Numerous countries preserve mythological versions of the witches' Sabbats. An instance of this practice exists in the story of Jane Maxie, a young servant girl from a small village in Devon, in southwestern England, who was rumored to be a witch. Under interrogation in 1638, Jane described witch gatherings every Midsummer Eve: "those that would be witches must meet the divell upon a hill and then the divell would licke them, and that the place was black." On the following Midsummer Eve, "the divell would meet them againe, and licke them as before" (Sharpe 1996, 77).

In some countries correlations were made between Midsummer Eve and the burning of witches by placing a witchlike doll on top of the traditional bonfire, or perhaps a witch's broom and hat, to be destroyed as symbols of evil. This tradition, however, is more recent, dating from the end of the nineteenth century, long after the last witches had been burned at the stake in the Western world. Such straw dolls could also symbolize winter.

In the far north of Europe, where midsummer brings the midnight sun, celebrations of the sun played a special role after the winter's long darkness. Confessions exist from Scandinavian witchcraft trials in which the witch's activities were directly related to Midsummer Eve celebrations. For instance, Danish court records and folktales described witches from Jutland who traveled as far as the church of Troms County, in Arctic Norway, to celebrate Midsummer Eve, riding northward on cats. Upon arrival at the church, they played card games, danced, ate, and drank. "To ride to Troms" was a common expression in Denmark and especially in Jutland. At Troms Church, the witches gathered to take part in obscene amusements with the Devil and to renew their satanic pacts (Kristensen 1901).

IN COMPANY WITH THE DEVIL AT THE GREAT MIDSUMMER EVE FEAST OF 1662

The persecution of accused witches and sorcerers in eastern Finnmark during the winter of 1662–1663 was the worst of its kind anywhere in Norway (Lilienskiold 1998). More than thirty women and some young girls under twelve years old were brought before the court in the course of a few months. Eventually, eighteen women were burned at the stake, and three others were tortured to death before sentencing. Mari Olsdatter (who had not yet turned twelve, according to reports) was among the prisoners, largely because her mother had been burned as a witch several years earlier. Mari began by telling of her visit to hell, along with many other local witches. Satan himself presided from a pond of sulfur, showing her the general "character and grandeur" of the place, according to court records. After the women had been shown around Satan's abode, a party was held at a local mountaintop called Domen on Midsummer Eve 1662. This time as well, Satan was the center of festivities, playing music for a circle dance on his red violin under the light of the flaming midnight sun on the top of Domen. Mari told in great detail about those who held hands while dancing. Following the dance, Satan served beer to the women from a silver bowl. This Midsummer Eve night at Domen came to an end when Satan accompanied each of the women homeward. Mari's confession and disclosure of who had taken part in the Midsummer Eve celebration with Satan resulted in the deaths of several women.

RUNE HAGEN;

TRANSLATED BY MARK LEDINGHAM

See also: CHARMS; COUNTERMAGIC; CUNNING FOLK; DEVIL; FLIGHT OF WITCHES; HELL; HERBAL MEDICINE; LAPLAND; LOVE MAGIC; MAGIC, POPULAR; NORWAY; POPULAR BELIEFS IN WITCHES; SABBAT; SHAKESPEARE.

References and further reading:

Henningsen, Gustav. 2000. "Om opfindelsen af ordet 'aquelarre.'" Pp. 244–254 in *Rätten: En festskrift till Bengt Ankarloo.* Edited by Lars M. Andersson, Anna Jansdotter, Bodil E. B. Persson, and Charlotte Tornbjer. Lund: Nordic Academic Press.

Hutton, Ronald. 2001. *The Stations of the Sun: A History of the Ritual Year in Britain.* Oxford: Oxford University Press.

Johansen, Jens Chr. V. 1991. *Da Djævelen var ude—trolddom i det 17.århundredes Danmark.* Odense: Odense Universitetsforlag.

Kristensen, Evald Tang. 1901. *Danske Sagn.* Vol. 6, part 2. Copenhagen: Gyldendal.

Lilienskiold, Hans H. 1998. *Trolldom og ugudelighet i 1600-tallets Finnmark.* Edited by Rune Hagen and Per Einar Sparboe. Tromsø: Ravnetrykk.

Monter, E. William. 1976. *Witchcraft in France and Switzerland: The Borderlands During the Reformation.* Ithaca, NY, and London: Cornell University Press.

Ryan, W. F. 1999. *The Bathhouse at Midnight: An Historical Survey of Magic and Divination in Russia.* University Park: Pennsylvania State University Press.

Sharpe, James. 1996. *Instruments of Darkness: Witchcraft in England, 1550–1750.* London: Hamish Hamilton.

MIDWIVES

The link between midwives and witchcraft is one of many issues involved in the witch hunts in which a clear disjuncture separates learned theory from actual practice. As men, and generally childless men, demonologists had little experience with midwives, so they speculated that these women's knowledge must come from the Devil, whom they repaid with the bodies of children. Most men and women—even those who accused others of witchcraft—had too much respect for the midwives on whose skills they depended to believe they were in league with Satan and knew very well that these skills came from earthly training and years of practice.

The *Malleus Maleficarum* (The Hammer of Witches) of 1486, Europe's most influential treatise on demonology and witch hunting, stated without doubt that witchcraft was particularly rampant among midwives: "No one does more harm to the Catholic Faith than midwives. For when they do not kill children, then, as if for some other purpose they take them out of the room and, raising them up in the air, offer them to devils" (Kramer and Sprenger [sic] 2001, 189). The *Malleus* recounted several stories of midwives who murdered infants, offering their unbaptized bodies for magical purposes, in particular the concocting of ointment that allowed witches to fly. The *Malleus* took some of its stories of midwife-witches from the earlier *Formicarius* (The Anthill) by Johannes Nider, and its examples were repeated verbatim in some later demonological works, including those by Jean Bodin, Martín Del Rio, and Henri Boguet.

Why did demonologists link midwives and witches? One reason was that learned authors used traditional myths of Jewish ritual murder, in which Jews supposedly used the bodies or body parts of Christian children in various ceremonies to create a stereotype of the activities of witches. Witches, like Jews, sought the blood or fat of innocent children, and what better source of this than midwives? Midwives also had access to other body parts associated with births that were judged to have magical powers: the placenta, the umbilical cord, and the caul (a piece of amniotic membrane that sometimes covers or is attached to an infant's head at birth, widely believed to have magical properties and to mark the infant as distinctive). Thus, more than other women, they were used to handling materials that had special power. This connection and their vital role in bringing children into the world explained to demonologists why Satan would be especially interested in recruiting them, for no other type of woman could be more helpful to his cause.

Some scholars of witchcraft have used the writings of demonologists about the evil of midwives as evidence that the witch hunts were primarily an attempt by male religious, political, and medical authorities to eradicate female healers, midwives among them. Midwives, they argued, were often "wise women" who had a wide knowledge of the healing and contraceptive properties of herbs and other materials, which they handed down orally as part of women's traditional culture. The witch hunts enabled male physicians to gain control of the birth process and male authorities to suppress women who were independent and skilled in birth control and abortion.

There are several problems with this line of argument. One is that the chronology is wrong. Though a few male midwives made inroads among the upper classes in England and France during the period of the witch hunts, most physicians were completely uninterested in obstetrical issues, and female midwives continued to handle almost all births in Europe and North America. City governments, rulers, and in some places religious authorities did concern themselves with midwives, but generally they attempted to recruit more women into the profession and train them adequately, not push women out. Women were barred from university medical training and formal apprenticeship as barber-surgeons, but this prohibition had begun long before the period of the witch hunts, and women's exclusion from medical schools continued into the late nineteenth or even twentieth centuries.

A second problem with viewing the witch hunts as a campaign against midwives is that doing so misrepresents the social and economic position of early modern midwives. Though midwives were generally middle-aged and older women—the population group most prevalent among those accused of witchcraft in many parts of Europe—the similarities stop there. Particularly in urban areas, midwives were well respected, quite well trained, and relatively well paid. In many villages, women elected or otherwise chose the midwives, a clear indication of esteem for their skills. They were generally the wives or widows of artisans or shopkeepers, not marginal and dependent members of society. In many parts of Europe they were literate, for midwives' manuals were published in many European languages beginning in the early sixteenth century—some written by midwives themselves—and city or religious authorities often expected midwives to be able to read the ordinances and oaths of midwifery that they issued. The era of the witch hunts saw a sharp increase in infanticide cases and increasing penalties for abortion, but the accused was almost always the mother, not a midwife. Midwives did appear in cases alleging infanticide or abortion through witchcraft, but as expert witnesses, called in to assess whether a woman had been pregnant or whether supernatural causes might have led to the death of an infant. They also appeared as witnesses in other types of court cases, such as rape, premarital fornication, and infanticide by natural means, and judges took their opinions very seriously.

A third, and the most significant problem with this line of argument is that it mistakes demonological theory for the actual course of the witch hunts. The learned authors of demonological works were apparently the only early modern people who believed that midwives were especially likely to be witches, for their number among the accused was strikingly small. In all the English witchcraft trials, only a few of the original sources identified the accused as a midwife, and in the unusually well-documented Scottish cases, which number in the thousands, less than 1 percent of the accused were midwives. In New England, only one midwife was suspected of witchcraft, and none was tried for it; Anne Hutchinson, the religious leader expelled from Massachusetts Bay Colony for teaching beliefs contrary to those of the Puritan leadership—and for doing so as a woman—was sometimes labeled a witch or midwife or both in later literature, but there is no evidence that she was either.

Even in the central European heartland of witch hunting, where demonological theory had the strongest impact, the statistical presence of midwives among those accused of witchcraft is negligible. There were a few spectacular cases, such as that of Walpurga Hausmännin, burned at the stake in 1587, who was accused of killing and eating unbaptized infants and causing stillbirths and the deaths of mothers in childbed. Her case was sensational enough to make it into one of the newsletters published by the Fugger family business; however, this merely indicates its unusual nature, not its typicality. A few of the midwives' ordinances that began to be issued in the fifteenth century—first in German cities and then elsewhere in Europe—did forbid midwives to use (in the words of a 1567 English ordinance) "any sorcery or incantation in the time of the travail of the woman," but many made no mention of magic at all, though they went on for many pages about training, procedures, and fees. Actual court cases against midwives followed the same pattern as the ordinances, for, like physicians and barber-surgeons, midwives were occasionally accused of negligence or malpractice, but these cases almost never involved charges of witchcraft.

MERRY WIESNER-HANKS

See also: CAUL; CUNNING FOLK; DEMONOLOGY; FOLKLORE; FUGGER FAMILY; GENDER; HAUSMÄNNIN, WALPURGA; INFANTICIDE; *MALLEUS MALEFICARUM*; MEDICINE AND MEDICAL THEORY; RITUAL MURDER.

References and further reading:
Ehrenreich, Barbara, and Deirdre English. 1973. *Witches, Midwives, and Nurses: A History of Women Healers.* New York: Feminist Press.
Forbes, Thomas Rogers. 1966. *The Midwife and the Witch.* New Haven: Yale University Press.
Harley, David. 1990. "Historians as Demonologists: The Myth of the Midwife-witch." *Social History of Medicine* 3: 1–26.
Horsley, Ritta Jo, and Richard A. Horsley. 1986. "On the Trail of the 'Witches': Wise Women, Midwives, and the European Witch Hunts." Pp. 1–28 in *Women in Germany Yearbook 3: Feminist Studies and German Culture.* Edited by Mariane Burkhard and Edith Waldstein. Washington, DC: University of America Press.
"Judgement on the Witch Walpurga Hausmännin." 1969. Pp. 75–81 in *European Witchcraft.* Edited by E. William Monter. New York: John Wiley and Sons.
Kramer, Heinrich, and Jacob Sprenger [sic]. 2001. *Malleus Maleficarum (1486).* Pp. 181–229 in *Witchcraft in Europe: 400–1700.* 2nd ed. Edited by Alan Charles Kors and Edward Peters. Revised by Edward Peters. Philadelphia: University of Pennsylvania Press.
Marland, Hilary, ed. 1993. *The Art of Midwifery: Early Modern Midwives in Europe.* London: Routledge.

MILAN

The city of Milan and its surroundings offer a good example of the way witch beliefs grew in northern Italy between the late Middle Ages and the end of the seventeenth century, with inquisitorial activities directed against magical practices increasing during the second half of the sixteenth century. Statistics are difficult to gather because the Holy Roman Emperor, Joseph II, ordered the destruction of all the Inquisition's records in 1788. Extant cases mention the executions of sixteen women and two men. This relatively modest number is due not only to the lack of information but also to the fact that a greater number of executions took place in towns and valleys around Milan.

Milan's first case of major interest involved a man called Giovanni Grassi of Valenza (Piedmont). He was arrested around 1375, brought to Avignon, and prosecuted by a Franciscan inquisitor who accused him of having dealings with the Devil. Grassi saved his life by confessing his crime. But ten years later he was arrested again in Milan and charged with similar accusations by a Dominican inquisitor in Sant'Eustorgio, where the Inquisition had its headquarters. Convicted as a second offender, or *relapsus*, Grassi was condemned to the stake and handed over to the city's *Podestà* (highest official), who duly burned him. In the very same years, Milan's Dominicans also judged two women, Pierina de Bugatis and Sibillia Zanni, for crimes linked to magical beliefs and deeds and condemned them to light penances. In 1390, like Grassi, they too were rearrested on the same charges. During their new interrogations, they confessed to participating in a *ludus* (game) paying homage to the *domina ludi* (Lady of the Game), called *Madona Oriente* (Lady of the East) or "Diana" or "Erodiade," borrowing these names from the now well-known *Canon Episcopi* (ca. 906). Their spells seemed different from those mentioned in later witchcraft trials: there were no confessions of killing babies, no blasphemy or descriptions of Sabbats; at one moment, Pierina mentioned a spirit called "Lucifello," who appeared and spoke to her in the shape of a man. Milan's new inquisitor seemed inclined to treat the two women's beliefs as real, beyond their unfortunate status as relapsed heretics. Both were condemned to death and handed over to the *Podestà*.

In the early fifteenth century, unlike the bloody repression of witches in the nearby diocese of Como, Milan offered little evidence of inquisitorial activity for either diabolism or *maleficia* (harmful magic). Around the mid-fifteenth century, we find many trials against men and women accused of heresy for beliefs and acts connected to magic and Devil-worshipping, but they took place in nearby valleys, not in Milan itself. These trials around 1450 were led by the inquisitor Luca di Lecco, whose sentences were not particularly severe, although several women were accused of having been seduced by the Devil to worship a *domina ludi,* now declared a demon, and of performing many heretical acts, such as stealing the Eucharist for their ceremonies. By the late fifteenth century, we find considerable confusion about the way to proceed in such cases, proved by the fact that both prosecutors and prosecuted addressed protests to the Duke of Milan, Francesco Sforza. The inquisitor most active at this time, Paolo dei Filiberti, was often supported by Francesco Sforza, who mentioned in his letters that babies were slaughtered and even eaten at the Devil's orders.

Around 1460, Girolamo Visconti, a scholarly friar at Sant'Eustorgio, using the tradition of trials accumulated since the late fourteenth century in his convent, wrote two treatises about *lamiae* and *striae* (witches), in which he affirmed the reality of beliefs and practices attributed to witches. Like other Renaissance Italians, Visconti decorated his account of this new phenomenon with words taken from classical antiquity.

After 1484, when the papal decree *Summis desiderantes affectibus* (desiring with supreme ardor) was promulgated, trials for witchcraft increased in Milan. Under the rule of Ludovico il Moro and at the very beginning of the sixteenth century, Milan and its surroundings experienced the activities of Rategno, Bernardo of Como, whose deeds as inquisitor of Como affected Milan; a mountainous place named Tonale appeared in sources during those years as one of the best-known Italian locations for Sabbats. Many trials held from 1483 through 1485 in Bormio, ruled by Como, were mentioned in Heinrich Kramer's *Malleus Maleficarum* (The Hammer of Witches, 1486).

During the first decades of the sixteenth century, many witchcraft trials took place in the Alpine valleys, especially in Valcamonica but also in Lugano and Mendrisio. These trials were all linked to the bishop of Como more than to Milan. A few cases were also reported in 1517–1518 around the city of Brescia and in two small towns, Orago and Lomazzo, not far from Milan. During the second half of the century, Milan's most distinguished figure was undoubtedly its cardinal-archbishop, St. Carlo Borromeo, who prosecuted witches with such intensity that his actions provoked a polite but firm intervention from the Roman Inquisition.

In Milan, the end of the sixteenth century and the first twenty years of the seventeenth century were still marked by witch hunting, with a handful of burnings being recorded in the city. The persecution of witches slowed and ended around 1640–1650. The last known execution occurred in 1641. Nevertheless, in the northern valleys, lay tribunals maintained a policy of ferocious persecution lasting until the beginning of the eighteenth century.

MARINA MONTESANO

See also: BORROMEO, ST. CARLO; *CANON EPISCOPI;* DOMINICAN ORDER; INQUISITION, ROMAN; ITALY; *MALLEUS MALEFICARUM;* RATEGNO, BERNARDO OF COMO; SPELLS.

References and further reading:
Farinelli, Giuseppe, and Ermanno Paccagnini. 1989. *Processo per stregoneria a Caterina de Medici. 1616–1617.* Milan: Rusconi.

Fumi, Luigi. 1910. "L'inquisizione romana e lo stato di Milano: Saggio di ricerche nell'archivio di Stato." *Archivio storico lombardo* 4, no. 13: 5–101.

Monter, William, and John Tedeschi. 1986. "Towards a Statistical Profile of the Italian Inquisitions, Sixteenth to Eighteenth Centuries." Pp. 130–157 in *The Inquisitions in Early Modern Europe: Studies in Sources and Methods.* Edited by Gustav Henningsen and John Tedeschi. DeKalb: Northern Illinois University Press.

Portone, Paolo. 1996. "Un processo di stregoneria nella Milano di Carlo Borromeo (1569)." Pp. 317–330 in *Stregoneria e streghe nell'Europa moderna.* Edited by Giovanna Bosco and Patrizia Castelli. Pisa: Pacini.

MILK

Milk has played a very important part in European witchcraft and popular magic, in pre-Christian and Christian mythology alike, generating a rich variety of magical measures and countermeasures. Innumerable beliefs and practices reveal the intimate connections between witches and milk. In Europe, milk witches spawned a rich variety of beliefs and rites, because village witchcraft grew from neighborhood conflicts, often between women. Cows and milk were basic for survival in early modern agriculture, and absolutely all work related to milk (except some cheese making) was done by women. Thus there was an automatic association among cows, milk, and the huge predominance of women among witches.

MYTHOLOGICAL FOUNDATIONS

Beneath these associations lay Indo-European mythical legacies regarding milk and cows and some beliefs and rites related to supernatural beings and milk dating from pre-Christian times. Certain Indo-European deities, particularly such gods of thunder as Indra, Zeus, or Jupiter, were due a sacrificial offering of milk (the belief that a fire that came from lightning can only be put out by milk survives in several parts of Europe). Indo-European linguists have reconstructed traces of the original myth (assaults of the lightning-god against monsters of the underworld in order to obtain stolen cows) from some legends in southeastern Europe that describe lightning striking a devil who is concealing a cow, sometimes under an elderberry tree or "devil's tree." The topos of a dragon that snatches milk or steals a cow also appears in the Balkans: killing the dragon restores the milk from dried-up cows. Pre-Christian mythologies about milk witches or milk fairies are known to practically all European peoples, and some demonic female figures have cow or milk attributes: the milk churn belonging to German, Czech, Hungarian, or Scandinavian witches (this is how they can be recognized on Christmas night); Romanian witches who travel to their Sabbat on a milk bucket or churn; Celtic fairies who steal cows and milk; Romanian and eastern Hungarian fairies and witches who can take the shape of a cow but can also saddle and thus ruin a cow; and Bulgarian witches who "pull the moon down" from the sky, which becomes a cow upon reaching the ground and can then be milked.

Features of pre-Christian mythologies persist in modern-day popular beliefs of various European peoples. A gift of milk is offered around the time of the winter solstice for the dead or demons who visit the living then (e.g., for the "Perchta" in southern Germany or Austria between Christmas and Twelfth Night). Among the peoples of the Balkans or among the Irish and the Scots, fairies of a definitely "deadly" character are associated with various milk rites, as are the pressing demons of the night called *mahr* or *mare* by Germanic peoples. In return for receiving milk, these beings increase the prosperity of the household and abstain from harming family members. Milk offerings associated with Bulgarian, Serbian, and Greek fairy cults occur in the context of healing rituals: healers offer the fairies a sacrifice containing milk when invoking them for assistance. Swiss and German folklore describes milk offerings given to the ghost of the house. Offering milk to a house snake, which impersonates the spirit of the ancestors, is recommended in most of Europe (if it is not fed milk, the head of the family will die). In the Balkans and some Slavic parts of Eastern Europe, the "fate women" who determined a baby's destiny at birth received an offering of food: on the first or third night after the birth, various foods, including milk, were prepared for them so that they would give the newborn a positive destiny.

MILK MAGIC AND FERTILITY RITUALS

The myth of vanquishing the cow-snatching demon—where the drought also ends when the cows are recovered—emphasizes the connections between rainfall and milk in Indo-European mythologies. Some beliefs of modern European peoples suggest that a magically induced absence or increase of rain induces a similar decrease or increase in milk yield. The practices of milk magic performed at sacred water springs, noted in German and French sources, draws on the same belief, as do the magical activities and practices of the rain magician or milk magician (the figure shows a witch milking the pillar and thus bringing rain). The correspondence between milk magic and rain magic is most clearly shown through the widespread beliefs in and rituals of dew picking in central and mainly southeastern Europe. The people of a village collect all the dew from the grass of the neighboring pasture by repeatedly pulling a tablecloth or other textile over the grass, usually during a spring or summer festival like Whitsun or Midsummer. The villagers thereby snatch the milk from the cows belonging to the neighboring village farmers; in accordance with the theory of limited goods, the increase in their milk yield exactly equals the drop in milk production from the neighbors' animals. Fertility rituals connected to the occasion of the first milking or to the first milk and manifesting in pouring or spraying water are known in a several places in both western and eastern Europe.

WITCHES DOING MALEFACTION TO COWS AND MILK

The theory of limited goods also explains why it was customary throughout Europe to attribute milk snatching to witches: by depriving others, one increased one's own milk yield. According to legends known all over Europe, witches stole milk from their neighbors' stables or gardens or acquired it by stealing objects related to the cow; by picking up its footprint or dung; or by milking such objects as a fencepost, a pillar of the house, or a gatepost: through the principle of participation magic, one acquires milk through an attribute of the cow or her owner. The witch who steals milk or damages the cow harms others for his or her private benefit—a general theme about milk witches throughout Europe, from France to Scandinavia or Romania. Everywhere such witches snatched milk or else spoiled it and the related dairy products.

Both in the Europe of the witchcraft trials and in more modern times, related legends described the milk witches' operating methods, the ways of identifying them, and the means of remedying their damage. Many beliefs associated damages to cows and milk with certain "witching days": Walpurgis (central and western Europe); Midsummer (central and eastern Europe); St. Luca (central Europe); or St. John's Day (essentially all of Europe). Legends mention witches sneaking into stables or stroking the cows. Particularly in western and northern Europe, witches with the evil eye can do harm by appearing unexpectedly at the time of calving or churning, drying up the milk of either a human mother or a cow by their jealous looks. All over Europe, witches sent helping animals or familiars—principally a cat or a frog—in order to snatch the milk (but one also finds rabbits or hedgehogs in western and northern Europe and snakes in eastern Europe).

Because of the witch's malefice, a cow gives no milk at all or its milk is bloody; the production of dairy products (e.g., churning butter) may fail, or the result is inedible. Even in contemporary Europe, such spells are considered realistic dangers in several places. Wherever the institution of village witchcraft and its accompanying beliefs and rites remained active (as in

A witch milks an axe handle, from Johann Geiler von Kaysersberg's sermons on witchcraft published as Die Emeis (The Ants), *1516. Witches were accused of stealing milk, a serious crime in an agricultural society. The cow in the background links cows, milk, and the prevalence of female witches. (Cornell University Library)*

some parts of present-day central and southeastern Europe), people knew and practiced innumerable magical methods to protect themselves against witches and prevent the spoiling of milk, as well as performed rites relating to milk on festive occasions. For example, on the first day the animals were herded out to pasture, villagers would protect them with prayers, spells, sacred water, sanctified poppies, a cross drawn over the stable, garlic tied to the cow's horn, thorny branches of rosehip, iron objects, or with millet scattered around the stable. It was a general principle in many places in Europe that no stranger should be present at the time of calving or churning.

Identifying the witch who had laid a curse on the milk, summoning her to the house and forcing her to cure the damage still formed part of the resolution of malefices within some twentieth-century European village communities. In most places, however, only folklore collections recorded these popular legends with a rich scale of variants. Essentially, these procedures required some technique of divination in order to identify the culprit and then force her to remove or cure the spell, usually carried out by a specialized witch doctor or healer, using various techniques to identify and symbolically harm some personal attribute of the suspected witch, who would then promptly appear at the house and be forced to remedy the spell. According to other widespread legends, the cats, frogs, snakes, and other creatures believed to be accomplices of the witch would be injured, thus provoking the witch to withdraw the spell. Other widespread legends from western and central Europe testify that it was also customary to harm the witch by analogy, damaging the milk or urine of the bewitched cow either by smoking it (hanging a boot containing the cow's urine over the smoke), beating the milk over the doorstep, immersing pointed or red-hot objects into the milk and stirring it, or even by spreading a coat or blanket over the cow and beating it.

ÉVA PÓCS;

TRANSLATED BY ORSOLYA FRANK

See also: EVIL EYE; FAIRIES; FAMILIARS; FOLKLORE; HUNGARY AND SOUTHEASTERN EUROPE, MAGIC; HUNGARY AND SOUTHEASTERN EUROPE, WITCHCRAFT; MAGIC, POPULAR; MIDSUMMER EVE; NIGHTMARES; SPELLS, WALPURGIS (WALPURIGS) NIGHT; WEATHER MAGIC.

References and further reading:
Eckstein, F. 1935. "Milch," "Milchhexe" and "Milchopfer." Pp. 243–367 in *Handwörterbuch des Deutschen Aberglaubens*. Vol. 6. Edited by Hanns Bächtold-Stäubli and Eduard Hoffmann-Krayer. Berlin: Walter de Gruyter.

Ivanov, V. V., and Toporov V. I. 1974. *Issledovania v oblasti slavianaskikh drevnostei: Leksicheskie i frazeologicheskie voprosy rekonstruktsii tekstov*. Moscow: Nauka.

Pócs, Éva. 1989. *Fairies and Witches at the Boundary of South-Eastern and Central Europe*. Folklore Fellows' Communications 243. Helsinki: Suomalainen Tiedeakatemia.

———. 1999. *Between the Living and the Dead: A Perspective on Witches and Seers in the Early Modern Age*. Budapest: Central European University Press.

Runeberg, Arne. 1947. *Witches, Demons and Fertility Magic: Analysis of Their Significance and Mutual Relations in West-European Folk Religion*. Helsinki: Societas Scientiarum Fennica.

Wall, Jan I. 1977–1978. "Tjumjölkande väsen. I. Äldre nordisk tradition, II. Yngre nordisk tradition." In *Acta Universitatis Upsaliensis*. Studia Ethnologica Upsaliensia series 3, 5.

MILLENARIANISM

In the most general terms, millenarianism or millennialism is the belief in a radical transformation of *this* world into one of justice, peace, and fellowship; it focuses on collective, this-worldly salvation. In Christian prophecy it is the expectation of a 1,000-year period (hence its name), mentioned in the Book of Revelation, during which Jesus is to rule and holiness is to prevail. On the surface, millennialism would seem to have little to do with witchcraft. But two forms of millennialism show distinct predilections for a discourse of magic and witchcraft.

As opposed to an egalitarian vision of the millennium in which the "saved" inhabit a world without class distinctions, where everyone lives by honest labor with none to harry them (Isaiah 2), many versions imagine a world of magical fertility in which labor is not necessary. These magical millennial visions appeal to those who believe that the spiritual world can defy the laws of nature.

Millennialism also spawns intense magical practices among those believers convinced that the advent of this millennium is imminent. Such movements of *apocalyptic* millennialists often perform rituals that will bring on the transformation. The Ghost Dance that spread though various Native American tribes at the end of the nineteenth century promised that its proper execution would prompt nature to shed the white man and his world as a snake sheds a skin.

In general, apocalyptic time (the period of transformation from the current "fallen world" to the redeemed millennial kingdom) encourages magical thinking, since these are by definition stupendous times, when the cosmic struggle between good and evil reaches its climax and definitive solution. Charismatic prophets regularly exhibit thaumaturgic capacities that demonstrate both their cosmic power and their benevolence. This increases the size and devotion of their following and sets in motion certain kinds of "idol worship," in which the messiah figure commands absolute obedience from a following that, despite their initial act of independence in breaking with their culture of origin and joining the dissident movement, no longer exercise independent judgment.

Such groups often meet with strong, even violent opposition from those in power (whether indigenous or imperialist), and among their ways of resisting repression, we find magical procedures that ensure immunity from the weapons of the enemy. Ghost Shirts were bulletproof, as were the very bodies of the Chinese Boxers (ca. 1900) who had gone through the proper initiation. The Anabaptist Thomas Münster, a leader of the German peasant revolt in 1524–1525 who preached the imminent end of the world, boasted that he would catch bullets in his sleeves. Such magical promises regularly led these movements into devastating failures when real bullets decimated the apocalyptic armies.

Apocalyptic time, however, also stimulates fear of malevolent witchcraft. Most apocalyptic scenarios contain cataclysmic phases in which vast destruction rains down upon humanity (e.g., *Revelation* 3–19). These tribulations result from the final and universal battle of good with evil, and, as a result, most apocalyptic expectations, whether they anticipate a coming millennium on earth or the end of the world, foresee cosmic battles. Such scenarios often begin with a metastasis of evil in the world, often led by an anti-messiah (Christian Antichrist, Muslim *Dajjal*). This evil figure (curiously like the mutant supervillains of comic books) has myriad minions who do his (almost never her) work in the world, preparing for his coming.

In the Christian West, from the fourteenth century onward, these apocalyptic fears often projected onto witches the role of minions of Antichrist. In their *anti*-apocalyptic phases, trying to discourage the sense of imminence, elites emphasized the terrors of the transition in order to discourage people from *wanting* the apocalypse to occur. In their apocalyptic phases, however, such elites often used the language of conspiracy and evil coming from below (chaos, anarchy), to fight against forces that threatened their dominion. This scapegoating technique targets certain people as the apocalyptic enemies. For Christians and Muslims, the primary apocalyptic scapegoat has been Jews, but at the end of the Middle Ages, Christianity added an ominous new enemy to its list of agents of Antichrist—a diabolic conspiracy of witches, primarily women.

Attacks on witches began in earnest in the early fifteenth century, in part because of an elaboration of a vast satanic conspiracy in which witches were perceived as agents in a cosmic plot by the Devil to destroy Christendom. The "witch's Sabbat," a parody and subversion of every element of Church ritual, was the centerpiece of the activity of the Devil and his servants, the witches. By the late fifteenth century, witchcraft accusations had become so common in some areas that Europeans could consider every "bad" thing that occurred (failed crops or business ventures, miscarriages, illnesses, accidents, etc.) as the *maleficia* (evildoings) of witches.

The apocalyptic dynamic here conflates the Devil's minions with the Antichrist's, and the panic behind the accusations sometimes reached frenzied levels, especially in Germany. The literary climax of this aggressive

paranoia came with the publication of the Dominican inquisitor Heinrich Kramer's *Malleus Maleficarum* (The Hammer of Witches) in 1486, with its ferocious misogyny and prurient fascination with the Devil's female "agents." Born of apocalyptic paranoia, the fear of witches became a hallmark of many subsequent apocalyptic episodes, especially in the early modern period, where a significant part of the elite embraced apocalyptic beliefs (Clark 1997). Indeed, in the sixteenth and seventeenth centuries, intense apocalyptic episodes (the early Reformation) occurred, and even after the early expectations had passed, both Catholic and Protestant authorities, permeated with the language of guilt, sin, and fear of the Devil, found the language of coercive purity aimed at exterminating witchcraft a particularly attractive solution to the persistence of evil. As late as 1692, Cotton Mather delivered an apocalyptic sermon on the text of Revelation 12:12 to account for the activities of the Devil and witches at Salem, Massachusetts.

Witch-hunting episodes also illustrate a key aspect of the dynamics of apocalyptic time. In periods of waxing and optimistic expectation, women often played prominent roles in millennial movements. But with the waning of such expectations (and hence the popularity of the movement), women's behavior, previously considered holy, became viewed as disorderly and dangerous. This perspective offered two hypotheses about the nature of early modern witchcraft persecutions: first, that their spread corresponded to more localized apocalyptic anxieties in the aftermath of earlier European-wide ones (early Reformation); and, second, that the ebbing of persecutions corresponded to an increasingly anti-apocalyptic attitude taken by elites. The "rationalism" that put an end to the participation of the educated elite in witch hunts may well have influenced the de-eschatologization of the Enlightenment.

RICHARD LANDES

See also: ANABAPTISTS; ANTICHRIST, THE; APOCALYPSE; BIBLE; DEVIL; ENLIGHTENMENT; JESUS; *MALLEUS MALEFICARUM*; MATHER, COTTON; ORIGINS OF THE WITCH HUNTS.

References and further reading:
Clark, Stuart. 1997. *Thinking with Demons: The Idea of Witchcraft in Early Modern Europe.* Oxford: Clarendon.
Cohn, Norman. 1975. *Europe's Inner Demons.* New York: Basic Books.
Delumeau, Jean. 1978. *La Peur en Occident, XIVe-XVIIIe siecles: Une cité assiégée.* Paris: Fayard.
Kieckhefer, Richard. 1976. *European Witch Trials: Their Foundations in Popular and Learned Culture, 1300–1500.* Berkeley: University of California Press.
Kramer, Heinrich, and James [sic] Sprenger. 1971. *Malleus Maleficarum.* New York: Dover.
O'Leary, Stephen. 1994. *Arguing the Apocalypse: A Theory of Millennial Rhetoric.* New York: Oxford University Press.
Wilson, Brian. 1973. *Magic and the Millennium: A Sociological Study of Religious Movements of Protest Among Tribal and Third World Peoples.* New York: Harper and Row.

MILLER, ARTHUR (1915–2005)

Famous for writing *The Crucible,* his 1952 play about the Salem witchcraft trials, Arthur Miller brought a contemporary American meaning to the term *witch hunt.*

Having grown up in New York, against the backdrop of the stock market crash of 1929 and the Great Depression, Miller rose to prominence in the 1930s as one of the outstanding playwrights of his generation, espousing President Franklin Roosevelt's attempts to improve social conditions. The onset of the Cold War and the unscrupulous "Red Scare" campaign waged by Senator Joseph McCarthy and the House Committee on Un-American Activities to discover Communists in the government and the entertainment industry caused him to reconsider the citizen's role in resisting irrational but state-sponsored social pressures. The abject recantation of his friend and mentor, Clifford Odets, before McCarthy's committee, combined with Odets's willingness to implicate others, finally compelled Miller to write *The Crucible.*

The play took as its theme the well-known cycle of witchcraft trials that had convulsed Salem, Massachusetts, between June and September 1692. The parallels between McCarthy's persecution of U.S. Communists and the Puritan-inspired witch hunts of the late seventeenth century were obvious, but Miller's skills as a playwright allowed *The Crucible* to transcend simple political allegory and become one of the most frequently produced plays in U.S. theater. Although he made good use of original sources (including the three-volume typescript of the trials, lodged in the Salem Court House), Miller pointed out that this play was "not history in the sense in which the word is used by the academic historian." The characters were "creations of my own, drawn to the best of my ability in conformity with their known behavior," while his aim as an author was to enable the reader "to discover . . . the essential nature of one of the strangest and most awful chapters in human history" (Miller 1978, 2). As a result, he increased the age of Abigail Williams in order to make her sexual relationship with John Proctor more plausible and palatable; he reduced the number of young girls charged to just five, in order to permit greater narrative clarity and fuller dramatic characterization; and he reduced the numerous judges present at the hearings to only two.

Miller provided an unhistorical although dramatically satisfying ending. He conveyed the impression that Proctor's noble death gave the lie to the allegations and that the trials had burned themselves out by autumn of 1692; but that was not the case. Prosecutions continued until April 1693, and their final abandonment—a month later—did not reflect either a rejection of a belief in the reality of the Devil or of the efficacy of witchcraft and demonic possession.

Despite such historical license, Miller's play plausibly recreated the simmering sexual and social tensions present in a tightly knit frontier community, where the problems created by greed, land hunger, and a domineering theocracy exploded—with devastating results—through the misconstrued actions of some thoroughly bored and repressed adolescents. Miller saw "bewitchment" as a mental state, here taking the form of mass hysteria that could be fomented by self-seeking and self-appointed "saviors" in order to gain power and influence over the frightened, the gullible, and the weak-willed.

In a case of life imitating art, Miller—probably on account of his authorship of *The Crucible*—was himself hauled before the House Committee in June 1956. He chose to echo the fictionalized sentiments of John Proctor, refusing to inform against his Communist friends and acquaintances and proclaiming that "I am trying to, and will, protect my sense of myself. I could not use the name of another person and bring trouble on him" (Martine 1979, 191). On May 31, 1957, he was found guilty of contempt of Congress, receiving a suspended jail sentence and a fine of $500. However, as the "inexplicable darkness" and dread engendered by McCarthyism began to dissipate, the U.S. Court of Appeals quashed his conviction in 1958.

JOHN CALLOW

See also: BEWITCHMENT; LITERATURE; SALEM; WITCH HUNTS, MODERN POLITICAL USAGE.

References and further reading.

Demos, John Putnam. 1982. *Entertaining Satan: Witchcraft and the Culture of Early New England.* New York and Oxford: Oxford University Press.

Martine, James J., ed. 1979. *Critical Essays on Arthur Miller.* Boston: G. K. Hall.

Miller, Arthur. 1957. *Collected Plays.* New York: Viking.

———. 1978. *The Crucible/Arthur Miller: Text and Criticism.* Edited by Gerald Weales. Harmondsworth, UK, and New York: Penguin.

Moss, Leonard. *Arthur Miller.* 1980. Boston: Twayne.

Scarre, Geoffrey, and John Callow. 2001. *Witchcraft and Magic in Sixteenth and Seventeenth Century Europe.* Basingstoke, UK: Palgrave.

MIRACLES

Two criteria are necessary to define an incident as miraculous: it must stand in contradiction to what the observer knows from experience to be the common or natural way things happen, and he or she must associate it with some numinous power. What is regarded as miraculous, therefore, depends on the education of the observer and the worldview of the society he or she lives in. The histories of all higher religions abound in records of miracles, the main effects of which may be described as power over animate and inanimate nature; healing or reviving humans and animals; punishing disbelievers and evildoers; changing psychic states; and contacting the supernatural through visions, apparitions, voices, or dreams.

For Christians, the belief in miracles is of course guaranteed through the many marvellous phenomena recorded in the Hebrew and Christian Bibles. Most wonders worked by the saints—or, theologically, by God acting through the saints' intercession—are imitations of the deeds of Jesus. However, if a miraculous phenomenon occurs within a dualistic religion like Christianity, the problem arises: which numinous power caused it, God or the Devil? The positive or negative effects of the action in question cannot provide an answer, because God also does painful things to people he wants to correct, whereas the Devil helps people in order to seduce them. Therefore many miracles of saints and misdeeds of witches, taken by themselves, reveal the very same structure. When, for example, Saint Bridgit of Sweden (d. 1373) learned that a respected clergyman did not believe her revelations, she prayed to Jesus, who promised to castigate the man. Soon he became depressed and died from gout. But causing gout by an evil spell was also a common accusation in witchcraft trials, as late as when the last sorceress's stake was kindled in Germany in 1749 for Maria Renata Singer. Several comparable instances could be cited, which were done in very similar ways both by holy and unholy women: influencing the weather, multiplying food, and contacting the dead. Perhaps the ambivalence between divine and devilish help is especially clear when we consider a piece of trial testimony against the *Vaudois* (Waldensians, but used to label witchcraft) of Fribourg in 1430. There a woman is mentioned who had served God so well that whenever she asked him to avenge an offense she had endured, he did so immediately. Was this the prayer of a saint or of a witch? Was the following miracle God's work or the Devil's, whom the woman venerated as God?

The same problem arose when a man or, more often, a woman claimed to have benefited from internal miracles, such as illuminations by the Holy Spirit or supernatural visions and apparitions. Were these true manifestations of the godhead or illusions caused by the evil one? This difficult question was one reason that the discernment of spirits became more and more elaborate in the later Middle Ages. But it remained unreliable. In 1391, Dorothy of Montau was on the verge of being burned as a sorceress, according to the judgement of the competent ecclesiastical jurisdiction, because many priests did not believe that her miraculous voices and visions came from God; today, the Catholic Church venerates her as the patroness of Prussia. Joan of Arc, who presumed to hear the voices of Saints Michael, Catherine, and Margaret, was burned as a witch in 1431 and achieved sainthood in 1920.

As soon as these manifestations are no longer interpreted within a religious scheme but considered as natural or psychic phenomena or frauds that had been misinterpreted in either good or bad faith, the question

of the miraculous becomes obsolete. This criticism started with the Reformation, which confined miracles to biblical times; it was continued by the Enlightenment and carried further by such modern sciences as psychology and parapsychology explaining away the incredible. Today, the belief in miracles survives as a dogma within text-based religions, such as Christianity, Judaism, and Islam. In Catholicism, two miracles are still necessary for canonization, and Pope John Paul II presided over the canonization of more saints than any other previous pontiff. Nevertheless, one suspects that most Christian theologians and clergy often ignore miracles. The number of officially accepted wonders is small in the present and usually related to special places of pilgrimage like Lourdes, where a group of theologians and surgeons are specially deputed to supervise very critically the operations of the supernatural.

Writing in the mid-eighteenth century, after the era of the witch hunts, the Scottish *philosophe* David Hume epitomized the Enlightenment view of miracles: "No testimony is sufficient to establish a miracle, unless the testimony be of such a kind, that its falsehood would be more miraculous than the fact which it endeavours to establish" (1748, pt. 1).

PETER DINZELBACHER

See also: BIBLE; DEVIL; DISCERNMENT OF SPIRITS; ENLIGHTENMENT; HOLINESS; JESUS; JOAN OF ARC; LIVING SAINTS; SUPERSTITION; VISIONS.

References and further reading:

Burns, R. M. 1981. *The Great Debate on Miracles.* Lewisburg: Bucknell University Press.
Dinzelbacher, Peter. 2001. *Heilige oder Hexen? Schicksale auffälliger Frauen.* 4th ed. Düsseldorf: Albatros.
Hume, David. 1748. "On Miracles." In *Enquiry Concerning Human Understanding.* London.
Mensching, Gustav. 1957. *Das Wunder im Glauben und Aberlauben der Völker.* Leiden: Brill.
Mullin, Redmond. 1979. *Miracles and Magic.* London: Mowbrays.
Swinburne, Richard. 1970. *The Concept of Miracle.* London: Macmillan.
"Wunder." 2001. Pp. 1311–1319 in *Lexikon für Theologie und Kirche.* Vol. 10. Freiburg: Herder.

MISCONCEPTIONS ABOUT THE WITCH HUNTS

Witchcraft attracts popular interest; everyone "knows" something about it. Even if this knowledge differs from scholarly knowledge, it may not be "wrong"; scholars and the general public may simply have different interests. Nor is scholarly knowledge necessarily "right." Research develops, new discoveries are made, and accepted theories are overturned.

Nevertheless, there are several widely held beliefs about the European witch hunt that can be regarded as incorrect in the light of current scholarship. Often these beliefs derive from the scholarship of earlier generations:

theories that have been overturned still linger on. Partly this is because nonscholars have no immediate access to the latest research, but also particular ideas continue to be repeated because they serve a contemporary purpose.

The first set of misconceptions derives from movements of thought in the eighteenth and nineteenth centuries: the anticlerical tendencies of the Enlightenment and the Romantic movement. Those appealing to modern rationality and truths derived from nature were often hostile to what they saw as domination of life by churches committed to outdated and artificial intellectual traditions. Witch hunting represented everything they disliked about organized religion. As the modern world has become more secularized, some of these anticlerical tendencies have been enhanced. The ideas they have produced are often effective, but some are misleading.

1. Role of the Inquisition. The institution that, above all others, has symbolized religious obscurantism and oppression is the Inquisition. Its dominance in the discussion has given rise to several related misconceptions. The first idea is simply that "the Inquisition" was the main body responsible for witch hunting. In fact, although a few inquisitors helped to develop the witch hunt in its early stages (for instance, by writing the *Malleus Maleficarum* [The Hammer of Witches, 1486]), the Portuguese, Spanish, and Roman Inquisitions effectively prevented witch hunts during the sixteenth and seventeenth centuries in southern Europe. Executions were overwhelmingly the responsibility of secular criminal courts.

The second idea is that the papal Inquisition, which had been established to persecute the Cathar and Waldensian (*Vaudois*) heresies, moved on to hunting witches in order to keep itself in business. However, the chronology does not support this belief. It used to be believed that there were mass witch hunts in the early fourteenth century, shortly after the suppression of Catharism, but they have been shown to be based on documents forged in 1829 by Étienne Léon de Lamothe-Langon.

The third idea is that the Inquisition burned witches in order to save their souls. In fact, the Inquisition's preferred aim was to reclaim heretics to the true faith *without* burning them. Those whom it burned (or rather, whom it handed over to the secular authorities for burning) were *impenitent* heretics or else repeat offenders. Burning did not save their souls but simply punished them for their crime.

2. Role of torture. Along with the emphasis on the Inquisition comes an emphasis on torture. Torture was, of course, extremely important in witch hunts, so this is not entirely a misconception. However, the tortures that are reported in popular accounts of witch hunting or displayed in "museums of torture" in various parts of the world, are usually the most extreme and dramatic physical ones; the false implication is that these were normal.

3. Inevitability of conviction. The idea of torture points to the idea that trials of witches were so stacked against the defense that convictions were the only possible outcome. In fact, about half of suspected witches actually endured torture without confessing—when it was done strictly according to the official rules, which was often not the case. Even during large-scale witchcraft panics, there were always some acquittals, and many other cases were dropped before reaching trial. The idea of inevitable conviction is common because people are receptive to the idea that witch hunting was cruel and barbaric.

4. Financial profitability. Another common idea is that witches were accused in order to make money. Usually it is said that the authorities themselves stood to profit, but sometimes accusations by neighbors are said to have been motivated by the neighbor's desire for the alleged witch's land or goods. It is true that some courts could confiscate a criminal's goods, but many other courts did not do so, and "confiscation" is a misleading term. Most witches were too poor to have any possessions worth coveting. A few active witch hunters like Matthew Hopkins received payment, but even he received only modest fees plus expenses; it was certainly not desire for money that made him a witch hunter. Some rich witches were accused because of resentment at their wealth and stinginess, but they were a tiny minority. The idea of witch hunting for money is attractive because it attributes to the witch hunters a motive that is readily understood in the modern world—but it is a modern myth projected onto our ancestors.

5. Swimming a witch. A misunderstanding of the "swimming test" (water ordeal) led some to believe that witches could be detected by dropping them in water. If they floated, they were guilty. If they sank, they were innocent—but they drowned. In fact, ropes were tied to suspects to pull them out of the water; moreover, this test had no legal value anywhere in Europe. This belief functions as an affirmation of our own cultural superiority: people today are cleverer or more sensible than the ignorant witch hunters. An early instance of a backlash against this belief from the 1850s comes from the Scottish explorer David Livingstone, who explained the swimming test to Africans as part of "the wisdom of my ancestors" in order to criticize some of their own traditional customs.

6. Witch hunting meant woman hunting. Witch hunting is often described as a more or less conscious device used by men for repressing women. In fact, although there is a clear relationship between women and witch hunting, it is quite complex. Feminist scholarship has done much to bring these issues, which traditional anticlerical scholars had ignored, to the forefront of the discussion; but the results have not gone as predicted. Witch hunters did not target women *as such,*

they targeted witches. At least 20 percent of all executed witches were men, and there are places where most of them were men. Moreover, the bulk of the testimony against female witches came directly or indirectly from other women.

7. The "Nine Million Witches" trope. As part of their stress on the enormity of the witch hunt, early feminist scholars were among those emphasizing the largest possible numbers for executions of witches. In the eighteenth century, Voltaire mentioned a speculative figure of 100,000 executions for witchcraft. A misreading by a late-eighteenth-century German archivist was extrapolated and inflated by Gustav Roskoff, a Viennese professor who published a widely read *History of the Devil* in 1869, into a statistical balloon of "9 million witches executed." A pioneering anticlerical feminist, Matilda Joslyn Gage, took it from Roskoff in 1893 and inserted it into early feminist discourse. Although this number was a wild guess ultimately based on completely erroneous research, it achieved a wide circulation because those wishing to emphasize the importance of witch hunting tended to pick the highest of the various figures available. In more recent times, the figure of 9 million was frequently repeated by Nazi propaganda (which otherwise seldom agreed with feminists) and, turned back against them, facilitated comparison with the standard figure of 6 million Jews murdered in the Holocaust. The true number of executions for witchcraft will never be known precisely, but the currently accepted scholarly estimate is under 50,000—close to Voltaire's figure. The importance of witch hunting does not lie primarily in the numbers executed, but in the climate of fear induced even by sporadic executions. "Overkill" seems the appropriate term here.

8. Midwives and healers. Two related misconceptions have to do with midwives. The first idea is that witch hunters especially targeted midwives when babies died. In addition to being a feminist idea, this one had an anticlerical element: the Church was believed to have been hostile to midwives because they tried to reduce the labor pains ordained for women to punish the sin of Eve. Some demonologies (including the earliest major one, the *Malleus Maleficarum*) did denounce midwives, believing that their access to babies gave them material for cannibalistic infanticide, but most ignored midwives. Some midwives were indeed accused of witchcraft, but too few to suggest that they were being targeted; most midwives seemed to have been well-respected people who were most unlikely to be accused by their clients or neighbors.

The second misconception involving midwives and healers is that an emerging male medical profession led an attack on traditional women healers—including midwives—by labeling them as witches. It appealed to an early generation of feminist historians in the 1970s, but no evidence supports it. Folk healers in early modern society could be either men or women. Some of them were accused of witchcraft, often when their cures went wrong, or they had a dispute with a client or a rival healer. But the role of the medical profession in witch hunting was peripheral—they were far less important than lawyers, for instance, and they were among the first important early skeptics about witchcraft.

9. Witchcraft as a surviving pagan cult. Modern pagans of the Wiccan movement have supported the idea that the witches who were hunted in early modern times practiced a pagan religion that had gone underground with the coming of Christianity. Its members worshiped a horned god, "Dianus," and were organized in covens of thirteen. When the Christian Church discovered this religion in the late Middle Ages, its members were persecuted for allegedly worshiping the Devil. Outline versions of this theory appeared occasionally in the nineteenth century, but it took enduring and detailed form in 1921 with a book by the Egyptologist Margaret Murray, *The Witch-Cult in Western Europe*. It came at the height of a vogue for "pagan" survivals and had a convincing appearance of deep scholarship. The book was in fact fraudulent—Murray's sources frequently did not say what she said they said—but that was not realized at the time. Murray's theory became influential, though it was never universally accepted. Historians familiar with the records of witchcraft trials frequently criticized it, but often they could say only that they had found no evidence for the theory in their own research. The theory even gained a fresh vogue in the 1960s among historians interested in popular movements. The painstaking work of exposing Murray's fraudulent use of sources was not undertaken until the 1970s (Cohn 1975).

By then, the modern Wiccan movement, whose founders wished to believe that they were inheriting an ancient tradition, had embraced Murray's theory. *Witchcraft Today* (1954), the key book by the movement's main founder, Gerald Gardner, announced that the author belonged to a coven of witches that had survived since pre-Christian times. The book had an approving introduction by Murray herself. Her theory thus gained a new lease on life, and the witch hunt became known as the "Burning Times" among Wiccans believing themselves to be successors of the witches. Some Wiccans still adhere to the theory, but many others have recognized that it cannot survive historical scrutiny.

10. Ergotism. Finally, we have an idea that depends on no past intellectual tradition but has achieved popularity through its very modernity. The idea is that the symptoms of demonic possession were caused by ergotism—eating rye contaminated by the ergot fungus. Those afflicted accused others of "bewitching" them, thus causing witch hunts. Some versions of the idea focus on Salem, whereas others extend it to all cases of demonic possession or even all witch hunting.

However, the ergotism theory has been discredited at Salem for various reasons, including its inability to explain why only the "afflicted girls" suffered from it (ergotism affects entire households, and men as much as women) and why their symptoms were often brought on by the presence of the accused witches. Nor has ergotism achieved much success in explaining cases of European demonic possession, which were rare exceptions to the normal pattern of witchcraft accusation based on neighborhood quarrels. However, the much-quoted fact that ergot is the source of lysergic acid diethylamide (LSD) adds to its attraction: people are fascinated by the idea that their ancestors also experienced drug-induced hallucinations. The idea's "scientific appearance gives it high status in a world dominated by technology and populated by millions of literate drug users. The theory was first popularized in 1976 by a *New York Times* article headed "Salem Witch Hunts in 1692 Linked to LSD-Like Agent."

In general, many of these ideas are attractive because they enable people to sympathize with the victims of witch hunting and to feel indignant at their cruel fate. It is perhaps natural to feel that there must have been some obvious fault in the witch hunters: they were wicked, ignorant, or both. Contemporary individualism has enhanced this tendency. Individuals who do not fit into the surrounding society and who struggle to overcome collective prejudice in order to realize their true worth are the heroes of numerous genres of modern culture. People identify with witches as misunderstood individuals of this kind. A willingness to empathize with people of the past, particularly victims of persecution, is laudable. However, historians wish to extend the same understanding to *all* the people whom they study—witch hunters as well as witches. Calling witch hunters wicked or ignorant cannot explain why they did what they did; moreover, many of them were clearly not ignorant, and some were considered pious rather than wicked. History is not an easy subject.

JULIAN GOODARE

See also: ACQUITTALS; BURNING TIMES; CONFISCATIONS OF WITCHES' PROPERTY; CONTEMPORARY WITCHCRAFT (POST-1800); DRUGS AND HALLUCINOGENS; ERGOTISM; FEMALE WITCHES; FEMINISM; GENDER; HISTORIOGRAPHY; HOPKINS, MATTHEW; INQUISITION, PORTUGUESE; INQUISITION, ROMAN; INQUISITION, SPANISH; LAMOTHE-LANGON, ÉTIENNE LÉON DE; MALE WITCHES; MIDWIVES; MURRAY, MARGARET ALICE; NUMBER OF WITCHES; POSSESSION, DEMONIC; SALEM; SWIMMING TEST; TORTURE; *VAUDOIS* (WALDENSIANS); VOLTAIRE; WITCH AND WITCHCRAFT, DEFINITIONS OF; WITCH HUNTS, MODERN POLITICAL USAGE.

References and further reading:
Cohn, Norman. 1975. *Europe's Inner Demons.* London: Chatto.
Harley, David. 1990. "Historians as Demonologists: The Myth of the Midwife-Witch." *Social History of Medicine* 3: 1–26.
Hutton, Ronald. 1999. *The Triumph of the Moon: A History of Modern Pagan Witchcraft.* Oxford: Oxford University Press.
Monter, E. William. 1972. "The Historiography of European Witchcraft: Progress and Prospects." *Journal of Interdisciplinary History* 2: 435–451.
Purkiss, Diane. 1996. *The Witch in History: Early Modern and Twentieth-Century Representations.* London: Routledge.
Simpson, Jacqueline. 1994. "Margaret Murray: Who Believed Her, and Why?" *Folklore* 105: 89–96.

MÖDEN, JOHANN (JAN) (CA. 1590S–1663)

Measured by sheer length of time and number of workplaces, *utriusque juris doctor* (doctor of both laws—civil and canon) Johann Möden seems one of the busiest jurists involved with seventeenth-century witchcraft persecutions in the Rhineland—an unusually energetic legal expert who hired his services out tirelessly in a dozen different places, working for Lutherans as well as Catholics. He epitomized the kind of entrepreneurial witch hunter that Friedrich Spee knew from personal experience.

Though we know much about his activities, his biography remains fragmentary. Möden was born at Koblenz in the 1590s, probably the son of a certain Herr Johann Möden who had lived in a high-status neighborhood since 1591. Matriculation registers show young Möden as a student from Koblenz (*Confluentinus*) enrolled at the Jesuit College of the University of Mainz in 1612 and 1613; in 1613 he began studying law at the University of Würzburg, where he probably received his doctoral degree in both civil and canon law. After Möden finished his studies, we know almost nothing about him, except that he married the daughter of a local official (*Schultheiss*) of Remagen and had his first child in 1619.

In 1627, Möden appeared on the regional scene of witchcraft persecutions. The outbreak of Archbishop Ferdinand's "war against the witches" (Schormann 1991) in the electorate of Cologne offered unprecedented opportunities, which Möden exploited ingeniously. Thus, we see him assisting the notorious Dr. Franz Buirmann in the town of Ahrweiler in 1628–1629 at trials that led to the death of at least twenty-six people. Möden soon became a *commissarius* (commissary) himself, working until 1633 in more than 100 trials in the various territories of the counts of Manderscheid-Blankenheim, Manderscheid-Gerolstein, and Manderscheid-Schleiden. His first engagement took place in the northern districts of Manderscheid-Blankenheim, very close to Cologne territory. Möden next moved to further similar business in the adjoining *Herrschaft* (estate) of Satzvey.

Though in the following years there was a notable decline in prosecutions, Möden and his colleague Buirmann moved their business to the Rhenish parts of the electorate of Cologne. Herman Löher, from Rheinbach, described their activities in his locality as well as in Meckenheim, where Möden was responsible for some seventy executions. In November 1637, Möden became acting mayor for one year of Münstereifel, where he had settled in 1629 and married his second wife about 1636. Although local notables became godparents for two of his children, Möden began to experience familial and economic decline. His second wife probably died by 1641, leaving him with enormous debts (he owed 1,465 Reichstaler to twenty-three creditors). We can therefore assume that Löher's description of Möden as needing money desperately because of his wife's obsession with pomp went beyond simple rhetoric.

In 1641–1642, Möden left Münstereifel, taking two of his seven children (the youngest born in 1640), and moved back to Koblenz. In professional terms, his decision proved useful. He conducted witchcraft trials at the Cologne exclave of Rhens from 1645 to 1647; in 1646, he started a long-lasting engagement in Winningen near Koblenz, a Lutheran exclave of the lower county of Sponheim. He also worked at the nearby lordship of Bürresheim in 1647 and gave his counsel on trials at the Sponheim county district town of Kastellaun in 1648. In 1649 he worked in the Cologne district of Altenahr and in 1653 in the county of Sayn-Hachenburg; in 1654 and 1656 he was again occupied with providing counsel for trials in Lutheran Kastellaun. When Winningen's persecutions finally ended in 1659, Möden disappeared as well. He died in Koblenz on February 24, 1663.

Möden practiced both as a Cologne-type commissary, exclusively in charge of the procedure, and later, in more southern territories, through the "mixed" method involving close cooperation with village committees and local officials. Like his colleague and mentor Buirmann, Möden combined working in a respectable field with earning respect, money, and a reputation for ruthlessness through a specialization in witchcraft trials. If a surplus of jurists existed in the seventeenth century, such careers as Möden's exemplify the possibilities of compensating for structural underemployment. A final assessment of his social achievement acquired in this manner is difficult. His and his first wife's popularity as godparents in Münstereifel could reflect prophylactic considerations by fearful neighbors. In his later Koblenz period (1641–1662), Möden never gained access to the inner circle of city councilors. After Trier's Archbishop-Elector Karl Kaspar von der Leyen (1652–1676) stopped witchcraft persecutions around 1653, Möden's ongoing business in neighboring territories could hardly give him any further respectability in his hometown. When he died, he left one adult daughter at home unmarried.

WALTER RUMMEL

Many thanks to Karin Trieschnigg (Münstereifel) for kindly offering me her overwhelming collection of information on the family history of Dr. Johann Möden.

See also: BUIRMANN, FRANZ; COLOGNE; COMMUNAL PERSECUTION; LÖHER, HERMAN; SPEE, FRIEDRICH.
References and further reading:
Bous, Robert, and Hans-Georg Klein, eds. 1998. *Quellen zur Geschichte der Stadt Ahrweiler 856–1812.* Bad Neuenahr-Ahrweiler: Selbstverlag der Gemeinde Bad Neuenahr.
Kettel, Adolf. 1995. "Hexenprozesse in der Grafschaft Gerolstein und in den angrenzenden kurtrierischen Ämtern Prüm und Hillesheim." Pp. 355–388 in *Hexenglaube und Hexenprozese im Raum Rhein-Mosel-Saar.* Edited by Gunther Franz and Franz Irsigler. Trier: Spee.
Löher, Hermann. 1676. *Wemütige Klage der frommen Unschültigen.* Amsterdam. Annotated edition by Thomas Becker. http://www.sfn.uni-muenchen.de/loeher (accessed October 20, 2002).
Rummel, Walter. 1991. *Bauern, Herren, und Hexen: Studien zur Sozialgeschichte sponheimischer und kurtrierischer Hexenverfolgungen.* Göttingen: Vandenhoeck and Ruprecht.
Schormann, Gerhard. 1991. *Der Krieg gegen die Hexen: Das Ausrottungsprogramm des Kurfürsten von Köln.* Göttingen: Vandenhoeck and Ruprecht.

MODENA

The prosecution of witchcraft at the northern Italian city of Modena (in Emilia) was carried out by the Inquisition, mainly in the sixteenth century, and followed the usual patterns for Mediterranean ecclesiastical tribunals. Modena's significance is simply that its inquisitorial records are better preserved than in most other Italian cities. Although significant energies were devoted to the repression of magic in all its different forms, there was little attention paid to diabolical witches, and apparently only one of them was ever executed here, in 1539. Although some key components of the cumulative concept of witchcraft (the Devil, the Sabbat) were present by the end of the fifteenth century, its prosecution remained a rare occurrence in Emilia, except for a real panic in nearby Mirandola in 1522–1523. After a long interval when the Roman Holy Office battled the spread of Protestantism, sorcery and magic reappeared among the priorities of the Modenese Inquisition toward the end of the sixteenth century. However, by this time, the Roman Holy Office had practically ruled out the prosecution of witchcraft through its cautious attitude.

An Inquisition tribunal established in Modena around the end of the thirteenth century was staffed by Dominican friars, dependents of the chief inquisitor for the duchy of Ferrara and Modena, then residing in Ferrara. Surviving trials from the Modenese branch include several early cases of magic attributed to demonic intervention, the most significant being that of Benvenuta Mangialoca, tried in 1370 for healing and divinatory magic using traditional popular remedies and the invocation of "spirits" (Biondi 1993). The court found her guilty of heretical magic, imposing relatively light spiritual penances but adding the humiliation of making her wear the special punitive robe of convicted heretics, with two yellow crosses. Her punishment characterized Inquisition policy toward illicit magic and witchcraft in the following centuries.

After a long gap (1382–1495), the Modenese Inquisition's records resume, first fragmentarily and then in almost complete form after 1517. The tribunal's activity increased under the determined leadership of Bartolomeo della Spina, author of the *Quaestio de strigibus* (An Investigation of Witches, 1523) and vicar of the Inquisition from 1518 to 1520 (Ginzburg 1990; Bertolotti 1991). A substantial number of trials from 1517 to 1520 revealed the pervasive presence of magic in everyday life and the pivotal role of the clergy in its practice. Male *stregoni* (wizards) mostly literate and middle class, figured prominently among those prosecuted for conjuring demons (generally using books of necromancy), foretelling the future, or finding hidden treasures. Female sorceresses, who were often of lower status, performed love magic and healing magic, usually derived from popular traditions.

All practitioners of magic required some consecrated objects or Catholic rituals to reinforce their spells or incantations. The Modenese clergy frequently practiced magical rituals themselves, although they were seldom prosecuted because they enjoyed widespread acceptance in the community and active support from the local Church. When, in 1517, the Inquisition tried the Cathedral exorcist, Don Guglielmo Campana, who had performed an endless series of diabolical incantations, both the bishop's vicar and the cathedral chapter mobilized in his favor, forcing the court to pronounce a favorable sentence (Duni 1999). People from very different backgrounds intersected through the practice of magic; the humanist and poet Panfilo Sassi and a sorceress from a mountain village, Anastasia la Frappona, were both tried in 1519.

In the early sixteenth century, Modenese inquisitors did not condemn magicians and sorceresses as members of a diabolical sect, but rather for overestimating the powers of Satan and therefore implicitly worshipping him through their practices. The gravest punishments were exile from Modena (up to ten years) or imprisonment (for two or three years), besides varied penances and such "shaming rituals" as standing in front of church for several Sundays wearing the garments of convicted heretics.

The relative lack of interest in witchcraft on the part of the Modenese Inquisition contrasted sharply with the treatment of convicted witches in Mirandola, a tiny city-state some 20 miles north of Modena ruled by Count Gianfrancesco Pico, where at least ten people were burned at the stake in 1522 and 1523. Although it is impossible to understand fully this dramatic event due to the total loss of trial records, it is clear that the witch hunt of Mirandola marked a turning point for the entire area. By the 1530s, the Modenese records contain increasing references to diabolical witchcraft,

an escalation culminating in 1539 with the trial of Orsolina Togni, *la Rossa* (the red one), the first Modenese witch to confess the full range of stereotypical activities (the Sabbat, sexual intercourse with the Devil, apostasy, etc.) and the only witch ever sentenced to death at Modena. The presence of diabolical elements continued in the following decades, reaching its most complete expression in 1564 with the trial of Antonia Vignola. However, witchcraft became less of a priority for the Inquisition, which devoted its energies to destroying Modena's strong and well-rooted Protestant community in the 1560s and 1570s: the number of trials for magic and witchcraft declined from almost five per year in 1517–1523 to less than one per year between 1530 and 1570 (thirty-three and thirty-eight, respectively).

In the last twenty years of the sixteenth century, when the threat of Protestantism had passed, Modena's Inquisition returned to repressing magical practices, but from a different perspective. Its inquisitors now scrutinized the entire range of popular "superstitions," from healing rituals to divinatory magic, seeing them as abuses of supernatural powers to which only the Catholic Church had legitimate access. The goal was to redirect the requests of the Modenese faithful for supernatural assistance from the sorceress and folk healer to the priest, who alone could guarantee the orthodoxy of the supernatural remedies applied. Unfortunately, some of Modena's lower clergy showed clear signs of professional inadequacy. Unlike the days of Don Campana in 1517, priests and friars were now frequently prosecuted for magic and the abuse of sacraments: there were twelve trials between 1580 and 1600 (O'Neil 1984). Increased attention was also directed to female practitioners, especially prostitutes accused of casting love spells and using "superstitious" *orazioni* or prayers (O'Neil 1987; Fantini 1999). Meanwhile, references to "diabolical" witches disappeared. Clearly connected to the changing policy of the Roman Holy Office with respect to witchcraft after the 1580s, this trend is difficult to chart with precision, especially given our fragmentary knowledge of the massive records extant for the seventeenth century, which, to date, have been almost untouched by historical investigators. But if Modena was anything at all like Siena, no maleficent witches will ever be found in its seventeenth-century inquisitorial records.

MATTEO DUNI

See also: CLERICAL MAGIC; INQUISITION, ROMAN; ITALY; POPULAR BELIEF IN WITCHES; SIENESE NEW STATE; SPINA, BARTOLOMEO DELLA.

References and further reading:

Bertolotti, Maurizio. 1991. "The Ox's Bones and the Ox's Hide: A Popular Myth, Part Hagiography and Part Witchcraft." Pp. 42–70 in *Microhistory and the Lost People of Europe. Selections* from *Quaderni Storici*. Edited by Edward Muir and Guido Ruggiero. Baltimore: Johns Hopkins University Press.

Biondi, Albano. 1982. "Lunga durata e microarticolazione nel territorio di un Ufficio dell'Inquisizione: il "Sacro Tribunale" a Modena (1292–1785). *Annali dell'Istituto storico italo-germanico in Trento* 8: 73–90.

Biondi, Grazia. 1993. *Benvenuta e l'Inquisitore: Un destino di donna nella Modena del '300*. Modena: Unione Donne Italiane.

Duni, Matteo. 1999. *Tra religione e magia: Storia del prete modenese Guglielmo Campana (1460?–1541)*. Studi e testi per la storia religiosa del Cinquecento 9. Florence: Olschki.

Fantini, Maria Pia. 1999. "Saggio per un catalogo bibliografico dai processi dell'Inquisizione: orazioni, scongiuri, libri di segreti (Modena, 1571–1608)." *Annali dell'Istituto storico italo-germanico in Trento* 25: 587–668.

Ginzburg, Carlo. 1990. "Witchcraft and Popular Piety: Notes on a Modenese Trial of 1519." Pp. 1–16 in *Myths, Emblems, Clues*. London: Hutchinson Radius.

O'Neil, Mary. 1984. "'Sacerdote ovvero strione': Ecclesiastical and Superstitious Remedies in Sixteenth-Century Italy." Pp. 53–83 in *Understanding Popular Culture: Europe from the Middle Ages to the Nineteenth Century*. Edited by Steven L. Kaplan. Berlin, New York, and Amsterdam: Mouton.

———. 1987. "Magical Healing, Love Magic, and the Inquisition in Sixteenth-Century Italy." Pp. 88–114 in *Inquisition and Society in Early Modern Europe*. Edited by Stephen Haliczer. London: Croom Helm.

Trenti, Giuseppe, ed. 2003. *I processi del tribunale dell'Inquisizione di Modena. Inventario generale analitico 1489–1784*. Modena: Aedes Muratoriana.

MOLITOR, ULRICH (1442–1508)

A jurist who served both at the episcopal court of Constance and later at the court of Sigismund, the count of Tyrol (often referred to as "Archduke Sigismund") Ulrich Molitor wrote an early treatise on witchcraft that stood as a counterpoint to the *Malleus Maleficarum* (The Hammer of Witches, 1486). Entitled variously *De Laniis et Phitonicis Mulieribus* (Concerning Witches and Fortunetellers) and *Tractatus de Pythonicis Mulieribus* (Treatise Concerning Women Who Prophesy), it first appeared in 1489 and was reprinted many times in both Latin (with *"Laniis"* changed to *"Lamiis"*) and German. Although Molitor accepted that anyone who actually made a pact with the Devil and renounced God deserved death for apostasy and idolatry, he also argued that the powers attributed to witches were illusory, emphasized the role of the Devil and the fact that his power depended ultimately on God's permission, and noted the ease with which the Devil could be resisted. Ironically, Molitor's book was the first treatise on witchcraft to be illustrated with woodcuts, which depicted as real the very activities his word denied. Born in Constance, Molitor studied at the universities of Basel and Pavia, from which he earned a degree in canon law in 1470. Returning to Constance, he served first as a notary and then as vicar in the episcopal court. In 1482, he began working at the court of Sigismund, becoming an adviser and then in 1495 or 1496 chancellor of Tyrol. In 1497, he became a procurator of the *Reichskammergericht,* the recently created imperial chamber court. In addition to his most famous work, *De Laniis,* Molitor wrote a number of legal texts and a comedy.

DE LANIIS

In 1485, the papal inquisitor Heinrich Kramer conducted an extensive investigation of witchcraft in the area around Innsbruck, the capital of the county of Tyrol. Although it ended with the acquittal of all seven suspects actually prosecuted, Kramer investigated approximately fifty people, including some from the archduke's household. Sigismund apparently remained relatively aloof from these proceedings, but was sufficiently disturbed by them that he commissioned Molitor to clarify the issues for him.

This Molitor proceeded to do in the form of a dialogue involving himself, the archduke, and another jurist named Konrad Schatz. This form was a standard scholastic device, and Molitor used it to deliver a standard Christian message. Drawing on these recent events, at almost the same time that Kramer was composing the *Malleus Maleficarum,* Molitor developed an alternative perspective deeply rooted in the *Canon Episcopi* tradition of denying the reality of most experiences attributed to witchcraft and magic while insisting on God's ultimate control over the rest. After some discussion, all three concluded that witches could not affect the weather, cause illness or impotence, change into animals, fly to the Sabbat, procreate with demons, or foretell the future. Of course, such things were possible if God permitted them; but only the Devil had this limited power, and he worked mainly through natural processes and his power to create illusions to deceive people into thinking they had magical powers. Molitor acknowledged that some people did turn from God to the Devil and asserted that a real pact deserved death for apostasy and idolatry, but he ended by noting the Devil could be easily defeated through Christian devotion.

Like the *Malleus, De Laniis* treated witchcraft as something particularly associated with women, perhaps because the great majority of suspects in the Innsbruck investigation were women, resulting from a long-standing folk tradition linking harmful magic particularly (though by no means exclusively) with women. Unlike Kramer, Molitor did not try to explain this association, noting only that women turned to the Devil because of poverty, despair, hatred, or some other temptation. He concluded by exhorting women to resist the Devil's blandishments by remembering the story of the virgin Justina, who fought off three demons with the sign of the cross.

ILLUSTRATIONS

De Laniis was the first book about witchcraft to be illustrated with woodcuts showing witches and the Devil engaged in various activities discussed in the text. Ironically, these pictures, which became models for future illustrations, depicted as real things those that Molitor's text argued were only illusions. Perhaps Molitor hoped the illustrations would draw credulous readers whose ideas would then be set straight by his words, but it seems almost certain that despite his skeptical text, the book became a wellspring of images that made witchcraft seem real, helping thereby to fix the impression that witches and their magic posed a real and potent threat to individuals and to the Christian community generally.

EDWARD BEVER

See also: ART AND VISUAL IMAGES; CANON EPISCOPI; FLIGHT OF WITCHES; GERMANY, SOUTHWESTERN; INNSBRUCK; KRAMER, HEINRICH; LAMIA; MALLEUS MALEFICARUM; PACT WITH THE DEVIL; TYROL, COUNTY OF; WEATHER MAGIC.

References and further reading:
Baroja, Julio Caro. 1964. *The World of the Witches.* Trans. O. N. V. Glendinning. Chicago: University of Chicago Press.
Broedel, Hans Peter. 2003. *The Malleus Maleficarum and the Construction of Witchcraft: Theology and Popular Belief.* Manchester, UK, and New York: Manchester University Press.
Lea, Henry Charles. 1939. *Materials Toward a History of Witchcraft.* Vol. 1. Edited by Arthur C. Howland. 3 vols. Philadelphia: University of Pennsylvania Press.
Maxwell-Stewart, P. G. 2001. *Witchcraft in Europe and the New World, 1400–1800.* New York: Palgrave.
Midelfort, H. C. Erik. 1972. *Witch Hunting in Southwestern Germany, 1562–1684: The Social and Intellectual Foundations.* Stanford: Stanford University Press.
Server Frühe Neuzeit. "Lexikon zur Geschichte der Hexenverfolgung: Ulrich Molitor." http://www.sfn.uni-muenchen.de/hexenverfolgung/frame_lexikon.html?art839.htm (January 21, 2003).

MONSTERS

Monsters are real or imagined entities that serve as a binary opposition in the process of defining what is human. Whether they are live, described, depicted, or used as figures of speech, monsters function as representations of the other face of humanity, some bestial or demonic alter ego that must be repudiated and effaced in order for the authentically human being to assert its civilized selfhood. They are ugly because they are deformed, literally "out of shape," deviating from the beauty of standardized corporeal order. Another fundamental meaning of the monster—perhaps the most important aspect for an anthropological understanding of its mythological and social significance—is its hybrid character. Monsters create confusion and horror because they appear to combine animal elements with human ones; they posit a possibility of animal origins, of bestiality. They thus represent a call to antisocial instincts and a threat of regression that the civilized self must struggle to overcome in order to maintain the precarious barrier of civilization.

Witches, beings who transgress the confines between human and nonhuman, are also a kind of monster. The monster shares a number of characteristics and functions with the witch: they both may have a connection with supernatural forces; their appearance may indicate an evil done or about to be done; they may appear in times of social crisis; their wicked origins are attested to by their telltale bodies; they may have an "unnatural" connection with animals; they may be agents of divine or diabolical retribution; they may tempt good people off their path of righteousness; a possessed person may be monstrously deformed; and they are both associated with powers of transformation, illusion, deception, and diabolic intervention. Both the witch and the monster are also categories of narrative and appear in narrative traditions in which their identity ranges freely from physical to moral qualities and back again. Finally, the categories of the monster and the witch take on negative or positive connotations over time and in different places. For example, the siren of antiquity (half-woman and half-bird or fish), symbolizing the extremely negative consequences of succumbing to the lure of feminine charms, appears today in the form of a widely merchandized mermaid, presented as a role model for little girls.

GENDER AND MONSTROSITY

Aristotle's scientific writings—authoritative texts well into the seventeenth century in Europe—established the medical precept that the cause of monsters was to be found in the struggle of the formal agent (male seed) to dominate the female matter. Depending on the strength, heat, abundance, or deficiency of the seed, its formative movement prevailed more or less efficiently over the generative secretion of the female (the menses). Because when it came to reproduction, "like should produce like," a baby that did not resemble its parents was already "a sort of monstrosity"; following this logic, the birth of a female was "a first departure" from a successful reproduction (Aristotle, *Physics* 4.767b–769b). Monstrosity was thus placed on a graduated scale of imperfection falling away from the realization of the intended perfect male form.

During its height of popularity in the early modern period, the pseudo-Aristotelian science of physiognomy, the art of reading a man's character from his physical features, further popularized the idea that, as one Italian author of the period put it: "Woman is a monster of nature, she is an imperfect man, as many Learned writers are pleased to determine, which we may deduce from all her parts" (Ghirardelli 1670, 624). Feminine qualities such as deceitfulness, vagueness, and capriciousness were thus considered monstrous signs of the naturally deformed female physiognomy.

FORM AND FUNCTION

The monster defines the limits of the human at both its "lower" and "upper" thresholds: half-animal or half-god, what is other is monstrous. A monster is "not human," then, and explicitly signals its foreign status with its body: too many limbs, or not enough, or not in the right place, or unnaturally formed. Certain characteristics of the monster are perhaps universal, but only those that describe the place it occupies in the social order and its relation to the interpretive community that defines it as such. In other words, a monster always indicates a transgression, a breakdown in hierarchy; it is quintessentially a symbol of crisis and undifferentiation. However, beyond these attributes a monster can take on any form: a baby born with birth defects, an extraordinarily talented or depraved person, a machine that moves or speaks, the state, women, peoples with different colored skin or unusual customs, an android, or an extraterrestrial.

The designation of a vulnerable member of the community as an agent of the sacred or the diabolical can provide an effective way to identify and contain the forces of evil or misfortune that could contaminate the entire community. Ritual slaying or ostracism of the dangerous element in the form of a sacrificial victim can act as a safety valve to tension that could otherwise erupt into destructive violence. From this perspective, both the monster and the witch have been viewed as scapegoats and their histories analyzed according to the scapegoat mechanism.

In addition to its mythological and poetic representations, the monster has appeared textually in the form of omens in prodigy books (Paré 1982), as a sign to be interpreted in the divination arts (Cicero, *De Divinatione*), as proof of the marvelous creativity of nature or God (Pliny, *Natural History Libri VII;* St. Augustine, *City of God*), as an object of scientific curiosity in the Aristotelian tradition, as illustrative figures in moralizing emblem books (Alciati 1985), and as a rhetorical figure or concept (Hobbes, *Leviathan*).

HISTORY OF THE MONSTER

In ancient times, the appearance of a monster, as an event happening outside the ordinary course of nature, was interpreted as an indication of divine will. *Monstrum* and *teratos,* the Latin and Greek roots of *monster,* did not signify a deformed being, but fell in the same category as other terms belonging to the divinatory sciences, only migrating later through association to the natural sciences. A *monstrum* (from *monere,* to warn or threaten) was by definition a terrible prodigy, not for what it was—a piteously deformed infant destined to die quickly by natural causes or by ritual sacrifice—but for what it foretold as a sign of coming calamity. How that sign was interpreted was purely a matter of historical context. For example, the ancient Chaldeans assigned one-to-one correspondences between limbs and exact events,

either auspicious or ominous portents: an extra finger meant abundant crops and so forth. The appearance of a monster thus presupposed an interpretive community, a social order to which it was addressed, and a priestly caste charged with deciphering its precise significance.

More recent "readings" of monstrous bodies, in addition to predicting political changes or calamitous wars, had precise propagandistic purposes. Martin Luther, for example, made great use of a famous monster baptized the *Mönchskalb* (the monk-calf), whose image appeared in numerous pamphlets as an emblem of Catholic depravity. Interpretation of monsters in the Renaissance was nothing less than an alternative political science, more popular and contemporary in nature than the erudite fare of princely counselors like Niccolò Machiavelli.

Monstrous births continued to inspire pious terror well into the modern period. In 1543 in Avignon, we are told, King Francis I ordered a woman to be burned along with her dog because she had given birth to an infant with canine features. The woman eventually confessed to having had intercourse with the dog; her monstrous progeny was thus interpreted as a sign of her wickedness and a divine punishment for her unnatural desires. As late as 1825, in Sicily, a baby girl born without a brain provoked such terror that those attending the birth threw her down a deep, dry well. She was saved only by order of the mayor (Taruffi 1881, 1:7:11).

Fear of monstrous births was also inspired by their supposed connection with demons, who were said to be responsible for parenting monsters through various techniques of "artificial insemination." In demonology texts, such as Francesco-Maria Guazzo's *Compendium Maleficarum* (A Summary of Witches) of 1608, demons and monsters were also linked by an obvious and relatively unproblematic correlation between moral depravity and corporeal deformation: the demon assumes a monstrous appearance; or to be more precise, demons *are* monsters, and monsters *are* demons. This association between evil and ugliness is widespread and deeply ingrained in the Platonic/Judeo-Christian tradition in which, conversely, truth and goodness are equated with beauty.

During the early modern period, monsters gradually lost their terrifying association with the forces of the sacred and became objects of wonder or curiosity to be put on exhibition in public squares and museums. Famous freaks of this period who traveled around Europe to show themselves included the double-bodied Lazarus and his brother Baptista who grew out of his side, and the giant Giovanni Bona. Stuffed animals made out of various animal parts pieced and sewn together to represent fantastic creatures such as hydras, basilisks, and dragons were sold by charlatans and were

David Ryckaert III (1612–1661), The Witch, *shows a Dutch witch battling and sending off monsters and demons in hell. The zoomorphic monsters remind us of their bestiality and opposition to humans. (Erich Lessing/Art Resource)*

in great demand. Scientific collections called "cabinets of curiosity" often contained specimens of monstrous animals or deformed human fetuses and even extended to live specimens such as the dwarves Sebastiano and Angelica Biavati, who lived their whole lives in a museum in Bologna on a permanent salary.

ZAKIYA HANAFI

See also: ANIMALS; CIRCE; DEMONOLOGY; DEMONS; DIVINATION; GENDER; GUAZZO, FRANCESCO MARIA; INFANTICIDE; LYCANTHROPY; MEDICINE AND MEDICAL THEORY; METAMORPHOSIS; PRODIGIES; SCAPEGOATS.

References and further reading:

Alciati, Andrea. 1985. *Emblems in Translation.* Edited by Peter Daly. 2 vols. Toronto: University of Toronto Press.

Findlen, Paula. 1994. *Possessing Nature: Museums, Collecting, and Scientific Culture in Early Modern Italy.* Berkeley and Los Angeles: University of California Press.

Ghirardelli, Cornelio. 1670. *Cefalogia fisonomica.* Bologna: Presso gli Heredi di Evangelista Dozza e Compagni.

Girard, René. 1977. *Violence and the Sacred.* Translated by Patrick Gregory. Baltimore and London: Johns Hopkins University Press.

Hanafi, Zakiya. 2000. *The Monster in the Machine: Magic, Medicine, and the Marvelous in the Time of the Scientific Revolution.* Durham, NC, and London: Duke University Press.

Impey, Oliver, and Arthur Macgregor, eds. 1985. *The Origins of Museums: The Cabinet of Curiosities in Sixteenth- and Seventeenth-Century Europe.* Oxford: Clarendon.

Niccoli, Ottavia. 1990. *Prophecy and People in Renaissance Italy.* Translated by Lydia G. Cochrane. Princeton, NJ: Princeton University Press.

Paré, Ambroise. 1982. *On Monsters and Marvels.* Translated by Janis L. Pallister. Chicago and London: University of Chicago Press.

Park, Katherine, and Lorraine Daston. 1982. "Unnatural Conceptions: The Study of Monsters in France and England." *Past and Present* 92: 20–54.

Taruffi, Cesare. 1881. *Storia della Teratologia.* Bologna: Regia Tipografia.

MONTAIGNE, MICHEL DE (1533–1592)

The best-known French author and thinker of the sixteenth century, Michel de Montaigne's collection of personal reflections, the *Essays,* was popular in his lifetime and has undergone hundreds of editions and translations.

His *Essays* continue to be read today, and scholarly interest in their author—including his famous digression ridiculing belief in witchcraft—remains high.

Montaigne's family came from the Bordeaux region; they were wealthy and well connected. He was a relative of two writers on demonology, Pierre de Lancre, and (through his Spanish Marrano mother) Martín Del Rio. Educated in classical humanism, Montaigne became a judge at the *Parlement* (sovereign judicial court) of Bordeaux in 1557. He served until 1570, when he sold his position to Florimond de Raemond and retired to his country estate, seeking tranquility in order to reflect and write during a time of brutal civil war. His early retirement was frequently interrupted by politics and military ventures as well as by two terms as mayor of Bordeaux, making him a participant in as well as an observer of the events of his turbulent age.

Based on a firm belief in the unknowability of God's intentions and his readings of the classics, he adopted a position of skepticism, summed up in his famous rhetorical question, "Que sçay-je?" (What do I know?). He attempted to avoid the extreme positions of his day because their adherents claimed true knowledge. Because humans could not know the mind of God, Montaigne argued that they should follow the religion of their country. Montaigne primarily blamed the Protestants for the chaotic civil war that raged for thirty-five years, but he also criticized Catholic zealots who similarly mistook their extreme opinions for facts. Montaigne was an early example of the Gallican Catholic *politique,* holding that it was unjustified to label dissidents as heretics and to kill people for such disagreements. This position, which ultimately prevailed under King Henry IV, was attractive to many of his contemporaries (and to modern readers) but aroused bitter hatred from zealous Catholics.

In his writing, Montaigne touched frequently on popular credulity. His essay, "On the Lame" (1588), addressed the belief in witchcraft and the penalties meted out to convicted witches. Montaigne revealed his basic skepticism toward the supernatural, stating, "All miracles and strange happenings hide away when I am about." He mocked the works of demonologists. "My local witches go in risk of their lives, depending on the testimony of each new authority who comes and gives substance to their delusions." He then told about observing and conversing with a group of old women who had been convicted of witchcraft, through the courtesy of an unnamed prince who wanted to overcome his distinguished visitor's skepticism. (In this context, he never mentioned his experience as a judge in the *Parlement* of Bordeaux, because witchcraft cases were unheard of there in the 1560s.) Montaigne concluded, "In the end, and in all honesty, I would have prescribed not hemlock for them but hellebore. 'Their case seemed to be more a matter of insane minds than

of criminal behavior.' [quoting Titus Livy] . . . After all, it is putting a very high value on your opinions to roast a man alive because of them" (Montaigne 1991, 1166–1169).

Montaigne's opinions on witchcraft inevitably caused controversy, because belief in the power of the Devil and witches was an important part of the fight against Protestant heresy. The position that witchcraft was only a fantasy of old women was attributed to Montaigne (sometimes coupled with such heretics as Johann Weyer) and was mentioned many times in demonological writings as a particularly dangerous idea that gave impunity to witches. Martín Del Rio, the most authoritative orthodox Catholic demonologist, sharply criticized Montaigne's views, calling him an unbeliever who endangered the fight against the Devil through his opinions.

Pierre de Lancre, despite his admiration for Del Rio, defended his distant kinsman Montaigne against Del Rio's criticisms, stating that Montaigne "did not present this proposition as true . . . no more than his other opinions. . . . leaving all things in doubt, where it seemed bold to decide them absolutely" (Lancre 1622, 339). Nevertheless, family honor aside, de Lancre was concerned that judges might let such views deter them from their responsibility to punish witches.

Montaigne lived and died as a Catholic. He traveled to Italy, where he visited the shrine at Loretto, met with Juan Maldonado, and had an audience with the pope. He was also careful to submit his work to papal censors. He died long before the religious wars ended and did not see Henry IV's triumph.

JONATHAN L. PEARL

See also: DEL RIO, MARTÍN; FRANCE; LANCRE, PIERRE DE; MALDONADO, JUAN; MIRACLES; SKEPTICISM; WARS OF RELIGION (FRANCE); WEYER, JOHANN.

References and further reading:
Lancre, Pierre de. 1622. *L'incredulité et mescréance du sortilege.* Paris.
Montaigne, Michel de. 1991. *The Essays of Michel de Montaigne.* Edited and translated by M. A. Screech. London: Penguin.

MONTER, WILLIAM (1936–)

Professor emeritus of early modern European history at Northwestern University in Illinois, where he taught from 1963 to 2002, Monter has exercised considerable influence on a generation of witchcraft research.

After completing a dissertation on Geneva, Monter became interested in witchcraft research during the Vietnam-protest era, while reading both Carlo Ginzburg's and Hugh Trevor-Roper's utterly contradictory accounts of it in 1967. By 1969, Monter published a collection of essays and sources titled *European Witchcraft.* Three years later, following Erik Midelfort's example, he provided a historiographical survey, dividing witchcraft into three major currents: rationalist, romantic, and social scientific. An active witness to the "ongoing renaissance in the historiography of European witchcraft" (Monter 1976, 9), Monter contributed one of the most important early comparative studies on a region labeled as "the borderlands during the Reformation," including Calvin's Geneva. Unlike Alan Macfarlane or Midelfort, Monter emphasized the importance of popular belief, and, unlike Keith Thomas, Monter's study paid close attention to regional differences between such territories as the Franche-Comté and the Swiss Canton of Fribourg (both Catholic) on the one hand, and Geneva and Bern (both Reformed) and Montbéliard (Lutheran) on the other. Monter succeeded in destroying stereotypes about uniform patterns of persecution or of patterns depending on the form of religion. Furthermore, he insisted on putting his results into a European perspective.

Two recurrent themes in his publications deserve comment: that the "witchcraft of the Germanic core of the Holy Roman Empire" could be taken as "normative" (Monter 1976, 191; Monter 2002) and that Geneva's Calvinists took a relatively moderate approach toward witchcraft (Monter 1976, 42–66). However, the Holy Roman Empire contained large territories with no executions of witches during the early modern period. Moreover, Geneva was located near the center of the Romance-speaking areas where the cumulative crime of witchcraft first emerged. The sixteenth-century urban republic was an angst-ridden society, driven by fears of plague-spreaders and witches; its "gentle Calvinists" killed more witches within their narrow confines than all popes in Rome together, or Luther's princes in Saxony, or most European towns.

Monter's publications are among the most illuminating on witchcraft and related subjects. His well-written survey *Ritual, Myth and Magic in Early Modern Europe* (1983) provided insights into the cultural fabric of different strands of Catholicism, Protestantism, and Judaism in all parts of Europe and their overseas colonies. It drew on recent research in all major European languages, and by treating witchcraft as one of many subjects, put it in perspective. In contrast to anthropologically oriented historians, Monter always emphasized the importance of "culture," popular as well as religious or intellectual. In numerous essays, he drew attention to the significance of such subjects as sodomy, child witches (1993), or male witchcraft (1997), with predominance in places like Normandy or the Alpine regions that can hardly be explained socially. Subsequently, he explored the group dynamics of a possessed Lorraine village with a parish priest who was a future saint, proposing it as a Catholic counterpart to Puritan Salem (Monter forthcoming).

Viewed as a whole, his publications combined the rational, romantic, and social-scientific approaches to witchcraft that he long ago identified in the historiography of witch hunting. Monter served on the editorial board of the *Encyclopedia of Witchcraft: The Western Tradition.*

WOLFGANG BEHRINGER

See also: HISTORIOGRAPHY.

References and further reading:

Monter, E. William. 1967. *Calvin's Geneva.* New York: John Wiley.
———, ed. 1969. *European Witchcraft.* New York: John Wiley.
———. 1972. "The Historiography of European Witchcraft: Progress and Prospects." *Journal of Interdisciplinary History* 2: 435–451.
———. 1976. *Witchcraft in France and Switzerland: The Borderlands During the Reformation.* Ithaca, NY, and London: Cornell University Press.
———. 1983. *Ritual, Myth, and Magic in Early Modern Europe.* Athens, OH: Ohio University Press.
———. 1987. *Enforcing Morality in Early Modern Europe.* London: Variorum Reprints.
———. 1988. "European Witchcraft: A Moment of Synthesis?" *The Historical Journal* 31: 183–185.
———. 1990. *Frontiers of Heresy: The Spanish Inquisition from the Basque Lands to Sicily.* New York: Cambridge University Press.
———. 1993. "Les enfants au sabbat: Bilan provisoire," Pp. 383–388 in *Le sabbat des sorciers en Europe, XVe-XVIIIe siècles. Colloque international E. N. S. Fontenay-Saint-Cloud, 4–7 novembre 1992.* Edited by Nicole Jacques-Chaquin and Maxime Préaud. Grenoble: Millon.
———. 1997. "Toads and Eucharists: The Male Witches of Normandy, 1564–1660." *French Historical Studies* 20: 563–595.
———. 1999. *Judging the French Reformation: Heresy Trials by Sixteenth-Century Parlements.* Cambridge, MA: Harvard University Press.
———. 2002. "Witch Trials in Continental Europe, 1560–1660." Pp. 1–52 in *The Period of Witch Trials.* Vol. 4 of *The Athlone History of Witchcraft and Magic in Europe.* Edited by Bengt Ankarloo and Stuart Clark. London and Philadelphia: Athlone and University of Pennsylvania Press.
———. Forthcoming. "The Catholic Salem: Mattaincourt." In *Witchcraft in Context.* Edited by Wolfgang Behringer and James Sharpe. Manchester, UK: Manchester University Press.

MOON

The moon has occupied a pivotal role in myth, religion, and magic, assuming a divine or at least anthropomorphic nature (sometimes male, sometimes female) in the majority of belief systems since prehistoric times. As a measurement of time, the moon and its cycles designated the various phases in the agricultural calendar as well as indicated appropriate times for the gathering of marine produce and sailing the seas. As a celestial force endowed with personality or divinity and associated with time, the moon and its movements were naturally regarded as exerting an influence on humans and their destinies, occupying a central position in the astrological system.

In terms of witchcraft and the occult, the moon has a revered and powerful function in the practice of

The moon presides over a witches' dance (from an eighteenth-century chapbook). The moon has been linked to witchcraft since antiquity. Meetings and activities were most effective when coordinated with the phases of the moon, especially a full moon as shown in this illustration. (Bettmann/Corbis)

magic. In ancient Greece, witches regularly invoked Selene, goddess of the moon, in their rites and incantations, often calling on her to assist their work by either shedding or concealing its light. Later in her myth cycle, Hecate also became associated with the moon. In both Greek and Roman literature, witches such as Medea were described as working with the moon, and the practice of drawing down the moon was a renowned art of Thessalian witches in particular. This magical art was sometimes presented in literature as the means to assist in the performance of rituals that required secrecy and, therefore, darkness. An alternative motivation for the act was presented in

the *Pharsalia* (6.505–6.506) by the Latin author Lucan (C.E. 39–65) who referred to a lunar fluid, emitted by the descending moon, that coated earthly foliage, endowing it with miraculous properties. In a similar vein, the ancients believed in the magical properties of stones from the moon, which were worn for a variety of purposes, including as amulets, and sold by magicians. Pliny, in his *Natural History* (37.164), also mentioned *glossopetra,* which fell from the sky during the waning of the moon and was used by "moon-diviners."

In early modern Europe, the moon continued to be regarded as a central part of a variety of forms of occult practice. The idea of drawing down the moon continued as a belief as illustrated in the speech of Hecate in Shakespeare's *Macbeth* (Act 3, Scene 5). In alchemy, the moon was a major cosmic force, representing the metal silver and the feminine principle as well as being an astrological influence that required acknowledgement in particular operations; by working under a waxing moon, for example, one obtained purer metals. In folk magic, the moon and its phases marked propitious times for the working of spells and similar endeavors such as summoning fairies or other supernatural beings. The links between the moon and witchcraft also continued, with consistent references in the literature of the persecution era to Satanism, its practitioners (and victims), and the lunar cycles. The *Malleus Maleficarum* (The Hammer of Witches, 1486) stated that devils, who could only operate through the medium of natural forces, "molest men at certain phases of the moon" (1:5). It regarded men who were vulnerable to such situations as lunatics, thereby reflecting the age-old folktale tradition of lunar-inspired madness. Such thinking was closely aligned with the belief in lycanthropy, a state of transformation often regarded as being determined by certain phases of the moon. Witches were believed to meet at times designated by the cycles of the moon, the full moon being an especially favorable time for gatherings. This association between the witch and the moon was particularly strong in the artwork of the persecution era (and beyond), with consistent images of a full or crescent moon watching over the predominantly female figures and their activities. In a Victorian magical text, Charles Leland's *Arcadia: Gospel of the Witches* (1889), the author wrote of witches gathering once a month "'when the moon is full" to worship the goddess Diana in a passage that clearly drew from ancient beliefs concerning the moon and one of its principal deities.

MARGUERITE JOHNSON

See also: ASTROLOGY; DIANA (ARTEMIS); DIVINATION; HECATE; LYCANTHROPY; *MALLEUS MALEFICARUM;* MENTAL ILLNESS.

References and further reading:
Barton, Tamsyn. 1994. *Ancient Astrology.* London: Routledge.
Flint, Valerie, Richard Gordon, Georg Luck, and Daniel Ogden. 1999. In *Ancient Greece and Rome.* Vol. 2 of *The Athlone History of Witchcraft and Magic in Europe.* Edited by Bengt Ankarloo and Stuart Clark. London and Philadelphia: Athlone and University of Pennsylvania Press.

MORA WITCHES

The large village of Mora was the first center of Sweden's great witch hunt of 1668–1676. Because the earliest and until recently the most widespread source of information about the entire affair was an account written by Mora's vicar, Elaus Skragge, his parish became the Swedish equivalent of Salem. Skragge's account, which covered the August 1669 hearings into suspected cases of witchcraft in the parishes of Älvdalen and Mora by the Witchcraft Commission, was translated into Dutch as early as 1670. It was published in German the same year; by the turn of the eighteenth century it had appeared in several editions, including English and French translations. There was a link to North America, where Cotton Mather was well aware of the Swedish witch hunt when discussing the possessed children of Salem (*Discourse on Witchcraft,* 1689; *The Wonders of the Invisible World,* 1693).

The early translations of Skragge's account have given rise to a greatly exaggerated view of the Blåkulla trials, due to misunderstandings and incorrect translations of the original text, which have influenced even relatively modern studies (e.g., Robbins 1959, 348). The first Dutch translation stated, with no support in the original, that eighty-four adults and fifteen children were put to death.

Skragge's account belonged to the initial phase of Sweden's great witch hunt, which afflicted Dalarna from 1668 to 1671. Official hearings began in Dalarna in the summer of 1668, when an eleven-year-old girl called Gertrud Svensdotter, who lived in the village of Åsen in the parish of Älvdalen, disclosed strange and terrible tales of widespread consorting with the Devil. Based on testimonies principally given by children, the local court passed eighteen death sentences, which were in due course referred to Svea High Court in Stockholm. In March 1669, it ratified seven death sentences, those passed on adults who had confessed their guilt, including two seventeen-year-old maidservants. Those whose death sentences were revoked included four children (Ankarloo 1990, 295). The death sentence was not usually passed on children under fifteen years of age, the only notable exception occurring in Stockholm in 1676, when the witch hunt finally came to an end. There a thirteen-year-old boy called Johan Grijs was executed because his perjury had caused a number of people to be sentenced to death.

From Älvdalen, rumors of witchcraft quickly spread to the neighboring parish of Mora. The increasing disquiet in the region resulted in a government decision to appoint a Witchcraft Commission, which held hearings in Mora in August 1669, presided over by Councillor Lorentz Creutz. The local community demanded the establishment of special courts of law. The Witchcraft Commission passed the death penalty only on those who had confessed (a prerequisite that was later abandoned at the culmination of the great witch hunt) and who proved to have had prolonged dealings with the Devil. This latter criterion enabled younger witches (for instance, two women in their twenties) to escape the death penalty. The hearings of the Witchcraft Commission lasted only a few days. The commission interrogated a total of sixty suspects in addition to an even larger number of children

(Ankarloo 1990, 295). In view of the large number of confessions that resulted, one suspects that torture was employed. The execution of those who had confessed took place on August 25, two days after the commission had departed from Mora. Of the twenty-three who had been condemned to death, fifteen were beheaded and then burned at the stake in Mora. Six others were executed in Älvdalen at the same time (Ankarloo 1990, 295). Hopes that the authorities would now take control of the situation proved to be in vain. The abduction of children to Blåkulla spread like wildfire, and other parishes requested government help to deal with the situation. Another Witchcraft Commission was appointed in 1671. A further fifteen people were executed (Ankarloo 1990, 296). That finally brought the witch hunt in Dalarna to an end, but in the rest of Sweden, the panic was only just beginning.

Julio Caro Baroja noted that one aspect of Elaus Skragge's account regarding the Blåkulla tales was unique in European tales of witches: namely, Satan's death and resurrection (Caro Baroja, 1965, 207ff.). The narrator of this occurrence was the afore mentioned Gertrud Svensdotter. The record of the proceedings described her tale in great detail because it contravened accepted theological doctrine. Anders Nohr Moraeus,

Witchcraft at Mora, Sweden, including the flight of witches to Blåkulla, child witches, sex with the Devil, and the execution of witches. (Anonymous, Sabbat der Hexen von Mora, 1739–1745. Directmedia Publishing GmbH: Berlin, 2003)

the cleric present at the hearing, therefore instructed the girl about the nature of God and explained how the Almighty does not change, become ill, die, or the like. The girl had described how Satan fell ill at Blåkulla and had lain on a bed in the banqueting hall, grunting, groaning, and appearing to be so ill that his guests had wept and mourned for him. Despite the efforts of one of the most experienced witches to cure him with liniments and cupping, he continued to lose strength. Finally, he was led out to another chamber, but a ghostlike image of him remained in the bed, as though it was his dead body. At this point, Satan's son-in-law entered the room together with his wife and two of his daughters, and with tears and weeping they carried him out, as though to be buried. However, Satan suddenly regained life; rushing back into the room, he danced around with one of the young witches in his arms to the delight of the guests.

This tale has been interpreted as a misunderstanding of the biblical theme of Jesus's death and resurrection. The mention of Satan's son-in-law is of particular interest. At the beginning of the witch hunt, a number of references described Satan with a wife and children. In Älvdalen, these clearly referred to the vicar's own family. At one point, Satan was referred to as "Lasse," a nickname for the vicar, Lars Elvius. In the section of the records referring to Satan's death and resurrection, the names of Satan's two daughters, Sara and Margeta, were crossed out, but they were in fact the names of two of the vicar's daughters.

Elaus Skragge's report of Gertrud Svensdotter's confession did not tell the entire story. The background to the Blåkulla trials took place in 1667, when Gertrud, then eleven years old, was herding goats together with a slightly younger boy on the banks of the river Österdalälven, near the village of Åsen. The children fought over a chunk of bread, and the boy, who came out the worst in the tussle, told the tale to his father so dramatically that before long the vicar, Lars Elvius, came to hear of it. The boy claimed that while the children were fighting, some of the goats had strayed out to an islet in the river, and Gertrud had fetched the goats by walking out on the water to the little island. In September 1668, the court concluded that Gertrud's walking on water was the first substantial indication of what turned out to be widespread witchcraft. It could equally well have become a miracle, but the record called it the work of the Devil. Satan had oiled the girl's feet so that she could wade out across the current without touching the riverbed.

In another episode from the girl's story, Satan showed Gertrud and the other witches "the whole world." In spite of the fact that they had calves to ride on, most of the journey was made by boat. During the boat trip, Satan instructed the youngest members of the party, including Gertrud, to keep the calves calm by scratching them on their necks while Satan himself rowed the boat with mighty strokes of the oars. During the boat ride, they noticed a man who stood and scooped salt from the water onto the shore. Satan and the witches took a supply of salt with them before proceeding onward. After some days, they reached the shore, from whence they flew onward, passing towns, villages, and churches. On their return, Satan confiscated all the salt, so the only thing that Gertrude and the others had to show from their long journey was exhaustion. Toward the end of the nineteenth century, at the time of a religious revival, stories of Blåkulla were heard again in the province of Dalarna. This time, however, the destination was called Josefsdal, an adaptation of the biblical valley of Jehosaphat, *Josafats dal* (*dal* means valley).

PER SÖRLIN

See also: ANGELS; BLÅKULLA; CARO BAROJA, JULIO; CHILDREN; CONFESSIONS; DEVIL; MATHER, COTTON; PANICS; ROBBINS; ROSSELL HOPE; SALEM; SWEDEN.

References and further reading:
Ankarloo, Bengt. 1990. "Sweden: The Mass Burnings (1668–1676)." Pp 285–317 in *Early Modern European Witchcraft: Centres and Peripheries*. Edited by Bengt Ankarloo and Gustav Henningsen. Oxford: Clarendon.
Caro Baroja, Julio. 1965. *The World of the Witches*. English translation. Chicago: University of Chicago Press.
Lagerlöf-Génetay, Birgitta. 1990. *De svenska häxprocessernas utbrottsskede 1668–1671: Bakgrund i Övre Dalarna. Social och ecklesiastik kontext*. Stockholm: Almqvist and Wiksell International. Summary in English.
Lennersand, Marie. 1997. "Androm till sky och skräck: Den rättsliga behandlingen av trolldomsprocesserna i Älvdalen och Mora 1668–1669." Pp 23–44 in *Vägen till Blåkulla: Nya perspektiv på de stora svenska häxprocesserna*. Edited by Linda Oja. Uppsala: Department of History, Uppsala University. Summary in English.
Monter, E. William. 1990. "Scandinavian Witchcraft in Anglo-American Perspective." Pp. 424–434 in *Early Modern European Witchcraft: Centres and Peripheries*. Edited by Bengt Ankarloo and Gustav Henningsen. Oxford: Clarendon.
Robbins, Rossell Hope. 1959. *The Encyclopedia of Witchcraft and Demonology*. New York: Crown.
Skragge, Elaus. 1683. *An Account of what happened in Sweden*. Translated by E. Horneck. In *Sadducismus Triumphtus*. By Joseph Glanvill. London, 1683.
Sörlin, Per. 1997. "The Blåkulla Story: Absurdity and Rationality." *Arv. Nordic Yearbook of Folklore* 53: 131–152.
Tegler, Kristina. 1997. "Till Blåkulla med kropp och själ: Schamanistiska föreställningar i svenska trolldomsprocesser." Pp 47–74 in *Vägen till Blåkulla: Nya perspektiv på de stora svenska häxprocesserna*. Edited by Linda Oja. Uppsala: Department of History, Uppsala University. Summary in English.
Wall, Jan. 1987. "Resorna till Josefsdal." *Svenska landsmål och svenskt folkliv* 110: 99–120. Summary in English.

MORAVIA

Witchcraft persecution in Moravia in the late Middle Ages and the early modern centuries has not been systematically researched, except for the northern Moravian witchcraft trials of 1678–1696. At present, the total number of known victims of the witch hunt in Moravia (including the northern Moravian witchcraft trials) was roughly 300 people, most of whom were executed. Considering the substantial losses of source material, especially records of town criminal courts before 1620, the real total was considerably higher.

Today part of the Czech Republic, Moravia (Morava) in the ninth and early tenth centuries was the center of the vast empire of Greater Moravia, which included Bohemia, Silesia, Slovakia, southern Poland, and northern Hungary. Later, Moravia became a margravinate in the Holy Roman Empire under the suzerainty of the princes and then kings of Bohemia.

Moravia's laws and juridical system in the medieval and early modern periods closely resembled those of Bohemia. Criminal courts in over 200 Moravian royal and patrimonial towns tried most of the region's witches until the battle of the White Mountain in 1620. Afterward, patrimonial courts took a more active part in prosecuting sorcery in Moravia alongside the town courts. The Land court, the only one with authority over all of Moravia, almost never heard any cases of sorcery. The Court of Appeal in Prague only established its authority to approve all death sentences from Moravian town and patrimonial courts in 1700. Like Bohemia, Moravia's first detailed legal regulation for the offense of witchcraft (sorcery) came only with the Josephina, the criminal code of Emperor Joseph I for Bohemia, Moravia, and Silesia, decreed in 1707, a time when witchcraft trials had almost ended in Bohemian crown lands.

Unlike Bohemia, Moravia lacks information about the activities of its fourteenth-century papal inquisitors. Moravia's most notorious inquisitor was certainly Heinrich Kramer (Institoris), author of the *Malleus Maleficarum* (The Hammer of Witches, 1486), who was named papal inquisitor to Moravia and Bohemia in 1500 by Pope Alexander VI at the instigation of the bishop of Olomouc, Stanislav Thurzo. Kramer settled in Olomouc, which boasted an important Dominican monastery, until 1505. He made no attempt to conduct witchcraft trials in Moravia; his task was rather to eradicate various Czech heresies. In April 1501, he published two tracts at Olomouc against them, but never began any inquisitorial trials against heretics in Moravia or Bohemia; his five years there were devoted to public disputes and literary polemics.

Inquisitorial procedure had long been known in Moravia, but as late as the first half of the seventeenth century it was used only by town courts in prosecuting capital crimes and then only in some southern Moravian towns owned by the capital city of Brno. Until the outbreak of the northern Moravian witch hunt in 1678, the offense of witchcraft meant simply *maleficium* (harmful magic)—mostly poisoning people or cattle, causing illness or damage to property, and sometimes administering love charms. There was no diabolism, no apostasy, and no participation in witches' Sabbats. Moravia's first known trial for harmful sorcery occurred around 1350 at Brno: the accused women were required to swear a purification oath. Sporadic trials against performers of harmful magic dotted the final quarter of the fifteenth century. Moravia's first known execution for this crime occurred in 1494 (four years before the first such instance in Bohemia) at the southern town of Uherské Hradiště, where a woman was sentenced to death for harmful sorcery, in addition to other crimes.

Only sparse information survives about Moravian witchcraft trials during the first half of the sixteenth century. Trials and executions increased gradually after mid-century. Before 1620, they were individual affairs, with one outstanding exception: the series of witchcraft trials from 1571–1576 in the patrimonial town of Velká Bíteš in southwestern Moravia, where at least twenty-two women were executed (fifteen of them in 1576) for harmful witchcraft, mainly poisoning humans or cattle or magically stealing milk. After 1620, Moravian witchcraft trials still usually remained individual affairs, even when mass witchcraft trials took place after 1651 in the neighboring principality of Neisse in Silesia, claiming hundreds of victims.

The single dramatic exception—by far the largest mass persecution of witches in Moravian history—was the northern Moravian witchcraft trials, which lasted from 1678 to 1696. They began at Easter 1678 in the lordship of Velké Losiny, after someone profaned the consecrated Eucharistic wafers, attempting to use them to perform magical spells. The guardian of Velké Losiny, Anna Sibyla (countess of Galle), called in a lawyer with vast experience in the field of witchcraft trials, Heinrich Franz Boblig (1612–1698), from the Moravian capital at Olomouc. Boblig came from a patrician family of Edelstadt; his father had been ennobled and served as mayor of the rich mining town of Zuckmantel in Silesia. He never completed his law studies (probably at Vienna University) and lacked a doctor's degree. By 1638, Boblig had become a judge in the Silesian principality of Neisse; his career culminated during the mass witchcraft trials, which took place there in 1651–1652. Sometime later, he moved to Olomouc. He came to Velké Losiny in September 1678 as chairman of the newly established special patrimonial court, charged with finding its alleged witches.

The first executions took place at Velké Losiny in August 1679. That same month, Boblig succeeded in becoming head of another newly established special patrimonial court of justice in the rich town of Šumperk (German Mährisch Schönberg), owned by a great Moravian and Silesian aristocrat, Prince Karl Eusebius of Lichtenstein. The dean of Šumperk, Christoph Alois Lautner (1622–1685), opposed the proceedings of this special patrimonial court (among the first people accused were Lautner's housekeeper and the wife of his friend, the former mayor Kaspar Sattler).

Lautner came from a rather poor family in Šumperk; his father had been a soldier during the Thirty Years' War. Lautner studied theology at Landshut in Bavaria, then philosophy and law at the University of Vienna, and theology again at the University of Graz (Styria). He was ordained a priest at Olomouc in 1656, where he remained as a chaplain before becoming a village priest at Dolní Moravice by Rýmařov in northern Moravia (1658–1663), then a dean in the Silesian town of Osoblaha (1663–1668), and finally dean of his native Šumperk. Lautner was an extraordinarily well-read priest. His rich library reflected his various interests; unlike Boblig, he even owned and read the *Malleus Maleficarum*. Boblig recognized a dangerous opponent in Lautner and soon charged him with witchcraft. Consequently, Lautner was arrested in August 1680 with the approval of the bishop of Olomouc, Karl II of Lichtenstein. The bishop immediately created a special commission ("committee of justice") for the purpose of investigating witchcraft charges against Lautner and some other clergymen from his diocese: it contained four men, including Boblig. Lautner remained imprisoned for five years.

Meanwhile, Boblig's tribunals in Velké Losiny and Šumperk passed death sentences and executed several dozen persons, mainly women. Lautner's housekeeper Susanna and Maria (the wife of Kaspar Sattler) were executed for witchcraft in December 1682. Sattler was put to death for the same offense, together with his daughter Elisabeth in August 1683. Dean Lautner was first interrogated in August 1680, and his examination was repeated many times. The bishop of Olomouc approved his torture in June 1684. After numerous postponements and delays, Lautner was condemned by the episcopal "committee of justice" in September 1685 to be defrocked and then burned at the stake. After the bishop of Olomouc approved this sentence, Lautner was burned on September 18, 1685, in the bishop's patrimonial town of Müglitz, in the presence of an enormous crowd. In all probability, Lautner was the only Catholic priest ever executed in Moravia or Bohemia for the offense of witchcraft. Boblig's witchcraft trials continued after Lautner's execution, lasting until 1696, but with less intensity. Overall, roughly 100 people (mainly women) died during these northern Moravia witch hunts, including 48 people from Šumperk (27 women and 21 men).

We do not know when the last death sentence for witchcraft was carried out in Moravia; it probably happened during the first half of the eighteenth century.

PETR KREUZ;

TRANSLATED BY VLADIMIR CINKE

See also: BOHEMIA; HOLY ROMAN EMPIRE; INQUISITORIAL PROCEDURE; KRAMER, HEINRICH; *MALEFICIUM*; ŚINDELÁŘ, BEDŘICH; TRIALS.

References and further reading:

Verbík, Antonín, and Ivan Štarha, eds. 1973. *Smolná kniha velkobíteśská 1556–1636* Brno: Blok.

Kočí, Josef. 1973. *Čarodějnické procesy: Z dějin inkvizice a čarodějnických procesu v českých zemích v 16.–18. století.* Prague: Horizont.

Kubíček, Antonín. 1902. "Jindřich Institoris, papežský inkvizitor v Čechách a na Moravě." *Časopis katolického duchovenstva* 63, 20–26, 115–120, 222–226, 320–325, 372–378, 491–500, 521–525.

Lambrecht, Karen. 1995. *Hexenverfolgung und Zaubereiprozesse in den schleslichen Territorien.* Cologne, Weimar, and Vienna: Böhlau.

Macek, Josef. 1999. *Jagellonský věk v českých zemích (1471–1526).* Vol. 4 Venkovský lid. Národnostní otázka. Prague: Academia.

Molnár, Amadeo. 1980. "Protivaldenská polemika na úsvitu 16. století." *Historická Olomouc a její současné problémy* 3: 153–174.

Rojčíková, Kamila. 2000. "Magické praktiky velkobíteśských čarodějnic." *Západní Morava* 4: 149–154.

Śindelář, Bedřich. 1970. "Konec,honu na čarodějnice¥ v tereziánské době u nás." *Sborník prací filozofické fakulty brněnské univerzity* C17: 89–107.

———1981. "Čarodějnictví a jeho pronásledování u nás do r. 1526." *Sborník prací filozofické fakulty brněnské univerzity* C28: 177–206.

———1986. *Hon na čarodějnice. Západní a střední Evropa v 16.–17. století.* Prague: Svoboda.

Spurný, František, Vojtěch Cekota, and Kouřil Miloš. 2000. *Šumperský farář a děkan Kryštof Alois Lautner, oběť čarodějnických inkvizičních procesu.* Šumperk: Městský úřad Šumperk a římskokatolická farnost v Šumperku.

Teichmann, Eduard. 1932. *Rennaisance und Hexenwahn mit besonderer Berücksichtigung der Verbrennung Lautners in Müglitz.* Hohenstadt: Burschofsky.

MORE, HENRY (1614–1687)

More was an English theologian and believer in the reality of apparitions, spirits, and witches. More belonged to a small band of philosophers known as the Cambridge Platonists because of their metaphysical interests and beliefs. Though fascinated by the spirit of inquiry in the occult sciences, More maintained a devout Christian faith. Astrology, for example, he dismissed as "a fanciful study built upon very slight grounds" (*Enthusiasmus Triumphatus*, 1656). He exerted an important influence on the debates about witchcraft in the second half of the seventeenth century, representing the conservative view that skepticism in such matters was dangerously linked to atheism. Over time, however, his opinions lost favor and would be branded "superstitious" by eighteenth-century free thinkers.

More was born at Grantham in Lincolnshire, the son of a minor gentleman. His parents were strict Calvinists, but as he grew up, More inclined toward a more moderate faith. He was educated at his local grammar school and in 1631 entered Christ's College, Cambridge, which was to remain his home and haven for the rest of his life. More was elected to a fellowship in 1639 and soon afterward took up holy orders. In the 1640s and 1650s, More remained staunchly loyal to the royalist cause but after 1660 refused all preferment and promotion offered in reward. Instead, More adhered to a life of contemplation, conversation, and composition; he was a prolific writer who translated his own work into Latin. He died in Cambridge in September 1687, much missed as an inspirational teacher.

More was remembered as a Christian mystic as well as a scientist in the providential tradition, an Anglican who spent his working life promoting a comprehensive natural theology suited to an age of science and experiment. The diverse subjects covered in his books included the doctrine of providence, the nature of the soul, idolatry, transubstantiation, the Kabbalah, and a commentary on the visions of the prophet Daniel. In 1653, More published his best-known contribution to witchcraft literature: *An Antidote Against Atheisme: or an Appeal to the natural Faculties of the Minde of Man, Whether There be no God.* It included the story of a Cambridge witch who refused to repent; at her execution, which More may have attended, an unnaturally strong gust of wind shook the gallows. He had certainly witnessed some trials of East Anglian witches in the mid-1640s. Despite its local anecdotal evidence, his book was also a serious work of theology, drawing upon such authorities as Jean Bodin, Johann Weyer, and René Descartes and lamenting that free thinking and discussion in religion was undermining God's order. He argued that because the existence of God and a spiritual realm was beyond question, then the power of witches must surely follow. Witches, in More's opinion, were powerless and poor but were tempted through weakness and impiety to follow the Devil's path. He believed that witches gathered in covens to make pacts with the Devil, a continental idea rarely known in England before his own time.

In his later years, More became a strong supporter of the credulous physician Joseph Glanvill (who had long admired More's own work). He reputedly edited Glanvill's polemical *Saducismus Triumphatus* (Sadducism Conquered) of 1681, which also connected skepticism with atheism; there is little doubt that More influenced it. Like Glanvill, More believed that accumulated testimonies demonstrating the reality of witchcraft would ultimately confound the skeptics and would offer a lasting antidote to atheism. The flaws in this line of reasoning were, first, that the data of hauntings and bewitchings could never be tested, and, second, that skeptics would never accept any evidence they considered to be ridiculous. As David Hume later argued, no testimony was sufficient to prove a miracle unless its falsity was more miraculous than the fact it sought to establish.

More died before his worst fears about the progress of atheism and the decline of the miraculous were realized;

but after 1700 it was clear that the occult medieval world of witches and spirits was crumbling as the foundation for Christian faith that More, Glanvill, and others of their generation believed it to be.

MALCOLM J. GASKILL

See also: ASTROLOGY; BODIN, JEAN; DECLINE OF THE WITCH HUNTS; DESCARTES, RENÉ; GLANVILL, JOSEPH; KABBALAH; MIRACLES; OCCULT; SKEPTICISM; SUPERSTITION; UNIVERSITIES; WEYER, JOHANN.
References and further reading:
Hall, A. Rupert. 1990. *Henry More: Magic, Religion, and Experiment.* Oxford: Blackwell.
Hutton, Sarah, ed. 1987. *Henry More (1614–1687): Tercentenary Studies.* Boston: Kluwer.
Sharpe, James. 1996. *Instruments of Darkness: Witchcraft in England 1550–1750.* London: Hamish Hamilton.

MOSES

Among the personages found in the Hebrew Bible, none was more venerated than Moses, and none, save perhaps Elijah, had a greater reputation for performing miraculous deeds and communing directly with God. Because his actions were considered part of the Israelite understanding of divinely shared power, Moses was not considered a magician or sorcerer or a practitioner of divinatory magic. Thus, when his staff was transformed into a snake (Ex. 4:2–3) or he struck the Nile with his staff and it turned into blood (Ex. 7:15–18) or he extended his rod to open the Red Sea (Ex. 14:13–31) or struck a rock to produce a stream of water (Num. 20:10–13), these events were seen as manifestations of God's power over creation, not a conjuration of forces by Moses. The storyteller, however, demonstrated a clear understanding of Egyptian magical practices in the narrative of the plagues (Ex. 7–11), indicating that, although magic was not part of the Israelite theological premise, the Egyptian audience for the match between Moses and the sorcerers would be impressed by the abilities of God's representative (compare Acts 7:22 for later tradition on this).

By tradition, Moses was the recipient of the divine judicial code contained in the Books of the Pentateuch that functioned initially for the Israelites and the later Jewish community as the basis for judicial procedure and their official system of justice. During the Christian era, the strength of this legal and authoritative tradition transformed these statutes into a divinely inspired set of injunctions upon which life was to be based and from which society's leaders could draw to solidify their own authority and preserve their people from error (Deut. 31:24–29). As a result, the laws against witchcraft (Ex. 22:18 [22:17]; Lev. 19:26; Deut. 18:10–14) were given the force of divine command and irrevocability because they were a part of the Mosaic code. In addition, the injunctions on these matters were used (along with the story of the suffering of Job and the principle of grace

in the New Testament) as the basis for the Protestant understanding of demonology and how to combat it.

During the Middle Ages and subsequently during the period of the Reformation, the figure of Moses became canonized into a dual character. He was both the quintessential lawgiver, having received through direct divine revelation the primal judicial code and the model for a divinely chosen secular leader. In the former role, he became the authoritative figure upon whom magistrates, judges, and exorcists based their commissions and upon whose code of justice they relied in dealing with criminals and those accused of witchcraft or dealings with demons. This was even the case with Protestants, who tended to rely more on the Gospels and Paul's concept of public office as a "divine ministry." The Protestant pastors of Strasburg, in their April 1538 treatise on witchcraft, enjoined godly rulers to "administer not their own judgment, but that of the Lord and they ought therefore to follow His Law" (i.e., the Mosaic code). Their combating of witchcraft therefore became a license to deal with social deviance, as they defined it, while using a theocratic underpinning as justification for their actions and beliefs.

As noted by the early-seventeenth-century English clergyman William Pemberton, Moses had two roles: he was a prophet of God and the ruler of God's people. In this latter capacity, he transmitted his authority down through the ages to kings and other rulers by means of God's instructions to Moses's successor Joshua (Josh. 1:1–9). Because these early leaders had been given the book of divine laws on Moses's death, it was attendant upon them to obey and enforce them vigorously. That model of leadership was in turn applied to later periods. Thus witchcraft, which violated both the first and third commandments (Ex. 20:3, 7), also threatened the entire system of law, and it became the paramount duty of secular leaders to eliminate it. In addition, and again based on the biblical narrative, Moses's achievements in combating magicians (Ex. 7:11—9:11) and usurpers of his power (Num. 16:27–33) became a portion of the argument, such as that made by Jean Talpin in 1567, that kings were to be venerated because of their ability to perform miraculous deeds, such as applying a healing touch to their subjects (compare Moses's raising a bronze serpent to cure his people of snakebite in Num. 21:8–9). As a result, the person and the tradition that surround Moses became singularly useful to religious and civil authority.

VICTOR H. MATTHEWS

See also: BIBLE; EXODUS 22:18 (22:17); JEWS, WITCHCRAFT, AND MAGIC; LAWS ON WITCHCRAFT (ANCIENT); MIRACLES.
References and further reading:
Clark, Stuart. 1997. *Thinking with Demons: The Idea of Witchcraft in Early Modern Europe.* Oxford: Clarendon Press.
Cryer, Frederick H. 2001. "Magic in Ancient Syria—Palestine— and in the Old Testament." Pp. 97–152 in *Biblical and Pagan*

Societies. Vol. 1 of *The Athlone History of Witchcraft and Magic in Europe.* Edited by Bengt Ankarloo and Stuart Clark. London and Philadelphia: Athlone and University of Pennsylvania Press.

Noegel, Scott E. 1996. "Moses and Magic: Notes on the Book of Exodus." *Journal of the Ancient Near Eastern Society of Columbia University* 24: 45–60.

Pemberton, William. 1619. *"The charge of God and the King: io iudges and magistrates, for execution of iustice": a sermon preached before Sr Henry Hobart Knight and Baronet, Lord Chiefe Iustice of the Common Pleas: and Sr Robert Haughton Knight, one of the iudges of the Kings Bench, at the Assises at Hartford.* London.

MOTHERHOOD

In local accusations, learned demonological treatises, and plays, the witch was often an inversion of what early modern people expected good mothers to be. Much like today, good mothers nurtured their children both physically and spiritually, cooked nutritious food for their families, and cared for them when they were sick. Unlike today, society also expected them to assist other women during childbirth. Conversely, witches poisoned their own or other people's children, nursed and nurtured demonic imps or animal familiars rather than children, dried up other women's milk or menstrual flows so that *they* could not mother, killed farm animals, and made food spoil. Issues of maternity and images of bad mothers emerge very often in witchcraft trials and the literature of witchcraft, including confessions by women admitting they were witches. This identification of witches with bad mothers was rooted in the circumstances of witchcraft charges, and may also be linked to deep-seated psychological ambivalence in people's emotions about mothers, as well as ambivalence about being a mother felt by mothers themselves.

Charges of witchcraft sometimes grew out of often long-standing quarrels among women, which generally emerged during activities in which women normally engaged. Women spent much of their time caring for children and animals and preparing food, often in the company of other women, and childbirth was experienced within a group of female relatives and friends. All these activities held possibilities for misfortune or tragedy: flocks of geese strayed into gardens and ruined them, cows lost their milk and the calves died, children became ill or injured, or mothers and children died in childbirth. Such incidents could easily be the origin of a witchcraft accusation, and the woman most likely to be accused was often one whom the others felt was somehow deficient in her own mothering: she was past child-bearing age, her own children had been sickly and died, or her own animals fell ill. Thus the accused had reason to project their own greatest shortcomings as mothers onto another woman who had bewitched them and their families. The male authorities who heard witchcraft cases largely shared women's ideas about what made a good mother. Although they added ideas drawn from demonological theory, they still described the witch's actions and character as those of a bad mother who had turned to Satan in her desire for revenge on other people's children.

Lyndal Roper and Deborah Willis have noted that psychoanalytical theory, especially that of Melanie Klein, could be helpful in exploring links between motherhood and witchcraft that went deeper than openly acknowledged notions of good and bad mothering. Klein's work centered on the experiences of early infancy, particularly the development of such negative feelings as envy, aggression, fear, and hate that accompany the love and attachment an infant feels toward its mother. These negative emotions were suppressed as children learned it was unacceptable to express them openly but remained part of the subconscious and might emerge later in fantasies about or aggression toward mothers or other people one expected to be nurturing, such as caregivers. Both Roper and Willis warned that psychological theory developed through analyzing modern people must be used carefully when looking at individuals who lived hundreds of years ago, but because envy and anxiety played such a central role in witchcraft trials, it is useful to consider why they are such powerful emotions. Explaining people's fantasies lies at the heart of both modern psychoanalysis and modern studies of the witch hunts, so an etiology for the witch hunts that incorporates the psychic and emotional state of those involved seems more accurate than one that does not.

As an aid to understanding certain aspects of witchcraft, recent medical research about the experience of motherhood may be even more useful than theories about infantile development. Physicians and psychologists have studied what is now labeled postpartum depression or postpartum psychosis, in which hormonal and other changes in the mother's body after birth can lead to serious clinical depression or even delusions about oneself and one's children. In a few ghastly recent examples, this psychosis has led mothers to kill or attempt to kill their own children, explaining this behavior as a desire to keep them from harm or prevent them from doing evil. This same language occasionally emerged in the confessions of early modern women accused of witchcraft, who reported that the Devil had tempted them to kill their own children, though they generally denied giving in to this temptation.

Women who *were* found guilty of killing their own children were also sometimes accused of witchcraft, with authorities arguing that only the Devil could lead a mother to kill her own child. In Belgium, such women were executed in even more gruesome ways than "normal" witches, such as being impaled on a stake before being burned or having the offending hand cut off before being drowned. It is impossible to tell, of course, whether such women suffered from what would currently be labeled "postpartum depression," but that is a distinct possibility; historians have frequently noted that behavior ascribed to divine or demonic forces in the early modern period is explained in medical or psychological terms today.

Given the sleep deprivation and other problems associated with new motherhood, many mothers who are not clinically depressed often feel ambivalence toward their infants, emotions that they feel guilty about and rarely express openly. Though the cultural context of the modern world and the world of the witch hunts is very different in many aspects, in both eras mothers were expected to be loving and nurturing, and those who were not were regarded as unnatural. Thus it is not surprising that women whose children had become sick or had died should have projected their negative feelings onto someone other than themselves, accusing a neighbor, acquaintance, or servant of witchcraft.

MERRY WIESNER-HANKS

See also: ACCUSATIONS; CHILDREN; CONFESSIONS; FAMILY; FEMALE WITCHES; FEMINISM; GENDER; INFANTICIDE; MIDWIVES; PSYCHOANALYSIS.

References and further reading:

Jackson, Louise. 1995. "Witches, Wives, and Mothers: Witchcraft Persecution and Women's Confessions in Seventeenth-Century England." *Women's History Review* 4: 63–83.

Leboutte, René. 1991. "Offense Against Family Order: Infanticide in Belgium from the Fifteenth through the Early Twentieth Centuries." *Journal of the History of Sexuality* 2: 159–185.

Roper, Lyndal. 1994. "Witchcraft and Fantasy in Early Modern Germany." Pp. 199–225 in *Oedipus and the Devil: Witchcraft, Religion, and Sexuality in Early Modern Europe.* By Lyndal Roper. London: Routledge.

———. 2004. *Witch Craze: Terror and Fantasy in Baroque Germany.* New Haven, CT, and London: Yale University Press.

Willis, Deborah. 1995. *Malevolent Nurture: Witch-Hunting and Maternal Power in Early Modern England.* Ithaca, NY, and London: Cornell University Press.

MOUNTAINS AND THE ORIGINS OF WITCHCRAFT

Was witchcraft a phenomenon concentrated in the mountainous areas of Old-Regime Europe? Over half a century ago, Fernand Braudel's influential *The Mediterranean and the Mediterranean World in the Age of Philip II* (1949) suggested that mountains constituted a world apart from civilization, the privileged shelter of witchcraft. Braudel's geographical determinism was later taken up by Hugh Trevor-Roper, who maintained that "mountains are the home not only of sorcery and witchcraft, but also of primitive religious forms and resistance to new orthodoxies" (Trevor-Roper 1967, 106); at high altitudes, thin air breeds hallucinations, and such natural phenomena as storms, cracking glaciers, or avalanches foster beliefs in the power of the Devil. No wonder that western Europe's great witch hunts began in the Swiss and French Alps and continued in other mountainous zones: the Jura; the Vosges; the Pyrenees (both the Spanish and French sides); the Valtelline; or the northern mountain valleys of Italian bishoprics like Milan, Brescia, or Bergamo. Historians have long debated the association between geography and witch hunts. Today, the "mountain theory" concentrates on two issues: the association between the Alpine region and the origin of the craze and an indirect corollary to the mountain theory, a climatic interpretation of witch hunting in general.

ORIGINS

Historical research currently agrees that the geographical birthplace of witch hunting was largely confined to western Alpine areas, including Dauphiné, the Pays de Vaud, Savoy, the Val d'Aosta, Fribourg, Lucerne, and Bern. Between 1375 and 1440, primarily in three dioceses of western Switzerland (Geneva, Lausanne, and Sion) Europe's first fully developed cases of diabolized witch hunting occurred. Trevor-Roper provided an early version of the acculturation thesis to explain this location. Witch hunting happened, he said, because Dominican inquisitors had reached into backward and incompletely Christianized mountain communities, which were also haunts of heretics. His interpretation was soon opposed by Jeffrey Russell, who maintained that "witchcraft descended from heresy more than from sorcery and first appeared in the lowland cities where heresy was strong, only later spreading into the mountains where it gained strength from the lingering practice of ancient sorcery" (Russell 1980, 72).

Subsequently, Arno Borst claimed that both interpretations needed reappraisal. Borst's argument hinged on two preliminary questions. First, was the early-fifteenth-century Alpine territory really a backward place? By 1400, Borst argued, the Alpine region had become a very active crossroads between Italy and northern Europe and had begun to gear its economy to distant European markets. Second, if from an economic and institutional point of view the Swiss federation resembled the modernity of northern Italian or upper Rhineland areas, why did the first significant trials take place in the Simme valley, high in the Bernese Alps?

Borst claimed that this very dynamic social change engendered a social and a spiritual crisis, producing witch hunts as one of its side effects. Using the account of the trial of a well-off peasant named Stadelin by a Bernese patrician Peter von Greyerz (a judge in the Simme Valley between 1392 and 1407) as retold by Johann Nider in his *Formicarius* (The Anthill, 1437–1438), Borst described the introduction of witchcraft in the valley. Some episodes revealed that Stadelin's rise in social status contrasted with several misfortunes (dead babies; damages to animals and crops) of his fellow villagers; his jealous neighbors eventually blamed him for causing them through the intervention of the Devil. In the end, the original forms of

Alpine witchcraft involved the clash between an open and dynamic society and a closed one.

Borst proposed three conclusions: (1) we cannot dissociate demonological theories built by intellectuals from the superstitions of Alpine villagers; (2) mountain culture cannot be blamed for the origins of the craze; but (3) the phenomenon of early witch hunting was nevertheless specifically Alpine. During the 1430s, as papal inquisitors and secular judges carried out the earliest methodical witch hunts in the Swiss and French Alps, several texts (Nider's tract, the anonymous *Errores Gazariorum,* the treatise of Claude Tholosan, and Martin Le Franc's *Defender of Ladies*) provided "important testimony to the revolution in thought about sorcery and witchcraft" (Kors and Peters 2001, 159) and marked the definitive formation of the idea of the witches' Sabbat (Ostorero, Bagliani, and Tremp 1999).

CLIMATE

When Peter von Greyerz asked Stadelin "how he was able to cause hailstorm and tempest, the criminal answered that he stood in a field saying certain words and begged the most powerful of all demons to send him a lesser demon to strike whatever Stadelin wished" (Kors and Peters 2001, 159). Here historians could spotlight some ways in which Christian doctrine was already transforming popular beliefs. But couldn't one of these Alpine *maleficia*—the weather-making witches—be associated with some more basic and deep seated cause, specifically with the cooling of the global climate known as the Little Ice Age, which afflicted Europe intermittently between 1430 and 1770? In fact, in some of the harsher phases of climate deterioration, agricultural failures led to disastrous food shortages, subsistence crises, and hunger that overlapped with some of the fiercest episodes of witch hunting.

Recently, Wolfgang Behringer has used the extreme sensitivity of sixteenth-century Germans to a series of agricultural disasters provoked by meteorological changes to explain this chronological coincidence. If the first major witch hunt (in Wiesensteig in 1563) "served as an example for radical eradication of 'the evil,' between 1562 and 1565 an interesting debate emerged about the possibility of weather-making. In a small Imperial city, Esslingen, an Evangelical preacher, Thomas Naogeorgus, supported popular demands for witch hunts and urged the magistrates to extend its persecution . . . as a kind of regulation of the weather" (Behringer 1999, 367). A scholarly debate ensued about whether witches could raise such disastrous hailstorms. Behringer found the connections between the Little Ice Age and witch hunting primarily within the Holy Roman Empire, but occasionally elsewhere:

> Where demographic pressure and economic depression lingered on, unstable governments were prone to new demands for persecution with every change due to the Little Ice Age. . . . Contemporary court records and broadsheets tell us about the importance of meteorological events as triggering factors in the background of these persecutions. . . . During the third decade of the 17th century, when the Thirty Years War occupied the governing elites, organized witch hunts in the ecclesiastical territories of the Empire reached their peak. The climax of witch hunting again coincided with some extraordinarily dramatic meteorological events. (Behringer 1999, 370)

Most recently, the geographic/mountain theory has been widened into a hypothesis contrasting the big climatic difference between areas of moderate witch hunting (Italy, Spain, Southwestern France) with the areas of severe hunts, finding the cold as a factor more vague but richer than mountain theory (Bechtel 1997, 770).

If the age of witch hunting overlapped with the Little Ice Age, the nexus between the two phenomena seemed to be limited to a very loose chronological coincidence in most European states. Places like England, Scotland, Spain, or sub-Alpine Italy were certainly agrarian societies that also endured colder winters, subsistence crises, and occasional meteorological disasters, but villagers' imaginations rarely connected unusually severe storms with witchcraft. In England, "the storm at sea which affected a single ship might sometimes be attributed to witchcraft, but on land the action of a tempest was usually too indiscriminate for such an interpretation" (Thomas 1973, 668). Similarly, in Scotland, witchcraft was blamed "occasionally for storm raising; it was rarely held to be responsible for large-scale disasters in which the suffering might be random" (Larner 2000, 82). In sixteenth- and seventeenth-century Spain, Aragonese considered mountains to be the shelter of bandits and witches, but there is no trace of weather-making witches (Tausiet 2000); if "ritual . . . for calling up storms were included in the repertoire of witches" during the Basque craze of 1609–1614 (Henningsen 1980, 88), it remained utterly marginal. In Italy, although accusations of causing hailstorms were rife in the northernmost Alpine valleys, no witches were ever reported to have caused damaging meteorological phenomena in the Sienese countryside, although agriculture there also suffered from many cold winters and wet summers. Historians have yet to explain this extremely uneven geographical distribution of witches' interference with the weather—or with such other human activities as sexual intercourse.

OSCAR DI SIMPLICIO

See also: ACCULTURATION THESIS; AGRARIAN CRISIS; DOMINICAN ORDER; HERESY; LITTLE ICE AGE; NIDER, JOHANNES; ORIGINS OF THE WITCH HUNTS; RURAL WITCHCRAFT; TREVOR-ROPER, HUGH; WEATHER MAGIC.

References and further reading:

Bechtel, Guy. 1997. *La sorcière et l'Occident: La destruction de la sorcellerie en Europe, des origines aux grands bûchers.* Paris: Plon.

Behringer, Wolfgang. 1999. "Climatic Change and Witch-Hunting: The Impact of the Little Ice Age on Mentalities." Pp. 335–351 in *Climatic Variability in Sixteenth Century Europe and Its Social Dimension.* Edited by Christian Pfister, Rudolf Brazdil, and Rüdiger Glaser. Dordrecht/Boston/London: Kluwer Academic Publishers.

Borst, Arno. 1992. "The Origins of the Witch-Craze in the Alps." Pp. 43–67 in *Medieval Worlds: Barbarians, Heretics, and Artists.* By Arno Borst. Translated by Eric Hansen. Chicago: University of Chicago Press.

Henningsen, Gustav. 1980. *The Witches' Advocate: Basque Witchcraft and the Spanish Inquisition.* Reno: University of Nevada Press.

Kieckhefer, Richard. 1976. *European Witch Trials: Their Foundations in Popular and Learned Culture, 1300–1500.* Berkeley: University of California Press.

Kors, Alan C., and Edward Peters, eds. 2001. *Witchcraft in Europe, 400–1700. A Documentary History.* 2nd ed. Revised by Edward Peters. Philadelphia: University of Pennsylvania Press.

Larner, Christina. 2000. *Enemies of God: The Witch-Hunt in Scotland.* 2nd ed. Edinburgh: John Donald.

Ostorero, Martine, Agostino Paravicini Bagliani, and Kathrin Utz Tremp, eds. 1999. *L'imaginaire du sabbat: Edition critique des textes les plus anciens (ca. 1430–ca. 1440).* Lausanne: Université de Lausanne.

Russell, Jeffrey B. 1980. *A History of Witchcraft: Sorcerers, Heretics, and Pagans.* London: Thames and Hudson.

Tausiet, María. 2000. *Ponzoña en los ojos: Brujería y superstión en Aragón en el siglo XVI.* Saragossa: Institucíon "Fernando el Católico."

Thomas, Keith. 1973. *Religion and the Decline of Magic: Studies in Popular Beliefs in Sixteenth- and Seventeenth-Century England.* Harmondsworth: Penguin.

Trevor-Roper, Hugh. 1967. "The European Witch-Craze of the Sixteenth and Seventeenth Centuries." Pp. 90–192 in *Religion, the Reformation and Social Change.* By Hugh Trevor-Roper. London: Macmillan.

MOURA, MANUEL VALE DE (D. 1650)

Vale de Moura wrote nine books, including *De incantationibus seu ensalmis* (On Incantations or Ensalmi [evil incantations]), published at Evora in 1620 (the only edition known). It was a long treatise about verbal magical healing, which briefly mentioned *maleficium* (harmful magic) and diabolical witchcraft. The author was obviously familiar with demonology; he described the diabolic pact, asserting that the Devil marks his followers and kills little children through witches. It was an erudite work filled with citations of Italian and Spanish theologians and canonists, Greek and Latin classics, the Church Fathers, and Holy Scripture.

Little is known about his biography. Vale de Moura was born in Arraiolos, studied theology at the Jesuit University of Evora, and later graduated with a degree in canon law from the University of Coimbra. In 1603, he entered the Inquisition as deputy (*deputado*) of the Evora tribunal.

The treatise *De incantationibus seu ensalmis* was divided into three sections. The first part attempted to refute the positions of João Bravo Chamisso, a lecturer at Coimbra University, who had asserted in 1606 that some words had intrinsic healing powers and that such power did not come from an implicit pact with the Devil. Vale de Moura presented a doctrine, which he believed defensible, regarding the legitimacy and efficiency of healing with words. He stated that the saints created blessings and holy words, to which the Lord gave His merits, and added that in the Hebrew Bible Solomon expelled demons from human bodies by pronouncing words. Vale de Moura suggested, following Cajetan and St. Thomas Aquinas, that many of these words had later been misused in vain ceremonies; although unapproved, they could still be tolerated because they resulted from Christian devotion. But, the author claimed, whenever it was not proved that natural effects or divine virtues underlay a healing ceremony, one might conclude that the healing originated in diabolical powers.

In the second part of *De incantationibus,* the author refuted the incorrect opinions presented in the first part and put forward his own doctrine. He condemned all healing of diabolical origin, stating that Devil's "benefits" were always injurious. He distinguished between sorcerers and *saludadores* (healers): the former act in ceremonies using words, holy objects, or herbs, and the latter act through personal virtue. He stressed that words had no intrinsic power to produce healing effects. Hence if they did produce such effects, they came from external virtues. He insisted that one must be careful about spells that supposedly resulted from divine revelation, as they might be either real or imagined and might sometimes come from God or good angels and other times from the Devil, especially when they were "fantastical" or "imaginary." Some effects were natural and were caused by excessive imagination. Vale de Moura believed those healed through their own supplications should not be condemned, as long as they made no pleas forsaking divine providence. Therefore, he says, it was permissible to cast spells, using holy words invoking God, in order to plead for health or tame a tempest, and always having steadfast faith that such pleas could be granted by God. However, the strongest argument Vale de Moura presented in his second part was that *all* healing through prayer was in general suspicious. Although holy words or church prayers were pronounced in such acts, they were nonetheless evil, for the Devil normally acted under the cover of sanctity.

The third part of Moura's book dealt more specifically with issues of jurisdiction over those who healed through spells. Vale de Moura asserted that only the Inquisition should be responsible for surveying such practices, because until proven otherwise, all healers were suspected of heresy and should therefore be prosecuted by the one court with jurisdiction over heresy. Moura's aim throughout was to limit the sacred field and to place it solely in the hands of its official representatives. Thus he stressed the efficiency of the Church's invocative prayer and exorcism when done by ecclesiastics and insisted that holy words should be pronounced only in holy places. Thus there was no need to turn to private prayers by laypeople.

The impact of Vale de Moura's work was not great. In Portugal, few quoted it, although some Spanish inquisitors followed his advice. Vale de Moura's positions were not immediately adopted by the Inquisition. However, there would come a time, in the first three decades of the eighteenth century, when healers would suffer much from Portugal's Holy Office.

JOSÉ PEDRO PAIVA

See also: CUNNING FOLK; DEL RIO, MARTÍN; DEMONOLOGY; DEVIL; DIABOLISM; INQUISITION, PORTUGUESE; PORTUGAL; SPELLS; WORDS, POWER OF.

References and further reading:

Caro Baroja, Julio. 1990. "Witchcraft and Catholic Theology." Pp. 19–43 in *Early Modern European Witchcraft: Centres and Peripheries.* Edited by Bengt Ankarloo and Gustav Henningsen. Oxford: Clarendon.

Fajardo Spinola, Francisco. 1992. *Hechiceria y brujeria en Canarias en la Edad Moderna.* Las Palmas: Cabildo Insular de Gran Canaria.

Machado, Diogo Barbosa. 1965. *Bibliotheca Lusitana.* Coimbra: Atlântida Editora.

Maggi, Armando. 2002. *Satan's Rhetoric: A Study of Renaissance Demonology.* Chicago and London: University of Chicago Press.

Paiva, José Pedro. 1997. *Bruxaria e superstição num país sem "caça às bruxas."* Lisbon: Editorial Notícias.

MUCHEMBLED, ROBERT (1944–)

A leading French historian of European witchcraft, Robert Muchembled has made numerous significant contributions to this topic at both the archival and synthetic levels.

A lifelong social historian working loosely within the French *Annales* tradition, Muchembled's earliest archival-based work on witch hunting deployed documentation from southern parts of the former seventeen provinces of the Netherlands, particularly the region of Cambrésis (Muchembled 1979, 159–261), in service of the "acculturation thesis." He incorporated this witchcraft research into a chapter ("The Repression of Witchcraft and the Acculturation of the Rural World") of his first book to be translated into English: a general survey titled *Popular Culture and Elite Culture in France, 1400–1700.* He has often employed witchcraft as an unusually vivid illustration of this process (e.g., Muchembled 1984). Over time, however, Muchembled has considerably softened the originally sharp contours of his dichotomy between a strongly dominant elite and their often-passive subjects. The evolution of his position on cultural history can perhaps best be seen in what is probably the best-known and most widely translated among his many books, *L'invention de l'homme moderne,* between its first (1988) and second (1994) editions, where a "society of compromises" deployed various strategies—adaptations, bricolage, resistances—to accommodate civilizing and confessional norms to which they supposedly conformed. Some of his works (e.g., Muchembled 1995) ranged widely across cultural history, blending chapters on Norbert Elias's court civilization, the role of women (a latent concern of most major witchcraft specialists), urban festivals and violence, French raconteurs as cultural mediators, village sociability, legal forms of social control—and, of course, witchcraft.

As a witchcraft scholar, Muchembled has exploited some significant archival discoveries. Three in particular stand out. First, he pioneered a "ground-up" perspective on witch hunting by uncovering some early-seventeenth-century petitions from the "better" (and richer) inhabitants of some Netherlands villages, encouraging their sluggish rulers to increase prosecutions of local witches by offering to pay the costs of such trials (Muchembled 1979, 192–196). Second, he explored the gruesomely macabre history of the child witches of Bouchain in Hainaut, the earliest (but unfortunately not the worst) known wave of trials and executions of witches well under the legal minimum age anywhere in Europe (Muchembled 1990). Third, he presented a richly documented microhistory of a relatively late witch-hunting episode in a tiny village of Francophone Flanders (Muchembled 1981); among other merits, this work first called attention to the role of feminine gossip in establishing the *publica fama* that often underlay witchcraft accusations.

At a synthetic level, one cannot ignore Muchembled's vigorous polemic with his prominent Italian colleague Carlo Ginzburg over the cultural origins and significance of the Sabbat, which produced some light as well as much heat (Muchembled 1990). Subsequently, Muchembled's most important contribution has been his effort to expand and reshape his sociopolitical analysis of witchcraft from his original southern Low Countries regional perspective to a more truly panoramic European level (Muchembled 1993). He has also shifted his cultural history perspective from the witch and her accusers to her supposed accomplice, the Devil (Muchembled 2000). Both endeavors have subsequently taken the form of lavishly illustrated coffee-table books (Muchembled 1994, 2002), each the best of its particular genre; the latter is a by-product of a television program on the Franco-German channel *Arte,* born from a critique that Muchembled's *Devil* discussed innumerable twentieth-century films but lacked any illustrations.

WILLIAM MONTER

See also: ACCULTURATION THESIS; CHILDREN; GINZBURG, CARLO; HISTORIOGRAPHY.

References and further reading:
Dupont-Bouchat, Marie-Sylvie, Willem Frijhoff, and Robert Muchembled, eds. 1978. *Prophètes et sorciers dans les Pays-bas, XVIe–XVIIIe siècle*. Paris: Hachette.

———. 1978. *Culture populaire et culture des élites dans la France moderne (XVe–XVIIIe siècles): Essai*. Paris: Flammarion. Trans. as *Popular Culture and Elite Culture in France, 1400–1750*. Translated by Lydia Cochrane. Baton Rouge and London: Louisiana State University Press, 1985.

Muchembled, Robert. 1979. *La sorcière au village (XVe–XVIIIe siècle)*. 2nd ed., 1991. Paris: Gallimard.

———. 1981. *Les derniers bûchers: Un village de Flandre et ses sorcières sous Louis XIV*. Paris: Ramsay.

———. 1984. "Lay Judges and the Acculturation of the Masses (France and the Southern Low Countries, 16th–18th Centuries." Pp. 55–65 in *Religion and Society in Early Modern Europe, 1500–1800*. Edited by Kaspar von Greyerz. London: Allen and Unwin.

———. 1987. *Sorcières, justice et société aux XVIe et XVIIe siècle*. Paris: Imago.

———. 1990. "Satanic Myths and Cultural Reality." Pp. 139–160 in *Early Modern European Witchcraft: Centres and Peripheries*. Edited by Bengt Ankarloo and Gustav Henningsen. Oxford: Clarendon.

———. 1993. *Le Roi et la sorcière: L'Europe des bûchers, XVe–XVIIIe siècle*. Paris: Desclée.

———, ed. 1994. *Magie et sorcellerie en Europe du Moyen Age à nos jours*. Paris: Armand Colin.

———. 1995. *Cultures et société en France, du début du XVIe siècle au milieu du XVIIe siècle*. Paris: SEDES.

———. 2000. *Une histoire du diable, XIIe–XXe siècle*. Paris: Seuil. Trans. as *History of the Devil: From the Middle Ages to the Present*. Translated by Jean Birrell. Cambridge, UK: Polity, 2003.

———. 2002. *Diable!* Paris. Seuil/Arte Editions.

MÜNSTER, PRINCE-BISHOPRIC OF

The largest ecclesiastical territory of the Old Reich in northwestern Germany, the prince-bishopric of Münster had relatively few witchcraft prosecutions in comparison to neighboring territories, such as electoral Cologne. The bishopric spread across an area of roughly 11,000 square kilometers (4,247.5 miles) and contained about 200,000 inhabitants by 1700. Between the mid-sixteenth century and the end of the seventeenth century, about 450 such cases can be proven; about 170 cases ended with the execution of the defendant. One-third of those executed were men, a relatively high percentage. However, because of the fragmentary nature of the sources, our information is very incomplete.

The first documented witch burning in this territory occurred in 1544; the last provable execution came in 1699, when a woman was sentenced to death for fortunetelling and witchcraft. Three local witch hunts can be discerned from documents surviving in regional archives. In 1624, twenty people were executed for witchcraft in the town of Lüdinghausen within a few months. In the county of Werne, in the southern part of the bishopric, the "witch craze" resulted in over sixty witchcraft trials, more than thirty of them in 1629. In 1629–1631, twenty-five accused witches died at the executioner's hands in the city of Coesfeld. Meanwhile, in the city of Münster, witchcraft trials are recorded from 1552 until 1644, with the worst persecutions occurring between 1627 and 1635.

The intensity of witchcraft prosecution differed by locality. The county courts, controlled by the government in Münster, pursued a relatively cautious policy with respect to witchcraft accusations that resulted in only a few trials, all carried out through a *processus ordinarius* (ordinary procedure). Only 27 of the 170 known executions were carried out by county courts; there were no mass prosecutions. However, some individual seigneurial courts became strongholds of prosecution, carrying out trials independently of the Münster government under the pretext of exercising their sovereign rights of criminal jurisdiction. These trials served as vehicles of self-assertion for local nobility and were mostly characterized by arbitrary procedures and infringements of legal requirements.

One peculiarity of the bishopric of Münster was the swimming test (the cold water ordeal), which was not only a mass phenomenon there but also was carried out in a unique way. The water ordeal, widespread in sixteenth- and seventeenth-century Westphalia, continued the medieval tradition of ordeals. It followed the usual rules: an accused witch was declared innocent if she sank but guilty if she floated on the water's surface, because the "pure water" refused the witch's body that had become ethereally light due to her sexual intercourse with the Devil. Local courts usually arranged the test during an ongoing trial, where the ordeal served as an "indicator for torture." However, in the bishopric of Münster the test took another form. Here, some noble courts developed regular water-ordeal centers, where every subject could voluntarily ask to undergo the swimming test, on condition of paying a large amount of money to the noble judge. Because more than 200 "independent" water ordeals can be proven in the bishopric between the years 1590 and 1650, we can speak of a mass phenomenon.

This peculiar practice, unique to Europe, resulted from the same constellation of legal conflicts that had stimulated the prosecutorial zeal of some seigneurial courts in the late sixteenth and the early seventeenth centuries. The local nobility was in fierce conflict with the government of the prince-bishopric, trying more and more vehemently to conserve its traditional jurisdictional rights in reaction to the threat from Münster, while the central government fought to standardize administration and jurisdiction. Witchcraft trials offered the local nobility a welcome method for upholding their right of criminal jurisdiction. Similar motives underlay the creation of water-ordeal centers at noble courts. The Münster government firmly opposed the swimming test, publishing several prohibitions of this practice. By systematically violating these prohibitions, the nobility (always by referring to their "good old right") expressed their resolve not to bow to the policy of the central government. This conflict between the nobility and the regional government was literally carried out on the backs of their subjects.

GUDRUN GERSMANN

See also: COLOGNE; ECCLESIASTICAL TERRITORIES (HOLY ROMAN EMPIRE); GERMANY, WEST AND NORTHWEST; ORDEAL; OSNABRÜCK, BISHOPRIC OF; SWIMMING TEST.

References and further reading:
Gersmann, Gudrun. 1998. "Wasserproben und Hexenprozesse: Ansichten der Hexenverfolgung im Fürstbistum Münster." *Westfälische Forschungen* 48: 449–481.

MURATORI, LUDOVICO ANTONIO (1672–1750)

A proponent of reason and enlightenment who ignored or discounted the anxieties of the educated elites and attributed belief in witchcraft to the ignorance and credulity of uneducated people, Muratori was an Italian antiquarian, historian, and critic, editor of several multivolume collections of fundamental medieval historical documents. Trained in philosophy and both civil and canon law and ordained a priest, he managed the Ambrosian Library in Milan before becoming librarian of Rinaldo I of Este's court in Modena.

As its title indicated, Muratori's *Della forza della fantasia umana* (On the Strength of Human Fantasy, 1745) examined the phenomena of witchcraft as examples of the power of the human imagination (or fantasy) to distort and falsify reality. Muratori's contempt for the intellect of common people was matched by his misogyny. He accepted the stereotype of the witch as female, and, following a strain of opinion dating from the *Canon Episcopi* (ca. 906), presumed that the phenomena of the Sabbat had no basis in external reality; these illusions were mostly suffered by women afflicted with a diseased and "filthy" imagination.

The most important chapter of Muratori's treatise was the tenth. There he described treatises against black magic as "a great forest where there is some truth, much simplemindedness, a great number of impostures" and concluded that "perhaps some people believe too little about this vile art, which horrifies anyone who is a true Christian. But on the other hand, there are great numbers of people who believe too much about it." Many phenomena attributed to demons by "incautious or weak fantasy" were either natural effects or outright fables (Muratori 1995, 100). Muratori did not contest the reality of demonic possession but called it a "truth mixed with many false suppositions"; most possession was

imaginary. "Exorcists certainly have power from God to cure those who are truly possessed; but they also have the misfortune to produce many imaginary [victims]; many are the tricks played by the frailty of female fantasy." Outbreaks of possession in Milan and elsewhere when relics were shown during Church services were a localized custom (*uso*) or "observance" rather than evidence of demonic presence. "When the relic is covered up, all that great noise ceases and there are no possessed persons left. . . . The ruined fantasy of one woman pulls a hundred along behind her" (Muratori 1995, 104).

The same applies to ghosts (*fantasmi*), which were frequently sighted during outbreaks of plague and other times of universal fright: Muratori advised his readers to investigate skeptically, "to spare themselves an imaginary [*sognato*, dreamed] but real evil, accompanied by the loss of tranquillity and health." Ordinary people should consult men who were wise and learned, rather than common rumors and the gossip and imaginations of silly women (*donniciuole*) (Muratori 1995, 104). It had also been proved that one person's imagination could not produce physical effects on another person through the evil eye; besides, it made no sense for someone to communicate a disease while not suffering from it herself. Muratori derived his disbelief in the evil eye from his understanding of communicable diseases. Mentioning it reminded him of some precautions he had omitted from his recent *Del governo della peste* (Treatise on Managing the Plague): in the presence of plague sufferers, one should not only cover one's nose and mouth but never swallow one's own saliva, instead spitting constantly, as tobacco chewers do. Accusations of the evil eye and other witchcrafts have fallen on many "poor old women, even good and innocent Christians" and parish priests often vainly oppose these "vain and injurious rumors" (Muratori 1995, 105).

Muratori's treatise continued a preoccupation with the power of imagination that had motivated discussions of witchcraft since the fifteenth century. In 1749, Girolamo Tartarotti investigated the question more nervously, insisting passionately that the unreality of witchcraft phenomena must not be construed as disproving the reality of demons or of magic.

WALTER STEPHENS

See also: *CANON EPISCOPI*; ENLIGHTENMENT; EVIL EYE; EXORCISM; GHOSTS; IMAGINATION; POSSESSION, DEMONIC; SKEPTICISM; TARTAROTTI, GIROLAMO.

References and further reading:
Bosco, Giovanna. 1994. "Ludovico Antonio Muratori." Pp. 197–198 in *Bibliotheca lamiarum: Documenti e immagini della stregoneria dal Medioevo all'Età Moderna*. Edited by Patrizia Castelli. Ospedaletto (Pisa): Pacini.
Cognasso, Francesco. 1949–1954. "Ludovico Antonio Muratori." Vol. 8, cols. 1523–1527 in *Enciclopedia cattolica*. 12 vols. Città del Vaticano: Ente per l' Enciclopedia Cattolica e per il Libro Cattolico.

Fido, Franco. 1996. "Muratori and Historiography." Pp. 344–345 in *The Cambridge History of Italian Literature*. Edited by Peter Brand and Lino Pertile. Cambridge: Cambridge University Press.

Muratori, Ludovico Antonio. 1995. *Della forza della fantasia umana*. Edited by Claudio Pogliano. Biblioteca della Scienza Italiana, VII. Florence: Giunti.

MURRAY, MARGARET ALICE (1863–1963)

Perhaps the most controversial twentieth-century author to investigate witchcraft, Margaret Murray's theories infuriated experts but persuaded much of the general public, inspiring much of the ritual and organization of modern neopagan witchcraft (the Wicca movement) from the 1950s onward.

Murray maintained that European witchcraft was an organized form of pagan worship originating in remote prehistory and surviving in secret throughout the Christian era. Its purpose was to ensure the fertility of crops, animals, and people by seasonal rituals and by periodic sacrifices of animals and human beings. She saw this as a joyful, life-enhancing religion that Christians had persecuted; she claimed it had had numerous secret followers, including several medieval kings and famous figures such as Joan of Arc. Although her theory gained very little support from professional historians, it reached the general public both through her entry in the authoritative *Encyclopedia Britannica* and indirectly through novels and films that exploited it.

Murray was born in Calcutta, where her father's business was based. She passed some of her childhood in England but received little formal education, despite her intelligence; her autobiography hinted that her life was one of middle-class inactivity and boredom throughout her teens and twenties. In 1894, when she was thirty-one, new horizons opened: she attended a course on Egyptology at University College in London and made such rapid progress that in 1899 she was appointed a junior lecturer in hieroglyphics on the recommendation of her tutor, Professor Flinders Petrie. The study of Egyptian antiquity became her life's work, and she earned considerable respect in this field.

The outbreak of war in 1914 disrupted academic life. Murray found herself with no students to teach and no possibility of fieldwork in Egypt. After a short spell as a nurse in a French military hospital, which badly affected her health, she turned to new studies, first the Grail legend and then witchcraft. She had "started with the usual idea that witches were all old women suffering from illusions about the Devil" but "suddenly realised that the so-called Devil was simply a disguised man" and immediately concluded that he was a masked priest of some ancient, primitive religion (Murray 1963, 104). Murray always treated this as her personal insight, achieved purely through reading primary sources; even

though others had previously put forward similar theories—including Jules Michelet, Charles Leland, and Karl Pearson, a professor at her own college.

Murray's theory about witchcraft was set out in an article in *Folk-Lore* in 1917 and then in a book, *The Witch-Cult in Western Europe*, in 1921. Witches, she said, everywhere worshiped the same deity, a phallic "Horned God" dating from prehistoric times; they followed exactly the same ceremonies on the same dates; and they were organized in groups of thirteen ("covens"), each group obeying a male leader who impersonated the god and had sexual rights over them. She believed that from time to time the leader (or a substitute) would be willingly burned to death to ensure the fertility of crops; here, she was influenced by Sir James Frazer's study of the "Killing of the Divine King" in *The Golden Bough*.

In one sense, her view of witchcraft was resolutely rational. Reading trial records and other writings from the time of the witch hunts, she seized upon anything for which she could devise a natural explanation, however implausible, and accepted it as proven fact; anything magical or supernatural she simply ignored. So, if a text described an encounter with a black, horned, and cloven-hoofed devil, she would take this to mean a man in black clothing wearing an animal mask and with a peculiarly shaped boot; if a witch confessed to riding to the Sabbat on a "little horse," she would accept the horse as real, even if the witch also stated that this "horse" was a wisp of straw. This selectivity seriously misrepresented her sources.

Her work also suffered from a total disregard for chronology and cultural context, mixing evidence from many countries and many centuries; that was common practice among comparative mythologists of her period and was not criticized at the time, though it is now seen as a serious flaw. Furthermore, she was an enthusiastic system builder, erecting rigid universal rules on very weak evidence. One of her most influential notions was the coven of thirteen, yet she herself admitted that only one witch actually mentioned this number; she resorted to dubious manipulations of figures in the attempt to prove that it was widespread. Similarly, the four seasonal festivals she claimed were held annually everywhere (Candlemas, Beltane, Lammas, and Halloween) were only mentioned as a group in one source. Murray ignored the fact that even in England several other dates are also mentioned (e.g., the Lancashire witches met on Good Friday).

However, some aspects of her book provided a welcome change from much conventional wisdom on the subject. Many writers had explained witch hunting as the result of ignorance, hysteria, and the use of torture to obtain confessions; a small minority, such as the eccentric Montague Summers, believed that Devil worship had actually occurred, with supernatural results. In comparison, Murray's interpretation seemed both novel and demystifying; it effectively eliminated both sides of this argument, opening the way to more rational discussion. This may explain why in 1929 she was invited to contribute the entry on "witchcraft" to the *Encyclopedia Britannica;* characteristically, she seized this opportunity to put forward her theory as if it were universally accepted.

Her second book, *The God of the Witches* (1933), written for a wider audience, was an emotional and openly anti-Christian defense of the "Old Religion" (not only was this term taken from Leland without acknowledgement, but her position was also disturbingly similar to contemporary Nazi propaganda on the topic of witchcraft). She painted a glowing picture of the devotion of witches toward their god and his human representative, expressed through feasts and dances, though reticent about their sexual orgies, which she had described in her earlier, more academic book. Such unpleasant activities as animal sacrifice and the killing of babies were mentioned only in passing, but the ritual killing of the coven leader was strongly emphasized.

Her third study of witchcraft, *The Divine King in England,* appeared in 1954, when she was ninety-two. It presented the sensational conspiracy theory that many kings, from Anglo-Saxon times to the early Stuarts, belonged to the "Old Religion" and had to be killed unless some prominent member of their family or court agreed to die as a substitute. In the same year, she also wrote an approving introduction for Gerald Gardner's *Witchcraft Today.* Gardner said that in 1939 he had been initiated into a coven in Hampshire whose practices were very like those Murray described; she took this as proof of her views, seemingly unaware of the alternative possibility that these "witches" (who were well-educated, middle-class people) could have simply read her books and copied what they found there.

Murray's last two books appeared in the year she died at the age of 100: an autobiography, and *The Genesis of Religion,* a rather sketchy work in which she first acknowledged the importance of goddesses in prehistoric cults.

Until the 1960s, most professional historians simply ignored Murray's work, presumably thinking her theory so self-evidently absurd as not to need rebuttal. However, a few historians (e.g., George Lincoln Burr in *The American Historical Review*) and folklorists (e.g., W. B. Halliday in *Folk-Lore*) had written strongly critical reviews of *The Witch-Cult.* In the late 1920s and the 1930s, C. L'Estrange Ewen researched numerous primary records of English witchcraft trials without finding any traces of an organized cult. But Murray simply ignored any adverse comments; her books grew steadily more dogmatic and extreme.

A time came, however, when historians finally realized how strong her influence was among the general public; her two main books had been reprinted in paperback, popular writers and novelists had taken her ideas on board, the Wiccans were citing her to prove that their religion was ancient paganism. Silence was no longer appropriate. Norman Cohn and Keith Thomas included a few pages savagely criticizing Murray in their analyses of the general history of witchcraft beliefs (Cohn 1975, 107–115; Thomas 1971, 514–517); Ronald Hutton, while exposing the flaws of her theory, described the cultural influences that shaped it (Hutton 1991, 301–306; Hutton 2000, 194–201).

From the point of view of historical and anthropological studies, Margaret Murray's theory has proved valueless; however, she played a significant (though unintentional) part in the growth of twentieth-century paganism in Britain and the United States and in the image of the witch in modern popular culture.

JACQUELINE SIMPSON

See also: BURR, GEORGE LINCOLN; CONTEMPORARY WITCHCRAFT (POST-1800); HALLOWEEN; HISTORIOGRAPHY; MICHELET, JULES; MUSIC; SUMMERS, MONTAGUE; THOMAS, KEITH.

References and further reading:

Cohn, Norman. 1975. *Europe's Inner Demons.* Falmer: Sussex University Press.

Hutton, Ronald. 1991. *The Pagan Religions of the Ancient British Isles.* Oxford: Oxford University Press.

———. *The Triumph of the Moon.* Oxford: Oxford University Press.

Murray, Margaret. 1921. *The Witch-Cult in Western Europe: A Study in Anthropology.* Oxford: Oxford University Press.

———. 1933. *The God of the Witches.* London: Sampson, Low, and Marston.

———. 1954. *The Divine King in England.* London: Sampson, Low, and Marston.

———. 1963. *The Genesis of Religion.* London: Routledge and Kegan Paul.

———. 1963. *My First Hundred Years.* London: William Kimber.

Oates, Caroline, and Juliette Wood. 1998. *A Coven of Scholars: Margaret Murray and Her Working Methods.* London: Folklore Society.

Simpson, Jacqueline. 1994. "Margaret Murray: Who Believed Her, and Why?" *Folklore* 105: 89–96.

Thomas, Keith. 1971. *Religion and the Decline of Magic.* London: Weidenfeld and Nicolson.

MUSIC

Music plays an important role in both ancient and modern religions, and it is therefore unsurprising that it should have strong associations with magic and witchcraft. Music has been used throughout the centuries in a number of ways to enhance rituals and to produce altered states of consciousness allowing, it is sometimes alleged, contact with supernatural deities. Beyond this, classical and modern composers have chosen the theme of "witchcraft" for large numbers of their works, some of which will be discussed below. However, finding examples before the early modern period can be extraordinarily difficult. One has to rely mainly on court documents and stage works from the sixteenth century, with an increasing abundance of material available up to the present time.

Margaret Murray was largely responsible for introducing witches' alleged musical activities to the public, which included them "singing most filthy songes" and generally performing "a kind of villanous musicke" (Michaëlis 1613, 336). Her descriptions of the music, mainly tortured out of Scottish and European victims, conformed to traditional folk gatherings gone awry, with dissonance and irregular rhythms suggesting the laws of misrule. Sixteenth- and seventeenth-century drama encouraged this tradition, with suitably exaggerated stage directions in such works as Ben Jonson's *The Masque of Queens* and, most famous of all, Henry Purcell's opera *Dido and Aeneas*. The infernal music theme continued in eighteenth- and nineteenth-century literature with such works as Robert Burns's *Tam o' Shanter* and Johann Goethe's *Faust,* both of which incorporated music and have received numerous musical settings. Twentieth-century written accounts of music appertaining to witchcraft have often repeated Murray's interpretations, adding personal biases in Montague Summers's and Dennis Wheatley's descriptions of demonic music. Significantly, it was Gerald Gardner who introduced magical elements into the witch's music (Scire 1999). This trend has been reinforced by the otherworldly music introduced by authors such as Kenneth Graham in the episode with Pan in *The Wind in the Willows* or Karen Ralls-MacLeod in *Music and the Celtic Otherworld.*

"ROUGH MUSIC" IN CLASSICAL AND ROMANTIC EUROPE

Considerably more material can be found in the classical music repertoire, where the witchcraft theme has always been and still is popular. Even a superficial survey uncovers hundreds of works, including many compositions that may be divided into vocal/choral and orchestral/instrumental.

Sixteenth- and seventeenth-century stage works used a variety of music by different composers, and thus there is, for example, confusion about who wrote what concerning William Shakespeare's *Macbeth* and Thomas Middleton's *The Witch.* In a more skeptical age, Purcell broke the mold of hideous music for witches with a stunningly beautiful anthem, *In Guilty Night,* but a century later Thomas Linley hinted at what the nineteenth century would provide in terms of harmonic and melodic dissonance in his *Ode on Witches and Fairies of Shakespeare.* Modeste Mussorgsky wrote a choral version of his famous *Night on Bald Mountain,* including the obligatory "Black Mass" scene, and Felix Mendelssohn, Robert Schumann, and Johannes Brahms also wrote choral and vocal works on similar

themes. The twentieth century saw a revival of Purcell's departure from the earlier haglike stereotypes. In an age of Wiccan themes, works such as John Corigliano's *Song to the Witch of the Cloisters* and Max von Schilling's poignant *Hexenlied* portrayed witches in a far more favorable light.

As one would expect, orchestral/instrumental music has obvious problems attached to it, since the absence of text forces one to rely on the composers' own program notes (when they exist). A few mainly anonymous witches' dances have survived from the seventeenth century, attached to productions of *Macbeth.* In the eighteenth century, Joseph Haydn's so-called *Hexen-menuet* (from his string quartet, the *Fifths)* had no real bearing on witchcraft whatsoever. However, in the nineteenth century, the expansion of the orchestra combined with interest in Gothic themes to create a dramatic increase in the number of works reproducing witchcraft themes. Hector Berlioz's *Songe d'une nuit du Sabbat* from his *Symphonie Fantastique* introduced violent syncopation, *col legno* (wood of the bow) playing, and general musical mayhem. This work was matched by Mussorgsky's famous *Night on Bald Mountain,* famously recycled in Walt Disney's *Fantasia,* and his "Baba Yaga" in *Pictures from an Exhibition.* Less well known were two contrasting works by Antonin Dvorak: *The Noonday Witch* and a piano piece for four hands called *The Witches' Sabbath.*

In the twentieth century, the Russian composer Anatol Lyadov wrote a jagged, infernal *Baba Yaga,* and Alexander Scriabin conceived a diabolical counterpart to his *Messe blanche* with the discordant *Messe noire* in 1913. Other twentieth-century works maintained the harsh sounds, including Franz Waxman's *Goyana* and Ian Ballamy's chamber work *Walpurgis Night.* Samuel Barber treated the theme more broadly to match the sorceress' range of emotions in *Medea's Meditation and Dance of Vengeance.* The influence of Igor Stravinsky's *Rite of Spring* (a pagan scenario, not a specific witchcraft event) could be seen in many works after its first performance in 1913. The complete opposite of the evil aspects of witchcraft was stressed in James MacMillan's *The Confession of Isobel Gowdie,* which painted a picture in orchestral terms of the grief and sense of guilt felt at the execution of so many innocent women in the "burning times."

The interpretation of witchcraft in classical music has varied throughout the centuries. The dissonance and rhythmic angularities at the start of the early modern period swelled in the nineteenth century and receded in the twentieth, sometimes replaced by far more favorable portrayals at a time when witchcraft was revived in benign forms. One constant feature is that male witches have been very poorly represented, with just a few to be found, mainly in operas.

MUSIC AND WITCHCRAFT TODAY

One might ask what music is actually used by witches for their rituals and ceremonies in the third millennium. The results of an extensive survey in 2001 conducted in England, with some input from the United States, provided useful information. According to circumstances and the availability of musicians, either recorded or live music is played before, during, and after rituals. Before a ritual, it is usually recorded, and its task is to relax the participants; examples mentioned were Enya and Loreena McKennitt. During the ritual, the recorded music used was mainly instrumental or wordless, because words of songs might clash with the primary emphasis of the rituals. When recorded, the music was chosen for a number of different reasons: to build up energy, to bind the group, to aid altered states of consciousness, to encourage the visitation of spirits—and practically, to obliterate external noises from traffic or other distractions. Examples were thus extremely varied, taken from the popular classical, folk, World, or New Age repertoire. Examples included Richard Wagner, Carl Orff (*Carmina Burana*), Clannad, Native American chants, Carolyn Hillyer, and Nigel Shaw. When musicians were available, live music used whatever instruments were available—often the acoustic guitar. Even if the group did not contain musicians, drumming and chanting were frequently employed to build energy and create a trance-like state of mind. After the ritual, music was also used for social purposes if live or as background sound for the feasting and possibly dancing that followed. Certain types of music were *not* popular at meetings: commercial pop, jazz, and "difficult" classical music. The reasons probably include the age of the participants, who were mainly above their mid-twenties and the feeling that such music was not suitable for joyful or emotional gatherings. It was of overriding importance to make music an important part of the religion, whether in its historical setting or in contemporary practices.

MELVYN J. WILLIN

See also: BURNING TIMES; MURRAY, MARGARET; OPERA; RENAISSANCE DRAMA, ENGLAND, SHAKESPEARE.

References and further reading:

Michaëlis, Sebastien. 1613. *Admirable Historie of the Possession and Conversion of a Penitent Woman.* London.

Murray, Margaret. 1921. *The Witch-Cult in Western Europe: A Study in Anthropology.* Oxford: Oxford University Press.

Ralls-MacLeod, K. 2000. *Music and the Celtic Otherworld.* Edinburgh: Polygon.

Sadie, Stanley, ed. 2001. *The New Grove Dictionary of Music and Musicians.* London: Macmillan.

Scire (Gerald Gardner). 1999. *High Magic's Aid.* Thame: I-H-O Books.

Stewart, R. J. 1988. *Where Is St George?* London: Blandford.

Willin, M. J. 2004. "Music in Pagan and Witchcraft Ritual and Culture." PhD diss. University of Bristol, UK.

N

NAPLES, KINGDOM OF

Relative to north-central Italy, the southern Kingdom of Naples participated only marginally in early witch hunts during the fifteenth and sixteenth centuries. Chronicles did not record any persecutions in the south; the vast demonological literature, both Italian and European, contained no traces of activity in the south compared to references to northern Italy, where the large numbers of trials and the zeal demonstrated by inquisitors such as those in Como merited commendation from Heinrich Kramer, the author of the *Malleus Maleficarum* (The Hammer of Witches, 1486). Except for a few late-sixteenth-century works such as Giovanni Lorenzo d'Anania's (Anania) *De Natura Daemonum* (Of the Nature of Demons, Venice, 1589), Leonardo Vairo's *De Fascino* (On Enchantments, Venice, 1583), and later, medical examiner Pietro Piperno's *De magicis affectibus horum dignotione, praenotione, curatione, medica, strata-gemmatica, divina, plerisque curationibus electis, et De Nuce beneventana maga . . .*(On Magical Ailments, Their Diagnosis, Prediction, and Treatment with Select Cures, Medical, Strategic, and Divine, and On the Walnut-Tree of Benevento; Naples, 1634), literature on the theme of witches remained underdeveloped and did not influence debate about their repression.

Although references to inquisitorial activity concerning witchcraft are scarce, it is possible to trace a general picture of the attitudes adopted by local ecclesiastical authorities toward witchcraft from documents conserved in the diocesan historical archives of Naples and from the sentences and abjurations conserved in the Trinity College Library in Dublin, which anticipated and in some ways inspired the changes in the official position outlined in *Instructio pro formandis processibus in causis strigum, sortilegiorum et maleficiorum* (Instruction for Conducting Trial Procedures Against Witches, Sorcerers, and Evildoers, ca. 1620).

Three witches (called *janare* or *magare* in southern Italy) were condemned to death in 1506 by the inquisitor-general of the Kingdom of Naples, and around 200 trials were initiated by Beneventan archiepiscopal curia, the outcome of which is unknown. Otherwise, nothing is known of the repression of witchcraft in southern Italy before trials were conducted in Naples in 1574, 1580, and 1590; between 1582 and 1601, 143 trials were held in the capital (Romeo 1990, 20, 166–167, 179). In the rest of the kingdom, trials against superstition were recorded at Bitonto in 1594; at Capua, where 130 cases of magic were tried between 1600 and 1715; and at Gallipoli, where three sorceresses were tried for witchcraft in 1600. Throughout this region, judges—regardless of the gravity of the errors confessed—merely required the accused to repent, recant their errors, and accept spiritual penances (D'Ippolito 1996, 425–437).

Documents from the Holy Office conserved at Trinity College Library in Dublin contain numerous cases in which subjects of the Kingdom of Naples appeared spontaneously before the tribunal of the Inquisition in Rome to confess they were sorcerers or necromancers, together with a few inquiries from local ecclesiastical tribunals in Naples, Lecce, and Teano. These trials also provide evidence that pagan spirituality was so profoundly imbued with official Christianity that it was experienced and practiced without any sense of wrongdoing. The judicial sentences indicate that the inquisitors were principally concerned with punishing the error of "believing that it is right to serve the work of the devil" (Trinity College Library, Dataria, Vol. 1228, ff. 111–114). The nature of these offenses, mostly entailing minor suspicions of heresy, and the primarily spiritual penalties imposed were never very severe (e.g., whipping, confinement to a cloister for regular clergy, formal imprisonment for a brief period, or, at worst, five years in the galleys). The Congregation of the Holy Office demonstrated a "southern" orientation that seemed far less rigorous than the attitude of Milan's famous cardinal-archbishop, St. Carlo Borromeo.

In general, the severity of southern Italian authorities against superstitions was restricted to their definitions of what constituted illicit use of the sacraments and sacramental objects. At the same time, ecclesiastical authorities sought to strengthen the thaumaturgical-defensive system of sanctioned traditional rituals (especially exorcism) and increase such forms of popular devotion as the cult of saints while limiting their repressive action to intimidating marginal and subaltern segments of society to discourage them (without much success) from engaging in magic spells and syncretistic practices. In the late sixteenth century, a "campaign of aggression and intolerance" was directed against superstitions, in line with Sixtus V's *Coeli et Terrae Creator* (Creator of Heaven and Earth, 1586) and *Immensa Dei Aeterni* (The Infinity of the Eternal God, 1587). Notwithstanding the gravity of the apostasies committed by the accused (participation in the Sabbat, homage to or pact with the Devil) and the atrocities they confessed (often spontaneously), no known cases involved accusations of diabolical witchcraft. The principal goal was instead to circumscribe and relativize the errors of the faithful: exorcism was preferable to burning at the stake because it transformed the witch into someone possessed by the Devil (Romeo 1990, 244).

Southern tolerance was also associated with the futile efforts of southern bishops to eradicate superstitions practiced by their clergy. Even after the Council of Trent, even higher-level southern monks lived in concubinage, moral laxity, and superstition. Numerous sentences from the Trinity College Library records detailed proceedings against members of the secular and regular clergy, including some cases against ordinary diocesan clerics accused of dealing with the Devil. A somewhat classical interpretation attributes such corruption among southern Italian clergy to the particular structure of the Church in the region, which was more receptive to it. This institution was controlled by laypeople and managed by refractory clergy who were often ignorant and superstitious, indifferent to the spirit of reform, and unresponsive to an inner religiosity founded on the purity of the evangelical message. These conditions are crucial to understanding the failure of the post-Tridentine Church's commitment to Christianizing the countryside. Ancient superstitions continued to thrive among the faithful. Southern bishops who lamented the presence of rites and cults of pagan origin frequently denounced them in the late seventeenth century and throughout the eighteenth century (Tamblé 1996, 545). Twentieth-century anthropologists and folklore scholars studied these same beliefs and practices.

PAOLO PORTONE;

TRANSLATED BY SHANNON VENEBLE

See also: BORROMEO, ST. CARLO; D'ANANIA (ANANIA), GIOVANNI LORENZO; INQUISITION, ROMAN; ITALY; *MALLEUS MALEFICARUM*; PIPERNO, PIETRO; SUPERSTITION.

References and further reading:

De Rosa, Gabriele. 1978. *Chiesa e religione popolare nel Mezzogiorno*. Rome-Bari: Laterza.
D'Ippolito, Lucia. 1996. *Spunti per una ricerca sulla stregoneria nel territorio della diocesi di Oria*. Pp. 425–437 in *Stregoneria e streghe nell'Europa moderna*. Convegno internazionale di studi (Pisa, 24–26 marzo 1994). Edited by Giovannea Bosco and Patrizia Castelli. Pisa: Pacini.
Monter, William. 2002. "Witchcraft Trials in Continental Europe 1560–1660." Pp. 1–52 in *The Period of the Great Witch Trials*. Vol. 4 of *The Athlone History of Witchcraft and Magic in Europe*. Edited by Bengt Ankarloo and Stuart Clark. London and Philadelphia: Athlone and University of Pennsylvania Press.
Monter, William, and John Tedeschi. 1986. "Towards a Statistical Profile of the Italian Inquisitions, Sixteenth to Eighteenth Centuries." Pp. 130–157 in *The Inquisitions in Early Modern Europe: Studies in Sources and Methods*. Edited by Gustav Henningsen and John Tedeschi. DeKalb: Northern Illinois University Press.
Romeo, Giovanni. 1990. *Inquisitori, esorcisti e streghe nell'Italia della Controriforma*. Florence: Sansoni.
Sallmann, Jean Michel. 1986. *Chercheurs de trésors et jeteuses de sorts: La quête du surnaturel à Naples au XVIe siècle*. Paris: Aubier.
Tamblé, Maria Rosaria. 1996. "Streghe, guaritrici, indovino." Pp. 541–565 in *Stregoneria e streghe nell'Europa moderna*. Convegno internazionale di studi (Pisa, 24–26 marzo 1994). Edited by Giovannea Bosco and Patrizia Castelli. Pisa: Pacini.

NASSAU-SAARBRÜCKEN, COUNTY OF

The county of Nassau-Saarbrücken, Lutheran since 1575, experienced only fifty-two witchcraft trials between 1578 and 1679, making it—like the Calvinist duchy of Pfalz-Zweibrücken—one of the territories in this region with a relatively mild pattern of witch hunting. Through strict regulation of the costs of witchcraft trials, the counts of Nassau-Saarbrücken succeeded in preventing the expansion and worst excesses of witch hunts, although they were not opposed in principle to the persecution of witches. Nassau-Saarbrücken's witchcraft trials were concentrated in areas subject to the criminal courts of the abbey of Wadgassen (nineteen trials), the lordship of Ottweiler (thirteen trials), and the lordship of Uchtelfangen (seven trials). In these three courts, other local lords shared criminal jurisdiction with the counts, although their respective rights were often in dispute. As in other German Protestant territories, women comprised almost all (95 percent) of the accused and executed witches in Nassau-Saarbrücken (Labouvie 1997, 45).

Summaries and statistics pertaining to the Nassau-Saarbrücken witchcraft trials have been studied as part of the Saar region (e.g., Hoppstädter 1959; Labouvie 1991, 1997). Unlike other major rulers in the Saar region (the elector of Trier, the duke of Lorraine, and the duke of Pfalz-Zweibrücken), the counts of Nassau-Saarbrücken ruled a relatively coherent territory as resident lords. They could thus exercise greater control over witchcraft trials than absentee rulers governing fragmented territories. The counts followed the Carolina (the 1532 code of criminal procedure for the Holy Roman Empire) on matters of evidence, the application of torture, and consultations with legal experts, and local customary laws (*Weistümer*) regulated the costs and length of trials and the arrest and imprisonment of suspects. The counts published no special witchcraft mandates: general ordinances of criminal procedure governed court fees, wages of court officials, payments to witnesses, and the use of torture. However, complaints from the count's subjects about increasing costs of witchcraft trials led to promulgation of an official mandate at the beginning of the seventeenth century, aiming to eradicate abuses and fix the level of wages and subsistence expenses of everyone involved in witchcraft trials.

Witchcraft allegations in Nassau-Saarbrücken between 1535 and 1734 were usually treated as cases of slander and did not trigger criminal proceedings—another reason for the relatively low number of witchcraft trials there. Unlike other Saar region territories, the terms for both female (*Hexe*) and male (*Hexenmeister*) witches were apparently established at an early date. Accusations of witchcraft came from both men and women, but with one exception, their targets were always women who were accused of making people ill or blind, bewitching dairying processes, or performing other serious acts of harmful magic.

The first known witchcraft trial took place in 1578 in Uchtelfangen following an accusation brought by court officials. The first witchcraft trials pursued with the help of organized village witch-hunting committees (*Hexenausschüsse*) also occurred in Uchtelfangen and nearby villages in the lordship of Ottweiler in 1595. Such witch-hunting committees were, however, much less widespread in Nassau-Saarbrücken than in other nearby states, for example, the duchy of Luxembourg, the electorate of Trier, or the territory of the imperial abbey of St. Maximin.

The witchcraft trials in the territory of the abbey of Wadgassen constituted a peculiar episode in the Nassau-Saarbrücken story. Although formally subject to the ultimate sovereignty (*Landeshoheit*) of the counts of Nassau-Saarbrücken, the abbey stood under the direct administrative authority (*Vogtei*) of the duke of Lorraine. This meant that it was forced—sometimes militarily—to seek advice in cases of witchcraft from the central legal tribunal in Lorraine (the *Change de Nancy*) rather than from the main court of the counts in Saarbrücken (the *Oberhof*). The dukes of Lorraine clearly pursued a long-term policy of establishing their own sovereignty over Wadgassen. Its witchcraft trials thus took place against a backdrop of conflicting priorities of its rival lords, whose territorial disputes were finally settled by treaty only in 1766.

Although the property of executed witches was not confiscated in Nassau-Saarbrücken, the trial costs were settled by surviving relatives, as the Carolina stipulated. Nonetheless, the question of paying trial costs when the property of the condemned witch was insufficient to cover them arose as early as 1595, at Uchtelfangen. Although the Carolina made the authorities meet the costs in such cases, the count of Nassau-Saarbrücken insisted that customary laws (*Weistümer*), which

required the heirs of the condemned to settle such costs, should be followed instead. His ordinance made it clear that trial costs must be settled at the local level, without intervention from the count's officials. Because neither local witch-hunting committees nor local lords were willing to take responsibility for paying the often horrendous costs involved in witchcraft trials, this ordinance significantly dampened local enthusiasm for witch hunting. In 1613, the count also repealed an earlier ordinance stipulating that witchcraft suspects must be kept only in prisons subject to his authority. Putting suspected witches in prisons belonging to lords of the relevant local criminal courts provided another means for the counts to avoid expenses in witchcraft trials.

The Thirty Years' War, which caused an 84 percent decline in population in Nassau-Saarbrücken, also brought its witchcraft trials to an end (Labouvie 1991, 252). A few trials occurred after 1648. In the last known case, a woman subject to the criminal court of Ottweiler claimed to be a witch in 1679. Legal advice on her case was sought from jurists at the University of Strasbourg, who recommended that the woman be questioned by clerics. Although the verdict is unknown, many indications suggest that she was treated mildly by the men who judged her.

RITA VOLTMER;

TRANSLATED BY ALISON ROWLANDS

See also: CAROLINA CODE (*CONSTITIO CRIMINALIS CAROLINA*); COMMUNAL PERSECUTION; GERMANY, WEST AND NORTHWEST; LORRAINE, DUCHY OF; LUXEMBOURG, DUCHY OF; PFALZ-ZWEIBRÜCKEN, DUCHY OF; POPULAR PERSECUTION; SAAR REGION; ST. MAXIMIN, PRINCE-ABBEY OF; TRIER, ELECTORATE OF.

References and further reading:

Hoppstädter, Kurt. 1959. "Die Hexenverfolgungen im saarländischen Raum." *Zeitschrift für die Geschichte der Saargegend* 9: 210–267.
Labouvie, Eva. 1991. *Zauberei und Hexenwerk: Ländlicher Hexenglaube in der frühen Neuzeit.* Frankfurt am Main: Fischer.
———. 1997. "Rekonstruktion einer Verfolgung: Hexenprozesse und ihr Verlauf im Saar-Pfalz-Raum und der Bailliage d'Allemagne (1520–1690)." Pp. 43–58 in *Hexenprozesse und deren Gegner im trierisch-lothringischen Raum.* Edited by Gunther Franz, Günter Gehl, and Franz Irsigler. Weimar: Rita Dadder.

NATIVE AMERICANS

Until very recently, virtually every native North American people believed in witches or evil shamans, who used their special access to potent spiritual power to attack enemies with disease, "accidents," bad luck in hunting, and other misfortunes. Witches were nearly as ubiquitous as life's troubles, and nearly anyone could be a witch; thus, people were always on the lookout for secret offenders who gave themselves away through antisocial behavior. Indians across time and space have held common beliefs about witches, contributing to a shared historical pattern in which communities split into factions advocating different approaches to colonial encroachment and then charged members of the rival faction with witchcraft. When such factions gelled around the revitalization programs of religious prophets, accusations sometimes escalated into actual witch hunts marked by systematic executions. Witch hunts have been rare since the early twentieth century, but belief in witches is still common in some Native American communities.

Quite unlike European beliefs about the supernatural, which divided power into good and bad as personified in God and the Devil, Native Americans believed that all power was double-edged, capable of being put to positive or negative ends depending upon the person who wielded it. Individuals gained access to spiritual power sometimes by communing with a spirit during a dream but most often through a vision quest. During the vision quest, an individual—almost always male—fasted, deprived himself of sleep, imbibed hallucinogens, and sometimes tortured himself until he pictured one or more spirits, usually in the form of animals or meteorological forces such as the wind. The spirit taught the vision seeker its song, gave him fetishes that could be used to call for power whenever it was needed, and explained what taboos would void this gift. The guardianship of an especially powerful spirit enabled the seeker to become a shaman with the ability to affect cures, rain, divination, or other social benefits. But he, and sometimes she, also could cause accidents or make people ill or insane by magically implanting poisonously enchanted objects as mundane as hairs or fingernails into the bodies of their victims or by capturing one of the victim's two souls as it lay exposed during dreaming. Until recent times and sometimes today still, American Indians attributed many, if not most, of their illnesses to such evildoing.

Among the Indian shaman's most important duties was diagnosing and treating witchcraft. The shaman would work himself into an ecstatic trance by fasting, dancing, contorting himself, and chanting, while people around him drummed and sang until he contacted his guardian spirits, who identified the root of the sickness. If the disease stemmed from an implanted magical item, the shaman would apply a tube to the violated area and suck out the object without breaking the skin. Sickness deriving from a captured dream soul required a more intricate cure because the shaman had to enter an even deeper trance to travel to the land of the dead to retrieve the patient's ghost. At other times, the shaman might trap the witch's dream soul in an insect or frog and then crush it dead.

Indians also depended upon their shamans to identify specific witches, who went to great ends to remain anonymous. Nevertheless, everyone knew what types of individuals turned to witchcraft. They were jealous, muttering underneath their breath at others' good fortune; hypersensitive, interpreting casual exchanges as insults; selfish, refusing to share food with their neighbors; and outcasts, who might be found wandering alone in the woods. Some of them either were the offspring of an incestuous relationship or participants in incest themselves. Others had been contacted during their visions by spirits oriented toward evil, such as Owl and Coyote in Apache belief, or the horned winged serpent found in Algonquian speakers' pantheon. Although the vast majority of Native American shamans were male and witches were defined as wicked shamans, a high percentage of accused witches were elderly women, as among Europeans. This disparity suggests an underlying hostility toward females who no longer could contribute to the group by reproducing or raising children and who, unlike old men, had little or no formal role in government, but sometimes tried to retain control over a household, apparently to their relatives' irritation.

Witchcraft suspicions were ubiquitous among Native Americans because of a tendency to read any violation of the people's unachievable consensus ideal as a sign of ill will. In the small-scale, face-to-face, and generally decentralized societies of Native America, cooperation was necessary to feed, defend, and govern. Therefore, everyone was under extreme pressure to suppress anger and disagreement with relatives and neighbors in favor of a moderate, pleasant attitude and willingness to share resources with anyone in want. For men, there were few outlets for social tension aside from war against foreign peoples and rough sport, and even fewer for women. Thus, when someone became sick or hurt following unsanctioned but inevitable family squabbles, love rivalries, or political disputes, people were quick to imagine that a witch on the other side was responsible.

The consensus ideal that bred suspicions of witchcraft also suppressed collective action against it. An accused witch was prosecuted only if community leaders agreed on the verdict. However, a witch was in grave danger when such consensus was achieved. A suspected witch was sometimes captured and tortured in order to remove his or her curses and then either warned, banished, or even killed. Customarily a witch was executed and left to rot unburied, but troubles with the witch did not end there. The witch's spirit lingered for a time in anticipation of finding a new host, and, if successful, it returned to plague the community with fresh vengeance.

The witch hunt has been one of the most violent manifestations of Native Americans' internecine responses to colonization, particularly epidemic disease, Christian missions, and harassment from Euro-American governments. European-introduced diseases like smallpox often wiped out most of an exposed community's population,

Chief of Florida Indians consulting a shaman before going into battle. Shamans were common among Native Americans, and functioned to attack enemies as well as to practice beneficent magic. (Ann Ronan Picture Library/HIP/TopFoto.co.uk)

leaving the traumatized survivors to try to determine what had happened. An unfamiliar disease causing such unprecedented mortality had to have a spiritual cause like witchcraft, as the Pima Indians of southern Arizona concluded in 1844–1845 when they killed four shamans in the aftermath of a cholera outbreak. Christian missionaries were less lethal than European diseases but nearly as disruptive. Indian neophytes neglected their people's customary rituals, broke their taboos, and partook of strange new religious forms and in the process turned themselves and their missionaries into obvious targets of witchcraft accusations.

The simultaneous appearance of disease and missionaries provoked particularly aggressive witch hunting, as in southern Ontario when the Hurons executed several French Jesuits and their followers during the 1630s and 1640s. However, witch hunts took their most dramatic forms when Indian societies came under intense pressure from white expansion, leading not only to epidemic disease and proselytization but also to land loss, warfare, alcohol abuse, economic dependency, and infighting. By the late eighteenth and nineteenth centuries, Indian communities in the path of American expansion typically divided into two factions: an accommodationist wing that agreed to land sales and reservations in exchange for annuities, peace, and trade benefits; and a "traditionalist" wing that advocated some version of pan-Indian cooperation (including violent resistance), religious revitalization, and rejection of the alcohol trade and land sales. Traditionalists received their inspiration from religious visionaries who claimed revelation from the "Great Spirit" and a special ability to identify witches. Not surprisingly, usually those witches were accommodationists and their leaders. Witch hunts of this type accompanied the rise of some of Native America's most famous prophets: the Delaware Neolin among Ohio River Valley tribes during the 1760s as a prelude to Pontiac's famous uprising; the Seneca Handsome Lake among the Iroquois of upstate New York during the 1790s; and, most notably, the Shawnee Tenskwatawa among the Great Lakes and Ohio Valley tribes and the Creek Indians during the early nineteenth century in conjunction with Tecumseh's campaigns against the United States. Few other witch hunts are so well documented, but they continued to mark intratribal politics well into the twentieth century.

Many Indian groups continue to believe in witchcraft, mostly along traditional lines with some concessions to outside influences. Christian Indians often associate witches with the Devil rather than traditional guardian spirits. Some people continue to attribute certain accidents, psychological disorders, and "traditional" ailments to witchcraft but acknowledge that "foreign" diseases can have other sources. They also believe that witches work only as individuals, not as part of the "witch societies" that were found during ancient times. Official executions of witches have been rare, but even into the late twentieth century, not unknown in some isolated cases. Most importantly, as the enduring antithesis of community values, the witch continues to define what those values are.

DAVID J. SILVERMAN

See also: SHAMANISM.

References and further reading:

Dowd, Gregory Evans. 1992. *A Spirited Resistance: The North American Indian Struggle for Unity, 1745–1815.* Baltimore: Johns Hopkins University Press.

Edmunds, R. David. 1983. *The Shawnee Prophet.* Lincoln: University of Nebraska Press.

Hultkratz, Åke. 1992. *Shamanistic Healing and Ritual Drama: Health and Medicine in Native North American Religious Traditions.* New York: Crossroad.

Sturtevant, William, ed. 1978–. *Handbook of North American Indians.* 12 vols. to date. Washington, DC: Smithsonian Institution.

Trigger, Bruce G. 1987. *The Children of Aataentsic: A History of the Huron People to 1660.* 1976. Reprint with a new preface, Montreal: McGill-Queen's University Press.

Walker, Deward E., Jr. 1989. *Witchcraft and Sorcery of the American Native Peoples.* Moscow: University of Idaho Press.

NAZI INTEREST IN WITCH PERSECUTION

Reports about the interest of SS (the *Schutzstaffel*— protection force or defense squad) leader Heinrich Himmler in research on witch persecutions were circulated as early as 1947 by the Berlin newspaper *Telegraf.* The information stemmed from an unknown librarian in Polish Poznan (formerly Posen), where a huge collection of books and some files from the SS were now stored, both giving credibility to such a project. In 1948 and 1951, further information came from a former concentration camp prisoner, Herbert Blank, who had been ordered by the SS to produce summaries of witchcraft trial documents. In 1952, an investigation dealing with the fate of German archival sources in Polish territory offered more hints about the project. However, information about Himmler's project vanished afterward, until Gerhard Schormann gave a firsthand account of the SS *H-Sonderkommando*'s (special unit H [*Hexen*-witches]) witchcraft-trial collection in his introduction to a short book (Schormann 1981). The news aroused widespread interest in Germany.

Since then, numerous scholars of both early modern Europe and Nazi Germany have used either the original material preserved in the Poznan archives or the copy on film kept by the Frankfurt Bundesarchiv. After the fall of the German Democratic Republic (GDR) in 1989, Jörg Rudolph discovered additional material in SS files, which had been kept secretly by the Stasi, the intelligence service of the former GDR, for political reasons. By 1999, a study group was able to present a collection of essays examining various aspects of the *H-Sonderkommando,* including, in addition to its political aims and ideological grounds, a critical assessment of the scientific value of the SS collection.

NATIONAL SOCIALIST VIEWS OF WITCHCRAFT AND WITCHCRAFT PERSECUTION

Though clearly reflecting his intention to use the witchcraft-trial material politically against both the Catholic Church and Protestant opponents, Himmler's interest was also deeply rooted in Nazi ideology. Like other intellectual National Socialists, the master of the extermination camps believed that the victims of late medieval and early modern witchcraft persecution had been pure descendants of the Germanic race. Witches were supposedly adherents and practitioners of a traditional Germanic religious cult, who for this very reason had fallen prey to persecutions instigated by Church authorities in their attempt to erase remnants of paganism. At bottom, this theory drew on anti-Semitism, pretending that the Catholic Church from its origins was penetrated by Jews and a "Jewish" commitment to destroy all racially superior beings.

Like so many other ideas and visions of National Socialism, the pagan interpretation of witchcraft stemmed from a long tradition of antimodern views. After the Enlightenment had disenchanted witch belief in the late eighteenth century, subsequent centuries, longing for romantic inspiration, discovered the "real truth" behind it. In France, Jules Michelet declared the witch to be the people's authentic medical service; in Germany, Jakob Grimm saw it as incorporating a lost Germanic culture. In England, Margaret Murray (1921) portrayed witchcraft as an ancient fertility cult. But nowhere did the materialization of the witch figure go farther than in Germany and Austria. When Hitler came to power in 1933, the neopagan vision of witchcraft displayed both a "white" interpretation and a "black" counterpart. The former claimed (like Michelet) that witches had been agents of popular medicine; the latter declared that people accused of witchcraft were really groups of Germanic warriors fighting demonic forces through ritual means. The military version, expounded by Vienna Germanist Otto Höfler, was, of course, highly agreeable to Himmler and his "Black Order," the SS, whereas the more peaceful "white" version, advocated by Himmler's political opponent, chief ideologist Alfred Rosenberg, fell prey to internal party rivalries.

Independently of these differences, both factions agreed that Christianity had been responsible for slaughtering millions of Germanic victims. Hence, research about witchcraft trials became an act commemorating "racial losses" and honoring the "ordeal of Germanic heroes," women and men alike. Given the apparent continuity of that confrontation, it also provided ammunition for an ongoing battle. Politically, therefore, witchcraft research figured as "scientific enemy observation," with full responsibility for the project falling on the SS secret service (SD) and centered at first in the *Amt II Gegnerforschung* (research on enemies) within the central SS administration, the Reichssicherheitshauptamt (National Central Security Department)

Work started in 1935, after Nazi publication of an ideologically revised version of a traditional peasant calendar claiming Church responsibility for millions of slaughtered heretics and witches had been successfully refuted as a scandalously ignorant historical fake. This failure made it obvious that historically accurate antireligious propaganda must henceforth be put on an organized scientific basis.

ORGANIZATION AND PERFORMANCE

The SS witchcraft research group (*H-Sonderkommando*) took pains to conceal its activities, as its abbreviation ("*H*" for "*Hexen*") showed. While the exploration of published literature continued, members began visiting archives within the Third Reich already in summer 1935, extending their investigations to occupied territories as well during the war. When doing so, they never officially revealed their membership in the SS, working under academic or private cover instead; otherwise, they would never have gained access to Church institutions, like the archiepiscopal archives in Trier.

Trial records and related documents were investigated following a fixed scheme, devised not only to establish the basic facts (number of victims, age, sex, and race(!)) but also to provide proof about who made the accusations and trials and especially about the responsibility of the churches. Secretaries later transferred the findings onto typed forms—hence the Polish title *Kartoteka* (card index) and organized it by localities, so that it could quickly be used to furnish local press campaigns. Within a more scientific framework, systematic studies were planned on racial and demographic aspects of the persecutions, on the use of torture, and on forgery in earlier historical accounts.

Though the project's ideological limits are plain, its perspective from below granted at least theoretically new insights, in particular by focusing on the social context (if one replaces "race" with "social rank"). Furthermore, the SS researchers were not so narrowminded as to overlook the close alliance between secular and Church officials within learned culture, but their ideology compelled them to use the notion of a separate (and racially conceived) people's culture. It is worthwhile to remember in this context that the idea of elite culture as opposed to popular culture would become a cherished approach of some social historians long into the 1980s, before yielding to rather more complex assumptions of differentiated intercultural relations. Meanwhile, the romantic image of witches being simply persecuted for being "wise woman" seems to be as lively as ever in feminist and neopagan circles. Truly modern, on the other hand, was the *H-Sonderkommando*'s intention to popularize its findings by exhibitions and articles in popular papers and by massive use of photographic material.

Despite its ambitious and modern aims, strategies, and approaches, the project's results were disappointing. With 33,846 cases recorded by the end of 1943, when project work ceased due to the course of war, results lagged far behind the 500,000 or even millions of victims that had been expected. About the role of the Church, apart from confirming what was already known about its propaganda, the evidence rather suggested the reverse, that is, the support persecutions enjoyed from ordinary German people. Obviously, early modern society had been more deeply penetrated by Christianity than the adherents of racial paganism believed. The search for traces of suppressed Germanic cults could not find substantial evidence.

Besides conceptual shortcomings and dead ends, the intellectual mediocrity, indeed dilettantism, of the *H-Sonderkommando* rendered its products useless for antireligious propaganda. Recent reexamination of the material in comparison with the archival sources (Lorenz et al. 1999) demonstrated countless errors, which opponents of Nazi paganism would have been able to reveal as well: mistaken identification of cases, misreading and confusion of names of the accused, misunderstanding of context, and ignorance of what was really happening in local persecutions.

No wonder then that none of its ambitiously planned studies could be finished. Significantly, a personal attempt by SS officer Dr. Rudolf Levin, a leading member of the group, to exploit his product on the academic market by presenting it as a *Habilitation* (second dissertation, necessary to earn tenure) at the University of Munich was defeated by the academic tribunal. Even crisis management by the group's gray eminence, prominent National Socialist historian and SS officer Professor Günther Franz, could not improve the situation.

The mediocrity of the group's philologists tells something about their motives for participating in the project: to exploit it as a vehicle for an academic career otherwise not accessible. The "modernists" within the group, however, those in charge of distributing the product to the public, used it as a chance to develop techniques crucial for their future careers in postwar German press and marketing. Thus, the head of the SS office on "scientific enemy observation," Professor Dr. Franz A. Six, became a leading figure in West German marketing in the postwar era.

Given the scholarly deficits of the SS witchcraft trial collection, its usefulness for current research is limited. Except for its photographic copies, transcriptions, and extracts of original documents, the *Kartotheka* cannot be used to substitute for otherwise lost archival material. However, it does have advantages as a means for surveying or checking sources and getting hints about some rather irregular findings, such as the sixteen witchcraft executions it reported as taking place in 1629 and 1630 in the village of Sehlem near Trier. These cases were documented only by a note in the Sehlem parish register, quite an exception to the contemporary doctrine denying condemned witches both Christian burial or even recording them. Given their generally superficial procedure, the SS researchers in this case surely relied on a local informant, probably someone working through parish registers for the sake of racial genealogy.

WALTER RUMMEL

See also: COMMUNAL PERSECUTION; HISTORIOGRAPHY; MICHELET, JULES; MURRAY, MARGARET ALICE; POPULAR PERSECUTION.

References and further reading:
Baumgarten, Achim R. 1994. "Hexenprozessforschung im Bundesarchiv." *Mitteilungen aus dem Bundesarchiv* 2: 75–83.
Behringer, Wolfgang. 1994. "Zur Geschichte der Hexenforschung." Pp. 93–146 in *Hexen und Hexenverfolgung im deutschen Südwesten.* Edited by Sönke Lorenz. Ostfildern: Cantz.
Hachmeister, Lutz. 1996. *Der Gegnerforscher: Die Karriere des SS-Führers Franz Alfred Six.* Munch: Beck.
Harmening, Dieter. 1989. "Himmlers Hexenkartei: Ein Lagebericht zu ihrer Erforschung." *Jahrbuch für Volkskunde.* Neue Folge 2: 99–112.
Lorenz, Sönke, Dieter R. Bauer, Wolfgang Behringer, and Jürgen Michael Schmidt, eds. 1999. *Himmlers Hexenkarthotek: Das Interesse des Nationalsozialismus an der Hexenverfolgung.* Bielefeld: Verlag für Regionalgeschichte.
Schormann, Gerhard. 1981. *Hexenprozesse in Deutschland,* Göttingen: Vandenhoeck and Ruprecht.
Sebald, Hans. 1989. "Nazi Ideology Redefining Deviants: Witches, Himmler's Witch-Trial Survey, and the Case of the Bishopric of Bamberg." *Deviant Behaviour* 10: 253–270.

NECROMANCY

Derived from the Greek words *nekros* (dead) and *manteia* (divination), necromancy is a form of divination in which the dead are used. Necromancy usually involves some form of direct interaction with a corpse (or parts thereof) to invoke spirits of the dead in order to obtain an omen. This magical act presupposes belief in the afterlife, belief in the life of the soul after the death of the physical body, and the conviction that the spirit of the deceased is endowed with supernatural wisdom or knowledge.

Throughout Western antiquity, necromancy was widespread, with records of its practice in Babylon, Egypt, Greece, and Rome. The oldest literary account of necromancy is in Homer's *Odyssey* (ca. 700 B.C.E.), in which the divine sorceress, Circe, instructed the hero Odysseus on summoning the deceased (primarily the ghost of the famous seer, Tiresias) for prophetic insight concerning his voyage home (X.488–540; XI.13–149). The Homeric passages contained many intricate details: the rites must be nocturnal and based around a pit and a fire; Odysseus must pour libations to a specified recipe; animals must be sacrificed and their blood drained for the ghosts to imbibe; and prayers must be recited to the ghosts and also to the gods of the underworld (who had to give their consent for the temporary release of the spirits). In a subsequent piece of Greek literature, the *Persians* (472 B.C.E.), the playwright Aeschylus described the practice of necromancy among the royal household of the Medes. This dramatic piece bore similar ritualistic traits to the Homeric description and reflected the Greek perception of Persians as exotic and inextricably linked with the practice of magic.

Roman sources regularly associated necromancy with the working of evil magic by wicked witches. The most infamous necromancer of antiquity was in Lucan's Latin epic *Pharsalia* (65 C.E.). Lucan's necromancer, the Thessalian sorceress Erictho, practiced hideous rituals involving the mutilation and consumption of corpses in her magical pursuit of divination. Although Lucan reveled in the repugnant details of Erictho's rites, the graphic detail of his portrayal was also partially designed to reflect the contemporary societal and political condemnation of magic. Beyond the literary tradition, the *Greek Magical Papyri* (PMG) contain spells concerning necromancy, such as PMG IV.2006–2125 (fourth century C.E.), which involved the conjuration of a ghost to assist a magician in a variety of endeavors, including divination.

The practice of necromancy is condemned in the Hebrew Bible, for example in Deuteronomy 18:10–11 (where the necromancer is listed alongside a series of magic practitioners), I Kings 28:8, and Isaiah 16:19. The most famous biblical account of necromancy concerns the witch of Endor (I Sam. 28), consulted by Saul during the war with the Philistines. Saul, dismayed at his situation and bereft at the belief that God had abandoned him, went to the necromancer at night and implored her to reanimate the spirit of Samuel. The woman summoned Samuel, who confirmed God's rejection of Saul and predicted the defeat and death of Saul and his sons. Theologians were intrigued by the account and various interpretations resulted. The Church Fathers Tertullian and St. Augustine regarded the apparition as real, but argued that it was the Devil who appeared to the necromancer, not the spirit of Samuel. In contrast, St. Jerome regarded the apparition as a hoax and the so-called pythoness a deceiver. Interpretations of the story by early modern writers were similarly divided; Jean Bodin, the French demonologist, supported the explanation of Tertullian and St. Augustine, but Reginald Scot argued that she was merely a ventriloquist.

In the early centuries of the Christian era, necromancy was a common magical practice, despite its condemnation by the Church. Tertullian warned against becoming involved in activities "in which demons represent themselves as the souls of the deceased" (*De anima* 57.2), an important statement in view of its premise that necromancy was not, in fact, the reanimation of the dead but a process that unleashed demonic forces masquerading as ghosts. This definition characterized the term *necromancy* in the early Christian era and subsequent centuries. By the Middle Ages, necromancy came to be associated with demonology and other forms of malevolent magic.

By the fifteenth century, from when a few necromancers' manuals survive (Kieckhefer 1997), this art was not necessarily associated with the aim of conjuring demons or devils for the primary purpose of divination, but it now encompassed a series of rituals for a variety of aims, including the acquisition of "love" and power in addition to the infliction of harmful magic on others, such as insanity and personal problems. Richard Kieckhefer (1989, 153) explained that a principal stronghold of necromancy was the "clerical underworld." The fact that clerics could be entrusted with the ritual of exorcism meant that they had access to specific texts that could also provide useful insights into the processes of invoking demons instead of driving them away. Clerics (and some members of higher ecclesiastical orders) also experimented with necromancy in order to verify certain aspects of their faith, such as the sacraments and purgatory. Various books on necromancy were available, including the *Table of Solomon* and the *Treasury of Necromancy*. The Dominican inquisitor Nicolas Eymeric, referred to the latter texts in his *Directorium inquisitorum* (Directory of Inquisitors, 1376); the books were, in fact, publicly burned by him (after he had read their contents). Eymeric recorded numerous rituals alleged to have come from texts such as the *Table of Solomon,* including inversions of Christian rites, such as genuflecting before the demons, baptizing icons or images, and perverting prayer formats. A century later, Joan Vicente, a cleric from Eymeric's region, used the *Table of Solomon* to perform necromantic rituals before the Inquisition caught him.

Not surprisingly, the Church took a severe position in regard to necromancy (among other forms of magic) and, in the late Middle Ages, numerous clerics were accused of practicing it. The contents of various texts on necromancy suggested that some formal education was required to perform necromancy's most intricate and learned procedures, but the practice of necromancy was not the exclusive domain of the clergy. In 1324, for example, Dame Alice Kyteler was eventually found guilty of practicing sorcery, including summoning demons and the use of body parts for various *maleficia* (evil acts). Although Alice Kyteler escaped being burned at the stake, her assistant, Petronella of Meath, was not so fortunate. In a less spectacular or threatening context, and one in keeping with the original meaning of the art, there are accounts of cunning folk participating in necromantic rites in order to acquire information concerning the diagnosis and treatment of disease. Likewise, ordinary folk summoned the deceased to visit them in their dreams for a series of reasons, including advice on matters ranging from their love lives to finances.

The curiosity that appears to have been a major component of early modern European experiments in necromancy was perhaps best captured in an account of his experience with this so-called black art by Benvenuto Cellini, an Italian goldsmith and sculptor. In 1523, Cellini hired a Sicilian priest to locate a missing woman and was invited to participate in a necromantic rite; he described his reaction: "I, who had a great desire to know something of the matter, told him, that I had all my life felt a curiosity to be acquainted with the mysteries of this art" (*Autobiography*, 64).

A half-century later, a practitioner of so-called high magic, John Dee, astrologer to Queen Elizabeth I, was fascinated with contacting spirits. He sought an alliance with Edward Kelley, an alchemist, medium, and necromancer. Together they created a system of occultism known as Enochian magic, the magic of angels and demons, subsequently influential in the development of the philosophies of the Golden Dawn. A more adept spiritualist than Dee, Kelly invoked spirits, while Dee recorded the rites. Although rumors abounded that both men had been involved in grotesque acts of necromancy entailing tomb robbing, more accurate accounts indicated the use of various magical implements, such as a scrying mirror, and the evocation of angels.

MARGUERITE JOHNSON

See also: AUGUSTINE, ST.; BIBLE; BODIN, JEAN; CIRCE; CLERICAL MAGIC; CUNNING FOLK; DEE, JOHN; DEMONOLOGY; DIVINATION; ENDOR, WITCH OF; EYMERIC, NICOLAS; GHOSTS; GREEK MAGICAL PAPYRI; HOMER; KYTELER, ALICE; RITUAL MAGIC; SCOT, REGINALD; TRITHEMIUS, JOHANNES; VICENTE, JOAN.

References and further reading:
Kieckhefer, Richard. 1989. *Magic in the Middle Ages.* Cambridge: Cambridge University Press.
———. 1997. *Forbidden Rites: A Necromancer's Manual of the Fifteenth Century.* Gloucestershire, UK: Alan Sutton.
Ogden, Daniel. 2002. *Magic, Witchcraft, and Ghosts in the Greek and Roman Worlds: A Sourcebook.* Oxford: Oxford University Press.

NETHERLANDS, NORTHERN

In the northern provinces of the Low Countries, the region that is now the Netherlands, trials for witchcraft were rare, with very few mass persecutions. The last Dutch witch was executed in 1608, making the Netherlands the first European state where witchcraft accusations ceased to be life-threatening. Both its economic situation and the attitude of its courts were instrumental in this remarkable development.

Until the outbreak of the Dutch Revolt in 1568, the northern provinces of the Low Countries were part of the Habsburg federation of seventeen provinces. After the Dutch Revolt, the northern provinces became an independent confederation, the Dutch Republic, which covered roughly the area of the present-day Netherlands. During the 1580s the southern provinces, located in what are now Belgium, Luxembourg, and parts of northern France, were reconquered by the Spanish army. But the war lasted for eighty years (1568–1648), during which time the boundaries of the new state shifted, depending on military developments.

Around 1500, the new demonology, making people who committed magical actions into accomplices of the Devil, reached the northern provinces of the Low Countries. But it should be emphasized that extreme views, such as those propagated in the *Malleus Maleficarum* (The Hammer of Witches, 1486), were never generally accepted there. Until the mid-sixteenth century, influential theologians maintained the traditional scholastic doctrine as articulated by St. Augustine and Thomas Aquinas. These scholastics distinguished between explicit and implicit pacts. The former was a capital crime, but the implicit pact was made without realizing its horrible implications and should therefore be discouraged by other, less radical methods. It resulted from superstitious practices and thus was merely a sign system through which humans informed demons about their wishes. Superstitious actions therefore implied a demonic covenant, but human beings could perform them while unaware of this implication. Because the laws of nature bound the Devil, these superstitious acts had at best a limited effect. He could create illusions and make people believe that they had, for instance, flown through the air in the company of other people and demons. All this was sheer illusion, however, and it was sinful to believe in its reality. In learned circles in the Low Countries, the *Canon Episcopi* (ca. 906) remained dominant until at least the mid-sixteenth century.

Before 1500, accusations of witchcraft rarely evolved into open trials in the northern Netherlands but were usually handled as minor offenses. Witchcraft was in theory already perceived as a capital crime, but tradition made it extremely difficult to attain a conviction. The *talio* (retribution) was still valid in this period; therefore, individuals who accused others of witchcraft ran the risk of being executed if they were unable to produce the necessary evidence. In at least one case (in Kampen 1515), a woman was indeed executed after failing to prove her allegations. Usually, the accused were allowed to buy off legal prosecutions by paying a fine or "composition." Only after the introduction of the inquisitorial procedure did the authorities start investigations on their own initiative. The Burgundian dukes and their Habsburg successors strongly supported this development and restricted the possibility of resolving such quarrels through compositions. During the first half of the sixteenth century, Roman law finally entered court practice in the Low Countries. In 1554, the Flemish jurist Joos de Damhouder published his *Praxis Rerum Criminalium* (Practice of Criminal Matters), which was almost immediately acknowledged as the best manual for judges and lawyers. It taught them how to interpret the laws of the *Codex Justiniani* (Justinian Code), including those regarding witchcraft. Damhouder viewed witchcraft as a form of lèse-majesté.

Another important element was the conviction of many jurists that the prince was responsible for the welfare of his people and therefore should ensure that the conduct of his subjects followed Christian standards. Not only the Habsburgs, but even their lifelong opponent Duke Charles of Gelderland saw it as their duty to fight the power of the Devil and his human followers. But the rapid growth of heresy already provided more demonically inspired offenders than they could punish. Although repeatedly instructing their local representatives to prosecute witches and sometimes even taking the lead in a campaign to wipe out these heinous people, as Duke Charles did in 1514, their major concern was to stem the rising Protestant tide. Obviously, both the Holy Roman Emperor Charles V and his enemy Charles of Gelderland desired the eradication of witchcraft; they wanted their law courts to prosecute witches and punish them if proven guilty. But witchcraft was a difficult crime to prove; there were usually no eyewitnesses to the crime, and material evidence was generally also lacking. The only way to prove the guilt of a suspected witch was by forcing her or him to confess. Torture was almost always needed to extract such a confession, but the usual torture devices were not sufficiently effective. In 1502, for instance, the sheriff of Haarlem arrested a woman who was subsequently tortured. But she managed to withstand the pain, despite the use of "exceptional severity," and in the end she was released. Only after Dutch hangmen had mastered special techniques, the so-called watching and walking, could they force witches into confession. It took several decades to learn this skill, but by 1550 it was known throughout the country.

In 1547, the countryside of the northeastern province of Groningen witnessed the first major outbreak of trials, during which twenty women and one man were executed. In the 1550s, a wave of prosecutions affected the region between the Rhine and the Meuse Rivers. The total number of victims cannot be established, since most trials took place in small, semiautonomous domains, where archives have been badly preserved. In the mid-1560s, especially in 1564, the number of trials rose once again, this time in the western province of Holland. Once again, we cannot establish an exact number of victims, because many relevant sources were lost during the tumult of the Dutch Revolt that began a few years later.

Despite this lack of precision, in the third quarter of the sixteenth century prosecutions seem to have reached their highest point in the northern Netherlands. Although the number of trials once again rose around 1590, this period was probably less bloody. After 1595, sizable persecutions occurred only in regions under Spanish control. In 1613, for instance, a persecution began in the region around Roermond, a small town today in the southeastern Netherlands, in which at least thirty-nine women and one man were executed. But in 1613, Roermond was under Spanish control. This is also true of the chain of trials in August and September 1595 that swept over northern and central Brabant, ultimately reaching Brussels, taking the lives of twenty-nine women and three men; the Dutch did not conquer northern Brabant until 1629.

Some areas (for instance, the northern province of Friesland) remained completely free of witchcraft trials, and in other regions prosecutions began relatively late. No trials occurred in central or northern Brabant until 1585, the year Antwerp surrendered to the Spanish. The region around Antwerp subsequently suffered an economic collapse and severe subsistence problems. In the densely urbanized and highly developed coastal provinces, popular fear of witchcraft was largely decided by economic conditions. The years 1589 and 1595

Execution of the witch Ann Hendricks in Amsterdam, where witchcraft trials seldom occurred. (TopFoto.co.uk)

witnessed the first trials and executions in this region, but in booming Holland they stopped in that same period. In 1564, for example, the number of trials suddenly rose in Holland—but only in towns that depended on trade and shipping, at a time when the sound was blocked because of a war between Sweden and Denmark, thereby severing connections to the Baltic and blocking the grain supply, called the "mother trade" by the Dutch. In 1563, Brussels banned all imports of English wool, and Queen Elizabeth responded by excluding ships from the Low Countries from English ports. Consequently, the economy of towns that depended on the trade with the Baltic and England collapsed. In 1564, particularly vulnerable places like Amsterdam and its surrounding countryside or the port of Delft suddenly became centers of witchcraft trials.

After 1585, the economic focus of northwestern Europe shifted to Holland and more specifically to Amsterdam, where an unprecedented economic boom began. The relative security of subsistence removed much of the fear of witchcraft. During the seventeenth century, many people immigrated from nearby parts of Germany affected by large-scale witchcraft panics. But none of them pressed for a prosecution of witches in their new domicile. Dutch authorities could now easily repel any attempt to influence their policy in this regard. For instance, when Amsterdam's Reformed ministers demanded in 1597 that the magistrates should suppress heresy and magic, they received the blunt answer that the Dutch had no desire to replace the Spanish Inquisition with Calvinist intolerance.

In the provinces of Holland and Zeeland, it became virtually impossible in the 1590s to convict someone for witchcraft if the defendant refused to confess freely. In 1593 the High Council, the appellate tribunal for the provinces of Holland and Zeeland, overturned a verdict of the court of Holland and Zeeland to torture two women. The High Council acquitted both women, and, as a result, it became virtually impossible to torture people suspected of witchcraft. A year later the court of Holland and Zeeland ruled in favor of a woman who had been convicted by a lower bench to undergo the swimming test (water ordeal). Its decision was based on advice from the professors of medicine and philosophy of Leiden University, which in turn was based on Johann Weyer's *De Praestigiis Daemonum* (On the Tricks of Devils, 1563). According to the professors, most women who were accused of witchcraft were melancholics and were therefore likely to be rather fat, which would keep them afloat. They also deemed it conceivable that the Devil would lift them up to prevent them from sinking. It should be noted that both the president of the High Council and the rector of Leiden University who drafted the university's advice were members of the Family of Love.

The Low Countries produced very few proponents of the prosecution of witchcraft, with the notable exception of Martín Del Rio. Traditional scholastics like Jacob van Hoogstraten represented an old-fashioned approach to demonology and as such were not founders of a skeptical tradition. However, later opponents from the Low Countries were skeptics who did not believe that the Devil was recruiting an army of human followers. Two prominent early examples of this skepticism are Johann Weyer (born in 1515 as Johan Wier in Grave, a small town not far from Nijmegen) and Cornelis (Cornelius) Loos (born in 1546 in the town of Gouda in Holland). The Erasmianism that dominated the intellectual climate in the Dutch Republic offered perfect surroundings for this skepticism.

There was a market here for vernacular books that denied the reality of the pact and the satanic cult. The first translation of Reginald Scot's *The Discoverie of Witchcraft* (1584) appeared in Leiden in 1609, albeit in an abridged form, which was reprinted in 1637 and 1638. In 1657 a translation of Friedrich Spee's *Cautio criminalis* (A Warning on Criminal Justice, 1631) was published. It should be added, though, that King James's *Daemonologie* (1597) also appeared in a Dutch translation in 1603, as did William Perkins's *A Discourse of the Damned Art of Witchcraft* (1608) in 1611. But the publication of works supporting the prosecution of witches was rather exceptional. A Puritan minister had made these translations of James's and Perkin's books, but they were never mentioned approvingly by leading Dutch Puritans; for instance, Gysbertus Voetius (1589–1676), professor of theology at Utrecht University after 1634 and the undisputed leader of Dutch Puritans, taught that it was morally wrong to prosecute somebody for witchcraft. Fully in line with the Dutch intellectual climate was the publication in 1660 of Weyer's *Opera omnia* (Complete Works). Original Dutch treatises on witchcraft were also meant to erode the fear of witchcraft; for example, Daniel Jonctys's plea to restrict the use of the rack (1651), Abraham Palingh's warning against a resumption of the trials (1659), Herman Löher's ego-document (a memoir, autobiography, diary, or personal correspondence in whose text the author is continuously present) (1676), and of course, Balthasar Bekker's voluminous rejection of demonic power (1691–1693).

Together with economic prosperity, an Erasmian tolerance that was broadly shared by secular authorities explains why the judicial search for witches ended so much sooner in the Dutch Republic than elsewhere in Europe. The republic was nominally Reformed, but secular authorities usually declined the Calvinist ministers' appeals to remodel society, if necessary by force. After 1594 the new jurisprudence regarding the crime of witchcraft spread from Holland and Zeeland to the other provinces; the last execution on the territory of the republic took place in 1608 in the town of Gorcum, the final victim a woman who had confessed to the local magistrates on her own initiative that she had committed a pact and had bewitched several people. At least 140 people lost their lives in witchcraft trials in the northern Netherlands, and that number rises to over 200 by including cases after the beginning of the Dutch Revolt in territories then under Spanish control but now part of the Netherlands. Considering that the population of these provinces rose from about 1 million to approximately 1.5 million between 1500 and 1600, the ratio of victims was remarkably low in comparison to other regions.

The early ending of the trials does not imply that belief in the reality of witchcraft also disappeared. Accusations of witchcraft or sorcery were still made long after legal prosecutions had ended (for that matter, they still are), and occasionally secular and ecclesiastical authorities had to deal with them, for example, through slander trials or similar procedures. Lynchings of supposed witches occurred in Amsterdam in 1624, Rotterdam in 1628, and at Huizen, a village southeast of Amsterdam, as late as 1746. People regularly asked church officials for help to undo what they saw as the effects of witchcraft. The only assistance that Reformed ministers could offer was prayers and communal fasting, but Catholic priests disposed of a far wider range of resources. In the 1580s the Catholic Church had crumbled away almost completely, but a small group of priests soon began building a network of clandestine parishes. These priests, the Jesuits especially, soon detected the value of exorcisms as propaganda and exploited this device to the fullest. Annual Jesuit reports to their superior in Brussels contained dozens of accounts about the exorcisms the Fathers applied to undo bewitchings of people, cattle, and houses and scores of other objects; to drive away demons; or to liberate people who had concluded a pact with the Devil.

Before, during, and after the trials, most accused witches were women, charged with a wide variety of destructive activities. However, in the eastern provinces about half of the accused were male. Most were suspected of attacking their enemies' cattle in the guise of werewolves. But in the trials, only a few men were formally charged with being werewolves. After 1610, lower courts were sometimes inclined to take action against supposed witches, but this never led to a conviction. In Holland, for instance, the fear of witchcraft revived again in the 1650s. In 1659, a woman was even formally accused of concluding a pact with the Devil and offering him her children. But in the end she was only put in the pillory and then released. In theory,

witchcraft remained a capital crime until the end of the Old Régime, but after 1608 this legal provision was only used to prosecute cunning folk and soothsayers, who were never put to death but only banished, and sometimes also flogged.

HANS DE WAARDT

See also: ACCUSATORIAL PROCEDURE; AMSTERDAM; BEKKER, BALTHASAR; *CANON EPISCOPI;* DECLINE OF THE WITCH HUNTS; DEL RIO, MARTÍN; ERASMUS, DESIDERIUS; FAMILY OF LOVE; HOOGSTRATEN, JACOB VAN; INQUISITORIAL PROCEDURE; JONCTYS, DANIEL; LÖHER, HERMAN; LOOS, CORNELIUS; LYNCHING; NETHERLANDS, SOUTHERN; PACT WITH THE DEVIL; PALINGH, ABRAHAM; PERKINS, WILLIAM; PURITANISM; ROMAN LAW; SCOT, REGINALD; SKEPTICISM; SPEE, FRIEDRICH; SWIMMING TEST; WATCHING AND WALKING; WEYER, JOHANN.

References and further reading:
Blécourt, Willem de. 1990. *Termen van toverij: De veranderende betekenis van toverij in Noordoost-Nederland tussen de 16de en 20ste eeuw.* Nijmegen: SUN.
Gijswijt-Hofstra, Marijke, and Willem Frijhoff, eds. 1991. *Witchcraft in the Netherlands from the Fourteenth to the Twentieth Century.* Rotterdam: Universitaire Pers Rotterdam.
James I. 1603. *Daemonologie, dat is, eene onderrichtinge tegen de tooverie.* Amsterdam: Claes Cornelisz and Laurens Jacobsz.
Jonctys, Daniel. 1650. *De pyn-banck wedersproken en bematigt.* Amsterdam: Hendrick Maneke.
Perkins, William. 1611. *Tractaet van de ongodlijcke toover-const.* Amsterdam: Jan Evertsz, Cloppenburch.
Scot, Reginald. 1609. *Ontdecking van tovery.* Leiden: Thomas Basson.
Spee, Friedrich. 1657. *De Waerborg om geen quaed hals-gerecht te doen.* Amsterdam: Jan Hendriksz and Jan Rieuwertsz.
Waardt, Hans de. 1991. *Toverij en samenleving: Holland 1500–1800.* Den Haag: Stichting Hollandse Historische Reeks.
Waite, Gary K. 2003. *Heresy, Magic, and Witchcraft in Early Modern Europe.* Houndmills, Basingstoke, Hampshire, UK; Palgrave Macmillan.

NETHERLANDS, SOUTHERN

In the historiography of witchcraft, the southern Netherlands (contemporary Belgium), which remained under Habsburg rule until the end of the eighteenth century, has usually been qualified as a region of terrible, centrally organized witch hunts during the sixteenth and seventeenth centuries, in total contrast to its neighbor, the so-called witch-free northern Netherlands. Recent archival research countered this statement and discerns a clear internal difference—chronologically as well as in terms of the intensity of prosecutions—between the Flemish-speaking part and the French- and German-speaking parts of the territory, which in general corresponds to present-day Belgium, minus the prince-bishopric of Liège.

TERRITORY (*SEE MAP*)

Before we look at the witchcraft trials in the southern Netherlands from 1450 to 1685, it is very

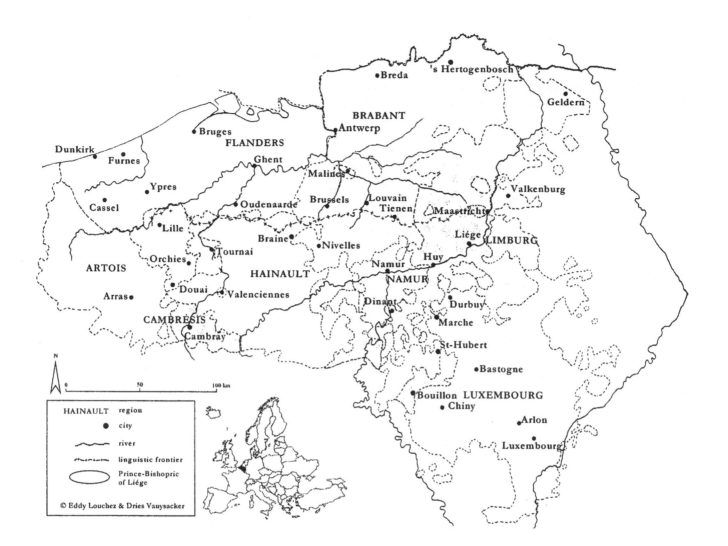

© Eddy Louchez & Dries Vanysacker

important to fix the territory of that region during this era. The southern (or Habsburg, or Austrian) Netherlands corresponds to the territory of the Low Countries that jurisdictionally did not belong to the Union of Utrecht after 1579. Regions that would later be connected with the Dutch Republic or (after Louis XIV) with France are here considered parts of the southern Netherlands. The territory of the southern Netherlands covered major regions such as Flanders, Artois (with Douai and Arras), Brabant (with Breda, Antwerp, Mechelen, Brussels, Louvain [Leuven], and 's Hertogenbosch), Maastricht, Roermond, Namur, Luxembourg, Limburg, Hainaut (Hainault), Lille-Orchies, Tournai, and Cambrai (Cambray). Recent research has shown that at least 2,564 (and perhaps even 1,000 more) witches were executed in the southern Netherlands during the period 1450–1685 (see Table 1). This number considerably exceeded the 160 witches executed in the northern Netherlands.

WITCHCRAFT TRIALS (1450–1685)

EARLY PHASE (1450–1480)

The ongoing impact of the famous trial of 1459 against the Waldensians in the city of Arras can hardly be overestimated. Fifteen persons were burned at the stake after they admitted to have taken part in obscene Sabbats and to have done homage to a black goat. The ever-increasing sorcery trials within the French-speaking regions south of the linguistic frontier were described in a similar way. Within the sources we find the words *sorcherie* (sorcery) and *vauderie* (Waldensian heresy) as inextricable synonyms: at Nivelles, a woman was banned in 1459 on suspicion of being a *vaudoise ou sorcière* (one who commits sorcery or heresy). Moreover, the crime of sorcery was increasingly mixed with fifteenth-century demonology. The pact with the Devil and his adoration by a sect had become standard items. The short-term consequences of the trials at Arras were substantial: already in 1460, large-scale inquiries were

TABLE N-1: TOTAL OF WITCHES EXECUTED IN THE SOUTHERN NETHERLANDS (1450–1685)

North of the linguistic frontier	South of the linguistic frontier (French-speaking)	South of the linguistic frontier (French- and German-speaking)
County of Flanders: 202	County of Artois, Cambrésis, Lille-Orchies, Tournai: 47	Duchy of Luxembourg: between 2000 and 3000
Duchy of Brabant: 57	County of Hainault: 28	
Limburg: 9	Duchy of Brabant: 31	
Roermond: 46	County of Namur: 144	
	Duchy of Luxembourg: minimum 2000	
in all: 314	in all: minimum 250	in all: between 2000 and 3000

begun at Tournai, Douai, and Cambray about possible witches. This exaggerated fervor to persecute forced officials to act. Episcopal inquisitors became aware of the fact they must cope with a new phenomenon. Several tracts were published; in 1477 Jean Tinctor had his tract against the Waldensians translated from French into Latin at Bruges. Preachers influenced the common people in the late fifteenth century using demonological interpretations of sorcery and thus articulating the cumulative concept of witchcraft to make them believe that witches belonged to an organized sect serving the Devil. Peculiarly enough, this belief or interpretation of the crime of sorcery made no headway in the Flemish (Dutch)-speaking part north of the linguistic frontier. In the county of Flanders, sorcery was still punished only in combination with poisoning.

FIRST PROSECUTION AND RELATIVE CALM (1510–1560/1570)

In 1495 Ysabeau Packet, of Huy in the prince-bishopric of Liège, was accused of flying to secret nocturnal gatherings with other witches. After a short jurisdictional procedure, she was burned at the stake on suspicion of harmful sorcery. Witch burnings soon spread to the neighboring county of Namur: between 1509 and 1555 at least forty-eight persons were executed at the stake and thirty-one others banished on suspicion of *vaudoisie et sorcellerie* (heresy or sorcery). Also, fortunetellers were severely persecuted. In the duchy of Luxemburg, at least thirty-three people stood trial on suspicion of witchcraft between 1509 and 1579. Fourteen of them—all women—were burned at the stake. In Artois, French-speaking Flanders, and Cambrésis, officers of justice for the first time concentrated intensively on female witches in the years 1510–1530. Also in the French-speaking part of Brabant, witches were executed between 1539 and 1543 at Limal and Jodoigne and twenty years later at Incourt, Villers, and, once again, Jodoigne. The county of Hainaut burned its first witch only in 1549, but between 1559 and 1576 at least fourteen others followed at Braine-le-Comte. After 1520, the county of Flanders intensified its prosecutions of

sorcery. It took until 1532 to burn the first witches—a man and a woman—at the stake on suspicion "of having given themselves to the enemy of Hell" (Vanysacker 1988, 151). The aldermen of the city of Bruges thus became the first in Flemish-speaking southern Netherlands to execute witches by fire. Moreover, it is striking that in the 1530s, six witches were burned or decapitated in Flanders. During the same period, several fortunetellers were reproached for having made a pact with the Devil. In cases of recidivism, no mercy was shown. Nevertheless, there were no mass executions: after 1538, Flemish stakes were extinguished, at least for witches (although large numbers of heretics were burned), for a period of fifty years, except for two executions at Oudenaarde (1554) and Furnes (1567).

The Flemish-speaking part of the duchy of Brabant avoided witch hunting for a long time. Of course there are accusations of sorcery, but the custom of buying off prosecutions from the officers of justice generally prevented trials. Real trials only started at the end of the sixteenth century at Kempen, 's Hertogenbosch, and Malines, as well in Inner and Northern Brabant. Two exceptions were Tienen, where seven women were burned from 1552 to 1554 and 1560 to 1564, and Kasterlee, where a woman was tortured to death during a witchcraft trial in 1565.

SECOND AND GREATER WITCH HUNT (1570–1685)

After a period of relative calm, which lasted longer in some regions than in others, around 1570 new prosecutions based on cumulative witchcraft began. Once again the regions south of the linguistic frontier, and especially the German-speaking territorial jurisdictions of the duchy of Luxembourg, were the pioneers. Recent research has claimed that there were around 2,500–3,000 witchcraft trials in the duchy of Luxembourg between 1560 and 1683; at least 2,000 ended with the execution of the accused. The jurisdictions of Bitburg, Arlon, Grevenmacher, Luxembourg, and Remich were especially zealous. The French-speaking regions of Luxembourg (Bastogne, Chiny, Durbuy, Virton, Marche, Saint-Hubert, and Bouillon) reached their highest point of persecutions between 1615 and 1630. War stopped most persecutions after 1630, except at Sugny, where eleven trials were held between 1657 and 1661. The last witch of the duchy of Luxembourg and of the whole southern Netherlands was executed in Anloy (near Bouillon) in 1685. Besides the county of Namur, where almost 100 witches died at the stake between 1560 and 1646, the French-speaking part of the duchy of Brabant also had its executions, especially at Nivelles and Genappe, with a minimum of twenty witches executed between 1572 and 1587 and another eight between 1594 and 1601. The county of Hainaut had its prosecutions: at Braine-le-Comte, there were twenty-eight trials between 1581 and 1613, with thirteen women burned at the stake. There were more sporadic prosecutions until 1640, the year in which the eighty-seven-year-old Anna Faulconnier died in jail.

Artois, Lille-Orchies, and Cambrésis had two peaks, in 1590–1600 and 1610–1620. After a period of relative calm, the stakes were once again lit in the decade 1630–1640. For twenty years, only female witches suffered, but from 1650 to 1660 many male witches were especially prosecuted. In the decade 1660–1670, witches again were exclusively female. In all, at least 245 people (203 women and 42 men) were prosecuted for witchcraft between 1550 and 1700. How many died is unknown, because the sources containing verdicts are lacking; we know only that at least 17 men and 30 women were executed. In the Artesian villages of Oisy and Arleux, there were at least 8 (perhaps 13) executions from 1612 to 1614, some of them Cistercian nuns at the abbey of Oisy-le-Verger. In Cambrésis, the villages of Quiévry, Bazuel, Rieux, Fressies, and Hem-Lenglet were especially known for their witch hunts. In addition, villages and cities such as Douai, Bouvignies (in 1679), Valenciennes, Bouchain, and Saint-Amand are to be mentioned.

North of the linguistic frontier, the actual witch hunts began only in 1589. In the duchy of Brabant, we find both the execution of Cathelyne van den Bulcke at Lier and trials against women and girls at Breda and 's Hertogenbosch, all in 1589. The county of Flanders opened in 1589 with the burning at the stake of Lievine Morreeuws in Furnes. For Brabant, Peelland, and Maastricht, the witch craze seems to have been relatively limited until around 1612, with forty-two executions. The year 1595 was especially bloody: from June until September, twenty-nine women and three men were executed in the Flemish-speaking part of Brabant. In the county of Flanders, the persecutions lasted until 1628, with at least 161 executions. The so-called *Westhoek*— with Furnes, Nieuport, Diksmuide, Sint-Winoksbergen, Dunkirk, Hondschote, Broekburg, Cassel, and Ypres— was the principal home of Flemish witches. Such great cities as Bruges (in 1595) and Ghent (in 1601) also had their "witch years." The region of Roermond, belonging to the southern Netherlands, had its witch hunt in 1613:

forty executions, with three more following in 1622. In the duchies of Limburg and Overmaas, Eysden had seven executions between 1609 and 1613, and Valkenburg had two executions in 1620.

Around 1630–1646, we see a new flash of prosecutions north of the linguistic frontier. Bruges and Malines had four and three executions, respectively, in 1634–1635 and 1642. The most striking characteristic of the witchcraft prosecutions in the county of Flanders is their late end: Nieuport still had four prosecutions between 1650 and 1652; Olsene two in 1661; Heestert three between 1659 and 1667; and Belsele burned the last witch in Flanders in 1684. In all, there were at least twenty-three northern executions after 1650.

Within the southern Netherlands we must distinguish between the prosecutions north and south of the linguistic frontier. Namur, Luxembourg, Lille-Orchies, Artois, and Cambrésis had their first serious hunts during the first half of the sixteenth century, immediately followed by Hainaut, but the county of Flanders—without forgetting a first phase of prosecutions around 1530–1540—and the Flemish-speaking part of the duchy of Brabant still awaited their first big trials. The real witch hunt north of the linguistic frontier started only around 1589, lasting until 1612 (Brabant) or 1628 (Flanders); a second cycle began around 1630–1645, and—surely for Flanders—the last executions came after 1650. North of the linguistic frontier there were possibly some 308 witches executed, with Flanders, Brabant, Roermond, and Limburg accounting for 202, 57, 46, and 9 witches, respectively. The essential difference between the Flemish-speaking regions of the southern Netherlands and the northern Netherlands lay more in the chronology than in the intensity of witchcraft prosecutions.

A totally different situation existed south of the linguistic frontier: there witchcraft persecutions began much earlier and were much more violent. After an early first phase, most regions experienced a second peak from 1570 until 1630. Some of them, certainly Artois and Cambrésis, continued their witch hunts deep into the seventeenth century. Nevertheless Namur, with 270 trials and 144 executions between 1509 and 1646, and especially the German-speaking parts of Luxembourg, with between 2,500 and 3,000 trials and at least 2,000 executions between 1560 and 1683, were by far the worst witch-hunting regions in the southern Netherlands. Their proximity to the Trier of Archbishop Johann von Schöneburg, who ordered hundreds of executions between 1581 and 1591, and the direct influence of the witchcraft tract of his suffragan Peter Binsfeld surely influenced the attitude of Namur and Luxembourg toward the crime of witchcraft.

CONCLUSIONS AND EXPLANATIONS
With the exception of some isolated cases, trials in which the pact between a "cumulative" witch and the

Devil stood central were all held in the southern Netherlands before local secular benches of aldermen or feudal courts, not before episcopal courts or central bodies like the Council of Flanders or the Council of Brabant. Witchcraft trials followed normal criminal procedure, but the judges, influenced by demonology, accepted the combination of facts and especially the *punctum diabolicum* (the Devil's spot or mark) as indications of guilt, which permitted arrests, torture, and even condemnations. Death by fire, the typical punishment for witchcraft, necessarily had to be preceded by the suspect's voluntary confession.

If 80 percent of the witches executed in the European witch craze were female, the southern Netherlands was no exception. In Flanders, exactly 80 percent (162 of 202) of those executed were women. In the Flemish-speaking part of Brabant this figure rose to 94 percent. In Hainault, *all* executed witches were women, and in Namur women constituted an overwhelming 92 percent. Only two regions showed a somewhat different picture: in Luxembourg, according to Marie-Sylvie Dupont-Bouchat's now-disputed figures, "only" 75 percent of the executed witches were female, and in the region around Cambray and Artois, only thirty of forty-seven known cases (64 percent) were women. This figure certainly has something to do with a relative scarcity of sources.

Recent publications have shown that despite excellent historical research, many fallacies persist about the witch hunt in the southern Netherlands. Thus, the statement that the central government decrees of July 20, 1592, and November 8, 1595, greatly stimulated the witch hunt, has become out of date. Those decrees did not mention cumulative witchcraft, and the central government, on the contrary, was reacting against excesses by local benches of aldermen. Also, the impact of the *Malleus Maleficarum* (The Hammer of Witches, 1486) on the prosecuting authorities in the southern Netherlands has been greatly exaggerated. Undoubtedly, the *Disquisitiones Magicae libri sex* (Six Books on Investigations into Magic, 1599/1600) of the Jesuit Martín Del Rio had far more impact on the witch hunt in his native region. It was this Catholic encyclopedia on witchcraft and on legal procedures in witchcraft trials, first published at Louvain, that made the theories of the *Malleus* known in the southern Netherlands a century after its publication.

In the Netherlands, witchcraft was far from exclusively a rural phenomenon. It began at Arras and spread to many large and small cities: Bruges, Malines, Ghent, Louvain, Antwerp, Breda, Roermond, Lille, Douai, Valenciennes, Nivelles, Bastogne, Durbuy, and Bouillon. Moreover, the influence of the learned city aldermen, who were well informed about the cumulative concept of witchcraft, which they studied in demonological tracts, was considerable. A letter from the aldermen of Bruges dated 1596 to their "ignorant" colleagues at Courtrai demonstrated this point. These learned aldermen, often humanists, spread the new cumulative concept of witchcraft throughout the region. An analysis of the private libraries of the aldermen of Bruges shows that they were acquainted not only with the *Malleus* or with the "primitive" demonology of their fellow townsman Joos de Damhouder (1507–1581), but also with the later demonological tracts of Paulo (Paulus) Grillando (Grillandus), Jean Bodin, Nicolas Rémy, and Del Rio. This presence of the learned witchcraft concept in Bruges can also be found in the torture sessions and in the formulation of verdicts by the magistrates. In the spread of modern witchcraft concepts and practices (e.g., pricking for a *punctum diabolicum* on the body of the witch), an active role was also played by the touring executioners. In the wake of these touring professionals, one could draw a chronology of witchcraft trials within several regions. Biographical studies on main figures (witches, aldermen, and executioners) could also be illuminating.

DRIES VANYSACKER

See also: ARRAS; BINSFELD, PETER; DEL RIO, MARTÍN; DEVIL'S MARK; EXECUTIONERS; EXECUTIONS; FEMALE WITCHES; LUXEMBOURG, DUCHY OF; TINCTOR, JOHANN; TRIER, ELECTORATE OF; URBAN WITCHCRAFT; *VAUDOIS* (WALDENSIANS).

References and further reading:

Aerts, Erik, and Maurits Wynants, eds. 1989. *Les sorcières dans les Pays-Bas Méridionaux (XVIe–XVIIe siècles).* Brussels: Archives Générales du Royaume.

Blécourt, Willem de, and Hans de Waardt. 1990. "Das Vordringen der Zaubereiverfolgungen in die Niederlande: Rhein, Maas und Schelde entlang." Pp. 182–216 in *Ketzer, Zauberer, Hexen: Die Anfänge der europäischen Hexenverfolgungen.* Edited by Andreas Bauert. Frankfurt: Suhrkamp.

Dupont-Bouchat, Marie-Sylvie, ed. 1987. *La Sorcellerie dans les Pays-bas. Aspects juridiques, institutionnels et sociales. De hekserij in de Nederlanden onder het Ancien Régime. Juridische, institutionele en sociale aspecten.* Heule: UGA.

———, Willem Frijhoff, and Robert Muchembled, eds. 1978. *Prophètes et sorciers dans les Pays-Bas, XVIe–XVIIIe siècle.* Paris: Hachette.

Gijswijt-Hofstra, Marijke, and Willem Frijhoff, eds. 1991. *Witchcraft in the Netherlands from the Fourteenth to the Twentieth Century.* Rotterdam. Universitaire Pers Rotterdam.

Monballyu, Jos. 1996. *Van hekserij beschuldigd: Heksenprocessen in Vlaanderen tijdens de 16de en 17de eeuw.* Heule: UGA.

———. 2002. "Die Hexenprozesse in der Grafschaft Flandern (1495–1692). Chronologie, Soziographie, Geographie und Verfahren." Pp. 279–314 in *Hexenprozesse und Gerichtspraxis.* Edited by Herbert Eiden and Rita Voltmer. Trier: Spee.

Muchembled, Robert. 1981. *Les derniers bûchers: Un village de Flandre et ses sorcières sous Louis XIV.* Paris: Ramsay.

———. 1994. "Terres de contrastes: France, Pays-Bas, Provinces-Unies." Pp. 99–132 in *Magie et sorcellerie en Europe du Moyen Age à nos jours.* Edited by Robert Muchembled. Paris: Armand Colin.

Roelants, Nienke, and Dries Vanysacker. 2005. "Tightrope Walkers on the Border Between Religion and Magic: Attitudes of Catholic Clerics North of the Linguistic Frontier in the Southern Netherlands Toward Superstition and the Crime of Witchcraft (1550–1650)." *Revue d'Hisoire Ecclésiastique* 100, nos. 3–4.

Vanhemelryck. 1999. *Het gevecht met de duivel: Heksen in Vlaanderen.* Louvain: Davidsfonds.

Vanysacker, Dries. 1988. *Hekserij in Brugge: De magische leefwereld van een stadsbevolking, 16de–17de eeuw.* Bruges: Van de Wiele—Genootschap voor geschiedenis.

———. 2000. "Het aandeel van de Zuidelijke Nederlanden in de Europese heksenvervolging (1450–1685): Een status quaesion-is." *Trajecta* 9: 329–349.

———. 2001. "The Impact of Humanists on Witchcraft Prosecutions in Sixteenth and Seventeenth-Century Bruges." *Humanistica Lovaniensia* 50: 393–434.

Voltmer, Rita. " . . .*Ce tant exécrable et détestable crime de sortilège.* Der 'Bürgerkrieg' gegen Hexen und Hexenmeister im Herzogtum Luxemburg (16. und 17. Jahrhundert)." *Hémecht; Zeitschrift für Luxemburger Geschichte* 56, no. 1: 57–92.

Waardt, Hans de. 1995. "Open en gesloten havens: Vervolging van toverij en toegang tot de zee aan het einde van de zestiende eeuw." Pp. 149–168 in *De Republiek tussen zee en vasteland: Buitenlandse invloeden op cultuur, economie en politiek in Nederland 1580–1800.* Edited by K. Davids, M. 'tHart, H. Kleijer, and J. Lucassen. Louvain: Garant.

NEW ENGLAND

Sixty-one trials for witchcraft are known to have taken place in seventeenth-century New England, in addition to those that occurred during the 1692 Salem witch hunt (Godbeer 1992, 235–237). The notorious Salem trials have often distracted attention away from the many other prosecutions for witchcraft that occurred throughout the seventeenth century in New England, from the 1638 indictment of Jane Hawkins in Boston to the 1697 acquittal of Winifred Benham and her daughter in Connecticut. Some formal complaints never came to trial, and many suspicions were never recorded but lurked nonetheless in the minds of towns-folk and villagers, warping their interactions with neighbors or acquaintances whom they suspected to be witches. Belief in the reality of witchcraft and fear of those who might be using occult powers to harm their enemies were part of everyday life in colonial New England. Prosecutions for witchcraft were the tip of a cultural iceberg.

In New England, a witchcraft trial generally took place only after a gradual and often lengthy process during which local suspicions had accumulated and hardened into conviction that a particular individual was indeed a witch. These suspicions resulted from the convergence of otherwise inexplicable misfortunes with problematic personal relationships. Puritan ministers encouraged their flocks to see individual suffering as a punishment from God for sin and inadequate faith. But in common with the English and other Europeans, colonists often preferred to explain illness or mishap for which there was no clear explanation in terms of malign occult forces that were apparently being wielded against them by their enemies. To blame a particular incident on witchcraft involved holding a specific individual responsible for one's misfortune. People today who seek external explanations for suffering and misadventure often blame impersonal forces such as corporate power or oppressive governmental agencies, as befits the largely impersonal nature of our society. Premodern men and women were much more inclined to point the finger at individuals, reflecting the intensely personalized environment in which they lived. Most New England communities contained no more than a few hundred adult residents, so that each individual interacted with neighbors in a wide variety of contexts. We deal regularly with all sorts of people who are otherwise unknown to us, but colonial New Englanders lived in communities where "every social transaction was personal in the fullest sense" (Demos 1982, 312).

Most allegations in witchcraft trials related to mysterious incidents that people explained in personal terms. Accuser and accused were usually neighbors with a history of disagreement. The accused had often requested a loan or gift, perhaps of food or a household implement; the accuser had refused but then felt guilty for having done so, especially since communitarian values were accorded great significance among early New Englanders. The person who had refused the original request now shifted guilt onto the aggrieved neighbor by blaming him or her for subsequent misfortunes such as a child's illness, the sudden death of livestock, or the inexplicable spoiling of food. The assumption underlying most accusations was that a person who felt aggrieved had resorted to witchcraft as a form of revenge.

There was no institutional outlet for the tension and hostility resulting from such disagreements. If a neighbor trespassed upon someone else's property or committed assault and battery, a law had been broken and the malefactor would be dealt with accordingly; but refusing to give a neighbor food or lend a tool was not a crime, so that the animosity that resulted could not be expressed or mediated directly through civil or criminal proceedings. Allegations of witchcraft provided an indirect outlet for feelings of guilt and hostility that resulted from confrontations of this kind. Such allegations made good sense in a culture that habitually explained human experience in both supernatural and intensely personal terms. The stress laid by Puritan ministers upon the ubiquity of evil and of temptations to commit evil doubtless fostered suspicions that witchcraft lay behind many misfortunes.

Not all New Englanders were equally vulnerable to accusations of witchcraft. When people feared that they had been bewitched and sought to identify the malefactor, they often blamed men and women in their local communities who already had a reputation for occult skill. These individuals (referred to by contemporaries as "cunning folk") were known for their expertise in magical divination and also healing techniques that combined spells or charms with simple herbal remedies. Though ministers condemned any such activities as dependent upon the Devil's assistance, many colonists were less concerned about issues of causation and valued the services provided by cunning men and women. Yet popular belief that occult power could serve both benevolent and malevolent purposes placed such practitioners in an ambiguous and vulnerable position: cunning folk might use their skills to harm as well as to help their neighbors and could easily become the target of suspicion if a disagreement in which they had been involved was followed by a mysterious stroke of bad fortune that befell the other party. Healers were especially susceptible to accusation if their patients grew sicker instead of recovering.

Women known for their "cunning" were much more likely than men to be accused of witchcraft. The power wielded by cunning folk was potentially dangerous whether in the hands of a man or a woman, but occult skill was especially threatening if the practitioner was female: the aura of power surrounding cunning folk contradicted gender norms that placed women in subordinate positions. Neither belief in the efficacy of folk magic nor its practice were gender specific: men as well as women resorted to and functioned as cunning folk. Yet suspicions that magical skill had been used for malicious ends were much more likely to be directed against female practitioners. Most accused cunning folk were women. Their prosecution testified not only to the ambiguous place that occult practitioners occupied within New England communities but also to specifically gendered fears.

An overwhelming majority (around four-fifths) of those New Englanders tried for witchcraft were women. As in old England, roughly half of the New England men charged with this crime were married or otherwise close to accused women: they were, in other words, guilty by association (Karlsen 1987, 47–48). Except in a few regions, such as New France and Iceland, witchcraft was perceived on both sides of the Atlantic as a primarily female phenomenon. Puritan ministers did not teach that women were by nature more evil than men, but they did see them as weaker and thus more susceptible to sinful impulses. Clergymen reminded New England congregations that it was Eve who first gave way to Satan and then seduced Adam, when she should have continued to serve his moral welfare in obedience to God; all women inherited that potential for collusion with the Devil from their mother Eve. Yet some women were much more likely than others to be accused of witchcraft. Throughout the seventeenth century, women became especially vulnerable to such allegations if they were seen as challenging their prescribed

place in a gendered hierarchy that Puritans held to be ordained by God.

Women who fulfilled their allotted roles as wives, mothers, household mistresses, and church members without threatening assumptions about appropriate female comportment were respected and praised as handmaidens of the Lord, but those whose circumstances or behavior seemed to disrupt social norms could easily become branded as the servants of Satan. Especially vulnerable were women who had passed menopause and thus no longer served the purpose of procreation, women who were widowed and so neither fulfilled the role of wife nor had a husband to protect them from malicious accusations, and women who had inherited or stood to inherit property in violation of expectations that wealth would be transmitted from man to man. Women who seemed unduly aggressive and contentious were also more likely to be accused; conduct that would not have struck contemporaries as particularly egregious in men seemed utterly inappropriate in women. Behavior or circumstances that seemed disorderly could easily become identified as diabolical and associated with witchcraft: the Devil had, after all, led a rebellion against God's rule in heaven.

Once New Englanders became convinced that a particular person was a witch and had accumulated sufficient evidence to justify a prosecution, they lodged a formal complaint with the authorities and so initiated a criminal prosecution. The penalty for witchcraft throughout the New England colonies was death, as laid down by Scripture. Yet convincing oneself and one's neighbors of an individual's guilt was not the same as convincing a court. Of the sixty-one known prosecutions for witchcraft in seventeenth-century New England, excluding the Salem witch hunt, sixteen at most (perhaps only fourteen) resulted in conviction and execution, a rate of just over one-quarter (26.2 percent). Four of these individuals confessed, which made the court's job much easier. If they are omitted, the conviction rate falls to just under one-fifth (Godbeer 1992, 158).

New England laws defined witchcraft in theological terms, demanding proof of diabolical allegiance. Yet whereas the Puritan authorities depicted witches as heretics and servants of the Devil, ordinary men and women were more inclined to think about witchcraft as a practical problem: believing that their misfortunes were due to witchcraft, they wanted to know who the witch was, and they wanted her punished. The evidence presented in witch cases rarely made any mention of the Devil. That disjunction between legal requirements and the nature of most popular testimony led to acquittal in most cases. That deponents did not adapt their testimony to fit legal criteria suggests that ordinary colonists were very much focused upon practical threats to their safety when thinking about witchcraft and also that at least some people were much less thoroughly schooled in official ideology than persistent stereotypes of early New Englanders would suggest.

Persons accused of witchcraft in seventeenth-century New England, excluding the Salem outbreak, were less likely to be convicted and executed than their counterparts across the Atlantic. The English statutes enacted against witchcraft in 1542 and 1563 had defined the crime as a hostile act rather than as heresy, so that the preoccupation of popular depositions with practical harm was less problematic. Continental law generally defined witchcraft in theological terms, but in many European countries, the courts used torture to extract the kinds of evidence that would justify conviction for diabolical heresy. The New England authorities, operating under English jurisdiction, had no legal recourse to torture when questioning defendants in witchcraft cases. (The Salem witch hunt was the only occasion on which New England courts gathered extensive evidence of diabolical allegiance; it was also the only occasion on which the authorities used psychological pressure and physical torture, illegally, to extract a large number of confessions.)

The depositions given against New England's accused witches generally fell into one of four categories. Most frequently, villagers and townsfolk described quarrels with the accused individual that had been followed by misfortune or illness for which there was apparently no natural explanation; the witnesses claimed that the alleged witch had afflicted them as a direct consequence of these arguments. Second, deponents claimed that the accused had a reputation for skill as a fortuneteller or healer; this established that the accused had occult powers that, it was implied, had also been deployed for malign purposes. Third, witnesses described having used countermagical techniques such as boiling the urine of a bewitched child; if a neighbor suffered an analogous injury or was drawn inexplicably to the house in which the experiment was taking place, that information was offered up to the court as incriminating testimony. And finally, neighbors of the accused would describe generally suspicious behavior, such as extraordinary and perhaps superhuman strength.

These depositions show beyond any doubt the fear that alleged witches aroused among their neighbors, but they were mostly unconvincing from a legal perspective. Magistrates and the learned ministers whom they consulted during many of these cases dismissed testimony relating "strange accidents" following quarrels as "slender and uncertain grounds" for conviction (Hall 1999, 348). Clergymen denounced countermagic as "going to the Devil for help against the Devil" (Godbeer 1992, 81) and warned that Satan was a malicious liar, which hardly encouraged magistrates to rely upon testimony describing countermagical experiments. They were occasionally willing to conclude that divination or other magical practices that ministers

condemned as diabolical proved collusion between the accused witch and the Devil, but even here magistrates were mostly reluctant to convict unless there was explicit mention of the Devil in a confession or hostile depositions.

New England magistrates were ready and willing to convict and execute accused witches, should the evidence against them prove convincing. But as in their handling of prosecutions for other capital crimes, the courts refused to convict unless the evidence satisfied rigorous standards of proof, which meant either a voluntary confession or at least two independent witnesses to an incident demonstrating the individual's guilt. It was difficult enough to secure two witnesses for sexual offenses that carried the death penalty, but the challenge was compounded when dealing with an invisible crime involving alleged collusion with supernatural agents. Only in a minority of cases were New England magistrates convinced that the evidence before them satisfied the established criteria for conviction. At other trials, their fastidious adherence to evidentiary standards resulted in acquittal. Judges sometimes pronounced accused witches to be "suspiciously guilty" but "not legally guilty" of the alleged crime (Godbeer 1992, 173). In some cases, they overturned jury verdicts, rejecting the instincts of local jurymen who were convinced of the accused person's guilt.

The neighbors and enemies of accused witches who had given what they considered to be damning testimony were often infuriated by the reluctance of magistrates to treat their depositions as legally compelling. Sometimes they would confer with each other, gather new evidence against the acquitted individual, and then renew legal charges. Three individuals were each prosecuted on three separate occasions; another five appeared in court twice on charges of witchcraft. All these cases resulted in acquittal. Repeat prosecutions expressed unshaken belief in an individual's guilt and also dissatisfaction with the courts' handling of witchcraft cases. That dissatisfaction sometimes resulted in extralegal retaliation: Mary Webster of Hadley, Massachusetts, was brutally assaulted in 1684, a year after her acquittal, when townsfolk became convinced that she had again bewitched one of her neighbors.

As the difficulty of securing a legal conviction for witchcraft became increasingly apparent, New Englanders became less and less inclined to initiate legal prosecutions against suspected witches: there were 19 witchcraft trials during the 1660s, but only 6 during the 1670s and 8 during the 1680s. That dramatic decline was not due to a lessening fear of witches, as would become clear in 1692, when official encouragement of witchcraft accusations in and around Salem Village unleashed a deluge of allegations. The witch hunt of 1692, which resulted in over 150 arrests and 19 executions, was atypical in its scale and intensity. Yet the fears and beliefs that underlay it merely expressed in extreme form assumptions and anxieties that were deeply rooted throughout New England culture.

The damaging controversy over the Salem court's reliance upon problematic testimony that led to the halt of the trials in the fall of 1692 reaffirmed and intensified judicial concerns regarding evidentiary issues. These combined with embarrassment as well as sincere distress over the problematic convictions of that year to discourage future prosecutions. Yet an end to witchcraft trials in New England by the end of the century did not signify an end to belief in and fear of witches. New Englanders continued to use counter-magic against suspected witchcraft throughout the eighteenth century and occasionally assaulted individuals whom they believed to be witches. In July 1787, as the Constitutional Convention was meeting in Philadelphia to design a new system of government that would embody Enlightenment principles, a mob outside in the city streets lynched a woman who was believed to be a witch.

RICHARD GODBEER

See also: ACQUITTALS; BERMUDA; COUNTERMAGIC; CUNNING FOLK; EVE; FEMALE WITCHES; GENDER; OCCULT; PERSONALITY OF WITCHES; PURITANISM; SALEM; TRIALS; WITNESSES.

References and further reading:
Demos, John Putnam. 1970. "Underlying Themes in the Witchcraft of Seventeenth-Century New England." *American Historical Review* 75: 1311–1326.
———. 1982. *Entertaining Satan: Witchcraft and the Culture of Early New England.* New York: Oxford University Press.
Godbeer, Richard. 1992. *The Devil's Dominion: Magic and Religion in Early New England.* New York: Cambridge University Press.
Hall, David D. 1985. "Witchcraft and the Limits of Interpretation." *New England Quarterly* 58: 253–281.
———. 1989. *Worlds of Wonder, Days of Judgment: Popular Religious Belief in Early New England.* New York: Knopf.
———. 1998. "Middle Ground on the Witch-Hunting Debate." *Reviews in American History* 26: 345–352.
———, ed. 1999. *Witch-Hunting in Seventeenth-Century New England: A Documentary History, 1638–1693.* Boston: Northeastern University Press.
Kamensky, Jane. 1997. *Governing the Tongue: The Politics of Speech in Early New England.* New York: Oxford University Press.
Karlsen, Carol F. 1987. *The Devil in the Shape of a Woman: Witchcraft in Colonial New England.* New York: W. W. Norton.
Reis, Elizabeth. 1997. *Damned Women: Sinners and Witches in Puritan New England.* Ithaca, NY, and London: Cornell University Press.
Weisman, Richard. 1984. *Witchcraft, Magic, and Religion in Seventeenth-Century Massachusetts.* Amherst: University of Massachusetts Press.

NEW FRANCE

During the seventeenth century, when witchcraft was a serious concern for the elites of Europe and New England, New France was a recently established, tiny community. In 1660, there were only around 3,000 Europeans in Quebec. This number rose to around 10,000 by the end of the century—only one-eighth of New England's population at this point. The largest cities in New France were small towns by French standards, with Montreal at 500 and Quebec City at 800 in 1663.

The French were not eager to emigrate. Both the severe weather and the fear of attacks from Indians discouraged immigration to New France. Many who voyaged to Quebec did not stay, so the colony's early population was especially transient and unstable. This was different from old France, where towns and villages had existed for centuries and most people stayed in their communities. Those who came to New France were mostly young, unattached males from the Paris region and northwestern France, who were more urban in origins than the mainly rural French population.

This frontier community imported much traditional folklore and culture, which included a strong role for the Devil, magic, and supernatural occurrences. One popular legend was the *Chasse Galerie,* which was a wild ride across the night sky by souls destined for damnation. This was a widely diffused European legend, with many local variants; in Quebec, the hell-bound riders used canoes rather than horses. Belief in the presence and power of the Devil was widespread. The inhabitants of the Ile d'Orléans, for example, feared that, if someone were dying at night, the Devil would intercept the friend or relative who went in search of a priest, so that he could gain possession of the soul of the person who died without absolution. If possible, they would send two carriages for the priest, expecting that at least one could get through. In addition, any unusual climactic condition like comets or strange sounds could be regarded as a diabolical portent.

Religious authorities, perhaps trying to get more priests dispatched to the colony, complained about the ignorance of the settlers as well as their unwillingness to attend Mass or pay their tithes. Still, Catholicism lay at the core of life in New France, with the same mixture of folklore and Christianity that flourished in old France. A church at Beaupré near Quebec City, dedicated in 1658 to Ste. Anne, soon became a scene of miraculous cures. In 1700, after a remarkable cure, Jean Salois hung his crutches on the chapel wall, beginning a tradition that persists to the present.

Unlike the situation in Europe and New England in this period, New France produced few cases involving witchcraft that were serious enough to come to the attention of the courts. In 1658, a disappointed suitor, René Besnard, cast a spell on the marriage of his former sweetheart by tying ritual knots in a string. This *nouement de l'aiguillette* (tying a knot, a ligature), widely practiced and feared in early modern France, was a traditional way of causing male impotence. The couple, frightened of the spell, could not consummate their marriage, and accused Besnard of causing "perpetual impotence . . . by *malefice.*" The court found him guilty, imposing a heavy fine and banishing him from Montreal. Both secular and religious authorities took this sort of spell casting seriously: the bishop of Montreal annulled the marriage. When both parties eventually remarried and, between them, had twenty-five children, it only confirmed the reality of the spell.

Another serious case, a few years later, involved another disappointed suitor. Daniel Vuil (or Will), a converted Protestant, was accused of causing the demonic possession of Barbe Hallay, who had rejected his marriage proposal. She was brought to Quebec City, where she was exorcized and freed of her demons through the care of the saintly Mother Catherine of Saint Augustine and the intervention of the martyred Father Jean de Brebeuf. Vuil was tried, convicted, and executed—though it is not clear whether it was primarily for blasphemy, for causing Barbe's possession, or for trading brandy with the natives.

In 1685, Jean Campagnard was charged with several instances of making people ill through witchcraft, including a young woman who refused his advances. The local court found him guilty, but the colony's appellate court, the Sovereign Council in Quebec City, established in 1663 as the equivalent of a French *parlement* (sovereign judicial court), overturned his conviction. These few cases do not compare to the record of New England, where sixty-one witchcraft trials took place and at most 36 witches were executed.

Several factors contributed to the remarkable paucity of witchcraft trials in New France. For one thing, by the time a viable community was established in Quebec, the French judicial elites were punishing very few people accused of witchcraft. Ordinary people still believed that witches were real and dangerous and accused their neighbors of trying to harm them by diabolical means, but the French judicial system was not responding strongly to these concerns.

Crucial differences also separated the social and demographic structures of New France and old France. Although most of its people lived by farming, Quebec's inhabitants did not replicate the society of French agricultural villages. The settlements in Quebec stretched along the Saint Lawrence River between Quebec City and Montreal, with properties averaging around 90 acres. Houses were built close to the river on each property, around 300 meters apart. Although conditions were very harsh, within a few years these *habitant* (resident) farmers were substantially better off than their French counterparts.

Most early immigrants to New France were male. In 1660, New France had over six single men for every available European woman. The royal government responded by sending shiploads of women to the colonies to marry and multiply. Not surprisingly, women, even widows with children, married with ease in Quebec. Marriages took place at much earlier ages, which tended to make families larger as well. Isolated older women were often accused of witchcraft in Europe, but this group did not exist in New France. The basic social unit there was the family farmstead, in which all the members worked together to clear the land, grow crops, and defend themselves against Indian attacks.

In Europe, most witchcraft accusations were made against women, supported by a long tradition of misogyny, but both old and New France emphasized male witchcraft. Quebec's three most serious cases all involved accusations against single men who had been disappointed in their attempts to marry. This was clearly the result of the unusual gender ratios in New France, where patterns of settlement and a shortage of women produced a society that, at least in its early stages, differed significantly from the old village communities of Europe. These factors apparently underlay the extraordinary scarcity of formal witchcraft trials in New France.

JONATHAN L. PEARL

See also: FRANCE; IMPOTENCE, SEXUAL; MALE WITCHES; NEW ENGLAND.

References and further reading:
Greer, Allan. 1997. *The People of New France.* Toronto: University of Toronto Press.
Moogk, Peter. *La Nouvelle France: The Making of French Canada—A Cultural History.* East Lansing: Michigan State University Press.
Pearl, Jonathan. 1977. "Witchcraft in New France in the Seventeenth Century: The Social Aspect." *Historical Reflections* 4: 191–205.
Seguin, Robert Lionel. 1971. *La Sorcellerie au Québec du XVIIe Siècle.* Montréal: Leméac.

NEW GRANADA

The New Kingdom of Granada (Nuevo Rein de Granada), corresponding to the modern states of Colombia and Venezuela and parts of Panama and Ecuador, was characterized by an especially high incidence of witchcraft trials in comparison with other Spanish American jurisdictions. In 1547 an *audiencia,* or high court, was established at the capital Santa Fe de Bogotá. The first archbishop came in 1553 to Santa Fe to assume the episcopal inquisitorial jurisdiction. From the foundation of the tribunal at Lima in 1570, New Granada was subject to the Peruvian Inquisition until September 26, 1610, when the third tribunal in Spanish America was installed in the city of Cartagena with jurisdiction over northern South America, Central America, and the Caribbean Islands. At the end of the seventeenth century, the Cartagena tribunal declined and was abolished after the proclamation of independence in 1811 and again in 1821 before the final achievement of independence of South America in 1824. Witchcraft trials occurred during the whole period of colonial rule, with peaks in the decades from 1610 to 1650 and at the beginning of the eighteenth century. Witchcraft, sorcery, and superstitions constituted the bulk of cases registered by the tribunal at Cartagena.

Witchcraft beliefs were widespread at all levels of New Granadan colonial society. In the period 1614–1690, 188 cases of superstitions were tried by the Cartagena Inquisition, of which 58 were witchcraft trials (Henningsen 1994, 19). Female defendants far outnumbered their male counterparts. After 1571, the indigenous population was exempt from the inquisitorial jurisdiction. Nevertheless, several witchcraft cases involving Amerindians can be traced even after the installation of the Cartagena tribunal. During the colonial period, a multiplicity of jurisdictions characterized the territory of the Cartagena Inquisition. In distant regions, both ecclesiastical and secular tribunals pronounced sentences in witchcraft cases. Also, the inquisitors were generally not very concerned with the superstitions of the poor, the Amerindians, or the slave population, even though the great majority of witchcraft accusations revolved around individuals of African descent. Often the accusations came from other members of the African population. Nonetheless, the ideas on witchcraft as recorded in trial documents correspond mainly to the European model of witches.

Witchcraft beliefs in sixteenth- and seventeenth-century New Granada included characteristic elements of both the European popular and demonological traditions: the witches were thought to be able to transform themselves into animals, fly through the air, and cause sickness and death through maleficent magic. Defendants reportedly took the shape of tigers, snakes, cats, and birds to fly at night. While their body remained lifeless at home, as if dead, their "soul" went through the air to suck the blood of children and to attend assemblies, where the witches venerated the Devil by kissing his anus. The tribunal at Cartagena was founded at a time when the *Suprema* (the supreme council of the Inquisition) in Madrid had ordered extreme caution to be exercised in dealing with witchcraft accusations. In periods of crisis, however, such as in the 1630s, the inquisitors at Cartagena gave full credit to the accusations. First, two women were arrested, and later, as the witch hunt spread throughout the province, a great number of people were imprisoned. Finally, two women of African descent were sentenced to die at the stake, but the *Suprema* ordered a copy of the documents to be brought to Spain and eventually revoked the sentence of the Cartagena tribunal. In the resulting auto-da-fé (act of the faith), held in 1634, twenty-one witches were punished, mostly by scourging.

IRIS GAREIS

See also: INQUISITION, SPANISH; NEW SPAIN; PERU; POPULAR BELIEFS IN WITCHES; SABBAT; SPAIN; SUPERSTITION.

References and further reading:
Ballesteros Gaibrois, Manuel. 2000. "La instalación del tribunal del Santo Oficio en Cartagena de Indias. Nuevas Noticias." Pp. 1025–1029 in *Historia de la Inquisición en España y América*. Vol. 3, *Temas y problemas*. Edited by Joaquín Pérez Villanueva and Bartolomé Escandell Bonet. Madrid: Biblioteca de Autores Cristianos, Centro de Estudios Inquisitoriales.
Ceballos Gómez, Diana Luz. 1994. *Hechicería, brujería e Inquisición en el Nuevo Reino de Granada: Un duelo de imaginarios.* Bogotá: Universidad Nacional de Colombia.
Escobedo, Ronald. 1993. "América y la Inquisición." Pp. 319–330 in *Los Inquisidores*. Vitoria-Gasteiz: Fundación Sancho el Sabio.
Henningsen, Gustav. 1994. "La evangelización negra: Difusión de la magia europea por la América colonial." *Revista de la Inquisición* 3: 9–27.
Lea, Henry Charles. 1922. *The Inquisition in the Spanish Dependencies: Sicily–Naples–Sardinia–Milan–The Canaries–Mexico–Peru–New Granada.* New York: Macmillan.
Medina, José Toribio. 1899. *Historia del Tribunal del Santo Oficio de la Inquisición de Cartagena de las Indias.* Santiago de Chile: Universo.

NEW SPAIN

In New Spain, witchcraft cases were subject to the jurisdiction of the Inquisition. Following the Spanish conquest of Mexico in 1520, a monastic and later an episcopal Inquisition was introduced in the vice-royalty of New Spain; until 1570, all sectors of the population were subject to them. In 1571, a branch of the Spanish Holy Office was installed at Mexico City with jurisdiction over Central America, the Spanish dependencies in North America, and the Philippines. It was not abolished until 1820. During its most active period, from 1571 to 1700, it investigated about 2,000 cases (Alberro 1988, 195), including a considerable number of sorcery and witchcraft accusations. Amerindians were exempt from the jurisdiction of the Mexican Inquisition but remained under the control of ecclesiastical courts after 1571. The similarity of procedures that characterized these institutions soon led to a confusion of competencies and jurisdictions. Other evidence indicates that monastic and secular tribunals, especially in distant rural areas, sometimes acted on their own, independently of the Mexican Inquisition, but did not always keep records of their witchcraft cases.

In the course of this long period, witchcraft trials underwent substantial changes in New Spain, due to a changing assessment of the crime of witchcraft. Witchcraft and sorcery were severely punished before 1570, but after the installation of the Inquisitorial tribunal, they were no longer considered heresy, but only superstition. With regard to the nature of witchcraft, trial documents suggested that in New Spain, the great majority of witchcraft and sorcery cases essentially involved individuals serving individual clients, either by magically curing people or inflicting harm on them.

From 1540 to 1700, the Mexican Inquisition tried 144 people for "superstition" (Henningsen 1994, 10, n. 1). No absolute data are available for the eighteenth century; but there is evidence of 60 cases qualified as "superstitious healing" being investigated by the Mexican Holy Office from 1701 to 1806, including 10 cases classified as sorcery (*hechicería*), and 5 as maleficent witchcraft (*brujería*) (Quezada 1989, cuadro 8). In addition, another source lists 125 different cases instituted by the Inquisition during the same period, including 20 cases of harmful witchcraft, 39 cases of sorcery, and 66 for other forms of superstition (Aguirre Beltrán 1963, 333–376). Evidently, more witchcraft cases were tried by the Inquisition in New Spain during the eighteenth century than in the seventeenth century, once all cases of superstition are included.

WITCHCRAFT TRIALS BY ECCLESIASTICAL INQUISITIONS

During the period before 1571, a peak in the frequency of trials occurred from 1536 to 1543, when Bishop Juan de Zumárraga served as apostolic inquisitor in Mexico. He conducted at least 152 trials, among which 23 dealt with accusations of sorcery and superstition (Greenleaf 1961, 14). The historical documents from these trials enable us to distinguish the witchcraft beliefs reflected in trials of Europeans, Africans, or the mestizo populations from those instituted against Amerindians. Accusations against the first group closely resembled the "superstitions" dealt with by other Spanish tribunals: divination (with or without invocations of the Devil), superstitious healing, and love magic (combined with incantations and the use of magic potions) were the most frequently mentioned offenses qualified as sorcery or superstition. Most defendants in this period (15 cases out of 20) were women (Greenleaf 1961, 112). All were slaves or belonged to the lower classes of colonial society. Trials from this period demonstrate vivid cultural exchanges among all ethnic groups of the colonial population, especially near the bottom of the social hierarchy. Spaniards, Africans, and Amerindians exchanged beliefs and practices of divination, magical healing, and love magic, and introduced such new elements as the use of Mexican hallucinogenic drugs. Intercultural contacts also connected practitioners of magic with their clients, as colonial magicians consulted Amerindian specialists in search of more effective practices or because of their knowledge of local herbal medicine.

However, a different picture emerged from the trials instituted against native Mexican people. The defendants—mainly men—were accused of sorcery and idolatry; of transforming themselves into such fierce animals as jaguars, lions, or dogs; or of making rain and producing similar effects by magical means. Contemporary colonial descriptions labeled these abilities of indigenous specialists as witchcraft. The trials, however, drew a clear distinction between sorcery and witchcraft: the former supposed an implicit pact with the Devil and the latter an explicit pact and denial of the Christian faith. Additionally, witchcraft was associated with harmful magic. Consequently, the offenses of the Amerindians were usually qualified as sorcery rather than witchcraft.

WITCHCRAFT TRIALS BY THE SPANISH INQUISITORIAL TRIBUNAL

Lacking jurisdiction over Amerindians, the Mexican branch of the Spanish Inquisition also instituted many more sorcery trials than witchcraft cases between 1571 and 1820. Like the "European" defendants of the episcopal inquisition, the great bulk of accusations again dealt with love magic, superstitious healing, and divination. Divination was practiced to find lost objects, for diagnostic purposes in magical curing, for advice in daily life, and to foretell the future. Practitioners could be male or female, but considerably more women were accused of love magic. Some cases were classified as maleficent witchcraft, an offense usually committed by individuals trying to harm another person. According to their ethnic descent, they preferred European, African, or Amerindian methods, including the native Mexican procedure of magically causing the death of a person by breathing in his or her direction.

Very few accusations corresponded to the contemporary European model of witchcraft. In 1614, however, witchcraft accusations suddenly increased in the northern Mexican town of Celaya, following the inquisitor's proclamation of the Edict of Faith (a list of types of heresy). The resulting inquisitorial trials, held a few years after a famous outbreak of witchcraft had preoccupied the Inquisition in Spain's Basque country, offered a vision of witchcraft similar to early modern Spanish ideas on witches (*brujas*) and their deeds. As in Spain, the majority of Mexican witchcraft defendants were women of low social status. Although women of different ethnic descent were implicated in the Celaya cases, most were descendants of Spanish colonists. They were accused of assembling at night outside the town, where they allegedly adored the Devil in the form of a billy goat with an obscene kiss. A strange detail of this Mexican version of the witches' Sabbat relates that the Devil, after the adoration, provided each of the witches with a portion of dung. His gift had special properties. Used as an ointment, it transformed the witches into animals (for example, geese) and enabled them to fly through the air; one woman became a parrot for her solitary nocturnal excursions. At the trials, the defendants prided themselves on their exploits, including their ability to transport other people through the air to distant places. Several male defendants related their encounters with the Devil and confessed to signing an agreement with him, written in their own blood. Despite these well-known elements of the European witch stereotype, the colonial Mexican version of witchcraft suffered from a lack of coherence, with certain characteristic elements still present in the popular imagination, while the general picture had fallen into oblivion.

IRIS GAREIS

See also: BASQUE COUNTRY; COURTS, ECCLESIASTICAL; DIVINATION; DRUGS AND HALLUCINOGENS; FEMALE WITCHES; FLIGHT OF WITCHES; KISS OF SHAME; LOVE MAGIC; NEW GRANADA; OINTMENTS; SABBAT; SORCERY; SPAIN; SUPERSTITION; WITCH AND WITCHCRAFT, DEFINITIONS OF.

References and further reading:
Aguirre Beltrán, Gonzalo. 1963. *Medicina y magia: El proceso de aculturación en la estructura colonial.* Mexico: Instituto Nacional Indigenista.
Alberro, Solange. 1988. *Inquisición y sociedad en México 1571–1700.* Mexico: Fondo de Cultura Económica (French Original 1988).
García-Molina Riquelme, Antonio. 1999. *El régimen de penas y penitencias en el Tribunal de la Inquisición de México.* Instituto de Investigaciones Jurídicas, Serie, Doctrina Jurídica, Núm. 7. Mexico: Universidad Nacional Autónoma de México.
Greenleaf, Richard E. 1961. *Zumárraga and the Mexican Inquisition, 1536–1543.* Washington, DC: Academy of American Franciscan History.
———. 1969. *The Mexican Inquisition of the Sixteenth Century.* Albuquerque: University of New Mexico Press.
Grunberg, Bernard. 1998. *L'Inquisition apostolique au Mexique: Histoire d'une institution et de son impact dans une société coloniale (1521–1571).* Paris and Montreal: L'Harmattan.
Henningsen, Gustav. 1994. "La evangelización negra: Difusión de la magia europea por la América colonial." *Revista de la Inquisición* 3: 9–27.
Huerga, Alvaro. 1993. "El Tribunal de la Inquisición de México." Pp. 351–386 in *Los Inquisidores.* Vitoria-Gasteiz: Fundación Sancho el Sabio.
Medina, José Toribio. 1905. *Historia del Tribunal del Santo Oficio de la Inquisición en México.* Santiago de Chile: Imprenta Elzeviriana.
Quezada, Noemí. 1989. *Enfermedad y maleficio: El curandero en el México colonial.* Mexico: Universidad Nacional Autónoma de México.

NEWBURY WITCH (1643)

Soldiers killed this anonymous woman during the English Civil War, possibly in the belief that she was a witch. Like many stories of witchcraft reported in the popular press, fact and fiction are difficult to separate. What may have been a very straightforward event was probably misinterpreted at the time and then subsequently embellished in order to make a sensational story or advance a political point.

In late September 1643, just after the Battle of Newbury in Berkshire, the royalist newspaper *Mercurius Civicus* reported that an angry old woman had left the royalist encampment outside Newbury and had crossed the River Kennet to present herself before the parliamentary army under the earl of Essex. There she had demanded to meet the general himself but had been denied. After a scuffle, she was arrested and charged with attempting to blow up the parliamentary army's magazine. It seems likely that she was executed as a spy or saboteur. At least, that was one version of what happened.

The following month saw this story change in at least three other newspapers. The most frequently repeated version was that parliamentary soldiers had been amazed to see an old woman sailing on a plank (or even, by some blasphemous miracle, walking on the water) and had captured her as a witch.

In wartime, it is likely that many suspected witches, including this one, suffered summary justice; England's worst panic, the Mathew Hopkins episode, lay in the near future. But her execution apparently did not go as planned. A cheap pamphlet published in 1643, *A Most Certain, Strange, and true Discovery of a Witch,* claimed that she caught the bullets fired at her and chewed them up, laughing and mocking the troops as she did so. They were now certain that she must be in league with the Devil and resorted to the customary magical countermeasure of "scoring the witch above the breath"; that is, cutting her forehead in the belief that drawing blood would rob the witch of her power. This done, a soldier placed his pistol beneath her ear and shot her at point-blank range, upon which, the pamphlet said, "she straight sank down and died, leaving her legacy of a detested carcass to the worms" (*A Most Certain, Strange, and true Discovery of a Witch,* 7) Though less gruesome than other wartime stories of this age, like Hans Jacob Christoph von Grimmelshausen's, the episode suggested that the carnage at Newbury had left British armies in a brutal state.

The pamphlet account, with a clear parliamentarian bias, also related that one of the soldiers who apprehended her first saw a tall, lean, agile woman traveling down the river. They set a trap for her. Some soldiers were afraid to touch her, but others obeyed the order to capture her and drag her before the military commanders. After they perceived that she was a witch, a firing squad of two marksmen was arranged. The first lead musket ball bounced off her body (as low velocity bullets sometimes did) and nearly hit the marksman in the face. Enraged, he ran at her with his sword. As the veins of her temple were cut, she realized that the Devil had deserted her. She stopped laughing and began instead to wail and moan, tearing at her hair.

Title page of pamphlet describing the witch of Newbury, caught walking on a plank in the water. (Glasgow University Library, Department of Special Collections)

At the dramatic climax, the propaganda message was delivered. The witch's last words were reported to be: "And is it come to pass, that I must die indeed? Why then, his excellency the earl of Essex shall be fortunate and win the field" (*A Most Certain, Strange, and true Discovery of a Witch,* 7). The defeat of a royalist witch was thus made into a prophecy of parliamentary superiority and provided proof that the Devil was on the king's side. The story of the witch of Newbury therefore revealed itself to have been a powerfully instructive fantasy or allegory, albeit one with little, if any, foundation in fact.

MALCOLM J. GASKILL

See also: ANTICHRIST; ENGLAND; HOPKINS, MATTHEW; PAMPHLETS AND NEWSPAPERS; WARFARE.

References and further reading:

Capp, Bernard. 1989. "Popular Culture and the English Civil War." *History of European Ideas* 10: 31–41.
Ewen, C. L'Estrange. 1933. *Witchcraft and Demonianism.* London: Heath Cranton.
Purkiss, Diane. 1997. "Desire and Its Deformities: Fantasies of Witchcraft in the English Civil War." *Journal of Medieval and Early Modern Studies* 27: 103–132.

NIDER, JOHANNES (CA. 1380–1438)

A Dominican theologian and religious reformer active in the early fifteenth century, Nider wrote some of the most extensive and influential early accounts of witchcraft. His major work on this subject, *Formicarius* (The Anthill), written in 1437 and 1438, was printed in seven separate editions between 1475 and 1692. It was also an important source of information for the infamous *Malleus Maleficarum* (The Hammer of Witches), written by the Dominican Heinrich Kramer and first published in 1486. The fifth book of the *Formicarius,* which dealt specifically with "witches and their deceptions" ("de maleficis et eorum deceptionibus"), was included in several later editions along with the *Malleus.* In addition to relating numerous stories of witchcraft in the *Formicarius,* Nider treated the topics of magic and sorcery in two other works, *De lepra morali* (On Moral Leprosy) and *Preceptorium divine legis* (Preceptor of Divine Law).

Born in the small Swabian imperial city of Isny in the early 1380s, Nider entered the Dominican Order at Colmar in 1402. At this time, Colmar (now in Alsace, France) was one of only two Dominican houses in German lands controlled by the so-called observant, or reform, movement. We can assume that Nider chose to enter the order at Colmar because he was attracted to the observant movement; he eventually became one of the most important observant Dominican leaders of his day. Following the normal course of Dominican education, Nider underwent his initial training at Colmar, then learned the liberal arts at a Dominican *studium generale* (house of studies; literally "general studies"), and finally received his theological education. He began studying theology in Cologne, possibly as early as 1410, but left before completing his degree and attended some sessions of the Council of Constance (1414–1418). In 1422, he petitioned to be admitted to study theology in Vienna, where he received his degree in June 1425.

Nider taught briefly at Vienna and then served as prior of the Dominicans in Nuremberg from 1426 or 1427 until April 1429, when he moved to Basel to undertake the reform of the Dominican priory there. While in Basel, he not only served as prior of the Dominicans but also became a leading member of the Council of Basel (1431–1449). He delivered the opening sermon of the council, served on its deputation for religious reform, and undertook several important missions to negotiate with the heretical Hussites in Bohemia. Moreover, under his leadership, several of the council's most important deputations and delegations met in his Dominican priory. In late 1434 or early 1435, however, Nider left Basel, returning to Vienna to teach theology. He was elected dean of the theological faculty in 1436. In 1438, he returned briefly to Basel, continuing on that summer to direct the reform of the female Dominican convent of St. Catherine in Colmar. Upon his return journey, he died at Nuremberg on August 13, 1438.

Although an active intellectual figure for slightly over ten years, from 1426 until 1438, and although frequently occupied during this period with numerous other duties, Nider was nevertheless a prolific author who wrote at least fifteen major treatises, as well as numerous sermons and letters. His topics ranged from the reform of the religious orders to heresy, as well as general moral guides and treatises on the care of souls. Yet he is mainly known as an authority on witchcraft, above all for his most important work, *Formicarius.* This long treatise was composed in the form of a dialogue between a theologian, who was clearly Nider himself, and a lazy but curious student who posed questions on a wide range of moral and spiritual matters. The treatise took its title and its organizing symbol from Proverbs 6.6 (which also served as its opening line): "Go to the ant, O lazy one, and consider its ways and learn wisdom." Throughout, the character of the student (the "lazy one" of the Proverbs) posed questions and demanded not just scholastic reasoning but also present-day examples to illustrate the theologian's points. Thus the dialogue of the *Formicarius* often became a collection of morally edifying stories probably intended for use in sermons.

Because of this format, when Nider turned to the topic of witchcraft, he presented not just a purely theoretical, scholastic account of the powers of demons and the workings of sorcery but actual stories of witches and witchcraft that he had heard from other authorities (he never seemed to have actually encountered a witch himself). Many of these stories were set in various locations in the western Alps, mostly the territory of Bern in the diocese of Lausanne, where some of the earliest true witchcraft trials were beginning to take place at this time. Many of Nider's stories of witchcraft came from a single source, the secular judge Peter of Bern, who had conducted numerous sorcery or witchcraft trials several years earlier in the Simme valley of the Bernese *Oberland.* Nider supplemented these accounts with information from a Dominican inquisitor of Autun who was active against witches, with personal discussions he had in Vienna with a former demonic magician or necromancer who had since reformed and now lived as a pious Benedictine monk, and with the account of certain delegates to the Council of Basel about the burning of Joan of Arc and several other women whom Nider regarded as witches.

The picture of witchcraft that emerged in the *Formicarius* contained most of the elements that became standard parts of the witch stereotype throughout the centuries of the great witch hunts in Europe. Nider described witches mostly as simple rustics who performed harmful sorcery of various sorts—causing infertility or illness in people or animals, killing small children, damaging or destroying crops, or magically stealing crops from their neighbors' fields. Witches performed this magic through the agency of demons, and the witches gained their power over demons by formally renouncing their faith and worshipping the Devil at secret nocturnal gatherings. At these ceremonies they also desecrated the cross and the sacraments, cannibalized the bodies of young children and babies, engaged in sexual orgies, and performed various other detestable acts. Notably, Nider's witches did not fly to these gatherings; night flight was never mentioned in the *Formicarius* except as a delusion.

Although in the course of his stories, Nider described both male and female witches and although he consistently used male pronouns when referring to witches in general, he is nevertheless the first major clerical authority to argue that women were more prone to witchcraft than men. Immediately after the discussion of Joan of Arc in the *Formicarius,* the lazy student expressed amazement that the weaker sex could be capable of such terrible crimes. Through the voice of the theologian, Nider responded that, shocking as it seems, learned authorities knew that it was not rare for women to wield such demonic power. He then explained how women were more prone to the temptations of the Devil, due mainly to their weaker physical, mental, and moral nature, and produced several biblical, patristic, and classical citations to this effect. Thus, women were more easily seduced into the crime of witchcraft than men. This section of the *Formicarius* served as a basis for the even more extreme misogyny of the later *Malleus Maleficarum.*

Interestingly, alongside tales of nocturnal conventicles and diabolic cults of witches, Nider also presented several accounts that lacked these more extreme flourishes. Most of these stories centered on the figure of a single "great witch," a man named Staedelin, of whom Nider heard from Peter of Bern. Although called a witch *(maleficus),* Staedelin was not presented as a member of any cult, and although his magic was demonic in nature, he does not appear to have surrendered his soul to the Devil or to have apostasized. Rather, these stories seemed much more "realistic" and probably more accurately depicted certain common magical practices and beliefs that existed before the emergence of the full stereotype of witchcraft. The *Formicarius,* therefore, seemed to represent almost the exact moment when the more developed stereotype of diabolic witchcraft superceded earlier ideas of simple demonic sorcery, at least in the minds of some clerical authorities.

Nider also discussed magic and witchcraft in sections of his moral treatises *De lepra morali* and *Preceptorium divine legis.* Lacking the narrative quality of the *Formicarius,* these treatises generally presented a more purely theoretical account of the supposed workings of demonic magic, particularly of the various powers and natural abilities of demons, and of the necessity and workings of the pacts that supposedly bound demons to the human sorcerers or witches who commanded them.

MICHAEL D. BAILEY

See also: BASEL, COUNCIL OF; DOMINICAN ORDER; FEMALE WITCHES; FLIGHT OF WITCHES; HUSSITES; JOAN OF ARC; KRAMER, HEINRICH; LAUSANNE, DIOCESE OF; *MALLEUS MALEFICARUM;* ORIGINS OF THE WITCH HUNTS; PETER OF BERN; SABBAT.

References and further reading:
Bailey, Michael D. 1996. "The Medieval Concept of the Witches' Sabbath." *Exemplaria* 8: 419–439.
———. 2001. "From Sorcery to Witchcraft: Clerical Conceptions of Magic in the Later Middle Ages." *Speculum* 76: 960–990.
———. 2003. *Battling Demons: Witchcraft, Heresy, and Reform in the Late Middle Ages.* University Park: Pennsylvania State University Press.
Borst, Arno. 1992. "The Origins of the Witch-Craze in the Alps." Pp. 101–122 in *Medieval Worlds: Barbarians, Heretics, and Artists.* Edited by Arno Borst. Translated by Eric Hansen. Chicago: University of Chicago Press.
Chène, Catherine. 1999. "Jean Nider, *Formicarius (livre II, chapitre 4 et livre V, chapitres 3, 4 et 7)."* Pp. 99–265 in *L'imaginaire du sabbat: Edition critique des textes les plus anciens (1430 c.–1440 c.).* Edited by Martine Ostorero, Agostino Paravicini Bagliani, and Kathrin Utz Tremp, with Catherine Chène. Lausanne: Université de Lausanne.
Tschacher, Werner. 2000. *Der Formicarius des Johannes Nider von 1437/38: Studien zu den Anfängen der Hexenverfolgungen im Spätmittelalter.* Aachen: Shaker.

NIGHT WITCH, OR NIGHT HAG

A witch believed to wander in the night is called a night witch or night hag.

The origins of the night witch can be traced back to ancient times. In Hebrew belief, for example, the female demon Lilith was associated with the night and its denizens. Lilith, the baby-snatching demon whose presence was a constant threat to mothers and their newborns, subsequently became a powerful force in early modern European demonology; her various powers included the ability to steal semen from sleeping men. In Roman literature of the imperial era, the image of the witch who worked her evil at night was prevalent. In the *Satyricon* (§ 63), Petronius (d. C.E. 65) described the work of the *strigae* (witches; etymologically connected with *strix,* or screech owl), whom he later called *nocturnae* (literally, "women of the night"). These night witches were described as having worked magic on a youth (replacing his innards with straw) and also causing insanity and later death to a valiant man who attempted to drive them away. The connotations of the night have contributed significantly to the belief in and depiction of the night witch, for it is at night that "life

is considered to be in a state of suspended animation, a necessary lull during the hours of the dominion of death" (Caro Baroja 1964, 5).

In Greece and Rome, ghosts and certain deities associated with witchcraft, such as Hecate, were thought to haunt crossroads and similar frightening places at night. Such beliefs remained and were altered and elaborated upon throughout the centuries. In the Basque region, for example, there are various stories about the nocturnal activities of witches, including ones not necessarily relating to evil acts, such as horseback rides in the dark hours. The witch's association with cats (in addition to owls and wolves) was partially based on the belief that witches, like cats, were particularly active at night. The conviction that witches could transform themselves into cats gave rise to various stories (and court cases) involving *maleficium* (harmful magic) directed against infants and children, as well as other random acts of evil. In 1608, Francesco Maria Guazzo, citing Nicolas Rémy, commented: "Remy (II, 5) writes nearly all those who came into his hands charged with witchcraft told him that they changed themselves into cats whenever they wished to enter other people's houses in secret, so that they could scatter their poison there by night" (*Compendium Maleficarum* [A Summary of Witches] 1.8).

The idea of the witch who transformed herself at night predated the early modern European age, as evidenced in the poem by Propertius (ca. 50–ca. 16 B.C.E.) in which he described the activities of a witch who "can change her form into that of a night-prowling wolf" (4.5.14). Similarly, Ovid (43 B.C.E.–C.E. 17) described the witch Dipsas, whom he suspected of performing shape-shifting magic to transform herself into a nocturnal bird (*Amores* 1.8.13–14). In the *Fasti* (6.131–146), Ovid described owl-like birds, which he suggested were old women transformed, who traveled at night in search of unprotected babies to devour. Norman Cohn (1993, 64) noted the existence of similar beliefs among the Germanic peoples prior to Roman and, later, Christian influences. During the Early Middle Ages, belief in the *strigae* continued throughout Germany, and the images that characterized their descriptions in Latin literature, namely, metamorphosis and cannibalism, were reflected in indigenous Germanic folktales. Those gripped by nightmares or suffering from night paralyses could also find an explanation in the presence and effects of the night witch. Sensations of heaviness, suffocation, and general discomfort were once ascribed to the night witch sitting on a person's chest (hence the term *night hag* or *old hag* syndrome).

The definitive expression of the activities of the night witch was, arguably, participation in the Sabbat, the gathering of witches in remote places that invariably took place at night. Again the motif of metamorphosis was prominent in the conceptualization of the Sabbat, with stories abounding of witches traveling to the specified location in the form of wolves, cats, owls, and bats. Belief in organized groups of witches flying to the Sabbat, which began to dominate the relevant literature of the fourteenth and fifteenth centuries, has its origins in earlier convictions about women of the night and nocturnal hags; for example, John of Salisbury, in his *Policraticus* (*The Statesman,* 1159) recorded gatherings in honor of Herodias, in which women (*lamiae,* a classical correspondent for *strigae*) banqueted on babies, "some of them being dismembered and gluttonously devoured" (2.17).

MARGUERITE JOHNSON

See also: CANNIBALISM; CATS; CROSSROADS; DIANA, FLIGHT OF WITCHES; GHOSTS; HECATE; JOHN OF SALISBURY; LAMIA; LILITH; METAMORPHOSIS; NIGHTMARES; PEOPLE OF THE NIGHT; SABBAT; STRIX, STRIGA, STRIA; WITCH AND WITCHCRAFT, DEFINITIONS OF.

References and further reading:
Caro Baroja, Julio. 1964. *The World of the Witches.* Translated by Nigel Glendinning. London: Phoenix Press.
Cohn, Norman. 1993. *Europe's Inner Demons: The Demonization of Christians in Medieval Christendom.* Rev. ed. London: Pimlico.
Gaster, Moses. 1900. "Two Thousand Years of a Charm Against the Child-Stealing Witch." *Folklore* 11: 129–161.
Ginzburg, Carlo. 1991. *Ecstasies: Deciphering the Witches' Sabbath.* Translated by Raymond Rosenthal. Harmondsworth: Penguin.
Ogden, Daniel. 2002. *Magic, Witchcraft and Ghosts in the Greek and Roman Worlds: A Sourcebook.* Oxford: Oxford University Press.
Stephens, Walter. 2002. *Demon Lovers: Witchcraft, Sex, and the Crisis of Belief.* Chicago and London: University of Chicago Press.

NIGHTMARES

The origin of the word *nightmare* can be found in the ancient Germanic and Nordic belief in the *mara,* a supernatural being, usually female, who lay on people's chests at night, suffocating and paralyzing them. The same concept is also present in Slavic cultures: we find the *zmora* in Poland, *kikimora* in Russia, and *morica* in Croatia, which suggests that the *mara* concept may have Indo-European roots. All these terms describe a sleep disturbance phenomenon classified today as sleep paralysis, which has been the subject of intellectual debate for nearly 2,000 years. The physician Galen, writing in the second century C.E., was the first to propose that the experience was caused by gastric disturbances. His explanation remained the dominant physiological explanation for the nightmare right down to the twentieth century. That great Elizabethan witchcraft skeptic Reginald Scot explained: "the mare, oppressing manie in their sleepe so sore, as they are not able to call for helpe, or stir themselves under the burthen of that heavie humor, which is ingendred of a thicke vapor proceeding from the cruditie and rawnesse in the stomach" (Scot 1972, 49).

Scot's views on the nightmare formed part of his attempt to debunk popular beliefs about witchcraft. Nevertheless, not only in England but also in many other parts of Europe, the nightmare experience was often attributed to the nocturnal visits of witches. It was widely believed that they came and straddled those whom they wished to torment, giving rise to the English expressions "hag-ridden" and "witch-ridden." The physical sensations of paralysis, pressure, and suffocation were frequently accompanied by aural hallucinations and visions of suspected witches.

Examples of people interpreting the nightmare experience in terms of witchcraft can be found in the court records of several European countries. Trial depositions from seventeenth century Augsburg, Germany, referred to witches' *trucken,* or pressing. In 1666 a pregnant woman named Anna Maria Cramer testified that a witch kept visiting her at night and lying upon her; in 1685 a man testified that his wife complained of feeling someone pressing her at night (Roper 1994, 209). When in 1609, Jean Grand Didier, from the duchy of Lorraine, went to sleep after having exchanged harsh words with a suspected witch, he felt a heavy weight upon him and saw several people in his bedroom, including the suspected witch, whom he imagined had tried to throttle him (Briggs 1996, 115–116).

In parts of western England, occasional accusations of witchcraft resulting from nightmare attacks still reached the courts in the nineteenth century; most concerned people prosecuted for assault after drawing blood from witches whom they believed were "hag-riding" them. In 1871, for example, a twenty-three-year-old farmer from the county of Dorset was sentenced to six months' imprisonment after having beaten an eighty-five-year-old woman he accused of persistently "hag-riding" him. In the previous decade, a Somerset couple, the Clapps, were prosecuted after having drawn blood from an elderly neighbor. The court heard how "between 12 and 1 o'clock, the old lady came into defendant's bedroom, and lay on her feet, when she suddenly felt her body grow stiff. After this complainant laid half across Mr. Clapp's chest, which he stated deprived him of the power of breathing, and rendering him quite helpless" (Davies 1997, 40–50).

The nightmare experience or sleep paralysis may seem to play only a minor role in witch accusations and beliefs, but the very physicality and perceived reality of such supernatural aggression was a potent confirmation of witchcraft. The nightmare experience represented an intimate, brutal assault. People awoke sore, sweating, and tired from the ordeal, and the vivid nature of associated hallucinations helped reinforce the supposed powers of witches.

OWEN DAVIES

In Henry Fuseli's most famous painting, The Nightmare
(*The Incubus*), *a demon lies on a woman's chest, suffocating and
paralyzing her. (Snark/Art Resource)*

See also: NIGHT WITCH, OR NIGHT HAG; SCOT, REGINALD.

References and further reading:

Briggs, Robin. 1996. *Witches and Neighbours: the Social and
    Cultural Context of European Witchcraft.* London:
    HarperCollins.
Davies, Owen. 1997. "Hag-Riding in Nineteenth-Century West
    Country England and Modern Newfoundland: An
    Examination of an Experience-Centred Witchcraft Tradition."
    Folk Life 35: 36–53.
———. 2003. "The Nightmare Experience, Sleep Paralysis, and
    Witchcraft Accusations." *Folklore* 114: 181–203.
Hufford, David J. 1982. *The Terror That Comes in the Night: An
    Experience-Centered Study of Supernatural Assault Traditions.*
    Philadelphia: University of Pennsylvania Press.
Jones, Ernest M. 1931. *On the Nightmare.* London: Hogarth Press.
Roper, Lyndal. 1994. *Oedipus and the Devil: Witchcraft, Sexuality,
    and Religion in Early Modern Europe.* London and New York:
    Routledge.
Scot, Reginald. 1972. *The Discoverie of Witchcraft.* London:
    William Brome. 1584. Reprint, New York: Dover.

NIGHTSHADE

Atropa belladonna is an excellent example of a poisonous
and medicinal herb believed to be used by witches in the
compounds called witches' brews. One finds it mentioned in various demonological and witchcraft texts
among the general lists of constituents of such
poisonous compounds. For example, Johann Weyer
mentioned the use of belladonna in witches' compounds
in his 1563 book *De praestigiis daemonum* (On the
Tricks of Devils). In Book 3, chapter 17, Weyer, himself
a physician and thus familiar with medicinal plants,
wrote that witches were thought to use belladonna,
hemlock, and aconite, among other poisons, citing
Italian examples from Giambattista Della Porta and
Girolamo Cardano, supplemented by an illustration of
nightshade's effects on the son of one of his Rhineland
colleagues. Traditional names for the plant reveal more
of this commonly held folklore. The plant has been
called Devil's cherries, naughty man's cherries, and
Devil's herb. The word *belladonna* perhaps derives from
the herb's ability to cause dilation of the pupils; women
used it in infusions to make their eyes look larger. There
was even a folk belief that the herb could take on the
form of a beautiful woman, which may offer another
source for the plant's name.

Witches used brews compounded with poisonous
herbs such as belladonna for various supernatural purposes. A witch might have administered belladonna as a
poison in a drink. One might also have compounded
poisonous herbs, including nightshade, with grease to
make a flying ointment. This last belief is supported by
the nature of the chemical constituents of nightshade,
which include hyoscyamine and atropine, as well as
scopolamine. Such drugs produce effects on the circulatory system and can make the individual who uses them
feel as though he or she is flying or floating. Aside from
its uses in witchcraft, belladonna was also considered an
herb that belonged exclusively to the Devil, who was
said to tend it personally. Folklore held that the Devil
was so fond of his belladonna that he rarely left it alone,
stopping his gardening duties only on Walpurgis Night
to attend the famous witches' Sabbat.

JANE P. DAVIDSON

See also: DRUGS AND HALLUCINOGENS; FLIGHT OF WITCHES;
HERBAL MEDICINE; OINTMENTS; POISON; WALPURGIS
(WALPURIGS) NIGHT.

References and further reading:

Davidson, Jane P. 1987. *The Witch in Northern European Art,
    1470–1750.* Freren, Germany: Luca.
Fletcher, R. 1896. "The Witches' Pharmacopoeia." *Bulletin of the
    Johns Hopkins Hospital* 147–157.
Grieve, M. 1931. *A Modern Herbal.* London: J. Cape.
Müller-Ebeling, Claudia, Christian Rätsch, and Wolf-Dieter Storl.
    2003. *Witchcraft Medicine: Healing Arts, Shamanic Practices,
    and Forbidden Plants.* Translated by Annibal Lee. Rochester,
    VT: Inner Traditions.
Weyer, Johann. 1998. *On Witchcraft: An Abridged Translation of
    Johann Weyer's* De Praestigiis daemonum. Edited by Benjamin
    G. Kohl and H. C. Erik Midelfort. Asheville, NC: Pegasus.

NODÉ, PIERRE

A Minim friar in Paris during the French Wars of
Religion, Nodé published a book in 1578,
Declamation contre l'erreur execrable des maleficiers

(Declamation Against the Execrable Error of Evildoers). Typical of the intellectual position of zealous Catholics in those troubled times, Nodé lamented that the chaotic conditions of his world were a sign of its imminent end. Like so many others, he considered the troubles caused by the rise and spread of Protestantism in France as the work of the Devil. It was incumbent on all believers in God (Catholics) to fight back and exterminate their enemies. Nodé appealed to the monarch, high nobles, and high court justices to join the battle wholeheartedly.

According to Nodé, witchcraft and magic were an epidemic in his time. Witchcraft involved such horrible sins as apostasy, blasphemy and *lese-majesté divine* or "treason against God." French Catholic demonologists frequently made this last charge (borrowed from French legal jargon condemning heretics) as an important argument for imposing the death penalty for witchcraft, even if the witches had harmed no one.

Nodé bemoaned the lack of commitment by the king and high nobles to eradicate heretics and witches. Judges had the responsibility and the duty to pursue actively these "diabolical monsters." As Nodé stated, "The civil law wishes their bodily death, the holy canons order their spiritual death, and God commands both against them so that this race of perverse malefactors is exterminated from Heaven and earth" (Nodé 1578, 46).

He was clearly angry and frustrated because French royal authorities were not taking this task to heart. French writers on demonology and heresy complained constantly that the French legal system did not pursue witches aggressively. Either "indiscreet pity" or incredulity was extremely dangerous. "It would be far better to exterminate such people from the earth and wipe out all memory of them," Nodé expostulated, "rather than wait for a great disaster and calamity" (Nodé 1578, 55).

Nodé's equation of the Protestant heresy with witchcraft, in the context of the anarchic conditions of the civil wars and the perceived presence on the apocalypse, was typical of these writers and preachers. The violence of the polemical wars matched the military violence of the times.

Following conventional wisdom, Nodé's work examined many aspects of the complex of beliefs comprising witchcraft: the transportation of witches over great distances, werewolves, maleficent crimes, and sexual dysfunction, always linking these evils to the current rise in heresy and unbelief. He also reported a very interesting case. Stating that the Devil could make people hate food, he told of a young woman who died after not eating for four months. The poor anorexic girl died in "extreme languor, dry as wood, thinner that a heron, pale as a sheet and thinner than parchment that shrivels near a fire" (Nodé 1578, 32). Some supernatural evil force must have caused something so extraordinary.

Throughout his tirade, Nodé trotted out clichés stressing the intimate connection between the heresy of the day and Satan's machinations that were central aspects of Catholic rhetoric during the Wars of Religion, hoping—vainly—to stimulate more active persecution of witches (and Protestants) by the state.

JONATHAN L. PEARL

See also: APOCALYPSE; BOUCHER, JEAN; DEMONOLOGY; FRANCE; HERESY; PROTESTANT REFORMATION; WARS OF RELIGION, FRANCE.

References and further reading:
Clark, Stuart. 1997. *Thinking with Demons: The Idea of Witchcraft in Early Modern Europe.* Oxford: Clarendon.
Nodé, Pierre. 1578, *Declamation contre l'erreur execrable des maleficiers.* Paris.
Pearl, Jonathan L. 1999. *The Crime of Crimes: Demonology and Politics in France, 1560–1620.* Waterloo, Ontario: Wilfred Laurier University Press.

NÖRDLINGEN, IMPERIAL FREE CITY

Thirty-three individuals—all but one of them women—were burned at the stake as witches in the Lutheran city of Nördlingen, Swabia, between 1589 and 1594. It constituted one of the most severe witch hunts seen in a Protestant imperial free city. The main reasons for this persecution were the zeal of the city councilors who tried the witches and the fact that they treated witchcraft as a *crimen exceptum* (the excepted crime), subject to none of the usual safeguards for the protection of the accused. Torture was therefore used to excess, usually forcing accused individuals to confess to witchcraft and denounce others as their accomplices. Records of virtually all trials, which formed part of a wave of witch hunts that occurred in Germany between 1585 and 1595, survive in Nördlingen's city archive.

Before 1589, Nördlingen had experienced only two witchcraft trials, in 1478 and 1534; both times, the alleged witches were released unpunished. The late-sixteenth-century persecution was triggered by Ursula Haider, a mentally unstable woman who in 1589 had the misfortune to nurse the three children of knifesmith Martin Hindenach, all of whom died of smallpox. Haider had claimed that she was plagued by the Devil even before 1589. Now she confessed that she had killed the second Hindenach child at the Devil's command, chiefly because its corpse had apparently bled as she held it: contemporaries believed that a body would bleed when touched by its murderer. She was arrested on suspicion of witchcraft on November 8, 1589. Under interrogation, she confessed to other acts of *maleficium* (harmful magic) and claimed that she had seen other Nördlingen women at witches' Sabbats, thus creating the potential for further trials. Haider was executed with two of the women she had denounced on May 15, 1590. That year, fourteen more Nördlingen women were arrested, mostly on the basis of denunciations: twelve were burned alive, one was burned after dying under torture, and one (Apollonia Rorendorfer) was released after refusing to confess.

Apart from one execution in 1592, there was a lull in the intensity of persecution from May 1591 until 1593, when sixteen more Nördlingen inhabitants were arrested. Thirteen of them (twelve women and one man) were executed, the bodies of two women who died under torture were burned, and one (Maria Holl) was released in 1594. The impetus for the 1593 trials came mainly from Nördlingen inhabitants who believed themselves to be victims of *maleficium*. Once restarted, however, the process of persecution again relied on denunciations for its continuation. Villagers from outside Nördlingen had a better chance of escaping execution: of nine women arrested as alleged witches at Goldburghausen, Itzlingen, and Sechtenhausen in 1590 and 1593, only one was executed. The council's "leniency" in these cases probably stemmed from its desire to avoid legal disputes with the count of Oettingen, who ruled the area around Nördlingen, over the right to try witches.

Nördlingen's witchcraft trials did not result from social conflicts: those executed came from a wide range of social backgrounds, from the poor and socially marginal to wives or widows of councilors. Nor did the council target particular individuals as witches: around one-third of all suspects were accused of *maleficium* by their fellow inhabitants, and suspects tended in the course of forced denunciations to name alleged Sabbat attendees on the basis of personal vendettas and preferences. However, the city councilors were responsible for the severity of the witch hunt. In 1589 they could either have dismissed Haider as insane or ignored her claims to have seen other women at Sabbats, thereby depriving the hunt of its momentum. They did neither because they were convinced of the reality of witches' Sabbats and of the need to rid Nördlingen of this evil. Crucially, they decided from the outset to treat witchcraft as a *crimen exceptum* and therefore to subject many accused women to extremely severe torture. Mayor Johann Pferinger and jurist Wolfgang Graf, both newly appointed in 1589 and desirous of making their mark, played leading roles in driving the witch-hunting zeal of the council. The active or tacit support of the persecution by a significant proportion of Nördlingen's inhabitants also helps account for its severity. Their anxiety about witchcraft may have increased before 1589 after a series of agrarian crises: it was doubtless heightened afterward by the sight of so many alleged accomplices of Satan burning at the stake.

The immense courage of Maria Holl was instrumental in finally ending Nördlingen's witchcraft trials. The wife of innkeeper Michael Holl, Maria was arrested on the basis of six denunciations on November 2, 1593. Despite suffering sixty-two bouts of torture with thumbscrews, leg-screws, strappado, and the rack, Maria refused to confess. On that basis and because her relatives from Ulm petitioned the Nördlingen council on her behalf, the council reluctantly released her on October 11, 1594. She was not the first Nördlingen woman to refuse to confess: Apollonia Rorendofer had shown similar steadfastness in the face of savage torture in 1590. However, Holl's case increased concern on the part of some councilors and inhabitants of Nördlingen that denunciations were an unsafe basis for pursuing witchcraft trials. After three more executions for witchcraft in 1598, there were no more witchcraft trials in Nördlingen. Maria Holl died at the age of eighty-five in 1634. By then one of the richest women in Nördlingen, she had outlived three husbands and all the men who had been involved in her trial for witchcraft forty years before.

ALISON ROWLANDS

See also: AGRARIAN CRISES; BAVARIA, DUCHY OF; *CRIMEN EXCEPTUM;* EXECUTIONS; GENDER; GERMANY; GERMANY, SOUTHEASTERN; GERMANY, SOUTHWESTERN; HOLY ROMAN EMPIRE; IMPERIAL FREE CITIES; *MALEFICIUM;* MENTAL ILLNESS; SABBAT; TORTURE; TRIALS.

References and further reading

Behringer, Wolfgang. 1997. *Witchcraft Persecutions in Bavaria: Popular Magic, Religious Zealotry and Reason of State in Early Modern Europe.* Translated by J. C. Grayson and David Lederer. Cambridge: Cambridge University Press.

Eschbaumer, Gloria. 1983. *Bescheidenliche Tortur: Der ehrbare Rat der Stadt Nördlingen im Hexenprozess 1593/94 gegen die Kronenwirtin Maria Holl.* Nördlingen: Buchhandlung Greno.

Friedrichs, Christopher R. 1979. *Urban Society in an Age of War: Nördlingen, 1580–1720.* Princeton, NJ: Princeton University Press.

Roper, Lyndal. 2004. *Witch Craze. Terror and Fantasy in Baroque Germany.* New Haven, CT, and London: Yale University Press.

Voges, Dietmar-H. 1994. "Reichsstadt Nördlingen." Pp. 361–369 in *Hexen und Hexenverfolgung im deutschen Südwesten* (Aufsatzband). Edited by Sönke Lorenz. Karlsruhe: Badisches Landesmuseum.

Wulz, Gustav. 1937; 1938/39. "Nördlinger Hexenprozesse." *Jahrbuch des Rieser Heimatvereins* 20: 42–72; 21: 95–120.

NORMANDY

Famous for the trial and execution of Joan of Arc in its capital, Rouen, this northern French province now seems most noteworthy in the history of European witchcraft as the leading punisher of male witches in western Europe. From the early 1540s until well after Louis XIV supposedly decriminalized witchcraft in France, Normandy's appellate court, the *Parlement* of Rouen, investigated primarily men for the crime of *sortilège* (diabolic magic). And, by French (or at least Parisian) standards, Norman judges punished them severely: although such other French *parlements* as Toulouse (1562) or Paris (1568) confirmed death sentences for witchcraft sooner than Rouen (1574), Norman parlementary records from the sixteenth and seventeenth centuries identified almost 400 accused witches and about 100 burnings for witchcraft. Almost three-fourths of these defendants were men, as were about two-thirds of those executed (Monter 1997, 572, 584).

The predominance of men among accused witches in Normandy increased over time. When the *parlement* first encountered one or two witches each year (1564–1578), men outnumbered women by only 15 to 10. But the disproportion between male and female witches grew steadily larger after 1600. Under Louis XIII, it surpassed 4 to 1, and by the late 1640s, when the *parlement* again averaged one or two witchcraft cases per year, women had almost disappeared. If certain types of women like old widows reappeared frequently among suspected witches elsewhere, so did certain types of men in Normandy. By far the most feared male witches in this cheese-producing region were shepherds, some of whom possessed veritable arsenals, featuring such items as toad venom and stolen Eucharists, suitable for performing both offensive and defensive magic. Priests were also heavily represented among Norman witches; between 1598 and 1647, seven Norman priests were burned for *sortilège,* another was given a life sentence to the galleys, and a half-dozen others were permanently banished from the Kingdom of France with loss of their benefices (Monter 1997, 582–583). A third dangerous occupational group was Normandy's blacksmiths, who exercised their skill in harming as well as healing horses.

The chronology and severity of Norman witchcraft persecution seemed unremarkable. Repression accelerated sharply here in the 1580s, as it did elsewhere in France. Between 1585 and 1610 the Rouen *parlement* judged over five witchcraft trials each year and upheld over 60 percent of lower-court death sentences for this crime; it ordered at least one witch burned every year until 1615 (Monter 1997, 572–573). However, this court placed little emphasis on the witches' Sabbat; although as many as ten witches were executed in the very worst years, they came from scattered places, and in Normandy no single episode ever grew into a serious panic. At the same time, Normandy experienced no scandals involving sadistic tortures, professional witch finders, "ducking" suspected witches (the swimming test, or water ordeal), or other clearly illegal practices; everything here seemed orderly and regular, except for the oddity that most accused witches were men. When the French phenomenon of bewitched convents finally reached Normandy in the 1640s, it was relatively unspectacular—and the most important female defendant (Madeleine Bavent) was never executed, despite her repeated confessions.

Although witch hunting had all but disappeared in most other parts of France by the time Louis XIV began his personal reign in 1661, Normandy kept putting its shepherd-witches on trial from 1670 until after 1700. Louis's government tried but ultimately failed to shut it down; despite the royal legislation supposedly decriminalizing witchcraft in 1682, the Rouen *parlement* was still burning them for sacrilege and "so-called *sortilège*" in 1694 and 1703, and sending them to the galleys even afterward. In 1718, Louis XIV's German sister-in-law remarked that "at Paris people don't believe in witches and we hear nothing about them; at Rouen they believe that witches exist, and there one always hears about them" (Monter 1997, 594).

Certainly the Norman *parlement* never displayed the scornful skepticism of their upriver Parisian colleagues about witchcraft. But compared with "offshore Normandy"—the Channel Islands, governed by England but speaking only French during the age of witchcraft trials—the *Parlement* of Rouen seems quite gentle in its treatment of witches. In terms of size and population, its judicial district was a hundred times greater than the Channel Islands (and its legal records are as rich as theirs), yet more women were burned as witches in the Channel Islands than in Normandy. The key to this grotesque discrepancy is that the Channel Islands enjoyed complete legal autonomy while Normandy had a scrupulous, if credulous, appellate court.

WILLIAM MONTER

See also: CHANNEL ISLANDS; FRANCE; JOAN OF ARC; LOUVIERS NUNS; MALE WITCHES, *PARLEMENT* OF PARIS

References and further reading:
Monter, William. 1997. "Toads and Eucharists: The Male Witches of Normandy, 1564–1660." *French Historical Studies* 20: 563–595.

NORTH BERWICK WITCHES

The cluster of witchcraft trials that occurred in Scotland in 1590–1591 in East Lothian and Edinburgh was sufficiently widespread and severe to merit the term "witch panic." From late November 1590 until December 1591 the hunt developed, as local magistrates and then the king and privy council uncovered what they believed to be conspiracy and treason by many women (and some men), led by the politically powerful earl of Bothwell.

The causes of the panic were long-term as well as immediate; some of the women and men who were interrogated, tried, and executed in 1590–1591 were accused of witchcraft activities stretching back as far as seventeen years. In 1586, Andrew Melville, the leading Presbyterian, returned from England along with fellow hard-line Protestants intent on creating a godly, disciplined nation. They soon established Presbyterian kirk sessions (parish disciplinary committees) in lowland and northeastern Scotland, where ministers and elders tried to enforce church discipline on a sometimes resistant population by investigating social disorder, sexual offenses, and popular magical practices. In certain areas, including East Lothian and Edinburgh, many people retained remnants of old Catholic beliefs and rituals. For the Kirk (the national—Presbyterian—Church of Scotland), Catholicism and magical beliefs were indistinguishable. The Kirk found an identifiable enemy in the North Berwick witch hunt: an underground network of witches inspired by the Devil and intent on overturning church and state.

The chain of events began in November 1590 when a servant girl who was a healer was accused by her master of witchcraft, tortured, and found to have the Devil's mark. The scope of the investigations widened, and a treasonable conspiracy involving some forty people was soon discovered against King James VI and his newlywed wife Anne. The network contained assorted practitioners of maleficent witchcraft, love magic, divination, and healing, including a long-established and respected healer, Agnes Sampson, and a schoolmaster, Dr. John Fian. Torturing some of the accused revealed a momentous tale of treasonable witchcraft. The accused came from a wide social range—peasants, servants, urban bourgeoisie, and aristocracy—and showed that belief in and practice of magic was prevalent throughout Scottish society.

The renegade earl of Bothwell, Francis Stewart, whose relations with the kirk and his cousin, the king, were highly unstable, was accused of involvement in the plot; he fled to escape trial and began an insurrection against James that ended with his forfeiture and banishment. Kirk and crown were temporarily allied against this supposed witchcraft conspiracy. James Carmichael, minister of Haddington, located in the area where many of the accused lived, helped King James. Carmichael was an ardent Presbyterian returned from exile with Melville, and one of the kirk's leading reformers and intellectuals.

A number of legal records of interrogations (sometimes under torture) survive from November 1590 to mid-1591. They produced stories that became more elaborate and coherent as the weeks passed, ultimately cohering into one story of a large-scale treasonous conspiracy involving personal appearances of the Devil at the witches' Sabbats. The stories mixed reality with fantasy: witches made pacts with the Devil and conspired to raise storms to prevent Anne's fleet from reaching Scotland and then James's from reaching Norway. After James and Anne returned safely, the witches planned James's death, using such familiar magical techniques as melting a wax image and poisoning his clothes. James was initially skeptical of the witchcraft threat but eventually took it seriously. Although later historians have been too ready to interpret the witchcraft conspiracy from the authorities' point of view, the evidence for its reality began to disintegrate by mid-1591, as witnesses

began to revoke their confessions, asserting them to be false and compelled by torture. There were indeed networks of acquaintance among those implicated in the accusations, but these ordinary links, some indeed based on shared practices of magic and witchcraft, were present in Scottish society from top to bottom.

Surviving trial records of the four most prominent accused witches show Scottish authorities reacting as the fearful and uncontrolled powers of magic, embodied in particular social types, threatened to overturn established social relations: a peasant wise woman with uncanny medical and political knowledge; a subversive schoolmaster in league with the Devil; respectable townswomen revolting against both class and sexual subordination; and Bothwell, who epitomized the sort of aristocratic rebellion against royal power that had plagued James for a decade and Scotland for generations. Socially insignificant accused witches were easily dealt with, but higher up the social scale, resistance to arrest and conviction mounted. In May 1591, Barbara Napier, a well-connected Edinburgh bourgeois, was acquitted of attending the North Berwick Sabbat, though she was convicted on other capital charges. James reacted angrily, and after threatening the assize with "wilful error" in blocking the operation of justice, he obtained a guilty verdict. The trial of Euphame MacCalzean, another wealthy Edinburgh woman from a well-connected legal family, involved a two-week long struggle to obtain a conviction and execution by the exceptionally cruel sentence of being burned alive.

The government seized the opportunity to destroy Bothwell that his contact with witchcraft offered. Bothwell was convinced that his enemy Chancellor Maitland was behind the witchcraft charges, and there is evidence that the government kept the main witness against Bothwell, a man later executed for witchcraft, in protective custody. Brought before the king and privy council in April 1591 to answer charges of treasonable conspiracy with a lately executed witch, Bothwell avoided trial in May when his peers refused to assemble to try him and escaped custody in June when Euphame MacCalzean was executed. In 1593, when he was finally tried for witchcraft, he was acquitted. When accused witches mentioned Bothwell in depositions, they clearly saw him as James's great adversary, so prominent that he became elided with the Devil himself.

Information about the witch hunt reached London in late 1591, while Scotland's witchcraft trials were still proceeding, with a pamphlet called *Newes from Scotland,* composed from materials probably supplied by Carmichael. Its lurid account of the witchcraft conspiracy offered maximum propaganda for King James, struggling heroically and single-handedly against diabolical agents, and contrasted James's

The North Berwick witches and witchcraft; nautical witchcraft, the Devil preaching, witches brewing in a cauldron, the earl of Bothwell reclining, witches eating and drinking in a cellar. (Fortean Picture Library)

divine-right legitimacy with the witches' diabolical subversion. It made no mention of Bothwell, who was still threateningly at large. The witch hunt also inspired James's *Daemonologie* (Demonology), probably written in 1591 but not published in Edinburgh until 1597, during a later witch hunt. James's account of witches' practices included details that he acquired from personally interrogating some of the North Berwick witches and that reappeared in trial records. *Daemonologie,* in orthodox fashion, made explicit the political threat to the established authorities that witchcraft represented. James's book had a baleful long-term effect on Scottish witch hunting by locating witchcraft within a theological framework and defining it as involving a pact with the Devil.

Historians have argued over what part, if any, Privy Council orders of 1591, 1592, and 1597 may have played in prolonging or exacerbating witch hunting after the North Berwick panic. What now seems clear is that the North Berwick witch hunt was a separate event from the next Scottish witch hunt of 1597 and that the government did not lose control of witchcraft prosecutions.

The witch hunt begun in North Berwick induced a brief lull in hostilities between Scotland's Presbyterian party and its monarch, while they cooperated in pursuing witches who represented each one's deepest fears: Catholic and magical beliefs and practices for the kirk, lawlessness and insurrection for James and his government. It was through witchcraft accusations that Bothwell's political threat was destroyed. When Parliament ratified Bothwell's forfeiture in 1592, it also finally gave the Kirk what it had long sought, legal sanction for Presbyterian church government, though the struggle between church and state would continue.

LAWRENCE NORMAND

See also: DENMARK; DEVIL'S MARK; IMAGE MAGIC; JAMES VI AND I, KING OF SCOTLAND AND ENGLAND; PACT WITH THE DEVIL; PANICS; SABBAT; SCOTLAND; WEATHER MAGIC.

References and further reading:

Dunlap, Rhodes. 1975. "King James and Some Witches: The Date and Text of the *Daemonologie.*" *Philological Quarterly* 54: 40–46.

Goodare, Julian. 2002. "The Framework for Scottish Witch-Hunting in the 1590s." *Scottish Historical Review* 81: 240–250.

Levack, Brian P. 1996. "State-Building and Witch Hunting in Early Modern Europe." Pp. 96–115 in *Witchcraft in Early Modern Europe: Studies in Culture and Belief.* Edited by Jonathan Barry, Marion Hester, and Gareth Roberts. Cambridge: Cambridge University Press.

Maxwell-Stuart, P. G. 1997. "The Fear of the King Is Death: James VI and the Witches of East Lothian." Pp. 209–225 in *Fear in Early Modern Society.* Edited by W. G. Naphy and P. Roberts. Manchester and New York: Manchester University Press.

———. 2001. *Satan's Conspiracy: Magic and Witchcraft in Sixteenth-Century Scotland.* East Linton: Tuckwell.

Normand, Lawrence, and Gareth Roberts. 2000. *Witchcraft in Early Modern Scotland: James VI's Demonology and the North Berwick Witches.* Exeter: University of Exeter Press.

Stafford, Helen. 1953. "Notes on Scottish Witchcraft Cases, 1590–91." Pp. 96–118 in *Essays in Honor of Conyers Read.* Edited by Norton Downs. Chicago: University of Chicago Press.

Wormald, Jenny. 2000. "The Witches, the Devil, and the King." Pp. 165–180 in *Freedom and Authority: Scotland c. 1050-c. 1650: Historical and Historiographical Essays Presented to Grant G. Simpson.* Edited by Terry Brotherstone and David Ditchburn. East Linton: Tuckwell.

Yeoman, L. A. 2002. "Hunting the Rich Witch in Scotland: High-Status Witch Suspects and Their Persecutors, 1590–1650." Pp. 106–121 in *The Scottish Witch-Hunt in Context.* Edited by Julian Goodare. Manchester and New York: Manchester University Press.

NORWAY

Almost all witchcraft trials in Norway, which was under Danish rule from 1388 to 1814, took place from 1551 to 1700. With few exceptions, they occurred after the implementation of the Reformation, which reached Norway from Denmark in 1537 after the king had turned Lutheran and Norway's last Catholic bishop had fled. Until the Reformation, the crime of witchcraft had been defined solely as *maleficium* (harmful magic); in medieval Norwegian (and Danish) laws, it deserved capital punishment only if it had caused death or injuries to people or animals. However, the medieval statutes on witchcraft in Norwegian customary law (*Landsloven,* or "Laws of the Lands") do not seem to have been applied until after 1540. The only case of medieval witchcraft dates from 1325, when a woman accused of love magic suffered penance ordered by the bishop of Bergen. In 1520, King Christian II introduced new laws involving harsher procedures in many criminal cases, including those involving witchcraft, that were not put into effect. Nevertheless, continental practice strongly influenced procedures in witchcraft cases as the death penalty came into use.

As one consequence of the Reformation, the Mosaic laws—including Exodus 22:18 (22:17; "Thou shalt not suffer a witch to live")—were introduced into criminal codes throughout Scandinavia. This process followed somewhat different courses in different states. In Sweden, the penalties of the Pentateuch were simply added to the existing law of the land as an appendix. In Denmark and Norway, the Mosaic prohibitions were introduced piecemeal during the century after 1540, with various articles punishing specific deeds; most of the Mosaic laws had been incorporated into the Norwegian legal framework by 1630.

Church and state cooperated closely in this confessional age: the king's laws about witchcraft were read from the pulpit every Sunday, and pastors reminded their congregations that the whole kingdom would suffer from God's wrath unless these creatures of the Devil were brought to justice and suitably punished. The Lutheran clergy cooperated closely with the new Lutheran regime to recommend strong actions against the enemies of God. Witches ranked among the very worst kind conceivable: a *crimen maiestatis laesae divina,* being a traitor to God, was even worse than being a traitor to the king. Such reasoning made it possible to legitimate the use of torture in witchcraft cases.

In 1584, the Danish king, responding to a petition from the Lutheran bishop of Stavanger, introduced the fully formed concept of demonology into the criminal code of Norway, ordering local authorities to prosecute all kinds of witchcraft, including "superstitious" healing practices that medieval legislation had ignored. This statute, introduced in the diocese of Bergen in 1593, seems to have been known throughout Norway. Finally, a new general witchcraft code was introduced for Denmark and Norway in 1617. It divided the crime into three parts: the pact with the Devil, *maleficium,* and healing practices. Death by beheading was to be employed on persons convicted of the first two categories.

WITCHCRAFT AND CRIME

Norway's recorded witchcraft trials began about 1540. Although there were no mass persecutions until after the enactment of the Witchcraft Code in 1617, an increasing number of trials took place after 1570. The best-known case involved Anna Pedersdotter, a clergyman's wife in Bergen, who, after two trials in 1575 and 1590, was burned at the stake. Bits and pieces of information show both torture and the water ordeal (swimming test) being used in Norwegian witchcraft cases since the sixteenth century, although Danish and Norwegian laws formally permitted neither.

The total number of cases known numbered about 880. In about 780 of these cases, a man or a woman was accused of some kind of witchcraft; the other 100 were defamation suits, initiated by a person who had come under suspicion for witchcraft in a local community.

These cases therefore might not be considered as ordinary witchcraft trials, but they nevertheless are of great interest in completing our knowledge of the ways witch beliefs were dealt with by the parties involved in Norwegian communities.

We know that approximately 310 persons suffered the death penalty for witchcraft in Norway; almost 90 percent of these executions took place during the years 1601–1670 (Næss 1990, 371). Allowing for lacunae in the documents, the total number was about 330. This number can be assessed relatively precisely because public accounts providing detailed information about all expenses paid for imprisonment, and executions have been preserved almost completely from most parts of Norway. Many witches were burned at the stake; but many others, having been "pardoned" by the regional governor or the king from being burned alive, were simply beheaded by the executioner's axe or sword. Typically, the vast majority of people, both among the accused and those suffering the death penalty, were women; only about one in five were men.

Despite all the attention it has received in recent research, witchcraft was far from the most common kind of offense involving capital punishment in post-Reformation Norway. One consequence of the introduction of Mosaic laws was that capital punishment became customary after convictions for murder or manslaughter, theft, adultery, incest, infanticide, bestiality, treason, or blasphemy. Minor sexual and moral offenses also received severe punishment. In Rogaland County, where most seventeenth-century records have been preserved, during the years 1610–1660 no fewer than 223 people were sentenced to die. Most had been convicted of incest (59), theft (54), manslaughter or murder (51), and infanticide (12); only 14 (or less than 7 percent) had been charged with witchcraft. However, 63 of them escaped, and 45 others were pardoned, receiving milder forms of punishment, often banishment from the county or the kingdom. Only 115 people were effectively put to death; but because witches were never pardoned and, being women, rarely escaped, 13 of them (over 11 percent) had been convicted of witchcraft. Because Rogaland contained about 6 percent of Norway's total population of about 440,000 inhabitants in the 1660s, it would seem that about 2,000 people were publicly executed, 216 of them for witchcraft, in this small country on the outskirts of Europe in the seventeenth century (Næss 1990, 369–370, 377). And it is worth remembering that the frequent use of capital punishment for many other crimes continued in eighteenth-century Norway, when no more witches were executed.

THE TYPOLOGY OF WITCHCRAFT

The stories told by the victims to Norway's bailiffs, sheriffs, priests, and judges provide a fairly comprehensive picture of the various concepts of witchcraft. The accusation of diabolism (pacts with the Devil and participation in the Sabbat) was invariably put forward during the interrogations by bailiffs and pastors urging the accused to confess. Details in Norwegian confessions obtained through the use of torture described meetings with the Devil and other witches on various widely scattered mountains like Domen (in far northern Finnmark), Dovre (in southern Norway), Lyderhorn (near Bergen), and even Blåkulla in Sweden. Because witches flew to the mountain closest to their own community, Blåkulla was mentioned solely in trials from southeastern parts of Norway close to the Swedish border.

There were a total of 789 specific accusations, including 263 for white magic, 398 for *maleficium*, and 128 for diabolism (Næss 1990, 373). The first group comprised various kinds of white magic and healing practices involving formulas and rituals; the use of herbs and strange substances like teeth, toes, and animal tails; and the use of "superstitious" prayers vaguely remembered from Catholic times, naming Jesus and Mary or other holy persons and distorted elements from biblical texts. The step from practicing white magic to suspicion of *maleficium* was often a short one. If the treatment of a patient by a wise woman brought about sickness or even death, she was quickly suspected by the public to be a witch. Over half of these accusations found in the cases tried involved *maleficium*. The evils allegedly done by the accused included the usual charges: manslaughter, killing or injuring of people or cattle, destruction of crops, impotency, and loss of wealth. Because fishing was an essential part of Norway's economy, its witches were also accused of causing storms and tidal waves that made ships sink and crews drown.

THE LEGAL SYSTEM

As elsewhere in Scandinavia, Norwegian criminal cases followed accusatorial procedures. The offended party indicted the aggressor. In cases involving the public interest, such as witchcraft, the bailiff acted as prosecutor. He could even begin a prosecution when only rumors of witchcraft were at hand. A case was proved when at least two independent witnesses had sworn on the Bible that the accusation was true. Such testimony was often difficult to obtain in witchcraft trials, so the court, often after a request from the bailiff, accepted it as sufficient proof if many people testified that they suspected the accused person of being a witch, even though they did not dare to swear to its truth. Accused witches found it difficult to employ the traditional means of defense, the compurgation, or oath of denial, by which a person in cases the court considered dubious could be acquitted if a certain number of people swore that they believed the accused to be innocent. Although the court gave several accused witches this opportunity, they found it impossible to persuade enough neighbors to swear to their innocence because they feared becoming charged with witchcraft themselves if they did so.

A bailiff had an enormous influence on the way criminal cases were handled. He acted as public prosecutor on behalf of the king and administered the court. The bailiff imprisoned accused persons; he was responsible for their examination; and he often brought in priests, or sometimes an executioner, in order to help secure a confession. The court justices were twelve local farmers, assisted by a secretary (*sorenskriver*) who gradually during the 1600s ended up as the real judge.

THREATS, TORTURE, AND CONFESSIONS

The large number of men and women being accused of *maleficium* and pacts with the Devil can only be accounted for by taking the practices employed by the authorities into account. Facing harsh interrogations, being threatened with going to hell by the pastors, being told what to confess under torture, many of the accused told the stories they knew in advance that they were expected to tell. Even though it was illegal to resort to torture before a sentence had been passed, courts nevertheless employed torture in several cases known to us so as to extract confessions from accused witches.

In order to further strengthen the evidence, suspects were submitted to the water ordeal. First documented in Norway in 1606, the water ordeal was recorded about forty times, although it was probably used much more frequently. Only a few instances are known in Norway in which courts searched for the Devil's mark on the accused's body. Defendants knew what suffering they might expect. According to the minutes of the judge, one imprisoned woman said to another: "Should you choose not to confess at once, they will try you on the water and next you will be put on the rack. After having extended your limbs they will increase your pains by pinching you with red-hot iron tongs." Another woman told the judge that she had willingly confessed at first because she preferred to shorten her life quickly instead of being exposed to the gruesome torture that awaited her.

REGIONAL DIFFERENCES: THE CASE OF FINNMARK AND CHAIN PROCESS

In most of Norway's eighteen counties, one finds that the number of persons burned or beheaded for witchcraft varied between six and fourteen. There were three exceptions: Hordaland killed twenty-two witches and Rogaland twenty-five; but Finnmark stands in a category by itself, executing about ninety-two witches, 30 percent of Norway's total. The relatively high figures from Rogaland and Hordaland reflect the fact that

witches were tried in these counties sooner than in the rest of Norway.

Finnmark, in the far north, had a very small population, no more than about 3,000 persons by 1600, both Norwegian and Sami. The latter ethnic group, however, was barely visible in Finnmark's witchcraft trials; its total of approximately 138 convicted witches includes only 27 Sami men and women (Hagen 1999, 44). Finnmark's contemporary authorities considered Norwegian women much more likely than the less-Christianized and nomadic Sami to practice *maleficium* and enter into pacts with the Devil. The governor, bailiffs, and pastors allowed frequent use of torture and the water ordeal in these cases. The consequences were horrifying: per thousand population, Norwegian women in Finnmark ranked among Europe's most intensely persecuted groups. Chains of accusations caused most of these arrests.

In Norway, no one willingly confessed to have made a pact with the Devil to perform evil. Persons convicted were strongly exhorted to denounce accomplices, who were then promptly indicted. Many local courts accepted such denunciations as independent accusations; two or more sufficed to pass a death sentence, even though this practice contradicted sixteenth-century laws. One case led to new trials due to denunciations from the first woman accused. The case against Gunvor Omundsdatter in Vardø in Finnmark in 1651 lasted for two years before she was burned at the stake, convicted of attending the Sabbat and causing storms that made ships and crews sink. A total of 21 other women were involved in this case, either because they denounced Gunhild or because she denounced them. The great majority of the approximately 92 people (almost all women) who suffered capital punishment in Finnmark were the victims of such chain processes (Hagen 1999, 44–45). In addition, three women died before sentencing, and one sami man was killed (by another man) during the trial. In total, we know the names of 353 persons denounced by other Norwegian witches. A majority of the death sentences in Norway resulted solely or partly from denunciations.

THE SOCIAL CONTEXT

Although high-ranking persons were occasionally accused and even convicted, as with Anna Pedersdotter at Bergen in 1590, the great majority of people indicted for witchcraft in Norway were old and on the same economic level as others in the community. Most of the accused, men or women, seem to have been from forty to sixty years of age, older than the average life span of people at that time. The typical process leading to accusations for witchcraft included quarreling with neighbors for many years over matters relating to accidents and deaths. Rumors of witchcraft led to suspicion and to accusations.

THE END OF NORWAY'S WITCHCRAFT TRIALS

The period of witch hunts in Norway largely coincided with Denmark's seventeenth-century wars. After the peace between Sweden and Denmark in 1660, relatively few persons were burned; Norway's last execution took place in 1695. After absolutism was introduced in Denmark in 1665, the largely Danish judges and other civil servants began to govern Norway by the 1670s, at both the central and local levels, in a far more modern and professional way than they had in previous decades. New rules imposed on local bailiffs and judges included stricter demands for documentation at all levels about each kind of case handled by a civil servant. The new generation of civil servants brought new and more critical attitudes about proof and evidence in all public matters. This attitude soon spread among judges and governors.

Meanwhile, Norway's old accusatorial legal system was replaced by an inquisitorial system, in which cases were decided by a judge's personal assessment of all evidence brought before him and after personal examination of both the accused and the witnesses. When this way of handling court cases was introduced in Norwegian witchcraft trials, it soon turned out that judges almost always found the evidence insufficient to sustain the accusations and consequently acquitted the persons accused. Although relatives of accused witches had formerly hesitated to defend them in public, from the 1660s onward several men appeared as defense council for the accused, further reducing the possibilities for starting a successful witchcraft trial. So, in a very short period of time, the whole mental climate about witchcraft changed dramatically in Norway.

HANS EYVIND NÆSS

See also: ACCUSATORIAL PROCEDURE; BLÅKULLA; DECLINE OF THE WITCH HUNTS; DENMARK; EXECUTIONS; EXODUS 22:18 (22:17); LAPLAND; LAWS ON WITCHCRAFT (EARLY MODERN); PEDERSDOTTER, ANNA; PROTESTANT REFORMATION; SWEDEN; SWIMMING TEST; TORTURE; TRIALS; WEATHER MAGIC.

References and further reading:
Alm, Ellen Janette. 2000. "Statens rolle i trolldomsprosessene i Danmark og Norge på 1500- og 1600-tallet: En komparativ undersøkelse." Hovedoppgave: Universitetet i Tromsø.
Alver, Bente Gullveig. 1972. *Heksetro og trolldom.* Oslo: Universitetsforlaget.
Botheim, Ragnhild. 1999. "Trolldomsprosessane i Bergenhus len 1566–1700." Hovedoppgave: Universitetet i Bergen.
Gilje, Nils. 2001. "'Djevelen står alltid bak': Demonisering av folkelig magi på slutten av 1500-tallet." *Tradisjon* 31: 107–116.
Hagen, Rune. 1999. "The Witch-Hunt in Early Modern Finnmark." *Acta Borealia* 1: 43–62.
———. 2002. "Harmløs dissenter eller djevelsk trollmann? Trolldomsprosessen mot samen Andres Poulson i 1692." *Historisk Tidskrift* 81: 319–346.
Knutsen, Gunnar W. 1997. "A Central Periphery? Witchcraft Trials in South-Eastern Norway." Pp. 63–74 in *Fact, Fiction, and Forensic Evidence: The Potential of Judicial Sources for Historical Research in the Early Modern Period.* Edited by Sølvi Sogner. Oslo: Historisk Institutt, Universitetet i Oslo.
———. 1998. *Trolldomsprosessene på Østlandet: En kulturhistorisk undersøkelse.* Oslo: Tingbokprosjektet.
———. 2003. "Norwegian Witchcraft Trials: A Reassessment." *Continuity and Change* 18: 185–200.
Lilienskiold, Hans Hanssen, Rune Hagen, and Per Einar Sparboe. 1998. *Trolldom og ugudelighet i 1600-tallets Finnmark.* Vol. 18, *Ravnetrykk.* Tromsø: Universitetsbiblioteket i Tromsø.
Mitchell, Stephen A. 1997. "Nordic Witchcraft in Transition: Impotence, Heresy, and Diabolism in 14th-Century Bergen." *Scandia* 63: 17–33.
———. 1998. "Anaphrodisiac Charms in the Nordic Middle Ages: Impotence, Infertility, and Magic." *Norveg* 41, no. 1: 10–42.
———. 2000. "Gender and Nordic Witchcraft in the Later Middle Ages." *Arv* 56: 7–24.
Næss, Hans Eyvind. 1982. *Trolldomsprosessene i Norge på 1500–1600-tallet: En retts- og sosialhistorisk undersøkelse.* Oslo: Universitetsforlaget.
———. 1984. *Med bål og brann: Trolldomsprsoesser i Norge.* Stavanger: Universitetsforlaget.
———. 1990. "Norway: The Criminological Context." Pp. 367–382 in *Early Modern European Witchcraft: Centres and Peripheries.* Edited by Bengt Ankarloo and Gustav Henningsen. Oxford: Clarendon.
Willumsen, Liv Helene. 1997. "Witches of the High North: The Finnmark Witchcraft Trials in the Seventeenth Century." *Scandinavian Journal of History* 22, no. 3: 199–221.
http://www.hf.uio.no/hi/prosjekter/tingbok/Bibliografi.html

NUMBER OF WITCHES

Wildly exaggerated figures are often cited for the number of witches executed in Europe, with a preposterous total of 9 million women still enjoying particular favor. This claim ultimately derives from an absurd calculation by an eighteenth-century anticlerical lawyer, Gottfried Christian Voigt, who multiplied up a mere twenty trials in one German city on the assumption that persecution levels had been constant across Europe for many centuries. It was given wider circulation by Gustav Roskoff's 1869 *History of the Devil,* much cited by Protestant and anti-Catholic writers, and was subsequently picked up by the German neopagan movement and by elements in the Nazi party.

American feminists seem to have relied on its appearance in a book by Matilda Joslyn Gage, *Woman, Church, and State* (1893), where she at least stated that only "the greater number" of this imaginary multitude were women. A connection is also made between "the burning times" and Margaret Murray's thesis of witchcraft as an ancient pagan religion under sustained attack from the western Christian Church, for which the idea of massive casualties over a long time span is a particularly convenient fiction. The myth of this early holocaust is probably indestructible, but historians are hampered in their responses by their inability to give any truly authoritative statistics based on the sources. Records of witchcraft trials across most of Europe are simply too patchy, so that reliable counting is only possible in a few exceptional jurisdictions, not on a national or European scale. Many of the suspiciously round figures given in contemporary sources also turn out to be far too high or lack any basis in fact at all. Few historians now subscribe to the idea of a massive persecution that traumatized either urban or rural society across the Continent, preferring instead to stress the localized, highly variable nature of the phenomenon.

The current estimates suggest a figure of, at the most, 50,000 legal executions in Europe (including Russia) between approximately 1400 and 1780, with perhaps 100,000 persons having been tried for witchcraft before properly constituted courts. The great majority of trials occurred in a much shorter period, around 1570–1630; in most of western Europe between 75 percent and 90 percent of trials took place over these years. In Poland and Hungary, by contrast, the trials peaked in the first half of the eighteenth century. Eastern Europe presents special difficulties because record destruction (above all in Poland) has been so serious, but the high figures once cited for Poland were generated by the same fallacious method that Voigt used in eighteenth-century Germany, that is, multiplying from a few local cases. Although a margin of error must always remain, it is hard to see how the figures could be plausibly increased by more than 20–30 percent on the most generous assumptions about missing evidence.

Unauthorized lynchings and the use of forms of popular justice such as the swimming test represent a separate problem, one that defies any statistical approach, despite the survival of occasional prosecutions of the perpetrators. On current evidence, there must at least have been hundreds of killings and very extensive witch-finding activities; total figures for lynchings may well have been in the thousands, although they are unlikely to have been so high as to alter the overall picture radically. Some of the most striking outbreaks of this kind were in countries like France, Spain, and England, which had low rates of legal executions, thus making unofficial local action an attractive and effective alternative. Rulers and governments always disapproved of such irregular procedures, and over the course of the seventeenth century they reacted with growing effectiveness to punish those involved where they could be identified. Nevertheless, a small number of physical attacks and killings persisted in parts of rural Europe until the late twentieth century.

The apparent lack of witchcraft persecution before 1400 may be deceptive because there could easily have been many trials in local courts and lynchings for which little evidence has survived. A scattering of references to individuals punished for witchcraft may well imply that such action was quite common. No reasonable estimate

of numbers can be given: the victims, unlike later witches, would not have been accused of belonging to a diabolical sect, although the local names for witches were already applied to some of them. Systematic persecution began with small numbers of trials in Savoy and the Dauphiné from around 1400, followed by bigger waves in the 1420s and 1430s. At the least, these Alpine regions must have seen several hundred trials in the decade after 1428, with a high ratio of capital sentences. These persecutions coincided with the emergence of the full-blown theory of a diabolical conspiracy, apparently propagated by the Dominicans. They were, however, followed by something of a lull over the next fifty years, when most trials seem to have been scattered local affairs, with the odd case involving twenty or more, as at Metz in 1456–1457 and Arras in 1459–1460. A second wave of larger-scale persecutions began in the 1480s and 1490s, again primarily around the Alps, continuing until about 1520 in the valleys on the Italian side. Although it is impossible to verify the figures from legal records, groups of trials involving up to sixty executions are said to have occurred in several places; the total cannot have been much short of 1,000 and could easily have reached 2,000. This second peak was again followed by a relative decline that lasted until the 1560s, despite scattered outbreaks like the one in Denmark in the 1540s.

In the 1560s, persecution began to increase again and soon reached unprecedented levels as it spread away from its Alpine heartland to cover virtually the whole of Europe. The vast majority of the trials in western and central Europe occurred in the half-century from 1580 to 1630, with a total of around 40,000 executions dwarfing anything seen before or since. The next fifty years were far milder, with most of the trials occurring in a few spectacular outbreaks (notably the Matthew Hopkins crusade in England, the 1661–1662 hunt in Scotland, the *Zauberer-Jackl* [Sorcerer-Jack] trials of Salzburg, the county of Vaduz between 1648 and 1680, and the Swedish hunt of 1668–1676). Each of these episodes involved hundreds of trials, but conviction rates were usually lower, so that the total of executions in these five instances may have been around 1,000. Elsewhere, growing judicial caution resulted in a massive reduction in the numbers of individual and small-scale trials, so that after 1630 the average rate of persecution probably fell to less than one-tenth of its peak levels in the preceding period. After 1680, there was no more than a trickle of isolated cases apart from the belated persecutions in eastern Europe.

For the period from the 1560s to the 1630s it becomes possible to analyze the statistics in more complex ways, notably to establish comparative rates of intensity across different regions. There are major problems of definition here because so much of Europe, notably in the Holy Roman Empire, was divided into very small political units unlike modern nation-states. The attribution of more than 20,000 executions to the German lands conceals an exceptionally varied picture. In a region with hundreds of separate territories, about 10,000 of these executions occurred in a dozen locations, some of them quite small, whereas other rulers displayed extreme caution or refused to convict witches at all. A simple comparative measure sets estimates of executions against total population for the end of the sixteenth century. On this reckoning there are striking differences between larger regions: modern Luxembourg had about 5 executions per 1,000 people; followed by Switzerland, with 4 executions; the Spanish (southern) Netherlands, with 2; Denmark, 1.75; Germany, 1.5; Scotland, 1.4; Hungary, 0.27; Italy, 0.2; and England and the northern Netherlands both about 0.13. France and Spain hardly register on the scale, at around 0.04 per 1,000 people. The differences become far greater when very small areas are included; modern Liechtenstein (the county of Vaduz) is way out in front, although per capita totals in a few smaller autonomous German territories were even higher, with the extraordinary figure of 100 per 1,000 inhabitants, 300 executions for a population of only 3,000. The electorate of Cologne led the middle-sized category at 10 (2,000 per 200,000 people), with the duchies of Lorraine and Luxembourg both over 5 (each around 1,600 per 300,000 inhabitants), and the electorate of Mainz not far behind. Although all these figures rest on calculations for both trials and total populations that are very approximate, the orders of magnitude seem fairly well established. Some of the lower figures, including those for the large monarchies of France, Spain, and England, are rather deceptive, because these regions had abnormally low rates of convictions and capital sentences. If the measure were in terms of trials rather than executions, their coefficient would move up quite sharply. Less than 10 percent of some 1,300 witches whose cases went to the *Parlement* of Paris (sovereign judicial court, with jurisdiction over approximately one-half of France) on appeal were executed, but hundreds were flogged or banished. In England the county of Essex was unusually active, with executions running at 0.82 per 1,000 people; if trials are considered, however, the figure was 4.

What the numbers also show are very different patterns. At one extreme were regions like Lorraine, Luxembourg, and the pays de Vaud, where there were no large crises, and trials were spread fairly evenly across several decades and quite wide areas. At the other extreme, there were the series of intense short-term persecutions, such as at the imperial abbey of St. Maximin, just outside Trier, where at least 400 people (out of a population of only 2,200) were executed as witches from 1586 to 1596. Alongside famous German cases

such as Bamberg (900) and Würzburg (1200), both with two surges within little more than a decade, one must place the Scottish and Danish witch hunts, the panic around Bouchain in the Spanish Netherlands, the Hopkins campaign in England, the various post-1650 cases mentioned above, and many others. Across much of Europe a mixed pattern is evident, with a series of isolated trials but also sudden bursts of more intense activity. In areas like the Franche-Comté or the Labourd, the victims were counted in scores rather than hundreds, but the dynamics were those of true witch hunts. The great persecution was thus a composite affair, which combined endemic suspicions within local communities with terrifying bursts of witch hunting, and the elites were heavily involved in the latter as both instigators and victims.

ROBIN BRIGGS

See also: CHRONOLOGY OF WITCHCRAFT TRIALS; HISTORIOGRAPHY; LYNCHING; MURRAY, MARGARET ALICE.
References and further reading:
Ankarloo, Bengt, and Gustav Henningsen. 1990. *Early Modern European Witchcraft: Centres and Peripheries.* Oxford: Clarendon.
Behringer, Wolfgang. 2004. *Witches and Witch Hunts.* Cambridge: Polity Press.
Levack, Brian. 1995. *The Witch-Hunt in Early Modern Europe.* 2nd ed. London: Longman.
Macfarlane, Alan. 1970. *Witchcraft in Tudor and Stuart England. A Regional and Comparative Study.* London: Routledge and Kegan Paul.
Monter, William. 2002. "Witch Trials in Continental Europe, 1560–1660." Pp. 1–52 and 122–146 in *The Period of the Witch Trials.* Vol. 4 of *The Athlone History of Witchcraft and Magic in Europe.* Edited by Bengt Ankarloo and Stuart Clark. London and Philadelphia: University of Pennsylvania Press.
Soman, Alfred. 1992. *Sorcellerie et Justice Criminelle: Le Parlement de Paris (16e–18e siècles).* Basingstoke: Ashgate Publishing. (Includes some articles in English.)

NUREMBERG, IMPERIAL FREE CITY

Nuremberg, one of the more important imperial cities of the Holy Roman Empire, unusual because of the skepticism of its leading citizens toward diabolical witchcraft and for the city's avoidance of witch hunts.

The inhabitants of Nuremberg (Nürnberg) embraced Lutheranism early on, despite the city's temporary role as the residence of the imperial government (*Reichsregiment*) in 1522–1524. By then, this rich town of about 30,000 inhabitants had reached maximal importance. Its merchants controlled mining activities in surrounding areas, and its craftspeople prospered in the metal industry and other handicrafts. Humanist Johannes Cochläus portrayed Nuremberg as the center of Europe, due to its geographic position as well as to the ingeniousness of its artisans: Erhard Etzlaub had recently invented maps indicating European travel roads; Peter Hele had invented the portable clock, useful for travelers and merchants; and there were of course Albrecht Dürer and his school, the most daring artists of their time, not to mention Hans Sachs, the shoemaker-poet, and the *Meistersingers.*

Nuremberg was presumably founded around 1000 as a royal castle, but when a royal mint was introduced soon afterward, a suburb developed. By 1200 Nuremberg had its own law and soon after became one of the first German towns with a self-governing council. It was already almost "free" when the council received high jurisdiction in 1320. During the reign of Emperor Charles IV of the Luxembourg dynasty, the "Golden Bull" of 1356 granted Nuremberg the right to host the first imperial diet of each emperor. After 1424, Nuremberg's prestige soared when emperor Sigmund decreed that this city would harbor the imperial symbols (*Reichsinsignien*), which indeed remained the case until 1796. As one of the few imperial cities, Nuremberg managed to get rid of all feudal remnants, simply by buying the Hohenzollern castle, and constructed its own territory, like an Italian city-state. Nuremberg's governing families indeed acquired noble status, and it was one of the few German towns where humanism was an urban phenomenon, with Willibald Pirckheimer as a figure of almost "national" importance. Nuremberg even founded a university at Altdorf, within its territory. However, the city suffered terribly during the Thirty Years' War and never again regained its former importance. Occupied by Bavarian and Prussian troops in the 1790s, it was swallowed by the Kingdom of Bavaria in 1806.

Nuremberg's attitude toward witchcraft was explored thoroughly by Harmut Kunstmann in 1970. The results of this legal dissertation were then surprising, because contrary to common expectations, Nuremberg experienced no witch hunts. Nuremberg's legal sources are exhaustingly rich, and it is unlikely that any trial escaped Kunstmann's attention. It held several dozen sixteenth-century sorcery trials (the death penalty was imposed for poisoning and sorcery in 1520), and there were frequent allegations of witchcraft among the populace, but Nuremberg's spirit of humanism and capitalism prevented any witch hunts. However, it had a few scattered witchcraft trials in a narrow sense, in which the city councilors proved to be extremely reluctant; one of them, Dr. Johann Hepstein, even ridiculed the existence of witches. Their attitude was reflected in contemporary art and literature: poet Hans Sachs also claimed that witchcraft was nothing but a devilish illusion, and the famous sketches of witches by Albrecht Dürer and his school should be interpreted likewise. Dürer was a councilor and part of Nuremberg's governing elite, in touch with leading humanists and Venetian and Dutch artists, and it is extremely unlikely that he believed in witchcraft in such an environment. Humanist Willibald Pirckheimer ridiculed recent ideas of witchcraft in his satire on Luther's opponent, Johannes Eck, *Eckius dedolatus* (Eck Cut Down). In 1536, the Nuremberg council issued a decree against "Sorcery, Witchcraft, and Divining" that explicitly designated these crimes as frauds. In 1590, a man was executed who had previously served the executioner of Eichstätt and had tried to launch a witch hunt in Nuremberg. Nuremberg's magistrates took this occasion to demonstrate the town's attitude toward witchcraft.

Like other upper German imperial cities, Nuremberg's situation reversed after the Thirty Years' War, when economic decline prevented any recovery of its former importance. New anxieties entered cities with populations that had shrunk to half their former size. In 1659, two women were executed for witchcraft, and a man was executed in 1660. But although it saw some serious cases until the end of the seventeenth century, Nuremberg had no more executions. All in all, this imperial free city represents the case of an urban environment where the rule of law prevailed and a skeptical attitude toward fantastical crimes was common. Nuremberg became a safe haven for refugees from the Franconian prince-bishoprics, and the town was sufficiently rich and self-confident to withstand all attempts by neighboring princes to force it into cooperation. Among urban elites, it was usually lawyers and artists rather than theologians who distanced themselves from popular beliefs about witchcraft and who maintained Nuremberg's position as a beacon of independence and freedom. And because Nuremberg dominated the imperial cities of the Franconian circle, its influence prevented atrocities among them, either through legal opinions (as in the case of the small imperial city of Weissenburg) or just by serving as an example generally.

WOLFGANG BEHRINGER

See also: DÜRER, ALBRECHT; GERMANY; GERMANY, SOUTHEASTERN; HEPSTEIN, JOHANN; HOLY ROMAN EMPIRE; IMPERIAL FREE CITIES; SKEPTICISM.

References and further reading:
Kunstmann, Hartmut Heinrich. 1970. *Zauberwahn und Hexenprozess in der Reichsstadt Nürnberg.* Nuremberg: Schriftenreihe des Stadtarchivs Nürnberg Bd. 1.

NUSS, BALTHASAR (1545–1618)

Count and judge at witchcraft trials, born in Brückenau, Nuss ranks among the most notorious German witch hunters. In Fulda, the largest prince-abbey in the Holy Roman Empire, at least 203 people died during the trials he led from 1603 to 1606. In contrast to most witch hunters, Nuss was eventually imprisoned for his crimes and finally beheaded in Fulda after spending twelve years in jail. In literature, he has commonly been referred to as "Ross," although court records invariably called him "Nuss."

Nuss (who had murdered a priest in his youth) owed much of his career to his mentor, Prince-Abbot Balthasar von Dernbach (1548–1606). When von Dernbach returned to Fulda after twenty-six years in exile, he appointed his old protégé, Nuss, to judge cases involving witchcraft. Nuss immediately began conducting trials in 1603. Würzburg's law faculty instructed the judge of the trial procedures to be followed, but Nuss violated these persecution-friendly rules. Especially spectacular was the trial of Marga Bien, whose husband complained about Nuss to the *Reichskammergericht* (imperial chamber court) but was ultimately unable to prevent her from being burned at the stake.

Nuss did make one grave mistake. In March 1604, he summoned six women belonging to Fulda's upper class, who had already fled with their families. Their summons was publicized in the particularly embarrassing form of an edict. However, none of them returned to Fulda, and several of their relatives filed suit for unlawful trial conduct against Nuss and von Dernbach in the *Reichskammergericht*. Before the court reached a decision, the prince-abbot died in spring 1606. His successor, Friedrich von Schwalbach, ended the witchcraft trials and fired Nuss. Three months later, after discovering that Nuss had embezzled 2,358 guilders, almost half the proceeds from the trial costs paid by the victims' families, Schwalbach had him arrested. The families of the six upper-class women accused in 1604 now returned to Fulda and filed suits against Nuss. After one year of imprisonment, Nuss's formal trial had not yet begun; the former judge appealed to the *Reichskammergericht*, which denied his request for release. After Nuss's second appeal in 1609, the court in Speyer reduced his sentence.

Prison conditions were such that Nuss and his wife produced four of their seven children while he was in jail. He suffered a series of strokes in jail and became increasingly handicapped, to the point at which he was eventually unable to walk and could barely speak. His wife lobbied Fulda's government on his behalf, but in vain. Nuss also received support from a nephew who was a lawyer in Frankfurt. In 1615, Würzburg's law faculty sentenced Nuss to indefinite state custody and ordered him to repay the money he had embezzled. This decision was not severe enough for the court in Fulda: instead, his files were sent to Ingolstadt as part of a second file sharing. In November 1618, Ingolstadt

sentenced Nuss to death. He was beheaded in Fulda at the age of seventy-three.

Nuss was the second German witch hunter to be executed. Five years earlier, Gottfried Sattler, a Bavarian witch judge in Wemding, had already been executed at Munich. A similar case also occurred later in Osnabrück. In 1650, Dr. Wilhelm Peltzer was jailed for his misconduct as that town's chief witch hunter. As with Nuss, the imperial chamber court became involved, but again without resolving the case; Peltzer died in prison, insane. Beheading a witch-hunting judge also proved to people that some witchcraft trials had been illegitimate and suggested that the traditional argument that God would not allow innocent people to be executed was apparently wrong. To Adam Tanner, the first major Jesuit opponent of witch hunting, Nuss's execution demonstrated the danger posed to innocent people by unjust judges. Friedrich Spee was also familiar with Nuss's case, citing Ingolstadt's death sentence (copied from Tanner) in his *Cautio Criminalis* (A Warning on Criminal Justice) of 1631. Spee could have learned about Nuss's witchcraft trials as early as 1612, during his Jesuit novitiate in Fulda. During the nineteenth-century *Kulturkampf* (culture war), Catholic scholars of witchcraft used the example of Balthasar Nuss to demonstrate that Catholic territories could end unjust witchcraft trials on their own and even punish those responsible.

PETER OESTMANN;

TRANSLATED BY JONATHAN STICKNEY

See also: FULDA, PRINCE-ABBEY OF; GERMANY, WEST AND NORTH-WEST; OSNABRÜCK, BISHOPRIC OF; *REICHSKAMMERGERICHT;* SATTLER, GOTTFRIED; SPEE, FRIEDRICH; TANNER, ADAM.

References and further reading:

Behringer, Wolfgang. 2000. *Hexen und Hexenprozesse in Deutschland.* 4th ed. Munich: Deutscher Taschenbuch.

Jäger, Berthold. 1997. "Zur Geschichte der Hexenprozesse im Stift Fulda." *Fuldaer Geschichtsblätter* 73: 7–64.

Oestmann, Peter. 1997. *Hexenprozesse am Reichskammergericht.* Cologne, Weimar, and Vienna: Böhlau, pp. 438–446.

Schormann, Gerhard. 1991. *Der Krieg gegen die Hexen.* Göttingen: Vandenhoeck und Ruprecht, pp. 115–120.

———. 1994. "Die Fuldaer Hexenprozesse und die Würzburger Juristenfakultät." Pp. 311–323 in *Hexenverfolgung und Regionalgeschichte.* Edited by Gisela Wilbertz et al. Bielefeld: Verlag für Regionalgeschichte.

O

OBRY, NICOLE (CA. 1550–?)

Nicole Obry (Aubry/Aubray) was the main actor in an extraordinary drama of demonic possession and exorcism in 1566. She was then fifteen or sixteen years old, the daughter of a baker in Vervins, a small town in northeastern France. In the fall of 1565, after seeing the ghost of her grandfather, she began to show symptoms that were diagnosed as demonic possession. She was exorcised in Vervins, but because all her thirty demons could not be made to leave her, she was brought to the diocesan capital at Laon in January 1566. Laon was a religiously mixed city, with an active Protestant minority. This was a very tense point in the religious wars. After the temporary end of organized religious warfare in 1563, propaganda and random violence continued. Organized warfare resumed in 1567, not long after this case was concluded.

In Laon, Nicole was exorcised in public (unlike any previous case of this sort in France), on a specially built scaffold in front of the cathedral. She was brought to the ceremonies in great processions, carried by eight or ten men who struggled to control her convulsions and deathlike trances. The exorcisms drew huge crowds. Her main demon was forced to identify himself as Beelzebuth, one of Satan's chief lieutenants. Speaking through Nicole, Beelzebuth also revealed that he was the prince of the Protestant heretics, referring to them as "my Huguenots" and delivering sermons against the heretics. The intimate connection between Protestants and the Devil became a recurrent theme in French Catholic polemic throughout and even beyond the age of the religious wars.

Laon's Protestants were skeptical from the outset. The prince of Condé, their military commander in the recent war and the most prominent Protestant nobleman in France, attempted to halt the exorcisms; he even tried to convert Nicole, but the king ordered her released. The exorcisms, now conducted personally by the bishop, continued. Interestingly enough, unlike many later French cases, no witch was accused of sending the demons into the possessed. The strongest weapon in the bishop's armory was the communion wafer, the Host. It is almost impossible to overemphasize the role of transubstantiation in France at this time. The ultimate charge against Protestants was that they fed consecrated Hosts to dogs; at the same time, superstitious (but Catholic) shepherds in northern France really did sometimes feed consecrated Hosts to animals precisely because of their supposed miraculous properties.

On February 8, 1566, Beelzebuth and the rest of the demons dramatically left Nicole's body in front of thousands of observers. A plume of smoke was observed rising from her body. This sensational spectacle was one of the most widely publicized acts of the early stages of the religious wars. It was regarded as a great Catholic victory, known across France as the "Miracle of Laon." Catholicism's ability to exorcise demons proved that the Catholic Church was the only true Christian church. Catholic polemicists seized on this incident because the supernatural power of the Host confirmed the correctness of the Catholic view of the sacraments. Pamphlets and books by Guillaume Postel, Jean Boulaese, Charles Blendec, and Florimond de Raemond described this miracle in order to attack Protestantism and defend the Catholic Church. Raemond, who had flirted with Protestantism, converted back to Catholicism as the result of witnessing the exorcism. For Postel, this miracle confirmed the role of consecrated priests and the traditional Catholic hierarchy.

This colorful event introduced the Devil as a key player in Catholic propaganda. For the next two generations, demonology in France was highly political, tied to Catholic attempts to demonize their adversaries. In 1599, supporters of the Catholic cause attempted to block the Edict of Nantes, the religious compromise that was to end violence, by recreating the "Miracle of Laon" in Paris. This attempt, however, proved a fiasco. Although Marthe Brossier was regarded as a fraud, people still continued to believe in demonic possession, and such spectacular public exorcisms as the Loudun nuns endured as popular theater in France far into the seventeenth century. Nicole Obry's miracle was quoted, if not repeated.

JONATHAN L. PEARL

See also: BROSSIER, MARTHE; DEMONOLOGY; DEMONS; EXORCISM; FRANCE; GHOSTS; LOUDUN NUNS; POSSESSION, DEMONIC; WARS OF RELIGION (FRANCE).

References and further reading:

Ferber, Sarah. 2004. *Demonic Possession and Exorcism in Early Modern France.* London and New York: Routledge.

Postel, Guillaume. 1995. *Summopere.* Edited by Irena Backus. Geneva: Droz.

Sluhovsky, Moshe. 1996. "A Divine Apparition or Demonic Possession? Female Agency and Church Authority in Demonic Possession in Sixteenth-Century France." *Sixteenth Century Journal* 17, no. 4: 1039–1055.

Walker, D. P. 1981. *Unclean Spirits: Possession and Exorcism in France and England in the Late Sixteenth and Early Seventeenth Centuries.* Philadelphia: University of Pennsylvania Press.

OCCULT

The term *occult* covers the qualities in nature hidden from ordinary human observation and understanding and the forbidden practices or rituals used to discover and manipulate these qualities. Occult practices include astrology (understanding the influence of the stars and planets on human lives), magic (the use of intrinsic and extrinsic, natural or supernatural powers to produce effects), alchemy (the study of the means to transform baser metals into gold), and divination (the means for understanding or divining a foreordained destiny). Typically, practitioners of the occult are in awe of the power of nature and are fascinated with the possibility of mastering it—usually for their personal gain. The occultist may also feel some sense of psychological, intellectual, or social superiority over others, or he or she may gain greater acceptance in societies that value occult knowledge (especially with regard to healing and protection against disease).

THE OCCULT, RELIGION, AND SCIENCE

Some historians have argued that magic, which involves the coercion of God, should be contrasted with religion, which involves the supplication of God by prayer. In practice, it is not always possible to distinguish the occult from religion. Both phenomena are based on a belief in the unity of nature, which includes God and the angels at one extreme and human beings and the terrestrial world at the other. In this sense, human beings are a special link in the great chain of being, and they can participate in some of the divine mysteries. Therefore, partial revelation of the occult was a key element in the Hellenistic cults of the ancient world. In contrast, Christians, who emphasized the fallen state of humanity and its tendency to sin, tended to regard the followers of these pagan religions as heretics and devil worshippers, and they attacked all attempts to delve into what they regarded as divine mysteries, such as the miracles of nature. As a result, the limits of natural knowledge were circumscribed and policed, and many occult practitioners were forced into silence or outward conformity. However, Christian occultists have claimed that they are serving God or that they derive their power from the divine. In many cases, the "spells" and symbols they employ in their rituals, as well as their aims, are similar to religious imagery and ritual.

Modern occultists tend to be associated with Satanism or with pseudoscience, although the nineteenth-century followers of the Order of the Golden Dawn were drawn to its mystical religiosity.

It is also important to note the relationship between the occult and science, for the two categories often seem historically indistinguishable. For example, mathematical knowledge was the basis for some medieval technology that appeared to imitate and master nature and shaded imperceptibly into natural magic. Sir Isaac Newton's (1642–1727) alchemical investigations complemented his search for the hidden quality that came to be known as gravity. The difference between the two is that all natural phenomena can be studied and understood, whereas the occult can never be fully understood or systematically investigated because the full source of its power is by definition hidden from the human mind. Moreover, occultists have usually formed private and closed social networks, and they sometimes withhold their arcane knowledge from the world.

Until secular authorities sanctioned them in the modern era (that is, since ca. 1750), occult texts circulated secretly, and many occult practitioners, including witches, were persecuted in the belief that all magic and most astrology were demonically inspired. However, there is a correlation between social status and the degree of tolerance of occultists. From the Middle Ages onward, magicians and astrologers could hold privileged positions at court. Indulgent princes and popes permitted learned men (as opposed to ignorant women) such as Michael Scot (ca. 1175–ca. 1235) and Michel de Nostredame (known as Nostradamus) (1503–1566) to practice their craft in relative freedom. For most people in the modern secular era, the occult has lost its potency and has become a matter of personal curiosity or an object of antiquarian or historical interest.

THE ANCIENT WORLD

The Greek philosopher Plato made a distinction between what was apparent and what was real in the universe, and he suggested how essential parts of nature were transmitted from the higher being by celestial intelligences known as *daemones*. In the *Timaeus* he discussed some of the numerological codes that formed the basis for an understanding of the world. His pupil Aristotle (384–322 B.C.E.), whose works heavily influenced the Western scientific and philosophical tradition up until the seventeenth century, thought that the natural world was ordered in a unified and fairly regular way. Therefore, nature's secrets were open to investigation and reasonable enquiry by humans in terms of the four essences (earth, air, fire, and water). However, both men provided occultists with some justification for secret or mystical forms of enquiry. For example, Aristotle allowed for the existence of a fifth essence inherent in the stars and planets that influenced earthly matters and provided the basis for astrology. Plato half-seriously suggested that initiation into pure philosophical truth could be compared with initiation into a mystery religion. Neoplatonists took up this suggestion more seriously and blended it with the religion of the first Iranian (Persian) empire, named after the prophet Zarathustra (better known by the Greek form of his name, Zoroaster), who saw all existence as the gradual realization of a divine plan. The Zoroastrian magi (priests) were adept in astrology and the arts of divination, and one branch of the occult was named after them: magic. Neoplatonists such as Plotinus (ca. 205–270), Porphyry (ca. 232–303), and Iamblichus (ca. 250–ca. 330) and the members of Hellenistic cults cultivated a form of gnosis (the special knowledge of spiritual mysteries). They read the revelations attributed to the Egyptian god Thoth, called Hermes Trismegistus (Thrice-Great Hermes), that concerned philosophy and the understanding or manipulation of astrology, alchemy, natural history, medicine, and magic. In this way, they argued that only a pious and sequestered magus assisted by the *daemones* could unlock natural and supernatural mysteries. Curses, spells, and enchantments that incorporate divine figures such as Isis have been discovered on stones, amulets, and scrolls from ancient Egypt and Greece also indicate the way in which occult power was associated with the divine will.

The Romans were heavily influenced by Greek writings on the occult, and they were no less fascinated by magic, astrology, and divination as transmitted by the books attributed to Hermes Trismegistus (known as the *Corpus Hermeticum*) or Pythagoras—a mathematician who was also considered to be the first practitioner of learned magic. Augury (divination) was widely used and was based on natural occurrences such as thunder and lightning, the flight of birds, and the movement of the planets. However, Pliny the Elder (ca. 23–79), like Cicero (106–43 B.C.E.), Seneca (ca. 4 B.C.E.–C.E. 65) and Galen (ca. 130–200), was skeptical about just how many marvelous things in nature, which seemed out of the ordinary course of nature described by Aristotle, could be ascribed to magic and other occult phenomena. Nevertheless, he recorded many examples of what would be called "natural magic" in his *Natural History*, thereby confirming a trend toward cataloguing the bizarre in nature and providing a basis for later occult investigations.

THE MIDDLE AGES

Early Christian writers such as St. Augustine of Hippo regarded Hellenistic cults as little more than centers of demonic magic. In Judeo-Christian thought, the benign Neoplatonic *daemones* who were neutral spirits intermediate between gods and human beings were recast as angels who had turned against God. Augustine discouraged speculation about the deeper mysteries of nature, such as monstrous births and other such omens, portents, and prodigies, and he deplored the way in which the practice of magic led people to ally themselves with Satan. As well as the often-quoted scriptural text of Exodus 22:18 (22:17; "Thou shalt not suffer a witch to live"), a locus classicus of such medieval hostility toward magicians was the story of Simon Magus of Samaria (Acts 8:9–24), whose iniquity stemmed from his attempts to rival the power of God in his miracle making. Subsequent Christian polemicists, following Augustine's views, fostered a distrust of intellectual curiosity, which was viewed as a dangerous and vain pursuit, leading as it did to pride, sin, and, ultimately, heresy (indeed, the occult was often associated with Judaism, and nocturnal assemblies of witches in the presence of the Devil were called "synagogues" for part of this period). Many members of the Latin Church, especially the scholars of the new universities known as the Scholastics, therefore attempted to set a limit on human knowledge. They left many of the deeper mysteries of the universe to God's will and understanding, and they condemned occult dabbling as a form of "superstition"—in the original sense provided by Saint Thomas Aquinas: a perversion of correct religious devotion.

However, stories of Jesus's miracles on earth, the wonder-working capabilities of prayer and adjurations, and the intensification of eucharistic devotion from the thirteenth century muddied the boundaries between *mira* (wonders) and *miracula* (miracles) and appeared to sanction some occult techniques based on mechanical and scientific knowledge and directed toward "holy" ends. This relationship was exacerbated from the twelfth century onward by the Europe-wide diffusion of Latin and vernacular translations of Arabic texts on the occult and science such as the *Picatrix* (the Latin translation of "The Aim of the Sage"). These collections of "secrets," which were supposedly imparted by a sage and often written in code or obscure language, may have encouraged readers to distinguish more sharply between natural magic and demonic magic and to increase interest in the former. However, such texts also opened the way for the study of necromancy (the conjuring of spirits), which was an explicitly demonic technique for controlling nature through Latinate incantations and quasireligious ritual, usually undertaken by educated clerics.

During the Middle Ages, horoscopes, medical self-help manuals, books of charms, manuals for divination, and alchemical manuscripts were read with increasing frequency by laypeople as well as clerics. These works comprised discussions of the influence of planets and stars on terrestrial affairs; recipes for procuring a lover; lists of enchantments for causing harm or ensuring personal protection; lists of protective amulets and gemstones; necromantic formulas and rituals; and instructions for the practice of oneirancy (the interpretation of dreams), chiromancy (the reading of palms), and onomancy (calculation through names). The effectiveness of such phenomena relied upon a variety of assumptions and claims. For instance, occult techniques and recipes were attributed to a classical authority or venerated figure such as Hermes Trismegistus, Virgil, or Albertus Magnus (Albert the Great, ca. 1200–1280), or to demons, as in the case of necromancy. It was often claimed that such spells had been employed successfully on many previous occasions, and there was an assumption that there was clearly some "occult" or hidden quality in the form of words, markings, or material used. In short, many people attributed a large number of occult phenomena to natural but obscure causes, practiced their art in secret or under royal protection at court, and ran an intermittent risk of secular or ecclesiastical prosecution, particularly if such arts caused harm to others.

THE OCCULT RENAISSANCE

From the beginning of the fifteenth century there was an increase in the production of these occult manuscripts. Moreover, after the establishment of printing presses in the cities and monastic or university centers of Europe, books of marvels and "secrets" as well as learned treatises on natural magic ranked among the most popular texts of the literate or listening public. Magic, astrology, and alchemy were openly studied and practiced at many late medieval and Renaissance courts, such as those of the emperors Frederick III (ruled 1440–1493) and Rudolf II (ruled 1576–1612); Pope Urban VIII (ruled 1623–1644); Cosimo de' Medici in Florence (1389–1464); and Elizabeth I of England (ruled 1558–1603). It has been argued that the occult sciences found favor in court because they provided a useful weapon in the armory of courtiers who sought to eliminate enemies and gain the ear of a ruler. However, astrologers such as William Lilly in seventeenth-century London cast horoscopes for maidservants as well as the nobility, and the vast literature about wonders and witches in northern Europe also suggests that there was a popular interest in the occult.

In contrast to the Middle Ages, this was an "age of wonders" when learned men and women sought to uncover the hidden powers of the universe by turning sharper eyes on nature (the macrocosm) and human experience (the microcosm). It is clear that this change was partly due to the revival of classical learning that lay at the heart of the Renaissance and was also a function of the longing for a more primitive, purified, and intensely mystical Christianity. The philological or historical investigations of this period were fueled by a

Heinrich Cornelius Agrippa von Nettesheim, De Occulta Philosophie (On Occult Philosophy), *1531—delineation of a horoscope chart founded on bodily characteristics. Divination was an important occult practice. (Bettmann/Corbis)*

desire for greater understanding of the Word of God. They also provided a basis for renewed interest in the Kabbalah (Hebrew mysticism), the *Corpus Hermeticum,* Aristotelianism, Neoplatonism, or the science of the ancients. A typical Renaissance magus such as the Florentine philosopher Marsilio Ficino (1433–1499) used his knowledge of Greek to translate works ascribed to Hermes Trismegistus. On the basis of this work and his Platonic studies, he outlined a form of astral magic that channeled the power of the stars and planets imprinted on the earth by celestial spirits. The German humanist and occult philosopher Heinrich Cornelius Agrippa von Nettesheim explored many of the texts and traditions employed by Ficino. In his *De occulta philosophia* (On Occult Philosophy; first complete edition, 1533), he defended the invocation of demons so long as they were good and the agents of divine miracles. The Neapolitan philosopher Giambattista Della Porta made a distinction between natural and demonic magic, and he aimed to uncover the natural properties in supposedly demonic magic. He explained that his popular *Magia naturalis* (On Natural Magic, 1558 and 1589; translated into English as *Natural Magick* in 1658) was intended to be a "survey of the whole course of nature" (Debus 1978, 13).

Renaissance occultists sought to understand the harmony in the universe and to use its powers to bring concord and unity to the political and religious divisions of Europe. Such philosophical and political arcana, although clearly attractive to rulers such as the Holy Roman Emperor Rudolf II, whose territories teemed with religious sects and whose court was filled with magi, were often condemned by the Church, and many magi were keen to distance themselves from accusations of sorcery. Therefore, Agrippa published a retraction of his ideas *before* he published the *De occulta,* and the Englishman Dr. John Dee, who practiced necromancy and studied mathematical or natural magic, defended himself against accusations that he was a "conjurer" by protesting that all of his studies had been directed toward God and emphasizing that many wondrous feats were naturally, mathematically, and mechanically contrived.

However, in seeking to reduce the scope of demonic magic and to lend authority to their own natural magic, the occultists undermined some of the theological bases for demonic magic and therefore the keystone in the Catholic and Protestant churches' campaigns against witchcraft. For example, Giambattista Della Porta supplied a naturalistic explanation for the demonic "witches' salve" (which was supposed to allow its users to fly to Sabbats or meetings). Consequently, he was investigated by the Inquisition and attacked by Jean Bodin in his book *De la Démonomanie des sorciers* (On the Demonmania of witches, 1580). These attempts to reduce the scope of the Devil's actions in the world were helpful to such early skeptics of witchcraft as Reginald Scot and Johann Weyer—a former student of Agrippa. However, the skeptics and occult connoisseurs had an unshakeable faith in Scripture and the learned texts of the occult heritage, and they betrayed an enormous condescension toward illiterate men and women whose healing techniques and claims to supernatural power they characterized as mere "superstition." Thus, their highly selective attacks on peasant beliefs strengthened the Church's authority to pursue witches and may have strengthened the social position and professional exclusivity of learned magicians, alchemists, and court astrologers.

THE MODERN SECULAR ERA

Technological and scientific discoveries in the sixteenth and seventeenth centuries, as well as the development of competing models of the cosmos, gradually undermined traditional beliefs about the world and discredited the authenticity of some of the ancient texts that formed the basis for occult activity. The growth of scientific academies in the seventeenth century further widened the scope for natural philosophical investigation, gradually stripping natural magic, astrology, and alchemy of their scientific credibility. The English politician and philosopher Francis Bacon (1561–1626) discussed occult qualities in nature, but he argued that true science should take the "mystery" out of things, and he thought it possible to reveal the causes of occult phenomena and to harness this knowledge for the benefit of the growing nation-state. Scientific pioneers were far from uniformly antioccultist; Galileo cast horoscopes for rich German students, and Isaac Newton expended enormous effort on alchemical experiments. One of Galileo's late-seventeenth-century successors as mathematician at the University of Padua continued to practice magic while maintaining an outward appearance of scientific "respectability." Other occultists contributed to modern technological developments. For instance, a mathematician and alchemist at the ducal court in Dresden made the discovery of porcelain manufacture in 1707.

The notion of occult powers continues to hold an attraction for many people. No doubt, there are some who still seek to understand and control the hidden forces in nature, and if the contents of the Internet and the lists of published books are reliable guides, there are probably many more who seek some form of occult "reenchantment" in a predominantly secular Western world.

STEPHEN BOWD

See also: AGRIPPA VON NETTESHEIM, HEINRICH CORNELIUS; ALCHEMY; AMULET AND TALISMAN; ASTROLOGY; AUGUSTINE, ST.; BODIN, JEAN; DEE, JOHN; DELLA PORTA, GIAMBATTISTA; DEVIL; DIVINATION; HERMETICISM; KABBALAH; MAGIC, LEARNED; MAGIC, NATURAL; MIRACLES; NECROMANCY; SCIENCE AND MAGIC; SCOT, REGINALD; SIMON MAGUS; SPELLS; SUPERSTITION; WEYER, JOHANN.

References and further reading:
Copenhaver, Brian P. 1988. "Astrology and Magic." Chapter 10 in *The Cambridge History of Renaissance Philosophy.* General editor, Charles B. Schmitt, editors Quentin Skinner and Eckhard Kessler, associate editor Jill Kraye. Cambridge: Cambridge University Press.
Daston, Lorraine, and Katharine Park. 1998. *Wonders and the Order of Nature, 1150–1750.* New York: Zone Books.
Debus, Allen G. 1978. *Man and Nature in the Renaissance.* Cambridge: Cambridge University Press.
Eamon, William. 1994. *Science and the Secrets of Nature: Books of Secrets in Medieval and Early Modern Culture.* Princeton, NJ: Princeton University Press.
Evans, R. J. W. 1973. *Rudolf II and His World: A Study in Intellectual History, 1576–1612.* Oxford: Oxford University Press.
Flint, Valerie. 1991. *The Rise of Magic in Early Medieval Europe.* Oxford: Clarendon.
Kieckhefer, Richard. 1989. *Magic in the Middle Ages.* Cambridge: Cambridge University Press.
Maxwell-Stuart, P. G., ed. and trans. 1999. *The Occult in Early Modern Europe: A Documentary History.* Basingstoke: Macmillan.
Ogden, Daniel. 2001. *Greek and Roman Necromancy.* Princeton, NJ: Princeton University Press.
Shumaker, Wayne. 1972. *The Occult Sciences in the Renaissance: A Study in Intellectual Patterns.* Los Angeles and Berkeley: University of California Press.
Thomas, Keith. 1971. *Religion and the Decline of Magic: Studies in Popular Beliefs in Sixteenth- and Seventeenth-Century England.* London: Weidenfeld and Nicolson.

Thorndike, Lynn. 1923–1958. *A History of Magic and Experimental Science.* 8 vols. New York: Columbia University Press.

Walker, D. P. 1958. *Spiritual and Demonic Magic, from Ficino to Campanella.* London: Warburg Institute.

Yates, Frances A. 1964. *Giordano Bruno and the Hermetic Tradition.* London: Routledge and Kegan Paul.

OFFENBURG, IMPERIAL FREE CITY

Eighty-nine accused witches lost their lives in this Catholic imperial free city in southwestern Germany, which belonged to the Circle of Swabia and shared a curial vote with the cities of Gegenbach and Zell am Harmerbach. Offenburg had approximately 2,400 inhabitants in 1803. Its early modern history was strongly influenced between 1550 and 1635 by its proximity to neighboring Ortenau and the consequent Austrian influence. Research on Offenburg's witchcraft trials goes back to Franz Volk's "excellent study" in 1882 (Midelfort 1972, 128). Chronologically, there were three distinct phases: before 1608, the wave of trials in 1608, and the great witch hunt from 1627 to 1630.

The first witchcraft trials were mainly isolated incidents; the city council remained relatively reserved. Although fifteen people were executed for witchcraft in neighboring Ortenau between 1595 and 1599, only four witches died in Offenburg during the same time. Consequently, Offenburg's guilds complained about the council's lax stance to the imperial commissioner, the governor of Lower Alsace. In 1599, he ordered the city to pursue witches, but nevertheless follow the Carolina (the imperial law code, 1532). After the Holy Roman Emperor Rudolf II and the *Reichshofrat* (imperial aulic court) confirmed this decision in 1602, Offenburg's next witchcraft trials began in 1603. The family of Barbara Pfäffinger, one of the accused, immediately got the *Reichskammergericht* (imperial chamber court) in Speyer to intervene on her behalf. While a messenger awaited permission to give the council the court's decision, Barbara Pfäffinger was already being secretly arrested and tortured. The council then justified its actions to the *Reichskammergericht* by saying that it had merely carried out the *Reichshofrat*'s decision. No large-scale witch hunt ensued.

Sixteen witchcraft trials, leading to between eleven and fourteen executions, took place in summer and fall 1608. Imperial Commissioner Earl Sulz approved the council's trial procedure. The council also addressed the *Reichskammergericht* in Speyer to protect itself before victims of the coming persecution could file suits and additionally sought advice from legal scholars in Freiburg and Hagenau. Nevertheless, Offenburg's 1608 witchcraft trials produced five suits against the city in the *Reichskammergericht*. In each case, the families of persecuted women complained about trial procedure and unbearable prison conditions. In fact, more witchcraft trials reached the *Reichskammergericht* from Offenburg than from any other imperial free city. After the court again intervened on behalf of the accused, the council terminated its trials at the end of 1608. However, Offenburg did not complain to the imperial aulic court about "obstruction" from the chamber court.

Almost twenty years later, Offenburg's witchcraft trials resumed in November 1627. Some women arrested in Ortenau denounced women in Offenburg for allegedly participating in the witches' Sabbat. Many of the accused were daughters of women burned as witches in 1608. Within three years, sixty people were put to death. There were three distinct phases within this trial wave: twelve people were executed between November 1627 and January 1628; seven further executions followed in mid-1628; and then, after a four-month break, forty more executions took place from late 1628 until early 1630, thirty-two of them in 1629.

The end of Offenburg's witchcraft trials has been mistakenly attributed in older literature to Swedish military occupation. However, the Swedish army reached Offenburg only in September 1632, but the decisive turning point had occurred in late 1629. After social boundaries had fallen at the witch hunt's apex when an influential alderman, Hans Georg Bauer, was executed, the trials lost momentum in December 1629, when a woman, Agnes Gotter (known in Offenburg as "Gotter Ness"), twice survived torture in a searing metal hot seat. Previously, no prisoner had ever survived this torture twice. Offenburg's uneasy magistrates released her and suspended further trials until after Christmas. In early 1630, two alleged witches already sentenced to death withdrew their confessions and were then released, bringing Offenburg's witch hunt to an abrupt end. Further trials took place in 1631, 1639, 1641, and 1642, but all were isolated incidents; there were no further large waves of persecution.

PETER OESTMANN;

TRANSLATED BY JONATHAN STICKNEY

See also: AUSTRIA; CAROLINA CODE (*CONSTITIO CRIMINALIS CAROLINA*); CONFISCATIONS OF WITCHES' PROPERTY; GERMANY, SOUTHWESTERN; IMPERIAL FREE CITIES; *REICHSHOFRAT*; *REICHSKAMMERGERICHT*; RUDOLF II, HOLY ROMAN EMPEROR.

References and further reading:
Midelfort, H. C. Erik. 1972. *Witch Hunting in Southwestern Germany 1562–1684: The Social and Intellectual Foundations.* Stanford: Stanford University Press.

Oestmann, Peter. 1995a. "Das Reichskammergericht und die Hexenprozesse—das Beispiel der Reichsstadt Offenburg." *Zeitschrift für Neuere Rechtsgeschichte* 17: 30–49.

———. 1995b. "Die Offenburger Hexenprozesse im Spannungsfeld zwischen Reichshofrat und Reichskammergericht." *Die Ortenau* 75: 179–220.

———. 1997. *Hexenprozesse am Reichskammergericht.* Cologne, Weimar, and Vienna: Böhlau.

Volk, Franz. 1882. *Hexen in der Landvogtei Ortenau und der Reichsstadt Offenburg.* Lahr: Verlag Moritz Schauenburg.

OINTMENTS

Early modern witch beliefs held that witches flew to the Devil's Sabbat by use of ointments that they smeared on themselves or on a broom or pitchfork. Demonologists like Martín Del Rio held that these ointments were efficacious only because of the action of demons, but skeptics like Giambattista Della Porta argued that they had natural properties that caused witches to dream that they could fly and participate in fantastic rites. Modern researchers have found that recipes for ointments contained in late medieval and early modern literature did include potent hallucinogens that were both extremely toxic and fat soluble, so utilization in the form of a fat-based salve was both possible and prudent. Although use of these unguents was not as widespread as the demonologists insisted or as some historians have argued, some late medieval and early modern Europeans used them to induce a profound trance state in which they vividly imaged fantastic experiences that seemed real and that demonologists interpreted as participation in diabolical rites. Furthermore, there is evidence that some people smeared these salves or closely related ones on an unsuspecting victim as a form of sorcery that would induce numbness, disorientation, delusions, and hallucinations.

Among the hallucinogenic plants native to the European continent, members of the *Solanaceae* family almost always became the active ingredients in recipes for witches' flying potions given by both demonologists and skeptics. The psychoactive alkaloids the plants contained are extremely toxic, and an overdose could easily lead to death. However, they were also fat soluble, and in that form readily absorbed through the skin, which was far safer than ingestion while still delivering a powerful dose. Probably any fat would have worked; but at least some of these recipes employed fat from babies or corpses, so they were one source of the idea that witches killed infants and dug up fresh graves.

Some users reportedly smeared the ointments all over their bodies, but they would have been absorbed particularly well through mucous membranes. A more efficient method involved smearing and then "riding" a broomstick or pitchfork, which would have concentrated the application in the anal and female genital areas. Because the ointments often induced a sensation of flight, this probably originated the notion that witches flew on broomsticks.

Many recipes called for a mixture of different *Solanaceae* plants, which themselves contained different combinations of psychoactive alkaloids. Because the different alkaloids probably induced somewhat different psychological effects, the recipes appear to have been tailored to promote specific experiences. Furthermore, the recipes contained other ingredients beside hallucinogens and fats, and specific purposes for them have also been suggested: wild celery to induce a deep sleep after the hallucinogenic fireworks and cinquefoil, parsley, or smallage to purify the blood and avoid a buildup of the toxins.

Hallucinogenic ointments also appear to have been used as weapons. Because the alkaloids in the *Solanaceae* block the neurotransmitter acetylcholine in the peripheral nervous system, smearing an ointment on the skin could well create a loss of feeling there, and the effects on the central nervous system would have created terrifying delusions and hallucinations in a victim who either had no idea what had happened or thought he or she had been attacked by a witch. The incidence of this tactic should not be overestimated, but because some early modern sorcerers are known to have practiced harmful magic and used poisons, the possibility in any particular case cannot be dismissed out of hand.

Not all recipes and pots of ointments brought forward as evidence of witchcraft appear to have contained powerful hallucinogens, and it is not clear whether they were simple frauds; they were produced simply to satisfy inquisitorial demands, to end the torments of torture; or they worked purely through the power of suggestion. These possibilities have led some historians to deny that they were used at all. However, we possess enough credible eyewitness accounts and instances in which physical ointments were found, to argue that some people did use such salves to induce profound trances in which they vividly imagined fantastic experiences (Sidkey 1997, 190–194). Although these instances did not constitute the diabolic conspiracy posited by demonology, they were probably one of its more important sources.

EDWARD BEVER

See also: DEL RIO, MARTÍN; DELLA PORTA, GIAMBATTISTA; DEMONOLOGY; DRUGS AND HALLUCINOGENS; FLIGHT OF WITCHES; INFANTICIDE; *MALEFICIUM;* POISON; SABBAT; STICKS.

References and further reading:
Del Rio, Martín Antoine. 1599. *Disquisitionum Magicarum.* Louvain: G. Rivius.
Della Porta, Giambattista. 1561. *Magiae Naturalis.* Antverpiae: Ex officina Christophori Plantini.
Duerr, Hans Peter. 1985. *Dreamtime: Concerning the Boundary Between Wilderness and Civilization.* Translated by Felicitas D. Goodman. Oxford: Basil Blackwell.
Harner, Michael J., ed. 1973. *Hallucinogens and Shamanism.* London: Oxford University Press.
Quaife, G. R. 1987. *Godly Zeal and Furious Rage: The Witch in Early Modern Europe.* New York: St. Martin's.
Schultes, Richard Evans, and Albert Hoffmann. 1980. *The Botany and Chemistry of Hallucinogens.* Springfield, IL: Charles C. Thomas.

Sidkey, H. 1997. *Witchcraft, Lycanthropy, Drugs, and Disease: An Anthropological Study of the European Witch-Hunts.* New York: Peter Lang.

OPERA

Since the birth of opera in its current form in Renaissance Italy, notably Florence, it has often been used as a medium to reflect human situations and emotions in exotic or unusual circumstances. It is therefore not surprising to find numerous references to witchcraft and related subjects—sorcery, magic, pagan rituals, and so on—in operatic works from the seventeenth century to the present. The repertoire contains a large number of different portrayals of witches that indicate a similarly wide range of emotions and characteristics. There were changes in these trends throughout the centuries, but at the time of the earliest operas the witches were portrayed as evil hags, often with grotesque qualities. These stereotypes were often accompanied by discordant music and harsh, exaggerated rhythms that highlighted their place outside society and concord. However, sorceresses often displayed more complicated traits, for example, grief at their rejection, usually by men, and finally anger and revenge. As we approach the present, operatic witches were treated increasingly sympathetically, expressing a broader view of femininity and regret at past abuses. Male sorcerers and wizards were uncommon, and with a few exceptions (above all, Faust), tend to be given less depth of character.

Henry Purcell's *Dido and Aeneas* was the earliest opera to provide specific parts for witches and to offer a leading role for a powerful sorceress. His witches had "horrid" music to accompany their dances and songs, employing unconventional harmonic and rhythmic features. His Dido was a majestic character whose music highlighted her importance in the plot. Although "furies" and "aerial spirits" appeared in other seventeenth-century operas (including Purcell's *The Indian Queen*), it was another classical sorceress, Medea, who inspired European composers at the time, notably Francesco Cavalli (*Jason*) and Marc-Antoine Charpentier (*Médée*). The emphasis on stage spectacle did not provide composers with much encouragement to explore detailed personalities. In the first half of the eighteenth century, this was still the case to some extent, but the famous German composer George Frideric Handel wrote approximately fifty operas, five of which might be termed "magical," containing characteristics normally associated with sorcerers and sorceresses, witches and wizards: *Rinaldo, Teseo, Amadigi, Orlando, and Alcina.* The latter's music displayed for the first time in opera a sorceress who was a fully formed character displaying majesty and passion, evil and vengeance.

In the latter part of the century, the towering figures of Joseph Haydn and Wolfgang Amadeus Mozart dominated, but neither wrote music specifically for witches. Of Haydn's approximately twenty operas, only one (*Armida*) portrayed a sorceress with any depth of feeling, and Mozart's Colas in *Bastien und Bastienne* was more a cunning man than a wizard. However, his justly famous *The Magic Flute* provided important parts for both the sorceress Queen of the Night and the sorcerer Sarastro. At the end of the century, Luigi Cherubini wrote the three-act opera *Médée,* preparing the way for the dramatic characterizations that would be demanded in the following centuries. Its use of minor chords, harsh chromaticisms, and the use of bass instruments enhanced the atmosphere, rising to a hellish fortissimo as Medea summoned the dark forces.

By arousing strong emotions and emphasizing the importance of the creative imagination, the Romantic movement had a direct influence on cultural taste in the nineteenth century. The world of legend and folklore became increasingly popular, with direct and indirect references to the supernatural and witchcraft. Throughout this century, most European countries produced composers who wrote operas on these themes. In Italy, the great tradition of bel canto reached new heights in terms of its portrayals of witches through the works of Arrigo Boito (*Mefistofele*); Giacomo Puccini (*Le Villi*); and above all Giuseppe Verdi, whose *Macbeth, Il Trovatore,* and *Un Ballo in Maschera* each contained many scenes providing his characters with important roles that the music enhanced. In *Il Trovatore,* Azucena, the daughter of a witch burned at the stake, sang a fiery invocation for the destruction of her enemies; in *Un Ballo in Maschera,* Ulrica's dark and austere role balanced the other personalities' lightness. Verdi specified himself how important he believed the witches' roles to be in *Macbeth.*

Apart from an orgy of evil spirits in Giacomo Meyerbeer's *Robert le Diable* that was reminiscent of a witches' Sabbat and its obligatory inclusion in Charles Gounod's *Faust,* there was little witchcraft activity in nineteenth-century French opera. This was similarly true of Russian opera, because the title of Pyotr Tchaikovsky's little-performed *The Sorceress* is totally misleading. A folklore theme can be found in Mikhail Glinka's *Russlan and Ludmilla,* where an evil sorceress (or fairy) Naina was feared for her evil powers, and there was an allusion to witchcraft in Nicolai Rimsky-Korsakov's *A May Night.* English opera provided very few examples apart from the comic works of W. S. Gilbert and Arthur Sullivan, including *The Sorcerer* and *Ruddigore or The Witch's Curse.* However, Germany produced a preponderance of such works.

The German operatic tradition of this period centered on three composers: Carl Maria von Weber, Englebert Humperdinck, and Richard Wagner. Although Weber's *Der Freischütz* did not contain witches per se, its overriding theme was so steeped in supernatural elements, including spell casting in the Wolf's Glen and the appearance of the Devil (Samiel), that its omission would be unthinkable. Humperdinck's *Hänsel und Gretel* (based on the Grimm brothers' *Kinde—und Hausmärchen*) and his *Königskinder* both featured witches in prominent roles. They were both somewhat stereotypical old hags, portrayed by the composer with awkward, leaping music that took on a particularly humorous quality in the former work because of its caricatural qualities. In the latter, the witch used *Sprechgesang* (speech-song), combining pitched notes with spoken dialogue. Wagner's works provided a very different picture, because intense characters who were given, in some cases, very deep and varied emotions, replaced the nameless hags. The three "Norns" in *Götterdämmerung* spun the web of destiny and had powers of divination similar to the witches in *Macbeth* or the Fates in Greek mythology. There was a connection to witchcraft in *Tannhäuser*, because the orgiastic aspects of the "Venusberg" revels could be associated with witches' Sabbats; Venus had an allure similar to Circe's, as both tried to prevent their men (Tannhäuser and Odysseus) from leaving them. In *Lohengrin*, the character Ortrud practiced sorcery for reasons of power, and in *Parsifal* one was introduced to a magician (Klingsor) and the impressive and complicated character of Kundry, who combined sexual and evil passion with pathos and regret.

The late twentieth century witnessed a decline in the number of operas being composed, partly because of the huge costs involved in staging such productions and also because of a reaction against the large-scale works of the nineteenth century. However, at the start of the century, this was not the case: such works as Antonin Dvorak's *Rusalka*, including a part for the witch Jezibaba, and *Armida* were composed. Sergey Prokofiev wrote two operas containing witchcraft issues, the comic *Love for Three Oranges* and the brutal and intense *Fiery Angel*. The latter contained an orgy scene in a convent, an interrogation by the Inquisition, and the final execution of the possessed woman (or witch). There are connections to be made here with Krzysztof Penderecki's *The Devils of Loudun* (1969), where similar atrocities took place. In Germany, Wagner's son Siegfried composed the deeply moving *Schwarzschwanenreich* on the theme of a woman abused and executed as a witch, and Richard Strauss included the sorceress Aithra in *Die Aegyptische Helena*. In the United States, Charles Cadman wrote *A Witch of Salem* in regret concerning the Salem witchcraft trials, and in Britain Sir Michael Tippett composed *The Midsummer Marriage* in praise of paganism, nature, and male–female polarity integral to modern witchcraft, Wicca.

MELVYN J. WILLIN

See also: CIRCE; CONTEMPORARY WITCHCRAFT (POST-1800); FAUST, JOHANN GEORG; MEDEA; MUSIC.

References and further reading:
Kobbé, G. 1987. *Kobbé's Complete Opera Book.* London: Bodley Head.
Price, C. 1986. *Dido and Aeneas: An Opera.* Norton Critical Scores. London: W. W. Norton.
Rosenthal, H., and J. Warrack. 1979. *The Concise Oxford Dictionary of Opera.* 2nd ed. Oxford: Oxford University Press.
Sadie, Stanley, ed. 1992. *The New Grove Dictionary of Opera.* London: Macmillan.
———, ed. 2001. *The New Grove Dictionary of Music and Musicians.* London: Macmillan.

ORACLES

Derived from the Latin noun *oraculum*, meaning a divine announcement or a prophetic declaration; and the Latin verb *orare*, meaning to entreat, pray and ask assistance, oracles, as this etymology indicates, are intrinsically linked with the spoken word—a proclamation understood to come from a divine or supernatural force and to be delivered to a chosen representative.

Oracles have played a long and highly significant role in both religion and magic, as illustrated by the Delphic oracle of ancient Greece, the preeminent seat of oracular power in the ancient Mediterranean. Situated in a deep cleft on the southwest spur of Mount Parnassus, the Delphic oracle was the principal seat of Apollo, the Greek god of prophecy. Here resided the Pythia, the priestess of Apollo, whose role was to commune with the god in order to answer questions put to her by inquirers. In typical oracular fashion and tradition, the utterances of the Pythia were ambiguous, partly because of the belief that the gods do not converse in the manner of mortals. Thus, oracles required specialized interpreters in the form of priests, who unraveled the ecstatic utterances of the divinely inspired priestess. Despite the influence of the Delphic oracle in the lives of both private individuals and state officials, its power began to be questioned by the fifth-century B.C.E., provoking a gradual decline in this once-great seat of oracular wisdom (although records from the site indicate that petitions were still made to it as late as the fourth-century C.E.).

The early Church Fathers railed against so-called pagan oracles, believing that they represented Satan's trickery. Although it was a tenet of Christian belief that only God possessed the omnipotence for oracular vision, this belief did not prevent the Devil from sometimes dispatching predictive information to give credibility to wicked practitioners of the magical arts. Because of this general repulsion toward non-Christian oracles, The Roman Emperor Constantine (274–337) ordered the ransacking of various shrines, such as those at Delphi and Dodona, and Emperor Theodosius (ca. 346–395) continued his policy.

In early modern Europe, the association among oracles, divination, devil worship, and witchcraft in general was cemented. Scholars cited such early Church Fathers as St. Augustine to argue that evil spirits could deceive humans into believing they could predict events. The *Malleus Maleficarum* (The Hammer of Witches, 1486), for example, described the evils of such pagan customs: "Another species of divination is practised by Pythons, so called from Pythian Apollo, who is said to have been the originator of this kind of divination, according to St. Isidore. This is not effected by dreams or by communication with the dead [necromancy], but by means of living men, as in the case of those who are lashed into a frenzy by the devil, either willingly or unwillingly, only with the aim of foretelling the future, and not for the perpetration of any other monstrosities" (Part 1, Question 16).

Despite such protests, the art of divination, expressly that of externally inspired utterances, flourished. The most famous prophet operating in a fashion similar to the oracular priestesses was the French physician Nostradamus (1503–1566). His method for attaining oracular insight was the technique of scrying, a method he believed to have been practiced by ancient Greek oracles:

> Gathered at night in study deep I sate,
> Alone, upon the tripod stool of brass,
> Exiguous flame came out of isolation,
> Promise of magic that may be believed.
> (*Century* 1.1)
> The wand in hand taken at the midst from
> BRANCHUS/the branches,
> The holm-oak damp from the water and the hem
> and the foot,
> A certain apprehension and voice, quivering
> through the wand's handles,
> Radiance divine. The augur settles close by.
> (*Century* 1.2)

Each of these quatrains was an invaluable source for Renaissance preparations to access oracular sight, provided by one of its most significant sixteenth-century practitioners. Nostradamus used a magical implement (a wand), similar to the forked rod employed for divining water, and a brass scrying bowl filled with water. The ceremony always took place at night; the seer stared into the bowl, then divided the water's surface with his wand and awaited the emanation of messages. His method corresponded quite closely to descriptions of ancient oracular practices recorded by the fourth-century Neoplatonic mystic, Iamblichus (ca. 250–ca. 330) in *De Mysteriis Aegyptiorum* (On the Egyptian Mysteries): "The woman also who conveys the oracles in verse at Branchidai, whether she is holding the wand that was first given by a divinity and becomes filled with the divine light . . . or whether she dips her feet or the border of her robe in the water, or receives the god by breathing in vapour from the water, she becomes by all these ways ready for the reception, and partakes of him from without" (Ficino 1972, 127). Marsilio Ficino's Latin translation of Iamblichus, printed at Venice in 1497 and reprinted at Lyons in 1547, gave Nostradamus his information, illustrating the Renaissance revival of ancient oracular traditions.

By the seventeenth century, the belief in oracles among intellectuals began to be seriously rejected, although it remained a topic of discussion (primarily treated as a remnant of the paganism of classical antiquity). Pierre Bayle (1647–1706), in the *Pensées diverses écrites à un Docteur de Sorbonne, à l'occasion de la comète qui parut au mois de décembre 1680* (Miscellaneous Thoughts Written to a Doctor of the Sorbonne on the Comet That Appeared in the Month of December, 1680, 1683) and in the *Dictionnaire historique et critique* (Historical and Critical Dictionary, 1697), and Bernard le Bovier Fontenelle (1657–1757), in the *Histoire des Oracles* (History of Oracles, 1687), both contributed significantly to philosophical skepticism and thereby to the disbelief in such ancient systems of supernatural prophecy.

MARGUERITE JOHNSON

See also: DIVINATION; *MALLEUS MALEFICARUM;* NECROMANCY; SIGHT, POWERS OF (SECOND SIGHT); SKEPTICISM.

References and further reading:
Aune, David E. 1983. *Prophecy in Early Christianity and the Ancient Mediterranean World.* Michigan: Eerdmans.
Ficino, Marsilio. 1972. *Iamblichus: De Mysteriis Ægyptiorum.* 1503. Reprint, Frankfurt: Minerva.
Fontenrose, Joseph. 1978. *The Delphic Oracle: Its Responses and Operations.* Berkeley: University of California Press.
Luck, Georg. 1985. *Arcana Mundi: Magic and the Occult in the Greek and Roman Worlds.* Baltimore and London: Johns Hopkins University Press.
Roberts, Henry C., trans. and ed. 1984. *The Complete Prophecies of Nostradamus.* Revised ed. London: Granada.
Ronan, Stephen, ed. 1989. *Iamblichus of Chalcis: On the Mysteries.* Translated by Thomas Taylor and Alexander Wilder. Sussex: Chthonios.

ORDEAL

Like many non-European peoples, the Indo-Europeans believed that numinous powers would intervene in juridical contentions and decide them, if certain rituals were followed. Only faint hints of such a belief existed in ancient Greece and Rome, where ordeals never became part of the official legal systems; it is remarkable that neither the Bible nor Roman law knew of any of the various types of ordeals used in the Middle Ages and beyond. It is strange that the most prominent legal ordeal mentioned in the Bible was never applied in Western Christian civilization. It was directed against a woman whose husband suspected her of infidelity, and required her to drink spoiled water; if she vomited it, she was stoned to death (Numbers 5: 11–31).

However, the Teutonic tribes must have used various kinds of ordeals before their conversion to Christianity, because their early medieval law codes (*leges barbarorum*) contained many provisions about *ordalia* or *judicia Dei* (the judgment of God). Ordeals were part of the official legal systems of early medieval kingdoms; in a capitulary of 809, Charlemagne even ordered everyone "to believe in the ordeals without any doubt." Though some popes showed a rather skeptical position on this question, several synods explicitly approved of ordeals (e.g., Mainz 847, Seligenstadt 1023, Reims 1119).

The usual way of proving something in an early medieval court was through collective oaths; only if this were not possible would the judgment of God be appealed to. Therefore, all ordeals except the duel were done in the presence and with the help of priests who sang paraliturgical formulas and blessed the necessary instruments, which were ecclesiastical property and whose use was permitted by episcopal privileges. Laypeople had to pay an additional fee for this ecclesiastical assistance, beyond the cost of a secular trial.

Depending on region, social standing, and the matter being disputed, a divine decision was sought through different kinds of tests. Among the ordeals affecting both parties, probably the oldest and most widespread one was the judicial duel (which, like the outcome of a battle, was interpreted as a manifestation of God's will). With very rare exceptions, it was reserved to male fighters—either the persons directly interested or paid champions. In the ordeal of the cross, plaintiff and defendant both stood with uplifted arms before a cross; whoever dropped his arms first lost his case. All other ordeals were one-sided and affected only the accused; most were based on the employment of "pure" elements of nature. The defendant had to walk through fire or over red-hot iron ploughshares or carry a piece of fiery metal a certain distance within a church. Or he had to plunge an arm into boiling water in order to find a small stone or ring thrown into the cauldron. It was not expected that even the innocent could do such things without being injured, but if he was indeed not guilty, his wounds should heal within three days. If they worsened, God had proved him guilty, and the court punished him.

Though generally the secular courts ordered these kinds of ordeals, it is clear that the assisting priest had much, if not decisive, power, because it was his task to judge whether a wound was healing or had become inflamed. When the ordeal by cold water (swimming test) was applied, the accused was bound and thrown into a pool: if the pure element of water refused to accept his body, that is, if he remained afloat, he was considered guilty. If he could manage to stay for some time under the surface, this was reckoned as a sign of his innocence. In the ordeal of consecrated bread or cheese, a large portion of one of them had to be swallowed, big enough to cause suffocation or to prove guilt if the accused hesitated because of a bad conscience. As a variant of this ordeal, reserved mostly to the clergy, a priest administered the Eucharist, which might cause similar problems to pious people (because they believed in the Eucharist). In some instances, lots were also used in ordeals; a special case was the Psalmbook, whose movement, when hanging from a thread, was expected to indicate the delinquent. Finally, the bier-right was based on the assumption that the corpse of a murdered person would begin to bleed afresh when the killer approached.

The practice of ordeals, which were sometimes sought by the accused themselves as a method of legal compurgation, seems to have had its heyday during the twelfth century. But this was also a period of a growing resistance within a new generation of academically trained intellectuals, among whom Peter the Chanter (d. 1197), master at Paris, played a leading role. They criticized the uncertainty and irrationality of such procedures, and the growing importance of the auricular confession led to the conviction that an avowal should also be indispensable in court. When the Fourth Lateran Council (1215) forbade priests to participate in ordeals, its action led to the increased application of torture as a means of finding the truth. Both the abolition of ordeals and the introduction of torture were based on papal decisions by Innocent III and Gregory IX. However, it took several decades until the council's canons were implemented into local law, and even afterward there are numerous records showing that ordeals—particularly the swimming test—continued to be practiced in a semiofficial way in several parts of Europe until the nineteenth century.

Like other people suspected of a major crime, presumptive heretics, sorcerers, and witches underwent ordeals, but infrequently. During the Middle Ages, the ordeal of fire seems to have been chosen most frequently in that case, perhaps in a form of anticipation, as burning was the conventional punishment for that crime. The *Longobard Edictum Rothari* (Lombard Law of Rothari, 198) prescribed a judicial duel when the accusation of sorcery was raised; the Thuringian Law (par. 55) allowed a woman suspected of poisoning her husband to clear herself by the ordeal of the red-hot ploughshares or through a champion fighting a duel for her. According to Addition 16 to the Laws of the Bavarians, the water ordeal was to be applied in cases of hexing (*maleficium*). During the High Middle Ages, ordeals were sometimes used in order to discover heretics, as we learn from St. Bernard of Clairvaux (1090–1153), who recorded the detection of a group of Cathars at Cologne by the *judicium aquae* (water ordeal) in a sermon (Super Cantica 66.5.12).

In 1484, Pope Innocent VIII still had to forbid Duke Sigismund of Tyrol to allow ordeals in cases of witchcraft. The *Malleus Maleficarum* (The Hammer of Witches, 1486) mentioned that the ordeal of the red-hot iron was used in Fürstenberg in the Black Forest in 1485, when a woman suspected of sorcery offered herself for compurgation with a red-hot iron and thereby won her case. But Heinrich Kramer, the author of this famous manual, opposed this method of proof and explicitly preferred torture. The judge, however, should propose the possibility of an ordeal, because the witch usually would agree, certain to be protected against harm by her demon. Her willingness to undergo an ordeal would betray her all the more (Malleus 3.17f.). In order to eliminate any help from the Devil, another popular juridical manual, the *Layenspiegel* (1509) by Ulrich Tengler, similarly did not accept the ordeal for witches, and the same position could be found in many later juridical texts.

Nonetheless, from the second half of the sixteenth century onward, the swimming test seems to have been used quite frequently in several parts of Europe to discover witches. Oudewater in Holland was famous for its witch ordeal scales, seemingly a postmedieval invention: if an accused person was lighter than expected, he or she was declared guilty. However, other types of ordeal fell into disuse after the sixteenth-century Reformations.

Beyond Europe, in parts of Africa and Madagascar, the poison ordeal was and is applied often at the suspicion of sorcery. If the substance (made from the fruit of the tanghin-tree) given by the witch doctor to the suspected person causes vomiting, he is innocent, if it produces vertigo or trance, his guilt is considered proved.

PETER DINZELBACHER

See also: COURTS, SECULAR; INNOCENT VIII, POPE; KRAMER, HEINRICH; LAWS ON WITCHCRAFT (MEDIEVAL); *LAYENSPIEGEL; MALLEUS MALEFICARUM;* SWIMMING TEST; TORTURE.

References and further reading:

Baldwin, John. 1994. "The Crisis of the Ordeal." *Journal of Medieval and Renaissance Studies* 24: 327–353.
Barthélemy, Domenique. 1988. "Diversité des ordalies médiévales." *Revue historique* 280: 3–25.
Bartlett, Robert. 1986. *Trial by Fire and Water.* Oxford: Clarendon.
Browe, Peter. 1932–1933. *De ordalibus.* 2 vols. Rome: Apud aedes Pont. Universitatis Gregorianae.
Gaudemet, Jean. 1965. "Les ordalies au moyen âge." *Recueil de la Société Jean Bodin* 17, no. 2: 99–145.
Glitsch, Heinrich. 1913. *Gottesurteile.* Leipzig: Voigtländer.
Grimm, Jacob. 1983. *Deutsche Rechtsaltertümer.* Vol. 2. Reprint, Darmstadt: Wissenschaftliche Buchgesellschaft, 563–604.
Lea, Henry Charles. 1971. *Superstition and Force: Essays on the Wager of Law, the Wager of Battle, the Ordeal, Torture.* 4th ed., rev. New York: B. Blom.
Müller-Bergström. 1927. "Gottesurteil." Pp. 994–1064 in *Handwörterbuch des deutschen Aberglaubens.* Vol. 3. Berlin: de Gruyter.
Nottarp, Hermann. 1956. *Gottesurteilstudien.* Munich: Kösel.
"Ordeal." 1917. Pp. 507–533 in *Encyclopaedia of Religion and Ethics.* Edited by James Hastings. Edinburgh: T. and T. Clark.

ORIGINS OF THE WITCH HUNTS

The first true witch hunts began in western Europe in the early fifteenth century. The earliest series of trials took place in Italy and in French- and German-speaking regions around the western Alps. Of course, concern about harmful sorcery had deep roots in medieval Europe, and both officially sanctioned prosecution and popular persecution had been brought to bear on its supposed practitioners long before. But only in the fifteenth century did the full stereotype of diabolical witchcraft develop, which would endure throughout the period of the major witch hunts in the sixteenth and seventeenth centuries.

Of particular importance for the ensuing hunts was the clear development, in the stereotype, of cultic and conspiratorial aspects of witchcraft. That is, witches were held to be members of organized groups engaging in a diabolically directed plot to undermine and destroy Christian communities and ultimately Christian civilization. Although individual trials for witchcraft might resemble earlier trials for harmful sorcery, full-fledged witch hunts were possible only after the notion that witches operated as part of an organized, conspiratorial cult began to become established. A hunt would develop out of a single trial or a relatively contained group of trials, either when authorities became convinced of the existence of large numbers of witches operating in a given area or when convicted witches would accuse, or be forced to accuse, others of membership in their sect. Ultimately, witch hunts arose due to the confluence of particular aspects of western European legal procedure, certain notions of demonic power and activity drawn from standard Christian demonology, and the widespread belief in the real efficacy of harmful magic or *maleficium.*

Concern over harmful sorcery and official sanctions against such magic were longstanding in medieval Europe, and legislation against what were perceived to be malevolent forms of magic existed in classical antiquity as well. In Christian Europe, condemnation and attempts to repress such magic arose from two distinct traditions, the religious and the secular. From the earliest days of Christianity, clerical authorities were convinced that much, if not most, supposed magical activity in the world was actually the result of demonic forces. Magicians who claimed to manipulate natural, if occult, forces were suspected instead of invoking and supplicating demons. Early Church Fathers such as St. Augustine condemned the practice of supposedly demonic magic as a serious crime against the Christian faith, and early Church legal codes condemned magic for this same reason. Throughout the Early Middle Ages, Christian penitentials, handbooks of penance used by priests in confession, contained condemnations of magic. The penalties prescribed for such practices, however, were by later standards relatively light. Christians who performed magic were to be made to recognize and confess their sins and do penance. In cases of extreme recalcitrance, excommunication might be required. Such penalties generally held force through the twelfth century. Thereafter, the Church's greater concern over heresy and the perceived need to combat heretics more actively began to feed into an increasingly severe response to magic.

In addition to clerical concerns and ecclesiastical legislation against magic, there was also a substantial body of secular legislation in the early medieval period. By no means were secular concerns distinct from ecclesiastical ones. Lay rulers generally accepted the clerical association of magic with demonic invocation and attempted to enforce Christian morality in their legal codes. Nevertheless, in the most general sense, it can be said that, although clerical concerns focused on the supposedly demonic nature of much magic, secular legislation was more concerned with the harmful effects to which magic could supposedly be put. Secular law codes were therefore more narrowly concerned with the crime of *maleficium,* or harmful sorcery. Many of these law codes prescribed execution as a potential punishment in cases involving malevolent magic. Such condemnation stemmed both from traditional Germanic laws against harmful sorcery and from the relatively stringent late-imperial legal codes against magic and magicians. Despite the existence of such legislation, however, prosecutions for harmful magic remained limited throughout the early medieval period. A key factor was the use of accusatorial procedure in most European courts prior to the twelfth or thirteenth centuries.

Under accusatorial procedure, an aggrieved party would initiate a case by making an accusation of a crime. This person then also assumed the responsibility of proving the guilt of the person or persons accused. If the accused was judged innocent, however, then the accuser was subject to punishment. This procedure served to limit the number of entirely specious accusations. With crimes that supposedly involved the use of magic, which was secretive by its very nature, clear proof of guilt was often impossible to attain. In these cases, the accused might be forced to undergo a judicial ordeal. In theory, this practice placed the determination of guilt or innocence in the hands of God. In fact, the practice was highly subjective, and certainly no accuser could be sure of ultimate vindication by these means. In sum, aspects of accusatorial procedure tended to stifle the potential for widespread accusations of harmful

sorcery and would have made difficult the sort of panic and chain-reaction accusations that typified later witch hunts. Beginning around the twelfth century, however, and continuing through the fourteenth and fifteenth centuries, European courts, both ecclesiastical and secular, increasingly moved away from accusatorial procedure and instead adopted inquisitorial procedure as their basic method of operation.

In contrast to accusatorial procedure, under inquisitorial procedure, the onus of proving guilt or innocence for a suspected crime fell on officials of the court rather than on the person who brought the initial accusation. In addition, the court could initiate an investigation or trial, even if no accusation of a crime had been made. In many ways, courts operating under inquisitorial procedure functioned in a more sophisticated way than those under accusatorial procedure in terms of the collection and evaluation of evidence. Yet in cases of suspected sorcery, still a highly secretive crime, visible evidence or eyewitnesses were almost always rare. In such cases, the best means of obtaining a conviction was through the confession of the suspected party. Because it was recognized that people would seldom willingly convict themselves of a serious crime, the use of torture was prescribed in order to extract the truth from suspects. Limitations and controls on the application of torture were established, but they could easily be ignored by overzealous magistrates eager for convictions. Especially in situations in which the nature of the crime aroused widespread anxiety or panic, as was the case with witch hunts, judicial controls on the use of torture were frequently set aside. Unrestricted torture allowed magistrates to extract confessions and to secure convictions for virtually any crime that they might suggest to the accused. The widespread use of inquisitorial procedure and of torture in the courts of western Europe therefore provided a necessary basis for the later functioning of witch hunts.

The existence of a legal and procedural basis alone, however, did not give rise directly to witch hunting. Rather, the basic level of concern over supposed magical activities had to increase among both religious and secular authorities, as did the conviction that practitioners of harmful sorcery were members of heretical and conspiratorial demonic cults. Initial signs of a new level of concern in these areas become evident in the early fourteenth century. The trial of Lady Alice Kyteler of Kilkenny, Ireland, is often seen as a sort of proto–witch hunt from this period. Lady Alice had married a succession of wealthy men. Her first three husbands died under mysterious circumstances, and when her fourth husband began to sicken, she was accused of bewitching these men and then murdering them through sorcery. In 1324, Bishop Richard Ledrede took up the case, and ultimately Alice and a group of suspected accomplices were convicted not just of using harmful magic but also of renouncing the Christian faith and gathering together as a cult to worship and offer sacrifices to demons. Although one member of this group was burned at the stake, Alice escaped punishment by fleeing to England, and her trial did not trigger any similar accusations in Ireland at the time. Nevertheless, the case revealed a connection being made between harmful sorcery and demonic invocation as well as the cultic worship of a demon.

A similar foreshadowing of later aspects of witch hunts can be seen in the trial of the Knights Templar for heresy, sodomy, and idolatry and the ultimate suppression of the Templars as a military and religious order. In actuality, the case was politically motivated. In 1307, officials of King Philip IV of France brought a range of charges against the Templars so that the royal government could seize the tremendous wealth and property controlled by the knights. Several key Templar leaders were arrested and questioned under severe torture. Ultimately, most confessed to a range of charges involving heretical beliefs and renunciation of the Christian faith, homosexual practices, and the worship of a demon in the figure of a head known as Baphomet. Succumbing to French pressure, Pope Clement V officially suppressed the order in 1312, and in 1314 the Templar grand master, Jacques de Molay, and other leaders were burned at the stake. Although charges of sorcery did not figure significantly in the trial of the Templars, the case nevertheless serves as an example of procedures that would later characterize witch hunts—extreme and unfounded accusations and false confessions secured through the use of torture (many Templars recanted their initial confessions, but this only exposed them to the charge of being relapsed heretics).

The cases of the Templars and of Alice Kyteler also revealed another important aspect of the rise of eventual witch hunts in western Europe, namely, that in the early fourteenth century, charges of harmful sorcery and the cultic worship of demons were being brought against relatively high-status defendants. Charges of the use of sorcery at princely courts occurred throughout the Middle Ages, but the number of clearly political sorcery trials seems to have risen in the early fourteenth century, thereby heightening concerns about the potential threat posed by harmful sorcery among powerful classes across Europe. Not even the papal court was immune. In 1258, Pope Alexander IV had ordered all papal inquisitors to refrain from involving themselves in cases of sorcery, unless the sorcery clearly entailed some form of heresy. In 1320, however, Pope John XXII, deeply concerned over matters of sorcery at least in part because he feared his own political enemies were using magic against him, ordered inquisitors to extend their investigations to include all matters of sorcery that seemed to involve the invocation and worship of demons, and in 1326 he formally excommunicated any Christian found guilty of practicing sorcery that involved invoking demons.

Concerns about the demonic, heretical, and ultimately cultic nature of much magical activity were rising among clerical authorities throughout the fourteenth century. In the early part of the century, the inquisitor Bernard Gui evinced a clear but still relatively slight concern over sorcery. In his inquisitorial handbook *Practica inquisitionis heretice pravitatis* (The Practice of the Inquisition of Heretical Depravity), written around 1324, Gui devoted only a small section to a discussion of sorcery, and, although he considered sorcery to be an aspect of heresy, did not discuss the nature of heretical sorcery in detail. Fifty years later, however, the inquisitor Nicolas Eymeric, in his handbook *Directorium inquisitorum* (Directory of Inquisitors), written in 1376, presented an extended argument about the necessarily heretical nature of demonic magic. The very act of invoking a demon, Eymeric argued, constituted an act of worship even if no other overt signs of worship were present. Hence, all acts of demonic magic automatically entailed idolatry and therefore were evidence of heresy. Eymeric's arguments proved definitive for many clerical authorities who came after him and provided the basis for inquisitorial action against suspected sorcerers throughout the entire period of the witch hunts.

Once the practice of supposedly demonic magic was firmly established as entailing the worship of demons and thus as a form of heresy, it was perhaps natural that suspected practitioners of sorcery should have become suspected also of operating in organized cults just as other supposed heretical groups were thought to do. Throughout the later fourteenth century and on into the fifteenth, the number of trials for harmful sorcery rose significantly, and critically, in the course of these trials, elements of diabolical heresy were grafted onto charges of simple *maleficium*. These elements of diabolism included the notion that witches were members of demonically organized cults that met secretly to feast, dance, and worship demons or the Devil. They also supposedly engaged in sexual orgies with each other, with demons, or with the Devil, and they performed a number of other horrific acts, such as murdering and eating babies or small children and desecrating the cross and the Eucharist.

The reasons for the rise in the number of trials during this period are uncertain. To some extent, the apparent rise may be a result of better survival of sources from this era. However, contemporary authorities clearly believed that sorcery and witchcraft were a growing threat in the world, which seems to have been reflected in an actual increase in the numbers of accusations and prosecutions. Many studies have revealed that accusations of witchcraft and witch hunts often originated in economic or social disruptions at the local level: agrarian failures; persistent inclement weather; new economic or commercial patterns in a region; or disputes between neighbors over property, social standing, or any number of issues. An overall rise in trials might be explained by a generalized economic or social crisis that exacerbated such local conflicts. Attempts to link particular rises in prosecutions for witchcraft to more generalized crises of this nature, however, have revealed disjunctures as often as they have uncovered clear connections.

Another general factor underlying growing concern over witchcraft in this period was the drive for religious reform originating in the Church. Many clerical authorities were convinced that Christian faith was declining in the late fourteenth and early fifteenth centuries, and that a general moral and spiritual rejuvenation was needed throughout Christian society. Extremely popular preachers such as Vincent Ferrer and Bernardino of Siena carried this reformist message to the people through the medium of popular sermons. The threat posed by witches to Christian society was a key theme employed by such men. Not surprisingly, a number of early witchcraft trials occurred in Dauphiné and western Switzerland in the wake of Ferrer's journeys through these regions, and Bernardino was associated with several witchcraft trials in Italy.

Most witchcraft trials in this period began with accusations of simple *maleficium* without any hint of other heretical or diabolical elements. Accusations were usually made by people against their close acquaintances or neighbors, in other words, people with whom they would have come into social or economic conflict, and these sorts of tensions generally underlay initial charges of *maleficium*. Once a case was brought to court, however, trained judges, ecclesiastical or secular but equally familiar with concepts of demonic magic and heresy, would introduce notions of diabolism. Once these notions were fully overlaid onto the supposed practice of harmful sorcery, the stereotype of witchcraft emerged, and actual witch hunts were possible. Thanks to the notion of witches operating as members of demonically organized, conspiratorial cults, accusations and trials could now originate not from individual conflicts, but from a general sense of threat to the community. A single accusation might fuel many more, and individual suspects could be expected, under torture or threat of torture, to name fellow members of the large cult of witches that authorities or the entire community might suspect was operating in a region.

The earliest series of witchcraft trials and witch hunts took place in the early fifteenth century in regions of Italy; in Savoy and Dauphiné; in the territories of the Swiss cities of Bern, Fribourg, and Lucerne; and in the diocese of Lausanne and Sion (roughly the present Swiss cantons of Vaud and Valais). In many of these regions, witchcraft trials grew directly out of earlier

trials of Waldensian heretics, and the mechanisms used by authorities to uncover and root out heretics were taken over and applied to witches as well. In particular, close cooperation between secular and ecclesiastical authorities seems to have typified many early witch hunts. At the same time, some of the first sources to describe the notion of cultic, conspiratorial witchcraft were being written in these regions. The Lucerne civic chronicler Hans Fründ described the supposed activities of a cult of witches in Valais in 1428. Around 1436, the French secular judge Claude Tholosan produced a treatise on witchcraft based on his experience conducting witchcraft trials in Dauphiné. Probably also in the middle of the decade, an anonymous clerical author, most likely an inquisitor, penned the *Errores Gazariorum* (Errors of the Gazars or Gazarii; i.e., Cathars, a common term for heretics and later witches), describing the errors of that heretical sect of witches, and in 1437 and 1438, the Dominican theologian Johannes Nider wrote extensive accounts of witchcraft, largely based on trials conducted by the secular judge Peter of Bern in the Simme valley of the Bernese *Oberland,* a mountainous region south of the city. Nider collected many of his accounts of witchcraft while at the Council of Basel, a great ecumenical council of the Church that met from 1431 until 1449 in the city of Basel, just to the north of the regions where the greatest early witch-hunting activity took place. This council, which drew clerics from across Europe, served as a sort of clearinghouse for ideas and concerns about witchcraft and helped to spread the initially fairly localized concern over cults of witches and the dynamics of witch hunting to other regions of Europe. Once the idea of conspiratorial cults of witches became widely established across Europe, witch hunts could and did occur in almost every region of the Continent.

MICHAEL D. BAILEY

See also: ACCUSATIONS; ACCUSATORIAL PROCEDURE; BAPHOMET; BASEL, COUNCIL OF; BERNARDINO OF SIENA; CHRONOLOGY OF WITCHCRAFT TRIALS; DAUPHINÉ, WITCHCRAFT TRIALS IN; *ERRORES GAZARIORUM;* EYMERIC, NICOLAS; FRÜND, HANS; GUI, BERNARD; HERESY; IDOLATRY; INQUISITION, MEDIEVAL; INQUISITORIAL PROCEDURE; ITALY; JOHN XXII, POPE; KYTELER, ALICE; LAUSANNE, DIOCESE OF; LAWS ON WITCHCRAFT (MEDIEVAL); MOUNTAINS AND THE ORIGINS OF WITCHCRAFT; NIDER, JOHANNES; ORDEAL; PETER OF BERN; SAVOY, DUCHY OF; SWITZERLAND; TEMPLARS; THOLOSAN, CLAUDE; TORTURE; TRIALS; VALAIS; VAUD, PAYS DE; *VAUDOIS* (WALDENSIANS); WITCH HUNTS.

References and further reading:

Bailey, Michael D. 1996. "The Medieval Concept of the Witches' Sabbath." *Exemplaria* 8: 419–439.
———. 2001. "From Sorcery to Witchcraft: Clerical Conceptions of Magic in the Later Middle Ages." *Speculum* 76: 960–990.
———. 2003. *Battling Demons: Witchcraft, Heresy, and Reform in the Late Middle Ages.* University Park: Pennsylvania State University Press.

Blauert, Andreas. 1989. *Frühe Hexenverfolgungen: Ketzer-, Zauberei- und Hexenprozesse des 15. Jahrhunderts.* Hamburg: Junius.

———, ed. 1990. *Ketzer, Zauberer, Hexen: Die Anfänge der europäischen Hexenverfolgungen.* Frankfurt: Suhrkamp.

Borst, Arno. 1992. "The Origins of the Witch-Craze in the Alps." Pp. 101–122 in *Medieval Worlds: Barbarians, Heretics, and Artists.* By Arno Borst. Translated by Eric Hansen. Chicago: University of Chicago Press.

Cohn, Norman. 2000. *Europe's Inner Demons: The Demonization of Christians in Medieval Christendom.* Rev. ed. Chicago: University of Chicago Press.

Kieckhefer, Richard. 1976. *European Witch Trials: Their Foundations in Learned and Popular Culture, 1300–1500.* Berkeley and Los Angeles: University of California Press.

———. 1989. *Magic in the Middle Ages.* Cambridge: Cambridge University Press.

Klaits, Joseph. 1985. *Servants of Satan: The Age of the Witch Hunts.* Bloomington: Indiana University Press.

Levack, Brian P. 1995. *The Witch-Hunt in Early Modern Europe.* 2nd ed. London and New York: Longman.

Peters, Edward. 1978. *The Magician, the Witch, and the Law.* Philadelphia: University of Pennsylvania Press.

———. 2002. "The Medieval Church and State on Superstition, Magic, and Witchcraft: From Augustine to the Sixteenth Century." Pp. 173–245 in *The Middle Ages.* Vol. 3 of *The Athlone History of Witchcraft and Magic in Europe.* Edited by Bengt Ankarloo and Stuart Clark. London and Philadelphia: Athlone and University of Pennsylvania Press.

Russell, Jeffrey Burton. 1972. *Witchcraft in the Middle Ages.* Ithaca, NY: Cornell University Press.

ORTHODOX CHRISTIANITY

Nearly all early modern witchcraft trials occurred in European and American regions where Roman Catholicism or Protestant denominations prevailed; state- or church-sanctioned witchcraft trials were less frequent in Orthodox Christian areas.

Orthodox churches are those Christian churches of the East and of eastern and southeastern Europe that accepted the primacy of Constantinople rather than Rome after the schism of the eleventh century. Slavic Orthodox churches, plus Moldavia and Wallachia, were founded by the missionary activity of the Greek Church from the ninth century onward. The Russian Church in Muscovy became the largest, and, after the fall of Constantinople in 1453, also the only substantial national Orthodox Church in an independent country. It was effectively autocephalous after its rejection of the reunion of the Orthodox churches with the Latin western Church that had been agreed in a Decree of Union at the Council of Florence in 1439, but was thereafter largely repudiated in most Orthodox areas. The Russian Church elected a metropolitan of Moscow in 1448 without reference to Constantinople and established the Patriarchate of Moscow in 1589.

The establishment of the Russian and southeastern European Orthodox churches was accompanied by other external cultural influences from Byzantium, including the magical and divinatory beliefs and practices that were a notable feature of Byzantine popular culture but excluding, for the most part, the intellectual interest in magic of such Byzantine philosophers as Michael Psellus (1018–ca. 1078). At the level of popular belief, Orthodox Christians had a good deal in common with Latin Christians, although the details of indigenous pagan survival differed. Literary evidence suggests that both in Byzantium and Russia, magic was usually regarded as demonic, and the notion of the pact with the Devil was familiar. At a more official level, the teaching of the Orthodox Church before the schism with Rome was essentially the same in matters of witchcraft and magic as that of the Latin Church.

Insofar as there was an official attitude, it derived from the opinions of the early Church Fathers and acts of the various early councils and synods, which tended to equate witchcraft with paganism. Reflecting the ambivalence of Jewish attitudes toward magic, divination, and witchcraft expressed in Scripture, the Church Fathers were not unanimous concerning the reality of witchcraft. Jewish views ranged from the outright condemnation of Exodus 22:18 (22:17; "Thou shalt not suffer a witch to live") and the "abominations" listed in Deuteronomy 18:10–14 to the frequent references to magical practices and belief in their efficacy. Patristic opinion did, however, agree in condemning magical practices and was supported in this by the tradition of Roman law. Among the early theologians who did appear to believe in the reality of witchcraft, St. Augustine of Hippo, with his extensive knowledge of the magic as well as the philosophy of the ancient world, did most to elaborate a theological view; but as a Latin, his writings had less influence in the East (where he was sometimes regarded with suspicion) than in the West. Augustine's works were unknown in Russia until relatively modern times.

The teaching of the early Church relating to magic and witchcraft, often found as condemnations in patristic sources (e.g., St. Basil and St. John Chrysostom) or expressed as prohibitions (especially to the clergy) in early collections of ecclesiastical law, was summarized at Constantinople in the acts of the Trullan Synod (692), which formalized the work of the fifth and sixth ecumenical councils (Constantinople II and III) but was later rejected by the Latin Church. This synod regulated marriage and sexual behavior. It also forbade association with Jews; mixed bathing; attending horse races, mimes, or animal shows; theatrical dancing; consulting diviners, sorcerers, cloud-chasers, or purveyors of amulets; celebrating the Calends, Vota, and Brumalia (Greek festivals in honor of Pan and Dionysius); wearing comic, satiric, or tragic masks; or jumping over fires at the beginning of the month. One cannot be sure how far this list represented genuine current concerns, but superstitions, astrology, amulets, and magical practices certainly occupied a large part of Byzantine life.

Apart from a revealing twelfth-century Greek commentary on the Trullan Synod by the Greek canonist and patriarch of Antioch, Theodore Balsamon (Fögen 1995), there was relatively little theological or canon-legal discussion of magic and witchcraft thereafter in the Orthodox churches; the acts of the Trullan Synod remained the basis of Russian ecclesiastical opinion on the subject until at least the eighteenth century. The reasons are not entirely clear. Certainly the belief in and practice of magic and witchcraft at all levels of society in the East was no less widespread than in the West and the official attitude of the Church no less hostile; in the later Byzantine era, legal jurisdiction in this field was firmly in the hands of the patriarchal court, and cases came up regularly.

By contrast, witchcraft became a matter of anxiety in the medieval Latin Church, where a considerable debate developed on the relation of witchcraft to heresy and demonology. This debate, which continued beyond the Reformation in both Catholic and Protestant churches, never occurred in the Eastern Orthodox churches. Although Byzantium certainly had numerous trials for practicing magic, Orthodox Christendom generally avoided the witch hunts and witchcraft trials of early modern western Europe. Indeed, the Orthodox churches under Turkish domination after 1453 could not promote witch hunts even had they so wished. Outside Muscovy, the other two Orthodox eastern Slav territories, the Ukraine and Belorussia, were under Polish rule until 1650, and the treatment of witches there was largely dependent on Polish practices and prevailing local laws.

In Kievan Russia from the tenth century onward and later in Muscovy, magicians were usually identified with practitioners of pagan rites; witchcraft, or any manifestations of magic or divination, were condemned in princely law codes and canon law collections as pagan, demonic, and "Hellenic" (i.e., Greek pagan). Russian penitentials, episcopal denunciations, and lists of banned books, often derived from the fourth-century *Constitutiones Apostolorum* (Apostolic Constitutions), were as varied as their Western counterparts; most Russian catalogs of sins, again like their Western counterparts, condemned sexual behavior, magic, poisoning, and employing demonic assistance. More than a millennium after the fourth-century *Canons of Laodicea* had condemned the practice of magic by the clergy, the acts of the *Stoglav* (Hundred Chapters) council, convened in Moscow by Ivan the Terrible in 1551 to deal with ecclesiastical abuses, specifically forbade the parish clergy, under pain of ecclesiastical ban, from involvement in magical practices. The *Stoglav* specifically classified magical practices and texts as heresy. Its decisions mostly cited the Trullan Synod and the various lists of "true and false books" that had their origin in the Greek Church but had been updated in Russia.

Information about punishments for witchcraft and magical practices is sparse and often contradictory. Russian chronicles described many occasions when pagan magicians were put to death by civil authorities or local communities, but perhaps as much for political as religious reasons. Ecclesiastical punishments for magical practices were often relatively mild, and early princely law in Kievan Rus' regarded magic and divination as matters mostly involving women and preferably corrected by husbands. The extensive manual of family and household management, the *Domostroi,* suggested that this view still prevailed in sixteenth-century Russia.

Muscovite Russia's first important attempt at a written legal code, Ivan the Terrible's *Sudebnik* of 1550, never mentioned witches, magic, or superstitious practices. A later version of it from 1589 mentioned witches when specifying levels of compensation for offenses against the honor (*beschestie*) of various social categories: witches came at the very bottom, with harlots. Male sorcerers were not mentioned, although they were certainly common in Russian society, implying that illicit magic still remained within Church jurisdiction. Codified Russian law changed in 1649 with the *Ulozhenie,* the code introduced by Tsar Aleksei Mikhailovich (which incorporated many provisions for offenses previously under canon law), and in 1715 with the military code (*Voinskii artikul*) of Peter the Great. These codes, either implicitly (in the *Ulozhenie*) or specifically (in the *Voinskii artikul*) made witchcraft a crime against the sovereign or state and punishable by death. Russia's criminalization of witchcraft and the evident fear of witchcraft among seventeenth-century tsars considerably diminished the Church's traditional role. Most accusations of malefic magic or witchcraft in Muscovite and early imperial Russia were now brought under the *slovo i delo gosudarevo* (word and deed of the sovereign) procedure, a kind of "hue and cry" designed to identify crimes against the sovereign.

The overlap between ecclesiastical and state jurisdiction and the close association of witchcraft, heresy, and treason can be seen in the accusations brought by senior bishops against Maxim the Greek (the ex-humanist Michael Trivolis) in his trials in 1525 and 1531. They charged him with having "evil intentions" toward the grand prince, communicating with the Turks in order to help them wage war against Russia, indulging in heresy and in Hellenic and Jewish black magic and witchcraft, and practicing sorcery against the grand prince. Half a century later, Prince Andrei Kurbskii, who had fled Muscovy, protested in a public epistle to Ivan IV that the tsar had "falsely accused the Orthodox of treason and magic and other abuses." Ivan replied: "As for your mentioning 'treachery and magic'—well, such dogs are executed in all countries." Ivan's court physician and astrologer Elisaeus Bomelius was tortured to death for treason; under interrogation, he implicated several highly placed persons, including Archbishop Leonid of Novgorod, whom he accused of running a coven of fifteen witches; Leonid was found guilty and disgraced, and the witches were burned.

The identification of witchcraft with heresy, evident in the common use in some parts of Russia of the word *heretic* for the more usual *koldun* (the male witch in most villages), meant that non-Orthodox, by definition "heretics," could often be accused of witchcraft. A striking example is the case of the False Dmitrii, the early seventeenth-century pretender to the Russian throne, who married a Polish noblewoman, adopted Polish manners, and briefly seized power in Moscow with Polish help. Contemporary accounts described him practicing "gypsy sorcery and every kind of devilish magic . . . like Julian the Apostate who did sorcery with devils" and "cast spells with devils"; indeed, he was reportedly buried as if he were a magician, and his Polish wife Marina, called an "evil heretic atheist," was popularly supposed to have escaped from a mob by turning herself into a magpie and flying away.

Nevertheless, these examples of witchcraft fears in sixteenth- and seventeenth-century Muscovy cannot compare to the scale of the witch hunts in many parts of western Europe. Despite infrequent clerical involvement and concern and the occasionally religious coloring of accusations, Muscovy and Orthodox Europe saw few religious polemics and had no ecclesiastical tribunals resembling western Inquisitions. However, they did prosecute "religious crimes," and their punishments could be severe; in the 1660s, Grigorii Kotoshikhin, a senior Russian official who fled to Sweden and wrote a hostile account of the internal politics and manners of the contemporary Russian court, stated that the *Razboinyi prikaz* (the ministry for suppressing crime and sedition) dealt with *koldovstvo* and *chernoknizhstvo* (sorcery and black magic), which it lumped together with blasphemy, theft of church property, sodomy, and false interpretation of Scripture. Kotoshikhin claimed that the penalty for all these crimes was to be burned alive (for men) or beheaded (for women).

The first article of the first chapter of Peter the Great's 1715 code of military law (*Voinskii artikul*) was entitled "On the Fear of God" and states that, depending on the nature of the offense, any soldier found to be an idol worshipper, black magician (*chernoknizhets*), gun charmer, or superstitious and blasphemous enchanter (*charodei*) would be placed under close arrest, put in irons, made to run the gauntlet, or be burned to death. It specifies that death by burning was the normal punishment for black magicians who had harmed anyone by sorcery or had dealings with

the Devil. Whoever had not harmed anyone or had dealings with the Devil should be punished by one of the other punishments and made to do public church penance. Its second article states that anyone who hired a magician or encouraged anyone else to do so in order to harm someone should be punished in the same way as the magician. Many cases were in fact punished with such lesser ecclesiastical penalties as public penance. Peter's military code was based largely on the Swedish military code introduced by Gustav II Adolf in 1621–1622, written when fear of witchcraft in Sweden was strong, and partly on the Carolina (*Constitutio Criminalis Carolina*), the 1532 law code of the Holy Roman Emperor Charles V. Peter's *Voinskii artikul* indirectly copied the old Roman law distinction between magic that harmed and magic that did not, and the punishment of the former by burning from article 109 of the Carolina (which omits the demonic/nondemonic distinction). The *Carolina's* requirement that confessions could be extracted by torture was already normal practice in Russia.

The confusion of civil and ecclesiastical law was compounded by Peter the Great's Church reforms. In his *Ecclesiastical Regulation* of 1721, Peter abolished the patriarchate of the Russian Orthodox Church and established a synod to govern it instead. Insofar as it served as a court, the synod was essentially a branch of the state apparatus and blurred the distinction between civil and ecclesiastical authority even further while depriving the Church of jurisdiction in many areas. In this period, the only specific Russian laws against witchcraft were found in Peter's military code, although in 1722 the synod obtained Peter's confirmation of its jurisdiction in cases relating to marriage, blasphemy, heresy, and *volshebnye dela* (magical matters). This created a curious situation, in which cases of harmful magic could be tried in the highest ecclesiastical court, the Synodal Court, under military law. Peter's Church reforms also required the clergy to report anything learned from penitents in confession, and bishops were obliged to send annual reports on superstitious practices in their dioceses.

The severe treatment prescribed by the state for those suspected of practicing magic and witchcraft continued after Peter's death. *Ukazy* (edicts) of March 20 and May 25, 1731, in the reign of the Empress Anna, prescribed death by burning for "deceivers" who practiced magic, and the knout, or in extreme cases death, as the punishment for consulting magicians (the phrasing indicated that male magicians were envisaged). The use of the word *deceivers* (*obmanshchiki*) suggested that the law now regarded witchcraft as a species of fraud, as elsewhere in Europe under the influence of the Enlightenment, even if the punishment was still associated with older views of magic and heresy.

W. F. RYAN

See also: AUGUSTINE, ST.; BALKANS; CAROLINA CODE (*CONSTITIO CRIMINALIS CAROLINA*); ENLIGHTENMENT; EXODUS 22:18, (22:17); HUNGARY AND SOUTHEASTERN EUROPE, MAGIC; HUNGARY AND SOUTHEASTERN EUROPE, WITCHCRAFT; JEWS, WITCHCRAFT, AND MAGIC; MAGIC, POPULAR; POLAND; RUSSIA; UKRAINE, WITCHCRAFT.

References and further reading:

Fögen, Marie Theres. 1995. "Balsamon on Magic: From Roman Secular Law to Byzantine Canon Law." Pp. 99–115 in *Byzantine Magic.* Edited by Henry Maguire. Washington, DC: Dumbarton Oaks Research Library and Collection, distributed by Harvard University Press.

Kieckhefer, Richard. 2000. *Magic in the Middle Ages.* Cambridge: Cambridge University Press.

Kivelson, Valerie. 1997. "Political Sorcery in Sixteenth Century Muscovy." Pp. 267–283 in *Cultural Identity in Muscovy, 1359–1584.* Edited by A. M. Kleimola and G. D. Lenhoff. Moscow: Its-Garant. English edition distributed by Slavica Publishers.

Maguire, Henry, ed. 1995. *Byzantine Magic.* Washington, DC: Dumbarton Oaks Research Library and Collection, distributed by Harvard University Press.

Ryan, W. F. 1999. *The Bathhouse at Midnight: An Historical Survey of Magic and Divination in Russia.* University Park: Pennsylvania State University Press.

Vogel, K. 1967. "Byzantine Science. XII. Superstition and Pseudo-Science." in *The Cambridge Medieval History.* Vol. 4, *The Byzantine Empire*; Pt. 2, *Government, Church, and Civilisation,* Chap. 28. Cambridge: Cambridge University Press.

Zguta, Russell. 1977. "Witchcraft Trials in Seventeenth-Century Russia." *American Historical Review* 82, no. 5: 1187–1207.

OSBORNE, JOHN AND RUTH (1751)

This elderly English couple was subjected to mob violence at Tring (Hertfordshire) in the summer of 1751. Ruth Osborne, aged about seventy, died as a result of the treatment meted out to her. One of the ringleaders, Thomas Colley, was subsequently convicted for murder at the Hertford assizes and executed at Tring on August 24, 1751, his body left to rot on a gibbet.

The incident has yet to be researched in detail, but it obviously opens up some important issues about witchcraft and witch beliefs in mid-eighteenth century England. There were several incidents of mob action against witches in Hanoverian England, but the Osborne case was unusually well documented because it prompted two printed pamphlets. The English witchcraft statutes had been repealed not long before (1736), but there was obviously widespread fear of and belief in witches among the population at large. Ruth Osborne had supposedly committed a number of acts of *maleficium* (harmful magic), and her husband, some fourteen years younger than she, had a reputation for being a wizard, so that none of the local farmers would employ him. In particular, a farmer turned innkeeper named John Butterfield was convinced that the Osbornes had killed his cattle by witchcraft, a tragedy that had led him to give up farming. Butterfield seems to have orchestrated the violence against the Osbornes; Colley claimed at his trial that it was the drink Butterfield supplied that caused him to take a leading part in the violence against the couple. This violence was well organized: the intention to "duck" the Osbornes (i.e., subject them to the swimming test) was announced publicly in a number of towns in the area, and some 5,000 people turned up to participate or watch. The Osbornes had taken refuge in the vestry of the parish church but were dragged out. Ruth was thrown into a pond, and Colley repeatedly pushed her further in with a stick. A local doctor subsequently called to the scene confirmed that she had died from drowning.

The pamphlet accounts of Colley's trial and of his subsequent execution very much followed the norms of polite Enlightenment society, stressing the dreadfulness of the events and the ill-advisedness of belief in witchcraft. It was particularly important to present Colley as coming round to a repentant and enlightened state of mind, in which he was able both to realize the enormity of his crime and accept that there was no such thing as witchcraft. In particular, an unnamed gentleman visited Colley in prison, hoping to convince him that his views on witchcraft were totally erroneous. Interestingly, Colley told this gentleman that he had witnessed a similar swimming of a witch, which also resulted in her death, in a neighboring county only a few years previously; because no legal action had been taken against any participants in that event, he thought such practices were legal. Throughout, one senses a tension between the rejection of witch beliefs among the educated, polite world of the gentry and their continuation among the population at large.

The authorities, obviously fearing that Colley might be rescued by mob action, had him accompanied to his place of execution by over 100 troopers from the Horse Guards. The soldiers were jumpy, and thinking they were being fired on, were thrown into confusion when one of their number accidentally discharged a pistol. In the event, there was no riot in support of Colley. Yet the pamphlet describing his execution recounted how the event attracted a large crowd of spectators, many of whom commented on the injustice of hanging a man for killing a witch.

JAMES SHARPE

See also: ENGLAND; PAMPHLETS AND NEWSPAPERS; POPULAR BELIEFS IN WITCHES; SWIMMING TEST.

References and further reading:

Anon. 1751. *The Tryal of Thomas Colley at the Assizes at Hertford on Tuesday the 30th of July 1751, before the Right Hon. Sir William Lee, Knight, Lord Chief Justice of the Court of King's Bench.* London.

Anon. 1751. *The remarkable Confession and last dying Words of Thomas Colley, executed on Saturday, August the 24th, at Gibblecot Cross, near Marlston (vulgarly called Wilston) Green.* London.

Carnochan, W. B. 1970–1971. "Witch-Hunting and Belief in 1751: The Case of Thomas Colley and Ruth Osborne." *Journal of Social History* 4: 389–404.

OSNABRÜCK, BISHOPRIC OF

An ecclesiastical territory situated in the northwest of the old Reich, the prince-bishopric of Osnabrück had approximately 120,000 inhabitants at the end of the eighteenth century. Because of the questionable situation of Osnabrück's sources, it is unclear when its witch hunt started. Its first provable witchcraft execution dates from 1501. Because many early records were lost in a fire that completely destroyed the city of Osnabrück in March 1613, we will never know how many witchcraft prosecutions were pursued here in the sixteenth century.

With regard to witch hunts, the bishopric of Osnabrück shows a distinct separation between parts of its territories that had high and low prosecution rates. Available sources suggested that very few witchcraft trials took place in the seven rural offices of the prince-bishopric, although a certain number of undetected cases must be added because of lost materials. Gisela Wilbertz, who produced the best work on this subject, mentioned ninety trials between 1538 and 1669. Over half of them (fifty-three) ended with the execution of the defendant; only four men were executed alongside forty-nine women. We can safely assume that only individuals were accused: the prince-bishopric of Osnabrück had no known mass trials.

However, the self-governing city of Osnabrück became a regional center of witchcraft prosecution: at least 276 people were put to death in several major witch-hunting waves between 1561 and 1639. By the mid-1580s, more than 130 people had already fallen victim to Osnabrück's witch hunts; soon afterwards, 22 women were sentenced and executed as witches in 1590 and 17 more women in 1592. Because of the fragmentary state of our sources, we cannot reconstruct the dynamics of any of Osnabrück's witch hunts.

The witch hunt in the city of Osnabrück reached a new peak between 1636 and 1639. The *spiritus rector* (driving force) behind this wave of prosecutions was the mayor, Dr. Wilhelm Pelzer, who was eventually removed from his position because of his judicial excesses and was imprisoned after 1651. The multiplication of witchcraft prosecutions in Osnabrück during these years must be seen against a background of two conflicts. One was the city's tenacious struggle with Gustavus Gustavson, an illegitimate son of the famous Swedish king Gustav II Adolph, attempting to protect its municipal autonomy against a foreign Protestant sovereign; the other involved internal city rivalries. Mayor Pelzer wanted to defend the city's independence against Gustavson at any price and used the witchcraft trials as a political measure. In the same way, he tried to

deprive his rival Dr. Modemann (a follower of Gustavson) of his power: Dr. Modemann's eighty-two-year-old mother, Anna Modemann, was accused of witchcraft along with other patrician women.

There was resistance within the city to Dr. Pelzer's arbitrary policies. Pastor Gerhard Grave, a relative of the executed Anna Modemann and preacher at the Church of the Virgin in Osnabrück, condemned from his pulpit, among other things, the use of the swimming test (cold-water ordeal) in witchcraft trials, regarding this ordeal as illegal. Pelzer took draconian measures to silence Grave, closing his church *cum maximo scandalo* (with very great scandal) in order to continue and intensify the use of the swimming test. For his part, Grave retaliated by making the events surrounding the water ordeal at Osnabrück into a pamphlet printed at Rinteln in the 1640s by Petrus Lucius. Today almost unknown, it was then considered a major attack against the water ordeal.

Another Osnabrück critic of the swimming test was Conrad von Anten, a lawyer at the *Reichskammergericht* (imperial chamber court), the highest appellate court in the Holy Roman Empire. His work about the *Mulierum Lavatio* (The Bathing of Wives), published in 1590, was based on personal experiences witnessing such persecutions; his own wife, Anna Schreiber, also from Osnabrück, had been accused and tortured as a witch. Based on his own experiences, von Anten's erudite treatise scathingly criticized the water ordeal for its degrading character. Besides publishing this book, von Anten also sued both the mayor and city council of Osnabrück in the *Reichskammergericht* for the annulment of his wife's *Urfehde,* her oath to the judge not to exact revenge against her accusers, and also for damages she suffered from personal injuries. Osnabrück's last witchcraft trial apparently occurred in 1639.

GUDRUN GERSMANN

See also: GERMANY, WEST AND NORTHWEST; HOLY ROMAN EMPIRE; MÜNSTER, PRINCE-BISHOPRIC OF; ORDEAL; *REICHSKAMMERG-ERICHT;* SWIMMING TEST; URBAN WITCHCRAFT.

References and further reading:
Stebel, Heinz-Jürgen. 1969. *Die Osnabrücker Hexenprozesse.* Osnabrück: Wenner.
Wilbertz, Gisela. 1983. "Die Hexenprozesse in Stadt und Hochstift Osnabrück." Pp. 218–221 in *Hexenprozesse: Deutsche und skandinavische Beiträge.* Edited by Christian Degn et al. Neumünster: Wachholtz.
———. 1978. "Hexenprozesse und Zauberglaube im Hochstift Osnabrück." *Osnabrücker Mitteilungen* 84: 33–50.

OVERBURY, SIR THOMAS (1581–1613)

Trials for the supposed murder of Thomas Overbury exposed the recourse to magic among the social and political elite of early seventeenth-century London.

Born into a prosperous Gloucestershire gentry family, the son of a successful judge, Overbury earned his BA at Oxford and then entered the Middle Temple in London to begin his legal training. In 1601, however, while visiting Edinburgh, he met and befriended another young gentleman, Robert Carr, at that time page to the earl of Dunbar. Carr came south with James VI and I in 1603 and became a leading royal favorite, becoming Viscount Rochester in 1610. Overbury, the more polished of the two, acted as a sort of mentor for Carr, hoping that Carr's rising fortunes would enhance his own.

By 1610, Carr was involved with Frances Howard, countess of Essex. The countess, whose life has formed the basis for several books (most recently Lindley 1993), planned to divorce her husband and marry Carr. Her granduncle, the earl of Northampton and leader of the powerful Howard faction, approved of this plan, but Overbury opposed it, fearing that his own influence over Carr would be replaced by that of the countess. Overbury had to be removed. His imprisonment in the Tower of London was engineered; both the new governor of the Tower and Overbury's jailer, Richard Weston, were Howard clients. While imprisoned, and probably without Carr's knowledge, Overbury was gradually poisoned. A woman named Anne Turner helped supply the poisons, Weston and an apothecary named James Franklin administered them, and a gentleman named Gervase Hewlys was also involved. Overbury died on September 14, 1613, his death being attributed by a consequent coroner's inquest to natural causes. Frances Howard divorced the earl of Essex on grounds of nonconsummation due to his impotence (the proceedings scandalized Jacobean high society) and married Carr, by this time the earl of Somerset, in December 1613.

By 1615, reports reached court that Overbury had, in fact, been murdered, and proceedings were opened against Turner, Hewlys, Franklin, and Weston that November, with the earl and countess of Somerset being tried in May 1616. All four commoners were convicted and executed; the earl and countess were found guilty but pardoned, being eventually freed in 1621.

The significance of the Overbury case in the history of witchcraft lies in some of the evidence that emerged during the trials of his murderers. It was revealed that in the period preceding her divorce, Frances Howard had consulted various cunning men and other magical practitioners, both to procure magical substances to render her husband impotent (apparently he had appropriate ointments rubbed onto his linen) and to win the love of Robert Carr. In particular, she had been an active client of the astrologer and quack doctor Simon Forman (1552–1611), who had built up a large practice, especially among well-connected ladies, knew many court scandals, and also had a reputation for dabbling in poisons. Like Anne Turner, he lived on the margins of court society and profited from its vices and was

therefore an excellent contact for Frances Howard. Turner became Frances Howard's confidante in 1610 and introduced her to Forman. The two women visited him on several occasions, turning for help after his death in 1611 to another magical practitioner named Savery. When at Turner's trial the judge produced damning evidence of magical dabblings, the packed audience was most scandalized by obscene copulating figures (supposedly aids to love magic) made of lead, brass, and wax, and various parchment charms, one of them with human skin attached to it. A crack in the scaffolding holding spectators while these exhibits were being shown fueled fears that the Devil was in the courtroom. There were reports of a list in Forman's handwriting naming those court ladies who had sought love potions from him.

The Overbury murder trials therefore made two important points. The first was that, even in the early seventeenth century, upper-class people were still willing to use magic to settle their problems and to consult magical practitioners, up-market cunning folk in effect, to help them. The second was that although witchcraft and associated beliefs are often thought of as essentially the products of a rural society, there was clearly a large, and still largely unresearched, network of cunning folk, astrologers, and other forms of magical practitioners in London. In both respects, Overbury's murder prefigured the Affair of the Poisons at Louis XIV's court over fifty years later.

JAMES SHARPE

See also: AFFAIR OF THE POISONS; CUNNING FOLK; ENGLAND; IMPOTENCE, SEXUAL; JAMES VI AND I, KING OF SCOTLAND AND ENGLAND; LOVE MAGIC; POISON; URBAN WITCHCRAFT.
References and further reading:
Lindley, David. 1993. *The Trials of Frances Howard: Fact and Fiction at the Court of James I.* London: Routledge.
McElwee, William. 1952. *The Murder of Sir Thomas Overbury.* London: Faber and Faber.

OXFORD AND CAMBRIDGE UNIVERSITIES

In contrast to the situation in other European states, where theology faculties were occasionally called upon to pronounce on witchcraft cases or on the concept of witchcraft more generally, English universities never offered professional opinions on witchcraft in specific instances. Moreover, the English common law, under which English witches accused on capital charges would be tried, was not studied at Oxford and Cambridge but rather at the Inns of Court in London ("civil," that is, Roman law, was offered at both universities, and it was there that ecclesiastical court judges gained their qualifications). Therefore, there was no law faculty to comment on witchcraft cases at English universities, and the Inns of Court do not seem to have been consulted institutionally about witchcraft.

Both English universities enjoyed parallel developments in the early modern period. After a post-Reformation slump, they enjoyed a boom for ninety years after 1550. Matriculations at the two institutions rose to over 900 annually by the 1580s. After a downturn in the 1590s, matriculations rose again to over 1,000 by the 1630s. They fell with the civil wars, and despite a recovery in the 1650s never regained their prewar levels in the late seventeenth and eighteenth centuries. The post-1550 boom was driven by a perceived need for a university-trained clergy, a goal virtually attained by the outbreak of war in 1642, and by a new fashionableness of a university education among the gentry.

Oxford and Cambridge Universities were, of course, responsible for spreading educated views of witchcraft both through theology and through the teaching of classical languages, because Greek and Roman literature furnished many examples of witchcraft and related phenomena. But Cambridge made two specific and important contributions to English witchcraft. The first was its role as a hotbed of advanced Protestant views during the Elizabethan and early Stuart periods. A by-product of this focus was the emergence of a number of clerical intellectuals who published works on demonology, usually along with other writings. The most influential of these intellectuals was William Perkins, whose important *Discourse of the Damned Art of Witchcraft* was published posthumously in 1608. Other Cambridge-based or Cambridge-educated demonologists included George Gifford, author of two tracts on witchcraft; Henry Holland, whose *Treatise against Witchcraft* was published in 1590; James Mason, author of *The Anatomie of sorcerie* of 1612; the physician John Cotta, whose *Tryall of Witch-Craft* appeared in 1616; and Richard Bernard, author of *A Guide to Grand Iury Men with respect to Witches* (1627), a book exemplifying a distinctive English demonological style. Cambridge's second great contribution was to foster,

in the 1640s and 1650s, what soon became a very influential body of Platonic and Neoplatonic thinkers. The most important of them was Henry More, a powerful and respected thinker, who was responsible for the emergence of Joseph Glanvill's *Saducismus Triumphatus* (Sadducism Conquered), an extremely important defense of the belief in witches and spirits, in its full form in 1681. More's own *Antidote against Atheisme* of 1653 pioneered the approach Glanvill and other later defenders of witch beliefs used by assembling apparently authenticated accounts of witchcraft, possession, and other supernatural happenings to prove the reality of the spirit world.

Oxford, however, had the distinction of direct involvement by a large body of its academics in a witchcraft case, the episode involving Anne Gunter, the daughter of a Berkshire gentleman who began showing signs of being bewitched in late 1604. Her case subsequently came to the attention of King James I, and she, together with her father, was subsequently tried for false accusations of witchcraft by the Star Chamber. Anne's sister Susan was married to Thomas Holland, then Regius Professor of Theology and Rector of Exeter College. Anne was lodged in the college for a while, and a number of academics, including some major university figures, gave evidence to Star Chamber, most of them arguing for the reality of her sufferings.

JAMES SHARPE

See also: COTTA, JOHN; DEMONOLOGY; ENGLAND; GIFFORD, GEORGE; GLANVILL, JOSEPH; GUNTER, ANNE; MORE, HENRY; PERKINS, WILLIAM; UNIVERSITIES.
References and further reading:
Lake, Peter. 1982. *Moderate Puritans and the Elizabethan Church.* Cambridge: Cambridge University Press.
Patrides, C. A., ed. 1969. *The Cambridge Platonists.* London: Edward Arnold.
Sharpe, James. 1999. *The Bewitching of Anne Gunter: A Horrible and True Story of Deception, Witchcraft, Murder, and the King of England.* London: Profile.

P

PACT WITH THE DEVIL

A purported contract, either implicit or explicit, between accused witches (and sometimes magicians) and the Devil, according to which a person pledged her or his soul to Satan in return for worldly gain, healing and magical powers, or arcane knowledge, was considered a pact with the Devil.

As an essential element of the cumulative or elaborated concept of witchcraft, the pact with the Devil gradually became one of four essential legal proofs (alongside *maleficium* [harmful magic], transvection and metamorphosis, and attendance at the Sabbat) in accusations of witchcraft. An explicit or express pact was not limited to a legal document, often supposedly composed in a person's blood, but also included an array of ritual acts of homage (e.g., kissing the Devil on the buttocks—the kiss of shame), with a material (e.g., monies that later turned out to be potsherds or clumps of dung) or sexual consideration literally reifying the covenant. Figuratively, the rituals were a perversion of feudal ceremonies associated with fealty (e.g., charter, kiss, exchange of a clump of earth) and marriage (e.g., dowry, consummation) concluded between legally (if not socially) equal partners; hence, the Devil was often iconographically depicted as a nobleman who propositioned the prospective witch. The ready familiarity of these legal and ritual concepts, their congruence with existing gender roles, and a strong literary tradition and the reintroduction of Roman law all help to explain the easy reception and centrality of the idea of the pact in late medieval and early modern Europe, especially on the Continent.

EARLY HISTORY

The Western tradition of contract law emerged in Roman jurisprudence in classical antiquity. One of the earliest inferences to the possibility of entering into a private commercial contract with the Devil is found among St. Augustine's works in the fourth century. However, not until a number of legendary incidents were translated into Latin in the ninth century did the idea become widespread. Foremost among these was the story of the monk Theophilus, known both on the Continent and among the late Anglo-Saxons. A Jewish magician persuaded Theophilus to transfer his allegiance to the Devil in a written agreement in return for magical powers—an early indication of the anti-Semitism inherent in diabolical belief structures.

During the twelfth and thirteenth centuries, scholastic theologians accentuated a view of all magic as demonic and implied the necessity of a Devil's pact as a precondition to gaining magical abilities. Previously, medieval necromancers operated under the assumption that they could command the spirits of the dead and the demons they summoned. However, Thomas Aquinas forcefully argued for a contractual reciprocity inherent in any concourse with the Devil, emphasizing the existence of tacit agreements or express pacts, either the implicit *pactum tacitum* or a *pactum expressum,* the latter literally a verbal or written contract. Reciprocity implied that the magician was guilty of apostasy, because mortals had little to offer Satan other than their service or their soul, thereby logically condemning all parties to pacts as demon worshipers and justifying their persecution by inquisitorial officials as heretics. Gradually, as demonologists came to view the contract as essentially one-sided rather than one conducted between equals, the relationship between necromancer and spirit shifted, and "as the master-magician was transformed into the servile witch, the sex of the malefactor changed from male to female" (Levack 1995, 35). Heiko Oberman's theory of an alternate and skeptical Augustinian tradition notwithstanding (a demonological *via moderna* [modern way], exemplified by the *Canon Episcopi* [ca. 906] and the Tübingen scholar Martin Plantsch), the Thomist *via antiqua* (old way) became the dominant ideology by the fifteenth century, echoed in the *Malleus Maleficarum* (The Hammer of Witches, 1486) as well as in later works by Martín Del Rio and others during the second (or bastard) scholasticism of the late-sixteenth and early-seventeenth centuries.

The especial significance of this tradition was to render all forms of magic suspicious and encourage their persecution. Initially, secular law codes (such as the Carolina, 1532) had condemned *maleficium* only, but by 1582, the pact with the Devil was recognized as a material element of accusations for witchcraft in the law codes of Württemberg, the electorate of Saxony, and the County Palatine of the Rhine. Medieval England, where reception of the *Malleus* was generally

Pact between Urbain Grandier and various devils, introduced as evidence in his trial in Loudun in 1634. The pact is in mirror writing because devils do everything opposite to Christians. (Reprinted from Mephistopheles: the Devil in the Modern World, *by Jeffrey Burton Russell, Cornell University Press, 1986)*

slow, was exceptional in this regard. Explicit mention of a diabolical compact remained completely absent from English law until 1604; the first English trial reference to an oral pact with the Devil dates from 1612; the first sworn evidence indicating a written pact dates from the investigations of Matthew Hopkins, witch-finder general, in the 1640s.

ELITE AND POPULAR BELIEFS

Some historians have suggested that there never were pacts with the Devil, but rather that they were imaginative inventions, part of the cumulative or elaborated concept of witchcraft developed by demonologists, jurists, and theologians and, hence, completely alien to the popular consciousness. In fact, there were actual persons who believed themselves possessed of extraordinary powers to heal, perform love magic, fly in out-of-body ecstasies, or engage in night battles against phantoms to defend agrarian fertility. There were also isolated individuals who contracted actual written pacts with the Devil. Obviously, the vast majority of those accused of contracting a pact probably did not do so, and in most cases, the implication is of a tacit or oral contract in any case. However, indications of written pacts should not be dismissed lightly for want of evidence, since their destruction as blasphemies was required, as reported by Martín Del Rio and others. Most contemporary demonologists—including the skeptical Johann Weyer—despondently confirmed their existence.

Additionally, although the evidence is extremely rare, archivists and historians have identified several surviving written pacts in the archives. The most famous of these are the pacts of Johann Haizmann with the Devil, discovered by the Viennese archivist Rudolf Payer-Thurn in 1920 and subsequently described in an article by Sigmund Freud. Convincing circumstantial evidence witnessed by contemporary legal investigations into four Devil's pacts have been located in the archives of the University of Tübingen alone, along with the actual written pact of the student David Leipziger, composed in 1596. Two pacts written in lemon juice by the demoniac Katharina Rieder in 1668 were discovered in Munich using quartz-lamp technology. A gender distinction readily emerges from an examination of these pacts. The pacts contracted by males for money or career advancement tend toward a Faustian model and were probably influenced by the first vernacular printed edition of the tale in 1587, which was immensely popular. However, the female Rieder-pact and its surrounding circumstances more closely resemble the witch model, to include copulation with the Devil, apostasy, and demonic possession, though here once again, given their timing, one should not preclude the possible influence of the Faust legend. A third influence can be traced to the common contemporary practice of contracting obligations with the saints, usually in return for individual healing or communal assurance for agrarian fertility—hence, legal condemnations of the practice of throwing saints' statues into rivers when communes felt they had failed to deliver on their presumed contractual obligations. In a literal inversion of the pact with the Devil, Elector Maximilian I of Bavaria contracted himself, his son, and his daughter-in-law to the Virgin Mary in their own blood in the mid-seventeenth century, and the contracts are still preserved at the dynastic cult shrine at Altötting.

SIGNS OF SKEPTICISM

As the publication of the Faust legend increased the likelihood of persons contracting actual written pacts, and just as persecutions for witchcraft approached their climax in western Europe, a number of skeptics entered into the debate on the cumulative concept of witchcraft, challenging its fundamental precepts. Foremost among these were Johann Weyer, who thoroughly debunked the efficacy of such contracts according to the precepts of Roman law and current medical theory in his *De praestigiis daemonum* (On the Tricks of Devils, 1563), and Reginald Scot, who refuted the possibility of pacts outright in his *Discoverie of Witchcraft* (1584). Weyer, sometimes considered to be the father of the modern insanity defense in Freudian psychoanalysis, developed the hypothesis of pacts as "leonine" contracts—that is, unfair contracts benefiting the Devil only, who failed to live up to his promises to the witch—thereby rendering them null and void, because they rested upon coercion. Weyer's arguments did suffer from certain inconsistencies because he too ultimately had to admit certain powers to the Devil, as well as to recognize the existence of attempted pacts, despite their legal invalidity. Nevertheless, Weyer's influence was great, as was that of Scot in England, so that by the mid-seventeenth century, numerous jurists, scholars, and theologians could successfully assert the illusory nature of pacts with the Devil, resulting in increased employment of the insanity defense in cases of witchcraft and especially demonic possession and suicide.

DAVID LEDERER

See also AQUINAS, THOMAS; AUGUSTINE, ST.; *CANON EPISCOPI*; DEL RIO, MARTÍN; DEMONOLOGY; DEVIL; FAUST, JOHANN GEORG; FREUD, SIGMUND; HOPKINS, MATTHEW; KISS OF SHAME; LAWS ON WITCHCRAFT (EARLY MODERN); MAXIMILIAN I, DUKE OF BAVARIA; NECROMANCY; POSSESSION, DEMONIC; ROMAN LAW; SCOT, REGINALD; SKEPTICISM; THEOPHILUS; WEYER, JOHANN.

References and further reading:

Clark, Stuart. 1997. *Thinking with Demons: The Idea of Witchcraft in Early Modern Europe.* Oxford: Clarendon.
Dülmen, Richard van. 1987. "Imaginationen des Teuflischen. Nächtliche Zusammenkünfte, Hexentänze, Teufelssabbate." Pp. 94–130 in *Hexenwelten: Magie und Imagination.* Edited by Richard van Dülmen. Frankfurt am Main: Fischer Taschenbuch.
Kieckhefer, Richard. 1989. *Magic in the Middle Ages.* Cambridge: Cambridge University Press.
Lederer, David. 2005. *Madness, Religion and the State in Early Modern Europe: A Bavarian Beacon.* Cambridge: Cambridge University Press.
Levack, Brian P. 1995. *The Witch-Hunt in Early Modern Europe.* 2nd ed. London and New York: Longman.
Mahal, Günther. 1981. "Fünf Faust-Splitter aus drei Jahrhunderten." In *Bausteine zur Tübinger Universitätsgeschichte* 1: 98–121.
Maxwell-Stuart, P. G. 2001. *Witchcraft in Europe and the New World, 1400–1800.* New York: Palgrave.
Midelfort, H. C. Erik. 1999. *A History of Madness in Sixteenth-Century Germany.* Stanford: Stanford University Press.
Oberman, Heiko A. 1981. *Masters of the Reformation: The Emergence of a New Intellectual Climate in Europe.* Cambridge: Cambridge University Press.
Thomas, Keith. 1971. *Religion and the Decline of Magic.* New York: Scribner's.
Zwierlein, Cornel Anton. 1999. "Das semantische Potential des Fauststoffes um die Wende vom 16. zum 17. Jahrhundert." Unpublished MA thesis, Ludwig-Maximilians-Universität München, Institut für Deutsche Philologie.

PADERBORN, PRINCE-BISHOPRIC OF

A prince-bishopric of the Holy Roman Empire with a population between 60,000 and 80,000, Paderborn was located in southeastern Westphalia in between two regions of intensive witchcraft persecution: the county of Lippe to the north and the electoral duchy (*Kurkölnisches Herzogtum*) of Westphalia to the southwest. Paderborn's power structure was split among three estates with extensive rights of self-determination: the cathedral chapter; the nobility; and representatives of its numerous, but largely agrarian, towns. The prince bishop's sovereign criminal justice system did not control the entire territory; sizable areas remained under the autonomous judicial authority of the cathedral chapter and of various noble families, the highest being the lords von und zu Büren and von Westphalen zu Fürstenberg.

Between 1510 and 1702, witchcraft trials against 260 persons are known to have taken place in Paderborn. In 204 cases, these trials ended in execution or death in prison; eighteen prisoners were released; and the outcome of the rest is unknown. Seventy percent of those prosecuted were women; children were occasionally prosecuted. These numbers are only a minimum. although both major noble rulers, von Büren and von Westphalen, left excellent sources, the area's other legal systems did not.

As early as 1500, the *Malleus Maleficarum* (The Hammer of Witches, 1486) was known among Paderborn's clergy. Isolated trials took place around 1510 and after 1555, before becoming endemic after 1572. Three main waves of persecution, similar to those in the duchy of Westphalia and other Catholic areas, occurred first in the 1590s and then between 1628 and 1631 and between 1656 and 1659. The first two immediately followed crises caused by extreme inflation or plague.

In 1598, the *Reichskammergericht* (imperial chamber court) intervened against Paderborn's cathedral chapter, thus preventing further executions, although the canons made reprisals against the relatives of the accused. In 1603 and 1604, Bishop Dietrich von Fürstenberg (ruled 1585–1618) caused a great stir by conducting trials against the prior, subprior, and two monks from the Augustinian convent in Dalheim, following allegations by confessed witches that all four clerics had participated in a witches' Sabbat. After one monk died during a year in prison, Würzburg's law faculty issued an opinion that saved the others' lives. This case, reminiscent of discussions going on at the same time in Bavaria, was still remembered at Paderborn and the abbey of Corvey as late as 1630; in a rather disguised manner, Friedrich Spee alluded to it in his *Cautio Criminalis* (A Warning on Criminal Justice, 1631).

The high point of persecution, around 1630, produced approximately ninety-five victims, fifty of whom were executed in Büren between March 17 and April 15, 1631, shortly before the *Cautio Criminalis* appeared in print in May 1631. Its author, Friedrich Spee, had taught moral theology at the Jesuit university of Paderborn since 1629. Spee had his share of enemies in Paderborn (including Suffragan Bishop Johann Pelcking), but he also had influential friends, who helped get his book published or recommended it. From 1619 to 1650, Paderborn's bishop was the archbishop of Cologne, Ferdinand of Bavaria, who had not visited Paderborn since the early 1620s. Because source materials are so scarce, it is unclear to what extent the archbishop's representatives and the estates used their administrative freedom either to promote or to prevent witch hunts in the prince-bishop's jurisdiction.

Between 1656 and 1660, a wave of demonic possession among young women in the town of Brakel aroused widespread attention after a Jesuit exorcist, Paderborn theology professor Bernhard Löper, turned the possessions into an uncontrollable epidemic. Löper used the exorcisms to demonstrate the superiority of Catholicism but could not expel the ghosts he had summoned, while the possessed and their families demanded a witch hunt against their enemies. Unsure how to judge the alleged demonic possession, Bishop Dietrich Adolf von der Recke (ruled 1650–1661) asked the Holy Office (the Congregation of the Inquisition) in Rome for guidance: one of his canons, Ferdinand von Fürstenberg, was close to the current pope, Alexander VII. A Roman exorcism expert advised Paderborn's clergy to reduce fear of the Devil and his powers through better pastoral care instead of heeding calls for witch hunts. After reading Löper's reports, Alexander VII doubted that the girls were possessed. But Roman skepticism about the credibility of the possessed and of witches' Sabbats found few supporters in Paderborn, especially when Löper denounced the bishop as a witches' lawyer. Von der Recke and his councilors then permitted witchcraft trials that eventually led to at least fifty executions from 1657 to 1659.

The trials began so slowly that a group of enraged men actually beat nine alleged witches to death on a public street. Paderborn's rulers caught the murderers, put them on trial, gave them death sentences, and following Rome's suggestion, put the more rabid of the possessed in solitary confinement in order to care for their spiritual needs.

These events ended Paderborn's last major wave of persecutions. Von der Recke's successor, the same Ferdinand von Fürstenberg (ruled 1661–1683), brought his Roman attitudes to Paderborn with him. In 1675 he authorized the execution of a man who used a consecrated Host to perform magic—a form of sacrilege punishable by death at Rome far into the eighteenth century. However, the situation in von Westphalen zu Fürstenberg's private jurisdiction was quite different. After a twelve-year-old boy was executed by cutting his arteries in 1694, one of the last witch hunts in Westphalia took place between 1700 and 1702, with twelve people accused and at least three women and two men receiving the death penalty.

RAINER DECKER;

TRANSLATED BY JONATHAN STICKNEY

See also: COLOGNE; ECCLESIASTICAL TERRITORIES (HOLY ROMAN EMPIRE); EXORCISM; FERDINAND OF COLOGNE; GERMANY; *MALLEUS MALEFICARUM;* POSSESSION, DEMONIC; *REICHSKAMMERGERICHT;* SPEE, FRIEDRICH.

References and further reading:
Decker, Rainer. 1978. "Die Hexenverfolgungen im Hochstift Paderborn." *Westfälische Zeitschrift* 128: 315–356.
———. 1994. *Die Hexen und ihre Henker: Ein Fallbericht.* Freiburg im Breisgau: Herder.
———. 2000. "Hexen, Mönche und ein Bischof: Das Kloster Dalheim und das Problem des Hexensabbats um 1600." *Westfälische Zeitschrift* 150: 235–245.
Schormann, Gerhard. 1977. *Hexenprozesse in Nordwestdeutschland.* Hildesheim: Lax, pp. 92–95.

PALATINATE, ELECTORATE OF

The widely dispersed territory of the electoral Palatinate, ruled by the older line of the Wittelsbach dynasty at Heidelberg, was situated in Germany between the upper and mid-Rhineland. Until the Thirty Years' War, the electorate also included the Upper Palatinate in northeastern Bavaria. Although the electoral Palatinate played a key role in supporting witchcraft trials in the late Middle Ages, it took the lead in opposing them during early modern times.

Soon after the new belief in diabolical witches had developed in the Swiss Alps during the first half of the fifteenth century, the electoral Palatinate became, as far as we know today, the first German territory to adapt this new belief and start its own witch hunts in 1446–1447. The Palatinate had both territorial and dynastic links with some core areas of the new witch beliefs. However, conditions for a favorable reception of a modern approach to witchcraft were exceptionally good at Heidelberg, especially with the university, which had demonologists such as John of Frankfurt and Nicholas of Jauer. Moreover, the Palatinate had been extremely active in purging heresy; the elector Palatine, its secular ruler, had played an active role, making considerable personal efforts. Even though theologians prepared the witchcraft cases, the electoral Palatinate adopted not the ecclesiastical procedure of witchcraft inquisition, but the secular witchcraft trial developed by Swiss cities. Final decisions and responsibility in the witch hunt belonged to the elector. More persecutions were documented in the Palatinate until the beginning of the sixteenth century.

However, when the first big wave of witch hunting in the early modern period began around 1560, the by-then-Calvinist Palatinate distanced itself from the common German trend by refusing to carry out witchcraft trials. This refusal remained characteristic afterward. It was due solely to the steadfastness of its administration that persecution of witchcraft never reached the electoral Palatinate from neighboring areas. Because this territory was in the middle of the main regions where witch hunts abounded, such external facts as the climate, geography, or economic position of the Palatinate cannot explain its opposition to the persecutions. And the Upper Palatinate, belonging to a different geographical region, also had no witchcraft persecutions while under the reign of the electors at Heidelberg. The absence of witchcraft trials was not a passive attitude, therefore, but an active policy of the electoral government to defend itself against internal and external opposition. From the outside, electoral policy was confronted with denunciations of Palatinate subjects by foreign witches and demands for persecutions by neighboring rulers. Serfs from the Palatinate became involved in foreign witchcraft trials and had to be defended, and many foreign subjects who fled to the Palatinate from persecutions in their home territories were allowed to settle. The intellectual elite of the electoral Palatinate included a strong group of supporters of the witchcraft trials, who demanded punishment especially for the apostasy and blasphemy of the witches. This group comprised most of the electorate's leading Reformed theologians and prevailed only at the end of the sixteenth century. The debates on the matter of witchcraft created a remarkable scientific discourse, including significant tracts by Thomas Erastus, Hermann Witekind, and Antonius Prätorius. Another dangerous demand for persecution came, as elsewhere in this region, from the populace. They made several accusations of witchcraft that could have started persecutions, but the Palatinate's administration refused all these demands.

Despite all the influence the prince-electors had on politics, the actual governing board was the Palatinate council (*Hofrat, Oberrat*) led by the chancellor. Extremely well-trained civil lawyers dominated this council. It acted as a unified organization that for the most part perpetuated itself, thereby ensuring a remarkable degree of continuity, despite several changes of confession (religion). So the refusal to persecute witches, once established in the 1560s, was maintained and even deepened over time. This policy drew important support from the faculty of law at Heidelberg University, where most councilors and government officials were trained. But of central importance for implementing this approach toward witchcraft was the Palatinate government's relatively good administrative control over punishing capital crimes. The *Hofrat* at Heidelberg, which oversaw all procedures of the lower courts, ultimately decided all important cases of criminal justice; usurpations of high justice by the populace, as in the electorate of Trier, were unimaginable.

The Reformed Church, established in the Palatinate in the 1560s, could not have been responsible for official disapproval of the persecution of witchcraft. Several Reformed territories in Europe (e.g., Scotland) had severe witchcraft persecutions. Opponents of the persecutions in the electoral Palatinate cannot be squeezed into one single intellectual tradition. Instead, one could develop a model for the electoral Palatinate showing several lines of tradition converging to build up an autonomous regional tradition, which is perhaps best described in Hermann Witekind's *Christlich bedencken und erinnerung von Zauberey* (Christian Thoughts and Memories about Sorcery, 1585). One finds traces of the so-called *Canon-Episcopi* tradition of southwestern Germany (Midelfort 1972), here in its Reformed version, as well as traces of the humanistic tradition led by Johann Weyer (who was highly regarded in the Palatinate), whose sons Dietrich and Johann reached very high positions in the electoral government. But one must also recognize that the attitude of the Palatinate opponents of witchcraft prosecution was mainly rooted in commonly accepted theological and legal norms; many traditional lines of the discourse on witchcraft that were opposed to the persecutions fit into this framework.

Strict observance of formal legal procedures in witchcraft trials saved the electoral Palatinate from rash executions by holding steadfast to ordinary methods (*processus ordinarius*). This demanded a considerable accumulation of proof before proceeding to torture, one nearly impossible to obtain in witchcraft trials. In the Palatinate, commonly used evidence like denunciations and the *mala fama* (bad reputation) were insufficient; the Devil's mark, the absence of tears, or the so-called water test (water ordeal; swimming test) were all inadmissible as evidence. Legal objections usually were in the foreground in official Palatinate arguments because they were unanswerable in imperial law. The electoral Palatinate was not completely alone in this policy. In most other large secular territories of the Holy Roman Empire, like the nearby duchy of Württemberg, an increasingly professional and centralized administration of law in the early modern state usually restricted the number of witchcraft trials and stopped any mass persecutions "to safeguard the dignity of the entire judicial apparatus" (Soman 1989, 14). But the existence of a powerful group strongly disapproving of the persecutions, like that found in the electoral Palatinate, was extremely unusual.

The specific difference here lay in a stronger criticism of the belief in witchcraft. Their fundamental opposition to the belief in witchcraft was based on the theocentric assumption of an almighty God, strongly emphasized by Reformed confessionalism, leaving little room for supernatural interference by diabolical agents. God alone ruled the world: sorcery was no more than an illusion of the Devil. The opponents of the persecutions therefore rejected any trials concerning supernatural elements like witches flying or fornicating with devils, because they were impossible. If the damaging effects of *maleficium* (harmful magic) were nonetheless legally punishable, this meant murder through poison or other offenses rationally possible. In the end, only separation from God and the pact with the Devil remained. But, as with all other forms of heresy, Palatinate authorities rejected the death penalty for spiritual crimes. In so doing they went beyond a Calvinist standpoint, as the opposition of Palatine theologians in the second half of the sixteenth century showed. However, using a missionary approach of "convert them, don't burn them," curiously like that of the Spanish Inquisition, Palatinate opponents of the persecutions demanded to lead those gone astray back to the true belief through pastoral care. In cases in which conversion was ineffective, as a last resort, banishment from the territory was the correct solution. The opponents of persecution supported disciplinary enforcements against people who practiced magic, but not with fire and sword, any more than for Anabaptists or refractory Catholics.

Because the approach toward witchcraft in the electoral Palatinate depended largely on its government, it became unsure when this region was occupied by Catholic troops in the course of the Thirty Years' War. From 1622–1623 until 1649, Spain and the emperor governed the part of the electorate west of the Rhine River, while Bavaria held those parts to the east. We can make no certain claims about witchcraft trials under Spanish occupation; but we have ample indications that from 1629 onward, a wave of witchcraft persecutions affected the Bavarian-ruled palatinate, apparently influenced by large persecutions in neighboring territories. Burnings occurred, although their exact numbers are unknown. The Bavarian government in Heidelberg, now controlling criminal justice, took up the persecutions with the support of Prince-Elector Maximilian. At that time, examples of witchcraft trials using procedures contrary to established laws occurred in the electoral Palatinate.

Interestingly, those forces in Munich opposed to witchcraft trials (who controlled Bavarian central administration) had no means to exert significant influence over these persecutions in far-off Heidelberg, for personnel and administrative reasons. The councilors and government officials that Bavaria installed in the Rhine Palatinate were mostly Catholic foreigners from the vicinity of the electoral Palatinate, distant from Bavarian traditions and therefore unaware of the moderate approach now dominant in Munich. So in the electoral Palatinate on the Rhine, the tradition against persecutions ended when its old government fled, while the Bavarians never extended their cautious approach to the Palatinate. Quite different however, was the situation in the Upper Palatinate, where no new persecutions occurred under the Bavarian government. Here the personnel from the electoral Palatinate remained largely intact, being replaced only slowly by Bavarians bringing Bavarian traditions with them. The radical rejection of persecutions by Calvinist authorities was thus gradually transformed into the cautious approach of the Bavarian Catholics, with minimal consequences.

After their return to Heidelberg in 1649, the Palatinate Prince-Elector Charles Ludwig and his government resumed the traditional rejection of persecutions, whose foundations were now strengthened and broadened by increasing religious tolerance and further humanization of penitential procedures.

JÜRGEN MICHAEL SCHMIDT

See also: ANABAPTISTS; BAVARIA, DUCHY OF; *CANON EPISCOPI*; DEVIL'S MARK; ERASTUS, THOMAS; GERMANY, SOUTHEASTERN; GERMANY, SOUTHWESTERN; *MALEFICIUM*; MAXIMILIAN I, DUKE OF BAVARIA; ORIGINS OF THE WITCH HUNTS; POPULAR PERSECUTION; PRÄTORIUS, ANTON; PROTESTANT REFORMATION; SWIMMING TEST; UNIVERSITIES; WEYER, JOHANN; WITEKIND, HERMANN.

References and further reading:
Behringer, Wolfgang. 1997. *Witchcraft Persecutions in Bavaria: Popular Magic, Religious Zealotry, and Reason of State in Early Modern Europe.* Translated by J. C. Grayson and David Lederer. Cambridge: Cambridge University Press.
Midelfort, H. C. Erik. 1972. *Witch Hunting in Southwestern Germany 1562–1684: The Social and Intellectual Foundations.* Stanford: Stanford University Press.
Schmidt, Jürgen M. 2000. *Glaube und Skepsis: Die Kurpfalz und die abendländische Hexenverfolgung 1446–1685* (Hexenforschung 5). Bielefeld: Verlag für Regionalgeschichte.
Soman, Alfred. 1989. "Decriminalizing Witchcraft: Does the French Experience Furnish a European Model?" *Criminal Justice History* 10: 1–22.
Thieser, Bernd. 1992. *Die Oberpfalz im Zusammenhang des Hexenprozessgeschehens im Süddeutschen Raum während des 16. und 17. Jahrhunderts* (Bayreuther Arbeiten zur Landesgeschichte und Heimatkunde, Bd. 2). 2nd ed. Bayreuth: Rabenstein.

PALINGH, ABRAHAM (1588/1589–1682)

Palingh was the author of the most prominent Mennonite book about witchcraft, *'t Afgerukt mom-aansight der tooverye* (The Mask of Witchcraft Pulled Off), published in 1659. Palingh was probably born in Beveren, a small town near Antwerp, and died at Haarlem.

The Spanish army's recapture of the provinces of Flanders and Brabant in the 1580s led to a Protestant exodus to places with more religious freedom. Palingh's family moved to Haarlem, a center of textile industry in Holland. His father, Andries Palinck, first appeared there in a document from 1602. Most Mennonites were craftspeople, and many of them were textile workers. Andries was a weaver and also one of the ministers of a Mennonite congregation in Haarlem. Except for a document from 1618 mentioning Abraham Palingh as consoler of the sick in this congregation, we know little about his early years. As an adult, he understood Dutch, French, and German but not Latin, which implies that he received only a primary education. He became a small trader in textiles; he married twice and had two sons, Andries and Jan. His profession brought him into contact with another textile trader, Herman Löher, whose *Hochnötige unterthanige wemütige Klage der Frommen Unschültigen* (Much Needed, Humble, and Woeful Complaint of the Pious Innocent) was published in 1676 and whose life history Palingh had summarized in his earlier book.

As a religious dissenter who could not read or speak Latin and did not belong to the most prosperous layer of craftspeople and shopkeepers, Palingh stood outside the cultural, economic, and political elites. But his book was nevertheless well received. After 1594 it was virtually impossible to prosecute anybody for witchcraft in the Dutch Republic. But in the 1650s, some local judicial authorities again showed some willingness to receive accusations of maleficent magic, leading Palingh to write his treatise in order to convince the courts and other authorities not to permit any renewal of witchcraft prosecutions. In February 1659, his book was indeed used by the defendant in a trial against a woman accused of having concluded a pact with the Devil.

In his book, Palingh mentioned several authors who supported the persecution of witches, but he countered their arguments using only biblical texts, mentioning no other authority except Erasmus, whose name appeared only once. He specifically refuted the views of Agricola of Sittard, Jean Bodin, William Perkins, and the Jesuit Paul Laymann. (Palingh was unaware that Laymann had not written the treatise he was attacking.) His line of reasoning was first and foremost practical. As a true Mennonite, Palingh argued that magic had no effect and that the Devil could not change the course of nature and therefore could not cause any disaster. He found the whole image of an anthropomorphic Devil who conversed with human beings ridiculous. As a merchant, he expressed amazement at the Devil's business policies as described by demonologists, finding it extremely stupid to invest time and energy training employees who would be executed shortly afterward. He also mocked the professional tactics of the Devil's followers, citing the habits of Livonian werewolves who, according to Bodin, had to pass through a river in January without wearing clothes in order to transform themselves into marauding animals. Palingh considered the idea of people preparing to dive naked into a river, in midwinter, in a northern country like Livonia, simply preposterous.

Fellow Mennonites apparently found Palingh's negation of the powers of the Devil quite acceptable. Unlike the Reformed minister Balthasar Bekker some thirty years later, Palingh was never attacked by coreligionists for denying that spirits could interfere with created matter. Incidentally, Bekker mentioned Palingh's work very favorably in his *De Betooverde Wereld* (The World Bewitched, 1691–1693). In the 1660s, Palingh also published two pamphlets defending the position of his congregation on problems then under discussion among Mennonites, matters having no connection with witchcraft or demonic powers. His participation in this debate suggested that the members of his congregation considered him a valuable defender of their views. His book was reprinted in 1725.

HANS DE WAARDT

See also: AMSTERDAM; ANABAPTISTS; BEKKER, BALTHASAR; BODIN, JEAN; DEMONOLOGY; DEVIL; ERASMUS, DESIDERIUS; LAYMANN, PAUL; LÖHER, HERMAN; MENNONITES; NETHERLANDS, NORTHERN; PERKINS, WILLIAM.
References and further reading:
Palingh, Abraham. 1659. *'t Afgerukt mom-aansight der tooverye*. Amsterdam: Jan Rieuwertsz.
Waardt, Hans de. 1992. "Abraham Palingh: Ein holländischer Baptist und die Macht des Teufels." Pp. 247–268 in *Vom Unfug des Hexen-Processes: Gegner der Hexenverfolgung von Johann Weyer bis Friedrich Spee*. Edited by Hartmut Lehmann and Otto Ulbricht. Wiesbaden: Harrasowitz.

PAMPHLETS AND NEWSPAPERS

Witchcraft pamphlets—in effect, occasional newspapers—were based on accounts by witnesses of witchcraft-related events or sometimes on court documents. They were important because they spread stories of witchcraft. Such pamphlets were a Europe-wide phenomenon that badly needs a comparative study. In Germany they reported trials such as that of the Pappenheimer family (1600), later translated for Dutch and English readers. The Swedish Mora trials (1668–1670) were publicized through a Dutch translation of a Swedish pamphlet, subsequently retranslated and anthologized by such English demonologists as Joseph Glanvill and read as far away as America; it was also translated into German and French. English pamphlets, currently the best-studied vernacular genre, cost from a penny to a few shillings in English money: although for many a substantial purchase, they were accessible to all but the poorest. Price depended on the number of pages and special features like illustrations. It seems likely that they were circulated among groups of people or read out to reach a wider, often illiterate, audience.

English witchcraft pamphlets offered a considerable range of form and diversity of content. The first to report a witchcraft trial was produced in three parts in London in 1566, although it is not clear whether the parts were sold separately. Based on pretrial examinations of suspects, an account of the courtroom testimony of their supposed victim, and the confession on the scaffold of the only person to be convicted and hanged, it tells the story of three women from Hatfield Peverell, a small Essex village, who were accused of a variety of *maleficia* (evil acts). Assize court records told us that one, Elizabeth Fraunces, pleaded guilty in court to paralyzing an infant (and was imprisoned accordingly), but the pamphlet records her pretrial confession. She admitted a far greater number of offenses than remain on record, some of them linked with her unwanted pregnancies and unwanted marriage. Apparently she was not prosecuted for these offenses, and so no trace of them remained outside the pamphlet, *The Examination and Confession of certaine Wytches* (London, 1566). The pamphlet gave us information we would otherwise lack and dramatized for us the gendered psychological issues behind a specific confession of witchcraft. By giving details of the suspect's life and of the dynamics of accusation and confession, it helped explain her willingness to confess in a way that other surviving records did not.

The pamphlet also deals with Agnes Waterhouse, who was named in a later pamphlet as Elizabeth's sister, and Agnes's daughter Joan. In the pamphlet, both are accused of afflicting a young girl, Agnes Browne, whose dramatically recreated court performance suggested to the reader that both women had preyed on this innocent. Agnes Browne had, she said, been tormented by a talking black dog with a monkey's face, which tempted her to suicide. Although assize records showed (and the pamphlet confirmed) that Agnes Waterhouse confessed to and was convicted of another offense and hanged, the court records and pamphlet differed in their account of Joan. Assize records showed that Joan was acquitted of bewitching Browne, but the pamphlet ended its report with the jury deliberating the case and implied that she would be found guilty. Here the pamphlet gives vividly represented detail of the case but fails to record fairly the outcome of the trial; it suggests, as pamphlets often do, that all the accused were guilty.

Agnes Waterhouse's scaffold confession also offered information, unavailable elsewhere, about those likely to be convicted of witchcraft. The pamphlet adds to assize records by telling us that Agnes was very poor, was sixty-four years old, and, before her death confessed that she prayed in Latin, suggesting an old, marginalized woman who had not accepted Protestantism. Like Elizabeth Fraunces, Agnes Waterhouse had gone begging in her community, and where charity had been denied, she said she had punished those who refused her. From this short pamphlet, the reader gains a wealth of information and conjecture about accusers, witches, and their communities, as well as—in this case—two poems and an epistle on witchcraft giving a pious commentary on the subject. It is also possible, by comparison with other records, to offer an assessment of the reliability of stories told in pamphlets.

Pamphleteers can be accused of sometimes sacrificing truthful reporting for a good story, but they also provided details that, where they can be checked, are often confirmed. They wanted to entertain purchasers but also to inform. They were usually anonymous, probably hack writers working for publishing houses in London, sometimes writing whole booklets, sometimes only prefaces for existing documents. Another pamphlet of 1566, *The Examination of John Walsh* (London), was an almost verbatim transcript of a still-surviving church court interrogation of a "cunning man," but the preface (probably by the publisher John Awdeley) added a violently anti-Catholic address to the reader that drew out suggestions in the main text that Walsh was a Catholic and had learned his craft from a priest. This may well illuminate the motives of his accusers and questioners, by associating him with worldwide popish superstitions scorned by proper Elizabethan Protestants.

A Scottish pamphlet of the early 1590s, *Newes from Scotland* (London, 1591), had a similar political undertone but illustrated more graphically the dangers of trusting journalistic sources. It was a narrative (rather than a document-based) account that reported the activities of a large number of witches who intended to harm the Scottish King James VI. These supposedly centered around a satanic ritual in North Berwick kirk. The pamphlet's detailed but highly selective account naively reflected the assumptions of the questioners, including the king. In short, it is invaluable as an official version of events: that the king of Scotland's authority and godliness were confirmed by the attack of Satan's agents upon him. It is, however, almost impossible for a modern reader to assess what really occurred: a very complex background of political feuding that undoubtedly influenced events went completely unreported, buried by propaganda.

Most pamphlets were fairly brief—eight or twelve pages—but they were sometimes lengthened by demonological or sociopolitical commentary. *A true and just Recorde* (London, 1582) was just over 100 pages long, and Thomas Potts's vast *The Wonderfull Discoverie of Witches* (London, 1612) was nearly 200. Both contained pretrial records relating to large groups of witches. The first was probably produced by and for Brian Darcy, a magistrate involved in questioning all the accusers and suspects; an assize court clerk, on the instruction of the judges, compiled the second. In both cases, an attempt was made to prove that there were a great number of witches at large:

the preface of *A true and just Recorde* favored legal reform to burn rather than hang witches, whereas Potts attempted to portray the judicial process as it stood as both merciful and just. Both pamphlets thus had an agenda and used large numbers of witchcraft cases as "data": illustrations of demonological and political arguments that might or might not be supported by a mass of relatively unmediated documents. Editorial tampering did, however, occur, and readers must be alert.

Witchcraft pamphlets were extremely important in circulating stories of witchcraft, upon which other cases or arguments about them might then be based. In 1619, a pamphleteer writing up *The Wonderful Discoverie of the Witchcrafts of Margaret and Phillip Flower,* an account of the murder by witchcraft of two children of the earl of Rutland, cited several pamphlets, including Potts's, among his sources to show that witches gave their souls to the Devil. As early as 1584, Reginald Scot in his *Discoverie of Witchcraft* discussed *A true and just Recorde,* among other accounts, both English and European, from which he drew the conclusion that there were no witches as conventionally defined. By 1718, Francis Hutchinson, the noted skeptic, had amassed a collection of instances of witchcraft in pamphlets and quoted at length in his *Historical Essay Concerning Witchcraft* from those reporting the hotly contested case of Jane Wenham (1712). With a much wider range of sources for the study of witchcraft, we are less inclined to regard pamphlets as straightforward reports, but they remain a uniquely valuable repository of stories about witchcraft.

MARION GIBSON

See also: CONFESSIONS; DEVIL BOOKS; ENGLAND; ESSEX; GLANVILL, JOSEPH; HUTCHINSON, FRANCIS; LANCASHIRE WITCHES; MORA WITCHES; NORTH BERWICK WITCHES; PAPPENHEIMER FAMILY; SCOT, REGINALD; ST. OSYTH WITCHES; WENHAM, JANE.

References and further reading:

Gibson, Marion. 1999. *Reading Witchcraft: Stories of Early English Witches.* London and New York: Routledge.
———. 2000. *Early Modern Witches: Witchcraft Cases in Contemporary Writing.* London and New York: Routledge.
Glanvill, Joseph. 1681. *Saducismus Triumphatus.* London.
Hutchinson, Francis. 1718. *An Historical Essay Concerning Witchcraft.* London.
Normand, Lawrence, and Gareth Roberts. 2000. *Witchcraft in Early Modern Scotland.* Exeter: Exeter University Press.
Rosen, Barbara. 1991. *Witchcraft in England, 1558–1618.* Amherst: University of Massachusetts Press.
Scot, Reginald. 1584. *The Discoverie of Witchcraft.* London.
Sharpe, James. 1996. *Instruments of Darkness: Witchcraft in England, 1550–1750.* London: Hamish Hamilton.
Thomas, Keith. 1971. *Religion and the Decline of Magic.* London: Penguin.

PAN

In Greek mythology, Pan was a rural god specifically in charge of forests, flocks, and shepherds. He was also a hunter and the inventor of a type of shepherds' pipe. He was born with horns, a goat's beard, feet, and a tail, and his body was covered with hair. His appearance was thus so frightening that even his own mother ran away at the sight of him, and when humans encountered him unexpectedly, they often fled in terror. Hence the Greek and then English word *panic.* The supposed derivation of his name from the Greek for "everything" is a false etymology.

Pan was not the only horned divinity in Europe. The Greek god Zeus was sometimes depicted with horns, for example, and the Gallic Cernunnos had stag's horns. During the Middle Ages, it became common for Jews to be depicted as having horns and a tail, and in a fifteenth-century manuscript, Waldensian heretics are shown worshipping Satan in the form of a goat. So the distinctive animal traits often associated with Satan, especially the presiding Satan of the witches' Sabbat, had precedents in both pagan mythology and popular hostile depiction of outsiders.

Artists of all kinds rapidly adopted the visual identification of Pan with Satan, and it became a cliché of his representation, even though written accounts of the Sabbat described the Devil as taking other animal forms as well, such as a dog, cat, or bull. Thus, the woodcuts in Francesco-Maria Guazzo's *Compendium Maleficarum* (A Summary of Witches, 1608) showed Satan in Pan-form receiving the worship of male and female witches, and Jan Ziaruko's engraving for Pierre de Lancre's *Tableau de l'inconstance des mauvais anges et demons* (Description of the Inconstancy of Evil Angels and Demons, 1612), one of the best known of the French demonological treatises, depicted Satan as an enthroned goat overseeing the detailed wildness of witches' behavior during a Sabbat. Once established, of course, the image was reproduced over and over again. The eighteenth-century occultist Eliphas Lévi (Alphonse Louis Constant) helped perpetuate it in a form that became famous: an androgynous winged Baphomet enthroned, with rearing horns, a goat face, and a pentagram in the middle of his forehead. Goya (Francisco José de Goya y Lucientes) too subscribed to the image. *Ensayos,* one of his *Capricho* series, showed witches practicing flying, watched over by an enormous black he-goat, and his most frequently reproduced picture had female witches worshipping a goat-shaped Satan.

Pan as Pan (rather than a type of Satan) was largely forgotten by literature, however, until the nineteenth century remade him into a divinity associated with the wilder and more exciting (that is, sexual) aspects of nature. From then on, English poets in particular used him as a shorthand image for their collective and individual thoughts about nature in the raw. Prose

Pan, a horned god who, because of his horns, gnat's beard, hairy body, and terrifying appearance, is associated with the Devil. (TopFoto.co.uk)

writers also took up the theme but transmuted the god into a symbol of aggressive rebellion against conventional morality, most notably perhaps in the early twentieth century when Aleister Crowley, identifying himself at one point with both Pan and the Egyptian god Seth, envisaged him as the god of homosexual passion.

But Margaret Murray finally returned Pan to his older self. In 1931, Murray published a book, *The God of the Witches,* a sequel to her *The Witch-Cult in Western Europe* (1921), which argued that the horned god was the oldest male deity in Europe and that his worship by men and women had been misinterpreted as the adoration of Satan by witches and therefore persecuted by the Church. Several scholars have demolished her theory, but the Pan image lingers on in the worship of the horned god by some modern Wiccans.

P. G. MAXWELL-STUART

See also: ART AND VISUAL IMAGES; BAPHOMET; CONTEMPORARY WITCHCRAFT (POST-1800); GOYA Y LUCIENTES, FRANCISCO JOSÉ DE; GUAZZO, FRANCESCO-MARIA; LANCRE, PIERRE DE; MURRAY, MARGARET ALICE; SABBAT.

References and further reading:
Hutton, Ronald. 1999a. *The Triumph of the Moon: A History of Modern Pagan Witchcraft.* Oxford: Oxford University Press.
———. 1999b. "Modern Pagan Witchcraft." Pp. 1–79 in *The Twentieth Century.* Vol. 6 of *The Athlone History of Witchcraft and Magic in Europe.* Edited by Bengt Ankarloo and Stuart Clark. London and Philadelphia: Athlone and University of Pennsylvania Press.
Merivale, Patricia. 1969. *Pan, the Goat-God: His Myth in Modern Times.* Cambridge, MA: Harvard University Press.
Russell, Jeffrey Burton. 1977. *The Devil: Perceptions of Evil from Antiquity to Primitive Christianity.* Ithaca, NY, and London: Cornell University Press.
Trachtenberg, Joshua. 1983. *The Devil and the Jews.* 1943. Reprint. Philadelphia and Jerusalem: Jewish Publication Society.

PANICS

There is much confusion about what constituted a witch panic. The most obvious examples occurred when very large numbers of accused witches were arrested and burned in one place within a short time. But when did a witch scare develop into something we could legitimately call a panic? One standard (Monter

1976, 89–92) suggested that ten deaths for witchcraft at one place in one year constituted at least a small panic, but there is no consensus among scholars. However, trying to measure witch panics seems like measuring exactly how many people are needed to make up a crowd. The larger witch panics were, the vaguer the estimates become about their actual size— almost exactly like newspaper or police estimates about the size of mass demonstrations. Nevertheless, we can offer a few plausible generalizations about when and where Europe's major witch panics occurred.

In Europe's worst witch panics, more than 100 witches were burned in relatively small regions within two or three years. Such episodes were extremely rare; so far as we know, they were confined to a handful of places in present-day Germany. The panic that lasted from October 1628 until March 1630 in the small town of Mergentheim provides a particularly well-documented and ghastly example (Midelfort 1972, 143–155). In all, exactly 117 witches were burned on 32 separate occasions (no more than 6 witches were ever burned together, probably because of limited jail facilities and the danger of controlling such conflagrations). Four more died in prison, probably from excessive torture. Although many accused witches were never imprisoned at Mergentheim, no imprisoned witch was ever acquitted until February 1630.

Some German witch panics were even larger and lasted considerably longer. Ellwangen, capital of a larger territory than Mergentheim, held seventeen execution days for witches in 1611 and seventeen more in 1612; the exact number who were burned in these two years is uncertain, but it probably exceeded 250. This panic continued into 1613, with six more execution days, and did not cease entirely until 1618 (Midelfort 1972, 98–115). Few cases surpassed Ellwangen in sheer ferocity. Perhaps Germany's worst witch panic afflicted the electorate of Cologne for nearly a decade after 1627, because the government orchestrated it through a network of special commissioners resembling a separate bureaucracy (Schormann 1991), but we have no reliable estimate of its exact dimensions.

Such large panics, with twenty or more burned in a single year, accounted for about 40 percent of the more than 3,200 witches known to have been executed between 1562 and 1666 throughout Baden-Württemburg, which included both Mergentheim and Ellwangen; years with ten or more executions accounted for 70 percent (Midelfort 1972, 72). It is likely that such ratios might be replicated on a macroscale. A rough estimate of Germany's eight or nine largest known witch panics, or "super-hunts," nearly all of them conducted (as at Mergentheim or Ellwangen) by ecclesiastical princes, suggests comparable results: in a country with over 300 separate governments, this handful of states apparently accounted for almost 40

percent of the more than 20,000 witches executed in Germany. Because Germany executed more than half of all witches throughout Europe, this handful of major panics probably accounted for at least one-fifth of all witches executed anywhere in Europe between 1560 and 1680.

At the same time, tiny villages occasionally suffered even more from witch panics than the very worst German cases. Consider the case of little Gollion, a completely unremarkable Protestant French-Swiss village of fewer than fifty households in the Pays de Vaud (Taric Zumsteg 2000). Within sixteen years (1615–1631), Gollion experienced six separate outbreaks of witch hunting, during which a total of twenty-five people were executed; nine of them died in one two-month span. Thus, within a generation, roughly one-fourth of Gollion's adults were burned as witches (almost 40 percent of them men). This ratio clearly surpasses even such disasters as Mergentheim, where, in a population of about 1,250 adults, about every tenth adult (and perhaps every sixth adult woman) was burned. However, Gollion is the worst case yet studied on such a microscopic level.

LARGE WITCH PANICS WITH FEWER BURNINGS

Major witch panics involving hundreds of burnings per year never occurred outside Germany. Sloppy scholarship has exaggerated their frequency elsewhere in Europe (and inside Germany as well) by accepting uncritically the numbers of witches burned found in sensationalist contemporary pamphlets, which deliberately exaggerated the extent of witches and witchcraft. These vast numbers of witches burned invariably shrink drastically upon closer inspection. For example, the well-known demonologist and judge Pierre de Lancre boasted of making several hundred Basque-speaking witches confess their crimes in 1609; well-known scholars (e.g., Trevor-Roper 1969, 112) deduced that this judge burned almost a hundred witches in only four months—but a careful reading of de Lancre's text identifies barely a dozen witches burned, including three priests (Monter 2002, 41–42). They were, however, enough to trigger a witch panic that soon involved two countries.

As the example of de Lancre suggests, simply counting the number of witches burned is not the only or always the best guide to using the phrase *witch panic* appropriately. It can be legitimately applied in parts of Europe outside Germany where fears of witchcraft obsessed entire regions for several years, even if large numbers of witches were not burned. The hysteria in Basque lands on both sides of the French–Spanish border between 1609 and 1614 provides the best example. Although probably only a dozen witches died on each side of the border, it has been called, with some justification, Europe's largest witch panic, simply because of its unprecedented scale: in addition to the hundreds of Basque confessions mentioned by de Lancre, the Spanish Inquisition eventually heard almost 2,000 spontaneous confessions of witchcraft, overwhelmingly from children. At least, that is what local interpreters told their employers, because neither the French judges nor the Spanish inquisitors understood Basque. It required sustained efforts by responsible authorities in both France and Spain to prevent their out-of-control officials from doing further damage and finally to calm things down.

The child-driven Swedish witchcraft hysteria lasting from 1668 to 1675 provides another equally well-known and instructive example of a truly large-scale witch panic. This panic spread extremely widely, eventually reaching most of northern Sweden and extending as far south as Stockholm. Exactly like the Basque episode, it involved thousands of children describing their experiences at the witches' Sabbat; unfortunately, in this instance, well over 100 witches were executed before it too could be brought to an end—by executing an adolescent accuser for perjury.

WHEN DID THEY BEGIN AND END?

Nothing resembling the Mergentheim panic occurred in fifteenth-century Europe. As early as the 1420s, large numbers of people were being arrested for witchcraft in Valais or Dauphiné; but local political circumstances and the repression of heresy often help explain such outbreaks, as they do in the first urban instance, the mid-fifteenth century *Vauderie* (Waldensianism, but used to label witches) of Arras. In general, it seems problematic to talk about witch panics in the age of the *Malleus Maleficarum* (The Hammer of Witches, 1486); when Inquisitor Heinrich Kramer arrested fifty women in the Tyrol in 1485, he certainly provoked an extreme reaction—but it was directed more against him than the accused witches (much later, something analogous apparently happened to de Lancre also).

Probably the last major witch panic in Europe was the *Zauber-jackl* (Sorcerer Jack) affair that affected the independent prince-archbishopric of Salzburg from 1677 to 1680; although slightly later than the Swedish case and located in Catholic rather than Protestant Europe, it was similarly child-driven. Here, however, adolescent boys were targeted as witches by the authorities rather than used by them to accuse others. Americans regard Salem Village in 1692 as a major witch panic; it does meet the criterion of twenty deaths in one place within a year, and it occurred even later than Salzburg. Although numerous witchcraft trials were held after 1700 in eastern Europe, no later episodes that deserve to be called major "witch panics" have yet been uncovered.

We know that firm actions by such high-level authorities as the Spanish Inquisition, the *Parlement* (sovereign judicial court) of Bordeaux, or Sweden's high court of appeals eventually stopped Europe's most widespread witch panics. However, relatively little work has been done so far on why Germany's major witch panics stopped. One explanation uses a list of the 160 people burned as witches on 29 occasions at Würzburg between 1627 and 1629 to argue that they stopped when they became dysfunctional after the traditional stereotype of a witch broke down (Midelfort 1972, 179, 182). In this instance, adult women formed 85 percent of the total in the first five burnings and almost 70 percent of the first fifteen groups. But in the next fourteen clusters, the stereotype collapsed completely: adult women now comprised less than one-fourth of the witches being burned, far outnumbered both by young children (mainly boys) and adult men. However, such clear examples seem unusual.

WILLIAM MONTER

See also: ARRAS; BASQUE COUNTRY; COLOGNE; ECCLESIASTICAL TERRITORIES (HOLY ROMAN EMPIRE); ELLWANGEN, PRINCE-ABBEY; GERMANY; INQUISITION, SPANISH; KRAMER, HEINRICH; LANCRE, PIERRE DE; MERGENTHEIM, ECCLESIASTICAL TERRITORY OF; MORA WITCHES; SALZBURG, PRINCE-ARCHBISHOPRIC OF; VAUD, PAYS DE; WITCH HUNTS; WÜRTTEMBURG, DUCHY OF; WÜRZBURG, PRINCE-BISHOPRIC OF.

References and further reading:
Midelfort, H. C. Erik. 1972. *Witch-Hunting in Southwestern Germany, 1562–1684: The Social and Intellectual Foundations.* Stanford: Stanford University Press.
Monter, William. 1976. *Witchcraft in France and Switzerland: The Borderlands During the Reformation.* Ithaca, NY: Cornell University Press.
———. 2002. "Witch-Trials in Continental Europe, 1560–1660." Pp. 1–52 in *The Period of the Witch Trials.* Vol. 4 of *The Athlone History of Witchcraft and Magic in Europe.* Edited by Bengt Ankarloo and Stuart Clark. London and Philadelphia: Athlone and University of Pennsylvania Press.
Schormann, Gerhard. 1991. *Der Krieg gegen die Hexen.* Göttingen: Vandenhoeck and Rupprecht.
Taric Zumsteg, Fabienne. 2000. *Les sorciers à l'assaut du village Gollion (1615–1631).* Lausanne: Zèbre.
Trevor-Roper, H. R. 1969. *The European Witch-Craze of the Sixteenth and Seventeenth Centuries and Other Essays.* New York: Harper and Row.
Wohlschlegel, Karin. 1995. "Die letzten Hexen von Mergentheim: Auswertung der Verhörprotokolle aus den Jahren 1628 bis 1631." *Würtembergisch Franken* 80: 41–115.

PAPACY AND PAPAL BULLS

In the development of witch persecution, the Roman papacy and its decisions on official doctrine played a central role. The nineteenth-century denominational approach to Church history presented the attitudes of the popes in a one-sided fashion, either polemically or apologetically. Overinterpretations resulted, rectified by subsequent research and the study of original texts during recent decades. On the whole, our evaluation of the papacy's role in creating and upholding the doctrine of witchcraft has become more nuanced, but no generally accepted academic consensus on the subject has yet been reached.

The papacy, which gradually developed from the increasing prominence of the bishop of Rome after the fifth century, reached its full stature in the tenth and eleventh centuries, becoming the ultimate authority of the Latin Church in all matters of doctrine, including the issues of demonology and witchcraft. In the Middle Ages, the legal decisions of the Holy See theoretically demanded absolute obedience, but papal infallibility in doctrinal issues was not entirely indisputable. Only after the end of the conciliar movement and the sixteenth-century Protestant Reformation was the pope's absolute doctrinal authority uncontested within the post-Tridentine Roman Catholic Church. Papal statements on the doctrine of witchcraft must also be understood in the light of the dogmatizing of the pope's power of jurisdiction and infallibility in 1870—a declaration that retroactively covered doctrinal statements made by previous Roman bishops and implied their universal validity.

In the Early Middle Ages, the entire western Church, including its popes, was preoccupied with overcoming the relics of paganism. Gregory I (ruled 590–604) attempted a synthesis of popular pagan desiderata with the claims of the Christian faith, particularly by nurturing reverence for relics of saints and the whole area of the miraculous; Christian churches were now built over the foundations of antique temples, thus creating a continuity of religious cults on sites that were not initially Christian. During Charlemagne's reign (768–814), the Frankish kingdom attempted to stamp out the remnants of paganism by issuing capitularies, which were accepted by the popes at imperial synods. Numerous regulations combated the practice of sorcery and opposed such judicial problems as vigilante justice against alleged sorcerers and witches. This attitude characterized Church and civil authorities until the High Middle Ages; papal bulletins on witchcraft were essentially restricted to specific issues, for example, a letter from Pope Gregory VII to King Harold of Denmark strictly prohibiting the lynching of alleged witches.

By the thirteenth century, several developments provoked a tighter organization of the Roman Church: the great Church law compilation, the *Decretum gratiani* (Gratian's *Concord of Discordant Canons*, known as the *Decretum,* 1130–1140 revision), and the first comprehensive textbooks and *summae* (summaries or compilations of theology or canon law) appeared, systematically recording theology in its entirety; in the thirteenth century, the Church was drawing up its own profile even as it began contending with heretical movements from within. The *Decretum gratiani,* accredited and advanced by the papacy, incorporated many stipulations concerning witchcraft, mainly compiled from early medieval texts; it laid the foundation for legal considerations that subsequently influenced the cumulative concept of witchcraft. Because the *Decretum gratiani* never mentioned such things as witches' Sabbats or a witchcraft sect and rejected the belief in witches flying, in accordance with the Frankish capitularies (*Canon Episcopi,* ca. 906), it rather restricted the evolution of the concept of witchcraft. However, canon law also contained sufficient clauses about heresy in general and its subsequent prosecution to provide substantial support for advocates of severe witch persecution.

An initial turning point toward more severe persecution of witchcraft occurred under Pope Alexander VI (ruled 1492–1503), who issued an ordinance to the Dominicans and Franciscans, to whom the new papal inquisition had been assigned, that sorcery and divination should be prosecuted only when accompanied by a strong suspicion of heresy. This ordinance, incorporated into the *Corpus iuris canonici* (Body of Canon Law, Bk. 6, c. 5, 2), implied certain parallels between sorcery or divination and heresy, which was the Church's primary enemy. Until the beginning of the fourteenth century, further instructions remained sporadic and specific, for example, in 1303, Boniface VIII (ruled 1295–1303) intervened against a bishop of Coventry accused of paying homage to the Devil, and in 1318, John XXII (ruled 1316–1334) took action against individual sorcerers. However, after the prohibition of the Templar order for political reasons, which was justified with the claim that the Templars formed a diabolical sect that must be eliminated, John XXII suddenly adopted a more radical attitude, thus multiplying anti-sorcery precedents.

John XXII resided at Avignon, in an environment rife with suspicion of witchcraft at the French and other courts, where the pope was seen as a possible victim of the black arts. Thus, he took a personal interest in the prosecution of alleged sorcerers. In 1320, the inquisitors of southwestern France (which harbored large concentrations of Cathars and Albigensians), received orders to deal severely with people who practiced divination, the black arts, and demonic sacrifices. Here, heresy became more closely associated with sorcery. His bull *Super illius specula* (Upon His Watchtower) in 1326 proved more fundamental and effective. For the first time, it considered a pact with the Devil as the worst crime of alleged sorcerers. Subsequently, demonological ideas predominated when describing practices previously classified as superstition.

It has justifiably been claimed that this papal bull contained no echoes of the cumulative concept of witchcraft, and this constitution never led to witchcraft trials like those of the fifteenth and subsequent centuries. Its significance lay in the unambiguous classification of all occult practices as heresy, because they involved homage to the Devil. An ominous step was taken from individual sorcerers toward the great diabolical conspiracy of sorcerers and witches, the existence of which was alleged by later inquisitors. At the same time, linking ecclesiastical trials for heresy with secular implementations of death sentences made sorcerers more vulnerable to the death penalty than previously. This policy was continued by John's successor Benedict XII (ruled 1335–1342), the former inquisitor Jacques Fournier. Although his instructions were generally restricted to resolving individual cases of sorcery, its associations with heresy became more firmly established. Subsequent popes showed relatively little interest in sorcery or witchcraft while the cumulative concept of witchcraft was being created, although some, including Martin V (ruled 1417–1431) and Eugenius IV (ruled 1431–1447), issued statements on the subject that prefigured aspects of subsequent bulls condemning witchcraft. Another decree directed at southern France and defining sorcery as heresy, employed the phrase *summis desiderantes affectibus* (desirous with supreme ardor), later made notorious by Innocent VIII (ruled 1484–1492). A bull of 1437 ordered severe measures against persons who made pacts with demons, worshipped them, and practiced harmful occult arts with their aid, even raising tempests. However, it was very general in character, being addressed to all inquisitors.

The most famous papal bull encouraging witchcraft persecution directly was the *Summis desiderantes affectibus* issued by Innocent VIII in 1484. It was composed at the specific request of Heinrich Kramer (Institoris), papal inquisitor for southern Germany, to help him overcome both ecclesiastical and secular resistance by supporting his enterprises with papal prestige. In one way, this bull was less significant than the standards of Eugenius IV on demonic witchcraft, because its instructions were merely regional rather than universal. Its use by Kramer in the introduction to his *Malleus Maleficarum* (The Hammer of Witches, 1486), giving his book a false appearance of papal approval, was at least as significant as the bull itself. At first glance, *Summis desiderantes affectibus* appears to be committed to a traditional, noncumulative concept of witchcraft. It never mentioned the notion of witches flying and placed no emphasis on women as the embodiment of witchcraft, which was so characteristic of the *Malleus Maleficarum*. Nevertheless, it contributed to the increase in witchcraft trials. Not only did it remind readers of the peculiar heinousness of the crime of witchcraft, justifying the Church's mission to hunt down and punish such offenders, but it also threatened to penalize anyone who resisted the Inquisition in this matter. For these reasons, the bull of Innocent VIII encouraged witch persecutions in the future. Opponents of the trials had to contend not only with the theological position of the *Malleus* but also with

papal promotion of inquisitorial trials against sorcerers and witches.

In the sixteenth century, inquisitorial witchcraft trials decreased drastically throughout northern Europe. The popes, however, were not silent on the problem of witchcraft. Julius II (ruled 1503–1513) encouraged stronger persecution of sorcerers in the diocese of Cremona, against the wishes of local clerics. Leo X (ruled 1513–1521) confronted the Republic of Venice, which sought to hinder papal inquisitors acting against witches and sorcerers. Adrian VI (ruled 1522–1523) confirmed a bull of Julius II regarding the inquisition of Lombardy. Some decrees of the Council of Trent dealt with witchcraft: the guidelines set out in the *Dominici gregis custodiae* (Guardians of the Lord's Flock, 1564) put all books on divination, sorcery, potions, prophesies, spells, and other magic practices on the Index (list of prohibited books).

During the great wave of frenzied witch hunting of the sixteenth and early seventeenth centuries, conducted mainly by Catholic prince-bishops in Germany, the papacy adopted moderate policies. Without ever directly questioning its demonological and judicial aspects, Rome displayed considerable skepticism about the cumulative, constantly intensifying concept of witchcraft. *Instructio pro formandis processibus in causis strigum, sortilegiorum et maleficiorum* (Instruction for Conducting Trial Procedures Against Witches, Sorcerers, and Evildoers) by Pope Urban VIII in 1635 prescribed the traditionally more cautious attitude of the Roman Inquisition for the German empire. Apparently written in reaction to the horrifying reports of massive witchcraft trials in Germany that had gradually reached Rome, it tried to prevent them by requiring proof of black magic before decreeing a death sentence and prescribed less severe punishments for harmless magic. However, Urban's distinctly moderate *Instruction* could not be enforced in many Catholic regions of Germany, where serious witch hunts continued for a long time with support from the local clergy. In regions to which Rome had direct access, relatively few prosecutions occurred.

Because of the legal and theological traditions of the Roman Catholic Church, certain elements of witchcraft theory endured into the nineteenth and twentieth centuries, although they had no practical significance. The *Corpus iuris canonici* remained valid until 1917, so that judicially speaking, the *impotentia ex maleficio* (weakness from harmful magic) delusion about witches flying was still an offense; sorcery, divination, and the like could still be considered heresies for which the Church could execute appropriate punishments. The scholastic concept of demonology was indirectly confirmed when Leo XIII declared Thomas Aquinas to be the normative theologian of Roman Catholicism, and the validity of earlier papal bulls became problematic after the promulgation of the dogma of infallibility of 1870. Such theoretical statements have had no practical consequences for many centuries, although occasional reports of severe exorcisms by Roman Catholic priests remain a phenomenon distantly related to the complex of the witch hunts.

JÖRG HAUSTEIN;

TRANSLATED BY HELEN SIEGBURG

See also: *CANON EPISCOPI;* GRATIAN; HERESY; INNOCENT VIII, POPE; INQUISITION, MEDIEVAL; INQUISITION, ROMAN; JOHN XXII, POPE; KRAMER, HEINRICH; LAWS ON WITCHCRAFT (MEDIEVAL); LYNCHINGS; *MALLEUS MALIFICARUM;* ORIGINS OF THE WITCH HUNTS; ROMAN CATHOLIC CHURCH; TEMPLARS; URBAN VIII, POPE.

References and further reading:
Behringer, Wolfgang. 1987. "'Vom Unkraut unter dem Weizen': Die Stellung der Kirchen zum Hexenproblem." Pp. 60–95 in *Hexenwelten: Magie, und Imagination vom 16.–20. Jahrhundert.* Edited by Richard van Dülmen. Frankfurt am Main: Fischer.
Clark, Stuart. 1997. *Thinking with Demons: The Idea of Witchcraft in Early Modern Europe.* Oxford: Clarendon.
Decker, Rainer. 2003. *Die Päpste und die Hexen: Aus den geheimen Akten der Inquisition.* Darmstadt: Wissenschaftliche Buchgesellschaft.
Diefenbach, Johann. 1886. *Der Hexenwahn vor und nach der Glaubensspaltung in Deutschland.* Mainz: Kirchheim.
Hansen, Joseph. 1900. *Zauberwahn, Inquisition und Hexenprozess im Mittelalter und die Entstehung der grossen Hexenverfolgung.* Munich: Oldenbourg.
———. 1901. *Quellen und Untersuchungen zur Geschichte des Hexenwahns und der Hexenverfolgung im Mittelalter.* Bonn: Georgi.
Kaufmann, Josef. 1903. "Die Stellung der Kirche zu den Hexenprozessen des 17. Jahrhunderts." Pp 59–69 in *Mitteilungen des Westpreussischen Geschichtsvereins* 2, no. 4.
Maier, Anneliese. 1952. "Eine Verfügung Johanns XXII. Über die Zuständigkeit der Inquisition für Zaubereiprozesse." Pp. 226–246 in *Archivum Fratrum Praedicatorum* 22.

PAPPENHEIMER FAMILY (1600)

Certainly the most famous clan of cesspool cleaners in early modern Europe, this wandering Swabian family became the principal target of a Bavarian crackdown on witches and other dangerous vagrants in 1600. They suffered punishments that were remarkably cruel even by contemporary standards.

There were several reasons for the exemplary sadism shown to this family of licensed beggars who also earned money as itinerant glaziers, tinkers, and cesspool cleaners. They and their chief "accomplices" were unusual witches: to begin with, most of them, including the ringleader, were men. The Pappenheimers were not Bavarians but foreigners; worse still, they were not members of a settled village community. After being arrested on charges that they had helped a convicted thief murder seven pregnant women in order to make "thieves' candles" from the fingers of unbaptized babies,

the Pappenheimers—father Paulus, mother Anna, two grown sons, and a ten-year-old boy—were taken to Munich by express order of Duke Maximilian and subjected to repeated bouts of relentless torture.

In an "indissoluble amalgam of falsehood and truth, which assembled rumors and reports from two decades" from various parts of Bavaria (Kunze 1987, 149, 154), the Pappenheimers ultimately became scapegoats for a variety of other crimes besides witchcraft. They admitted close to 100 murders, almost ten per year, although not a single corpse was ever found (they explained that they always burned them); they further confessed setting dozens of fires and committing several hundred thefts, many of them from churches. (They claimed they sold such sacrilegious goods to Jews, who were prohibited from living in Bavaria, however.) And of course, the Pappenheimers confessed to witchcraft. Before they were through, they had denounced almost 400 "accomplices," once naming 99 of them at a single torture session; following customary stereotype, 80 percent were women, and 10 percent of the women were midwives (Kunze 1987, 342f, 345).

The chief engineer of the Pappenheimer family's destruction was the ambitious leader of Bavaria's witchcraft "zealots," the chancellor of the court council, Dr. Johann Sigismund Wagnereckh (ca. 1570–1617), whose ideological commitment compensated for his modest standing within Bavarian society. Like Duke Maximilian, Wagnereckh had studied at Ingolstadt during the 1590 witch hunt. He not only directed the Pappenheimers's questioning under torture, but when a tailor arrived at court with a petition to free some of their imprisoned "accomplices," Wagnereckh immediately had him arrested and tortured, and he soon confessed to witchcraft also.

Because Duke Maximilian desired to show his government's teeth to Bavaria's "dangerous classes" by enforcing his drastic laws against them to the fullest, the executions in June 1600 of Paulus Pappenheimer, his wife and their two adult sons, together with two of their Bavarian "accomplices" (including the unfortunate tailor-petitioner), makes truly gruesome reading. At the place of execution, the body of each was torn six times with red-hot pincers, the mother had her breasts cut off, the five men had their arms and legs broken on the wheel, and finally Paulus became one of very few western European criminals to be impaled on a stake, like Vlad the Impaler's Moldavian victims. After these preliminaries, all six were burned alive. For sheer savagery, no other single episode of early modern Europe's theater of judicial terror ever quite matched it.

These brutalities were widely publicized. Woodcuts, printed broadsheets, and chronicles reported them. Bavarian Jesuits passed the news to their demonological colleague Martín Del Rio, who mentioned it in his next edition of his *Disquisitiones Magicae libri sex* (Six

Books on Investigations into Magic). "A chronicler of Freising included them in his world chronicle a few years later among the most important events of the century," while "as late as 1744 they were referred to in a book published at Leipzig" (Behringer 1997, 232). Although six more "conspirators," including the Pappenheimers's ten-year-old son, were burned at another spectacle at Munich in December 1600, the Pappenheimers's fate did not begin any Bavarian witch hunt: as soon as some of the arrested "accomplices" came from respectable Bavarian families, their relatives protested and the whole investigation was quietly dropped.

WILLIAM MONTER

See also: BAVARIA, DUCHY OF; DEL RIO, MARTÍN; EXECUTIONS; GERMANY, SOUTHEASTERN; MAXIMILIAN I, DUKE OF BAVARIA; TORTURE.

References and further reading:

Behringer, Wolfgang. 1997. *Witchcraft Persecutions in Bavaria: Popular Magic, Religious Zealotry and Reason of State in Early Modern Europe.* Translated by J. C. Grayson and David Lederer. Cambridge: Cambridge University Press.

Kunze, Michael. 1981. *Der Prozess Pappenheimer.* Ebelsburg: n.p. (law dissertation, Univ. of Munich).

———. 1987. *Highroad to the Stake: A Tale of Witchcraft.* Chicago: University of Chicago Press.

PARACELSUS, THEOPHRASTUS BOMBASTUS VON HOHENHEIM (CA. 1493–1541)

Paracelsus was a prophet, philosopher, alchemist, and Renaissance magician.

The fascination of the Swiss Paracelsus stems both from what is known and from what remains unknown about his bizarre and nomadic life as an eccentric and rebellious physician. At times he was considered an impostor, at other times a prodigious healer of fatal diseases who was accused of practicing diabolical arts. His works combined high culture and popular traditions, wide-ranging scientific interests, and an unusual reliance on everyday experiences and myths. Throughout his life, he refused to pursue a normal, professional career, attacked the university teaching of his day, and attempted to revolutionize both the medical and natural sciences by promoting the virtues of alchemy within the context of an original philosophical interpretation of the universe and of illness. Paracelsus challenged the Aristotelian and classical paradigm by introducing new principles of knowledge, which he adopted from the Hermetic tradition and from popular health care. He believed in witchcraft, demons, and evil spells; in the witches' Sabbat; and in their ability to take animal shape. Nevertheless, the originality of his ideas led him to reject the practice of burning witches at the stake, which he deemed an inadequate response to a phenomenon that was, after all, "natural."

LIFE AND WORKS

Theophrastus von Hohenheim, also known by his grandfather's name as Bombast, but only later as Paracelsus (which perhaps meant "beyond Celsus," one of the most renowned naturalists of antiquity), was born about 1493 in Einsiedeln in central Switzerland. His father, Wilhelm Bombast de Riett, was a physician and the illegitimate son of a Swabian aristocrat. When the family moved to Villach in Carinthia, Theophrastus first came into contact with the world of the mines. He also started taking lessons with religious teachers, one of whom may have been Johannes Trithemius, who was suspected of having practiced black magic. From 1507 to 1511, Paracelsus attended lectures at several European universities but soon became bored listening to the commentaries of distinguished professors. He therefore chose to travel Europe, perhaps as an army surgeon following military troops. Around 1520, he wrote his first work, the *Eleven Treatises on the origins, causes, symptoms, and treatment of the diseases,* and in 1524 he moved to Salzburg. He was sympathetic toward the peasant revolts and soon obtained some fame for his prophecies. Despite his interest in theology, ethics, and politics, he never joined any organized religious group. In 1526, the city of Strasbourg offered him citizenship, and he began practicing medicine, meanwhile dedicating himself to writing a vast work on medicine, which he never completed, and several treatises, including the *Libri Archidoxis* (Archidoxes of Magic: Of the Supreme Mysteries of Nature, of the Spirits of Planets, Secrets of Alchemy, Occult Philosophy, Zodiac Signs).

During the following year, Paracelsus moved to Basel, where he cured the publisher Johann Froben and the humanist scholar Erasmus. Yet this brief period of fortune did not last. Paracelsus started a career as a public teacher but soon made enemies at the local university because of his incessant attacks against mainstream medicine. Consequently, he was reduced once again to living almost as a traveling pauper, which did not, however, prevent him from acting as a prophet and from writing numerous texts, which mostly remained in manuscript form until after his death. They include a work on syphilis, the *Paragranum* (an outline of his theories garnished with some severe attacks on mainstream medicine) and the *De divinis operibus et secretis naturae* (On Divine Works and the Secrets of Nature), a collection of treatises written after 1529 and printed between 1589 and 1590, which probably was to become the first volume of his unfinished *Philosophia Magna* (Great Philosophy). Paracelsus completed his *Paramirum* during a stay in the Swiss City of St. Gallen, in 1531–1532, where he was a guest of the humanist and mayor Joachim Vadian. Subsequently, Paracelsus

Eminent Renaissance magician, physician, alchemist, Hermeticist, and philosopher Paracelsus (Theophrastus Bombastus von Hohenheim) believed in witchcraft but disapproved of executing witches. (Archivo Iconografico, S.A./Corbis)

grouping him with other philosophers and naturalists such as Pietro Pomponazzi and Marsilio Ficino.

The final years of the sixteenth century saw the beginnings of Paracelsus's fame, largely thanks to the writings of Petrus Severinus (*Idea Medicinae Philisophicae,* 1571) and Oswald Croll (*Basilica Chymica,* 1609) and to the publication of his works. There was a fashion for *spagyric* medicine, a form opposed to official Galenic practices that followed Paracelsus's example in allowing the treatment of syphilitic patients with chemical compounds (the term is derived from two Greek words referring to the extraction and elaboration of metals). Paracelsus was particularly respected in England (Francis Bacon was among his admirers), as well as elsewhere in Europe, where his fame grew, despite disapproval and censorship, thanks to the Rosicrucian sect. Daniel Sennert, a professor at Wittenberg, wrote a work in 1619 in which he hoped to reconcile the Galenic tradition and Paracelsus's chemistry. Joan (Jan, Jean) Baptista van Helmont (1579–1644), known for his revolutionary discoveries in the field of illnesses, adopted some important concepts from Paracelsus. Johann Wolfgang von Goethe gave Paracelsus and his assistant Oporinus immortal fame when he chose them as models for his Faust and for Wagner. Paracelsus's twentieth-century admirers included the psychoanalyst Carl Jung and Marguerite Yourcenar, who chose some of his features for the protagonist Zénon of her *L'Oeuvre au noir* (The Abyss, 1968). The poets Robert Browning and Ezra Pound also dedicated works to Paracelsus.

THE INTERPRETATION OF NATURE AND OF WITCHCRAFT

Classical Western medicine, inspired by Hippocrates, Galen, and the Arabs and operating within the framework of Aristotelian natural philosophy, assumed that illnesses resulted from an imbalance of the bodily fluids (blood, yellow bile, black bile, phlegm) and of the fundamental physical qualities (hot, cold, dry, and humid). Paracelsus, on the contrary, stated that the universe was a web of relations linking human beings, nature, and the stars (which did not influence behavior on earth). In order to cure the sick, he argued, it was necessary to observe the sky, live virtuously, know alchemy, and understand the secrets of plants and minerals, which were revealed in their *signatura* (signs). The appearance of a particular herb, for instance, indicated its use for medical treatment. All of life, according to Paracelsus, stemmed from the union of three essential metals (sulfur, salt, and mercury), which, through their combustion and corruption or by being in disharmony with one another, determined the course of an illness. Medical treatment required wisdom, close observation, and the application of similar substances (a principle rejected by traditional medicine, like his use of chemical compounds). Other

dedicated himself mostly to social questions and to caring for the poor. Moving between Austria, Switzerland, Tyrol, and Germany, he wrote various works on politics, theology, surgery, astronomy, professional diseases, and thermal cures. In 1537, he was received at the imperial court, where, despite his fame, he failed to obtain favor. Returning to Villach, he wrote the *Trilogy of Carinthia,* his first violent diatribe against Galen's disciples. Poor, ill, and unable to publish his writings, Paracelsus died in Salzburg in 1541.

FORTUNE

The first person to write about Paracelsus was his disciple and assistant Johannes Oporinus (1507–1568), who became a publisher in Basel and printed several of his master's manuscripts. Oporinus described Paracelsus as both sophisticated and vulgar, ingenious and coarse, attracted by the pleasures of wine but not by those of the flesh. The first to condemn him was Thomas Erastus (in 1572), a theologian and physician, who was profoundly convinced of the existence and power of witches. In a severe attack on Paracelsus's works, Erastus defined him as a follower of Satan, factors also influenced diseases: the power of imagination, God, demons, and human intentions, which could take the form of evil spells or witchcraft.

Paracelsus did not reject popular medicine, nor did he attribute madness, physical deformity, mental illness, and fatal diseases to such remote causes. In a world he believed to be populated by spirits, half-human figures, dwarfs, and nymphs (some of them benign and even friendly toward human beings), there was also space for witchcraft, which he treated in the short treatise *De sagis et eorum operibus* (On Witches and Their Works, a text that formed part of *De divinis operibus*). Without referring to the pact with the Devil, he argued that witches were born as such because of a certain predisposition and because of their astral "ascendant." Just like devils, they performed their harmful deeds with the help of the secret forces of nature. Only the virtuous could resist the Devil, whereas witches (whom he described stereotypically) usually followed their instructions, thus causing storms, illnesses, and sexual mishaps. Devils and witches (who could fly and also take different shapes with the help of ointments) held their meetings on top of the remote Heuberg (in the Swabian Alps), where they fornicated, reproduced, held their rites, and prepared evil deeds.

They could, however, be fought by physicians through the use of opposite magical practices, which Paracelsus considered legitimate. He disapproved of witchcraft, devils, and their spells and considered them worthy of punishment, but he was also opposed to burning witches on the stake, arguing that they should be educated and taken care of instead. Later in the sixteenth century, Johann Weyer argued this position far more convincingly. Ever since Erastus, many scholars have asserted that, by combining popular traditions with a strong opposition to the dominant culture, Paracelsus helped to naturalize black magic. Although this statement is not untrue, it must also be said that, by abandoning official explanations of illness, he helped to shape an attitude common among physicians at the end of the sixteenth century (precisely when Paracelsus's works began to reach a wider audience): they rejected Galenism, feared the Devil, and explained certain fatal diseases through their belief in witchcraft.

VINCENZO LAVENIA

See also: ALCHEMY; COUNTERMAGIC; ERASTUS, THOMAS; FAUST, JOHANN GEORG; HERMETICISM; MAGIC, LEARNED; MAGIC, NATURAL; MEDICINE AND MEDICAL THEORY; SCIENCE AND MAGIC; TRITHEMIUS, JOHANNES; WEYER, JOHANN.

References and further reading:

Debus, Allen G. 1977. *The Chemical Philosophy: Paracelsian Science and Medicine in the Sixteenth and Seventeenth Centuries.* 2 vols. New York: Science History Publications.

Grell, Ole P., ed. 1998. *Paracelsus: The Man and His Reputation, His Ideas and Their Transformation.* Leiden: Brill.

Pagel, Walter. 1982. *Paracelsus: An Introduction to Philosophical Medicine in the Era of the Renaissance.* 2nd ed. Basel: Karger.

Sudhoff, Karl, and Wilhelm Matthiesen, eds. 1996. *Theophrast von Hohenheim Paracelsus: Medizinische, naturwissenschaftliche und philosophische Schriften.* Bd. 1–14, facs. ed. 1922–1933. New York and Zurich: Hildesheim.

Webster, Charles. 1982. *From Paracelsus to Newton: Magic and the Making of Modern Science.* Cambridge: Cambridge University Press.

PARIS, UNIVERSITY OF

The University of Paris, a main center of scholastic theology and philosophy during the Middle Ages, took a leading role in condemning the practice of magic. In September 1398, the theology faculty of the university, meeting in the Church of St. Mathurin, approved a set of twenty-eight articles declaring the practice of ritual magic to be heretical. In 1402, Jean Gerson the theologian, political theorist, and devotional writer who was chancellor of the university at the time, included the document in a somewhat altered form in his treatise against magic, *De erroribus circa artem magicam* (Concerning Misconceptions about Magical Arts). The articles were later used to condemn the practice of witchcraft.

The faculty took this action in response to what the document referred to as "newly arisen superstitions." The practice of ritual magic—the summoning up of demons in order to put them at the service of human beings—had flourished during the thirteenth and fourteenth centuries, especially at the universities and at the courts of European rulers. In the thirteenth century, William of Auvergne claimed that he had seen magical books when he was a student at the University of Paris, and in 1277 the archbishop of Paris had condemned "books, rolls, or booklets containing necromancy or experiments of sorcery, invocation of demons, or conjurations hazardous for souls" (Kieckhefer 1990, 157). Magicians defended their rituals on the grounds that they were commanding demons, and they insisted that they were not violating Catholic doctrine. In making this pronouncement, the faculty intended to "assure that this monstrosity of horrid impiety and dangerous contagion will not be able to infect the Christian realm, which formerly has been free from such monstrosities" (Weyer 1991, 577).

Citing St. Augustine's condemnation of superstitious observances, the faculty attacked "this wicked, pestilential, death-dealing abomination of mad errors, along with all the attendant heresies" (Weyer 1991, 577). The theologians declared that the claims made by ritual magicians to justify their practices were erroneous and in some cases blasphemous. The second article, for example, declared it to be idolatrous to give or offer demons anything in their honor. The third article declared it to be idolatry and apostasy to make an implicit or explicit pact with demons. By "implicit pact" the theologians meant every "superstitious ritual, the effects of which cannot be reasonably traced to either God or nature" (Levack 2004, 48). Other articles condemned offering incense and smoke and making sacrifices and immolations to demons. Yet another denied that images made of bronze, lead, or gold, of white or red wax, or of other material, when baptized, exorcized, and consecrated, had tremendous powers on those days of the year identified in magical books. The twenty-third article condemned the claim that some demons are good, that others are omniscient, and that still others are neither saved nor damned.

The Paris faculty made its pronouncement just before the first trials for witchcraft took place at the *Parlement* of Paris (sovereign judicial court, with jurisdiction over approximately one-half of France). The articles did not say anything about witchcraft as it came to be defined during those trials. The faculty was concerned about theological justifications of ritual magic, not the practices of the women and men who allegedly used magic to bring widespread harm to their neighbors and who also worshipped the Devil in nocturnal orgies. Nevertheless, the Paris faculty's condemnation of magic as heretical and idolatrous provided authoritative support for later condemnations of witchcraft, especially since it included references to *maleficia* (harmful magic) as well as pacts with the Devil. The *Malleus Maleficarum* (The Hammer of Witches, 1486) made numerous references to it. In the sixteenth century the condemnation was reprinted in the preface to Jean Bodin's *De la démonomanie des sorciers* (On the Demon-Mania of Witches, 1580), and quotations from it appeared in Lambert Daneau's *Les sorciers, dialogue tres-utile et necessaire pour ce temps* (Witches, a Very Useful Dialogue and One Necessary for the Present Time, 1574) and Martín Del Rio's *Disquisitiones Magicae libri sex* (Six Books on Investigations into Magic, 1599/1600). Johann Weyer, the sixteenth-century skeptic regarding witchcraft, also devoted the final chapter of his massive *De Praestigiis daemonum* (On the Tricks of Devils, 1563) to this document. It provided support for Weyer's own condemnation of ritual magic.

BRIAN P. LEVACK

See also: DEMONS; GERSON, JEAN; IDOLATRY; IMAGE MAGIC; RITUAL MAGIC; SUPERSTITION.

References and further reading:
Bodin, Jean. 1580. *De la démonomanie des sorciers.* Paris.
Gerson, Jean. 1973. *Oeuvres complètes.* Vol. 10. Paris.
Kieckhefer, Richard. 1990. *Magic in the Middle Age.* Cambridge: Cambridge University Press.
Levack, Brian P., ed. 2004. *The Witchcraft Sourcebook.* London and New York: Routledge.
Peters, Edward. 1978. *The Magician, the Witch, and the Law.* Philadelphia: University of Pennsylvania Press.
Weyer, Johann. 1991. *Witches, Devils, and Doctors in the Renaissance: Johann Weyer,* De Praestigiis daemonum. Edited by George Mora. Binghamton, NY: Medieval and Renaissance Text and Studies.

PARLEMENT OF PARIS

The *Parlement* (sovereign court) of Paris, the most prestigious court in France, had an enormous influence on witchcraft trials in the kingdom. Its authority in criminal cases stretched over nearly half the country. Although the records of the appeal hearings before it are rather brief, they do extend over virtually the entire period of serious witchcraft persecution, enabling historians to draw important conclusions about both the court's own practices and events across a wide region.

The statistics reveal a sharp increase in trials from the 1570s to a plateau that lasted until the 1620s; they also indicate that the *parlement* released many suspects and commuted the majority of death sentences, even though the lesser courts were relatively lenient. The Parisian judges were very concerned about procedural irregularities, eventually moving to enforce an automatic appeal in all witchcraft cases. From around the time this right was fully effective (1624), the court had virtually abandoned death sentences for witchcraft, setting a pattern that several other *parlements* followed, before the royal government ultimately put a stop to all trials across France.

The Paris *parlement* was an elaborate organization, with overlapping political, judicial, and financial roles and a complex internal hierarchy. By the early seventeenth century, it held over 200 judges who had inherited or purchased their positions; they formed a *Grand' Chambre,* five chambers of *Enquêtes,* and two of *Requêtes.* The *premier président* (presiding magistrate) was an enormously influential figure in national politics, so this appointment was closely guarded by the crown, and a *procureur-général* (public prosecutor) and two *avocats-généraux* (deputy prosecutors) were also charged with representing the royal interest and were known as *les gens du roi* (the king's men). The major business of the *parlement* was that of supervising legislation and managing the application of property law, with criminal jurisdiction as a relatively secondary function. The hearing of criminal appeals was delegated to a special chamber called the *Tournelle,* staffed on a rotating basis by councilors from the other chambers. The *ressort* (jurisdiction) of the *parlement* covered a huge area, stretching from Poitou and the Auvergne to Champagne and Picardy, or close to half of France, and all those convicted of serious crimes in lesser courts within this area were entitled to appeal for a final hearing in Paris. Before Jean-Baptiste Colbert sponsored a new criminal code in 1670, the rules were essentially those specified in the 1539 Ordinance of Villers-Cotterets, which defined the use of the so-called inquisitorial procedure. Under this system, preliminary hearings gathered evidence from witnesses and through an interrogation of the suspect; if specified standards of proof for an immediate conviction were not met, a court might still decide there were sufficient grounds to subject the accused to torture. When the *Tournelle* heard cases on appeal, the defendant appeared in person, accompanied by papers from his original trial, which were passed to a councilor who acted as *rapporteur*, summarizing the case and making a recommendation to his colleagues, who often also interrogated the accused.

This system meant that appeals were often a costly business, requiring the accused to be brought to the *Conciergerie* in the Parisian *palais de justice* (the seat of the *parlement*) under guard and then held there until the case was decided. Nevertheless, the *parlement* was eager to assert its authority in this fashion, especially when it suspected that the lesser courts had committed procedural abuses. The Parisian judges had a very keen sense of their own status and the prestige of their institution; furthermore, they saw themselves as embodying the higher rationality of the educated elite. They also had a distinctive position where religious values and secular ones overlapped. The court remained strongly Catholic during the Wars of Religion and then split in two between 1589 and 1594, with some councilors remaining in Paris under the Holy (Catholic) League, while the majority formed a royalist *parlement* at Tours. Despite such differences of opinion, the great majority of councilors seem to have favored a moderate Gallican position, hostile to encroachments by either the papacy or the institutional French Church.

The councilors' suspicions of ecclesiastical interference on all fronts almost certainly predisposed them toward a pragmatic rationalist position on issues such as witchcraft. It is unclear whether this was already true in 1491, when the *parlement* struck an early blow against local abuses by posthumously rehabilitating the accused from the sensational affair of the *Vauderie* of Arras thirty years before. This involved a curious jurisdictional anomaly, because Arras—which belonged to the duke of Burgundy, not the king of France—was subject to the Parisian appellate system (Cohn 1975, 230–232). Very early in the major period of persecution, in 1587–1588, the revelation of numerous abuses in trials from the Ardennes led the *gens du roi* to propose that all witchcraft cases should automatically be appealed before the *parlement*. The political crisis of the following years prevented an immediate decision in this sense, but between 1600 and 1604, a new series of abuses led to the formal adoption of this position. Finally, in 1624, the court took effective steps to implement its decision by circulating a printed text to all lower courts, on the eve of its less public move to abandon death sentences for witchcraft (Soman 1992, VII and XII).

The painstaking research by Alfred Soman revealed that the *parlement* heard a minimum of 1,288 appeals from convicted witches between 1540 and 1670; if cases of magicians are included, the number rises to 1,481 (Soman 1992, XIII, 42). Just over 40 percent of the witchcraft suspects had been condemned to death in the lower courts, but the *parlement* confirmed only one-quarter of these sentences, so that just above 100 individuals went to the stake, barely 10 percent of appellants. Two-thirds ended up either banished or released, in roughly equal proportions. These proportions did not change dramatically over the period; the two statistical features that stand out are an increase to 20 percent executed in the 1590s and then a downward trend after 1610. Just over half the appellants were men, in proportions varying from roughly two-thirds in the western part of the *ressort* to one-third toward the eastern border, and there is little evidence of gender bias in the sentences handed out. Most remarkably, of 185 suspects sent to the torture chamber, only one actually confessed, a woman who was merely shown the instruments of torture in 1587. Although statistical precision is impossible because the surviving documents are so laconic about details of cases, the local cunning folk (*devins* and *devineresses*) appear to have been prominent among the accused. The *parlement* clearly took a cautious view of witchcraft charges from the very start, which quite rapidly developed into more extensive skepticism. There was some continuity with attitudes toward other crimes, because the court was inclined to moderate sentences generally, but one should note that in another great persecution that began in the late sixteenth century, some 70 percent of death sentences for infanticide were confirmed (Soman 1992, passim). Witchcraft charges seem to have caused special disquiet for two key reasons: the high level of local abuses apparent from the very start, and the legal difficulties of proof when direct evidence from eyewitnesses was virtually ruled out by the very nature of the alleged crime. The *Tournelle* evidently feared that such charges could become a convenient method for settling scores between peasants whom they saw as both superstitious and mendacious.

The repeated evidence that local judges broke the rules, denied the accused their rights, and even resorted to the wholly illegal swimming test could only increase misgivings in the *parlement*. A series of reprimands were handed down whenever such misbehavior was detected; judges might be called to Paris to explain themselves, or special restrictions were placed on the rights of individual courts to hear certain types of cases. A marked drop in the number of witchcraft appeals after the late 1620s suggests that awareness of this watchfulness from the *parlement* had a major effect on the subordinate courts. This must have been reinforced in 1641, when the *lieutenant de justice* and two other officials of the court at Bragelonne were convicted of murdering a suspected witch and were hanged in the *place de Grève* in Paris; news of this drastic punishment was publicized throughout the whole *ressort*. In a further case from eastern France, the *seigneur* (lord; rural estate owner), *procureur fiscal* (fiscal representative or attorney), and another individual from Viviers-sur-Artaut were hanged in effigy in 1647, having fled after a suspect was lynched (Mandrou 1969, 354–356; Soman 1992, XII, 197). By this time, few observers could doubt either the skepticism of the *parlement* or its determination to enforce its authority. In a fascinating conversation from 1643, the *curé* (chief parish priest) of Nanterre recorded asking his friend, the councilor Laisné, why the court no longer convicted witches; he was told that it was very difficult to secure adequate proof, so they convicted them solely for any proven harm they had done or for open sacrilege (Mandrou 1969, 360–361). This policy was still applied in the last major series of cases heard by the *parlement* in 1687–1691, involving nine shepherds from the Brie region accused of poisoning animals and of sacrilege; four were sent to the galleys, three banished, and two sentenced to death (Mandrou 1969, 500–507). Such relative severity, in an exceptional set of circumstances, should not be allowed to obscure the notable success of the *parlement* in securing the rule of law and damping down any threat of mass persecution under its jurisdiction.

ROBIN BRIGGS

See also: APPEALS; ARDENNES; ARRAS; CUNNING FOLK; DECLINE OF THE WITCH HUNTS; FRANCE; INFANTICIDE; INQUISITORIAL PROCEDURE; LYNCHING; MANDROU, ROBERT; PROOF, PROBLEM OF; SKEPTICISM; SWIMMING TEST; WARS OF RELIGION (FRANCE).

References and further reading:

Cohn, Norman. 1975. *Europe's Inner Demons.* London: Chatto Heinemann.

Mandrou, Robert. 1969. *Magistrats et sorciers en France au XVIIe siècle: Une analyse de psychologie historique.* Paris: Plon.

Pearl, Jonathan L. 1999. *The Crime of Crimes: Demonology and Politics in France, 1560–1620.* Waterloo, Ontario: Wilfred Laurier University Press.

Shennan, John H. 1969. *The Parlement of Paris.* London: Eyre and Spottiswoode.

Soman, Alfred. 1992. *Sorcellerie et Justice Criminelle: Le Parlement de Paris (16e–18e siècles).* Basingstoke, UK: Ashgate Publishing. (Includes some articles in English.)

PAULUS, NIKOLAUS (1853–1930)

A Catholic priest from the Alsatian village of Krautergersheim, Paulus managed to produce innovative pieces about the role of women in witchcraft persecutions despite a lack of formal academic training, publishing one of the first essays to explore the gender issue seriously. Inspired by the Catholic historian Johannes Janssen (1829–1891), Paulus spent years in Munich libraries and archives studying sixteenth-century confessional theology. Driven by the Catholic minority position in the German *Kulturkampf,* or culture wars, under the Prussian-dominated German Second Empire, all of Paulus's essays were utterly biased.

Paulus's other writings treat such topics as witchcraft trials in Rome or the participation of Lutheran authorities in witch hunts. Most of his pieces were republished at Munich in 1910 in a collection entitled *Hexenwahn und Hexenprozess vornehmlich im 16. Jahrhundert* (Witch Craze and Witch Trials, Especially in the Sixteenth Century).

WOLFGANG BEHRINGER

See also: GENDER; HISTORIOGRAPHY.

References and further reading:

Behringer, Wolfgang. 1994. "Zur Geschichte der Hexenforschung." Pp. 93–146 in *Hexen und Hexenverfolgung im deutschen Südwesten.* Edited by Sönke Lorenz. Ostfildern: Cantz.

PEDERSDOTTER, ANNA (1590)

The trial of Anna Pedersdotter, widow of the Lutheran theologian Absalon Pedersen Beyer, is the most famous prosecution in the history of Norwegian witchcraft. The charges against Anna arose out of the opposition that had developed in the town of Bergen to the efforts by her husband and other clergymen to destroy Roman Catholic images. Instead of charging the clergy, who often had influential patrons, their opponents accused their wives. In 1575, a year after Absalon's death, charges of witchcraft were brought against Anna in a secular court at Bergen, but she was acquitted.

In 1590, however, Anna was charged once again with witchcraft. The family of the woman engaged to Anna's son objected that, although Anna had been acquitted, her neighbors still suspected her. The case against Anna was therefore reopened. The main charges brought against her were for practicing maleficent magic. Anna was accused of inflicting illnesses on various persons who had crossed her, including the wife of a cabinet-maker whom she had falsely accused of witchcraft. The husband of a woman who had contracted a fatal illness claimed that Anna had bewitched her when she picked up a coin that Anna had dropped at her feet. Anna was also charged with causing the death of a young boy by giving him a bewitched cookie. As the trial developed, however, Anna was also charged with devil worship. Her servant, Elena, testified that Anna had turned her into a horse and had ridden her to the Sabbat at a mountain called Lyderhorn. At this location, a famous meeting place of witches in Norwegian folklore, a group of witches allegedly plotted to raise a storm to destroy all ships arriving at Bergen. At subsequent meetings, it was charged, they plotted to burn the town or cause it to be flooded. A man in white, who claimed that God would not allow it, dispersed this assembly of witches.

The charges of diabolism introduced at Anna's second trial seem relatively bland compared to those that emerged in many German, French, and Swiss trials. The Sabbat Anna allegedly attended involved no promiscuous sexual activity, infanticide, cannibalism, or blasphemous misuse of the Eucharist. Nor was Anna tortured to make a confession, as happened in a few other Norwegian witchcraft trials. Anna's conviction was based mainly on charges of maleficent magic, not devil worship. Even the confessions of two previously executed witches, who had claimed that they had seen Anna at the Lyderhorn, said more about her magical powers than her activities at the Sabbat. The court was also persuaded that a storm that had arisen when Anna was supposedly at the Lyderhorn was caused by her magical powers.

The case of Anna Pedersdotter owes its modern-day fame to a play by the Norwegian author Hans Wiers-Jenssen, an English translation of that play, *Anne Pedersdotter*, by John Masefield (1917), and a Danish film, *Day of Wrath*, directed by Carl Theodore Dreyer (1943). The play and the film took numerous artistic liberties with the historical record but nonetheless addressed two important themes in the history of witchcraft. First, they explored the ways in which tensions within families, in particular, relations between mothers and daughters-in-law, could result in witchcraft accusations. In the play and the film, Absalon's mother, Merete Beyer, had never approved of her son's second marriage to the young and beautiful Anna. When Anna fell in love with Martin, Absalon's son by his first marriage, the relationship between Anna and Merete deteriorated. When Absalon died suddenly upon discovering that his wife and son were having an affair, Merete charged Anna with having caused Absalon's death by witchcraft. Second, the play and film also explored the way in which Anna gradually came to the realization that she was a witch. Having learned from her husband that her own mother had been accused of witchcraft and spared by Absalon's intervention, she began to believe that she had acquired her mother's powers. Her success in winning Martin's affection and in wishing her husband's death reinforced this realization, leading her to confess at the end of the play.

BRIAN P. LEVACK

See also: BEWITCHMENT; CONFESSIONS; FAMILY; FILM (CINEMA); NORWAY; PROTESTANT REFORMATION; SABBAT; WEATHER MAGIC.

References and further reading:
Bainton, Roland. 1977. *Women of the Reformation: From Spain to Scandinavia*. Minneapolis: University of Minnesota Press.
Day of Wrath. 1943. Directed by Carl Theodore Dreyer. Hen's Tooth Video.
Wiers-Jenssen, Hans. 1917. *Anne Pedersdotter: A Drama in Four Acts*. Translated by John Masefield. Boston: Little, Brown.

PEÑA, FRANCISCO (CA. 1540–1612)

Peña is known for editing in 1578 a revised and updated edition of Nicolas Eymeric's authoritative *Directorium inquisitorum* (Directory of Inquisitors, 1376), which became the first in a series of annotated transcriptions of treatises on inquisitorial procedure.

Born in Villaroya de los Pinares, in the Aragonese province of Teruel, Spain, Peña studied at the University of Valencia, earning a master of arts degree. Peña probably left Valencia for Rome during the pontificate of Pius V, armed with an official recommendation from King Philip II to the papal court. He pursued his studies at the University of Bologna, earning his doctoral degree in 1573. Afterward, Peña continued his theological and juridical studies. In 1581 he edited Ambrogio Vignate's *Tractatus de haeresi* (Treatise on Heresies), along with *Allegatio in materia di haeresi* (Allegations in Matters Concerning Heresies) by Juan Lopez de Vivero. In 1584 followed, among other publications, an edition of Bernardo of Como's *Lucerna inquisitorum haereticae pravitatis* (A Lantern for Inquisitors of Heretical Depravity). Peña's own treatise, *Introdutio seu praxis inquisitorum* (Introduction, Or the Practice of the Inquisitors), was not printed until 1655, when it first appeared in Cesare Carena's *Tractatus de officio sanctissimae inquisitionis* (Treatise of the Holy Inquisition).

From the time Sixtus V appointed him auditor of the papal Rota in 1588 (he became its dean in 1604) until his death, Peña worked in Rome as a judge, also becoming a patron for young men commencing their careers at the papal court. During this period, Peña served both as a consultant to the Spanish embassy in Rome and as a papal adviser on Spanish affairs.

Despite his noteworthy diplomatic service for the Spanish crown in Rome, Peña's modern fame rests largely on his edition of the *Directorium inquisitorum*. The exact circumstances surrounding the decision ordering Peña to revise this fourteenth-century inquisitorial guide are unclear. Papal sponsorship was probably part of a general need to revise and update antiquated ecclesiastical texts and decrees for use by the Congregation of the Holy Office. Gregory XIII approved the revised edition, and other papally sponsored texts of this period also confirm this assumption. Peña worked on Eymeric's *Directorium* for several years, and his commentaries constantly pointed out textual variations among the different manuscripts. Peña's edition of the *Directorium* was a one-volume text divided into three parts. The first short part included 26 lengthy commentaries by Peña, and its larger second part contained 83 commentaries. Its final section, the actual handbook of inquisitorial procedure, contained 131 questions from Eymeric and 180 commentaries from Peña. The work was completed by a selection of papal decrees collected by Peña, a summary, and an index of topics. Peña took a particular interest in the subject of witchcraft and referred to much of the orthodox literature from previous centuries, especially the *Malleus Maleficarum* (The Hammer of Witches, 1486).

LOUISE NYHOLM KALLESTRUP

See also: EYMERIC, NICOLAS; INQUISITORIAL PROCEDURE; *MALLEUS MALEFICARUM;* RATEGNO, BERNARDO OF COMO.

References and further reading:
Borromeo, Agostino. 1983–1984. "A proposito del *Directorium inquisitorum* di Nicolàs Eymeric." *Critica Storica* 4: 499–548.
Buchberger, Michael, and Walter Kasper, eds. 1995–. *Lexikon für Theologie und Kirche* 8: 17. Freiburg.
Del Col, Andrea, and Giovanna Paolin, eds. 2000. *L'Inquisizione romana: Metologia delle fonti estoria istitutionale.* Trieste: Università di Trieste.
Martin, Ruth. 1989. *Witchcraft and the Inquisition in Venice, 1550–1650.* Oxford: Blackwell.
Pastor, Ludwig von. 1925. *Geschichte der Päpste seit dem Ausgang des Mittelalters.* Vol. 9. Freiburg im Breisgau: Herder-Druck.
Peters, Edward. 1975. "Editing Inquisitors' Manuals in the Sixteenth Century: Francisco Peña and the *Directorium Inquisitorum* of Nicholas Eymeric." *The Library Chronicle* 40: 95–107.
Van Der Vekene, Emil. 1973. "Die gedruckten Ausgaben des 'Directorium inquisitorum' des Nicolaus Eymerich." *Gutenberg-Jahrbuch 1973* 12: 286–298.

PEOPLE OF THE NIGHT (*NACHTVOLK*)

When Carlo Ginzburg first presented his famous *Benandanti* (do-gooders) in 1966, many scholars initially suspected that it somehow proved the existence of a sect of witches. These charismatic individuals from early modern Friuli experienced ecstasies and worked as healers and witch finders. They supposedly fought imaginary air battles against witches to defend the crop harvest and decide the fate of their communities (Ginzburg 1983). Shamanistically gifted individuals have also been discovered in many corners of Europe. In field studies on Dalmatian islands in the early 1950s, *Krsniki* were still considered opponents of witches and were feared and sought for their divinatory powers (Boskovic-Stulli 1960).

Starting from the Hungarian *Táltos* (shaman), Gábor Klaniczay collected similar ideas throughout eastern Europe, from the Friuli over the Balkans down to the Black Sea, demonstrating that Ginzburg's seemingly bizarre findings formed part of a much wider puzzle (Klaniczay 1990), thereby making possible a new access to the world of European fairy tales, where archaic folklore meets literature. The nocturnal ride with Diana, the journey to Venus's mountain, the game of the good society (*ludus bonae societatis*), strange goddesses, and contact with the deceased, together with gaining prophetic or healing powers, are present in early modern sources as well as non-European cultures (Ginzburg 1991).

The traditional theological device for interpreting such phantoms was the famous *Canon Episcopi* (ca. 906). This key text influenced later notions, although it remains unclear whether learned references or personal experiences were added to texts such as the instruction by the Dominican Bernard Gui, in the chapter on sorcery of his handbook for inquisitors, to ask women whether they believed they flew with the fairies on certain nights (Hansen 1901, 48). Many traces of popular beliefs exist in trial records of inquisitors or secular courts, including two Inquisition trials from Milan in 1384 and 1390 in which women confessed nocturnal flights with a "Good Lady" as their own real experiences (Muraro 1976). Nicholas of Cusa (1401–1464), philosopher and bishop of Brixen, discovered beliefs in a *domina Richella* in remote Alpine valleys, noting in sermons of 1457 that she was called *Holda* in German (*Nicolai Cusae Cardinalis Opera*, 2 [Paris 1514], fol. 170v–172r). A Danish folklorist found traces of a fairy cult recorded in sixteenth- and seventeenth-century trial records from Sicily by the Spanish Inquisition (Henningsen 1990). Although there is room for argument, such images open the gates to Europe's *Dreamtime*, a sphere, according to Australian Aborigines, where the boundaries between myths and reality or past and present become fluid (Duerr 1985). Numerous motifs of fairy tales, as classified in Antti Aarne and Stith Thompson's "Motif-Index of Folk Literature," appeared in trial records as experienced "facts." Vladimir Propp (1968) concluded that the roots of fairy tales were connected with layers of human consciousness, where linear perceptions of time and Euclidean space became meaningless.

Chonrad Stoeckhlin, a shaman-type diviner in the northern Alpine valley of Oberstdorf, who involuntarily triggered a large-scale witch hunt in the prince-bishopric of Augsburg in 1586, claimed to fly with the *Nachtschar* (phantoms of the night) to certain places during the Ember nights (Ember Days were those of special prayer and fasting at the beginning of the four seasons), and during these ecstasies he gained knowledge about the identity of the witches (Behringer 1998). Hitherto unknown to historians of witchcraft, the *Nachtschar* is inextricably intertwined with the notion of the *Nachtvolk,* or night people, in folklore research. When Austrian and Swiss folklorists began collecting folk narratives and fairy tales, they found an astonishing variety of stories about "people of the night" in an area reaching from the Oberstdorf valley where Stocckhlin lived into western Austria and all across Switzerland into Valais, the very region where the witches' Sabbat was discovered in the fifteenth century, then partly ruled by the duchy of Savoy. Research into such forms of folk belief could therefore fill gaps in our understanding of the invention of the witches' Sabbat.

The "people of the night" emerge almost everywhere in local narratives from Vorarlberg, the Grisons, and Valais (Beitl 1965). However, ethnographic field studies had independently detected them in the late nineteenth and early twentieth centuries (maps in Liebl 1971, 258–259). Unlike terrifying stories of the "wild hunt," where demonic creatures frighten and threaten those who watch them, the "people of the night" fascinated observers with music of unearthly beauty and never harmed anyone. They could even perform the miracle of the bones, restoring devoured cattle to life the morning after their orgiastic nightly festivities, feasting and dancing at remote Alpine locations. They invited observers to their nocturnal gatherings and invested them with such supernatural abilities as fortunetelling and healing.

According to folk belief, the "people of the night" are the "good society"; they harm only when they feel attacked but otherwise bring people good luck. Sometimes they resemble a fairy society, but other narratives make them seem part of the Otherworld. Well into the seventeenth century, the "people of the night" were not confined to fairy tales: a good number of ecstatics actually claimed to have seen them, received regular visits from them, flew with them, or even belonged to the *Nachtvolk* themselves. A citizen of Lucerne, Renward Cysat (1545–1614), collected dozens of stories from his friends in order to attack this widespread superstition. But Cysat's polemic made it perfectly clear that those whose houses the night people visited were envied and considered lucky by their neighbors. This case serves to show how belief systems were reduced to fairy tales and may also indicate that it was more than inquisitors' fantasies that formed the idea of witchcraft.

WOLFGANG BEHRINGER

See also: AUGSBURG, PRINCE-BISHOPRIC OF; *BENANDANTI; CANON EPISCOPI;* DIANA (ARTEMIS); FAIRIES; FLIGHT OF WITCHES; FOLKLORE; GINZBURG, CARLO; GRIMM, JACOB; GUI, BERNARD; HOLDA; SHAMANISM; STOECKHLIN, CHONRAD; *TÁLTOS.*

References and further reading:

Aarne, Antti, and Stith Thompson. 1987. *The Types of the Folktale: A Classification and Bibliography.* Helsinki: Academia Scientiarum Fennica.

Bächtold-Stäubli, Hans, ed. 1934. "Lincke, Nachtvolk, -schar." In *Handwörterbuch des deutschen Aberglaubens.* vol. 6, cols. 805–809.

Behringer, Wolfgang. 1998. *Shaman of Oberstdorf: Chonrad Stoeckhlin and the Phantoms of the Night.* Translated by H. C. Erik Midelfort. Charlottesville: University Press of Virginia.

Beitl, Klaus. 1965. "Die Sage vom Nachtvolk: Untersuchung zu einem alpinen Sagentypus (Mit Verbreitungskarte)." Pp. 14–21 in *Fourth International Congress of Folk Narrative Research in Athens: Lectures and Reports* Edited by Georgios A. Megas. Athens.

Boskovic-Stulli, Maja. 1960. "Kresnik-Krsnik." *Fabula* 3: 275–298.

Büchli, Arnold. 1947. "Wilde Jagd und Nachtvolk." *Schweizer Volkskunde* 37: 65–69.

Duerr, Hans Peter. 1985. *Dreamtime: Concerning the Boundary Between Wilderness and Civilization.* Oxford: Blackwell.

Ginzburg, Carlo. 1983. *The Night Battles: Witchcraft and Agrarian Cults in the Sixteenth and Seventeenth Centuries.* Baltimore: Johns Hopkins University Press.

———. 1991. *Ecstasies. Deciphering the Witches' Sabbath.* New York: Random House.

Hansen, Joseph, ed. 1901. *Quellen und Untersuchungen zur Geschichte des Hexenwahns und der Hexenverfolgungen im Mittelalter.* Bonn: C. Georgi. Reprint. Hildesheim: Georg Olms, 1963.

Henningsen, Gustav. 1990. "'The Ladies from Outside': An Archaic Pattern of the Witches' Sabbat." Pp. 191–215 in *Early Modern European Witchcraft: Centres and Peripheries.* Edited by Bengt Ankarloo and Gustav Henningsen. Oxford: Clarendon.

Klaniczay, Gábor. 1990. *The Uses of Supernatural Power: The Transformation of Popular Religion in Medieval and Early Modern Europe.* Princeton: Princeton University Press.

Liebl, Elsbeth. 1971. "'Totenzug' und Geisterheere und ähnliche Erscheinungen." Pp. 753–767 (maps 258–259) in *Atlas de Folklore Suisse: Kommentar,* pt. 2, sec. 7. Basel.

Luck, Georg. 1935. "Totenvolk und Nachtschar." Pp. 26–31 in *Rätische Alpensagen.* Chur: Schweizerische Gesellschaft für Volkskunde.

Muraro, Luisa. 1976. *La Signora del Gioco,* Milan: Feltrinelli.

Propp, Vladimir. 1968. *Morphology of the Folktale.* Austin: University of Texas Press.

PERKINS, WILLIAM (1558–1602)

Perkins's place in witchcraft history is assured by his large work of demonology, *A Discourse of the damned art of Witchcraft: so farre forth as it is revealed in the Scriptures, and manifested by true Experience,* published at Cambridge six years after the author's death, having initially been written as a series of sermons presumably delivered during the 1590s. It was brought to press and prefaced with an "Epistle Dedicatorie" by an obscure Cambridge-educated clergyman, Thomas Pickering, then minister of Finchingfield (Essex), who was also responsible for editing and publishing a number of Perkins's other works in the years following his death.

The leading English Protestant theologian of his day, Perkins was born in rural Warwickshire and entered Christ Church College, Cambridge, where the great Protestant scholar and preacher, Lawrence Chaderton (1536–1640), taught him. Perkins, on his own account, experienced a somewhat dissolute youth before reforming himself and going on to become a fellow of his college and establish himself as a gifted preacher and prolific writer. In the sixteenth and seventeenth centuries, continental Protestant authors frequently cited his works, which had been translated into Latin and several European languages. In England, they were widely read and influential well into the eighteenth century.

The *Discourse* lay firmly in the mainstream of Protestant demonology, although it had an unusually heavy reliance on Scripture rather than on other forms of authority. Perkins seldom referred to classical authors, the Church Fathers, other demonologists, or contemporary cases. Rather than *maleficium* (harmful magic), Perkins stressed the centrality of the demonic pact as the central issue in witchcraft (although, like other Protestant demonologists, he was slightly embarrassed by the lack of any scriptural reference to it). Like many other authors, he deplored the popular tendency to attribute a wide range of misfortune to witchcraft rather than to divine providence. Perkins was very much concerned with popular "superstitions," which impeded correct religious understanding, and lost no opportunity to ridicule Catholic practices he regarded as either superstitious or just as devilish as witchcraft.

In particular, he took a very strong line against cunning folk, those "good" witches to whom the ignorant population (Perkins's term) flocked so eagerly. Perkins felt that cunning folk, like other conjurors and magicians, derived their powers from the Devil as surely as did the malefic witch. Thus, Perkins could assure his readers that "this must always be remembered, as a conclusion, that by Witches we understand not those onely, which kill and torment but all Diviners Charmers, Iugglers, all Wizzards, commonly called wise men and wise women" (p. 256). Such magical practitioners were, indeed, worse than malefic witches, because they pretended to do good and therefore deluded the ignorant populace and led them further from godliness. Perkins, in fact, ended his *Discourse* by stating that "death therefore is the iust and deserved portion of the good Witch" (p. 257).

English court records suggest that Perkins's recommendation in this respect was not taken to heart by those responsible for administering English witchcraft trials: cunning folk usually suffered the relatively light penalties of penance before the ecclesiastical courts and fines before secular courts. But, more generally, Perkins's opinions on witchcraft remained influential for over a century, and English advocates of witch hunting drew considerable comfort from the fact that so eminent a man had written in support of their cause. In his justification of the Salem trials of 1692, *The Wonders of the Invisible World*, Cotton Mather cited Perkins's work extensively, and close study would probably reveal citations among continental Protestant writers on witchcraft. Further proof of the status of the *Discourse* comes from its place as the prime target of an important skeptical work, Sir Robert Filmer's *An Advertisement to the Jury-men of England, touching Witches: Together with a Difference between an Hebrew and an English Witch* (London, 1653). Filmer, an advocate of absolute monarchy and a royalist in the Civil War, especially attacked Perkins's emphasis on the pact, which Filmer obviously regarded as similar to Puritan views on covenant theology, to which this royalist gentleman was extremely hostile.

JAMES SHARPE

See also: CUNNING FOLK; DEMONOLOGY; ENGLAND; FILMER, SIR ROBERT; MATHER, COTTON; PURITANISM; SUPERSTITION.

References and further reading:
Breward, Ian, ed. 1969. *The Work of William Perkins.* Appleford, Abingdon, Berks: Sutton Courtenay.
Clark, Stuart. 1997. *Thinking with Demons: The Idea of Witchcraft in Early Modern Europe.* Oxford: Clarendon.
Estes, Leland. 1988. "Good Witches, Wise Men, Astrologers, and Scientists: William Perkins and the Limits of the European Witch Hunt." Pp. 154–165 in *Hermeticism and the Renaissance: Intellectual History and the Occult in Early Modern Europe.* Edited by Ingrid Merkel and Allen G. Debus. Washington, DC: Folger Shakespeare Library.

PERREAUD, FRANÇOIS (1572/1577–1657)

A Huguenot minister of attested probity and reliability, Perreaud wrote two short treatises on demonology published together as *Démonologie ou traité des demons et sorciers, ensemble l'Antidemon de Mascon* (Demonology, or a Treatise on Demons and Witches, including the Anti-Demon of Mâcon) in Geneva in 1653. The first, *Démonologie,* served as a kind of lengthy, self-contained introduction to the second, *L'Antidemon de Mâcon,* which provided a long and mostly circumstantial account of a poltergeist haunting, to which Perreaud and his whole household had been subjected for just over three months at the end of 1612. The latter treatise caught the eye of Sir Robert Boyle, a future member of the Royal Society, who heard the details from Perreaud himself and as a result sponsored an English translation, which appeared in 1658.

DÉMONOLOGIE

The *Démonologie* began with a short preface in which Perreaud explained that in 1652 he visited Bern for the first time for fifty years and there congratulated the city on passing a law against witches. Attacks at the hands of Catholics who blamed the Reformed religion for an infestation of witches in the Pays de Vaud and personal experience of an evil spirit caused him to write his treatise in order "to explain by reliable grounds and principles what one must believe [in relation to witches], the strength and weakness of evil spirits, and the proper remedies and safeguards one may take against them" (Perreaud 1653, 3).

The treatise was divided into twelve short chapters and read like an extended sermon. Perreaud argued that Scripture and human experience all over Europe prove that both good and bad angels exist and that evil spirits were necessary in God's scheme of things to punish sin and test the faith of believers. Maintaining that witches did not exist was merely one of Satan's tricks. Nevertheless, it was as dangerous to be overcredulous as it is to be unbelieving. Certain phenomena, such as unexpected hailstorms and tempests, might have natural explanations. Deliberate fraud must not be discounted. Malicious accusation, too, was always possible. Demons, however, could act only with God's permission; so if storms do occur, they are likely to be signs of God's anger at our sins.

The word *demon* meant "someone who knows," Perreaud said—actually, it came from a Greek word for an intermediary spirit or deity—and demons possessed two qualities: the power to know and the power to act. Thus, demons could predict the future, because they were immensely skilled at interpreting signs and drawing correct inferences from past actions. But they worked principally through illusions and might persuade people to believe their illusions by manipulating their imaginations or affecting their sight and hearing. Consequently, witches merely imagined they flew to their Sabbats because Satan made use of their proclivity to melancholia to manufacture illusions in their brains.

Demons could do things that were impossible for humans, such as making dead bodies move and speak believably or creating false bodies from congealed air for the same purpose. If witches did in fact fly, it was because they were carried by evil spirits who bore them up, much as a wind carried heavy objects through the air. Satan's aim in all this was the destruction of humanity. He misled people through idolatry as manifested in the Church of Rome or those who claimed to cure diseases by popular magic. The end of the world was not far off, so Satan was constantly inventing new stratagems to ensnare and destroy the faithful. He could not be restrained by superstitious means such as crosses or holy water. A strong faith in God, prayer, vigil, and fasting were the appropriate weapons for a true Christian.

There was nothing in Perreaud's treatises that was in the least novel or unorthodox, and little (save his conclusion) that was distinctively Protestant. Protestant demonologists often quoted from Catholic sources as texts worthy of credence, and Perreaud cited Pierre de Lancre more than once. As an example of the demonological genre, therefore, Perreaud's treatise was limited. As a prefatory sermon to his account of his poltergeist experience, however, it was of immediate interest, because it took on the air of a personal conversation between Perreaud and the reader, a warning of the dangers from preternatural forces whose attentions he himself suffered, and a reassurance to anyone who might find him- or herself one day in a similar position not to

be disconcerted or frightened, because these events were not beyond our courage or our endurance.

P. G. MAXWELL-STUART

See also: DEMONOLOGY; DEMONS; FLIGHT OF WITCHES; IDOLATRY; IMAGINATION; LANCRE, PIERRE DE; POLTERGEIST; VAUD, PAYS DE; WATER, HOLY.
References and further reading:
Labrousse, Elisabeth. 1996. *Conscience et Conviction: Etudes sur le xviie siècle.* Paris: Universitas, and Oxford: Voltaire Foundation, pp. 16–41.

PERSONALITY OF WITCHES

Unfriendly, abusive, and, to a lesser degree, antisocial or deviant people run a particular risk of being suspected witches in cultures that believe in witchcraft. Witches are thought to be people who have secretly turned against their communities, engaging in antisocial activities and inflicting harm on their neighbors, so people who believe in them are naturally prone to suspect people who manifest hostility or evince alienation from the community. Early modern European theories about witchcraft were somewhat atypical because they stressed the range of people who might become witches, but they also emphasized hostile and antisocial behaviors. Early modern popular suspicions targeted people, usually women, whose behavior and attitudes made them seem most likely to be responsible for harm suffered by others in their community. However, in early modern Europe as elsewhere, because witches were thought to practice their rites secretly and to inflict harm through occult means, the essential issue was not the suspect's overt behavior but his or her inner orientation. Although cultural images generally emphasized the witch's hostility and perversity, actual witch suspects were not necessarily belligerent or antisocial. Most theories about why people in a broad range of societies feel so threatened by the presumed hostility of witches approach the issue as one of victimization due to cognitive malfunctions on the part of the accuser, manifesting the displacement of other social processes or the dictates of a culturally prescribed narrative. Consideration of the role of personality in witch beliefs, however, raises the possibility that witchcraft beliefs were a way to categorize and cope with people whose habitual use of harmful ritual magic or malevolence in interpersonal disputes threatened the integrity of small-scale communities and the well-being of their members.

CULTURAL IMAGES OF WITCHES' PERSONALITIES
Twentieth-century anthropological studies found that the idea that particularly hostile or otherwise antisocial people were thought to be witches was extremely widespread. In Africa, for example, the Azande believed that

witches were spiteful or dour and quarreled with, threatened, and extorted favors from others. In North America, the Navajo held that witches were particularly mean spirited, while the Tangu of New Guinea said witches were surly, selfish, and unsociable, and took without reciprocating. This lack of respect for the social rules of reciprocity was seen to manifest not only hostility to the other person but also an antisocial disregard for the conventions that held society together. Similarly, the Navajo suspected not only hostile people but also people whose ambition or willfulness disrupted the smooth functioning of society, and the Nupe, Gisu, and Mandari in Africa considered any atypical behavior to be suspect. The Azande added dirtiness and other disregard for socially prescribed hygiene to hostility in their concept of witchcraft. These cultures and the innumerable others that included witchcraft beliefs naturally varied greatly in the specific social norms they thought witches breached and to a lesser extent in the specific ways witches expressed hostility. Nevertheless, the association of a hostile personality with witchcraft is very strong across cultures, and the association of witchcraft with more diffuse socially disruptive behaviors, while less strong, is still significant.

Late medieval European theologians describing witches in their demonologies were primarily concerned with their supposed clandestine activities and so discussed their personalities mainly in regard to their motives for becoming witches. Because they wanted to show how widely the Devil cast his net, they emphasized the range of reasons people succumbed to his temptations and, by implication, the variety of people who might be witches. Even so, though, their characterizations conformed broadly to the cross-cultural norms. For example, the *Malleus Maleficarum* (The Hammer of Witches, 1486) emphasized five personality characteristics that were supposed to lead people into witchcraft: malice, vengefulness, lust, avarice, and gloominess. The first two are forms of hostility, the last two have direct counterparts in witch beliefs of some other cultures, and the middle one, lust, was considered particularly antisocial (sinful) in medieval Christian morality. Even when such learned discussions tried to emphasize the breadth of types of people who became witches, they still conformed broadly to cross-cultural conceptions.

PERSONALITIES OF WITCH SUSPECTS

Anthropological accounts of witchcraft in various cultures have suggested that in practice, suspected witches did not necessarily display overt hostility or perversity, for some suspected people seemed friendly and conformed to social strictures, whereas others who were combative or deviant may not have been considered witches. However, these discrepancies did not mean that personality was unimportant, just that what was at issue was not so much a suspect's overt behavior and attitudes as his or her inner convictions. Thus, a friendly persons' friendliness had to be shown to be hypocritical in order for an allegation of witchcraft to carry weight. Conversely, a moderately belligerent or antisocial person's behavior did not become evidence of witchcraft if it was understood to be the full manifestation of that person's character.

We actually have better information about what kinds of late medieval and early modern people were suspected from popular practices than from demonologies written by learned men, because our main sources for the former are trial records. Records of mass panics are not much help: suspects were drawn in because of testimony obtained through torture, and the courts conducted proceedings in an atmosphere of mass hysteria. Records of small trials of one or only a few suspects are more useful. Although elite fears influenced small trials, they offer a relatively straightforward record of proceedings that were often initiated by commoners, almost always drew on their knowledge and ideas, and were generally conducted according to proper judicial procedures. These records suggest that popular beliefs were closer to the cross-cultural norm than the learned discussions. Most trials began because the accusers thought they had been harmed rather than because they were concerned about a diabolical conspiracy: thus many of the accused were people, especially women, who had reputations for chronic contentiousness. More generalized antisocial behavior sometimes led to a trial but more often played a role as supporting evidence about a suspect's reputation. Some suspects had good reputations and apparently amiable dispositions, but as long as standard judicial procedures were followed, they were far less likely to be tortured, convicted, or executed than suspects with long histories of belligerence.

These European trial records also contain significant information about people who have been less prominent in anthropological research, people who freely confessed to being witches. Social scientists' assessments of them have generally taken the fact of confession to be prima facie evidence of a pathological personality and therefore tended not to probe what these people were like apart from their willingness to confess. Their most common assessments have been that confessed witches were either mythomanics, hysterics, or just senile. However, the disappearance of hysteria as a psychological diagnosis, recent reconsiderations of the appropriateness of using modern Western psychological categories to classify people in other times and places, and a new understanding of the influence of cultural expectations on perceptions and experience make such judgments dubious; stories that sound bizarre to modern Westerners may not indicate pathology in another cultural context. In their personalities, beyond a readiness to implicate themselves, confessed witches actually appear on the whole to have been fairly typical witch suspects, known for their combativeness and general antisociability. If anything, a higher proportion were people who conformed to their culture's image of witches, because that image would have informed their self-definition as witches.

PERSONALITY AND INTERPERSONAL RELATIONS IN SMALL-SCALE SOCIETIES

Social scientists have traditionally looked to witches' personalities to help explain why they were victimized, seeing them as objects of clerical misogyny, scapegoats for social-historical turmoil, explanations for otherwise inexplicable personal misfortune, exemplars of social boundaries, obstacles to patriarchy, or as characters in culturally constructed narratives. In all these approaches, the crucial elements were the accusers and their motives; the suspects' personalities mattered only insofar as they served to focus the victimization process. Looking at the problem from the point of view of the suspects' personalities, however, suggests another line of reasoning. First, in most societies, some people actually did consciously employ harmful ritual magic or unconsciously project malevolent attitudes as tactics in interpersonal disputes. Second, malefic ritual magic often did involve, and unconscious projection of a menacing persona may well have involved breaking social norms or other perverse actions that toughened the "witch's" psyche while intimidating others. Third, people who engaged in harmful magic or who chronically projected a malevolent attitude may have caused harm through physical agents or psychological manipulation; they definitely strained the bonds of community that were vital for the survival and prosperity of small preindustrial communities. Consequently, although witchcraft beliefs exaggerated, distorted, and even invented many of the activities and dangers ascribed to witches and were definitely abused, there was probably real survival value for the small-scale communities on the margin of subsistence where witch beliefs generally originated and flourished in identifying and placating, isolating, disciplining, or eliminating people who consciously utilized harmful magic or those who unconsciously projected a malevolent persona in interpersonal disputes.

EDWARD BEVER

See also: ACCUSATIONS; ANTHROPOLOGY; BEWITCHMENT; CONFESSIONS; DISEASE; FEMALE WITCHES; GENDER; *MALEFICIUM; MALLEUS MALIFICARUM;* MELANCHOLY; MENTAL ILLNESS; POPULAR BELIEFS IN WITCHES; PSYCHOANALYSIS; RITUAL MAGIC; SCAPEGOAT WITNESSES.

References and further reading:

Bever, Edward. 1982. "Old Age and Witchcraft in Early Modern Europe." Pp. 150–190 in *Old Age in Preindustrial Society.* Edited by Peter Stearns. New York: Holmes and Meier.

Briggs, Robin. 2002. *Witches and Neighbors: The Social and Cultural Context of European Witchcraft.* 2nd ed. Oxford: Blackwell.

Harner, Michael. 1972. *The Jivaro: People of the Sacred Waterfall.* London: Robert Hale.

Levack, Brian P. 1995. *The Witch-Hunt in Early Modern Europe.* 2nd ed. London: Longman.

MacFarlane, A. D. J. 1970. *Witchcraft in Tudor and Stuart England.* New York: Harper and Row.

Newell, V. 1970. *The Witch Figure.* London: Routledge and Kegan Paul.

Sanders, Andrew. 1995. *A Deed Without a Name: The Witch in Society and History.* Oxford: Berg.

PERU

In Peru, witchcraft cases were tried by the Inquisition, first by the episcopal Inquisition and from 1570 by the tribunal of the Holy Office sitting in Lima. This tribunal was abolished in 1818. All sectors of the colonial population except the Amerindians were subject to the Inquisition. From the beginning until the end of Spanish colonial rule in Peru, the native population was exempt from the jurisdiction of the Inquisition but remained under the control of ecclesiastical courts. The Lima inquisitorial tribunal subsumed witchcraft (*brujería*) and sorcery (*hechicería*) trials under the greater category of "superstition." Consequently, the Peruvian Inquisition imposed no death penalty for witchcraft during the colonial period. An extremely broad geographic area fell under the jurisdiction of the Lima tribunal: When the tribunal was established in 1570, all South American Spanish possessions were subject to the Peruvian inquisitorial court. In 1610, after the foundation of a tribunal at Cartagena, the northern part of South America came under a separate jurisdiction, but all regions south of the vice-royalty of New Granada (modern Colombia, Venezuela, and parts of Panama and Ecuador) remained subject to the Lima tribunal. Evidently, the enormous geographical extent of this court's jurisdiction made more effective control possible only in the urban centers of the vice-royalty. To a certain degree, this situation may have accounted for the fact that in Peru, witchcraft and sorcery cases were mainly an urban phenomenon. Generally, the defendants had a low social status and—with regard to the total number of cases—there was a clear majority of trials instituted against women.

STATISTICAL DATA

From 1570 until 1818, that is, during the whole period of its existence, the Lima tribunal instituted 1,566 cases for matters of faith, of which 209 were subsumed under the category of superstition. That is, 13.3 percent of the total number of trials (Millar Carvacho 1998, 230). The majority of the superstition cases were sorcery (*hechicería*) trials. No witchcraft (*brujería*) trials are reported in the records of the Peruvian Inquisition. For the first period of inquisitorial activities in Peru, from the Spanish conquest in 1532 until the foundation of the Lima tribunal in 1570, no exact data are available. In any case, there is no evidence of important witchcraft or sorcery trials. From 1570 until the end of the 1580s, sorcery or witchcraft had lesser importance than in the next period from 1590 to 1700. The highest incidence of sorcery cases in this period was recorded for the 1590s. In that decade, twenty-six persons were tried, twenty men and six women (Castañeda Delgado and Hernández Aparicio 1989, 374). At the end of the sixteenth century, the pope urged the Spanish Inquisition to prosecute all sorcery accusations under suspicion of heresy. In 1629, a special edict was published inviting denunciations of those who practiced witchcraft and sorcery (Medina 1887, 2:35–40), which produced an increasing number of accusations and trials. At the same time, Peru's economic crisis of the 1630s may also have played a part in the increasing inquisitorial activities against all sorts of superstition, as more people probably consulted sorcerers in search of help in a desperate situation. The next period, which continued through the eighteenth century until the end of the Peruvian Inquisition in 1818, was characterized by a high percentage of sorcery trials. Behind bigamy cases, which occupied the first place with 26.15 percent, the Lima Inquisition's ninety superstition cases held second place with 23.07 percent (Hernández Aparicio 1993, 391).

DEFENDANTS AND OFFENSES

Most of the defendants were women of a low social status, often widowed, abandoned, or unmarried, who therefore lived at the margin of colonial society. Thus, the majority of the offenders were accused of trying to improve their situation or that of their clients. For example, magical practices were employed to bring a husband back to his wife or to procure a new partner for a client. Many cases also revolved around the precarious financial situation of clients and defendants. In accordance with the mixed ethnic profile of the people involved in sorcery cases, the magical practices were mainly based on contemporary European love magic but at the same time included indigenous Peruvian incantations and magical procedures, such as the use of medicinal plants in magical healing. Since the early seventeenth century, the offenses described in the sorcery trials show that by this time, European and Amerindian elements had merged into a new colonial Peruvian model of magic. African elements were less dominant, although a considerably high proportion of the defendants were of African descent. The majority of the defendants were classified as Spanish or Creole, followed by the so-called quadroons (cuarterones), Europeans with one-fourth African ancestry. Although male defendants more often used magical procedures in search of fortune and wealth, female defendants more frequently practiced love magic and magical healing.

FORM AND NATURE OF MAGIC IN PERU

Magical procedures were quite similar despite differences in gender or in the ethnic or social profile of the defendants: Invocations of demons or of saints who specialized in different kinds of magic were often combined with various incantations, the fabrication of charms, and magic potions. In cases of love magic, the practitioners frequently addressed Saint Martha or the "limping devil" (diablo cojuelo), whereas St. Cyprian was invoked in healing sessions. Spanish spells were often used in combination with typical Peruvian materials, such as coca leaves. The use of coca leaves in divination, magical curing, and sorcery was widespread within all levels of society, including with Spanish, Creole, or African women. Coca leaves were also regularly consumed as a stimulant. In magical procedures, coca leaves were often addressed as Incas (pre-Columbian rulers of Peru), Coyas (Inca-princesses), or as "mother Coca" (Mama Coca); in other words, the practitioners, mostly of European descent, invoked an Andean deity. Despite the invocations of the Devil or specific demons, all these cases were defined as sorcery, not witchcraft. Some male and female defendants were even accused of signing contracts with the Devil in order to secure his help in their endeavors to find treasure or love or simply to improve their situation. The Peruvian Inquisition classified these offenses mainly as fraudulent superstitions, notwithstanding the fact that the defendants were accused of an implicit or an explicit pact with the Devil. Peruvians accused of witchcraft were not charged with several activities attributed to early modern European witches: they did not allegedly attend nocturnal assemblies to worship the Devil, perform harmful magic, or fly through the air.

Only a few witchcraft trials are recorded in the viceroyalty of Peru. They were instituted not by the Inquisition but by a parallel institution, the so-called Extirpation of Idolatry. Founded in 1610 in the archbishopric of Lima to prosecute cases of idolatry, sorcery, and witchcraft among the Amerindian population, this ecclesiastical court tried a few Amerindians as witches (brujos). These individuals were thought to possess the ability to fly through the air, transform themselves into animals, especially birds, and perform similar deeds. Furthermore, they were accused of bloodsucking witchcraft or of practicing other kinds of harmful magic. All these elements formed part of the native notion of witchcraft in the Andes and were reported in seventeenth-century Spanish colonial historical sources. As a new element, the Spaniards introduced the witches' Sabbat from the European demonological tradition. Eighteenth-century indigenous testimonies reflected the fusion of the early modern European and the native Peruvian notions of witchcraft. Records of witchcraft and sorcery trials from the late colonial period instituted by ecclesiastical courts against Amerindians show that even in some rural regions, distant from the capital of the colony, several characteristic elements of the European demonological tradition had merged with popular ideas on witchcraft into an hybrid Peruvian concept, almost identical to the demonological stereotype of witches.

IRIS GAREIS

See also: FEMALE WITCHES; IDOLATRY; INQUISITION, SPANISH; INVOCATIONS; LOVE MAGIC; MAGIC, POPULAR; NEW GRANADA; NEW SPAIN; SORCERY; SPAIN; SUPERSTITION.

References and further reading:
Castañeda Delgado, Paulino. 1993. "Características de los procesados en el tribunal de Lima: 1570–1818." Pp. 407–424 in *Los Inquisidores*. Vitoria-Gasteiz: Fundación Sancho el Sabio.
Castañeda Delgado, Paulino, and Pilar Hernández Aparicio. 1989. *La Inquisición de Lima (1570–1635)*. Vol. 1. Madrid: Editorial Deimos.
———. 1995. "Los delitos de superstición en la Inquisición de Lima durante el siglo XVII." *Revista de la Inquisición* 4: 9–35.
Gareis, Iris. 1993. "'Brujos' y 'brujas' en el antiguo Perú: Apariencia y realidad en las fuentes históricas." *Revista de Indias* 53, no. 198: 583–613.
———. 1997. "Popular Religion and Identity in Colonial Lima." Pp. 105–122 in *Religion and Identity in the Americas: Anthropological Perspectives from Colonial Times to the Present*. Edited by Brigitte Huelsewiede and Ingo W. Schroeder. Bonner Amerikanistische Studien 28. Moeckmuehl: Sauerwein.
Henningsen, Gustav. 1994. "La evangelización negra: Difusión de la magia europea por la América colonial." *Revista de la Inquisición* 3: 9–27.
Hernández Aparicio, Pilar. 1993. "La actividad procesal en la Inquisición de Lima: 1570–1818." Pp. 387–406 in *Los Inquisidores*. Vitoria-Gasteiz: Fundación Sancho el Sabio.
Medina, José Toribio. 1887. *Historia del Santo Oficio de la Inquisición de Lima (1569–1820)*. 2 vols. Santiago de Chile: Imp. Gutenberg.
Millar Carvacho, René. 1998. *Inquisición y sociedad en el virreinato peruano: Estudios sobre el Tribunal de la Inquisición de Lima*. Santiago de Chile: Ediciones Universidad Católica de Chile.
Osorio, Alejandra B. 1997. "El callejón de la soledad: Vectors of Cultural Hybridity in Seventeenth-Century Lima." Pp. 198–229 in *Spiritual Encounters: Interactions Between Christianity and Native Religions in Colonial America*. Edited by Nicholas Griffiths and Fernando Cervantes. Birmingham: University of Birmingham Press.

PETER OF BERN (FL. CA. 1400)

A Swiss lay magistrate, Peter of Bern was mentioned several times by Johannes Nider in his *Formicarius* (The Anthill, 1437–1438) as an accomplished witch hunter.

Formerly identified as the patrician Peter of Gruyères (or von Greyertz), active 1392–1406 in the upper Simme valley (Simmenthal) of Switzerland; Peter's identity now appears problematic. Regional archives between 1392 and Nider's *Formicarius* show at least three judges named Peter (Hansen 1901, 91 n. 2; Borst 1992, 108–120; Chène 1999, 223–231). In short, we are not certain who exactly Peter was.

The tales that Nider claimed Peter told him featured two varieties of evildoers: a sect of apostate infanticidal cannibals, male and female, with most of the characteristics later attributed to "witches"; and a dynasty of individual males, who conformed to the older stereotype of the necromancer or sorcerer (Chène 1999, 243–244). Nider conflated several confessions that Peter extorted from his defendants with more recent information he had learned at the Council of Basel, reinterpreting Peter's stories in the light of current ideas to help shape a more "modern" notion of witchcraft beliefs (Bailey 2003, 41–45).

The most famous confession introduced the witches' "cauldron." According to Nider, Peter forced a defendant to confess that her sect of heretics stealthily killed babies in their cradles, so that they seemed to die of natural causes. Later the children were exhumed and boiled in a cauldron, according to an unspecified ritual. When ingested, the broth provided magical knowledge and power, conferring leadership over the "sect." From the sediment in the cauldron, the heretics prepared unguents useful to their arts. (Heinrich Kramer would interpret this unguent as the "flying" ointment that induced demons to transport witches aerially.) Peter forced another defendant to embellish the story, describing ingestion of the broth as the central moment in an initiation that included renunciation of Christianity and ritual homage to the Devil. Peter's tales of protowitches showed influences of late medieval myths identifying Cathar and Waldensian heresies as cannibalistic secret societies (Borst 1992, 115–118, following Cohn 1975).

The central moment of the initiation was counter-Eucharistic: by drinking a broth made from the flesh of murdered babies, the novice witch absorbed heresy through powerful mental images. The ceremony was also an antibaptism, requiring formal renunciation of baptism; not coincidentally, the broth was normally made from babies lacking baptism. By asserting that witches mostly victimized unbaptized babies, Nider (through Peter of Bern), like other early theorists, implied that baptism protected babies from harm, including witchcraft.

Yet the theory was not perfect: to explain why witches sometimes killed baptized babies, Peter blamed parents for not reinforcing baptismal protection with nightly prayers and signs of the cross. Peter was even more obsessed by the efficacy of sacramental crossing than by baptism. One tortured defendant confessed striking victims with hail and lightning yet admitted being powerless against anyone protected by the sign of the cross. Peter crossed himself constantly, and so when he injured himself badly in a fall, he attributed the lack of divine protection to his own negligence: losing his temper and even naming the Devil, he canceled the protection gained earlier by crossing himself. This comforting scenario was corroborated by the "confession" of a man Peter burned at the stake (Stephens 2002, 190–206, 241–252).

Nider's portrayal of Peter's obsessive interest in infanticide, cannibalism, ritual, and demonic encounters reflected deep insecurities about the efficacy of the Church's sacraments and sacramentals, particularly baptism, the Eucharist, and the sign of the cross. Nider's detailed anecdotes of Peter's exploits, intended to allay widespread clerical anxieties, probably exacerbated them, particularly after Heinrich Kramer quoted them in *Malleus Maleficarum* (The Hammer of Witches, 1486).

WALTER STEPHENS

See also: BASEL, COUNCIL OF; CANNIBALISM; CAULDRON; INFANTICIDE; KRAMER, HEINRICH; *MALLEUS MALEFICARUM;* NIDER, JOHANNES; OINTMENTS; ORIGINS OF THE WITCH HUNTS; SACRAMENTS AND SACRAMENTALS; *VAUDOIS* (WALDENSIANS).

References and further reading:
Bailey, Michael D. 2003. *Battling Demons: Witchcraft, Heresy, and Reform in the Late Middle Ages.* University Park: Pennsylvania State University Press.
Blauert, Andreas. 1989. *Frühe Hexenverfolgung: Ketzer-, Zauberei- und Hexenprozesse des 15. Jahrhunderts.* Hamburg: Junius.
Borst, Arno. 1992. *Medieval Worlds: Barbarians, Heretics, and Artists in the Middle Ages.* Translated by Eric Hansen. Chicago: University of Chicago Press.
Chène, Catherine. 1999. Commentary to "*Formicarius* (livre II, chapitre 4 et livre V, chapitres 3, 4, et 7)," edited by Catherine Chène. Pp. 201–265 in Martine Ostorero, Agostino Paravicini Bagliani, and Kathrin Utz Tremp. *L'imaginaire du sabbat: Edition critique des textes les plus anciens (1430 c.–1440 c.).* Lausanne: Université de Lausanne.
Cohn, Norman. 1975. *Europe's Inner Demons: An Enquiry Inspired by the Great Witch-Hunt.* New York: Basic Books.
Hansen, Joseph, ed. 1901. *Quellen und Untersuchungen zur Geschichte des Hexenwahns und der Hexenverfolgung im Mittelalter.* Bonn: Carl Georgi.
Nider, Johannes. 1971. *Formicarius (Vollständige Ausgabe der Inkunable Köln o[hne] J[ahre].* Introduction by Hans Biedermann. Cologne: 1480. Reprint, Graz: Akademische Druck.
Stephens, Walter. 2002. *Demon Lovers: Witchcraft, Sex, and the Crisis of Belief.* Chicago: University of Chicago Press.

PFALZ-ZWEIBRÜCKEN, DUCHY OF

Thorough research into the witch persecutions that occurred in the duchy of Pfalz-Zweibrücken is not yet complete, but it appears that there were only a few episodes of witch hunting in this initially Lutheran and then Calvinist territory from 1575 to 1590 and 1629 to 1633. As elsewhere in western Germany, the persecution was concentrated mainly in areas in which jurisdictional rights were divided among different lords (as was, for example, the case at the criminal court of Neunkirchen/Nahe, where there were about thirty-six witchcraft trials) and in areas in which rights of lordship were a matter of dispute (such as those subject to the criminal court of Hornbach, where there were approximately thirteen trials). In those parts of the Nahe and Saar regions that were subject to the territorial authority of Pfalz-Zweibrücken, witch hunts were pursued by the combined efforts of *Hexenausschüsse* (witch-hunting committees organized at the village level) and minor lords with rights of criminal jurisdiction. In those territories bordering the duchy of Lorraine, however, witchcraft trials were investigated ex officio; this happened at the criminal court of Hornbach. No trials are known to have occurred in the areas bordering Alsace and the Palatinate, such as Amt (district) Bergzabern. As was the case in other Protestant territories, women were clearly the main focus of witchcraft trials in Pfalz-Zweibrücken. Only a tiny proportion of the trial records have survived; references to trials can, however, be found in records of ecclesiastical visitations and in the trial records of the *Reichskammergericht* (imperial chamber court).

THE ATTITUDES OF THE DUKES OF PFALZ-ZWEIBRÜCKEN TOWARD WITCH PERSECUTION

As early as 1532, Duke Wolfgang of Pfalz-Zweibrücken (1532–1569) asked the Lutheran reformer Johannes Schwebel for advice about how to proceed in cases of accusations of witchcraft. In response, Schwebel advocated a cautious approach, recommending only the legal prosecution of allegations of murder and harm caused by magical means. Schwebel's answer was in line with the precepts of clause 44 of the Carolina (the code of criminal legal procedure issued by Charles V for the Holy Roman Empire in 1532). The Carolina's definition of the crime of sorcery and its regulations regarding trial procedures and the settling of trial costs constituted the main influences on witchcraft trials in Pfalz-Zweibrücken under the next two dukes, Johann I (1569–1604) and Johann II (1604–1635), who did not promulgate any ordinances relating specifically to the conduct of witchcraft trials. A clear process governed all criminal cases. The ducal chancellery authorized the arrest, interrogation, and torture of alleged witches, sometimes including a detailed list of questions that were to be put to the suspect. On the whole, the chancellery lawyers adopted a "wait-and-see" attitude toward accusations of witchcraft and encouraged local officials to treat such accusations with moderation. Despite their efforts, witchcraft trials became endemic during the rule of Duke Johann I between 1574 and 1590 (in Hornbach and Neunkirchen/Nahe), although Johann consistently tried to limit the spread of the trials by ordering arrested women released on bond, by concerning himself especially with the issue of the correct settlement of trial costs, and by attempting to prevent trials that were not carried out in accordance with the Carolina. Johann I's moderate stance led opponents to bring lawsuits against him at the *Reichskammergericht* in 1592 and 1594, accusing him of being extremely skeptical with regard to witchcraft trials. His insistence on strict adherence to the Carolina was met with particularly vehement opposition from minor lords who possessed rights of criminal jurisdiction.

WITCHCRAFT TRIALS AT THE CRIMINAL COURT OF NEUNKIRCHEN/NAHE: A CASE STUDY

The criminal court of Neunkirchen/Nahe belonged to the count of Veldenz and was held as a fief by the dukes of Pfalz-Zweibrücken: the four villages of Neunkirchen, Gonnesweiler, Selbach, and Eckesweiler were subject to its jurisdiction. The lords of Sötern in part held rights of jurisdiction. As a result of the involvement of *Hexenausschüsse*, seventeen witchcraft trials occurred in Gonnesweiler in 1580, in the course of which ten women were executed. In 1589, working in conjunction with the local *Hexenausschüsse*, Georg Wilhelm of Sötern had six women of Selbach arrested: four of them were forced through horrific torture into making confessions of witchcraft and were subsequently executed. Georg Wilhelm and the *Hexenausschüsse* forced the relatives of the executed women and the two remaining women (who were released) to meet the extremely high trial costs of approximately 900 florins. The six families thus affected were ruined financially and reduced to begging for a living.

Duke Johann I of Pfalz-Zweibrücken then intervened against this clear breach of the law and forced the *Hexenausschüsse* and Georg Wilhelm to reimburse the families for their forfeited property. Georg Wilhelm and his son, Conrad, promptly brought a lawsuit against Johann I at the *Reichskammergericht*. The verdict is unknown, but no more witches were tried at the criminal court of Neunkirchen until 1629, again on the initiative of local *Hexenausschüsse* and the lord of Sötern, Johann Reinhard. At least nine people were executed in 1629–1630. In 1633, further trials were pursued against six individuals featuring the imposition of excessive costs, fraud, bribery, and the manipulation of legal proceedings. Local witch-hunting committees were also active in the Pfalz-Zweibrücken areas of Meisenheim, Lichtenberg, and Zweibrücken.

REASONS FOR THE PFALZ-ZWEIBRÜCKEN TRIALS AND THEIR CESSATION

The first witchcraft trials in Pfalz-Zweibrücken were triggered by the intensification of ecclesiastical visitations, during which popular magical practices, previously categorized as "superstitions," were criminalized and linked with the crime of witchcraft. Despite this, relatively few accusations of sorcery ended in witchcraft trials, primarily because the moderating influence of the ducal chancellery prevented the escalation of witch hunts. The trials at the criminal court of Neunkirchen/Nahe were in all probability triggered by the mass persecution of witches in the neighboring territory of the electorate of Trier in the late sixteenth century. Strict adherence to the Carolina and the close links between the dukes of Pfalz-Zweibrücken and the authorities in the Palatinate, who were opposed to witch hunts, ensured that mass witchcraft trials never occurred throughout the duchy. Members of the collateral line of Pfalz-Birkenfeld also adopted a critical attitude toward witchcraft trials. The devastating effects of the Thirty Years' War, which wiped out almost 90 percent of the population of the Pfalz-Zweibrücken territories in the Saar region, ensured that no further witchcraft trials took place there.

RITA VOLTMER;

TRANSLATED BY ALISON ROWLAND

See also: CAROLINA CODE (*CONSTITIO CRIMINALIS CAROLINA*); COMMUNAL PERSECUTION; FEMALE WITCHES; GERMANY, WEST AND NORTHWEST; HOLY ROMAN EMPIRE; PALATINATE, ELECTORATE OF; POPULAR PERSECUTION; *REICHSKAMMERGERICHT*; SAAR REGION; SORCERY; TRIER, ELECTORATE OF.

References and further reading:

Baumgarten, Achim R. 1987. *Hexenwahn und Hexenverfolgung im Naheraum: Ein Beitrag zur Sozial- und Kulturgeschichte.* Frankfurt am Main: Peter Lang, pp. 43–90.
Labouvie, Eva. 1991. *Zauberei und Hexenwerk: Ländlicher Hexenglaube in der frühen Neuzeit.* Frankfurt am Main: Fischer.
Schmidt, Jürgen-Michael. 2000. *Glaube und Skepsis: Die Kurpfalz und die abendländische Hexenverfolgung, 1446–1685.* Bielefeld: Verlag für Regionalgeschichte.
Übel, Rolf. 1992. "Ein Hexenprozess im Herzogtum Pfalz-Zweibrücken." *Pfälzer Heimat* 43: 71–78.

PICO DELLA MIRANDOLA, GIANFRANCESCO (CA. 1469–1533)

Author of the best-known Italian Renaissance dialogue on witches, Gianfrancesco was the son of Galeotto I of Mirandola and of Bianca Maria d'Este, illegitimate daughter of Niccoló III of Ferrara, and the nephew of the famous Renaissance philosopher Giovanni Pico della Mirandola. Only six years younger than his uncle, Gianfrancesco thrived on the cultured society that Giovanni frequented. After Giovanni died in 1494, Gianfrancesco wrote a biography that introduced the first edition of his uncle's works (Bologna 1496). Although they agreed in some matters, including their views concerning judicial astrology, their philosophical positions were generally very different.

We know little about Gianfrancesco's childhood; he may have studied in Ferrara or Milan, where he participated in a tournament at the Sforza court in

January 1491. Two months later, Gianfrancesco married a Neapolitan heiress, Giovanna Carafa, and used her dowry to purchase the hereditary title to the tiny principality of Mirandola from his uncle Giovanni. From 1491 to 1499, Gianfrancesco dedicated himself to studying humanist philosophy, meeting the most important contemporary intellectuals and politicians, and composing numerous literary and philosophical works that were published at the beginning of the sixteenth century. His letters circulated in manuscript form before being translated into French in 1498 and into English by Thomas More in 1510. The friendships established through his uncle's connections in the cultured court societies of Bologna, Ferrara, Florence, and Mantua were very important to Gianfrancesco's career. But the most important influence was his encounter with the friar Girolamo Savonarola, whom Gianfrancesco met in 1491. In 1497, Gianfrancesco defended Savonarola twice in response to attacks by a Franciscan monk, Samuel de Cassini (Cassinis); the next spring, he composed a third defense in the vernacular directed at Florentine public opinion, but his work could not save Savonarola from being burned at the stake in May 1498. Gianfrancesco never stopped defending Savonarola, nor did he stop inviting disciples like Pietro Bernardini or Fra Luca Bettini to stay with him. He worked on composing a *Vita Hyeronimi Savonarolae* (Life of Girolamo Savonarola) until his death.

In 1499, Gianfrancesco's father, Galeotto I, died. Gianfrancesco's life became enwrapped in a long twisting struggle to claim the hereditary principality as Galeotto's eldest son, while his mother—aided by the French and the Milanese—favored Gianfrancesco's younger brothers. In 1502, after a long siege, the castle of Mirandola fell into the hands of his brothers; Gianfrancesco was imprisoned and later exiled. For eight and a half years, Gianfrancesco traveled to various Italian cities, serving the emperor and the pope while remaining in contact with important German humanists. The recovery of the castle of Mirandola became part of a plan to conquer the city for the Papal States by Pope Julius II, who personally conducted its siege and capture from December 1510 to January 1511. Gianfrancesco's satisfaction was brief; the Milanese commander Gian Giacomo Trivulzio soon seized Mirandola and expelled the heirs. In 1514, with the mediation of the imperial vicar, they reached an agreement, giving the land and some rural villas to the brothers.

Gianfrancesco composed a dialogue about witches, *Strix, sive de ludificatione daemonum* (The Witch, or the Deceptions of Demons), published in Bologna in 1523, with the practical purpose of justifying a violent repression he had recently conducted in Mirandola against numerous witches in 1522 and 1523, earning an indignant reaction from the population of the castle and the nearby villa. Although created for specific personal political purpose, his treatment became immediately popular. A vernacular translation by Fra' Leandro Alberti appeared in Bologna in 1524; *Strix* was translated again in Tuscany in 1555, appearing in the canonical work of Turino Turini. Gianfrancesco's text was also included in a collection of theoretical works published in Padana during the first half of the sixteenth century, alongside works by two Dominicans, Silvestro Prierias and Bartolomeo della Spina, both inquisitors and papal theologians.

One can immediately distinguish Gianfrancesco's account by its originality. He wrote not as an inquisitor but as a scholar who attended these trials in his capacity as count of this small principality and wanted to answer an important question: was this "cult of Diana," consisting of ten people in Modena and Mirandola, the same bacchanal pagan assembly of antiquity described as a superstition by the *Canon Episcopi* (ca. 906) and included in Gratian's *Decretum* (Concord of Discordant Canons, known as the *Decretum*, 1130–1140 revision), or was it instead a new form of heresy? Gianfrancesco argued in dialogue form, with the participation of four people: Fronimo (the scholar, wise and sensitive, that is, Pico himself) and Dicasto (the judge, modeled after the Dominican inquisitor Girolamo Armellini) in conversation with Apistio (an unidentifiable skeptic), who at the conclusion became Pistico (the believer), now persuaded of witchcraft's satanic nature; a witch is offered in order to testify about the "cult of Diana." In a text rich with the quotation and reinvention of pagan ceremonies, the author linked modern witches' Sabbats with many antiquated beliefs, but differentiated them in some important rituals, especially the presence of devils. Modern witchcraft differed from the beliefs described by the *Canon Episcopi,* but the origins of both heresies were embedded in ancient paganism. Recent studies about the historical context in which these witches were tried have illuminated the jurisdictional conflicts among the inhabitants of Mirandola that aggravated the cruelty of the repression; but Gianfrancesco's dialogues demonstrated that this persecution of witches was motivated above all by intellectual and ideological convictions.

GABRIELLA ZARRI;

TRANSLATED BY JESSICA BOTHWELL

See also: *CANON EPISCOPI;* CASSINI (CASSINIS), SAMUEL DE; DIANA(ARTEMIS); GRATIAN; PRIERIAS, SILVESTRO; SPINA, BARTOLOMEO DELLA.

References and further reading:

Biondi, Albano, ed. 1989. *Gianfrancesco Pico della Mirandola, Libro detto Strega o delle illusioni del demonio nel volgarizzamento de Leando Alberti.* Venice: Marsilio.
Bonomo, Guiseppe. 1985. *Caccia alle streghe: La redenza nelle streghe dal sec: XIII al XIX con particolare reiferiment all'Italia.* 3rd ed. Naples: Palumbo.

Burke, Peter. 1976. "Witchcraft and Magic in Renaissance Italy: Gianfrancesco Pico and his *Strix.*" Pp. 32–53 in *The Damned Art.* Edited by Sidney Anglo. London: Routledge and Kegan Paul.

Herzig, Tamar. 2003. "The Demons' Reaction to Sodomy: Witchcraft and Homosexuality in Gianfrancesco Pico della Mirandola's *Strix.*" *Sixteenth Century Journal* 34, no. 1: 53–72.

Schmitt, Charles B. 1967. *Gianfrancesco Pico della Mirandola (1469–1533) and His Critique of Aristotle.* The Hague: Martinus Nijhoff.

Vescovili, Graziella, and Graziella Federici Vescovina. 1998. "Gianfrancesco Pico: La vanitá dell'astrologia e la stregoneria." Pp. 213–228 in *Giovanni e Gianfrancesco Pico: L'opera e la fortuna di due studenti ferraresi.* Edited by Patrizia Castelli. Florence: Leo Olschki.

Zambelli, Paola. 1997. *L'eredità pichiana in mano agli inquisitori: il caso di Gianfrancesco.* Milan: Mondatori, pp. 177–210.

PIEDMONT

The early history of witchcraft in the Piedmontese state was dominated by developments that occurred mainly in its western and northern French-speaking parts, including the Val d'Aosta. The central role of the dukes of Savoy-Piedmont in helping create the doctrine of the witches' Sabbat at the time of the Council of Basel is now well-known (Ostorero et al. 1999), and considerable evidence about fifteenth-century trials in the northwestern parts of Savoy-Piedmont has been preserved at Turin among the fiscal records of ducal officials. However, this entry will focus primarily on the Italophone territories comprising the present-day Piedmontese region, created after the unification of the Kingdom of Italy in 1860, when Nice and Savoy went to France.

During the time of recorded trials for sorcery and witchcraft (local records date from 1292), the House of Savoy subjugated many local lordships. In the thirteenth century, Piedmont was composed only of Turin, Aosta, and Savoy, but in the fifteenth century included within its borders Cuneo, Vercelli, Biella, Ivrea, Tenda, and Nice. The state added Asti, Alba, and Saluzzo in the sixteenth and seventeenth centuries. In the first decades of the eighteenth century, when Piedmont's rulers became kings, it annexed (through international treaties with France, Austria, Spain, and England) Alessandria, Tortona, the Lomellina and Novara (taken from the duchy of Milan), and the Monferrato of Acqui and Casale (taken from the duchy of Mantua). The present Piedmont region took form only after the unification of the Kingdom of Italy, when the territories of Nice and Savoy went to France, and Liguria (acquired in 1815) broke away from the Piedmont.

In his constitutions of 1430, the Savoyard Pope-Duke Amadeus (Amedeo) VIII (1383–1451, ruled 1416–1451) established the death penalty for heretics and casters of harmful spells (*sortileges*); by that date, Domenican Friars had not yet assigned inquisitors to Torino, Vercelli, Alessandria, Novara, Savigliano, and Ivrea. As late as 1673, Duke Carlo Emanuele II reaffirmed the death penalty for anyone who cast spells and charms. Important information has also been obtained by consulting both state and municipal archives, which sometimes document expenses for building scaffolds or stakes (Centini 1995, 31–32) or still keep important trial records (Merlo et al. 2004). From published documents (Centini 1995, 32–52), we learn that the oldest case of witchcraft known in Piedmont dates back to 1292: a woman from Villafranca, who was forced to pay a fee for *sortilegia in visione stellarum* (casting spells while stargazing). A certain Lorenza di Cumiana was the first sorceress burned at the stake, in 1321; Bertolotto, her accomplice, was hanged.

Many fourteenth- and fifteenth-century trials were held, often in Alpine regions: the valleys of Lanzo and Susa, the Canavese, Bardonecchia, Pinerolo, Cuneo, Mondovi. Overall, between 1292 and 1417, twenty-six persons were put on trial (eight of them men) and seven received death sentences. Between 1421 and 1445, many more charges and sentences are documented: thirty-one people were investigated (eleven of them men), with twenty-five death penalties. Between 1461 and 1479, we find thirty-five accused people (including seven men) and nineteen executions. Because of inaccuracies in the sources, we exclude thirty-two mountain dwellers accused of casting spells in Savoy in 1436, several women who were tried as witches in the Canavese between 1350 and 1390, and almost forty townsfolk in Andezeno in the late fifteenth century, where Catharism overlapped with accusations of devil worship, promiscuity, etc.

During the sixteenth and the seventeenth centuries, the phenomenon seemed to decrease in the modern Piedmontese geographical area; for example, only four witches were tried at Turin during the lengthy French occupation before 1559. Between 1530 and 1682, not counting sketchy data, we note only thirty-three sentences (only five concerning men) and fourteen executions.

Overall, from 1292 to 1742, we have—besides many uncertain cases—a total of 242 people under investigation for witchcraft in Piedmont, including 120 women and 30 men; capital sentences and deaths in prison totaled 82. Centini (2004) found for the period from 1329 through 1740 a total of 102 people under investigation; trials, 79; capital sentences, 49; amputations, 2; fines paid, 12.

In Piedmont, the bishops' ancient power to judge in matters of faith, including heresy and witchcraft, was never taken away; the records of diocesan synods from the 1550s offer substantial evidence about practices of popular magic; the bishops assigned punishments to witches, magicians, wizards, and fortunetellers (Corrain and Zampini 1970). Although dossiers of trials held before episcopal courts have disappeared from many diocesan archives, some information can be extrapolated from annals and chronicles. One set of court records from the bishop of Acqui (which became Piedmontese only in the eighteenth century) includes fifty-seven persons put on trial for illicit magic between 1585 and 1727. They include thirty-six men and only twenty-one women; most of these men were soldiers, quartered in Monferrato during the time of the succession wars around 1630. Their punishments never exceeded canonical penances, fines, and gifts to charities (Panizza 1994, 178–179).

St. Bernardino of Siena, during one of his sermon campaigns in Piedmont (probably in 1417 or 1418) alleged that Piedmontese witches had already killed five inquisitors in previous years, so that no one wanted to serve in those places and "*mettervi mano*" (meddle with them). Bernardino explained how such *male genti* (evildoers) performed the nefarious practice of the *barilotto*—communal drinking from a keg of wine polluted with the pulverized corpse of a baby, which was passed around and shared during their Sabbat as a sign of their fealty to Satan. The gray friar's passionate exaggerations, however, did capture a kind of local Piedmontese color: the fact that it was, historically and geographically speaking, in the front line among those territories between France and Italy where Catharism had existed in the Western Alps.

The confessions of Piedmontese sorcerers under investigation revealed their desire to master the magical arts, sometimes as a way to manipulate the ruling powers. Magic spells bedeviled the court of Savoy as far back as the time of Pope-Duke Amadeus, and similar spells continued to be cast on the lives of the Savoy kings, deeply worrying the Turinese court in the first thirty years of the eighteenth century. Another good late example was the 1752 case of several residents of Alessandria who were involved in various underground activities, including trafficking in books of magic and necromancy, stealing various body parts from hanged men, and making talismans that their friends (men, mostly soldiers) used mainly to look for hidden treasures in the hills (Panizza 1989, 36–37). Testimony about witchcraft in seventeenth-century rural Piedmont, beyond its traditional contexts of popular magic, offered tantalizing bits of evidence about the survival of practices and rituals apparently connected to ancient heresies that once flourished in the mountains (Gremmo 1994, 12–17, 22, 50).

GIAN MARIA PANIZZA;

TRANSLATED BY DANIELLA CATELLI

See also: BERNARDINO OF SIENA; ITALY; MOUNTAINS AND THE ORIGINS OF WITCHCRAFT; ORIGINS OF THE WITCH HUNTS; RURAL WITCHCRAFT; SAVOY, DUCHY OF.

References and further reading:
Centini, Massimo. 1995. *Streghe, roghi e diavoli: i processi di stregoneria in Piemonte.* Cuneo: L'Arciere.
Corrain, Cleto, and Pierluigi Zampini. 1970. *Documenti etnografici e folkloristici nei sinodi diocesani italiani.* Bologna: S.I.R.A.B. S.r.l.
Gremmo, Roberto. 1994. *Streghe e magia. Episodi di opposizione religiosa popolare sulle Alpi del Seicento.* Biella: Edizioni ELF.
Loriga, Sabina. 1994. "A Secret to Kill the King: Magic and Possession in Piedmont in the Eighteenth Century." Pp. 88–109 in *History of Crime: Selections from "Quaderni Storici."* Edited by Edward Muir and Guido Ruggiero. Baltimore and London: Johns Hopkins University Press. Originally published as "Un Secreto per far morire la persona del re: magie e protezione nel Piemonte del 1700." *Quaderni Storici* (1983): 529–552.
Merlo, Grado Giovanni. 2004. *"Lucea talvolta la luna." I processi alle "masche" di Rifreddo e Gambasca del 1495.* Cuneo: Società per gli studi storici della Provincia di Cuneo.
Muzio, Domenico Francesco, O.P. 1730. *Tabula Chronologica Inquisitorum Italiae, et Insularum Adiacentium ex Ordine Praedicatorum Compilata, et Notis Historicis Illustrata,* unpublished manuscript, in the Municipal Library of Alessandria (MS 67).
Ostorero, Martine, et al., 1999. *L'Imaginaire du sabbat. Edition critique des textes les plus anciens (1430 ca.–1440 ca.).* Lausanne: Cahiers Lausannois d'Histoire Médiévale, 26.
Panizza, Gian Maria. 1989. "Abominevoli esperimenti in luoghi secreti: magia e sortilegi popolari ad Alessandria a metà Settecento." *Rassegna Economica della Provincia di Alessandria* 42/1: 33–40.
———. 1994. "Da alcuni tenuta donna da bene, et da alcuni tenuta una strega": i procedimenti contro gli accusati di stregoneria negli atti del Foro ecclesiastico conservati presso l'Archivio Diocesano di Acqui (1585—1727)." *Rivista di Storia Arte e Archeologia per le Province di Alessandria e Asti* 103: 155–192.

PIPERNO, PIETRO

Seventeenth-century Italian philosopher and physician from Benevento, Piperno was author of *De magicis affectibus horum dignotione, praenotione, curatione, medica, stratagemmatica, divina, plerisque curationibus electis, et De Nuce beneventana maga . . .* (On Magical Ailments, Their Diagnosis, Prediction, and Treatment, with Select Cures Medical, Strategic, and Divine, and On the Walnut Tree of Benevento), published at Naples in 1634 in five books and reprinted in 1647 with an added sixth book. The appendix was reprinted in 1640 at Naples, along with a treatise in Italian on the same subject (*Della superstitiosa noce di Benevento: Trattato historico . . .* [On the Magical Walnut Tree of Benevento: A Historical Treatise]), containing sensational anecdotes.

Reasoning from effects to causes, the work enlisted the symptomology of diseases to prove that demons exist. It discussed witchcraft as the means whereby demons caused disease and possible remedies, both natural and supernatural (e.g., exorcism, prayers, blessed amulets), for curing ailments. Like other treatises that defended the reality of demons against skeptical detractors, Piperno's book addressed the vexed question of the relative power of the human imagination. His "extremely unoriginal" (Mori 1994, 181) work relied heavily on citations from sixteenth-century demonologists and exorcists. An appendix discussed the infamous walnut tree of Benevento, the supposed meeting place of witches and demons, mentioned by St. Bernardino of Siena and other fifteenth- and sixteenth-century writers on witchcraft. According to Piperno, the tree emitted natural, intoxicating effluvia that predisposed witches to commit the horrors of the Sabbat.

Piperno's son Nicolò composed a play on the legend of the tree, *La noce maga di Benevento . . .* (The Magical Walnut Tree of Benevento), which was staged in 1665 and 1666 at Benevento and Rome and published in 1682.

WALTER STEPHENS

See also: BENEVENTO, WALNUT TREE OF; ITALY; SABBAT.

References and further reading:

Mori, Giovanna. 1994. "Pietro Piperno." Pp. 181–183 in *Bibliotheca lamiarum: Documenti e immagini della stregoneria dal Medioevo all'Età Moderna.* Edited by Patrizia Castelli. Ospedaletto (Pisa): Pacini.

Piperno, Pietro. 1634. *De magicis affectibus horum dignotione, praenotione, curatione, medica, stratagemmatica, divina, plerisque curationibus electis, et De Nuce beneventana maga. . . .* Naples: Roncalioli. 1647. Reprint, Naples: Colligni.

———. 1640. *Della superstitiosa noce di Benevento: Trattato historico, con il trattato in lingua latina scritto gli anni passati dall'istesso autore. . . . Seconda impressione . . . emendata.* Naples: Gaffaro.

Thorndike, Lynn. 1958. *A History of Magic and Experimental Science.* New York: Columbia University Press, vol. 8, pp. 547–549.

PITTENWEEM WITCHES

A small fishing village on the coast of Fife in Scotland, Pittenweem, like most other Scottish villages and towns, accumulated a history of magical operators, often dubbed witches, and dealt with either by the local kirk session (parish disciplinary committee) or by the criminal courts. Because of the nature of the records, Pittenweem's witches emerged quite late, at the end of the seventeenth and the beginning of the eighteenth century. Several complaints involved villagers consulting witches rather than being witches themselves. In January 1693, Margaret Greenhorn, a servant, was referred to the presbytery for consulting a man about things lost, and the minister investigated her again five years later on a similar charge. In May 1697, Agnes Adamson was rebuked for consulting, and the minister took the occasion to lament "how common this scandalous sin is of consulting persons reputed sorcerers anent things secret or lost" (Ms. record, Scottish Record Office, CH2/183, p. 143). Not that parishioners always accepted their rebukes mildly. In April 1698, Jean Durkie was accused of consulting; when the session censured her, she cursed both minister and elders roundly. In May 1704 she was in trouble again for asking a woman (Nickolas Lowson) to teach her how to be a witch.

It was in this year, 1704, that Pittenweem began to suffer its most notorious (but atypical) witchcraft episode. In March, it was alleged that sixteen-year-old Patrick Morton, the son of a local blacksmith, had annoyed Beatrix Laing, long reputed to be a witch, by refusing to make her some nails. Next day, while passing her house, Patrick noticed a wooden vessel with some water and a fire coal in it, which he took to be a magical charm directed against himself. At once he became so weak that he took to his bed, and there he lay for several weeks, becoming more and more emaciated as time passed. Then at the beginning of May he started to have fits. His body would distort itself into remarkable and unnatural positions, and his tongue would be drawn back right into his throat. Even so, he was able to let people know the names of those he claimed were inflicting these magical torments upon him: Nickolas Lowson, Beatrix Laing, Janet Cornfoot, Margaret Wallace, Isobel Adamson, Margaret Jack, and Thomas Brown, all of whom were arrested and imprisoned, probably in the church steeple, the common place of confinement in places that did not have a town jail.

They were examined by the kirk session on May 29, 1704, and four of them confessed they had made a pact with the Devil, renounced their baptism, and attended meetings along with several others whom they named. This was serious, so the affair was referred to the presbytery, then to the General Assembly, and finally to the Privy Council of Scotland, which was asked for a commission to try the accused. The Privy Council sent three men to Pittenweem to investigate, as a result of which they decided not to proceed with prosecutions and ordered the prisoners' release. The women were set free. Thomas Brown, however, had died in prison. It appears that the local minister had been reading to Patrick Morton an account of the recent Bargarran case in which a young woman had accused several people of bewitching her. We cannot be sure when the minister started his reading, but Patrick did not begin to exhibit signs of demonic possession until halfway through his illness, so it looks as though Patrick may have faked his symptoms in imitation of "the Bargarran imposter," as the young woman involved in that case was called.

The release of the prisoners did them little good. Emotions were running high in Pittenweem, and Beatrix Laing continued to be persecuted by the townsfolk, who imprisoned her for five months and then, when she escaped, prevented her from returning to her own house. She was thus forced to live as a beggar.

Another of the accused, Janet Cornfoot, suffered much more. Escaping from Pittenweem to a nearby village after being tortured, she was sent back by its minister. On her return, a mob lynched her, first pelting her with stones while she was hanging from a rope and finally pressing her to death beneath a heavy door heaped with stones. This outrage reached the ears of the Privy Council, which ordered the arrest and prosecution of those involved, particularly the local magistrates who had signally failed to keep order. Despite a flurry of indignant pamphlets, nothing was done; the council did not pursue the matter further.

P. G. MAXWELL-STUART

See also: BEWITCHMENT; LYNCHING; POSSESSION, DEMONIC; SCOTLAND.

References and further reading:

Anonymous. 1820. *A True and Full Relation of the Witches at Pittenweem.* . . . 1704. Reprinted in *A Collection of Rare and Curious Tracts on Witchcraft.* Edited by D. Webster. Edinburgh.

Goodare, Julian, ed. 2002. *The Scottish Witch-Hunt in Context.* Manchester: Manchester University Press, pp. 43–44, 175, 179–181, 202–203.

Ms. record. 1704. Scottish Record Office: CH2/183.

PLAGUE

From earliest times, epidemic disease has been associated with preternatural and supernatural forces and powers. Most Europeans, whose understanding of disease, famine, and war was largely drawn from the Bible, were convinced that epidemics were not purely natural phenomena. Disease was frequently seen as a tool God used to chastise wicked people. Certain biblical passages (but rarely the book of Job) facilitated this understanding of disease.

The plagues of Egypt included epidemic disasters God employed to force Pharaoh to free the children of Israel. However, these stories communicated more to medieval and early modern Christians than just God's power over his creation. The biblical account also stressed the ability of Pharaoh's "magicians" to perform acts that mirrored—though never defeated—the miracles Moses performed (Exod. 7:6–11:10). Because many of these miracles were connected with disease, commentators deduced that God was directly involved with large-scale epidemics. Similar conclusions could be drawn from the death of 24,000 Israelites from plague for their sexual immorality and idolatry in consorting with Moabites and worshipping Baal (Num. 25:1–9)—another direct connection between plague and God's wrath. Israel's enemies were beset with plague and were also struck by famine after capturing the Ark of the Covenant (1 Sam. 5:1–6:18). The obvious conclusion was that epidemics were associated with God's wrath and that disease could be averted by avoiding an evil that had aroused God's anger.

Christianity made the link between disease (and the ability to prevent or cure it) and religion even more explicit. Jesus and the Apostles proved their divine mandate by their miracles, most of which cured physical or psychological ailments (disease and possession). Moreover, introducing demons and an explicit Satan (absent in the Hebrew Bible) powerful enough to tempt Jesus in the wilderness added a new and menacing dimension to beliefs about illness. The Christian Church continued these ideas through the cults of martyrs and saints, placing great emphasis on their power over disease and even death. Also, saints' lives often revolved around conflict with Satan or his demonic minions. Evil personified was closely connected with illness.

The historical record also persuaded Christians that humans played an active part in propagating epidemic disease. Although Thucydides believed that the great plague that struck Athens during the Peloponnesian War (431–404 B.C.E.) was natural, he noted that others attributed it to evil forces, especially intervention by Athenian enemies. During the great pandemic that ravaged the Byzantine Empire, Emperor Justinian (ca. 482–565) clearly believed that the plague resulted from tolerating heresy and sexual immorality, especially homosexuality. More importantly for western Christians, during this pandemic, Rome was saved through a procession led by Pope Gregory I (540–604). The appearance of the Archangel Michael (still commemorated on top of Hadrian's Tomb) halted the advance of the disease and confirmed the power of prayer and procession in controlling plague.

PLAGUE AND SCAPEGOATS

Into this environment of disease, the demonic, and religion, the Black Death erupted from 1347 to 1351. During numerous subsequent outbreaks, various reactions emerged that affected future responses to plague. From France to Switzerland and Germany, Christians persecuted Jews as plague spreaders. This intensification of earlier anti-Semitism included accusing Jews of poisoning wells to cause plague. The pope and most of the ecclesiastical hierarchy categorically condemned such charges as irreligious nonsense. But the methodology and rationale behind the accusation are fascinating: Jews were accused of conspiring with lepers (ritually impure outcasts), the infidel rulers of Islamic Spain, and, most important, with Satan himself—that is, with internal and external enemies as well as the Great Enemy. These coconspirators provided the poisons used by the Jews. Thus, from the very first outbreaks of plague in the late 1340s, Christians were convinced that its "causes" lay within, including such "enemies" as Jews, Muslims, lepers, unbelievers (heretics), and such immoral people as prostitutes or homosexuals.

This persecution became a fixed pattern. Avoiding an impending outbreak or ending one required identifying and eradicating those responsible for provoking God's wrath. Then the survivors relied on penance, prayers, processions, and fasts to appease God. In other words, confronting a basically untreatable epidemic disease, western Europeans attempted to identify those who had "caused" it and thereby limit or eliminate it by sacrificing them. Moreover, plague remained enduringly connected to evil (the demonic).

PLAGUE-SPREADING CONSPIRACIES

Two later plague outbreaks revealed the capacity of Europeans to differentiate between evil people and demonic pacts. From about 1530 to about 1640, a region centered on Geneva, stretching from Lyons to Milan and from Neuchâtel to Turin, experienced frequent accusations that individuals had conspired to spread plague. Interestingly, the governments involved consistently refused to consider the conspirators "demonic." Many features of these conspiracies suggested witchcraft. For example, the conspirators used greases and powders to spread the plague. They took an oath saying, "if I reveal any details, may my soul be given to Satan." And most of them were poor, marginalized women.

Nevertheless, other features encouraged a purely natural understanding of these conspiracies. Barber-surgeons, who mixed the greases and powders or gave instructions for preparing them, led the conspirators. The conspiracies never involved orgiastic rituals and never met Satan. Their goal was to allow plague workers greater opportunity to loot the homes of wealthy people. Thus, even though the conspirators' behavior somewhat resembled a demonic pact, the magistrates consistently saw a purely natural conspiracy based on simple greed.

Only twice did Catholic clerics attempt to interpret plague-spreading behavior as demonic witchcraft, and Catholic officials took neither seriously. In Lyons, a Catholic writer alleged that the plague spreaders were Protestants allied with Satan, but the royal governor and magistracy ignored his charge. In Milan, during the 1630 outbreak made famous by Alessandro Manzoni, some clerical chroniclers implied a demonic connection behind the conspiracy. However, they merely suggested that plague spreading was "diabolical" (evil), not witchcraft involving a demonic pact. Plague-spreading conspiracies remind us that the early modern world was not determined to find supernatural causes for every natural event—even a plague outbreak. Although everyone involved in plague-spreading conspiracies believed that the presence and progress of plague was providential and almost certainly a sign of God's displeasure, no immediate or necessary links were made to demons and witches.

Explicit charges of spreading plague are largely absent from witchcraft accusations, although witches were routinely accused of causing disease and ill health in both animals and people. Even when Geneva simultaneously experienced plague, a plague-spreading conspiracy, *and* a witch hunt in the 1570s, the link was rarely made explicit, if at all. One possible explanation is that plague was seen first and foremost as a direct expression of divine judgment and chastisement rather than an evil that God simply allowed. Protestant theology precluded ascribing that much power to Satan, let alone his earthly minions (witches). History and Scripture suggested that life's greatest disasters—massive earthquakes, large-scale famines, devastating floods, horrendous epidemics—were acts of divine providence; Satan might be the prince of this world, but there were limits to his power. Thus, even if an occasional connection was made between individual witches and a specific plague outbreak, it never created a witch hunt. It was simply considered an extreme example of *maleficium* (harmful magic), less important than the judges' emphasis on the stereotypical aspects of demonic pacts and Sabbats.

WILLIAM G. NAPHY

See also: BIBLE; DEVIL; DISEASE; GENEVA; HOMOSEXUALITY; MIRACLES; MOSES; POISON; SCAPEGOATS.

References and further reading:
Briggs, Robin. 2002. *Witches and Neighbours: The Social and Cultural Context of European Witchcraft.* 2nd ed. Oxford: Blackwell.
Cunningham, Andrew, and Ole P. Grell. 2000. *The Four Horsemen of the Apocalypse: Religion, War, Famine and Death in Reformation Europe.* Cambridge: Cambridge University Press.
Dixon, L. 1995. *Perilous Chastity: Women and Illness in Pre-Enlightenment Art and Medicine.* Ithaca, NY: Cornell University Press.
Edwards, J. 1988. *The Jews in Western Europe, 1400–1700.* Manchester: Manchester University Press.
Elmer, Peter, ed. 2004. *The Healing Arts: Health, Disease, and Society in Europe 1500–1800.* Manchester: Open University Press.
Ginzburg, Carlo. 1983. *Night Battles.* London: Routledge.
Kiple, Kenneth, ed. 1997. *Plague, Pox, and Pestilence.* London: Weidenfeld and Nicolson.
Naphy, W. G. 2002. *Plagues, Poisons, and Potions: Plague-Spreading Conspiracies in the Western Alps, c. 1530–1640.* Manchester: Manchester University Press.
Siraisi, Nancy G. 1990. *Medieval and Early Renaissance Medicine. An Introduction to Knowledge and Practice.* Chicago: University of Chicago Press.
Stephens, Walter. 2002. *Demon Lovers: Witchcraft, Sex, and the Crisis of Belief.* Chicago: University of Chicago Press.

PLANTSCH, MARTIN (CA. 1460–1533/1535)

Considered one of the most prominent representatives of a moderate understanding of witchcraft during the transition to early modern times, Plantsch studied theology at Tübingen under Gabriel Biel (ca. 1410–1495), who is generally considered the most significant late scholastic representative of the *via moderna* (modern way). A strict nominalist (nominalism postulates the freedom of the divine will as the highest principle), Plantsch became university principal at Tübingen in 1490 and lectured as doctor of theology after 1494.

Prompted by a witchcraft trial in Tübingen in 1505, Plantsch undertook a thorough theological investigation of the subject of witchcraft, producing a series of sermons that were printed in 1507 as an *Opusculum de Sagis Maleficiis* (A Brief Work on Evil Witches). This extensive piece of work, the style of which was more academic-scholastic than rhetorical, considered all the prevalent contemporary aspects of the doctrine of witchcraft. Like the lawyer Ulrich Molitor, who had some impact shortly before, Plantsch upheld certain aspects of the belief in witches, such as their ability to work *maleficia* (harmful magic) and influence the weather, but rejected the notion of witches actually flying and the resulting consequences. Thus, Plantsch must be ranked among the initiators of the *Canon Episcopi* (ca. 906) tradition, which was particularly widespread in southwestern Germany. Further aspects of his nominalist viewpoint included his claim that God's permission was necessary for any actions by witches and his admonition to victims of witchcraft not to use any countermagic. However, Plantsch's scholastic background was evident in the fact that he adopted such aspects of medieval demonology as incubi and succubi.

To what extent Plantsch was actually involved in propagating these ideas is difficult to evaluate, but his reputation as principal and theology professor at Tübingen University and as a gifted preacher undoubtedly gave him a certain level of influence. Furthermore, Plantsch was in contact with such well-known figures in both theology and the arts as Johannes Reuchlin; another humanist, Heinrich Bebel, wrote a short poem for the preface to Plantsch's *Opusculum*. Because of his close relationship with Reuchlin, Philip Melanchthon may have acquired his comparatively moderate attitude toward witchcraft during his studies at Tübingen. In the late medieval dispute on the "new" understanding of witchcraft, Plantsch presented his views as the "Catholic truth." Like the *Malleus Maleficarum* (The Hammer of Witches, 1486), but with more formal authority and correctness, the Tübingen professor of theology declared his attitude toward the issue of witchcraft to be correct doctrine—a view, however, at odds with the *communis opinio* (common opinion).

JÖRG HAUSTEIN;

TRANSLATED BY HELEN SIEGBURG

See also: *CANON EPISCOPI;* DEMONOLOGY; INCUBUS AND SUCCUBUS; *MALLEUS MALEFICARUM;* MOLITOR, ULRICH.

References and further reading:

Clark, Stuart. 1997. *Thinking with Demons: The Idea of Witchcraft in Early Modern Europe.* Oxford: Clarendon.

Mentzel-Reuters, Arno. 1995. "Notanda reliquit doctor Martinus Plantsch: Leben und Werk eines Tübinger Theologen (ca. 1460–1533)." *Bausteine zur Tübinger Universitätsgeschichte* 7: 1–44.

Midelfort, H. C. Erik. 1972. *Witchcraft in Southwestern Germany 1562–1684: The Social and Intellectual Foundations.* Stanford: Stanford University Press.

Oberman, Heiko A. 1981. *Masters of the Reformation: The Emergence of a New Intellectual Climate in Europe.* New York: Cambridge University Press.

Plantsch, Martin. 1507. *Opusculum de sagis maleficis.* Pforzheim: Anshelm. Online facsimile: http://141.84.81.24/cgi-bin/plantsch/plantsch.html.

PLEIER (PLEYER, BLEIER), CORNELIUS (1595–16??)

Pleier was a physician who published the *Malleus judicum* (The Hammer of Judges), an anonymous pamphlet opposing witchcraft trials, in 1628.

The son of a Lutheran cleric in Coburg, Pleier received his doctorate at Basel in 1620; he was named municipal physician of Coburg in 1622 and professor at the local *Gymnasium Casimirianum* in 1623. In 1624, he became municipal physician at Kitzingen am Main but lost his position in 1629 during the bishop of Würzburg's recatholicization. Pleier later converted to Catholicism. His exact date of death is unknown.

Pleier was responsible for two medical publications. The anonymous pamphlet, allegedly written by a "Catholic Christian," entitled *Malleus judicum, Das ist: Gesetzhammer der unbarmherzigen Hexenrichter, Auss dem besten Ertz Göttlicher, Natürlicher und Weltlicher Rechten* (Hammer of Judges, in Other Words, a Legal Hammer Against Pitiless Witchcraft Judges, Taken from the Best Divine, Natural, and Human Laws) appeared between 1626 and 1629. The copy in the state library of Bamberg contains a handwritten remark naming Pleier as the author. Pleier based his work on Johann Weyer's *De praestigiis daemonum* (On the Tricks of Devils, 1563) and frequently cited Hermann Witekind's (pseud. Augustin Lercheimer) *Christlich bedencken und erinnerung von Zauberey* (Christian Thoughts and Memories about Sorcery, 1585) and Anton Prätorius's *Von Zauberey und Zauberern Gründlicher Bericht* (A Thorough Account of Magic and Magicians, 1598). In polemical form, Pleier criticized judges, torture, and cruel prisons and demanded "Christian reforms" instead of executions from the authorities. The well-known witchcraft commissioner Heinrich von Schultheis voiced his objections to the *Malleus judicum* in 1634, which entered the collection of Johann Reiche in 1703.

GUNTHER FRANZ;

TRANSLATED BY JONATHAN STICKNEY

See also: PRÄTORIUS, ANTON; SCHULTHEIS, HEINRICH VON; SKEPTICISM; WEYER, JOHANN; WITEKIND, HERMANN.

References and further reading:
Franz, Gunther. 1992. "Der *Malleus Judicum, Das ist:*
Gesetzhammer der unbarmhertzigen Hexenrichter von Cornelius
Pleier im Vergleich mit Friedrich Spees *Cautio Criminalis.*" Pp.
199–222 in *Vom Unfug des Hexen-Processes: Gegner der*
Hexenverfolgung von Johann Weyer bis Friedrich Spee. Edited by
Hartmut Lehmann and Otto Ulbricht. Wiesbaden:
Harrossowitz.
———. 1994. "Der *Malleus Judicum, Das ist: Gesetzeshammer der*
unbarmherzigen Hexenrichter von Cornelius Pleier und andere
Gegner der Hexenprozesse von Johann Weyer bis Friedrich
Spee." Pp. 27–47 in *The Salem Witchcraft Persecutions.* Edited
by Winfried Herget. Trier: Wissenschaftlicher.

POISON

Poisons have been strongly associated with witchcraft and sorcery throughout the world since antiquity, because they manifest a desire to cause harm; involve secret, often ritual, preparations; and work through a hidden, or occult, process. Even though the defining feature of magic and witchcraft is spiritual or supernatural agency, they actually make extensive use of physical substances. They may be incorporated into secret rituals performed at a distance, but they may also be used to "carry" a spell by being brought to or concealed near the target or by being introduced directly into the victim's body. Such substances may contain intrinsically toxic chemicals or psychoactive agents that are not inherently toxic but open the victim to suggestion; they may even be chemically inert, deriving their power purely from the sorcerer's confidence in and the victim's fear of their magical properties. The inherent uncertainty of allegations of poisoning along with the important role of psychological factors in many cases have led some social scientists to treat fear of poisoning as more significant than the use of poisons. There is no question that such fear is an important phenomenon in its own right, but strong evidence from both anthropology and history suggests that this fear is rooted in the fact that poisons have been used as a real and potent form of interpersonal attack in a wide variety of social settings.

Anthropologists have found varying degrees of association between sorcery and poison in Australia, Oceania, Africa, and the Americas. In some cases, sorcerers use chemically active agents in connection with magic rituals while attributing the poison's power at least as much to the magic as to the substance's intrinsic properties. In other cases, poisons are understood to work without magic, and sorcerers may use them separately, or even as a backup if their regular spells do not seem to be working. In the West, the connection between magic and poisoning goes back to antiquity. There is a linguistic link between poison and magic in both the Greek word *pharmakon* and the Latin *veneficium* (poisoning), and the association was made by the second-century *Epistle of Barnabas,* St. Augustine, Isidore of Seville, and the Venerable Bede. During the High Middle Ages, magicians flourished at courts, with their intense rivalries and intrigues, and some practitioners provided poisons along with more esoteric services. Similar practitioners operated at the popular level as well, and there is considerable evidence that both specialized sorcerers and ordinary people continued to employ poisons in the early modern period. Allegations of poisoning were among the most common accusations precipitating witchcraft trials, and in German courts the term *veneficium* came to be used routinely as a term for witchcraft.

The types of poisons used included both refined products like arsenic, rat poison, and lye, and locally occurring fauna such as ergot-infested wheat, toxic mushrooms, and parts of various flowering plants. The efficacy of the former was basically a function of dosage, so anyone who could purchase them could use them. Employing the latter was more difficult because the plants had to be located and in some cases picked at a particular stage of growth, the potent parts had to be known, and they had to be prepared in a way that made them effective while not alerting the person consuming them. Poisons were most commonly introduced in food or drink served, lent, or bestowed as a gift, but they could also be secretly introduced into the victim's food stocks or, in Germany, beer cask, which was often kept open near the door. Another form of delivery of psychoactive agents was as a salve smeared on the victim's skin, which caused local numbness and general disorientation that could easily be interpreted into a variety of somatic complaints. The generally surreptitious nature of poison contributed to a strong element of suspicion in neighborly relations in early modern Europe, and it was not uncommon for people to routinely feed pieces of food received from neighbors to household animals before consuming the rest themselves.

The gradual substitution of *veneficium* for "witchcraft" in legal terminology not only reflected the important role of poisons in witchcraft beliefs but also contributed to the gradual decline of witchcraft prosecutions. First, it led to the separation of the physical crime, which even leading skeptics like Johann Weyer and Reginald Scot considered a felony, from the religious and spiritual offenses. Second, the continued prosecution of poisonings and the increased regulation of poisons reduced one of the most common fears that had contributed to witchcraft suspicions.

EDWARD BEVER

See also: AFFAIR OF THE POISONS; HEMLOCK; *MALEFICIUM;*
NIGHTSHADE; OINTMENTS; PLAGUE; POTIONS.

References and further reading:
Arendt-Schulte, Ingrid. 1994. *Weise Frauen—böse Weiber: Die*
Geschichte der Hexen der Frühen Neuzeit. Freiburg: Herder.
Beckmann, Dieter, and Barbara Beckmann. 1990. *Alraun, Beifuss,*
und andere Hexenkräuter. Frankfurt and New York: Campus.

Bever, Edward. 2002. "Women, Witchcraft, and Power in the Early Modern Community." *Journal of Social History* 36, no. 4: 955–988.

Fiume, Giovanna. 1997. "The Old Vinegar Lady, or the Judicial Modernization of the Crime of Witchcraft." Pp. 65–87 in *History from Crime*. Edited by Edward Muir and Guido Ruggiero. Translated by Corrada Curry et al. Baltimore: Johns Hopkins University Press.

Kieckhefer, Richard. 1976. *European Witch Trials: Their Foundations in Popular and Learned Culture, 1300–1500*. Berkeley: University of California Press.

Robischeaux, Thomas. 2001. "Witchcraft and Forensic Medicine in Seventeenth Century Germany." Pp. 197–216 in *Languages of Witchcraft*. Edited by Stuart Clark. New York: St. Martin's.

POLAND

Witchcraft prosecutions peaked in the Polish Crown lands between 1650 and 1750, about a century later than most of Europe, with the exception of Hungary or Russia. Estimates of the number of deaths attributable to the prosecutions have ranged from a few thousand to 30,000. The subject has received relatively little scholarly analysis, and serious research has been hampered by the loss of many court records during World War II. The Polish-Lithuanian Commonwealth of the early modern period included territory that now comprises much of Ukraine and Belarus, plus Lithuania and parts of Latvia. In the fourteenth and fifteenth centuries, witchcraft trials were held before clerical courts, where death sentences were not usually passed. From the sixteenth century, however, jurisdiction passed increasingly to secular courts, where the death sentence (burning at the stake) was common. Legal persecution ended in Poland only in 1776, with the repeal of the witchcraft statutes. However, illegal reprisals persisted into the nineteenth and even twentieth centuries. One of the most obvious explanations for the late peak in the number of trials is the crises and invasions that Poland experienced in the late seventeenth and early eighteenth centuries. The best extant records come from the area around Poznań, known as *Wielkopolska* (Greater Poland), and from Gdansk (Danzig), Cracow, Lublin, and Bydgoszcz.

GEOGRAPHY AND STATISTICS

The statistics quoted by the majority of historians of the European witchcraft prosecutions have been derived from Bogdan Baranowski's estimate of a total of 15,000 deaths, found in the French summary of his work *Procesy czarownic w Polsce w XVII i XVIII w.* (Witchcraft Trials in Poland in the Seventeenth and Eighteenth Centuries). Baranowski, using a figure of 1,250 Polish towns, supposed that each town court tried an average of four cases of witchcraft during the period and sentenced two people to death from each trial. He added 5,000 deaths to reflect the illegal murders of people suspected of witchcraft, making a total of 15,000 deaths

throughout the period (Baranowski 1952, 178). His calculations included only the territory known as the Crown lands of Poland, excluding both Silesia and the Grand Duchy of Lithuania. However, in an epilogue to the first Polish translation of Kurt Baschwitz's work *Czarownice: Dzieje procesów o czary* (Witches: A History of Witchcraft Trials), published in 1963, Baranowski revised his statistics down to a few thousand. Trials for sorcery or magical practices were also heard prior to the sixteenth century, but according to extant records, the peak of the persecution was between 1650 and 1750 (from work carried out on *Wielkopolska*). There appear to have been more trials in the western areas of Poland and fewer in areas to the east, where Orthodoxy replaced Catholicism as the predominant religion. This geographical and chronological diffusion may be merely a reflection of the extant records rather than an accurate account of the prosecutions.

The percentage of cases in which the death sentence (burning at the stake) was passed varied substantially geographically, from close to 100 percent in some towns of Greater Poland to under 50 percent in those privileged towns (e.g., Cracow and Lublin) where appellate systems were in place. However, in private towns (that is, owned by a noble, a king, or the Church), final jurisdiction was often in the hands of the manorial lord. Therefore, because charges were often instigated by him or at his instruction against his peasants, the sentences were frequently carried out on the morning following the trial. Those tried were almost exclusively peasants, because only their peers could try the nobility. Occasionally minor noblewomen appeared in trials, but that was rare.

In the nineteenth century, an attempt was made to centralize the archival collections, and many records were moved to Warsaw to the Archiwum Główne Akt Dawnych (AGAD; Central Archive of Old Records). Due to extensive bombing during World War II, up to 90 percent of these records were destroyed. Thus, where records have not survived, our information is necessarily based on the work of authors writing before 1939 who were familiar with the lost sources. Another collection of primary material comes from an unexpected source, which has barely begun to be used in Poland: during World War II, the *H-Sonnderkommando* (Special Unit H [*Hexen* = witches]), under instructions from Heinrich Himmler, extended their collection of witchcraft trial records into the occupied territories. This collection, known as the *Himmlerkartoteka* (Himmler card index), is held in Poznań, with a copy in Berlin.

CHRONOLOGY OF THE TRIALS

The earliest literary mentions of individuals employing witchcraft in Poland appeared in the chronicles of Marcin Bielski and Jan Długosz. They tended to describe individuals whose practices were more commonly regarded as sorcery or slanders against women. In many trials before fifteenth-century clerical courts, the accused was charged with causing impotence, divination, or illness. In other cases, men sought to dissolve marriages because their wives had reputations as witches. In Poland, as in the West, clerical courts almost never passed death sentences (although the first execution in Poland, in 1511, occurred in an ecclesiastical court, with the initial execution pronounced by a secular court in 1544); instead, the accused were required to apologize, swear not to repeat the crime, and pay a suitable fine. Banishment became more common in the sixteenth century, when the charges made against those accused of witchcraft became more elaborate. Rituals that had previously been encouraged even by the town authorities (for example, in Biecz, a well-known witch called *Mater Diabolica* [diabolical Mother] Zachariaszek had been hired as late as 1600 to find stolen goods) now became unacceptable. In the secular trials from the sixteenth century, especially those from Kalisz and Poznań, starting in 1544, charges were generally made against the so-called cunning folk. Confessions included descriptions of invocations of a pseudoreligious nature to the Virgin Mary and the saints and the use of herbs to restore ruined beer or to make cows produce more milk.

At the court of the Polish king Sigismund II Augustus (ruled 1548–1572), rumors of the deployment of witchcraft took on a political nature (as in Russia). They never reached any judicial court but instead served to ruin the reputations of those involved. The accusations were leveled first at the king's mother Bona Sforza, an Italian (a typical xenophobic tactic against foreigners). Foreigners were more often perceived to use magic in the context of warfare. A witch employed by Bona was arrested on the orders of King Sigismund, who was ready to try her and sentence her to death. She was taken to Brest, but the king was also on his way there. His astrologer Proboszczewicz advised him that he would be in danger from fire in that city, so he moved the witch to Dubnik, where the sentence was carried out. In turn, the king's wife, Barbara Radziwiłłówna, was accused of employing love magic to seduce the king. Sigismund Augustus appears to have been particularly susceptible to these practices, because his later mistresses, Susanna Orłowska and Barbara Giżanka, were also thought to have been witches.

This sample of 251 trials involved 511 defendants, 96 percent of whom were female. The largest outbreaks came at Kalisz (1650–1680), Gniezno (1670–1690), and Grodzisk (1710–1720). There was a steady trickle of trials heard at Kleczew. The maximum number of deaths (24) occurred between 1707 and 1711. From this sample, only four places, including Poznań, heard more than twenty trials.

After the major disruptions of Poland's mid-seventeenth century "deluge," witch hunting gathered momentum during the late seventeenth and early eighteenth centuries. The reasons suggested include cultural backwardness, although in light of Poland's intellectual achievements in the Renaissance and highly developed relations with western Europe, this is a debatable viewpoint. A better reason employs the social-strain gauge theory of witchcraft: the wars and economic disasters that ravaged Poland left behind a new level of fear and suspicion, increased by severe competition for resources. In this heightened atmosphere, accusations of witchcraft were more likely to surface and be pursued vigorously.

ACCUSATIONS

By the late sixteenth century, Polish witchcraft trials began to contain mentions of the Devil. Eventually, suspicion of concrete harm or *maleficium* was no longer required for a charge to be brought; that of making a pact with the Devil sufficed. Accusations displayed many features common to western European witchcraft, such as love magic, causing harm to people or animals, and attendance at the Sabbat. Charges also included inflicting devils upon someone, which could be done through food or drink. A particularly Polish feature was that of *koltun*, or a condition of matted hair, known as *Plica Polonica*, which was also believed to be the result of bewitchment. Victims would not cut off their hair for fear of death or blindness. Court charges involving *koltuń* persisted well beyond the repeal of the witchcraft acts in 1776.

In a collection of trials from Grodzisk, Greater Poland (1707–1737), and also at Kleczew, the accused admitted to stealing the Host and then beating it until it bled and the Christ Child appeared. The blood was then used in various spells. This echoed the bleeding

TABLE P-1 PRELIMINARY SURVEY OF TWENTY-FIVE TOWNS IN WIELKOPOLSKA

Dates	Trials	Accused Women/Men
1500–1575	6	6/0
1576–1600	8	10/0
1601–1625	15	18/3
1626–1650	14	25/1
1651–1675	36	81/1
1676–1700	78	188/5
1701–1725	47	75/5
1726–1750	38	62/5
1751–1775	6	16/0
1776–1800	3	9/1

Host accusations, usually leveled against Jews in Germany, Poland, and elsewhere in the medieval period. Coincidentally, the peak in the number of witchcraft trials coincided with an increase in accusations of the blood libel (the baseless charge that Jews used Christian blood for religious purposes) in Poland. Usually powders of varying colors were used to harm people, animals, or crops, but sometimes manure and other elements were said to have been buried under the intended victim's threshold.

The witches' gathering, or Sabbat, took place on *Łysa Góra* (Bald Mountain). However, like Sweden's Blåkulla, this did not refer exclusively to the mountain bearing that name in the *Góry Świętokrzyskie* (Holy Cross Mountains). In the trial records, it indicated any local area that was a supposed meeting place. Feasts of abhorrent food were served, weddings were celebrated between witches and devils, and the witches usually were reported to have had sex with their devils. In contrast to popular belief, Polish trial records rarely mentioned diabolic ceremonies, orgiastic behavior, or boiling babies for their fat. Moreover, the traditional concept of the Devil's pact was replaced by sexual consummation between an individual devil and a witch. These devils were often named and described as brightly clothed. The Devil's mark is rarely found in trial accounts, but there are descriptions of the Devil biting the accused in a particular finger. Silence during torture was ascribed to the presence of the Devil, who purportedly prevented the accused from confessing.

THE CRIME OF WITCHCRAFT

Witchcraft was prohibited and punished in several statutes, the first of which appears to come from the Synod of Buda in 1279. A provincial law was passed that forbade anyone other than a bishop to give penance to a practitioner of witchcraft. In the fifteenth and sixteenth centuries, episcopal courts heard most of the cases. Jurisdiction was removed ostensibly from the secular courts and placed under the clerical authorities under the Cracow Constitution of 1543; subsequent royal decrees from 1672 and 1713 confirmed this. Nonetheless, municipal secular courts held most Polish witchcraft trials because they involved material harm. Village courts were ordered to refer such cases up to municipal courts, and indeed the statute of 1745 forbade village judges from trying such cases on pain of death. Many town courts in Poland used Magdeburg Law, which was often quoted in cases, along with some modern legal authorities, including the Flemish jurist Joos de Damhouder and the Saxon jurist Benedict Carpzov (II). Polish courts also had the custom of referring to the breaking of the biblical commandments, especially Exod. 22:18 (22:17; in the King James Version, "Thou shalt not suffer a witch to live").

There was a similar pattern to the case procedure. Another individual usually brought charges against the accused. The accused witch was questioned and then tortured. After torture, her confession was confirmed, and often the torture was repeated. The use of torture was apparent in virtually every case from *Wielkopolska,* even those involving children. It took such forms as burning the accused with straw, racking, and burning candles under the arms or against the lips. It was supposed to be employed only three times, but there were many exceptions to this rule. Those who died in the course of torture were often declared to be witches, buried under the gallows, and denied burial in consecrated ground.

A controversial case, said to have taken place at Doruchów in 1775, has been the subject of much speculation (Tazbir 1966). An eyewitness account that appeared in 1835 described the case. The author gave a full description of the trial, torture, and execution of fourteen women. No trial record is extant, although there is a reference to the trial of six women in the same area in 1783. It was said that disgust at the Doruchów case hastened the end of the legal persecution. In the *Sejm* (Parliament) of 1776, torture and the trying of witches were forbidden by statute, at the representation of the castellan of Biecz, Wojciech Kluszewski.

However, there was another controversial claim involving an even later case, from 1793, sometimes mentioned as the last case in Europe. Its inclusion in Georg Wilhelm Soldan's work has ensured exposure. It was said in 1801 that when a Prussian commission arrived at a certain town in Poland in 1793, it saw the remains of stakes and was told by the town magistrate that two witches had been burned there. The account has been contested by Polish historians, who have dismissed it as German propaganda because the vague terminology used in describing the event provokes doubt about its authenticity. However, there were accounts of slander cases and even lynchings involving witchcraft long after that date, including the famous case of Krystyna Ceynowa of Chaupy, who was drowned in 1836 after several duckings (the swimming test). Other women were still occasionally ducked in ponds or rivers in the nineteenth century.

POLISH DEMONOLOGY

Descriptions of demonology, witchcraft, and magical remedies appeared in a variety of Polish printed sources, from early treatises to the calendars and encyclopedias of the late eighteenth century. The most important work was the first translation into any European vernacular of *Malleus Maleficarum,* under the title *Młot na czarownice* (The Hammer of Witches) by Stanislaw Zambkowicz, secretary to the castellan of Cracow, in 1614. The author translated only the second part and provided a short introduction. He dedicated the book to Prince Ostrogski and published it in Cracow. The printing house of Wojciech Regulus in Poznań published several works that were influential in the witchcraft debate. Among those was an anonymous work, which was an adaptation of, or heavily influenced by, the work of Friedrich Spee, titled *Czarownica powolana* (A Witch Denounced) in 1639. It was the most famous among several works attacking abuses perpetrated by the judiciary in witchcraft trials. Daniel Wisner, Serafin Gamalski, Bishop Józef Andrzej Zaluski, and Bishop Kazimierz Florian Czartoryski also attacked the judiciary. Of particular note are the works by Jan Bohomolec and Benedykt Chmielowski.

WANDA WYPORSKA

See also: ACCUSATIONS; BARANOWSKI, BOGDAN; CAROLINA CODE; CARPZOV, BENEDICT; CHRONOLOGY OF WITCHCRAFT TRIALS; CONFESSIONS; COURTS, ECCLESIASTICAL; COURTS, SECULAR; CUNNING FOLK; DANZIG (GDANSK); DEVIL; EXECUTIONERS; EXECUTIONS; HUNGARY; JEWS, WITCHCRAFT, AND MAGIC; LAWS ON WITCHCRAFT (EARLY MODERN); LITHUANIA, GRAND DUCHY OF; LOVE MAGIC; LYNCHING; *MALEFICIUM; MALLEUS MALEFICARUM;* NAZI INTEREST IN WITCH PERSECUTION; ORTHODOX CHRISTIANITY; PACT WITH THE DEVIL; POZNAŃ; PRUSSIA; RITUAL MAGIC; RITUAL MURDER; RUSSIA; SABBAT; SEXUAL ACTIVITY, DIABOLIC; SILESIA; SOLDAN, WILHELM GOTTLIEB; SOURCES FOR WITCHCRAFT TRIALS; SWIMMING TEST; TORTURE; TRIALS; UKRAINE, WITCHCRAFT TRIALS; ZIARNKO, JAN.

References and further reading:
Baranowski, Bogdan. 1952. *Procesy czarownic w Polsce w XVII i XVIII wieku.* Łódź: Lodzkie Towarzystwo Naukowe.
———. 1963. Epilogue to Kurt Baschwitz., *Czarownice: Dzieje procesów o czary.* Warsaw: PWN.
Brzezińska, Anna. 1993–1996. "Accusations of Love Magic in the Renaissance Courtly Culture of the Polish-Lithuanian Commonwealth." *East Central Europe* 20–23: 117–140.
Carpzov, Benedict. 1684. *Practicae novae rerum criminalium imperialis saxonica in tres partes divisa.* Viteberg.
Czartoryski, Bishop K. F. 1669a. *Instructio circa judicia sagarum judicibus eorumque consiliariis accomodata Romae primum 1657.* Swarzewice.
———. 1669b. *Mandatum pastorale ad universum clerum et populum Dioecesis suae de cantelis in processu contra sagas adhibendis die XI Aprilis.* n.p.
Długosz, Jan. 1711–1712. *Historia Polonica Libri XII.* Cracow.
Gamalski, Serafin. 1742. *Przestrogi duchowne sędziom, inwestygatorom i instygatorom czarownic.* Poznań.
Kaczmarczyk, Zdzislaw, ed. 1980. *Volumina legum, przedruk zbioru praw staraniem XX: Pijarów w Warszawie od roku 1732 do 1793.* Warsaw: Wydawnictwa Artystyczne i Filmowe.
Koranyi, Karol. 1927. "Czary i gusła przed sądem kościelnemi w Polsce w XV i w pierwszej polowie XVI wieku." *Lud* 26: 1–24.
Kramer, Heinrich, and Jakub [sic] Sprenger. 1614. *Młot na czarownice.* Translated by S. Zambkowicz. Cracow: Szymon Kempini.
Soldan, Wilhelm. 1843. *Geschichte der Hexenprozesse.* Stuttgart and Tubingen.
Tazbir, Janusz. 1966. "Z dziejów falszerstw historycznych w Polsce w pierwszej polowie XIX wieku." *Przeglad Historyczny* 57: 580–598.
Wisner, Daniel. 1639. *Tractatus brevis de extramagi, lamii, veneticis.* Poznań.
Wyporska, Wanda. 2003. "Witchcraft, Arson, and Murder—the Turek Trial of 1652." *Central Europe* 1: 41–54.
X. A. R. 1835. "Relacja naocznego świadka o straceniu 14-tu mniemanych czarownic w drugiej połowie 18-go wieku." *Przyjaciel Ludu* 2, no. 16.
Załuski, Bishop Józef. 1766. *Objaśnienie błędami zabobonów zarażonych oraz opisanie niegodziwości, która pochodzi sądzenia przez próbę pławienia w wodzie mniemanych czarownic jako takowa próba jest omylna różnym dowodami stwierzone.* Berdyczów.

POLTERGEIST

A spirit or ghost that makes itself known by loud noises or movements is known as a poltergeist.

In some witchcraft trials one could observe a poltergeist pattern: inexplicable sounds are heard, inanimate objects move of their own accord, and people are lifted into the air in inexplicable ways. A well-known example is the case against the drummer of Tedworth, who was held responsible for the strange phenomena in the home of John Mompesson, a magistrate of Tedworth, Wiltshire. The phenomena continued from March 1662 to April 1663, and began after Mompesson, in connection with a forgery trial, had confiscated the drum of a vagrant confidence trickster, William Drury. The magistrate kept the drum in his own home after releasing Drury. The situation became even more annoying when the strange phenomena continued in Mompesson's home after the drum had been destroyed, particularly affecting his ten-year-old daughter. In the meantime, the confidence trickster had been sentenced in Gloucester to transportation to Virginia for stealing pigs, but he escaped by jumping overboard from the convict ship. At the beginning of 1663 he reappeared with his trickery and a new drum a few miles from Tedworth. Mompesson had him arrested and charged with practicing witchcraft; although several of the local gentry testified against him, Drury had to be acquitted for lack of evidence. The celebrity of the case was due first and foremost to the Reverend Joseph Glanvill, chaplain to Charles II and a Fellow of the Royal Society, who went to Tedworth to investigate the matter and later described it in his *Sadducismus Triumphatus* (*Sadducism Conquered,* 1681), which gave the author a reputation as a father of modern psychical research.

An unspecified number of similar cases can be found among European witchcraft trials. From Denmark we have the famous case of the haunted house in Køge (*Køge Huskors*), where a rich merchant's house in this Zealand city was haunted by what we would call poltergeist manifestations. They did not cease until 1613, after seven local witches had been burned. During their trial they confessed that they had conjured the Devil up from a well and sent him into the merchant's house in the form of a rat. Many years later his widow wrote an account of the events, which was later published by the minister Johan Brunsmand in 1674 and translated into both Latin (1693) and German (1696).

The last Danish witchcraft trial, which took place in 1708 at the district court of the estate of Schelenborg on Funen island, also involved poltergeists; fourteen-year-old Anna Lauridsdatter was finally sentenced to the workhouse for life, and an adult woman, Karen Madsdatter, whom she had named as her mentor, was condemned to the stake. On the farm where Anna was a servant, heavy flour bags, kneading troughs, and many other objects were observed flying around without anyone being able to see who was moving them. At the Funen County Court, though, the judges partly overturned the local court's verdict. The adult woman was acquitted but was sentenced to make a public apology for the scandal she had caused with her false confession. The lower court's conviction of the young girl, however, who would not retract her statement, was upheld. She insisted that she had renounced Christianity and that the Devil, in the shape of a dog or a cat, had carried out her sorceries at the farm after she had invoked him. The enlightened high court judges tried in vain to get Anna Lauridsdatter to admit that she had performed these acts herself, but although she had been caught in the act several times, she denied it vehemently.

The descriptions of poltergeist phenomena in these trials were fairly constant. What changed were the explanations. During the witch persecutions, they were explained as witchcraft and the work of the Devil. During the Enlightenment, authorities tried to expose the phenomena as fraud or lies— as something that had not taken place in reality. Today they are sometimes explained by a parapsychological theory that claims that such phenomena always happen in connection with young women on the threshold of their teenage years, which are apparently related to certain psychical forces that are released in that connection.

GUSTAV HENNINGSEN;

TRANSLATED BY JAMES MANLEY

See also: GHOSTS; GLANVILL, JOSEPH; SALEM; SPECTRAL EVIDENCE.

References and further reading:

Bæksted, Anders, ed. 1953. *Johan Brunsmand: Køge Huskors.* Copenhagen: Danmarks Folkeminder (with English summary).
Brunsmand, Johan. 1696. *Das geängstigte Köge oder eine wahrhafte und denkwürdige Historie von einer entsetzlichen Versuchung des leidigen Satanas.* Leipzig.
Henningsen, Gustav. 1988. "Witch Persecution After the Era of the Witch Trials: A Contribution to Danish Ethnohistory." *Arv* 44: 103–153.
Robbins, Rossell Hope. 1959. *The Encyclopedia of Witchcraft and Demonology.* London: Peter Nevill.
Rogo, D. Scott. 1979. *The Poltergeist Experience.* New York and Harmondsworth: Penguin.

POMPONAZZI, PIETRO
(1462–1525)

Born in Mantua, this Aristotelian philosopher of the Renaissance studied at the University of Padua, where he earned his degree in 1487 and taught natural philosophy from 1488 until 1509 before moving to Ferrara and then to Bologna in 1511, where he died in 1525. Often (although incorrectly) denounced as an "atheist" who denied the immortality of the soul, he was also extremely skeptical about the supernatural phenomena that underpinned witchcraft theory in his age.

Pomponazzi owed much to Aristotle, as his numerous works show. At Bologna, he wrote his most famous (or notorious) work, *De immortalitate animae* (On the Immortality of the Soul, 1516). Here the original elements in Pomponazzi's position were derived from Aristotelian philosophy. He affirmed that no philosophical arguments derived from reason could demonstrate the hypothesis of the soul's immortality. Many works were written to refute Pomponazzi's conclusions. Although he never actually denied the immortality of the soul, his analysis led some of his followers to reject the dogma. Pomponazzi claimed to accept the authority of the Church in all matters of faith but refused to allow such considerations to influence his judgments in the realm of philosophy, whose autonomy he staunchly defended. He sought to reconcile his position with the dogmas of the Church by distinguishing between faith and knowledge, asserting that what is true in theology may not be true in philosophy. Some denounced him as a heretic.

With respect to witches and demons, Pomponazzi's main work is *De naturalium effectuum causis sive de incantationibus* (Of the Causes of Natural Effects, or of Incantations), written in 1520. Pomponazzi sought and found natural explanations for apparently wondrous events. He accepted the existence of angels and demons, but he argued the existence of natural causes to explain many apparently supernatural events. Pomponazzi was enough of a Christian to say that demons exist, but enough of an Aristotelian to deny that they can act on humans. By describing a natural world that had no need of demons, Pomponazzi influenced witchcraft skeptics such as Johann Weyer, Reginald Scot, and others. But, although he took a generally skeptical stance about the possibility of witchcraft, we should not exaggerate his radicalism; Pomponazzi accepted astrological influences and believed that words used in incantations or characters in talismans worked through some power of imagination (*vis imaginativa*) flowing from operator to patient.

Through such arguments, he revealed his desire to investigate nature in order to discover the real causes of odd events and to reject all ideas of occult causation. Any marvels or apparently strange events were, therefore, due to natural laws. Pomponazzi repeatedly claimed that his theories relied on Aristotle in exactly the same way as he had done with the immortality of the soul, yet he declared his desire to subject all his arguments to the Church's approval (however, *de incantationibus* was printed at Protestant Basel in 1556 through the efforts of an exiled Italian scientist, Guglielmo Grataroli).

Likewise controversial was Pomponazzi's book, *De fato libero arbitrio, praedestinatione et providentia Dei* (Of Arbitrary and Free Will, Predestination, and the Providence of God), written at the very moment (1520) when Martin Luther was so dramatically challenging free will, but not published until 1567. It dealt with determinism and predestination, another of Christianity's important but insoluble dilemmas. Here Pomponazzi first affirmed determinism but later managed to combine and reconcile traditional and progressive features. Thus, human free will coexisted with God's foreknowledge without being incompatible or contradictory. He maintained that divine omniscience did not preclude free will. His attempts to save human freedom without rejecting St. Augustine were unconvincing but original. Among Pomponazzi's many critics who wrote treaties against Pomponazzi's theories, the outstanding ones were Gasparo Contarini and Agostino Nifo.

MICHAELA VALENTE

See also: AQUINAS, THOMAS; CARDANO, GIROLAMO; DELLA PORTA, GIAMBATTISTA; SCOT, REGINALD; SKEPTICISM; WEYER, JOHANN.

References and further reading:
Nardi, Bruno. 1965. *Studi su Pietro Pomponazzi.* Florence: Le Monnier.
Pine, M. L. 1986. *Pietro Pomponazzi: Radical Philosopher of the Renaissance.* Padua: Antenore.
Pomponazzi, Pietro. 1567. *Opera.* Basel: Henricpetrina.
———. 1957. *Libri quinque de fato: De libero arbitrio et de praedistinatione.* Edited by Richard Lemay. Lucani: In Aedibus Thesauri Mundi.
———. 1997. *Gli incantesimi.* Edited by C. Innocenti. Scandicci: La nuova Italia.
———. 1999. *Trattato sull'immortalità dell'anima.* Edited V. Perrone. Florence: Olschki.
South, James B. 1999. *Sub voce* in *Encyclopedia of the Renaissance.* 6 vols. Edited by Paul F. Greudler. New York: Scribner's, 5: 116–118.
Walker, D. P. 1958. *Spiritual and Demonic Magic from Ficino to Campanella.* London: Warburg Institute.
Wonde, J. 1994. *Subjekt und Unsterblichkeit bei Pietro Pomponazzi.* Stuttgart: Teubner.
Zanier, G. 1975 *Ricerche sulla diffusione e fortuna del* De incantationibus *di Pomponazzi.* Florence: La Nuova Italia.

PONZINIBIO, GIOVANNI FRANCESCO/GIANFRANCESCO (FIRST HALF OF THE SIXTEENTH CENTURY)

In his *Tractatus subtilis, et elegans, de lamijs, et excellentia utriusque iuris* (Subtle and Elegant Treatise on Witches and the Excellence of Both Civil and Canon Law), written in 1519–1520, this somewhat skeptical lawyer from Piacenza denied the witches' flight to their nightly reunions because, he argued, demons no longer possessed powers after Jesus's death and so could not carry witches through the air. Although he dismissed Sabbats as nothing more than the fantasies and illusions of ignorant people from the lower social classes, he at the same time recognized that Sabbat-like gatherings must exist because the worship of the Devil formed the antithesis of the Christian religion and the sacraments. Ponzinibio was in no way a disbeliever in sorcery. He stated that men could be bewitched by incantations and *maleficia* (harmful magic) or by the evil eye. Thus he posited that it was untrue that witches carried the Sacrament to the Sabbat, offered it to the demon, and did the other things recorded in inquisitorial trials; and that it was not true that witches entered houses at night to suck children's blood, because a just God permitted no one to be injured unjustly and that everyone, even unborn children, had a guardian angel.

As a civil lawyer, Ponzinibio was profoundly angered by the injustices of inquisitorial procedure, whether applied to heretics or to sorcerers who had been defined by the theologians as heretical. So Ponzinibio attacked the whole system in his treatise: according to him, civil law had the same authority as canon law to discuss theological questions. He was very critical of the procedures used in witchcraft trials, urging judges to verify the authenticity of the accuser's testimony and the defendant's confessions, in addition to ignoring everything about the Sabbat and witches flying there.

By asserting the equality of Roman law with canon law even in theological matters and the consequent necessity of adding lay assessors to inquisitors, Ponzinibio aroused the wrath of inquisitors and theologians. Within a few years, the Dominican Bartolomeo della Spina criticized him vehemently in *Tractatus de pre-eminentia sacre Theologiae super alias omnes scientias* (Treatise on the Supremacy of Sacred Theology over All Other Sciences). For centuries, Spina pointed out, university faculties of theology had always ranked theology as the supreme science, by which such questions as witchcraft should be decided. In 1525, in three succeeding *Apologiae in Ponzinibium de lamijs* (Defense from Ponzinibio's On Witches), Spina refuted the lawyer's theories, relying on the Bible, the Church Fathers, and the *Malleus Maleficarum* (The Hammer of Witches, 1486). In his second *Apology,* Spina accused Ponzinibio of being a heretic, demanding that he renounce his theories and that inquisitors burn his treatise. Nevertheless, Ponzinibio's tract was reprinted (by Protestant heretics) at Frankfurt in 1592, together with Paolo Grillando's

Tractatus de haereticis et sortilegiis (Treatise on Heretics and Sorcerers).

DRIES VANYSACKER

See also: FLIGHT OF WITCHES; GRILLANDO, PAULO; INQUISITORIAL PROCEDURE; *MALLEUS MALEFICARUM;* ROMAN LAW; SABBAT; SPINA, BARTOLOMEO DELLA.
References and further reading:
Bonomo, G. 1959. *Caccia alle streghe: La cedenza nelle streghe dal secolo XIII al XIX, con particolare riferimento all'Italia.* Palermo: G. B. Palumbo, pp. 366–373.
Bosco, Giovanna. 1994. "Giovanni Francesco Ponzinibio (XV–XVI sec.)." Pp. 120–121 in *Bibliotheca Lamiarum: Documenti e immagini della stregoneria dal Medioevo all'Età Moderna.* Ospedaletto: Pacini editore.
Clark, Stuart 1997. *Thinking with Demons: The Idea of Witchcraft in Early Modern Europe.* Oxford: Clarendon.
Lea, Henry Charles. 1957. *Materials Toward a History of Witchcraft.* Edited by Arthur C. Howland. 3 vols. New York and London: Thomas Yoseloff, 1: 377–382.

POPULAR BELIEFS IN WITCHES

Some wicked women . . . believe and profess that, in the hours of night, they ride upon certain beasts with Diana, the goddess of pagans, and an innumerable multitude of women, and in the silence of the night traverse great space of earth, and obey her commands as of their lady, and are summoned to her service on certain nights. But if only they alone perished in their faithlessness, without drawing many other people with them into the destruction of infidelity, for an innumerable multitude . . . believe this to be truth. . . . (Kors and Peters 2001, 62)

With frustration, the *Canon Episcopi* (ca. 906) illustrated the existence of some deep-rooted and centuries-old popular beliefs about witches. Time and again, we must ask some essential questions about witches: Who were they? What did they look like? What were they supposed to do? Why did people believe in their powers? And, not least, did witches really exist?

DEFINITION

For most early modern people, a witch was someone who had performed some hostile act. But historians are wary of adopting restrictive definitions that could mislead them in understanding the surviving sources. An analysis of the language used in the trials can take us far because contemporaries often used a term like *witch* interchangeably with other dramatis personae. Specialized practitioners, similar to a sorcerer, a healer, or a soothsayer, acted in opposition to the witch. In this broader sense, *witch* could be extended to almost any operator within a complex ideology that was basically designed to explain unexpected misfortune. Therefore,

in this larger meaning, a witch could refer to any person with specific abilities for casting spells, magical healing, fortunetelling, or finding lost objects.

THE MALEFICENT WITCH

From a deep reading of witchcraft trials, two black-and-white opposed categories emerge: the just and the wicked, the forces of good who fight against the forces of evil. Theologians ruminated on the reciprocal necessity of these binary opposites. Tuscan villagers expressed such a vision of the world with the oft-repeated expression, "since I can distinguish the good from the evil." A witch, then, might be seen simply as the personification of a "primary factor" intrinsic to human nature: the evil. But throughout early modern Europe, the witch usually remained only a bit player, not a protagonist. In daily life within the village communities of old Europe, it was generally necessary to coexist with witches, even if sometimes it became unavoidable to destroy such evil people.

APPEARANCE, SEX, AND AGE

The nineteenth- and twentieth-century archetypal fairy-tale witches were old, female, and ugly. This picture resembled the sixteenth- and seventeenth-century stereotype shared by all social classes, although it tended to collapse during the largest witch hunts, whose victims included men, young women, and even child witches. Though this stereotype remained generally valid in ordinary situations, ugliness should be discounted from the identikit of a witch; behavior and personality were the determining criteria orienting people's judgment. No wonder that in order to distinguish witches from harmless neighbors, contemporaries often resorted to other devices, like looking for the Devil's mark or using the water ordeal (swimming test).

It remains emphatically true that, so far as we can determine, most witches were indeed females beyond childbearing age. As to age, 173 women in a sample of 304 witches from such diverse places as Geneva, Essex, Württemberg, the Department of the Nord in France, and Salem were older than fifty (Levack 1995, 142). But such statistics must be squared with the important fact that a good number of people tried as witches had been suspected for many years, even decades. As to gender, an identikit should not ignore the fact that in many countries (including Germany, the heartland of witch hunting), men amounted to over 20 percent of accused witches or that in some places they might even have been a majority.

THE MAKING OF A WITCH

The witch was a social construction, and his or her identity was the outcome of complex relations with his or her social environment. Because historians, inquiring about the origin of a witch's evil reputation, usually face severe deficiencies in their source materials about the witch's early life, general explanations can easily become overly schematic. It has been suggested that "once we start aggregating, the variables multiply so fast that chaos theory, with its pattern of unpredictability, is the scientific model which best fits the case" (Briggs 1996, 53). What can be said about the kinds of people who were most vulnerable to accusations of witchcraft? Meticulous research suggests that most witches cannot be described as "outsiders," migrants (such as shepherds), forest dwellers, peddlers, or wandering beggars. Instead, the great majority of suspects were long-term neighbors of their accusers, inserted within the dynamics of a village community. The popular belief that the power of a witch was handed down by blood from parents to child within certain families did not contradict the assertion that witchcraft was an art that had to be learned.

PERFORMANCES

In a way, witches were performers, and witchcraft was a performance art. Maleficent witches possessed the power to commit a great variety of social crimes; we badly need a comparative profile of these *maleficia*. Future research must sort out and analyze basic uniformities in order to describe and, if possible, explain the huge range of local peculiarities. It appears a thorny task to distinguish power on an individual basis (England, Tuscany, Hungary, Scotland) from power on a collective basis (mostly Germany and northern Europe). Witches mostly performed their misdeeds against neighbors through the intrinsic powers of their speech, touch, or gaze. The words spoken by witches—which in most instances were religious in origin—were perceived as powerful but did not require any special knowledge or information. Most attacks of witchcraft can be summed up as a set of words (often curses) spoken in a crisis by someone with a dubious reputation. In sixteenth-century Lorraine, Jean Regnauldin had earned the enmity of a suspect woman by testifying against her on a previous occasion, so she uttered threats against him, wishing that he might have the bar of a door across his stomach. That night "something like a person climbed on his bed and grasped him by the throat with such force and violence that he thought he was about to be strangled" (Briggs 2002b, 14). The nightmare of being attacked in one's own bed was a recurrent feature in witchcraft reports. During the Basque craze (1609–1614) or in Sweden (1668–1676), this phenomenon even took the dimension of a vast Sabbat-dream epidemic.

COEXISTING WITH WITCHES

Maleficent witches were pivotal constituents of an ideology that functioned in a symbiosis with other performers, such as the white witches or "cunning folk" (randomly female or male) who were consulted as counterwitches, healers, and diviners. Willem de Blécourt, adapting the chessboard metaphor from anthropologists, maintained that within the web of relations that regulated communal conflict, if any one piece was separated from the others, its meaning became incomprehensible. Some magical specialists performing within the spectacle of witchcraft were also called witches, through a process of lexical assimilation shared by the Roman Inquisition and Protestant authorities. Antiwitch procedures were extremely widespread but basically uniform throughout Europe, and they mainly targeted divinatory and curative magic. The counterwitch, as well as the witch, was believed to possess special powers rather than knowledge. Their power was strengthened by a secrecy that their customers were careful to respect, lest something go wrong with the counterspell. Because the objects and words (most often specific prayers) considered to have special power were practically limitless, customers did not ponder much about the meaning of these magical techniques, provided they were effective—and the ubiquity of countermagic throughout Europe should convince historians that such methods frequently worked.

White magic certainly remains a demanding topic for researchers. The power of the healer was two-edged and therefore a source of both hope and fear. Although a white witch might occasionally have been accused of casting spells, this "symbiotic" coexistence between the harmless witch and the malefic one hid many pitfalls. Historians must be wary of being sidetracked by the popular contention that those who know how to heal also know how to harm, an idea consequently implying that a white witch who failed to perform a remedy might eventually be suspected of witchcraft. Unfortunately, many witchcraft trial depositions cannot tell us how often accused witches had been active healers in their villages or were merely evildoers compelled to lift spells that they themselves had cast.

Moreover, the strong antimagic healing campaign by both secular and ecclesiastical hierarchies in the late sixteenth century may have caused an anomalous drift in the system. This blurring in the sources could probably be reduced by carrying out a closer scrutiny of the reputation enjoyed by the witch doctor within the community in normal times, uncorrupted by the distorting mirror of witchcraft trials. In truth, cunning men might have been consulted with trepidation, but were they really accused by their neighbors of using their power maliciously? In the villages of late-sixteenth-century Siena, for instance, several female healers generally considered by their neighbors as godly persons (*spirituale*) were denounced to the inquisitors for magical healing because their customers were refused absolution by their confessors for not doing so. But such healers were never suspected of committing the sort of deeds attributed to a neighborhood maleficent witch (*strega*). And no such ambiguity ever affected the behavior of Tuscany's most powerful cunning folk and soothsayers, all males, who had a regional reputation and were never accused of harmful witchcraft.

DESTROYING WITCHES

In most regions of early-seventeenth-century Europe, "it was not a meaningless coincidence when a small child, who had previously been healthy, fell ill and died, nor an inexplicable misfortune when a pig began to sicken" (Henningsen 1980, 30). Such things were sometimes attributed to an evil acquaintance. But if all steps for controlling the witch through ordinary ritualized procedures failed, the quality of the human village relationships acquired a dramatic Mozart-like *re-major* tonality, as people resolved to charge the witch formally and demand retribution for the harm they had suffered.

ACCUSATIONS FROM BELOW

It is now generally acknowledged that the impulse to prosecute maleficent witches usually came from ordinary people. But why were some misfortunes, such as the sudden death of a baby, explained in personal terms by blaming a neighbor as the perpetrator, and others not? The etiology of witchcraft led the victim to locate the misfortune in the web of social relations and to personalize the responsibility. Therefore, it is hardly surprising that the motif of retaliation permeated so many witchcraft trials so deeply, appearing as a corollary of personalistic thought. Witchcraft accusations should be seen in relation with this particular misfortune syndrome. The patients of the Oxford physician Richard Napier rarely accepted chance as a cause of their misfortune. Would they have accepted the concept of divine providence proposed by British clerics then, or even a century later? Much like in the time of the *Canon Episcopi,* "there is little evidence that popular beliefs changed in response to religious instructions, either before or after decriminalisation, and there is much to suggest that they continued in their earlier form. Indeed, the frequency with which local communities took illegal counter-actions against suspected witches suggests strongly that popular witch beliefs persisted for many generations after the trials had stopped" (Levack 1999, 46). Still, historical research struggles discontentedly with a lack of consensus about whether or not the impulse to prosecute witches also stopped from below.

DEVIL WORSHIPPING AND "ALLIED BELIEFS"

Researchers are today in agreement that throughout Europe, on the Continent as well as in the British Isles, popular classes thought in terms of *maleficium* (harmful magic): for them, a witch was someone with the super-natural ability to harm others. On the whole, demonic elements remained marginal at the popular level. Most essential ingredients in the formation of witch beliefs, for example, the English belief that witches kept "familiars" in their houses who sucked their blood or the Basque belief that such spirits were usually toads, came from pagan religion and folklore. Although the role of imps in continental Europe badly needs research, the casebooks of the Oxford physician Richard Napier point to a widespread notion of imps and spirits, described as being like mice, cats, dogs, bees, toads, and so on. Were such ideas part of pre-Christian lore, like weather spirits or forest gods? Napier's patients often appear convinced that they embodied both a good spirit and an evil spirit. Fairies as well could be either wicked or mischievous people. No doubt, villagers inhabited a mental world where religious rituals coexisted with other important areas of allied beliefs, including the presence of witches, ghosts, and fairies. It was a world lacking homogeneity, even if there were probably interconnections of strands of beliefs (Larner 2000) that historians can reconstruct only with difficulty. Beliefs about fairies exemplify this ambivalence: they were liminal creatures, midway between good and evil, and had to be treated with caution. Occasionally, historians encounter archaic fantastic beliefs revolving around particular people, basically all performing some form of magical healing, like the *Krsniki* (Christians) in Slovenia, the *Benandanti* (do-gooders) in Friuli, the *Nachtschar* (phantoms of the night) in the Bavarian Alps, the *donas de fuera* (women from outside) in Sicily, or the *táltos* (shamen) in Hungary. The extravagant popular perceptions (Behringer 1998) of these healers might be local variants of a Europe-wide belief in fairies. Such archaic survivals include tales of ecstatic experiences of flight in unconscious states.

This enormous variety of European convictions and magical practices (to which many others could be added, including such basic notions as cannibalism or metamorphoses into animals) certainly pose serious challenges to historical reconstruction. With current technology, future trends of research can compare thousands of witchcraft trials in order to facilitate a detailed morphological analysis of such archaic survivals, mapping their geographical and chronological variations—and possibly provide an explanation of their meaning for ordinary people. In the eight centuries between the *Canon Episcopi* and Voltaire, were these pre-Christian notions altered under the pressure of the conquering medieval and post-Reformation Christianity? We know that the specific concept of the witches' Sabbat was formed shortly before 1450 in a large Alpine area, where such notions were still thriving in the early modern period. It remains unclear how far this new demonological doctrine represented a willful "mistranslation" and appropriation of popular notions by literate clerics and laypeople. But popular beliefs in malevolent spirits fitted extremely well with the Christian image of demons, and such customs as folk dances played a role in the construction of the Sabbat.

We know that during the heyday of witchcraft trials, some important confessions about the nocturnal rides, pacts with the Devil, the repudiation of Christianity, secret nocturnal meetings, desecration of the Eucharist and the crucifix, sexual orgies—even about sacrificial infanticide and cannibalism—were not made under torture or extreme psychological pressure. How should we interpret such unforced confessions? With hundreds of voluntary Basque confessions to explain, Gustav Henningsen maintained that during a witchcraft trial, an accused person not infrequently suffered a reversal of identity, accepted the negative personality pattern, combined his or her imagination with what he or she already knew about witches, and fabricated the confession expected of him or her.

DID WITCHES REALLY EXIST?
The horns of this dilemma concern the question of the self-awareness of being a maleficent witch, as well as the recurring theme of the existence of some sectarian organization practicing the complete inversion of Christianity. In the *Malleus Maleficarum* (The Hammer of Witches, 1486), the belief that witches formed a sect with its own rites of initiation and abjuration was expounded systematically. Despite the earnest insistence of some contemporary Wiccans, the evidence does not support the widespread contention that the witches of old Europe formed organized groups to perform rituals or for any other purpose. Apart from the fact that "witches" did exist as living healers, and apart from the fact that people "knew" who they were, did the maleficent village neighborhood witch live up to her role? Was she aware, did she internalize such an identity? Keith Thomas suggested that some of them used witchcraft to improve their condition when all else had failed; it is also possible that some Scottish suspects of witchcraft "accepted their own reputation and even found ego-enhancement in the description of a 'rank witch' and the power that this gave them in the community" (Larner 2000, 94).

OSCAR DI SIMPLICIO

See also: CONFESSIONS; COUNTERMAGIC; CUNNING FOLK; DEVIL; DIVINATION; FAIRIES; FAMILIARS; GHOSTS; LYCANTHROPY; MAGIC, POPULAR; METAMORPHOSIS; MORA WITCHES; NIGHTMARES; OINTMENTS; PEOPLE OF THE NIGHT; PERSONALITY OF WITCHES; RURAL WITCHCRAFT; SABBAT; SORCERY; VAMPIRE; VISION; WITCH AND WITCHCRAFT, DEFINITIONS OF; WORDS, POWER OF.

References and further reading:
Behringer, Wolfgang. 1998. *Shaman of Oberstdorf: Conrad Stoeckhlin and the Phantoms of the Night.* Charlottesville: University Press of Virginia.

Briggs, Robin. 1996. "'Many Reasons Why': Witchcraft and the Problem of Multiple Explanation." Pp. 49–63 in *Witchcraft in Early Modern Europe: Studies in Culture and Belief.* Edited by Jonathan Barry, Marianne Hester, and Gareth Roberts. Cambridge: Cambridge University Press.
———. 2002a. "Shapeshifting, Apparitions, and Fantasy in Lorraine Witchcraft Trials." Pp. 1–21 in *Werewolves, Witches, and Wandering Spirits: Traditional Beliefs and Folklore in Early Modern Europe.* Edited by Kathryn A. Edwards. Kirksville, MO: Truman State University Press.
———. 2002b. *Witches and Neighbours: The Social and Cultural Context of European Witchcraft.* 2nd ed. Oxford and Malden, MA: Blackwell.
Demos, John Putnam. 1982. *Entertaining Satan: Witchcraft and the Culture of Early New England.* Oxford and New York: Oxford University Press.
Di Simplicio, Oscar. 2000. *Inquisizione, stregoneria, medicina: Siena e il suo stato (1580–1721).* Monteriggioni (Siena): Il Leccio.
Henningsen, Gustav. 1980. *The Witches' Advocate: Basque Witchcraft and the Spanish Inquisition.* Reno: University of Nevada Press.
———. 1990. "'The Ladies from Outside': An Archaic Pattern of the Witches' Sabbat." Pp. 191–218 in *Early Modern European Witchcraft: Centres and Peripheries.* Edited by Bengt Ankarloo and Gustav Henningsen. Oxford: Clarendon.
Kors, Alan C., and Edward Peters, eds. 2001. *Witchcraft in Europe, 400–1700. A Documentary History.* Revised by E. Peters. 2nd ed. Philadelphia: University of Pennsylvania Press.
Larner, Christina. 2000. *Enemies of God: The Witch Hunt in Scotland.* 2nd ed. Edinburgh: John Donald.
Levack, Brian P. 1995. *The Witch-Hunt in Early Modern Europe.* 2nd ed. London and New York: Longman.
———. 1999. "The Decline and End of Witchcraft Prosecutions." Pp. 1–94 in *The Eighteenth and Nineteenth Centuries.* Vol. 5 of *The Athlone History of Witchcraft and Magic in Europe.* Edited by Bengt Ankarloo and Stuart Clark. London and Philadelphia: Athlone and University of Pennsylvania Press.
Macdonald, Michael. 1981. *Mystical Bedlam: Madness, Anxiety, and Healing in Seventeenth-Century England.* Cambridge: Cambridge University Press.
Monter, William. 1976. *Witchcraft in France and Switzerland: The Borderlands During the Reformation.* Ithaca, NY, and London: Cornell University Press.
Muchembled, Robert. 1990. "Satanic Myths and Cultural Reality." Pp. 139–160 in *Early Modern European Witchcraft: Centres and Peripheries.* Edited by Bengt Ankarloo and Gustav Henningsen. Oxford: Clarendon.
Pócs, Éva. 1999. *Between the Living and the Dead: A Perspective on Witches and Seer in the Early Modern Age.* Budapest: Central European University Press.
Sharpe, James. 1997. *Instrument of Darkness: Witchcraft in England, 1550–1750.* Harmondsworth: Penguin.
Thomas, Keith. 1973. *Religion and the Decline of Magic: Studies in Popular Beliefs in Sixteenth- and Seventeenth-Century England.* Harmondsworth: Penguin.
Trevor-Roper, H. R. 1967. "The European Witch-Craze of the Sixteenth and Seventeenth Centuries." Pp. 90–192 in *Religion, the Reformation, and Social Change.* By Hugh Trevor-Roper. London: Macmillan.

POPULAR PERSECUTION

The term *popular witch persecutions* demands precision. Given the widespread belief in the malevolent character and power of witches in Latin Christianity, it seems almost trivial to conclude that persecutions, especially in times of crisis and disorder, were profoundly popular. Similarly, it is plain that governmental judicial action against witches relied on this popularity to produce evidence supporting specific accusations, apart from the rather unusual self-propelling persecutions, based primarily or exclusively on evidence produced by torture (as, for example, around 1627 at Bamberg and Wurzburg in Franconia), in which the confession of alleged "accomplices" sufficed to nurture further trials.

But German witchcraft trials usually had a social basis and responded to popular demands. Due to their preoccupation with judicial procedures, older historical perspectives and especially traditional legal history disregarded such social contexts. But even witch hunts started by the authorities with so-called general inquisitions only *reacted* to rumor and unrest among their subjects, who already knew which suspects should be accused, condemned, and burned. With the overwhelming evidence produced by social historical research since the 1970s and the corresponding shift in perspective, one cannot seriously maintain the simplistic notion that witch hunting proceeded essentially from "above" (Horsley 1979). Regardless of their mode of introduction (whether by private accusation or official inquisition), witchcraft trials relied upon a broad variety of popular incentives. Leaving aside the role of propaganda (invariably from elite culture), persecutions always combined pressure from below and (re)action from above.

The question, then, is, what qualified a witch hunt as "popular" in terms of active participation and not only in terms of attitudes? What were the features of popular participation, apart from furnishing the authorities with accusations and evidence? How can we assess the relationship between subjects and authorities, once the latter gave way to the demands of the former, and, finally, what was the impact of such cooperation on the trials?

LEVELS, STRUCTURES, PATTERNS

Long before formal charges were presented, popular action against witches started with socially ritualized strategies of reconciliation or countermagic, which frequently involved a specialist. If such actions failed and formal appeal to the authorities was impossible, such forms of self-help as beating or even lynching could be practiced. Continuous protests over years, particularly public scolding, seem to have been frequently practiced.

When seeking aid from official justice instead of militant self-help, individuals approached a local court or a local official with specific charges or at least a general demand for action against suspects. It was most desirable to make the authorities not only start inquiries but also transform the charges into *ex officio* accusations (magisterial approach). Private accusers could thus avoid the responsibility of paying for any financial and physical damage if the accused was found innocent. However, especially in territories of medium size, the authorities, though basically willing to support inquiries, preferred to keep such accusations private, with all financial risks remaining fully on the original accuser. Such considerations could deter accusers from pursuing further action until the community assumed full judicial and financial responsibility.

Partly because of such peculiar problems and partly because of the scope of action the population demanded, witch hunts often started only after subjects and communities had delivered formal addresses to the authorities. Thus, in 1598, the jurors of the county of Vaduz (modern Lichtenstein) demanded a public audience day to present their charges against specific persons. While getting official approval for persecutions, such meetings and petitions also arranged the terms to fit popular interests: complete competence to local officials without central supervision, extensive use of torture to speed up procedures and minimize the risk of liberating prisoners, and generous confiscation standards to avoid having communities pay the sizable costs of such operations.

In pursuing these ends, interested groups (e.g., parents of bewitched children in Swedish Mora, provincial estates in Vaduz or Jülich-Berg, and whole village communities in several parts of the Holy Roman Empire) confronted magistrates and rulers with their demands. To overcome governmental or magisterial resistance, proponents drew extensively on Christian discourse (e.g., references to Exod. 22:18 [22:17]), reminding authorities of their duties before God, threatening divine wrath, and painting terrible scenes of the consequences of the witches' reign. Political pressure also played a role: subjects threatened to withdraw their oath of loyalty, and peasants threatened emigration (Scotland, the electorate of Trier) if the trials they demanded were not granted. More subtle strategies presented such demands on occasions of raising taxes or addressed princes by emphasizing the efforts in neighboring territories, thus exploiting political and confessional rivalry. If local officials supported princely objections against unrestricted persecutions, physical action reinforced verbal efforts: complaints about "hard pressing" from subjects often appeared in reports about such situations, although they also served to justify local officials in doing what they wanted anyway.

In several western regions of the Holy Roman Empire, including the southern Netherlands, popular promotion of witch hunts went as far as creating communal committees. Formally and legally, they acted as a collective accuser, financially backed by the community, thus relieving individual accusers from the responsibility of paying the costs in case trials ended without condemnation. In practice, these committees did much more than present formal charges to courts or officials: their members collected evidence, hired notaries and lawyers, arranged for hearing witnesses, and even arrested and guarded the accused themselves. They exploited such functions to the point of continuing formal interrogations with their own methods, thus ensuring a high degree of success. Finally, the committees organized executions and accounted for all costs.

These committees represented the triumph of popular witch hunting. In certain regions of the electorate of Trier and in the nearby duchy of Luxembourg, they also produced numerous "unauthorized" trials, coming close to legalized lynching and social tyranny. But even when they were subjected to governmental control, the close alliance between village committees and local authorities guaranteed that the former had the final say: these committees of peasants, through continuous abuses of power and massive social support, determined who was to be accused. In rare cases, some victims obtained revenge (their justice), either by themselves denouncing their opponents as alleged accomplices or by their families demanding a similar fate for other members of the community through a simple but conclusive analogy.

This picture would be incomplete without considering the contribution made by instigators fueling popular fears about witches. Government ordinances trying to calm popular temper for reasons of political expediency were quick to denounce the "restless subjects" responsible for such disorder. But members of elite culture, like local priests (for example, in Cambrésis or Luxembourg) or preachers, sometimes assumed the role of instigators as well. In major western monarchies, which never tolerated such village committees, traveling witch finders made a temporary career of promoting and organizing real campaigns in villages and regions (Essex, Languedoc, Catalonia), drawing heavily on popular support. The Jesuit Friedrich Spee even reported entrepreneurial witch hunters in the electorate of Cologne who sent subordinates to villages stirring up peasant support for persecutions, so that their master's "accidental" arrival there sufficed to start trials. Nevertheless, the role of such figures should not be exaggerated: English villagers had less need of Matthew Hopkins than he had of them.

The range and success of popular persecutions demonstrated how local conditions could override governmental policies. Hence, the crucial importance of local officials, notaries, and clerks, who protected committees against critical supervision from above. Town magistrates and minor lords were important allies as well. Political reasons sometimes induced magistrates to start witch hunts to appease the population (for example, in Reutlingen and Lemgo), whereas minor lords realized that supporting popular demands for trials could help to defend or even extend their judicial rights against the territorial princes' desire for governmental centralism. Not surprisingly, therefore, popular pressure was rarely directed against feudal lords. Such alliances between parts of the population and local authorities created a type of unauthorized and technically illegal trials (Voltmer 2002; Kamen 1993).

Judicial localism did not interfere with inquisitorial procedure. On the contrary, the latter actually furthered social participation by using social evidence (e.g., testimonies about a suspect's reputation) in witchcraft trials. However, when localities successfully avoided the requirements of imperial law and allowed local courts and village jurors to exercise their traditional rights and customs, popular input on the trials increased.

Judicial localism prevailed in most European states (for example, Poland), where we know of intense popular influence on persecutions. It therefore seems to have been an essential prerequisite to fulfill what at least part of the population wanted. However, we should not overlook the dissenting minorities, which for obvious reasons had to disguise themselves behind silence. Much scandal was required, often bloodshed, before governmental interest in local affairs encouraged those groups to express their opinions, thus revealing that "popular" persecutions were almost never unanimously popular.

WALTER RUMMEL

See also: ACCUSATIONS; BUIRMANN, FRANZ; COMMUNAL PERSECUTION; CONFESSIONS; COUNTERMAGIC; HOLY ROMAN EMPIRE; HOPKINS, MATTHEW; LYNCHING; MÖDEN, JOHANN; POPULAR BELIEFS IN WITCHES; SPEE, FRIEDRICH; STEARNE, JOHN; WITCH FINDERS; WITCH HUNTS.

References and further reading:
Briggs, Robin. 2002. *Witches and Neighbours: The Social and Cultural Context of European Witchcraft.* 2nd ed. Oxford: Blackwell.
Dillinger, Johannes, Thomas Fritz, and Wolfgang Mährle. 1998. *Hexenverfolgungen in der Grafschaft Hohenberg, der Reichsstadt Reutlingen und der Fürstprobstei Ellwangen.* Stuttgart: Steiner.
Horsley, Richard. 1979. "Who Were the Witches? The Social Roles of the Accused in the European Witch Trials." *Journal of Interdisciplinary History* 9: 689–715.
Kamen, Henry. 1993. *The Phoenix and the Flame: Catalonia and the Counter Reformation.* New Haven: Yale University Press.
Levack, Brian P. 1984. "The Great Scottish Witch Hunt of 1661–1662." *Journal of British Studies* 20: 90–108.
———. 1987. *The Witch Hunt in Early Modern Europe.* London: Longman.
Rummel, Walter. 1991. *Bauern, Herren, und Hexen. Studien zur Sozialgeschichte sponheimischer und kurtrierischer Hexenprozesse 1574–1664.* Göttingen: Vandenhoeck and Ruprecht.

————. 2003. "Das 'ungestüme Umherlaufen' der Untertanen: Zum Verhältnis von religiöser Ideologie, sozialem Interesse und Staatsräson in den Hexenverfolgungen im Rheinland." *Rheinische Vierteljahresblätter* 67: 121–161.

Schormann, Gerhard. 1981. *Hexenprozesse in Deutschland.* Göttingen: Vandenhoeck.

Tschaikner, Manfred. 1990. "Hexenverfolgungen in Dornbirn." *Dornbirner Schriften Schriften:* 3–79.

Voltmer, Rita. 2002. "Monopole, Ausschüsse, Formalparteien: Vorbereitung, Finanzierung und Manipulation von Hexenprozessen durch private Klagekonsortien." Pp. 5–67 in *Hexenprozesse und Gerichtspraxis.* Edited by Herbert Eiden and Rita Voltmer. Trier: Spee.

Walz, Rainer. 1993. *Hexenglaube und magische Kommunikation im Dorf der frühen Neuzeit: Die Verfolgungen in der Grafschaft Lippe.* Paderborn: Schöningh.

Wilbertz, Gisela, Gerd Schwerhoff, and Jürgen Scheffler, eds. 1994. *Hexenverfolgung und Regionalgeschichte-Die Grafschaft Lippe im Vergleich.* Bielefeld: Verlag für Regionalgeschichte.

PORTUGAL

Portugal was a country without "witch hunts." It experienced thousands of recorded witchcraft accusations, much surveillance by judicial authorities, and considerable repression, but there was no "witch hunting." Although various tribunals (secular, episcopal, and, after 1536, the Inquisition) prosecuted several thousand people, only around ten cases of capital punishment are known between the mid-sixteenth century and the end of the eighteenth century. Most sentences involved exile, confinement, fines, and shaming rituals (e.g., public exposure at church doors or wearing distinct clothing). In other words, repression was not harsh. Hence, in the early modern period, Portugal avoided the witch panics and fears that afflicted many other parts of Europe. Most Portuguese victims were healers and sorcerers who practiced love magic or divination, not women accused of going to Sabbats or bringing death or illness to their neighbors. On the other hand, judicial prosecution reached its peak here in the first half of the eighteenth century, at a moment when persecution had practically ended in the places where witch hunts had been most violent.

A number of factors combined to produce such an unusually mild degree of repression: first, the education received by Portuguese elites at Coimbra University, with its strongly neo-Scholastic Thomist basis; second, a united, prestigious, and powerful Portuguese Church, undisturbed by the Protestant Reformation; third, the Church's patient Christianization of rural Portugal throughout the early modern era; fourth, a well-established anti-Jewish tradition throughout Portuguese society, which concentrated the Inquisition's attention on combating crypto-Jewish converts; and, finally, the specificity of Portuguese judicial procedure, namely, the absence of any attempt to treat witchcraft as an "excepted" crime (*crimen exceptum*).

In Portugal, forms of superstition were treated as crimes *mixti fori* (of mixed courts). In other words, those who practiced such superstitions could be prosecuted by the crown courts, by ecclesiastical courts, and, from 1536, by the Inquisition. Crimes of heresy were reserved for the latter.

The earliest legislation for this type of crime was ecclesiastical. The Braga Synod of 1281 prohibited divination or any other "deeds of magic." In fact, episcopal surveillance was maintained throughout the fourteenth and fifteenth centuries, as can be seen in provisions of the Lisbon and Braga Synods of 1393 and 1439, respectively. Episcopal legislation increased after the beginning of the sixteenth century; diocesan constitutions introduced specific sections on how to deal with the problem of "superstitions," especially forbidding divination. Convicted magicians were excommunicated, as they had been in the Middle Ages. Nonetheless, during the sixteenth century, these constitutions referred only briefly to crimes of superstition. The use of holy objects in witchcraft, invocation of evil spirits, divination, and magical healing practices were forbidden, but the sentences proposed were lighter than in previous royal legislation. By the seventeenth century, the list of forbidden practices was extended and the degree of seriousness attributed to them increased. (The first constitutions regulating such practices came from the diocese of Guarda, printed in 1621.) Monetary fines, imprisonment, and exile were some of the means at the disposal of the ecclesiastical judges ruling on these cases.

Crown competence over illicit magical practices began with legislation in the reign of King João I; his royal edict of November 1385 forbade a series of practices, including pacts with the Devil, charms, and divination, all punishable by exile. Afterward, all the kingdom's law compilations included provisions on this matter. The *Ordenações Afonsinas* (issued by Afonso V in 1446) suggested capital punishment for those practicing witchcraft, with lesser sentences for divination and other forms of superstition. The *Ordenações Manuelinas* (issued by Manuel I in 1512) added more detailed descriptions of the condemned practices and classified punishable crimes into four levels. The first included the most serious crimes, such as using holy objects for purposes of illegal magic, invoking evil spirits, or performing love magic, all of which deserved capital punishment. The second encompassed divination, as well as possessing objects linked to the world of the dead and using them to harm others; such offenses were punishable by exile, branding on the face by hot irons, and monetary fines. The third group covered healing practices, and the fourth forbade healing or blessing animals without possessing a special license from the king or the bishops. Such minor cases were punishable by monetary fines and exile, depending on the accused person's social condition. Manuel's code completed Portugal's secular legal framework for these crimes; the *Ordenações Filipinas,* issued in 1603 by Filipe II (Philip III of Spain), added nothing new.

The Inquisition's ordinances (*Regimentos*) defining the extent of its justice did not originally cover such matters. The first to do so were the ordinances of 1640, although there were some earlier letters from Portugal's inquisitor-general, Cardinal Henrique, which included provisions about divination. The 1640 ordinances forbade witchcraft, divination, and superstition whenever diabolical machination was presumed to exist. In case of a relapse, capital punishment was foreseen, always to be executed by royal courts. Less serious crimes were punishable by exile, prison, whippings, and defamation. In 1774 Portugal's last Inquisition ordinance was published, marking the end of state repression of magic and superstitious deeds by envisaging them as "idealistic and fantastical crimes" and declaring their perpetrators "impostors" who needed to be reeducated.

However, this legal framework tells us nothing about how royal or inquisitorial prosecutions were carried out in practical terms. Little is known about practices of royal justice, because all original documentation has been lost. We know that several kings (Duarte, Afonso V, João II, João III, and Sebastião) issued letters of pardon to witches prosecuted by royal courts. Other documents reported royal investigations of the practice of such crimes and told us of witches in crown prisons, but none bore specific information about such actions. However, one extremely violent episode of repression against witches was carried out by a royal court: in 1559, a trial ordered by the duke of Aveiro's judge sentenced six women to the stake in Lisbon. It was followed by an official inquiry in the Lisbon area, ordered by the Queen-Regent Catalina, which subsequently resulted in another execution. That was as close as Portugal ever came to a witch hunt.

The actions of Portugal's ecclesiastical courts are better known. Both bishops in their dioceses, mainly during their pastoral visits, and the Inquisition through the prosecution of the practitioners of such deeds left copious traces of their intervention (the Inquisition's first trials against sorcerers were held in 1541). As far as the number of prosecutions is concerned, bishops were apparently much more active: between the sixteenth and eighteenth centuries, several thousand individuals were prosecuted. In the diocese of Coimbra, our best-known example, around 2,000 cases were denounced during the bishop's visits between 1640 and 1770. Although it investigated many fewer cases, the Holy Office's treatment of these crimes was far more severe. Nonetheless, of the 912 cases brought before its three courts between 1540 and 1774 (370 at the Coimbra tribunal, 288 at Lisbon, and 254 at Évora), only four were "released to the secular arm," that is, sentenced to

death: a man at Évora in 1626, a woman at Coimbra in 1694, another man at Lisbon in 1735, and another woman at Évora in 1744.

The first half of the eighteenth century marked the summit of repression in Portugal, as the number of cases prosecuted both by episcopal justice and the Inquisition increased greatly, especially the persecution of healers. At this time, Christianization campaigns condemned practices and beliefs that were widely disseminated among the Portuguese; but they were carried out with much patience, seldom employing violent measures.

JOSÉ PEDRO PAIVA

See also: BEWITCHMENT; BRAZIL; COURTS, ECCLESIASTICAL; *CRIMEN EXCEPTUM;* CUNNING FOLK; DIVINATION; GEOGRAPHY OF THE WITCH HUNTS; INQUISITION, PORTUGUESE; LOVE MAGIC; SUPERSTITION; WITCH HUNTS.

References and further reading:
Bethencourt, Francisco. 1987. *O Imaginário da magia: Feiticeiras, saludadores e nigromantes no século XVI.* Lisbon: Projecto Universidade Aberta.
———. 1990. "Portugal: A Scrupulous Inquisition." Pp. 403–422 in *Early Modern European Witchcraft: Centres and Peripheries.* Edited by Bengt Ankarloo and Gustav Henningsen. Oxford: Clarendon.
———. 1994. "Un univers saturé de magie: L'Europe méridionale." Pp. 159–194 in *Magie et sorcellerie en Europe du Moyen Age à nos jours.* Edited by Robert Muchembled. Paris: Armand Colin.
Paiva, José Pedro. 1992. *Práticas e crenças mágicas: O medo e a necessidade dos mágicos na diocese de Coimbra (1650–1740).* Coimbra: Livraria Minerva.
———. 1997. *Bruxaria e superstição num país sem "caça ás bruxas."* Lisbon: Editorial Notícias.
Ribeiro, Márcia Moisés. 2003. *Exorcistas e demônios: demonologia e exorcismos no mundo luso-brasileiro.* Rio di Janeiro: Campus.
Souza, Laura de Mello. 1993. *Inferno atlântico: Demonologia e colonização séculos XVI–XVIII.* São Paulo: Companhia das Letras.
———. 1993. "Autour d'une ellipse: Le Sabbat dans le monde luso-brésilien de l'Ancien Régime." Pp. 331–343 in *Le Sabbat des sorciers (XV–XVIII siècles).* Edited by Nicole Jacques-Chaquin and Maxime Préaud. Grenoble: Millon.

POSSESSION, DEMONIC

The western Christian tradition shares with many other religions a belief that evil spirits can inhabit the body, causing dramatic physical and behavioral changes. Possession is sometimes said to be caused by witchcraft or a curse; at other times, its agonies are seen as God's punishment of a person's own sin. Devils can also possess a person spontaneously, with God's permission. In early modern Europe, the diagnosis of possession occurred on its largest scale in Christian history. Alleged witches were executed for causing possession, and some demoniacs assumed the role of oracles, as their "demons" discoursed on religious controversies or foretold the future.

SYMPTOMS OF POSSESSION

Most theologians agree that possession is a condition of the body manipulated by demons, not of the soul. Symptoms of demonic possession in the New Testament have influenced understandings of the phenomenon throughout Christian history: they include loss of sight (Matt. 12:22), hearing (Mark 9:25), or speech (Mark 9:17, 25–29; Matt. 12:22); superhuman strength (Luke 8:29; Mark 5:3–4); mania or suicidal tendencies (Mark 9:17–22); and falling "as if dead" (Mark 9:26–27). Beyond biblical precedents, criteria for diagnoses of possession have derived from an accumulation of authorities: Francesco Guazzo's *Compendium Maleficarum* (A Summary of Witches, 1608) listed around fifty possible signs of possession, including speaking in languages unknown to the sufferer, grotesque bodily distortions, and strange movements under the skin. For the female possessed, symptoms of the Devil's presence have been seen in the light of assumptions about natural female capacities and limitations: uncanny strength, knowledge of theology or foreign languages, talking in a "manly" voice, blaspheming, or a fondness for drinking songs are all recorded as typical symptoms of diabolic activity in women. Revulsion in the face of Christian symbols or rituals has often been depicted as decisive evidence that demons, not a natural ailment, are the cause of the person's condition. In the early modern period, naturalist explanations maintained that all signs of possession, however strange, could have physical causes such as melancholy or "the mother" (hysteria). Indeed, the Catholic Church traditionally advised clerics to consider medical explanations of apparent possession to prevent frivolous or fruitless exorcisms. Historically, almost all mysterious or spectacular conditions, especially those with a mental or behavioral aspect or those that follow an unpredictable course, have at some time been seen as signs of possession.

However, we cannot assume that everyone diagnosed as possessed really did present with those symptoms or traits that were recorded as decisive. Aside from the fact that many accredited symptoms of possession seem implausible to most modern readers, historical actors have often "seen" possession for quite specific, if unconscious, reasons. By the time we reach surviving accounts of diagnosed demoniacs, their condition has usually progressed from an amorphous collection of physiological and psychological disturbances to a neatly categorized set of responses to preselected criteria, designed to help clerics and physicians decide what to do with them and who should treat them.

Many of those diagnosed as possessed were probably suffering from something, if only a kind of delirium. A modern association of possession with different forms of mental illness, such as posttraumatic conditions, does not seem out of order; but for historical cases, it raises complex and ultimately unsolvable questions about the limits of retrospective diagnosis. Suggestions that apparent possession might be caused by food poisoning do not stand up to critical scrutiny. In the last analysis, possession remains for Christians a spiritual affliction that can only be legitimated through clerical diagnosis and cannot therefore be reduced to the spiritual equivalent of some biologically identifiable disease. Rather, its epidemiology in any given era is related to the significance attached to its perceived causes and claimed cures.

REASONS AND CAUSES

Christian belief holds that, with God's permission, possession can occur when a demon or demons enter the body of a person made vulnerable through her or his own sin; when demons are sent by outsiders, notably witches; or when demons attack human beings of their own accord to spread their malice. Whatever its precipitating cause, a diagnosis of possession is usually recorded for some exemplary purpose, as a medium of divine instruction. For example, possession fulfils the purpose of exposing the sin of witchcraft; it can be a torment sent to test the faithful or punish sin; or a successful exorcism can show the Devil's fear of the Christian deity. All these causes share the notion that God "uses the powers of evil to promote His own wise and mysterious purposes" ("Demonic Possession," *Catholic Encyclopedia*). In Christian history, therefore, possible public responses to possession, especially in the form of exorcism, have mattered almost as much as the reasons for its diagnosis.

Jesus's exorcisms served publicly to prove his divinity, and gospel accounts do not dwell on the moral condition of the possessed. New Testament demoniacs were not generally represented as suffering for their or others' sins: they were simply victims of "unclean spirits." Nor were possessing demons yet assimilated with the image of the Devil as the Hebrew Bible's adversary of God: they were still incursions from a morally ambiguous spirit world, which could only be influenced by spiritually gifted people. Through the mouths of biblical demoniacs, "devils" gave reluctant testimony of Jesus's divinity (Matt. 8:29; Mark 1:24–25; Mark 5:7; Luke 4:34, 41; Luke 8:28). These examples and the story of the girl possessed of a "spirit of divination" (Acts 16:16–18), have underscored the historical notion that the possessed are granted special insight, including an understanding of holy mysteries. Because John 8:44 refers to the Devil as the "Father of Lies," however, theological commentators have generally argued that, although devils may sometimes speak the truth, they will also "mix honey with poison," adding evil fabrications to lead the faithful astray.

In antiquity, possession and exorcism contributed to the spread of Christian cults. Many early Christian proselytizers undertook exorcisms to demonstrate the special claims of the new religion, and the behavior of some demoniacs was a litmus test for the authenticity of holy relics. The primary function of these "seismographs of sanctity" (Brown 1977, 13) was not to be healed by exorcists; rather, their "devils" might be almost permanent fixtures at new holy sites, there to proclaim wildly the invisible potency of an apparently mundane object, such as a saint's bone or garment.

In the context of Christian martyrdom, possession offers the opportunity to display a martyr's willingness to endure the Devil's torture from within. Historical accounts sometimes parallel possession with the torments of St. Anthony or even Job, who were not possessed but whom demons tormented to test their faith. Possession in this sense overlaps with *obsession,* a term that usually meant torment by devils from the outside but that is also used interchangeably with (or even, in many Latin texts, instead of) *possession.*

By the later Middle Ages, possession was increasingly understood as something suffered either as punishment for one's own sins or as the consequence of another's sins. Early modern commentators listed as typical causes of possession such sins as infidelity, the use of magic, contempt for religion, and causing harm to others. Parents cursing children was also cited as a common cause. The fact that possession could be punishment for using magic, however, alerts us to the possibility that witches themselves might be seen as possessed, even though they were also believed capable of causing possession in innocent victims. The moral position of the possessed, whether victims or sinners, is rarely clear: their standing depends on the significance God assigns to their possession; so possession in Christianity has more than one potential meaning or function.

EARLY MODERN POSSESSION
The early modern era has been called the "golden age of the demoniac" (Monter 1976, 60). Although a vast "hinterland" of possession (Clark 1997, 390) apparently existed throughout the Middle Ages and beyond, what was distinctive about this period is the simultaneous proliferation of many different forms of possession, interpreted and exploited for a wide range of purposes. Possession occurred across Europe and in its colonies, among members of the Catholic, Lutheran, and Reformed churches. The rise in publicized possessions intersected with several social phenomena, including local campaigns against so-called superstition, fear of witchcraft and the occurrence of witch hunts, interconfessional conflict, heightened anxiety about the end of the world, a rise in public prophesying, and the pursuit of holiness through direct divine inspiration. In this era, all these phenomena—none of which was entirely new—were inflected by an intense fear of demons: in combination, they helped generate a virtual epidemic of possession.

Possession affected individual adults and children. It occurred among sexually mixed groups of all ages, as well as in female convents. Some individual demoniacs claimed attention through dramatic public exorcisms, making scandalous witchcraft accusations or prophesying. Catholics used exorcism most extensively; but widespread anxieties about the encroachments of the Devil in the world and the peerless example of Jesus's own exorcisms meant that even those churches following strictly biblical precedents might legitimately employ exorcism as a form of proselytism. A conservative estimate, based on published sources alone, would suggest that several hundred cases of possession were diagnosed, involving hundreds of exorcists to remedy them, with many thousands of people witnessing major public exorcisms.

Although our knowledge of publicized cases tells us about the uses of possession for those who were not possessed—exorcists and their public—the experiences of the possessed themselves are of primary importance. It is hard to say why so many people in this era experienced what came to be seen as possession: even now, explanations of psychosomatic afflictions are rarely simple, and the geographical diversity and multiple forms of possession in this period make conclusive analysis especially difficult. At a time of such turbulent change, any number of circumstances could have induced real psychological discomfort, especially among socially marginal figures. In this regard, the story of Françoise Fontaine, whose first signs of possession appeared after royal soldiers raped her during the French religious wars, may stand for many. Publicized possessions also appear to have fed an unconscious awareness of the possibility of becoming possessed oneself. Critics of possessions leveled charges of "copycat" displays, and although the causes of outbreaks were doubtless more complex, knowledge of role models cannot be discounted as an influence.

WITCHCRAFT
From the late fourteenth century, campaigns against alleged superstition led to a growing "demonization" of popular healing methods, with several apparent implications for the history of possession. The clerical view that local healers might be guilty of witchcraft appears to have encouraged local people to seek help from priests. Villagers also appear to have become more inclined to see witchcraft and demons in otherwise inexplicable diseases, in many cases pointing to a diagnosis of possession. The notion that a witch had to be identified before bewitchment of any kind could be cured fed into this impulse. Priests influenced by demonology also appear to have been more interventionist in diagnosing possession. For example, in 1565, Nicole Obry's family originally accepted her self-diagnosis that the spirit of her dead grandfather

possessed her and used such remedies as holy water and pilgrimages to help her. Only when a Dominican diagnosed the presence of a demon and proceeded to public exorcism did her story reach beyond her village. In the late sixteenth century, the wide dissemination of exorcism manuals among senior and junior clergy alike probably contributed to a wider diagnosis of possession at the local level.

Most people believed that devils could enter one's body and that witches could make this happen. Although some critics doubted that witches could send devils into other people, arguing that this attributed too much power to witches, Jean Bodin argued that it was possible, with God's permission. (Bodin 1580, fol. 76r and 160v). In cases of possession, witchcraft now became by far the most common diagnosed cause. Contemporary commentators noted the phenomenon: Father Gerard Grudius, describing the exorcisms he performed at Annonay in 1581, remarked "It is a great pity to see today that witches have such power, which is a bad sign" (quoted in Benedicti 1611, 70). Another exorcist at Loudun wrote in 1634: "In these unfortunate times we see that most possessions occur through malefice, God permitting that demons afflict the bodies of the most innocent through the intervention of witches and magicians" (Tranquille 1634, 68.)

Rather than simply expelling demons, clerics used exorcism in witchcraft show-trials to elicit information from the "possessing" devils. The Roman Ritual of 1614, published in part to curb such excesses, nonetheless explicitly permitted interrogation of the possessed, since the more one learned about the Devil's modus operandi, the easier it became to expel him. Exorcists stretched this concession by continually asking "demons" for testimony about the source of their victim's affliction. Because this apparent solicitation of the Devil offended some observers, exorcists reinforced demonic testimony with evidence from the possessed, speaking "as themselves" between bouts of demonic activity. Thus, the scriptural example of devils correctly identifying Jesus together with the pervasive Renaissance idea of the Devil as a natural magician who could do, see, and know beyond human capacities served as counterweights to fears of demons telling lies. In several notorious cases, mainly in France, the "devils" of the possessed told about the location of magic charms, which they said had to be found before they would leave the bodies of their victims. Such exorcisms sometimes lasted for months or even years, as "devils" postponed their departure dates. Thus, possession became a virtual profession for some, physically draining and frequently coerced.

POSSESSION AND PROPAGANDA

The premium on signs of direct divine action and intense rivalry between Christian churches in this period enabled exorcists to make demonic possession a high-profile public issue. The possessed, successfully exorcised, took a prominent role in trying to convince audiences of the rightness of one church or another: marginalized Jesuits and Puritans in England used the possessed to show God's favor, and Catholic zealots on the Continent mobilized the possessed against Protestant and Catholic doubters alike. The logic of asking demons to defend a claim of divine favor was shaky, but the very paradox of "devils" being forced to acknowledge the power of God acting through a particular cleric or church made these performances convincing to many observers. (The risks to credibility were obvious, however, even to broadly sympathetic viewers. When an exorcist in the Catholic Low Countries ordered a devil to admit that the Catholic Church was the true church, another Catholic critic wrote that "if the bedevilled had said the contrary, they would have made a marvellous parade of it" [Lottin 1985, 129–130]). The displays of demoniacs also appeared to many as clear signs of the advent of the Antichrist, a harbinger of the Last Days, with possession offering significant evidence of Satan's malice loosed on the world (Clark, 1997, part III).

Each exorcist relied on the possessed to exhibit enough demonic revulsion and torment to prove his charismatic power to confront the Devil. Symbiotic relationships developed between the possessed and exorcists, who exhibited what psychologists call "codependency" and possibly a degree of mutual exploitation. Skeptics, voicing opinions heard since antiquity, compared their public displays to traveling shows or bear baiting and made accusations of sexual liaisons between female possessed and their exorcists. The demoniacs were often socially marginal figures—young women and youths—but they rarely came from the very lowest social strata and usually enjoyed at least minimal support among the elite. The possessed in sixteenth-century Augsburg, for example, included maids of elite families, whose exorcisms demonstrated the power of Catholic ritual in a confessionally divided city (Roper 1994).

POSSESSION AND SPIRITUALITY

European Catholicism underwent a major spiritual revival in the early modern period, with a rising cult of so-called living saints, charismatic figures who became a focus of veneration. Such people had characteristics in common with the possessed: possession was seen as a phenomenon akin to ecstasy, characterized by trance states and a capacity to expose otherwise inaccessible knowledge, such as news from purgatory or other people's hidden sins and private thoughts. Insofar as such displays by the possessed were deemed licit, these people functioned as a type of church-sanctioned witch, in a time when traditional witches were being persecuted. Indeed, the possibility of witchcraft accusations against the possessed (and ecstatics) was ever-present. And although demonic possession offered some of these people, mostly women, an opportunity to display God's favor through their visible capacity to suffer, a sense of taint surrounded possession. Ecstasy and possession were considered legitimate only if the suffering was entirely involuntary, so any signs of personal pride in public success could create suspicions of witchcraft. No clear line separated possession, ecstasy, and witch status: categories were determined in an ad hoc manner, often subject to such extrinsic factors as patronage. Exorcists sometimes used their rite to test ecstatics, with the aim of summoning any devils lurking behind apparent displays of holiness; even St. Teresa was exorcised to ensure her holiness was not demonic. Possessed women and ecstatic mystics were extremely ambiguous figures: their resistance and suffering made them appear holy in times that craved holiness, but they were also highly suspect in times that saw the Devil everywhere.

It is not difficult to situate demonic possession in convents within the context of the increasingly rigorous religious standards imposed by the post-Tridentine Catholic Church; it is less easy to draw a line between possession as a conscious or unconscious response to this environment. At one extreme of the religious spectrum, a desire for self-mortification led some religious women to overdo their physical suffering in a way that simply turned their minds. This happened in possession cases in New Spain, at Lille in 1613, and at Montdidier, under the influence of Madeleine de Flers, an ecstatic who was allegedly possessed herself but who was also said to have caused other nuns to fall into possession. Other nuns appear to have pretended to be possessed or convinced themselves they were possessed to escape religious life, and this possibility was noted by contemporary authors. And one possessed woman in Germany "seems to have found in demon possession a way of expressing the two violently contradictory ways she felt about religion" (Midelfort 1989, 113–127)

FRAUD AND SKEPTICISM
In the thirteenth century, Abbot Caesarius of Heisterbach had a monk in one of his dialogues remark, "I do not deny that some have pretended to be possessed for worldly gain, but in many cases there is no pretense" (Caesarius von Heisterbach 1929, 333). Yet it is impossible to know how many demoniacs have been consciously fraudulent: the question is clouded both by the problem of perception in a Christian culture—one needs to believe in order to see—and because most recorded confessions of fraud tended to follow some kind of threat or coercion. The many proofs and signs of possession also make it open to suspicion of fraud: demoniacs in the early modern era quaked seemingly on cue in the presence of mundane items (such as unblessed water) presented to them as holy, and the stop–start quality of symptoms in the presence of

clerics was interpreted as collusion. Nor did those seen as possessed always embrace the diagnosis: Louise Capeau at Aix protested that she was not possessed, and the duke of Jülich-Cleves was a unique case of a major ruler who underwent exorcism for six months against his wishes in 1604. In both cases their protests were interpreted as proof of the Devil's presence. It could be said that a secularist search for the "reality" behind the displays of the possessed misses the point. The historical reality was what the documents described: situations of extreme passion, confusion, coercion, and suggestibility. Pressure to prove fraud arose within specific politico-confessional contexts, giving diagnoses a significance beyond the immediate question of how to treat the possessed. Literature voicing skepticism about demonic possession, originally embedded in such contexts, became part of a growing tradition that has helped shape both outright modern rejection of possession and ambivalence among Christians. Ironically, though, there are modern examples of secular doctors sending people who claim to be possessed to exorcists, who are sometimes able to cure them, as if by placebo.

SARAH FERBER

See also: AIX-EN-PROVENCE NUNS; AUGSBURG, IMPERIAL FREE CITY; BEWITCHMENT; BIBLE; BODIN, JEAN; CARPI, POSSESSION IN A POOR CLAIRE'S CONVENT; CONVENT CASES; DARRELL, JOHN; DEMONS; DEVIL; EXORCISM; FÉRY, JEANNE; GUAZZO, FRANCESCO MARIA; GUNTER, ANNE; JESUS; LIVING SAINTS; LOUDUN NUNS; LOUVIERS NUNS; MELANCHOLY; MENTAL ILLNESS; NEW SPAIN; OBRY, NICOLE; ORACLES; PADERBORN, BISHOPRIC OF; RANFAING, ELISABETH DE; SALEM; VALLÉES, MARIE DES.

References and further reading:
Benedicti, Jean. 1611. *La Triomphante victoire de la vierge Marie, sur sept malins esprits, finalement chassées du corps d'une femme, dans l'Eglise des Cordeliers de Lyon.* Lyons: Pierre Rigaud.
Bodin, Jean. 1580. *De la demonomanie des sorciers.* Paris: Jacques du Puys.
Brown, Peter. 1977. *Relics and Social Status in the Age of Gregory of Tours.* Reading: University of Reading Press.
Caesarius von Heisterbach. 1929. *The Dialogue on Miracles.* Translated by H. von E. Scott and C. Swinton Bland. Introdution by G. G. Coulton. 2 vols. London: Routledge.
Certeau, Michel de. 2000. *The Possession at Loudun.* Translated by Michael B. Smith. Foreword by Stephen Greenblatt. Chicago: University of Chicago Press.
Cervantes, Fernando. 1991. "The Devils of Querétaro: Skepticism and Credulity in Late Seventeenth-Century Mexico." *Past and Present* 30: 51–69.
Clark, Stuart. 1997. *Thinking with Demons: The Idea of Witchcraft in Early Modern Europe.* Oxford: Clarendon.
Ferber, Sarah. 2004. *Demonic Possession and Exorcism in Early Modern France.* London: Routledge.
Gentilcore, David. 1992. *From Bishop to Witch: The System of the Sacred in Early Modern Terra d'Otranto.* Manchester and New York: Manchester University Press.
Guazzo, Francesco Maria. 1988. *Compendium Maleficarum.* 1608. New York: Dover.
Lottin, Alain. 1984. *Lille: Citadelle de la Contre-Réforme? (1598–1668).* Dunkirk: Westhoek-Edition.

———. 1985. "Sorcellerie, possessions diaboliques et crise conventuelle." Pp. 111–132 in *L'Histoire des faits de la sorcellerie.* Publications de Centre de Recherches d'Histoire Religieuse et d'Histoire des Idées, 8. Angers: Presses de l'Université d'Angers.

MacDonald, Michael, ed. 1991. *Witchcraft and Hysteria in Elizabethan London: Edward Jorden and the Mary Glover Case.* Introduction by Michael MacDonald. London and New York: Tavistock/Routledge.

Mandrou, Robert. 1968. *Magistrats et sorciers en France au XVIIe siècle: Une analyse de psychologie historique.* Paris: Seuil.

Midelfort, H. C. Erik. 1989. "The Devil and the German People: Reflections on the Popularity of Demon Possession in Sixteenth-Century Germany." Pp. 98–119 in *Religion and Culture in the Renaissance and Reformation.* Edited by Steven Ozment. Ann Arbor: Sixteenth Century Essays and Studies 10.

———. 1994. *Mad Princes of Renaissance Germany.* Charlottesville: University Press of Virginia.

Monter, E. William. 1976. *Witchcraft in France and Switzerland: The Borderlands During the Reformation.* Ithaca, NY, and London: Cornell University Press.

O'Donnell, M. J. "Demonic Possession." *Catholic Encyclopedia.* http://www.newadvent.org/cathen/12315a.htm (accessed December 3, 2003).

O'Neil, Mary R. 1984. "'Sacerdote ovvero strione': Ecclesiatical and Superstitious Remedies in Sixteenth-Century Italy." Pp. 53–83 in *Understanding Popular Culture.* Edited by Steven L. Kaplan. Berlin: Mouton.

Pearl, Jonathan L. 1999. *The Crime of Crimes: Demonology and Politics in France 1560–1620.* Waterloo, Ontario: Wilfrid Laurier University Press

Roper, Lyndal. 1994. 'Exorcism and the Theology of the Body.' Pp. 171–198 in *Oedipus and the Devil: Witchcraft, Sexuality, and Religion in Early Modern Europe.* London and New York: Routledge.

Sharpe, James. 1999. *The Bewitching of Anne Gunter: A Horrible and True Story of Football, Witchcraft, Murder, and the King of England.* London: Profile.

Tranquille, Father. 1634. *Briefve intelligence de l'opinion de trois Docteurs de Sorbonne et du livre du P. Birette Touchant les Diables Exorcisez.* In *Veritable relation des ivstes procedvres observees av faict de la possession des Vrsulines de Loudun: Et au procez d'Vrbain Grandier.* By Father Tranquille. La Flèche: George Griveau.

Twelftree, Graham H. 1993. *Jesus the Exorcist: A Contribution to the Study of the Historical Jesus.* Tübingen: J. C. B. Mohr (Paul Siebeck).

Walker, Daniel P. 1981. *Unclean Spirits: Possession and Exorcism in France and England in the Late Sixteenth and Early Seventeenth Centuries.* London: Scolar.

Weber, Alison. 1993. "Between Ecstasy and Exorcism: Religious Negotiation in Sixteenth-Century Spain." *Journal of Medieval and Renaissance Studies* 23, no. 2: 221–234.

POTIONS

From the Latin *potare*, meaning "to drink," potions are a fundamental element of witchcraft and magic, having an ancient history in both literary depictions of the occult arts and their actual practice. In ancient Greece, the use of *pharmaka* (drugs or potions) was not always magical, and the term *pharmakeia* (the administering of drugs or potions) can be divided into three main categories: magical uses, poisoning without magic, and the practice of medicine or healing.

The first recorded use of *pharmaka* by a witch occurs in book 10 of Homer's *Odyssey* (seventh-century B.C.E.), describing the sorceress Circe administering *kaka pharmaka* (evil drugs) and *pharmaka lygra* (dangerous drugs) to Odysseus's men, the results of which transformed them into pigs. In addition to the magic of transformation, Circe practices the art of rejuvenation, which is also achieved by using another potion or *pharmakon* to return the men to their previous form, but with a more youthful demeanor. The other major practitioner of potions in Greek literature was the sorceress Medea, whose magical poisons were the cause of several often-violent deaths throughout her myth cycle, including death by self-combustion. The *Argonautica* by the poet Apollonius (second-century B.C.E.) depicts Medea's early career as a sorceress in the art of *pharmakeia.* She kept a casket full of *polla pharmaka* (many drugs), some of which healed and some of which killed; in one particularly evocative passage in book 3, Apollonius describes one of Medea's potions called *pharmakon Prometheion* (the charm of Prometheus). This potion came from a magical plant that sprang from the fluids released from the Titan's veins while he was being perpetually torn open by an eagle, a punishment by Zeus for his insolence. To prepare this potion, one had to bathe in seven streams, sing rituals to Hecate, then be clothed in black, and cut the plant in darkness. This process clearly illustrates the symbiotic relationship between potion making and ritual, and Appollonius's description emphasized the ancients' differentiation between such occult arts and the more straightforward work of the herbalist.

The tradition of actual potion making in antiquity was best illustrated by the *Greek Magical Papyri* (PGM), which offered a collection of spells from Greco-Roman Egypt between the second-century B.C.E. and the fifth-century C.E. Herein were recipes for numerous magical outcomes, involving the use of a variety of substances ranging from basic ingredients to such exotic, hard-to-find, and expensive substances as myrrh, crocodile teeth, and body parts of wild animals (for example, a wolf's head). One of the recurring spells from the *Papyri* was a love potion or philter (e.g., PGM 4:2441–2621), a spell of attraction consisting of various animal and insect parts, including "the fat of a speckled goat that is a virgin" and "moon beetles" as well as frankincense and onions. The recipe told the spell caster how to prepare the ingredients, such as thorough pounding in a mortar and placement in a lead container. The instructions for the potion's use were complex, involving the enactment of the spell at a precise location (a high roof) and a specific time (moonrise) together with a series of lengthy invocations to Hecate in her various guises.

The use of potions, particularly for love, was sufficiently widespread in antiquity that authors opposed to magic regularly advised unsuspecting men against allowing women to dabble in such things. For example, Plutarch's *Moralia* 139.5 (second century C.E.) warns husbands to be wary of love potions (*philtra*), which he aligned with sorcery (*goeteia*) because they could, at the very least, undermine male authority in the household. The inherent danger of such magic was illustrated in the references to the adverse affects on the object of the spell: Suetonius (69–140 C.E.) describes how the Roman Emperor Caligula went insane after imbibing a philter dispensed by his wife, Caesonia.

The use of potions in early modern Europe, as in antiquity, involved a sometimes-vague definition in terms of the practitioners, blurring the lines of classification among healers (or doctors), herbalists, poisoners, and witches. The stereotypical view of the woman healer or herbalist executed or ostracized on charges of witchcraft testified to this skewed taxonomy; as Scotland's Sir George Mackenzie observed in 1678: "Not only witches but even naturalists may give potions that incline men and women to lust" (*Laws and Customs of Scotland in Matters Criminal*). Nevertheless, evidence of making potions was a topos of witchcraft literature, trials, and records. Amid numerous accounts of potion making was a reference to the use of human parts, "especially the bodies of those who have been punished by death or hanged," in Francesco Maria Guazzo's 1626 *Compendium Maleficarum* (A Summary of Witches, book 2, chap. 2). Guazzo continued in the same vein: "For not only from such horrid material do they [witches] renew their evil spells, but also from the actual appliances used at executions, such as the rope, the chains, the stake, and the iron tools." He also described some of the ingredients used in deadly potions, including "leaves and stalks and roots of plants; from animals, fishes, venomous reptiles, stones and metals," and explained that "sometimes these are reduced to powder and sometimes to an ointment" (2:3). Such deadly potions and, more significantly, those who used them, were often blamed for spreading outbreaks of the plague, as exemplified by an incident in Geneva in 1545, when a witch hunt was orchestrated after a man had confessed to having started a pestilence by anointing the foot of a hanged man as well as several door bolts with such a potion.

One of the most common beliefs connected the use of potions in witchcraft with the witches' flight. Ointments used for flying supposedly included the fat of children as well as assorted narcotics. Among the most detailed account of flying potions was that given by Jean de Nynauld in 1615 in his *De la lycanthropie, transformation, et extase des sorciers* (Lycanthropy,

Metamorphosis, and Ecstasy of Witches). Nynauld specified, however, that the potions used only gave the impression of flying: for such a sensation, a witch could take belladonna (deadly nightshade), eat the brain of a cat, or if a more exotic potion was unavailable, get drunk. For the hallucinogenic effect of travel to a Sabbat, Nynauld explained that a witch could prepare a potion also composed of baby fat plus, among other ingredients, the juice of water parsnip and, again, belladonna (which does produce hallucinogenic effects). Despite the doubts by authors such as de Nynauld that witches could actually fly, popular belief in many countries maintained they could—aided, of course, by Satan. Artwork both before and during the persecution era consistently combined the image of the witch with potion making and flying, specifying the flight-inducing powers of the witches' concoctions. In a chiaroscuro woodcut by Hans Baldung [Grien] of 1510, four witches were depicted: three involved in the process of potion making and one, in the air, riding a demonic goat. The stereotypical implication of the image was the direct association between the airborne witch and the potion of her "sisters," the vapors of which curled into the air, whirling about in a "flying" motion.

The more fantastic accounts of witchcraft include many references to the Devil's role in providing both potions and powders to the witch. The powders often came in different colors, each denoting the substance's specific use. Alternatively, the witch could make her own potions or powders, sometimes at the Sabbat, from such ingredients as toad venom, body parts (particularly from stillborn babies), and stolen Hosts. The belief that such substances could heal as well as harm indicated the contradictory societal perceptions of the witch's powers; she could be sought by a desperate client to provide a cure beyond the abilities of more official healers or medical practitioners, thereby simultaneously signifying the role of the witch as a potentially viable alternative to the curing powers of God.

Potions, along with amulets and spells, were also believed to prevent or ease the pain of torture. This, unfortunately, often led to the torture of the accused being prolonged, usually until a full confession was obtained.

MARGUERITE JOHNSON

See also: AMULET AND TALISMAN; ART AND VISUAL IMAGES; BALDUNG [GRIEN], HANS; CIRCE; DRUGS AND HALLUCINOGENS; FLIGHT OF WITCHES; *GREEK MAGICAL PAPYRI;* HECATE; HEMLOCK; LOVE MAGIC; MEDEA; NIGHTSHADE; OINTMENTS; PLAGUE; POISON; SPELLS.

References and further reading:
Betz, Hans Dieter, ed. 1992. *The Greek Magical Papyri in Translation.* Vol. 1. 2nd ed. Chicago: University of Chicago Press.
Briggs, Robin. 2002. *Witches and Neighbours: The Social and Cultural Context of European Witchcraft.* 2nd ed. Oxford: Blackwell.

Faraone, Christopher A. 1999. *Ancient Greek Love Magic.* Cambridge, MA: Harvard University Press.

Harner, Michael J. 1973. "The Use of Hallucinogenic Plants in European Witchcraft." Pp. 125–150 in *Hallucinogens and Shamanism.* Edited by Michael J. Harner. Oxford: Oxford University Press.

Robbins, Rossell Hope. 1959. *The Encyclopedia of Witchcraft and Demonology.* London: Spring Books.

Sullivan, Margaret A. 2000. "The Witches of Dürer and Hans Baldung Grien." *Renaissance Quarterly* 53: 332–401.

Zika, Charles. 1989–1990. "Fears of Flying: Representations of Witchcraft and Sexuality in Early Sixteenth-Century Europe." *Australian Journal of Art* 8: 19–48.

POZNAŃ

Poznań, the capital of Wielkopolska (Greater Poland), is famed as the location of both ecclesiastical and secular courts that heard some of Poland's earliest witchcraft trials (fifteenth century) and the purported last trial in Europe in 1793. This case remains a subject of controversy; Polish historians have dismissed it as German propaganda in the wake of the partitions of Poland, but its inclusion in Wilhelm Soldan's widely used history has ensured subsequent citation. It was reported in 1801 that when members of a Prussian commission reached a certain town in Poland in 1793, they saw the remains of stakes, and the town magistrate told them that two witches had been burned there. Polish historians are convinced that the vague terminology used to describe the event makes its authenticity dubious. This case was mentioned in the *Himmlerkartoteka* (Himmler card index), a collection of trials gathered by the *H-Sonnderkommando* (Special Unit II [*Hexen* – witches]) on the orders of Heinrich Himmler, whose more than 30,000 cards are now housed in the state archive in Poznań. The archive also contains records from the *województwo* (palatinate) of Wielkopolska (Greater Poland).

CASES

Accusations of witchcraft were heard by Poznań's ecclesiastical courts as early as 1430 (*Acta* number 1016), and over a dozen sentences were passed down over the next century. Cases were brought on charges of countermagic, preventive practices against illness, causing illness, attempted murder by female spouses, increase of crop output, and causing impotence. Poison was still largely synonymous with witchcraft, as a case from 1517 reveals (*Acta* number 1709). Witchcraft accusations were also used as a mechanism to dispose of unwanted spouses, as illustrated by the case of Malgorzata Zawarta, whose husband accused her of witchcraft. It was also claimed that she used the finger of a hanged man to improve beer fermentation. She was sentenced to death but was later pardoned (*Acta* number 1016). An ecclesiastical court probably passed the first death sentence in 1511, but they were rarely carried out. The majority of cases ended in recantation or another form of punishment, such as an offering to the Church. Ecclesiastical courts continued to hear cases until the mid-sixteenth century. Secular courts (despite jurisdiction having passed officially to the ecclesiastical courts in 1543) heard their first cases of witchcraft in 1544, those of Dorota Gnieczkowa (sentenced to death at the stake) and Agnieszka of Żabikowo. In a similar fashion to the cases heard before ecclesiastical courts, accusations consisted largely of pouring wax to divine the identity of a thief, washing cows with herbs to protect the milk yield, or other harmless practices. In the seventeenth and eighteenth centuries, trials began to include details of diabolic practices, and death at the stake was the usual sentence.

DEMONOLOGY

Poznań contained printing houses of various Christian confessions, which published some of the most important treatises, as well as many legal codices, including *Speculum Saxonum* (Law of the Saxons); Chelmno Law; Magdeburg Law; Polish Crown Law; and a collection of Roman, Canon, and Saxon laws. Of particular note was Wojciech Regulus's publishing house, responsible for the publication of an anonymous work in 1639, *Czarownica powolana* (A Witch Denounced). It was considered by some to be the first vernacular translation of Friedrich Spee's famous *Cautio Criminalis* (A Warning on Criminal Justice) of 1631, but it differed from Spee's work in many respects. It was published in the same year as Daniel Wisner's *Tractatus brevis de extramagi, lamii, veneticis* (Brief Treatise on Magic, Witches, and Poisoners), which also criticized the abuses committed by the judiciary during witchcraft trials. This work, significantly, was dedicated to Łukasz and Krzysztof Opaliński. The latter wrote a satirical verse ridiculing the tendency to attribute all misfortune to witches, who were generally harmless peasant women. Another work critical of judicial abuses was Serafin Gamalski's *Przestrogi duchowne* (Clerical Warnings), published posthumously in 1742. The author claimed to have heard the confessions of those accused of witchcraft and was convinced of their innocence. A common feature of these Poznań authors was their emphasis on the large number of witchcraft executions, which, however, is not corroborated by the extant trial records.

WANDA WYPORSKA

See also: BARANOWSKI, BOGDAN; CLERGY; COURTS, ECCLESIASTICAL; DEMONOLOGY; NAZI INTEREST IN WITCH PERSECUTION; POLAND; SPEE, FRIEDRICH.

References and further reading:
Baranowski, Bogdan. 1952. *Procesy czarownic w Polsce w XVII i XVIII wieku.* Łódź: Łódzkie Towarzystwo Naukowe.

Karpiński, Andrzej. 1995. *Kobieta w mieście polskim w drugiej połowie XVI i XVII wieku.* Warsaw: IHPAN.

Koranyi, Karol. 1927. "Czary i gusła przed sądem kościelnemi w Polsce w XV i w pierwszej połowie XVI wieku." *Lud* 26: 1–24.

Soldan, Wilhelm. 1843. *Geschichte der Hexenprozesse.* Stuttgart and Tubingen.

Ulanowski, Bogdan, ed. 1894–1903. *Acta capitulorum nec non iudiciorum ecclesiasticorum selecta.* Cracow: Wydawnictwo Komisji Historycznej Akademii Umiejętności w Krakowie.

Wyporska, Wanda. 2004. "Motive and Motif: Representations of the Witch in Early Modern Poland." PhD diss. Oxford University.

PRÄTORIUS, ANTON (1560–1613)

A German Reformed parson, in 1598 Prätorius published the important treatise *Von Zauberey und Zauberern Gründlicher Bericht* (A Thorough Account of Magic and Magicians), which clearly opposed witchcraft persecution and demanded abolishing torture immediately; he was one of the first authors in Germany to propose this radical solution.

We know little about his early years or his education. After 1581, he was recorded as teaching in Lippstadt, later becoming headmaster of the Latin school in Kamen. He appeared in 1587 as a Lutheran deacon at Worms and in 1589 as a Reformed deacon at Oppenheim in the electoral Palatinate. In 1592, Prätorius became parson of Dittelsheim, a Palatine village, moving in 1595 to Offenbach am Main in the county of Isenburg-Büdingen. From 1596 to 1598, he held the post of court chaplain at Birstein before returning to the electoral Palatinate as parson of Laudenbach, where he remained for the rest of his life.

The cause that provoked Prätorius's treatise against witchcraft persecution was the abominations of the trials he had personally witnessed because of his position as court chaplain in Birstein. In 1597, he was directly involved in the trials against four women accused as witches. Despite vigorous intervention in their favor, he was unable to save their lives. Shaken by this experience, Prätorius wrote his book and returned to serve in the electoral Palatinate, which rejected persecution. Prätorius originally published his treatise under the name of his son Johannes Scultetus. When the book sold out quickly and was republished in 1602 and 1613 in rewritten editions, he used his own name. (Another edition in 1629 simply reprinted the 1602 edition.)

Prätorius was skeptical of the belief in witchcraft, not only criticizing the procedures of its persecution but also denying the reality of witchcraft. He named Benedikt Pererius, Johann Georg Goedelmann, Otto Melander, and especially Hermann Witekind from the electoral Palatinate as his most important predecessors and role models. Moreover, the electoral Palatinate's rejection of witchcraft persecutions obviously influenced Prätorius through his contacts and employment.

Prätorius showed an intimate knowledge of most contemporary treatises on witchcraft but commented on them only briefly. He founded his arguments mainly on the Bible, following common exegetical practices among Reformed theologians. Like other skeptics, Prätorius's viewpoint was theocentric: God is almighty; only he could override the laws of nature in his creation, and neither the Devil nor wizards possessed any physical powers that transcend nature. Physical harm through magic thus could not be real. Nor were any of the three elements (the witches' flight, participation in the Sabbat, and sexual intercourse with the Devil) that constituted witchcraft in the strict sense; all of them existed only in fantasy. Here Prätorius did not rely on the Bible alone but founded his argument also on the empirical reasoning of Hermann Witekind, typical of Reformed discourse in Germany.

According to Prätorius, all witches were guilty of the spiritual crime of apostasy and the diabolical pact. Their crimes were most horrible and would be punished by God with eternal damnation if the sinner did not repent. This did not, however, justify the death penalty by secular justice. Although unlike Witekind, Prätorius relied mostly on the Hebrew Bible and affirmed the validity of the Mosaic laws, he emphasized with Johann Weyer that the death penalty of Exodus 22:18 (22:17) was not directed indiscriminately against all kinds of sorcerers, but only against poisoners. With any spiritual crime, the sinner could always repent, after which God no longer desired his physical destruction. In principle, sorcery must be punished by secular justice, but in cases of conversion, not with the death penalty. He thus adopted the social-disciplinary position of his predecessors, not deterring sorcery post facto through criminal justice but preventing it by restoring true Christian faith and conduct among the people.

Concerning procedural law, Prätorius began by rejecting the idea of witchcraft as a *crimen exceptum* (excepted crime). For him, correct legal proceedings began with humane conditions of incarceration. His critical descriptions of the often-inhumane conditions of early modern imprisonment could be considered standard. However, his arguments against torture were quite revolutionary: based on his personal experiences in prosecuting witchcraft, Prätorius demanded nothing less than the immediate abolition of torture in European criminal proceedings. None of his predecessors had demanded this in such radical fashion. This achievement secured Prätorius an important place in the history of German criminal law, even though he did not argue for open assessment of evidence as a replacement for torture, thus making his argument less forceful.

JÜRGEN MICHAEL SCHMIDT

See also: EXODUS 22:18 (22:17); GOEDELMAN, JOHANN GEORG; PALATINATE, ELECTORATE OF; SKEPTICISM; WEYER, JOHANN; WITEKIND, HERMANN.

References and further reading:

Dresen-Coenders, Lène. 1992. "Antonius Praetorius." Pp. 129–137 in *Vom Unfug des Hexen-Processes: Gegner der Hexenverfolgung von Johann Weyer bis Friedrich Spee.* Edited by Hartmut Lehmann and Otto Ulbricht. Wiesbaden: Harrassowitz.

Hegeler, Hartmut. 2002. *Anton Praetorius: Kämpfer gegen Hexenprozess und Folter.* Unna: Eigenverlag.

Karneth, Rainer. 1997. "Hexen, Hexenverfolgung und ein vermeintlicher Alzeyer Kritiker-Antonius Praetorius." *Alzeyer Geschichtsblätter* 30: 37–76.

Prätorius. Antonius. 1613. *Von Zauberey und Zauberern Gründlicher Bericht. Darinn der grawsamen Menschen thöriges/feindseliges/schändliches vornemmen: Und wie Christliche Oberkeit in rechter Amptspflege ihnen begegnen/ihr Werck straffen/auffheben/ und hindern solle/ und könne . . ..* Heidelberg.

Schmidt, Jürgen Michael. 2000. *Glaube und Skepsis: Die Kurpfalz und die abendländische Hexenverfolgung, 1446–1685.* Hexenforschung 5. Bielefeld: Verlag für Regionalgeschichte.

———. 2001. "Praetorius, Antonius." In *Lexikon der Europäischen Hexenverfolgung.* Edited by Gudrun Gersmann, Jürgen Michael Schmidt, and Margarete Wittke. http://www.sfn.uni-muenchen.de/hexenforschung (cited September 10, 2002).

Schwerhoff, Gerd. 1986. "Rationalität im Wahn, Zum gelehrten Diskurs über die Hexen in der frühen Neuzeit." *Saeculum* 37: 45–82.

PRÄTORIUS, JOHANNES (1630–1680)

Prätorius (whose real name was Hans Schultz, and who should not be confused with Anton Prätorius, who used the pseudonym Johann Scultetus) was a graduate of Leipzig University, a polymath, and a Baroque poet. Under numerous, deliberately amusing pseudonyms (such as Steffen Läuscpeltz, or "Stephen Lice Fur"), he published more than fifty treatises and collections of myths and fairy tales, dealing predominantly with occult themes and folk beliefs or superstitions. In his *Blockes-Berges Verrichtung* (Performance at the Blocksberg), published in 1668, Prätorius provided a compilation of popular and learned ideas about magic, sorcery, and witchcraft. As a result of its use by Johann Wolfgang von Goethe and the brothers Grimm, this compilation also influenced nineteenth-century German literature.

Prätorius was born in the Lutheran village of Zethlingen in Sachsen-Anhalt. After attending grammar school at Halle, he matriculated at the University of Leipzig. He pursued various branches of study in the natural sciences, graduating with a master of arts degree in 1653. After giving several unsalaried lecture series on astrology, chiromancy (or palmistry), and geography at the university, he was named poet laureate, a title he valued very highly, in 1659. Remaining in Leipzig until he died of the plague a few days after his fiftieth birthday, he used the resources of the university's library (housed in the so-called *Paulinum*) as the basis for his many treatises and anthologies. The works of Prätorius had considerable influence on other German writers; Hans Jacob Christoph von Grimmelshausen had already drawn on them before Prätorius's death, and Goethe, Friedrich von Schiller, and Clemens Brentano also valued the treatises of Prätorius as treasure troves of material to be utilized in their own publications (Goethe, for example, drew on the *Blockes-Berges Verrichtung* in creating his immortal Walpurgis Night scene in part 1 of *Faust,* published in 1808). Prätorius's collection of stories about the Silesian mountain spirit Rübezahl remains well-known to this day.

After Prätorius had announced its publication several times, in 1668 finally appeared the *Blockes-Berges Verrichtung/oder ausführlicher geographischer Bericht von den hohen trefflich alt- und beruhmten Blockes-Berge. Ingleichen von der Hexenfahrt und Zauber-Sabbathe, so auff solchen Berge die Unholden aus gantz Teutschland jährlich den 1. Mai in Sanct Walpurgisnacht anstellen sollen* (Performance at the Blocksberg, or Detailed, Geographical Report of the High, Excellent, Old, and Famous Blocksberg. Also Treating of the Witches' Journey and Magical Sabbat, That the Witches from All over Germany Supposedly Attend Every Year on This Mountain During Walpurgis Night, the First of May). Prätorius used a travel narrative, written by another author in 1653, to begin the German version of his treatise; it described a journey over the Blocksberg (which lay in the Harz region) and other nearby places. The rest of the work was divided into two main parts. Here Prätorius used the *Blocksberg* of the title (also known in German as the *Brocken*), presented as the chief meeting-place of German witches, as a thematic introduction to a broader discussion of witchcraft belief. Prätorius devoted the first part of the work to describing various sinister places, such as those where witches supposedly gathered, and accursed caves, lakes, or mountaintops that were supposedly haunted by ghosts and spirits.

The second part of the work was divided into eight chapters. Here Prätorius presented "reports" about the flights of witches and the supposed activities of witches at their gatherings, or Sabbats, and told stories of various horrible occurrences that had allegedly involved the practice of harmful magic. He went into great detail on the themes of the Devil's sexual relationships with witches and of incubi, succubi, and changeling children, drawing on the Tannhäuser legend of the *Mons Veneris* (Venusberg, or Venus Mountain), written by Heinrich Kornmann in 1614. Prätorius also discussed the possibility that witches could change themselves into animals. He concluded the work with a collection of popular stories about ghosts and spirits, including tales of the mountain-spirit Rübezahl and of the "furious army," a horrific-looking group of spirits of dead men who were believed to travel at night, marauding and generally terrifying the living.

The *Blockes-Berges Verrichtung* offered a compendium or textbook of witchcraft, aimed at an interested public. In composing it, Prätorius used a vast range of ancient, medieval, and contemporary writings and treatises, including authors from both sides of the debate about witchcraft belief. Prätorius drew uncritically on their work, using any stories that seemed to fit best into his own compilation. Thus, he drew both on the work of the skeptic Johann Weyer and used material from the hard-line *Malleus Maleficarum* (The Hammer of Witches, whose author he mistakenly cited as Jacob Sprenger). He took information pell-mell from Catholics and Protestants—Johann Geiler von Kaysersberg, Ulrich Molitor, Olaus Magnus, Girolamo Cardano, Paulo Grillando, Jean Bodin, Nicolas Rémy, Lambert Daneau, David Meder, and Benedict Carpzov, among others. Prätorius was genuinely convinced of the real corporeal existence of the Devil and the demons and evil spirits who served him; he believed that witches really made pacts with the Devil and had intercourse with him, changed themselves into animals, flew to Sabbats, and performed harmful magic.

RITA VOLTMER;

TRANSLATED BY ALISON ROWLANDS

See also: GRIMM, JAOCB; SABBAT; WALPURGIS (WALPURIGS) NIGHT.
References and further reading:

Dünnhaupt, Gerhard. 1991. "Praetorius, Johann, Zetlingensis (1630–1689)." Pp. 3145–3193 in *Personalbibliographien zu den Drucken des Barock.* 2nd ed. By Gerhard Dünnhaupt. *Bibliographischen Handbuches der Barockliteratur,* vol. 5. Stuttgart: Anton Hiersemann.
Möhring, Wolfgang, ed. 1979. *Johannes Prätorius. Hexen-, Zauber- und Spukgeschichten aus dem Blocksberg: Mit Holzschnitten des 15.–17. Jahrhunderts.* Frankfurt am Main: Insel.
Waibler, Hellmut. 1979. "Johannes Prätorius (1630–1680): Ein Baraockautor und seine Werke." *Archiv für Geschichte des Buchwesens* 20: 953–1151.

PRICKING OF SUSPECTED WITCHES

A common way of detecting the "Devil's mark," an insensitive spot that would not bleed when pricked with a pin, was called pricking. If such a mark was found, it provided important evidence for prosecuting a witch.

The insensitive spot was only one kind of Devil's mark. Other marks were detected by means other than pricking: a protruding teat with which English witches were believed to suckle their "familiar" (the witch's mark); an area of discolored skin, sometimes perceived as the shape of a small animal or as the imprint of the Devil's claw; a mark in the eye, which a few witch detectors claimed to have special powers to see; or simply a mark that the suspect confessed to possessing and that therefore required little or no physical verification.

Physical verification by pricking was often a lengthy process involving an experienced pricker and numerous witnesses. The suspect would be blindfolded, partially or wholly stripped, and pricked with pins until a spot was found where a pin could enter undetected. Sometimes their body hair would be shaved. The pins varied in length from two fingers' breadth to 3 inches, occasionally more. In one French case from 1624, a pin of four fingers' breadth sank into a suspect's buttock irrecoverably. Jean Bodin, citing Revelation 14:9, expected the mark on the forehead or hand. In practice, prickers found marks in a variety of locations, with the back, shoulder, buttock, or thigh being common. Theologically the Devil's mark was equivalent to Christian baptism, which could be administered only once, but two or more marks were often found.

Church ministers or gentlemen supervising pretrial investigations might do their own pricking of suspects. The court might commission physicians, surgeons, or quasi-medical men (such as barbers). Executioners' anatomical expertise could be used for pricking as well as judicial torture. Judges or court officials might do their own pricking. A few courts commissioned women prickers; one Franche-Comté case called them *chirurgiennes.* Some regions had itinerant professional prickers; in 1621, a hangman based at Rocroi, near the French border with the Netherlands, admitted he had done this service for pay 231 times.

With practice, it was probably easy to find insensitive spots. Many "marks" were probably birthmarks or warts, both of which could be insensible. Most suspects were older people who had spent a lifetime in physical labor and whose nutrition was sometimes poor; many of them had old scars or circulatory or arthritic problems associated with losses of local sensation. It would be interesting to know what proportion of witchcraft suspects might have had physical features vulnerable to the pricker. One Scottish pricker in northern England claimed to find marks on twenty-seven out of thirty suspects brought to him, which might be some indication. This pricker, however, was a professional and, like his colleague at Rocroi, seems to have been a fraud.

With amateur prickers, the problem was more likely to be self-deception; if they were convinced that the mark existed, they would be less rigorous in their search. Did the pin *really* enter so deeply and was there *really* no pain? Occasions when the suspect felt and expressed pain were sometimes recorded, but they represented failures on the pricker's part; probably most such occasions were passed over silently. Some suspects' claims to feel pain were rejected because they could not identify the spot precisely enough or simply because no blood flowed from it. Ultimately, pricking depended more on belief and perception than on physical evidence.

Technically, pricking was not "torture." The aim of judicial torture was to inflict pain in order to secure a

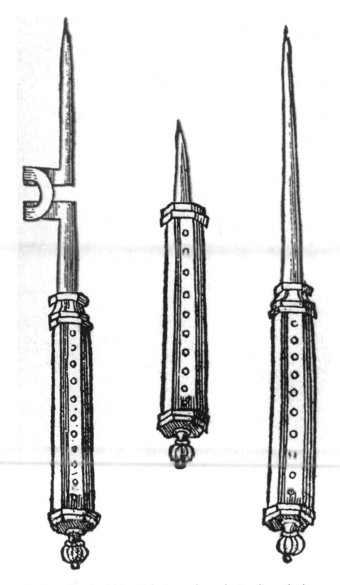

Courts employed pricking with pins to detect the Devil's mark, the insensitive spot on a witch's body where the Devil had marked his servant. (TopFoto.co.uk)

confession: pricking, by contrast, aimed to inflict *no* pain in order to secure physical evidence. Some pricking may have been connected with the popular belief that scratching them to draw blood could counteract witches' magic, and here pain would be expected. In practice, pricking was a coercive procedure that could help to break down a suspect's resistance and make a confession easier to obtain. Numerous witches began to confess after they were told that a mark had been found. This was particularly important for women, for whom being stripped, shaved, searched intimately, and pricked by men could be a form of symbolic rape.

Unlike the swimming test, which resembled a judicial ordeal (an appeal to God to display the truth), pricking seems to have had no medieval antecedents and has not been traced back further than the mid-

sixteenth century; unfortunately, many reports of the finding of the "mark" leave the discovery method unspecified. Pricking undoubtedly gained in importance during the early seventeenth century, above all in Protestant regions, where the Devil's mark seemed relatively more important than among Catholics. For example, the Inquisition did not use pricking.

The belief that the Devil might remove his mark in order to protect witches may have been a largely Catholic one. In 1631, the Jesuit Friedrich Spee complained that if the pricker failed to find a mark, the judge would decide that the Devil had removed it in order to protect the witch. This could occasionally be used against a suspect, enabling the prosecution to claim that a suspect was still guilty even though no mark had been found, which seems to have happened with another Jesuit, Urbain Grandier, in Loudun in 1634. But more often, the belief in the mark's erasability seems to have discouraged courts from seeking it. Some suspects even volunteered to be pricked in the belief that it would prove their innocence.

Usually of lower-class origins, professional prickers were among the few people who clearly stood to profit financially from witch hunting. During periods of intense witch hunting, they could make a windfall profit by offering their services to worried local authorities. They flourished particularly in seventeenth-century Scotland, where about ten professional prickers are known. Payment by results opened a temptation to outright fraud, for which five Scottish prickers were prosecuted or reprimanded. Two turned out to be women dressed as men. The activities of an unnamed Scottish pricker in the north of England in 1650 are particularly well documented. He pricked many women brought to him through neighborhood denunciations, charging 20 shillings apiece, and his evidence seemed to have been central in their trials. He had presumably begun his career in the Scottish panic of 1649. He was executed for fraud in Scotland after reportedly confessing responsibility for the deaths of 220 witches (the Rocroi hangman, who may hold the European record by discovering a mark 231 times, was sentenced to perpetual service in the galleys by the *Parlement* of Paris).

In 1631, Friedrich Spee warned that prickers should be watched carefully because they were prone to fraud: they would cry out that a mark had been found, or would use a retractable bodkin. An illustration of such a bodkin was published by Reginald Scot in 1584, though he cited it as a general proof of the possibility of fraud in witchcraft accusations and did not specifically mention pricking. Most prickers seem to have preferred ordinary needles, rather than bodkins with handles. The exposure of frauds fueled skepticism about prickers by the mid-seventeenth century, even among the medical profession: for example, Genevan surgeons searched over a dozen suspected witches after 1622 but never found an unambiguous Devil's mark. The practice was never banned but faded away along with the witchcraft trials.

JULIAN GOODARE

See also: BODIN, JEAN; DEVIL'S MARK; EVIDENCE; FAMILIARS; LOUDUN NUNS; PROOF, PROBLEM OF; SCOT, REGINALD; SPEE, FRIEDRICH; SWIMMING TEST; TORTURE; WITCH'S MARK.

References and further reading:
McDonald, Stuart W. 1997. "The Devil's Mark and the Witch-Prickers of Scotland." *Journal of the Royal Society of Medicine* 90: 507–511.
Monter, E. William. 1976. *Witchcraft in France and Switzerland: The Borderlands During the Reformation.* Ithaca, NY: Cornell University Press.
Neill, W. N. 1922. "The Professional Pricker and His Test for Witchcraft." *Scottish Historical Review* 19: 205–213.
Pihlajamäki, Heikki. 2000. "'Swimming the Witch, Pricking for the Devil's Mark': Ordeals in the Early Modern Witchcraft Trials." *Journal of Legal History* 21: 35–58.
Soman, Alfred. *Sorcellerie et justice criminelle: Le Parlement of Paris (16e–18e siècles).* Bath: Variorum

PRIERIAS, SILVESTRO (CA. 1456/1457–CA. 1527)

Theologian and inquisitor best known as the first Roman respondent to Martin Luther, Silvestro Mazzolini da Prierio or Prierias (as he is usually called, after his birthplace in Piedmont, Italy) wrote several influential works on witchcraft and demonology that helped fuel witch hysteria in early modern Europe.

Born in 1456 or 1457, Prierias entered the Dominican order in 1471, joining the reformed Observant branch of Lombardy. After studying philosophy and theology at the *studium generale* (house of studies) in the convent of San Domenico in Bologna, he began his teaching career there in 1489 as master of studies, later serving also as its regent master (1499–1502). In 1508 came appointments as both vicar general of his Lombard Dominican congregation and inquisitor for Brescia, Crema, and environs, a position the friar held until 1511, when he was transferred to Sant'Eustorgio in Milan as inquisitor for the busier territories of Milan, Piacenza, and Lodi. The Observant Dominicans lost control of Sant'Eustorgio in 1512, and Prierias moved to Cremona as prior of the convent of San Domenico. In 1514, he was sent to teach theology in Rome where, in the following year, Pope Leo X appointed him to the chair of theology at the University of Rome, while also naming him master of the sacred palace (i.e., official theologian of the papal curia) as well as Roman inquisitor, responsible for all inquisitorial activities of the tribunal at Santa Maria sopra Minerva. In 1518 the pope assigned to Prierias the task of evaluating the orthodoxy of Martin Luther's *Ninety-Five Theses;* the Dominican's resultant critique, the *Dialogus* (Dialogue), as well as subsequent elaborations and responses, set in motion the process that soon led to Luther's condemnation as a heretic. Prierias died in Rome, most likely in 1527.

Among Prierias's other major works are the 1503 *Rosa aurea* (Golden Rose), a preacher's handbook reprinted nineteen times in the sixteenth century, and the 1514 *Summa summarum de casibus conscientibus* (Complete Compendium of Cases of Conscience), better known as the *Summa silvestrina* (Silvester's Compendium), a theological, moral and canonical handbook for confessors, reprinted twenty-nine times.

Most important for our subject, however, are his early treatises on the Devil, demonic possession, and exorcism, the *Tractatus de diabolo* (1502, reprinted 1573); the *De strigimagarum, demonumque mirandis* (Concerning the Prodigies of the Witch-Magicians and Demons, 1521, reprinted 1575); and the various relevant entries (e.g, *Haeresis, Maleficium, Superstitio* [Heresy, Sorcery, Superstition]) in the *Summa silvestrina,* some of which represent the core of Lenten sermons collected in his *Quadragesimale aureum* (Golden Lenten Sermon Series) of 1515.

Prierias's interest in demonology and witchcraft surfaced early in his Dominican career and remained a constant preoccupation thereafter. Already as regent master in Bologna, if not sooner, he participated in exorcisms and witchcraft trials and summarized the fruit of this experience in *De diabolo.* Prierias's approach was consistently hard-line; his goal, to overcome the leniency toward witchcraft and related activities encouraged by traditional interpretations of the Church's central legal text on the matter, the *Canon Episcopi* (ca. 906), which consigned such phenomena merely to the realm of personal delusion and harmless superstition. Prierias acknowledged that in earlier centuries this may have been true but warned that recent times had seen the birth of a new, internationally organized sect of heretics consisting of antinomian, devil-worshipping women and men who, through nocturnal flight, gathered for orgiastic Sabbats, engaged in sorcery, and wrought acts of malevolence against private citizens and the established Christian order.

Prierias told us that he wrote his longest work on the subject, the *De strigimagarum,* because he had encountered alarming skepticism among his peers while serving as judge in a Roman witchcraft trial. Besides its intransigence, *De strigimagarum* was noteworthy for the neologism introduced by its author, namely, the term *strigimagus,* created to enforce the view that the two hitherto distinct categories of persons, the common witches (*striges*) and the more prestigious scientific-philosophical magicians (*magi*), were in fact equally diabolical and deserving of elimination. However, beyond this, the work added little to earlier works by other writers or by Prierias. Ultimately, Prierias's efforts helped to heighten Christendom's awareness and fear of this "new sect" of witches. However, the theologian-inquisitor was only partially successful in his own homeland: although early modern Italy prosecuted witches, their punishments were usually lenient, and actual executions were few, relative to the rest of Europe.

FRANCO MORMANDO

See also: *CANON EPISCOPI;* DEMONOLOGY; DOMINICAN ORDER; ITALY.
References and further reading:
Lehner, Francis Christopher. 1967. "Mazzolini, Sylvester." Vol. 9, pp. 524–525 in *The New Catholic Encyclopedia.* Prepared by an editorial staff at the Catholic University of America. New York: McGraw-Hill.
Tavuzzi, Michael. 1997. *Prierias: The Life and Works of Silvestro da Prierio, 1456–1527.* Durham: Duke University Press.
Wicks, Jared. 1996. "Prierias, Sylvester Mazzolini." Vol. 3, pp. 341–342 in *The Oxford Encyclopedia of the Reformation.* 4 vols. Edited by H. J. Hillerbrand. New York: Oxford University Press.

PRODIGIES

Prodigies are phenomena—natural or supernatural, but often marvelous or wonderful—that are interpreted as signs of future events, usually disastrous.

"Prodigies" include monsters, deformed births, comets, wars, famines, pestilence, earthquakes, ghosts, dreams, demons, and witches. Belief in prodigies rests on belief in a theocentric (God-centered) and unified universe. In this way, the divine plan may include unusual events or creatures on earth that people interpret as punishments or as spurs to action and moral reformation. Similarly, aberrations in the natural order are considered to be the result of human discord and sin. Such wonders can also be given scientific or natural explanations, but in the Western tradition, theological or eschatological (related to the Last Judgment and the end of the world) explanations have predominated. The literature of prodigies is large, reaching its peak in Europe during the religious and political unrest of the early modern period between 1450 and 1750.

PRODIGIES IN ANTIQUITY

Such classical authors as Aristotle, Virgil, Seneca, Pliny the Elder, and Plutarch recorded numerous prodigies. Cicero attempted to categorize and explain prodigies in *De divinatione* (On Divination). He explained that the meaning of "prodigy" derives from the way in which such wonders "predict" (*praedicunt*), but argued that some wonders should not be given a prodigious interpretation.

The Judeo-Christian tradition is full of prodigious events. For example, in the Hebrew Bible, plagues of locusts, frogs, and caterpillars rain down upon such wicked kings and nations as Pharaoh and the Philistines. In the New Testament, the Gospels of

Matthew, Mark, and Luke also provide lists of prodigies and portents of future calamities. Jesus's warning of the impending days of vengeance (Luke 21:25), "And there shall be signs in the sun, and in the moon, and in the stars," was often cited by medieval and early modern doomsayers. Moreover, according to the Revelation of St. John, the four horsemen who would appear at the Apocalypse would rain down war, famine, and plague on the earth. Indeed, a medieval prophetic legend, the Fifteen Signs before Doomsday, described a succession of prodigies that would appear in the fortnight before the Last Judgment. The book of Revelation also describes how the binding up of Satan at the second coming of Jesus would last 1,000 years. As a result, medieval and early modern Europeans believed that an upsurge in prodigies, including false prophecy, magic, and witchcraft, was caused by the Devil, who was angered at the thought that he had little time left and was hastening to do as much damage as he could. The approach of the millennium was also signaled by the appearance of the Antichrist, with whom many prodigies were associated. St. Augustine, following Pliny the Elder and Cicero, found the preoccupation with the evils that were supposed to follow specific wonders disagreeable, because it detracted from the more general wonder and beauty of God's plans and led people to expect an imminent Apocalypse. However, later medieval and early modern writers enthusiastically embraced the biblical emphasis on prodigies as divine messages and signs of things to come.

MEDIEVAL AND EARLY MODERN PRODIGIES

Much of the classical tradition of prodigy literature was transmitted through the writings of the encyclopedist Isidore of Seville and Albertus Magnus (ca. 1200–1280), as well as by the authors of numerous texts on herbs (herbals) and strange animals (bestiaries). Although the scope for wonderful yet essentially regular species widened as natural causes were investigated under the influence of Arabic and Greek texts, most medieval writers accepted God's prerogative to suspend the normal laws of nature and produce prodigies. Therefore, singular events such as the conjunction of planets (e.g., Mars and Saturn in 1484), bright comets (e.g., Halley's Comet of 1066), and snow in summer or plagues of mice were interpreted as threatening and divine messages.

Religious disputes and political tensions contributed to a spate of prodigy literature during the sixteenth century. There was an enormous range of texts, from single-sheet woodcuts of monstrous births with a brief interpretation—such as that of a two-headed child born to Jewish parents in Venice in 1575—to large and apparently disorganized encyclopedias of prodigies such as Conrad Wolffhart's (pseud. Lycosthenes) 1557

Prodigiorum ac ostentorum chronicon, quae praeter naturae ordinem (Chronicle of Prodigies and Portents That Are Outside the Order of Nature). It was translated into English and updated in 1581 by Stephen Bateman as *The Doome warning all men to the Judgemente*. Some of the prodigies that they described had precise scriptural foundations. For instance, a seven-headed monster was interpreted as a clear warning of the seven-headed mount of the whore of Babylon described in Revelation 17:3–18. Other prodigies, such as an earthquake in the Italian city of Venice in 1511 in which certain statues on public buildings were damaged, were given more localized political interpretations by witnesses.

Prodigies were often related to providences (punishments of the ungodly), and consequently the early modern fascination with such curiosities was sharpened by confessional strife. Protestants and Catholics directed the accusation of being Antichrist against each other. For instance, Martin Luther considered the Roman papacy to be Antichrist, whereas Catholics viewed Luther as the Antichrist or at least one of the signs of his coming. The advent of the Antichrist was also taken as the surest of many signs that the struggles of the English Reformation were part of the last and decisive confrontation between good and evil described in Revelation.

Because witches and prodigies both had eschatological significance and scriptural justification, they were often discussed in the same breath. In addition, early modern men and women believed that many prodigies had demonological causes and associated them with the final struggle between good and evil. One demonologist detected signs of the Antichrist's activities in the rise of witchcraft, explaining in 1623 that the Antichrist had in fact been born twelve years before. According to the influential Catholic theologian St. Robert Bellarmine (1542–1621), the Antichrist would be a "noted magician" (magus). Conrad Wolffhart and Stephen Bateman both cited witchcraft trials in their books as signs of mankind's future destruction.

The English politician and philosopher Francis Bacon (1561–1626) dismissed such prodigies as "monstrous births" as irregular but naturally occurring variations. Popular skepticism about prodigies is particularly evident from the mid-seventeenth century, when the prodigious interpretation of comets, for instance, was often condemned as a facet of vulgar superstition or of overzealous Christian belief. However, "scientific" explanations of the return of comets could still coexist with a divine, if less frequently used, prerogative to warn men and women of future doom. In the modern "scientific" age, one catches a few echoes of the eschatological understanding of natural events in recurring fears about "apocalyptic" disasters such as asteroid impact and global warming.

STEPHEN BOWD

See also: ANTICHRIST; APOCALYPSE; ISIDORE OF SEVILLE, ST.; MILLENARIANISM; MONSTERS; OCCULT; ORACLES.
References and further reading:
Barnes, Robin Bruce. 1988. *Prophecy and Gnosis: Apocalypticism in the Wake of the Lutheran Reformation.* Stanford: Stanford University Press.
Céard, Jean. 1977. *La Nature et les prodiges: L'Insolite au XVI siècle en France.* Geneva: Droz.
Daston, Lorraine, and Katharine Park. 1998. *Wonders and the Order of Nature, 1150–1750.* New York: Zone Books.
Hanafi, Zakiya. 2000. *The Monster in the Machine: Magic, Medicine, and the Marvelous in the Time of the Scientific Revolution.* Durham and London: Duke University Press.
Kappler, Claude. 1980. *Monstres, démons et merveilles à la fin du moyen âge.* Paris: Payot.
Niccoli, Ottavia. 1990. *Prophecy and People in Renaissance Italy.* Translated by Lydia G. Cochrane. Princeton, NJ: Princeton University Press.
Schenda, Rudolf. 1962. "Die deutschen Prodigiensammlungen des 16. und 17. Jahrhunderts." *Archiv für Geschichte des Buchwesens* 4: cols. 637–710.
Walsham, Alexandra. 1999. *Providence in Early Modern England.* Oxford: Oxford University Press.
Wilson, Dudley. 1993. *Signs and Wonders: Monstrous Births from the Middle Ages to the Enlightenment.* London: Routledge.

PROOF, PROBLEM OF

The issue of proof is central to any analysis of the witch hunts. Investigators who argue that the hunts were campaigns to control certain types of people imply that proof of witchcraft was not particularly important in the persecutions. In this view, if authorities wished to discourage women from asserting their views, for example, they would attack assertive women, with the accusation of witchcraft a mere cover. But if the hunts are considered as efforts to uncover criminals responsible for actual, perceptible damage to humans, animals, or property, proof must play a large role in any discussion.

Questions of evidence and proof in the courts are also related to the use of torture. Understanding it as a repressive mechanism or as a warning to others not to engage in certain behavior also supports the conclusion that the witch persecutions were largely ways of marking acceptable social boundaries. But insofar as the application of torture in criminal cases on the European Continent and Scotland (it was rarely used in Scandinavia or England) may be seen as an attempt, however crude, to get at the truth, then the hunts become drives to eliminate perceived evildoers. The two major Continental law codes in force during the witch hunts, the German *Carolina* of 1532 and the 1539 French statutes of Villers-Cotterets, made clear that torture was to be used only in specific circumstances, when several clues (*indicia*) appeared to connect a suspect to a crime. For instance, Hans is found stabbed to death, Fritz owns a knife that fits the wounds, and the two men were seen arguing shortly before the homicide. If Fritz does not confess voluntarily, the courts might order him tortured.

To pass a guilty sentence in a capital case, Continental courts usually insisted on "complete proof," which was either the testimony of two eyewitnesses or a confession, sometimes dubbed the "Queen of Proofs." These standards appeared along with the new "Romano-canonical," or inquisitorial courts, beginning in the eleventh century. The requirement of complete proof could often be satisfied only through a confession; hence, on the Continent, pressure mounted to obtain one when *indicia* existed. In all types of criminal cases, a suspect's generally poor reputation constituted an *indicium.* But *indicia,* especially in troubled times or in a jurisdiction operating without the supervision of appellate courts, might be as minor as an ugly appearance.

Juries in England did not require "complete" proof, so courts there had little need to use torture. However, standards for conviction were not necessarily higher. In fact, courts in both old and New England sometimes found defendants guilty of witchcraft on the basis of reputation and circumstantial evidence, for example, that a quarrelsome woman passed by a baby who fell ill and died.

Whether or not torture was used in judicial proceedings, witchcraft was regarded as an extremely serious crime throughout Europe and North America from roughly 1430 far into the 1700s. It was simultaneously like and unlike other capital crimes. No other offense was ostensibly carried out with the help of a supernatural power, yet the damage that resulted was similar to the injuries inflicted for other reasons. Detailed case studies of witchcraft trials have shown that although the charge of allying with the Devil usually received close attention from authorities, witnesses focused on the damage defendants had allegedly done to creatures and things. Thus, suspects in witchcraft trials received much the same treatment as in other felony cases. However, the means of identifying suspects was often different, because people who had supposedly attended a witches' Sabbat might be pressed under torture to name others who had taken part. Yet even this chain reaction effect was not peculiar to witchcraft trials; members of a gang of thieves, for instance, might have undergone similar treatment. These two kinds of charges seem interwoven in at least one large case, the *Zauberer-Jackl-Prozess* (Sorcerer-Jack-Trial) held at Salzburg from 1677 to 1680.

Lower courts might quickly turn to torture and accept its results, especially if great fears of witches affected a given area. Higher courts often had higher standards of evidence. Removed from the emotional ground of unexplained destruction and from the reputation anyone bore in a face-to-face community, appellate justices based their decisions on written evidence, sometimes supplemented by personal interrogation of defendants. French appellate courts (*parlements*), for instance, began to overturn all death sentences for witchcraft by local tribunals in the 1620s. Similar trends appeared later in Denmark, Sweden, and Scotland.

Likewise, urban courts displayed more skepticism about proofs of witchcraft than their rural counterparts. No convictions are recorded for Frankfurt, Germany, for example, although several cases dragged through the city's courts for years. Conviction rates in Geneva were much lower than in close-by rural areas. The issue of reputation was less important in a city than in a village; in the former setting, high mobility meant that status rested largely on documents or direct testimony about actions. Circumstantial evidence figured less strongly in places where hundreds of people might have been nearby when someone's baby died unexpectedly. What might be called the social geography of evidence was terribly, perhaps even decisively, important.

For various reasons, standards of proof in witchcraft cases declined in many parts of western Europe during the witch hunts. Fear of witches might heighten suspicion of anyone, whether a social deviant or not. If a vehement witch hunter stirred an area into action against witches, news of trials close by sometimes prompted both local peasants and officials to read events in the worst possible light.

Some well-documented hunts show that lowered standards of evidence evoked widespread objections; in turn, such criticisms helped to end trials in many locations. Prompted in some instances by the vehement objections to the misuse of torture that Friedrich Spee made in 1631, seventeenth-century German judges finally found that they could no longer tell who was a witch, because anyone could be accused, and given the harsh methods of the torture chamber, almost anyone could be made to confess. Once the number of people handled in this way reached a certain level, it became clear that innocent residents had been convicted. At that point, the problem of what constituted reliable proof was unmanageable, and hunts collapsed on the spot.

The witchcraft trials of 1692 in Salem, Massachusetts, provide another vivid example of this trend. Earlier in New England, juries had infrequently returned guilty verdicts in witchcraft cases, and when they did, judges sometimes overturned them. But in a tense atmosphere of political insecurity and Indian attacks, juries in Salem Village accepted "spectral evidence" as proof of witchcraft in one fatal year. Witnesses testified that defendants' specters had attacked them, even when the accused had demonstrably been elsewhere. But in 1693 the members of one jury repudiated their decisions of the previous months, saying that they had relied on "such evidence against the accused, as, on further consideration and better information, we justly fear was insufficient for the touching the lives of any" (Kors and Peters 2001, 437).

In place after place, the witch hunts subsided over the issue of proof, despite continuing references to the power of the Devil and his minions. When large numbers of people were accused (several hundred were named, at least unofficially, in the Salem affair) and the standards of proof were quite low, anyone might be convicted. Witch hunts sometimes fell, in effect, from their own weight.

A focus on how standards of proof in witchcraft cases declined and finally rose suggests that the trials were not about disciplining any category of people; they resembled other contemporary criminal processes in their examination of evidence, except that panics about witchcraft were more likely than other crimes to afflict a given area. Witches could allegedly fly and gather anywhere in great numbers in an instant, so that their danger seemed acute to many Europeans, particularly when assiduous witch finders, news of other trials, or general anxiety highlighted their activities. The erection of new social boundaries or definitions cannot be correlated with witch hunts. Sometimes they occurred where such change never happened, but in regions of great social realignment they may have been minor or completely absent. Instead, the witch persecutions centered on the issue of proof.

ROBERT W. THURSTON

See also: CONFESSIONS; DECLINE OF THE WITCH HUNTS; EVIDENCE; GERMANY, SOUTHWESTERN; INQUISITORIAL PROCEDURE; NEW ENGLAND; SALEM; SPEE, FRIEDRICH; TORTURE.

References and further reading:
Boguet, Henri. 1602. *Discours des sorciers: Tiré de quelques procez, faicts de deux ans en ça à plusieurs de la même secte, en la terre de S. Oyan de Ioux, dicté de S. Claude au comte de Bourgogne: Avec une instruction pour une iuge, en faict de sorcellerie.* Lyon: Iean Pillehotte.
Briggs, Robin. 2002. *Witches and Neighbors: The Social and Cultural Context of European Witchcraft.* 2nd edition. Malden, MA, and Oxford: Blackwell.
Karlsen, Carol F. 1987. *The Devil in the Shape of a Woman: Witchcraft in Colonial New England.* New York: W. W. Norton.
Kors, Alan C., and Edward Peters, eds. 2001. *Witchcraft in Europe, 1100–1700: A Documentary History.* 2nd ed. Revised by Edward Peters. Philadelphia: University of Pennsylvania Press.
Langbein, John H. 1977. *Torture and the Law of Proof: Europe and England in the Ancien Regime.* Chicago: University of Chicago Press.
Midelfort, H. C. Erik. 1972. *Witch Hunting in Southwestern Germany, 1562–1684.* Stanford: Stanford University Press.
Soman, Alfred. 1985. "Criminal Jurisprudence in Ancien-Regime France: The Parlement of Paris in the Sixteenth and Seventeenth Centuries." Pp. 43–75 in *Crime and Criminal Justice in Europe and Canada.* Edited by Louis A. Knafla. Waterloo, Canada: Wilfrid Laurier University Press.
Spee, Friedrich von. 1649. *Cautio Criminalis,* German edition. Frankfurt-am-Main.
Thurston, Robert W. 2001. *Witch, Wicce, Mother Goose: The Rise and Fall of the Witch Hunts in Europe and North America.* London: Longman.

PROTESTANT REFORMATION

The Reformation, which began in Germany by 1520 and quickly spread to the whole of central, western, and northern Europe, had considerable impact on the history of European witchcraft trials. By the mid-fifteenth century, the concept of witchcraft had already acquired clear contours, and the first substantial prosecutions of this new "sect" had already begun. Meanwhile, the Inquisition's longstanding preoccupation with older kinds of heretics took a back seat in Germany, where such trials had petered out entirely long before the Reformation began. Both ecclesiastical and secular authorities who retained their allegiance to Rome turned their undivided attention to fighting the Reformation.

The Reformation did not end the witch hunts; instead, most of the new Protestant churches evolved distinctive theological frameworks for persecuting alleged witches. After its consolidation at the Council of Trent (1545–1563), the Roman Catholic Church refurbished its late medieval doctrines. By the late sixteenth century, alleged witches and sorcerers were persecuted with varying intensity by every confessional denomination, except the underground Anabaptist sects. The climax of the witch persecution occurred between the Peace of Augsburg (1555) and the Peace of Westphalia (1648). Certain historians have extended the Reformation period into the seventeenth century, which suggests that the Reformation was an essential element in the increased frenzy against witches. However, it is more helpful to distinguish between the pre-1560 reformations and the subsequent confessional period (late sixteenth and early seventeenth centuries), when conditions were entirely different in the Holy Roman Empire, where most witch hunts occurred.

Except in Upper Germany, where Heinrich Kramer had already conducted extensive witchcraft prosecutions, Protestantism generated a reserved attitude toward witchcraft trials. The phenomenon was approached primarily through expositions of the first commandment, as a continuation of earlier attacks on superstition by medieval preachers. Their aversion to Dominican Scholasticism and to the papal Inquisition contributed to the fact that the early reformers, at least Martin Luther and the Swabian reformer Johann Brenz, opposed the cumulative concept of witchcraft. With Philipp Melanchthon and Jean Calvin, humanist influences increased their skepticism toward certain elements of the concept of witches. Because the Reformation was predominantly concerned with the beliefs and practices of laypeople, forms of superstitious practices came under constant scrutiny. Early Protestants widened their interpretation of violations of the first commandment to include reverence paid to saints and idolizing elements of creation, as well as to astrology and everything that distracted people from real faith in God. Every Christian was exposed as a radically superstitious being.

The background for this was the idea, shared by all streams of the Reformation, of human beings' inherent sinfulness and consequent inability to obtain righteousness before God with their own strength, necessitating complete dependence on God's forgiveness and grace. In the early stages of the movement, all Reformers favored spreading the Gospel without force, and Luther's rejection of civic punishment for heresy was one reason for his criminal conviction in 1520. Finally, the strongly eschatological aspect of the early Reformation assumed that the end of the world was imminent and led to a strong conviction that the reformation of the Church was the last great event in world history, one that would transform the whole Church in accordance with God's will. In Luther's later works, we find the assertion that sorcery and superstition had decreased when the Gospel began to "run its course," but that evil was again increasing, since the Reformation had not prevailed everywhere.

The concept of witchcraft survived the Reformation not because, as liberal nineteenth-century Protestantism asserted, some medieval "relics" were unintentionally retained. Rather the Reformation was subject to a premodern interpretation of the world to a significantly greater degree than "enlightened" or "disenchanted" Protestant theology was willing to admit. When Ernst Troeltsch distinguished "old" and "new" Protestantism around 1900, his principal criterion was the strong supernaturalism of old Protestantism. This, in fact, explained why concepts of sorcery and witchcraft, varied though they were, could be retained in Protestantism until the eighteenth century.

Further developments in the Reformation movement strengthened this phenomenon. In 1530, the failure of an attempted consensus between different reform movements within the church became apparent, and separate church structures soon evolved in German Protestant territories, England, and the Scandinavian countries. Their disciplinary regulations generally included clauses prohibiting sorcery but did not define this concept. In every Protestant region (as in places retaining allegiance to Rome), regulations treated witchcraft, divination, and similar violations of the first commandment as serious religious offenses.

At the same time, there was growing pressure to apply religious discipline in order to display the success of the respective confession and to enforce its requirements. The particular Protestant emphasis on the prohibition of even harmless sorcery and the misuse of Christian symbols and subject matter (often called white magic) enormously widened the circle of possible offenders. On the one hand, this element of Reformed doctrine encouraged witchcraft trials and was adopted later by the Catholics; on the other hand, the Reformation stressed the individual believer's direct relationship to God, an aspect that discouraged mass persecution. Thus with regard to sorcery, the central message of the Reformation was that people should not blame misfortune or affliction on witches and sorcerers but accept that even unnatural sickness was due to the direct will of God. In following decades, this argument of the requirement of God's permission for witchcraft combined with widespread rejection of the concept of witches flying and holding Sabbats—both of which are specific to the Reformation—reduced the prospects for large-scale witch hunts in Protestant Europe.

By the end of the Reformation movement around 1555, a theological system had developed that conformed to its original ideas but left the issue of witchcraft unresolved. Therefore, during the subsequent confessional period, a relatively open discussion of the doctrine of witchcraft was possible within Protestantism, in sharp contrast to the doctrinal tradition of the Roman Catholic Church after the condemnation of Cornelius Loos in the 1590s. Protestant opponents of the witchcraft trials such as Johann Weyer, Anton Prätorius, Johann Matthäus Meyfart, and numerous others were not considered outsiders by supporters of severe witch persecution. However, by 1600 the concept of witchcraft had changed within Protestantism, because Protestant (and in particular, Lutheran) theology had reverted to the Scholastic interpretation of Aristotle and now accepted the cumulative concept of witchcraft, including the notion of witches flying and holding Sabbats.

Nevertheless, even orthodox books on doctrine, such as those of Johann Gerhard, contain no statements that exceed God's permission for practicing witchcraft. Much Protestant exegetical literature of the confessional period interpreted the biblical statements on witchcraft with a reservation not unlike that of the Early Middle Ages; in addition, the great increase in the philological knowledge of Protestant exegetes encouraged doubts about the validity of the contemporary concept of witches. Thus the theological spectrum of the Reformation was considerably broad; by the late sixteenth century, a cautious graduation separated the strong Lutheran theology as expressed in the *Formula Concordiae* (Formula Concord) of 1577, Melanchthonian Lutheran theology, and Reformed Calvinism, which already partly rejected elements of supernaturalism and thus started a theological development that led to a radical rejection of the fundamentals of the witch hunts. However, witchcraft trials occurred in nearly all territories and states of the various Protestant denominations, with the Calvinist electoral Palatinate being the most important exception. Within

Germany, the focal point of witchcraft persecution, Reformed territories usually conducted fewer trials than Lutheran states.

Church historians have evaluated the Reformation's role in the history of witchcraft trials from various perspectives. In the early nineteenth century, Protestant historians firmly rejected any notion of confessional "guilt" for mass prosecutions; in the late nineteenth century, Catholics claimed exactly the opposite, that the Reformation laid the foundation for the hysteria about witches. The consensus from these debates is that the Reformation undoubtedly permitted a continuation of witchcraft trials and that this was not unintentional and was theologically motivated. However, relatively recent empirical studies (Midelfort 1972) suggested that, at least in Germany, Catholic territories pursued these prosecutions with somewhat greater intensity than most Protestant territories. One reason for this lay in the theological emphasis on an inscrutable divine Providence that characterized the Reformation; in addition, Protestantism had several leading figures, not all of whom were interested in witchcraft trials. However, a comprehensive study of the influence of the Reformation on the history of witchcraft trials, based on the insights gained over the last fifty years, is still a desideratum for historians of Christianity and of the witch hunts.

JÖRG HAUSTEIN;

TRANSLATED BY HELEN SIEGBURG

See also: ANABAPTISTS; APOCALYPSE; BRENZ, JOHANN; CALVIN, JOHN; HOLY ROMAN EMPIRE; KRAMER, HEINRICH; LOOS, CORNELIUS; LUTHER, MARTIN; MEYFART, JOHANN MATTHÄUS; PALATINATE, ELECTORATE OF; PRÄTORIUS, ANTON; SUPERSTITION; WEYER, JOHANN.

References and further reading:

Behringer, Wolfgang. 1987. "'Vom Unkraut unter dem Weizen': Die Stellung der Kirchen zum Hexenproblem." Pp. 60–95 in *Hexenwelten: Magie und Imagination vom 16.–20. Jahrhundert.* Edited by Richard van Dülmen. Frankfurt am Main: Fischer.

Clark, Stuart. 1997. *Thinking with Demons: The Idea of Witchcraft in Early Modern Europe.* Oxford: Clarendon.

Diefenbach, Johann. 1886. *Der Hexenwahn vor und nach der Glaubensspaltung in Deutschland.* Mainz: Kirchheim.

Haustein, Jörg. 1990. *Martin Luthers Stellung zum Zauberer- und Hexenwesen.* Stuttgart: Kohlhammer.

Midelfort, Erik H. C. 1972. *Witch Hunting in Southwestern Germany, 1562–1684: The Social and Intellectual Foundations.* Stanford: Stanford University Press.

Paulus, Nikolaus. 1910. *Hexenwahn und Hexenprozess, vornehmlich im 16. Jahrhundert.* Freiburg im Breisgau: Herder.

Waite, Gary K. 2003. *Heresy, Magic, and Witchcraft in Early Modern Europe.* Basingstoke, UK: Palgrave.

PRUSSIA

Witchcraft trials were common in early modern Prussia, being held in at least fifty places, but the destruction of the Prussian archives in the twentieth century prevents an accurate estimate of the number of trials and executions. However, sources do exist in the Polish state archives in Gdańsk and in Bydgoszczy and in the library of the Polish Academy of Sciences in Gdansk (Danzig).

The political and ethnic history of this region, like so much else in eastern Europe, is complex. The Teutonic Order, which forcibly Christianized this territory, favored German colonization in the area. In effect, the population that developed mixed native Prussians with Germans, Poles, and Pomeranians. After Poland's King Casmir IV defeated the Teutonic knights in 1466, their lands were divided into Royal Prussia, which was incorporated directly into Poland, and a vassal-state ruled by the order. The latter part became the duchy of Prussia in 1525, when the grand master of the Teutonic Order converted to Protestantism. This entry examines the territory of ducal and Royal Prussia proper and excludes the Brandenburg section of the Prussian state. Ducal and Royal Prussia's population in the sixteenth century was between 500,000 and 800,000; by the late eighteenth century, Prussia's population was between 2 and 2.5 million.

THE LAW

Although the Chełmno Law was commonly recognized, it had no uniform codification and hence was locally applied in the three most popular revisions, its Lidzbark, Nowe Miasto, and Toruń versions. All Prussian laws penalized witchcraft with death by burning. The Teutonic knights, who were technically friars, ran ecclesiastical courts, which commonly heard cases of misdeeds against God and religion, witchcraft included, before and after accepting Polish suzerainty in 1466. Because witchcraft was treated relatively mildly under canon law (fines or penance usually involving public display of the sentenced clad in humiliating attire, commonly in front of the church at the time when the locals gathered for Mass), sorcery cases increasingly reached municipal and other secular courts; many autonomous Prussian towns passed so-called Willkür (discretion; arbitrary action), city and village statutes against witchcraft. Some of these statutes stipulated that witches be burned alive, some sent the witch to the block before burning, and some decreed banishment for life. After 1532, ducal Prussia followed the Carolina (the *Constitutio Criminalis Carolina*), the imperial law code promulgated in that year, and Royal Prussia recognized it on an auxiliary basis. Prussian laws were not reformed until the mid-eighteenth century. In 1746, King Frederick IV granted Samuel von Coccei the authority to reform the Prussian legal system, and a royal decree in 1750 made all death sentences, corporal punishments, and torture subject to royal approval, although torture was not abolished until 1754, well after the end of witchcraft trials. The motivation for this judicial reform was state centralization, not humanitarian considerations. Royal Prussia abolished witchcraft as a crime only in 1776, due to the constitution adopted by the Polish parliament.

TRIALS IN PRUSSIA

Because of the ruination the Prussian archives suffered in World Wars I and II, the history, intensity, and extent of witchcraft trials in Prussia can be reconstructed only fragmentarily; occasionally an older work (Lilienthal 1861) provides information that has since been destroyed. Our earliest surviving Prussian evidence comes from the bishopric of Chelmno, where sorcerers were given ecclesiastical penances and occasionally banished. Exile was a means to maintain peace and order within a village; as late as 1724, the need to do this was stated explicitly as the grounds for a sentence of banishment given by a local court in Starogard.

Of course, witches were frequently put to death: for example, the Cistercians had two women beheaded and burned at Oliwa in 1662 (Rozenkranz 1993) and three more in 1664 (Bogucka 1997). On rural estates owned by self-governing towns, witchcraft convictions seem much more frequent and severe. In the towns, such trials appear even more numerous. The accusations were absolutely stereotypical: casting spells on humans or animals, acting in alliance and fornicating with the Devil, and producing poisons. Despite massive destruction, surviving sources indicate that witchcraft trials were held in some fifty Prussian localities (Bągart, Biały Bór, Braniewo, Bydgoszcz, Chojnice, Czerniejewo, Fordon, Gdansk, Głębock, Gniew, Grudziądz, Jantar, Kętrzyn, Królewiec, Kwidzyń, Młynary, Mrągowo, Nowe, Nowy Dwór Gdański, Olecko, Oliwa, Orneta, Ostróda, Pasłęk, Pieniężno, Prabuty, Pszczółki, Puck, Rębielicz, Romankowo, Rudno, Skarszewy, Staniszewo, Starogard, Stary Targ, Straszyn, Subkowy, Szestno, Szczodrowo, Szczytno, Szpengawsk, Tczew, Toruń, Trąbki, Tropy, Tuchola, Ujeścisko, Wejherowo, Włocławek, and Zalewo).

Any figures for Prussian witchcraft trials can only be estimates. Furthermore, the number of people convicted for witchcraft cannot be determined because the materials in our possession frequently mention the initiation of a trial or represent only fragments of court files, without final sentences. However, some fragmentary information suggests that witchcraft trials were relatively frequent in Prussia, the only largely Germanophone Baltic region, just as they were in other Germanic enclaves in eastern Europe. In 1571, according to Hans Spatte's reliable chronicle from Gdansk, Prussian prisons held 134 women convicted of witchcraft, and 60 of them were burned (Simson 1902). This fairly early and possibly greatly exaggerated number of

arrests could have been caused by a massive hunt for Prussian folk healers who might have bewitched the young mentally ill Prince Albrecht. A record of criminal cases for the year 1595 lists 655 trials in Prussia, including 50 for witchcraft (this figure of 8 percent is relatively high in comparison with other German evidence, but not remarkable) (Wunder 1983).

A few localities produced numerous trials. For example, Fordon (now a district of Bydgoszcz), a place with only 271 inhabitants in 1674, held 73 witchcraft trials between 1675 and 1747, mostly coming from three neighboring villages (Żołędowo, Jastrzębie, and Niemcz). Another town of equal size, Nowe, recorded 28 persons accused of witchcraft. In one quite small Prussian city, Braunsberg, over 120 witchcraft trials are known before 1772. Its Old Town banished several sorcerers between 1534 and 1604 before burning its first witch in 1605 and its last in 1670; its New Town (whose records began only in 1600) burned its first witch in 1610 and its last one in 1686. Overall, trials came in small clusters (a maximum of 6) and under half of those tried (58 of 122) were executed. In Braunsberg, witches agreed that the Devil had no nostrils (Lilienthal 1861, 99). Prussia's last witchcraft trial took place in 1767, with the last execution for witchcraft in 1767 (in Oliwa).

Despite the formal abolition of witchcraft prosecution imposed in the second half of the eighteenth century, attempts to put witches on trial in Prussia were made as late as in the nineteenth and even twentieth centuries. When unsuccessful, such attempts sometimes ended in lynchings. In 1811 a woman accused of witchcraft (in connection with the great fire of the town) was executed by burning in Reszel. The court, however, did not consider the case in terms of witchcraft, but arson. In 1836, a woman suspected of witchcraft in the village of Chałupy was dunked, and she drowned. The justice administration judged the lynching severely and sentenced the ringleader to prison for life. Several claims of witchcraft were filed with the court of Puck as late as in the pre–World War II period. The court, however, dismissed the suits; witchcraft trials then disappear from the records. All that remains of the trials are local topographical names, such as Łyse Góry (Sabbat Hills), Góry Czarownic (Witch Hills), and Stawy Czarownic (Witch Ponds).

KRZYSZTOF SZKURŁATOWSKI

See also: COURTS ECCLESIASTICAL; DANZIG (GDANSK); DECLINE OF THE WITCH HUNTS; ECCLESIASTICAL TERRITORIES; GERMANY, NORTHEASTERN; LAWS ON WITCHCRAFT (EARLY MODERN); POLAND; ROMAN CATHOLIC CHURCH; TRIALS.

References and further reading:
Bogucka, Maria. 1997. *Żyć w dawnym Gdańsku.* Warsaw: Wydawnictwo Trio.
Janicka, Danuta. 1992. *Prawo karne w trzech rewizjach prawa chełmińskiego z XVI wieku.* Torun: Towarzystwo Naukowe w Toruniu.

Koranyi, Karol. 1927. "Czary i gusła przed sądami kościelnemi w Polsce." *Lud* 26: 1–25.

Langbein, John. 1976. *Torture and the Law of Proof.* Chicago: University of Chicago Press.

Łaszewski, Ryszard. 1974.*Wymiar sprawiedliwości we wsiach województwa chełmińskiego w 16 i 17 wieku.* Torun: Uniwersytet Mikołaja Kopernika.

———. 1988. "Prawo karne w dobrach biskupstwa chełmińskiego w pierwszej połowie XVIII wieku." Pp. 365–435 in *Księga pamiątkowa 750- lecia prawa chełmińskiego.* Toruń: Uniwersytet Mikołaja Kopernika.

Lilienthal, Johann A. 1861. *Die Hexenprozesse der beiden Städte Braunsberg, nach den Criminalacten des Braunsberger Archivs.* Königsberg.

Maisel, Witold, and Z. Zdrójkowski, eds. 1985. *Prawo Starochełmińskie.* Torun: Uniwersytet Mikołaja Kopernika.

Reich, Felix. 1940. *Hexenprozesse in Danzig und in den west-preussischen Grenzgebieten.* Munich: Universität München.

Rozenkranz, Erwin. 1993. *Gdańska archeologia prawna.* Gdańsk: Wydawnictwo Uniwersytetu Gdanskiego.

Salmonowicz, Stanisław. 1987. *Prusy: Dzieje państwa i społeczeństwa,* Poznań: Wydawnictwo Poznańskie.

Simson, Paul. 1902. "Ein Beitrag zur Geschichte des Zauberwahnes in Danzig." *Mitteilungen des Westpereussichen Geschichtvereins* 1:76.

Szkurłatowski, Krzysztof. 1997. "Proces inkwizycyjny przeciwko czarownictwu w praktyce sądów sołtysich województwa malborskiego na przełomie XVII i XVIII wieku na tle rozwoju europejskiego prawa karnego." *Rocznik Elbląski* 15: 45–53.

Wunder, Heide. 1983. "Hexenprozesse im Herzogtum Preussen während des 16. Jahrhunderts." Pp 179–203 in *Hexenprozesse: Deutsche und skandinavische Beiträge.* Edited by Christian Degn, Hartmut Lehmann, and Dagmar Unverhau. Neumünster: Karl Wachholtz Verlag.

Zygner, Leszek. 1998. "Kobieta-czarownica w świetle ksiąg konsys-torskich z XV i początku XVI w." Pp. 91–102 in *Kobieta i rodzina w średniowieczu i na progu czasów nowożytnych.* Torun: Uniwersytet Mikołaja Kopernika.

PSYCHOANALYSIS

Because psychiatry is traditionally associated with pastoral care and demonic possession with hysteria and insanity, psychoanalysis has proven a particularly fruitful interdisciplinary method for investigating the witch hunts in late medieval and early modern Europe. Psychoanalysis is the psychiatric method of studying the individual subconscious as a case history in order to diagnose disorders of the mind. The reasons for its usefulness as a historical tool are essentially twofold.

First, since the nineteenth century, seminal figures in psychiatry repeatedly and consciously referred back to the witch hunts and demonology as historical examples to justify their own contemporary theories. They eulogized the sixteenth-century skeptical witchcraft theorist Johann Weyer as the father of modern psychiatry, struggling against ignorance and superstition. In 1801, Phillipe Pinel praised Weyer in his *Traité médico-philosophique sur l'alienation mentale ou la manie* (Medical-Philosophical Treatise on Mental Alienation).

To his fellow "enlightened" physicians, Pinel explained the therapeutic value of exorcism: it offered an emotional shock treatment to cure deluded sufferers of demonic possession through cathartic ceremonies imbued with strong emotional connotations. The first man to hold an academic chair of psychiatry in France, Jean-Martin Charcot, coedited *Demoniacs in Art* (1887), which contained artistic representations of the possessed from the fifth to the eighteenth century. With a romanticized perception of Weyer, Charcot developed an analytic method known as "retrospective medicine," using his own theories about hysteria to analyze historical cases of possession.

Sigmund Freud, the foremost pioneer of psychoanalysis, learned about retrospective medicine while studying with Charcot in Paris in 1885. Freud also read widely in early modern medicine, theology, interpretations of dreams, and demonological literature. He developed a lifelong admiration for Weyer and incorporated the tenets of retrospective medicine into his own analyses of hysteria. Later, Freud made a detailed study of the demonic possession of Johann Christoph Haizmann, a seventeenth-century painter—arguably the first work of psychohistory. Since that time, numerous scholars, with varying degrees of success, have applied psychoanalytic methods and categories to explain subconscious motivations among witch hunters, accused witches, and demoniacs. Two noteworthy examples studied witch persecutions in early modern New England (Demos 1982) and offered a gender analysis of witchcraft trials in Augsburg (Roper 1994).

A second reason why a psychoanalytic perspective has enriched historical analysis of the witch hunts lies in the precocious sixteenth-century evolution of psychiatry and psychology as subjects of systematic investigation. Casuists and demonologists of all confessions (Weyer, for example, was Protestant) undertook such investigation; however, the Catholic Society of Jesus produced many early prominent leaders in this field. Indeed, Martín Del Rio, a prominent Spanish Jesuit and demonologist, coined the term *psychiatry*. In his *Florida Mariana* (The Flowers of Mary) of 1598, Del Rio specifically described Jesus as a psychiatrist (*psyche* + *iatrus* = "healer of souls") who authorized his representatives on earth to heal troubled or afflicted souls through various cathartic religious rituals and sacraments (e.g., baptism, auricular confession, pilgrimage, exorcism, etc.); Del Rio and other theologians literally touted such methods as "spiritual medicine." Widely recognized by contemporaries throughout Europe as "spiritual physic," its practitioners (referred to by the Italian exorcist, Giralomo Menghi, as *medici spirituale*) supplemented ordinary "physicians of the body" (*medici coporale*). In Catholic Europe, "spiritual physicians" were no mere allegory to "real" doctors; their domain was officially recognized by jurists and even by physicians. Their perceived efficacy in treating both psychic and somatic illnesses agreed with orthodox perceptions of natural philosophy, Galenic humoral pathology, Aristotelian physics, and the Catholic casuistry of moral theology. As a relatively coherent psychiatric system, "spiritual physic" had strong social and moral components.

The twisted path from "spiritual physic" to modern psychoanalysis is complex, but there is a continuous emphasis in both on sexuality, sin, morality, and emotions. The earlier form provides some important keys to supplement the potential of psychoanalysis for studying the historical mentality behind witchcraft trials, especially how the closely related rituals of judicial confessions and torture aided in construction of the self. Finally, "spiritual physic" offers a frequently ignored historical argument that psychoanalysis, as a scientific method, has been linked for many centuries with medicine and pastoral care.

DAVID LEDERER

See also: DEL RIO, MARTÍN; DEMONOLOGY; EXORCISM; FREUD, SIGMUND; MEDICINE AND MEDICAL THEORY; MENTAL ILLNESS; POSSESSION, DEMONIC; WEYER, JOHANN.

References and further reading:
Demos, John P. 1982. *Entertaining Satan: Witchcraft and the Culture of Early Modern New England.* Oxford: Oxford University Press.
Lederer, David. 2001. *Madness, Religion and the State in Early Modern Europe.* Cambridge: Cambridge University Press.
Roper, Lyndal. 1994. *Oedipus and the Devil: Witchcraft, Sexuality, and Religion in Early Modern Europe.* London and New York: Routledge.
Vitz, Paul C. 1988. *Sigmund Freud's Christian Unconscious.* New York: William B. Eerdmans

PURITANISM

A movement that shaped many of the ideas English demonologists held in the late sixteenth and seventeenth centuries, Puritanism also lent support to the prosecution of witches in England during the 1640s and in New England in 1692. Conversely, under some circumstances, Puritanism made it more difficult for courts to convict witches.

The term *Puritan* is applied to English Protestants of the late sixteenth and early seventeenth centuries who sought to make the English Church more fully Protestant and thus bring it into greater conformity with the Reformed or Calvinist churches on the European continent. Puritans were dissatisfied with the Elizabethan Settlement of Religion of 1559, claiming that it left the Church only partially reformed. They sought therefore to remove the vestiges of popery from English religious services, such as the wearing of vestments by the clergy, genuflection, the use of the sign of the cross, and bowing at the mention of the name of Jesus.

Puritans were divided on the issue of church government. Moderate Puritans were willing to work within the established episcopalian system of church government (i.e., a hierarchy of archbishops, bishops, and archdeacons), but more radical groups advocated the introduction of either a presbyterian system, in which a hierarchy of clerical synods and assemblies governed the church, or a congregational system, in which individual congregations possessed considerable autonomy and were only loosely associated in a national church. Presbyterians attempted without success to introduce their system of church government during the reign of Queen Elizabeth I (1558–1603). Only during the Puritan Revolution of the 1640s did the Westminster Assembly authorize the introduction of presbyterianism. That system, however, was soon replaced by a congregational structure of church government during the 1650s. Members of Protestant sects that wished to separate from the Church of England are generally not classified as Puritan, and after 1660 it is customary to refer to the heirs of Puritans, such as Presbyterians, Congregationalists, Baptists, and Quakers, as dissenters rather than Puritans.

Puritans were often identified by their religious fervor and the intensity of their commitment to religious reform. They were the "godly" ministers and laymen, the more zealous or "hotter" sort of Protestants, "saints" who were confident that they were members of the elect. As members of a godly community, Puritans practiced a rigorous moral discipline and sought to impose that same discipline on others. Because Puritans remained within the Church and only occasionally were prosecuted for nonconformity, it is often difficult to distinguish between them and the more orthodox English Protestants who are later referred to as Anglicans. Nevertheless, many prominent English demonologists between 1587 and 1646 (e.g., Henry Holland, George Gifford, William Perkins, Alexander Roberts, Richard Bernard, and John Gaule) acquired reputations as godly ministers and were sometimes referred to as Puritans. Theologically these men were all staunch Calvinists who resisted the efforts of Arminians (named for the Dutch theologian Jacobus Arminius) to weaken or modify the central Calvinist doctrine of predestination. Perkins, whose status as one of the most respected English theologians survived long after his death in 1602, provided inspiration for an entire generation of Puritan divines, including the most famous New England demonologist, Cotton Mather.

These "Puritan" demonologists agreed on most major questions regarding witchcraft and diabolism. First, like all good Calvinists, they proclaimed the sovereignty of God and the dependence of all demonic activity on divine Providence. The Devil worked only with the permission of God, and witches exercised no power of their own. Second, they emphasized the demonic or spiritual nature of the witch's crime, focusing on the pact with the Devil rather than on *maleficium* (harmful magic), which was the exclusive concern of the English witchcraft statute of 1563 and the primary concern of the statute of 1604. Their concern with the diabolical nature of witchcraft, which usually did not include references to the witches' Sabbat, also led them to argue that the white magic performed by healers and cunning folk, which they classified as superstition, was just as dangerous as *maleficium*. Third, these ministers, like many Protestant demonologists on the Continent, identified witchcraft with Roman Catholicism. This tendency was reinforced by the Protestant classification of Catholic religious ceremonies as magical and the Protestant claim that many witches were papists. In his *Treatise against Witchcraft* (1590), Holland compared saint worship to devil worship and the sign of the cross to witchcraft. Finally and most distinctively, these Puritan demonologists placed a strong emphasis on the Apocalypse and the identification of witchcraft as the work of the Antichrist and the Devil during the final days. Roberts, for example, in *A Treatise of Witchcraft* (1616), declared that witchcraft was one of the dreadful evils prophesied for "these last days and perilous times" (Clark 1997, 325). The most powerful expression of this apocalyptic witchcraft literature was Cotton Mather's *Memorable Providences Relating to Witchcrafts and Possessions* (1689), in which he claimed that demonic possession and witchcraft were signs of the Devil's activity during the final days.

The most obvious disagreements among these English "Puritan" demonologists concerned their recommendations for proceeding against witches. Gifford, Bernard, and Gaule all urged considerable caution after observing miscarriages of justice in their native counties. The others took a harder line, including Perkins, who in *A Discourse of the Damned Art of Witchcraft* (1608) listed numerous proofs of diabolical activity that could result in a witch's conviction. He urged the execution of witches without exception because they depended on Satan as their God. Roberts defended the prosecution of Mary Smith in King's Lynn, Norfolk. The main concern of most of these godly ministers, however, including Perkins, was to prevent their parishioners from falling into theological error, not bringing accused witches to justice.

Puritanism did, nevertheless, inspire some ministers and lay magistrates to prosecute witches as part of a campaign to purge society of its diabolical contaminants. These efforts became most evident in England when Puritans gained control of the church and local government during the English Civil War. The largest witch hunt in England's history, the campaign Matthew Hopkins and John Stearne conducted in East Anglia in 1645–1647, can be attributed at least in part to Puritan

zeal. The religious orientation of Hopkins cannot be ascertained, although his reference to the marriage of the Devil to witches according to the order prescribed in Book of Common Prayer (the service book of the English Church) suggests Puritan sympathies. John Stearne, however, who served as Hopkins's assistant, was clearly a zealous Puritan layman, and in his treatise, *A Confirmation and Discovery of Witchcraft* (1648), Stearne described the prosecution of witches as a spiritual duty. Puritanism was pervasive in Essex at that time that Hopkins and Stearne were actively trying to discover witches. Many of the parishes in that county had replaced "scandalous" ministers with godly Puritans during the early years of the Civil War. A widespread iconoclastic campaign in Essex and Suffolk to destroy statues and paintings that Puritans considered idolatrous provides further evidence of the strength of Puritanism in the area where Hopkins and Stearne were most active. Millenarian sentiment was also strong in all Puritan counties during these years, especially in Essex. The strength of Puritanism in these areas helps to explain why local communities invited Hopkins and Stearne to discover the local witches they feared were in their midst and why those same communities encouraged or facilitated their prosecution.

In New England, where Puritanism was dominant from the settlement of Massachusetts Bay Colony by nonseparating Congregationalists in 1628 until the end of the seventeenth century, the connections between Puritanism and witchcraft were different from what they were in England. Owing to Puritan influence, the crime of witchcraft in Massachusetts was defined in demonic terms, and consequently witches could not be convicted without evidence of having made a pact with the Devil. This definition of the crime led to the acquittal of a great majority of witches accused by their neighbors of *maleficium* before 1692. In that year, however, the fits experienced by a group of young girls in Salem Village led the Salem community to attribute their afflictions to witchcraft, thus initiating a large witch hunt in which more than 150 individuals were arrested and 19 executed. Puritanism contributed to the Salem witch hunt in three related ways. First, the Puritan belief that God spoke to his chosen people of Massachusetts through signs and events in their daily lives—the remarkable providences that Mather discussed in his treatise of 1689—led them to interpret the afflictions of the girls and also the Indian war that had recently devastated the colony as signs of God's disfavor. The sermons of Samuel Parris, the minister in Salem Village, and his predecessor Deodat Lawson prior to the trials also encouraged their parishioners to believe that the misfortunes lay within the community itself and were the result of God's punishment. The accusation and prosecution of witches at Salem can thus be seen as a Puritan response to these supernatural signs of divine anger. Second, the girls whose fits triggered the episode were brought up in pious Puritan families (some were members of the Parris household), suggesting a link among Puritan religiosity, demonic possession, and witchcraft accusations. Third, residents of Salem Village made many of the accusations against people who had apparently assimilated the commercial values of nearby Salem Town and who therefore posed a threat to the traditional Puritan values that the farmers of Salem Village were struggling to maintain.

The trials originally won the support of the Puritan ministers of the Boston area, under the leadership of Cotton Mather, who in a letter to the governor of the colony on June 15 urged the vigorous prosecution of the witches. In the end, however, it was a sermon by the Puritan minister Increase Mather, Cotton's father, in October that helped to stop the trials. The sermon, which was soon published as *Cases of Conscience Concerning Evil Spirits Personating Men* with endorsements by fourteen Massachusetts ministers, called for procedural caution in the trials on the grounds that the Devil might have made the girls see the specters of innocent people afflicting them. This skepticism regarding the validity of spectral evidence, itself a reflection of Puritan beliefs regarding the nature of demonic power, led to the termination of the trials and the release of the witches still in prison. The contrasting positions taken by Increase and Cotton Mather during the Salem witchcraft trials demonstrate that the relationship between Puritanism and witchcraft in New England, just as in England, cannot be expressed in simple terms. A determination to rid the world of the Devil's confederates may have led many Puritans to support the prosecution of witches, but the Puritan belief in the limitations of demonic power by a sovereign God ultimately helped to bring them to an end.

BRIAN P. LEVACK

See also: APOCALYPSE; DEMONOLOGY; DIABOLISM; ENGLAND; ESSEX; GAUTE, JOHN; GIFFORD, GEORGE; HOPKINS, MATTHEW; *MALEFICIUM;* MATHER, COTTON; MATHER, INCREASE; NEW ENGLAND; PERKINS, WILLIAM; PROTESTANT REFORMATION; SALEM; SPECTRAL EVIDENCE; STEARNE, JOHN.

References and further reading:
Boyer, Paul, and Stephen Nissenbaum. 1974. *Salem Possessed.* Cambridge, MA: Harvard University Press.
Clark, Stuart. 1997. *Thinking with Demons: The Idea of Witchcraft in Early Modern Europe.* Oxford: Clarendon.
Godbeer, Richard. 1992. *The Devil's Dominion: Magic and Religion in Early New England.* Cambridge: Cambridge University Press.
Hunt, William. 1983. *The Puritan Moment: The Coming of Revolution in an English County.* Cambridge, MA: Harvard University Press.
Norton, Mary Beth. 2002. *In the Devil's Snare: The Salem Witchcraft Crisis of 1692.* New York: Knopf.
Perkins, William. 1608. *A Discourse on the Damned Art of Witchcraft.* Cambridge: Cantrel Legge.
Sharpe, James. 1996. *Instruments of Darkness: Witchcraft in England 1550–1750.* London: Hamish Hamilton.
Teall, J. L. 1962. "Witchcraft and Calvinism in Elizabethan England." *Journal of the History of Ideas* 23: 22–36.
Thomas, Keith. 1971. *Religion and the Decline of Magic.* London: Weidenfeld and Nicolson.

INDEX

Note: Page numbers in bold indicate main entries.

Idolatry, 89–90, **534–536**
    See also Bible; Devil; Ritual magic
Il messaggiero (Tasso), 1108
Iliad (Homer), 507–508
Illness, 221, 283–285
    See also Disease; Medicine and medical theory
Image magic, **536–538**
Imagination, **538–540**
Imperial free cities, 65–67, **540–544,** 831–832,
    841–842, 850–851
    See also Holy Roman Empire
Impotence, sexual, **544–546,** 978, 1010
    See also Magic, popular
Imps, 40
    See also Demons; Fairies
Incantations, 1077–1078, 1168
Incarnation, 114
Incubus and succubus, **546–548,** 1131, 1189
    See also Demons; Sexual activity, diabolic
Index of Prohibited Books, 46, 320, 551, 559, 578,
    688
Indians. *See* Native Americans
Indiculus Superstitionum et Paganiarium, **548–549**
    See also Sorcery; Superstition
Infanticide, **549–550,** 789–790, 896–897, 1149,
    1202
    See also Cannibalism; Children; Sabbat
Infants, 175–176
Ingolstadt, University of, **550–551**
    See also Bavaria; Gregory of Valencia; Jesuits;
        Universities
Innocent III, Pope, 207, 289, 457, 554, 555, 855,
    1115
    See also Papacy and papal bulls
Innocent IV, Pope, 554
    See also Papacy and papal bulls
Innocent VIII, Pope, **551–552,** 856, 880
    See also Kramer, Heinrich; Papacy and papal bulls
Innsbruck, **552–553**
    See also Austria; Kramer, Heinrich
Inquisition, 49, 276–277, 318–319, 631, 637, 771,
    774–775, 968, 969
    Brazilian, 143–144
    confessions and, 204–206
    courts, 225–227
    Dominican, 289–290
    medieval, 553–556
    Mexican, 823–825
    Peruvian, 822
    popular culture and, 108

Portuguese, 556–557, 919–920, 1133
Roman, 26–27, 169–170, 195, 224–225, 558–560,
    1034–1036, 1047, 1130, 1133
Spanish, 54–56, 82–83, 93–97, 173, 189, 276–277,
    381, 560–562, 644, 991, 1032, 1047, 1130, 1133
Venetian, 562–563
Inquisitorial procedure, 5–6, **563–565,** 1116, 1133,
    1134, 1212
Instrucio pro formandis, 559
Interrogations, 1134
    See also Trials
Inversion, 1226
Invocations, **565–567**
    See also Demons; Ritual magic
Ireland, **567–568,** 613–615
    See also Quteler, Alice
Isidore of Seville, St., **568–569,** 618
Islamic witchcraft and magic, **569–573**
Isolani, Isidoro, **573–574**
    See also Italy
Israel, 117
Italy, 109–110, 112–113, 245–246, 294–295, 438,
    558–569, 562–563, 573–574, **574–579,**
    763–765, 774–776, 832–833, 898–902,
    951–952, 1032–1036, 1057, 1108–1109,
    1125–1126, 158.169, 158.170
    See also Benevento, Walnut Tree of; Mountains and
        origins of witchcraft; Origins of witch hunts;
        Roman Inquisition
    drama, 294–295
    Milan, 763–765
    Modena, 774–776
    Naples, 801–802
    Piedmont, 900–901
    Sicily, 1032–1034
    Venetian Inquisition, 562–563
Ivanhoe (Scott), 1022, 1112

J

Jabir ibn Hayyan, 571
Jackals, 288–289
Jackson, Elizabeth, 600
Jacquier, Nicolas, 93, **581–582**
Jailers, **582–583**
    See also Executioners
James VI and I, King of Scotland and England, 1,
    186, 189, **583–586,** 662, 812, 835, 974, 1010,
    1017, 1019, 1097, 1188
    See also England; North Berwick witches; Scotland

875, 877, 989–990, 990, 1087, 1204, 1213, 1235, 1236

See also Demonology; France

Langton, Walter, **623–624**

See also England

Languedoc, 48, 141, 152, 187, 189, 276, 289, 318, 319, 388, 389, 458, 465, 512, 513, 555, **624–625**

See also France

Lapland, 373, 374, 473, **625–627**

See also Finnmark; Norway

Larkham, Thomas, 952

Larner, Christina, 233, 496, 627–628

See also Historiography; Scotland

Latvia, 323, 325, 412, 415, 416, 628–630

Lausanne, diocese of, 368, **630–632**, 1126–1127

See also Origins of witch hunts; Switzerland

LaVey, Anton, 1003

Laws on witchcraft, 72–74, 585, 855–856, 861–862, 919–920, 938–939, 1143–1145, 1212

ancient, **632–634**, 970–971

Carolina Code, 8–9, 8–9, 56, 71, 72, 168–169, 168–169, 430, 505–506, 629, 636, 637, 934–935, 934–935, 1008, 1128, 1130, 1143, 1145, 1212, 1228

early modern, 634–640

medieval, 640–644

Lawyers, 2, 3, 38, 59, 66, 67, 99, 100, 101, 103, 126, 175, 200, 202, 204, 206, 228, 233, 252, 260, 262, 273, 305, 331, 332, 343, 359, 361, 386, 388, 389, 422, 423, 441, 444, 450, 455, 459, 461, 483, 494, 506, 533, 550, 551, 555, 565, 599, **644–645**

See also Trials

Layenspiegel (Tanner), 63, 66, 565, 567, **645–646,** 1142–1143

See also Germany

Laymann, Paul, 251, 261, 299, 587, 588, 599, **646–647,** 1129, 1130

Le Champion des dames (Le Franc), 647

Le Franc, Martin, 93, 164, 194, 328, **647–648**

See also Origins of the Witch Hunts

Lea, Henry Charles, 154, 477, 495, **648–649**

See also Historiography

Leach, Edmund, 696–697

Learned magic, 12, 34, 35, 51, 93, 167, 192, 198, 241, 242, 448, 490, 574, 700–704, 1209

See also Hermeticism; Ritual magic

Legal system. See Courts, ecclesiastical; Courts, secular

Legends, 24, 38, 41, 75, 236, 249, 383–384, 383–384, 502

Leiden University, 439, 812

Lemgo, 274, 432, 435, 476, 653–654, 918, 1210

Lemnius, Levinus, **649**

Leo XIII, Pope, 54, 161, 880

See also Papacy and papal bulls

Leo X, Pope, 688, 749, 880, 932

See also Papacy and papal bulls

Leopold I, Emperor, 50, 51, 507, 608, 953–954

Leprosy, 128

See also Disease

Letters on Demonology and Witchcraft (Scott), 1022

Levack, Brian, 172, 332, 356, 485, 519, 520, 650–651

See also Historiography

LeVey, Anton, 125

See also Satanism

Leviathan (Hobbes), 498–499

Leviticus, 117–118, 256, 291, 641

Liable accusers, 6

Lichtenstein, principality of, 50–51, 415, 501, 786, 917, 953–954, 1153–1154

See also Hohenems, Franz Karl von; Kempten, prince-abbey of; *Reichshofrat*

Lilith, 117, 119, 120, 379, 382, 523, 525, 548, 651–652, 828

See also Demons

Lille nuns, 160, 301, **652–653**

See also Convent cases; Exorcism; Possession, demonic

Lilly, William, 65

L'incredulité et mescéance du sortilege (Lancre), 623

Lippe, county of, 19, 20, 430, 432, 436, **653–654**

See also Germany, West and Northwest

Literature, **654–658**, 1021–1022, 1114, 1145, 1145–1146

See also specific authors and texts

Lithuania, 325, 326, 412, 414, **658–660**

Litterae annuae, 587

Little Ice Age, 22, 105, 106, 425, 506, 507, 577, 579, **660–664,** 791, 1187, 1211

See also Agrarian crises; Weather magic

Living saints, 158, 445, 503, 573, 574, 578, **664–665,** 1164–1165

Llorente, J.A., 94

Lloyd, Temperance, 336, 337

Lo Stregozzo (Veneziano), 62

Locke, John, 373, 1048

See also Enlightenment

Maria Theresa, Holy Roman Empress, 74, 507, 602, 639, **729–731,** 1049, 1097, 1098
 See also Austria; Decline of the Witch Hunts; Swieten, Gerard van
Marital status, 1054
 See also Family of love; Female witches
Mark of the Devil. *See* Devil's mark
Marlowe, Christopher, 23, 273, 342, 353, 463, 957
Martson, John, 958
Mary II, Queen, 974
Mary, Queen of Scots, 583
Mary, the Virgin, **731–732, 1113–1114**
Masque of Queenes (Jonson), 958
Materials Toward a History of Witchcraft (Lea), 648
Mather, Cotton, **732–734,** 768, 783, 941, 942–943
 See also Demonology; New England; Salem
Mather, Increase, **734–736,** 1075
 See also New England; Salem; Spectral evidence
Max III Joseph, 102
Maximilian I, Duke of Bavaria, 638, **736–737,** 881
Maximilian I, Holy Roman Emperor, **737,** 1136
Mayer, Andreas Ulrich, 103
McCarthy, Joseph, 359, 769
Mechanical philosophy, 193, 314, 358, **737–739**
Mecklenburg, Duchy of, 393, 418, **739–741**
 See also Germany, Northeastern
Medea, 61, 119, 176, 190, 479, **741–742**
Meder, David, **742**
Mediators, 524
Medicine and medical theory, 179, 546, 578, 600, 649, **742–747,** 883–884, 1195
 See also Magic, Popular; Weyer, Johann
 disease and, 283–285
 folk, 128–129
 herbal, 484–485
 midwives, 762–763
Mediterranean Inquisitions, 3, 4, 276, 331, 557
Meinders, Hermann, 6
Melancholia paintings, 231
 See also Art and visual images; Cranach, Lucas
Melancholia paintings (Geiler), 1006
Melancholy, 274, 314, 321, 395, 448, 506, 516, 570, **747–749**
 See also Mental illness; Weyer, Johann
Melanchthon, Philipp, 352, 463, 481, 905, 936, 937, 1198
Melibea, 177, 294
Memorates, 383
Memorial der Tugend (Schwarzenberg), 61
Memory Prompts to Virtue (Breu), 145–146

Menghi, Girolamo, 340, 460, 559, 578, **749–750,** 940
Mennonites, 36, 37, 536, 601, **750–751,** 873
 See also Gender; Protestant Reformation
Mental illness, 31, 253, 263, 289, 493, 747–749, **751–752,** 1195
 See also Freud, Sigmund; Medicine and medical theory; Melancholy; Psychoanalysis; Weyer, Johann
Mergentheim, ecclesiastical territory of, **752–753,** 877
 See also Ecclesiastical territories
Merian the Elder, Matthäus, 62
Merlin, 40, 546, 753–754
 See also Magus
Merry Devil of Edmonton, 958
Mersenne, Marin, 402
Merzig-Saargua, 986
Metamorphoses (Golden Ass), 51, 379
Metamorphosis, 40–41, 161, 191, 260, 261, 281, 406, 448, **754–757,** 1044, 1123, 1139, 1202–1203
 See also Lycanthropy
Metamorphosis (Kafka), 656
Metonymy, 1224
Mexican Inquisition, 823–825
Meyfart, Johann Matthäus, **757–758,** 1129
Michelet, Jules, 460–461, 494, 495, **758–759**
 See also Female witches; Historiography
Middle Rhine, 429–431
Middleton, Thomas, 43, 1017, 1028
Midelfort, H. C. Erik, 105, 357, 496, **759–760,** 978
 See also Germany, Southwestern; Historiography
Midsummer Eve, 325, **760–762**
Midwives, 67, 153, 175, 358, 360, 407, 477, 478, 516, 519, 526, 528, **762–763,** 772
 See also Female witches; Gender
Milan, 21, 26, 29, 67, 139, 219, 225, 319, 351, 372, 384, 456, 464, 558, 574, 575, 576, 598, **763–765**
Milk, 13, 40, 42, 59, 60, 84, 115, 195, 239, 325, 347, 350, 351, 383, 406, 409, 410, 433, 450, 521, 522, 525, 526, 528, 529, 629, **765–767,** 1139, 1142
 See also Magic, popular
Millenarianism, 47, 358, **767–768**
 See also Antichrist; Apocalypse; Devil
Miller, Arthur, 359, 369, 370, **769**
 See also Literature; Modern Political Usage; Salem; Witch hunts
Milton, John, 1002

O

Wright, Joan, 182–183
Württemberg, duchy of, **1227–1230**
Würzburg, prince-bishopric of, 991, 1210,
    1230–1232
    See also Ecclesiastical territories